International Directory of
COMPANY
HISTORIES

International Directory of
COMPANY HISTORIES

VOLUME 46

Editor
Tina Grant

ST. JAMES
PRESS®

Detroit • New York • San Diego • San Francisco • Cleveland • New Haven, Conn. • Waterville, Maine • London • Munich

International Directory of Company Histories, Volume 46

Tina Grant, Editor

Project Editor
Miranda H. Ferrara

Editorial
Erin Bealmear, Joann Cerrito, Jim Craddock, Stephen Cusack, Peter M. Gareffa, Kristin Hart, Melissa Hill, Margaret Mazurkiewicz, Carol A. Schwartz, Christine Tomassini, Michael J. Tyrkus

Imaging and Multimedia
Randy Bassett, Robert Duncan, Lezlie Light

Manufacturing
Rhonda Williams

LIBRARY OF CONGRESS CATALOG NUMBER 89-190943
ISBN: 1-55862-464-3

BRITISH LIBRARY CATALOGUING IN PUBLICATION DATA

International directory of company histories. Vol. 46
I. Tina Grant
33.87409

Printed in the United States of America
10 9 8 7 6 5 4 3 2 1

CONTENTS _____

Company Histories

PREFACE

The St. James Press series *The International Directory of Company Histories (IDCH)* is intended for reference use by students, business people, librarians, historians, economists, investors, job candidates, and others who seek to learn more about the historical development of the world's most important companies. To date, *IDCH* has covered over 5,475 companies in 46 volumes.

Inclusion Criteria

Most companies chosen for inclusion in *IDCH* have achieved a minimum of US$25 million in annual sales and are leading influences in their industries or geographical locations. Companies may be publicly held, private, or nonprofit. State-owned companies that are important in their industries and that may operate much like public or private companies also are included. Wholly owned subsidiaries and divisions are profiled if they meet the requirements for inclusion. Entries on companies that have had major changes since they were last profiled may be selected for updating.

The *IDCH* series highlights 10% private and nonprofit companies, and features updated entries on approximately 45 companies per volume.

Entry Format

Each entry begins with the company's legal name, the address of its headquarters, its telephone, toll-free, and fax numbers, and its web site. A statement of public, private, state, or parent ownership follows. A company with a legal name in both English and the language of its headquarters country is listed by the English name, with the native-language name in parentheses.

The company's founding or earliest incorporation date, the number of employees, and the most recent available sales figures follow. Sales figures are given in local currencies with equivalents in U.S. dollars. For some private companies, sales figures are estimates and indicated by the abbreviation *est.* The entry lists the exchanges on which a company's stock is traded and its ticker symbol, as well as the company's NAIC codes.

Entries generally contain a *Company Perspectives* box which provides a short summary of the company's mission, goals, and ideals, a *Key Dates* box highlighting milestones in the company's history, lists of *Principal Subsidiaries, Principal Divisions, Principal Operating Units, Principal Competitors,* and articles for *Further Reading.*

American spelling is used throughout *IDCH*, and the word ''billion'' is used in its U.S. sense of one thousand million.

Sources

Entries have been compiled from publicly accessible sources both in print and on the Internet such as general and academic periodicals, books, annual reports, and material supplied by the companies themselves.

Cumulative Indexes

IDCH contains three indexes: the **Index to Companies**, which provides an alphabetical index to companies discussed in the text as well as to companies profiled, the **Index to Industries**, which allows researchers to locate companies by their principal industry, and the **Geographic Index**, which lists companies alphabetically by the country of their headquarters. The indexes are cumulative and specific instructions for using them are found immediately preceding each index.

Suggestions Welcome

Comments and suggestions from users of *IDCH* on any aspect of the product as well as suggestions for companies to be included or updated are cordially invited. Please write:

The Editor
International Directory of Company Histories
St. James Press
27500 Drake Rd.
Farmington Hills, Michigan 48331-3535

ABBREVIATIONS FOR FORMS OF COMPANY INCORPORATION

A.B.	Aktiebolaget (Sweden)
A.G.	Aktiengesellschaft (Germany, Switzerland)
A.S.	Aksjeselskap (Denmark, Norway)
A.S.	Atieselskab (Denmark)
A.Ş.	Anomin Şirket (Turkey)
B.V.	Besloten Vennootschap met beperkte, Aansprakelijkheid (The Netherlands)
Co.	Company (United Kingdom, United States)
Corp.	Corporation (United States)
G.I.E.	Groupement d'Intérêt Economique (France)
GmbH	Gesellschaft mit beschränkter Haftung (Germany)
H.B.	Handelsbolaget (Sweden)
Inc.	Incorporated (United States)
KGaA	Kommanditgesellschaft auf Aktien (Germany)
K.K.	Kabushiki Kaisha (Japan)
LLC	Limited Liability Company (Middle East)
Ltd.	Limited (Canada, Japan, United Kingdom, United States)
N.V.	Naamloze Vennootschap (The Netherlands)
OY	Osakeyhtiöt (Finland)
PLC	Public Limited Company (United Kingdom)
PTY.	Proprietary (Australia, Hong Kong, South Africa)
S.A.	Société Anonyme (Belgium, France, Switzerland)
SpA	Società per Azioni (Italy)

ABBREVIATIONS FOR CURRENCY

$	United States dollar	KD	Kuwaiti dinar
£	United Kingdom pound	L	Italian lira
¥	Japanese yen	LuxFr	Luxembourgian franc
A$	Australian dollar	M$	Malaysian ringgit
AED	United Arab Emirates dirham	N	Nigerian naira
		Nfl	Netherlands florin
B	Thai baht	NIS	Israeli new shekel
B	Venezuelan bolivar	NKr	Norwegian krone
BFr	Belgian franc	NT$	Taiwanese dollar
C$	Canadian dollar	NZ$	New Zealand dollar
CHF	Switzerland franc	P	Philippine peso
COL	Colombian peso	PLN	Polish zloty
Cr	Brazilian cruzado	PkR	Pakistan Rupee
CZK	Czech Republic koruny	Pta	Spanish peseta
DA	Algerian dinar	R	Brazilian real
Dfl	Netherlands florin	R	South African rand
DKr	Danish krone	RMB	Chinese renminbi
DM	German mark	RO	Omani rial
E£	Egyptian pound	Rp	Indonesian rupiah
Esc	Portuguese escudo	Rs	Indian rupee
EUR	Euro dollars	Ru	Russian ruble
FFr	French franc	S$	Singapore dollar
Fmk	Finnish markka	Sch	Austrian schilling
GRD	Greek drachma	SFr	Swiss franc
HK$	Hong Kong dollar	SKr	Swedish krona
HUF	Hungarian forint	SRls	Saudi Arabian riyal
IR£	Irish pound	W	Korean won
K	Zambian kwacha	W	South Korean won

International Directory of

COMPANY HISTORIES

AVC Advocat

Advocat Inc.

---

277 Mallory Stations Road, Suite 130
Franklin, Tennessee 37067
U.S.A.
Telephone: (615) 771-7575
Fax: (615) 771-7409
Web site: http://irino.com/avc

Public Company
Incorporated: 1980 as Diversicare Inc.
Employees: 5,620
Sales: $196 million (2000)
Stock Exchanges: OTC
Ticker Symbol: AVCA
NAIC: 623110 Nursing Care Facilities

Based in Franklin, Tennessee, Advocat Inc. operates assisted-living facilities for the elderly as well as nursing homes. The company concentrates on serving smaller communities in 12 mostly southern states and four provinces in Canada. Changes in reimbursement levels from Medicare have led to serious financial difficulties for the company, resulting in its stock being delisted by both the New York Stock Exchange and Toronto Stock Exchange.

Company Origins: 1980

The driving force behind Advocat is its chairman and CEO, Dr. Charles W. Birkett, who became involved in the nursing home industry in 1980. Born in Canada, he completed his medical training at the University of Toronto in 1960. He gained management experience at Sterling Drug Ltd of Aurora, Ontario, ultimately becoming a vice-president and the medical director of the firm. He supplemented his practical business experience by returning to school, earning an MBA from York University in 1972. Birkett then went to work as a senior consultant for Hickling-Johnston Ltd, a Toronto company that offered consulting services to the Canadian health-care industry. He was named a partner in the firm in 1975 and eventually became a vice-president and director. In 1980, Birkett left Hickling-Johnston to help found a corporation called Diversi-

care Inc., devoted to the "assisted living" field. It would lead to the eventual creation of Advocat.

The first step for Diversicare was to acquire a financially troubled Toronto complex that included 246 nursing home beds, Although the building also featured 287 apartments for seniors, only a handful of those residents actually employed services from the nursing home staff. Birkett described this early venture in a 1996 article he wrote for *Nursing Homes,* explaining that the Diversicare team did not recognize a connection between independent seniors and those requiring greater care: "What we had, in, fact, were two separate concepts— independent living and nursing home care—sharing a building. . . . Within three years we came to recognize how very little we knew about the elderly, especially those who didn't need nursing home care. Once we achieved that realization, we were able to develop a new mind-set, one that made it possible to begin to learn what this continuum of care concept—elderly residents moving from independence, to frailty, to infirmity—is all about." Moreover, Birkett came to realize that "much of the definitions, organization, and development of health care has been for the convenience of the provider. That is most definitely the wrong mind-set." Although Diversicare applied many of these early lessons in the 1980s, the company continued to view assisted living facilities and nursing homes as separate endeavors, each requiring a different approach. According to Birkett, "We saw the nursing home business as one of expense control and the assisted living/retirement housing business as one of revenue maximization." As a result Diversicare was organized into two divisions.

In 1983, Diversicare was acquired for its real estate portfolio by Counsel Corp., a Toronto-based company that had been formed in 1979 and had been primarily involved in financial services and real estate development. Counsel's entry into the assisted living industry was not that unusual, however, because a number of real estate developers viewed the business simply as an extension of the housing market rather than a part of the health-care industry. Birkett stayed on as president of Diversicare, in addition to becoming a director on Counsel's board.

Diversicare expanded to the U.S. market, establishing a subsidiary based in Clearwater, Florida, then in 1988 made a major acquisition, purchasing Wessex Corp, a Franklin, Tennessee, health-care services company. The nursing home business of Wessex was the primary reason for the deal, but a home health-care business called American HomePatient was also included. Two years earlier, Atlanta-based American Home Patients Centers Inc. acquired Wessex in a $21 million stock swap, then assumed its name, merged management teams, and relocated to Franklin. Counsel elected to operate American HomePatient as a subsidiary of Diversicare, which now moved its headquarters to Franklin, a more central location for the company's U.S. facilities than was Clearwater.

The health-care business, at the time, was not a significant contributor to Counsel, which by 1989 boasted $2 billion in assets and generated $350 million in annual revenues. The fortunes of the conglomerate soon suffered, however, as a recession ensued and the bottom fell out of real estate prices. Because the corporation's U.S. health-care business continued to show healthy growth, Counsel decided in 1991 to spin-off Diversicare, taking it public in 1991.

The $15 million raised in the initial public offering of Diversicare was earmarked for an expansion program, which the company actively pursued in 1992. Diversicare began the year with 24 facilities in four states and ended with 53 facilities in ten states. All of the company's purchases were located in southern states, with the exception of the acquisition of Duracare Medical Equipment in Tempe, Arizona. For the most part, however, the plan was to expand by moving into secondary markets, with populations between 50,000 and 250,000, and where Diversicare operations were already in place in an adjacent state. The demographics of the United States, with an aging population, looked promising for the future, especially in the home health care side of the business. Moreover, the nursing home industry was highly fragmented, with a majority of the businesses being single facilities and family owned, a situation that offered opportunities for public companies to greatly enhance market share.

Advocat Formed in 1994

Counsel now decided to split up the businesses of Diversicare. In 1994, the nursing home management operation was spun off as a new company called Advocat, with Birkett as CEO, and Diversicare subsequently changed its name to its remaining subsidiary, American HomePatient. Advocat was then taken public in May 1994, raising $5.2 million. In addition, the new company arranged a $17.5 million line of credit, of which $10 million was budgeted for acquisitions of long-term care facilities. By the end of the year, Advocat acquired a 134-bed nursing home, as well as securing leases on six other nursing homes with a total of 625 beds and three other nursing homes under construction and scheduled to open in mid-1995.

Advocat entered its first full year with a certain number of acquisitions it wished to achieve. Prices were considered too high, however, and it was not until December 1995 that the company found a property, a 169-bed Texas facility, that management felt was reasonably priced. The company had better success with a new 40-bed Alzheimer's unit that it opened in Corpus Christi, Texas, in February 1995, the result of market research on local needs. It was also an extension of the lessons Birkett learned during his early years with Diversicare, a matter of focusing on the entire range of patient care, from independence to infirmity. Within six months the Alzheimer facility was fully occupied and making a significant contribution to the balance sheet. As a result of the company's inability to make acquisitions, it fell short of its overall financial goals for the year. Nevertheless, Advocat topped $133 million in net revenues for 1995 and posted a net profit of more than $4.4 million.

Acquisition prices were more in line with Advocat's expectations in 1996, and as a result the company was extremely active, adding four facilities in both the United States and Canada. The company purchased a 60-bed nursing home in St. Petersburg, Florida; an 86-bed nursing home in Hartford, Alabama; a 130-bed nursing home in Little Rock, Arkansas; and a 74-unit continuum-of-care center located in Brantford, Ontario. In addition, Advocat opened a new 60-bed nursing home and expanded existing facilities. In all, the company added 350 beds and $10 million in annual revenues. For the year, revenues showed a significant increase over the previous year, reaching almost $159 million, with net income reaching $4.7 million. Advocat also took steps in 1996 to offer new patient services, such as rehabilitation and fitness programs, medical alert services, adult day care, and specialized recreational programs. The company formed a strategic relationship with Prism Health Group of Boston to research some of these potential services.

Advocat made its largest acquisition in 1997, when it paid $32 million for the assets of the Pierce Management Group, the largest operator of assisted-living facilities in North Carolina. Under terms of the transaction, Advocat purchased 15 rest homes and gained leases to 14 others, with the option to purchase 12 of them after five years. Management viewed the Pierce acquisition as a base from which to build a U.S. presence in the assisted-living services market, one that Advocat's Canadian operations had been involved in for many years. The new facilities, mostly located in rural areas, added approximately 2,000 patients and was expected to increase Advocat's annual revenues by $26 million.

The pursuit of acquisitions and establishing new businesses, however, would be superceded by adverse developments in 1997. Advocat settled a wrongful death suit involving one of its Alabama facilities, but state regulators then cut off Medicare and Medicaid payments to two of the company's Alabama nursing homes after finding that the facilities lacked adequate staffing, used inappropriate physical restraints, and served food at improper temperatures. As a result, one facility was decertified for 69 days and the other for 91 days before inspectors deemed the company was in compliance. Not only did the loss of Medicare and Medicaid payments have a negative impact on year-end results for Advocat, the bad publicity also caused the price of its stock to drop. Management maintained that Alabama officials overreacted and that intermediate penalties should have been imposed rather than immediately turning to decertification. Nevertheless, Advocat conducted a review of its seven Alabama facilities and took steps to improve relationships with that state.

Balanced Budget Act of 1997 Hurts Nursing Home Industry

A far more important development in 1997, one that would affect the entire industry, was the Federal government's passage of the Balanced Budget Act of 1997, which included a number of cost-saving measures for Medicare and Medicaid. Nursing homes were now required over the next three years to transition to a prospective payment system (PPS). In effect, PPS set standard reimbursement rates for Medicare and Medicaid services, thus forcing management to cut operational expenses to offset reduced revenues from the government programs. The actual effects of these changes would not be immediately apparent. In the meantime, Advocat posted another record year in revenues, exceeding $177 million in 1997, although net profits fell to $3 million, due in large part to the Alabama losses.

As Advocat moved to convert its facilities to PPS, it became clear that the reduced Medicare and Medicaid reimbursement levels combined with more stringent regulations were going to severely hurt its business. The company spent $2.5 million on a new information system to help it better manage its costs in response to PPS, but even greater efficiencies could not compensate for the lower reimbursement rates. Fortunately for Advocat, its Canadian operations were not affected, and its new assisted-living facilities in North Carolina were performing well. As a result, revenues grew to $205.2 million in 1998, although the company posted a $3 million loss on the year. Advocat faced an uncertain future, and Birkett, according to press accounts, was now very much interested in selling the company. Attempts to find a new partner with deep pockets, however, proved fruitless.

The financial situation would only worsen for the nursing home industry in 1999. Reduced Medicare and Medicaid payments and the costs incurred from increased regulation were debilitating enough, but an increased level of litigation drove up the cost of liability insurance. As a result, a large number of nursing home operators were forced into bankruptcy. Even with the benefit of its Canadian business and assisted-living operation, Advocat suffered through a disastrous 1999. Net revenues fell to $182 million and the company lost more than $21.6 million. Just to survive the year Advocat required forbearance from its major landlord and banker. Unable to meet equity and capitalization requirements of the New York Stock Exchange, Advocat, whose stock lost 75 percent of its value in the previous year, was delisted and its shares forced to trade over the counter. In order to free himself to focus on these financial difficulties, Birkett hired Charles H. Rinne, an executive with considerable experience in the nursing home industry, to serve as president and chief operating officer and take over the day-to-day operational responsibilities.

Conditions improved only slightly in 2000. Advocat managed to avoid defaulting on loans, and by the end of the year was able to consolidate its debt and renegotiate its leases. Net revenues for the year improved to $196 million, and the company was able to cut its net loss to $3.85 million. Some of the Medicare and Medicaid cutbacks were restored, but the changes would not be felt until 2001. Advocat, and the nursing industry as a whole, looked for relief from a new president in 2001, hoping that the regulatory burden might be eased. The cost of liability insurance, on the other hand, appeared as if it would only grow worse, especially in Texas and Florida. Clearly, the company faced an uncertain future, yet the demographics had not changed: America was aging and Americans were living longer. As a result, the long-term prospects for Advocat remained somewhat optimistic.

Principal Subsidiaries

Advocat Ancillary Services, Inc.; Diversicare Assisted Living Services, Inc; Diversicare Canada Management Services Co., Inc.; First American Health Care, Inc.

Principal Competitors

Beverly Enterprises Inc.; Life Care Centers; Manor Care Inc.

Further Reading

Birkett, Charles, "Moving into Assisted Living," *Nursing Homes,* February 1996, p. 22.
"Diversicare Inc," *Wall Street Transcript,* May 17, 1993.
"Diversicare Sells Subsidiary to Continue Home-Care Push," *Modern Healthcare,* March 14, 1994, p. 20.
"Dr. Charles W. Birkett," *Wall Street Transcript,* March 31, 1997.
Mallett, Gina and David North, "We Make House Calls," *Canadian Business,* January 1996, p. 73.
Russell, Keith, "Advocat Makes Exec Changes," *Nashville Business Journal,* June 25, 1999.

—Ed Dinger

Aeronca Inc.

1712 Germantown Road
Middletown, Ohio 45042
U.S.A.
Telephone: (513) 422-2751
Toll Free: (800) 991-1387
Fax: (513) 422-0812
Web site: http://www.aeroncainc.com

*Wholly-Owned Subsidiary of Magellan Aerospace
    Corporation*
Incorporated: 1928 as Aeronautical Corporation of
    America
Employees: 225
Sales: $31.92 million (2000 est.)
NAIC: 33251 Hardware Manufacturing; 336412 Aircraft
    Engine and Engine Parts Manufacturing; 336413
    Other Aircraft Parts and Auxiliary Equipment
    Manufacturing; 336415 Guided Missile and Space
    Vehicle Propulsion Unit and Propulsion Unit Parts
    Manufacturing

Once a maker of a famous line of light planes, Aeronca Inc. has developed into a leading sub-contractor specializing in high-tech brazed and conventional aerospace structures. Aeronca has had a part in many of the largest U.S. aircraft programs, including the Space Shuttle and B-1 bomber. Aeronca's product line includes engine and nacelle components, aircraft and space structures, and missile control surfaces.

1928 Origins

Aeronca lays claim to being the first U.S. company to market a true light airplane. The company's C-2 model helped popularize flying in the country; it is in fact credited with launching the U.S. general aviation industry.

Before the C-2, writes Jay Spenser in his history of the ''Flying Bathtub,'' American aircraft manufacturers aimed their products at ''professionals'' and very wealthy ''sportsmen.''

There were no flying clubs as in Europe. However, after the introduction of light planes, flying schools began to proliferate.

The revolutionary plane was unassuming in every detail. Its lines have been compared to that of a pelican or bathtub. Its engine, propeller, and wings were relatively small; the plane's weight was only a little over 400 pounds. However, it was simple to fly and inexpensive to maintain.

French-born designer Jean Roche had conceived the basis for the C-2 as a teenager in New York City. Nevertheless, the search for a manufacturer for his light plane took years, in spite of its patented pivotal airfoil system, which gave it very stable flying characteristics.

The Aeronautical Corporation of America seemed to be the answer to Roche's dream. Incorporated in November 1928, the company's board included such eminent citizens as I.C. Keller of the Dow Chemical and Drug Company and Ohio senator Robert A. Taft, son of the former president. Aeronca, as the firm came to be called, boasted assets of $500,000 but lacked a product, factory, and designer. The board soon chose a headquarters at Cincinnati's new Lunken Airport.

Roche was introduced to the company by his friend Conrad Dietz, an Ohio businessman who had unsuccessfully attempted to sell Aeronca his own design for a bi-plane that the company considered old-fashioned. The fact that Roche had become senior aeronautical engineer for the Army Air Service helped him secure a chance to demonstrate his machine to the company.

Aeronca gave Roche shares in its stock to obtain rights to build the plane. Production began after the company hired a local aviation expert to re-engineer the design for factory production. Aeronca hired factory space from the failing Metal Aircraft Company, then acquired it outright after Metal Aircraft went bankrupt following the stock market crash of October 1929. Roche had contracted Detroit's Govro-Nelson Company to build the engines, which at first produced only 26 horsepower.

Aeronca first publicly introduced the plane in November 1929. Many imaginations were captured with the idea of a plane that cost only $1,495 (this was reduced to $1245 by June

Company Perspectives:

Aeronca consistently is in the industry forefront in the design and manufacture of lightweight, high strength engine and airframe structures. Typically, our products are challenged by the most severe temperature and operating environments.

1931). Aeronca sold 90 aircraft in 1930. In 1931, the company introduced the C-3 "Collegian" or "Duplex" models, which were 36-horsepower, two-seat versions of the single-seat C-2 "Scout."

By the mid-1930s, Aeronca lead the country in making light planes for personal use. Success had its imitators, writes Spenser; the "flivver-plane movement" soon spawned nearly two dozen competitors.

The company officially changed its name to Aeronca in 1941. During World War II it produced many aircraft under license, including the Grasshopper, a light liaison and observation craft; the PT19 and PT23 primary flight trainers; and gliders. The firm also produced parts for the B-17 bomber and C-46 cargo plane.

The Company Exits the Light Plane Business in 1951.

Aeronca introduced several popular small planes for the postwar civilian market, including the Champion, Chief, Super Chief, and Defender. Its Arrow model updated its design tradition by incorporating a low wing and retractable landing gear. Unfortunately, a recession hit the industry hard during the late 1940s. Although production at one point exceeded 50 planes per day, Aeronca left the light plane business in 1951. The company had manufactured 17,408 aircraft of 55 different models in little over twenty years. Ten thousand of the Champion (or Aeronca 7) series were produced in the company's last five years of aircraft production. (Another company, Champion Aircraft, resumed production of this series between 1955 and 1964 under the names Traveler and Challenger.)

Aeronca had already been developing a new specialty: brazing and bonding heat resistant aircraft components. Aeronca's high temperature, brazed honeycomb structures shielded the command modules used in the Apollo lunar space program and, decades later, the Space Shuttle.

Diversification in the 1970s and 1980s

Donald A. Bordlemay was named Aeronca president and CEO in September 1976. He replaced Roy J. Benecchi, who was retiring early due to illness. After posting a net loss of $7.7 million in 1976 on sales of 31.6 million, Aeronca edged $1.4 million into the positive in 1977 as sales rose to $34.5 million. During the year, the company decided to stop manufacturing its line of Microtron air filters and to terminate some contracting operations. In 1976, the company had sold its foreign subsidiary at a loss.

At the time, Aeronca's operations consisted of two segments. One segment included assemblies and sub-assemblies; components and parts for commercial airplanes, military airplanes, and space vehicles; and panels for surface ships, aircraft engines, and general aviation aircraft. The other segment included terminal boxes, air handling, Agitair and other environmental control systems and components.

Aeronca briefly stepped back into the construction of complete aircraft in 1978. That January, the company won a contract from Minneapolis-based Foxjet International to build prototypes for the new Foxjet four-place twin-turbofan-powered business jet. Aeronca had several clients in the business jet industry, including Gates (maker of the Learjet business aircraft), Dassault-Breguet (the Falcon), and Rockwell (the Sabreliner). Delays in production of the Foxjet prototype, which client and builder blamed on each other, resulted in this contract being terminated by October 1978.

Aeronca was headquartered in Charlotte, North Carolina, during the 1980s. President and chief operating officer Joe L. Miller was appointed CEO in March 1981. He added the title of chairman in January 1983.

By August 1981, the company was formulating plans to launch a new microcomputer software division. The new unit was dubbed Execuware. Its Next Step database software, introduced in April 1983, was designed to allow business managers to utilize IBM Personal Computers without relying on computer programmers. The software sold for about $345. Execuware soon came out with client management, real estate analysis, and financial analysis software (priced between $90 and $150).

Aeronca's sales were $43.8 million in 1983. In 1984, Aeronca dropped plans to acquire Continental Scale Corp. of Bridgeview, Illinois, due to a disagreement over price. The company did acquire a four-year-old California operation called CompositAir, which had sales between $2 million and $5 million a year. It developed several new applications for composite materials, such as airline seat components, X-ray tables for the medical industry, and industrial components for the papermaking industry. Aeronca sold CompositAir's assets to Ferro Corp. in March 1987.

Aeronca Joins Fleet in 1986

Aeronca Inc. was acquired by Fleet Aerospace Corp. in September 1986. Fleet, a publicly-traded company based in Toronto, produced a variety of high-tech components for the aerospace industry. Aeronca had initially fought the takeover. In the process, Fleet filed suit challenging an Ohio law that banned suitors from acquiring more than 20 percent of a company's shares without the approval of its stockholders.

Fleet was soon overextended, and began selling off subsidiaries. It sold Aeronca's California operations to Aerostretch Acquisition Inc. in December 1990. In November 1992, Bill J. Wade, president of both Fleet Aerospace and Aeronca, resigned. Earl T. O'Loughlin, a retired USAF general, was then named president of Fleet, while James O. Stine was named executive vice-president and general manager of Aeronca.

Key Dates:

1928: Aeronautical Corporation of America is founded.
1929: The pioneering C-2 light plane is introduced.
1941: The company officially abbreviates its name to Aeronca and enters war production.
1946: Numerous new models of aircraft are brought out after the war.
1951: Aeronca exits light plane production.
1986: Fleet Aerospace (later called Magellan) acquires Aeronca.
2000: Bolstered by new contracts, Aeronca expands its facilities.

In March 1995, the company received a large order from Southwest Airlines to produce aluminum replacement engine fan cowl doors for the airline's fleet of Boeing 737s, which were originally fitted with high-maintenance plastic composite cowl doors. The deal was worth C$21 million to C$28 million. The U.S. Air Force later awarded Aeronca a C$10.4 million ($7.5 million) contract for similar work on its fleet of C-141 military transports. In August 1995, Aeronca won a C$16 million ($12 million) contract from McDonnell Douglas to provide fuselage components for the MD-11 aircraft. The program had a potential total value of C$97 million ($73 million).

The name of Aeronca's parent company changed from Fleet Aerospace Corporation to Magellan Aerospace Corporation in October 1996. Aeronca was also producing components for fighter aircraft and missiles for the U.S. government and Japanese Defense Agency.

In September 1999, Textron Marine & Land Systems awarded Aeronca a contract to produce propeller ducts for an amphibious assault vehicle being developed for foreign sales. Aeronca had already produced ducts for the U.S. Navy's fleet similar vehicles.

Expansion in 2000

Fueled by a new $29 million jet exhaust systems contract, Aeronca began an $11 million, 60,000-square-foot expansion and renovation of its Middletown, Ohio, facilities in 2000. At the same time, the company was tearing down an existing 250,000-square-foot building, freeing another nine acres for development. Aeronca was investing millions to engineer and develop a new exhaust system for the Airbus A340 and brand new A318 aircraft in collaboration with Hispano-Suiza Aerostructures. Aeronca was also fulfilling a similar $23 million follow-up contract for the Boeing 747 and 767 aircraft. The projects were expected to add 75 badly needed high-tech jobs to traditionally blue collar Middletown after years of downsizing by Aeronca. City and state governments were giving Aeronca considerable tax credits in connection with the expansion.

Principal Competitors

BF Goodrich Aerospace; Bombardier Aerospace; Hexcel Corporation; The NORDAM Group; Orkal Industries LLC; Vought Aircraft Industries, Inc.

Further Reading

Abel, Alan, *The Best of Paul Matt: A Collection from the Historical Aviation Albums,* Terre Haute, Ind.: SunShine House, 1988.

''Aeronca May Get Bid for Leveraged Buyout Totaling $18 Million,'' *Wall Street Journal,* August 26, 1985, p. 1.

''Aeronca to Build Foxjet,'' *Aviation Week & Space Technology,* January 23, 1978, p. 18.

Baker, Don, ''Middletown Expansion Set,'' *Dayton Business Journal,* October 13, 2000.

Dodd, Leon P., Jr., ''Aeronca's Flight Towards Continuous Process Improvement,'' *Journal for Quality and Participation* (Cincinnati), October/November 1995.

Downie, Don and Julia Downie, *The Complete Guide to Aeroncas, Citabrias and Decathlons,* Blue Ridge Summit, Pa.: Tab Books, 1984.

Grey, C.G., and Leonard Bridgman, eds., *Jane's All the World's Aircraft, 1931,* London: Sampson, Low, Marston & Company, 1931.

Heck, Mike, ''Know Your Client Knows Its Job,'' *Interface Age, Computing for Business,* March 1984.

——, ''Make Giant Strides with Next Step,'' *Interface Age: Computing for Business,* December 1983.

Hollenbaugh, Bob, *Aeronca: A Photo History,* Aviation Heritage, 1995.

Kemper, Kevin, ''Hook Field Ready to Fly with Growth,'' *Dayton Business Journal,* October 23, 2000.

''New Foxjet Facility,'' *Aviation Week & Space Technology,* October 23, 1978, p. 20.

Renstrom, Roger, ''Southwest Airlines Replacing Plastic Cowls with Aluminum,'' *Plastics News,* April 10, 1995, p. 23.

Smith, G., ''Ever the Champ,'' *Air Progress,* September 1987.

——, ''Flying Bathtub,'' *Air Progress,* June 1987.

Spenser, Jay P., *Aeronca C-2: The Story of the Flying Bathtub,* Washington, D.C.: National Air and Space Museum/Smithsonian Institution Press, 1978.

—Frederick C. Ingram

Air China

Beijing Capital International Airport
Beijing
China
Telephone: 86-10-6456-3201
Fax: 86-10-6456-3831
Web site: http://www.airchina.com.cn

State-Owned Company
Incorporated: 1988
Employees: 15,000
Operating Revenues: $1.38 billion (1997)
NAIC: 481111 Scheduled Passenger Air Transportation;
481112 Scheduled Freight Air Transportation; 48819
Other Support Activities for Air Transportation

Air China is China's principal international airline, and is the designated flag carrier of the People's Republic. Based in the capital of the world's most populous country, the airline has occupied a special place in the hearts of aircraft manufacturers and foreign airlines eager for access to the untapped potential of the Asian market. Air China's logo, made up of the letters "VIP" styled into the form of a phoenix, reflects the carrier's aspirations regarding customer service. The airline flies a young fleet of about 70 planes, carrying about 16 million passengers a year.

Origins

Air China was one of several airlines created out of the Civil Aviation Administration of China (CAAC) in the mid-1980s. This body, and its predecessors the China Civil Aviation Administration (CCAC) and the Chinese Civil Aviation Bureau (CAB), had directed China's civil air service since 1949. At first dependent on Soviet aviation technology, by the 1980s the Chinese were fielding fleets of modern Western jets as they began to compete with Western airlines on international routes.

Difficulty adapting to new marketplace competition and a series of accidents between 1979 and 1983 created pressure for the organization to change. The CAAC was reorganized in late 1984, producing the following four regional divisions: Eastern, Southern, Southwestern, and Northwestern. Air China, based in Beijing, was given chief responsibility for intercontinental flights, and took over the CAAC's long haul aircraft (Boeing 747s, 767s, and 707s, as well as medium-haul 737s) and routes when it was granted its autonomy on July 1, 1988. Because of the commercial importance of Guangzhou (formerly Canton), China Southern was also cleared for international flights, along with Shanghai-based China Eastern.

The CAAC remained in existence as a kind of governmental overseer. It still controlled aircraft purchasing and worked very closely with its newly independent branches. The government also made its voice known to domestic passengers—an official letter of recommendation was a prerequisite for booking a flight until 1993.

At its launch in 1988, Air China operated 32 international routes to 31 destinations, and also connected 30 cities within China. It was China's largest carrier, and the only one allowed to carry China's national flag. In 1989, Air China posted a net profit of $106 million on revenues of $383 million. (The carrier had 6,000 employees at the time.) In that same year, Air China entered a joint venture with Lufthansa German Airlines, which provided 40 percent of the capital, or $220 million, to create the Beijing Aircraft Maintenance Center (Ameco Beijing). It specialized in the upkeep of the Boeing aircraft that comprised Air China's fleet. The venture was expanded with another $218 million (¥1.2 billion) in 1992. Ameco Beijing employed nearly 4,000 people, a little fewer than 50 of them from Lufthansa. *Air Transport World* reported the company preferred to source its needs through joint ventures due to the country's lack of hard currency. Its Beijing Air Catering was 40 percent owned by a large Hong Kong caterer.

Expanding in the 1990s

Air China's president, Xu Bai Ling, had years of experience piloting China's most distinguished visitors. An early priority for the airline was repairing a reputation damaged by delays, cancellations, or poor in-flight service. In the early 1990s, CAAC launched an incentive program to foster improvements. Air China hired consultants from Singapore Airlines, which was

Key Dates:

1984: Civil Aviation Administration of China (CAAC) is reorganized, creating four divisions, one based in Beijing.
1988: Air China becomes autonomous from CAAC.
1989: Lufthansa enters maintenance joint venture with Air China.
1991: CAAC launches incentive program to improve in-flight service and on-time performance.
1994: Operating revenues exceed $1 billion.
1997: CAAC delays Air China IPO due to Asian financial crisis.
1998: Excess capacity leads China's airlines to billions in losses.
2000: Air China chief Wang Li'an's "trans-Millennium" flight garners attention for the airlines as an effective public relations stunt.
2001: CAAC's ten airlines agree on merger plans.

known for its stellar cabin crews. It also hired a few Russian planes and crews to fly certain routes.

Operating revenues for Air China were $1.05 billion in 1994, producing a net income of $36 million. In 1997, the airline reported sales of $1.38 billion (¥11.5 billion). The fleet had grown to 65 aircraft and the carrier was flying 144 routes overall. By October 1997, Air China was planning a public stock offering. China Eastern Airlines and China Southern Airlines had listed on the Hong Kong and New York exchanges earlier in the year. Air China delayed plans based due to poor financial performance and a downturn in business caused by the Asian financial crisis.

Rumors of a state-prompted merger between Air China and China Southern Airlines abounded in 1999. By this time, China Southern, based in the commercial center of Guangzhou, had become the country's largest carrier. At the time, China had 30 airlines, and Beijing wanted to group them into several, more globally competitive units. Altogether, mainland airlines lost more than ¥6 billion in 1998. *Flight International* observed that a merger with China Southern could give Air China access to the Hong Kong and New York stock markets.

About 16 million passengers flew Air China in 1998. The October 1999 opening of a new terminal at Beijing Capital International Airport, where Air China operated the vast majority of flights, promised not only to relieve travelers of cramped conditions but also to allow Air China to devote more resources to its lucrative ground handling business for international carriers. One-fifth of Air China's 15,000 employees worked in ground handling.

Although the Chinese aviation industry as a whole was expected to earn ¥1 billion ($120 million) in profits in 1999, Air China and other individual airlines were struggling to break even and mitigate their collective losses of 1998, which totaled $300 million. Air China was not publicly traded and was not quite as open with its own sales figures as China Eastern and China Southern.

New Frontiers in the New Millennium

To demonstrate the airline's faith in its Y2K preparations, Air China chief Wang Li'an and several other top officers personally piloted several flights at the turn of the millennium. As reported in the *China Daily,* this decision generated a considerable amount of positive publicity in China. Wang had worked for the CAAC for more than 40 years before being appointed Air China's director-general in early 1999.

Early in 2000, Air China teamed with China National Aviation Co. Group (CNAC), the CAAC's Hong Kong-listed commercial arm, to establish a Hong Kong branch (95% owned by Air China). Direct flights to London from Hong Kong soon began. Air China faced competition at its home base from Air France, which increased its four flights a week to Beijing, begun in 1997, to daily service. British Airways also wanted to increase its frequencies (it was operating 18 flights a week to China).

In mid-2000, the CAAC repeated earlier calls for a consolidation of the ten airlines it controlled into three. (Air China, China Southern, and China Eastern were to each acquire the smaller airlines.) Apart from the ten CAAC airlines, there were another 24 smaller carriers that had been formed by provincial or private interests.) Price wars had proved so destructive that the government banned discounting. However, no deadlines or plans for financial support for ailing carriers were made. To aggravate the airlines' financial troubles, the CAAC blocked a proposed merger in September 2000 between Air China and China Southern on anti-competitive grounds.

In January 2001, the CAAC's ten airlines announced they had agreed on a merger plan. Air China was to acquire China Southwest Airlines and China International Airlines, the country's fourth strongest domestic airline. This was to create a group with assets of ¥56 billion (HK$ 52.5 billion), including 118 aircraft.

Air China had completely dropped plans to merge with China Southern and was soon reported to be planning its own

$500 million floatation on the New York and Hong Kong stock markets. The funding was to help Air China, which had been eclipsed in recent years by China Eastern and China Southern, to grow sufficiently enough to justify its status as a national flag carrier.

Later in the year, the influential Star Alliance, founded by United Air Lines and Lufthansa, was reported to be considering inviting Air China to join in the alliance. This would raise Air China's profile considerably, as well as connecting to the world's largest network of air routes, reported the *South China Morning Post.* However, China's airlines were negatively impacted by the September 11, 2001 terrorist attack on New York and Washington. According to China Eastern chairman Ye Yigan, the incident was expected to cost the top three airlines ¥3.35 billion ($405 million) due to a drop in passenger demand and higher operating costs.

Principal Competitors

Cathay Pacific Airways Limited; China Eastern Airlines Corporation Limited; China Southern Airlines Company Limited.

Further Reading

"Air China Launches New Service, Works on Image," *USA Today,* October 9, 1991, p. 8B.

"Air China to Stand Alone," *Airfinance Journal,* March 1995, p. 8.

Bangsberg, P.T., "Lufthansa, China Plan More Funds for Aircraft Maintenance Venture," *Journal of Commerce,* June 24, 1992, p. 2B.

Bradbury, Nicholas, "Troubled But Hopeful," *Asset Finance & Leasing Digest,* June 1994, p. 23.

"CAAC Blocks China Southern Merger with Air China," *AFX-Asia,* September 28, 2000.

Chan, Christine, "Link-Up Possible Between Mainland Flagship and Southern Airline; Rumours Fly of Giant Merger," *South China Morning Post,* Bus. Sec., July 9, 1999, p. 4.

Chang, Leslie, "China Intends to Merge 10 Airlines Into Three," *Wall Street Journal,* July 24, 2000, p. A21.

"China: Person of the Week; Making the Trans-Millennium Flight, Wang Creates a Marketable Image," *China Daily,* December 12, 1999, p. 8.

Davies, R.E.G., "Airlines of the New China," *Airlines of Asia Since 1920,* London: Putnam Aeronautical Books; McLean, Va.: Paladwr Press, 1997, pp. 403–24.

Flynn, Ann Amelia, "China's Airlines Take Wing," *China Business Review* (Washington), May/June 1993, p. 14.

Harding, James, "Air China Plans Overseas Float," *Financial Times* (London), October 15, 1997.

Holland, Tom, "China Break-In," *Far Eastern Economic Review,* October 25, 2001, p. 41.

"It's a Jungle Up There: China Tries to Tame Its Unruly Aviation Sector," *ChinaOnline,* October 25, 2000.

Lo, Joseph, "Star Alliance Beckons Air China," *South China Morning Post,* Bus. Sec., May 24, 2001, p. 2.

McGregor, Richard, "Call for Mergers Leaves Chinese Carriers Up in the Air," *Financial Times* (London), August 1, 2000.

Ng, Eric, "Air China Set to Announce Lead Bank for Listing," *South China Morning Post,* Bus. Sec., July 16, 2001, p. 4.

"Rise of the Phoenix," *Ground Handling International,* July 1999, p. 55.

"Ten Chinese Airlines Prepare for Takeoff of Mergers, Alliances," *China Online,* January 11, 2001.

Vandyk, Anthony, "Air China: New Name, New Heights," *Air Transport World,* February 1991, p. 54.

—Frederick C. Ingram

Aldila Inc.

12140 Community Road
Poway, California 92064
U.S.A.
Telephone: (858) 513-1801
Fax: (858) 513-1870
Web site: http://www.aldila.com

Public Company
Incorporated: 1972
Employees: 1,250
Sales: $39.6 million (2001)
Stock Exchanges: NASDAQ
Ticker Symbol: ALDA
NAIC: 33992 Sporting and Athletic Goods Manufacturing

Aldila Inc. has been one of the world's leading producer of graphite composite golf club shafts since the early 1970s. It manufactures hundreds of different shaft models, many of them custom-designed for specific golf club manufacturers. Aldila's customers, which include industry leaders such as Callaway, Taylor Made, Ping, and Titleist. Since 1994, Aldila has itself produced much of the graphite prepreg used in the manufacture of its shafts. Since 1998, the company has operated a facility in Evanston, Wyoming, that produces carbon fiber, one of the raw materials the company utilizes in its shafts. Although much of the carbon fiber the firm makes is used in the manufacture of its own products, Aldila also sells some of it to third parties. Aldila participates in a joint venture with SGL Carbon Group to produce carbon fiber. Calloway Golf president Richard C. Helmstetter once described Aldila as one of the graphite shaft industry's "very first and true innovators."

Company Beginnings

Aldila was founded in 1972 by Jim Flood, a man who has been called the Thomas Edison of modern golf. In addition to the graphite golf shaft, Flood also invented the Basakwerd putter, the Power Pod, Slinger Irons, and an automatic head maker for woods. Flood was already working with golf equipment as an eighth grader working at the Cherry Hills Country Club near Denver, Colorado, where he performed minor repair work on clubs that members had damaged. By 1960, he had begun working as an investment broker, but his interest in golf remained unabated. Eventually he moved to San Diego, where a friend happened to describe graphite composite, a light, strong, flexible metal used to make the wings of the F-111 fighter plane. Flood's interest was piqued—his first thought was that the material would probably make excellent golf club shafts. It would produce a shaft that was much lighter than the steel ones that were used almost universally. He obtained some graphite samples and began tinkering with ideas for a new golf club, using fishing rods, glue, and his daughter's hair drier. Flood has no training in engineering, and when he formed his new company to introduce his first graphite shaft in April 1972, none of his employees did either. Products were designed relying on trial and error.

The new company, Aldila Inc., took its name from an Italian song of the 1960s that translated roughly as "far beyond." At first the firm was little more than a workshop, ringing up about $36,000 in sales during its first year of operations. The turning point came when Flood set up an Aldila booth at a golf trade show in Florida. Working his booth by himself, he there spoke with a Japanese man who said he wanted to buy gold club shafts. How many, Flood asked? Ten thousand, the Japanese man replied. The large order forced Aldila to grow quickly. Within a few weeks the number of employees grew from 15 to 150, while the company's production space had to be boosted from 1,500 square feet to 30,000, and not much later to 60,000. Its annual sales soon jumped to $12.5 million.

New Owners and Hard Times

Jim Flood was interested in creating innovative golf equipment, not in managing a multi-million dollar business, and in 1975 he sold Aldila to John Moler and John Hine, Sr. During the late 1970s and 1980s the company experienced difficulty making its product profitable. The new graphite shafts had a tendency to break when striking the ball, and their design thus had to be improved. There was resistance from professional players to graphite shafts for a number of years as well, which in turn slowed their acceptance among the mass-market for golf equipment. Another hindrance to widespread popularity of graphite clubs was their hefty price tag in the early years. In 1988, Aldila was sold again, this time to two Chicago investors, Gary Barbera and Vince Gorguze, a takeover specialist who had already acquired a number of small to mid-sized companies.

In the late 1980s, metal woods caught on among golfers, a trend that marked another turning point for the firm. Metal heads were heavier than traditional wood heads, which meant a lighter shaft was needed. Graphite shafts fit the bill. Manufactured using eight to sixteen sheets of a hybrid comprised of graphite polymers, plastics, epoxy, and rare elements like boron, the sheets wrapped around a metal core and were then oven-treated. The resulting shafts were much lighter than traditional steel-shafted clubs. As a result, golfers could swing the clubs faster, and the extra speed was transmitted to the ball, which consequently traveled a greater distance. By that time, graphite shaft technology had reached a stage of development where professional players were willing to use them. By the end of the 1980s, Aldila's credibility was further boosted by endorsements it received from golf pros Payne Stewart and Nancy Lopez. In the first six months of 1988, Aldila had sales of almost $4 million. So attractive were the properties of graphite that Aldila hoped to introduce other products that utilized it, such as baseball bats and bicycle frames. Another decade would pass before the first of those products would materialize.

By 1991, Aldila's annual sales had climbed to more than $40 million. Although sales of golf equipment were beginning to slump nationwide, Aldila's workforce of 500, up from 200 in 1988, was producing at full capacity. The firm had over 2,400 customers, which included many of the most famous golf club manufacturers, including Taylor Made, Karsten, Wilson, Spalding, and Callaway Golf, the maker of the Big Bertha driver. As the 1990s began, the company had claimed over 50 percent of the graphite shaft market in the United States.

Public Offering and Expanded Operations

Aldila was sold for a third time in January 1992 to DJ-Forstmann Little & Co., the nation's second largest leveraged buyout firm. Based in New York City, Forstmann, which owned a portfolio of companies such as sports card maker Topps, General Instrument (a manufacturer of high tech equipment), and Gulfstream Aerospace, paid $83.1 million for the company and left the old management team in place. In April 1993, Forstmann announced that Aldila would make an initial public offering of 2.3 million shares. Forstmann would continue to hold about 59.1 percent of Aldila's outstanding shares and the management team approximately 11.5 percent. The proceeds from the offering were to be used to pay off much of the

$31 million bank debt Forstmann incurred when it bought Aldila. Analysts at the time saw Aldila as a standout offering at a time when many less than desirable companies were going public. The only question mark was Aldila's large accounts receivable, which had grown from $171,000 in 1992 to $3.27 million in 1993.

The stock was first offered on the NASDAQ in June 1993 with an opening price of $14 a share. Within the first two days of trading, the company's share price rose 52 percent to $21.25, and by mid-September it reached $31.50. So bullish was Aldila's stock that, in January 1993, the company's board of directors approved a two-for-one stock split. Aldila's sales rose in 1993 as well, reaching $62.6 million, an increase of 31 percent from the previous year. As the 1994 fiscal year got under way, Aldila was predicting a year of 20 percent growth. In 1994, Aldila started manufacturing the sheets of graphite for its shaft production rather than purchasing them from on outside vendor. The firm, which by then was using nearly four percent of the world's carbon fiber, also hoped to be able to create other products that used this material. As part of the plan, the company began shopping around in Utah and Wyoming for a site to build a facility to produce the carbon fiber it needed for its shaft production.

Golf Industry Slump of the Mid-1990s

The company's fortunes took a downturn in July 1994. The price of Aldila stock began to drop when rumors began making the rounds that Callaway Golf Co., the maker of the popular Big Bertha driver and a company that purchased nearly all of its graphite shafts from Aldila, was going to start buying a significant number of its shafts from other manufacturers. Callaway denied the rumors, saying it expected Aldila to remain its biggest supplier of shafts. However, six months later, in January 1995, Callaway formally announced it was sharply cutting its orders from Aldila, a move that sent Aldila's stock into a plunge that saw its value cut in half, from $10 to $5 in a single day. In July the firm made up some of its lost ground when it signed a three-year contract to produce 80,000 shafts a month for Taylor Made Golf's Burner Bubble metalwoods. Aldila's sales suffered nonetheless in 1995, dropping to $56.5 million from $79.8 million in 1994. Sales recovered slightly in 1996, rising to $58.4 million.

In May 1996, Aldila finalized a deal to purchase G. Loomis Products, a Woodland, Washington-based company, for an undisclosed amount. Loomis, the top maker of graphite shafts for irons used by players on the Professional Golf Association tour (Aldila was the number one maker of graphite shafts for woods on the tour), also made fishing rods, fishing rod blanks, and other tubular structures. The acquisition came because Aldila was looking to expand its technology base. Purchasing Loomis presented an opportunity to do that without the time and cost of developing it in-house. In May 1997, Aldila announced that Evanston, Wyoming, would be the site of its new 50,000-square-foot manufacturing plant, which would employ about forty workers. Production of carbon fiber began in early 1998.

Aldila sales dropped again in 1997 to $55.7 million. In response to the decline, the Aldila board of Directors passed a plan in November 1997 to close the company's operations and

Key Dates:

1972: Aldila Inc. is founded.
1975: Aldila is sold to John Moler and John Hine, Sr.
1988: Gary Barbera and Vince Gorguze purchase the company.
1992: Aldila is acquired by the DJ-Forstmann Little & Co.
1993: Company goes public.
1994: Aldila begins producing graphite composite for its golf club shafts.
1996: Aldila acquires G. Loomis Products.
1997: Aldila begins construction of plant to manufacture carbon fiber in Evanston, Wyoming.
1997: Headquarters and company operations are consolidated in Poway, California.
1998: SGL Carbon Group acquires a 50 percent interest in Aldila; the two companies form joint venture for production of carbon fiber.

headquarters in Rancho Bernardo, California, and consolidate everything at its facility in Poway, where graphite fiber production was handled. SGL Carbon Group, the world's largest producer of carbon and steel products, acquired a 50 percent interest in Aldila's carbon fiber subsidiary for about $7 million in cash. The purchase was intended to forge a partnership that would enable Aldila to manufacture more carbon fiber. The companies' joint venture, formed to produce products for recreation, industry, and aerospace, was based at Aldila's Evanston plant. Around the time the deal was being made, Aldila was briefly implicated in an investigation by the U.S. Justice Department into price-fixing in the graphite industry. The investigation focused on an alleged artificial shortage of graphite in the early 1990s created to inflate prices. Aldila, however, had not begun making its own carbon fiber until 1994 and used most of its production to make golf club shafts. Although the company was subpoenaed in the investigation, the government gave it a verbal assurance that it would not be targeted by the grand jury. On the other hand, SGL Carbon, Aldila's joint venture partner, pled guilty to price-fixing and was fined a record $135 million.

By 1999 the golf industry was beginning to pull out of a slump that had plagued it since the mid-1990s. Aldila's sales, however, continued to decline in 1999, dropping by over 25 percent, from $62.5 million in 1998 to $45.1 million. In 2000, however, the firm was buoyed, posting $55.9 in sales. That same year, the company had a record 46 percent increase in golf club shaft shipments, and in the first quarter of 2001 it managed to nearly double its earnings from the same quarter of the previous year. Moreover, Aldila finally began to diversify its

product line, producing hockey sticks in 2000. Still, challenges ensued in 2001, with sales again falling, to $39.6 million. Despite a less than attractive financial showing, the company, now debt free, remained optimistic and proud in particular of its product line, including the new Aldila ONE shaft.

Principal Subsidiaries

Carbon Fiber Technology LLC.

Principal Competitors

Royal Precision Inc.; True Temper Sports; Toray Industries, Inc.

Further Reading

"Aldila and SGL Carbon Complete Joint Venture to Produce Large Tow Carbon," *Business Wire,* November 1, 1999.

"Aldila Files 2.3 Million Share Initial Public Offering," *PR Newswire,* April 23, 1993.

"Aldila Inc. Sold to Forstmann," *San Diego Union-Tribune,* December 17, 1991.

"Aldila Says Not Target Of Fed's Carbon Fiber Investigation," *Dow Jones Business News,* August 25, 1999.

Antilla, Susan, "Forstmann Little's Next Coup?" *New York Times,* May 2, 1993, pp.C3, C15.

Bauder, Don, "Callaway-Aldila Rumor Stinks," *San Diego Union-Tribune,* March 17, 1995, p. C3.

Brown, Michael, "Aldila Down For Second Day Amid Market Rumors," *Dow Jones News Service–Ticker,* July 5, 1994.

Cushman, Tom, "Off-the-wall Inventions by Flood Are Par None in His Golf Laboratory," *San Diego Union-Tribune,* February 5, 1992.

Faust, Fred, "Zoltek Sues Engineer Over Trade Secret Dispute," *St. Louis Post-Dispatch,* May 5, 1997.

"Forstmann Little Closes Buy Of Golf Club Shaft Manufacturer," *Dow Jones News Service—Ticker,* January 13, 1992.

Riggs, Rod, "Aldila to Buy Golf-shaft Maker Loomis," *San Diego Union-Tribune,* p.C2.

"Shares Of Aldila Rise 52% On First Day Of Trading," *New York Times,* June 9, 1993, p. D3.

Sloan, Allan, "Quiet Killing vs. a Noisy Beating," *Newsday,* May 2, 1993, p. 84.

Spaulding, Richard, "Aldila, Golf-Club Shaft Maker, Sold to Two Chicago Investors," *San Diego Union-Tribune,* September 26, 1988.

"Taylor Made, Aldila Sign Letter of Intent for Manufacture of Bubble Shafts for Woods and Irons," *Business Wire,* July 19, 1995.

"Three Golf Firms Tee Up Stock Issues; Hoping to Ride Winning Streak," *St. Louis Post-Dispatch,* September 15, 1993, p. C8.

"2.3 Million Share Of Aldila Common Stock Priced At $14 Per Share in Initial Public Offering," *PR Newswire,* June 7, 1993.

—Gerald E. Brennan

ALLTEL Corporation

One Allied Drive
Little Rock, Arkansas 72202
U.S.A.
Telephone: (501) 905-8000
Fax: (501) 905-5444
Web site: http://www.alltel.com

Public Company
Incorporated: 1960 as Mid-Continent Telephone
    Corporation
Employees: 27,257
Sales: $7.6 billion (2001)
Stock Exchanges: New York Pacific
Ticker Symbol: AT
NAIC: 51331 Wired Telecommunications Carriers;
    513322 Cellular and Other Wireless
    Telecommunications; 513321 Paging

The ALLTEL Corporation is a telecommunications conglomerate that provides bundled services, including local telephone, wireless, long-distance, paging, and Internet services to over 10 million customers in 24 states. As the sixth-largest local telephone company in the United States, ALLTEL provides local service to more than 2.6 million customers in the Southeast and Midwest regions of the United States. The firm also operates as the nation's seventh-largest wireless concern with 6.6 million customers. Along with is telecommunication activities, the company provides financial services, operations management and networking solutions, and publishes telephone directories. ALLTEL got its start as a grouping of local Ohio telephone companies that branched out to other fields after the deregulation of the telephone industry in the 1980s. The firm then grew rapidly during the 1990s through a series of strategic acquisitions.

Early History

The company that became ALLTEL was founded in 1960 by Weldon W. Case, whose grandfather, Weldon Wood, had founded the Hudson Underground Telephone Company of Hud-

son, Ohio. Wood bought the town's two existing telephone companies with his savings and a $25,000 bond sold to local businessmen; he merged the companies in 1910. Case's father went into Wood's business, and Case's first job, in 1934, was as a member of a line construction crew. During World War II, Case served in the Army Signal Corps, and upon his return he became manager of the family business, at that time called Western Reserve Telephone Company. While he was away, his family's holdings had been augmented by the West Richfield Telephone Company, whose owner had been unable to staff it adequately and had been forced to sell.

In the late 1940s, under Case's supervision, the Western Reserve Telephone Company introduced dial service in Aurora, Ohio. By 1954, the company had added automatic dialing for long-distance calls. Two years later the company made its first move to expand when it purchased 15 percent of the Elyria Telephone Company of Elyria, Ohio, a concern almost twice as large as Western Reserve. Case was put in charge of managing this company and served in that capacity for the next ten years.

In 1960, Case decided to merge the Western Reserve and Elyria holdings, creating a company with the explicit intention of purchasing other telephone properties. After the American Telephone & Telegraph Company (AT&T) objected to Case's idea of calling the new company the Mid-America Telephone System, the company was named Mid-Continent Telephone Corporation. The new enterprise kept its home base in Hudson, Ohio.

Mid-Continent joined five small Ohio telephone companies, which served a total of 50,000 customers. Although the new company assembled a central administrative staff of specialists in public relations, engineering, finance, and other fields, the bulk of the work of running the individual phone companies was left up to the local employees. The company's subsidiaries consequently were able to preserve their autonomy, and the build-up of a large central bureaucracy was prevented.

During the 1960s, Mid-Continent multiplied by ten the number of phones it served, as the company's size doubled regularly at three-year intervals. Most of this growth came through acquisitions, as the company bought 90 other telephone companies in its first 20 years in existence. By the end of the 1970s, Mid-Continent served 700,000 customers in 13 states. It had become the country's fifth-largest independent telephone network. In addition, the company had acquired two small cable television concerns.

During the time that Mid-Continent was growing rapidly, another telephone company in the Midwest was also building a network of holdings. The Allied Telephone Company of Little Rock, Arkansas, had been founded by Hugh Wilbourn and Charles Miller, who had worked as contractors in the telephone business in the early 1940s. In 1943, they purchased the Grant County Telephone Company, which operated a toll line that ran from Sheridan to Pine Bluff, Arkansas, connecting 275 magneto telephones. After World War II, Wilbourn and Miller put together a network of four small telephone operating companies in Arkansas. During the next 30 years a steady stream of acquisitions helped Allied expand to serve customers in six states.

The Formation of ALLTEL Corporation: 1983

Both Allied and Mid-Continent had entered unregulated areas of the telecommunications industry, and their activities fit well together. Given these factors, the companies decided to join forces. Mid-Continent and Allied merged on October 25, 1983, and the new enterprise was named the ALLTEL Corporation. ALLTEL began with assets of $1.35 billion, making it the fifth-largest American telephone company. The company expected consolidated revenues of $600 million. Case, who had been president of Mid-Continent, became chairman and chief executive officer of ALLTEL, and his counterpart at Allied, Joe T. Ford, became the company's president.

ALLTEL's formation came at a time of transition in the telephone industry. At roughly the same time that the company began, AT&T—the giant company that had dominated the American phone industry for much of its history—was broken up into eight smaller companies under court order. This opened up a broad spectrum of new opportunities and services, both regulated and unregulated, to companies in the telephone industry. In some ways, the transformation of the industry provided a more challenging business environment. Telephone companies now faced competition in areas where they never had before. For instance, the sale of telephone equipment and the sale of long distance service were now businesses hotly contested by a number of entrants in the field. In order to remain profitable and grow in the face of this encroachment into the company's traditional fields of operation, ALLTEL's leaders determined that the company must diversify its operations in the telecommunications field.

Growth Through Diversification: 1980s

The company started out with some assets to build on. In addition to its fledgling cable television operation, ALLTEL got interests in the manufacture of telecommunications supplies from Mid-Continent and Allied; it also inherited Mid-Continent's $10 million investment in the Argo Communications Corporation, a new domestic and international telecommunications common carrier. With the greater financial strength that it commanded after its merger, the company planned to increase its holdings in non-regulated areas of the telephone industry, taking advantage of technological breakthroughs to offer services such as mobile phones based on cellular radio. The company looked to diversify its operations through acquisitions. "We'll keep examining opportunities as they present themselves," Case told the *Wall Street Journal,* "either in the regulated or non-regulated part of the business."

In making purchases, ALLTEL sought out properties in fields and geographical areas that the company already knew well—areas where it was confident that it could provide sound management and high-quality service. In addition, of course, ALLTEL sought out enterprises that would provide a good rate of return on its investment.

In the months following the company's creation, ALLTEL continued to make acquisitions in its traditional field of operation, buying three West Virginia local telephone companies to add to the service area of its subsidiary Mountain State Telephone Company. In 1984, the company bought three Pennsylvania telephone networks and merged them into its Brookville Telephone Company. ALLTEL thereby fostered growth in its local telephone operations, which are subject to regulation and are the unglamorous mainstay of its business. ALLTEL also continued to upgrade the quality and efficiency of its local telephone network, investing $160 million in switching equipment in 1985 alone.

By 1985, ALLTEL's non-regulated activities included its subsidiary ALLTEL Mobile Communications, which offered cellular phones and wide area paging in 11 major cities, including Cleveland, Ohio; Detroit, Michigan; Pittsburgh, Pennsylvania; and Charlotte, North Carolina. In September of 1985, this unit purchased the MCI Communications Corporation's MCI Airsignal, Inc., a radio paging system based in northern Ohio.

The company's most profitable subsidiary was ALLTEL Supply, Inc. Based in Atlanta, Georgia, this company acted as a distributor of telecommunications equipment across the country, dispensing the products of more than 500 manufacturers. In addition, ALLTEL profited from its ALLTEL Publishing unit. This company coordinated the sales, advertising, printing, and distribution of 119 local telephone directories in nearly 20 states.

Within three years of its founding, ALLTEL had also made major investments in several parts of the telecommunications industry with emerging technologies and fast-growth potential. By buying into these ventures instead of starting its own operations in these fields, or taking others over completely, the company minimized its risk by refraining from a large investment of capital. In addition to its holdings in the Argo long-distance company, ALLTEL became part owner of the Lite and Microtel long-distance companies, which made use of fiber-optic tech-

Key Dates:

1960: Weldon W. Case forms Mid-Continent Telephone Corporation.

1983: The company merges with The Allied Telephone Company; the new company is named ALLTEL Corporation.

1985: ALLTEL continues expansion efforts and acquires MCI Airsignal Inc.

1992: ALLTEL buys Computer Power Inc. and begins mortgage processing.

1996: The Telecommunications Act of 1996 is passed; the company begins offering long-distance service.

1999: ALLTEL completes its $1.8 billion purchase of Aliant Communications Inc.

2001: ALLTEL buys 600,000 telephone lines in Kentucky from Verizon Communications Inc.

nology and satellite transmission. The company also purchased nine percent of the shares of Comdial—an enterprise in Charlottesville, Virginia, that used robots to manufacture phones—and eight percent of the stock of Telecom Plus International—an independent installer and supplier of business phone systems. In addition, ALLTEL owned a minority interest in ten of its competitors in the mobile cellular phone industry.

Although ALLTEL's president told a group of investors in late 1986 that the company was no longer aggressively seeking new businesses in non-regulated fields at that time, the company did continue to add to its current holdings. In 1987, ALLTEL acquired radio paging services covering Ohio and Kentucky, which it later sold. In the following year, the company bought CP National, a West Coast-based telephone operations and military communications firm, for around $300 million. With this extension of its services, the company now provided 1.2 million telephone lines in 25 states.

Also in that year the company added to its cellular holdings when it purchased Cellular America. In 1989, ALLTEL signed an agreement to merge with the HWC Distribution Corporation, an electric wire and cable supply concern. The company spent $143 million to acquire the property, which complemented its ALLTEL Supply, Inc. subsidiary. The steady pace of major purchases continued when ALLTEL branched out from its core telecommunications interests to buy into the information processing business, purchasing Systematics, a manufacturer of computer software for financial institutions, for $528 million in May of 1990. Ten months later the company announced that it would merge its own data processing functions into the new company. In addition to these expenditures, the company announced that it would spend more than $200 million to upgrade its local telephone operations.

Cellular Communications and Information Services: Early to Mid-1990s

In 1991, four years after company founder Case stepped down as ALLTEL's chief executive officer, making Ford its chairman as well as president, ALLTEL announced that it would switch its corporate headquarters from Hudson, Ohio, the small town that had been Case's lifelong home, to Little Rock, Arkansas, the historical base of Ford's company, Allied Telephone. By this time, growth in ALLTEL's core businesses had begun to slow, although the company's profits overall remained strong. The recession of the early 1990s reduced returns from ALLTEL's local telephone operations, in particular after the company suffered several negative regulatory decisions finding that ALLTEL had earned more than its allowed rate of return in several states. In addition, profits from the company's equipment distribution business slumped in 1991.

In response to these factors, ALLTEL began to look elsewhere for its future earnings growth. The company focused on two fields: cellular communications and information services. With Systematics, its subsidiary in information services, ALLTEL controlled the industry leader in software development and the management of data-processing services. In addition to its thriving United States business—running back-offices for banks—the company began to seek out clients overseas. To further enhance its activities in this field, ALLTEL purchased Computer Power, another data processing firm that specialized in mortgage processing, for $270 million in 1992. Although revenues from this sector of the company's business grew quickly, high costs associated with ALLTEL's entry into the field kept profits down.

In its cellular operations, ALLTEL continued to acquire new networks, and the company also moved to link the holdings it did have, joining areas of coverage in Sunbelt cities with the less populated areas around them. Since the company found that customers were less likely to make calls on their cellular car phones when they were deep within urban areas and coping with increased traffic and congestion, ALLTEL expanded its route along major interstates, finding success on the roads leading south from Atlanta to Florida, and from Little Rock to Dallas. Due in part to these moves, ALLTEL's number of cellular phone users increased dramatically in 1991. By the end of that year, operations outside the local telephone market accounted for more than half of ALLTEL's revenues. In 1993, the firm opened its first wireless retail store.

The company continued to strategically position itself in the increasingly competitive telecommunications industry into the mid 1990s. Indeed, The Telecommunications Act of 1996 gave way to increased competition at the regional level. As such, the company bolstered its offerings, and in 1996 the firm branched out into providing long-distance services. The following year, the company began to offer its Little Rock customers bundled services by merging its long-distance, wireless, and Internet business operations into one unit, ALLTEL Communications. During 1998, it also began competing with regional Bell operating firms in various markets by offering local phone services to businesses as a competitive local exchange carrier (CLEC).

Strategic Acquisitions: Late 1990s and Beyond

The company also began to grow rapidly by making a series of key acquisitions. To further strengthen its wireless holdings, ALLTEL purchased 360 Communications Co. in 1998 for $4.2 billion. The deal gave ALLTEL access to wireless markets in certain parts of Virginia and North Carolina as well as in the

Midwest, Nevada, and parts of New Mexico. A company spokesperson commented on the acquisition in an *Arkansas Business* article, claiming that the two companies fit "like hand in glove." Indeed, by combining assets, ALLTEL tripled its cellular customer base and became the seventh-largest wireless provider with revenues of nearly $5 billion.

The purchase attracted industry acclaim for both Ford and the company. Ford was named *Arkansas Business* magazine's "Newsmaker of the Year" while ALLTEL was ranked 49th in *Business Week*'s "100 Best Performing Information Technology Companies in the World." Several acquisitions followed after the 360 deal. During 1999, Aliant Communications Inc. was purchased for $1.4 billion and added Nebraska to ALLTEL's growing list of states that it serviced. The firm also bought Georgia-based Standard Group Inc., BellSouth Mobility's Alabama-based wireless operations, Liberty Cellular of Kansas, and Colorado-based Durango Cellular Telephone Company. By now, ALLTEL's coverage area had grown to include 24 states and its revenues had reached $6.3 billion.

ALLTEL entered the new millennium on solid ground. During 2000, Bell Atlantic and GTE Corp. were forced to divest certain operations in order to complete their merger, which formed Verizon Communications Inc. As such, ALLTEL formed a wireless exchange with the two companies in 13 states, which added 690,000 new clients to its growing customer base. The firm also acquired additional wireless customers in Louisiana from SBC Communications Inc. in a deal that expanded its reach along the Gulf Coast. In 2001, ALLTEL acquired nearly 600,000 Verizon customers in Kentucky for $1.9 billion.

ALLTEL then made an ambitious and unsolicited attempt that year to acquire CenturyTel Inc., but the competitor privately refused the offer. ALLTEL then went public with its bid in hopes of promoting shareholder negotiation. CenturyTel however, publicly refused the offer a second time. Nevertheless, ALLTEL left its offer on the table in hopes that a deal would come to fruition and position ALLTEL as one of the leading telecommunications providers in the United States.

At that time, the telecommunications industry as a whole appeared to be ripe for consolidation and increased merger activity as the Federal Communications Commission (FCC) began to loosen regulations on the amount of spectrum a carrier could own in an area. According to a November 2001 *Business Week* article, "Many wireless service providers have been bumping up against the capacity limits of their systems within existing spectrum allocations. This electromagnetic spectrum used to transmit voice calls and data is getting crowded. The result: service glitches that result in dropped calls and service complaints." New FCC rulings would bump current spectrum allocations from 45 megahertz (Mhz) to 55 Mhz. This had the potential to entice wireless providers to combine forces to increase their spectrum holdings, especially as wireless data applications—including e-mail, text messaging, and wireless Web access, which required increased spectrum—became increasingly popular and attractive to those customers who had typically been using wireless phones for voice applications. In fact, Morgan Stanley predicted that the U.S. wireless industry

would grow from $53 billion in 2000 to $98 billion in 2003 as more customers demanded wireless data services.

While ALLTEL continued to look for promising alliances and lucrative acquisitions, many analysts began to speculate that ALLTEL itself would become a takeover target. Its revenues were climbing towards the $8 billion mark after it had substantially increased its holdings through merger and acquisition activity over the past several years. Whether ALLTEL would continue to grow independently through acquisition or by way of a merger or takeover, however, remained to be seen.

Principal Subsidiaries

ALLTEL Alabama, Inc.; ALLTEL Arkansas, Inc.; ALLTEL Carolina, Inc.; ALLTEL Communications, Inc.; ALLTEL Communications Service Corporation; ALLTEL Florida, Inc.; ALLTEL Georgia, Inc.; ALLTEL Georgia Communications Corp.; ALLTEL Kentucky, Inc.; ALLTEL Mississippi, Inc.; ALLTEL Missouri, Inc.; ALLTEL Mobile Communications, Inc.; ALLTEL Mobile Communications of the Carolinas, Inc.; ALLTEL New York, Inc.; ALLTEL Ohio, Inc.; ALLTEL Oklahoma, Inc.; ALLTEL Pennsylvania, Inc.; ALLTEL South Carolina, Inc.; ALLTEL Wireless Holdings, L.L.C.; 360 Communications Company; 360 Communications Company Investment Company; 360 Paging, Inc.; Aliant Cellular, Inc.; Aliant Communications Co.; Aliant Wireless Holdings, Inc.; Baton Rouge Cellular Telephone Company; Cellularfone, Inc.; Centel Cellular Company of Laredo; Empire Cellular, Inc.; Georgia ALLTELCOM Co.; Georgia ALLTEL Telecom, Inc.; Georgia Telephone Corporation; KIN Network, Inc.; Liberty Cellular, Inc.; Louisiana Cellular Services, Inc.; Radiofone, Inc.; Standard Group, Inc.; Teleview, Inc.; The Western Reserve Telephone Company; Wireless Telecom, Inc.; ALLTEL Communications Products, Inc.; ALLTEL Communications Products International, Inc.; ALLTEL Corporate Services, Inc.; ALLTEL Distribution, Inc.; ALLTEL Holding, Inc.; ALLTEL International Holdings, Inc.; ALLTEL Investments, Inc.; ALLTEL Management Corporation; ALLTEL Mauritius Holdings, Inc.; ALLTEL Publishing Corporation; ALLTEL Publishing Listing Management Corporation; ALLTEL Information Services, Inc.; ALLTEL Information Services Limited (United Kingdom); ALLTEL International Resource Management, Inc.; ALLTEL Mortgage Solutions Limited (United Kingdom); ALLTEL Wholesale Banking Solutions, Inc.; Advanced Information Resources UK Ltd.

Principal Competitors

BellSouth Corp.; SBC Communications Inc.; Verizon Communications Inc.

Further Reading

Byrne, Harlan S., "ALLTEL Corp.: Cellular, Information Services Ring the Bell for Fresh Growth.," *Barron's*, November 18, 1991.

Case, Weldon W., *ALLTEL Corporation: Twenty-Five Years of Growth and Dedication to Excellence*, New York: The Newcomen Society of the United States, 1985.

Cuff, Daniel F., "ALLTEL Selects Chairman," *New York Times*, October 26, 1983.

Kharif, Olga, "Will Wireless Outfits Exchange Rings?," *Business Week*, November 29, 2001.

Lee, Simon, "Key Word of ALLTEL Is Convergence," *Arkansas Business*, April 7, 1997, p. 1.

Lovel, Jim, "Ford Leads ALLTEL to Banner Year," *Arkansas Business*, December 28, 1998, p. 1.

McCartney, Scott, "ALLTEL Agrees to Buy Aliant for $1.4 Billion," *The Wall Street Journal*, December 21, 1998, p. B10.

"Never Blink," *Telephony*, October 15, 2001, p. 38.

Parham, Jon, "ALLTEL's Joe Ford Predicts More 'Huge Opportunities'," *Arkansas Business*, February 14, 2000, p. 1.

Smith, David, "ALLTEL Adds 2.6 Million Cellular Customers with 360 Degrees," *Arkansas Business*, July 6, 1998, p. 10.

Smith, David, and John Haman, "ALLTEL's Buy of 360 Degrees Fits 'Like Hand in Glove,' " *Arkansas Business*, March 23, 1998, p. 1.

Spicer, Malcolm, "Familiar Refrain: ALLTEL Grows, RBOC Shrinks," *Wireless Insider*, August 7, 2000.

—Elizabeth Rourke
—update: Christina M. Stansell

AMERICAN GENERAL

American General Corporation

2929 Allen Parkway
Houston, Texas 77019
U.S.A.
Telephone: (713) 522-1111
Toll Free: (800) 242-1111
Fax: (713) 523-8531
Web site: http://www.agc.com

Wholly-Owned Subsidiary of American International Group, Inc.
Incorporated: 1926 as American General Insurance Company
Employees: 7,500
Total Assets: $11 billion
NAIC: 524113 Direct Life Insurance Carriers; 524292 Third Party Administration of Insurance and Pension Funds; 522291 Consumer Lending

American General Corporation (AG) is one of the nation's largest insurance and financial services organizations. The company is the second-largest issuer of life insurance in the United States. It operates a substantial business in retirement planning, designing group retirement plans and also managing annuities. It ranks as the third-largest writer of annuities and number one in issuing fixed annuities in the nation. Through its financial services division, AG runs one of the country's largest networks of consumer lending branches. It provides a variety of loans, from consumer loans to home mortgages. American General also manages investments for institutions and for individuals. Beginning in the 1980s, American General developed a reputation for buying other insurance companies—a practice unprecedented in the industry—and assimilating them profitably. This strategy of growth through acquisition became a corporate hallmark, and AG's assets quadrupled during the 1980s. After continuing its acquisition spree in the 1990s, AG was itself bought up in 2001 by American International Group, Inc. (AIG). AIG is a U.S.-based international insurer, operating in approximately 130 countries.

Roots in the Early 20th Century

The history of AG may be traced to Gus Sessions Wortham, a native of Houston, Texas, who established the John L. Wortham & Son Agency insurance firm with his father early in the twentieth century. Gus was managing the agency when his father died in 1924, and, the following year, he formed his own business after the Commission of Appeals of Texas ruled that single insurance companies could combine lines of business, allowing multi-line underwriting of both fire and casualty insurance. With the backing of several business associates and the John L. Wortham & Son Agency, Gus formed one of the nation's first multi-line insurance companies on May 8, 1926: the American General Insurance Company. Operations began on June 7, 1926.

With the help of Wortham's experience and business instincts, AG earned an underwriting profit in its first year of operation. The company paid its first dividend on common stock during its third year, shortly before the stock market crash of 1929. Despite the effects of the Great Depression and numerous economic downturns in the ensuing decades, dividends were paid every year, without reduction or interruption, into the 1990s.

AG, like the city of Houston in general, saw tremendous growth through the 1930s. The company's capital and surplus topped the $1 million mark by 1936; three years later, the company was licensed to operate in nine states, including Texas, and had assets of nearly $2.2 million. In 1939, AG established its first subsidiary, The American General Investment Corporation, which was the company's first foray beyond fire and casualty insurance. The American General Investment Corporation eventually expanded its original offerings—financing for automobiles and real estate projects—to become a main link in the company's mortgage and real estate business segment. In 1945, AG made its first acquisition, implementing the growth strategy for which it would later become unique in the industry. The acquired company, Seaboard Life Insurance Company, was a successful Houston-based life and health insurer that predated AG by one year.

Postwar Acquisitions

In 1953, AG hired Benjamin N. Woodson away from the National Association of Life Underwriters, where he was man-

<table>
<tr><td>

Company Perspectives:

American General is dedicated to enriching the communities where we live and work. We mobilize our resources, time, and talents to improve the quality of life for our communities through a focused involvement in education advancement, health and human service, cultural enrichment, and character development.

</td></tr>
</table>

aging director. At AG, Woodson focused on expansion into the national market, using his extensive business contacts to find and acquire other companies. The company's emphasis during the 1960s was on expanding its life and health insurance segment. Toward that end, AG purchased life insurance companies in Nebraska, Hawaii, Oklahoma, Pennsylvania, and Houston, as well as a fire and casualty company in Marshall, Texas.

A milestone was reached in 1964 when AG purchased the Maryland Casualty Company, a Baltimore-based property and liability company dating to 1898. Through this acquisition, long a goal of Gus Wortham, AG doubled its size and became a major property and casualty insurer in all 50 United States as well as in Canada. Moreover, construction of a new 24-story AG headquarters building was begun one mile west of downtown Houston, on the banks of Buffalo Bayou. The corporation moved in 1965, and this location eventually included 36 acres and five office buildings by 1990.

The New York life insurance market became AG's next territory, with the acquisition of Patriot Life Insurance Company in 1966. The following year, the Variable Annuity Life Insurance Company (VALIC) attracted AG's interest. VALIC was noted for innovations in sales of tax-deferred annuities to the employees of nonprofit organizations. AG acquired majority stock in VALIC by 1975, and VALIC eventually became a wholly-owned subsidiary. At the end of 1968, AG surpassed $1 billion in assets when it acquired a 65-year-old regional insurer, the Life and Casualty Insurance Company of Tennessee. That year, AG bought one-third of California-Western States Life Insurance Company (Cal-West), increasing its share to 63 percent over the next few years. Cal-West was a large but struggling company, and a new, dynamic 38-year-old president and CEO was striving to achieve a turnaround in the company's fortunes.

AG showed increasing interest in the man who was engineering Cal-West's rebound: Harold Swanson Hook. Hook had been raised on his family's dairy farm outside of Kansas City, Missouri, and, upon graduating from the University of Missouri, he was hired as an assistant to the president of National Fidelity of Kansas. Within five years, the 31-year-old Hook made industry history as the youngest insurance company president in the nation. Hook later served as president of U.S. Life Insurance in New York, and he became known for his successful development of management programs. His success in bringing Cal-West back to profitability drew notice from AG, and he was hired by AG in 1975 as president, overseeing the network of acquisitions made by Woodson. Hook became chairman and CEO when Woodson retired in 1978.

Doubling in Size in the 1980s

Emphasizing the importance of size to a company's success in the insurance industry, Hook focused on acquisition as the most efficient policy in a growth strategy. As he told *Business Week* in 1983, "Our competitive advantage is our ability to acquire, integrate and control complex operations." To this end, Hook applied his theories of management in a system taught to more than 80 percent of AG's employees, usually by graduates of Hook's Main Event Management Corporation in Sacramento, California. Hook contended that this implementation of a uniform philosophy and language accounted for AG's remarkable record with regard to acquisition, assimilation, and management. The company successfully integrated more than 20 companies during the 1980s, and the company's name was changed to American General Corporation to reflect its wider concerns.

Between 1982 and 1984, the corporation doubled in size, launching what it called "the most aggressive acquisition program" in insurance industry history. In 1982, under this program, AG made what was the largest single life insurance company acquisition in history at the time, with its purchase of NLT Corporation. NLT was the parent company of the National Life and Accident Insurance Company of Nashville, Tennessee. When AG failed to receive approval from the state of Tennessee to purchase the ten percent stock maximum, AG offered a stock swap. However, NLT refused and, in turn, made a bid for AG. AG rejected the bid and filed suit to stop the takeover proceeding, announcing what was dubbed the "godfather offer" in that it was difficult to refuse: a $46 per share merger proposal. This $1.5 billion, two-step merger was completed in late 1982. In response to initial concerns over the new company's debt load, Hook shaved NLT staff by one-third and divested overlapping and irrelevant subsidiaries, increasing cash flow more than $50 million. NLT was reportedly 70 percent absorbed within six months of the purchase.

That year, AG also acquired Credithrift Financial of Indiana, entering into the consumer credit business, which was later bolstered by the addition of General Finance Corporation. Another important acquisition during this time included the insurance properties of Gulf United Corporation, purchased for $1.2 billion.

In 1988, AG's consumer finance operations were doubled by the acquisition of the consumer finance division of Manufacturers Hanover. In order to rid the firm of its most cyclical units and concentrate on the faster-growing operations, AG shed its property-liability insurance business, as well as its group life and health insurance operations. On May 26, 1989, AG sold its property liability segment to Zurich Insurance Company—a multi-line, Swiss-based insurer—for $740 million. An agreement for the sale of AG's group insurance operations to Associated Insurance Companies for total consideration of up to $195 million, including $175 million in cash, was announced on September 21, 1989.

AG was the subject of a takeover bid in April 1990, when the Torchmark Corporation offered $6.3 billion to acquire AG. The bid was withdrawn within days, after receiving a chilly reception, and Torchmark then undertook a proxy battle to win five

Key Dates:

1926: The company begins operating.
1945: Seaboard Life Insurance is acquired.
1964: The company doubles its size by purchasing Maryland Casualty.
1988: The consumer finance division of Manufacturers Hanover is acquired.
1990: The company thwarts a takeover bid by Torchmark.
2001: The company is acquired by AIG.

seats on AG's 15-member board. Once again, AG rebuffed Torchmark, but its slim 60 percent victory persuaded the American General board to take action. At the May 2, 1990 annual meeting, Hook announced that AG was putting itself up for sale, and that he expected the company to fetch more than $7 billion. The board's decision to put AG on the block was made, according to Hook, because ''we recognized that . . . we were in play. We wanted to be in control of the process.'' Hook also noted that if an acceptable offer was not received in several months, the company was prepared to dismantle and sell its subsidiaries.

AG's stock soared during the proxy battle, but by the time Hook took the corporation off the auction block late in 1990, its price had plummeted to a six-year low. Hook agreed to sell portions of the company in September but rejected Torchmark's $3.6 billion bid for the home-service (door-to-door) life insurance as too low. During this time, Hook kept AG's options open, while continuing to streamline operations and expand through acquisitions. Divesting its real estate segment, AG acquired New Jersey Life Insurance Co.'s 28,000 policies worth $3 billion in 1993. Another aspect of American General's retrenchment involved a long-term stock buyback: from 1987 through 1992, the company invested over $1.5 billion to repurchase about 29 percent of its outstanding shares.

After having its home service insurance operations up for sale for nearly three years, AG announced its decision to remain in that segment of the business and expand those operations through acquisitions. AG consolidated this division in Nashville, Tennessee, reducing its workforce by over 25 percent, automating many processes, and overhauling the organizational structure, which had been in place since the subsidiary was founded.

More Growth and a Sale in the Late 1990s

In the mid-1990s, AG referred to itself as ''a company for all years,'' a designation based, in part, on its consistent stockholder returns and overall financial stability. In 1993, the company's ratings for both debt-paying and claims-paying ability were among the strongest in the industry. The company provided financial services to over six million households in all 50 states, Puerto Rico, the Virgin Islands, and Canada. Moreover, AG led its principal markets, ranking as the largest provider of voluntary savings plans to employees in public education; one of the largest consumer finance branch office networks, serving over two million customers; and the seller of more life insurance policies than any other shareholder-owned life insurance

organization in the United States. But the company was not content to settle at its current size. By 1994, AG's market capitalization had grown to $5.7 billion, and CEO Hook told investors he would double that by the year 2000. The company's acquisition strategy continued even as Hook stepped aside and Robert Devlin became CEO in 1996. Devlin added ten new people to the top rank of management, and then kept on much as his predecessor had. Between 1994 and 1997, the company made five acquisitions, spending over $3 billion. It bought up Franklin Life for $1.2 billion in 1995. That company, based in Springfield, Illinois, had a substantial business in upper-income life insurance. Later that year AG paid out some $362 million for the Independent Insurance Group, based in Jacksonville, Florida. It also picked up Home Beneficial, an insurer based in Richmond, Virginia, in 1996 for $665 million. In another major deal, AG spent $1.8 billion for USLife Corp. in 1997, another insurer with a major market share in life insurance for wealthier clients. With this acquisition finalized, AG became the third largest life insurer in the United States, calculated in terms of number of policies sold. AG had bought 40 percent of Western National Life Insurance in 1994. In 1997, the company acquired the remaining portion of that company. This deal vaulted AG to the number three spot nationwide as a writer of individual annuities. In spite of the rapid pace of acquisitions, AG was able to assimilate its new purchases and save operating costs by cutting redundant units. The new companies it acquired in the mid-1990s also changed the tenor of the company somewhat. AG had long profited from insurance sold the old-fashioned way, door-to-door. With its new acquisitions, a higher percentage of its sales came through other distribution channels—for example, from banks. Working through banks and independent insurance agents was on the whole less costly for the company than paying its own door-to-door sales people.

Another change for AG in the late 1990s was its first foray into the Mexican market. The company had previously operated in Canada and in Puerto Rico and the Virgin Islands. In 1997, AG bought a 40 percent stake in a joint venture with a Mexican financial services company to administer public and private pensions in that country. Its domestic pension and retirement planning subsidiary, Valic, meanwhile continued to prosper. Between 1994 and 1997, Valic approximately doubled its sales, bringing them to $1.7 billion in 1997. It was the leading company in the overall education market and held the number two spot for pension and retirement planning in the higher education market. Valic also held the number three spot in the health care market.

American General had a banner year in 2000. Operating earnings rose 13 percent, and AG's assets under management rose about six percent to $114 billion. The company performed strongly in all its divisions. The company soon found itself, as it did ten years earlier, the object of a complex takeover. In early 2001, AG received a bid from the large British insurer Prudential PLC. AG's board voted to accept the offer in March, but the deal was soon quashed when AG received a bigger offer from another company, American International Group. AIG, based in New York, had a large overseas insurance business, though it was far less known in its home country. AIG listed its stock in London, Paris, Tokyo, and on the Swiss Exchange, as well as in New York, and it operated in 130 countries worldwide in a wide variety of financial services fields. Among its many business lines, the company leased airplanes, invested in real estate, handled retirement plans, and engaged in consumer finance. AG agreed to pay $600 million to Prudential to get out of its previous agreement and cemented the merger with AIG in August 2001. AG folded many of its operations into its new parent's. The alliance of the two companies gave AIG a much bigger slice of the North American market, while AG hoped to benefit from AIG's expertise abroad.

Principal Divisions

Life Insurance; Retirement Services; Consumer Finance.

Principal Subsidiaries

Variable Annuity Life Insurance Co.; American General Finance, Inc.

Principal Competitors

Prudential Financial; John Hancock Financial Services Inc.; CUNA Mutual Life Insurance Co.

Further Reading

American General Corporation: History 1926–1986, Houston: American General Corporation, 1986.

Byrne, Harlan S., "American General," *Barron's*, December 21, 1992, pp. 39–40.

——, "Winning Policies," *Barron's*, December 15, 1997, p. 23.

Connolly, Jim, "Amer. Gen'l to Buy Other 55% of Western Nat'l," *National Underwriter*, September 22, 1997, p. 61.

——, "American General's Buying Spree Continues Apace," *National Underwriter*, December 12, 1994, p. 23.

Friedman, Amy S., "American General Makes Entry into Mexican Pension Mkt," *National Underwriter*, November 17, 1997, p. 49.

Ivey, Mark, "Harold Hook: A Hunter Who Feels Hunted," *Business Week*, April 22, 1991, pp. 92, 94.

Niedzielski, Joe, "American General Will Acquire Home Beneficial," *National Underwriter*, January 6, 1997, p. 49.

——, "Am. General's Independent Deal Affirms Strategy," *National Underwriter*, October 30, 1995, p. 4.

Panko, Ron, "Four Companies, Four Strategies," *Best's Review*, February 1998, pp. 37–39.

Schmitt, Frederick, "Amer. General to Buy USLife for $1.8 Billion," *National Underwriter*, February 17, 1997, pp. 1, 62.

Thomas, Trevor, "AIG Closes American General Acquisition," *National Underwriter*, September 3, 2001, p. 49.

——, "Winning American General Makes AIG Major Player in U.S. Life Industry," *National Underwriter*, May 21, 2001, p. 48.

—Carol I. Keeley
—updates: April Dougal Gasbarre and A. Woodward

American Home Mortgage Holdings, Inc.

520 Broadhollow Road
Melville, New York 11747
U.S.A.
Telephone: (516) 949-3900
Toll Free: (800) 991-0979
Fax: (516) 908-3628
Web site: http://www.mortgageselect.com

Public Company
Incorporated: 1999
Employees: 1,006
Total Assets: $58.3 million (2000)
Stock Exchanges: NASDAQ
Ticker Symbol: AHMH
NAIC: 522292 Real Estate Credit

American Home Mortgage Holdings, Inc. is a Long Island-based holding company involved in the residential mortgage loan business through two wholly-own subsidiaries: American Home Mortgage Corp. and Marina Mortgage Company, Inc. The company concentrates its efforts on selling to new home buyers rather than homeowners looking to refinance. It offers a broad range of mortgage products, including Fannie Mae-eligible loans, adjustable rate mortgages, jumbo loans, FHA-insured and VA-guaranteed loans, and non-prime loans. In addition, American Home offers home equity, second mortgage loans, construction loans, and bridge loans. The company generally sells the loans that it originates, usually within a month, rather than holding onto them for long-term investment. (Co-op loans made in New York City are held until properties reach occupancy.) Although buyers include Fannie Mae, thrifts and smaller banks, securities dealers, and real estate investment trusts, American Home sells most of its loans to major institutional investors. In 2000, for instance, the company sold 24.5 percent of its loans to Fleet Mortgage Corp., 20.4 percent to Chase Manhattan Mortgage Corporation, and 14.7 percent to Wells Fargo Funding. American Home's line of loan products are offered through three divisions: Retail, Wholesale, and Internet. The Retail operation accounts for 75 percent of all sales.

Selective acquisitions since the company went public in 1999 has extended American Home's reach to the Midwest and West Coast of the United States, growing to a network of 55 community offices in 13 states. The company also does business through joint ventures with mid-size real estate brokerage firms: 50–50 arrangements in which the venture sells loans that it originates to American Home, which in turn sells them to its institutional buyers. The company's Wholesale Division works with a network of more than 75 independent mortgage brokers, who refer borrowers by submitting completed loan applications for an underwriting determination. American Home's Internet division, MortgageSelect.com, accounts for less then 20 percent of the company's loans, but holds great promise for the future. It was the Internet model, in fact, that served as the focal point of the company's initial public offering. Rather than spending money to build a brand out of MortgageSelect, American Home seeks out destination website partners to offer mortgage services to their visitors who do not leave the host site. For customer support, the company maintains three call centers. This private label approach to the Internet minimizes the amount of money American Home spends to acquire a loan, giving it a significant advantage over online rivals.

American Home Mortgage Corp. Established in 1988

American Home's president, CEO, and chairman, Michael Strauss founded the business in 1988. Originally from Chicago, he earned a B.S. in business administration from Washington University in St. Louis, Missouri, then moved to New York City. At the outset, American Home was little more than a one-man business operating out of Manhattan. Strauss soon moved to the Long Island city of Melville, where he would be able to recruit from a work force experienced in the mortgage industry. Over the course of the next ten years Strauss built his business, taking a regional approach to growing the volume of loans originated while adding sales personnel. By 1994, American Home had four branches and originated $220 million in loans. By 1998, that volume approached $1.2 billion and the number of branches increased to 12, with locations in New York and six eastern states. Revenues for 1998 totaled more than $20 million, and the company posted a $4.87 million profit. Not only did Strauss reach a juncture at which he felt the need to

Company Perspectives:

American Home Mortgage's continued success is based on three main drivers of growth: accretive acquisitions, a successful model for online profitability, and organic growth in its branch offices.

expand beyond his East Coast base of operations, he also took note of the way the Internet was beginning to have an impact on mortgage lending. He decided that by establishing an Internet mortgage lending business he would be able to quickly realize his desire for expansion.

Strauss introduced MortgageSelect.com in January 1999, making 14 loans for a total of $2.7 million. By July, the business was already turning a profit, a rarity among Internet startups. By October, it was originating more than $60 million in loans per month. American Home's strategy of co-branding with partners was clearly working, with the company able to forge relationships with a number of major Web sites, including Microsoft's HomeAdvisor, E-Loan, GetSmart, LendingTree, Consumer Financial Network, RealEstate.com, LoanWeb, Iown.com, and Genesis2000. It was on the immediate strength and long-term promise of MortgageSelect that Strauss centered his effort to take American Home public.

In conjunction with the initial public offering, American Home Mortgage Holdings, Inc. was formed on June 15, 1999. In October 1999, the company completed its IPO, underwritten by investment bank Friedman, Billings, Ramsey & Co., offering 2.5 million shares of common stock at $6 per share. Not only did Strauss intend to use the money raised to bolster the infrastructure on the new Internet venture, he wanted to pick up smaller brick-and-mortar mortgage companies to increase market share. He publicly stated that there were two types of acquisitions he was interested in: mortgage or Internet operations that a bank was looking to sell off and traditional mortgage companies. According to Strauss, ''These are companies that are unable to realize as high a price for the loans that they create as we are, or companies that don't have the same technology platform.'' Unlike major mortgage lenders like Citigroup, Chase Manhattan, Washington Mutual, and Wells Fargo that were on the prowl for firms that generated between $5 billion and $20 billion worth of mortgages, Strauss was focusing on acquisition targets that generated between $500 million and $1 billion in annual loans originated. Well off the radar screen of the major players, these firms, many of which were struggling to survive, were available at modest prices.

Marine Mortgage Company Acquired in 1999

The first addition to American Home came quickly when in December 1999 it acquired Irvine, California-based Marina Mortgage Company in a $7.3 million stock and cash transaction. Marina, involved in the home mortgage business since 1979, was a significant West Coast retail lender that brought with it 13 offices in California and one in Arizona, thus adding significantly to American Home's limited presence in the West. Moreover, Marina had its own Internet division, Consumer First

Mortgage, which provided a West Coast call center to MortgageSelect. American Home finished 1999 generating revenues of nearly $25 million and a profit of over $3.8 million, despite the cost of starting its Internet operation.

In June 2000, American Home gained a major toehold in the Midwest, acquiring Chicago's First Home Mortgage Corp. in a stock and cash transaction worth over $7 million. First Home, founded in 1987, was one of the largest independent mortgage lenders in the metropolitan Chicago area. In addition to Illinois, First Home included branch offices in three other states. American Home continued its buying spree later in 2000 when it purchased four branch mortgage offices from New York-based Roslyn National Mortgage Corporation. American Home gained a presence in the Mid-Atlantic region with the addition of Roslyn operations in Columbia, Maryland and Vienna, Virginia, while adding to its Northeast business with offices in West Hartford, Connecticut, and Patchogue, New York. In essence, American Home was able to transform these unprofitable acquisitions by stripping them down to their sales forces, then relying on its own back-office operations. American Home's strategy proved to be extremely effective. In 2000, the company increased revenues by 135 percent to $58.3 million and reported net income in excess of $5.3 million. Total loan origination also increased in volume by 126 percent to $3 billion. MortgageSelect.com contributed 17 percent of the company's core business, ranking third among active online lenders.

American Home continued to expand offline in 2001. It acquired ComNet Mortgage Services, the residential mortgage business of Commonwealth Bank, based in Norristown, Pennsylvania. The deal added five branches offices located in Pennsylvania and Maryland. In addition, Commonwealth agreed to provide mortgage loans and services from American Home to its 60 branch locations in Southeastern Pennsylvania. The transaction was expected to add as much as $350 million a year to American Home's volume of loans. To fund further acquisitions with the expressed hope of doubling the amount of loans it originated for the year to $6 billion, the company made a secondary offering of stock in July 2001, turning again to Friedman, Billings, Ramsey & Co. It sold 2.4 million shares at $10.25 per share, netting $23.1 million.

Several weeks later, in August 2001, American Home used some of the capital it raised to purchase Valley Bancorp and its wholly-owned subsidiary Valley Bank of Maryland in a $5.5 million cash and stock transaction. Originally established in 1952 as the Baltimore Building and Loan Association, Valley Bank served the suburban Baltimore market through a full service branch office located in Owings Mills, Maryland, in addition to an administrative office in Hunt Valley, Maryland. As of June 20, 2001, the bank held $37 million in deposits and approximately $47 million in assets. Aside from increasing American Home's footprint in the Mid-Atlantic region and boosting the volume of loans originated, Valley Bank was a federal savings bank that brought with it a highly valuable charter that would benefit American Home on a number of levels. Because of its deposits, Valley Bank would be able to supply some of the funding that American Home had been borrowing from major banks such as Morgan Stanley Dean Witter Mortgage Capital and First Union National Bank. Strauss estimated that by drawing on the resources of Valley

```
┌─────────────────────────────────────────────────┐
│                   Key Dates:                    │
│                                                 │
│  1988:  Michael Strauss establishes American    │
│         Home Mortgage Corporation.              │
│  1999:  MortgageSelect.com is launched; a       │
│         holding company is formed and taken     │
│         public.                                 │
│  2000:  The company originates $3 billion in    │
│         mortgages.                              │
│  2001:  Valley Bancorp is acquired.             │
└─────────────────────────────────────────────────┘
```

Bank, American Home could save at least 150 basis points on a loan. ''We're in a business that's dominated by thrifts and banks, and our costs to carry and fund loans is higher than our competitors,'' he told *American Banker* shortly after the Valley Bancorp acquisition. ''This makes us competitive with our peer group.'' In addition, Valley Bank's federal charter also provided American Home with some tax breaks in New York. The company was on pace to originate $7 billion in mortgages in 2001, establishing a growth rate that was quickly garnering attention. After generating $500 million in loans in 1998, American Home began to grow by more than 100 percent, reaching $1.3 billion in 1999 and $3 billion in 2000. At that rate the company was in line to reach $25 billion a year within a few years.

American Home Solutions Launched in 2001

Most of American Home's growth in loans originated was still the result of its brick and mortar operations. Nevertheless, the company remained committed to its MortgageSelect business, which it continued to believe held great long-term promise. The Internet side of American Home produced several positive developments in 2001. A new online venture, American Home Solutions, was launched in June of that year. Described as an online homebuyers concierge service, the American Home Solutions Web site offered mortgages via MortgageSelect as well as a wide variety of discounts through partnerships with such companies as General Electric, ProCheck, ImproveNet, Allied Moving Services, Select Comfort, Covenant Insurance Company, PeaPod.com, Coldwater Creek, and MarthaStewart.com. Registered visitors to the site were then able to take advantage of discounts on appliances, paint, and hardware; moving trucks; home security systems; home inspection services; homeowners' insurance; home furnishings; nursery services; and even grocery shopping services. In addition to being available to anyone with access to the Internet, the site was also created as a tool for real estate agents to help them provide greater service to clients.

For American Home, the new Web site was just another way to increase potential traffic for MortgageSelect, which in 2001 established important new relationships with both traditional banks and online ventures. In the first half of the year, MortgageSelect signed outsourcing agreements with three new banking partners: Sterling Bank, Madison Bank, and Insurers Bank. Furthermore, it became the key lender on Planet Realtor. By the end of 2001, MortgageSelect added a number of other financial institutions, including The Bank of Lexington, Community Bank of the Cumberlands, Bank of Frankewing, Security Bank & Trust, Farmers & Merchants Bank-Trezavant, and Farmers & Merchants Bank-Adamsville. In September 2001, Mortgage-Select signed a multi-year agreement with Microsoft to be the exclusive mortgage provider on its HomeAdvisor site. In December 2001, MortgageSelect announced that it had reached a agreement with the popular The Motley Fool financial site to serve as the exclusive mortgage provider to its online Home Center.

With the addition of Valley Bank and its thrift charter, and an Internet model that was proving both profitable and flexible, American Home was well positioned to realize Strauss' long-term goal of being sheltered from the cyclical nature of the mortgage business, which fluctuated with the rise and fall of interest rates. As American Home continued to grow as a major provider of mortgages, another issue loomed: How much longer could its founder, filling all the top management positions, continue to run the company before turning over some of the responsibility to others?

Principal Subsidiaries

American Home Mortgage Corp.; Marina Mortgage Company, Inc.

Principal Competitors

Champion Mortgage Co.; Countrywide Credit Industries Inc.; Prism Financial Group; Bank of America Corporation; E-Loan Inc.

Further Reading

Bergsman, Steve, ''Bricks and Clicks,'' *Mortgage Banking,* August 2000, pp. 36–41.

Hochstein, Marc, ''Web Lender Cuts Costs by Not Pushing Its Brand,'' *American Banker,* November 23, 1999, p. 9.

Julavits, Robert, ''American Home CEO Says Bank Comes With Bonus,'' *American Banker,* August 31, 2001, p. 13.

Padgett, Tania, ''Top 100/Providing That At Times Smaller Can Be Better/American Home Mortgage Outshines Big Players,'' *New York Newsday,* June 4, 2001, p. C10.

Shinkle, Kirk, ''A Tech-Heavy Offering But Old-School Success,'' *Investor's Business Daily,* July 12, 2001.

Wipperfurth, Heike, ''American Home Builds On Its Foundation,'' *Crain's New York Business,* October 15, 2001, p. 59.

—Ed Dinger

American States Water Company

630 East Foothill Boulevard
San Dimas, California 91772-9016
U.S.A.
Telephone: (909) 394-3600
Fax: (909) 394-1382
Web site: http://www.gswater.com

Public Company
Incorporated: 1929 as American States Water Service
    Co. of California
Employees: 489
Sales: $197.5 million (2001)
Stock Exchange: New York
Ticker Symbol: AWR
NAIC: 221310 Water Supply and Irrigation Systems

American States Water Company is a holding company whose main subsidiary, Southern California Water Company, supplies water to more than 245,000 customers in California. American States supplies an additional 10,000 customers in Arizona. While the delivery of water accounts for 92 percent of the company's revenues, American States also distributes electricity in one service area and its American States Utility Services subsidiary operates and maintains municipally owned water and wastewater systems on a contract basis. American States operates out of the Southern California Water Company headquarters located in the Los Angeles suburb of San Dimas.

American States Founded in 1929

The delivery of water was crucial to the growth of Southern California. In 1905, shortly before the invasion of the film industry, Los Angeles was a city of just 300,000 people and further growth was jeopardized by a lack of additional water supplies. Thanks in large part to legendary engineer William Mulholland and the Los Angeles Aqueduct he built, water from the north flowed into the region. The local distribution of that water, however, was less well organized. By the 1920s, most Southern California communities formed their own water-

works, leaving just a few, scattered private water companies. Eventually a group of Chicago investors decided to consolidate some of these smaller operations and run them under central management with private funding.

The Chicago investors formed a holding company on April 16, 1928, naming it American States Public Service Company with the intention of investing in utility companies across the country. After some study the new company decided that the Southern California water market presented an excellent opportunity. A public utility engineer named John C. Rath was dispatched to the Los Angeles area and given the authority to purchase small water companies. From March 1928 to October 29, he purchased 33 properties at a cost of nearly $5.8 million. The water companies were spread across Los Angeles County and Orange County, held by two separate local holding companies set up by Rath: the Los Angeles and Suburban Water Company and the Orange County Water Company. His most significant acquisition was the $640,000 purchase of the Los Angeles Water Service Company. Before he left the area to take on other projects for the parent company, Rath made one other contribution to the new water enterprise: he engaged the engineering firm of Olmstead & Gillelen, where he met a young sanitary engineer named Cornelius Prugh Harnish. C.P. Harnish would be associated with the new water company for the rest of his life, including 14 years as its president.

The Chicago corporate parent assigned the task of creating an operational structure out of Rath's acquisitions to Ephraim Ewing Towles. To consolidate the two holding companies set up by Rath, he created the American States Water Service Company of California, incorporated on December 31, 1929. An office was set up in Los Angeles and Harnish was hired as general manager and chief engineer. The new water company began its operations with 43,000 customers located in 31 communities, with only a portion of its systems inter-connected.

Only a few months prior to the incorporation of American States, the New York Stock Exchange suffered the crash that would usher in the Depression of the 1930s. The water business remained profitable, however, with American States earning more than $600,000 on revenues of nearly $1.5 million in its first full year of operation. Nevertheless, its Chicago holding company did not fare well overall. A change in management led to the termination of Towles, despite having successfully launched the California enterprise. By 1936, the holding company was well on its way to bankruptcy and the America States water business, looking to distance itself, changed its name to the Southern California Water Company. American States Public Service Company emerged from receivership in 1938 and changed its name to American States Utilities Corporation. It continued to own a vast majority of stock in Southern California Water and maintained effective control. Ralph Elsman was named president of the water company, but because he elected to remain in San Jose, California, to also run the San Jose Water Works, he turned over operational control of Southern California Water to Harnish, who put his expertise in sanitary engineering to good use by greatly improving the system's water quality.

Elsman soon came into conflict with executives of the parent corporation because he advocated selling the properties of Southern California Water to municipalities. The issue divided the board and was only resolved when several Omaha-based investors gained control of the company and ousted Elsman. Walter Whitworth, who had previously headed Southern California Water in the 1930s, took over again. He immediately changed course, withdrawing an offer Elsman made to sell a property to Huntington Beach, and even added two more small water companies to the system: Manchester Heights Water Company and Gould Water Company.

Southern California Water Gains Independence in 1947

Conflicts with the parent corporation continued into the 1940s. In 1942, the Omaha investors who controlled the holding company, gained control of Southern California Water and removed Whitworth. The valuable Harnish, however, stayed on. He was instrumental in a 1943 effort that consolidated the company's operations, which until this point were an inefficient patchwork collection of water systems, with separate billing and delivery capabilities. The reorganization of Southern California Water not only produced greater efficiencies and allowed the company to lower the rates it charged customers, but it ultimately resulted in improved profits. With the post-World War II building boom in Southern California about to begin, the company was in a much better position for future prosperity, although it would face other challenges in the years following World War II. In 1946, the City of Los Angeles announced that it wanted to acquire most of the company's water delivery properties within the city, a move made possible by condemnation rights afforded local communities by California state law. Because Los Angeles properties represented about 30 percent of the company's total holdings, Southern California Water re-

sisted the city's bid. During the five years of negotiations that ensued, the company would finally be free of American States Utilities Company, which was ordered dissolved by the SEC. In November 1947, the matter was finalized and Southern California Water began a separate existence. Harnish, who assumed the presidency of the company late in the year, would lead the company into a new era.

The number of customers served by Southern California Water under Harnish's leadership increased steadily, growing from 85,000 in 1948 to 97,000 by 1951. That number would soon drop by 30,000 and revenues decrease by approximately 26 percent when negotiations with the City of Los Angeles were finally concluded in June 1951 and the company agreed to a $3,342,9444 purchase price for the properties the city wanted. Harnish took advantage of the cash, however, investing in improvements to the system as well as acquiring water properties in the Norwalk district of Los Angeles County that added 16,000 customers. He also reorganized the divisions of the company, resulting in a streamlined operation. In addition, Harnish was heavily involved in the development of a new master plan with the Metropolitan Water District of Southern California to ensure a reliable source of potable water for the future.

By the end of the 1950s, Southern California Water more than recovered the ground it lost in the sale of its property to the City of Los Angeles, with the number of customers it served growing to 114,000. Moreover, revenues, which totaled almost $2.75 million in 1952, increased to $6.5 million in 1959. With the company on a solid footing, Harnish, who was approaching his 68th birthday, decided in March 1960 that it was time to retire and turn over the presidency to new leadership. He remained on the board, however, and continued to exert a positive influence through the 1970s. His replacement, Philip F. Walsh, had been with the company for 21 years, so that despite lacking an engineering degree he was well prepared to lead Southern California Water.

During the 14-year tenure of Walsh at the helm, Southern California Water was extremely active in acquiring private water companies as well as selling off systems to municipalities. The company also applied to the state for rate increases on a steady basis. In 1968, Walsh turned to the state's Public Utilities Commission to find a new manager of the company's Rate and Valuation Department; the individual he appointed to this position, William V. Caveney, would one day become president of Southern California Water. At the same time, Walsh, whose health was starting to fail due to lung cancer, began to groom his immediate successor, William Franklin, an electrical engineer by training. Gradually Walsh turned over control of the organization to Franklin and finally he succumbed to cancer in 1973 at the age of 59. Southern California Water enjoyed a prosperous era under Walsh, with annual revenues growing by more than 140 percent to nearly $17.4 million. Like Walsh, Franklin had been hired by Harnish in 1939 and had a deep commitment to the company. He assumed the presidency of the company during a difficult period, as the nation suffered through a recession that resulted in high interest rates as well as inflationary pressures. Because of spiking energy costs, he was forced to constantly request rate increases, while at the same time trimming debt and keeping a close eye on the balance sheet. Despite trying circumstances, the company was able to

Key Dates:

1928: American States Public Service Company begins acquiring small California water companies.
1936: The company changes name to Southern California Water Company.
1951: The City of Los Angeles uses condemnation laws to acquire one of the company's major systems.
1976: California Cities Water Company is acquired.
1998: A holding company, American States Water Company, is formed.
2000: Chaparral City Water Co. of Arizona acquired.

top $20 million in annual revenues in 1975. The following year Southern California Water made one of its largest single acquisitions, the $3.4 million purchase of the California Cities Water Company, which added more than 20,000 customers.

Well over 60 years of age, Franklin tabbed Caveney as the man to succeed him at Southern California Water, at first naming him an executive vice-president in 1978. Then, in 1980, when he turned 65, Franklin named Caveney the new president of the company, but stayed on as CEO and chairman of the board. At the end of another two-year period, Caveney became the chief executive as well, with Franklin continuing on as chairman. As the first president without ties to the company's earliest years, Caveney was in a position to understand the time had come for fundamental changes at Southern California Water. He recognized the need for capital expenditures and increased the budget accordingly. He also convinced the board to contract a consulting firm to take a look at the company from the outside and recommend a succession plan. The resulting plan suggested that Southern California Water had two viable options: either sell the company or recruit skilled executives to take the company to the next level. Selling the company was never seriously considered, and Caveney began to beef up his management team.

The Mid-1980s Bring Conflicts With Local Communities

During the mid-1980s, Southern California Water came into conflict with many of the communities it served. Upset over ever increasing rates, several municipalities threatened to use the state's condemnation laws to take over local water systems. The most contentious situation involved the city of Big Bear Lake in Bear Valley, whose water company had been one of the original properties purchased by John Rath in 1928. Southern California Water was offered $10.4 million for the system, which the company appraised at $27 million. After several years of litigation, in 1989, the suit was settled and Southern California Water was awarded $29 million in total compensation. The case had a galvanizing effect on other state water companies, which aggressively lobbied for a change in the law. In 1992, California passed a "Necessity Bill," requiring communities to provide a justification for condemnation as well as fair compensation.

In 1990, revenues for Southern California Water reached $87.34 million. In that same year, Caveney turned over day-to-

day responsibilities and the presidency to Floyd Wicks. As had been the case with Franklin, he stayed on as chairman and also retained the CEO position for a two-year transitional period. Wicks was one of the new breed of executives Caveney had brought into Southern California Water in recent years. A trained engineer, Wicks had 15 years of experience with Consumers Water Company in addition to time in the public sector. He joined Southern California Water in 1988 as Vice President of Operations, a job that gave him a strong overview of the organization. His first priority as president was to bolster the staff. Compared to other water companies Southern California Water, with its 39 separate water systems, was understaffed. The California Public Utilities Commission questioned the validity of this sudden rise in employment and in 1992 initiated an audit. Rather than resist, Caveney and Wicks decided to offer the company's full cooperation with the outside firm hired to conduct the study. Two years later an audit report was released, and rather than criticizing the company for high staffing levels, it suggested that Southern California Water actually needed additional personnel. In addition, it made 114 recommendations for change. Management replied by unequivocally accepting every recommendation, most of which were improvements to the organization. As a result Southern California Water initiated sweeping changes in all of its systems and, in the process, modernized its information technology infrastructure and positioned the company to compete in a new era for the water industry.

The United States water industry was traditionally a highly fragmented business, with tens of thousands of private and municipal water systems spread across the country. During the mid-1990s a period of consolidation ensued, as many of the private companies, which comprised 20 percent of all water systems, were acquired by larger concerns. Moreover, municipalities increasingly turned over the operation of their water and wastewater systems to the private sector. Much of this activity was fueled by major French companies that following World War II had been forced out of electricity and gas by nationalization and subsequently devoted all of their resources to water, the only remaining utility available to them. After decades of growth and mergers, the resulting French behemoths targeted the United States, forming partnerships with domestic companies to gain a significant share of America's water and wastewater business. Southern California Water was the second largest investor-owned water company in California and the fifth largest in the nation. It was not considered a small company, but it clearly faced a future in which it had no choice but to grow larger. On July 1, 1998, a new holding company with an old name was formed, American States Water Company. Southern Water became a subsidiary, as did American States Utility Services, a business set up to manage community water and wastewater systems.

American States acquired its first water system in over ten years when in December 2000 it purchased the Peerless Water Co. In March the company expanded outside of California for the first time in its history, buying the Chaparral City Water Co. of Arizona for $31.2 million. Investors began to take notice of American States, which traded on the New York Stock Exchange, but they were more likely to view it as an attractive takeover candidate than as a company with prospects for greater growth. Entering 2002, American States remained independent, but whether it would remain so remained very much an open question.

Principal Subsidiaries

Southern California Water Company; American States Utility Services, Inc.; Chaparral City Water Company.

Principal Competitors

Western Water Co.; California Water Service Group; Los Angeles Department of Water and Power; Southwest Water Co.

Further Reading

"American States: Not Treading Water," *Business Week,* September 18, 2000, p. 172.

Byrne, Harlan S., "Precious Fluids," *Barron's,* August 19, 1996, p. 18.

——, "Steady Flow," *Barron's* January 26, 1998, pp. 14–15.

Gordon, Mitchell, "Pumping Profits," *Barron's National Business and Financial Weekly,* June 16, 1986, p. 48.

Harnish, C.P., *Southern California Water Company History,* Los Angeles: Southern California Water Company, 1976, 268 p.

Moore, Brenda L., "For Investors, There May Be Gold in Water," *The Wall Street Journal,* May 17, 2000, p. CA1.

Morris, Robert R., *Southern California Water Company,* San Dimas, Calif.: Southern California Water Company, 1999, 129 p.

—Ed Dinger

Applied Materials, Inc.

3050 Bowers Avenue
Santa Clara, California 95054-3299
U.S.A.
Telephone: (408) 727-5555
Fax: (408) 748-9943
Web site: http://www.appliedmaterials.com

Public Company
Incorporated: 1967
Employees: 17,000
Sales: $7.34 billion (2001)
Stock Exchanges: NASDAQ
Ticker Symbol: AMAT
NAIC: 333295 Semiconductor Machinery Manufacturing;
334413 Semiconductor and Related Device
Manufacturing

Applied Materials, Inc. operates as the leading manufacturer and supplier of products and services to the global semiconductor industry. The first company within the industry to surpass $1 billion in sales of semiconductor equipment, Applied Materials has 90 locations in 13 countries across the globe. In 2000, the majority of the firm's sales stemmed from the Asia-Pacific region, while North America and Europe accounted for 27 percent and 15 percent of sales, respectively. The firm is involved in the manufacture of systems that execute chemical vapor deposition (CVD), physical vapor deposition (PVD), epitaxial and polysilicon deposition, rapid thermal processing (RTP), plasma etching, electrochemical plating, ion implantation, metrology, and chemical mechanical planarization (CMP). The company also produces equipment that is used for mask pattern generation, as well as systems used to manufacture flat panel displays (FPDs).

Origins and Rapid Growth: Late 1960s–70s

Applied Materials was founded in 1967 to manufacture chemical vapor deposition systems for semiconductor wafer fabrication. The semiconductor industry itself, however, which makes the microcircuitry used in all electronics products, dates back to the invention of the first transistor during the early 1950s by scientists working at Bell Telephone Laboratories. With the advent of the transistor, it was possible to make electronic circuitry smaller and this, in turn, led to the manufacture of products which were lighter weight, more compact, and more energy efficient. During the late 1950s, semiconductor chip makers who initially both designed and built their own production equipment began to contract with vendors that supplied the equipment used to make their miniaturized devices. This trend helped to develop the semiconductor equipment industry. In the modern world, semiconductor manufacturing technology revolutionized the industrialized nations, providing the basis for all electronic products ranging from advanced fighter aircraft instrumentation to consumer goods such as radios and digital clocks. Indeed, it is not an overstatement to say that economies and national cultures have been dramatically affected by the semiconductor industry.

Within this historical context, Applied Materials' place in the development of the semiconductor manufacturing industry was unique. From 1967 to 1973, company revenues grew at a pace of more than 40 percent annually, and its total market share of the semiconductor equipment industry reached 6.5 percent. With such rapid market expansion and such enviable financial success, in 1972 the company decided to go public. In 1974, management decided to acquire Galamar Industries, a manufacturer of silicon wafers. During the mid-1970s, however, a severe recession had a very negative effect on the entire semiconductor industry. Applied Materials was hit especially hard, suffering a 45 percent drop in sales in 1975. Despite the drop in sales, management pursued prospects for growth, entering into a joint venture with Fairchild Camera and Instrument Corporation to construct a silicon production site in the same year.

Persistent financial problems related to non-semiconductor areas throughout 1976 and 1977 necessitated both organizational and management changes. James C. Morgan, formerly a partner in a private venture capital firm and with extensive experience in management at Textron's high-technology divisions, became president and chief executive officer. Morgan immediately shut down the unprofitable Galamar Industries, sold its share in the silicon manufacturing center, and concen-

Company Perspectives:

Our mission is to be the leading supplier of semiconductor fabrication solutions worldwide—through innovation and enhancement of customer productivity with systems, process modules, and service solutions.

trated on improving its area of expertise in the semiconductor industry. In 1978, Applied Materials reported an increase in sales of approximately 17 percent. And in 1979, sales grew by a phenomenal 51 percent over the previous year.

Expansion Amid Industry Downturns: 1980s

Applied Materials, under the guidance of Morgan, continued its expansion strategy and acquired the ion implantation division of British-based Lintott Engineering, Ltd. in 1979. The company also formed Applied Materials Japan, Inc., a joint venture created to increase the company's share of the growing Japanese semiconductor equipment market. Sales reached $69.3 million in 1980, but by 1982 the company was once again hit hard by a worldwide recession in the semiconductor industry. At the end of that year, Applied Materials reported a loss of $9.4 million on total sales of $88.2 million.

The company's commitment to research and development, however, helped it weather the recession much better than many other vendors. The introduction of the AME 8100 Series Plasma Etch Systems revolutionized the dry etching of semiconductors. The quick market acceptance of this product and an agreement reached with the General Electric Venture Capital Corporation (GEVENCO) supplying a $20 million investment helped the company ride out the remainder of the recession. By 1983, the company was financially healthy once again; sales broke the $100 million mark. With 30 percent of its total sales originating from Japan, management steered a course to increase participation in the Japanese semiconductor market and started construction of a technology facility which would not only include a state-of-the-art research and development laboratory but also incorporate the most advanced technology for processing semiconductor wafers.

In 1984, increased demand for semiconductors pushed worldwide sales up a record 45 percent to approximately $26 billion, and Applied Materials benefited from this strong upturn to report sales of $168.4 million, a 60 percent surge over 1983. Yet in 1985, the cyclical nature of the semiconductor industry was again apparent when worldwide sales decreased by almost 20 percent. This downturn led to the worst recession ever for the semiconductor equipment industry and, as the recession deepened in 1986, many of the company's major customers began to reduce their equipment budgets. As a result, revenues continued to decline although Applied Materials was still performing better than most other companies in the semiconductor equipment market.

Advances in Technology: Late 1980s–Early 1990s

A large part of Applied Materials' success during the recession was due to the development of leading-edge technology.

In 1986, the company introduced the Precision Etch 8300A, featuring major improvements in contamination control and higher than previous levels of automation. In 1987, the company introduced the Precision 5000 CVD, a new system which met the industry's need for significant improvements in the low-temperature deposition of dielectric materials. Orders for this new technology helped Applied Materials improve its financial position, as did a public stock offering which brought in an additional $54.7 million. In the same year, James W. Bagley, Applied Materials senior vice-president of operations since 1981, with over 15 years of previous experience in engineering and project management at Texas Instruments, was appointed president and chief operating officer. Morgan, after serving 12 years as president, remained chief executive officer and chairman of the company's board of directors.

The combination of Applied Materials' commitment to new product introduction and a renewed demand in the worldwide semiconductor equipment market made 1988 a record year for the company. Net sales of $362.8 million more than doubled the previous year's sales figures. By continuing to introduce new products and by improving the technology and applications in its existing product lines, revenues jumped to $501.8 million in 1989. With the previous addition of a service center in Beijing, China, and a regional office in Seoul, Korea, during the mid-1980s, in 1989 the company continued to build upon its presence in the Pacific Rim with the construction of new facilities in Japan. After ten years, over 40 percent of the company's revenues were coming from the Asia/Pacific market.

New product development was the cornerstone of management's strategy for improving the company's market position in the early 1990s. In 1990, the company introduced the Endura 5500 PVD in order to enter a new market, physical vapor deposition. In 1991, the firm announced its intention to enter the market for Thin Film Transistor Liquid Crystal Display manufacturing equipment. Shipments for systems which manufacture these flat panel displays started in 1993. In 1992, Applied Materials was beginning to reap the benefits of its strategy for product introduction and its expansion in Japan and the Pacific Rim. Total revenues were reported at $751.4 million, backlog orders at $254 million, and net income at $39.5 million. The geographical distribution of sales broke down as follows: 40 percent in the United States, 30 percent in Japan, 18 percent in Europe, and 12 percent in the Pacific Rim.

In 1993, Applied Materials entered into an agreement with Komatsu, Ltd., a Japanese firm, to form a new company named Applied Komatsu Technology, Inc. The company was created in order to develop, manufacture, and market systems that were employed in producing FPDs. Operating with facilities in both the United States and Japan, it was agreed upon that company headquarters were to be established in Japan. In October 1993, the company announced its first product, the AKT 1600 PECVD, for chemical vapor deposition of thin films employed in manufacturing Thin Film Transistor structures in FPDs. The development of this technology had broad applications ranging from desktop and laptop computers to any electronic products that use high quality, color displays.

The strategy of Applied Materials in establishing partnerships like the one with Komatsu proved extremely profitable for

Key Dates:

1967: Applied Materials is established.

1972: The firm goes public.

1979: Sales grow 51 percent over the previous year; Applied Materials Japan is formed.

1982: Sales drop due to a worldwide recession in the semiconductor industry.

1986: Applied Materials introduces the Precision Etch 8300A.

1988: Sales double over the previous year, reaching $362.8 million.

1993: Company partners with Komatsu Ltd. to develop, manufacture, and market systems for producing flat panel displays; the company's sales exceed $1 billion.

1998: Copmpany launches its Equipment and Process Integration Center (EPIC).

2001: The company restructures due to a decline in the semiconductor industry.

the firm. Joint ventures increased the company's market share in Japan because the new operation functioned like a Japanese firm and relied on Japanese employees to provide the manufacturing base, marketing skills, and sales techniques required to do business in that country. In addition, the intimate relationships created with valued Japanese customers helped to sell Applied Materials' products when the customer decided to open a plant in the United States or somewhere overseas. The success of this strategy was the reason why nearly one-third of all Applied Materials sales involved Japanese semiconductor customers in the early 1990s.

Applied Materials continued to focus on establishing long-term relationships with users of semiconductor equipment in the 1990s and also took advantage of foreseeable trends in manufacturing technology. For example, as the semiconductor industry produced more and more circuits with smaller geometries, particulate contamination in what is called the ''cleanroom'' became a major concern requiring contaminant-free manufacturing environments. One solution to this problem of particulate contamination was the trend toward through-the-wall equipment design, where manufacturing equipment was completely encased in an airtight shell (a ''cleanroom'' environment) with only one access port which connects the equipment to the wafer fabrication facility. Applied Materials focused on developing new and highly reliable equipment for semiconductor customers to use within this ''cleanroom'' manufacturing environment.

In 1993, Applied Materials reached one of its long-term goals: it became the first company within the semiconductor equipment industry to hit the $1 billion mark in revenues. Total sales in 1993 amounted to $1.08 billion. One critical element in the company's financial success was the 13 percent of total revenue, or $140.2 million in fiscal 1993, invested in research and development. The commitment of a significant portion of its revenue to developing new technology historically provided stability and helped the company weather the cyclical periods of growth and recession in the semiconductor industry. This com-

mitment was also recognized throughout the industry. In 1996, Morgan was awarded the National Medal of Technology by President Bill Clinton.

Continued Growth: Late 1990s and Beyond

During the mid- to late 1990s, Applied Materials continued to focus on developing new technology and creating close working partnerships with customers by means of global expansion. The company also made several key acquisitions that secured its position as the number one semiconductor equipment manufacturer in the world. In early 1997, the firm completed the purchase of Opal Inc. and Orbot Instruments Ltd., both Israel-based companies involved in inspection equipment and metrology. Morgan commented on the acquisitions in a 1996 *Electronic News* article, stating, ''Our entry into the market for metrology and inspection equipment is consistent with our long-term standing strategy of serving our global customers with a broader array of enabling technology required to economically manufacture new generations of advanced semiconductor devices.''

Meanwhile however, the semiconductor industry once again found itself embroiled in a downturn, this time related to an economic crisis in Asia and oversupply and falling prices in several key industries including the personal computer market. While Applied Materials was forced to cut jobs, it continued to forge ahead. In 1998, the company opened its Equipment and Process Integration Center (EPIC) in Santa Clara, which was used to launch new products and services that supported the Copper Interconnect Equipment Set Solution (ESS). During the 1990s, copper began to replace aluminum as the main electrical conductor for the interconnect circuitry in chips. As chips became increasingly smaller, copper became more effective in carrying current through the circuitry, mainly because it had a lower resistance than aluminum and could carry more current to a smaller area.

That same year, Applied Materials also acquired Consilium Inc., a supplier of manufacturing execution system (MES) software used by the semiconductor industry. In 1999, the firm purchased the remaining interest in its joint venture with Komatsu Ltd. and also acquired Obsidian Inc., a firm whose chemical mechanical planarization technology fit into Applied Materials' burgeoning product line. That year, revenue surpassed $5 billion.

Applied Materials entered the new millennium on solid ground. It made a significant purchase at the start of 2000, announcing its intent to acquire Etec Systems Inc. for nearly $1.8 billion. Upon completion of the deal, Applied Materials stood as the leader in the mask pattern generation market—the company defines a mask pattern generation system as one that uses a laser or electron beams to write each layer of a semiconductor chip's design onto a piece of chrome-coated quartz glass, which is called the mask or photomask. A series of completed masks are then used to transfer the chip's design onto the semiconductor wafer.

During that time, 300mm became the new standard wafer size in the semiconductor industry, replacing 200mm wafers. As the industry shifted to manufacturing chips on 300mm wafers—

these new wafers had a larger surface area and could hold 2.5 more chips—the company launched its 300mm wafer systems product line, the broadest line in the industry. The firm expected that it would be key in the firm's growth over the next five years.

The year 2000 proved to be a record year for Applied Materials. Fueled by the growth of the Internet and communications industries, the company secured $12.3 billion in new orders. Revenue reached $9.6 billion, nearly doubling over the previous year. During 2001 however, the industry entered into yet another downturn and chipmakers cut back on investments in new technology that was provided Applied Materials. As such, the firm announced that it anticipated that worldwide semiconductor capital spending would decline during 2001. The firm itself cut back on spending and began company-wide layoffs.

Applied Materials historically weathered downturns well, and continued to prepare for the next upswing. During 2001, it began a $30 million advertising campaign entitled "Information for Everyone." Management eyeballed the campaign as crucial to building name recognition outside of the semiconductor industry. The firm also set plans in motion to acquire Global Knowledge Services Inc. in late 2001. Global's data mining services were expected to go hand-in-hand with Applied Materials' inspection and defect reduction products. New orders for 2001 declined to $6.10 billion while sales fell to $7.34 billion.

While the slowdown in the semiconductor industry continued into early 2002, Applied Materials remained optimistic. With the worldwide semiconductor market expected to exceed $312 billion in 2003, and the market for semiconductor fabrication equipment slated to reach $38 billion by 2004, Applied Materials appeared to be well positioned for future success amid a turbulent industry.

Principal Subsidiaries

Etec Systems Inc.; Consilium Inc.; Obsidian Inc.; Applied Komatsu Technology, Inc.; Applied Materials France; Applied Materials GmbH (Germany); Applied Materials Israel Ltd.; Applied Materials Japan; Applied Materials Europe; Applied Materials Korea; Applied Materials Taiwan; Applied Materials Asia-Pacific (Singapore).

Principal Competitors

Tokyo Electron Ltd.; KLA-Tencor Corp.; Lam Research Corp.

Further Reading

"Acquisition: Applied Materials to Acquire Consilium in Stock Swap," *EDGE: Work-Group Computing Report*, October 19, 1998.

"Applied Rolls Products for Copper Interconnect," *Electronic News*, November 9, 1998, p. 12.

Bank, David, "Applied Materials to Cut Staff 15%, Salaries," *Wall Street Journal*, August 26, 1998, p. B6.

Chappell, Jeff, "AMAT Sets Record Quarter and Year," *Electronic News*, November 20, 2000, p. 10.

"Chipmaking: 'Long-Term Opportunity Is So Vivid Today'," *Business Week Online*, July 16, 2001.

Cohen, Charles, "Applied Materials Combines the Best of East and West," *Electronic Business*, May 6, 1991, pp. 52–4.

Dorsch, Jeff, "Applied To Take Over AKT Venture," *Electronic News*, October 4, 1999, p. 2.

Erkanat, Judy, "Applied Buys Opal, Orbot," *Electronic News*, December 2, 1996, p. 1.

——, "Applied Moves on 3 Product Fronts," *Electronic News*, June 24, 1996, p. 46.

Haber, Carol, "Applied Is Feeling the Pain As Industry Slowdown Deepens," *Electronic News*, May 18, 1998, p. 56.

Lineback, Robert J., "Applied Cuts Growth, Spending Projections," *Electronic Engineering Times*, February 19, 2001, p. 43.

Pitta, Julia, "The Realist," *Forbes*, May 13, 1991, pp. 116–17.

Ristelhueber, Robert, "Applied Rides Acquisition Route to Dominance," *Engineering Electronic Times*, January 24, 2000, p. 45.

—Thomas Derdak
—update: Christina M. Stansell

Artesyn Technologies Inc.

7900 Glades Road, Suite 500
Boca Raton, Florida 33434-4105
U.S.A.
Telephone: (561) 451-1000
Fax: (561) 451-1050
Web site: http://www.artesyn.com

Public Company
Incorporated: 1984
Employees: 9,200
Sales: $494 million (2001)
Stock Exchanges: NASDAQ
Ticker Symbol: ATSN
NAIC: 334417 Electronic Connector Manufacturing;
    334414 Electronic Capacitor Manufacturing; 334415
    Electronic Resistor Manufacturing; 334419 Other
    Electronic Component Manufacturing

Artesyn Technologies Inc.—formerly known as Zytec Corporation until its 1998 merger with Computer Products Inc.—is a leading designer and manufacturer of power conversion products and communications subsystems which convert, distribute, and regulate the electricity needed to operate computers, peripherals, office equipment, and communications technology. The Florida-based company is one of the largest power supply producers in the United States and has earned a reputation for quality within the industry and with the high-tech original equipment manufacturers (OEM's) which are its customers. Among those customers are Alcatel, Cisco Systems, Compaq, Dell Computer, Ericsson, Hewlett-Packard, Lucent Technologies, Nortel, Siemens, Motorola, Ciena, and Sun Microsystems. Along with its U.S. interests, Artesyn has plant operations in Austria, Germany, Hong Kong, Hungary, Ireland, and the UK.

Roots in Control Data Corporation

In the mid-1960s, as part of its vertical integration strategy, Control Data Corporation (CDC) opened a power supply plant in Redwood Falls, Minnesota, a small town about 100 miles southwest of Minneapolis. The factory produced power supply units for CDC subsidiary Magnetic Peripherals Inc. (MPI),

which manufactured large magnetic disk drives. Engineering, purchasing, inventory control, and production schedules for the Redwood Falls plant and other small-town "feeder plants" manufacturing components and subassemblies for CDC were centralized in the Twin Cities.

In the early 1980s, CDC was faced with rapidly advancing electronics technology and intense competition in the marketplace. In response, CDC implemented a new business strategy. The company began to sell off its low-tech manufacturing operations—such as power supply units, cables, and circuit boards—and turned its resources to product development. From a different perspective, the community of Redwood Falls was at risk of losing its largest employer (the plant had once employed more than 500 people), when the region was already being rocked by an agricultural crisis.

CDC offered to sell the plant to a long-time employee, peripheral products manager Ronald D. Schmidt. His initial response to the idea was negative, but he became interested in acquiring the company when he was assigned to work on a plan to jointly operate the power supply operation with another large computer company. When the joint venture failed to materialize and a buyout offer made by plant employees was rejected by CDC, Schmidt asked John M. Steel, another peripheral products manager, and Lawrence J. Matthews, head of component development at Magnetic Peripherals, to enter into a leveraged buy out of the plant.

CDC invested $500,000 for 22 percent of the company: an investment to be phased out over a three-year period through a discounted employee repurchase of stock. Schmidt, Steel, and Matthews raised $200,000, and CDC's financial subsidiary, Commercial Credit Co., kicked in $5.5 million in financing. Production would continue in Redwood Falls with the management and engineering offices located in the Twin Cities. Zytec was incorporated in January 1984 with Schmidt at the helm. Initially, CDC continued to provide Zytec with purchasing, inventory, and some corporate support services as well as orders for power supplies.

The Difficult Path to Independence

Schmidt, Steel, and Matthews planned to broaden their business by diversifying into other power supply markets, including minicomputers, engineering workstations, telephone switches,

---

Company Perspectives:

As a leading supplier of power conversion products and communication subsystems, we strive to focus our efforts on high-growth applications within four key markets: computing and storage; carrier and enterprise networking; wireless infrastructure; and network access. Through a combination of dedicated design, manufacturing, and service facilities in nine countries, we have the global reach to service the world's leading OEM's.

---

and medical testing and diagnostic machines. The new owners also made a commitment to use Dr. W. Edward Deming's 14 points for management—a philosophy which often received credit for reviving Japan's post-World War II economy—as a framework for making manufacturing changes. In the meantime, the newly independent company was operating under increased demand, while working to establish its own purchasing and production systems and building a warehouse for inventory. Nearly all of Zytec's first year revenues of $66 million were generated from its business with MPI.

The optimism associated with its initial surge of growth and plans for the future was squelched by a dramatic slump in the computer industry and existing manufacturing problems. Zytec began 1985 with $11 million in parts on its shelves and $6 million in unfinished product in the plant. Cycle times—the time from introduction of materials on the plant floor to shipment of product—were getting longer and cutting into already slim profit margins.

In the midst of the developing crisis, Schmidt worked to familiarize managers with Deming's concepts. He also brought on board people who were experienced in implementing Statistical Process Control (SPC) and Just-In-Time (JIT) manufacturing techniques: SPC involved the continuous monitoring of the production process in order to identify problems quickly, while JIT involved introducing and moving materials through the manufacturing process with maximum efficiency. Zytec also adopted a Total Quality Commitment (TQC) management approach, which gave all employees some level of responsibility for establishing, tracking, and achieving production goals and objectives.

However, in June 1985, after several earlier cutbacks on new orders, MPI abruptly stopped all shipments. The computer industry had weakened, and sales on CDC's large disk drives had plummeted even further. Production at the Redwood Falls plant was completely shut down for two weeks. Zytec gradually resumed operation, with employees taking salary cuts of 10 to 20 percent. According to George Dixon in Corporate Report Minnesota, "Later that summer Control Data slowly began to place more orders. By then, however, Zytec had begun to get its ruinous inventory and work-in-progress problems under control." They survived the period, according to Schmidt, by living off their inventory. Sales for 1985 had fallen to $48.5 million with losses of $2.3 million.

Reorganization and Renewal in the Late 1980s

Zytec's revamping was put into full gear in 1986. Employee training was accelerated. The factory was reorganized into

manufacturing cells to streamline the production process. Quality control techniques were integrated into corporate areas as well as on the manufacturing floor and in the warehouse. Zytec returned to profitability in 1986, but revenues were still falling and the vast majority of orders were still coming from CDC.

San Francisco-based Micro-Tech Consultants, which served the power supply industry, estimated 1986 sales by independent producers to be more than $1.6 billion. With approximately $45 million in sales, Zytec was ranked seventh among U.S. firms. The industry consisted of many small producers with access to the same basic technology, operating under few industry standards, and most often producing custom made power supplies for a single large customer.

Power supplies, an essential element of electronic equipment, basically did the following: switch alternating current (AC) to the direct current (DC) used by electronic systems, provide various levels of DC voltage to subsystems and components, and monitor and regulate voltages to protect the equipment from power surges. However, the stress on the product caused by continuous use, the high level of manual construction, and the dearth of investment in technology had saddled the power supply industry with a reputation for product failure.

By 1987, Zytec was gaining notice, not for its failures but for its successes. The manufacturer had become more competitive with overseas power supply producers in terms of cost, quality, scheduling, and delivery times. Currency exchange rates had also started to favor domestic businesses, and the company gained such customers as Fujitsu America, Tandem Computers Inc., Unisys Corp., Abbott Laboratories, AT&T, IBM, Eastman Kodak, Network Systems, Sun Microsystems, and StorageTechnology. Zytec continued to refine its operations, invest in technological advancements, and diversify its markets over the next few years.

In 1991, Zytec won the Malcolm Baldrige National Quality Award, the Minnesota Quality Award, and the IBM Market Driven Quality (MDQ) Gold Award. The privately held company's revenue grew by nearly 30 percent in spite of a recession. Zytec also expanded internationally with the acquisition of an Austrian power supply manufacturing plant.

By the beginning of 1992, Zytec had 21 customers; less than five percent of business was with CDC. Zytec planned to go public that year, but the initial public offering was canceled due to inconsistent earnings coupled with an unfavorable market for smaller companies. Zytec did win another honor: Industry Week magazine named the Redwood Falls plant one of "America's Ten Best Plants." David Altany of Industry Week said Schmidt's and Zytec's commitment to Deming's quality principles set them "apart from the pack." Nevertheless, the company's bottom line was still wavering: Austrian operations lost nearly $4.5 million and largely contributed to the year-end loss of $3.3 million.

Zytec finally went public in November 1993. The stock was sold at $10.375 for a total of $9.2 million. The Austrian plant still generated a small loss in 1993, but the company's earnings were on an upswing. Zytec-designed and collaborative power supplies, the product segment with the highest profit margin but the longest development time, brought in 78 percent of revenues in 1994. Customer-designed power supplies, a low-risk and

Key Dates:

1984: Ronald D. Schmidt, John M. Steel, and Lawrence J. Matthews buy Control Data Corp.'s (CDC) Minnesota-based power supply plant through a leveraged buyout and incorporate under the name Zytec Corp.
1991: The company wins several awards, including the Malcolm Baldridge National Quality Award.
1993: Zytec goes public.
1996: The company's net income reaches $7.9 million; a distributed power architecture (DPA) office is established in Richardson, Texas.
1998: Zytec merges with Computer Products Inc. to form Artesyn Technologies Inc.
2001: The company undergoes restructuring efforts during a market downturn.

low-margin segment of business, contributed 13 percent of revenues. The remaining nine percent was generated by the repair and service end of the business. Zytec's power supply repair operation was the largest in the United States: they handled the products of more than 200 manufacturers. The bulk of the service business was dedicated to one customer, Hewlett-Packard, via Zytec's California repair facility. Overall, Zytec's revenue for 1994 grew by 41 percent to $128 million.

Mid-1990s Forces Affect Zytec and the Industry

In the mid-1990s, the power supply market remained highly fragmented with over 350 manufacturers. According to a 1995 John G. Kinnard & Co. report, two industry trends were likely to benefit Zytec. Many original equipment manufacturers—which accounted for about half of the power supply market—were shutting down their internal power supply operations finding it more economical to purchase the product rather than to manufacture it themselves. In addition, as power supplies became more complex and the industry became more automated, increased design and capital costs made it more difficult for the smaller independent power supply manufacturers to be competitive. Only a small percentage of U.S. manufacturers—Zytec among them—had annual revenues of more than $100 million while the vast majority of U.S. power supply makers had annual sales of less than $10 million.

A different trend in the electronics industry, one of demand outstripping capacity, had a negative effect on Zytec in 1995. A shortage of power semiconductors shut down production on several key projects early in the year. Zytec compensated by seeking out additional suppliers and redesigning some products, but the supply problem kept year-end earnings down in spite of significant revenue growth.

Schmidt, Steel, and Matthews, the leaders of the buy out from CDC, still owned about 35 percent of the company in 1995; other employees owned an additional 10 percent. Since the IPO, Zytec stock had hovered around the initial offering price, but in 1996 the stock experienced some volatility: first, due to earnings estimates, and then later because of an online

bulletin board notice. Other activity included two stock splits and a postponed public offering.

The opening of a new manufacturing plant in Broomfield, Colorado, and an expansion of the plant in Redwood Falls helped alleviate Zytec's capacity problems. Zytec also acquired a magnetic components plant, the primary supplier for its Austrian operation, from the Hungarian government in 1996.

Zytec's 1996 revenues were $228 million. Net income rose 103 percent—if a one-time tax gain was excluded—to $7.9 million. In its 1996 10-K report, Zytec contributed its recent surge in sales to sole-provider opportunities with original equipment manufacturers for the Internet and data communications marketplace. Zytec also reported that its service and logistics business had been doubling each year, and the company was seeking additional customers in that growing area.

As more complex electronics technology drove the need for smaller and more efficient power supply systems such as the ones Zytec manufactured, the company focused on its product offerings. By the mid-1990s, they had hundreds of components and performed advanced diagnostic and power management functions. In 1996, Zytec established a distributed power architecture (DPA) office in Richardson, Texas. DPA is a process that allows greater flexibility when adding electronic components or upgrading hardware. The developing technology had been commonly used in telecommunications and was finding expanded applications in data networking, large volume data storage, and high-end data processing markets. Based on industry forecasts, Zytec expected the DPA technology to be an important expansion of its business in the future.

1998 Merger with Computer Products Inc.

The power source industry remained highly fragmented, however, with over 350 manufacturers in North America alone. With little room for major growth, power supply product firms began eyeing consolidation through acquisition as key to remaining competitive. A Zytec competitor, Computer Products Inc. (CPI), had done just that, spending most of the mid-1990s buying up smaller companies. CPI then set its sights on Zytec. Finally, in 1997, Zytec agreed to team up with CPI in perhaps the most significant move of its history. When the merger was completed in 1998, the newly combined company became a leading power supply product manufacturer with over 6,000 employees. The firm's name was changed to Artesyn Technologies and headquarters were moved to Boca Raton, Florida. Joseph O'Donnell—CPI's CEO—took the same position at Artesyn and co-chaired the firm with Schmidt. O'Donnell commented on the firm's name change in a 1998 *South Florida Business Journal* article, stating that ''the new company we are forming is the largest for power systems and power supply in the communications industry. We build the power that drives workstations and personal computers. The 'Art' part of Artesyn describes the craftsmanship we provide in our products. 'Syn' stands for the synergy of the two companies.''

Eyeing the communications industry as key for future growth, Artesyn focused its energies on supplying products related to both wireless and Internet infrastructure. As part of its strategy, the firm released new products including the SimScope, a Web-based power supply design simulation tool. The company then purchased Spider Software Ltd., a Scottish manufacturer of products used to facilitate communication between various networks, computers, and wireless and fixed wire telecommunications instruments like pagers, routers, servers, and telephones. The acquisition—completed in 2000—gave Artesyn a strong foothold in this growing sector of the industry. The firm's purchase of Azcore Technologies that same year also bolstered its holdings in DC-DC converters used in DPA technology. During 2001, the company acquired Real Time Digital, a manufacturer of digital signal processor (DSP) software and high-density DSP board products used to control information from circuit-based public telephone networks to packet-based Internet networks.

Strategic Alliances for the New Millennium

While revenue climbed to $690.1 million in 2000, increasing from $594.2 million recorded in 1999, Artesyn began to experience hard times during 2001 and into 2002. In June 2001, the firm announced that it planned to cut its employee base by as much as 15 percent and also implemented a cost-cutting strategy in order to combat weakening market conditions that caused the firm's sales and profits to plummet. In December of that year, Artesyn sold is Solutions division to Solectron Corporation for $33.5 million. As revenues continued to fall during 2001, Artesyn turned to Bruce Cheng, founder of Delta Electronics Inc., a leading power supply, electronic component, and video display manufacturer. An investment group led by Cheng pumped $50 million into Artesyn and also brought the potential for possible joint ventures and partnerships between the two businesses.

While many of the markets that Artesyn operated in remained weak, O'Donnell remained optimistic about future profit gains. Claiming that the firm's restructuring operations were successful, the CEO stated in a January 2002 press release that the company's objective was "to emerge from this slowdown as a much stronger competitor" and that he believed that Artesyn was "well-positioned to benefit from the eventual pickup in end market demand." However, whether Artesyn would emerge profitable on its own or through another strategic merger remained to be seen.

Principal Subsidiaries

Artesyn International Ltd. (Cayman Islands); Artesyn North America, Inc.; Artesyn Netherlands B.V. (Netherlands); Artesyn Technologies Communications Products, Inc.; Artesyn Delaware, Inc.; Azcore Corporation; Artesyn Asset Management, Inc.; Artesyn Communication Products Investment Inc.; Artesyn Communication Products, LLC; Artesyn Delaware LLC; Real Time Digital, Inc.; Artesyn FSC, Inc. (Barbados); Artesyn Austria GmbH; Artesyn Austria GmbH & Co. KG; Artesyn Holding GmbH; Artesyn Technologies Asia Pacific Ltd. (Hong Kong); Artesyn Ireland Ltd.; Artesyn Cayman LP; Artesyn Holdings (Ireland) Ltd.; C.P. Power Products (Zhong Shan) Co., Ltd. (China); Artesyn (U.K.) Ltd.; Artesyn Communications Products UK Ltd. (Scotland); Spider Software Ltd. (Scotland); Spider Software, Inc.; Artesyn France S.A.R.L.; Artesyn Germany GmbH (Germany); Artesyn GmbH & Co. KG (Germany); Artesyn Elektronisch Gerate Beteiligungs-und Germany Verwaltungs GmbH; Artesyn Hungary Elektronikai kft; Artesyn Technologies Intellectual Property (Hungary); Licensing Liability Company; Artesyn Energy Systems S.P.A. (Italy).

Principal Divisions

Power Group; Communications Products Group.

Principal Competitors

Emerson Electric Co.; Lucent Technologies Inc.; Power-One Inc.

Further Reading

Alexander, Steve, "Online Mention by Motley Fool Takes Zytec Stock on Wild Ride," *Star Tribune* (Minneapolis), May 9, 1996, p. 1D.

Altany, David, "America's Best Plants," *Industry Week*, October 19, 1992, p. 62.

Chabot, Lucy, "Artesyn Acquires Real Time Digital," *South Florida Business Journal*, February 16 2001, p. 19A.

——, "Artesyn Cuts Jobs, Revises Estimates," *South Florida Business Journal*, June 8, 2001, p. 15A.

"Corporate Capsule: Zytec Corp.," *Minneapolis/St. Paul CityBusiness*, July 12, 1996, p. 26.

Dixon, George, "Keizen!" *Corporate Report Minnesota*, December 1987, pp. 56–60.

Gross, Steve, "Pendulum Swings Toward U.S. for Maker of Computer Parts," *Star Tribune* (Minneapolis), February 4, 1988, p. 1D.

——, "Zytec Cancels Offering, Cites Unsettled Market," *Star Tribune* (Minneapolis), June 23, 1992, p. 3D.

Jones, Jim, "A Quest for Quality," *Star Tribune* (Minneapolis), October 2, 1991, p. 1D.

Krause, Renhardt, "Plugging into Net to Jolt Power Supply Sales," *Investor's Business Daily* (Los Angeles), July 5, 1996.

Larson, Mark, and Mike McCarthy, "Zytec Blasts Off in Lincoln," *Business Journal Serving Greater Sacramento*, October 28, 1996, p. 1.

Mankikar, Mohan, "Anatomy of a Merger," *Electronic Engineering Times*, September 15, 1997, p. 82.

Peterson, Susan E., "It's Easy to Miss Zytec's CEO, But Not His Success," *Star Tribune* (Minneapolis), February 24, 1992, p. 1D.

——, "Zytec Corp. Wins Baldrige National Quality Award," *Star Tribune* (Minneapolis), October 10, 1991, p. 1D.

"Quality with a Capital 'Z,'" *Minnesota Enterprise*, January 1992, p. 6.

Rayner, Bruce C.P., "Zealous Zytec Takes On the World with JIT," *Electronic Business*, November 1, 1987, pp. 130–38.

"Serving Your Multinational Needs with Our Multinational Resources," Boca Raton: Zytec Corp., February 1997.

"Solectron Buys Artesyn Solutions," *Electronic News*, December 10, 2001, p. 4.

Varma, Kavita, "Merger Will Double Computer Products," *South Florida Business Journal*, January 8 1998, p. 3A.

Youngblood, Dick, "Investment Is Key to Successful Global Competition," *Star Tribune* (Minneapolis), June 7, 1987, p. 1D.

——, "The Control Data Legacy: More Than 70 Businesses Trace Roots to Company," *Star Tribune* (Minneapolis), June 3, 1992, p. 2D.

——, "Zytec Puts Its Quality Effort on the Line and It Pays Off," *Star Tribune* (Minneapolis), June 13, 1994, p. 2D.

"Zytec '95 Sales Up 33%," *Electronic News*, March 4, 1996, p. 49.

—Kathleen Peippo
—update: Christina M. Stansell

Asiana Airlines, Inc.

Asiana Town
Kangseo P.O. Box 98
47 Osae-Dong
Kangseo-ku
Seoul
Korea
Telephone: +82 (2) 669-3183
Toll Free: (800) 227-4262
Fax: +82 (2) 669-3170
Web site: http://us.flyasiana.com

Public Company
Incorporated: February 17, 1988
Employees: 6000
Sales: W 1.78 trillion ($1.41 billion) (1999)
Stock Exchanges: KOSDAQ
Ticker Symbol: 20560
NAIC: 481111 Scheduled Passenger Air Transportation;
    481112 Scheduled Freight Air Transportation; 481211
    Nonscheduled Chartered Passenger Air
    Transportation; 481212 Nonscheduled Chartered
    Freight Air Transportation; 48819 Other Support
    Activities for Air Transportation

Asiana Airlines, Inc., Korea's second national airline, has carved out an impressive place for itself during its relatively brief time in the skies. Founded by the Kumho Group as a chiefly domestic carrier. Asiana has invested in new planes from the start and has sought to compete on quality rather than price. Asiana flies a fleet of more than 50 planes to 50 destinations in 13 countries and has extensive cargo and catering operations in addition to its passenger business.

Origins

Asiana Airlines was formed in February 1988. Korea's new-found prosperity was creating rising consumer demand for airline tickets, notes aviation historian R.E.G. Davies, and the transitioning of the country from Third World to industrial made having a single national airline (Korean Airlines Co. Ltd., or KAL) seem an obsolescent idea. With KAL unable to maintain market share in the face of unprecedented demand, Korean president Chun Doo Hwan granted a license for a second national airline to the Kumho Group. This was to be headquartered in the southern city of Kwangju in the Chollanam-do Province, an area somewhat removed economically and politically from the Korean mainstream.

The Kumho Group worked its way into aviation literally from the ground up, starting in taxis in 1946 before moving on to buses and, finally, planes. It was also the country's largest tire producer. Kumho founder In Chon Park, a former police officer, dreamed of founding an air empire. However he died in 1984 before this could be realized.

His son, Dr. Park Seong-Hwang, Kumho Group chairman and former transport minister, saw the dream through as Asiana's first chairman. A former economics professor trained at Yale, he helped secure $36.5 million in start-up capital for the new venture, 35 percent of it came from the Korean Development Bank.

Asiana began scheduled services the week before the government lifted restrictions on foreign travel on January 1, 1989. The pent-up demand was immense. Asiana began with domestic routes based on hubs in Seoul and Cheju. Within a year and a half, it was also flying to four Japanese destinations. In fact, Asiana was able to provide passengers from provincial cities in Japan better international connections in Seoul than they could obtain using Japan's own international airports, noted *Business Week.*

With domestic fares already low in Korea, Asiana competed on service quality. It operated relatively new planes from the beginning, starting with Boeing 737s leased from Ireland's GPA Group. Asiana ordered still more planes in April 1989. This show of confidence continued in September 1990, when the very young airline ordered or optioned $6 billion worth of planes from Boeing.

Asiana's revenues were less than $100 million in 1989, and the carrier lost $46 million. Losses of about $90 million were

Company Perspectives:

The company's mission is to become recognized worldwide by our customers, shareholders, and employees as the best airline in the world. We will focus our energy on performing services that are consistent with our mission by de-centralizing authority, empowering employees, exceeding customers' expectations, and continually improving by providing on-going education. To assist with our mission, we will focus on the following guiding principles: safety will not be compromised; be customer driven, both externally and internally; develop the attitude that conformance to customer expectations has top priority; understand that improvement includes everyone in all parts of the organization; bring all employees into the decision making process; trust people and their ability to contribute to the mission; place emphasis on prevention and problem solving work; treat each other with dignity and respect.

posted the next two years, though revenues reached $150 million in 1990 and doubled in 1991. The company had about 3,000 employees at the time.

Spreading Its Wings in 1991

In early 1991, Asiana's international network spread to Taipei, Hong Kong, Bangkok, and Singapore—all important commercial centers. That November, the carrier launched an ambitious passenger/freight service to Los Angeles via Boeing 747. By the end of 1992, Asiana had also added separate routes to San Francisco and New York. The carrier would have preferred Chicago over San Francisco, but it was already served by KAL and the U.S. government would not allow Asiana to fly there as well. International flights accounted for 65 percent of Asiana's revenues of $404 million in 1992.

Asiana's international expansion outpaced the Korean government's ability to hammer out air traffic agreements with other countries. Korea and China were working on a bilateral agreement covering the Beijing-Seoul route in early 1993; China only wanted to allow one of Korea's airlines to operate between the two cities. Guidelines established in 1990 had only permitted Asiana to fly to Japan, Southeast Asia, and the U.S., but these rules were soon bent.

Routes to two very different destinations were launched in July 1993: Ho Chi Minh City and Honolulu. Unfortunately, Asiana also experienced its first crash that month when one of its Boeing 737s hit a mountain on the Korean coast. By this time, Asiana had a fleet of 29 new Boeing aircraft flying 6 million passengers a year to 16 domestic and 19 international destinations. It had 6,000 employees. The company planned to double in size within seven years.

Profitable in 1994

Asiana's president since 1991, Park Sam-Koo, was the younger brother of company founder Park Seong-Hwang. Park Sam-Koo banned smoking from all planes upon learning the majority of passengers preferred nonsmoking seats. Such deci-

siveness, noted *Business Week,* helped the carrier carve out its place in a competitive market and post its first profit in 1994—W 14.2 billion ($18 million) on sales of W 792.5 billion ($993 million). The airline had lost $200 million during the previous five years. Kumho periodically infused capital into the airline to keep it running. The group did dilute its holdings; it owned 75 percent of Asiana in 1993.

Asiana signed a code-share agreement with Northwest Airlines Corp. in August 1994, operating trans-Pacific routes in tandem with Northwest and giving it access to passengers transferring from the U.S. carrier's extensive network. In 1995, Asiana began operating a Shanghai-Seoul service in collaboration with China Eastern Airlines, which had previously partnered with KAL on that route. However, in November 1996, the South Korean government halted a space-sharing arrangement with Virginia-based Gemini Air Cargo on the New York-Seoul route, contending that this represented a wet lease, which was illegal in South Korea. In a wet lease, one company provides planes, fuel, and crew for another.

By the end of 1996, Asiana was flying cargo flights to three countries, including service to Delhi and Macao, where Asiana shipped cargo on barges from nearby Hong Kong. Cargo accounted for a quarter of Asiana's revenues in 1996.

In the fall of 1997, Asiana became one of several Pacific Rim airlines to sign a code-share agreement with American Airlines, which was attempting to expand its presence in the East. Sabena, Austria Airlines, and Air China were other code-share partners.

Crisis in the Late 1990s

Asiana and Korean Air both suffered during the Asian financial crisis as both the Korean won and passenger counts fell. Asiana logged a loss of W 53.6 billion on revenues of 684 billion for 1997. Both airlines began selling off planes to reduce their debt; Asiana had borrowed $3 billion to expand its fleet. One analyst quoted in *Business Week* gave the company a 50–50 chance of going bankrupt.

Both Asiana and Korean Air also petitioned the government to allow a greater percentage of ownership from foreign investors. Since Korean Air was publicly traded, the government allowed it to be half-owned by foreigners, though it was only 21 percent foreign-owned at the time. Asiana was limited to 20 percent foreign ownership and was in fact 19 percent owned by foreign interests since Swiss-based Pacific Investment Capital had invested in parent company Korean Air Transportation Co. in 1996.

A new bilateral agreement between the U.S. and Korea in 1998 opened the US market to Korean carriers. Asiana soon was posting profits again, thanks in part to a focus on high-yield routes to China and Japan and the recovery of the national economy. A string of accidents at rival Korean Air boosted Asiana's passenger loads. In 1999, Asiana recorded a net profit of W 109.6 billion on sales of W 1.78 trillion, after losing W 141.5 billion on sales of W 1.54 trillion the year before.

Asiana launched an initial public offering on the local KOS-DAQ exchange on December 24, 1999. The carrier earmarked the capital to restructuring its debt. The airline, along with the rest of

Key Dates:

1988: Korea's Kumho Group forms Asiana Airlines.
1989: Korean government lifts foreign travel restrictions.
1990: Asiana orders $6 billion worth of new Boeing aircraft.
1991: U.S. operations commence.
1997: Asian financial crisis hits Korean business traffic hard.
1998: New bilateral agreement further opens U.S. market to Korean carriers.
1999: Asiana lists on the KOSDAQ exchange.
2000: Asiana participates in historic flight to North Korea.
2001: Asiana trims routes and staff and receives government assistance.

the Kumho Group, was helping to pay for the development of Inchon International Airport. After the IPO, Kumho Group's ownership in Asiana fell from 66.7 percent to 47 percent.

Challenges Beyond 2000

Unfortunately, the carrier could not maintain its good results. It posted a net loss of W 156 billion for 2000, thanks largely to higher fuel prices and a weaker currency. Another cause for concern was the re-entry of more foreign carriers, such as All Nippon Airways, into the Korean market.

Asiana started a high-speed delivery service in the spring of 2000 that paired its planes with motorcycles. In June of that year, Asiana was tasked with carrying a South Korean delegation to Pyung Yang in a historic first flight to North Korea since the country was divided in 1945.

As part of its effort to attract lucrative business travelers, Asiana installed sleeper beds in its first class cabins, which were limited to only a dozen seats. In-flight entertainments systems were also top rate, and Asiana compared its business class cabin to other airlines' first class. A generous mileage program and excellent on-time performance were two other key selling points for the business client.

Flight attendants and ground staff staged a strike at Asiana in June 2001. That summer, Asiana was protesting a ruling by the U.S. Federal Aviation Administration that lowered Korea's air safety rating, preventing any of its carriers from expanding or changing operations to the U.S. Asiana felt it was being unfairly penalized, as its own safety record was above average.

Asiana continued to vie aggressively for trans-Pacific cargo business. In June 2001, it launched a service to carry fresh fruit and seafood from Seattle to Asia. In late September, the carrier announced cutbacks to its Los Angeles service at the same time as it was trimming 360 jobs from its 8,600-strong workforce. Asiana also cut routes in Asia and Europe.

The Korean government announced a W 250 billion ($192 million) bailout package for both Asiana and Korean Air in November 2001. Asiana was to receive a low-interest loan for W 110 billion ($85 million).

Principal Operating Units

Air Transportation; Catering; Communication; Construction; e-business; Electricity; Engineering; Facilities; Ground Handling; Logo Products.

Principal Competitors

All Nippon Airways; British Airways; Cathay Pacific Airways; Fed Ex; Japan Airlines; Korean Airlines Co. Ltd.; Singapore Airlines; United Airlines.

Further Reading

Arceo-Dumlao, ''Sunday Biz 'Sleepers' and a Generous Mileage Program Sell This Airline,'' *Philippine Daily Inquirer,* February 4, 2001.

''Asiana Faces Growth Setback as Seoul Fumbles in Air Talks,'' *Business Times* (Singapore), Shipping Times, March 26, 1993, p. 20.

''Asiana Lists on Kosdaq as Profits Rise,'' *Airfinance Journal,* November 1999, p. 12.

''Asiana on Brink of Corporate Overhaul by Selling Fleet,'' *Airfinance Journal,* February 1998, p. 6.

''Asiana President Summoned; KAL Gets New Safety Head,'' *Airfinance Journal,* February 2000, p. 5.

Bangsberg, P.T., ''Korean Airlines Shedding Planes to Pare Their Debt,'' *Journal of Commerce,* April 29, 1998, p. 13A.

——, ''South Korean Air Carriers Spread Their Wings, Put Focus on Cargo,'' *Journal of Commerce,* November 1, 1996, p. 8B.

Barnett, Chris, ''Korean Competitor; Asiana Airlines Fights for Market Share as It Seeks Waiver from FAA Ruling,'' *Journal of Commerce,* September 10, 2001, p. 39.

Bociurkiw, Michael, ''South Korea's Asiana Sets a Scorching Pace,'' *South China Morning Post,* Bus. Sec., August 25, 1993, p. 4.

Cameron, Doug, ''Asiana Stays for the Long Haul,'' *Airfinance Journal,* March 1995, p. 30.

Cheesman, Bruce, ''Asiana Airlines: Korean Upstart Comes of Age,'' *Asian Business,* September 1993, p. 17.

Clifford, Mark, ''Upstart Still Rising: Airline Is Group's Loss Leader,'' *Far Eastern Economic Review,* April 18, 1991, p. 64.

Clifford, Mark L., Brian Bremner, and Hugh Filman, ''The Airlines That Fell to Earth,'' *Business Week,* July 13, 1998, p. 126.

Darlin, Damon, ''Two Sons Rise in the East,'' *Forbes,* September 26, 1994, p. 58.

Davies, R.E.G., ''Airlines of South Korea,'' *Airlines of Asia Since 1920,* London: Putnam Aeronautical Books; McLean, Virginia: Paladwr Press, 1997, pp. 515–32.

Donaghue, J.A., ''Asiana's Competitive Code,'' *Air Transport World,* July 1996, p. 30.

Flint, Perry, ''All Dressed Up and No Place to Go,'' *Air Transport World,* May 1991, p. 22.

Jones, Dominic, ''On the Rebound?'' *Airfinance Journal,* December 1999, pp. 34–36.

Kayal, Michele, ''Open Skies Could Put Korea in the Cockpit; Drop in Cargo Rates to US Feared as Lines Aggressively Add Capacity,'' *Journal of Commerce,* April 29, 1998, p. 1A.

——, ''South Korea Halts US Airline,'' *Journal of Commerce,* November 27, 1996, p. 1B.

Lee, Dexter, ''Asiana Flying High with First Profit,'' *Business Times* (Singapore), Shipping Times, August 29, 1995, p. 2.

Levere, Jane L., ''Business Travel; The American Airlines Pact with Asiana Is Part of a Strategy to Increase a Pacific Rim Presence,'' *New York Times,* October 22, 1997, p. D11.

''Market Development Award: Asiana,'' *Air Transport World,* February 1997, pp. 47–8.

Moorman, Robert W., ''The Other Korean Airline,'' *Air Transport World,* June 2000, pp. 57–9.

Nakarmi, Laxmi, Joyce Barnathan, and Hiromi Uchida, "Clouds Part for Asiana," *Business Week,* March 20, 1995.

"New Korean Airlines Gives Boeing $1 Billion Order," *Los Angeles Times,* Bus. Sec., April 11, 1989, p. 2.

"Passenger Service: Asiana," *Air Transport World,* February 2001, p. 35.

Pasztor, Andy and Jeff Cole, "Asiana Air's Pilots Face U.S. Bribery Inquiry," *Wall Street Journal,* July 10, 1996, p. A2.

Proctor, Paul, "Asiana Nears Profitability After Bankruptcy Scare," *Aviation Week & Space Technology,* May 31, 1999, p. 36.

Rainat, Joyce, "A Cabbie's Legacy," *Asian Finance,* March 15, 1991, p. 12.

"Strike Takes Heavy Toll on South Korea's Embattled Airlines," *Business Recorder,* June 14, 2001.

Westlake, Michael, "Fly in the Ointment: South Korean Carriers Vie for Passengers," *Far Eastern Economic Review,* September 3, 1992, p. 55.

Wong Joon San, "Asiana Airlines to Increase Cargo Services to Territory," *South China Morning Post,* Freight and Shipping, June 1, 1997, p. 6.

—Frederick C. Ingram

Avon Products, Inc.

1345 Avenue of the Americas
New York, New York 10105-0196
U.S.A.
Telephone: (212) 282-5000
Fax: (212) 282-6049
Web site: http://www.avon.com

Public Company
Incorporated: 1886 as the California Perfume Company
Employees: 43,000
Sales: $5.9 billion (2001)
Stock Exchanges: New York
Ticker Symbol: AVP
NAIC: 32562 Toilet Preparation Manufacturing; 45439 Other Direct Selling Establishments

The oldest beauty company in the United States, Avon Products, Inc. has grown from a modest line of perfumes sold door-to-door to one of the world's leading brand of cosmetics. It manufactures and sells cosmetics, fragrances, toiletries, accessories, apparel, and various decorative home furnishings. Avon employs a unique direct-selling method, which was greatly responsible for its incredible success in the 1950s and 1960s, when women were easily found in the home for sales purposes. After unsuccessful efforts at diversification into the health-care service industry left the company with massive debts in the late 1980s and early 1990s, Avon began to refocus on its roots: beauty products and direct selling. The company's products are sold through catalogs, mall kiosks, its prestigious day spa in Trump Tower in New York, the Internet, and in J.C. Penney stores. Its products are also sold directly to customers in nearly 143 countries by 3.5 million independent sales representatives, making Avon the number one direct sales company in the world.

Early Years as the California Perfume Company

The beginnings of Avon Products, Inc. can be traced to the mid-1880s, when a door-to-door book salesman named David H. McConnell attempted to bolster declining sales by offering small samples of perfume to housewives who would listen to his sales pitch. It soon became clear, however, that his customers were more interested in the perfume, and McConnell left the book-selling business to create an entire line of perfumes to be sold door-to-door. He brewed the perfume in a pantry-sized space in New York City, naming the product line the "Little Dot Perfume Set," which consisted of five scents: white rose, violet, lily of the valley, heliotrope, and hyacinth. His endeavor was named the California Perfume Company in an effort to invoke images of the beauty and excitement of that state.

McConnell's intent was to build a business around quickly used products sold directly to the consumer through use of the national network of sales agents he had organized during his years as a bookseller. The nation's first Avon Lady was Mrs. P.F.E. Albee of Winchester, New Hampshire, the wife of a U.S. senator. Within the first six months of operation, Albee had assembled a solid base of 100 salespeople and their customers; within 12 years, Albee had recruited and trained nearly 5,000 representatives.

In addition to new scents, other products were quickly added to the California Perfume Company's product line. Popular early items included spot remover, Witch Hazel Cream, machine oil, mending cement, Almond Cream Balm, food flavorings, Tooth Tablet, and carpet cleaner. In 1896, ten years after the company was conceived, McConnell hired Adolf Goetting, a noted perfumer who had been in the business for 25 years. The following year, a new laboratory was built in Suffern, New York, and the first illustrated catalog was produced. By the company's 20th year, its product line had expanded to include more than 100 items, and in 1914 the company's rapid expansion was marked by the opening of an office in Montreal, Canada.

The Early 1900s: Avon Is Born

The first products in the California Perfume Company's line of Avon Products—a toothbrush, cleanser, and vanity set—appeared in 1920. The Avon name was inspired by the area around the Suffern lab, which McConnell thought resembled the countryside of William Shakespeare's home, Stratford-on-Avon, England. Never wavering from its strategy of door-to-door sales and catalogs filled with low-cost home and beauty products, the company surpassed the $2 million sales mark in 1926, the year of its 40th anniversary.

By the end of the 1920s, the company was doing business in 48 of the United States and in Canada. During this time, thousands of female sales representatives, under Albee's supervision, were partaking in one of the first opportunities for American women to experience a degree of economic freedom without upsetting their culturally accepted role as homemakers. The company launched three-week sales campaigns and a "specials" strategy in 1932. Five years later, in 1937, McConnell died and was replaced by his son, David H. McConnell, Jr., who headed the company for the next seven years. Under his supervision, the company's growth remained steady. In 1939, the California Perfume Company was renamed Avon Products, due to that product line's immense popularity and success.

During World War II, cosmetic production slowed while nearly half of the staff in the Suffern lab devoted themselves to wartime production of such things as insect repellent, pharmaceuticals, and paratrooper kits. In 1944, W. Van Alan Clark replaced McConnell as the company's chairman. The new Avon then instituted several changes during the 1950s, the most notable of which was its entry into overseas markets and the rapid expansion of its sales force.

Postwar Expansion in the 1950s and Beyond

Following the war, many more housewives began seeking extra income and work that did not interfere with family life. In the early 1950s, the Avon sales force almost quadrupled in size. Sales representatives' territories were downsized by several hundred homes, a strategy that enabled more representatives to be added and sales to increase sixfold over the following 12 years. Avon advertisements appeared on television for the first time, including the famous slogan, "Ding Dong, Avon Calling," which was first televised in 1954. That same year, Avon opened offices in Venezuela and Puerto Rico, marking its first venture into what would become a very lucrative Latin American market. It also penetrated the European market in 1957 with the institution of Avon Cosmetics, Ltd. in the United Kingdom.

Under the leadership of W. Van Alan Clark, Avon also saw changes such as the rapid expansion of foreign sales and Avon's listing on the New York Stock Exchange in 1964. Clark was replaced by J.A. Ewald in 1966, who was followed by W. Hicklin

a year later. Under Hicklin, the traditional three-week sales cycle was changed to two weeks to improve sales. The three-week campaign was still used overseas, particularly in Asia, a market which was entered by Avon in 1969 through the opening of operations in Japan. Japan remained one of Avon's key foreign markets, along with Brazil, Mexico, and the United Kingdom.

The 1970s presented Avon with its greatest challenges in the company's history. Though sales topped $1 billion in 1972, and its profitable costume-jewelry line—begun in 1971—had made Avon the world's biggest jewelry manufacturer in just five years, Avon's growth stalled in 1973. The company was hit hard by a recession and the mass entry of women into the workforce. The direct-selling system, Avon's innovation and strength, was nearly toppled by social changes that management had not anticipated. The status of the U.S. dollar reduced the company's international profits; recession and inflation crippled its high-sales decanter products line; in 1975, about 25,000 Avon Ladies quit; and Avon products were outpaced by retail cosmetic firms offering jazzier products to women with new attitudes. All of these factors converged and led to troubled times—and Avon's eventual restructuring.

In response to these hardships, the most visible change Avon made was to become more sensitive to its market. Sales representatives began to follow women into the workplace, where about 25 percent of Avon's sales are made today, and new businesses such as direct-mail women's apparel were tested. Changes were also made to the cosmetics product line and its overall pricing as a result of market studies. Fred Fusee, who had advanced through the manufacturing side of Avon to become its chairman in 1972, was replaced in 1975 by David W. Mitchell, whose years with Avon had been spent in marketing. Mitchell worked to solidify Avon's presence in the beauty business via consumer and product research, product development, and promotion. Avon's image was overhauled to give it a more contemporary appeal, advertising time was more than tripled, and sales were revamped.

In 1979, Avon made another strategic move to update its product offerings through the purchase of Tiffany & Company, the upmarket jeweler, for $104 million. The Tiffany purchase set the tone for the next decade: diversification through acquisition. This included an ill-fated billion-dollar plunge into the health-care industry and a later entry into the prestige-fragrance market.

The 1980s: Diversification Through Acquisition

In 1983, Hicks Waldron, who had previously helped turn around General Electric, left his post at R.J. Reynolds to become Avon's chairman. Shortly before Waldron's appointment, Avon had purchased Mallinckrodt, a chemical and hospital supply company. Waldron followed this purchase with the acquisition of Foster Medical Corporation in 1984. Initially thriving in the home and health-care equipment field, Foster became the fastest-growing division of Avon. Just as the company began to celebrate its success, however, Foster was devastated by Medicare cost-containment efforts. At the same time, Tiffany's profits were steadily declining—in part because customers had become alienated by the introduction of lower-priced merchandise—and the Tiffany subsidiary was sold in 1984.

Key Dates:

1886: David H. McConnell establishes the California Perfume Company.
1897: A new laboratory is built in Suffern, New York, and the company's first illustrated catalog is produced.
1914: The company opens an office in Montreal, Canada.
1920: The Avon Products line is launched.
1939: The company is renamed Avon Products Inc.
1957: Avon enters the European market and forms subsidiary Avon Cosmetics Ltd. in the United Kingdom.
1964: The company goes public.
1995: Justin Pty Ltd. is acquired; sales reach $4.5 billion.
1999: Andrea Jung becomes the first female CEO of Avon.
2001: Retail brand beComing is launched in J.C. Penney retail outlets.

Avon then tried to focus on health care for the elderly with the 1985 acquisitions of the Retirement Inns of America and The Mediplex Group, both of which were nursing home operations. Unfortunately, only 15 percent of Avon's sales came from its health-care holdings that year. This failure, combined with the fact that annual profits overall were about half of what they were in 1979, caused Waldron to rethink his strategy and abandon the diversification plan. Mallinckrodt was sold in early 1986 and Foster in 1988, both at a great loss to Avon, and plans to sell the remaining health-care divisions were announced. The company sold Retirement Inns of America in 1989 and The Mediplex Group in 1990. Avon's brief health-care industry foray left it $1.1 billion in debt.

Diversification into prestige fragrances later proved to be a more stable endeavor. First came a joint venture with Liz Claiborne in 1985, followed by the acquisitions of Parfums Stern and Giorgio, Inc. in 1987. Parfums Stern, which produced Oscar de la Renta, Perry Ellis, and other designer perfumes, was a chief competitor of Liz Claiborne, and before long Claiborne dissolved its agreement with Avon. Strapped for cash, Avon then sold Parfums Stern in early 1990. Giorgio remained a top-selling national brand well into the 1990s, however, and under the parentage of Avon introduced several new products in the Giorgio line.

Gaining Financial Stability: Early to Mid-1990s

Waldron retired in 1989, and his successor, James E. Preston, immediately faced several takeover attempts. Avon fought off a bid by Amway Corporation in partnership with Irwin L. Jacobs, a Minneapolis, Minnesota-based raider who then launched a takeover attempt himself. While these efforts receded in the early 1990s, a new suitor appeared in the form of the Chartwell Association, an investment group that included the chief financial officer of Mary Kay Cosmetics. Interestingly, the Avon sales force proved to be the greatest deterrent to these takeover bids; in massive letter-writing campaigns, the sales representatives told aggressors that they will be unwilling to work for them.

In 1990, Avon continued to focus on rejuvenating its domestic sales figures, while selling approximately 40 percent of Avon Japan to the Japanese public for $218 million in revenues. Mean-

while, the company entered further into the business of selling items in the United States through direct-mail means, using full-color catalogs to promote its products. These measures helped the company increase 1990 sales to $3.45 billion, marking an increase of over $150 million from the previous year.

As Avon began to stand on firmer ground financially, it was able to focus once again on expanding its scope worldwide. The early 1990s were spent establishing sales headquarters and networks in other countries, while also continuing to boost sales in the United States. Avon entered the sales market in Poland in 1992 through the recruitment and training of more representatives to work in direct sales capacities there. The company also entered the Russian market in 1993. Annual sales broke the $4 billion mark that year, and the per-share price of Avon's stock rose to over $32. The company also began selling its product on the Internet, taking advantage of the increasing popularity of the information superhighway.

In 1994, Avon sold off its Giorgio product line, which was becoming a less important asset as time went on. The company instead focused on promoting products carrying its own name. It further strengthened its standing in the foreign market in 1995 with the addition of a sales office in India, and the acquisition of Justin (Pty) Ltd. in South Africa, the country's second largest direct-selling cosmetics company. 1995 sales topped off at almost $4.5 billion.

Expansion continued as Avon also began selling sportswear and apparel for women in its direct-mail catalogs after finalizing a joint venture with fashion designer Diane Von Furstenberg to introduce a line of moderately-priced casual wear. Avon tied the addition in with the company's corporate sponsorship of the 1996 Summer Olympics in Atlanta, Georgia, and a multi-million dollar advertising campaign that named sports figures such as Jackie Joyner-Kersee as ''Just Another Avon Lady.'' Also in 1996, Avon introduced ''Lifedesigns,'' a corporation developed to offer goal-setting and management seminars to women. Early the following year, Avon also purchased Discovery Toys, Inc., a direct-sales marketer of educational toy products for children. Discovery Toys continued operations separate from those of Avon, with the hope that Avon's immense global sales network would help the small company attain higher sales and thus contribute to its new parent's yearly revenues. The sales from this unit did not reach expected levels, however, and Discovery was sold in 1999.

Rebuilding the Avon Brand: Late 1990s and Beyond

Avon entered the late 1990s trimmed of its unwieldy diversification into the health-care industry. The company continued to hire sales representatives throughout the world to sell products directly to consumers, while also working to expand various other sales outlets. The majority of its efforts during the last years of the decade, however, were spent fine-tuning its brand as it faced fierce competition and slowing American sales. By this time, Avon products had developed a somewhat stodgy image and held little appeal to young women. In 1998, revenue grew by just three percent—far from the company's goal of reaching levels of eight-to-ten percent annual growth by 2000.

As a result, the firm began to devote millions to various advertising campaigns. In an attempt to launch the Avon brand with more of a trendy, upscale appeal, the firm opened a day spa, The Avon Centre, in Trump Tower in New York City. Avon's president at the time, Andrea Jung, commented on the company's objective in a 1999 *Fortune* article, stating that the firm wanted to position Avon as a "world-class beauty brand" and that it needed to "change people's minds about Avon." Jung—who joined Avon in 1994—was named CEO in 1999, becoming the company's first female CEO.

Under her leadership, Avon began its brand turnaround and also focused on bolstering U.S. revenues, which accounted for nearly 30 percent of company sales in 2000. The company started to make sweeping changes to its advertising, manufacturing, packaging, and selling strategies. Adopting the tagline, "The Company for Women," Avon set out to increase market share, break into new selling channels, and prove that the faltering Avon Lady and her products could enter the new millennium with a fresh, innovative appeal.

During 2000, Avon increased its advertising budget to $90 million—nearly doubling what it spent in 1999—and also invested in revamping its Web site. It signed celebrity tennis stars Serena and Venus Williams to its "Let's Talk" ad campaign. The firm also spent heavily in research and development, increasing its budget in 2000 by 46 percent over the previous year, and pushed to reduce the time it took to launch new products on the market. During that year, the firm introduced Anew Retroactive, an age reversal cream. Avon Wellness, a line of nutritional, aroma therapy, fitness, and relaxation products, hit the market in 2001. The company also began its foray into store branding by teaming up with J.C. Penney to position its retail brand beComing in a department store setting. Jung also tapped Avon's newly elected president Susan Kropf to overhaul the company's manufacturing and distribution operations. Kropf cut the number of Avon suppliers from 300 to 75 and completely automated the ordering processing. Her efforts saved the company $400 million and reduced errors in shipments and customer orders.

While Jung—named chairman in 2001—pressed for further growth for 2002 and beyond, she faced several challenges. While company stock had increased by 70 percent since her election to CEO in 1999, it began to fall after the September 11th terrorists attacks on the U.S. Consumer spending slowed, and foreign markets such as Argentina faltered due to economic crises. During 2001, the company posted revenues of $5.9 billion, a small 4.9 percent increase over the previous year. Jung, while optimistic, prepared for the challenging future. "The next couple of years are going to be no walk in the park," she commented in an October 2001 *Fortune* article. "This turnaround is far from complete. I'm probably thinking that we need to be even bolder and faster."

Principal Subsidiaries

Cosmeticos Avon S.A.C.I. (Argentina); Avon Cosmetics Australia Proprietary Limited (Australia); Avon Products Pty. Limited (Australia); Avon Cosmetics Vertriebsgesellschaft m.b.h. (Austria); Arlington Limited (Bermuda); Stratford Insurance Co., Ltd. (Bermuda); Avon Holdings, Ltd. (Bermuda); Productos Avon Bolivia Ltda. (Bolivia); Avon Cosmeticos, Ltda. (Brazil); Avon Industrial Ltda. (Brazil); Avon Canada, Inc. (Canada); Avon Fashions, Inc. (Canada); Avon Mode Inc. (Canada); Cosmeticos

Avon S.A. (Chile); Avon Products (Guangzhau) Ltd. (China) (73.85%); Avon Products (China) Co. Ltd. (73.85%); Avon Cosmetics, Spolecnosti S. Rucenlm Omezenym (Czech Republic); Avon Capital Corp.; Avon International Operations, Inc.; Avon-Lomalinda, Inc.; Productos Avon S.A. (Dominican Republic); Productos Avon Ecuador S.A. (Ecuador); Productos Avon, S.A. (El Salvador); Avon S.A. (France); Avon Cosmetics GmbH (Germany); Productos Avon de Guatemala, S.A. (Guatemala); Productos Avon, S.A. (Honduras); Avon Cosmetics (FEBO) Limited (Hong Kong); Avon Cosmetics Hungary KFT (Hungary); Avon Service Center, Inc.; Avon Beauty Productos India Private Limited (India); P.T. Avon Indonesia (Indonesia; 92%); Albee Dublin Finance Company (Ireland); Avon Limited (Ireland); Avon Cosmetics S.p.A. (Italy); Avon Products Company Limited (Japan; 66%); Live & Life Company Limited (Japan; 68%); Avon Cosmetics SIA (Latvia); UAB Avon Cosmetics (Lithuania); Avon Cosmetics (Malaysia) Sendirian Berhad (Malaysia; 70%); Avon Cosmetics, S.A. de C.V. (Mexico); Avonova, S.A. de C.V. (Mexico) (49%); M.I. Holdings Inc.; Avon Americas, Ltd.; Avon Overseas Capital Corp.; Avon Cosmetics Limited (New Zealand); Productos Avon de Nicaragua, S.A. (Nicaragua); Avon Cosmetics A/S (Norway); Productos Avon S.A. (Peru); Productos Avon S.A. (Panama); Avon Cosmetics, Inc. (Philippines); Avon Products Mfg., Inc. (Philippines); Beautifont Products, Inc. (Phillipines); Avon Cosmetics Polska Sp. z o.o (Poland); Avon Cosmeticos, Lda. (Portugal); Avon Cosmetics Spal s r.o (Slovak Republic); Avon Beauty Products Company (Russia); Justine/Avon (Pty) Ltd. (South Africa); Avon Cosmetics, S.A. (Spain; 75%); Avon Cosmetics (Taiwan) Ltd. (Taiwan); Avon Products Limited (Taiwan); Avon Cosmetics (Thailand) Ltd. (Thailand); California Manufacturing Co. Ltd. (Thailand); Eczacibasi Avon Kosmetik Urunleri Sanayi ve Ticaret A.S. (Turkey) (50%); Avon Cosmetics (Ukraine); Avon Cosmetics Limited (United Kingdom); Avon European Holdings Ltd. (U.K.); Cosmeticos Avon De Uruguay S.A.; Avon Cosmetics de Venezuela, C.A.

Principal Competitors

L'Oreal SA; Mary Kay Inc.; Revlon Inc.

Further Reading

Brooker, Katrina, "It Took a Lady to Save Avon," *Fortune*, October 15, 2001, p. 202.

Cardona, Mercedes M., "Becoming a Store Brand," *Advertising Age*, September 10, 2001, p. 70.

"Earnings Fall at Avon," *United Press International*, February 6, 2002.

The Greatest Beauty Story Ever Told, New York: Avon Products, 1986.

Hayes, Linda, "The Changes in Avon's Makeup Aren't Just Cosmetic," *Fortune*, August 13, 1979.

Kleinfield, Sonny, *Staying at the Top*, New York: New American Library Books, 1986.

Klepacki, Laura, and Pete Born, "Avon's Star Return," *WWD*, December 15, 2000, p. 10.

McLean, Bethany, "Not Your Mother's Avon: A Middle American Icon Gets Sort of Cool," *Fortune*, May 24, 1999, p. 44.

"Remaking the Avon Lady," *Money*, February 1, 2000, p. 46.

—Carol I. Keeley
—updates: Laura E. Whiteley and
Christina M. Stansell

Bank of America.

Bank of America Corporation

Bank of America Corporate Center
100 North Tryon Street
Charlotte, North Carolina 28255
U.S.A.
Telephone: (704) 386-1845
Toll Free: (800) 299-2265
Fax: (704) 386-6699
Web site: http://www.bankofamerica.com

Public Company
Incorporated: 1904 as Bank of Italy; 1960 as North
    Carolina National Bank
Employees: 142,724
Total Assets: $621.7 billion (2001)
Stock Exchanges: New York
Ticker Symbol: BAC
NAIC: 551111 Offices of Bank Holding Companies;
    52211 Commercial Banking

Bank of America Corporation was formed in the 1998 merger of NationsBank Corporation and BankAmerica Corporation. It operates as the third-largest bank in the U.S. with over 4,200 retail consumer banking locations in 21 states and the District of Columbia. The company is ranked number one in terms of deposit market share in Texas, California, Florida, Georgia, North Carolina, and Washington. Bank of America has four main business segments, comprising Consumer Banking, Commercial Banking, Global Corporate and Investment Banking, and Asset Management. Through these segments, the firm provides financial products, services, and solutions to customers in 48 states and 38 countries across the globe.

The History of BankAmerica Corporation

BankAmerica was founded in 1904 as the Bank of Italy. Its credo was radical at the time: to serve ''the little fellows.'' From its humble beginnings in a former tavern, BankAmerica grew to become a force that revolutionized U.S. banking. With deregulation, however, its traditional emphasis on the general consumer created problems for the bank.

Amadeo Peter Giannini, founder of BankAmerica, became one of the most important figures in twentieth-century American banking. Giannini, an Italian immigrant, was seven when his father died. By age 21, he had earned half ownership of his stepfather's produce business. He married into a wealthy family, and profits from the produce business, combined with shrewd real estate investments in San Francisco, enabled him to retire at age 31.

His retirement was brief. When his father-in-law died, he left a sizable estate, including a directorship of a small San Francisco savings bank. When Giannini failed to convince the board of this bank that the poor but hardworking people who had recently come to the West Coast were good loan risks, he resigned his position and set out to start his own bank—a bank for ''people who had never used one.''

The year, 1904, was an inauspicious one; an up-and-down economy and the financial irresponsibility of many banks during this period gave banking such a bad name that the government was eventually prompted to create the Federal Reserve system, in 1917. But Giannini's bank was atypical. His policy of lending money to the average citizen was unheard of in the early 1900s, when most banks lent only on a wholesale basis to commercial clients or wealthy individuals.

Giannini raised capital for his new bank, called the Bank of Italy, by selling 3,000 shares of stock, mostly to small investors, none of whom were allowed to own more than 100 shares. Although Giannini never held a dominant share of stock, the extreme loyalty of these and subsequent stockholders allowed him to rule the bank as though it were closely held. His innovative policies made the Bank of Italy and its successor, the Bank of America of California, the most controversial bank in the United States. The nation watched with wary eyes as he created a system of branch banking that made it the world's largest bank in a mere 41 years.

During the famous San Francisco earthquake of 1906, Giannini rescued $80,000 in cash before the bank building burned by hiding it in a wagon full of oranges and bringing it to his house for safekeeping. With this money he reopened his bank days before any other bank and began making loans from a plank-

---

Company Perspectives:

Bank of America seeks to build broad, deep and long-lasting relationships with its customers by providing a full range of banking, investing and insurance products and services, and to create value for customers by delivering financial solutions within the context of each customer's complete banking relationship and financial situation, as one company with one customer experience. Middle-market and large corporate clients also benefit from the company's relationship-based approach, with client managers coordinating delivery of a broad range of products and services, including (but not limited to) commercial lending, treasury management, debt and equity capital raising, risk management and mergers and acquisitions advisory services.

---

and-barrel counter on the waterfront, urging demoralized San Franciscans to rebuild an even better city.

Giannini's original vision led naturally to branch banking. Expense made it difficult for small depositors to travel long distances to a bank, so Giannini decided his bank would go to them, with numerous well-placed branches. Accordingly, the Bank of Italy bought its first branch, a struggling San Jose bank, in 1909.

Giannini made up the rules as he went; he was not a banker, and his was the first attempt ever at branch banking. Going his own way included loudly denouncing the ''big interests,'' and he repeatedly offended influential members of the financial community, including local bankers, major Californian bankers, and many state and federal regulators, who were already uncertain about how to handle an entirely new kind of banking. Some did support Giannini's vision though, including William Williams, an early California superintendent of banks, and the Crocker National Bank, which lent money to a subsidiary of the Bank of Italy expressly for acquiring branch banks.

The Formation of Bank of America of California and Transamerica: Late 1920s

The bank grew rapidly; in 1910 it had assets of $6.5 million. By 1920, assets totaled $157 million, far outstripping the growth of any other California bank and dwarfing its onetime benefactor, Crocker National. Further expansion was stymied, however, by the state of California and by the new Federal Reserve system, which did not allow member banks to open new branches. Giannini shrewdly sidestepped this regulation by establishing separate state banks for southern and northern California (in addition to the Bank of Italy) as well as another national bank, and putting them all under the control of a new holding company, BancItaly. Finally, in 1927, California regulations were changed to permit branch banking, and Giannini consolidated his four banks into the Bank of America of California.

With California conquered, Giannini turned to the national scene. He believed that a few large regional and national banks would come to dominate American banking by using branches, and he intended to blaze the trail. He already owned New York's Bowery and East River National Bank (as well as a chain of banks in Italy); next he established Bank of America

branches in Washington, Oregon, Nevada, and Arizona, again before branch banking was explicitly permitted.

Federal regulators, objecting to Giannini's attempts to dictate the law, took exception to some of his practices. In response, Giannini created another holding company in 1928, to supplant BancItaly. The new company was called Transamerica, to symbolize what Giannini hoped to accomplish in banking.

Giannini knew he needed a Wall Street insider to help him realize his dream of nationwide branch banking, and he thought Elisha Walker, the head of Blair and Company, an old-line Wall Street investment-banking firm, was just the man. So, in 1929, the year Bank of America passed the $1 billion mark in assets, Transamerica bought Blair.

A year later, Giannini consolidated his two banking systems into the Bank of America National Trust and Savings Association, under the control of Transamerica. Sixty years old and in poor health, he relinquished the presidency to Walker, retired for the second time, and went to Europe to recuperate. It was again a short retirement. His stay ended abruptly in 1931, when he received news that Walker was trying to liquidate Transamerica.

Giannini headed straight for California, where three-quarters of the bank's stockholders remained. What followed was one of the most dramatic proxy fights in U.S. history. Giannini crisscrossed California, holding stockholder meetings in town halls, gymnasiums, courthouses, and other public spaces. A poor public speaker, he hired orators to drive home the message that Walker and eastern interests, the dreaded ''big guys'' Giannini had battled against for years, were trying to ruin the bank. The campaign succeeded and the stockholders returned control of the Bank of America to Giannini.

The bank had suffered, though. By the end of 1932, deposits had shrunk to $876 million, from a high of $1.16 billion in 1930. No dividend was paid that year, for the first time since 1905, and the battle had cost Giannini his New York banks. Depositor confidence had to be rebuilt.

Giannini's presence seemed to be just the right thing. By 1936, Bank of America was the fourth-largest banking institution in the United States (and the second-largest savings bank) and assets had grown to $2.1 billion. The bank continued to innovate, instituting a series of new loans called Timeplan installment loans. Timeplan included real estate loans, new and used car financing, personal credit loans from $50 to $1,000, home appliance financing, and home-improvement loans, all industry firsts.

As the Bank of America became more influential, Giannini took on bigger and bigger foes, among them the Federal Reserve, Wall Street, the Treasury Department, the Securities and Exchange Commission (SEC), Hans Morgenthau, and J.P. Morgan, Jr. Eventually, the enmity Giannini aroused in his war against the American financial establishment cost the bank its chance for nationwide branch banking. The beginning of the end came in 1937, when the Federal Reserve made its first attempt to force Transamerica and Bank of America to separate.

Postwar Growth

World War II brought tremendous growth to the Bank of America. As people and businesses flocked to California during

Key Dates:

1874: Several prominent Charlotte, North Carolina, citizens form The Commercial National Bank.

1887: The Citizens Bank of Savannah, Georgia, begins operation.

1904: Amadeo Peter Giannini forms the Bank of Italy in San Francisco, California.

1906: Citizens Bank merges with Southern Bank to form Citizens and Southern (C&S) Bank.

1909: Bank of Italy buys its first branch, a struggling San Jose bank.

1927: California regulations allow for branch banking; Giannini consolidates his holdings into the Bank of America of California.

1928: Giannini forms holding company Transamerica.

1929: Bank of America surpasses $1 billion in assets; Blair and Company is purchased.

1930: Giannini consolidates his banking systems into the Bank of America National Trust and Savings Association, which falls under control of Transamerica.

1945: Bank of America becomes the world's largest bank during World War II.

1957: The Federal Reserve forces Transamerica to separate from Bank of America.

1960: The North Carolina National Bank (NCNB) is created.

1968: BankAmerica Corporation is created as a holding company for Bank of America N.T. & S.A.

1975: BankAmerica's assets reach $60 billion.

1981: BankAmerica begins to experience a loan crisis; NCNB expands into Florida.

1984: Two major institutions, Virginia National Bankshares and First and Merchants, merge to form Sovran Financial Corp.

1987: BankAmerica begins restructuring efforts.

1990: C&S and Sovran merge.

1991: NationsBank Corp. is formed from the merger of NCNB and C&S/Sovran Corp.

1992: BankAmerica Corp. and Security Pacific Corp. merge.

1997: NationsBank announces the purchase of Barnett Banks Inc.; BankAmerica acquires Robertson, Stephens and Company L.P.

1998: BankAmerica and NationsBank merge in a $62 billion deal and offically adopt the name Bank of America Corporation soon thereafter.

2001: Kenneth D. Lewis is named chairman and CEO; the company focuses on brand recognition.

---

the war, the bank more than doubled in size: in 1945, with assets of $5 billion, it passed Chase Manhattan to become the world's largest bank.

As California began to rival New York as the most populous state, Bank of America continued to expand. Giannini continued to battle, and win, against the big interests, until his death in 1949. From radical outsider to the leader of what *Business Week* called the "new orthodoxy" of banking—the trend toward serving average consumers—Giannini's was one of the most innovative careers in twentieth-century banking.

He was succeeded as president of Transamerica by his son, Lawrence Mario, long a top official at the bank, who continued in his father's tradition. In 1952, however, Lawrence Mario succumbed to lifelong health problems. Following the deaths of the Gianninis, Bank of America slowly made itself over. New chief Clark Beise moved to decentralize operations, encouraging branch managers to assume more responsibility for their branches. This approach paid off with tremendous growth; by 1960, assets totaled $11.9 billion. The bank continued to innovate. In 1959, it was the first bank to fund a small-business investment company. It was also the first U.S. bank to adopt electronic and computerized record-keeping; by 1961, operations were completely computerized. Other new programs included student loans, an employee loan-and-deposit plan that let workers transact bank business through their offices (a response to increased competition from credit unions), and the first successful credit card, BankAmericard, the predecessor of Visa.

In addition, Bank of America stepped up its international presence, becoming one of only four U.S. banks with significant impact on international lending. It also began to pursue wholesale accounts, to supplement its traditional retail base. Finally, in 1957,

the Federal Reserve forced Transamerica to separate from Bank of America, an event the two institutions had anticipated.

Bank of America's efforts to become a "department store of finance" in the late 1950s and early 1960s marked the last significant period of innovation in the bank's history until the 1980s. It was a time when the bank strove to sell the widest variety of banking services to the widest possible market. Beise felt there was more room for innovation, saying in 1959 that "there are new frontiers to develop," but warning that "we are constantly fighting against the attitude of entrenched success." It was a battle that the Bank of America lost, as it eventually became a conservative, stodgy, and inflexible institution.

The Formation of BankAmerica Corporation: 1968

In 1968, BankAmerica Corporation was created as a holding company to hold the assets of Bank of America N.T. & S.A. and to help the bank expand and better challenge its arch-rival, Citibank. This came just before banking deregulation, which affected Bank of America more adversely than was predicted. Bank of America's branch banking system was a major problem, since it gave the bank the highest overhead in the banking industry. Through this period the retail division provided 50 percent of the bank's profits. It was not until interest rates exploded in the 1970s that the bank's bulk of low-interest-bearing mortgages became damaging, as it was for many savings and loans.

As the largest bank in the world, the Bank of America was a natural target for groups with statements to make during the 1960s. It became the first major employer in California to sign a statement of racial equality in hiring. At the time, the Bank of America had more than 3,500 minority employees—more than 10 percent of its workforce. The bank also responded to complaints from women's groups by creating a $3.8 million fund for training female employees in 1974, and set itself the goal of a 40 percent-female workforce.

By 1970, Bank of America had established a $100 million loan fund for housing in poverty-stricken areas and purchased municipal bonds that other California banks would not touch. This was in keeping with the tradition Giannini had established when he bought rural school bonds and bonds for the Golden Gate Bridge at a time when no other bank would buy such issues.

A.W. "Tom" Clausen succeeded Rudy Peterson as chief executive officer (CEO) in 1971. He presided over Bank of America's last tremendous growth spurt—assets jumped 50 percent (to $60 billion) just between 1973 and 1975. Bank of America was the only one of the 20 largest U.S. banks to average 15 percent growth between 1971 and 1978; its seemingly unstoppable growth earned its management great praise during the 1970s.

Restructuring: 1980s

When Clausen left Bank of America in 1981 to head the World Bank, Bank of America had $112.9 billion in assets. Clausen was replaced by 40-year-old Samuel Armacost. Soon the Bank of America began to fall apart. Energy loans, shipping loans, farming loans (Bank of America was the largest agricultural lender in the world) and loans to third-world countries all started to go bad. Bank of America, whose large deposit base had traditionally made it exceptionally liquid but had also given it trouble in maintaining proper capital reserves, was ill prepared to meet the crisis. Suddenly, the biggest bank in the world had no money. It could not even raise capital in the stock market because its stock price had plummeted at a time when most bank stocks were rising.

Armacost started a general campaign to cut costs. The bank dropped a third of its 3,000 corporate clients, sold subsidiaries and its headquarters building, closed 187 branches, and began to lay off employees, something it had never done before. In 1986, the wounded BankAmerica became the target of a takeover bid from a company half its size. First Interstate Bancorp offered $2.78 billion for the nation's second-largest banking group. A few days after this bid was made public in early October, Armacost resigned and was replaced by none other than Tom Clausen, the man many blamed for BankAmerica's troubles in the first place. Clausen resisted the takeover, but Joe Pinola, Interstate's chairman, was determined, and by the end of October had sweetened the deal to $3.4 billion. Clausen was equally determined to prevent BankAmerica's takeover. He rejected First Interstate's bid and battened down the hatches for a hostile assault. In the end, Clausen was able to rally shareholders behind him and thwart First Interstates' plans.

In 1987, BankAmerica set about restructuring its operations. Clausen sold nonessential assets—including the Charles Schwab discount securities brokerage and Bank of America's Italian subsidiary—and refocused the bank's attention on the domestic market. New services, including advanced automated teller machines and extended banking hours, lured Californian customers back. In addition, the bank went after the corporate business it had neglected in the early 1980s. Clausen cut back substantially

on staff, cleaned up the nonperforming loans in Bank of America's portfolio, and hired a number of exceptional managers to execute BankAmerica's new directives. By the end of 1988, the bank was in the black again. Though still plagued by a good deal of exposure to Third World debt, BankAmerica was able to record a profit of $726 million, its first in three years.

By 1989, BankAmerica's recovery was so strong that it was able to declare its first dividend since the fourth quarter of 1985. Industry analysts called the recovery the biggest turnaround in the history of U.S. banking. Retail operations were expanded in Nevada with the acquisition of Nevada First Bank, and in Washington with the purchase of American Savings Financial Corp. by the subsidiary Seafirst Corp., the largest bank in the Pacific Northwest. During this year, BankAmerica was the first major bank in California to announce that it would open all its branches on Saturdays and extend weekday hours for greater consumer convenience.

Acquisitions and Mergers: 1990s

In 1990, BankAmerica showed further evidence of its recovery by announcing that its revenues exceeded $1 billion for the first time. Industry analysts theorized that the bank had the cleanest loan portfolio of the nation's big banks. Acquisitions included Woodburn State Bank of Oregon, Western Savings and Loan branches in Arizona, and Benjamin Franklin and MeraBank Federal Savings, the largest S&Ls in Oregon and Arizona, respectively. The bank also opened a new international branch in Milan, Italy.

In 1990, BankAmerica surpassed Chase Manhattan to become the second-largest bank holding company in the nation. Also, in keeping with the bank's policy of community responsibility, it began an Environmental Program that included activities directed toward saving paper and other materials through recycling, and energy and water conservation.

Seeking to expand its operations beyond its branches in seven western states, the bank added branches in two more states with the 1991 acquisitions of ABQ and Sandia Federal Savings banks of New Mexico, and Village Green National Bank in Houston. Another purchase was a subsidiary of GNA Securities that had operated an investment program in the bank's branches since 1988. The program, called Bank of America Investment Services, offered mutual funds and tax-deferred annuities. In spite of the nation's economic recession at this time as well as higher deposit insurance premiums and higher credit losses and non-accruals, BankAmerica was able to post its third straight year of record earnings—more than $1 billion.

Expanding services to customers continued with the opening of full-service branches in grocery stores in southern California. In addition, to allow customers access to money anytime and anywhere, the bank opened several hundred new Versateller ATM's for a total of 2,300 in nine states.

After nine months of preparation, the merger of BankAmerica Corp. and Security Pacific Corp. became final on April 22, 1992. After the merger BankAmerica became the nation's second-largest bank. The joining of the California banks was the largest merger in the history of banking at the time and created an institution with nearly $190 billion in assets and $150 billion in deposits. The merger was part of a national trend of bank consolidation that sought to strengthen troubled and even healthy institutions. For BankAmerica, the merger offered an opportunity to become more efficient and save money—an estimated $1.2 billion annually within the next three years. The merger also helped the bank expand into new markets and geographic locations. By the end of 1992, consumer banking services were provided in ten western states, trust and consumer financial services were provided nationwide, and commercial and corporate banking operations were located in 35 countries worldwide.

Acquisition activity continued with the purchase of Sunbelt Federal Savings, which held 111 branches in 76 cities in Texas; HonFed, the largest thrift in Hawaii; and Valley Bank of Nevada, which made BankAmerica the largest depository institution in that state. However, the persistent national recession, combined with a recession in the state of California, caused a decline in earnings reported for 1992.

Domestic expansion continued in 1993 with the acquisition of First Gibraltar of Texas and with an agreement to make a $1 million equity investment in Founders National Bank, the only African-American-owned bank on the West Coast. Additional overseas expansion occurred when BankAmerica received approval from the People's Bank of China to upgrade its Guangzhou representative office into a full-service branch, the first U.S. bank to have such a branch. Consolidation of consumer and commercial finance units was undertaken, and one year after the merger, the bank had consumer operations in much of the United States, wholesale offices in 37 nations, retail branches in ten western states, and consumer finance company operations in 43 states.

As BankAmerica moved into the mid-1990s, it focused on many of the policies it had begun in the 1980s. Under the leadership of David Coulter—named chairman and CEO in 1996—BankAmerica's strategies included development of new products and services for consumers; geographic diversification into such fast-growing economies as Asia and Latin America, which would enable the bank to better withstand the economic cycles of the domestic market; community investments; environmental programs; and loans to students and those with low income. BankAmerica also continued to hope for changes in laws and regulations that would allow interstate banking and more effective competition with non-bank institutions providing similar financial services. The company got its wish when federal laws began to allow banks to participate in the securities industry. As such, BankAmerica purchased investment banking firm Robertson, Stephens & Co. in 1997 for $540 million.

The History of NationsBank Corporation

NationsBank was one of the United States' largest banking and financial companies. Based in Charlotte, North Carolina, the company grew at breakneck speed through the late 1980s and early 1990s to claim a spot as one of the nation's top five financial institutions. Industry analysts credit this phenomenal growth to the company's foundation of bold, aggressive management and thorough, professional planning. They also credit the company's success to the personality and leadership of Hugh L. McColl, Jr., who served as NationsBank's CEO from 1983 to 1998 and then as Bank of America Corp.'s chairman

and CEO to 2001. McColl's style, that of a southern-born and bred ex-Marine, contrasted sharply with that of most members of the banking community and contributed to NationsBank's image as one of the mavericks of the banking world.

NationsBank was officially formed on December 31, 1991, with a merger between the $69 billion asset North Carolina National Bank Corporation (NCNB) and the $49 billion asset C&S/Sovran Corporation. The merger created the fourth-largest banking company in the United States. McColl became the first president and chief executive officer of NationsBank and Bennett A. Brown became the first chairman.

The two companies entered the merger having both completed a decade of rapid growth that was typical of the banking industry in the 1980s. NCNB and C&S/Sovran both followed the common industry pattern of numerous mergers and acquisitions in the 1980s. After expanding into South Carolina and Florida in the early to mid-1980s, Charlotte-based NCNB took an unprecedented leap forward through a unique expansion into Texas in 1988. The FDIC selected NCNB to manage the restructured subsidiary banks of First RepublicBank Corporation of Texas. Atlanta-based C&S Bank had banking offices throughout Georgia, Florida, and South Carolina. In 1990, this company merged with similarly sized Sovran Financial of Norfolk, Virginia. Sovran had banking offices throughout Virginia, the District of Columbia, and Maryland, as well as in Tennessee and Kentucky. After these two companies merged, the resulting organization established dual headquarters in Atlanta and in Norfolk.

The Growth of NCNB

NCNB traces its illustrious history back to the Commercial National Bank, which was organized by several prominent Charlotte citizens in 1874. Its initial start-up capital was $50,000. A series of mergers with other North Carolina financial institutions in the 1950s ultimately led to the creation of North Carolina National Bank on July 1, 1960. At the time of its formation, NCNB had 1,300 employees, 40 offices in 20 North Carolina communities and assets of $480 million. The bank continued to acquire smaller institutions, and by 1969 NCNB had grown to 91 offices in 27 North Carolina counties with deposits of more than one billion dollars. Ten years later, it stood as the state's largest bank.

In the mid-1950s, however, when the nation talked about banking in the state of North Carolina, most people were talking about Wachovia Bank and Trust Company, NCNB's arch-rival. Based in Winston-Salem, Wachovia had offices from the mountains to the coast and exercised considerable political clout in the capitol city of Raleigh. Bankers at other institutions stood in envy of Wachovia. Many bankers thrived on the competition, and some, such as Addison Reese at American Commercial Bank—one of NCNB's predecessor institutions—in Charlotte, considered that competition the reason for going to work each morning.

At the time, Reese believed that North Carolina banking was poised for a change and nothing could stop him from meeting Wachovia's threats. North Carolina's banking laws were more liberal than in most states. They had been on the books since the early 1800s, when a Wilmington, North Carolina, bank appealed to the state legislature for permission to open an office about ninety miles away in Fayetteville. The legislature complied with the bank. Unlike law-makers in most states, the North Carolina legislature saw no reason to restrict branch banking during the intervening 150 years. In retrospect, many people believe that it was the close competition with backyard rival Wachovia that spurred NCNB's rapid growth.

North Carolina National Bank broke new ground when it expanded into Florida in 1981 with its purchase of First National Bank of Lake City, Florida. At the time, it became the first non-Florida bank to expand its retail services into the state. After a quick approval of the purchase by the Federal Reserve Board of Governors, NCNB rapidly purchased several other Florida banks.

In 1986, NCNB benefited from a change in North Carolina's interstate banking laws. With the advent of reciprocal interstate banking in the Southeast, North Carolina National Bank moved into South Carolina with the purchase of Bankers Trust Company. In 1985, it acquired Southern National Bankshares of Atlanta and Prince William Bank of Dumfries, Virginia, in 1986. North Carolina National Bank moved into Maryland in 1987 with the purchase of CentraBank of Baltimore. In 1989, NCNB acquired full ownership of First RepublicBank in Texas. During this period of growth, North Carolina National Bank established several "firsts" in its industry. For example, NCNB was the first U.S. bank to use commercial paper to finance the activities of nonbank subsidiaries; to open a branch in London; to operate a full-service securities company; and to list its common stock on the Tokyo Exchange.

The Development of C&S/Sovran

The C&S/Sovran side of the NationsBank puzzle traces its roots back to the 1860s. The company that would eventually become Sovran opened its doors in Richmond during that decade. At the time, its customer base included Confederate Army commander Robert E. Lee. More than a century later, in 1984, two major institutions—Virginia National Bankshares and First and Merchants—merged to form Sovran Financial Corporation. At the time, it was the largest banking merger in Virginia's state history.

Sovran's management team decided to merge with D.C. National Bancorp, headquartered in Bethesda, Maryland, in 1986. By November of 1987, Sovran was moving west by merging with Commerce Union, a 71-year-old bank holding company based in Nashville. Commerce Union's business at the time spanned Tennessee and had a presence in Kentucky. The merger gave Sovran strongholds in both of those states.

Around the time Sovran Bank's foundations were being laid, the Citizens Bank of Savannah, Georgia, opened its doors in the temperate coastal city on November 2, 1887. At the time, the bank had $200,000 in startup capital. In 1906, it merged with its crosstown rival, Southern Bank, to form Citizens and Southern Bank. The resulting organization became the state's largest financial institution. It began to spread rapidly across the state of Georgia. Citizens and Southern began opening offices in South Carolina in 1928, but the company sold its operations there in 1940 when it anticipated federal rules preventing banks from owning branches in multiple states. The resulting C&S

Bank of South Carolina was rejoined with Citizens and Southern in 1986 when the Georgian giant bought them back. That acquisition, along with the purchase of Landmark Banks of Florida in 1985, helped Citizens and Southern double its size within eighteen months during the mid-1980s.

C&S can also claim several firsts in the industry. Among the highlights in C&S history are being the first bank to figure "to the penny" balances, one of the first to offer checking accounts in the South and to issue its own credit card, and the first bank in the nation to offer 24-hour access to its services via automated teller machines. The nation's first ATM machine was set up in Valdosta, Georgia, under the C&S banner.

In spring of 1989, C&S was successful in resisting a takeover bid by NCNB. At the time, C&S cited what it considered a low price offer and concerns about NCNB's recent entry into the then-depressed Texas banking market. Soon thereafter, C&S and Sovran merged in a deal finalized on September 1, 1990.

The C&S/Sovran and NCNB Merger

The banking environment, however, was in the midst of tremendous change. Large banks were continuing to consolidate. As a result, smaller banks were under constant pressure to find new ways to improve their efficiency and productivity and reduce their workforces. In addition, the nation as a whole experienced a downturn in the real estate market—an area responsible for much of an average bank's business. The newly merged C&S/Sovran (the merger was announced in the spring of 1989 and consummated in the fall of 1990) was suffering from the recession in the Southeast, and it had been particularly hard hit by mounting losses on loans in the District of Columbia metropolitan area. Real estate loans made up 32 percent of the bank's $34 billion portfolio at the end of 1990, with Washington, D.C., accounting for 21 percent of the real estate total. C&S/Sovran's stock price had dropped from $35.88 at the close of the first quarter in 1989, when NCNB announced its merger intentions, to $15.63 at the close of the fourth quarter in 1990. Under these circumstances, North Carolina National Bank renewed its offer to merge with C&S/Sovran.

Prior to reissuing his offer, McColl gathered with his advisors. According to Howard Covington and Marion Ellis in the book *The Story of NationsBank: Changing the Face of American Banking*, McColl told Senior Vice-President C.J. "Chuck" Cooley, "I am going to buy C&S/Sovran. I don't know when. I don't know how." He instructed Cooley to hire the best talent available and deliver a complete psychological profile on C&S/Sovran's key players, including Bennett Brown and Dennis Bottoroff. Cooley handled the job himself, and several weeks later, he handed McColl a profile of Brown as well as a profile of McColl himself, as seen by Brown.

Cooley told his boss that the keys to Brown's relationships with people were honesty, sincerity, warmth, and friendliness. To McColl's chagrin, however, each of those traits was opposite the characteristics that McColl portrayed to Brown. From Brown's vantage point, McColl was arrogant, crude, and ungentlemanly. After hearing Cooley's report, McColl and several other advisors began an intense series of role-playing sessions. McColl was schooled to avoid the use of militaristic terms and other verbal and nonverbal examples of his usual aggressive style. His staff coached him to become softer, more receptive, and friendlier in his approach.

Meanwhile, McColl's confidence was growing as C&S/Sovran's problems continued to multiply. The credit problems in the D.C. area increased, and the bank's board split badly between an Atlanta faction and a Tennessee and Virginia faction. News filtered down to the NCNB leaders that although both factions preferred to remain independent, a merger with NCNB was the second choice among those on both sides. With this knowledge, McColl renewed his merger efforts with Brown.

On June 20, McColl departed Charlotte in the NCNB plane for Atlanta to make Bennett Brown a second offer. The two banking leaders sat down in Brown's home to discuss the terms of the deal. Brown's concerns were predictable: he wanted to know about leadership, cuts in personnel and staff, the name of the new bank, and—most important—the price.

McColl supplied the right answers to all of Brown's questions. The merged bank would carry the name NationsBank, which eased concerns about the North Carolina flag flying over Georgia. Shortly after NCNB's Texas acquisitions, the marketing group began experimenting with new names that would better reflect the company's size and geographic diversity, as well as be more acceptable in new markets. At that time, the company began working with the Naming Center in Dallas. The Naming Center enlisted the work of academic linguists who worked with Latin teachers and poets to develop names rather than generating them by computers.

On the list of prospective names was the word "Nation." Using poster-sized flash cards, the company combined two of them to create the single word "NationsBank." Everyone was surprised when lawyers determined that the new name was not in use anywhere else in the world, and it soon cleared marketing surveys conducted nationwide. Ironically, NationsBank consistently scored as one of the most recognized and highly regarded names in banking, although it had never been used before. The corporate identity firm of Seigel and Gale in New York then developed a graphic look for the word that would reinforce its characteristics.

As for the issue of leadership, McColl wanted Brown to take the chairmanship, while he retained the title of CEO and president. McColl also pulled a sheet of paper from his coat that illustrated an exchange of 0.75 shares of NCNB stock for each share of C&S/Sovran. That exchange would mean a total payout of $3.99 billion for C&S/Sovran's shareholders. Brown was receptive to the deal, but could not supply McColl with a firm answer.

It was on June 25 that the news about the probable merger broke in the Charlotte community. Even the national media focused on the possibility of this mega-deal between these banks in the South. C&S/Sovran's leadership soon received the second offer with enthusiasm. Among other issues, NCNB had proven the wisdom and success of the large Texas acquisition, and C&S/Sovran was seeking the efficiencies and economies of scale inherent in a merger of this magnitude. The merger was approved by the Federal Reserve on November 29, 1991, and NationsBank officially opened its doors on January 2, 1992. At the time of the union, North Carolina National Bank was the

tenth-largest bank in the United States, and C&S/Sovran was the twelfth largest. Together, they thrust each other to a position among the top three banking leaders in the United States.

The new entity quickly went to work to establish its presence in its chosen corporate headquarter city of Charlotte. Already, NCNB's office buildings jutted into the southern skyline, but as NationsBank the company decided to build a new headquarters building. The result of this goal was the new NationsBank Corporate Center, a pristine sixty-story tower designed by architect Cesar Pelli. At the time it was built, it became the tallest building in the Southeast, and NationsBank firmly established itself as one of the nation's financial heavyweights. As tribute to the man who led this building effort, many Charlotte onlookers began to call the new Corporate Center the "Taj McColl."

The new bank had more domestic deposits than New York's Citibank, market capitalization to rival J.P. Morgan & Company, more branch offices than almost any other competitor, and assets of nearly $120 billion. In addition to serving as a leader in the financial world, in the early 1990s NationsBank served as a role model to the larger corporate community as well. Nationwide, it was known as a company that exercised not only sound management practices, but cultural consciousness as well. Under McColl's leadership, NCNB had already established flexible hours for working parents and a pre-tax child care expense reimbursement fund. Maternity leave was extended to six months, and the concept was expanded to include time off for new fathers. These ground-breaking policies attracted the attention of the *Wall Street Journal*, which in its centennial issue edition in 1989 selected NCNB as one of twelve companies in the world to watch in the future. *Fortune* magazine also chose McColl as one of the year's twenty-five most fascinating business people—the only one selected from the banking industry—in its January 1989 issue.

The company's financial strength also served as a resource for the many communities it supported. Charlotte itself was one of the nation's fastest growing metropolitan areas, due largely to the growth and visibility of NationsBank. In 1994, the company had 1,800 branch offices, which made it the second-largest branch network in America. By providing traditional banking products to retail and corporate customers, as well as investing in innovative products and services, the company's assets had grown to $165 billion.

As the banking industry continued to consolidate and change during the mid-1990s, NationsBank made several key purchases. In 1996, the company announced the $9.6 billion acquisition of St. Louis, Missouri-based Boatmen's Bancshares Inc. McColl commented on the purchase in a 1997 *St. Louis Business Journal* article, claiming that "it brings NationsBank into contact with 100 million Americans, 40 percent of the population. That's exciting to us. Also, I'm a classical strategist. It denies it to the enemy, the enemy being everyone else." NationsBank then went on to purchase Barnett Banks Inc., Florida's largest bank. The $15.5 billion deal was completed in January 1998.

The 1998 BankAmerica and NationsBank Merger

NationsBank, which had completed over 70 deals since 1980, made another aggressive move in 1998 when McColl approached BankAmerica's Coulter about merging the two companies. Both McColl and Coulter knew that by joining forces, the combined entity would be the first coast-to-coast banking company in the United States with $572 billion in assets and offices in 22 states. Coulter agreed to a "merger of equals" and on April 13, 1998, BankAmerica announced that it would team up with NationsBank in a $62 billion merger. It soon became apparent however, that NationsBank would be the dominant partner.

The merged entity, whose name officially became Bank of America Corporation, took headquarters in Charlotte and served 30 million households in the U.S. as well as customers in 38 different countries. McColl took control of the new company as chairman and CEO. Coulter, however, resigned his presidency in the Fall of 1998 amid speculation that he and McColl had come into conflict over some of BankAmerica's previous bad loans and lost earnings. McColl—slated to retire after the deal—had his work cut out for him upon completion of the merger, as he tried to integrate both BankAmerica and Nations-Bank, as well as the purchases both companies had made just before their merger. Industry analysts began to speculate that perhaps McColl may have taken on more than he could handle with the BankAmerica deal.

During 1999 and into 2000, Bank of America was plagued with integration problems which forced it to post lower than anticipated revenue growth, net income, and earnings. The company cited credit problems and bad loans as culprits in its lackluster financial performance. As such, Bank of America began to restructure in order to streamline operations. Nearly 10,000 jobs were cut, mostly in middle management. The firm also began to refocus on customer service.

McColl retired in April 2001 and left Kenneth D. Lewis to take over as chairman and CEO. Under new leadership, Bank of America turned its efforts to independent growth, which had taken a back seat to deal-making activity for years. "Our priority is organic growth. Our strategy is to deepen, to expand relationships . . . and to focus on quality of service," claimed Bank of America's chief financial officer James Hance in a 2001 *American Banker* article. The company also went to work on its brand image, increasing its 2002 advertising budget to $145 million—an increase of 50 percent over the previous year.

When the dust settled around the BankAmerica-Nations-Bank deal, the new Bank of America stood as the third largest bank in the U.S. and the thirteenth-largest U.S. corporation. Many analysts argued the firm had yet to reach the potential created by the 1998 merger and looked to Lewis to implement strategies that would secure increased earnings and positive financial results. While Bank of America appeared to be well positioned for success amid the turbulent and ever-changing banking industry, its ability to integrate the purchases of the 1990s remained key in securing future profits.

Principal Subsidiaries

American Financial Service Group, Inc.; BA Merchant Services, Inc.; BA Mortgage, LLC; Banc of America Advisors, Inc.; Banc of America Business Finance Corporation; Banc of America Capital Management, Inc.; Banc of America Commercial Corporation; Banc of America E-Commerce Holdings, Inc.; Banc of America Investment Services, Inc.; Banc of America Securities LLC; Bank of America Capital Corporation; Bank of America (Asia) Limited (Hong Kong); Bank of America (Polska) S.A.; Bank of America Brasil Holdings Ltda.; Bank of America Canada; Bank of America International Limited (UK); Bank of America, S.A. (Spain); BankAmerica Acceptance Corp.; Barnett Bank Premises Company–Brickell; Boatmen's Financial Services, Inc.; C&S Premises, Inc. CSF Holdings, Inc.; Fleetwood Credit Corp.; NationsBanc Charlotte Center, Inc.; NationsBank Trust Company of New York; NCNB Corporate Services, Inc.

Principal Competitors

Citigroup Inc.; J.P. Morgan Chase & Co.; Wachovia Corp.

Further Reading

"BankAmerica Corp.," *Wall Street Journal*, February 4, 1993, p. B6.

BankAmerica Environmental Progress Report, BankAmerica Corporation, 1992.

Bank of America Milestones, 1989–93.

Boraks, David, "B of A, Its Deals Done, Turns Attention to Brand-Building," *American Banker*, August 13, 2001, p. 1.

Brooks, Rick, and Martha Brannigan, "Coulter Quits BankAmerica President Post," *Wall Street Journal*, October 21, 1998, p. A3.

Calvey, Mark, "Executive of the Year: BankAmerica CEO Develops Power Within," *San Francisco Business Times*, January 9, 1998, p. 1.

——, "NationsBank Takes Command," *San Francisco Business Times*, April 17, 1998, p. 1.

Covington, Howard E., and Marion A. Ellis, *The Story of NationsBank: Changing the Face of American Banking*, Chapel Hill: The University of North Carolina Press, 1993.

Haber, Carol, "Robertson Deal Latest in Bank Moves on Wall St.," *Electronic News*, June 16, 1997, p. 64.

Hector, Gary, *Breaking the Bank: The Decline of BankAmerica*, Boston: Little, Brown, 1988.

James, Marquis, and James, Bessie R., *Biography of a Bank: The Story of Bank of America, N.T. & S.A.*, New York: Harper, 1954.

Manning, Margie, "McColl Scales New Heights with Boatmen's Buy," *St. Louis Business Journal*, January 6, 1997, p. 1.

"The Megamergers of 1998: At B of A, Dealmaking Gives Way to Discipline," *American Banker*, October 25, 2001, p. 1.

"NationsBank-BankAmerica—A Coast-to-Coast Pioneer," *American Banker*, April 14, 1998, p. 1.

"NationsBank to Pay $15.5B for Florida's Barnett," *The Financial Post*, August 30, 1997, p. 9.

"New BankAmerica Debuts," *BankAmerican*, April 22, 1992, p. 1.

Nicolova, Rossita, "Birth of National Giant Bank of America Announced," *The Kansas City Business Journal*, October 2, 1998, p. 5.

Stewart, Thomas A., "Where the Money Is," *Fortune*, September 3, 2001, p. 153.

Zuckerman, Sam, "B of A Adopting SecPac's Orphan NonBank Units," *American Banker*, April 6, 1993, p. 1.

—Wendy Johnson Bilas
—updates: Dorothy Kroll and Christina M. Stansell

Bank of Montreal

119 St. Jacques
Montreal, Quebec H2Y 1L6
Canada
Telephone: (514) 877-7373
Fax: (514) 877-7399
Web site: http://www.bmo.com

Public Company
Incorporated: 1822
Employees: 32,000
Total Assets: $238 billion (2001)
Stock Exchanges: New York
Ticker Symbol: BMO
NAIC: 52211 Commercial Banking

The Bank of Montreal is one of the largest banks in Canada. It also has a substantial presence in the United States. The bank operates over 1,200 branches spread across North America, Europe, Latin America, and Asia. Bank of Montreal owns Harris Bankcorp, the fourth largest bank in the Chicago area. Another major subsidiary is the investment firm BMO Nesbitt Burns. Nesbitt Burns is a premier international equity trading company. Bank of Montreal also owns the New Jersey-based investment firm CSFBdirect Inc. That company is part of Bank of Montreal's wealth management division, which focuses on affluent individual investors. In a joint venture with Royal Bank of Canada, Bank of Montreal runs the largest credit card processing company in Canada, Moneris Solutions Corp. Bank of Montreal offers a full array of banking products, with over 30 different lines of business.

Canada's First Bank

Until the late 20th century, Canada's banks were on the whole stodgy, sheltered, and highly regulated institutions. The Bank of Montreal was among the fustiest and most traditional of them all. But two singular events in the 1970s and 1980s—the arrival of an aggressive new CEO in 1975 and the deregulation of the Canadian banking industry in 1985—shook up this old bank and forced it to deal with the increasing complexity and internationalization of the financial world. By 2000, the bank

had a global presence and was rapidly expanding both in Canada and the United States.

If any bank had a right to be stodgy and traditional, it was certainly the Bank of Montreal, whose roots stretch back to the early 19th century. It first opened for business in 1817 on St. Paul Street, in the heart of Montreal's business district, as the Montreal Bank. It did so without an official charter and was forced to rely on American investors for nearly half of its initial capital. But within five years the new bank had proven its worth to the community, and it was granted a charter in 1822 as the Bank of Montreal. By then, all but 15 percent of its capital stock had been repatriated.

During its early years, the bank engaged in bullion and foreign-currency trading in addition to its lending activities. In 1827 and 1828, it was forced to omit its dividend for the first and last time after the bulk of Quebec's fur-trading activity shifted to the Hudson Bay, depressing the local economy and causing a number of loan defaults. During this time, however, the Bank of Montreal also began its long financial and managerial association with the expansion of Canada's canal and railway systems. In the late 1830s, it prospered despite political upheaval. The Bank of Montreal acquired the Toronto-based Bank of the People at that time; thus, when Upper and Lower Canada were united into the Province of Canada in 1841, its total assets exceeded C$4 million.

During the early 1860s, the Bank of Upper Canada, which was then the Canadian government's official banker, slid inexorably toward failure, and in 1864 the Bank of Montreal was appointed to take its place. It continued in this capacity until the establishment of the Bank of Canada in 1935. The bank also began to expand its branch network when Canada achieved full political unity in 1867, opening two offices in New Brunswick. It opened a branch in Winnipeg, Manitoba, in 1877 and followed the Canadian Pacific Railway westward as railroad construction opened up the prairie for settlement. Bank of Montreal branches appeared in Regina, Saskatchewan, in 1883; Calgary, Alberta, in 1886; and Vancouver, British Columbia, in 1887.

The bank already had two foreign offices by this point; it had opened one in New York in 1859 and another in London in

1870. The Bank of Montreal used its foreign representation to expand into investment banking in the late 1870s. It joined a syndicate of London bankers in underwriting loans to the province of Quebec and the city of Montreal. In 1879, it underwrote a Quebec securities issue and floated it on the New York market. And in 1892, it became the Canadian government's official banker in London, underwriting all of the national government's bond issues on the London market.

Expansion in the Early 20th Century

At the turn of the century, the Bank of Montreal embarked on an acquisition spree that would make it Canada's largest bank by the outbreak of World War I. It improved its position in the Maritime Provinces and northern Quebec by acquiring the Exchange Bank of Yarmouth, the People's Bank of Halifax, and the People's Bank of New Brunswick. In 1906, it bought out the bankrupt Bank of Ontario.

In 1914, the Bank of Montreal had C$260 million in assets, 179 offices, and 1,650 employees. Nearly half of its mostly male workforce enlisted in the military at the outbreak of war, but the hiring of women in large numbers made up for the loss. In fact, the war had a rather salutary effect on the bank's finances due to the sale of war bonds, which were quite popular. World War I also marked the end of the London market's role as the Canadian government's main source of external financing, as the London securities markets were closed to foreign issues from 1914 to 1918, and the Bank of Montreal and the government began to float their bond issues in New York.

An economic crash in 1920 followed a short postwar boom, and the crisis forced Canadian banks to consolidate. The Bank of Montreal had already acquired the British Bank of North America in 1918; it bought the Merchants Bank of Canada in 1922 and the Montreal-based Molsons Bank in 1925. These acquisitions increased its branch network to 617 offices, more than three times what it had been during the war.

The depression that struck Canada in the 1920s, however, was not as serious as the Great Depression of the 1930s. In 1933, Canada's gross national product was almost half of what

it had been in 1928, and the number of unemployed increased nearly thirteen-fold. Bank of Montreal's assets were worth nearly C$1 billion in 1929, then dropped below C$800,000 for five consecutive years. The Depression finally ended with the outbreak of World War II, during which the Bank of Montreal, just as it did during the previous war, lost large numbers of employees to the armed services and also made money from the sale of war bonds.

The years after World War II brought prosperity and rapid economic development to Canada. Canadian banks also prospered, but in a regulated and noncompetitive atmosphere. "It was sort of a clubby affair," Bank of Montreal executive vice president Stanley Davison told *Fortune* in 1979. Canadian law limited the interest banks could charge on their loans to 6 percent, and power in the banking industry was concentrated in a group of five major banks, of which the Bank of Montreal was one. During this time, however, the Bank of Montreal also earned itself a reputation for stodginess and an unwillingness to adapt to change. In the mid-1960s its earning performance began to weaken. Then, in 1967, an amendment to the Canadian Bank Act eliminated the interest-rate ceiling, opening up new opportunities in the area of consumer and small-business lending. The Bank of Montreal was caught unprepared to keep pace with its competitors.

Its financial performance was further eroded by a costly but necessary computerization program. The Bank of Montreal's accounting procedures seemed not to have changed much since the age of the quill pen; when CEO Fred McNeil assumed his post in 1968, he asked a personnel department executive for a copy of the departmental budget and the executive replied: "Budget? No one has ever asked us to prepare one." But computerizing the bank swallowed up more and more money. Its projected cost in 1969 was C$80 million, and the figure was repeatedly revised upward for several years thereafter. In 1972 the bank started a credit card program, and the start-up costs added even more financial liability. The Bank of Montreal was the last of Canada's five major banks to bring out a credit card.

Renewed Vigor in the 1970s–80s

Into this state of affairs stepped William Mulholland, who was named CEO in 1975, when McNeil became chairman. Mulholland was an American. Formerly a partner at the prominent investment bank Morgan Stanley, in 1969 he was named president of Brinco Limited, a Canadian mining company. After taking the top job at the Bank of Montreal, he dodged the controversy over an American heading up one of Canada's largest banks by promising to consider adopting Canadian citizenship.

Mulholland's aggressive and uncompromising management style was once described as "chewing through underlings with a chainsaw" by *Canadian Business* magazine, and a number of senior executives left the bank during his tenure. But the bank's condition also improved immediately after he took office. Mulholland closed down 50 unprofitable branches during his first five years in office, revised the Bank of Montreal's internal pricing system to reflect the cost of funds more accurately, and modernized procedures for asset and liability management. He was also unafraid to bring in outside help, as he did when he recruited IBM executive Barry Hull to get the computerization

<table>
<tr><td colspan="2">Key Dates:</td></tr>
<tr><td>1817:</td><td>The bank begins operations as Montreal Bank.</td></tr>
<tr><td>1822:</td><td>The bank is officially chartered.</td></tr>
<tr><td>1864:</td><td>Bank of Montreal becomes the Canadian government's official bank.</td></tr>
<tr><td>1914:</td><td>Bank of Montreal is established as largest bank in Canada.</td></tr>
<tr><td>1975:</td><td>William Mulholland becomes CEO.</td></tr>
<tr><td>1984:</td><td>The bank acquires Chicago's Harris Bank.</td></tr>
<tr><td>1987:</td><td>The bank acquires brokerage firm Nesbitt Thomson.</td></tr>
<tr><td>1993:</td><td>The bank begins major expansion drive in U.S.</td></tr>
<tr><td>1998:</td><td>Bank of Montreal's merger with Royal Bank of Canada is not approved.</td></tr>
</table>

program on track. The bank opened its first computerized branch office in 1975, and all 1,240 of its branches were plugged into the computer system by 1979.

The Bank of Montreal also sought to internationalize under Mulholland, joining a trend in which just about every one of the world's major financial institutions participated since the late 1960s. In 1978 it purchased a 25.1 percent interest in Allgemeine Deutsche Creditanstalt, a medium-sized West German bank. Also in 1978, the Bank of Montreal tried to expand into the American retail banking market when it began negotiating the acquisition of 89 branch offices from Bankers Trust Company. Mulholland forged ahead with the deal despite analysts' misgivings, but negotiations broke down in 1979 and the deal was never consummated.

The Bank of Montreal suffered in the early 1980s under the strain of loans to Latin America and to oil and real estate interests in western Canada that went sour. However, in 1984, it finally obtained entry into the American retail market when it acquired Harris Bankcorp, then the third-largest bank in Chicago, for $547 million. As with the Bankers Trust bid, banking analysts expressed their doubts over the deal; the Bank of Montreal paid $82 per share for Harris stock, or nearly twice its previous price. But two years later, the analysts had changed their opinion entirely. The Harris acquisition made the Bank of Montreal one of the leading foreign institutions involved in U.S. commercial and industrial lending and enhanced its foreign exchange capabilities. The strong performance of regional bank stocks in 1985 and 1986 also made the deal seem like a bargain in retrospect.

In 1985, the Progressive Conservative government of Prime Minister Brian Mulroney decided to deregulate Canada's financial system, a move that blurred the traditional lines between insurance, banking, and securities brokerage. Companies that had been restricted to one business were allowed to diversify into others, increasing competition among individual firms but also the power of holding companies seeking to build financial service empires. One immediate consequence of deregulation was a surge in merger-and-acquisition activity involving Canadian securities firms. Growing foreign investment in North America helped accelerate this trend, as did an increasing demand for stocks among domestic small investors (one brokerage executive told *Barron's:* "It wasn't too long ago that the average Canadian's idea of a

balanced portfolio was a savings bond and a lottery ticket"). The Bank of Montreal responded by acquiring Nesbitt Thomson, Canada's fourth-largest brokerage firm, in 1987.

Cracking the U.S. Market in the 1990s and After

William Mulholland made way for a younger successor, Matthew W. Barrett, in 1987. However, the bank continued in the direction Mulholland had set for it. It grew in Canada, offering more services, and expanded across the border, mostly through its Harris Bancorp subsidiary. In 1993, the bank announced a major push to grow Harris. Harris got a new CEO that year, whose job was specifically to oversee the expansion plan. By 1993, Harris accounted for about 30 percent of Bank of Montreal's earnings. The parent company thought that figure could rise to 50 percent over the next decade. The company planned to invest some $600 million to $700 million to triple the number of Harris branches, of which there were 40 in 1993. The plan called for increasing Harris's presence in the Chicago area and in seven surrounding states. This Midwestern region by itself had a gross national product twice that of Canada as a whole. Bank of Montreal planned to become a leading bank in the area, and so make itself an integrated cross-border "truly North American" bank. The ten-year plan got off the ground quickly. In 1994, Harris acquired Suburban Bancorp Inc., headquartered in Palatine, Illinois. With the addition of Suburban's 30 offices, Harris was already over halfway to its goal of tripling its branches. The bank also moved beyond its original focus of growth in the Midwest. Harris had had a trust banking business in Florida since the early 1980s. In 1997, it moved to change its trust charter to allow it to do commercial banking in Florida in a joint venture under the name Harris Bank/Bank of Montreal. The rationale for the move was to attract the 90,000 Chicagoans and 409,000 Canadians who wintered in Florida.

Back in Canada, Bank of Montreal proposed a giant merger which would have made it Canada's largest bank. The idea was for Bank of Montreal to combine with its rival Royal Bank of Canada. At the same time, two more of Canada's leading banks, Canadian Imperial Bank of Commerce and the Toronto-Dominion Bank, also proposed merging. This would have left the two newly merged banks in control of some 70 percent of Canadian banking. Bank of Montreal argued that the consolidation would help protect Canadian consumers. The newly enlarged Canadian banks would be able to compete successfully with behemoth American banks who were increasingly encroaching on Canadian turf. If Royal and Bank of Montreal merged, the new bank would be one of the top 25 banks globally, and so it would be better able to compete worldwide. But the Canadian government balked at the deal. In December 1998, Canada's finance minister ruled that the mergers could not go through, citing "an unacceptable concentration of economic power in the hands of fewer, very large banks." Bank of Montreal chafed at the setback, yet it still found ways to increase its business, both in Canada and abroad.

Soon the two would-be merger partners, Bank of Montreal and Royal Bank of Canada, proposed a different deal. In a joint venture, they would run a credit card processing company, or so-called merchant acquirer, called Moneris Solutions Corp. Canadian law required banks to handle only one credit card. Bank of Montreal was the leading MasterCard bank, but it was not allowed to issue Visa cards. To process merchants' credit card deposits, the bank had to go through a complicated process of sorting and sending the Visa slips elsewhere. The two banks got the government go-ahead to combine their services and launched Moneris in December 2000. The company expected to process 30 percent of all Canadian credit card transactions. Its 330,000 clients made it the largest credit card processing company in Canada and number five in North America.

By 2001, Harris Bank had 140 branches and roughly $6 billion in assets. It kept up its acquisition charge, buying the First National Bank of Joliet in 2000, as well as Village Bank of Naples, Florida, and the Century Bank, in Scottsdale, Arizona. Bank of Montreal announced a new goal for its U.S. subsidiary in 2001, which was to focus on top urban markets. This meant the bank was looking for takeover targets in Texas; California; Atlanta, Georgia; and Florida, as well as in cities in the Midwest. Between 1999 and 2001, Bank of Montreal made six acquisitions in the U.S., ending 2001 with the major purchase of CSFBdirect Inc. This was a subsidiary of Credit Suisse First Boston, with a huge client base of affluent individual investors. The purchase meshed with the wealth management services offered by Bank of Montreal's Nesbitt Burns brokerage subsidiary and Harris Bank's investment services. The bank combined these operations under its Private Client Group division, which managed some $149 billion in total assets as of October 2001.

Principal Subsidiaries

Harris Bankcorp, Inc.; BMO Nesbitt Burns; Moneris Solutions Corp. (50%).

Principal Competitors

Royal Bank of Canada; Toronto-Dominion Bank; Canadian Imperial Bank of Commerce.

Further Reading

"Bank of Montreal Taps Barrett as President, Heir to Mulholland," *Wall Street Journal*, September 23, 1987, p. 1.

"Bank of Montreal to Begin Midwest Expansion," *Wall Street Journal*, June 17, 1993, p. B7.

Denison, Merrill, *Canada's First Bank: A History of the Bank of Montreal*, 2 vols., New York: Dodd, Mead, 1966.

Elstein, Aaron, "Canada Bars 2 Megadeals, Sees Threat to Competition," *American Banker*, December 15, 1998, p. 1.

Holloway, Andy, "Plastic Surgery," *Canadian Business*, September 17, 2001, p. 96.

Kassner, Pam, "Harris, Suburban Bancorp, Bank of Montreal Merger Agreement—A Major Step in North American Strategy," *PR Newswire*, April 18, 1994, p. 1.

Murphy, Patricia A., "A New Arrival from the North," *Credit Card Management*, September 2000, pp. 30–36.

Plunkett, Marguerite M., "Harris Starting Fla. Expansion," *Palm Beach Post*, December 3, 1997, p. 9B.

Reilly, Patrick, "Mapping Bank of Montreal's Expansion Plan," *American Banker*, November 1, 2001, p. 1.

Simon, Bernard, "For the Big Canadian Banks, Profit Is Retail and Domestic," *New York Times*, November 28, 2001, p. W1.

Weber, Joseph, "Why Canada Should Lighten Up on Foreign Banks," *Business Week*, December 7, 1998, p. 130.

—update: A. Woodward

The Bank of New York Company, Inc.

One Wall Street
New York, New York 10286
U.S.A.
Telephone: (212) 495-1784
Fax: (212) 635-1799
Web site: http://www.bankofny.com

Public Company
Incorporated: 1968
Employees: 18,861
Total Assets: $77.2 billion (2000)
Stock Exchanges: New York
Ticker Symbol: BK
NAIC: 52211 Commercial Banking; 52392 Portfolio
   Management; 52393 Investment Advice

The Bank of New York Company, Inc. operates as a leading financial holding company in the United States, with total assets surpassing $80 billion. With 350 branches in the New York metropolitan area and offices in 26 countries, the Bank of New York has business interests in securities servicing and global payment services, corporate banking, retail banking, private client services and asset management, and financial market services. During 2000, the company secured its ninth consecutive year of record financial performance.

Certain corporations come to bear the impress of a single, dominant individual, and for more than 200 years the Bank of New York has exemplified the fiscal policies, character, and even the temperament of its chief founder, Alexander Hamilton. The patrician lawyer was famous for his brilliant theories of finance, for his personal elegance, and for his staunch conservatism; his bank must be said to share all three characteristics. The Bank of New York has remained a pillar of strength during this country's many panics and depressions, able to weather the financial storms that have sunk so many more aggressive institutions by preserving a conservative lending policy and high liquidity. Indeed, so blue-blooded is the bank's history that one is tempted to ascribe its long-established, understated strength

less to sound fiscal strategy than to what its founder would have called ''good taste.''

There are simply certain things the Bank of New York does not do, has never done, and will never permit—or would not have, that is, until the year 1982, when its new chairman, J. Carter Bacot, began a program of acquisition and restructuring designed to pull his aristocratic bank into the decidedly plebeian twentieth century and beyond. Bacot succeeded in his task; the bank was rated the tenth-largest financial institution in the United States by the early 1990s and had acquired a very modern reputation for iron competitiveness. His successor, Thomas A. Renyi, also continued the acquisition strategy, securing the Bank's position as a leader in the securities servicing and global payment services sector of the banking industry. Whether the Hamiltons, Roosevelts, and Rikers—whose names grace the list of past bank directors—would be entirely pleased with these changes is open to some doubt, but their approval was probably not of much interest to Mr. Bacot or Mr. Renyi.

Development: 1784–1800s

The period immediately following the Revolutionary War was a time of fiscal chaos for the newly-independent states. Incredibly enough, at that point there was only one bank in all of North America, which had opened its doors in Philadelphia in 1781. The colonies had long depended for their medium of exchange on a haphazard mix of barter, wampum, foreign coins, and a vast array of colonial currencies, none of them of much value beyond the immediate vicinity of their printing. In such a confused climate it was difficult to transact business, and in 1784 a group of men in New York decided to create a bank that would help stabilize the precarious situation, in a profitable manner. The leader of this group of citizens was Alexander Hamilton, the distinguished former congressman, revolutionary colonel, and co-author of the *Federalist Papers*. Though only 27 years old, Hamilton was already looked upon as a brilliant statesman with special expertise in the areas of economics and banking. At a time when the country lacked not only banks but also banking laws, Hamilton devised the constitution for what would soon be called the Bank of New York, insisting on a host of policies that were soon adopted as standard practice for all modern banks. In particular, he and the other directors agreed that the bank would sell its original stock for specie only—that is, its capital would consist of gold and silver instead of the land mortgages then backing most of the shaky colonial currencies. Having quickly raised $500,000 in capital, the bank's 13 directors elected General Alexander MacDougall as president and opened its doors at 159 Queen Street on June 9, 1784. New York City finally had its first bank.

The original bank directors included many of the city's leading businessmen: Isaac Roosevelt had made a fortune refining sugar, creating the wealth which later would help raise two of his descendants to the presidency of the United States; MacDougall was not only a successful merchant but had risen to the rank of major general during the war; and Comfort Sands was one of the city's most prominent shippers and importers. The list of shareholders was equally impressive, leading one early social scientist to note that of the 15 New York families reputed to keep carriages in 1804, four of them were at some time represented on the bank's board of directors. From the beginning, the bank's aristocratic heritage helped it gain the confidence of the city's business community.

Prospering immediately, the bank began a string of consecutive dividend payments never to be broken. It was also helpful that its young founder, Hamilton, became the secretary of the treasury of the United States in 1789, fostering a long intimacy between the bank and both state and national governments. Hamilton relied on "his bank" to perform services useful to the new and struggling government, such as loaning it $200,000 in 1789, and two years later buying up large quantities of government bonds to keep their price from falling sharply. In return, as secretary of the treasury, Hamilton did his best to protect the bank during difficult times, fighting to keep government funds in the bank even after the new Bank of the United States (also his creation) established a branch in New York. In this he was ultimately not successful, but it is clear that the bank enjoyed what would now be considered unethical treatment at the hands of its founder.

In 1789, the bank moved to its present location at the corner of Wall and William Streets. By that time, the American banking system had begun to evolve and stabilize its financial markets, and by 1800 the bank had its first competitor in New York, Aaron Burr's Manhattan Company. The city was growing at a frantic pace, however, and there was plenty of business for the plethora of banks soon to follow. The Bank of New York always had the advantage over its rivals of being the first and most prestigious of the New York banks, enabling it to adopt a posture somewhat above the fray of the marketplace. At a time when the young country was being rapidly populated with a variety of shaky frontier banks, the Bank of New York was able to further its reputation for prudence by moving slowly and thoughtfully toward a portfolio of well-secured, stable loans. In 1822, the bank significantly increased its resources and strengthened its image overseas by borrowing $250,000 from two London banks. Already it was known in Europe not only as the largest bank in New York, but also as the safest bank in the United States.

Surviving National Panics and the Civil War

In 1830, a number of the bank's directors helped to found the New York Life Insurance and Trust Company, a similarly patrician corporation which 100 years later would merge with the bank. The 1830s were marked by continued economic growth, often fueled by excessive speculation in the newly created banks and industrial companies. The pyramiding of securities reached such a point that when the Bank of England shut off all credit to the United States, it sparked the national panic of 1837, one of the worst in American history. In what would become its typical fashion, the bank rode out the storm easily, having never indulged in dubious loans and always keeping a larger-than-normal amount of cash on hand. It therefore had fewer non-performing loans than many other banks, as well as liquid capital to allay the anxieties of its depositors, thus avoiding both prongs of the panic. Such conservative banking policies, which often earned for the bank adjectives like "stodgy" or even "inert," became considerably more appealing in times of panic and depression, and largely account for the bank's continued existence over the past 200 years.

In 1853, New York banks took an important step when they formed the New York Clearing House Association, an instrument through which the banks could settle their daily accounts with each other in a single, secure location. But the clearing house soon took on another, more important function—that of bringing together all banks and pooling a part of their assets became a line of defense against the danger of massive deposit withdrawal during panics. Any bank facing a grave depletion of funds could receive a loan from the clearing house to keep it afloat until the crisis had passed. Unfortunately, it required another panic to illustrate this potential of the clearing house. As it did 20 years before, the Bank of New York came through the panic of 1857 without suffering any real damage.

The greatest challenge was yet to come, however. By the late 1850s it was clear that civil war was inevitable and for New York banks this was particularly ominous. Over the years, New York had become the center of the booming cotton and clothing trade between England and the southern states, with shipments in each direction stopping at the port of New York and often changing hands there. At the time of the outbreak of the Civil War in 1861, southern planters owed various northern banks an estimated $300 million, making the banks' attitude toward the war more complicated than geography might imply. Furthermore, in 1861, as today, New York banks dominated finance in all of the United States: some $92 million of the country's $126 million in total deposits rested in the vaults of Manhattan banks. The support of the New York bankers was therefore crucial to the success of the Union cause.

of 1884, the other New York banks looked to the Bank of New York as a haven, relying on its cash reserves for critical loans and on its overall leadership for guidance and support. Toward the close of the nineteenth century, the bank was, as it had been a hundred years before, New York's largest and most respected financial institution, its list of shareholders a veritable roll call of the city's most famous families. In a time of stupendous economic growth, however, it was not long before the bank lost its claim to being the city's largest, settling instead, as the twentieth century began, for the title of most elegant.

Expansion During the Early 1900s

The turn of the century saw the bank's increasing involvement in foreign-exchange banking, especially in Latin America. Herbert Griggs, who in 1901 began what would become the longest tenure as president in the bank's history, brought to the position much expertise and interest in the foreign-exchange business, further accelerating the bank's expansion in that area. Even though the bank was no longer New York's largest, the early decades of this century were highly profitable ones for the company as World War I became something of a bonanza for the American economy in general and banks in particular. From a net income of about $400 million in 1900, profits rose to some $820 million in 1917, the year of America's maximum war effort. All of the important New York banks worked closely with the government to finance the war; the Bank of New York by itself loaned about $38 million, and also offered various other services to Washington. The loans were highly profitable, and by the end of the war the bank was more than ready for the 1920s.

Along with the rest of the nation, the bank was soon doing more business than ever. In the heady atmosphere of that decade, even the staid Bank of New York began to hunger for a dramatic increase in its capital—for a way to recoup some of the ground it had lost to younger and more aggressive rivals. In 1922, the bank announced its merger with the New York Life Insurance and Trust Company. The merger was a natural fit, and with little strain the two companies became the Bank of New York and Trust Company, relocating in 1928 to a new 32-story building immediately adjacent to the old bank headquarters. Deposits at the new bank, now once again chartered under state (as opposed to national) banking law, totaled $78 million and continued to climb during the bountiful years leading up to October 1929.

As its history might predict, the bank sailed through the great panic of that year with little damage. Even the worst of all modern depressions could not upset the carefully managed portfolio at the Bank of New York, which actually increased its total deposits during the slump's most dangerous early years. While 4,600 banks across the country closed their doors, the Bank of New York took an asset depreciation of $6 million without breaking stride, continuing to rack up profits every year and paying its normal, healthy dividends on time and without anxiety. The bank actively supported President Roosevelt's radical attempts to halt the economy's slide. Later the Bank of New York worked along with the nation's other financial institutions in funding the enormous war effort from 1941–45. In times of crisis such as these, the bank's long and stable history gave to it a special importance in the eyes of the business world.

Key Dates:

1784: Alexander Hamilton and others establish the first bank in New York City.

1822: The bank bolsters its image overseas by borrowing $250,000 from two London banks.

1830: The New York Life Insurance and Trust Company is founded.

1853: The New York Clearing House Association is formed.

1865: The Bank of New York begins participating in the National Banking Act.

1917: Profits rise to $820 million during World War I.

1922: The firm merges with the New York Life Insurance and Trust Co.

1948: The company merges with Fifth Avenue Bank.

1969: The firm officially adopts the name Bank of New York Company, Inc.

1988: The Bank of New York operates as the tenth-largest bank holding company in the U.S.

1994: The company expands into China.

1995: The bank continues with international expansion and forms the New York Fund Management Ireland Ltd. in Dublin.

1999: The bank sells its factoring business to General Motors Acceptance Corp.

Despite the huge losses involved, the financiers threw themselves behind the North without reservation. In August 1861, Secretary of the Treasury Salmon Chase asked a group of banks for a $150 million loan to equip the Union Army, which he quickly got; the Bank of New York eventually held about $3 million in government paper. Unfortunately, Chase insisted on receiving specie for the government notes, assuming that the gold would circulate through the economy and back to the banks. It is no surprise, however, that the gold was promptly snatched up and held by a populace faced with the uncertainties of war, leaving to the various state currencies the role of basic fiscal exchange. Since these were of little use beyond the borders of their issuing states, the federal government was soon forced to print its first "greenbacks" in 1862. To ensure that these were accepted as sound currency, congress passed the National Banking Act the following year. This important measure for the first time regulated all subscribing banks under a federal code, stipulating that if a bank left one-third of its capital with the government, it could loan up to 90 percent of that amount in the form of the new federal currency or other securities. The danger posed by grossly undercapitalized banks was thus reduced, and in July 1865 the Bank of New York joined the rapidly growing system, becoming the Bank of New York, N.B.A.

The bank came through the war with its usual health intact, actually raising dividends from three to five percent by 1865. The postwar years followed a pattern of frenzied boom period leading to over-speculation, panic, and depression. Though severe, the panic of 1873 and the lean years afterward also had little effect on the bank's overall strength; once again, its conservative loan philosophy spared it the worst effects of typical boom-and-bust cycles. Both in 1873 and in the less acute crash

Postwar Growth: Mergers and Acquisitions

After World War II, the Bank of New York underwent a gradually accelerating transformation into a more modern financial institution, most obviously in the form of a series of mergers and acquisitions. In 1948, the bank merged for the second time, joining forces with the Fifth Avenue Bank of mid-town Manhattan; in the mid-1960s it added Empire Trust Company. In 1968, the bank was incorporated as The Bank of New York, Inc., and the next year added the ''Company'' now in its name when it absorbed six subsidiaries. Between 1969 and 1974, the bank acquired four more small banks. Its next large acquisition came in 1980, when it bought the Empire National Bank; in 1987, it bought the Long Island Trust Company. More significant than any of these moves, however, was the 1982 elevation of J. Carter Bacot from president to chairman of the bank. It was Bacot's vigorous leadership that had, in the words of one financial analyst, ''dragged BONY into the 20th century.'' A relatively young 49 when he took over, Bacot showed little patience with the bank's traditional posture of high-toned inertia.

Bacot's changes were in four basic areas. He sold off the bank's upstate retail branches, concentrating all of its retail business in the greater New York metropolitan area, especially in more affluent Long Island and in the counties north of New York City. Second, Bacot was far more daring in his loan philosophy, dealing more quickly and in larger amounts than the bank had usually allowed. Loans of up to $60 million became common as the bank focused its portfolio in the areas of commercial industry, Wall Street securities firms, utilities, and the oil and gas industries. Third, the chairman ended the bank's long ambivalence about the role it wanted to play in the financial world, giving up all pretensions to investment banking and the capital markets to concentrate on becoming a large regional bank. Much of the bank's income was generated by processing the daily transactions of securities brokers, an activity which, strictly speaking, was not even in the banking field. Finally, in 1987, Bacot confirmed the bank's place in the rough and tumble of modern business when he initiated a year-long hostile takeover bid for S.B. Irving Trust Bank Corporation, a Wall Street neighbor whose $24 billion in assets were slightly larger than those of the purchaser. When the dust had settled, and Irving Trust was merged with the Bank of New York on December 30, 1988, Bacot had created the nation's tenth-largest bank holding company, one well-positioned for further expansion.

The takeover was universally praised by financial analysts—except those at Irving, which fought the takeover—who felt that the two banks' similar interests would mesh together quite well. All in all, a very tidy merger, and not one anyone would have expected of the bank before its recent sea change. While the frankly aristocratic traditions of the Bank of New York lingered on in one form or another, Bacot was convinced that even blue blood could be made to circulate faster than was once thought seemly.

Continued Growth: 1990s and Beyond

Bacot lead the company through much of the 1990s expanding through acquisition and diversifying into various banking operations. In 1990, the bank acquired the factoring business of Bankers Trust Co. The following year, it canceled its proposed stock issue, leaving its acquisition plans in question. Doubt concerning the company's ability to finance further expansion was quelled however, with the 1992 purchase of the New York branches of Barclays Bank plc. Growth continued in 1994, when the company established a branch office in Shanghai, China and then the following year with the formation of Dublin-based Bank of New York Fund Management Ireland Ltd.

During 1995, the bank also made several key acquisitions including Meridian Trust Co., the municipal bond administration operations of Hibernia National Bank, Investors Bank and Trust Co.'s trust servicing operations, and BankAmerica Corp.'s securities processing business. The company also extended its reach into the global custody market with the purchase of such operations from both J.P. Morgan and Nations-Bank. The pattern continued into 1996, with the acquisition of certain assets from First Hawaiian Bank, Investors Fuduciary Trust Co., and Wells Fargo & Co. The bank also bolstered its international operations by opening offices in Abu Dhabi, United Arab Emirates.

Thomas A. Renyi—named company president in 1992—took over as CEO in 1996. Working with Bacot, the duo had orchestrated over 33 acquisitions from 1993 to 1998. During 1998, Renyi was named successor to retiring Bacot. That year, the bank made an unsolicited $24 billion bid for competitor Mellon Bank Corp. The proposal was dropped, however, when the Mellon board rejected the offer, claiming they did not have confidence in Renyi as a leader. The abrupt refusal did not put a damper on the new chairman's business strategy, as he quickly began laying the groundwork to shift the company's focus to securities processing and custody portfolios. Beginning in 1998, the bank began selling off its less profitable businesses, including that of its credit card business, which was sold to Chase Manhattan Corp. In 1999, it also sold its asset-based lending and factoring business to General Motors Acceptance Corp. for $1.8 billion. Renyi commented on the sale and the bank's business goals in a 1999 American Banker article, stating that ''this transaction further advances our overall strategy, which is to focus on our higher-growth, fee-based activities, including securities servicing, cash processing, and fiduciary services.''

Also part of that strategy was the continued push for international expansion. Eyeing the European market as a significant growth opportunity, the Bank acquired the global custody business of Royal Bank of Scotland Plc. The 1999 purchase secured the company's position as the leading provider of securities processing and investor services over competitors Chase Manhattan and State Street Corp.

The bank continued to focus on its goal of becoming the leading financial asset service company into the new millennium. During 2000, the company made ten acquisitions including that of Ivy Asset Management, Harris Trust, SG Cowen Securities, Schroder & Co., BHF Securities, and GENA. As market conditions weakened in the U.S. during 2001, the company began a loan disposition program for 25 credit relationships including 24 with emerging telecommunications firms and one with an energy trading company rumored to be the bankrupt Enron Corp. While profits fell during the fourth quarter of 2001, management remained confident that the bank would remain a leader in the banking industry. With assets surpassing $80 billion, the company stood well positioned to continue its long-standing history of success.

Principal Subsidiaries

The Bank of New York; The Bank of New York (Delaware); The Bank of New York Trust Company of Florida N.A.; BNY Asset Solutions LLC; BNY Capital Funding LLC; BNY Capital Markets Inc.; BNY Clearing Services LLC: BNY ESI & Co. Inc.; BNY Investment Center Inc.; BNY Midwest Trust Co.; BNY Trust Company of Missouri; BNY Western Trust Company; Estabrook Capital Management LLC; Ivy Asset Management Corp.; BNY International Financing Corp.; The Bank of New York Europe Ltd.; The Bank of New York Capital Markets Ltd.; The Bank of New York (Luxembourg) S.A.; The Bank of New York Trust Co. (Cayman) Ltd.; AIB/BNY Fund Management (Ireland) Ltd.

Principal Competitors

Citigroup Inc.; J.P. Morgan Chase & Co.; State Street Corp.

Further Reading

"The Bank of New York Company Inc. Completes Acquisition of Ivy Asset Management," *PR Newswire*, October 4, 2000.

"4Q Earnings: Regions Up; No Surprises From PNC, Bank of N.Y.," *American Banker*, January 18, 2002, p. 20.

Moyer, Liz, "Bank of N.Y. Calls Mellon Intransigent, Drops Offer," *American Banker*, May 21, 1998, p. 1.

——, "Bank of N.Y.'s CEO Sticks to His (Profitable) Knitting," *American Banker*, June 30, 1999, p. 6.

——, "Deal to Make Bank of N.Y. World Leader in Custody," *American Banker*, March 24, 1999, p. 1.

——, "Renyi: A New Chairman Off to a Stunning Start," *American Banker*, April 23, 1998, p. 22.

Nevins, Allan, *History of the Bank of New York and Trust Company*, New York: Bank of New York, 1934.

Streeter, Edward, *Window on America*, New York: Bank of New York, 1959.

Timmons, Heather, "Bank of N.Y. Selling Unit to GMAC for $1.8 Billion," *American Banker*, June 9, 1999, p. 1.

—update: Christina M. Stansell

Bell Helicopter Textron Inc.

P.O. Box 482
Fort Worth, Texas 76101
U.S.A.
Telephone: (817) 280-2011
Fax: (817) 280-2321
Web site: http://www.bellhelicopter.com/

Wholly-Owned Subsidiary of Textron Inc.
Incorporated: 1957 as Bell Helicopter Corporation
Employees: 8,600
Sales: $1.5 billion (2001 est.)
NAIC: 336411 Aircraft Manufacturing; 54171 Research
    and Development in the Physical, Engineering, and
    Life Sciences

Bell Helicopter Textron Inc. is the largest maker of helicopters in the world, and the company has been one the industry's most significant pioneers. A vintage Bell Model 47 helicopter is even part of the permanent collection of the Museum of Modern Art in New York City. In its first half century of business, Bell produced 34,000 helicopters. Its whirlybirds are active in 124 countries.

Origins

The helicopter has existed in human imagination at least since Leonardo da Vinci conceived his helical air screw. However, a practical model would not be produced for another five hundred years. American inventor Arthur Young is credited with building one of the first viable helicopters in the early 1930s.

Although closely identified with helicopters, Bell's history goes back to the Buffalo, New York-based Bell Aircraft Corporation, which by the 1940s was producing revolutionary fixed-wing aircraft for the U.S. military. These designs included the P-39 Airacobra, a ground attack aircraft, and America's first jet plane, the P-59 Airacomet.

After years of experimentation with scale models, Arthur Young showed Lawrence D. "Larry" Bell, Bell Aircraft's founder, a home movie of his research in September 1941. Bell

was taken with Young's helicopter design and established a small shop in Gardenville, New York (a former Chrysler auto dealership vacated in wartime) to accommodate its production. By June 1945, this operation had been incorporated into the main Bell Aircraft plant, which had moved to nearby Niagara Falls Airport.

The first prototype was called the Bell Model 30, a one-seat, 165-horsepower helicopter capable of reaching 100 m.p.h. in level flight. The first example was christened *Genevieve* on December 18, 1942. Within a year, the dramatic rescue of a Bell pilot, who had crashed testing one of the company's new jets over snowbound upstate New York, had already generated national publicity for the program. The first production model was called the Bell Model 47B, which began deliveries to the U.S. Army in 1946.

The Model 47 was praised for its simple, elegant design, and ultimately landed a spot in the permanent collection of the Museum of Modern Art in New York City. The craft was durable, too: hundreds of Model 47s remained in service fifty years after their introduction.

However, after the war, helicopters proved a hard sell. Bell Aircraft's total sales volume fell from $317 million in 1944 to $11 million in 1946. Despite pioneering America's first jet aircraft, the country's air forces did not pick it as a manufacturer after the war (though the company did eventually win contracts to supply Boeing and Convair).

A personal helicopter market also failed to materialize, and even selling its two-seat Model 47B at $25,000 each (three times the price of a four-seat airplane), the company was losing money on them. The price was raised to $39,500 each in late 1948, yet soon reduced to $23,500 in the face of competition from the Hiller 360 helicopter.

Though originally intended for the commercial market, the first Bell helicopters produced would go to the military. Most of the helicopters produced in the 1940s went to the agricultural market, where they excelled in crop dusting applications.

In the late 1940s, Bell created subsidiaries to market helicopters and operate them in oil exploration duties. In spite of a

Company Perspectives:

As the world's pre-eminent provider of vertical take-off and landing aircraft, Bell Helicopter Textron is committed to provide every customer with products and services of the highest quality. Our Strategy is to win and keep customers by producing the most reliable helicopters in the world and by being the most responsive company in the industry to our customers' needs. We will aggressively improve our cost competitiveness and provide our customers the best value in our products of today and our products of tomorrow.

nineteen-week strike by the UAW (United Auto Workers), in 1949 Bell Aircraft posted its first profitable year since the end of the war, earning $204,000 on sales of $11.8 million. Employment more than doubled during the year, to 4,000 workers. More than 11,000 were employed by the end of 1951, spurred by the outbreak of the Korean War. Bell's sales reached $147 million in 1953.

The success of the rotary-wing aircraft had justified the creation in January 1951 of a separate helicopter division, headquartered in Fort Worth, Texas. In March, this division moved to facilities in Kenmore, New York, originally built for Curtiss Airplane Company.

Helicopter Division sales reached $48 million in 1955. By the time of Larry Bell's death in 1956, the company had developed a number of innovative rotorcraft variants, including the XH-13F turbine helicopter and the XV-3 Convertiplane, which pioneered the tilt-rotor concept that would later be used in the V-22 Osprey. In 1957, the Bell Helicopter Corporation was established as a wholly owned subsidiary of Bell Aircraft. It was acquired in July 1960 by Textron Inc., along with other Bell Aircraft units, for $22 million. Their former parent company, Bell Aircraft, then changed its name to Bell Intercontinental Corporation, while the Bell Helicopter Corporation was renamed the Bell Helicopter Company. At this time, Edwin Ducayet succeeded Harvey Gaylord as Bell Helicopter's president.

Choppers Over Korea and Vietnam

Helicopters were first used extensively on the battlefield during the Korean War, where they excelled at evacuating wounded soldiers. A dedicated medical evacuation helicopter was commissioned by the U.S. Army in 1955, resulting in the MU-1 Iroquois, more popularly known as "Hueys." This chopper, much larger than the Model 47, would be armed and used for attack as well as rescue and medevac duties in Vietnam. A larger and more powerful version, the Model 205 or UH-1D, was ordered in 1960 and entered production in August 1963. It could carry 12 troops and six stretchers, approximately 4,000 pounds in total cargo.

In 1960, Bell lost an Army contract for a light observation helicopter (LOH) to Hughes, a newcomer to the industry. Bell incorporated its research for this bid into the commercial Model 206A JetRanger helicopter, which would dominate the market for light turbine helicopters into the 1990s. A military version of this, the OH-58A Kiowa, won the Army's LOH contract when

Hughes raised the unit price for its second batch of choppers. Deliveries of the OH-58A began in May 1969, though the commercial variant did not enter production until 1977.

Bell developed other military helicopters during the 1960s. The UH-1G Cobra attack helicopter, armed with a 7.62mm minigun in a chin turret and rocket mounts on stub wings, began production in October 1966. The UH-1 spawned more powerful variants such as the Model 214 KingCobra. Iran acquired the first KingCobra in 1975. Bell continued to develop this program after the US withdrew from the country a few years later.

Bell Helicopter's sales increased phenomenally during U.S. military action in Vietnam, when production totaled 14,000 helicopters. The company had revenues of $150 million in 1962, $60 million of it civil. In 1967, Bell's revenues were more than $2 billion, with civil sales accounting for just $385 million.

After peaking at $1.81 billion in 1970, Bell's military sales fell to just $300 a million a year by 1975. Still, its transition to peacetime was much less shocking than that of rival Sikorsky and Boeing Vertol, both of which required substantial bailouts from their corporate parents, notes *Whirlybirds* author Jay Spenser. Jim Atkins, appointed Bell Helicopter president in 1972, directed the company's postwar diversification.

The government of Iran's record $500 million order for 490 civil and military helicopters, announced in December 1972, helped keep Bell's order books full. (However, this success may have encouraged the U.S. Army to prop up other helicopter manufacturers: Hughes would win the bid to replace the Super-Cobra with its AH-64 Apache, and Sikorsky's Blackhawk became the military's replacement for the venerable Huey.) Unfortunately, this contract, which included plans for a co-production venture in Iran, were scuttled by that country's civil unrest within a few years. Further, it later emerged that the commander of the Iranian air force held an interest in a company that received a $3 million commission in the deal.

By 1976, Bell Helicopter had become Textron's largest division. In 1982 the name was changed to Bell Helicopter Textron Inc. (BHT). The next year, Bell Helicopter Textron Canada was formed. Its plant at Mirabel, Quebec, opened in 1985. The Canadian unit would build all of Bell's commercial helicopters, with rotors and transmissions supplied by the Fort Worth plant.

Teaming Up in the 1980s

Bell partnered with Boeing to win a Navy contract to design a Joint Services Advanced Vertical Lift (JVX) aircraft in 1983. Based largely on Boeing research, this program would develop into the V-22 Osprey tiltrotor, an aircraft whose rotors could point either up or forward to fly as an airplane or hover as a helicopter. The hybrid helicopter/planes boasted twice the speed and range capability of a traditional helicopter, but could land in much smaller areas than fixed-wing aircraft. Later in the decade, Bell teamed with McDonnell Douglas to bid on an Army light helicopter contract, which it lost to a Boeing/Sikorsky team in 1991.

Leonard M. "Jack" Horner, son of H.M. "Jack" Horner, the former head of Sikorsky parent United Technologies

---

Key Dates:

1941: Bell Aircraft backs Arthur Young's pioneering helicopter research.
1946: The Bell Model 47 helicopter enters production.
1951: A separate division is created for helicopters.
1953: Helicopters push Bell's annual sales to $147 million
during Korean War.
1957: Bell Helicopter Corporation established.
1960: Textron buys Bell Helicopter.
1967: Annual revenues reach $2 billion during Vietnam
War.
1983: Canadian unit formed to focus on civil helicopters.
1992: Controversial Bell/Boeing V-22 tiltrotor project
proceeds.
2000: A new plant in Amarillo, Tx. opens, dedicated to
tiltrotor production.

Corporation, became Bell Helicopter's fourth president in 1984. At the time, Bell Helicopter had 7,200 employees and was posting operating income of $30 million a year.

In March 1985, Textron announced it was putting the company up for sale in order to raise $500 million to offset the cost of its recent purchase of major military supplier Avco Corporation. However, this sale was canceled four months later after the US Army announced it was investigating the company for ''accounting deficiencies.'' Bell ultimately agreed to refund the government $90 million to settle an impending fraud case alleging the company over-billed for spare parts.

Controversy also followed the V-22 Osprey program, which suffered crashes and cost overruns. By late 1992, noted the *New York Times,* the program had cost $3.6 billion, and another $1.5 billion had been released to the program—more than double the V-22's original $2.4 billion estimate. Estimates for a proposed production run of 612 Ospeys over ten years exceeded $22 million. Half of the parts for the Boeing and Bell's V-22 were subcontracted to 2,000 other companies.

The Clinton administration supported the V-22 as both a means to transport small army units rapidly to remote battlefields and, in the civil arena, a way to help relieve congestion at the nation's crowded airports. Critics doubted the plane's high fuel and maintenance costs would make it viable for commercial passengers.

The Model 407, a replacement for the fantastically successful Model 206 JetRanger, was introduced in 1995. Commercial sales were particularly strong in South America, where Bell doubled its business in the mid-1990s, stealing market share from rival Eurocopter.

Terry Stinson, a member of the Stinson family of aviation pioneers, became Bell Helicopter's president and CEO in 1997. The next year, Bell bought three of Boeing Helicopter's commercial helicopter lines. Boeing had only been selling 30 commercial helicopters a year; just over a tenth of the number Bell was selling. Nevertheless, the deal gave Bell the broadest product line in the market. On the high end of the range, Bell

Helicopter was taking orders for a civilian version of the V-22 known as the 609, with a base price of $8 million each. One of the company's smaller turbine helicopters, the 206, sold for just $750,000.

New Markets for the New Millennium

Bell revived a joint venture project that had been shelved in favor of the V-22 program. This joint venture, with the Italian firm Agusta S.p.A., which manufactured some Bell choppers under license, developed a larger commercial helicopter called the AB139 that was scheduled to be available for sale in 2002 at a price of between $6 million and $7 million. Bell had exited the market for large helicopters in 1990, when it stopped building its Model 214ST. Agusta had also been chosen as a partner in the commercial version of the V-22 tiltrotor called the Bell/Agusta 609.

One important export market for Bell's military helicopters was Turkey, which used them to fight Kurdistan Workers' Party (PKK) terrorists in the country's southeastern region. In 2000, Bell beat out Italy's Agusta and a joint venture between Russia's Kamov and Israeli Aircraft Industries to tentatively win a $4.5 billion order for 145 attack helicopters. The winning model, the AH-1Z King Cobra, was an upgrade of the Super Cobra the company had sold to Turkey in the early 1990s.

A V-22 crashed in April 2000, killing all 19 Marines aboard a training flight. The resulting investigation placed most of the blame on human error. A second fatal accident in North Carolina followed in December, after which the Marines grounded their fleet. A Marine Corps investigation blamed this on a combination of a failed hydraulic line and a software glitch.

Bell opened a new $40 million V-22 Osprey plant in Amarillo, Texas, in November 2000. The town had offered millions in incentives to lure the plant, which was supported by the state's congressmen. The new plant was not unionized, unlike Bell's other plants in Fort Worth, Arlington, and Grand Prairie. Bell also devoted about a third of its 6,300 Texas workers to making parts for the tiltrotor aircraft.

By the middle of 2001, Bell had received a handful of orders for its civil Model 609 tiltrotor aircraft—though no prototype had yet been built—and remained optimistic about prospects for the V-22, of which 14 had been delivered. Tiltrotors accounted for $432 million of Bell's 2000 revenues. ''We're going to change the way people fly,'' was the catchphrase of new Bell Helicopter president John Murphey. Indeed, under development was an even larger version of the V-22 known as the Quad Tiltrotor, designed to carry six times the payload of the Osprey.

Principal Subsidiaries

Bell/Augusta Aerospace (75%).

Principal Divisions

Bell Helicopter Textron Canada.

Principal Competitors

Agusta S.p.A.; Eurocopter; MD Helicopters Inc.; Robinson Helicopter Company; Sikorsky Aircraft.

Further Reading

"Bell Helicopter to Repay $90 Million to US in Fraud Case," *Los Angeles Times,* March 10, 1988, Bus. Sec., p. 1.

Berry, John, "Helicopter Pact Halted by Iran," *Washington Post,* December 28, 1978, p. D9.

Biddle, Wayne, "Army Cuts Bell Copter Payments," *New York Times,* July 13, 1985, p. A29.

——, "Textron to Sell Bell Helicopter," *New York Times,* March 5, 1985, p. D1.

Bryce, Robert, "Vicarious Consumption; A Grand Entrance, In Your Own Helicopter," *New York Times,* November 22, 1998, p. C11.

Bulban, Erwin J., "Bell Stresses AAH In-House Development," *Aviation Week & Space Technology,* June 9, 1975, p. 35.

Cox, Bob and Dan Piller, "Fort Worth, Texas-Based Helicopter Maker's Chief Upbeat on Osprey Prospects," *Fort Worth Star-Telegram,* April 12, 2001.

Crudele, John, "Textron Ends Effort to Sell Unit," *New York Times,* July 20, 1985, p. A31.

"A Deal That Could Bend the Buy American Act," *Business Week,* September 24, 1979, p. 63.

Dworkin, Andy, "Bell Helicopter Textron Acquires Pair of Boeing Helicopter Lines," *Dallas Morning News,* February 26, 1998.

——, "Competitors Seek Piece of Bell Helicopter's Action in Latin America," *Dallas Morning News,* April 21, 1998.

——, "Fort Worth, Texas-Based Aviation Company Unveils New Helicopter," *Dallas Morning News,* June 12, 1999.

——, "Turkish Government Contract Poses Dilemma for Bell Helicopter, Others," *Dallas Morning News,* August 17, 1996.

Fairbank, Katie, "Bell Helicopter Textron Relocates Assembly of V-22 Osprey to Amarillo, Texas," *Dallas Morning News,* November 30, 2000.

——, "Fort Worth, Texas-Based Helicopter Manufacturer Bets on Hybrid Aircraft," *Dallas Morning News,* May 6, 2001.

Kuzela, Lad, "Giving Management Finger-Tip Control," *Industry Week,* July 11, 1983, p. 38.

"The Pentagon Defends Its Hot New Helicopter," *Business Week,* April 19, 1976, p. 112.

Spenser, Jay P., *Whirlybirds: A History of the U.S. Helicopter Pioneers,* Seattle: University of Washington Press, 1998.

"Textron Unit Admits $1.7 Million in Questionable Funding Abroad," *Aviation Week & Space Technology,* August 27, 1979, p. 103.

Uchitelle, Louis, "An Odd Aircraft's Tenacity Shows Difficulty of Cutting Arms Budget," *New York Times,* November 2, 1992, p. A1.

"Unrest in Iran Threatens Bell Helicopter Programs," *Aviation Week & Space Technology,* December 11, 1978, p. 24.

Whittle, Richard, "Europe Still Enthusiastic About Aircraft Technology Despite Problems in US," *Dallas Morning News,* June 23, 2001.

——, "Osprey Makers Hope to Pitch Larger Helicopter-Airplane Hybrid," *Dallas Morning News,* July 8, 2001.

"Why Did Bell Win the Helicopter Tender?" *Turkish Daily News,* July 24, 2000.

—Frederick C. Ingram

Berkeley Farms, Inc.

25500 Clawiter Road
Hayward, California 94545
U.S.A.
Telephone: (510) 265-8600
Fax: (510) 265-8754
Web site: http://www.berkeleyfarms.com

Wholly-Owned Subsidiary of Dean Foods Company
Founded: 1910
Employees: 557
Sales: $158 Million (1997)
NAIC: 112120 Dairy Cattle and Milk Production; 311511
Fluid Milk Manufacturing; 311512 Creamery Butter
manufacturing; 311520 Ice Cream Manufacturing

Berkeley Farms, Inc. processes and markets a complete line
of fluid milk and other dairy products in northern California.
The company obtains milk from independent dairy farms in
northern California and from its own dairy ranch in the San
Joaquin Valley and uses milk free of recombinant bovine
growth hormone (rBGH). Berkeley Farms produces and distributes more than 135,000 gallons of milk daily, including whole,
2 percent lowfat, 1 percent lowfat, and nonfat milk, and chocolate and strawberry flavored milk. Milk is sold in packaging as
small as a one-half pint chug and as large as a five-gallon bag-
in-box, used in food service institutions. The company's line of
dairy products include ice cream and ice cream novelties, heavy
whipping cream, sour cream, butter, cottage cheese, yogurt,
buttermilk, and seasonal egg nog. Berkeley Farms owns Bud's
Ice Cream, its brand of premium ice cream, with many flavors
named after San Francisco landmarks, such as Golden Gate
Vanilla, Alcatraz Rock Road, and Market Street Mint Cup. The
company distributes its products to supermarkets, independent
grocers, convenience stores, large discount stores, and food
service businesses throughout California. Companion products
for distribution include eggs, fruit drinks, and popular brands of
orange juice and other fruit juices.

Company Origins

Berkeley Farms founder John Sabatte immigrated to the
United States in 1895 at the age of 17. He found employment in
an Oakland, California, restaurant, quickly becoming the maitre
d'. Several years later, after a prolonged illness, Sabatte turned
to milk distribution, working with an uncle. He and a business
partner purchased a milk distribution route in South Berkeley in
1908 and named their business the South Berkeley Creamery.
At that time milk distribution involved transporting raw milk in
large containers and transferring it to containers owned by the
customers. The company purchased milk from farmers in Alameda and Contra Costa counties and transported it by horse-
drawn cart in ten-gallon milk cans. At the customer's home,
they ladled milk into pitchers.

When Sabatte started his own business in 1910, he retained
the company name. The company expanded to serve new distribution routes, requiring Sabette to relocate the Creamery to
Oakland, near South Berkeley. Sabatte operated the business
with the help of his wife, Mary Sarraute Sabette, who was also a
French immigrant. In addition to caring for their five sons, she
prepared meals for the company's ten employees who lived
on-site and, later, helped with the milk bottling operation.

During the 1910s and 1920s, technology transformed the
milk processing and distribution business. Compulsory pasteur-
ization required milk processors to install appropriate equipment, which meant that the milk remained fresh longer. The use
of Ford Model T's to deliver milk and the ease of distribution
that came with milk storage in bottles allowed the creamery to
expand its distribution over greater distances. The creamery
expanded its product offering to include a complete line of dairy
products, such as whipping cream, sour cream, ice cream, and
buttermilk, then under the brand Lady Berkeley. By 1932, the
company employed twenty men and served 11 delivery routes.

The Great Depression brought great difficulties to the California dairy industry. Retail stores engaged in a price war for
milk, selling a quart for as low as a penny. To guarantee higher
prices from milk processors, dairy farmers dumped their milk.
The State of California stabilized prices by enacting a law that
set a minimum resale price on milk at $0.12 per quart for home

delivery and $0.09 per quart at retail stores. Despite the challenges of the era, the South Berkeley Creamery grew to serve 28 routes with 40 employees in 1940. Home delivery of milk was at its peak during the 1930s, 1940s, and into the 1950s. By 1947, the company needed to relocate to a larger milk processing facility in Emeryville, which was near Berkeley. The new, $500,000 plant processed 10,000 gallons of milk per day initially and was expanded several times over the next 50 years.

Sabatte's five sons were instrumental in the growth of the creamery and took leading positions at the company. George P. became transportation manager; Albert M., sales manager; Frank E., general manager; John A., ice cream and milk plant operations manager; and Remond C., office and restaurant manager. In 1953, the Sabatte sons took full control of the company, and four years later John Sabatte died.

In 1955, the company operated branch distribution centers in Hayward, San Mateo, and Walnut Creek. The company counted 240 delivery routes and 305 employees. Berkeley Farms fountain restaurants provided another outlet for the company's dairy products, particularly its ice cream. In addition to serving basic American diner food, Berkeley Farms restaurants served ice cream dessert specialties, such as the popular Berkeley Farms Derby, made with chocolate and black walnut ice cream topped with fudge, nuts, and a cherry. The restaurants offered hand packed or pre-packed ice cream for customers to take home. Berkeley Farms fountain restaurants opened throughout the company's milk delivery territory, including Alameda, Walnut Creek, Navoto, and Tracy. The South Berkeley Creamery became Berkeley Farms in 1956.

Adapting to Industry Changes in the 1950s–60s

During the 1950s, home delivery of milk declined in the face of increased competition from retail grocers, as dairies owned by supermarkets competed with companies like Berkeley Farms. Berkeley Farms felt the effects of retail competition. The company hired James Plessas, Inc. in 1965 to develop advertising for the company. The firm developed what may be the longest running and most memorable advertising slogan in the San Francisco Bay Area. To the tagline, "Farms in Berkeley?," a cow responded, "Mooooo." Berkeley Farms had the advertisement painted on its delivery trucks and used it in radio and print advertisements. In 1970, the radio advertisements featured the voice of Mel Blanc, a native of San Francisco and famous for providing the cartoon voices of Bugs Bunny, Elmer Fudd, Porky Pig, and many other Loony Tune characters.

By 1967, the decline in home delivery milk sales caused the Sabattes to call a meeting of family members involved in the business, including several grandchildren of the founder, to chart the future of Berkeley Farms. They determined to adapt to the changing conditions of the dairy industry by repositioning the company for the institutional and grocery wholesale milk business. Berkeley Farms sought new customers among supermarkets, small grocers, convenience stores, and food service providers, and they phased-out its home delivery service.

The founder's grandchildren were involved in the renewal of the company, with sons taking positions in sales and dairy operations and daughters in the office and restaurant operations. Donald Sabatte managed operations in Hayward and San Mateo and expanded business into Santa Clara and Monterey counties, eventually becoming executive vice-president as he became responsible for labor and operations. Norman Sabatte sought new business in Contra Costa County and Gary Sabatte in the highly competitive San Francisco market.

Changes at Berkeley Farms involved expansion to adjacent markets through acquisition of other small dairy companies, beginning with Tomales Bay Creamery in 1968 and the Christopher Dairy in 1970. Later acquisitions included the Edelweiss Dairy, Arden Farms, and Adohr Farms. In 1975, Berkeley Farms began operations of a dairy cattle ranch in Firebaugh in San Joaquin Valley, managed and partly owned by Sabatte granddaughter Michelle. The company owned a closed herd of Holsteins, employing dairy experts and nutritionists to care for the animals. Berkeley Farms grew its own feed on 1,500 acres to ensure its nutritional value for the herd. Also, the company practiced integrated pest management to minimize use of pesticides on cattle feed crops.

By 1986, Berkeley Farms listed at number 58 of the top 100 private companies in the San Francisco Bay area, recording $98 million in revenues the previous year. Growth continued steadily to $115 million in 1989, when the company had 450 employees.

In 1990, Berkeley Farms concentrated on expanding its ice cream business when Roger and Randy Sabatte formed a separate ice cream division. As premium ice cream with rich flavor and high butterfat content became popular among consumers, Berkeley Farms tried to develop and promote its Lady Berkeley premium ice cream, but without success. Instead, in 1991 the company purchased most of the assets of Bud's Ice Cream, a well-known, premium ice cream maker founded in San Francisco in 1932. In recent years, the Bud's brand had been weakened by competition from new brands, such as Haagen-Daz, Dreyers Grand, and Breyers, and by less consumer awareness as the owners decreased spending on advertising. In 1990, a group of Wisconsin investors purchased Bud's Ice Cream, then in bankruptcy.

Berkeley Farms purchased the company's brand name, ice cream formula, product line, trademarks, and a production facility in South San Francisco. Ownership by Berkeley Farms gave Bud's Ice Cream access to distribution throughout California. The investment group retained control of 140 ice cream parlor franchises in California and a joint venture to operate Bud's in China, where it was the only ice cream brand with a license

to do business, and in Thailand. Berkeley Farms shared in the profits of the overseas ventures as well as in Bud's gourmet quality egg nog, produced in the United States.

Berkeley Farms followed the acquisition of Bud's with an advertising campaign to reestablish the brand name quickly. Advertising included radio spots, print ads in Bon Appetit and Better Homes and Gardens magazines, and limited television exposure. The company sought to establish new markets for the product, particularly with small grocers not yet committed to Haagen-Daz or other brands of premium ice cream. Bud's became the only ice cream served at the 75 Penguin Frozen Yogurt Shops in California. Plans for national distribution began with entry into Nevada and Arizona markets. In 1993, Bud's introduced Mocha Bean Crunch ice cream, a coffee flavored ice cream with chocolate-covered coffee beans, as its signature product.

Late 1990s: A New Facility and New Ownership

In the late 1990s, Berkeley Farms required a new facility for its milk processing, packaging, and distribution operations. The company maintained its commitment to remain in the San Francisco Bay area and found a 20-acre site in Hayward. Berkeley Farms completed construction on the $55 million project and relocated operations in March 1998. The 228,000-square-foot facility processed 135,000 gallons of milk per day, with a capacity to process 200,000 gallons per day, the largest rBGH-free milk processing facility on the west coast. The nine packaging lines included the addition of a new plastic bottle filler, with a capacity to fill 105 gallon-bottles per minute, and two new fillers for table-top milk cartons. Berkeley Farms planned to relocate ice cream production to the Hayward site; at a cost of $15 million, the facility would make 30,000 gallons of ice cream per day.

State-of-the-art technology involved an automated order entry and picking system (SAM) to simplify distribution in the 50,000-square-foot refrigerated milk holding room. SAM used an automated vision sortation device which directed stacks of plastic milk cases to one of 26 conveyor lanes. Each lane had the capacity to carry 136 six-high stacks of plastic cases, a total of 21,000 plastic milk cases per lane. SAM handled half-gallon, school-size milk cartons, plastic gallon bottles. The system allowed four people to unload for distribution more than 4,000 plastic milk cases per hour. Order preparation for yogurt, cot-

tage cheese, and other dairy products were handled manually in a different area. Over those lanes, light displays informed order pickers the amount of product needed for each order.

In November 1998, Dean Foods Company, the largest processor of milk in the country, acquired Berkeley Farms, in part to capitalize on the new plant. Berkeley Farms continued to operate as they had before the change in ownership, adding $158 million in annual revenues to Dean Foods $3.3 billion in revenues. In May 2000, Dean Foods closed the San Leandro milk processing plant and consolidated operations at the Hayward plant. Also, the company installed three packaging lines for filling chugs (re-sealable, single-serving, plastic milk bottles) in half-pint or one-pint sizes. In March 2000, the company installed a new cooler at the Hayward plant to support distribution of the new chugs line. The Krispy Kreme chain of donut shops carried Berkeley Farms chugs in stores in northern California.

While Berkeley Farms continued to use the long-running tag line, "Farms in Berkeley?" to advertise the company, Dean Foods hired a new advertising agency and initiated an advertising campaign using the tag line, "Pure. California." Advertising outlets included radio, newspaper inserts, and outdoor locations, such as bus shelters.

Principal Competitors

California Dairies, Inc.; Horizon Organic Holding Company.

Further Reading

"Berkeley Farms," *Dairy Foods*, September 1998, p. 72.
"Bud's China First to Jointly Produce Ice Cream in China," *San Francisco Business Times,* November 16, 1990, p. 13.
Carlsen, Clifford, "The Scoop on Bud's Ice Cream: National Expansion Under Way," *San Francisco Business Times,* July 2, 1993, p. 1.
Carroll, Jon, "What Did I Know? When Did I Know It?" *San Francisco Chronicle,* November 17, 1989, p. E 18.
"Cool Cooler," *Dairy Foods,* March 2000, p. 45.
"Dean Foods Building Position as National, 'On-the-Go' Dairy," *Feedstuffs,* September 27, 1997, p. 6.
"James Plessas, Inc." *Ice Cream Reporter,* April 20, 2000, p. 8.
Marzec, Michael and others, "Top 100 Private Companies," *San Francisco Business Times,* November 9, 1987, p. 17.
Nelson, Eric, "Wisconsin Buyers See Cool Promise in Bankrupt Bud's," *San Francisco Business Times*, April 23, 1990, p. 5.
Pender, Kathleen, "Berkeley Farms to Acquire Bud's," *San Francisco Chronicle,* June 15, 1991, p. B1.
Reiter, Jeff, "Juices and Drinks with a Twist," *Dairy Foods,* February 1995, p. 52.
Saekel, Karolo, "Faux Whipped Cream Challenges the Real Thing," *San Francisco Chronicle,* January 17, 1990.
Schroeder, Kathryn, "Johnson, Allies Win," *ADWEEK Southwest,* July 24, 2000, p. 10.
Simonds, Shelly, "Farmers Cowed Over Hormone Use," *San Francisco Business Times,* October 7, 1994, p. 3.
Tanaka, Wendy, "Berkeley Farms' New Start Bay Area Dairy Sold to Out-of-State Competitor," *San Francisco Examiner,* September 16, 1998, p. B1.

—Mary Tradii

Business Post Group plc

Express House, 464 Berkshire Avenue
Slough, Berkshire SL1 4PL
United Kingdom
Telephone: (+44) 1753-819-918
Fax: (+44) 1753-819-022
Web site: http://www.business-post.com

Public Company
Incorporated: 1971
Employees: 1,452
Sales: £123.71 million ($175.2 million)(2001)
Stock Exchanges: London
Ticker Symbol: BPG
NAIC: 492210 Local Messengers and Local Delivery

Business Post Group plc is one of the fastest-growing parcel delivery companies in the United Kingdom. Based in Slough, Berkshire, the company has claimed more than five percent of the U.K. market for express mail delivery, with over 90 percent of its revenue derived from next-day delivery service. The company's network of 60 depots—both company-owned and franchised—and a fleet of 1,200 vehicles give it national coverage and allow it to offer an extensive range of delivery services, including early-morning, evening, and weekend delivery. Business Post's 20 company-owned depots act as regional hubs for its 40 franchised locations. Franchising enabled the company to quickly extend its reach throughout the United Kingdom; the company believes that the franchise system has also helped create a network of highly motivated, quality-conscious personnel. Through partnerships—previously with Air Express International, but since September 2001 with Federal Express—the company can also offer international delivery services. The company developed a similar partnership with Germany's Eurodis to cover road-based deliveries on the European continent. The United Kingdom remains the company's single largest market, however, generating 90 percent of its nearly £124 million in sales. Business Post has also targeted the growing e-commerce market for growth, launching subsidiary Homeserve.net to offer home delivery services to Internet-based businesses. The company has also gained the home delivery contract with the United Kingdom's leading personal computer manufacturer, Tiny Computers. By making significant investments in updating its information technology infrastructure since the late 1990s, Business Post has expanded its services to include in-cab bar coding systems, web-based POD (proof of delivery) and tracking services, as well as web-based dispatching facilities. Business Post's shares are listed on the London stock exchange. Founder Peter Kane and family own 51 percent of the company's shares; brother and co-founder Michael Kane holds 13 percent of the company's shares. Both Kanes have retired from active management of the company, although Peter Kane has taken on the role of non-executive chairman since July 2001. Day to day operations are led by CEO Paul Carvel.

Postal Strike Opportunities in the 1970s

Peter Kane originally started out as a cab driver, forming his own company to serve his hometown of Harrow, near London. A strike by the British postal service in 1971 offered Kane a new opportunity—that of delivering parcels instead of people. Kane, then just 23 years old, formed Business Post Group in 1971 and focused on serving the Harrow-area business community, offering parcel and overnight mail delivery services. Kane was soon joined by his younger brother Michael Kane. Together the brothers built Business Post into a nationally operating company.

Business Post's growth started in earnest in the second half of the 1980s. From 1987, the company, which moved its headquarters to nearby Slough, began to expand regionally and then nationally, opening transport hubs in Reading, then heading north to Birmingham. The still-small company, unable to finance a rapid expansion with its own funds, chose instead to develop its network of depots through a system of franchises. By the beginning of the 1990s, the Kane brothers had built Business Post into a steadily growing national parcel delivery service. The company's chief target market remained the business sector, its infrastructure revolving around 20 company-owned regional hubs, which in turn served its growing network of franchised depots that typically targeted local markets. By the end of the decade the company's franchise network had grown to 40 depots. In 1990 the company began to extend its range of services, particularly by entering into a partnership agreement with Airborne Express that enabled the company to offer its customers international delivery services.

Fast Growth in the 21st Century

The Kane brothers sought further expansion for the company in the mid-1990s. In order to fuel its growth, Business Post went public in 1993. While the Kane brothers reduced their shares by about 20 percent, Peter Kane himself maintained a stake of some 60 percent in the company. The successful floatation valued the company at £60 million, as the company's sales were nearer the £40 million mark.

The public listing of Business Post enabled it to continue its growth: the company opened new depots and expanded existing hubs to serve a steadily increasing clientele. Going public also gave Peter and Michael Kane the opportunity to step back from active management, as the brothers took on non-executive positions with the company. Neil Benson now took over as chairman, seconded by Michael Jones as managing director. In 1995, Peter Kane sold off 4.5 percent of his holdings in the company, reducing his stake to 56 percent. The company meanwhile continued to make steady sales gains, reaching £65.5 million by 1996.

Business Post entered the Eurodis alliance in 1995, giving it access to that group's European road-based delivery service infrastructure. Back home, the company strengthened its position as a national parcel delivery provider with the opening of a new national hub in Heartlands, Birmingham, in 1997. Construction of the facility cost more than £7 million.

The company continued to enjoy rising revenues, topping £80 million for the year 1997. Yet the following year proved a difficult one for Business Post. In July 1998, the company issued a profit forecast of some 18 percent growth. By August 1998, however, the company, which until then had seen an unbroken rise in both sales and profits, was forced to issue its first profits warning, crushing its share valuation. This move was followed by the ouster of Jones, together with its finance director, who had sold off his entire stake in the company shortly before the collapse in the company's share price, netting him more than £4.5 million.

Peter and Michael Kane returned to active leadership of the company, working to restore not only its performance but its

reputation among the shareholder community by embarking on a vast modernization program as it implemented a new cutting-edge information technology and aligning itself with the growing potential of the e-commerce community, culminating with the launch of a new subsidiary, Homeserve.net Ltd., specifically directed to servicing the delivery needs of Internet-based retailers.

Homeserve.net received a quick boost soon after its launch in January 2000, when it was picked by the United Kingdom's largest computer manufacturer, Tiny Computers, as its principal carrier for the country. The contract helped boost Homeserve .net's portion of group sales to 10 percent, reflecting the rising proportion of residential deliveries made by the company. As Peter Kane declared, "This is an exciting development for Business Post and establishes Homeserve.net as a major player in the fast-developing home delivery market."

In 2000, Kane stepped down again from active management of the company he had founded in 1971, appointing Paul Carvell in his place. Kane nonetheless remained an active participant in the company's affairs, not only as its single largest shareholder, but also, following chairman Neil Benson's decision to step down in July 2001, as non-executive chairman. At the same time Michael Kane also returned to a non-executive position.

Business Post's revenues continued to make steady gains at the turn of the century, rising to £114.3 million in 1999 and then topping £123 million in 2000. Nonetheless, the weakness in the high-technology market spelled difficulty for the company, as its major customers, including Tiny Computers, began to see a drop off in computer and related sales. Business Post found a temporary means to bridge that gap in the first half of 2001 when, in response to a new strike by the Royal Mail service, the company began delivering its customers' first-class mail. This pointed the way to a potential new market as the British government made plans to deregulate mail service in the United Kingdom.

Business Post received a fresh boost in May 2001 when it signed an agreement with Federal Express that called for the world-leading parcel delivery company to handle Business Post international deliveries, while Business Post agreed to take over deliveries for those places in the United Kingdom not served by Federal Express. The agreement was expected to add another 10 percent to the company's sales. As the company completed the implementation of its new information technology infrastructure, it also continued to build its satellite facilities, including the opening of a new hub in Ilford, London, the expansion of its Swansea regional hub, and the construction of a new 38,000-square-foot facility in Leicester, opened in summer 2001. Having grown to claim more than five percent of the United Kingdom's parcel delivery market by the beginning of new century, Business Post plans to remain one of the U.K. market's major players in the years to come.

Principal Subsidiaries

Business Post Ltd.; Homeserve.net Ltd.

Principal Competitors

FedEx Corporation; United Parcel Service Inc.; Deutsche Post AG; DHL Worldwide Express, Inc.; Consignia plc; Exel plc; Air Express International plc; TNT Post Group N.V.

Further Reading

Davies, Ross, ''Business Post on Fast Track to Cutting Costs,'' *Evening Standard*, November 10, 1998.

''Business Post's Customers Send Fewer Packages,'' *Financial Times*, May 28, 1999.

Lea, Robert, ''Profits Drop But Business Post Upbeat,'' *Evening Standard*, December 5, 2000.

Lindsay, Robert, ''Business Post Faces Computer Blow,'' *Evening Standard*, May 24, 2001.

Lister, David, ''Exchange Probe as Post Sounds Alert,'' *Evening Standard*, September 16, 1998.

—M. L. Cohen

buy.com, Inc.

27 Brookline
Aliso Viejo, California 92656
U.S.A.
Telephone: (949) 389-2000
Toll Free: (888) 880-1030
Fax: (949) 389-2800
Web site: http://www.buy.com

Wholly Owned Subsidiary of SB Acquisitions, Inc.
Incorporated: 1996 as BuyComp.com
Employees: 150
Sales: $787.7 million (2000)
NAIC: 454110 Electronic Shopping and Mail-Order Houses

With a mission to provide the "Lowest Prices on Earth," and a trademarked description as "The Internet Superstore," buy.com Inc. provides a wide range of goods through its buy.com web site. As of the beginning of 2002, buy.com offered the following categories of products to businesses and consumers: computers, software, books, magazines, videos, DVDs, games, music, electronics, and wireless. With no brick-and-mortar store behind it, buy.com was one of a handful of pure-play Internet retailers to achieve substantial sales. For the year 2000, revenues reached $787.7 million, a 32 percent increase over 1999 sales. Buy.com was never able to turn a profit, though, and Wall Street drove down the company's stock price to less than $1 a share, causing it to be de-listed from the NASDAQ in August 2001. Founder Scott Blum, who had left the company before it went public in 2000, re-acquired all of the stock of buy.com in November 2001 for $.17 a share, or $23.6 million. He took the company private, making it a wholly owned subsidiary of his holding company, SB Acquisitions, Inc.

BuyComp.com: 1997–98

Scott Blum, an entrepreneur and junior college dropout, founded BuyComp.com in October 1996 to sell computer products at a discount. Blum was something of a serial entrepreneur, having founded his first company when he was 19 years old.

After he sold that company, he founded Pinnacle Micro, a computer memory company that went public in 1991. Blum left Pinnacle in 1996 after the company got in trouble with the Securities and Exchange Commission (SEC) for booking revenues for items before they were shipped.

BuyComp.com was selling about $1 million worth of computer products a day when it changed its name to buy.com in November 1998 and launched its new Web site, www.buy.com. Buy.com offered a wider range of products, including videos, DVDs, books, and computer games, as well as computer products. These products were offered as a result of buy.com's acquisition of SpeedServe, the Internet division of Ingram Entertainment, which buy.com completed with the help of $60 million in venture capital financing from Japanese software distributor Softbank. Both Ingram Entertainment and Softbank gained a minority interest in buy.com and seats on its board of directors.

With the acquisition of SpeedServe, buy.com set up specialty stores for each product line. It rebranded SpeedServe's BookServe, GameServe, and VideoServe sites as Buybooks.com, Buygames.com, and Buyvideos.com. In many cases, buy.com was selling products such as DVDs and videos for less than retailers could buy them from distributors or the movie studios. In the future buy.com would follow a pattern of creating specialty stores for new product lines. Before the end of 1998, the company purchased the rights to more than 2,000 domain names beginning with the word "buy."

Buy.com's business model required it to sell products at the lowest possible price. In fact, the company did not plan to make money on its margins, the way traditional retailers did. Rather, it hoped to attract enough traffic at its Web site to make consumer goods manufacturers want to advertise there. In order to sell products at the lowest possible price, Blum spent more than a year perfecting search agents that would determine the lowest prices being offered on the Web. Buy.com also did not carry any inventory, relying on wholesalers to ship products directly to its customers.

Buy.com got off to a fast start in 1998. Its sales of $125 million beat Compaq Computer Corp.'s 15-year-old-record of $111 million for a company in its first year.

Company Perspectives:

Buy.com, The Internet Superstore and low price leader, offers its approximately 4 million customers nearly one million products in a range of categories including computer hardware and software, electronics, wireless products and services, books, and more. Individuals and businesses can shop quickly and easily at buy.com 24 hours a day, seven days a week. Buy.com was named the ''Best E-Commerce Site'' by PC World *magazine (June 2001), ''Best Overall Place To Buy'' by* Computer Shopper Magazine *(January 2001), the No. 1 electronics e-tailer in the PowerRankings by* Forrester Research, Inc. *(November 2000), and a ''Best of the Web'' in the computer and electronics category by* Forbes *magazine (Spring 2000 and Fall 2000).*

Buy.com Expands Amid Customer Complaints in 1999

By February 1999, buy.com was selling about $2 million worth of goods a day. For the year, sales rose to nearly $600 million. The company added an online music store that promised every title on ''The Billboard 200'' for $9.95, excluding 2-CD and box sets. In mid-1999, the buy.com Web site was redesigned to let customers buy products from its different specialty stores all in one shopping cart.

While buy.com was building customer loyalty on the basis of price, it was falling short in the area of customer service. Disgruntled customers began to set up protest Web sites with names like Buycrap.com and Boycottbuy.com. *Sm@rt Reseller* magazine published a survey by ResellerRatings.com that said more than 60 percent of online shoppers felt that buy.com's sales staff was not knowledgeable about its products nor was it easy to deal with. More than 80 percent said exchanges were handled in an unprofessional manner, and only about half would recommend buy.com to a friend.

In March 1999, Gregory Hawkins, an executive at Ingram Micro, became buy.com's president and CEO. As part of an effort to improve customer service and transactions, he invited a group of unhappy customers to the firm's headquarters in Orange County, where he promised to hire customer service representatives to improve customer relations. One area of particular concern was buy.com's billing practices regarding out of stock merchandise. Buy.com would bill a customer's credit card for the purchase, even if the item was out of stock. If the order remained unfulfilled, buy.com would credit the customer's account, in some cases days or even weeks after the order was placed. Another rift with customers occurred when buy.com made a mistake in listing the price of a computer monitor, pricing it $400 less than was intended. Buy.com refused to honor the erroneous price, which resulted in a lawsuit on behalf of customers who ordered the monitor, and the initial ruling in the case went against buy.com.

Through heavy advertising buy.com built its brand in 1999. Early in the year it advertised on professional football's Super Bowl television broadcast. In its fourth quarter, the company spent an estimated $25 million on advertising to boost holiday sales. When Nike Inc. ended its seven-year sponsorship of the Professional Golf Association's developmental tour, buy.com agreed to sponsor the tour for five years beginning in 2000.

Operating as a Public Company: 2000–01

Buy.com's initial public offering (IPO) took place on February 8, 2000. The company sold 14 million shares at $13 per share and raised $182 million. Investors appeared unaffected by buy.com's failure to turn a profit and bid the stock up to $35 a share on the first day of trading before it closed at $25.12 a share. For 1999, buy.com reported revenue of $597.8 million, more than four times that of 1998, and a loss of $130.2 million, compared to a loss of $17.8 million for 1998.

Prior to buy.com going public, founder Scott Blum resigned from the company, in part because of his previous company's problems with the SEC. Hawkins became buy.com's president, CEO, and chairman. The company's IPO enabled buy.com to issue 1.12 million shares to the PGA Tour as part of its sponsorship agreement, along with a cash payment of $8.5 million. The agreement also required a 1999 payment of $6.4 million and a $17 million letter of credit from buy.com. When buy.com's financial problems became more acute in 2001, the PGA Tour attempted to drop buy.com as the primary sponsor of its developmental tour, but buy.com remained the tour's sponsor in 2002. At the beginning of 2001, buy.com sued the PGA Tour for breach of contract when the PGA Tour named USA Networks' Electronic Commerce Solutions to design and operate the tour's online store.

Buy.com's attempts in 2000 to expand into new products and services were not always successful. Its specialty travel store, called Buytravel.com, operated from February 2000 through November 2000 before shutting down. The company also opened a new business superstore that offered more than 55,000 office products. A new sports store powered by Global Sports offered active wear and sporting goods. Buy.com's License Online Program launched in April 2000 and offered software licenses on Microsoft's complete line of licensing products. The program was later expanded to include software from other companies, including Symantec, Computer Associates, Executive Software, and Trend Micro.

Buy.com expanded into international markets in 2000 by opening Web sites in the United Kingdom and Australia, both of which were accessible from buy.com's home page. These proved to be short-lived, however, and the Australian operations were discontinued in November 2000. Following a disappointing 2000 holiday season, buy.com's operations in the United Kingdom were sold in March 2001 to Britain's department store group, John Lewis Partnership, who would continue to operate it as a co-branded site. As of the beginning of 2002, visitors to buy.com's home page were given the option of selecting either the United States or the United Kingdom for their online shopping.

Wireless phones, service, and accessories were added to buy.com's product mix in mid-2000 with the acquisition of online retailer Telstreet.com for about $8 million in stock. Buy.com opened its wireless store in October 2000. Customers could shop for cellular phones and accessories, cellular plans, Web-enabled phones, and similar products from companies such as Ericsson, Nokia, Motorola, Mitsubishi, AT&T, Nextel, and Verizon. In the second half of 2000, buy.com began offering wireless access to its Web site through agreements with Spring PCS and AT&T Wireless, and customers with Web-enabled mobile phones could access and shop at the buy.com Web site.

Problems in 2001

Buy.com's cash position came to the attention of analysts as early as mid-2000, when investment banker Goldman, Sachs & Co., financial magazine *Barron's,* and stock market Web site TheStreet.com reported that buy.com was in danger of running low on capital by the end of 2000 or early 2001. In November 2000, Merrill Lynch & Co. issued a warning that buy.com was funding its operations from a dwindling supply of cash. By late November, the company's stock was trading around $2 a share.

Throughout 2000, buy.com was unable to reduce its losses. At the beginning of the year it raised its prices slightly and reported a positive gross margin of 4.3 percent in the first quarter. For the first half of the year, sales reached $400.8 million, with a loss of $66.4 million. The company's third quarter net loss was $21.4 million on sales of $190.2 million. A disappointing holiday season resulted in sales of $196.7 million for the fourth quarter, about $23 million under estimates, and a net loss of $36 million. For the year, buy.com reported a net loss of $133 million on sales of $787.7 million.

At the beginning of 2001, buy.com projected it would deliver positive operating cash flow by the fourth quarter of the year. The company planned to refocus on its core products, including computer hardware and software, consumer electronics, and wireless products, plus a general clearance category. Cutbacks and cost-cutting measures included shutting its sports store in March, discontinuing its Canadian store operation in February, and laying off 125 employees—more than half its 230-person workforce—in the first quarter. Buy.com's cost-cutting measures were expected to save about $70 million annually.

Buy.com's top management also changed in the first quarter of 2001. Hawkins and chief financial officer Mitch Hill resigned for unspecified reasons, apparently forced out by the company's board of directors. Donald Kendall, a long-term member of buy.com's board, became chairman, and board member James B. Roszak was named interim CEO. Robert Price was hired as

chief financial officer. *E-Commerce Times* speculated that the management change could signal a new beginning for buy.com as well as a possible search for a white knight. The white knight turned out to be company founder Scott Blum.

Buy.com's first quarter revenue of $124.6 million was 40 percent less than the previous year's first quarter, and the company reported a $45 million quarterly loss. It redesigned its Web site in May 2001 and added an enhanced search engine, new product menus, and a cleaner user interface. The site more heavily promoted the company's most popular merchandise and increased the visibility of related products and accessories.

Second quarter revenue dipped even more, down more than 50 percent from the previous year to $94.9 million, compared to $193.2 million in 2000. The company's net loss was $5.7 million, compared to $33.6 million in 2000. More than 80 percent of buy.com's sales during the quarter were computer hardware and software. With its stock trading below $1 a share, the company was de-listed from the NASDAQ in August. An additional 50 jobs were cut, reducing the company's workforce to 65 employees. Around this time it was announced that Scott Blum would repurchase buy.com for $23 million, or $.17 a share, and provide interim financing of $9 million. A two-member office of president was created, with CFO Robert Price and Kevin Baxter, senior vice-president of corporate development, jointly serving as president.

Blum wasted no time in cranking up buy.com's advertising and promotion, even before his acquisition of the company was finalized on November 27, 2001. He brought back the ''Lowest Prices on Earth'' guarantee, which had been dropped in 2000 as the company's losses mounted. Thinkbig Marketing Group, also based in Aliso Viejo and partly owned by Blum, was selected to create a new advertising campaign. By the fourth quarter of 2001, buy.com's cost-cutting measures seemed to be having an effect, increasing gross margins to 12 percent from 7 percent the previous year. According to *Forbes Global,* Blum predicted that buy.com would turn a profit in the first quarter of 2002.

Principal Competitors

Amazon.com, Inc.; eBay; Priceline.com.

Further Reading

''The Beat Goes On,'' *Golf World,* November 2, 2001, p. 10.
Benz, Matthew, ''Buy.com,'' *Billboard,* August 25, 2001, p. 56.
Brady, Mick, ''Measuring Amazon Vs. Buy.com,'' *E-Commerce Times,* August 2, 2000.
Brown, Ken Spencer, ''Buy.com Hikes Prices to Outlast Flood of Failing Firms,'' *Los Angeles Business Journal,* June 12, 2000, p. 7.
''Buy.com Shuts Its Travel Site, Will Explore Other Avenues,'' *Travel Weekly,* December 7, 2000, p. 38.
Campbell, Scott, ''Buy.com Loses One in Court, but Precedent Is Unclear,'' *Computer Reseller News,* July 12, 1999, p. 6.
——, ''Buy.com Meets Unhappy Customers,'' *Computer Reseller News,* April 26, 1999, p. 56.
——, ''Buy.com: Not All It's Cracked Up To Be,'' *Computer Reseller News,* April 19, 1999, p. 7.
''Changes at the Top of Buy.com,'' *InternetWeek,* February 19, 2001, p. 9.
Chen, Christine Y., ''All I Want for Christmas Is a Pulse,'' *Fortune,* November 27, 2000, p. 194.

Davis, Jessica, and Dan Neel, ''Pure-Play E-Tailers Retrench,'' *Info-World,* February 5, 2001, p. 10.

Enos, Lori, ''Buy.com Cuts Staff in Half,'' *E-Commerce Times,* February 28, 2001.

——, ''Buy.com Sells UK Operations to British Retailer,'' *E-Commerce Times,* February 6, 2001.

——, ''Top Execs Depart Buy.com,'' *E-Commerce Times,* February 13, 2001.

''The Everything Website,'' *Fortune,* December 7, 1998, p. 35.

''First One's Free,'' *PC/Computing,* August 1999, p. 91.

Foster, Ed, ''Dubious Marketing Ploys at Buy.com Expose the Seamy Side of E-Commerce,'' *InfoWorld,* May 3, 1999, p. 99.

Gurley, J. William, ''The Lowest Prices on Earth,'' *Fortune,* January 11, 1999, p. 150.

Hardy, Quentin, ''The Death and Life of Buy.com,'' *Forbes Global,* January 21, 2002.

Henshaw, Jean, ''Greg Hawkins,'' *Internet World,* September 15, 2000, p. 50.

''Is It Adios for Buy.com?,'' *Online Reporter,* September 3, 2001.

''John Lewis Acquires Buy.com UK Operations,'' *New Media Age,* February 8, 2001, p. 3.

Kemp, Ted, ''Embattled Buy.com Redesigns Website,'' *TechWeb,* May 12, 2001.

Milliot, Jim, ''Buy.com Hopes to Net $138 Million in Public Offering,'' *Publishers Weekly,* November 8, 1999, p. 16.

Nee, Eric, ''Meet Mister Buy (Everything).com,'' *Fortune,* March 29, 1999, p. 119.

Panettieri, Joseph C., ''Customer Boycott Bites Buy.com,'' *Sm@rt Reseller,* April 5, 1999, p. 25.

Regan, Keith, ''Buy.com Says Goodbye to Australia,'' *E-Commerce Times,* November 21, 2000.

——, ''Buy.com Slashes Workforce as Sales Plummet,'' *E-Commerce Times,* August 15, 2001.

——, ''Founder to Buy Back Buy.com,'' *E-Commerce Times,* August 13, 2001.

Russell, Geoff, ''Tour Refuses to Sell out on Buy.com,'' *Golf World,* October 20, 2000, p. 4.

Sacirbey, Omar, ''Buy.com Signals E-Tailings Long Farewell?,'' *IPO Reporter,* February 7, 2000.

Sirak, Ron, and Tim Rosaforte, ''Wanna Buy.com a Tour?'' *Golf World,* February 25, 2000, p. 70.

Sirak, Ron, ''A Tour Named Sue,'' *Golf World,* March 9, 2001, p. 4.

Streitfeld, David, ''Warning Issued on E-Retailers,'' *Washington Post,* November 9, 2000, p. E01.

Villa, Joan, ''Customers, Revenue Rise at Buy.com,'' *Video Business,* October 30, 2000, p. 28.

Vogelstein, Fred, ''Whoa! Has Buy.com Got a Deal for You!'' *U.S. News & World Report,* February 15, 1999, p. 46.

''We're Still Here!,'' *Business Week,* October 29, 2001, p. EB8.

Wilson, Wendy, ''Buy.com Buys SpeedServe,'' *Video Business,* November 23, 1998, p. 1.

——, ''Web Sites Launch New Looks in Bid for 'Stickiness'.'' *Video Business,* June 7, 1999, p. 28.

—David P. Bianco

Cap Rock Energy Corporation

500 West Wall Street, Suite 400
Midland, Texas 79701
U.S.A.
Telephone: (915) 683-5422
Fax: (915) 756-2866
Web site: http://www.caprockelec.com

Private Company
Incorporated: 1999
Employees: 91
Sales: $57.1 million (2000)
NAIC: 221122 Electric Power Distribution

Based in Midland, Texas, Cap Rock Energy Corporation buys electric power at cost and distributes it to more than 34,000 customers in approximately 30 counties across Texas. Additionally, the firm operates an electric cooperative and manages a municipal electric utility. By the end of 2001, Cap Rock's operations had grown to include the McCulloch Division in Brady, Texas; the Hunt-Collin Division in Celeste, Texas; the Lone Wolf Division in Colorado City, Texas; and the Stanton Division in Stanton, Texas.

Rural America without Power: 1939

Cap Rock Energy's roots stretch back to 1939 when the company was founded as the Cap Rock Electric Cooperative. Like many electric cooperatives, it was founded because of the needs of rural citizens. Cities and towns across America enjoyed the benefits of electric power soon after it was invented. However, such was not the case for the nation's rural areas, where it was not economically feasible to run costly power lines to serve a handful of customers. This presented numerous difficulties for farmers and their families, who were forced to continue farming manually, light their homes with kerosene lamps, and rely on old-fashioned methods to perform domestic tasks like washing and ironing clothes. It also caused many farmers' children to break tradition and seek life in lighted cities. Aside from relying upon wind-chargers—and thus being at the mercy of the weather—rural residents had few options for obtaining electricity.

Less than ten percent of farms were equipped for electric power in 1929. As Peggy Luxton explained in *Preserving Our Heritage—Facing Our Future*, electric utilities and the holding companies that controlled them "continued to ignore the rural areas of the nation, except for those which were heavily populated, easy to reach, and well off economically—conditions necessary to assure early profits." Eventually, in May of 1935, the federal government paved the way for rural electrification when President Franklin Roosevelt established the Rural Electrification Act. A year later the act was passed, the Rural Electrification Administration was established, and a lending program was implemented that improved conditions for electrical co-op's.

In 1935, the Agricultural Census indicated that less than ten percent of the nation's 6.8 million farms enjoyed electric power. This was in addition to a large number of non-farm rural homes. In the following years, conditions slowly improved. Actually getting electric service established in rural areas was the challenge. Municipalities and private utility companies were considered for this task. However, for various reasons—including opposition to the Rural Electrification Administration by private industry—nonprofit cooperatives emerged as the solution. Although private power companies did much to thwart the success of rural electric cooperatives, which only made things difficult for rural customers, many survived and prospered.

Getting Organized: 1939–1949

Citizens in the west Texas counties of Howard and Martin eventually heard about the REA and the loans it offered to help rural areas establish electric service. On July 22, 1939, a small group of them met to form a committee, the purpose of which was to form an electric cooperative. H.W. Deavenport was elected committee president and Riggs Shepperd was named secretary. The committee retained H.N. Roberts, an engineer from Lubbock, Texas, who was given instructions to draw up plans for an electrification project. Additionally, the committee decided to print 500 customer contracts and easements so that everything would be in order once the REA approved their loan application. Many of the committee members were from the area of Stanton, Texas, which sits on the edge the Caprock, an escarpment that separates the state's low rolling plains from the

Cap Rock Electric is united in its commitment to support and improve the lifestyle and business of our customers and community as the energy supplier of choice, with vision and leadership in enhancing customer ownership through value-added, high quality service based on progressive market development and a diversified energy and resource supply.

high plains. Accordingly, the new organization was named Cap Rock Electric Cooperative.

By August 1939, an application had been sent to the REA for a project that would involve 500 members and 205 miles of electric lines. In the meantime, the REA worked with Cap Rock to get organized and sign up members. Cap Rock also named its first board of directors. Deavenport, a farmer from Martin County, was its first president. Glenn Cantrell, a farmer from Howard County, later succeeded Deavenport. Although some residents were skeptical, Cap Rock's small band of leaders went to work signing up new customers. A vacant storefront on East Second Street in Big Spring, Texas, was selected as the co-op's first headquarters.

Cap Rock received a contract from the REA on July 8, 1940. After its original loan application for $144,000 was approved, it was possible for the new co-op to establish its first electric line, which was to stretch 125 miles. Cap Rock obtained power at wholesale from Texas Electric Service Co. (TESCO) at a location north of Big Spring, Texas. Power lines slowly began to run to farms. In preparation, a crew of 12 electricians worked to install meters and wire homes for electricity. On December 10, 1940, the co-op's first 25 customers received electric power. Rates for residential, commercial, and small-power service were set by the REA.

In 1940, Cap Rock hired O.B. Bryan as its first manager. Bryan would do much for Cap Rock in the following years. As the 1940s proceeded, Cap Rock worked to expand its service area by having contractors build new lines. Cap Rock's employees maintained the lines, working from two pick-up trucks. In 1941, Cap Rock instituted group purchasing of various electric appliances for its members, which then totaled about 125. In July 1942, the co-op moved its headquarters to a location on North St. Peter Street in Stanton, Texas. When World War II challenged the nation's human and material resources, the REA convinced the War Production Board that providing electricity to farms was essential to increasing food production. However, material shortages made this a challenging task for Cap Rock, which needed wire and poles, materials difficult to obtain in wartime, in order to expand.

By 1945, expansion was a realistic prospect, and Cap Rock grew as fast as new lines could be installed. In March 1947 alone, 159 people signed up for service. This level of demand also was happening in other regions. Eventually, it led to shortages and layoffs due to lack of work. In June 1947, two-way radio was instituted at Cap Rock, significantly improving safety and efficiency. By the end of the 1940s, more than 75 percent of the nation's farms had electricity thanks to projects financed by the REA. Cap Rock also was in fine shape. A new

office building and warehouse were scheduled for completion in 1949, and James D. Eiland was hired to handle public relations.

Cap Rock Expands: 1950s

During the early 1950s, Cap Rock served more than 2,000 customers. When the decade began, the co-op's directors voted to start a telephone cooperative called Wes-Tex Telephone Cooperative. By 1952, O.B. Bryan served as managing director of Wes-Tex, in addition to his responsibilities at Cap Rock. Four years later, the cooperative would be able to actually offer telephone service. In addition to the telephone initiative, Cap Rock Refrigeration Cooperative, started during the 1940s, was among the nation's most successful. As Luxton explained, "In addition to slaughtering, processing, and storing meat for local people, the Cap Rock locker plant purchased and slaughtered beef calves and hogs for sale to the people in a wide area of west Texas."

Besides offering electric service, Cap Rock Electric was doing much to benefit its members during the early 1950s. For example, when individuals purchased new electric ranges, Cap Rock supplied breaker boxes, outlets, cable, and even the labor required to install them. Bylaws were changed so that any remaining monies, after operating expenses were paid, were annually returned to members through a capital credits plan. Cap Rock also provided loans to members for things like the plumbing, wiring, and installation of irrigation systems. The co-op's employees also enjoyed new benefits; a retirement plan was introduced in 1957 along with merit increases for some workers.

Cap Rock's reach extended to ten counties in west Texas by 1952. In addition to its residential base, the co-op was serving a growing number of oil field meters and oil company camps. According to Luxton, customers included "2,684 farms, ranches, schools, churches, stores, and oil field installations on 1,588 miles of service line in an area 70 miles wide and 120 miles long." Half-way through the decade, the co-op had outgrown its headquarters. In late 1955, construction began to add about 1,600 extra square feet to the building, which now was home to Wes-Tex, at a cost of $27,717. This growth came despite efforts by competing firms that falsely labeled co-op's as socialist institutions that did not pay taxes.

Propaganda Attacks: 1960s

When the 1960s arrived, almost all (96 percent) of the nation's farms had electric power. Cap Rock continued to grow. In 1960, the co-op received approval to expand and remodel its headquarters at a cost of $191,415. The project was completed in July of 1961. Other important developments included Manager O.B. Bryan being named to the board of Texas Electric Cooperatives Inc. (TEC) in 1968. The following year, Cap Rock submitted an application to join the National Rural Utilities Cooperative Finance Corp. (CFC), a private bank that the nation's co-op's had formed.

During the 1960s, Cap Rock continued to implement measures for the benefit of its members. Among these initiatives were "zero billing," whereby people were billed for even numbers of kilowatt hours; a toll-free telephone number that was shared with Wes-Tex; and a depository where Cap Rock and Wes-Tex customers could drop off payments after hours. Cap Rock also continued to issue capital credits to its membership

Key Dates:

1939: A group of farmers form Cap Rock Electric Cooperative, an electric cooperative.
1950: Cap Rock's directors vote to start a telephone cooperative called Wes-Tex Telephone Cooperative.
1989: Cap Rock forms Capstar Communications Inc.
1999: Non-profit Cap Rock Electric Co-op Inc. forms Cap Rock Energy Corp. and begins the transition to becoming an investor-owned, for-profit organization.
2000: Cap Rock serves 34,000 customers in 28 Texas counties.

base, which numbered 5,634 by the end of 1964. At that time, Cap Rock delivered electricity to 13 Texas counties across 2,460 miles of power lines.

The 1960s presented several challenges for Cap Rock and other co-op's around the country. First, private electric companies continued to attack the nation's rural co-op's through lobbying efforts and propaganda, touting them as socialist threats to free enterprise. Organizations such as the Edison Electric Institute, the Electric Companies Advertising Program, and the National Association of Electric Companies carried out national advertising and lobbying campaigns backed by million-dollar budgets. In response, the National Rural Electric Cooperative Association launched its own national campaign called Tell the National the Truth, or TNT. Along with other co-op's across the country, Cap Rock contributed ten cents per member to help fund the effort. Despite these and other challenges, the demand for electricity remained strong when the 1960s concluded, painting a bright picture for the road ahead.

Challenging Times: 1970s

Although the 1960s ended on an optimistic note, the entire nation faced difficult challenges during the 1970s. The wholesale price of energy skyrocketed, coupled with double-digit inflation. The increased energy costs began in 1974 when TESCO, Cap Rock's supplier, increased its rates by 15 percent. By the decade's end, the energy crises was in full swing. In 1979, for the fourth time in its history, the co-op was forced to adjust its rates. Between 1940 and 1979, these adjustments amounted to a net increase of 45.4 percent. Due to changing circumstances within the federal government, and specifically the REA, the cost of borrowing money also increased during the 1970s. This added to the overall difficulties experienced by co-op's. Materials like wooden poles and aluminum conductors were once again in short supply, and their associated costs rose accordingly. Despite these challenges, Cap Rock's customer base grew to 11,451 by the end of the decade, and power was delivered over 3,843 miles of power lines.

In addition to the energy crisis and its related challenges, several other developments unfolded at Cap Rock during the 1970s. Cap Rock Refrigeration Cooperative folded in 1970. That same year, Wes-Tex announced that it would become a separate co-op located in a different facility. In 1971, Cap Rock joined other Texas co-op's in a data processing program that

allowed things like capital credit payments and billing to be handled at a data center located in Austin, Texas. On August 1, 1973, James D. Eiland replaced O.B. Bryan as Cap Rock's manager. A 1940 graduate of Texas A&M University, Eiland worked for the Census Bureau in Washington and as a hospital administrator prior to joining Cap Rock.

One positive thing for Cap Rock during the 1970s was its stellar safety record. In 1972, the co-op received a certificate of commendation from the National Safety Council when it went 260,446 man-hours without any injuries. In 1974, Cap Rock received the General Electric Outstanding Safety Achievement Award. In 1977, for the seventh consecutive year, the Texas Job Training and Safety Program recognized Cap Rock's employees, who went 835,000 man-hours without a lost-time accident.

New Horizons: 1980s

When the 1980s arrived, Cap Rock continued to focus on its members. In 1980, the co-op issued capital credits for the 24th consecutive year. In 1983, it began allowing customers to pay their bills by credit card. The following year, an average payment plan was implemented, followed by a bank draft service in 1985. Two years later, Cap Rock formed a member advisory committee that helped to determine a 5.2 percent rate increase, implemented in 1986. By that time, members had three locations where they could pay their bills. Cap Rock began offering satellite TV service to members in 1987. Two years later it formed two corporations: Capstar Communications Inc., which was devoted to offering satellite services, as well as a corporation devoted to traditional electric offerings.

In addition to basic improvements like a new Pitman Polecat truck in 1980, Cap Rock continued on a path of general expansion. In 1983, the co-op purchased a former Dr. Pepper bottling plant adjacent to its headquarters and used the area for storage. The following year, a computer system was installed. In 1988, Cap Rock opened a new dispatching office that was equipped with an array of high-tech capabilities for monitoring service.

One change for Cap Rock during the 1980s was co-generation, whereby, as Luxton explains, power is "generated with steam as a by-product of a manufacturing process." Cap Rock entered into an agreement with Panda Energy Corp. that called for construction of a co-generation facility. This would allow Cap Rock to obtain power from a source other than TESCO, which was both supplying the co-op with wholesale power and competing for the co-op's customers.

In August of 1980, James Eiland was appointed secretary-treasurer of the Association of Texas Electric Cooperatives (TEC) and named to the association's board of directors. In June of the following year, Eiland retired as Cap Rock's manager. His successor was Rodger Burch, who had much prior experience with electric cooperatives. Burch graduated from New Mexico State University, where he was involved in a cooperative education program. His father was a long-time manager of the San Patricio Electric Cooperative. Burch was succeeded by Cap Rock Assistant Manager David W. Pruitt in July 1987. A graduate of both Texas A&M and Texas Tech University, Pruitt had previously worked for two other electric cooperatives besides Cap Rock. He was named CEO of Cap Rock in 1988.

Throughout the 1980s, electric cooperatives endured a challenging relationship with the Reagan administration. This made it difficult for electric cooperatives to obtain financing from the REA and required them to pay higher interest rates—as much as 21 percent—on short-terms loans from other lenders. This came in addition to high wholesale energy costs, which by 1982 accounted for approximately 73 cents of each revenue dollar. To make matters worse, Cap Rock was forced to contend with customers who tampered with electric meters and stole electricity, as well as those who left the state with unpaid electric bills.

Despite these challenges, Cap Rock prospered through the 1980s. In 1987, the co-op took advantage of a special opportunity and refinanced all of the money it had borrowed from the REA through the National Rural Electric Cooperative Finance Corp. The move enabled Cap Rock to receive a discount of $11.5 million on its principal of $27.4 million. This had a positive effect on the co-op's bottom line, and by the decade's end it had evolved into a multi-million dollar corporation.

Growing for the Future: 1990 and Beyond

In 1992, Cap Rock signed an agreement to purchase the majority of its power at wholesale from Amarillo, Texas-based Southwestern Public Service Co. (SPS). At that time, the co-op was still buying power at wholesale from its competitor, Texas Utilities Electric Co., which then was the nation's fifth largest utility. By 1995, the changeover had occurred and Cap Rock, which was still a non-profit organization, had formed a for-profit subsidiary called NewCorp Resources to handle the acquisition of bulk power.

During the 1980s and 1990s, mergers and acquisitions occurred as a result of growing competition. These cut the number of Texas electric cooperatives in half. Cap Rock was involved in voluntary mergers with two other Texas cooperatives in the early 1990s. In 1991, it acquired Lone Wolf Electric Cooperative, followed by Hunt-Collin Electric Cooperative in 1992. Cap Rock then relocated its headquarters to a modern office building in downtown Midland Texas and began to form joint ventures with other energy companies and diversify into re-

sources like natural gas. In 1999, Cap Rock merged with Mc-Cullough EC. When the new millennium arrived, it had been involved in more mergers than any other U.S. electric cooperative. In February 2000, Cap Rock announced its intent to buy the Arizona and Vermont electric utility operations of Citizens Utilities. However, the deal—which would have added about 91,500 meters to Cap Rock's customer base—fell through in March 2001 when Cap Rock could not obtain financing.

By 1993, Cap Rock supplied power to 25,000 meters in a service area that was similar in size to the state of Maryland. At that time it had revenues of approximately $40 million. In early 2000, the non-profit Cap Rock Electric Co-op Inc. was on its way to becoming an investor-owned, for-profit organization called Cap Rock Energy Corp. This was the result of a decision made at the co-op's October 1998 meeting. In early 2000, Cap Rock was serving 34,000 customers in 28 Texas counties. It had evolved from the simple needs of rural Americans into a multi-million dollar corporation poised to meet future challenges.

Principal Competitors

Brazos Electric Power Cooperative Inc.; El Paso Electric Company; TXU Corporation; Reliant Energy Inc.

Further Reading

Aldridge, James, "South Texas Electric Co-Op's to Consolidate Operations," *San Antonio Business Journal*, August 17, 2001.

"Cap Rock Co-op Becomes Cap Rock IOU," *Electricity Daily*, February 23, 2000.

"Cap Rock Co-Op Sets Up a Subsidiary to Buy Bulk Power Outside of ERCOT," *Southeast Power Report*, May 19, 1995.

"Cap Rock Co-op to Link with SPS," *Electrical World*, November 1993.

Collier, Steven E., "Off and Running," *Public Utilities Fortnightly*, June 1, 1993.

Luxton, Peggy, *Preserving Our Heritage—Facing Our Future. A 50-Year History of Cap Rock Electric Cooperative*, Lubbock, Tex.: 1989.

"Using Innovative, Practical Ideas to Stay Competitive," *Electrical World*, May 1992.

—Paul R. Greenland

Carroll's Foods, Inc.

2822 West Highway 24
Warsaw, North Carolina 28398
U.S.A.
Telephone: (910) 293-3434
Fax: (910) 293-3199
Web site: http://www.carrollsfoods.com

Wholly Owned Subsidiary of Smithfield Foods, Inc.
Founded: 1936
Employees: 2,500 (est.)
Sales: $500 million (1999 est.)
NAIC: 11221 Hog and Pig Farming; 11233 Turkey
   Production

Based in Warsaw, North Carolina, Carroll's Foods, Inc. has been a subsidiary of Smithfield Foods since 1999, following a long-term association with the Virginia-based meat packer. Carroll's is one of the largest hog producers in the world, sending nearly 3 million hogs to market each year. It operates its own farms, as well as partners with contract farmers to raise its animals in North Carolina and Virginia. In addition, Carroll's maintains joint ventures with hog producers in Brazil and Mexico. The company is also one of America's largest producers of turkeys. It owns a 49 percent stake in Carolina Turkeys (a joint venture with Goldsboro Mills), one of the country's largest processors of turkey, selling under the Carolina brand as well as private labels.

Carroll's Foods Emerges During the Depression Era

Carroll's Foods was founded by Otis S. Carroll, whose father owned a general store in a town named Turkey, a few miles from Warsaw. He accumulated land during the lean years of the Depression. In addition to leasing his land to tenant farmers, Carroll opened a grain mill in 1936 on a site outside of Warsaw where Carroll's Foods headquarters would one day be built. He also took advantage of excess feed to raise broiler chickens and hogs. Far from being a stereotypical farmer, Carroll was a risk-taker with a bent for enterprise. In 1967 he decided to bring in a younger associate to help with the mill and

introduce some new ideas. He hired a 32-year-old feed salesman named Bill Prestage, who worked for Central Soya Inc. of Fort Wayne, Indiana, and would one day become a 50 percent partner. It was Prestage who convinced Carroll to raise turkeys for the entire year, rather than just for the holidays, and to drop chickens.

Prestage was also instrumental in the company developing new feed for its turkeys, pelletizing the mix to improve digestibility. The result was less waste and higher profits. While competitors required five pounds of feed to produce one pound of turkey, Carroll's only needed 3.3 pounds. With that edge, the company stopped selling its grain and by 1969 dedicated it all to the raising of its turkeys and hogs. The company also proved innovative in the production of hogs, applying some of the factory system techniques used in the raising of broilers and turkeys. The factory system had been applied to chickens for some twenty years. Because of red meat rationing during World War II, the demand for eggs and chicken had increased significantly. Battery cages arranged in rows and tiers became standard, as did the practice of using confinement sheds for broiler chickens. Moreover, poultry underwent vertical integration. Companies such as Tyson and Perdue began to acquire all sectors of production: breeder and commercial flocks, eggs, hatcheries, feed mills, medications, slaughter, processing, and delivery. Small farmers were also contracted to maintain the chickens. Carroll's Foods would be in the vanguard of businessmen who transferred these techniques to hog production.

Traditionally hogs had been reared in a mud pit with corn feed haphazardly spread across it. Not only did this arrangement limit the size of an operation, it made the animals susceptible to such diseases as cholera that could decimate an entire herd. Such would be the case in 1969 for Murphy Family Farms, a rival of Carroll's and future acquisition of Smithfield. In response to this crisis, Murphy turned to contract farming, moving piglets from one contractor to the next at particular stages when the animals would be likely to pick up diseases from older animals. Carroll's contribution to the new way of raising hogs was to create a controlled environment: buildings with a metal grating over a concrete floor and a lagoon in which wastes could be properly treated. Old-timers may have called them "hog

Company Perspectives:

Efficiency, consistency, and product quality, as well as the safety of our associates and animals are four of Carroll's primary goals. Our success in achieving these goals relies heavily on the integral working relationship of each department within our company. Therefore, communication, team work, dependability, leadership, and self-motivation are imperative qualities in our pork and poultry business.

parlors,'' but these structures were a key element in creating a factory system. Aside from insuring the quality of the animals, it also provided Carroll's with other tangible benefits. By increasing the number of hogs it could raise, Carroll's enjoyed the economies of scale in its purchase of feed and vitamins, resulting in the company becoming one of the lowest-cost producers of pork as well as turkey.

Sonny Faison Joins Carroll's in 1974

Revenues of $2.8 million in 1968 grew to $16 million by 1974, at which point a pair of events occurred that changed the direction of Carroll's. The company was about to open its first 1,000-sow hog farm and was in the midst of constructing a new feed mill when grain prices skyrocketed because of a crop failure, putting the company in a precarious position. Rather than take a step back, Carroll and Prestage decided to make an even greater commitment to the hog business, increasing their investment by turning to a genetically pure breeding stock rather than a mixed lot of sows. Also in 1974 the company added a new member to the management team, Sonny Faison. He was a Wake Forest graduate who became an accountant and worked as a controller for a North Carolina furniture factory before joining Carroll's. Not only did Faison greatly improve the company's accounting systems, as a non-farmer he also came into the business with a fresh perspective. He recognized that because the company could not control its selling price, the key to prosperity was controlling costs by knowing precisely the breakdown of those costs. Computers now joined hog parlors as essential ingredients in the modern production of hogs.

Faison emerged as president of the company after Carroll died and his daughter, Joyce Carroll Mathews, inherited his share of the business. Prestage wanted to go it alone and offered to buy out Joyce. According to company lore, Prestage wrote down a price, supposedly $6 million, on a slip of paper, which he then presented to Joyce in an envelop. He would either buy her out at that price, or she could acquire his share of the business for the same amount. To his surprise, Joyce decided to pay the $6 million for complete control. Faison had apparently convinced her that he could effectively run the business for her. Prestage would eventually start his own turkey and pork producing company, Prestage Farms, while Faison continued Carroll's movement towards vertical integration in response to outside developments. At the time, the company sold most of its turkeys to one packer, Marval Poultry Co., but when Marval was acquired by turkey grower Rocco Enterprises in 1982, Carroll's was suddenly dependent on a rival, which could now squeeze it on price. In response, Carroll's joined forces with another North Carolina turkey grower, Goldsboro Milling Co., to create Carolina Turkey Co. and build a $50 million processing plant. The business would be successful, but because Carroll's gained a processing capability late in the game, it would require some time to grow the Carolina Turkey brand name.

Faison then tried to learn from the company's experience with turkeys to protect its position with pork. To get a jump on the other major North Carolina pork producers, Murphy Farms and Prestage Farms, in 1986 Carroll's entered into a hog producing deal with Smithfield Foods, agreeing to sell all of its hogs to the packer at market price. As part of the deal, Carroll's bought 13 percent of Smithfield's stock, which in effect provided the company with some of the benefits of vertical integration. Historically, hog prices were subject to four-year cycles. When prices were low, Carroll's would now benefit through Smithfield's increased processing profits. Moreover, Faison gained a seat on Smithfield's board to help protect Carroll's interests.

Like Carroll's, Smithfield was established during the Depression. Joseph Luter and his son, Joseph Luter II, both worked for Gwaltney, a Smithfield, Virginia, pork packer, and decided to strike out on their own. They raised $10,000 to start Smithfield Packing Co. in 1936 and opened a plant across the street from their old employer. Joseph Luter III was originally uninterested in becoming involved in the family business, opting instead to pursue the law. While a senior at Wake Forest University, however, his father died. Upon graduation in 1962 he returned home to take the reins of Smithfield Packing. When a conglomerate bought the business for $20 million four years later, Luter stayed on as manager but was fired in six months. Nevertheless, he had become a rich, young man. He started up a Virginia ski resort, Bryce Mountain, and spent considerable time in New York. In December 1974 he learned that Smithfield was deep in debt and losing money. He told *Forbes* in a 1992 profile, ''For a company like this to lose money in December, it's like Budweiser losing money in July.'' He decided to drop the ski lodge and reacquire the family business.

With Smithfield stock trading at 50 cents a share, Luter made a deal with creditors to run the company for $50,000 a year with the option of buying 10 percent of the stock at $1 a share. Luter cut debt by unloading nonpork businesses and within a year returned the company to profitability. He then began to take advantage of the hog price cycle to acquire stock when the price of Smithfield shares was depressed because of high commodity prices. Under Luter, Smithfield acquired other brand name processors (including Gwaltney), whipping them into shape through cost-cutting measures. Although midwestern packers had long dominated the field, Smithfield, augmented by Gawltney's operations, was gaining the upper hand. Not only was it closer to the heavily populated East Coast, placing half of the U.S. population within a day of delivery, Smithfield was becoming less reliant on Midwest hogs. After signing the deal with Carroll's, it received a major share of its hogs from its partner. It also established its own pork producing operation in North Carolina, Brown's of Carolina. Smithfield would enjoy an ongoing advantage as North Carolina made rapid strides in overtaking midwestern states in hog production. In 1986, North Carolina was the seventh largest pork producer, and by 1996 it would be second only behind Iowa. While North Carolina hog producers like Carroll's were able to ramp up production through expansion of the factory system, midwestern states passed anticorporate farming laws in an effort to protect family farms. Ironically, contract farming in North Carolina served as a way to retain family farms. Producers like Carroll's provided contract farmers with guaranteed income that allowed them to borrow sufficient capital in order to convert to hog production. Loans were then paid off in a matter of years and the farmers could look forward to a profitable future.

Carroll's and Smithfield Forge a Relationship in 1991

Carroll's and Smithfield signed a joint hog-production agreement in 1991 in an effort to bring a leaner hog to market, buying the North American license to a genetically new pig developed by the National Pig Development Co. of East Yorkshire, England. In total the partners spent approximately $15 million to buy the rights, fly in 2,000 sows, and build a specialty North Carolina facility to house them. It was estimated that the NPD pig featured half the back fat of other pigs and significantly leaner hams and bacon. Not only would the leaner pigs mean more sellable meat per animal, resulting in less costs associated with trimming, the product would be able to command a premium price. Because the leaner pork would have a different texture than consumers were accustomed to, Carroll's also bred the NPD pig with other varieties in order to gain some flexibility in finding a leaner pork that would appeal to consumers.

Although Carroll's deals with Smithfield gave it the benefits of vertical integration, it remained vulnerable to commodity price swings in a way that Smithfield was not. In 1998, hog prices plummeted, reaching lows not seen since 1971, down more than 60 percent over 1997 prices. Despite a 7 percent increase in U.S. consumption of pork and a 32 percent increase in exports, the market was glutted, caused by a convergence of factors. Not only did family farmers and larger concerns like Carroll's overproduce hogs, the Midwest also harvested a large, high quality corn crop. Because the corn prices were low, hogs producers held onto their stock longer, resulting in animals that were heavier than normal. Another major factor was the closing of some Midwest packers who had been losing money. The loss of production capacity meant that there were more hogs available than could be slaughtered. Moreover Canadian hogs increased the amount of hogs available to processing plants.

While hogs farmers were in danger of going out of business, processors like Smithfield enjoyed robust profits, especially since strong consumer demand for pork products maintained prices at the grocery stores in spite of the low prices for hogs.

In February 1999, Smithfield announced that it would buy its strategic partner, Carroll's, America's second largest hog producer, for $500 million. Carroll's would be run as an independent business with Faison staying on as its president and chief operating officer. Carroll's would therefore be insulated from further price swings, and Smithfield would become the world's largest hog production and processing company. It would gain a number of advantages because of its increased size, including the ability to price its products six months out because its costs would be known. When the deal was finalized three months later, the deal would shrink considerably, with Smithfield paying $107 million in stock and assuming $231 million in debt. Although it was originally thought that Smithfield would sell off Carroll's turkey operations, it decided to also retain that business.

Smithfield's dominance in the production of hogs grew even larger in 1999 when it acquired Murphy Family Farms of North Carolina, the country's largest hog company. The company was founded by Wendell Murphy who graduated from North Carolina State in 1960 with a degree in agriculture. As Otis Carroll had done, Murphy became involved in hogs through the ownership of a mill, which he bought in 1962 after he and his wife scraped together $3,000 and his father, a tobacco farmer, guaranteed a $10,000 loan. He raised pigs on the side, using ground corn left over from the mill. By 1968 he devoted his business solely to the raising of hogs. As discussed earlier, a 1969 cholera epidemic that decimated his herd led him to focus on contract farming that allowed him to become the top U.S. hog producer. No matter how large the company had become, however, the depressed hog prices of the late 1990s was slowly driving Murphy out of business, just as it was the smallest hog farmer. Murphy had failed to develop its own packing operation and in order to maintain operations was forced to go deep into debt. The Smithfield deal included almost $290 million in stock and $170 million in debt assumption.

Carroll's, as well as Murphy's, lost a bit more of its autonomy in 2001 when Smithfield consolidated all of its production units into a management company named Murphy-Brown LLC in order to realize cost savings in purchasing, transportation, logistics, and better utilization of its management talent. Nevertheless, the three children of Joyce Carroll Mathews, who inherited the business after their mother's death, benefitted from the stock they owned in giant Smithfield that was three times the size of its nearest rival and gaining worldwide stature.

Principal Divisions

Hog Production; Turkey Production.

Principal Competitors

ConAgra Foods; Hormel; Perdue; Prestage Farms.

Further Reading

Dailey, David, "Hog Heaven," *Business North Carolina,* April 1994, p. 30.

David, Gregory, "Bionic Pigs?" *FW,* November 8, 1994, p. 32.

Koselka, R., "$OINK, $OINK," *Forbes,* February 3, 1992, p. 54.

Parker, Akweli, "Norfolk, Va.-Based Smithfield Foods to Buy Hog Producer," *Virginian-Pilot,* February 26, 1999.

Rhee, Foon, "Glut of Hogs Puts North Carolina Farms in Jeopardy," *Charlotte Observer,* December 23, 1998.

Roth, Daniel, "The Ray Kroc of Pigsties," *Forbes,* October 13, 1997, p. 115.

"Smithfield Gets Carroll's; Big Pork Producer Buys Rival," *Morning Star* (Wilmington, N.C.), February 26, 1999.

—Ed Dinger

China National Petroleum Corporation

Liupukang
Beijing
People's Republic of China
Telephone: (010) 6209 5129
Fax: (010) 6209 5126
Web site: http://www.cnpc.com.cn

State-Owned Company
Incorporated: 1988
Employees: 1.5 million
Sales: RMB 403.83 billion ($48.79 billion) (2000)
NAIC: 211111 Crude Petroleum and Natural Gas
Extraction; 213111 Drilling Oil and Gas Wells; 22121
Natural Gas Distribution; 32411 Petroleum Refineries;
48611 Pipeline Transportation of Crude Oil

China National Petroleum Corporation (CNPC) is a ministry-level institution responsible for exploring and developing onshore oil and natural gas resources. It owns more than 20 oilfields and overseas onshore oil and natural gas reserves. The company's most precious domestic assets have been bundled into PetroChina Limited Co., which began trading shares on the Hong Kong and New York stock exchanges in April 2000. PetroChina is the world's fourth largest publicly-listed oil company. CNPC accounts for two-thirds of China's petroleum and natural gas output. The central government has traditionally bought nearly half of its crude output at controlled prices for allocation to Sinopec, the national refining company. CNPC owns 25 small oilfield refineries itself. Apart from substantial holdings within China, the company is exploring or developing oilfields in the Americas, Africa, the Middle East, and elsewhere in Asia.

Origins

The origins of the China National Petroleum Corporation go back to the earliest days of Communist China. China's first oil joint venture was launched on March 27, 1950, by an agreement with the Soviet government to establish the Sino-Russian Petroleum Co. Ltd. in order to develop Xinjiang's Dushanzi Oil Mines.

On April 23, 1950, the Chinese government created the General Bureau of Petroleum Administration within the Ministry of Fuel Industry to oversee production and construction in the country's petroleum industry. The Ministry of Petroleum Industry (MOPI) was created five years later.

An exploration well struck oil in the Karamay Oilfield in Xinjiang's Junggar Basin on October 29, 1955. Several other productive oilfields were discovered in the next fifteen years, located in Qinghai, Heilongjiang Province, and Shandong Province.

A reorganization of the government's petroleum, coal, and chemistry sectors created the Ministry of Fuel and Chemistry Industries on June 22, 1970. In August of the same year, construction began on China's first long distance pipeline, running from Daqing to Fushun.

The Ministry of Fuel and Chemistry Industries was replaced with the Ministry of Petroleum and Chemistry Industries in January 1975. That June saw the construction of the Qinhuangdao to Beijing Oil Pipeline. Soon China would be a major world producer.

In March 1978, the Ministry of Petroleum Industry (MOPI) was restored, replacing the three-year-old Ministry of Petroleum and Chemical Industries. By the end of the year, the country would be producing 100 million tons of oil a year.

Before 1983, according to Haijiang Henry Wang, China's petroleum industry was in disarray. Its ownership was highly fragmented, divided among various corporations and government bodies. To consolidate the industry, two new companies were created in 1982 and 1983—the China National Offshore Oil Corporation (CNOOC) and the China National Petrochemical Corporation (Sinopec). Sinopec had authority over most refining facilities, except for certain smaller ones based at oilfields. For its part, MOPI had been given new importance under the new national energy plan and announced the ambitious goal of achieving 3.0 million barrels per day by 1990 (the figure was actually attained five years later).

One key constraint was a lack of capital and technology. To overcome this, in the mid-1980s the Chinese government cleared the way for cooperative projects with foreign companies in the south of the country, areas that China's existing equipment had been unable to exploit effectively. The first such contract was signed on May 28, 1985 between the China National Oil Development Corporation and the Australian CSR Company. On September 17, 1988, the China National Petroleum Corporation was established to replace the Ministry of Petroleum Industry (MOPI).

Looking Abroad in the 1990s

A restructuring in early 1993 added two new joint-venture trading companies to the traditional international trading monopoly controlled by the China National Chemicals Import and Export Corporation (Sinochem). China National United Oil Corporation (called ChinaOil or SinOil) paired Sinochem and CNPC to export crude oil. The China International United Petroleum and Chemicals Corporation (Unipec) was a joint venture between Sinochem and Sinopec, China's national refining company, to market refined products.

Wang Tao, the chairman of CNPC at the time, planned to use the extra profits from the new export joint venture to fund new domestic refineries as well as more exploration and development abroad through the China National Development Company, which had been established in 1981 but was under-funded.

In the early 1990s, CNPC was producing 140 million tons of crude a year from its domestic wells. With the Chinese economy the fastest growing in the world, the company set off on a global search for oil. CNPC became the first Chinese company to acquire overseas oilfield development rights in 1993. On March 5, the company obtained operational rights in Thailand. On July 15, the company obtained rights to part of the North Twing Oilfield in Alberta, Canada. Rights at the nearby Tarara Oilfield were obtained in October. CNPC soon ventured into Latin America in partnership with Petroleos del Peru. Sites in Papua New Guinea were also being explored.

The liberalization of trade in China was accompanied by an economic boom. This reduced the amount of petroleum products available for export. In 1990, the price of crude oil was regulated between 174 and 500 yuan per ton, the equivalent of $5 and $14 per barrel, given an official exchange rate of 4.78 yuan per dollar. In 1995, the exchange rate had gone to 8.31 yuan per dollar, and the price of crude was between 700 and 1200 yuan per ton, or about $11.50 and $19.70 per barrel.

A recalculation of crude oil prices by the Chinese government in 1994 allowed CNPC to show a profit for the first time in several years. However, the company remained concerned about its future due to increasing exploration and development costs.

According to the China Petroleum Information Institute, CNPC was operating a total of 9,479 wells in 1995, about ten percent of them exploratory wells. Daqing, China's largest oilfield, accounted for 2,851 of the total.

The company obtained rights to the Muglad Basin in September 1995 and March 1997. After a round of competitive bidding, two oilfields in Venezuela were added to the list in July 1997. This deal was worth $358 million.

In October 1997, CNPC acquired a 60 percent holding in the Aktyubinsk Oil Company, gaining access to oilfields in western Kazakhstan. CNPC paid $325 million for its shares and agreed to invest another $4 billion over 20 years, mostly to build a proposed pipeline to China. It outbid a consortium led by U.S. oil group Amoco. During 1997, CNPC also secured a $1.3 billion contract to develop Iraq's Al Ahdab oilfield upon the lifting of United Nations sanctions.

CNPC accounted for 89 percent of China's crude oil production in 1996. The China National Offshore Oil Corporation (CNOOC) accounted for another ten percent, while the Ministry of Geology and Mineral Resources (MGMR), local governments, and joint ventures between CNOOC and foreign companies shared the remaining 1 percent.

The China National Star Petroleum Corporation (CNSPC) was created in 1997 to develop both onshore and offshore oil and, particularly, natural gas resources on a commercial basis, through partnerships with foreign companies. It gave the existing state-owned oil companies a new competitor and was formed due to a lack of progress in staving off an impending oil shortage.

1998 Restructuring

CNPC was created as an upstream conglomerate but had plans to expand its downstream (refining) sector by 2000 by forming integrated refining-petrochemical centers in Karamay, Dushanzi, Daqing, Zhongyuan, and Bohai Bay. In a 1998 restructuring of the national oil industry, CNPC acquired 19 companies from the China Petrochemical Corporation (Sinopec), including several refineries, while Sinopec acquired 12 of CNPC's companies, including several oilfields. After the swap, CNPC and Sinopec became known as "Northern" and "Southern" companies, respectively, due to the location of their assets, which in CNPC's case totaled $57.2 billion. CNPC accounted for two-thirds of both China's petroleum and its natural gas output.

In January 1999, CNPC merged 10 pipeline enterprises into its China Oil and Gas Pipeline Bureau subsidiary, which was also given authority over four engineering construction companies, two research and design centers, a personnel training center, and a hospital. This gave the bureau assets of 23 billion yuan ($2.77 billion), including 13 oil or gas pipelines.

CNPC completed its first long-distance crude pipeline built overseas at the end of May 1999. It linked the Muglad oilfield to Port Sudan over a distance of 1.05 kilometers. By this time, China was importing 20 percent of the oil it used. This figure was projected to increase to 40 percent by 2010. The country's oilfields in the north and northeast were maturing, noted Britain's *Financial Times,* and its more recently discovered fields in the west had proved disappointing, both in terms of yields and in the cost of shipping the oil to the east coast economic centers.

By June 1999, CNPC had begun to restructure subsidiaries and trim jobs in preparations for a partial flotation. *China Daily* noted the company was plagued with an unnecessarily large number of employees, duplicated construction, high costs, and heavy debts, all a relic of the centralized planning regime. The company's offshore oil exploration counterpart, CNOOC, was also planning an IPO but canceled it in October. That did not dissuade CNPC management from pursuing their own flotation.

In November 1999, CNPC announced the establishment of a new limited liability company, China National Petroleum Co., Ltd. (China Petroleum or PetroChina), engaged in a variety of upstream and downstream activities. A few subsidiaries, already listed on the Hong Kong or mainstream China stock markets, were transferred to China Petroleum, with the exception of China (Hong Kong) Oil Co., Ltd., which retained its position in the stock market. PetroChina was thus endowed with CNPC's most valuable assets. It would have 480,000 employees, while CNPC would retain the bulk of the other one million, most of whom were likely to be laid off.

CNPC's net profits for 1999 were about 17 billion yuan ($2 billion), more than two and a half times greater than the previous year's. Sales income was about 330 billion yuan ($39.8 billion). The company pumped 107 million tons of crude oil and 16 billion cubic meters of natural gas during the year. A government crackdown on refined oil smuggling and CNPC's own restructuring efforts were credited with the positive results.

An IPO in 2000

Before its planned flotation on the Hong Kong and New York stock markets, PetroChina based the compensation of its top managers on performance, making it one of the first Chinese companies to adopt such a Western-styled incentive system. In spite of this, the PetroChina initial public offering (IPO) was disappointing.

CNPC had planned to raise $7 billion in what would have been China's largest IPO to date. However, the company only took in HK$22.5 billion ($2.9 billion) from the offering, even after the Chinese government pressured its mainland enterprises listed in Hong Kong to buy shares in the issue. One big subscriber was the British oil giant BP Amoco PLC, which agreed

to invest up to $1 billion for a 20 percent holding. Several U.S. pension funds boycotted the issue due to alleged human rights abuses and terrorist connections in Sudan, where CNPC was participating in a joint venture (PetroChina itself had no overseas assets), as well as environmental damage in Tibet. PetroChina shares fell markedly after listing on the New York and Hong Kong exchanges in early April 2000.

Principal Subsidiaries

Aktyubin Oil Company (Kazakhstan; 60.3%); China National Petroleum (PetroChina) Co., Ltd. (90%); China National United Oil Corporation (50%); China (Hong Kong) Oil Co., Ltd.; China Petroleum International Engineering Company; PetroChina Company Limited (90%).

Principal Competitors

China National Chemicals Import and Export Corporation (Sinochem); China National Offshore Oil Corporation (CNOOC); China National Star Petroleum Corporation (CNSPC); China Petrochemical Corporation (Sinopec); Petroliam Nasional Berhad.

Further Reading

China Petroleum Industry, 1995, China Petroleum Information Institute, 1996.
"CNPC Merges Pipeline Enterprises," *China Daily,* January 25, 1999.
"CNPC Regrouping," *China Chemical Reporter,* November 29, 1999.
"CNPC to Strengthen Exploration for Oil, Gas," *China Business Information Network (CBNet),* January 25, 1999.
"CNPC Ventures Need More Funds," *China Daily,* August 2, 1999, p. 5.
Corzine, Robert, "From Minor to Major: Formerly Monolithic State Oil Companies Are at Last Challenging the Western Majors on Their Home Turf," *Financial Times,* August 19, 1997, p. 13.
——, "The Lure of the East: China, a Vast Potential Market for Kazakh Oil," *Financial Times,* July 23, 1997, p. 4.
Gesteland, Lester J., "PetroChina Falls in New York, Hong Kong," *China Online,* April 10, 2000.
Harding, James, "Chinese Oil Giant Finalises Plan to Raise Up to $10 Billion," *Financial Times,* June 29, 1999, p. 1.
Ho Swee Lin, "China Oil Company to Revive Withdrawn Offering," *Financial Times,* November 26, 1999, p. 15.
——, "Chinese Issue Disappoints," *Financial Times,* March 31, 2000, p. 30.
——, "Investors to Tread Warily in China Oilfields," *Financial Times,* December 23, 1999, p. 8.
——, "Western Wiles to Woo the Market," *Financial Times,* March 14, 2000, p. 18.
Kynge, James, "China Anxious to Ensure That Oil Supplies Are More Secure," *Financial Times,* May 6, 1999, p. 6.
Landler, Mark, "China's No. 2 Oil Company Prepares to Go Public," *New York Times,* October 12, 2000, p. W1.
——, "Stakes in China Suddenly Seem Less Appealing," *New York Times,* March 31, 2000, p. C1.
Ling Zhuang, "Joys and Worries in Operations of CNPC and Sinopec," *China Chemical Reporter,* October 6, 1998.
McMahon, William J., "PetroChina's Roadshow Kicks Off as Detractors Drill Its Prospects," *China Online,* March 28, 2000.
"National Petroleum Corp. Signs Up for Oil Exploration in Three Continents," *South China Morning Post,* November 22, 1993, p. 2.
"Oil Giant Rakes in Big Bucks," *China Daily,* December 29, 1999, p. 1.

"Sinopec, CNPC Reduce Gas Prices, Begin Market Competition in Shanghai," *China Online,* August 15, 2001.

"Slick Maneuvers: China's Petroleum Shake-Up Dashes Competition Hopes," *Far Eastern Economic Review,* July 2, 1998, p. 61.

"Slick Move by Petroleum Firm Creates Oil Giant," *China Daily,* November 9, 1999, p. 5.

Walker, Tony, "China Creates Third State Oil Company; New Operation to 'Commercialise' Oil Bureaux and Research Institutes in Attempt to Revive Sector," *Financial Times,* January 27, 1997, p. 4.

——, "Survey of China," *Financial Times,* November 18, 1993.

Wang, Haijiang Henry, *China's Oil Industry & Market,* New York: Elsevier, 1999.

Yuan, Sy, Yi-kun Chen, and Ann M. Weeks, "An Update on China's Oil Sector Overhaul," *China Business Review,* March/April 2000.

—Frederick C. Ingram

Chubu Electric Power Company, Inc.

1 Higashi-shincho
Higashi-ku
Nagoya 461-8680
Japan
Telephone: (052) 951-8211
Fax: (06) 962-4624
Web site: http://www.chuden.co.jp

Public Company
Incorporated: 1951
Employees: 18,851
Sales: ¥2.25 trillion ($17.83 billion) (2001)
Stock Exchanges: Tokyo Osaka Nagoya
NAIC: 221111 Hydroelectric Power Generation; 221112
Fossil Fuel Electric Power Generation; 221113
Nuclear Electric Power Generation; 221119 Other
Electric Power Generation; 221121 Electric Bulk
Power Transmission and Control; 221122 Electric
Power Distribution

Chubu Electric Power Company, Inc. ranks third among the ten major Japanese electric power companies in terms of generating capacity, energy sales, revenues, and total assets. The company serves over 16 million consumers in a 39,000-square-kilometer area in the center of Japan ("Chubu" means "central"). The Chubu region is located on the main island of Honshu, between Tokyo and Osaka, and consists of a prosperous coastal plain with excellent harbors and rich farmland. Inland are the mountain ranges known as the Japanese Alps which rise to 3,000 meters above sea level. The rivers cascading down these mountains provide an abundant and steady source of hydroelectric power. Today the Chubu region accounts for 20 percent of Japan's industrial output. Chubu Electric maintains headquarters in Nagoya, Japan's fourth-largest city, and also operates eight regional offices in Japan and representative offices in Washington, D.C., and London. During fiscal 2001, the company secured electric energy sales of 123 billion kilowatt-hours, while its total generating capacity was 31.7 million kW.

Company Origins: 1950s

Chubu Electric was established in May 1951, a few months before the Japanese Constitution was promulgated and the year before the U.S. occupation ended. It was one of nine companies formed at the same time as part of the restructuring of Japan's energy industry after World War II. In addition to these nine companies, Okinawa Electric Power acted as a regional supplier to Okinawa prefecture. Except for Okinawa, the power systems of these companies were interconnected to ensure stable and efficient service for the entire country. In recognition of the public nature of electric power utilities, rates and other important factors were under the supervision of the Ministry of International Trade and Industry (MITI), although the industry itself was private.

At the time of its formation, Chubu Electric was given responsibility for supplying electricity to Aichi, Gifu, Mie, and Nagano prefectures, as well as that portion of Shizuoka prefecture west of the Fuji River. Its shareholders' equity was ¥29.4 billion, and its generating capacity was 1.03 million kW. It soon emerged, however, that this capacity was inadequate. Because of the age of the company's equipment, which it had inherited from the restructuring, its actual generating capacity was in fact only 600,000–700,000 kW. To make matters worse, the Korean War created a sudden surge in demand for electric power as Japan became a rear-base for the U.S. Army. In order to tackle this problem the company adopted a dual approach by conducting a publicity campaign for energy savings and by constructing new power plants, both hydroelectric and coal-fired. Construction of the Hiraoka hydroelectric plant in 1952 was followed by the construction of the Oigawa hydroelectric plant and the Mie and Shin-Nagoya coal-fired plants. By the latter half of the 1950s, supply and demand finally balanced out. This expansion of Chubu Electric's generating power required spending ¥210 billion over ten years, which was mainly covered with financing from the Japan Development Bank and with foreign capital.

In September 1959, a typhoon struck Chubu Electric's operating region, badly damaging one of the company's plants and flooding another on the coast for several months. Using the slogan "Electric power is the generator of recovery," the company responded with an all-out restoration effort. The efforts of the company to cope with this disaster earned it an award from the Disaster Committee Headquarters—it was the only award of this kind given to a private-sector company—and formed the basis of its approach to future disasters.

Meeting Increased Demand: 1960s

The 1960s were a period of marked economic growth in Japan, highlighted by the 1964 Tokyo Olympics and the improvement of the country's infrastructure with the opening of the Tokaido bullet train and the Tomei and Meishin highways, which linked up major industrial areas in central Japan with Tokyo. Because it occupied part of the Pacific coast belt, the Chubu region attracted the heavy chemicals industry and demand for electric power increased by more than 10 percent per annum. For several years, the growth rate in this area was one of the highest in Japan.

To meet the increasing demand, the company introduced a large volume of new oil-fired generating capacity. In 1960, fossil-fuel-fired plants contributed more than half of the company's electricity output for the first time, and subsequently new coal-fired plants with capacities of over 4 million kW were built around the Ise Bay, in Yokkaichi, Owashi, Chita, Nishi Nagoya, and Atsumi. At the same time this base was supplemented with hydroelectric plants—Hatanagi Unit 1 and Takane Unit 1—to meet peak demand.

In addition to developing new electricity sources, the company expanded its grid, constructing a 270,000 volt (V) transmission line around Ise Bay and strengthening its links with other utilities. Because oil prices remained stable during this period of rapid economic growth, the company did not need to revise its rates between 1954 and 1964.

In the 1970s, problems stemming from the period of high economic growth began to emerge. Environmental pollution had been a growing problem in Japan since the late 1950s, when people began to suffer from mysterious and horrific diseases. Because the symptoms of those affected became so widespread, developing "Citizens' Movements" (Shimin-Undo) were able to coerce the government and industry into tackling the problem. In response to the pollution problem, Chubu Electric promoted dual measures—for fuel and plant—concerning atmospheric pollution, noise, and waste water. These included reducing the sulfur content of its fuel. As with the later oil crises, Japan managed to turn adversity to advantage with the pollution problem and was to become one of the worlds' leading nations in terms of pollution control.

Diversification Amid Oil Crises: 1970s–80s

The first oil crisis hit in October 1973, a product of the fourth Middle East War. The price of crude oil—oil-generated electricity accounts for about 30 percent of Chubu's generation—rose above $10 a barrel, and after the second oil crisis in 1979, above $30. Chubu Electric revised its rates three times—in 1974, 1976, and in 1980—and largely managed to overcome the difficult times. A three-tiered rate system was introduced for household use, and a special rate for industrial users was introduced as the company promoted the concept of energy saving.

The oil crises proved a major turning point in Japan's economic development. The industrial emphasis moved from heavy chemicals to manufacturing, assembly, and knowledge-intensive industries. The rate of growth in demand for electric power, which had been 10 percent per annum, steadily increased. In response, Chubu Electric adopted what was called a "positive management" policy aimed at restructuring its business. Subsequent stabilization and decline in oil prices and the appreciation of the yen, reducing fuel costs further, meant that with little pressure on its balance of revenues and expenditures the company was able to reduce its rates four times up until April 1989, following the recommendations of MITI's Electricity Utility Industry Council.

In the early 1970s, the company began promoting diversification of its energy sources, mainly into nuclear power and Liquefied Natural Gas (LNG). The promotion of these power generation methods was perceived by the company to reduce environmental pollution, especially carbon dioxide emissions. Its first nuclear power plant, Hamaoka Unit 1, started operation in March 1976, five years after construction began. Construction of Units 2, 3, and 4 followed. In December 1973, at the height of the oil crisis, Chubu Electric entered into a contract with Indonesia for long-term supplies of LNG, and in March 1978 it commenced operation of two exclusively LNG-fired plants, Chita Units 5 and 6. It also promoted switches to LNG at Chita Units 1 to 4, Yokkaichi and Kawagoe. As a result, LNG's share of power generation reached 33 percent in 1989.

During the 1970s and 1980s, customer needs grew more sophisticated. Chubu Electric met the demand with various measures to introduce new technology and reduce costs. Measures included construction of a second 500,000 kilovolt (kV) transmission line, the introduction of super-high voltage lines for urban areas, enhancement of protection against lightning, the introduction of optical communications, improvement of information capabilities, and automation of facilities. In addition, the thermal efficiency of Yokkaichi Unit 4 and Kawagoe Unit 1, which started in 1989 using the latest technology, was raised to over 40 percent, compared with an industry average for the nine companies of 38.8 percent, within a year.

To meet increasingly varying customer needs, Chubu Electric promoted equipment for late-night consumption of electricity, heat pumps, 200-volt household appliances, office building air conditioning, area heating and cooling—the leveling-off of demand over peak and trough times in a particular area—and electric heat for industrial use and institutional kitchens.

In conjunction with these measures, Chubu Electric inaugurated a Challenge program in 1984 aimed at rationing and

---

Key Dates:

1951: Chubu Electric is established as Japan's energy industry restructures.
1952: The Hiraoka hydroelectric plant is constructed.
1976: The firm's first nuclear plant, Hamaoka Unit 1, becomes operational.
1992: The firm partners with Italy-based Ente Nazionale per L'Energia Electricia.
1999: Chubu begins laying fiber optic cables for household use.
2000: The retail sector of Japan's electric power industry begins to deregulate; the subsidiary LNG Chubu Co. Ltd. is established.

---

quality control, supported by Action Challenge Circles—information- and finance-gathering organizations set up abroad to facilitate these two functions. It established offices in Washington, D.C., in 1982 and London in 1985, and diversified its activities, principally into telecommunications and heat supply. In 1988, the company embarked on a program to update its corporate image and prepare itself for the twenty-first century.

Focus on Environmental Protection and Diverse Power Sources: Early 1990s

Chubu Electric also continued to implement anti-pollution measures at its thermal power plants. Greater use of low-sulfur fuel oils, flue-gas de-sulfurizers, and LNG reduced sulfur-oxide pollution. Flue-gas de-nitrification, use of low-nitrogen fuels, and boiler modification greatly suppressed generation of nitrogen oxides. Also, all company power plants became equipped with electrostatic precipitators which remove soot from flue gases with a high collection efficiency of 90 percent or more. Measures being adopted to prevent water pollution by power plants included the purification of discharge water by such methods as coagulating sediment, neutralization, and filtration.

To deal with noise and vibration problems, consideration was given to the use of low noise apparatus and the installation of noise suppression devices. Also, where necessary, installation of machinery was confined to indoor or underground sites. In addition, the grounds of power plant sites were landscaped with greenery. The amount spent on thermal power protection in fiscal year 1990 came to ¥40.8 billion ($258.2 million). However, Chubu Electric's overall policy on environmental protection considered that a rational balance must be kept between environmental protection and the stable supply of energy necessary for sustained economic growth.

Chubu Electric also continued to diversify power sources, improve overall energy efficiency, and develop carbon dioxide removal techniques. Due to rising crude oil prices and the depreciation of the yen in the early 1990s, power generation costs were rising. To maintain the current level of rates charged to consumers, the company began to implement radical cost reduction measures by upgrading operations.

During this time period, Chubu set forth several strategic goals. Between the years 1991 and 2000, Chubu Electric

planned to reach a capacity of 10.86 million kW. Of this, 10.3 million kW was to come from sources developed by Chubu Electric—2.24 million kW from nuclear power, 6.1 million kW from coal, 700,000 kW from LNG, and 1.26 million kW from hydroelectric sources. These numbers changed through the years however, as demand increased.

Chubu Electric also believed that nuclear power generation was needed to ensure adequate power supplies and a sufficient diversity of sources. In addition to the 1.137 million kW Unit 4 reactor under construction at Hamaoka, the Units 1 and 2 at Ashihama—each with a planned output capacity of 1.1 million kW—were expected to provide power for the early 21st century. Plans for the Ashihama nuclear power plant however, were later dropped due to residential protests.

Active development of thermal power, also considered necessary, centered primarily on coal. In addition to the Unit 1 to 3 generators under construction in the early 1990s at Hekinan, each with an output of 700,000 kW, plans for the Unit 1 and 2 generators at Shimizu, each with a capacity of one million kW, were also implemented.

With a view to fully exploiting indigenous Japanese energy resources, construction work on hydroelectric plants was proceeding at six sites with a combined total capacity of 1.095 million kW. As for existing hydroelectric plants, remodeling or improvement plans were also in operation.

Power supply was to be stabilized in relation to demand over the next ten years, with the prospect of maintaining an additional 8–9 percent of demand in reserve capacity. The proportion of power supplied by nuclear power plants was expected to increase from 18 percent recorded in 1990, to 22 percent by the year 2000, while oil-fired power was expected to decrease from 40 to 24 percent during the same period, in accordance with an accelerated trend toward reduced dependence on petroleum.

Chubu Electric also planned to make improvements to supply reliability. In 1990, the Chubu trunk transmission line system was composed primarily of 500 kV lines, and electricity was distributed around the load centers, or high-consumption areas, of Nagoya. Power transmission facilities began to be expanded to cope with factors such as increasing power demand, progress in development of new power sources, and growing urbanization.

In the early 1990s, developments included the installation of a second 500 kV outer loop line. In addition, the 275 kV system within the city of Nagoya was being expanded. Specific measures to improve reliability included further lightning protection for transmission lines and reinforcement of lines linking substations, as well as automation of troubleshooting and service restoration procedures. The funds required for the implementation of the above-mentioned projects were set to total ¥618 billion during the fiscal year 1991 and ¥649 billion in 1992.

While Chubu was focused on improving operations in the early 1990s, it was also gearing up for the partial deregulation of electric utilities in Japan. The company began to forge partnerships with international firms, including a 1992 joint venture with Italy's public electric utility Ente Nazionale per L'Energia Electricia. As part of the deal, both companies shared personnel as well as information about the electric power industry in each country.

Weakening demand from its industrial customers and a slowing of the Japanese economy during 1992, however, resulted in lackluster sales growth. In fact, in 1992 the company's growth levels were the lowest they had been since 1982. Sales and profits continued to fall in 1993 due to a cooler than usual summer, increased depreciation costs for its nuclear power plants, and the continuing economic slowdown. In 1994, however, a heat wave bolstered demand and despite continued rate cuts, Chubu's revenues surpassed ¥2 trillion for the first time in its history.

While sales continued to rise, the firm's profits did not fare as well because of increased facility repair costs. In 1995, the company reported a drop in profits of 6.7 percent to ¥89,290 million. Nevertheless, Chubu was determined to prepare for its future. In 1996, the company adopted a new set of business policies that were designed to ensure its arrival into the 21st century as a electric power enterprise. Included in the new strategy was a focus on Chubu's customer relationships and its environmental practices.

Partial Deregulation in Japan: Mid-1990s and Beyond

During this time, the electricity industry in Japan was undergoing major changes. In 1995, changes in the Electricity Utilities Industry Law allowed competition to enter into the electricity generation and supply market. Then, in 1996, a wholesale electric power bidding system enabled non-electric power companies to sell electricity to electric power companies. Finally, in March 2000, retail sales of electricity was partially deregulated, allowing large-lot customers—those demanding large amounts of electricity—to choose their power supplier.

The intent of deregulation was to foster competition, which in turn would lower the electricity costs in the country. The deregulation was slow to change the Japanese industry, however, and during 2001 Chubu and the nine other regional companies still controlled 99 percent of the market. In fact, only six Japanese-based companies—other than the original ten—supplied power to large customers, including retail stores and office buildings. This accounted for a .2 percent share of the overall market.

Amid the deregulation, Chubu continued to solidify its position in the Japanese market. In late 1999, the company announced plans to lay fiber optic cable that would connect over three million households in Nagoya and other cities in the Chubu region (the company was the first Japanese utility to install fiber optic cable for household use). Chubu then planned to lease these cables to telecommunications firms looking to use the lines for cable television and Internet applications. During 2000, the firm partnered with Iwatani International Corp. to form LNG Chubu Co. Ltd. The new venture was created to withstand increased competition expected from further deregulation in the industry.

Another strategic alliance was formed in 2001 with Toyota Tsusho Corp. Both companies, along with Tomen Corp.,

planned to build and operate a coal-fired facility in Thailand, which was slated to be the largest such facility operated by an independent power provider. The deal also marked the first time that Chubu become involved in a international power generation venture.

Meanwhile, demand began to falter once again due to the slowing of the Japanese economy along with many other international economies. As such, Chubu stopped operations at two of its thermal power plants and began to implement a cost cutting program that would shave off nearly 20 percent of its expenses related to power generation and distribution by 2005. Despite these challenges brought on by fluctuating economies and increased deregulation, Chubu management remained dedicated to increasing its sales and developing new business in the environmental and technology sectors.

Principal Subsidiaries

Chuden Kogyo Co. Ltd.; Eiraku Development Co. Ltd.; Eiraku Auto Service Co. Ltd.; Chuden Bldg. Co. Inc.; Chubu Plant Service Co. Ltd.; C-Tech Corp.; Techno Chubu Company Ltd.; Chita LNG Co. Ltd.; Chubu Telecommunications Company Inc.; CTI Co. Ltd.; Toenec Corp.; Aichi Electric Co. Ltd.

Principal Competitors

The Kansai Electric Power Company Inc.; The Tohoku Electric Power Company Inc.; The Tokyo Electric Power Company Inc.

Further Reading

"Anti-Nuke Vote Sends Gov't on Defensive," *Mainichi Daily News,* November 20, 2001.

"Chubu Elec, Toyota Tsusho to Join Thai Power Plant Project," *AsiaPulse News,* August 17, 2001.

"Chubu Electric Expects Big Profit Jump," *Jiji Press Ticker Service,* February 25, 1992.

"Chubu Electric Power's Profits Revenues Fall," *Jiji Press Ticker Service,* May 24, 1994.

"Chubu Electric Power's Sales Level Off in '92," *Jiji Press Ticker Service,* January 26, 1993.

"Chubu Electric to Tie Up With Italian Firm," *Japan Economic Newswire,* July 14, 1992.

"Higher Costs Squeeze Chubu Electric's Profit," *Jiji Press Ticker Service,* November 24, 1992.

"Japanese Utilities Chill-Out With Eco-Ice," *Petroleum Times Energy Report,* September 1, 1997, p. 7.

"Japan's Chubu Electric Aims to Cut Costs 20% by FY05," *AsiaPulse News,* April 24, 2001.

"Japan's Chubu Electric Scraps Nuclear Power Plant Plan," *AsiaPulse News,* February 23, 2000.

"Japan's Chubu Power to Lay Fiber Optics for 3.4 Mln Households," *AsiaPulse News,* December 22, 1999.

"Leaky Reactor—Shaky System," *Mainichi Daily News,* November 15, 2001.

Mullen, Theo, "Government and Market Pressures Cut Prices in Japan," *Electrical World,* July 1997, p. 37.

Yamamoto, Daisuke, "Profile: Japan's Electric Power Industry," *AsiaPulse News,* November 2, 2001.

—Julian James Kinsley
—update: Christina M. Stansell

CKE Restaurants, Inc.

401 West Carl Karcher Way
Anaheim, California 92803-4349
U.S.A.
Telephone: (714) 774-5796
Fax: (714) 490-3695
Web site: http://www.ckr.com

Public Company
Incorporated: 1966 as Carl Karcher Enterprises, Inc.
Employees: 35,500
Sales: $1.7 billion (2001)
Stock Exchanges: New York
Ticker Symbol: CKR
NAIC: 722211 Limited-Service Restaurants

CKE Restaurants, Inc., known as Carl Karcher Enterprises Inc. for much of its history, owns and franchises restaurants. From its beginnings as a hot-dog cart run by company founder Carl N. Karcher, CKE has grown into a firm with 441 company-owned and 530 franchisee-owned Carl's Jr. restaurants, and 751 company-owned and 1,706 franchisee-owned Hardee's. Since its 1997 purchase of the Hardee's chain, CKE has been involved in a re-franchising program, selling its corporate-owned restaurants to franchisees in order to pay down debt. The company also sold its Taco Bueno chain as part of its strategy to return to profitability.

Early History

Carl N. Karcher was born in 1917 in Upper Sandusky, Ohio, the third of eight children. Karcher's great-grandfather had immigrated to the Ohio Valley from Germany in 1840, leading to a growing population of Karchers in northwest Ohio. It was the Karcher who left Ohio, however, who set Carl Karcher on the road to entrepreneurial success. Karcher had been helping on his father's farm since he quit school after the eighth grade. But when his uncle offered him a job at his Anaheim, California, feed and seed store in 1937, Karcher and his brother, Ralph, set off for the West Coast.

Karcher did not remain with his uncle for long. By 1939, Karcher had secured a job as deliveryman at the Armstrong

Bakery in Los Angeles and had married Margaret Heinz. On his 75-mile delivery route, Karcher noticed the growing number of hot-dog carts and stands on various Los Angeles street corners. When a customer offered him the chance to purchase one for himself, Karcher acted quickly. Over his wife's objections, he secured a $311 loan using their new 1941 Plymouth as collateral. Fifteen dollars in cash provided the rest of the $326 needed to buy the cart and put Karcher in business on July 17, 1941.

Karcher located his cart at Florence and Central in South-Central Los Angeles, across the street from a Goodyear plant busy with wartime work. First day receipts were $14.75 from the sale of hot dogs, chili dogs, tamales, and soft drinks. Karcher displayed his knack for innovation when he started to offer curb-side service, enabling his customers to remain in their cars.

In May 1942, Karcher bought a second hot-dog cart—with the full support of his wife this time—which he relocated near a service station on another busy intersection. Later in the year a third was added, also near a service station. The next year Karcher added a fourth unit, which was not a cart but a stand—a small building with five stools placed around an outside counter for on-premise eating.

Though Karchers' enterprise was successful, Margaret Karcher wished to be closer to her family in Anaheim. Carl Karcher decided to expand his business; he soon found a Bob's Restaurant for sale, not far from where Margaret's family lived. Eager to move into the family restaurant sector, Karcher bought the facility's furnishings and equipment for $4,200 and signed a 12-year lease at $120 per month. The Karchers purchased a house down the street from the restaurant.

In January 1945, the newly named Carl's Drive-in Barbeque opened in Anaheim, serving a variety of sandwiches, chicken fried steak, barbecued ribs, and hamburgers. The hamburgers proved to be particularly popular and were added to the hot-dog stand menus after 15-inch grills were installed at each location in 1946. At Carl's Drive-in, Karcher installed a large neon sign with a flashing star on top to draw attention to a menu that was "out of this world." The star later evolved into the "happy star" logo that became synonymous with the Carl's Jr. chain.

Company Perspectives:

We are moving toward an operating strategy in which CKE provides the brand leadership, but operates a smaller percentage of restaurants. We believe this strategy at both Carl's Jr. and Hardee's will, in the longer term, provide better management, improved restaurant operations, and present a stronger financial picture.

Carl's Jr. Launch Highlights 1950s

In the late 1940s and early 1950s, Karcher's enterprises became increasingly sophisticated. The hot-dog carts and tiny stands evolved into larger hamburger stands with warehouse rooms to store supplies on-site, brick exteriors, and an overhang as standard features.

The 1950s were a time of increasing affluence in America and eating out became more common. At the same time the pace of life was quickening, providing the right ingredients for the explosion of what would later be called "fast food." Karcher recognized these trends and decided to create mini-versions of the full-service Carl's Drive-in Barbeque, calling the smaller spinoffs Carl's Jr. The first Carl's Jr. opened in Anaheim in 1956, followed quickly by a second in nearby Brea. Each Carl's Jr. had about a thousand square feet of space, two customer windows—one to place orders and another to pick them up— and a small patio with redwood picnic tables for on-site eating. The Carl's Jr. menu was much more varied than the typical quick-service restaurant of the time—notably McDonald's. Carl's Jr. served hot dogs, shrimp baskets, hamburgers, tacos, and even pizza. The star logo was featured at each site, though now personified with the addition of a freckled, smiling face; this "happy star" wore booties and held a shake in one hand and a hamburger in the other. Carl Karcher asked his brother Don to manage the Carl's Jr. operations.

By the end of the 1950s, there were four Carl's Jr. restaurants in Orange County, one of which had briefly experimented with a drive-thru years before drive-thru's became standard fast-food restaurant features. Other Carl's Jr. innovations of the time were not so quickly abandoned. An inside take-out window and an enclosed patio were both quickly accepted by the public, as was the procedure of paying for one's order before receiving it— unheard of at the time but later standard practice in the industry.

Reorganization in the 1960s

The 1960s were a time of slow growth and missteps for the operations of Carl Karcher. Karcher owned five separate corporations when, in 1964, he hired management consultant Irving J. Mills as a consultant. Under Mills's guidance, the five corporations were consolidated in 1966 under Carl Karcher Enterprises, Inc. The firm was divided into two branches. Don Karcher became vice-president of field operations, overseeing all restaurants, while another brother, Frank, became vice-president of services, overseeing purchasing, construction, financing, real estate, and public relations.

Mills next suggested that Karcher Enterprises needed a theme to differentiate itself within the exploding fast-food scene. Designers and architects developed a railroad-themed concept called Carl's Whistle Stop and three opened in 1966 in La Habra, Garden Grove, and Long Beach. The Whistle Stops were among the first fast-food restaurants with ordering areas that were enclosed and air-conditioned. They failed, at least in part, because they were ahead of their time. People mistook the Whistle Stops for coffee shops because the order windows were hidden inside and because of the buildings' architecture. This confusion led Karcher to convert the Whistle Stops to Carl's Jr. restaurants, with outside walk-up windows. Within a few years, enclosed, air-conditioned ordering areas became the industry norm and the converted Whistle Stop units were changed back to their original inside ordering area style.

A second failure of the mid-1960s came when the company decided to expand by purchasing three full-service, Scottish-themed coffee shops called Scot's. They were never successful, however, and were sold soon after the Whistle Stops were converted. Mills soon parted ways with the company, which proceeded to return to its roots.

Carl's Jr. Revamped in the Late 1960s

In 1968, Carl Karcher Enterprises had 25 restaurants in operation when Karcher decided to refocus on the Carl's Jr. brand. His concept of a "new" Carl's Jr. featured a more attractive exterior with used brick and a tiled roof; upgraded interiors with carpets, cushioned booths, and music; and a re-tooled ordering procedure whereby customers still ordered and paid for food at an outside walk-up window but now were served their food at tables by employees—so-called partial dining room service. Most of these changes were firsts for the fast-food industry. The most radical change, however, was a streamlining of the menu in order to offer quicker service— Karcher decided to offer only hamburgers, hot dogs, french fries, malts, and soft drinks.

Despite numerous objections raised by others at Karcher Enterprises, the first revamped Carl's Jr. opened in Fullerton in 1968 and met with immediate success. This restaurant was the first in the company to rack up $1,000 in a single day's sales. It also helped Karcher Enterprises's 1968 sales reach almost $5 million.

Other Carl's Jr. restaurants were soon converted to the new format and the company embarked on an expansion plan which enabled it to reach the 40-restaurant mark by the end of the decade. The Carl's Jr. "happy star" logo appeared in San Diego County and the San Fernando Valley for the first time. To support the expansion, advertising increased, featuring the star and the slogan "It's Out of This World."

As growth increased, Karcher Enterprises became more concerned with quality control and training. The company developed its first procedures manual to ensure that customers received the same product from all Carl's Jr. restaurants and created a training department to make training more uniform.

Expansion in the 1970s

Carl's Jr. transformed into a major regional chain during the 1970s. In that decade, Carl Karcher Enterprises grew from 40 restaurants to 289, from 300 employees to 8,500, and from

$5.6 million in annual revenue to $138.6 million. Carl's Jr. and additional innovations led the way.

In 1974, Carl's Jr. successfully reintroduced the drive-thru abandoned a decade earlier. Two years later, the industry's first soup and salad bar appeared in a Carl's Jr.; this innovation was rolled out chain-wide three years later. Carl's Jr. expanded outside Southern California for the first time in 1975, when seven units opened in Northern California. The following year, Karcher Enterprises built a 29,000-square-foot corporate headquarters in Anaheim, then two years later added a $5-million, 145,000-square-foot commissary and warehouse adjacent to the headquarters. The company also began to manufacture most of the products it sold.

During the late 1970s, several of the older Carl's Jr. units were remodeled, and some were upgraded with drive-thru's. In 1977, the 200th Carl's Jr. opened. With the chain's expansion going so well, the company decided it was time to expand outside California. After a year spent investigating possible areas, Las Vegas, Nevada, was identified as the best site for the first out-of-state unit. This was a logical choice because of the city's proximity to Southern California and because 60 percent of Las Vegas tourists came from Southern California. In June 1979 the first Carl's Jr. in Nevada opened.

Karcher Enterprises suffered one notable failure in the 1970s when it decided to start its own chain of Mexican fast-food restaurants, called Taco de Carlos. Attempting to cash in on the increasing popularity of Mexican food, the company opened the first Taco de Carlos in 1972 and had 17 of them operating by decade-end. The chain was never given the attention necessary for success and was abandoned in the early 1980s and all of the units were sold, 12 of them to Del Taco for $2.2 million.

Setbacks Plague Company in the 1980s

Carl's Jr. had become the largest privately held, non-franchised restaurant chain in the United States by the 1980s. After the successes of the 1970s, management boldly set goals for the year 1990: 1,000 Carl's Jr. restaurants and $1 billion in annual revenue. Unfortunately, the company would fall far short of these figures. In 1980, Carl Karcher promoted Don

Karcher to president and chief operating officer of Karcher Enterprises. Carl Karcher remained chairman and CEO.

To reach their lofty goals, the Karchers needed to accelerate Carl's Jr.'s expansion program. To help finance the expansion, they decided to take the company public, raising $13.79 million through the October 1981 initial public offering. In 1981, the 300th Carl's Jr. opened. The following year the Carl's Jr. chain entered its third state when a Yuma, Arizona, restaurant opened in June. That same year several locations began to offer 24-hour service. In 1984, Carl's Jr. was franchised for the first time, an unusually long-delayed entry into franchising for a fast-food chain.

In the mid-1980s, Carl's Jr. ran aground from overexpansion and excessive tinkering with the menu. Earlier in the decade the chain had successfully introduced a Western Bacon Cheeseburger and a Charbroiler Chicken Sandwich. Then in an attempt to be a cross between a fast-food restaurant and a coffee shop, four charbroiler dinners were added to the menu in 1983—top sirloin steak, boneless chicken breast, rainbow trout, and ground beef steak. Each came with a choice of baked potato, fried zucchini, or wedge-cut potatoes and garlic toast. The dinners were served on platters rather than paper plates, and customers were provided with silverware, not plastic utensils. Unfortunately, the charbroiler dinners created a host of problems: the need to install dishwashers, traffic backups at the drive-thru's thanks to the length of time it took to prepare the dinners, and general customer confusion over what Carl's Jr. was. In 1985, the chain abandoned the dinners in another return to roots; restaurants signs which had read "Carl's Jr. Restaurant" were changed back to "Carl's Jr. Charbroiled Hamburgers." Prices were cut and all-you-can-drink beverage bars were added.

Compounding the company's difficulty was the chain's expansion into Texas, which began in 1984, just as the state economy was entering a prolonged depression. Texas had been chosen as the first state in a national roll-out of the Carl's Jr. brand. The three dozen units established there never came close to meeting sales expectations, and by early 1987 Carl's Jr. had pulled out of the state entirely, taking a $15 million writeoff as a result and posting a loss for fiscal 1986. The company decided to limit the areas where it would build company-owned stores to California and Arizona and also converted a number of company-owned units to franchised units. Over the next few years, national expansion was placed on the back burner; instead more than 200 older Carl's Jr. restaurants were remodeled.

By 1988, the chain included 383 units and Carl Karcher Enterprises posted record earnings of $16 million. Carl Karcher credited the turnaround in part to the 1986 hiring of Raymond Perry as vice-president of operations; Perry had more than 20 years of restaurant experience, including serving as president of Straw Hat Pizza.

The Securities and Exchange Commission (SEC) filed a lawsuit against Carl Karcher in April 1988, alleging that in late 1984 he had tipped off relatives to an upcoming announcement that profits were expected to drop by half. Karcher vigorously denied the insider-trading charges, but in July 1989 he and six relatives agreed to settle the case by paying a total of $664,245 without admitting guilt. In related insider-trading cases, Al

DeShano, the company's accountant, agreed to pay $24,794; six other Karcher family members, including Don Karcher, settled with the SEC for $187,561.

As if all these problems were not enough, the Carl's Jr. chain had the added burden of a chairman and CEO who took public positions on controversial issues. Carl Karcher was a dedicated conservative Republican and had served as the party's finance chairman for Orange County, one of the most conservative counties in the country. His support for right-wing Republican John Schmitz, who had tried in the 1970s to ban homosexuals from teaching in public schools, came to the attention of gay rights groups. And Karcher's adamant opposition to abortion—a result of his devout Catholicism—led to demonstrations at Carl's Jr. restaurants organized by abortion rights groups in the late 1980s and early 1990s. In 1991, opposition from gay and abortion rights groups led students at California State University, Northridge, to narrowly vote down the establishment of a Carl's Jr. on their campus.

Meanwhile, Carl's Jr. brand expanded internationally for the first time. In 1988, a license agreement was signed with the Friendly Corporation of Osaka, Japan, to develop at least 30 Carl's Jr. restaurants in Japan by 1993. Two years later a license agreement with Malaysia-based MBf International (later known as MBf Holding Berhad) called for 16 restaurants to be built in the Pacific Rim—including Malaysia, Singapore, Hong Kong, Australia, New Zealand, Taiwan, Thailand, the Philippines, and Indonesia—over five years. In 1995, a new joint venture agreement with MBf was signed and called for 130 Carl's Jr. units to be built in a five-year span. In October 1990, Carl Karcher Enterprises signed an agreement with a third licensee, Valores Matalicos, to expand the chain into Mexico.

Management Chaos in the Early 1990s

The early 1990s were marked by turbulence in the management ranks at Carl Karcher Enterprises. Perry had been considered an heir apparent to the aging Karcher, but was abruptly dismissed from his number three position in 1991. Then Don Karcher died of cancer the following year. Carl Karcher began to lose control of the company board at the same time he was experiencing personal financial difficulties. In December 1992, Karcher attempted to simultaneously regain control and solve his money woes through a $103 million leveraged buyout of Carl Karcher Enterprises that he proposed with the Los Angeles investment firm Freeman Spogli & Co. The deal might have earned him $43 million. The board rejected the offer, then the following month appointed Donald Doyle, former head of Kentucky Fried Chicken USA, CEO and president, with Karcher remaining chairman. In addition to the management upheaval, chain-wide sales were beginning to level off thanks to fierce competition in the industry and the company posted a fiscal 1993 loss of $5.5 million, the first loss since fiscal 1986.

Karcher and Doyle clashed throughout 1993, most notably over a Karcher proposal to test dual-branded restaurants featuring both Carl's Jr. fare and that of the ailing Mexican food chain Green Burrito, run by Anaheim-based GB Foods Inc. If approved by the board, Karcher's financial problems would have reportedly been solved. In August the board rejected the proposal, which led Karcher to threaten a proxy fight to oust certain board members.

In October, the board voted Karcher out as chairman for interfering with long-term management strategy, replacing him with long-time board member Elizabeth A. Sanders.

Two months later, Karcher was back on the board but with the more or less honorary title of chairman emeritus. To regain his seat and to solve his financial woes, Karcher struck a deal with a partnership led by William P. Foley II, an entrepreneur who had built Fidelity National Title into the nation's fourth-largest title insurance company. Foley's partnership paid off Karcher's $23 million bank loan in exchange for the 3.8 million shares of company stock posted as collateral. The partnership then controlled about 25 percent of the stock, gaining Foley a seat on the board.

For the next several months, Sanders and Doyle led Carl Karcher Enterprises and decided that for Carl's Jr. to better compete its traditional premium pricing strategy should be changed to one based on lower prices. When sales continued to drop during fiscal 1994, Foley stepped in to challenge Doyle's leadership. Doyle soon resigned, Foley was appointed chairman and CEO and brought in Bay Area franchisee Tom Thompson as president and COO. Also in 1994, the new board received shareholder approval for a new corporate structure which created a parent company called CKE Restaurants, Inc., with subsidiary Carl Karcher Enterprises, Inc. in charge of the Carl's Jr. chain.

Mid-1990s Transformation into Multi-Brand Empire

In July 1994, the CKE board reversed course and approved a test of dual Carl's Jr.-Green Burrito restaurants. Then, in a further twist, CKE decided early in 1995 to abandon the dual branding with Green Burrito and instead develop a dual concept with its own Mexican concept called Picante Grill. GB Foods subsequently sued CKE, calling the new concept a "knock-off." Finally, in June 1995, the two parties settled their differences and agreed to develop a minimum of 140 dual-branded locations. Twenty-two of them were operating in fiscal 1996 and posted sales 25 percent higher than when the units were simply Carl's Jr. outlets. Also in 1995, the company signed a deal with UNOCAL 76 Products Company to open Carl's Jr. restaurants within ten UNOCAL Fast Break convenience stores and gasoline stations in California. Remarkably, Foley and Thompson had turned the Carl's Jr. chain around.

The defining move toward improvement came in mid-1995, when the chain abandoned value pricing and developed a new advertising campaign which emphasized quality and quantity through the slogan "If it doesn't get all over the place, it doesn't belong in your face." According to a company annual report, ads featured "big, messy, juicy burgers dripping on a variety of targets including a basketball player's high-tops, a motorcycle cop, and an unsuspecting pigeon." Backed by the campaign, same-store sales began increasing for the first time in five years.

With Carl's Jr. on the rebound, CKE officials confidently looked outside the company for undervalued restaurant properties for acquisition or investment. In April 1996, CKE spent $4.1 million for a 15-percent stake in the struggling Rally's Hamburgers, Inc., operator of a chain of nearly 500 Rally's double drive-thru's. This stake was increased to 18 percent later in 1996, and CKE also began managing 28 Rally's in California and Arizona. The two companies also agreed not to compete against each other in the same markets—Rally's was primarily located in the southeastern United States—and Rally's borrowed Carl's Jr.'s "messy" advertising strategy to turn around its fortunes.

CKE acquired Summit Family Restaurants Inc., which operated the 104-unit JB's Restaurant chain, six Galaxy Diners, and 16 HomeTown Buffets as a franchisee. CKE quickly made Summit profitable again and spun off its Star Buffet Inc. line in September 1997, but just as quickly determined that it did not want to focus on family dining and divested most of these holdings during the late 1990s.

In October 1996, CKE bought Casa Bonita Incorporated from Unigate PLC for $42 million in cash, gaining the 107-unit Taco Bueno fast-food chain and two Casa Bonita family restaurants, which featured entertainment. The deal returned CKE not only to the Mexican food sector that the company abandoned when it gave up on Taco de Carlos but also to that nettlesome state of Texas, which was where Casa Bonita was headquartered and where it operated 67 Taco Bueno units.

Continuing a whirlwind year, in November 1996 CKE became involved with another struggling double drive-thru hamburger chain when it purchased $12.9 million of Checkers Drive-In Restaurants, Inc.'s senior secured debt. CKE followed up by acquiring a 10 percent stake in the 475-unit Checkers in February 1997. In April CKE helped to craft a proposed merger of Checkers and Rally's, which was completed in 1999 and created the largest double drive-thru quick service restaurant system in the U.S. CKE then sold its Rally's restaurants back to Checkers.

CKE's stock split three-for-two in January 1997, and the company announced an amendment to its dual-brand agreement with GB Foods whereby the original 140-unit commitment was increased to a minimum of 306 stores, with a minimum of 60 restaurants to be converted each year over a five-year span. But the company announced a real blockbuster in April 1997 when it said it would acquire Hardee's Food Systems Inc. from Imasco Ltd. of Montreal for about $327 million—the number seven burger chain buying the number four chain. Hardee's, yet another struggling burger chain, boasted 3,100 units located in 41 states and ten foreign countries and had 1996 revenues of almost $3 billion. Its U.S. units were strongest in the Midwest and Southeast, which meshed well with Carl's Jr.'s predominance in the West. CKE began to test dual-branded Carl's Jr.-Hardee's units, with Hardee's teaming with Carl's Jr.'s lunch and dinner sandwiches.

After a few years of Foley's leadership, CKE was barely recognizable as the same company. Fiscal 1997 revenue reached a healthy $614.1 million, while net income was a record $22.3 million. Bob Wheaton, a CKE executive that was named Star Buffet's CEO claimed in a 1997 *Restaurant Business* article that "the key to CKE's success has been a real simple strategy. Identify strong but underperforming brands that can be acquired at a reasonable price, where both operating discipline and economies of scale, as well as creative marketing, can improve margins."

Further Reorganization: Late 1990s and Beyond

The glow of success was short-lived, however, when the company soon realized the debt burden incurred by the Hardee's purchase would eventually take its toll on its bottom line. Along with its growing debt, the company faced staunch competition in the fast food industry. As both Hardee's and Carl's Jr. reported unfavorable sales results in 1998, stock price began to falter. In response, CKE launched a re-franchising program where it began to sell its corporate-owned restaurants to franchisees and also began to introduce new menu items in an attempt to boost restaurant traffic. The firm also began to convert the Hardee's chain into Star Hardee's, which combined both Hardee's and Carl's Jr. menu items.

Bad times continued into the new millennium. During 2000, CKE sold nearly 400 restaurants and closed underperforming locations. It also sold its Taco Bueno chain to an equity buyout group for $72.5 million. In fiscal 2001, the company posted a $194.12 million loss after recording a $29.12 million loss in the previous year. Andrew Puzder—elected CEO and president in 2000—along with chairman Foley, remained dedicated to pulling CKE from debt and continued with the re-franchising program. Their efforts seemed to payoff when, in August 2001, Hardee's reported a same-store sales increase for the first time in years—the sales increase was one percent. By December, the company claimed to be back on track to profitability with little-to-no existing long-term debt.

In early 2002, the company announced plans to acquire the Santa Barbara Restaurant Group Inc., which owned and franchised the Timber Lodges, Green Burrito, and La Salsa restaurant chains. The firm claimed the proposed purchase was in line with its restructuring campaign. It also continued to focus on brand development—which touted its restaurant's quality and service—offering new menu products and remodeling its stores. Both Puzder and Foley claimed CKE was close to securing profits; however, whether or not the company would return to its glory days of the mid-1990s remained to be seen.

Principal Subsidiaries

Carl Karcher Enterprises, Inc.; Hardee's Food Systems Inc.

Principal Competitors

Burger King Corp.; McDonald's Corp.; Wendy's International Inc.

Further Reading

Alva, Marilyn, "Star Man: Bill Foley Knew Nothing about Restaurants. So How Did He Work Miracles with the Ailing Carl's Jr. Chain?," *Restaurant Business*, October 10, 1996, pp. 90–3, 96, 100.

Barrett, Amy, "One Burned-Up Burger Baron: Why Carl's Jr. Founder Carl Karcher Was Ousted by His Own Board," *Business Week*, October 18, 1993, pp. 62–63.

Barrier, Michael, "Building on a Better Burger," *Nation's Business*, January 1988, pp. 63–4.

Bell, Alexa, "Carl's Quandary: Now 75, Carl Karcher Must Decide Who'll Carry the Family Torch," *Restaurant Business*, July 1, 1992, pp. 52–3, 56–7.

Bellantonio, Jennifer, "CKE Shares Up Steeply as Firm Slashes Debt, Sells Restaurants," *Los Angeles Business Journal*, December 3, 2001, p. 32.

Brooks, Steve, "A Star Is Born; How CKE's New Spin-Off Is Making Its Mark by Buying Up Lagging Buffet Chains," *Restaurant Business*, December 1, 1997, p. 21.

Carlino, Bill, "CKE Acquires Taco Bueno, Makes Push into Texas, Okla.," *Nation's Restaurant News*, September 9, 1996, p. 1.

"CKE Divests 121 Hardee's Units to Franchisees," *Nation's Restaurant News*, August 7, 2000, p. 3.

"CKE Launches Retrofit for Hardee's," *Food Institute Report*, February 8, 1999.

"CKE Loses $194 Million After Shutting Stores in FY 2001," *Nation's Restaurant News*, May 7, 2001, p. 16.

Gomez, James M., "Carl's Jr. Founder Ousted as Chairman of Burger Chain," *Los Angeles Times*, October 2, 1993.

Hamstra, Mark, "CKE Crafts Merger of Checkers, Rally's," *Nation's Restaurant News*, April 7, 1997, pp. 1, 6.

Hamstra, Mark, and Bill Carlino, "CKE Restaurants Inc. to Acquire Hardee's, Roll Out Carl's Jr. Brand," *Nation's Restaurant News*, May 5, 1997, p. 5.

Knight, B. Carolyn, *Making It Happen: The Story of Carl Karcher Enterprises*, Anaheim, Calif.: Carl Karcher Enterprises, 1981.

——, *Never Stop Dreaming: Fifty Years of Making It Happen*, San Marcos, Calif.: Robert Erdmann Publishing, 1991.

Liddle, Alan, "CKE Trims Hardee's Corporate, Moves HQ," *Nation's Restaurant News*, November 22, 1999, p. 1.

Lubove, Seth, "Inexperience Pays: Bill Foley Didn't Know How to Run a Restaurant Chain, But He Learned Quickly How Not to Run One," *Forbes*, September 23, 1996, pp. 60–1.

Martin, Richard, "CKE Buying JB's Parent for $37M," *Nation's Restaurant News*, December 11, 1995, pp. 1, 74.

Sepctor, Amy, "The Long, Hot Summer? CKE Wilts as Sales Slide," *Nation's Restaurant News*, June 21, 1999, p. 1.

Smith, Rod, "CKE Completes Taco Bueno Sale, Hands Rally's Units to Checkers," *Feedstuffs*, June 21, 2001, p. 7.

——, "CKE To Acquire Restaurant Chain Owning Timber Lodge Steakhouses," *Feedstuffs*, January 7, 2002, p. 7.

Veverka, Mark, "CKE, Grilled on McDonald's News, Is a Good Bargain Now, Experts Say," *Wall Street Journal*, March 12, 1997.

Woodyard, Chris, "The Commercial Life of Happy Star Karcher," *Los Angeles Times*, November 10, 1991.

—David E. Salamie
—update: Christina M. Stansell

Classic Vacation Group, Inc.

One North First Street, Suite 300
San Jose, California 95113
U.S.A.
Telephone: (408) 882-8455
Fax: (408) 287-9272
Web site: http://www.gvg.com

Public Company
Incorporated: 1998
Employees: 490
Sales: $132.9 million (2000)
Stock Exchanges: American
Ticker Symbol: CLV
NAIC: 561520 Tour Operators

Classic Vacation Group, Inc. pioneered consolidation of wholesale travel vacation providers when it formed with the acquisition of several leading companies in the late 1990s. Its financial difficulties led to a dismantling of the company, as minor subsidiaries were sold in late 2001 and early 2002. In January 2002, Expedia, Inc., an Internet-based travel company, purchased the primary subsidiary, Classic Custom Vacations, which had become one of the largest wholesale vacation providers in the nation under Classic Vacation Group. Expedia paid $52 million, $5 million in cash and $47 million stock. Three Cities Research, the primary note-holder for Classic Vacation Group, and Thayer Capital Partners, the primary stockholder, planned to sell the Expedia stock and to pay common shareholders at least $0.26 per share from the proceeds. They planned to liquidate remaining assets and to distribute those proceeds to the public shareholders as well.

Wholesale Travel Providers: 1998

Classic Vacation Group originated with the recapitalization of Allied Bus Corporation, which was then renamed Global Vacations Group (GVG). Roger Ballou formed GVG to consolidate wholesale vacation package providers into a larger, streamlined public company. Ballou brought 19 years experience in the travel industry, including such positions as former CEO of Alamo Rent-a-Car and former president of American Express Travel Services. Ballou's background enabled him to attract investors and experienced executives to GVG. He hired J. Raymond Lewis, past president of Certified Vacations, Inc., as COO, and Walter Berman, former CFO of American Express Travel, for the same position at GVG. Thayer Capital Partner, headed by Fredric Malek, formerly president of Marriott Hotels and Resorts and Northwest Airlines, invested $75 million to fund acquisitions.

The predecessor of GVG, New York City-based Allied Bus Corporation, doing business as Allied Tours, provided escorted bus tours to European visitors to the United States. Founded in 1959, Allied marketed the tours to wholesale travel operators overseas; these operators sold the travel packages through retail travel agents. Eventually Allied added independent air-hotel packages and fly-drive packages, and offered vacation packages to Hawaii, Canada, Mexico, and the Caribbean. Allied expanded to wholesale companies in Asia and Central and South America, becoming one of the largest providers of in-bound, wholesale travel. In 1993, Allied began to offer escorted bus tours to travel agents in the United States. In 1997, Allied recorded $24.3 million in revenues, and a net loss of $1.1 million.

Concurrent with the capital investment of Thayer Capital in late March, GVG began to consolidate wholesale travel companies with the completion of two acquisitions. GVG purchased Haddon Holidays, Inc. of Mount Laurel, New Jersey, for $7.7 million. In business since 1975, Haddon provided upmarket vacation packages to Hawaii, Australia, and New Zealand. The company's travel products included escorted or independent travel packages, offering airfare, hotel, ground transportation, and sightseeing options to independent travelers. Haddon recorded $7.1 million in revenues and $88,000 net income in 1997. GVG expected to benefit from Haddon's exclusive contract with United Airlines to continue its plans for streamlined expansion. Executive vice-president Cheryl Van Horn stayed with Haddon under the new ownership.

In April, GVG acquired Classic Custom Vacations, Inc. in San Jose, California, for $18.5 million. As the name suggests, Classic tailored vacation packages according to the customer's

Key Dates:

1998: Global Vacations Group forms to consolidate wholesale vacation providers.
1999: Problems related to merger of MTI and Globetrotters cause financial losses.
2000: Executive changes lead to appointment of new CEO.
2001: The company relocates to San Jose and takes the name Classic Vacation Group.
2002: Expedia, Inc. acquires Classic Custom Vacations and CLV discontinues operations.

needs, offering airfare, car rental, brand-name hotels, and sightseeing trips. The company arranged customized sightseeing tours and excursions as well. For 20 years Classic Hawaii was the company's primary travel destination. In 1995, Classic Custom introduced Classic America, to 20 U.S. destinations, and in 1998, introduced Classic Europe, to Italy, Greece, and Turkey. Classic reported $42.9 million in revenues in 1997 and $1 million in net profit. GVG retained Ron Letterman as president of Classic Custom.

In May 1998, GVG purchased two wholesale travel operators offering mid-priced vacation packages. For $27.2 million GVG purchased most of the assets of MTI Vacations of Oak Brook, Illinois. In addition to providing wholesale vacation packages for travel to Hawaii, MTI also handled Amtrak-sponsored vacation packages and reservations for Hyatt vacation packages. They also operated credit card reward fulfillment programs. In 1997, MTI earned $2.3 million in net income from $29.2 million in revenues.

GVG acquired Globetrotters, Inc., of Cambridge, Massachusetts, for $5.8 million. Globetrotters offered vacations packages to Florida, Mexico, the Caribbean, as well as other destinations, offering accommodations at brand name hotels. GVG merged the operations of the two companies, transferring Globetrotters to MTI's computer reservations platform and to the reservations center near Chicago; however, GVG planned to operate the division under the Globetrotters brand. Globetrotters president Bill Maulsby remained in that position, overseeing the newly combined unit.

Through its acquisitions GVG created a two-tiered marketing system. GVG merged Haddon and Classic Custom, though it continued to use both brand names for upmarket travel planning. MTI and Globetrotters provided mid-priced vacation packages. The consolidation of these companies created a foundation for high volume, high margin operations for vacations packages that sold at retail for $750 and up per person. GVG sought to simplify operations by limiting hotel and car rental suppliers to the most recognized and trusted brands, thus reducing the number of vendors and obtaining low-cost, high-volume rates which could be translated into competitive pricing. Also, the company simplified by discontinuing certain travel packages at Globetrotters.

While Ballou did not intend for GVG to develop so rapidly, he found more opportunities for acquisition than anticipated.

GVG was the first to attempt a consolidation of wholesale travel providers, forming a prototype that other companies followed. Private travel companies sought the competitive edge of assimilation into a larger company. Selling $507 million in wholesale travel in 1998, GVG subsidiaries recorded $114.9 million in combined revenues for the entire year. Under GVG ownership, that meant $90.4 million in revenues and $4.7 million in net income for 1998. Approximately 50 percent of revenues originated from travel vacations to Hawaii.

Initial Public Offering and Acquisitions

GVG's rapid growth led Ballou to advance the anticipated initial public offering of stock, moving it forward about 18 months to July 1998. GVG offered 3 million shares of stock at $14 per share and raised $36.2 million, after expenses. GVG became the first vacations wholesaler to be listed on the New York Stock Exchange.

The stock offering provided funds for working capital and for additional acquisitions. In March 1999, GVG purchased Long Island-based, family-run Friendly Holidays for $10.2 million in cash plus an additional payment, up to $2.8 million, depending on operating results. With revenues of $13 million in 1998, Friendly provided mid-range, wholesale travel to the Caribbean, Mexico, Central America, and South America. The company planned to use Friendly as a lead negotiator for volume inventory for these destinations, including a Globetrotters Mexico package. GVG retained the Friendly Holidays brand but integrated operations into its Chicago reservations system.

In April, GVG acquired both International Travel & Resorts and Island Resort Tours for $5 million, plus an additional payment, up to $1.7 million, based on future earnings. International Travel & Resorts provided representation and marketing services for three- to five-star, independent hotels in the Caribbean and private-label representation for hotel groups in the Caribbean, Mexico, Central America, mainland United States, and Hawaii. GVG also hoped to extend hotel representation services to Europe and South America. Island Resort Tours offered vacation packages to several Caribbean islands, so GVG integrated that company into operations at Globetrotters/MTI Vacations.

In promoting its wholesale travel packages, GVG fostered preferred supplier relationships with its travel agent customers, notably American Automobile Association, Carlson Wagonlit Travel, American Express Travel, Vacation.com, Leisure Travel Group, and Giants. GVG changed its commission structure to reward cumulative sales by travel agents, offering commission overrides based on sales from its different brands, with higher percentage rates given for more expensive travel packages. For 1999, travel GVG offered a $50 bonus for every five reservations made with Classic Custom or Haddon.

Using the capabilities of its travel wholesale subsidiaries, GVG began to expand its travel products line in 1999. Friendly introduced vacation packages with airfare to Rio de Janeiro and Globetrotters added vacation packages to popular American ski resorts and to Europe. Classic Custom expanded its travel options to Italy and added travel packages to Spain and Portugal, where Classic Custom chose 26 luxury resorts based on distinctiveness, service, and location. In 2000, Classic Custom began to offer travel packages to England and France. GVG created private label travel packages for Meridian Corporation under the name Better Homes and Gardens Vacations, using the popular magazine as a base for advertising. The joint venture offered national hotel brands to popular destinations, including New York, Florida, Hawaii, California, and Mexico.

Computer capability was a primary concern at GVG, creating simplified reservations systems for its retail travel agent customers, as well as for direct consumer sales on the company website. In June, the company purchased most of the assets of Trase Miller Solutions. Trase Miller designed and implemented Trips Pro, GVG's reservation system, and back office and market support systems, including the website and online booking. Also, GVG became the first operation to offer travel packages on Yahoo! Travel, the premier online travel site. GVG brand travel packages were made available on the front page of the new Specials area.

GVG launched a new auction website, vacations4auction .com, and began to offer tour products on FairMarket.com. Bids for vacation travel began as low as $1 for low season travel to Hawaii, Caribbean, Europe, and certain U.S. cities. The bidding period lasted ten days, being open to travel agents and consumers.

By summer 1999, problems with the integration of MTI and Globetrotters became apparent. The problems related to merging operations and converting Globetrotters to the Trips Pro reservation system, resulting in poor service to travel agents and lost business. Also, Globetrotters lost some of its original customer base due to delays in executing new promotional packages. Lower sales impacted the cost-structure of its hotel room inventory, resulting in higher room costs for Globetrotters. Lower earnings at Globetrotters led to lower stock prices and executive changes. Maulsby resigned and Cheryl Van Horn, then senior vice-president of strategic planning, took over as president of Globetrotters. In addition, travel sales had declined industry-wide. Allied tours reported lower revenues as the weak economies in Asia and Latin America reduced travel to the United States from these areas. In 1999 GVG reported revenues of $129 million and net loss of $3.5 million.

GVG Restructures Operations: 2000

By June 2000, GVG's stock price dropped to approximately $3.00 per share and the company's market capitalization fell to $38.7 million, below the New York Stock Exchange minimum of $50 million. GVG raised $27.5 million in funding from Three Cities Research, a private, venture capital firm. The investment consisted of nine percent, seven-year subordinated notes to convertible at $5.25 per share. GVG used the funds to pay debt and for working capital. Thus, the company gained approval to retain its position on the Exchange, with quarterly reviews. Ray Lutz, president of the Globetrotters private label operations, took over Globetrotters in June 2000.

In August, the company decided to merge the Friendly Holidays, Haddon, and Globetrotters brands into Classic Custom under Ron Letterman, also named vice-chairman of GVG's board. At the same time, GVG discontinued the pilot program

for Better Homes and Gardens Vacations. The restructuring left the company with four operating divisions: private label travel and reservations; Allied Tours; Island Resort Tours, including International Travel & Resorts; and Classic Custom. The change made Classic Custom the third largest wholesale travel company in the industry.

Classic Custom adapted to the new structure by extending its vacation packages to include mid-priced hotels. Since Classic Custom offered 75 percent of the same hotels as Globetrotters, this allowed the company to eliminate overlap with Globetrotter. Classic Custom then added new hotels to expand availability. GVG halted new sales of Globetrotters trips to Florida by September and to other destinations by the end of the year. GVG transferred Globetrotters to the personal computer reservations system used by Classic Custom, but it continued to use the Globetrotters reservation center in Chicago. GVG continued to use Trips Pro for private label vacation reservations. While GVG cut staff, including management, Classic Custom hired 45 reservation agents.

Restructuring the company resulted in a write-down of $35 million in tangible and intangible assets related to Trips Pro and employee severance. GVG expected saving to add up to $8 million to operating income. For 2000, GVG reported a 5.5 percent increase in revenues, to $132.9 million, and a net loss of $44.7 million. GVG executives and stock analysts attributed some of the company's problems to the rapid growth and slow assimilation of the acquisitions. The financial benefits of volume business took too long to manifest. Moreover, GVG leaders made different decisions than they might have as a private company, perhaps taking fewer risks out of concern for shareholder value.

Financial difficulties prompted a series of changes at GVG, beginning with executive leadership. Ballou resigned in August, followed by CFO Jay Stuart in October. Malek, of Thayer Capital, became interim CEO until the board promoted Ron Letterman to the position in November. Debbie Lundquist, CFO at Classic Custom, took that position at GVG. One of Letterman's first decisions was to shift GVG stock trading to the less restrictive American Stock Exchange in January 2001, citing that exchange as better suited to the size of the company and its shareholder base. GVG became Classic Vacation Group (CLV) in May 2001 and relocated to Classic Custom's offices in San Jose.

The September 11th terrorist attack on the World Trade Center in 2001 further exacerbated financial problems at CLV, as all travel and new reservations came to an immediate halt and customers cancelled travel reservations. In October, CLV laid off 220 of 710 employees. CLV attempted to offset the decline in sales by offering travel agents a 20 percent commission on tours booked by the end of the year. Also in October, CLV obtained $24.5 million in financing from CVG Investment, LLC, an affiliate of Three Cities Research and Thayer Capital. In addition to providing working capital, the funds allowed CLV to initiate a stock repurchase plan with the intention to take the company private. CLV initiated a tender offer of $0.15 per share; the stock traded at approximately $0.65 per share at that time.

The tender offer began the dismantling of CLV. Stephen Hicks, the original owner of International Travel & Resorts and

Island Resort Tours, repurchased those companies from CLV for $500,000 in November. The tender offer was extended into late January 2002 to accommodate other divestitures. In January, Kouni Holdings, a travel services company in Switzerland, purchased Allied Tours. The senior management team of Globetrotters and other investors purchased Globetrotters. By that time the subsidiary comprised Amtrak Vacations and a credit card rewards fulfillment program, Hyatt vacations reservations having been transferred to Classic Custom Vacations.

The final demise of CLV occurred when Expedia, Inc., an Internet-based travel company, acquired Classic Custom Vacations, retaining Letterman as president. Expedia paid $52 million, $5 million in cash and the balance in stock for the retirement of $47 million in debt. Expedia assumed $30 million in liabilities involving customer deposits and other working capital accounts. Three Cities Research, the primary noteholder for CLV, and Thayer Capital Partners, the primary stockholder, planned to sell the Expedia stock and to pay common shareholders at least $0.26 per share from the proceeds. They planned to liquidate remaining assets and to distribute those proceeds to the public shareholders as well.

Principal Competitors

American Express Company; Liberty Travel, Inc.; Pleasant Holidays, LLC.

Further Reading

Barseghian, Tina, ''Commissions Will Change at GVG,'' *Leisure Travel News*, April 12, 1999, p. 33.

''Classic Offers 'Best Sale of the Year' Part Two—$250 Airfare Credit, Free Car and Free Nights in Hawaii,'' *Business Wire*, September 5, 2000.

''Classic Vacation Group Announces Sale of Globetrotters Vacations, Inc. Subsidiary,'' *Business Wire*, January 23, 2002, p. 2396.

''Classic Vacation Group to Sell Classic Custom Vacations to Expedia; Public Shareholders to Receive Cash Payment of $0.26 Per Share,'' *Business Wire*, January 23, 2002, p. 2393.

''Classic Sets 20% pay through 2001,'' *Travel Weekly*, October 22, 2001, p. 54.

Cogswell, David, ''A Year in the Public Eye,'' *Travel Agent*, July 5, 1999, p. 36.

——, ''Global Vacations Group to Merge Several Operations,'' *Travel Agent*, August 7, 2000, p. 5.

Cogswell, David, Martin Elder and James Ruggia, ''Smooth Operators,'' *Travel Agent*, January 4, 1999, p. 60.

Cube, Christine, ''Global Packs Up D.C. Digs,'' *Washington Business Journal*, December 1, 2000, p. 8.

Deady, Tim, ''Travel Companies on Road to Going Public,'' *Washington Business Journal*, May 22, 1998, p. 3.

''Despite Setbacks, GVG Forges Ahead,'' *Travel Weekly*, August 28, 2000, p. 1.

''Global Vacation Group Launches New Auction Web Site, Joins New Auction Network as Featured Vacation Provider,'' *Business Wire*, September 20, 1999, p. 1432.

''Global Vacation Group, Meredith Corporation Team Up To Create Better Homes and Gardens Vacations,'' *Business Wire*, May 25, 1999, p. 1550.

''Global Vacation Group Raises $27.5 Million in New Funding; Company Issues 9 Percent Subordinated Convertible Notes to Investment Group,'' *Business Wire*, June 21, 2000, p. 2462.

''Global Vacation Group Signs Agreement with Yahoo!; Becomes First Package Vacation Provider on Yahoo! Travel Specials Area,'' *Business Wire*, July 28, 1999, p. 1070.

''Global Vacation Group to List Stock on American Stock Exchange,'' *Business Wire*, January 5, 2001, p. 2428.

''Online Travel Firm Expedia Acquires California-Based Vacation-Package Company,'' *Knight-Ridder/Tribune Business News*, January 24, 2002.

Shillinglaw, James, and Kristian Schiller, ''On the Rebound with Ron,'' *Travel Agents*, December 18, 2000, p. 34.

''Tender Offer for Classic Vacations Group Extended,'' *PR Newswire*, January 7, 2002.

Tice, Kerry, ''Classic Expands Its Europe Program,'' *Leisure Travel News,* May 17, 1999, p. 4.

——, ''Globetrotters to Limit Focus of Suppliers,'' *Leisure Travel News*, January 4, 1999, p. 9.

——, ''GVG Buys More, and Enters Hotel Biz,'' *Leisure Travel News*, April 5, 1999, p. 4.

——, ''GVG Buys Trase Miller,'' *Leisure Travel News*, June 7, 1999, p. 4.

——, ''GVG Gets Friendly,'' *Leisure Travel News*, March 22, 1999, p. 1.

—Mary Tradii

Cordis Corporation

14201 N.W. 60 Avenue
Miami, Florida 33014
U.S.A.
Telephone: (305) 824-2000
Toll Free: (800) 327-7714
Fax: (305) 842-2440
Web site: http://www.cordis.com

Wholly Owned Subsidiary of Johnson & Johnson
Incorporated: 1957 as Medical Development Corp.
Employees: 3,500
Sales: $200 million (2001 est.)
NAIC: 339112 Surgical and Medical Instrument
    Manufacturing; 334510 Electromedical and
    Electrotherapeutic Apparatus Manufacturing

Cordis Corporation, a Johnson & Johnson (J&J) company, operates as a leading developer and manufacturer in the circulatory disease management industry. The company operates three main business segments including Cardiology Systems, Endovascular, and Interventional Neuroradiology. Cordis's products include guidewires, balloons, catheters, and stents that are used to treat circulatory system problems, including coronary artery disease and cerebral aneurysms.

Plagued throughout its relatively brief history by product recalls and marketing missteps, Cordis appeared to have found a profitable niche in the cardiac catheter industry in the early 1990s. Sales more than doubled during the first half of the decade, from $202.6 million in 1990 to more than $443 million in 1994, whereas net profits multiplied from $20.1 million to $50.2 million. Johnson & Johnson made a hostile bid for control of the fast-growing firm late in 1995 and won the takeover battle early in 1996 with a $109 per share stock swap valuing Cordis at $1.8 billion. Under J&J's direction, Cordis spent the remainder of the 1990s focusing on interventional medicine, minimally invasive computer-based imaging, and electrophysiology.

Postwar Origins

The medical device company was founded in Miami, Florida, by Dr. William Murphy. The son of Nobel laureate Dr. William Parry Murphy, Murphy was immersed in medicine from his youngest days. A 1984 *Inc.* article by Eugene Linden noted, "So total was the medical environment of his youth that it never occurred to him not to go into medicine." The younger Murphy also realized early on that he had a particular aptitude for mechanical engineering. The self-described "tinkerer" even designed his own medical devices as a teen.

After pursuing a dual education in medicine and engineering, Murphy was involved in the creation of the first artificial kidney. He also served briefly at Miami's Dade Reagents Inc., but when that company was bought out by American Hospital Supply Corp., it became clear to the ambitious Murphy that his career at this big, relatively anonymous company was limited. So Murphy formed Medical Development Corp. in 1957. One of the first products he developed was a "lumbar puncture tray," a disposable set of needles and tools used for spinal taps. Noticing that doctors performing this procedure often used dull and sometimes burred needles, making the test difficult and often painful, Murphy developed the concept of using a disposable kit, meaning that each patient would get a sterile, sharp needle. The doctor-engineer-entrepreneur developed several elaborations on this basic concept, patented them, and licensed the core concept to Mead John & Co. He used the $300,000 in royalties that accrued over the next couple of years to finance research and development at his own company. Ironically, the disposable procedural tray business would grow to $60 million per year by the early 1980s.

Realizing that his strengths lay more in research and development than operational management, in 1959 Murphy induced John Sterner to serve as president of his small, but growing, company, which had moved from its original garage headquarters to a house. Sterner, a physicist, introduced Murphy to venture capitalist General Georges F. Doriot, whose American Research and Development Corp. would invest nearly a quarter of a million dollars in the start-up business.

By 1960, Murphy had changed the business's name to the more distinctive Cordis ("of the heart"), a moniker that indicated the primary focus of the company's efforts. During the decade, Cordis became involved in the relatively new field of cardiac pacemaking, which utilizes a small, usually battery-operated electronic device known in the industry as a pacer to stimulate the heartbeat with electrical charges. By the early

Company Perspectives:

We believe our first responsibility is to the doctors, nurses and patients, to mothers and fathers and all others who use our products and services. In meeting their needs everything we do must be of high quality. We must constantly strive to reduce our costs in order to maintain reasonable prices. Customers' orders must be serviced promptly and accurately. Our suppliers and distributors must have an opportunity to make a fair profit. We must experiment with new ideas. Research must be carried on, innovative programs developed and mistakes paid for. When we operate according to these principles, the stockholders should realize a fair return.

1970s, Cordis ranked second only to Medtronic among America's pacemaker manufacturers. Cordis introduced its first remotely programmable pacemaker in 1973 and launched improved electrodes (which make the actual connection to the heart muscle) by mid-decade.

Despite infusions of more than $500,000 in cash in its first few years, Cordis had a rocky start. Under Murphy, the company was so devoted to research and development that it was not until 1980 that it achieved a positive net operating cash flow. Murphy and Sterner were forced to sell their stock to keep the firm afloat; by 1984, they held less than five percent between them.

Quality Control Crisis in the 1970s

Cordis found itself facing poor quality control, both within its own manufacturing operations and in components from an important supplier, in the mid-1970s. Flawed circuits from supplier CTS Corp. and an internal rejection rate that soared to 30 percent contributed to the U.S. Food and Drug Administration's (FDA) issue of a product advisory against Cordis in 1974. Cordis's share of the pacemaker market declined from 20 percent in 1975 to 13 percent in 1978. With sales and net worth plummeting, too, corporate executives were compelled to cut salaries by 20 percent across the board.

The supplier, CTS Corp., agreed to keep Cordis afloat via a $5 million injection of capital in exchange for control of nearly one-fourth of the pacemaker manufacturer's stock. For its part, Cordis promised to buy back the shares at a premium, which it was able to do in 1977. Hoping to reinvigorate the company after its near-death experience, Murphy and Sterner brought in a new president, Dr. Norman Weldon, in 1979. Characterized by Forbes as "a husky Indiana farm boy turned biochemist, economist, and businessman," the 40-something Weldon had served as CTS's president before moving to Cordis. For two years, Sterner, Murphy, and Weldon formed a management troika that focused on a costly restructuring of Cordis's manufacturing and marketing operations. Among other things, Weldon organized the company's first independent marketing department and boosted the sales force by 30 percent. The restructuring cost dearly. Cordis lost $8.3 million in 1981 and by that time had racked up $89 million in debt.

A Second Dilemma Mars the Early 1980s

Cordis's luck appeared to be changing in the early 1980s. Four years after a competitor launched the first lithium-powered

implantable pacemaker, Cordis introduced its first lithium model in 1979. The Miami company's version featured an encapsulated battery that purported to be smaller, yet more efficient, than its predecessors. Just three years later, Cordis won FDA approval for an innovative "physiological" or "synchronous" pacemaker, which issued electric pulses only when needed by regulating two chambers of the heart instead of one. At the same time, several competitors—including Intermedics, which had supplanted Cordis as number two in pacemakers in 1979—were reeling from a kickback scandal.

Cordis took good advantage of the situation, increasing sales by more than 75 percent, from $117.7 million in 1984 to $207 million. It also recovered from a net loss of $8.2 million to more than $10 million in profits during the period. Furthermore, it regained the number-two rank among pacemaker manufacturers.

In the meantime, however, engineers at the company had discovered two potentially devastating problems with the lithium-powered pacer. First, they learned that their method of encapsulating the battery had a high potential for corrosion and, possibly, leakage. Though not legally obligated to do so at the time, Cordis modified the battery and notified both the doctors and the FDA about the possibility that the device could become corrupted. The close monitoring of the 8,500 patients who had already received the pacers revealed a second, more serious problem; a totally unforeseen chemical reaction was sapping the power of the batteries. The FDA ordered recalls of Cordis's pacemakers in 1983 and 1985 and prohibited the company from testing and selling new products for 18 months.

Cordis's sales were more than halved from 1984's $207 million down to just $80 million in 1986. The company sold the pacemaker division, which had at one time contributed more than half its annual revenues, in 1987 and reached a $5.7 million settlement with claimants two years later. CFO Robert Strauss succeeded Weldon as president and CEO upon the latter's resignation in 1987.

Under Strauss, Cordis fell back on a secondary business interest, diagnostic cardiac catheters, in the late 1980s. These fine-gauge tubes are used in angiography, the injection of special dyes into blood vessels and the heart chambers to conduct tests for impairment of this vital muscle. By 1990, Cordis had captured 40 percent of the global angiography market, and this business segment constituted 85 percent of the company's total revenues.

Rapid Growth Marks the Early 1990s

During the first half of the 1990s, Strauss guided what investment bankers Hambrecht & Quist characterized as a "metamorphosis" from a "troubled, unfocused, regulatory-hindered Cordis [to] a streamlined one." Moreover, Strauss's reorganization planned to transform it from a firm focused almost exclusively on development of new technology to one emphasizing customers' needs. Having eradicated the company's pacemaker obligations, Strauss focused on maintaining the company's leading share in angiography catheters and diversifying into the larger and more profitable therapeutic heart catheter market. Commonly known as angioplasty, this therapy uses specialized catheters to ream out blockages in the arteries around the heart, or, in the case of balloon angioplasty, to expand the artery to allow increased blood flow.

CEO Strauss hoped to increase Cordis's share of the therapeutic catheter market from two percent in 1991 to 15 percent by mid-decade, but he faced daunting competition from well-established giants in the medical business, including market-leading Eli Lilly & Co. and Pfizer Inc. He reorganized Cordis's staff into product-oriented teams focusing on balloon catheters, interventional catheters, steerable guidewires, and diagnostics, thereby encouraging the development of a comprehensive line. He used competitive pricing and dynamic marketing to make Cordis the industry's fastest growing competitor in the early 1990s. By 1994, the company had captured ten percent of total U.S. angioplasty sales—short of Strauss's ambitious goal, but an impressive expansion nonetheless.

Perhaps more important, the company made dramatic inroads into the global heart catheter business, achieving a third-ranking 17 percent of the worldwide angioplasty market by the middle of 1994. By that time, overseas sales constituted more than 50 percent of Cordis's total annual revenues. Strauss also reduced the company's debt from $31.6 million in 1990 to a mere $1.1 million by the end of 1993. Sales increased from $202.6 million in 1990 to more than $443 million in 1994, while net income multiplied from $20.1 million to $50.2 million.

Product Development Under Johnson & Johnson: Late 1990s and Beyond

Cordis's speedy growth attracted the attention of health care giant Johnson & Johnson, which initiated a highly unusual (for this industry, at least) hostile takeover of the Miami manufacturer in October 1995. Eager to create a total cardiac package of products, J&J offered $100 per share in cash for a company that was then trading at $81. Cordis initially resisted the assault, but in November it agreed to a stock swap valued at $1.8 billion. Cordis became a J&J company in February 1996. The merger combined J&J's cardiac stents—minuscule steel tubes that repair damaged arteries—with Cordis's balloon catheters, which were used to deliver the stents, forming a globally significant manufacturer of cardiac devices.

Under the leadership of its new parent, Cordis spent the remainder of the 1990s developing new products. In 1997, the company formed its Endovacular division to focus on vascular disease treatments. In an attempt to bolster J&J's share of the stent market, Cordis also began to manufacture several different stent's including the Palmaz-Schatz Crown Stent, the CrossFlex hybrid stent, and the S.M.A.R.T. stent.

Cordis also made several key acquisitions and formed strategic partnerships during this time period. In 1997, the firm teamed up with Cardiometrics Inc. in a co-distribution agreement involving Cardiometrics' testing products. Cordis also settled a patent dispute with Medtronic Inc. by forming a patent cross-license agreement for certain stents and stent delivery systems. In 1998, the firm acquired various assets of IsoStent Inc., including the BX Stent. The following year, AngioGuard Inc. was purchased, giving Cordis access to the firm's technology that was developed to protect the heart and brain during medical procedures.

The deals continued into the new millennium. In 2000, Cordis resolved another patent dispute, this time with Guidant Corp. Under the terms of the agreement, Cordis was able to provide its U.S. customers with rapid exchange catheters, which were used in interventional cardiology procedures, including angioplasty and stent placement. Cordis also acquired Atrionix Inc., a developer of catheter-based systems used in the treatment of atrial fibrillation—a disruption in the heart's normal sinus rhythm. In 2001, TERAMed Inc., a developer of catheter-based systems utilized to treat abdominal aortic aneurysms, was purchased.

The most significant moves for the company during the late 1990s and into the new millennium, however, were its attempts to reinvent itself in the stent market. In 1994, J&J had introduced the coronary stent and saw sales of the product increase rapidly to $500 million by 1996. Nevertheless, its prosperity was short-lived. By 1997, its 95 percent market share had fallen to just five percent and revenues had dropped to $200 million. *Forbes* commented on J&J's falter in a 2001 article, claiming that the company had "angered doctors with high prices, ignored demands for better technology, and wrongly assumed its patents would stall rivals. When competitors invaded in 1997, doctors were only too happy to switch."

Cordis, headed by Robert Croce, began to develop new stents and increased its sales force by 40 percent. Along with the less profitable Crown and CrossFlex stent released in the late 1990s, Cordis launched the Bx Velocity stent in 2000, which proved to be the success J&J needed to regain market share. In 2001, the Velocity Hepacoat stent was introduced. This stent was coated with a blood thinner that prevented blood clots from forming and quickly became responsible for nearly 20 percent of company stent sales.

Cordis then put plans in motion to launch a drug-coated stent that would prevent restenosis, a reclogging of the artery that occurred in 25 percent of patients that receive stents. By this time, stents were used in 80 percent of angioplasties performed in the U.S. and accounted for $1.4 billion in annual sales. J.P. Morgan Chase predicted that the release of the new stent could potentially increase U.S. market sales to $3 billion. Cordis, which received FDA approval for its SIRIUS study of the

Sirolimus pharmaceutical-coated Bx Velocity Coronary stent, hoped to launch the breakthrough product in 2003, which would position it ahead of competitors by one year. Cordis chose the name SIRIUS—which means brightest star in the heavens—to symbolize the advantages of the new restenosis-preventing stent. The release of this new product had the potential to position both Cordis and J&J at the forefront of the stent market. Whether or not that potential would be realized, however, remained to be seen.

Principal Subsidiaries

Cordis Medizinische Apparate GmbH (Germany); Cordis Europa NV (Netherlands); Cordis S.A. (France); Cordis S.a.r.l. (Switzerland).

Principal Competitors

Boston Scientific Corp.; C.R. Bard Inc.; Guidant Corp.; Medtronic Inc.

Further Reading

Abelson, Reed, "Cordis Corp.," *Fortune*, June 5, 1989, p. 176.

"Cardiometrics Inc.," *Health Industry Today*, July 1997, p. 14.

"Catheters Unclog Cordis' Growth," *Florida Trend*, January 1994, p. 8.

"Cordis," *BBI Newsletter*, August 1999, p. 186.

"Cordis," *BBI Newsletter*, March 2001, p. 80.

"Cordis: Building Marketing Muscle To Pump Up Strength in Biomedicine," *Business Week*, December 20, 1982, p. 63.

"Cordis Completes Enrollment in Landmark U.S. Trial," *PR Newswire*, August 30, 2001.

"Cordis Faces Import Sanctions, Begins Heart-Valve Recall," *South Florida Business Journal*, May 18, 1992, p. 7.

"Cordis Quality Starts with Suppliers," *Florida Trend*, May 1988, pp. 50–52.

"Cordis Receives Approval for New Catheter," *South Florida Business Journal*, March 19, 1990, p. 6.

Davis, Philip M., "Beware of Corporate Criminal Conduct," *Design News*, November 7, 1988, p. 214.

Engardio, Pete, "Why Cordis' Heart Wasn't in Pacemakers," *Business Week*, March 16, 1987, p. 80.

Farley, Dixie, "Firm Pleads Guilty to Selling Faulty Pacemakers," *FDA Consumer*, September 1989, pp. 38–9.

"Johnson & Johnson Launches Hostile Bid for Miami Firm," *The Atlanta Constitution*, October 20, 1995, p. F6.

Keller, Katrina, "Cardiac Comeback," *Forbes*, April 30, 2001, p. 164.

Linden, Eugene, "The Role of the Founder: Murphy's Law," *Inc.*, July 1984, pp. 90–6.

McGough, Robert, "Choppy Waters," *Forbes*, September 12, 1983, p. 183.

——, "Mr. Clean," *Forbes*, April 23, 1984, pp. 141–42.

Miller, Susan R., "Snag Slows Down Cordis Deal with Johnson & Johnson," *South Florida Business Journal*, December 29, 1995, pp. 3–4.

Nesse, Leslie Kraft, "Change in Cordis' Structure Leads to Increased Sales, Profits," *South Florida Business Journal*, June 10, 1994, pp. 8–9B.

——, "Cordis in Licensing Agreement," *South Florida Business Journal*, June 17, 1994, pp. 3–4.

Painewebber Inc., "Cordis Corp.—Company Report," The Investext Group, November 25, 1994.

Paltrow, Scot J., "Cordis Stock Plunges on J&J Delay," *Los Angeles Times*, December 28, 1995, p. D2.

Petruno, Tom, "Johnson & Johnson Makes Bid for Cordis," *Los Angeles Times*, October 20, 1995, p. D2.

Raloff, J., "Keeping Pace," *Datamation*, January 1984, p. 38.

Resnick, Rosalind, "Cordis Recovers; Can It Catch Up?," *Florida Trend*, June 1991, pp. 41–3.

Waresh, Julie, "Back to the Drawing Board," *South Florida Business Journal*, August 14, 1989, pp. 1–2.

——, "Spin-offs Lift Burden from Cordis Corp.," *South Florida Business Journal*, December 12, 1988, pp. 5–6.

Westlund, Richard, "Cordis Corporation: A Wellness Program with 'Heart,'" *South Florida Business Journal*, June 9, 1995, p. 12B.

—April Dougal Gasbarre
—update: Christina M. Stansell

Cotton Incorporated

6399 Weston Parkway
Cary, North Carolina 27513
U.S.A.
Telephone: (919) 678-2220
Fax: (919) 678-2230
Web site: http://www.cottoninc.com

Not-For-Profit Company
Founded: 1970
Employees: 164
Sales: $60 million (2000)
NAIC: 81391 Business Associations

Cotton, Incorporated is a marketing and research company funded by over 30,000 producers and importers of upland cotton and cotton products in the United States. Cotton Inc. holds a 60 percent market share of the U.S. retail fiber market and is the world's best-selling fiber. The company is overseen by the U.S. Department of Agriculture and maintains offices in Mexico and the Far East.

History of Cotton Growers

In Postbellum America, making a living as a cotton farmer became more difficult than ever. The end of the Civil War, and consequently, the end of free labor in slaves, meant the cost of farming cotton rose. In the late 1800s and early 1900s, a series of natural disasters conspired to further challenge farmers. First, there was the infection of boll weevils, and then the flooding of the Mississippi River in 1927, and in the early 1930s, there was a drought. As disasters wiped out much of the U.S. cotton crop, cotton prices remained stable in the 1920s and dropped in the 1930s. Between 1924–29, cotton brought in an average of $1.5 billion per year; in 1932, the figure was $465 million.

When Franklin D. Roosevelt took over the presidency of the United States in March 1933, his focus was to relieve and help the citizens through the worsening Depression. One of the acts signed by the president as part of his "first New Deal," was the Agricultural Adjustment Act. The goal of the Act was to match supply and demand, which in turn was to stabilize prices and create a livable income for farmers. Cotton farmers were paid to not grow cotton, or to reduce the amount of cotton grown, until the surplus was eliminated from the market. Although the Act was later found to be unconstitutional, it was important in that for the first time, it organized cotton farmers to work together for their common benefit. Though the Act was considered successful in raising farm family incomes, in 1935 cotton farmers were still earning 40 percent less than they had in 1925.

Due to some failures of government programs and the record output of cotton in 1937, farmers took action and formed their own industry organization. Those who created the first industry organization recognized that production was only half of the problem; cotton farmers had to find a way to influence demand for their product.

Early Organization for Cotton Interests

The formation of the National Cotton Council (NCC) in 1938 brought new hope to the diverse people who farmed cotton throughout the United States. The NCC was designed to speak on behalf of all cotton interests: producers, ginners, warehousemen, merchants, and cottonseed crushers, with the stated goal of "increase(ing) the consumption of cotton and products thereof." In order to protect each disparate interest, each interest had veto power and any resolution had to be passed by a two-thirds vote from each interest. The NCC would be the first stand-alone commodity-specific organization. It was fortunate for the commodity that it chose to stand together as one; as a global economy began to emerge and synthetic fabrics were discovered, cotton would be challenged even more than before.

By the 1950s, the U.S. cotton growers' supremacy was over. U.S. cotton farmers were producing the same as they had in 1920, yet foreign growers were producing 3.5 times as much in the 1950s as they had in 1920. During the same time period, production on man-made and synthetic fibers rose from 32,000 to 5.5 million bale-equivalents. The rise in synthetic fiber production was part of the reason that cotton's share of apparel sales dropped from an 88 percent share in 1920 to a 66 percent share in 1957. Another factor was that people were spending

Company Perspectives:

From agricultural, fiber and textile research, market information, and technical services, to the FABRIC OF OUR LIVES television advertising campaign, fashion forecasts and retail promotions, we keep one goal in mind: To ensure that cotton remains the first choice among consumers in apparel and home products.

less on clothing; Americans reportedly spent nine percent of disposable income on clothing in the 1930s, and in 1956 that figure was little more than six percent.

Problems arose in the NCC, mainly due to the disparate interests of the five main groups. Millers, for example, did not have the same interests as growers. Millers could make clothing and other products from synthetic fibers as well as cotton; in many cases, it was easier and cheaper for millers to use synthetics. As a result, in 1960, a subsidiary of NCC was formed: the Cotton Producers Institute of the National Cotton Council (CPI). Funded by a levy of $1.00 per bale on producers, the CPI worked exclusively on the interests of cotton growers, mainly through research and promotion. Through the next decade, CPI worked tirelessly but with less money than the competition, and the same problem persisted: lack of marketing savvy to increase consumer demand. CPI next decided to break with NCC and installed J. Dukes Wooters, a marketing vice-president for *Reader's Digest*, as head of the organization. One of the first acts of the newly independent CPI was to move the operations from Memphis to New York City, with research and development settled in Raleigh, North Carolina.

Cotton Incorporated is Formed

After the formal break, CPI decided it was time for a new name to go along with the new image. The name Cotton Incorporated was first used in 1971. The first job of the new Cotton Inc. was to convince producers they should service the needs of customers; in this case, customers did not just mean buyers of finished cotton apparel and products but also millers and manufactures. Part of the early marketing strategy was to convince manufacturers to produce garments with a blend of fibers. Instead of shirts made from synthetic fibers, Cotton Inc. convinced manufactures to make blended garments, such as 65/35 cotton/polyester blends. Cotton also began focusing on fashion and market research.

The emphases on sales, fashion, and research made the market for cotton edge upwards, and Wooters decided to update cotton's image with a clean, modern logo. Commissioned in 1973, the logo featured ''cotton'' in lower-case letters and a white cotton ball growing out of the double 't's. With Wooters' ingredients in place, the share of cotton rose from 33 percent in 1973 to 36 percent in 1976.

By the time Cotton Inc. was up and running, the generation that fought the war had adapted to synthetic fibers and cherished them as easy to wear, easy to care products. Wooters thus decided to focus on their children, the so-called baby-boomers. Children and teens in the late 1960s and early 1970s had

rebelled in many ways, one of which was in their taste for clothing. Among the more popular fashion trends were t-shirts and jeans, both strong cotton markets. The trick was not only to market to a baby-boom generation that preferred cotton products, but to continue to sell them on the fiber as they grew older.

The trouble with marketing cotton to the end-user, the wearer of apparel, was that a lot of money and energy would have to be invested before a payoff was realized. Cotton Inc. poured money into television advertisements, hoping to create a demand from consumers of manufacturers. While spending began in 1971, it was not until 1980 that the demand for cotton was truly felt. During this time, the boomers and the actors in the Cotton Inc. commercials aged together, and Cotton Inc. played on the boomers' feeling that natural and simpler was better. The patience paid off as the demand continued into the 21st century.

The high point in marketing for Cotton Inc. came with the ''Fabric of Our Lives'' campaign, which began in 1989. The tag line was used into the 21st century as a tie-in for different Cotton Inc. commercials.

In addition to end-users, Cotton Inc. also had to create demand from mills and manufacturers of apparel and other cotton products. Synthetic and man-made fibers held distinct advantages over natural fibers, including cotton. Supply of synthetic fibers could be constant; there was no crop to wait on. Synthetic fibers could also be customized to different mills' specifications, and synthetics were uniform in strength, length, and color.

In order to compete with the advantages of synthetics, Cotton Inc. invested money in research and development. The first job was to set a standard for cotton quality. Although cotton had always been judged by certain standards, these were highly subjective and varied. In the mid-1950s a process began—a long one—for trying to bring uniformity and objectivity to determining the quality of cotton. The development of high-volume instrumentation (HVI) began in 1965, initiating high-speed testing to the process. Through the years, this quality determination system evolved into an industry standard for testing length and strength. HIV systems were installed in mills as early as 1969, and the systems slowly began taking their place in mills and classing offices. As late as the 1970s, cotton was largely inspected and classified by hand; by 1991 the whole U.S. cotton crop was classified by HVI.

This revolution pulled cotton closer to its competitors as far as mills were concerned. Now they had cotton they could buy based on objective criteria. The next step was to produce cotton with uniformity that mimicked the uniformity of synthetics. Research produced software, called the Engineered Fiber Selection (EFS) system, that could analyze data derived from HVI. This gave mills information quickly and efficiently about every bale of cotton they processed. Cotton Inc. began and continued to serve as host at the Engineered Fiber Selection (EFS) conference annually, which showcased the previous year's research and development, as well as new cotton fiber management systems.

The Future for Cotton

In 1996, Hurricane Fran inflicted damage along the east coast of the United States. Assessing damage at its own research facility at some $750,000, Cotton Inc. decided to build a new

Key Dates:

1970: Cotton Incorporated is created to combat loss of market share due to consumers' infatuation with synthetic products.

1973: The Seal of Cotton logo is born.

1975: Cotton Inc. opens a research dyeing and finishing laboratory for the development of new and improved cotton products.

1976: A fiber processing laboratory with state-of-the-art equipment is opened.

1982: Cotton Inc. opens two international offices, in Osaka, Japan, and London, England.

1987: Company introduces garment wrinkle-resistant finishing.

1989: The Fabric of Our Lives television advertising campaign debuts on Thanksgiving Day.

1994: Cotton Inc. hosts its first Crop Management Seminar for crop management consultants to discuss pesticides and management techniques.

2000: Cotton Inc. opens its new World Headquarters, a 125,000–square-foot research, development and office complex in Cary, North Carolina.

facility, combining two facilities into one, and having research and development and corporate functions under one roof. The new facility, located in Cary, North Carolina, was a 125,000-square-foot site, with a cost of $17 million. Although much was combined, the promotion, marketing, and fashion staffs remained in New York City.

The fiber industry overall suffered some declines in 2000 and looked forward to a better year in 2001. Although cotton was not as badly affected as markets for some synthetic fibers, it did suffer from low cotton futures and large supplies. Still, cotton continued to hold a 60 percent market share, and Cotton Inc. representatives felt that whatever synthetic fibers were developed, cotton could compete. Cotton Inc. was determined to keep reminding the public that cotton was a better fiber and developing functional finishes to cotton, such as water repellency, UV resistance, flame resistance, and other consumer-friendly finishes. By 2000, cotton held the top spot of the home fabrics market, with a 64.5 share, an increase of 1.3 percent from 1999, and up 3.9 percent since 1997. In individual categories, cotton's share of sheet set sales went from 63.3 to 70.8 percent from 1997 to 2000; mattress covers from 37.3 to 44.8 percent; and sheets from 66.2 to 67.8 percent. The market share for towels stayed at 96 percent from 1997 to 2000.

During this time, a portion of the Cotton Inc. research center was focused on fashion, with many colors and styles of cotton fabrics produced as samples for the top fashion houses. In mid-2000, Cotton introduced new woven constructions of cotton materials in six categories. TableWear featured textures for use in tablecloths and napkins; Decorative 1 showcased Bedford cords for upholstery; Decorative 2 introduced a dual-twill weave and Angelina sparkle yarn; Sheers Curtains introduced a fancy mock leno weave; Top-the-Bed collection featured Grecian honeycombs and twills with honeycomb weaves; and the Drapery group introduced dobby weaves, honeycomb weaves and novelty yarns.

After the terrorist attacks on the east coast of the United States in September 2001, Cotton Inc. partnered with Jones Lang LaSalle, a management company of retail malls across the country, to raise money for the families of the tragedy. Called "Share the Spirit," the program offered teddy bears with American flag t-shirts for a minimum donation of $5 and a $50 minimum purchase of cotton products. Proceeds went to The New York Police and Fire Widows' and Children's Benefit Fund.

Clothing made from organic fibers, including cotton and wool, grew by 11 percent from 1996 through 2001. Analysts projected that sales of organically grown fiber clothing would increase 44 percent from 2000 through 2005. The Organic Trade Association (OTA) had long fought to have products made with organic fibers recognized by various government and trade bodies. In June 2000, Cotton Inc. reversed its policy of recognizing only conventionally grown cotton, allowing the use of its Seal of Cotton to be licensed for products sold as organically grown. However, the new criteria from Cotton Inc. maintained that "the prospective licensee must not, either individually or as a part of a collective effort, publicly denigrate, criticize, or otherwise negatively comment about cotton, cotton products, or cotton production systems." The OTA protested, finding that the mandate prohibited them from pointing out what they felt were superior features of organically grown cotton.

Cotton Inc. continued to tailor their approach to advertising and marketing to different cultures. In 2001, 62 percent of women surveyed in the United States said they would rather dress comfortably than fashionably, and 70 percent said they would rather be comfortable than fashionable when they are out shopping. In Europe, especially among older women, fashion ranked higher than comfort. In the same survey, it was found that European and Japanese women preferred to change outfits throughout the day, as events warranted, while women in the United States were more likely to wear one outfit throughout the day. One other important difference in demographics was that women in the United States were more likely to think clothes made from natural fibers were of better quality, whereas women from Japan and Europe did not agree. Cotton Inc. thus had its work cut out for it on foreign soil.

At the end of 2001, Cotton Inc. introduced new commercials, building on the Fabric of Our Lives campaign. The new 30-second spots were part of a $20 million advertising campaign and featured ordinary people dancing in their cotton clothing. Past ad campaigns were targeted towards women ages 18 to 49; this campaign focused on women ages 18 to 34. Moreover, the new commercials focused exclusively on cotton apparel, unlike past campaigns, which also featured lines, bedding, and towels. Cotton Inc. wanted to focus more on younger women, who were still developing their buying habits. Continuing to promote the advantages of cotton, Cotton Inc. was a major advertiser during the Winter Olympics in February 2002.

Principal Competitors

E.I. du Pont de Nemours (DuPont); Celanese AG; Milliken & Company, Inc.

Further Reading

Bishop, Susan, ''Cotton Incorporated Opens New World Headquarters,'' *HFN,* May 1, 2000, p. 18.

''Cotton Inc. Launches $17 Million Research Center,'' *DNR,* April 24, 2000, p. 17.

''Cotton Incorporated Unveils New Woven Constructions,'' *HFN,* June 12, 2000, p. 22.

''Cotton Prices Rising After Five Years,'' *DNR,* February 5, 2000, p. 92.

''Home Goods Are Cottoning More to Cotton These Days,'' *HFN,* March 5, 2001, p. 29.

Jacobson, Timothy Curtis, and George David Smith, *Cotton's Renaissance: A Study in Market Innovation,* Cambridge: Cambridge University Press, 2001.

Maycumber, S. Gray, ''Cotton Ads Target Younger Audience,'' *DNR,* November 12, 2001, p. 44.

——, ''Fiber Outlook: Bumpy Road Getting a Little Smoother,'' *DNR,* January 28, 2000, p.8.

''News in Brief: Cotton Incorporated and Jones Lang LaSalle,'' *DNR,* November 5, 2001, p.7.

Nicksin, Carole, ''Cotton Incorporated Ads Dance to a Whole New Beat,'' *HFN,* November 19, 2001, p. 29.

''OTA Seeks 'Fair and Equitable' Treatment for Organic Agriculture,'' *PR Newswire,* July 5, 2000.

''Sales of Organic Fiber Products Continue to Grow,'' *PR Newswire,* January 4, 2002.

—Lisa Musolf Karl

CryoLife, Inc.

1655 Roberts Boulevard Northwest
Kennesaw, Georgia 30144
U.S.A.
Telephone: (770) 419-3355
Toll Free: (800) 438-8285
Fax: (770) 426-0031
Web site: http://www.cryolife.com

Public Company
Incorporated: 1984
Employees: 340
Sales: $87.7 million (2001)
Stock Exchanges: New York
Ticker Symbol: CRY
NAIC: 621991 Blood and Organ Banks

CryoLife, Inc., headquartered in Kennesaw, Georgia, is an industry leader in the biomedical development and commercial adaptation of ultra-low temperature preservation or "cryo-preservation," the process by which viable cardiovascular and orthopaedic human tissues (primarily heart valves, leg veins, and cartilage) are preserved for use in vascular or orthopaedic surgery. It provides this biomedical service in the United States and Canada, where it "harvests" such donor tissues from hospitals and coroners, then, for a fee, processes and stores them. By law, the company cannot directly sell human body parts, but it can process and preserve them for a fee. Their end users, surgical transplant patients, pay the relevant fees when the stored tissues are implanted. The company specializes in vascular products, including heart valves and conduits, but it also stores and provides cartilage and tendons for orthopedic surgery. Through its CryoLife International, Inc. and CryoLife Europa, Ltd. subsidiaries, it also markets its products and services in 42 countries spread across the globe. Among other significant products, CryoLife has developed its SynerGraft line, tissued engineered heart valves and vascular graft replacement products, and BioGlue, a bioadhesive bonding product for use in aortic dissections. Through its AuraZyme Pharmaceuticals unit, formed in 2001, the company also develops and markets light-activated drug-delivery systems. CryoLife's CEO, president, and chairman is Steven G. Anderson, one of the company's co-founders.

1984–92: CryoLife Emerges

CryoLife came into being in 1984, when Ray H. Holloway and Steven G. Anderson partnered to found it. Holloway, who had been selling mechanical hearts, saw the open-ended potential of using preserved heart values in transplant surgery after the University of Alabama had begun using such cryopreserved valves rather than the artificial products he was then marketing. He teamed up with Anderson, who had served as a marketing executive for Intermedics, a pacemaker manufacturer. The new enterprise became the first biomedical company to develop, for commercial use, the low temperature "cryopreservation" of tissue for surgical implant.

One of the chief obstacles to early success was the negative, even unsavory aura of cryogenics, prompted in part by Robin Cook's best selling novel *Coma* (1977) and the movie adaptation of that work released in 1979. But there was resistance within the medical community as well. According to Anderson, quoted in a 1987 article in *Business Atlanta*, the problem was that, although "the technique was well-documented," it was still "stuck in the research lab," of benefit to no more than 100 people a year.

The first CryoLife valve implant—the recipient was a young child—occurred in October 1984 at New York's Columbia-Presbyterian Hospital. Because of the hospital's reputation as a leading medical center, it gave the new company a helpful infusion of credibility, leading other major hospitals to start participating in the CryoLife program.

Still, initially, the company struggled to survive. Its first year's revenues were a balance sheet embarrassment. Over the next year they rose to $911,000, almost reaching a breakeven point. Through that first rough hoeing, Anderson searched for some investors, but found the financial world even a tougher turf to work than the medical profession. Anderson could find no backers in Atlanta, but he finally lucked out in Nashville, Tennessee, where he was able to convince Lucius Burch that CryoLife was a legitimate enterprise with tremendous potential. In December 1985, the Massey-Burch Group put up $1 million and obtained warrants for an additional $1.4 million in stock. With that capital backing, in 1986 CryoLife generated revenues of $3.2 million and turned a profit of $230,000.

In order to train surgeons in the use of its valves, CryoLife sponsored courses on working with homographs, and it soon attracted important, even eminent physicians. One, for example, was Dr. Ellis Jones, professor of thoracic surgery at Emory University in Atlanta. He took the course in 1986, and within a year successfully installed 18 CryoLife preserved valves.

The heart valves treated and stored by CryoLife came from the hearts of patients that physicians judged were brain dead. They were donated by hospitals and only involved hearts for which no suitable heart transplant recipients could be located within a time span that would allow them to be used for a full heart transplant. At the time CryoLife was founded, about 85 percent of all donated hearts had to be discarded because of the logistical problem of getting them to heart-transplant patients on time. CryoLife provided an alternative. Removed hearts were air-freighted to Marietta, where the heart valves were surgically removed and, if deemed acceptable, placed in a liquid-nitrogen bath for over 90 minutes, methodically taking the deeply frozen valves to a temperature of minus 196°C. They were then either stored by CryoLife or shipped back to the donating hospital. In 1987, its fee for this service ranged from $1,955 to $2,295.

By 1990, CryoLife had begun expanding its tissue preservation technique to include veins, and in the next year petitioned the FDA to approve an innovative method of freezing whole blood. At the time, the company was using 10 to 12 percent of its annual revenues for research and development, or up to three times the industry's average. The company would continue to diversify and expand through the rest of the decade.

1992–95: Going Public and Developing New Products

In December 1992, the FDA classified human heart valves for transplantation as medical devices subject to premarket approval application before their commercial distribution. In response, CryoLife requested the FDA's permission to conduct IDE (investigational device exemption) clinical testing for its allograft CryoLife heart valve. In June 1993, permission for its clinical study was expanded to allow up to 35 patient implants at each of 10 primary medical centers plus up to 1,200 implants at 440 secondary centers. In order to help finance its expansion and its R&D, CryoLife also went public in 1993 and began trading on the New York Stock Exchange.

By the time that CryoLife had made its formal application for the FDA's premarket approval (in November 1993), over

900 surgeons had already implanted more than 14,000 valves preserved by CryoLife. The valves were widely recognized as an important valve replacement alternative for women of child-bearing age and children with congenital heart defects. CryoLife's 1993 revenues, reflecting the impact of that recognition, had reached $21.2 and had put the company well on its path to solid annual earnings.

CryoLife's R&D efforts continued to pay significant growth dividends for the company. In April 1994, it opened its new combined bioadhesive laboratory and pilot production facility. The laboratory was built to make FibRx, a fibrinogen-based bioadhesive designed to control hemorrhaging during surgery. CryoLife research scientists developed an efficient single-syringe formulation for effective and expedient use during operations. Studies using animals began immediately, and human trials were set for early 1995 at major medical centers, though they were later delayed until the fourth quarter of 1996.

The company's performance was strong in the mid 1990s. For example, in 1995, its revenues reached approximately $29.2 million, a 23 percent increase over its 1994 revenues of $23.8 million. Some of the increase resulted from the sale of the company's Viral Inactivation Process, but there was also strength in all of the company's revenue producing sectors. One area of great growth was in the cryopreservation of orthopaedic tissue for use in knee reconstructive surgery. In 1995, it generated an increase in revenues of 145.6 percent over its figure for 1994.

1996 and Beyond: Further Expansion and Diversification

Between 1995 and 1997, CryoLife took some other major steps in product development and diversification. First, in 1995, it acquired the rights to the O'Brien Stentless Aortic Porcine Bioprostheses, a vital key in the development of its SynerGraft technology. In simple terms, the new technology allowed a porcine heart valve, depopulated of its porcine heart valve cells, to replace a human heart valve in transplant surgery. In early experiments with animals, the transplanted porcine valves showed that they could be repopulated with new cells and new tissue architecture biochemically generated by their recipients.

By the fall of 1998, CryoLife had shipped almost 31,000 heart valves for surgical use, with only one documented instance of contamination caused by a fungus. It had also built an imposing network of 280 tissue banks, which was sufficient for supplying most of the company's tissue and organ needs. In return for that support, CryoLife provided training in cadaver dissection and heart packaging as well as promotional help for the tissue banks and their services. With few serious competitors, it also claimed an 80 percent share of the human heart valve trade.

By 2000, CryoLife was logging record revenues and earnings, partly driven by the company's expansion and diversification. Importantly, the roll out of CryoLife's BioGlue surgical adhesive in both domestic and overseas markets had begun playing a strong role in generating the company's growing sales. BioGlue had begun selling in foreign markets since March of 1998, but it was not until January 2000 that the FDA, under its Humanitarian Device Exemption (HDE) regulations, gave its approval for the domestic use of BioGlue in aortic dissections. Although the FDA's authorization included the caveat that the adhesive could only be used in conjunction with sutures or staples, CryoLife knew that it had finally jumped an imposing hurdle in the development of a major biomedical product.

By the fall of 2000, BioGlue had been approved for vascular and pulmonary repairs in 41 countries, although in the United States it was still available only in life-threatening situations under the FDA's guidelines. However, by that time, CryoLife had received FDA approval for expanding clinical trials for using BioGlue for all cardiac and vascular repairs. Meanwhile, advances in the use of porcine heart valve for human implantation argued that CryoLife's investment in that process would soon prove justified. Early in 2000, in operations in Brisbane, Australia, CryoLife's SynerGraft porcine valves repopulated with human cells were successfully used in two transplant operations. In the following August, bolstered by news of four additional SynerGraft implants in Australia, the company submitted an FDA application for an Investigational Device Exemption (IDE) that would allow it to begin human clinical trials of its SynerGraft valves and procedures in the United States.

While on hold, waiting for the FDA to act on its application, CryoLife's SynerGraft technology was making progress elsewhere. In October, the company announced that it had received product certification for SynerGraft's use in the European Union. In that same month, the company sold all the remaining assets of Ideas For Medicine, Inc.(IFM), its wholly owned subsidiary, to Horizon Medicine, Inc. As part of its diversification strategy, CryoLife had originally acquired IFM, which made surgical instruments, in 1997, but within a year sold IFM's product line to Horizon Medical Products. However, Horizon defaulted on a supply contract that was part of its sales agreement obligations, and CryoLife was forced to reassume control of IFM in 1999. The divestiture was finally completed when Horizon, reorganized, bought the subsidiary for a price that could climb as high as $5.9 million, depending on whether or not all the contractual terms were met.

At the start of the new century, CryoLife's future prospects were excellent. In its special, very challenging field, it had garnered a solid reputation for its excellent R&D. It was also on a very solid footing financially. In the decade ending in December 2000, the company's revenues had climbed to $77.1 million, up from $15.3 million in 1991, the last year in which the

company recorded a bottom-line loss. Especially from 1996 on, the company's marketplace performance was excellent, with profit margins running between 9.2 percent and 10.7 percent, except in 1999, when they dipped down to 6.7 percent.

Not that CryoLife had completely trouble-free sailing. It had some problems, and not just delays necessitated by waiting out the FDA. During 2000, for example, it had to weather some negative publicity that resulted from exposé journalism claims that profits were being made from the "sale" of organs and tissues harvested from volunteer, uncompensated donors. In 2001, it also faced litigation when the Colorado State University Research Foundation filed suit against the company for its failure to credit a university professor for patents on a surgical process that the plaintiffs alleged CryoLife used in its SynerGraft processes. Such problems were but motes to trouble CryoLife's business eye, however, for the company was clearly on the move.

Among other things, it was further diversifying its business. In 2001, it formed AuraZyme Pharmaceuticals. A wholly owned subsidiary of CryoLife, AuraZyme's chief raison d'être was to foster the commercial development of the company's new light-activated drug delivery systems, engineered for the treatment of cancers, heart problems, strokes, and blood clots. Gerald Seery, who had been CryoLife's vice president of marketing since 1995, assumed the AuraZyme's posts of president and CEO.

As much as anything else, the formation of AuraZyme illustrates a major fact that will help shape CryoLife's destiny: it is in an industry with a wide-open potential for expansion made possible by the tremendous milestones now being reached in medicine and related technologies. CryoLife has already shown and should continue to show that it can stay in step with new advances, making the sky its proverbial limit.

Principal Subsidiaries

CryoLife International, Inc.; CryoLife Europa, Ltd.; AuraZyme Pharmaceuticals.

Principal Competitors

ATS Medical, Inc.; Baxter International Inc.; Datascope Corp.; Guidant Corporation; Regeneration Technologies, Inc.; St. Jude Medical, Inc.

Further Reading

Allison, David, "CryoLife Creating Heart Pacemaker with Human Cells," *Atlanta Business Chronicle*, April 3, 1989, p. 1.
"CryoLife, Inc. Advances Application of Its Tissue-Engineered Human Heart Valves," *Canadian Corporate News*, August 11, 2000.
"CryoLife, Inc. Open New Surgical Adhesives Facility," *PR Newswire*, April 13, 1994.
"CryoLife, Inc. Submits Premarket Approval (PMA) Application to FDA on Cryopreserved Heart Valves," *PR Newswire*, November 10, 1993.
Henderson, C.W. "FDA Application Filed for SynerGraft Heart Valve," *Blood Weekly*, August 17, 2000, p. 14.
Troop, Paul, "When Science Fiction Becomes Science Fact," *Business Atlanta*, October 1987, p. 142.
Upbin, Bruce, "King of Hearts," *Forbes*, November 2, 1998, p. 214.

—John W. Fiero

Deltic Timber Corporation

210 E. Elm Street
P.O. Box 7200
El Dorado, Arizona 71731-7200
U.S.A.
Telephone: (870) 881-9400
Fax: (870) 861-6457
Web site: http://www.deltic.com;
http://www.chenal.com

Public Company
Incorporated: 1996
Employees: 526
Sales: $106 million (2001)
Stock Exchanges: New York
Ticker Symbol: DEL
NAIC: 321113 Sawmills; 111998 All Other
Miscellaneous Crop Farming

Deltic Timber Corporation, headquartered in El Dorado, Arkansas, harvests and mills lumber on its 368,000 acres of Arkansas timberland, rich in Southern Pine. The company operates two sawmills: the Ola Mill, in central Arkansas, and the Waldo Mill, in south Arkansas. The lumbering and milling operation account for over 80 percent of the company's annual revenue. The company also owns a 50 percent interest in Del-Tin Fiber L.L.C., which manufactures and markets a medium density fiberboard, and through a subsidiary, Chenal Properties Inc., Deltic also manages a 4,300-acre master-planned residential and corporate community in Chenal Valley, the premier upscale development in the Little Rock real estate market. Until 1996, when it was spun off as a separate corporation, Deltic, then named Deltic Farm & Timber Co., was a subsidiary of Murphy Oil. Heirs of Murphy Oil founder C.H. Murphy Sr. still own about 27 percent of Deltic Timber. Altogether, Deltic owns about 413,000 acres, including about 36,000 acres of farmland in northeastern Louisiana.

1907–70: From Murphy Oil Corporation to Deltic Timber

Because Deltic Timber Corporation originated as a subsidiary of Murphy Oil Corporation, its roots go back to 1907, when Charles H. Murphy Sr., an entrepreneur, first started accumulating pine wood acreage in Arkansas for investment purposes. Murphy was a south Arkansas banker and land baron, something like a modern-day venture capitalist long before that role was defined. Oil was only one of Murphy's varied interests, but one that began to pay dividends when fields in Shuler, Arkansas, and Ezzell, Texas began producing crude.

During the pre-World War II years, long before using land for lumbering, Murphy began buying up additional acreage. Notably, in the 1920s, he acquired considerable property at public sales, not just in Arkansas, but elsewhere as well. Still, oil was not Murphy Sr.'s focal interest. It was, his son, Charles H. Murphy Jr. who wanted to be an oil man pure and simple, and after serving in the armed forces during the first half of the 1940s, he entered the business with a missionary's zeal and over the next several years built a legendary reputation in the industry. He was prompted by what became the foundation for Murphy Oil–the 1944 discovery of oil in the Delhi Field in Richland Parish, Louisiana.

The Delhi Field, first worked in conjunction with Sun Oil, eventually produced over 213 million barrels of oil. Its early promise led Charles Jr. to take some very aggressive steps. In 1952, two years before his father died, he took Murphy Oil public and proceeded to grow and diversify the company over the next half century. In 1953, he created a subsidiary, Ocean Drilling and Exploration Co.(ODECO) to drill offshore for both his own company and others. Thereafter, he became intrigued with the idea of expanding Murphy Oil into global markets. He invested in Venezuelan oil exploration, and in the mid-1960s moved into oil producing areas in Southeast Asia. Among ODECO's industry's successes was its development of the Sassan Field off the Iranian coast in the Persian Gulf, in which it held a 25 percent share, and its part in the discovery and development of the large Ninian Field, off the British coast, in the North Sea.

Company Perspectives:

The company is focused on expanding its land base, increasing timber harvest levels, and enhancing manufacturing capabilities.

During those years, although his focus was on oil exploration and production, Charles, Jr., did take at least one significant step that would figure importantly in the future of Deltic Timber Corporation: in 1957, he acquired 85,000 acres in a public land trade and added them to the company's holdings.

1971–96: Deltic Farm and Timber Company Is Formed

With an uncanny degree of prescience, in the 1970s, Murphy Oil began diversifying its operations. Although its focus was and would remain on oil exploration and production, it branched into some new ventures, including the cutting and milling of timber on large tracts of land it had acquired over its long history. It was in 1971 that the Deltic Timber Corporation, originally named Deltic Farm and Timber Company, Inc. and formed as a subsidiary of Murphy Oil, commenced its sawmill operations. Although an oil man tried and true, Murphy knew the potential of the timber and milling business, and between 1976 and 1984, he authorized the acquisition of another 138,000 acres of pine-forest land. By 1984, Deltic Timber was operating two saw mills, one at Ola in central Arkansas, and the other at Waldo, in southern Arkansas.

In 1985, Deltic started up its real estate operation for the purpose of developing and managing its timberland located in Chenal Valley, smack in the middle of Little Rock's growth corridor. Four years later, it began its annexation of real estate, with the incorporation of 2,180 Chenal Valley acres.

Deltic Timber's parent, Murphy Oil, entered a financial slump in the early 1990s. From 1991 to 1996, it returned only an average of about seven percent on its equity, far below the average 11 percent for all comparable integrated oil companies. Refining and marketing, which accounted for over half of the company's revenue, were not the traditional core businesses of Murphy Oil, and in the 1990s they fared badly. In August of 1996, as part of an effort to reverse Murphy Oil's declining fortunes, Claiborne Deming sold off nearly all of Murphy's producing properties in the United States, for which the buyers, a group of institutional investors, paid about $50 million. Then, in September, he made plans to spin off Deltic Timber, whose assets at that time were estimated to be worth about $260 million. The result was that Murphy Oil was left with exploring and production operations in the Gulf of Mexico, Canada, and the North Sea fields near Britain, the core activities that had made the Murphy family's fortune.

Prior to being spun off, Deltic Farm & Timber Co. had expanded its operations. Among other steps it took, in 1995, in a new business venture, it entered into a joint ownership arrangement with Temple-Inland Forest Products Corp., a subsidiary of Temple-Inland Inc., to begin construction of the Del-Tin Fiber LLC medium density fiberboard (MDF) plant in the Newell community near El Dorado. The large plant, boasting nine acres under roof, was designed to process about 430,000 tons of raw materials annually, turning out about 150 million feet of fiberboard.

1997 and Beyond: Deltic Timber Goes Public and Expands

Emerging as an independent company, Deltic Timber Corporation began taking several further steps to grow the company and develop other business possibilities. One of its first steps was to raise capital by going public. It also increased its acreage, timber harvest, mill capacity, and real estate operations.

Late in 1996, Deltic had implemented a timberland acquisition program designed to allow the company to increase its timber harvest and its inventory. It aim was to increase its acreage holdings in the southern part of the United States, where most of the timberland was still privately owned.

Between 1992 and 1996, as a subsidiary of Murphy Oil, Deltic's timberland had remained stable at around 342,000 acres, all of which were located in Arkansas and northern Louisiana. In 1997, it increased its holding to about 360,000 by buying an additional 17,000 acres. At that point, most of Deltic's operating income was generated from its forest products business and agriculture, with just nine percent coming from its real estate development.

However, it was in real estate that Deltic started its most significant growth. In June 1997, the company announced plans for developing two new residential communities, one just outside Little Rock and the other just outside Hot Springs. Like Deltic's Chenal Valley developments, these were planned as upscale communities, though not on a matching scale. Clearly, Deltic's real estate division was playing an increasingly important role in the company's business. In 1998, although that division's $16 million in net sales only represented about 15 percent of Deltic's total revenue of $107 million, its operating income was $5 million, or 27 percent of Deltic's overall operating income of $18.3 million.

In that same year, 1998, Deltic purchased an additional 16,300 acres of pine timberland in Arkansas from RII Timberland Partners I, LP. That acquisition increased the company's timberland holdings to almost 400,000 acres. It was also in 1998 that the Del-Tin MDF plant finally began operations.

In the following year, 1999, the company announced plans to sell or exchange some of its agricultural land in Louisiana in order to acquire additional southern pine timberland. It also planned to convert some of its Louisiana farm land directly into timberland. In that year, too, Deltic got into an annexation fight with the Little Rock board of directors. The issue was the annexation of Deltic's final portion of its 4,700-acre Chenal Valley development in west Little Rock. The company wanted to use the last 1,200 acres for developing approximately 700 home sites and constructing a second 18-hole golf course for Chenal Country Club, but some city board members were concerned about the capital costs involved in additional annexations. Despite objections, the board approved Deltic's request but left some concern about future annexation efforts.

Although Deltic's net income for 2000 rose to $13.6 million in 2000, up from $10.9 million in 1999, its revenues declined

Key Dates:

1907: C.H. Murphy, Sr., purchases investment land.
1946: Charles Murphy takes reins of Murphy Oil.
1971: Deltic Farm & Timber Company begins milling operations.
1985: Company begins its Chenal Valley real estate operations.
1995: Deltic announces plans to build Del-Tin, a medium density fiberboard (MDF) plant with Temple-Inland Forest Products Corp.
1996: Murphy combines its real estate and agricultural operations and spins them off as Deltic Timber.
1997: Deltic goes public.
1998: Del-Tin commences operations.

from $124.2 million to $109.5 million, prompting CEO and president Ron Pearce to acknowledge that the company's financial performance was "disappointing." Deltic's milling operations produced sales that were at or near the lowest in ten years, in part because of downtime at the company's two mills. Although capital projects and two ice storms were partly responsible for the temporary shutdowns, poor market conditions also played a major role.

The timber business depression continued into 2001. In February, Deltic temporarily shut down its jointly owned Del-Tin plant, giving as reasons a weakened MDF market and the high cost of natural gas. While the plant was closed, the plant's owners made a $2.8 million modification in its heating system. Meanwhile, in order to counter the timber market downturn, Deltic continued to expand its program of selling tracts of land that could be priced high enough to offset their value as timberland. Between 1956 and 1999, Deltic and its original parent, Murphy Oil, had purchased over 67,000 acres in west Pulaski County, Arkansas, paying an average price of about $350 per

acre. By 2001, land in the same area was selling for an average of $6,400 an acre for undeveloped land and an average of $85,000 an acre for land within Deltic's Chenal Valley development. The value of the land offered a strong incentive for growing Deltic's real estate operations. As the company's mission statement indicates, Deltic entered the new century determined not just to weather bad market conditions, but also to expand its timberland holdings, increase its harvests, and upgrade its manufacturing capabilities.

Principal Subsidiaries

Chenal Properties Inc.

Principal Competitors

Georgia-Pacific Group; Louisiana-Pacific Corporation; Plum Creek Timber Company; Potlatch Corporation; Tembec Inc.; Weyerhaeuser Company.

Further Reading

Chaney, Don, " 'The Avenue Chenal' Plans Announced," *Arkansas Business*, June 12, 2000, p. 8.

Haman, John, and Smith, David, "Deltic Timber Plans Two Upscale Developments," *Arkansas Business*, June 2, 1997, p 30.

Mack, Toni, "Roots: The Third Generation in His Family to Run Murphy Oil, Claiborne Deming Is Bringing It Back to the Business That Made the Murphys Rich," *Forbes*, October 7, 1996, p. 60.

"Murphy Subsidiary Plans New $80 Million Pant–Del-Tin Fiber Operation Near El Dorado Will Add Over 100 Jobs in Region," *Arkansas Business*, October 30, 1995, p S18.

Parham, Jon, "Deltic Timber to Grow Forest Products Business," *Arkansas Business*, November 29, 1999, p. 8.

Smith, David, "Deltic Faces Annexation Fight; 1,230-Acre Addition to Chenal to Include Golf Course, 700 Homes," *Arkansas Business*, June 14, 1999, p 1.

"Timber Companies Cutting Operations," *Arkansas Business*, February 5, 2001, p 11.

—John W. Fiero

Denison International plc

Masters House
107 Hammersmith Road
London W14 OQH
United Kingdom
Telephone: (+44) 20-7603-1515
Fax: (+44) 20-7603-8448
14249 Industrial Parkway
Marysville, Ohio 43040
United States
Telephone: (937) 644-4500
Web site: http://www.denisonhydraulics.com

Public Company
Incorporated: 1932
Employees: 1,072
Sales: $153.1 million
Stock Exchanges: NASDAQ
Ticker Symbol: DENHY
NAIC: 332911 Industrial Valve Manufacturing

Denison International plc is a specialist producer of hydraulic fluid power components and systems. With corporate headquarters in both London, England, and Marysville, Ohio, Denison is a world player in its market. More than half of its sales are generated in Europe, while more than one-third of sales are produced in the United States. The company operates manufacturing facilities in the United States, the United Kingdom, France, German, Italy, and Finland, and operates sales and distribution facilities in more than 15 countries. Denison Hydraulics, the company's main operating subsidiary, concentrates on the high-margin specialty hydraulics components, including piston pumps and motors, vane pumps and motors, manifolds, radial piston motors, and valves. Vane and piston pumps account for nearly 60 percent of the company's turnover, while valves add nearly 21 percent to Denison's sales of $153 million (2000). The company has been taking steps to join in on the consolidation of its highly fragmented industry at the turn of the century, acquiring Finland's Lokomec Oy and Italy's Riva Calzoni Oleodinamica. Originally founded in the United States,

Denison was acquired by a private investment group that incorporated the company in the United Kingdom before listing it on the NASDAQ stock exchange in 1997. Denison is led by CEO and president David Weir.

Fluid Power in the 1920s

The origins of Denison International can be traced back to the pioneering days of the U.S. automotive industry. The company began operations as the Cook Motor Company, based in Delaware, Ohio, in 1900. Cook's original focus was on the development of heavy-duty gasoline-powered industrial engines. Cook's motors were large, single-cylinder models—its 50hp engine weighed some three tons.

When its original owner sought to retire after World War I, the Cook Motor Company was taken over by William Denison. Despite the dwindling market for gasoline engines—as newer more powerful diesel engines began to take over as the primary industrial engine type—the Cook Motor Company continued to produce engines until the 1930s.

Luckily for his company, Denison proved somewhat of an inventor. By 1920, he had recognized the need to take the company into a new direction and began experimenting with new types of power designs. Denison turned his attention toward developing fluid power systems—which became known as "hydrOILics." In 1925, Denison produced his first hydraulics machine, a "car pusher" designed to push a car loaded with clay products through a kiln. The Denison hydraulics machine quickly captured a leading position in the ceramics industry, holding at one point some 80 percent of the market for car pusher devices.

The Cook Motor Company, however, was heading toward financial disaster as its business collapsed during the Great Depression of 1929. By the beginning of the 1930s, the company had gone bankrupt. At that time, however, hydraulic power systems, which offered considerable advantages over existing mechanical power transfer methods, was developing into an entirely new market segment. Hydraulics technology proved highly flexible, capable of being incorporated into large-scale, heavy-lifting systems while also proving useable for small, high-precision tasks.

Key Dates:

1900: The Cook Motor Company is founded in Delaware, Ohio.
1925: Bill Denison acquires Cook and invents the hydraulic car pusher.
1931: Cook goes bankrupt and Denison reorganizes the company as Denison Engineering.
1955: American Brake Shoe (ABEX) acquires Denison.
1968: ABEX merges with Illinois Central and becomes IC Industries.
1986: Denison is sold to Hägglund & Söner.
1988: Hägglund & Söner is broken up and Denison becomes part of newly formed Hägglunds Denison Drives AB.
1991: Denison Drives is split into two companies, Hägglunds Drives and Denison Hydraulics.
1993: Denison Hydraulics is acquired by group of private investors and is incorporated in the United Kingdom as Denison Hydraulics International.
1997: The company goes public on NASDAQ exchange as Denison International plc.
2001: Denison launches new Premier range of mobile piston pumps.

Based on his hydraulics expertise—the Denison company was to go on to produce more than 600 patents during the twentieth century—Bill Denison resurrected his company, reorganizing and reincorporating it as the Denison Engineering Company in 1931. The company had abandoned its engine operating and now concentrated on the development of hydraulic systems and components for the ceramics industry.

Yet Denison appeared to have rebuilt his company only to see it collapse again. In 1933, the company's manufacturing plant was destroyed by a fire. Denison quickly found a solution, renting out a nearby property owned by the Budd-Ranney Company. Denison now entered an operating contract with Budd-Ranney; two years later, Denison acquired Budd-Ranney.

Throughout the 1930s, Denison remained at the forefront in developing new hydraulics technology. One of the major new directions for the application of fluid power systems was in the design of machine presses, which vastly increased the productivity of industrial processes. Denison was approached by the United States military for help in developing machine presses for weapons and aircraft component production.

With the U.S. military as a primary customer, Denison expanded rapidly during the years of World War II. The company established a network of manufacturing plants in the Columbus, Ohio region, including a research center and a dedicated aircraft test facility. By the end of the war, Denison had become a leading player in the U.S. hydraulics industry. A major product for the company was the Multipress.

The company continued to produce for the Military—introducing high-speed and lightweight pumps for aircraft in 1945—but increasingly turned toward the civil sector for growth. Denison had diversified into the design and engineering of components for hydraulics systems, launching production of piston-type pumps in 1941. In 1945, Denison extended its components business with the production of hydraulic valves, and in 1952 the company launched its first vane pumps, which formed the basis of such automotive developments as power steering and automatic transmissions. Meanwhile, the U.S. Government remained an important customer; in 1954 the company inaugurated a dedicated facility for the production of aircraft pumps in conjunction with the U.S. government.

Specialty Hydraulics for the 21st Century

Denison Engineering was acquired by American Brake Shoe in 1955. The following year, American Brake Shoe moved production of aircraft pumps to Rochester, New York. At the end of the 1950s, production of the Denison-branded pumps was moved to California. In 1958, Denison began manufacturing pressure control valves.

The company, which had limited sales largely to the U.S. market, began looking more and more toward the international market for growth. In 1959, the company opened its first sales and service facility in Germany in order to support its growing European market sales. Back at home, American Brake Shoe began construction of a new manufacturing plant in Marysville, Ohio. Completed in 1962, the Marysville plant initially concentrated on piston pump production before being expanded to include production of the company's Multipress line. Meanwhile, Denison's international sales grew strongly, and in 1963 Denison inaugurated a manufacturing plant in Hilden, Germany, and later opened plants in Burgess Hill, England, and in Vierzon, France.

American Brake Shoe changed its name to ABEX in 1966, then merged with Illinois Central in 1968, changing its name to IC Industries. Denison remained an active brand name, however, and by the beginning of the 1970s had come to focus on high-margin specialty hydraulics products. In 1971, the company launched production of poppet vales. The company also launched a new subsidiary in that decade, Denison Transmission, which brought out a line of small-sized hydrastatic drives in 1975. By the beginning of the 1980s, Denison had extended its product line into components and systems designed for marine use.

In 1986, IC Industries sold its Denison division to Swedish conglomerate Hägglund & Söner (later Hägglunds AB), a major producer of military vehicles, among other products. Hägglunds was also a prominent producer of hydraulic motors and that business was combined with its new Denison acquisition to form Hagglunds Denison, a world leading manufacturer of hydraulic pumps and valves. Two years later, Hägglund & Söner was broken up into independent companies, one of which became Hägglunds Denison Drives AB.

Hägglunds Denison Drives was hit hard by the recession of the late 1980s and early 1990s, and was forced to shut down a number of its operations, including its factories in Columbus and Delaware, Ohio. Denison's operations and headquarters were then transferred to the Marysville site. In 1991, Hägglunds, which by then had come under the control of Wallenberg family investment vehicle Incentive, split into two entities, Hägglunds Drives and Hägglunds Denison.

Incentive then sold Denison to three private investors—J. Colin Keith, Anders Brag, and E.F. Gittes—who incorporated the company in the United Kingdom as Denison Hydraulics International in 1993. The slimmed-down company posted more than $100 million in sales that year. Denison's new owners brought Denison to the stock market, listing its shares on the NASDAQ exchange in 1997. At that time, the company took on the name of Denison International plc, with executive offices in both Marysville and London.

Denison continued its long tradition of innovation, preparing to launch a new series of open loop piston pumps for heavy duty industrial applications. Meanwhile, the company, which had traditionally produced products for industry uses, had begun to expand into the mobile market. By 1998, the mobile market accounted for 37 percent of the company's sales, which topped at $145 million that year.

Part of Denison's motivation for its expansion was the ongoing consolidation of much of the world's industry. As the company's chief competitors—including Rexroth, Parker Hannifin, and Eaton—began leading a consolidation of the hydraulics industry, which remained heavily fragmented at the turn of the century, Denison was determined not to be left behind.

In 1998, Denison made its first acquisition when it bought Finland's Lokomec Oy, Scandinavia's largest maker of hydraulic manifolds. Denison expected to be able to export Lokomec's product through its own worldwide network. By the end of the 1990s, Denison operated manufacturing facilities in five countries, with sales and distribution offices in a total of 15 countries. While the United States represented Denison's largest national market at more than one-third of sales, more than half of Denison's revenues were produced across Europe. The Asian market represented another fast-growing segment of Denison's sales.

Denison made a new acquisition in 2000, purchasing Italy's Riva Calzoni Oleodinamica. That acquisition gave Denison an expanded range of high-torque, low-speed radial piston hydraulic motors, enhancing the company's ability to offer its customers total hydraulics systems solutions. The following year, Denison launched a new line of mobile piston pumps. Building on a century of innovation, Denison had attained a leading position for itself in the worldwide specialty hydraulics market.

Principal Subsidiaries

Denison Holdings Limited (UK); Denison Financial Holdings Limited (UK); Denison Hydraulics U.K. Limited; Denison Hydraulik Svenska Ab (Sweden); Denison Hydraulik Danmark AS (Denmark); Merifire Oy (Finland); Denison Lokomec Oy (Finland); Denison Hydraulics Benelux B.V. (Holland); European Distribution Centre Denison B.V. (Holland); Denison Hydraulik GmbH (Germany); Denison Hydraulics France S.A.; Denison Hydraulics S.A. (Spain); Denison Hydraulics Italy S.r.l.; Denison Hydraulics Inc. (Japan); Denison Hydraulics Limited (Hong Kong); Shanghai Denison Hydraulics ENGG. Ltd.; Denison Hydraulics SEA Pte Limited (Singapore); Denison Hydraulics (Proprietary) Limited (Australia); Denison Hydraulics Canada Incorporated; Denison Hydraulics Inc. (USA); Denison Hydraulics FSC, Inc. (Barbados).

Principal Competitors

Rexroth PLC; The Oilgear Company; Hydrakraft; Interpump Group S.P.A.; Parker Hannifin Corporation; Eaton PLC; Atos SA; Bosch AG.

Further Reading

Brezonick, Mike, ''Making a Move in the Mobile Markets,'' *Diesel Progress*, March 2000.
''Denison International Announces Acquisition of Lokomec Oy,'' *Business Wire*, December 29, 1998.
''Denison International Ends Year with Solid Performance,'' *Business Wire*, February 20, 2001.
''History of Denison Hydraulics,'' Dension International corporate web site, http://www.denisonhydraulics.com.

—M.L. Cohen

DENSO

DENSO Corporation

1-1, Showa-cho
Kariya City
Aichi 448-8661
Japan
Telephone: (81) 5 6625-5511
Fax: (81) 5 6625-4537
Web site: http://www.globaldenso.com/

Public Company
Incorporated: December 16, 1949 as Nippondenso
  Company
Employees: 86,000
Sales: ¥2.02 trillion ($16.25 billion) (2001)
Stock Exchanges: Tokyo Osaka Nagoya
Ticker Symbol: NZOY
NAIC: 333319 Other Commercial and Service Industry
  Machinery Manufacturing; 333618 Other Engine
  Equipment Manufacturing; 336312 Gasoline Engine
  and Engine Parts Manufacturing; 336322 Other Motor
  Vehicle Electrical and Electronic Equipment
  Manufacturing; 33633 Motor Vehicle Steering and
  Suspension Components (except Spring)
  Manufacturing; 336399 All Other Motor Vehicle Parts
  Manufacturing

A well-established spin-off of Toyota Motor Corporation, the DENSO Corporation (originally incorporated as the Nippondenso Company) is Japan's leading producer of automobile components and the world's fourth largest. Its products include air conditioners and heaters, electrical and electronic control products, fuel management systems, radiators, meters, and filters. General Motors leaders acknowledged DENSO as a model for GM spin-off Delphi Automotive. As the second-largest member of the Toyota Group, more than half of DENSO's products go to Toyota Motor Corporation (TMC), which owns better than 20 percent of DENSO stock. DENSO also supplies nearly all other major Japanese automakers as well as numerous U.S. manufacturers, including Ford, General Motors, and Chrysler, and major European auto manufacturers such as Volvo, BMW, and Fiat. The company's emphasis on quality control and improved manufacturing efficiency throughout its history, its aggressive international expansion program, and its well-funded research-and-development activities since the 1960s have produced steady sales growth and allowed DENSO to capture dominant positions in many of its world markets.

Origins

Nippondenso rose to its international presence from Toyota Motor Corporation's in-house electrical and radiator operations, which began after Toyota Automatic Loom Works formed an automobile division in 1933. In 1936, the Japanese government passed legislation to promote domestic production of automobiles. Loom Works separated its automobile division from the rest of the company, and the motor division developed an in-house electrical-parts factory.

The inability of Loom Works to adequately fund automobile production on its own and the fact that legislation had made automobile production potentially profitable led to the 1937 establishment of Toyota Motor Corporation. Soon afterwards, the Toyota Group was reorganized around Toyota rather than Loom Works. The limited number of Japanese independent parts manufacturers in the late 1930s, especially those that produced electrical parts, led to the development of parts makers with close ties to automobile manufacturers. Shortly after Toyota Motor Corporation was formed, it built a factory in Kariya to produce starters and coils. In 1943 a radiator plant was added, and the two factories eventually became the basis for Nippondenso.

Japan's involvement in World War II contributed heavily to the development of Toyota and its affiliates through wartime contracts. After Japan surrendered to the Allies in 1945, the automobile industry was reshaped by the Supreme Command for the Allied Powers, and Toyota was compelled to spin off Nippondenso as an independent company.

Nippondenso Company was incorporated on December 16, 1949 as an automotive electrical-equipment maker with ¥15 million in capital and 1,445 employees. Torao Hayashi was named

---

Company Perspectives:

Mission: *Contributing to a better world by creating value together with a vision for the future.* Management Principles: *Customer satisfaction through quality products and services, global growth through anticipation of change, environmental preservation and harmony with society, corporate vitality and respect for individuality.* Individual Spirit: *to be creative in thought steady in action, to be cooperative and pioneering, to be trustworthy by improving ourselves.*

---

president. Nippondenso's first products as an independent company included starters, ignition coils, distributors, voltage regulators, radiators, meters, oil coolers and cleaners, horns, dynamos, windshield wipers, and car heaters.

In March 1950, Nippondenso announced it would cut personnel in response to recession. A two-month strike resulted and was resolved after Toyota president Kiichiro Toyoda and the company's managing director and executive vice-president resigned. Shortly thereafter, 1,760 employees retired voluntarily.

In the 1950s, Nippondenso used standardization and quality control to rise to the top of its field. Hayashi and other top executives initially viewed quality control as a means to standardize and to procure U.S. military contracts. Nippondenso also looked to foreign cooperative agreements during the decade as a way of improving standardization techniques, gaining technological knowledge, and expanding product lines.

Quality Control in the 1950s and 1960s

Following the recommendations of U.S. and Japanese quality-control experts, Nippondenso established a program that combined design, processing, and cost controls. In 1950, Nippondenso formed an inspection department that learned statistical quality-control methods. The following year use of control charts was initiated, and in 1952 random sampling and other testing methods were adopted. In 1954, the company embarked on a five-year quality control program, which included compiling a training manual for employees and subcontractors. The program initially targeted improvements in standardization and inspections. In 1956, Nippondenso established a quality-control staff office and an independent committee to oversee quality-control programs.

Beginning in 1953, Nippondenso entered a three-year technical agreement with Robert Bosch of West Germany for the production of electronic parts, fuel injection pumps, and spark plugs. As a result of the Bosch tie-up, Nippondenso's product line was expanded in the latter part of the decade to include car air conditioners, engine regulating equipment, fuel injection systems, and diesel engines.

In 1957 and 1958, Nippondenso de-emphasized finished product inspection and focused quality-control efforts on improved process-control methods. At the same time, it extended quality-control techniques into design and prototype-manufacturing areas. In 1958, Nippondenso purchased precision measuring equipment and automatic inspection devices to help

workers control quality themselves. By the end of the decade sales had grown 23 times from 1950 levels and surpassed ¥10 billion.

In 1960, Nippondenso began working with integrated-circuit (IC) technology and developed an electromagnetic fuel pump fitted with a diode transistor. Two years later the company created an IC device that dims headlights automatically.

In 1961, Nippondenso implemented a second five-year quality control plan that was designed to strengthen the company's management. Later that year, long-range planning efforts of the Quality Control Committee, established in 1956, along with supervisors for planning, development, and production-line activity, were recognized when Nippondenso received the prestigious Deming quality-control award.

Beginning in the latter half of the 1960s, Nippondenso expanded in a number of areas; in 1965, new domestic plants were established in Hiroshima and Ikeda to manufacture radiators, radiator-fan motors, and oil coolers. Two years later Nippondenso's fourth plant, a starter and alternator production facility, was opened in Anjo.

Between 1965 and 1966, three new domestic manufacturing and sales subsidiaries were formed: Nippon Wiper Blade Co., Ltd. in Saitama Prefecture, GAC Corporation in Nagano Prefecture, and Asahi Manufacturing in Aichi Prefecture. These companies produced windshield-wiper parts, small motors for automobiles, bus air conditioners, lead wires for automobile components, and central air conditioning systems. In the following year, Nippondenso also began exporting automotive components in order to supply the growing number of Japanese automakers assembling automobiles in East and Southwest Asian countries.

North American Offices Established 1966

Nippondenso's interest in marketing supplies to major U.S. automakers and an increase in Japanese-made cars exported to the United States led to the 1966 establishment of the company's first overseas facilities, which were branch offices in Chicago and Los Angeles. About the same time, liaison offices were opened in New York and Montreal. New products featuring increased automation were also introduced by Nippondenso during the mid-1960s. These included power seat and power window motors, automatic door locks, and a mechanical cruise-control system.

In 1967, Hayashi became the company's first chairman of the board. Tatsuo Iwatsuki, a former vice-president and managing director who had been with the company since its incorporation, became president.

The company made a commitment to integrated-circuit technology in 1968 with the opening of its IC Research Center, the first of its type in the automotive industry. That same year it set up the Electronics Product Division to assemble printed circuit boards. The rapid growth of Nippondenso, especially in the latter half of the 1960s, resulted in an eightfold sales increase from 1960 to 1969. By the end of the decade the company recorded annual sales in excess of ¥90 billion.

Key Dates:

1937: Newly formed Toyota Motor Corporation builds starter and coil factory in Kariya.
1949: Nippondenso Company is formed from two existing Toyota plants.
1950: Quality control methods begin to be adopted.
1953: Nippondenso begins technical agreement with Bosch.
1957: Nippondenso refocuses on process control methods.
1959: Annual sales reach ¥10 billion.
1965: New plants open in Hiroshima and Ikeda.
1966: Nippondenso establishes offices in the U.S. and Canada.
1967: The company opens a starter and alternator factory in Anjo.
1968: Nippondenso opens auto industry's first integrated circuit research facility.
1969: The company's annual sales exceed ¥90 billion.
1971: International growth prompts the formation of overseas subsidiaries.
1979: The company's annual sales reach ¥500 billion.
1985: Nippondenso Technical Center is established in Southfield, Michigan.
1987: The company's sales pass ¥1 trillion and subsidiaries are established in Taiwan and Thailand.
1996: The company's name is shortened to DENSO Corp., reflecting global orientation.
2001: DENSO buys out the remaining interest in Purodenso Company.

Accelerating Globally in the 1970s

In the 1970s, Nippondenso stepped up the pace of its international expansion, research, and product development. In 1970, the company established Nippon Soken near the Nishio plant for basic automotive-component research. Also in that year the new Nishio plant in Japan began manufacturing a number of the company's principal products, including car heaters and air conditioners, radiators, radiator-fan motors, fuel injection pumps, and electronic fuel injection components. Four years later another domestic plant opened in Takatana to produce meters, oil filters, machinery, and tools.

Between 1971 and 1976, the company bolstered its worldwide presence by establishing nine overseas subsidiaries. In 1971, Nippondenso formed its first overseas subsidiary, Nippondenso of Los Angeles, to assemble and sell air conditioners and import and sell rebuilt electrical automotive equipment and spark plugs. From 1972 onward, Nippondenso formed subsidiaries in Australia and Asian nations in response to more stringent domestic content regulations.

As business with U.S. automakers expanded in the early 1970s, Nippondenso established additional import and sales subsidiaries in North America. In 1972, Nippondenso Canada was established in Toronto. Three years later, Nippondenso Sales, Inc. was set up in Detroit. In 1973, Nippondenso's first European subsidiary, Nippondenso (Europe) B.V., was established in Amsterdam to import and sell air conditioners and air conditioner compressors. Also in 1973, Iwatsuki was named chairman of the board. Takaaki Shirai, another former vice-president and managing director, was named president.

Nippondenso responded quickly to changing market needs in the 1970s. After the 1973 oil crisis struck and fuel economy became an international issue, Nippondenso refocused its research-and-development programs and produced an engine control system. After air pollution became a growing concern later in that decade, Nippondenso produced an electronic fuel injection system that regulated exhaust emissions. The two developments enhanced the company's reputation and boosted sales. So did the push toward smaller, fuel-conserving cars, which increased demand for the compact Nippondenso-made components.

Other Nippondenso innovations during the decade included an electronically controlled automatic transmission developed in conjunction with Toyota in 1970. More electronically controlled systems followed, including a spark advance system, knock control system, and idle speed control system. IC-based technology produced an electronic fuel injection system, new igniters, regulators, and speed sensors. The decade's innovations also included an anti-skid device, electronic cruise control, a power trunk opening computer, and such non-automotive applied electronics products as industrial manufacturing robots, an automatic fire extinguisher, and a portable refrigerator. The 1975 introduction of a new spark plug with a patented U-groove electrode, marketed by Nippondenso of Los Angeles, boosted U.S. sales and contributed to Nippondenso's firm establishment in the spark plug market.

Also in 1977, Takaaki Shirai became chairman of the board, and was succeeded as president by Fubito Hirano. Hirano, like other presidents before him, had climbed the corporate ladder via the offices of managing director and vice-president. By the end of the decade 8.4 percent of net sales were coming from overseas operations. Sales over the previous ten years had grown by 500 percent, to better than ¥500 billion. The sale of automobile air conditioners and heaters continued to pace earnings, followed by growing sales of electrical components.

New Ventures, New Products in the 1980s

Sales continued to climb throughout the 1980s, although earnings slipped mid-decade due to the high value of the yen. During the decade, the company focused on product diversification, international expansion, and the construction and automation of factories.

In 1980, Nippondenso formed its first South American subsidiary, in Brazil. That same year, the company entered Malaysia with the formation of Nippondenso (Malaysia) SDN./BHD. Three years later a second Malaysian subsidiary was established. Products of the three new sales and manufacturing subsidiaries included air conditioners, air conditioner compressors, windshield washers, alternators, starters, and radiators.

In 1982, Hirano was named chairman of the board and Kengo Toda, a former vice-president and managing director, was named president. That same year Nippondenso opened a domestic plant in Daian to produce distributors, spark plugs, magnetos, sensors, and actuators.

Nippondenso bolstered its European presence in 1984 with the formation of Nippondenso (Deutschland) GmbH, an import and sales subsidiary established for air conditioners, air conditioning compressors, sensors, emission devices, and actuators. Another import and sales subsidiary, Nippondenso (U.K.) Ltd., was formed in 1984 to handle windshield washers, emission control products, and air conditioner parts.

Nippondenso's new products during the first half of the 1980s focused on automobile components emphasizing comfort, safety, and improved driving capabilities. Comfort-related items included a knee warmer, a seat heater, and a mosquito killer. Expanded electronics technology produced an electronically controlled diesel injection system, an electronic suspension control system, and a traction-control system. Nippondenso, which had a history of producing a majority of its specialized manufacturing equipment itself, also entered the automation business during the early 1980s, with the introduction of a magnetic stripe card reader recognition system and a bar-code scanner.

In 1985, Nippondenso posted its fifth consecutive year of increased sales and earnings, reaching all-time highs of ¥954 billion and ¥42.8 billion, respectively. Company officials attributed financial gains largely to increases in overseas production and domestic sales. Nippondenso's strongest push in overseas expansion during the decade was in the United States. In 1984, the marketing and service joint venture A-B Nippondenso was formed when Nippondenso and Allen-Bradley Company of the United States agreed to cooperate on factory automation. The agreement called for cooperation in the development and sales and service of electronics products and was designed to help Nippondenso advance in factory automation and to help Allen-Bradley, a major manufacturer of control devices and factory automation systems, enter the Japanese market.

In 1984, the wholly owned subsidiary Nippondenso Manufacturing U.S.A. was formed in Battle Creek, Michigan, for the manufacture and sale of radiators, car heaters, refrigerators, cooling units, condensers, and windshield washers. The $18 million Nippondenso Technical Center U.S.A., in Southfield, Michigan, was established in 1985. The center's goal was to provide engineering services for U.S. customers, test product designs, and perform other research-and-development activities. That same year Nippondenso developed its second comprehensive domestic testing facility at its corporate headquarters. The new Kariya facility was equipped with laboratories to simulate weather for visibility evaluation, and to simulate driving.

Net sales continued to grow in 1986 and 1987 and passed ¥1 trillion, but net profits declined as a result of the rapidly appreciating value of the yen. Net earnings fell better than ¥10.4 billion in 1986 and ¥1 billion the following year. In 1987, Toda was promoted to chairman, and Taro Tanaka assumed the duties of president. Two domestic plants in Toyohashi and Kota were also opened in 1987.

In the late 1980s, rapid expansion continued, accompanied by increased net earnings. Between 1987 and 1989 five major U.S. subsidiaries were formed, including three joint ventures. In January 1989, Michigan Automotive Compressor, Inc. was formed as a joint venture between Nippondenso and Toyoda

Automatic Loom Works, for the manufacture and sale of air conditioning compressors and magnetic clutches. In September of that year, Nippondenso established Purodenso Company in Jackson, Tennessee, as a 50–50 joint venture with Purolator Products Company of Tulsa, Oklahoma, to produce and sell air cleaners and oil filters for Toyota, Saturn Corporation, and others. Two months later Nippondenso and Robert Bosch GmbH founded Associated Fuel Pump Systems Corporation as a 50–50 joint venture to produce fuel pumps for Big Three and Japanese automakers operating in the United States.

Nippondenso also continued expansion outside of North America in the late 1980s. In 1987, manufacturing and sales subsidiaries were established in Taiwan and Thailand. Nippondenso Tool and Die (Thailand) Co., Ltd. was Nippondenso's first offshore producer of dies, and Nippondenso Taiwan Company was set up to produce electrical automotive equipment, radiators, and automotive heaters and air conditioners for Toyota's subsidiaries in Taiwan.

In the first broad-based cooperation agreement among Japanese auto-parts makers belonging to different groups, Nippondenso agreed in 1987 to help an Isuzu Motors affiliate with radiator production techniques. Nippondenso Finance (Holland) B.V. was also established in 1987. This subsidiary was to carry out group finance and fund-raising activities in the European market. In 1988, Nippondenso struck a deal with Champion Spark Plugs to produce 20 million spark plugs annually under the Nippondenso brand name.

In 1989, Nippondenso and Japan's Shinwa Tsushinki Company agreed to cooperate on the development of mobile communications. That same year, Nippondenso and Valeo, the largest French automotive components manufacturer, together established VND in Spain, to produce and sell distributorless ignition coils.

In 1989, Nippondenso also acquired IMI Radiators of the United Kingdom. The new subsidiary, which specializes in production of oil coolers, intercoolers, and radiators for European automakers, was renamed ND Marston. Nippondenso also formed Australian Automotive Air, Pty. Ltd. in 1989 to manufacture condensers, cooling units, and electric fans for car air conditioners.

Nippondenso's growing interest in the home, office, and factory automation markets resulted in a number of new products in the latter half of the 1980s, including a programmable controller for manufacturing equipment, marketed through A-B Nippondenso. Nippondenso also introduced new factory automation products, including a compact bar-code handy scanner, marketed as the world's smallest and lightest, and a bar-code handy terminal, which combined scanning, storing, and transmission functions. Security systems making use of finger print-reading devices, a hands-free automobile telephone, and an automobile facsimile transceiver were also introduced. Other new automobile components included a navigation system and a traction-control system.

After a profit decline in 1986 and 1987, Nippondenso closed the decade with a rebound in earnings, which climbed to a high of ¥48.3 billion in 1989, while net sales reached ¥1.3 trillion. Sales continued to be paced by car air conditioners and heaters, which accounted for about 36 percent of revenues, and electrical automotive equipment, which represented about 20 percent of sales.

Going Global in the 1990s

Nippondenso entered the 1990s by breaking into the Italian market with the January 1990 formation of Nippondenso (Italia), for the import and sale of starters and alternators. In February 1990, Nippondenso's tenth domestic plant began operations in Agui, producing machinery and tools.

Nippondenso's plans for the future were represented in the company's motto: "to be pioneering, innovative, and creative." Further international expansion was planned with the goal of establishing a comprehensive global presence and a leading share in at least 15 of its major product markets, concentrating on improvement of electronic components, communications systems, ceramics actuators and heaters, factory-automation systems, information devices, environmental cooling control systems (for factories, offices, and trains), and refrigeration systems for perishable-food delivery trucks.

A global recession eventually cut into sales of Japan's luxury autos, with a corresponding decline for Nippondenso, which had invested ¥3 billion in air conditioners and navigation systems for Toyota's Lexus line. The recession also resulted in automakers putting more pressure on Nippondenso to reduce prices. Exchange rate fluctuations were another factor in a three-year slide in profits. More parts were being sourced in America, both by Japanese carmakers and by Nippondenso itself. On a more promising note, by the end of 1991, Toyota was responsible for only half of Nippondenso's total sales.

Tsuneo Ishimauru, an engineer and 30-year company veteran, was appointed president in March 1991. Diversification was a key feature of his plan to keep the company profitable. However, non-parts operations only accounted for four percent of sales in 1993. Car heaters, air conditioners, and electrical control parts were each accounting for about a third of sales.

In late 1994, an equally owned joint venture (Yantai Shougang Nippondenso Co.) was created to produce auto air conditioners in China. Nippondenso Mexico S.A., formed in September 1994, was preparing to supply measuring instruments to Chrysler Corp. Yet another Asian subsidiary, DENSO International Singapore Pte. Ltd., was formed in 1995.

Nippondenso shortened its name to DENSO Corp. in October 1996, reflecting its global orientation. The automotive industry's prospects were proving better outside Japan at that point.

DENSO was investing in intelligent traffic system projects such as automated toll systems. Increasing restrictions on diesel engine exhaust prompted to increase capacity for production of its line of fuel injection systems for diesel engines. The company was also increasing production of components in England to supply European makes.

In the late 1990s, DENSO aimed to increase sales to the Big Three automakers in the U.S. Sales to Japanese transplants—the factories set up by Japanese carmakers in North America to meet regulatory quotas—helped make DENSO's North American unit a $2.7 billion company in 1997 (the parent company's revenues were $13 billion). However, GM, Ford, and Chrysler accounted for only a fraction of sales. At the same time, the auto-parts divisions of GM (Delphi Automotive) and Ford (Visteon) were looking to increase their own business with Japanese automakers. Chrysler Corp. was DENSO's biggest customer in the U.S. Its merger with Germany's DaimlerBenz AG caused DENSO some concern, as consolidating companies typically sought to reduce trim their lists of suppliers.

In 1999, DENSO acquired the climate control division of Magneti Marelli S.p.A. of Italy for $430 million. In June 2001, it bought out ArvinMeritor's 50 percent interest in Purodenso Company, a $110 million maker of air, oil and fuel filters in Jackson, Tennessee.

President and CEO Hiramu Okabe aimed to make DENSO Corporation the leader in all the market segments it served. Unlike his American counterparts, Okabe was not quick to close or sell underperforming units, considering them instead candidates for further investment. At the time of DENSO's fiftieth anniversary in December 1999, the company had a dozen market leading automotive products. It also had a winning bar code terminal. (One of its optical scanners read DENSO's new QR—"quick response"—language of data-rich two-dimensional symbols instead of just vertical stripes.) Okabe wanted the company to have 25 number one products by 2005. He aimed to increase non-automotive sales to 20 percent of the total from seven percent in fiscal 1998.

The developing market for navigation systems provided DENSO with a chance to expand its U.S. market via its unique range of expertise in a number of related areas, including cellular telephones and voice-activation technology. DENSO could offer a complete driver's information/entertainment system to automakers for a retail price of $2,000 each.

In May 2001, DENSO announced it was ceasing production of mobile phones, which it had begun producing in 1992. That year alone, the company lost ¥10 billion ($82 million) on the venture. In the same year, plans were announced to merge its bar code scanner and factory automation units and spin them off as DENSO Wave, Inc.

Principal Subsidiaries

American Industrial Manufacturing Services, Inc. (United States; 50%); ASMO North America LLC (United States); Associated Fuel Pump Systems Corporation (United States; 50%); Australian Automotive Air Pty. Ltd. (Australia); Chongqing Denso Co., Ltd. (China; 94.2%); Denso Abdul Latif Jameel Co., Ltd. (50%); Denso Automotive Deutschland G.m.b.H. (Germany); Denso Barcelona S.A. (Spain); Denso Europe B.V. (Netherlands); Denso do Brasil Ltda. (Brazil; 75.9%); Denso Haryana Pvt. Ltd. (India); Denso Finance Holland B.V.; Denso India Ltd. (52.9%); Denso Industrial da Amazonia Ltda. (Brazil); Denso International America, Inc. (United States); Denso International Asia Pte. Ltd. (Singapore); Denso International Australia Pty. Ltd.; Denso International Europe B.V. (Netherlands); Denso International Singapore Pte. Ltd.; Denso International (UK) Ltd.; Denso Kirloskar Industries Pvt. Ltd. (India;

89%); Denso (Malaysia) Sdn. Bhd. (72.7%); Denso Manufacturing Argentina S.A. (97%); Denso Manufacturing Canada, Inc.; Denso Manufacturing Czech s.r.o.; Denso Manufacturing Hungary Ltd.; Denso Manufacturing Italia S.p.A. (Italy; 80%); Denso Manufacturing UK Ltd.; Denso Manufacturing Michigan, Inc. (United States); Denso Manufacturing Midlands Ltd. (United Kingdom); Denso Manufacturing Polska Sp.z.o.o. (Poland); Denso Manufacturing Tennessee, Inc. (United States); Denso Manufacturing Vietnam Co., Ltd. (95%); Denso Maquinas Rotantes do Brasil Ltda.; Denso Marston Ltd. (United Kingdom); Denso Mexico S.A. de C.V. (95%); Denso PS Corporation (Republic of Korea; 40%); Denso PS Electronics Corporation (Republic of Korea; 51%); Denso Sales Belgium N.V.; Denso Sales California, Inc. (United States; 80%); Denso Sales France S.A.R.L.; Denso Sales India Pvt. Ltd.; Denso Sales Italia S.R.L.; Denso Sales Korea Corp; Denso Sales Sweden AB; Denso Sales UK Ltd.; Denso Taiwan Corp. (80%); Denso (Thailand) Co., Ltd. (51.3%); Denso Thermal Systems S.p.A. (Italy); Denso Tool & Die (Thailand) Co., Ltd.; Denso Wireless Systems America, Inc. (United States); Flexdrive Industries Limited (Australia); GAC Corporation de Mexico S.A. de C.V. (49%); Korea Wiper Blade Co., Ltd. (75%); Kyosandenki America, Inc. (United States); Michigan Automotive Compressor, Inc. (United States; 40%); Nippon Wiper Blade (Malaysia) Sdn. Bhd. (80%); North Carolina Asahi, Inc. (United States); NWB U.S.A., Inc. (85%); Philippine Auto Components, Inc. (Philippines; 95%); Premier Instruments & Controls Ltd. (India; 12.5%); P.T. Asmo Indonesia; P.T. Denso Indonesia Corp. (58.3%); P.T. Hamaden Indonesia Manufacturing; Subros Limited (India; 13%); Tianjin Asmo Automotive Small Motor Co., Ltd. (China; 43%); Tianjin Denso Air-Conditioner Co., Ltd. (China; 51%); Tianjin Denso Electronics Co., Ltd. (China; 85.9%); Tianjin Denso Engine Electrical Products Co., Ltd. (China; 40%); TBDN Tennessee Company (United States; 49%); TD Deutsche Klimakompressor G.m.b.H. (Germany; 35%); Techma U.S.A., Inc.; Yantai Shougang Denso Co., Ltd. (China; 30%).

Principal Divisions

Electric Systems Group; Electronic Systems Group; Environmental Systems; Industrial Systems; Powertrain Control Systems Group; Thermal Systems Group.

Principal Operating Units

Automotive Business; New Business.

Principal Competitors

Delphi Automotive Systems Corporation; Robert Bosch GmbH; Visteon Corporation.

Further Reading

"Auto-Parts Maker Faces Profit Squeeze; Nippondenso Struggles to Cut Costs as Clients Push for Lower Prices," *Nikkei Weekly*, Finance Sec., February 21, 1994, p. 16.

"Bigger Is Better at Denso," *Economic Times* (India), December 3, 1999.

Butters, Jamie, "Japanese Auto-Parts Manufacturer's Strategy Does Not Include Retreat," *Detroit Free Press*, October 26, 2001.

Chappell, Lindsay, "Denso Serves as Delphi's Role Model," *Automotive News*, March 10, 1997, p. 20.

Cusumano, Michael A., *The Japanese Automobile Industry: Technology and Management at Nissan and Toyota*, Cambridge: The Council on East Asian Studies, Harvard University, 1985.

Do Rosario, Louise, "Riding the Slipstream: Business Ties Help Japan's Leading Car-Parts Maker," *Far Eastern Economic Review*, December 26, 1991, p. 72.

"Japan's Denso Aims for 25 Top-Ranked Products in 2005," *Asia Pulse*, December 17, 1999.

"Japan's Denso to Stop Making Mobile Phones," *Asia Pulse*, May 13, 2001.

Kamiya, Shotaro, *My Life With Toyota*, Toyota City: Toyota Motor Sales Company, 1976.

Moran, Tim, "Denso Committed to High-Voltage Future," *Automotive News*, March 12, 2001, p. 24G.

Nozawa, Koji, "Nippondenso President Sees Market for Auto Parts Still Expanding Globally; Company Changing Its Name to Reflect International Nature," *Nikkei Weekly*, Industry Sec., September 30, 1996, p. 9.

"Poor Sales of Luxury Autos Hit Parts Makers' Profits," *Japan Economic Newswire*, September 18, 1992.

Robinson, Aaron, "Denso Plans Growth in America," *Automotive News*, March 13, 2000, p. 38D.

Simison, Robert L., "Denso Is Wary of Consolidations Among Car Makers," *Wall Street Journal*, September 20, 1999, p. B11H.

——, "Japan's Denso, Auto-Parts Supplier, Pushes to Boost Sales to U.S. Big Three," *Wall Street Journal*, March 6, 1998, p. B9C.

Toyoda, Eiji, *Toyota: Fifty Years In Motion*, Tokyo: Toyota Motor Company, 1987.

Toyota: A History of the First 50 Years, Toyota City: Toyota Motor Corporation, 1988.

Vasilash, Gary S., "Denso's Clever New Code," *Automotive Manufacturing & Production*, February 1998, pp. 60–1.

—Roger W. Rouland
—update: Frederick C. Ingram

Detroit Tigers Baseball Club, Inc.

Comerica Park
2100 Woodward Avenue
Detroit, Michigan 48201
U.S.A.
Telephone: (313) 471-2000
Fax: (313) 471-2560
Web site: http://detroit.tigers.mlb.com

Wholly-Owned Subsidiary of Ilitch Holdings, Inc.
Founded: 1901
Employees: 320
Sales: $120.8 million (2000 est.)
NAIC: 711211 Sports Teams and Clubs

The Detroit Tigers Baseball Club, Inc. operates a Major League Baseball team that is a charter member of the American League, making it one of the longest-lived in the game. The team's many historical highlights include the tenures of legendary players Ty Cobb, active from 1905–26, as well as Hank Greenberg and Charlie Gehringer in the 1930s and 1940s, Al Kaline and Willie Horton in the 1960s and 1970s, and Lou Whitaker, Allen Trammell, and Cecil Fielder in the 1980s and 1990s, along with World Series wins in 1934, 1945, 1968, and 1984. In 2000. the team began play at a new stadium in downtown Detroit named Comerica Park. The Tigers have been owned since 1992 by Mike Ilitch, founder and owner of Little Caesar Enterprises, Inc. and owner of the National Hockey League Detroit Red Wings.

Beginnings

The birth of the Detroit Tigers dates to 1901, when baseball entrepreneur Ban Johnson sought teams around the United States to participate in his newly-created American League. Using as their basis nine players from Detroit's existing Western League team, County Sheriff James Burns and manager George "Tweedy" Stallings formed the Tigers, who took their moniker from a nickname Stallings' previous team had been given by a local sportswriter. In addition to the nine carry-overs, additional players were obtained from disbanded National League teams (the N.L. having recently shrunk from 12 to eight clubs).

April 25, 1901 was the day of the new team's first contest, and Detroit's Bennett Park saw an overflow crowd of more than 10,000 witness the Tigers' 14–13 victory over Milwaukee. At first the Tigers had no permanent home, playing weekday and Saturday games at Bennett Park and Sunday contests at Burns Park, as city laws prevented games on Sunday and Burns Park was located just outside the city limits. The team's first season ended with a respectable fourth-place finish, but manager Stallings was subsequently ousted, reportedly due to clashes with co-owner Burns. Burns himself soon joined his manager when he was forced by Ban Johnson to sell the team to insurance man Samuel F. Angus. Like Burns, Angus was required to cede a controlling 51 percent share of Tiger stock to Johnson, as were all American League owners during these early years.

With new manager Frank Dwyer in place, the 1902 season was less successful, seeing the team reach a seventh place finish. Dwyer soon gave way to another new manager, and over the next several years the Tigers were led by new men each season. In 1905, the struggling team acquired a player who would later make baseball history—one Tyrus Raymond "Ty" Cobb. Playing on a minor league team in Augusta, Georgia, where the Tigers prepared for the season at their spring training camp, Cobb's skill and highly aggressive style caught the attention of manager Bill Armour, who arranged for his acquisition in exchange for a pitcher and $750 in cash.

Early 1900s: Navin and Jennings Lead the Tigers to Success

Like that of his predecessors, owner Samuel Angus' tenure was a brief one, and by 1907 the team's presidency and ownership were in the hands of Frank Navin, who had joined the organization in 1902 as bookkeeper and had moved up the ladder by steadily acquiring ownership shares. The manager seat's game of musical chairs was ended in 1907 when ex-Baltimore Oriole Hugh Jennings took the job. The team began to click under Jennings, and with the legendary Cobb now in full flower the Tigers won the American League pennant in 1907, 1908, and 1909, though they fell short of a World Series victory against the opposing National League teams. Cobb led the league in batting, runs batted in, and total hits each of these years, and the entire Tiger roster had the highest combined batting average in the league.

Key Dates:

1901: The Detroit Tigers are formed and play their first season.

1905: Future baseball legend Ty Cobb is signed, beginning his 21-year career with the Tigers.

1907: The team wins its first American League pennant for new owner Frank Navin.

1912: Navin builds a new ballpark to house team's growing legion of fans.

1935: The team wins its first World Series; Navin dies and the team is taken over by Walter Briggs.

1945: A second World Series victory is claimed when the Tigers beat the Cubs in 7 games.

1956: Briggs family sells team to investors led by Jim Fetzer and Fred Knorr.

1960: Fetzer buys out his other partners and renames team's home Tiger Stadium, formerly Briggs Stadium.

1968: Tigers win their third World Series; season attendance tops two million for the first time.

1983: The team is purchased by Dominoes Pizza owner Tom Monaghan for $43 million.

1984: The Tigers win a fourth World Series over the San Diego Padres.

1992: The team is sold for $85 million to Mike Ilitch, owner of Little Caesar's Pizza.

2000: The Tigers move into a Comerica Park, a newly-built stadium in downtown Detroit.

The excellence of the Cobb-era Tigers sparked growing fan interest, and the team's home games were often sold out. An expansion of Bennett Park in 1911 proved to be only a temporary measure, and in 1912 it was torn down and a new 23,000-seat facility, Navin Field, built on the same site. That same year the baseball season was marred by an incident in which the volatile Cobb ran into the stands and beat up a spectator who had been taunting him. After the umpire ordered Cobb off the field, the rest of the team also left the diamond, and then decided to go on strike. Unable to convince them to return, the Tigers were forced to play a game against Philadelphia with a pick-up team, getting trounced 24–2. The next game was cancelled, and then management convinced the players to return, though they were each fined and Cobb was suspended for ten games.

Ty Cobb consistently led the league in batting during these years, topping the mythical .400 batting average mark in both 1911 and 1912. He went on strike in 1913 after his request for a raise was turned down, eventually settling for $12,000, $3,000 less than he had asked for. Despite Cobb's stellar play, by the end of the 1910's the team was in a prolonged slump, and manager Jennings was dismissed after the 1920 season. His replacement was one of the few people who could get along with the aggressive, hot-tempered Ty Cobb—Cobb himself. Though the star was able to hold his personality in check well enough to manage his players, there was still plenty of tension on the field, and Cobb's long record of violent behavior continued unabated with incidents such as a post-game fight with an umpire that led to another suspension.

Nevertheless, Cobb was able to motivate his team to success, and the Tigers played well under his tenure, nearly winning the pennant again in 1924, a year that saw attendance top 1 million for the first time. He finally left the team in November of 1926 and played his final two seasons with the Philadelphia Athletics. During the 1920s the Tigers had been helped by strong batters such as Harry Heilmann, but were hindered by a dearth of good pitchers and several bad trade deals in which future stars were bartered away for less stellar performers.

The 1930s: First World Series Win

After Cobb's departure the team saw several more changes of managers as its success in the standings remained erratic. Things got better in 1934 when the Tigers purchased Mickey Cochrane from Philadelphia for $100,000 to manage and play catcher, after attempts to hire Yankee legend Babe Ruth had failed. An intense competitor like Cobb, Cochrane was also a better "people person" and proved an instant success, leading the Tigers to a pennant win in 1934 and a pennant and a World Series win in 1935. Among the legendary players who contributed to the team's success in this era were pitcher "Schoolboy" Rowe and sluggers "Goose" Goslin, Charlie Gehringer, and Hank Greenberg, the latter one of the rare Jewish major leaguers, a full decade before Jackie Robinson broke the color barrier for blacks.

The success of the 1934–35 seasons brought record revenues for the team, with attendance again topping a million during the latter year. Owner Frank Navin was only briefly able to appreciate his team's championship status, however, dying at the age of 64 in November 1935. Upon his death his partner, William Briggs, took over sole ownership of the Tigers. Briggs soon set about expanding the stadium, and by 1938 it had a capacity of 53,000, more than double the original figure.

The team's 1935 championship season was followed by several less successful ones, and in 1938 Cochrane was relieved of his job in mid-season and replaced with Del Baker. The team's energy seemed to be revived, and the 1940s started off on a high note with another pennant win. The war years were difficult ones for the Tigers, however, with many players inducted into the armed forces, including sluggers Gehringer and two-time American League Most Valuable Player Greenberg, who served overseas from 1941 through 1945. Greenberg's return in July of 1945 brought the team back up to nearly full strength, and it was the war veteran who put another pennant win on ice by blasting a grand slam home run with two outs in the ninth inning of the next-to-last game of the season. That year the team brought home its second World Series trophy, though it would be the last one for more than two decades.

The postwar years were ones of great fan interest, with an average of 1.6 million tickets sold each year between 1945 and 1950. The Tigers gave up their status as one of the two remaining major league teams to play home games exclusively in daylight when Briggs Stadium (as it was now known) hosted its first night game on June 15, 1948 under electric lights.

The team went through a difficult period during the 1950s. 1952 saw the Tigers' worst season ever, with only 50 wins and 104 losses, and also the death of Walter Briggs, Sr. His son,

Walter Jr. (''Spike''), took over the team's presidency, but four years later the Briggs family sold the team for $5.5 million to a group of 11 radio and television executives led by John Fetzer and Fred Knorr. The Tigers continued to struggle, however, and after a number of personnel and management changes John Fetzer bought out his partners to claim sole ownership, and also renamed the team's home Tiger Stadium.

A Return to Form in the 1960s

The 1960s proved to be a considerably better decade for baseball in Detroit than the previous one had been. With the team rallying under new manager Mayo Smith, 1968 proved to be ''The Year of the Tiger'' in Detroit, as the team won the pennant and then the World Series. Among the many highlights of the year were league Most Valuable Player Denny McLain's 31 pitching wins (the first time since 1934 any pitcher had topped 30). The Tigers won 103 games, a team record, and saw attendance hit two million for the first time ever. Stars of the team, in addition to McClain, included sluggers Al Kaline and Willie Horton, as well as key Series pitcher Mickey Lolich.

In 1969, Major League Baseball expanded, adding four new ball clubs and creating two divisions in each league, necessitating a post-season playoff series to determine the pennant winner. Detroit was placed in the Eastern division, which was a tough one that featured top competitors New York and Boston, as well as Cleveland, Washington, D.C., and Baltimore. Expectations were high in the wake of the World Series victory, but Detroit could not get on track and finished 19 games out of first place. 1970 was even worse, with the team failing to make even a .500 won-lost percentage. The Tigers subsequently traded self-destructing pitching star Denny McLain and several others. McLain was seemingly his own worst enemy, having endured suspensions during the season for gambling, pouring ice water on two reporters, and carrying a handgun.

The downward spiraling Tigers again sought a new manager, hiring Alfred Manuel ''Billy'' Martin after the 1970 season to replace Mayo Smith. The scrappy Martin put some spark back in the team, and it won the division in 1972, though losing the playoffs to Oakland. However, a year later Martin, too, was dismissed after one too many disagreements with Tiger higher-ups. Once again the manager's chair became a musical one, as the Tigers sought a leader who could bring consistent victories, but the team found itself enduring several last-place seasons. The year 1976 saw a new pitcher with an unorthodox style ignite fan interest, though the team's final standings were second to last. Mark ''The Bird'' Fidrych won 19 games for the team while talking to the ball, shaping the pitcher's mound with his hands, and performing other antics. At the end of the decade the team finally found a manager who would stick around when George ''Sparky'' Anderson was installed in the dugout.

The 1980s saw dramatic changes take place in the world of baseball. The influence of big television broadcasting contracts, among other things, gave professional players a sense that they were being underpaid, and the ''free agent'' market for top players changed the dynamic of the game forever, as star athletes no longer stayed with a team at the behest of management, but moved wherever the most money could be had. In June

1981, the players went on strike and the season was suspended for 50 days, with 53 Tiger games ultimately cancelled.

Ownership Changes in the 1980s

At the end of the 1983 season, John Fetzer sold the Tigers to Dominoes Pizza magnate and rabid Tiger fan Tom Monaghan for an estimated $43 million. The well-heeled Ann Arbor, Michigan, pizza maker soon outbid several other suitors for the services of free agent infielder Darrell Evans, the first time the financially conservative Tigers had taken such a step. Monaghan's tenure began with a season that saw the Tigers lead their division from opening day onward, racking up a record 104 wins. The team's momentum continued with a playoffs sweep and then a 4-to-1 win in the World Series over San Diego. The 1984 season also brought the Tigers record attendance of 2,704,794.

The team could not quite keep the momentum going, however, and despite a division win in 1987, by 1989 they were in last place, with just 59 wins versus 103 losses. After the season was over, Monaghan again brought out his checkbook and won the services of several free agents, including slugger Cecil Fielder. The post-season break also saw changes in the front office, when long-time Tiger president Jim Campbell left his post to assume the board chairmanship, and recently retired University of Michigan football coach Bo Schembechler was appointed to the top job. He was immediately faced with problems when the players, making threatening noises, were locked out by the owners during spring training. The issues were resolved a few weeks later, forcing a late start to the pre-season exhibition game schedule. The season was an improvement, though the Tigers still posted a losing record.

New acquisition Fielder earned his keep, belting 51 home runs and accounting for 132 runs batted in, the best in both categories in the major leagues that year. The 1990s saw the Tigers continuing to struggle on the field. In August 1992, another Michigan pizza franchiser, Mike Ilitch of Little Caesar's, stepped in to buy the team from Monaghan for an estimated $85 million. Monaghan's decision to sell was caused in part by his clashes with Detroit officials over his intentions to move the Tigers out of the downtown area. Ilitch, who had played baseball for a Tiger farm team in the 1950s, already owned the Detroit Red Wings hockey team, which he had built into one of the National Hockey League's most profitable franchises. Tigers president Bo Schembechler, who had never meshed well with the team's organization, also departed at this time. A major P.R. gaffe of the new regime was the decision to ask long-time Tiger radio broadcaster Ernie Harwell to retire, allegedly to bring a more updated sound to the team's broadcasts. The fans howled with disgust, and the genial, southern-accented Harwell was soon brought back to the microphone.

In 1994, the continually expanding major leagues were subdivided into three divisions per league, with the Tigers shifted to the five-team Central. Another player strike cut off the team's season at 115 games, and baseball's annual World Series was cancelled for the first time since it had begun in 1905. The Tigers were still stumbling, finishing last in their division during the shortened year, before a diminishing fan base that yielded the worst attendance figures in the major leagues. The once optimistic Ilitch now seemed disheartened, stating, "I think if I had known the shape baseball was in specifically . . . I don't think I would have bought the club."

The strike continued throughout the off-season and into the start of the 1995 baseball schedule. Manager Sparky Anderson took a leave of absence as the team scrambled to find players from their farm teams to fill in, only returning after the players and owners agreed to "no settlement," but to play ball. It would be his last season with the team—his 17 years comprising the longest tenure of any manager in Tiger history. He was replaced by the young and relatively inexperienced Buddy Bell.

Seeking a New Stadium in the 1990s

In 1995, the team appointed a new president and chief executive officer, John McHale Jr., who soon began working hard to line up funding for construction of a new ballpark to replace the outdated Tiger Stadium. The team's longtime home, which had been sold to the city for $1 in 1978, was one of the oldest stadiums still in use, and had none of the fancy skyboxes and luxury amenities favored by corporations for entertaining. Many previous replacement efforts had failed, including Monaghan's, but this time Ilitch offered more of his own money for the project, and the deal was approved. After securing assistance from both the city and the state of Michigan, construction on the new stadium was started in downtown Detroit, on Woodward Avenue near the lavishly restored Fox theater, also owned by Ilitch.

While the stadium deal was being negotiated, the Tigers were still mired in the league cellar. During the mid-1990s, players shuffled in and out of the lineup with great regularity, another factor that contributed to a downturn in fan interest. The Tigers, like all major league teams, had a "farm system" of associated minor-league teams which served to develop young players and provide backups in case of injuries. In 1996, the team signed an affiliation agreement with the Grand Rapids-based West Michigan Whitecaps, who were enjoying great popularity. The Whitecaps would be the Tigers' first Michigan-based farm team in more than 40 years. Other Tiger-affiliated teams at this time included the "Triple-A" league Toledo Mud Hens (just across the border in Ohio, and closer to Detroit than Grand Rapids), the Jamestown, New York-based Jammers, the Jacksonville, Florida, Suns, and two Lakeland, Florida-based teams called the Tigers who played in different leagues (Lakeland having served as the Tigers' spring training location since 1934).

In 1999, the Tigers became a part of Ilitch Holdings, Inc., as Mike Ilitch restructured his financial empire. At season's end he hired another new manager, luring seasoned leader Phil Garner from Milwaukee with an estimated $1 million offer. He replaced former Tiger star Lance Parrish, a first-time manager who had taken Buddy Bell's place in September of 1998.

In 2000, the team made the transition to Comerica Park, whose name reflected a sponsorship agreement with a Detroit-based banking corporation. The first season in the $361 million stadium was another disappointing one, with the Tigers finishing below .500 yet again, 16 games out of first place. Ticket sales were given a boost by the move, however, jumping from just over 2 million the year before to more than 2.5 million.

Shortly after the next season began, team president and CEO John McHale, Jr. left to join the Tampa Devil Rays, and Ilitch took over his roles. A replacement was named in November, when Florida Marlins general manager Dave Dombrowski was appointed to head the organization. Shortly after he assumed control, the Tigers announced an across-the-board decrease in ticket prices, with the cheapest seats (only 319 of which were available) going for $5, and most priced between $20 and $30. Some prices now included free drinks and hot dogs or pizza slices, or coupons good for rides on the stadium's carousel and Ferris wheel. The team also appointed 1960s legends Al Kaline and Willie Horton to jobs helping with spring training and with the Tigers' minor league teams. The Tigers' centennial year of 2001 was another frustrating one, ending with a .391 won-lost percentage, next-to-last in the American League central division.

After 100 years in operation, The Detroit Tigers were looking to the future with a new stadium and general manager, and hopes for rebuilding the team into a pennant contender once again. With sports fan and downtown Detroit booster Mike Ilitch behind it, the ball club's recent lack of success would hopefully soon give way to a return to fighting trim.

Principal Competitors

Chicago White Sox Ltd.; The Cleveland Indians Baseball Company, Inc.; Toronto Blue Jays Baseball Club; Kansas City Royals Baseball Corporation.

Further Reading

Anderson, William M., *The Detroit Tigers: A Pictorial Celebration of the Greatest Players and Moments in Tigers' History*, Detroit: Wayne State University Press, 1999.

Lam, Tina, "Celebration Marks End of Long Road," *Detroit Free Press*, April 11, 2000.

——, "Ilitches Give Reins to a Daughter, Son," *Detroit Free Press*, June 20, 2000.

McGraw, Bill, "Ilitch's Local Success is Legendary," *Detroit Free Press*, June 20, 2000.

——, "Tigers of Different Stripes," *Detroit Free Press*, July 30, 1992.

McGraw, Bill, and John Lowe, "Ilitch Strikes Deal to Buy Tigers," *Detroit Free Press*, July 29, 1992.

—Frank Uhle

Deutsche Bahn AG

Potsdamer Platz 2
D-10785 Berlin
Germany
Telephone: (49) (30) 297-0
Fax: (49) (30) 297-61980
Web site: http://www.bahn.de

State Owned Company
Incorporated: 1920 as Deutsche Reichsbahn
Employees: 222,656
Sales: EUR 15.5 billion ($14.5 billion) (2000)
NAIC: 485112 Commuter Rail Systems; 482111 Line-
Haul Railroads; 48821 Support Activities for Rail
Transportation

Headquartered in Berlin, Deutsche Bahn AG (DB) is Germany's state-owned railway company. DB operates passenger and freight transport services, carrying some 1.7 billion passengers and hauling some 300 million tons of freight a year within Germany and to other countries. The company operates five business divisions: the passenger transport division consists of DB Regio AG, which operates commuter trains in Germany's urban centers, and DB Reise & Touristik AG, which manages mid-and long distance passenger transport and the company's tourism business; DB Cargo AG, the company's division for freight transport; DB Station & Service AG, which maintains the company's 5,794 train stations and related services; DB Netz AG, which is responsible for DB's 36,588 kilometers of railroad tracks; and DB Immobilien GmbH, which oversees the company's real estate. In addition, DB is involved in numerous other activities, including catering services on trains through its MITROPA subsidiary; local bus service in the western part of Germany; trucking, bridge, and tunnel construction; and power generation and advertising. DB also has a 18 percent stake in the phone company it uses, Mannesmann Arcor AG & Co, which ranks second in Germany's telecommunication market.

United in 1920 and Split Up in 1945

The history of Germany's railway is closely connected with the history of the country. As a part of the strengthening of central government during the Weimar Republic, the railways of the different German states were centralized in 1920 under the umbrella of Deutsche Reichsbahn, which in 1924 became Deutsche Reichsbahn-Gesellschaft. The Reichsbahn emerged as Germany's single largest employer. Including pensioners and the employees' families, some three million people belonged to the "Reichsbahn-family"—about five percent of the population. Reichsbahn was not merely their employer, it was their way of life. They lived in Reichsbahn-owned neighborhoods and joined Reichsbahn's many leisure clubs.

During the Nazi administration and throughout World War II, the Reichsbahn submitted to the government's criminal plans and had a crucial function in transporting Jews bound for death in the concentration camps, soldiers and war supplies to the front, and slave laborers and prisoners of war back to the homeland. In 1945, after the war had ended, Germany was divided into four occupied zones, each with an independent railroad network. The railroad company in the zone occupied by Soviet troops, which in 1949 became the German Democratic Republic (GDR), took over the old name Deutsche Reichsbahn. Beginning October 1, 1946, the Reichsbahn railroad lines in the American and British zones were placed under the control of a common central administration, based in Bielefeld. By September 7, 1949, the name Deutsche Reichsbahn was changed in the American and British occupied zones to Deutsche Bundesbahn (DB). In January 1951, the railroad in the French occupied zone was merged with DB. The formal merger of the DB took place when the Federal Railroad Act came into effect on December 18, 1951. The integration of the railroads of the Saar began in 1957 and was concluded in 1959 when the Saarland joined the Federal Republic of Germany.

Because of war damage, DB and Deutsche Reichsbahn began operating under extremely adverse conditions. Not only had buildings, permanent ways—tracks, points, bridges, and signal boxes—and fleets suffered badly during the war. As had happened at the end of World War I, the railway assets were used as

Company Perspectives:

If you want to experience the true Germany, travelling by rail offers a lot of attractive possibilities. Whether you are on a business trip or on holiday you are connected with nearly every town in Germany and you can reach every region comfortably and quickly.

reparation payments and numerous railroad tracks and other installations were dismantled, especially by the Soviets. DB had to carry out repairs and reconstruction predominantly by itself and had to bear the costs of paying maintenance and interim payments—grants to cover refugees' losses and help them to resettle—to railway workers expelled from central and eastern Germany and to their surviving dependants, as well as to those entitled to war maintenance. These and similar non-operating overheads were later transferred to the state budget. Furthermore, the alignment of the network, which before the war had run predominantly in an east to west direction, no longer corresponded to the traffic flows and now ran mainly in a north to south direction. The realignment of the network through building new stretches of track required much time and expenditure.

Struggling Against Competition

When the railroad first emerged in the 19th century, it had no competition and soon dominated cross-country transportation. However, especially after World War II, the automobile evolved as the new preferred means of transport for passengers as well as for freight. In the GDR, Deutsche Reichsbahn was granted a quasi- monopoly by the state, and freight transport on the road was limited and regulated by the government. In West Germany the picture was somewhat different. Beginning in 1950, largely owing to the increasing popularity of road transport, but also due to the declining significance of the coal and steel industry, DB's relative importance in the transport markets began to lessen. The company's market share of freight transport declined from over 60 percent in 1950 to about 40 percent in 1970 and 29 percent in 1990. In passenger business, DB had 6 percent of the total riders in 1990 as compared with 36 percent in 1950. In passenger transport, the motor car dominated the market with a market share of around 82 percent.

The evolution of new freight structures had an adverse effect upon the railroads as changes in Germany's industrial structure led to a dramatic increase in the proportion of goods better suited to road transport. The West German government accelerated this development with policies that favored roads over the rails. Between 1960 and 1992, DM 450 billion from the federal budget fueled freeway construction, but a mere 12.5 percent of that sum was channeled into the railroad network. In the 1950s and 1960s, DB's volume of freight carried grew considerably, from 203.2 million tons in 1950 to a historic peak of 351.8 million tons in 1974. From then on, the amount of freight transported declined. By 1990, freight volume totaled 275.1 million tons. The picture was somewhat different for passenger transport. While the number of rail passengers, including those using the suburban lines, dramatically diminished, and while there was a downward trend in the number of rail passengers

from the 1960s, passenger train services operated, including suburban lines, rose from 30.2 billion passenger-kilometers in 1950 to 38.5 billion in 1970, reaching 43.6 billion in 1990. The number of passengers rose from 1.28 billion in 1950 to a high of 1.47 billion in 1957, but since then tended to decline. In 1990, 1.04 billion people traveled by rail. However, riders on the state-subsidized S-Bahn rapid transit suburban services in and around densely-populated regions quintupled between the early 1970s and 1990.

DB tried in many ways to make its services more attractive in order to withstand competition from road transport. One of the most significant investments to enhance the competitiveness of the railroads was the increased electrification of the network. In 1950, it was envisaged that the electrified lines taken over from the Deutsche Reichsbahn be extended by 4,500 kilometers to a total of 6,000 kilometers. By the mid-1980s, this target projection was exceeded. The electrified network comprised around 11,700 kilometers in 1990. By then, more than four-fifths of DB's transport services operated on the electrified lines, which made up around 40 percent of the total network. Diesel trains ran on the non-electrified lines, while steam locomotives ceased to operate in spring 1977.

Apart from a few smaller stretches of new line, DB's major new construction program began as late as August 1973 with the commencement of work on the new line between Hanover and Würzburg. This line, along with the link between Mannheim and Stuttgart, were to replace the winding and heavily-used stretches through the mountain ranges of central western Germany. Work was delayed due to protracted planning and approval procedures and numerous legal proceedings. The two lines did not go into full service until the beginning of June 1991. The new Hanover-Würzburg line permitted the operation of freight traffic at maximum speeds of up to 160 kilometers per hour and InterCargoExpress services were able to cover the Hamburg to Munich corridor on night runs. The first closure of certain branch lines occurred at the end of the 1950s, but the network was not greatly reduced over the next 50 years.

Beginning in the 1970s, DB concentrated on speed and regularity of long-distance services. The Intercity (IC) system linked densely-populated areas with high rider volumes. IC trains began operation in winter 1971–72 on four lines, with trains leaving at two-hour intervals. In 1979, the interval for IC services was reduced to one hour, and in 1985 a further line was added. In freight business, too, DB reoriented its services to concentrate increasingly on the transporting of goods between industrial centers, where the high volume of traffic permitted the use of through trains. DB also reduced the number of part-load stations—terminals where freight trains carrying less than full loads are handled; reorganized the marshaling—or shunting—system, and in 1984 established the InterCargo overnight service. Since then, the eleven most important industrial centers in Germany have been connected by overnight services. For regional freight distribution, DB used trucks, of which it had between 3,000 to 4,000 under contract.

DB's involvement in inter-modal transport also helped to improve local collection and delivery services. The technology of piggyback transport and container transport, where only the transport vessel is changed, superseded the Culemeyer Stras-

Key Dates:

1920: Deutsche Reichsbahn is founded.
1924: The company becomes Deutsche Reichsbahn-Gesellschaft.
1937: Deutsche Reichsbahn-Gesellschaft is dissolved by the Nazis.
1949: The Deutsche Bundesbahn is founded in West Germany.
1990: The treaty for the reunification of Germany calls for the technical and organizational merging of the two railways.
1994: Deutsche Bundesbahn and Deutsche Reichsbahn are merged to Deutsche Bahn AG.
2000: The German government initiates a "future of the rail" task force.

senroller (wagon-carrying road trailer), the so-called private siding, a line leading off a main line to an industrial plant for collection and deliveries of freight. The container business was operated by DB's subsidiary Transfracht Deutsche Transportgesellschaft, founded in 1969. Despite the considerable growth rate in the volumes carried by inter-modal services, in 1989 piggyback and container traffic represented only around 8 percent of DB's total rail freight business.

Struggling Against Debt

DB had experienced financial difficulties since its foundation. In parallel with its decreasing economic importance and declining market shares, the company's revenues fell. Since its incorporation, DB made a profit only once, in 1951, and with the exception of 1955, the company's losses increased year by year. In 1960, the deficit stood at DM 13.5 million. By 1965, however, it had exceeded DM 1 billion. The company had received financial resources from the West German federal government since the beginning of the 1950s. According to the federal minister for transport, grants allocated to the DB between 1952 and 1960 amounted to DM 5.9 billion. In 1965, DB received equalization payments from the state of more than DM 1 billion. From the beginning of the 1960s, financial aid from the federal government was increasingly determined by both national and European Community (EC) legislation. This included equalization payments for the public sector, in particular to cover losses due to the imposition of cheap fares for commuter and school traffic, and equalization payments to offset losses due to the disadvantages suffered by DB in the competitive field—in particular, the enormous increases in social security payments, as DB ran its own superannuation scheme, as well as government ownership obligations such as interest payments and repayments for loans taken on by DB.

DB's deficits and the state's subsidies added up to almost DM 14 billion annually. It was not surprising, therefore, that DB came to be described as a drain on the budget. In 1974, Hans-Otto Lenel wrote in volume 25 of the ORDO-Jahrbuch that "the Deutsche Bundesbahn has been one of the biggest headaches in transport policy for more than one and a half decades." This statement has lost none of its relevance.

From the beginning of the 1980s, DB's statement of accounts made a distinction between the commercial sector, the public sector, and the state-financed sector. The commercial sector included particularly long-distance passenger and freight services. The public sector, subsidized by the government, included those services operated by DB which were unprofitable to run but had to be provided in the interest of the general public. This sector included short-distance passenger services. The state-financed sector included the provision of infrastructure.

An inheritance from its early history, DB's main financial challenge was its excessive personnel—not only the company's sheer number of workers, but the fact that many of them were civil servants who could not be laid off and who were eligible for high retirement benefits. To bring about DB's financial recovery, the company focused on the reduction of its workforce, which had reached a historic peak in 1948 at 602,000. Soon afterward, strategies to eliminate redundancy decreased DB's average annual work force to 530,000 in 1950, after which the number of employees diminished further. Until 1969, the number of employees fell to 398,000. The beginning of the 1980s brought an accelerated reduction in staff to 246,000 by the end of 1990. Expenditure on personnel represented around 70 percent of DB's total outlay. On the other hand, the railway had a chance to compete with road and air-based transport only if it invested considerably in its infrastructure, which was financed by loans. The interest payments on DB's huge debt consumed 15 to 18 percent of its revenues. As a result, the railway's debt more than tripled between 1970 and 1990.

DB's Struggle for Independence until 1990

Since 1920, the German railway had traditionally been a state-owned institution—a government agency and at the same time an economic enterprise. Thus, its ability to compete on equal terms with other carriers and its adjustment to economic developments and changes in structure were considerably restricted. The 1951 Federal Railroad Act stipulated that DB was to carry out its public service duties within the framework of a commercially run company. In general, the duties of operation, transportation, and fares were included under the generic term of public services. DB was obliged to provide rail transport, even on unprofitable sections of its network. The closure of lines required formal procedures in which various political bodies were involved. DB was also obliged to adjust its capacities to take account of transport demand at peak times. DB's fares were set by the minister for transport until the 1961 amendment of the transport laws—the so-called minor transport policy reform—gave DB greater freedom to set prices. However, fare changes still required the approval of the minister for transport. Until this change in the law, DB's freight rates had to be in line with those for long-distance road haulage and inland shipping. DB's freight rates were governed by the *Reichskraftwagentarif*, from 1989 known as the long-distance road haulage tariff, which hindered DB's competitiveness in the road haulage market.

The deterioration in DB's financial situation could not be prevented even by various plans for reform and restructuring. As early as 1958, the DB board of directors requested that DB be given more leeway to adapt to commercial market requirements. Prerequisites for this were equality in conditions after reform and restructuring in the transport field and the relaxation of the legal and financial relations between the state and the federal railroad. In 1960, the Brand Commission, established by the government to examine the state of affairs at DB, advocated a stronger commercial orientation in the field of transport; the discontinuation of the policy whereby only civil servants could be board members, managers of the business divisions at the DB headquarters, or presidents of the regional headquarters; and clarification of the financial relations between the railroad and the state.

In 1967, the government put forward the Leber Plan, its transport program for 1968 to 1972 which gave special attention to road haulage, planned line closures, and managed reductions in staffing. In 1969, the advisory committee to the minister for transport proposed that financial responsibility for the public service sector be imposed on the regional administrations requiring the provision of DB services. In the 1970s, the minister for transport set various objectives, the government commissioned projects, and the DB board put forward its conception for an optimum commercial network. These plans envisaged, amongst other things, the closure of lines leading to a halving of the network, DB's concentration on long-distance traffic, and staff reductions. In 1983, the government agreed to the guidelines presented by the minister for transport for DB's consolidation, according to which increases in productivity, investments, the closure of lines, and reductions in personnel were to lead to a 40 percent reduction in overall expenditure by 1990. In addition, a ceiling was set on government grants which were already authorized and running.

Beginning in the 1980s, managers from the private sector could be appointed to DB's board. Despite all these measures, government policy still did not allow DB the necessary freedom of action. As a result, DB's commitments toward public service duties were dominant until the end of the 1980s. Altogether there were no less than 16 initiatives for railway reform between 1949 and 1990, none of which was able to yield the desired results.

Reunited in 1994—the New Railway Reform

Two German railways co-existed for some 50 years—and started cooperating when tensions between the two governments relaxed somewhat in the 1980s—until the unexpected fall of the Berlin Wall in November 1989 gave way to the re-unification of the two German states. The treaty for the reunification of Germany included the takeover of the Deutsche Reichsbahn (DR) by the federal government and called for the ultimate technical and organizational merging of the two railways. In February 1993, the German government enacted new legislation which became known as the *Bahnreform*, and in December of the same year the necessary changes in the *Grundgesetz*, Germany's constitution, passed the governing bodies. In 1994, Deutsche Bundesbahn and Deutsche Reichsbahn were merged to Deutsche Bahn AG (DB) which was again owned solely by the state. The new entity got a fresh start, since the federal government took over DM 67 billion in debt and pledged to reimburse DB for the investments necessary to upgrade the former East German railroad to the Western standard. In addition, DB's public service obligations, in particular the obligation to provide affordable regional passenger transport, were transferred to the German states. A new agency,

the *Eisenbahnbundesamt* (EBA) was established to oversee all railway activities. DB was first split into five subdivisions and later organized into five business divisions.

However, the railway's problems did not disappear. Although its workforce was reduced by about one third, DB still had 203,615 employees on its payroll in 2000, and roughly a quarter of them were civil servants. Eastern European trucking companies which charged significantly less than established firms intensified competition in the freight transport market, and some of DB's biggest clients, such as the Post Office and large automakers, started moving their freight transports to the road. Half of all bridges in the railroad network were more than 75 years old, and two-thirds of the tunnels were over 100 years old. Between 1994 and 1998, DB invested DM 72 billion but was criticized for channeling much of the money into prestigious projects favored by politicians, instead of securing and improving the functioning of the existing infrastructure.

Throughout the 1990s, DB's chairmen demanded more entrepreneurial freedom—and wore themselves out in the task. Heinz Dürr, chairman of DB's board since 1991 and a driving force behind the new railway reform, was succeeded by a former civil servant at the Chancellor's Office, Johannes Ludewig, in 1997. By then, DB was again heavily in debt. In June 1998, the worst catastrophe in DB's history happened when a defective wheel caused an ICE to crash into a bridge at high speed near the German town of Eschede, killing 101 passengers. Besides the serious damage of DB's image, insiders estimated the long-term cost of the accident in the hundreds of millions. Ludewig was replaced by Hartmut Mehdorn, a manager from the private sector, in December 1999.

In the second half of the 1990s, new guidelines from the European Union required that railroads be independent of the state, that their infrastructure and use be separated, and that the use of the railroad tracks be made available to outside companies. While German politics seemed to go along with these guidelines, DB's management stressed the importance of an integrated railway system under its control. In 2000, DB's top management was united under one roof in the new ''Bahn Tower'' headquarters in Berlin. In that year, passenger transport accounted for roughly 70 percent of DB's revenues while freight transport contributed one quarter of the total. The new CEO described the state of affairs in the company's 2000 Annual Report: ''The situation assessment showed that—at halftime of the rail reform program—we still have tremendous deficits to overcome in infrastructure, our rolling stock, and our railway stations. It also showed us that the most difficult years of rail reform and restructuring are still to come.'' When he presented new prognoses of potential losses in the billions, it became clear that the initially planned IPO was not realistic. The German government initiated a ''future of the rail'' task force in December 2000, and management consultants from Arthur Andersen started to investigate DB's balance sheets for past sins. In early 2002, the establishment of an additional government agency to ensure fair competition on Germany's railroads was still pending.

Principal Subsidiaries

DB Regio AG; DB Cargo AG; DB Netz AG; DB Reise & Touristik AG; DB Station & Service AG; DB Energie GmbH;

S-Bahn Berlin GmbH; DB Anlagen und Haus Service GmbH; Deutsche Gleis- und Tiefbau GmbH; Deutsche Eisenbahn-Reklame GmbH; Deutsche Bahn Immobiliengesellschaft mbH.

Principal Competitors

Société Nationale des Chemins de Fer Français; Preussag AG; Vivendi Environnement SA.

Further Reading

''Anhaltende Talfahrt der deutschen Staatsbahnen; Hoffen auf die 'schwarze Null' im Jahr 1994,'' *Neue Zürcher Zeitung,* May 27, 1994, p. 36.

''Anklage wegen ICE-Unglück in Eschede,'' *Die Welt,* November 10, 2001.

''Bergungsarbeiten in Eschede vor Abschluß,'' *Die Welt,* June 8, 1998, p. 1.

''Bundesregierung nimmt Bahn AG an die Kandare—Regierungschefs tagen,'' *dpa,* December 13, 2000.

''Die Bahn will den 'Innovationsschub' mit hohen Schulden finanzieren,'' *Frankfurter Allgemeine Zeitung,* October 31, 1994, p. 22.

''Die Deutsche Bahn AG hat einen Gewinn von 350 Millionen DM erzielt,'' *Frankfurter Allgemeine Zeitung,* January 18, 1995, p. 14.

''Die Deutsche Bahn AG schreibt eine 'schwarze Null,' '' *Frankfurter Allgemeine Zeitung,* December 23, 1994, p. 16.

''Doch keine unabhängige Wettbewerbsaufsicht für die Bahn,'' *Frankfurter Allgemeine Zeitung,* January 8, 2002, p. 15.

Gall, Lothar and Manfred Pohl, *Die Eisenbahn in Deutschland,* Munich, Germany: Verlag C.H. Beck, 1999, 496 p.

Hamm, Walter, ''Das huschende Milliardengrab,'' July 29, 1997, p. 11.

Lambrecht, Matthias, ''Mit Volldampf bergab,'' *Die Woche,* July 17, 1998, p. 11.

Nolte, Paul, ''Stationsvorsteher haben nichts im Kopf als ihre Pensionsberechtigung,'' *Frankfurter Allgemeine Zeitung,* October 12, 1999, p. L46.

''Schuldenzug ist nicht zu bremsen. Bundesbahn fährt aus Krise nur mit neuem Finanzierungssystem,'' *Süddeutsche Zeitung,* December 30, 1992.

Schwenn, Kerstin, ''Mehdorns Zwischenprüfung,'' *Frankfurter Allgemeine Zeitung,* March 13, 2001, p. 17.

——, ''Weg vom Abstellgleis,'' *Frankfurter Allgemeine Zeitung,* December 16, 1999, p. 17.

''Schwerstes Unglück seit Eschede,'' *Die Welt,* February 7, 2000.

''Verkehr; Unternehmen Zukunftsangst,'' *Focus,* November 13, 2000, p. 30.

—Berthold Busch
—update: Evelyn Hauser

1·800·Mattress.
mattress.com

Dial-A-Mattress Operating Corporation

31-10 48th Avenue
Long Island City, New York 11101
U.S.A.
Telephone: (718) 472-1200
Toll Free: (800) 482-6554
Fax: (718) 482-6554
Web site: http://www.mattress.com

Private Company
Incorporated: 1976
Employees: 350
Sales: $90 million (2000)
NAIC: 731104 Marketing Utilities

Conducting business as 1-800-Mattress, Dial-A-Mattress Operating Corporation is a Long Island City retailer that popularized the selling of mattresses over the telephone. In recent years, Dial has expanded its 24-hour offerings to include bedding and other products and turned to the Internet to augment its telemarketing operations. The company sells brand name and private label mattresses, promising two-hour delivery in its primary markets. Sales outside of the New York City area are handled by franchises or through more than 500 partnerships with retailers across the country, for which Dial receives a commission. Although Dial's business is predicated on the belief that customers are willing to purchase mattresses without first seeing them, the company has opened a number of showrooms where mattresses are available for sale and from customers to see, touch, or feel.

Dial-A-Mattress Founder
Emigrates to America in 1968

Napoleon Barragan, founder and chief executive officer of Dial, was born in 1941 on a farm in Bilovan, Ecuador. Instead of farming he turned to teaching, eventually leaving Ecuador for Columbia, where he established a language school. In 1968, he sold the business in order to move to New York City with his pregnant wife and child. According to Barragan, he arrived with little more than ten dollars to his name and settled in a Queens neighborhood where friends and family also lived. While his wife, Kay, worked as an Avon Lady, Barragan took on manufacturing jobs, including work in a carpet factory and on the assembly line of a shoe factory. In 1973, he became a salesman in a furniture store, learned the business, and soon became the sales manager. By 1976, he scraped together enough money to open his own furniture store in a 1200-square-foot site on bustling Jamaica Avenue. This area of Queens was a major transportation hub and home to a large number of retailers— major department stores as well as mom-and-pop operations. Barragan's small storefront was located near York College, part of the City University system, prompting him to name his business College Furniture Discounters. Because he lacked the money to change the signs at this and a future location, he relied on the names of former businesses, Lerner's Sleep and Two Fingers Furniture.

With no credit or cash reserves, and relying on the sale of inexpensive furniture (such as seven-piece bedroom sets priced at $299), Barragan struggled to keep his business afloat and support his family. He worked 12 hour days and resorted to every sales strategy he could think of to move his merchandise, including the placement of one of his mattresses at a neighborhood fruit and vegetable shop with a hand-lettered sign that stated "Buy This Mattress!" An arrow directed customers to his nearby furniture store. On Sundays, when the store was closed, Barragan sold off some of inventory on the flea market circuit. Barragan's constant search for a better way to sell furniture culminated in a break-through moment on a New York subway car in September 1976. While reading *The New York Post*, he noticed an advertisement for Dial-A-Steak, a company that offered home delivery of cooked steaks. It was little more than a clever twist on a long-standing New York practice of food delivery, but the ad struck a chord with Barragan, and he immediately decided to try selling furniture over the telephone. After considering his stock, he settled on mattresses as the item best suited for his telemarketing idea. It was by no means, however, an obvious choice. Retailers had always assumed that most people would want to try out a mattress before purchasing it, but there were a number of factors that favored Barragan's idea. Mattress sales in New York were dominated by major department stores (Abraham & Straus, Bloomingdale's, and

Company Perspectives:

With its astounding success, 1-800-Mattress continues to develop an international presence and as in the United States has many imitators around the world.

Macy's), each with enough clout to force the major mattress manufacturers (Simmons, Sealy, and Serta) to produce exclusive products of what were essentially the same item. The result was a confusing array of choices and prices that fluctuated wildly, depending on which retailer was conducting a sale at any given time. Moreover, delivery could take up to six weeks. Part of Barragan's concept for selling mattresses over the phone included prompt delivery, just like Dial-A-Steak and the corner deli. Unwittingly, he would be tapping into a changing American lifestyle, where time and convenience would become crucial considerations.

Late-Night Television Ads Begin in 1978

Barragan launched his telephone retail business by placing a small ad in *The Village Voice,* promoting his cheapest line of mattresses: $29 for twin, $39 for full-size, and $49 for queen-size. Soon he began to receive telephone orders, growing to a high enough volume that he had to limit his delivery area to select parts of Queens and Brooklyn. Although Barragan's main business continued to be his furniture store, the extra revenue from telephone sales allowed him to move to a larger location in Queens on Steinway Street and to open a second store in the Harlem section of Manhattan. To boost Dial's mattress sales, in 1978 he turned to late night television, creating the company's first television commercial with New York Broadcast Services, whose Tom Pirrone coined what would become Dial's signature tagline: "Dial 1-800-MATTRESS, and leave off the last 's.' That's the 's' for savings." At the time, however, Dial relied on a local exchange rather than a 1-800 number. Nevertheless, late night television, which Dial chose simply because of low ad rates, proved to be an ideal time to sell to people in need of a new mattress.

Barragan was unable to accommodate late night calls, which always followed the running of its television commercials. At the time, he had two salespeople working with him in the Steinway store, and together they called back customers who had left messages the night before. During regular business hours, in between waiting on walk-in customers, they also took phone orders, although they continued to rely on the answering machine when everyone was busy. Dial fueled its growth by adding radio spots, allowing the company to expand its reach. Barragan acquired additional phone numbers for other area exchanges, so that print ads became crammed with the various combinations. Moreover, Dial's many satisfied customers spread the word about the company's bargain prices and strong service.

Barragan's early emphasis on prompt delivery, which became same day delivery and ultimately a two-hour guarantee, was perhaps just as important as the telephone concept. The key was convenience: not only could customers place their orders from home, they did not have to take off a day from work to accept delivery. Moreover, they had the right to refuse delivery

if the mattress failed to meet their expectations. At first Barragan relied on his own truck for delivery, although he and his salespeople were also known to deliver mattresses strapped to the roof of their cars. Eventually he would engage a number of independent truck drivers who were paid in cash. Because a large number of its customers paid for their mattresses in cash, Dial had enough currency on hand to pay its drivers as well as other staff, allowing everyone to under-report their tax liabilities. Although this was a common practice among small businesses struggling to make ends meet, Barragan continued to rely on it even after Dial emerged as a successful and highly visible business in the late 1980s.

Dial's reputation for solid customer service was also the result of its evolving telemarketing style, which was greatly influenced by an employee, Joe Vicens, who only began working the phones after he strained his back loading trucks. On Vicens' first day, Dial enjoyed its best sales day. He now became the person assigned to return messages left the night before and the first one to take phone orders during the day. His intuitive technique would soon be understood and adopted by Dial as standard policy. In essence, Vicens listened and asked questions to determine what the customer needed, rather than focussing on what he wanted to sell. Moreover, he was friendly and knew the products he was selling. However simple, it was an effective technique. Even as Dial computerized its operations, the company would make sure that its "Bedding Consultants" were thoroughly acquainted with the products they were selling, as well as the Dial-A-Mattress telephone style developed by Vicens.

Dial-A-Mattress Makes 1991 Move to Long Island City

In the early years of its operation, Dial relied on no-name mattresses. The major manufacturers simply refused to sell quality mattresses to what they considered a maverick operation, fearful that they would alienate buyers at traditional department stores and larger retail operations. Dial's customers, however, often requested brand name mattresses. Around 1984, Dial resorted to buying quality mattresses from Jack's Furniture in Manhattan, and later Cosmo's Furniture in Queens. Because Dial bought in quantity, it received a discount. The profit margin was smaller than with house brands, but at least Dial was now able to meet the specific requests of its customers. Eventually the leading mattress manufacturers noticed that Jack's Furniture and Cosmo's Furniture were selling an usually high number of mattresses, and they learned about the ties to Dial. By the mid-1980s Barragan was finally able to convince the manufacturers to directly sell their mattresses to Dial.

Dial placed increasing emphasis on television and radio spots, cutting back on print, so that by 1986 virtually all of the company's advertising was electronic. After hiring radio shock-jock Howard Stern to do Dial-A-Mattress ads on his morning program, sales surged. Many of the calls came from outside the boroughs of New York City, prompting Barragan to expand Dial's delivery area to a 50-mile radius. He stopped selling furniture and instead used his Steinway store to warehouse mattresses. In late 1987 he leased 5,000 square feet in the Ridgewood section of Queens, a space cut out of three adjoining brownstones where Dial was now able to have warehouse space, a call center, and a small showroom. Staff was spread out over three shifts in order to answer the telephones 24 hours a day. To accommodate his growing business, Barragan also sought to gain control of the 1-800-MATTRES telephone number, which would allow customers to call a single toll-free number and eliminate the various exchange-specific numbers to simplify Dial's advertising. While in the midst of securing the number, however, he learned that a New York businessman named Anthony Page had somehow managed to gain control of the number. Following litigation, in a landmark decision a court granted Dial the use of ''mattress'' with any exchange. Although Page retained the 1-800-MATTRES number, he was prevented from using it. An accommodation was eventually reached and at the cost of $500,000 Dial gained control use of the toll-free number.

To support his dream of creating a national enterprise, Barragan now invested heavily in computer systems. This endeavor was spearheaded by Joel Stewart, a Dial supplier who became the company's comptroller in 1988. Sales transactions that had been done on paper were now computerized, which not only improved inventory control but allowed Dial to better gauge the effectiveness of its advertising. The information resulted in smarter media buys. Nearly ten percent of Dial's sales were earmarked for advertising, fueling a period of rapid growth for the company. Despite reaching a new level, however, Dial continued its practice of relying on cash transactions and under-reporting tax liabilities, as employees were able to determine how much of their salary they preferred by check and how much in cash.

In 1988, Dial generated $4 million in revenues, an amount that doubled the next year, then grew to $12 million in 1990 and $16 million in 1991. By now Dial controlled 10 percent of New York's mattress business. Even a national recession that strained so many sectors of the economy proved to be a good business environment for the mattress discounters. In 1991, Barragan moved his expanding operations to Long Island City, located in Queens, the company's current location. The new 70,000-square-foot facility featured a high-tech telemarketing room where 90 bedding consultants worked around the clock, answering approximately 4,000 calls a day. Barragan and his rags-to-riches story was also gaining media attention, resulting in an appearance on the ''Donahue'' television show as well as an invitation to the White House.

Barragan aspired to greater heights by teaming up with distributors and selling some franchises in order to gain national reach for Dial, while also exploring the possibility of taking the business overseas. Moreover, he considered using 1-800 numbers to sell products other than mattresses. He teamed with a Brooklyn baker to create Dial-A-Bagel to sell New York bagels over the telephone and deliver them by Federal Express. Other telemarketing products he considered included pet beds, cosmetics, vacuum cleaners, computers, and carpets. Newspapers also reported that Barragan was thinking of taking Dial public. To assist him in his far-ranging plans, Barragan hired Jay Brzezanski, an experienced executive from Federated Department Stores, to become the company's chief financial officer.

On March 18, 1993, 35 employees from the New York State Department of Taxation and Finance, search warrant in hand, descended upon Dial to collect some 90 boxes of potential evidence, including a computer back-up tape that would ultimately reveal the company's accounting discrepancies. Officials estimated that Dial evaded over $300,000 in sales tax during the period of October 1988 and December 1992. Moreover a paper trail revealed that 150 employees received cash payment for which they did not pay income tax, including Barragan and other executives. Ultimately Barragan reached a plea bargain with officials. To gain immunity for his employees, who would be allowed to file amended tax returns, he agreed in the fall of 1994 to plead guilty to grand larceny in the second degree, subject to a $1 million fine and a year in prison. In addition, because he had never become an American citizen, Barragan faced deportation. In the end, he spent just 36 hours in confinement and served out the rest of his term in a individualized monitor program that allowed him to continue to run his business during the day and live in his own home at night.

Barragan's conviction clearly hurt Dial on a number of levels. Many of its competitors in mattress telephone sales, who had risen in recent years to challenge Dial, did not hesitate to turn Dial's notoriety to their advantage. Lenders were also reluctant to fund the business, and plans to go public were shelved, even denied to have ever existed. Nevertheless, Dial continued to grow, reaching $75 million in annual revenues in 1995 before beginning to slip. Primarily due to increased competition, sales fell to $70 million in 1996, prompting cuts in management salaries. Poor conditions then continued in 1997, resulting in Barragan laying off staff for the first time in Dial's history. He also cut his own salary by 50 percent.

To regain momentum in the late 1990s, Dial began to sell furniture. Barragan returned to the furniture business, launching 1-800-4-FURNITURE. Dial, which actually began selling mattresses over the Internet as early as 1994, also made a concerted effort to sell its products on-line. Coming full circle, Barragan opened a number of New York-area showrooms where customers could try out Dial's mattresses. He also continued to display an innovative spirit, creating what he called ''mobile showrooms,'' converted school buses that traveled to customers' homes or offices in New York City. Revenues improved to $80 million in 1998, then settled at $90 million in 1999 and 2000. In July 2000 Dial, opened its first superstore. Although Barragan and Dial faced difficult conditions, there was little doubt that he would continue to seek out new and innovative ways to continue to grow a prosperous business.

Principal Divisions

1-800-Mattress; 1-800-4-Furniture.

Principal Competitors

J.C. Penney Company Inc.; Mattress Discounters; Mattress Giant; Sears Roebuck and Co.; Select Comfort Corporation; Sleepy's; e-mattress.com.

Further Reading

Barragan, Napoleon, *How To Get Rich With A 1-800 Number,* New York: ReganBooks, 1997, 284 p.

Croghan, Lore, "Dial-A-Mattress Squeezed," *Crain's New York Business,* May 5, 1997, p. 1.

Fiedelholtz, Sara, "Entrepreneur Dials a Pile of New Business Idea," *Crain's New York Business,* July 27, 1992, p. 13.

Furman, Phyllis, "Stuffing a Mattress With Money," *Crain's New York Business,* March 13, 1995, p. 1.

Hoke, Hank and Pete Hoke, "Barragan Family Sleeps Well at Night," *Direct Marketing,* October 1993, p. 52.

McCune, Jenny C., "A Perfect Sleeper," *Small Business Reports,* July 1994, p. 24.

Messina, Judith, "Dial-A-Mattress Number Up?," *Crain's New York Business,* September 26, 1994, p. 1.

Taneja, Sunil, "Bedtime Story," *Chain Store Age,* July 1999, pp. 50–4.

—Ed Dinger

Digex, Inc.

14400 Sweitzer Lane
Laurel, Maryland 20707
U.S.A.
Telephone: (240) 264-2000
Fax: (301) 847-5215
Web site: http://www.digex.com

Public Company
Incorporated: 1991
Employees: 1,455
Sales: $168.1 million (2000)
Stock Exchanges: NASDAQ
Ticker Symbol: DIGX
NAIC: 514191 On-Line Information Services; 541513
    Computer Facilities Management Services; 541611
    Administrative Management and General Management
    Consulting Services

Digex, Inc. began the 1990s as an Internet service provider (ISP). Its enhanced data services made it a desirable takeover target for larger telecommunications companies, and in 1997 Digex was bought by competitive local exchange carrier (CLEC), Intermedia Communications, Inc. With Intermedia as its parent company, Digex expanded its Web hosting capabilities and became a separate public company in 1999, with Intermedia retaining control of the company. When Intermedia was acquired by long-distance carrier WorldCom, Inc. in 2001, Digex became a key component of WorldCom's business plan.

From ISP to Web Host: 1991–98

Digex, Inc. was founded in 1991 by Doug Humphrey, a Maryland entrepreneur, as an Internet service provider (ISP). By 1995, sales had reached $10.7 million, and Digex made plans to go public. Humphrey hired Chistopher McCleary, a telecommunications executive, as CEO, with Humphrey remaining as chief technology officer. In October 1996 Digex held its initial public offering (IPO) at $10.13 a share.

In June 1997, Intermedia Communications Inc., a competitive local exchange carrier (CLEC) that offered local and long-distance telephone service in competition with the regional Bell operating companies (RBOCs), announced that it would acquire Digex for $150 million, or $13 a share. From Intermedia's point of view, Digex was a desirable strategic acquisition because of its enhanced data services. At the time Digex was providing Internet access as well as Web site management and hosting services to more than 2,000 customers. Its first quarter revenue in 1997 was $8.7 million, and the company had 450 employees. Following the acquisition, Christopher McCleary remained as Digex's chairman, president, and CEO.

Later in 1997, Digex expanded its Web hosting capabilities by opening a second data center in Cupertino, California, to complement its original data center in Beltsville, Maryland. The new data center offered high availability through Web servers in different geographic locations. As a result, data would be delivered more quickly to Web site visitors. The second data center also added load balancing and site mirroring for Digex customers.

For the rest of 1997 and 1998, Digex gained high-profile corporate clients for its Web hosting services. When Martha Stewart Living (www.marthastewart.com) launched in September 1997, it was managed by Digex. Site traffic was estimated to be 2,000 concurrent users and 6,000 hits per minute, requiring Digex to add more servers. Other clients included J. Crew, Kraft, Mercedes-Benz, and Nike. Digex's strategy was to focus on larger organizations with well-defined needs and to provide them with a high level of customer support. According to *Network Computing,* Digex's customers reported a high level of satisfaction in the area of problem resolution.

At the 1997 Internet World trade show, Digex introduced three new Web hosting services: Insurance Server, Distribution Server, and Disaster Server. The Insurance Server provided failover support when a customer's server went down, regardless of where the server was located. Distribution Server utilized Digex's data centers in California and Maryland and provided customers with a Web server at each location. Visitors to customers' Web sites would then be routed to the closest server, thus reducing response time for site visitors and providing backup in case of an outage. The Disaster Server provided customers with backup within a guaranteed number of hours. It was designed for customers who did not want to administer two separate Web sites.

Also at Internet World, Digex introduced a new testing service that allowed customers to beta test their Web site in a production environment for a discounted fee. In addition, the company created a professional services group to expand its consulting services. Digex consultants would work with business customers on the development, testing, implementation, and maintenance of their Web sites. Specific services that were offered included developing an architecture and planning the site, stress testing, site migration planning, high-availability design, and performance analysis and tuning. By mid-1998 Digex had finished building its Web site performance testing lab, enabling the company to work with clients before and after they launched their Web site. The testing lab allowed stress testing a site to determine when and why it would go down.

Digex Spin-Off: 1999

At the beginning of 1999, Digex was focused on Web hosting and was operating more than 1,000 servers. Its plans called for the construction of additional data centers in the United States and Europe. In five years the company expected to be operating more than 20,000 servers. At the time, the market for Web hosting was projected to reach $15 billion in 2002, according to a study by Forrest Research, compared to less than $1 billion in 1998. In mid-1999, Digex moved into a new headquarters with 109,000 square feet and triple the Web hosting capacity of its previous headquarters. It was around this time that Mark Shull joined Digex as president and CEO. He was formerly in charge of GTE's Web hosting business unit.

In mid-1999, Intermedia spun off Digex as a public company, offering 49 percent of the company's stock to the public. There was a high degree of interest among investors in Internet-related companies at this time, and it was expected that going public would increase the value of Intermedia's investment in Digex. Digex's revenue had grown from $2.8 million in 1996 to $22.6 million in 1998, and revenue for the first quarter of 1999 was $9.4 million. Digex had yet to turn a profit, showing losses of $16.5 million in 1998 and $22.9 million in 1997. It had about 550 top-tier clients and operated some 1,300 servers. Following the IPO in mid-1999, Digex's stock rose to a high of around $160 a share in March 2000. From its peak, though, the stock tumbled over the next two years and was trading in the $2 to $4 range at the end of 2001.

For the rest of 1999, Digex introduced new, enhanced services. These included the SmartSecurity service, which monitored security information sites and sent e-mail notifications to customers when a security threat, such as a computer hacker, was detected. SmartBackup, another new service, guaranteed data recovery in four hours, compared to previous guarantees of two days. Digex also offered a SmartReporting service for both Windows NT and Sun Solaris servers. SmartReporting allowed Digex's clients to access Web site activity logs and see what their own customers were doing at their Web sites. SmartMonitoring was a new service that alerted Digex to any performance problems, and SmartAdmin gave Digex more network, software, and hardware administration capabilities.

Web Hosting Makes Digex an Acquisition Target: 2000–2001

At the beginning of 2000, Digex hosted more than 600 corporate Web sites and managed more than 2,000 application and database servers. Approximately 80 percent of the company's revenue came from Web hosting, another 15 percent from application service providers (ASPs), and about five percent from consulting. Digex's ASP business involved partnering with developers to bring more applications to the Web rather than competing directly with other ASPs. Digex provided an enabling platform and operations for its ASP partners, who then would market to their enterprise customers. Digex also offered its ASP partners the ability to test the reliability of their Web-enabled applications before offering them directly to corporate customers. Around this time Microsoft, Compaq, and Sun Microsystems were all making substantial investments in the ASP market. In January 2000, Microsoft and Compaq jointly invested $100 million in Digex to develop application hosting services using Microsoft software platforms and Compaq servers. The ASP market was projected to reach $22 billion by 2003, according to *PC Week*.

By 2000, Digex had gained recognition as an industry leader in Web hosting services through its high-profile clients. Its ad campaigns focused on well-known Digex customers such as J. Crew, Martha Stewart Living, Fila, and TWA. *Network Computing* magazine included Digex among the top Internet service providers. In mid-2000, the company launched a $7 million ad campaign that featured basketball star Shaquille O'Neal. The company also received a $4 million grant from the state of Maryland to create more than 1,000 jobs over the next four years.

In September 2000 WorldCom Inc., the second-largest long-distance telephone company in the United States, announced it would acquire Digex's parent company, Intermedia Communications, for $6 billion, including $3 billion in stock and $3 billion in assumed debt. WorldCom's bid for long-distance provider Sprint had been denied by regulators two months prior to its announced acquisition of Intermedia. The primary reason for WorldCom's interest in Intermedia was Digex and the higher profit margins associated with Web hosting services.

WorldCom's acquisition of Intermedia, which would not close until July 1, 2001, gave WorldCom control of Digex. Intermedia owned 55 percent of Digex's equity and controlled 94 percent of the company's voting interest. The acquisition

Key Dates:

1991: Digex is founded as an Internet service provider by Doug Humphrey.
1996: Digex becomes a public company.
1997: Digex is acquired by Intermedia Communications, Inc. and begins offering Web hosting services.
1999: Digex is spun off from Intermedia and becomes a separate public company.
2000: Worldcom announces it will buy Intermedia for $6 billion in order to gain control of Digex.
2001: Worldcom's acquisition of Intermedia closes, with conditions imposed by the U.S. Department of Justice.

marked WorldCom's entry into the Web hosting market, where Digex's Web hosting services would complement WorldCom subsidiary UUNet Technologies' managed services offerings to corporate customers. The acquisition accelerated WorldCom's ability to roll out new managed services by a year to a year-and-a-half. Although Digex already owned its own Internet network backbone, UUNet operated one of the most widely deployed Internet networks in the world, with more than 2,500 points of presence providing Internet connectivity in more than 100 countries. Digex also gained direct access to WorldCom's 28 data centers then under construction. Around this time Digex moved its headquarters from Beltsville to Laurel, Maryland.

The results of Digex's alliance with Microsoft and Compaq were unveiled in October at the Internet World show in New York. The new managed hosting platform, dubbed xFrame, was built on Compaq servers and Microsoft software. It enabled customers to access XML-based data from any of Digex's four data centers worldwide and let software developers write Digex-enabled applications. The xFrame platform remained in beta testing with about ten customers before it was more widely deployed in January 2001.

Mydigex.com, a new portal for Digex customers, was also scheduled to debut in January 2001. It provided Digex customers with access to a wide range of information, including server performance statistics, traffic use, bills and invoices, asset management, new orders, upgrade status, and more. Basic services were offered to customers at no charge, with advanced services such as high-level reporting metrics and stress testing having a fee. Analysts viewed the new portal as an attempt to improve customer relationships by offering value-added services and overcome the reluctance on the part of some enterprises to outsource more of their Web sites and applications.

Before the end of 2000, Digex launched a new data center in London, England, as the first stage of its plan to enter the European market. Although WorldCom's takeover of Intermedia was not yet complete, WorldCom formed a partnership with Digex and added Digex's managed hosting services to its expanded Web hosting product suite. Among the Digex managed services included in the deal were site architecture and configuration, leased hardware and software, server monitoring, and backup and recovery.

For the year 2000, Digex's revenue increased 181 percent, from $59.8 million in 1999 to $168.1 million in 2000. However, its losses also increased substantially, from $65 million in 1999 to $143 million in 2000. The company reported that it did not expect to reach profitability until 2003.

WorldCom Takeover: 2001

During the first quarter of 2001, Digex prepared for the anticipated acquisition of Intermedia by WorldCom by rolling out its infrastructure and operational standards at the WorldCom data center in Virginia. Digex's first quarter revenue more than doubled to $52.1 million, compared to $25.8 million for the first quarter of 2000. The company's loss grew from $25.6 million in the first quarter of 2000 to $44.2 million in the first quarter of 2001. Despite first-half losses totaling $57.8 million, Digex actually expanded its workforce by more than 100 workers in the first half of 2001 to 1,455 employees.

Meanwhile, the U.S. Department of Justice ruled that it would allow WorldCom to acquire Intermedia, but WorldCom would have to sell all of Intermedia's assets except Digex. That ruling was later modified to require WorldCom to sell all of Intermedia's Internet assets. In January, the Federal Communications Commission (FCC) approved the takeover and endorsed the Justice Departments stipulations. In March, a Delaware court approved WorldCom's settlement of a lawsuit brought by Digex's minority shareholders. Under the terms of the settlement, WorldCom agreed to give Digex shareholders about $165 million worth of WorldCom stock, with half going to shareholders of record on September 1, 2000, and the other half to shareholders of record when the acquisition closed. WorldCom also agreed to pay up to $250 million to cover Digex's expenses and to provide $900 million in loans to Digex.

WorldCom's acquisition of Intermedia closed on July 1, 2001. The deal was valued at $4.1 billion due to a drop in the value of WorldCom's stock since the acquisition was first announced. It was clear that Digex, which would remain a stand-alone company, was a key part of WorldCom's business plan. WorldCom planned to reduce its reliance on long-distance voice revenue and increase its presence in the lucrative data and Internet services business. With WorldCom's financial backing, Digex planned to expand its capacity and enter new markets with very low levels of capital investment.

Principal Competitors

AboveNet Communications, Inc.; Digital Island, Inc.; Exodus Communications, Inc.; Genuity, Inc.; GTE Corp.; IBM Global Services; Verio Inc.

Further Reading

Briody, Dan, "Heavyweights Vie to Define the ASP Model," *InfoWorld,* January 17, 2000, p. 20.
Callahan, Sean, "Digex Wages Shaq Attack," *B to B,* June 5, 2000, p. 30.
Cirillo, Rich, "Visionary–Digex: Working Faster for ASPs," *VARbusiness,* November 22, 1999, p. 60.
"Digex and WorldCom Link Up," *Communications Today,* November 14, 2000.

"Digex Launches in UK Ahead of Euro Push," *New Media Age,* November 9, 2000, p. 16.

"Digex Posts $13.6 Mn 2Q Loss, Expects Slowing Revenue," *Communications Today,* August 2, 2001.

Follett, Jennifer Hagendorf, "Tightening the Belt," *Computer Reseller News,* May 7, 2001, p. 134.

Fonseca, Brian, "Web Hosting Hand-Holding," *InfoWorld,* October 30, 2000, p. 10.

Gerwig, Kate, "Digex to Ease Growing Pains of Web Sites," *InternetWeek,* March 23, 1998, p. 31.

——, "Putting Web Sites to the Stress Test," *InternetWeek,* June 8, 1998, p. 35.

Goo, Sara Kehaulani, "Digex Loss Widens in Quarter and Year as Revenue Soars," *Washington Post,* February 2, 2001, p. E5.

Hurley, Hanna, "ISPs Improving Service and Support," *Network Magazine,* February 1998, p. 24.

"Intermedia to Buy Internet Provider DIGEX for $150M," *Telecommunications Report,* June 9, 1997, p. 4.

Jones, Jennifer, "WorldCom's Hosting Play," *InfoWorld,* January 22, 2001, p. 12.

Kady, Martin, III, "WorldCom-Backed Digex Hires—Yes, Hires—155 in '01," *Washington Business Journal,* May 25, 2001, p. 22.

Koblentz, Evan, "Compaq, Microsoft Help Digex," *eWeek,* October 16, 2000, p. 16.

Lapolla, Stephanie, "Web Hosting and Then Some," *PC Week,* September 15, 1997, p. 167.

Madden, John, "Digex Hosts Apps, Securely," *PC Week,* January 3, 2000, p. 32.

"Mark Shull—President and CEO, Digex," *VARbusiness,* November 13, 2000, p. 82.

Mateyaschuk, Jennifer, "Site Security Gets Tougher," *InformationWeek,* July 12, 1999, p. 36.

Moozakis, Chuck, "Intermedia Fills out WorldCom Lineup," *InternetWeek,* September 11, 2000, p. 12.

Munson, Christian T., "Another Era for Digex," *Washington Business Journal,* February 19, 1999, p. 1.

——, "Beltsville's Digex to Say Hello Again to IPO Arena," *Washington Business Journal,* April 30, 1999, p. 17.

Rogers, Amy, "Martha Decorates the Web," *InternetWeek,* September 15, 1997, p. 33.

Rooney, Paula, "IT Trio Takes Wraps off XML Platform," *TechWeb,* October 26, 2000.

——, "Microsoft, Digex, Compaq to Unveil xFrame," *TechWeb,* October 4, 2000.

Shipley, Greg, "Enterprise-Class ISPs: The Big Eight Revealed," *Network Computing,* May 15, 1998, p. 116.

Spangler, Todd, "Everyone Wants to Attend ASP Party," *Inter@ctive Week,* January 17, 2000, p. 14.

Stern, Gary M., "N@me Recognition," *Electronic Business,* May 2000, p. 116.

Sullivan, Bruce, "Digex Banks on WorldCom's Deep Pockets," *Communications Today,* May 3, 2001.

Sullivan, John, "WorldCom on the Rebound," *Boardwatch Magazine,* November 2000, p. 126.

"Sunny Days for Three Firms," *Washington Techway,* June 26, 2000, p. 13.

Torode, Christina, "Digex Gains Backbone Via Acquisition," *Computer Reseller News,* September 11, 2000, p. 10.

Wallace, Bob, "Digex to Host J.P. Morgan Site for Millionaire Investors," *InformationWeek,* March 27, 2000, p. 167.

Ward, Keith, "A Managed Success Story: Digex, Inc.," *ENT,* March 26, 2001, p. 1.

White, Suzanne, "Digex," *Washington Business Journal,* September 29, 2000, p. 22.

Williamson, Richard, "WorldCom Enters Web Hosting," *Inter@ctive Week,* September 11, 2000, p. 18.

"WorldCom Clears FCC Hurdle," *Communications Today,* January 19, 2001.

"WorldCom Closes Intermedia Deal," *Communications Today,* July 3, 2001.

"WorldCom, Intermedia Working It," *Communications Today,* February 20, 2001.

"WorldCom to Buy Digex, Intermedia in $6B Deal," *Washington Business Journal,* September 8, 2000, p. 21.

"WorldCom to Settle Lawsuit with Tampa, Fla., Firm's Web-Hosting Subsidiary," *Knight-Ridder/Tribune Business News,* April 7, 2001.

—David P. Bianco

Dionex Corporation

1228 Titan Way
Sunnyvale, California 94085-3603
U.S.A.
Telephone: (408) 737-0700
Fax: (408) 730-9403
Web site: http://www.dionex.com

Public Company
Incorporated: 1980
Employees: 805
Sales: $186.8 million (2001)
Stock Exchanges: NASDAQ
Ticker Symbol: DNEX
NAIC: 334513 Instruments and Related Products
  Manufacturing for Measuring, Displaying, and
  Controlling Industrial Process Variables

Located in Sunnyvale, California, in the heart of Silicon Valley, Dionex Corporation has been in the business of designing, manufacturing, and marketing analytical instruments since the mid-1970s. The company made its reputation with ion chromatography (IC) products, employing a revolutionary technique that permitted chemists to quickly separate, identify, and measure ionic components (or charged molecules) in complex chemical mixtures, even at very low levels of concentration. IC replaced more time-consuming wet chemical methods and found a ready market. Dionex IC products are used in such applications as environmental monitoring and the quality control of substances used in food, beverages, drugs, and cosmetic products. Its customers include corporations, research laboratories, and government agencies, both in the United States and around the world. Because Dionex's devotion to the constant improvement of IC technology, it controls more than 70 percent of a $200 million worldwide market, the same share it held twenty years earlier. Dionex is a much smaller player in the field of high-performance liquid chromatography (HPLC), a $2 billion market in which the company holds just a one percent share. HPLC uses light to separate and measure molecules. Furthermore, Dionex makes separation products that rely on the Accelerated Solvent Extraction technology it invented in the

mid-1990s. ASE dramatically speeds up the extraction of organic compounds for analysis from such complicated samples as soils, polymers, and processed foods. What previously required hours, or even days, can now be accomplished in minutes using ASE. The technology is used, for example, to detect the presence of PCB's in soil. Every year since going public in 1982, Dionex has posted record sales and earnings. In addition to offices located throughout the United States and a worldwide distribution network, the company owns subsidiaries located in Austria, Belgium, Canada, China, Denmark, France, Germany, Italy, Japan, the Netherlands, Switzerland, and the United Kingdom.

Developing Ion Chromatography in the 1950s

The idea for IC grew out of the Dow Physical Research Laboratory in Midland, Michigan, during the late 1950s. One of the early pioneers of the technology was Hamish Small, who was born and educated in Northern Ireland and worked several years for the United Kingdom Atomic Energy Authority before immigrating to the United States in 1955 and taking a job with Dow Chemical. According to Hamish's writings, there was no corporate mission at Dow to develop IC, just a belief that inorganic ion analysis would be an improvement over wet chemical techniques: Inorganic chromatography, as it was called then, was just a dream shared among such colleagues as Bill Bauman, Bob Wheaton, and Mel Hatch. Each was active, in one way or another, in ion exchange technology; none was trained as an analytical chemist. IC, however, gained little ground over the next decade. The researchers used water as an eluent and employed electrical conductivity to detect and measure ions in a single process. It was not until late 1971, according to Hamish, that he and his colleagues developed a chromatographic method that used ion exchange as the separation mode and conductivity monitoring as the means of detection. Once certain particles were ionized, however, it was necessary to find a way to see them through the noise. Thus, a suppressor device was introduced, a column of ion exchange resin that allowed the ionized particles to stand out. The final hurdle was to find the most suitable eluent. At first, sodium hydroxide was employed but an accidental discovery led the researchers to finally settle on a carbonate-bicarbonate solution, which would become the standard anion eluent for many years to come.

Aside from the laboratory challenges, the researchers faced resistance from Dow management, which at first did not recognize the importance of the new technology. After months of internal lobbying by researchers, IC became accepted within Dow, and once it showed commercial promise, a number of executives wanted the company to develop IC products. Hamish was not enthusiastic about that possibility, foreseeing the relatively tiny boat being swamped, and was relieved at the decision to seek an entrepreneurial licensee outside of the company.

At this stage, at least by today's standards, IC was still a crude process, yet it was already clear that what took chemists hours to accomplish could now be done in mere minutes. The company that appreciated the importance and commercial possibilities of the IC technology and purchased exclusive rights from Dow was the Palo Alto, California, firm of Durrum Instrument Corp., makers of analytical instruments. Durrum was owned by International Plasma Corp. of Hayward, California, established in 1969 to produce gas plasma processing equipment. It acquired Durrum in 1974.

Durrum established a separate business unit for its new IC products, naming it Dionex, derived from Dow Ion Exchange. To provide legal protection, Dow's patent department was active in securing a number of patents that were important to the growth of the new venture. In September 1975, the first commercial IC instrument made its public debut at the fall meeting of the American Chemical Society, demonstrated in the back of a rented van. It was also introduced to the scientific community in a paper published in *Analytical Chemistry*. At first the instruments were only capable of analyzing simple anions and used mostly to detect sulfates. Nevertheless, Dionex's claims seemed too good to be true to many chemists. Once the company proved that its product indeed saved time and money, however, it began to log steady sales and build a solid customer base. Dionex forged a close relationship with its customers and began to work with them to develop new methods, and eventually new products, to address problems that IC was particularly suited to solving. That customer interaction would become a cornerstone of Dionex's future research and development efforts, maintained to this day. For a number of years Dionex also continued to work closely with the Dow researchers in further improvements on IC technology.

A. Blaine Bowman Leads a 1980 LBO

The IC business unit was spun-off in 1978. While the business of its subsidiary grew, Durrum by 1980 reduced its emphasis on other products, and the parent corporation sold off the gas plasma processing equipment business to SmithKline. Dionex Corporation was then incorporated in California in 1980 to purchase the Dionex assets, a leveraged buyout(LBO) led by A. Blaine Bowman, a Durrum executive. Bowman had both a scientific and business background. He earned an undergraduate degree in physics from Brigham Young University and an M.B.A. from Stanford. Before joining Durrum as an executive vice-president in 1977, he worked as a Product Engineer at Motorola Semiconductor Products Division. After generating less then $1 million in revenues from the sale of IC products in 1977, the new Dionex reached 16 million in sales in 1981. In December of 1982, Bowman took the company public. Dionex would be reincorporated as a Delaware company in 1986.

Under Bowman, Dionex began its impressive string of record sales and profits, fueled in large part by devoting as much as nine percent of revenues to an ongoing research and development program. The first major improvement to the IC technology was realized in 1981, when Dionex introduced fiber suppressors. Instead of the operator taking time to remove the suppressor device and regenerating it with a chemical solution, fiber technology made possible continuous regeneration. Dionex also introduced in 1981 its series 2000i ion chromatographer, the first metal-free system, a far more versatile product that eliminated contamination caused by corrosive eluents. In 1984, Dionex took a major step when it offered the first PC-based IC workstation and the first on-line IC system from process analysis. The company also gained approval from the Environmental Protection Agency for its AS4 column in the analysis of anions in drinking water. Dionex's research efforts then produced a revolutionary breakthrough in IC technology with the 1986 introduction of its MicroMembrane suppressors, which now made gradient elution possible meaning the types of ions that could be analyzed grew substantially. To fully take advantage of the MicroMembrane suppressor, Dionex introduced its 4000I system in 1986.

Expansion and Acquisitions: Late 1980s and Beyond

Aside from technological advances, Dionex also expanded its business operations in the early 1980s, forming subsidiaries in Europe. By fiscal 1985, the company was generating more than $35 million in annual revenues. By the end of fiscal 1987, sales would top $50 million. Profits also showed continual improvement. Despite having no debt and substantial cash in hand, however, Dionex showed little interest in external growth. The only exception was the 1988 acquisition of Lee Scientific, maker of superficial fluid chromatography equipment, which allowed the company to enter into a related market.

To support its steady sales growth, Dionex employed a two-prong marketing strategy. In addition to direct sales calls, it improved its customer base in already established applications by using direct mailings and advertising in trade publications and at seminars and workshops. By continuing to work closely with its customers to solve specific problems, Dionex created new applications to be exploited commercially. In effect the company's marketing and research and development efforts converged. By 1993 annual revenues topped the $100 million level.

Most customers in the early 1990s were clearly interested in increased productivity, and Dionex responded with a series of affordable and reliable products that allowed a greater sampling capability, as well as ease of use. In 1990 the company introduced the DX-100, a low-cost system geared toward routine ion analysis applications. A year later came the DX-300, suitable for gradient and microbore applications. In 1992, Dionex introduced its Self-Regenerating Suppressor feature, which eliminated the need for chemical regenerants, replaced instead by water. Hamish, long since retired from Dow, collaborated with Dionex researchers in 1995 to help incorporate the AutoSuppression feature in future products and ultimately lead to what the company called its Just Add Water technology.

Some of the most important advances in IC systems were the result of improved software. In fiscal 1994, Dionex introduced its PeakNet Windows-based software, which was incorporated into a new line of PC-based IC workstations. Improved versions of PeakNet would result in even more productive systems.

In the 1990s, Dionex began to expand beyond its traditional IC products. In fiscal 1995, it introduced a new technology, Accelerated Solvent Extraction. The resulting systems would be used around the world for a multitude of environmental, industrial, and food and beverage applications. Although Dionex was engaged in small niches of the $2 billion high-performance liquid chromatography market, in 1998 it fully entered the business by acquiring a small German company, Softron GmbH, at the cost of $24.7 million. The Softron technology was combined with a Chromeleon software system to produce Dionex's Summit HPLC System for use by scientific, pharmaceutical, and industrial laboratories in analyzing chemical compounds. Moreover, Softron, with $10 million in annual revenues, provided a European customer base on which to build.

In fiscal 1998, Dionex topped $150 million in revenues while posting a $28.7 million profit. By fiscal 2001, revenues would improve to $176.8 million and net income to $31.4 million. During that year Dionex would also make one of the rare acquisitions in its history, the $12 million purchase of LC Packings B.V., a Dutch maker of liquid chromatography systems used in Proteomics and drug discovery research. The

Packings acquisition improved Dionexs position in the HPLC market. In a released statement, Bowman noted, "This will greatly improve our access to the leaders in Protoemics research, and our insight into the quickly developing needs of the major pharmaceutical and biotechnology companies doing this important work." Far from content with its success, Dionex was introducing more new products than ever before. It was also expanding its worldwide distribution channels. In January 2001, it increased it direct sales subsidiaries by opening offices in Denmark and China.

Despite boasting record profits each year since going public in 1982, Dionex remained virtually unknown to a vast majority of individual investors, with most of its stock owned by institutions. The company's business was difficult for most people to understand, a major reason why the price of Dionex stock was undervalued when compared to its competitors or to the market in general. The company had made money in both good times and bad, and appeared well positioned to continue its pattern of growth well into the future. Under Bowman, Dionex gained a solid reputation with its customers, who displayed their loyalty to the company by returning to buy more products. Good relations were maintained by not only having Dionex employees install its products, but with strong after-sales support as well. Moreover, an ever-widening network of distributors and foreign distributors allowed Dionex to spread its risk, with more than 60 percent of all sales coming outside of the United States. The company could also expect to improve significantly on its share in the HPLC market, with a short-term goal of becoming the third largest player. Perhaps the biggest challenge to Dionex in the years ahead would simply be its ability to recruit the number of trained and qualified technical people needed to keep pace with the company's growth.

Principal Subsidiaries

Dionex Softron GmbH; LC Packings Nederlands B.V.

Principal Competitors

Alltech Associates; Hewlett-Packard Company; Perkin-Elmer Company; Varian Associates; Shimadzu Corporation; Thermo Instruments; Waters Corporation.

Further Reading

"A. Blaine Bowman," *Wall Street Transcript,* September 30, 1999.

Autry, Ret, "Dionex," *Fortune,* July 2, 1990, p. 93.

Bowman, A. Blaine, "Dionex: Building on a Strong Past," *International Scientific Communications,* February 2000, p. 120.

"Dionex Corp.," *Barron's,* January 9, 1989, pp. 36–7.

Small, Hamish and Blaine Bowman, "Ion Chromatography: A Historical Perspective," *American Laboratory,* October 1998, p. 56C.

—Ed Dinger

DMI Furniture, Inc.

One Oxmoor Place, Suite 205
101 Bullitt Lane
Louisville, Kentucky 40222
U.S.A.
Telephone: (502) 426-4351
Fax: (502) 429-6285
Web site: http://www.dmifurniture.com

Public Company
Incorporated: 1911 as Huntingburg Furniture Company
Employees: 371
Sales: $97.14 million (2001)
Stock Exchanges: NASDAQ
Ticker Symbol: DMIF
NAIC: 337122 Nonupholstered Wood Household
    Furniture Manufacturing; 42121 Furniture Wholesalers

DMI Furniture, Inc. manufactures, imports, and markets furniture for the home and office. The company operates in four divisions: DMI Office Furniture, DMI Desk Company, Wynwood, and Home Styles. DMI Office Furniture offers complete collections of office furniture. DMI Desk markets both residential and home-office desks. Wynwood and Home Styles both carry lines of home furnishings, with Wynwood products being more upscale and Home Styles more casual.

Headquartered in Louisville, Kentucky, DMI owns and operates three furniture production plants and one sawmill in southern Indiana. In addition to manufacturing its own furniture, the company also imports from producers in Asia and Latin America. DMI sells its products through independent sales representatives in the United States, Puerto Rico, Canada, Mexico, the Caribbean, and Saudi Arabia. The majority of sales are to furniture chain stores and independent stores, wholesale clubs, catalog retailers, and independent distributors.

Early to Mid-1900s: Inception and Steady Growth

The company that is today DMI Furniture was first established as the Huntingburg Furniture Company in 1911 in Hunt-
ingburg, Indiana, a small town in the far southern part of the state. Its three founders—Edwin Fish, George Brown, and Harry Gabriel—were local businessmen who viewed furniture manufacturing as a promising enterprise for the area, due to the abundance of native timber. Incorporating their new business, the three men built a one-story brick building in downtown Huntingburg, hired some twenty-five workers, and began producing bedroom furniture. By June 1912, the company was profitable.

Throughout the 1920s, Huntingburg Furniture expanded its operations. In 1920, the company enlarged its original facility by purchasing the adjacent property. In 1928, still operating solely out of its Huntingburg plant, the company expanded its capabilities significantly when it purchased an additional plant in Ferdinand, Indiana. This second plant, which eventually came to be called the Stylemaker Furniture Company division, was remodeled for furniture manufacturing and enlarged with a 11,000 square foot, two-story addition. It employed approximately 90 production workers.

More expansion followed. In 1936, the year Huntingburg Furniture celebrated its 25th anniversary, two of the company's directors acquired a third manufacturing facility. They leased the plant, located in Huntingburg, to the company, enabling it to again increase capacity. That same year, the company purchased its second property in Ferdinand, Indiana—a former flour mill—for $2,700. By that time, Huntingburg Furniture had managed to amass considerable capital reserves—some $99,000.

The fast-growing furniture company made still two more expansions before the 1930s ended. In 1939, it purchased a two-story building in Huntingburg. Another former mill, the new facility was fitted out for furniture manufacturing, and soon began operations. That same year, the company purchased a warehouse in Huntingburg, which it converted into a furniture showroom.

The 1940s brought more growth. In 1941, the company expanded its offices to accommodate a growing administrative and clerical staff. In 1943, it acquired the Indiana Wood Industries, in English, Indiana, which it converted and renamed English Furniture Works. By the middle of the decade, the company's increased furniture production had resulted in an

---

Company Perspectives:

We are a vertically integrated manufacturer, importer, and marketer of office and residential furniture, and a leader in our primary product lines: home office and computer work-stations; desk chairs; commercial office furniture collections; casual lifestyle furniture; and collections of better quality, wood residential furniture.

---

increased need for dimensioned lumber parts—lumber that was pre-cut into precise, standard lengths and widths, such as two feet by four feet. To ensure its supply at a reasonable cost, Huntingburg Furniture partnered with another investor to organize and incorporate the Wood Cellulose Products Company. Based in Chattahoochee, Florida, the company served as supplier of dimensioned wood parts.

In 1946, Huntingburg Furniture sold one of its Ferdinand plants to a new furniture company starting up in the area. That same year, it acquired a former tomato canning factory in Marengo, Indiana, which soon became the Marengo Furniture Company.

Meanwhile, the company was exploring the prospects for business further afield. In 1946, Huntingburg Furniture purchased a former military airfield in Dothan Alabama. Dothan was located in the far southeastern corner of Alabama, approximately twenty miles from both Florida and Georgia. One of the most heavily forested areas of the United States, Alabama, like southern Indiana, seemed hospitable to the furniture industry. Huntingburg Furniture established the Napier Furniture Company on the former airfield, and it began operations in 1947.

1950s to Mid-1960s: Decentralization and Further Expansion

At the mid-point of the century, Huntingburg Furniture had grown to include seven production plants, plus a share of the dimensioned lumber producer in Florida. The company had also established trucking distribution centers, with company-owned fleets for moving finished product to its network of dealers. Huntingburg Furniture's manufacturing operations were grouped into four divisions: Huntingburg Furniture Company Plant, Stylemaker Furniture Company, English Furniture Works, and Napier Furniture Company.

Up until 1953, bookkeeping and record keeping for all the various plants were centralized in the Huntingburg office. In 1953, however, due to the geographic dispersion of the various plants, the company decided to establish separate offices for its four divisions. Managerial responsibility was also decentralized at this time, and the company hired a manager for each plant.

Huntingburg Furniture kept up a steady rate of expansion throughout the 1950s. In 1954, the company acquired a lumber company in Ferdinand, Indiana, which produced crating lumber and dimensioned lumber. The property was renamed, somewhat whimsically, the Wonderland Manufacturing Company. In 1956, Huntingburg Furniture constructed a 20,000-square-foot warehouse in Huntingburg, just east of one of its manufacturing

plants. In 1957, the company acquired a former pottery production facility in Huntingburg which it used the following year to house a newly acquired subsidiary: Fawn Lake Shops. Fawn Lake was a manufacturer of novelty tables and other decorative pieces.

In 1958, Huntingburg Furniture entered a new area of manufacturing and marketing: dining room furnishings. The company converted its former showroom to a production plant for the new venture, and created a division named Paragon Furniture Company. Also in 1958, the company bought out its partner in the Wood Cellulose Products Company for $200,000, becoming the sole owner of that subsidiary. The following year, as the 1950s drew to a close, Huntingburg Furniture purchased a new office building in downtown Huntingburg and moved its home office to that location. By that time, the company and its subsidiaries employed more than 800 workers, and had a sales volume of $7.8 million.

While the 1960s were to bring real change to Huntingburg Furniture, the decade started out with business as usual, which, for the expansion-minded furniture maker, meant acquiring new land and facilities and continuing to grow. In 1961, the company took several steps forward, including enlarging its Stylemaker Furniture plant in Ferdinand, Indiana, and broadening its delivery capabilities by acquiring a fleet of tractors and vans that had previously been operated by a local trucking line. Also in that year, the company acquired the land and buildings formerly owned by a furniture company and a panel company in Gettysburg, Pennsylvania. The facilities were put into operation producing bedroom furniture and given the name Timely of Gettysburg.

Two years later, in 1963, Huntingburg Furniture contracted with a landowner in Crockett, Texas, to establish the company's first operation in that state. Under the terms of the contract, the owner of the land agreed to build an 80,000-square-foot manufacturing plant and to lease it to Huntingburg Furniture at a set price for 25 years. The company also prepared to make further expansions to its Huntingburg operation by purchasing several acres of land on which to build a fabricator plant. Also in 1963, several of Huntingburg Furniture's subsidiaries—including Fawn Lake Shops, Napier Furniture Company, Wood Cellulose Products Company, and Timely of Gettysburg—were merged into the parent company.

Mid-1960s to 1970: Dolly Madison Industries

In 1964, Huntingburg Furniture's officers ordered an appraisal of the company's value. When the appraisal was completed in July, the results were good: The total fair market value of the company and all its assets was $5.25 million—$3.5 million more than the book value of the company's fixed assets. Armed with this news, Huntingburg's board of directors began exploring the possibility of taking the company public. In the course of talking with underwriters, however, they learned of a holding company in New York that was interested in acquiring Huntingburg Furniture outright.

The company was Rittmaster & Co., and it owned, among other things, Dolly Madison Foods—the maker of Dolly Madison ice cream. Rittmaster offered $6 million in cash for Hunt-

Key Dates:

1911: Edwin Fish, George Brown, and Harry Gabriel form the Huntingburg Furniture Company to produce bedroom furniture.
1928: Huntingburg Furniture expands its capacity by purchasing a second manufacturing plant, in Ferdinand, Indiana.
1936: The company adds its third and fourth manufacturing facilities in Huntingburg and Ferdinand, Indiana.
1945: The company purchases partial ownership in Wood Cellulose Products Company.
1963: Huntingburg Furniture merges several of its subsidiaries into parent company.
1964: Dolly Madison Foods acquires Huntingburg Furniture.
1970: Dolly Madison files for Chapter 11 reorganization.
1977: The company emerges from reorganization as DMI Furniture, Inc.
1998: The company forms Home Styles and DMI Office Furniture divisions.

ingburg Furniture, which was to become a division of Dolly Madison Foods. In September of 1964, Huntingburg's shareholders voted to okay the sale of the company.

During the first few years of its new ownership, the furniture company continued to expand with even greater vigor. In 1965, it acquired the assets of Carter Furniture Company, a Salisbury, North Carolina-based maker of upholstered furniture, office furniture, and stereo, television, and sewing machine cabinets. This acquisition added four manufacturing plants and in excess of $5 million in annual sales.

By the end of 1965, Dolly Madison Foods was engaged in a range of non-food related businesses. Over the course of the year, the company had not only acquired Huntingburg Furniture, but had also obtained a company that converted wood waste into fertilizer and mulch and had established a new division for leasing furniture. In early 1966, the company changed its name to better reflect the diversity of its operations, becoming Dolly Madison Industries, Inc.

In 1966, Dolly Madison expanded many of its furniture-making facilities, including the Stylemaker plant in Alabama, the saw mill in Indiana, the Timely plant in Pennsylvania, and one of the newly acquired Carter plants in North Carolina. The following year, the company saw good results in its new furniture leasing division; revenue more than doubled and earnings increased by 30 percent. Encouraged by this performance, the leasing division was expanded and turned into its own subsidiary—American Furniture Leasing, Inc.

Their leasing success notwithstanding, 1967 was a difficult year for Dolly Madison Industries. Sales in the furniture division did not increase enough to make full use of all the newly added manufacturing capability. Sales were also soft in the foods division, while operating costs increased. These factors

combined to drive year-end earnings down by 50 percent, from $1.5 million in 1966 to $755,658 in 1967.

In 1968, Dolly Madison Industries embarked on an acquisition campaign that was to more than triple its size by the end of the decade. The businesses it acquired during this period—some thirty-five in all—included several small furniture retail chains, various producers and distributors of foodstuffs, a carpet company, an upholstery plant, a maker of steel kitchen cabinetry and furniture, and a maker of ice cream and milk vending machines.

1970s to the Mid-1990s:
Bankruptcy and Reorganization

The company's efforts to become a super-conglomerate did not work as planned. In 1970, with $38 million in debt and a slowdown in furniture sales, the company filed for Chapter 11 bankruptcy protection. At the time the company went into reorganization, it consisted of 18 furniture manufacturing plants, 56 retail furniture stores, fourteen furniture leasing centers, and a host of food-related businesses.

During the course of the reorganization, which lasted for seven years, all of the food-related subsidiaries—and some of the furniture-related ones as well—were sold or dissolved. In 1977, when the company emerged from bankruptcy, its new name reflected its single focus: DMI Furniture, Inc.

The company's troubles were not over, though. Again pursuing an overly ambitious course of expansion, the company suffered through years of loss. According to an August 21, 1994 article in the *Louisville Courier Journal*, DMI lost $18 million in the first nine years after it emerged from bankruptcy. By the spring of 1986, the board of directors needed to install a new CEO for the struggling firm, someone who could turn things around. They found their leader Donald Dreher, the company's former financial officer, who stepped in as interim CEO. Although Dreher's stay was not intended to be a permanent one, it soon became apparent that he was the right man for the job. Under his leadership, DMI almost immediately began to improve. From 1987 through the middle of the 1990s, the company enjoyed record sales and did not post a loss in any quarter.

Part of DMI's turnaround was attributable to its ability to lower production costs by moving the bulk of its home office furniture manufacturing to China. In the early 1990s, the company first began importing product from Asian factories. While clearly cost-effective, the sourcing was not without its problems. One of the first hurdles DMI faced was an uneven level of quality in the finished product. To overcome this problem, the company took a more hands-on approach with its Asian producers, establishing an office in southern China with its own managers and inspectors. As it was able to ensure consistent quality, DMI moved more and more of its home office furniture production to China.

Late 1990s: New Divisions

At the midpoint of the 1990s, DMI was operating two furniture manufacturing plants in Huntingburg, Indiana, one in Ferdinand, Indiana, and one in Gettysburg, Pennsylvania. The company also had a saw mill and dimension parts plant in Ferdinand and a fabrication plant in Huntingburg. Its products include low- and medium-priced bedroom furniture, accent furniture, and home and office desks, conference tables, and chairs.

In late 1995, DMI idled its production plant in Gettysburg, and in 1996 sold the property. The following three years were marked by changes in DMI's product line and its structure, as the company both expanded its offerings and made clearer distinctions between the various markets it was trying to reach. In September of 1997, DMI launched a new division to produce and market a higher-end line of furniture. The division, named Wynwood, offered upscale bedroom, dining room, home office, and occasional furniture.

Just a month later, the company introduced another new division—DMI Desk Company. DMI Desk was formed to focus on home office furnishings and to help the company separate and expand its existing desk and home office furniture lines. In January of 1998, the company created their Home Styles division. Aimed at a younger, less affluent consumer, the Home Styles line included casual furnishings—including futon-style pieces, glider rockers, and kitchen islands and carts—that were affordable and easy to assemble.

Late 1998 saw still another division added to the rapidly growing DMI portfolio: DMI Office Furniture. This division, like DMI Desk, was designed to help the company better focus its sales efforts on the specific market it was trying to reach. Previously, office furniture had been marketed as part of its overall DMI Furniture product mix; by setting it apart, DMI hoped to achieve greater penetration of its distribution channels.

In 1999, DMI closed its Ferdinand, Indiana manufacturing plant, citing underused capacity. The company's sawmill and dimension mill in Ferdinand remained open. During the last few years of the century, it appeared that DMI's multiple-division strategy was paying off. Sales increased by 15 percent from 1997 to 1998, by 25 percent from 1998 to 1999, and by 30 percent from 1999 to 2000. Growth in the Home Office division was particularly strong, accounting for approximately 36 percent of the total sales increase in 1999 and 48 percent of the 2000 increase.

New Century, New Challenges

DMI's performance suffered somewhat in 2001, with both net sales and income declining—the latter by a sizable amount. This earnings nosedive was due not only to an overall economic slowdown, but also to costs associated with the company's decision to discontinue its manufacture of fully assembled, promotional-priced bedroom furniture. DMI recorded a pre-tax charge of $775,000 for inventory, bad debt, and severance pay for laid-off workers as part of the closing.

As 2001 drew to a close, DMI, like so many other companies, struggled against the ill effects of a recessionary economy. Even so, the company believed that the changes it had made over the previous few years had served to position it well for the future. In a November 2001 press release, Donald Dreher acknowledged that economic conditions were likely to damage the company's performance in the short term, but said he was optimistic about DMI's long-range prospects, stating that "we continue to believe in the operating strategy that drove the record setting performance in fiscal 1999 and fiscal 2000. . . . As the economy improves, we believe our domestic and Asian infrastructure can capitalize on the changing dynamics in the furniture industry and deliver long-term value to our investors."

Principal Subsidiaries

DMI Management, Inc.

Principal Divisions

DMI Office Furniture; DMI Desk Company; Wynwood; Home Styles.

Principal Competitors

Chromcraft Revington, Inc.; Furniture Brands International, Inc.; LifeStyle Furnishings International Ltd.

Further Reading

Gadzdziak, Sam, "DMI Reaps Big Dividends from Big Changes," *Wood & Wood Products*, July 1998, p. 65.
Ward, Joe, "Out of the Woods: After Years of Struggling with Its Identity, DMI Furniture Has Found a Profitable Niche," *Louisville Courier-Journal*, August 21, 1994, p. 1E.

—Shawna Brynildssen

Documentum, Inc.

6801 Koll Center Parkway
Pleasanton, California 94566-7047
U.S.A.
Telephone: (925) 600-6800
Toll Free: (800) 232-9250
Fax: (925) 600-6850
Web site: http://www.documentum.com

Public Company
Incorporated: 1990
Employees: 893
Sales: $197.6 million (2000)
Stock Exchanges: NASDAQ
Ticker Symbol: DCTM
NAIC: 511200 Software Publishers

Documentum, Inc. is a Pleasanton, California, company that develops, markets, and supports content management software. Its products allow businesses to create, personalize, organize, and share a wide variety of documents in differing formats simultaneously over the Internet as well as corporate intranets. Documentum customers include some of the largest corporations in the world, including AT&T, Bayer AG, Dow Chemical, Ford Motor Company, Pfizer, and United Airlines. The company has 25 offices located around the world, with a presence in such major cities as New York, Los Angeles, London, Munich, Paris, and Tokyo.

Documentum Origins in 1990

Documentum grew out the research efforts of Xerox Corporation's prolific Palo Alto Research Center. Established in 1970, PARC brought together prominent researchers to explore ''the architecture of information,'' resulting in many important advances in the computer world: the first commercial mouse, graphical user interfaces, bit-mapped displays, laser printing, the ethernet network, object-oriented programming, and much of the protocols essential to the Internet. Although the purpose of PARC was to develop new products for Xerox, internal conflicts between researchers and executives over funding and product strategy resulted in the departure of key personnel, who took with them important future technologies (such as the inventor of the Ethernet and founder of 3Com, Bob Metcalfe, and the inventor of graphic user interface, Alan Kay). While Xerox benefited from such developments as laser printing, far too many of PARC's advances were commercially exploited by collaborators, the most spectacular examples being 3Com, Apple Computer and Microsoft. The latter two used the ''point and click'' technology of graphical user interface as the key element of their personal computer operating systems. Frustrated by its inability to capitalize on its own research, and stung by criticism in the press and the book *Fumbling the Future: How Xerox Invented, Then Ignored, the First Personal Computer* by Douglas K. Smith and Robert C. Alexander, Xerox in 1989 formed Xerox Technology Ventures, essentially a venture capital program that would fund and spin-off start-up companies based on PARC research. The initiative was launched and run by a former Xerox executive vice-president named Robert Adams. Establishing Documentum was one of XTV's earliest efforts, based on in-house software developed in the early 1980s for Xerox's laser printing division. The document management technology was brought to Adams' attention and he recruited technical engineer Howard Shao to launch the new company. Shao had been involved with product development at database company Ingres. To help him in the start-up he brought in a coworker from Ingres named John Newton.

Documentum was incorporated in Delaware in January 1990, with Adams serving as chairman and Shao as chief executive. Not only did Xerox provide $3.5 million in seed money it allowed the new company to work rent-free in the back of a Hayward, California, warehouse. Moreover, Xerox lent its credibility to Documentum, giving the start-up access to the chief information officers at Fortune 500 companies. For the first several months the company was staffed by just Shao and Newton, but within two years it had assembled a team and was able to ship its first product, a beta version of its Enterprise Document Management System, which produced $500,000 in revenues for 1992. EDMS was intended to improve the productivity of major corporations by helping them to organize and manage their unstructured information, from text to images. While traditional relational databases managed structured data,

Company Perspectives:

With its proven ability to manage an unlimited volume of dynamic content, Documentum content management technology is an essential component of a scalable e-business infrastructure.

essentially information suited for tables, approximately 80 percent of a company's information, according to Documentum, consists of unstructured information. Given that a company's storehouse of information could expect to grow exponentially over time, the problem of managing documents and providing employees with a way to access them and work on them was clearly an opportunity for a company like Documentum.

New Leadership in 1993

With a developmental version of EDMS on the market, Shao recognized that it was time to step aside in favor of a chief executive with the skills to take Documentum to the next level, as well as boasting the credentials necessary to raise the next round of funding. It took Shao a year to recruit the man he wanted, Jeffrey Miller. Not only did Miller have a technical background, earning an undergraduate degree in electrical engineering and computer science, he held an MBA and had years of marketing experience. The early years of his career, from 1976 to 1983, were spent in various positions at Intel. He then gained experience with a start-up when he became the vice president of marketing at Adaptec in 1983. Miller next served as a division president at Cadence Design Systems from 1991 until mid-1993 when he joined Documentum. With Miller on board, Shao was able to assume the position of vice-president in charge of product development.

Miller was instrumental in developing a clearer focus on the business of Documentum. While at Cadence he had become familiar with the marketing theories of Geoffrey Moore, author of *Cross the Chasm,* who focused on how a company could enter a new marketplace, especially a high-technology marketplace, by concentrating on a specific application for a specific industry. For Miller, a start-up like Documentum offering a unique product was an ideal opportunity to apply Moore's principals, and he hired Moore to serve as a consultant for a month in late 1993. Moore conducted sessions with Documentum's employees, 30 at a time, during which they identified 75 business processes in specific industries that would be greatly improved by using the company's document management technology. In the end, the process narrowed the candidates down to one business process to target: the burdensome task of preparing a new drug application to the Food and Drug Administration. Because such an application included hundreds of thousands of pages, it required a considerable amount of time to compile and organize. Documentum estimated that a pharmaceutical company lost $5 million in revenues on a major drug for each week it took to complete the approval process. If Documentum could shave off time by helping to organize the application material, pharmaceuticals would gladly buy its product. Not only would Documentum become entrenched in an important industry, it would establish a base from which to target adjacent markets.

Documentum customized its software to address the FDA application process, then courted major pharmaceuticals Merck and Glaxo. Once they became customers, other pharmaceuticals bought in. As a result Documentum increased revenues from $2 million in 1993 to more than $10 million in 1994, 70 percent coming from pharmaceuticals. With the pharmaceutical business in hand, Documentum expanded its staff significantly in 1994 to bolster support and its direct-sales force. It then hired the former CFO of Borland International, Alan Henricks, to anchor the company's improved operational structure. The company also took steps to enhance its limited European distribution operations by setting up offices in London, Paris, and Munich.

In 1995, Documentum targeted an adjacent market to the pharmaceuticals: the commodity and specialty chemical industry. From there it was able to move into the discreet manufacturing sector, customizing its technology for aerospace, electronics, and automotive manufacturers, which resulted in customers such as General Motors and Sun Microsystems. Documentum was then in a position to tackle the adjacent market of engineering and construction. The result of this island-hopping strategy was that in 1995 revenues would grow to nearly $25.5 million and the company would post its first profit, $1.26 million. A year later sales would increase to over $45 million with profits of $4.5 million.

Documentum Goes Public in 1996

In 1996, Documentum became the first of the XTV ventures to go public. In February, the company raised $43.2 million on the sale of 1.8 million shares at $24 per share. By early May, it was priced above $45. Although Documentum was now an established business, it had to worry about challenges from large relational database companies, such as Oracle, as well as the possibility that a giant software company like Microsoft might decide to enter the market once a standard architecture had been established. Moreover, the dramatic rise of the Internet forced Documentum to essentially reinvent itself. In addition to employees accessing internal materials, businesses now had to also cater to countless Internet visitors. The increasing reliance of corporations on the combination of the Web and intranet systems, however, provided Documentum with an important driver for future growth. Early in 1996, the company introduced Accelera, which allowed customers to access Documentum's document repository with a Web browser. But in order to take full advantage of the possibility of document management on the Internet, other enhancements would be required, such as security.

In addition to modifying its technologies to the Internet, Documentum began to transition itself from a document management company to a company dedicated to knowledge management, of which document management was just a component. Simply arranging content would no longer be sufficient; management systems needed to understand the content they were organizing. To support this goal, Documentum acquired Relevance Technologies, a San Francisco content-mining developer, for $36.5 million. Its core technology, Semantic Modeling Architecture, permitted users to locate unstructured text-based information in both internal and external sources. With this expertise, Documentum planned to incorporate a stand-alone search tool into its products, allowing them to manage email documents as well as a variety of Internet material. The

Key Dates:

1989: Xerox Technologies Ventures is created.
1990: XTV funds Documentum start up.
1993: Jeffrey Miller is named CEO.
1996: The company goes public.
1998: Relevance Technologies is acquired.
2001: Miller is named chair; David De Walt is named CEO.

Relevance purchase resulted in a $23.5 million loss in 1998 on revenues of $123.8 million.

Documentum continued to add online capabilities to its products in 1999 and forged alliances with other companies in order to focus on content management that could power e-business. As a result of these expanded offerings, Documentum lost an additional $8.4 million in 1999 on revenues of $128 million. In the first half of 2000 the company was particularly aggressive in creating relationships with both systems integrators and technology partners. For instance, in March 2000, Macromedia Inc. and Documentum formed a partnership to integrate Documentum's content management system with Macromedia's Dreamweaver 3 Web authoring platform. Alliances with systems integrators included PriceWaterhouseCoopers and IXL. For these companies Documentum's technology became a key component in an overall e-business solution for customers. Miller made clear his long-term goals for the company in a June 2000 interview in *The Wall Street Transcript:* "The first mountain we want to climb is to become the undisputed leader in the content management business. . . . In a few years that's a $3–$5 billion marketplace, so whoever's going to get the leadership share there is going to be a very large, successful company, and we think we've got a great shot to do that." Many investors were encouraged by the steps Documentum was taking, and as a result bid up the company's stock in 2000. For the year, the company returned to profitability, posting net earnings of $8.7 million while significantly increasing revenues to nearly $198 million.

Early in 2001, Documentum made some changes to top management. Miller became chairman, replacing Adams who remained as chairman emeritus. Although Miller retained his CEO title, executive vice-president David De Walt became the company's president and chief operating officer. The company also began to experience a downturn in its business, due in large measure to a weak economy that caused many corporations to cut spending on major information technology projects. High-end software purchases such as Documentum suites were simply put on hold by corporate customers. After the company reported poor first quarter results, investors began to sell off Documentum shares. For the first time in its history the company was forced to cut overhead. In addition to imposing a hiring freeze, it reduced its work force by 12 percent, totaling some 140 jobs.

In August 2001, De Walt took over the reins as Documentum's chief executive, although Miller retained his chairmanship. De Walt was well suited to leading the company that was now emphasizing its e-business applications. He had been brought in two years earlier as an executive vice president to serve as the general manager of Documentum's e-business unit. Like Miller, he also combined a scientific background with business expertise. He earned a computer science and electrical engineering degree from the University of Delaware before doing graduate work in finance at the University of California at Berkeley. Although he brought new enthusiasm to the job, in light of economic conditions there was little De Walt could do in the short-term. In October, he oversaw a second round of layoffs, this time cutting close to 6 percent of Documentum's work force, approximately 57 positions, mostly in sales and marketing. Although times were difficult, Documentum had a solid business that, unlike an ephemeral dot-com company, produced revenues and had proven itself capable of posting healthy profits. With the eventual turnaround of the economy and increased corporate information technology (IT) budgets, there was every reason to believe that Documentum would quickly return to growing its business. With the ever increasing proliferation of information in the world, the need to manage it would only continue to accelerate.

Principal Subsidiaries

Documentum International, Inc.; Documentum Software Europe Ltd. (United Kingdom); Relevance Technologies, Inc.; Nohon Documentum K.K. (Hong Kong); Documentum GmbH (Germany); Documentum F.S.C.

Principal Competitors

Broadvision Inc.; FileNET; Hummingbird; Microsoft Corporation; Oracle Systems Corporation.

Further Reading

Avalos, George, "Pleasanton, Calif.-Based Document Software Firm Waits for Next Big Wave," *Knight-Ridder Tribune News,* June 25, 2001.

Beckett, Jamie, "A Formula for Success," *San Francisco Chronicle,* June 4, 1998, p. D1.

Gianturco, Michael, "Make That Paper Go Away," *Forbes,* January 12, 1998, p. 88.

Ginsberg, Steve, "More than Copycats," *San Francisco Business Times,* April 18, 1997, p. 8A.

"Jeffrey A. Miller," *The Wall Street Transcript,* June 26, 2000.

Kahn, Hal, "Documentum Crossed over the 'Chasm' to Success," *Knight-Ridder/Tribune News Service,* January 16, 1996.

Morrissey, Jane, "Startup Fills Doc-management Niche," *PC Week,* June 20, 1994, p. 123.

Mullin, Rick, "Documentum Crosses the Chasm," *Journal of Business Strategy,* May-June 1996, p. 50.

Schwartz, Susana, "Turning the Page," *Intelligent Enterprise,* May 15, 2000, p. 14.

—Ed Dinger

DoubleClick Click

DoubleClick Inc.

450 West 33rd Street
New York, New York 10001
U.S.A.
Telephone: (212) 683-0001
Fax: (212) 889-0062
Web site: http://www.doubleclick.net

Public Company
Incorporated: 1996
Employees: 1,929
Sales: $405.6 million (2001)
Stock Exchanges: NASDAQ
Ticker Symbol: DCLK
NAIC: 541810 Advertising Agencies

DoubleClick Inc., based in New York City, offers a variety of Internet marketing and advertising services. It originally acted as a broker that sold banner ads to a large network of Web sites and also used its proprietary DART technology to determine what ads to deliver to individual visitors. To keep pace with the evolution of Internet advertising, and to maintain its dominant position in the industry, DoubleClick has evolved into a broader based operation divided into five strategic business units. DoubleClick TechSolutions helps Web sites and marketers to deliver targeted ads. DoubleClick Media sells ads to the company's network of Web sites, which attract nearly half of all Internet traffic. The company's Direct Marketing unit makes use of consumer information gathered by Abacus, a 1999 acquisition. The Abacus database includes detailed information on nearly 90 million consumers drawn from catalogers. DoubleClick's Email Marketing Solutions uses its DARTmail technology to help advertisers target potential customers and create email advertising campaigns. Finally, DoubleClick's online research company, Diameter, provides tools to marketers to evaluate and maximize their online advertising efforts.

DoubleClick Formed in 1995

Although chairman Kevin J. O'Connor and Dwight Merriman are generally regarded as the cofounders of DoubleClick, in fact the company was originally a division of the Poppe Tyson advertising agency. In business for decades, New York-based Poppe Tyson was a traditional television and print ad agency that concentrated on industrial clients until its 1993 acquisition of a modest Silicon Valley online advertising agency, Carlick Advertising. In April 1995, Poppe Tyson created a division named DoubleClick in order to sell ads on the Internet. Operating out of California, DoubleClick created a network of Web sites on which advertisers could purchase banner ads. Member Web sites were required to sign exclusive deals with DoubleClick and allow the broker to coordinate the delivery of ads for the entire network. The goal, as always in advertising, was to reach a maximum number of potential buyers of a particular product while minimizing waste. In order to select an appropriate banner ad for a Web site visitor, however, DoubleClick required better technology than it possessed. O'Connor and his partner Dwight Merriman would fill that need.

Until 1996, O'Connor had never worked in advertising. Fascinated with technology since childhood, he earned a degree in electrical engineering from the University of Michigan, then dropped out of a Ph.D. program to become involved in the rise of the personal computer industry in the early 1980s. He recognized the future importance of the PC in a business world then dominated by mainframe computers, and he started a software company, Intercomputer Communications Corp., to develop a way for PC's to communicate with mainframes. Investors, however, did not share his vision for the PC, forcing O'Connor to scrape together his seed money by appealing to family and friends, as well as tapping into savings and even resorting to personal credit cards. Instrumental in developing the technology that contributed to making Intercomputer successful was Merriman, a computer science graduate from Miami University of Ohio. By early 1995, O'Connor sold his business to a larger rival, Attachmate Corporation. Both he and Merriman went to work for an Atlanta computer software company, Digital Communications Associates, ultimately quitting their jobs in order to start a new business together. As he had done some fifteen years earlier with personal computers, O'Connor recognized the future importance of the Internet and wanted to become part of the new medium. He and Merriman reportedly spent eight months brainstorming in a basement, developing 100 product ideas. O'Connor recalled that in September 1995, "all the stars lined up, and we realized advertising was going to be the key part of the Internet and we had the product that could solve a key problem." At the time, it was far from certain whether the Internet would develop into a subscription-based medium or be supported by advertising. Moreover, O'Connor understood that what differentiated the Web from television, radio, and print was its potential to deliver advertising to target customers, thereby eliminating a great deal of waste.

1995 Operations Merger

In 1995, O'Connor and Merriman created the Internet Advertising Network in Atlanta. Its first product offering was Internet Address Finder, which located email addresses. More importantly, the company was developing a way to target banner ads. Even though the goal was narrowcasting, O'Connor recognized the importance of selling ads to a network of Web sites in order to achieve the kind of mass exposure that advertisers required. In late 1995, the DoubleClick unit of Poppe Tyson was well on its way to creating the kind of network that O'Connor needed, while he and Merriman were developing the kind of ad delivery software that DoubleClick required. A ten-minute telephone conversation between O'Connor and his counterpart at DoubleClick paved the way for a merger of the two parties in early 1996. As part of the transaction, Poppe Tyson spun off its Internet unit, and O'Connor took over as the chief executive officer of the combined company, which retained the better-sounding DoubleClick name. Merriman became its chief technical officer. Poppe Tyson's corporate parent, advertising firm Bozell, Jacobs, also provided $2 million in capital.

O'Connor and Merriman moved to New York, setting up shop in the section of Manhattan that had become known as Silicon Alley. Within three months the new DoubleClick was selling ads to a network of 30 web sites, as well as continuing work on its ad delivery software. The initial product was called ClickBoosters. Essentially a robotic media planner, ClickBoosters was able to determine which Web pages generated the most traffic while spotlighting visitors that had yet to be exposed to a particular banner ad. It was assumed that new viewers of an ad were more likely to "click through," or actually visit the advertising site linked to the banner. The goal was to deliver fresh ads to Web visitors, a rough first step in targeted Internet advertising.

By the end of 1996, DoubleClick unveiled a more sophisticated system called DART (Dynamic Advertising Reporting and Targeting), which it used for its own network and made available to other Web sites for a fee. DART was able to garner far more specific information about consumers than ClickBoosters, in effect creating a digital shadow of the person behind the computer who visited a particular Web site. DART accomplished this by taking advantage of the "cookie" file used by Web browsers that allowed Web sites to store information on the hard drive of a visitor's computer. This small text file records information about a visitor ranging from site passwords to site preferences. Cookies have limited access to a computer, and allowing one Web site to create a cookie does not permit a different site to read that cookie. Users also have the ability to block the creation of a cookie, although many sites will not function without it. Aside from not knowing they can block cookies, a large number of computer users are simply unaware that information about their Web usage is being generated and stored on their computers. For DoubleClick, access to cookies placed by affiliated Web sites allowed it to take the next step in targeted Internet advertising. The company had limited information on the Internet activity that took place on specific computers, identified only by IP addresses, but it was enough to significantly improve the company's ad delivery business.

Late in 1996, DoubleClick signed an exclusive deal to deliver ads for Alta Vista, a major Web search engine and portal owned by Digital Equipment. Alta Vista would immediately become the greatest single source of revenues for DoubleClick. During its few months of operation in 1996, DoubleClick generated $6.5 million in revenues while posting a loss of $3.2 million. It was a successful enough start, however, to attract venture capitalists, and in mid-1997 the company was able to raise $40 million by selling half of its stock, a record amount for a New York start-up at that time. Not only did the company repay money owed to Bozell, DoubleClick spent $25 million to redeem shares held by some investors. During 1997, DoubleClick also took steps to expand its footprint in an emerging industry by establishing sales offices around the world (including Canada, the United Kingdom, Australia, and Japan), in addition to forming business partnerships to create Web networks in Latin American, Spain, Portugal, and Scandinavia. Gaining a dominant position was important, as the Internet grew at a fast clip in 1997. By the end of the year over 29 million people used the Web in the United States, and over 50 million worldwide. The price of PC's also continued to fall, putting them well within reach of most households, a development which promised to spur even greater growth for the Internet. For advertisers, the demographics of Web users were particularly attractive: almost half held a college degree, two-thirds were aged 18–44, and the mean household income was $53,000. DoubleClick's 1997 results reflected the steady growth of the Internet, with revenues increasing to $30.6 million. Due to its rapid expansion, DoubleClick also saw its net loss increase to $8.4 million.

In February 1998, DoubleClick was in the vanguard of New York new media start-up companies that went public. Underwritten by Goldman Sachs, DoubleClick's initial offering raised $62.6 million at $17 per share. Trading on the NASDAQ, the stock quickly rose in value, nearly doubling within a month to make DoubleClick into a $4 billion company. Although the company was not close to making a profit, it was gaining market share and becoming the dominant player in its field. By the end

---

Key Dates:

1995: Advertising agency Poppe Tyson forms Double-Click as a division of its company.
1996: DoubleClick is spun-off and merged with Internet Advertising Network.
1998: The company goes public.
1999: Abacus is acquired.
2000: Kevin Ryan is named CEO.
2001: The company's European division is sold off.

---

of 1998, DoubleClick's network grew to more than 1,300 Web sites. As a result, revenues increased to $80.2 million, with a $18.2 million net loss. Investors, however, remained sanguine about DoubleClick's long-term prospects, as evidenced by a successful secondary offering of 2.5 million shares of stock priced above $34 in December 1998.

In March 1999, DoubleClick raised another $200 million by selling convertible subordinated notes. Flush with cash the company was able to launch further international operations and make several strategic acquisitions in 1999. It acquired software maker NetGravity for more than $550 million in stock, a deal that filled in a major gap in DoubleClick's business. NetGravity offered software to Web sites that preferred to sell and deliver their own ads. Now DoubleClick could do business with customers who did not want to be part of its network of DART-managed Web sites. DoubleClick also became involved in e-mail advertising in 1999, a move that it supported by acquiring Opt-in Email.com, a privately held e-mail marketing firm. The most expensive and strategically important acquisition in 1999, however, was the $1.7 billion stock-for-stock purchase of Abacus Direct corporation, a leading information and research provider to the direct marketing industry. Abacus managed the nation's largest proprietary database of consumer catalog buying behavior, containing five years of purchasing history of nearly 90 million U.S. households, updated weekly. Shortly before the acquisition, moreover, Abacus had formed an alliance with other market research companies to create a cooperative database, the Abacus Publishing Alliance, to gain access to even more consumer information. For DoubleClick, Abacus promised to take ad delivery to the next logical step: matching the digital shadows produced by cookies with actual names, addresses, and buying histories. Rival companies were also moving in this direction, but when privacy advocates and the media soon protested the linking of consumer information, the ensuing firestorm of controversy was almost entirely focused on DoubleClick and O'Connor, who had been forthcoming about his company's intention of exploiting consumer information.

The Focus of Controversy in 2000

DoubleClick was clearly caught off guard by what turned into a public relations nightmare. Despite continuing to grow at an accelerated clip, generating $258.3 million in revenues for 1999, DoubleClick watched the price of its stock fall from a high of $135 in January 2000 to $81 in mid-February, when on top of private law suits the company found itself the subject of a Federal Trade Commission probe, as well as investigations

from the states of New York and Michigan. By early March 2000, O'Connor was contrite, telling the press, ''I made a mistake in moving ahead with these plans with no privacy standards in place.'' He announced that DoubleClick would not move forward with linking consumer names to Web activity, at least until the establishment of government and industry privacy standards. Consumers were also promised an ''opt-out'' mechanism to allow them to maintain privacy of their records. Furthermore, O'Connor appointed the former New York Consumer Affairs Department commissioner, Jules Polonetsky, to serve as DoubleClick's chief privacy officer. Rival firms followed suited, naming their own CPO's.

DoubleClick's changes did little in the short run to improve the company's public image, with critics maintaining that DoubleClick had instituted cosmetic changes, that opt-out provisions were mere window dressing, and DoubleClick was simply delaying its long-term plans to marry Abacus information with Web usage. In fact, DoubleClick, other Internet firms, and individual Web sites were already gathering consumer names on a voluntary basis, through product and site registration as well as contests that offered an inducement to reveal desirable information. Whatever DoubleClick's long-term plans may have been for Abacus, in the short run results for the unit were disappointing, accounting in large part to a free fall in the company's stock price. By mid-October 2000 DoubleClick shares traded at $12, down from a 52 week high of $135.25.

In the midst of its travails in 2000, O'Connor relinquished his role as chief executive officer, retaining the chairmanship of the corporation while Kevin Ryan, president and chief operating officer, became CEO. Ryan, a former investment banker, had previous media experience at United Media Inc. DoubleClick was not alone among Internet start-ups in transferring power from visionary founders to more seasoned executives, although DoubleClick's change appeared to be a more logical, fluid transition of power. Ryan maintained that he would continue to work closely with O'Connor, who would now focus on the future direction of DoubleClick, making sure it adapted to the ever-changing new-technology world.

In December 2000 DoubleClick cut staff for the first time in its history, laying off more than 150 employees. Although revenues grew to $505.6 million in 2000, almost double the $258.3 million generated the year before, DoubleClick's loss increased to $156 million, a significant increase over the $55.8 million the company lost in 1999. Moreover, there was no certain date at which the company would finally become a profitable venture. Nevertheless, DoubleClick was in a much stronger position than its competitors, which did not have DoubleClick's $900 million in the bank to see it through a difficult period in which the economy soured, investments dried up, and the Internet continued to search for its place among the mass media.

After enduring another round of layoffs in 2001, DoubleClick began to reposition itself as an online advertising infrastructure company. It established Diameter, a research unit designed not only to service Internet advertisers and marketers but to also compete against the audience measurement businesses of Nielsen NetRatings and Media Metrix. To bolster this endeavor, DoubleClick acquired@plan, an online market research Company, and signed a deal with comScore Networks to develop Web measurement tools. Through a series of acquisitions, DoubleClick also established a presence in email marketing, a field that held great promise. To improve the bottom line, DoubleClick sold off its European operation, which had accounted for a major portion of the company's operating losses. By the end of 2001, DoubleClick had shifted its emphasis away from banner and pop-up ads, the effectiveness of which had severely eroded as more consumers chose to ignore them, to become a full-service Internet marketer. There were few certainties in the new media world, and although the Internet was clearly established, many observers believed it would eventually converge with television. DoubleClick was betting that the Internet would remain a separate medium and, given its market share and cash in hand, the company hoped to be the last one standing among online advertising firms and finally emerge as a highly profitable business.

Principal Divisions

DoubleClick TechSolutions; DoubleClick Media; Direct Marketing; Email Marketing Solutions; Diameter.

Principal Competitors

24/7 Real Media; AOL Time Warner Inc.; L90, Inc.; Modem Media, Inc.; Terra Lycos, Inc.; Yahoo! Inc.; yesmail.com.

Further Reading

Angwin, Julia, "DoubleCLick Keeps Two Steps Ahead of Rivals," *Wall Street Journal,* April 26, 2001, p. B6.

Beatty, Sally Goll, "Poppe Tyson Leads the Charge of Agencies Signing on the Internet," *Wall Street Journal,* February 2, 1996, p. B3.

Brown, Eryn, "The Silicon Alley Heart of Internet Advertising," *Fortune,* December 6, 1999, pp. 166–68.

Edmonston, Peter, "DoubleClick Isn't Deterred by Ad Slump," *Wall Street Journal,* November 5, 2001, p. B9.

Messina, Judith, "New Media's Hot Play," *Crain's New York Business,* June 16, 1997, p. 1.

Moukheiber, Zina, "DoubleClick Is Watching You," *Forbes,* November 4, 1996, p. 342.

Petersen, Andrea, "A Privacy Firestorm at DoubleClick," *Wall Street Journal,* February 23, 2000, p. B1.

Petersen, Andrea and Jon G. Auerbach, "Online Ad Titans Bet Big in Race to Trace Consumers' Web Tracks," *Wall Street Journal,* November 8, 1999, p. B1.

Reeves, Scott, "Offerings in the Offing: To DoubleClick or Not to DoubleClick?," *Barron's,* February 16, 1998, p. 34.

Rewick, Jennifer, "DoubleClick Plans Its First Layoffs Ever, Signaling Depth of Online-Ad Slowdown," *Wall Street Journal,* December 5, 2000, p. B8.

Rothenberg, Randall, "An Advertising Power, but Just What Does DoubleClick Do?" *New York Times,* September 22, 1999, p. 14.

Schrage, Michael, "The IQ Q&A: Kevin O'Connor," *Adweek,* January 18, 1999, pp. A12–A18.

Warner, Melanie, "DoubleClick," *Fortune,* July 8, 1996, p. 104.

Weber, Thomas E., "New Software Helps Advertisers Get Through Tangled Web Pages," *Wall Street Journal,* October 23, 1996, p. B5.

—Ed Dinger

EDO Corporation

60 East 42nd Street, Suite 5010
New York, New York 10165
U.S.A.
Telephone: (212) 716-2000
Fax: (212) 716-2050
Web site: http://www.edocorp.com

Public Company
Incorporated: 1925 as Edo Aircraft Corp.
Employees: 1,500
Sales: $260 million (2000)
Stock Exchanges: New York
Ticker Symbol: EDO
NAIC: 334511 Search, Detection, Navigation, Guidance, Aeronautical, and Nautical System and Instrument Manufacturing

Long Island-based EDO Corporation, with corporate offices in Manhattan, manufactures an array of highly engineered products, mostly catering to defense customers, which account for approximately 70 percent of all sales. EDO is organized into three segments: Defense, Communications and Space Products, and Engineered Materials. Defense products include bomb racks, electronic surveillance and jamming systems, underwater communication systems, sonar sensors, and helicopter-towed minesweepers. EDO's Communications and Space products include antenna products used on military as well as private aircraft, and sensor and communication products used by NASA and commercial satellites. EDO's Engineered Products consist of electro-ceramic products and fiber composite structural products.

EDO Aircraft Corporation Founded in 1925

EDO's founder was Earl Dodge Osborn, a little-remembered aviation pioneer. Born in 1893, Osborn graduated from Princeton University in 1915. Before America entered World War I, he traveled to Europe to be part of the American Ambulance and Commission for Relief. He was wounded at the Battle of

Verdun in 1917 and awarded the Croix de Guerre before subsequently enlisting in the 78th Division of the American Expeditionary Force. After the war Osborn learned to fly and became a passionate supporter of aviation, in particular the seaplane. He went to work for the Aeromarine Airways Company, a pioneering effort to transport passengers via seaplanes. Osborn was also gaining a reputation as a writer, becoming editor and publisher (and ultimately owner) of *Aviation* magazine from 1924 to 1929. In 1925, at the age of 32, he decided to become involved in the manufacture of low-powered seaplanes, establishing EDO Aircraft Corp., the name derived from the initials of his name. He set up shop with 14 employees on the shore of Flushing Bay in a small building in College Point, a small town located on the outskirts of New York City. Years later, La Guardia Airport would be built across the water.

Shortly after the Wright Brothers launched the aviation industry, inventors like the Frenchman Henri Fabre and American Glenn Curtiss developed planes that could take off and land on water, which made any sizeable body of water a potential airstrip. Early seaplanes relied on wooden floats, or pontoons, which were not only heavy but were susceptible to water damage after long-term use. Osborn opted to construct his floats out of aluminum, which was lightweight, strong, and durable. Although his Malolo single engine plane was the first to employ aluminum floats in 1926, Osborn quickly realized that there was no demand for such a low-powered seaplane. With seaplanes opening up remote locations around the world to aviation, however, he recognized that there was a sizeable market for his aluminum floats. EDO's first production floats were designed for the popular WACO 9 biplane, which lacked the power to lift out of the water using wooden floats. Subsequently, EDO improved its floats by fluting the bottoms, an innovation that greatly increased a plane's ability to lift out of the water and made the reputation of the new company. EDO's aluminum floats soon became the equipment of choice for all seaplanes, which, because of the lightweight floats, improved performance and gained even greater usage. The company's work force grew to 100 by the end of the 1920s, when EDO produced eight different models of floats that were used on 25 different makes of airplanes. EDO floats would play an important role in many of the early speed and endurance records, as well as feats of

Company Perspectives:

EDO Corporation is a supplier of highly engineered products for governments and industry worldwide. Our advanced electronic, electromechanical, and information systems and engineered materials are products which are critical to the mission success of our customers.

exploration. In 1930, the first non-stop flight from New York to Bermuda was accomplished by a seaplane fitted with EDO floats. In 1933, Admiral Richard Byrd explored the South Pole in a Curtiss Condor biplane using EDO's floats. Lincoln Ellsworth in 1935 flew similar flights over the North Pole in a Northrop Gamms equipped with EDO aluminum floats. Although EDO had competition in the manufacture of floats, it had no true rivals, finishing the 1930s as the world's leading maker of this product.

EDO Becomes a Defense Contractor

It was World War II and the need to put a large number of planes on floats that would lead to the U.S. military becoming EDO's major customer. Even before the attack on Pearl Harbor that precipitated the entry of the United States into the conflict, EDO was geared up for the war effort. The company, with its beefed-up work force of more than 1,000, had already begun the task of fitting a wide variety of military aircraft, from fighters to huge cargo planes, with aluminum floats. The most common usage of EDO floats was on the Kingfisher aircraft, which was carried by virtually every large ship in the U.S. Navy and was launched by catapults to conduct scouting and rescue missions. The Kingfishers were especially effective at picking up downed aviators, saving countless lives throughout the war.

During World War II, EDO also performed sheet metal work on a subcontract basis for airframe manufacturers. This experience led the company to return to airplane manufacture when the war was over. EDO designed and built a seaplane to replace the Kingfisher, and although it was a great improvement, the military only bought 10 aircraft, due to the emergence of the helicopter, which now took over rescue operations for the military. Moreover, the rise of the passenger airline industry and the building of airports caused the demand for seaplanes to fall, and consequently the need for EDO floats declined. The company was forced to contract its work, cutting the number of its employees from a wartime high of 2,400 to just 400. Osborn also became less active in the running of EDO, turning over much of the day-to-day operations to executives he hired away from Bendix.

Postwar Diversification

Unable to rely solely on the manufacture of aluminum floats, EDO began to diversify after the war. Its sheet metal operation built aluminum step stools as well as doors for blueprint machines. Despite its production of these commercial products, EDO nevertheless became increasingly dependent on government contracts, most of which at this time were connected to the company's sheet metal capabilities. It manufactured a line of aluminum boats, including the A-3 rescue boat that could be dropped from a B-29 bomber and was large enough to accommodate 15 people, a 32-foot cargo launch, and an 18-foot arctic skiff. EDO also used its sheet metal expertise to produce collapsible, lockable crates to hold the possessions of soldiers shipping overseas. EDO expanded into a new area, electronics, but focused on water technology, where the company already had a solid reputation. It began to design and manufacture underwater detecting systems and equipment, becoming heavily involved in the development of SONAR (SOund, NAvigation, and Ranging).

In recognition of its changing business, EDO Aircraft Corp. restructured itself and changed its name to EDO Corporation in 1947. Although the company continued to produce aluminum floats, its new electronics division became increasingly more important to EDO's future. During the 1950s, the company developed 36 sonar systems and became a leader in the use of sonar for ocean depth sounding. EDO also developed LORAN (LOng RAnge Navigation), which superceded older sonar systems and became standard equipment for navies around the world. The company then modified LORAN for use in the air, and the major airlines of the world adopted the EDO system. Meanwhile, EDO continued to make aluminum floats, introducing its 2000 series for use with the small Piper Super Cub private airplane. Fitted with EDO floats, the Super Cub was able to travel to any remote part of the globe that featured a river or lake. Later in the 1950s EDO floats also became available for use on the popular Cessna 180.

In 1953, Osborn decided to retire from the company he founded, although he remained a director. A man of varied interests, he became heavily involved in the leadership of the Institute for International Order, which would become later known as the World Policy Institute, an organization devoted to using public education to promote peace through the offices of the United Nations. In 1956, EDO's management took the company public and began to expand. That same year, EDO acquired King Laboratory, Inc., which would eventually become EDO Western Corp. In 1958, EDO acquired a Utah ceramic manufacturing company in order to secure a supply of ceramic transducers needed in its sonar equipment. It also created EDO Electro-Ceramic Products, which would become a major supplier to the U.S. Navy. With so much of its business now devoted to defense, EDO created the EDO Commercial Corporation to market its aluminum floats and aircraft loran systems. The company added to this division with the 1969 acquisition of Fiber Science, Inc., which produced composite water and waste tanks for commercial airliners.

During the late 1950s and 1960s, EDO became more heavily involved in general avionics, instrumentation, and flight control. Serving as subcontractor for Grumman, the company eventually played an important part in the 1969 Apollo moon landing. EDO probes were used to indicate when the Lunar Excursion Module had touched down, in effect becoming the first part of the craft to reach the moon.

Defense Contributions: 1970s–80s

It was not until the 1970s that EDO began to win major defense contracts in the United States as well as with NATO

Key Dates:

1925: Earl Dodge Osborn establishes EDO Aircraft Corp.
1926: EDO introduces first aluminum floats for airplanes.
1933: EDO floats are used by Admiral Byrd in Antarctic exploration.
1947: The company's name is changed to EDO Corp.
1953: Osborn retires.
1956: The company goes public.
1969: EDO sensors record Apollo touchdown on moon.
1973: EDO helicopter-towed minesweeping system used in Vietnam.
1988: Osborn dies at the age of 95.
2000: AIL Technologies acquired; Neil Armstrong is named chairman.

---

countries. A major turning point came in 1971 when the U.S. Navy decided to replace minesweeping ships with helicopters. Using its sonar expertise, EDO developed the MK105 helicopter-towed mine detection system, which would be used for the first time in 1973 in the clearing of Vietnam's Haiphong Harbor and become standard equipment ever since. EDO's "Towed Array" and "Side Scan" sonars were also applied to commercial underwater drilling and mining operations. In addition, EDO Electro-Ceramics Products began to find commercial uses for its piezo-electric technology, which converted acoustic energy to electrical energy and vice versa, and was important in underwater military applications. EDO now applied it to medical imaging products and fuel level sensors for aircraft. In the 1980s, piezoelectric materials would be used in such products as camera actuators and fish finders, then in the 1990s find applications in automotive sensors, pest control devices, and even sports equipment.

Although a downturn in the single-engine aircraft business led to EDO taking a $9 million writeoff in 1982 and a $1.7 million loss for the year, when the company unloaded certain electronics operations, EDO greatly benefited from the military buildup of the early 1980s. EDO's finances were helped in large part by up-front payments on a $170 million contract to build ejection release systems, used for either bombs or fuel tanks, for the Tornado fighter aircraft. The company was able to pare its long-term debt to less than $5 million and buy back almost a quarter of its stock, which it distributed as a dividend to shareholders. Although EDO was now a cash-rich company, and it talked about using the money to make select acquisitions, it spent just $5 million to pick up three small companies. By the summer of 1985, EDO, which had generated sales of just $123 million the year before, was sitting on $90 million in cash, and investors were beginning to question management's long-term vision.

In 1986, EDO made the largest acquisition in its history as a company, paying $13.5 million in cash to acquire Barnes Engineering Co., a manufacturer of electronic parts; however, with Barnes' stock price lagging well behind the value of EDO's assets, the move did little to repair a growing rift between the company and its investors. Concerning the management team, an independent analyst, Bob Ince, was quoted in a July 1987 *Crain's New York Business* article as saying, "These guys have been there forever. They strike me as very sleepy." In fact,

Osborn, who was now well into his 90s, still attended occasional board meetings. The average age of the board, not counting Osborn, was 67. The company, despite its quality products, was also criticized for not aggressively promoting itself in Washington. It has also allowed itself to become a prime candidate for a hostile takeover, and many of its shareholders began to openly desire such a development.

In December 1988 Osborn died at the age of 95. With the end of the Cold War and declining defense appropriations, the company that bore his name was now forced to transition into a new era. With revenues falling in the early 1990s, it created EDO Sports, employing its expertise in the manufacture of golf club driver heads as well as high-tech carbon-based bicycle spokes for racers. EDO also became involved in the natural gas vehicle business, acquiring Automotive Natural Gas Inc., a leading supplier of natural gas refueling stations. In November 1993, the company finally moved to shake up management, however incrementally. Its 82-year-old chairman, William R. Ryan, stepped down after 21 years, replaced by 68-year-old Gerald Albert, who stayed on as CEO. Frank A. Fariello, 59, was named president. EDO also changed its corporate by-laws to impose an age limit of 70 for officers and 73 for directors, which would result in seven of the 12 board members retiring within the next three years.

1990s and Beyond

EDO's attempts at diversification did not fare well, resulting in losses of $17 million in 1993 and $24 million in 1994. Fariello took over as CEO and began the process of unloading unprofitable ventures and cutting jobs, returning the company's focus to the defense business. Instead of directly competing with large defense contractors, however, he sought to become a supplier to such companies as Lockheed Martin and Boeing. EDO returned to profitability in 1995 and reached $7.2 million in earnings by 1998. Fariello then began to build the business by making strategic acquisitions, picking up Technology Services Group for $4.2 million, Specialty Plastics, Inc. for $5.5 million, Zenix Products Inc. for $700,000, and M Technologies Inc. for $4.5 million. Fariello also sold off some assets that no longer fit in with EDO, including Barnes Engineering Company.

In 2000, EDO made its most significant transaction with the merger of AIL Technologies, another Long Island defense company. The origins of AIL reached back to World War II, when the company was created to manufacture a submarine detection system. Although AIL would increase EDO's annual revenues to over $200 million, it would also add some $35 million in debt. In the long-term, the acquisition would broaden EDO's product line and strengthen its position as a supplier to major defense contractors. EDO also added AIL's prestigious chairman—Neil Armstrong, the first man to walk on the moon—to its fold. In November 2000, he succeeded Fariello as EDO's chairman.

Armstrong and EDO entered 2001 expecting to cope with an environment of shrinking defense budgets. The September 11 terrorist attacks on the World Trade Center and the Pentagon, however, promised to change business conditions. EDO's stock had already been rising during the course of the year, following the company's successful integration of AIL, and rumors of a possible takeover bid. After September 11, EDO stock jumped an additional 57 percent, reaching $31 by early October. Only days after the attacks, EDO filed for a $4 million secondary offering of stock to fund further acquisitions. With America's "war on terror" promising to be of uncertain duration, there was every expectation that EDO, repositioned in the defense arena, would prosper in the foreseeable future.

Principal Subsidiaries

AIL Technologies; EDO Western Corporation; EDO Electro-Ceramic Products; M Technologies Inc.; Specialty Plastics.

Principal Competitors

DRS Technologies Inc.; Sparton Corporation; United Industrial Corporation.

Further Reading

Davisson, Budd, "If It Floats . . . ," *Air Progress,* July 1989, p. 8.

Frederickson, Tom, "Local Firms Gain Ground in War Effort," *Crain's New York Business,* October 15, 2001, p. 56.

Gandel, Stephen, "Defense Company Finds Way to Protect Itself, *Crain's New York Business,* January 17, 2000, p. 14.

Harrington, John, "EDO's Best Offense Is Good Defense," *Crain's New York Business,* May 7, 2001, p. 42.

Mirabella, Alan, "Exec Leading EDO Consumer Charge," *Crain's New York Business,* December 20, 1993, p. 11.

Sternberg, Bill, "Investors Ponder War on Defense Firm," *Crain's New York Business,* July 6, 1987, p. 3.

——, "War Begins in Queens Over EDO Defense Firm," *Crain's New York Business,* July 14, 1988, p. 1.

"What Now? (EDO Corp.)," *Forbes,* June 3, 1985, p. 108.

—Ed Dinger

EMC²

where information lives

EMC Corporation

171 South Street
Hopkinton, Massachusetts 01748-9103
U.S.A.
Telephone: (508) 435-1000
Toll Free: (877) 362-6973
Fax: (508) 497-6961
Web site: http://www.emc.com

Public Company
Incorporated: 1979
Employees: 19,000
Sales: $8.87 billion (2000)
Stock Exchanges: New York
Ticker Symbol: EMC
NAIC: 334112 Computer Storage Device Manufacturing;
     334413 Semiconductor and Related Device
     Manufacturing; 334412 Bare Printed Circuit Board
     Manufacturing

EMC Corporation operates as the leading provider of information storage systems, software, networks, and services. Its main product lines include the Symmetrix Information Storage Systems, the CLARiiON Information Storage Systems, Information Storage Software, and Information Storage Services. EMC was started in the late 1970s, and grew rapidly through aggressive sales practices. In the mid-1980s, the company experienced some trouble with its technology, but regained a leading place in its industry in the 1990s through the early introduction of a new generation of computer memory technology. In 1994, EMC co-founder Richard J. Egan was named the "National, Master Entrepreneur of the Year," an award sponsored by *Ernst & Young, Inc.* magazine, and Merrill Lynch, for his lifetime achievement as an entrepreneur. During the 1990s, EMC stock grew by 80,575 percent—the highest single-decade performance of any listed stock in the history of the New York Stock Exchange.

By 2000, EMC's customers included 93 percent of Fortune 500 financial institutions, 98 percent of the Fortune 100, and 90 percent of the Business Week 50. With sales topping $8.8 billion in 2000, the firm controlled 34.6 percent of the information storage systems market and 25.5 percent of the storage management software market. The company was named the "Most Admired Company" in the computer peripherals industry in both 1999 and 2000 by *Fortune* magazine.

Egan began his career as an electrical engineering student at the Massachusetts Institute of Technology (MIT). While there, he worked on a team that helped to develop a guidance system for the Apollo lunar mission. The device designed by Egan's team helped the space capsule to return safely to earth after landing on the moon. After graduation from MIT, Egan founded a company called Cambridge Memories, later known as Cambex, which manufactured storage devices for computers. Under Egan's leadership, this company's revenues grew into the multi-millions.

After leaving Cambex, Egan worked as a technical consultant to other big computer firms, such as Honeywell. In 1979, he founded EMC along with partner Roger Marino. Like Cambex, EMC's main product was devices that allowed computers to store information. Egan created circuit boards that could be installed in popular computer models, in order to dramatically increase a pre-existing computer's memory. In this way, EMC's products were able to extend the life of mini-computers, allowing users to upgrade and keep on using old equipment, rather than having to buy a new machine.

Emphasis on Sales Approach: Early 1980s

Rather than put EMC's main emphasis on research and development or engineering expertise, Egan focused the company's energy on sales. To fill out his staff, he recruited bright young college graduates who had played competitively on sports teams in school. In addition, to foster team spirit and competitiveness in his salesmen, Egan set up EMC's sales offices in a bullpen configuration. Different sales regions were designated by pennants, which indicated the relative standing of the regions. In the center of the room, a brass bell was hung. Anyone who gained an order of $10,000 or more got to ring the bell. In contrast, EMC also strove to keep costs down in its engineering and technical support divisions.

In the early 1980s, such decisions brought EMC rapid growth, and the company became the subject of a case study used by students at the Harvard Business School. The company's sales and profits continued to grow through the middle of the decade. By June 1985, however, EMC's continued success had attracted the unfavorable notice of a competitor, and the company was sued for patent infringement by the Digital Equipment Corporation (DEC) which also made memory boards. This suit was eventually settled in October 1987, when EMC was granted a license for the DEC technology in question, and in January 1989, EMC paid DEC $100,000 to settle the legal action.

Shortly after this suit was filed, EMC added to its product line again, as the company introduced new four- and eight-byte memory cards in July 1985. In August of that year, the company also augmented its offerings for the Hewlett-Packard 3000 computer.

In May 1986, EMC announced that it would offer stock to the public for the first time. The company planned to raise capital by selling 2.2 million shares. Five months later, the company announced that it had formed a new unit, Network Intelligence, Ltd., to develop software that would seek out and remove defects in local area network programs. At the end of the year, EMC reported record profits of $18.63 million.

EMC then expanded the market for its products, when Marubeni Electronics began to sell EMC memory boards for upgrading existing computers in Japan. In addition, EMC continued to introduce new products, announcing that it expected the bulk of its future growth to come from products designed to enhance the memory of large-scale and mid-range computers.

Toward this end, EMC introduced a new class of products, disk drives, in mid-1987. The company rolled out a disk drive and controller for use in IBM 9335-compatible machines in June of that year, and, two months later, introduced an optical disk subsystem for use in DEC VAX computers, which boosted the storage capacity of these machines, as well as a similar system for use with machines built by the Prime Computer company. Next, EMC augmented its line of disk drives for computers made by other companies yet again, when it rolled out a product designed to be used in Hewlett-Packard RISC-based Spectrum computers.

Pushed by these new products, EMC's sales took a giant leap in 1987, as sales gained 90 percent over the previous year, to reach $127 million. Profits had grown to $24 million, and EMC was named the seventh hottest growing company in America by *Business Week* magazine. Over the course of early 1987, the company's stock hit a high of $29 a share.

Problems Arise: Late 1980s

By September 1987, however, EMC had hit a snag, as its new line of disk drives, which contained a small, inexpensive circuit board made by NEC Corporation, proved to be defective. When problems with the drives arose, EMC's response was to ship out new disk drives to customers through overnight mail. Because the replacement drives, which were much more expensive, were bulky and delicate instruments, they had to be delivered and installed by an EMC employee. In order to make this possible, the company was compelled to maintain inventories of the replacement drives at all of its 23 regional sales offices. In addition, its small staff of service representatives was severely taxed by the glut of problems.

As a result of these conditions, EMC's cost of doing business rose dramatically. The company's low-overhead philosophy, which had kept its investment in technical and service areas low, meant that the company was not well prepared to cope effectively with the crisis of its defective disk drives. By the end of April 1988, EMC's results had started to show the impact of this situation, as earnings over the previous three months dropped from $5.8 million to $1 million, despite the fact that sales rose by 57 percent. This reflected the fact that EMC felt compelled to keep shipping the problem drives, even after difficulties with the product had been identified, in order to keep up with sales targets.

EMC, which had experienced smooth sailing up until this point, came in for criticism as a result of these problems. The company's investors claimed that they had been kept in the dark and not notified early enough by EMC management about problems with the disk drives. "The company is in the doghouse," one financial analyst told *Business Week,* as the price of EMC's stock plummeted to $7 per share, half the level it had been in the wake of the stock market crash of 1987. "Their engineering and technical support is something they always skimped on," a competitor observed in *Business Week.*

In response to the difficulty with its disk drives, EMC's management made a number of changes. The company located two additional suppliers for the defective part made by NEC, and it also tried to beef up its engineering division. Responding to criticism that the company had focused on sales to the detriment of quality, Egan admitted that EMC should have tested the drives more thoroughly before shipping them out. In June 1988, EMC announced that it would raise the price of its products by five to 15 percent, due to the cost of the computer chips they housed. In addition, EMC brought in a new president and chief executive officer, Michael Ruettgers. "We had some serious quality and service problems," this executive later told the *New York Times,* adding, "We were overwhelmed."

As EMC attempted to respond to the problems its rapid growth had engendered, the company continued to augment its product line. In October 1988, EMC brought out a new magnetic disk subsystem for use in DEC VAX machines. One month later, the company also introduced a solid state disk drive for use in IBM 3080 and 3090 model computers.

```
┌─────────────────────────────────────────────────┐
│                 Key Dates:                      │
│                                                 │
│ 1979:  EMC is founded by Richard J. Egan and Roger │
│        Marino.                                  │
│ 1985:  The firm launches four- and eight-byte memory │
│        cards.                                   │
│ 1986:  The company goes public.                 │
│ 1987:  Sales grow 90 percent over the previous year to │
│        $127 million.                            │
│ 1988:  EMC reports a $7.82 million loss due to problems │
│        with its disk drives.                    │
│ 1991:  Sales rebound as the firm rolls out its new product │
│        line that uses RAID technology.          │
│ 1993:  Epoch Systems Inc. and Magna Computer Corp. are │
│        acquired.                                │
│ 1994:  Sales exceed $1 billion; Array Technology is pur- │
│        chased.                                  │
│ 1997:  EMC is ranked 16th in Business Week's Top 50 list │
│        of America's best-performing companies.  │
│ 1999:  Joseph M. Tucci is elected president and chief oper- │
│        ating officer; the company introduces the EMC En- │
│        terprise Storage Network.                │
│ 2000:  EMC's market share in the information storage sys- │
│        tems industry grows to 34.6 percent.     │
│ 2001:  Ruettgers is named executive chairman and Tucci │
│        takes over as CEO.                       │
└─────────────────────────────────────────────────┘
```

Despite the contribution of these new products, EMC's disk drive problems continued to plague the company, causing EMC to report a net loss for 1988 of $7.82 million. In January 1989, EMC responded to its falling financial returns by cutting costs, as the company reduced its staff by one-third, letting 60 people go. This move was part of a larger shake-up directed by EMC management in the company's sales and engineering operations.

Two months later, EMC introduced another new product, in an effort to shore up its sales. The company's latest disk drive offering was designed to be used with computers manufactured by the Wang company. Four months later, the company made a large sale, signing an agreement with Storage Technology to supply $100 million worth of EMC's solid state memory storage subsystems for resale. These products were designed to be used with IBM-compatible machines.

New Product Development: Early 1990s

In October 1989, EMC also announced plans to market a new generation of memory boards that relied on a larger chip. This effort was part of the company's overall strategy of moving into new markets, with a new class of products. By the end of 1991, EMC was able to report improved financial results, as the company returned to profitability, with earnings of $2.7 million.

During this time, EMC's efforts to roll out new products started to bear fruit, as it announced the introduction of a new IBM-compatible disk system based on a 24-gigabyte computer chip, that used RAID technology. RAID, which stood for "redundant arrays of inexpensive disks," used a large number of small, commonly manufactured disk drives, such as the hard drive found in many personal computers. These separate memory cells were linked by special software to provide fast, reliable storage of very large quantities of data. This type of storage system contrasted with the product of EMC's main competitor, IBM, which relied on a single, complex, expensive disk drive for computer memory. With its RAID technology, EMC entered the field that would provide the bulk of its growth in the first half of the 1990s.

As EMC began to roll out its new line of products, the company's financial fortunes continued their improvement. At the end of 1990, EMC reported sales up 30 percent from the previous year, to $171 million, yielding earnings of $18.2 million. "EMC was on a roller coaster in the 1980s," one analyst told the *New York Times,* noting that "They're a more mature company today."

With that maturity, however, came further legal troubles. In November 1990, EMC lost a court battle with Cambex, Egan's first firm, over trade secrets involving add-in computer memory upgrade boards for use in the IBM 3080 model line. The company was ordered to pay Cambex $2 million. One month later, in December 1990, EMC announced that it would appeal this verdict.

In addition, in March 1991, EMC and two other computer companies were sued by the IBM Credit Corporation, the branch of IBM that leased large computers. IBM charged that EMC had misappropriated IBM Credit property by removing original parts and replacing them with others when it upgraded computers rented by IBM leasing customers. When customers returned the computers they had rented from IBM, they did not contain the same parts they had when IBM sent them out. EMC maintained that the suit was simple harassment over a practice that had long been permitted.

EMC continued to roll out new products for use with IBM computers. In March 1991, the company announced that it would incorporate software made by the Midrange Performance Group that performed minicomputer analysis. One month later, EMC also began shipping a new subsystem based on the IBM 9336 midrange disk drive.

EMC then completed an agreement with Sun Data that allowed this company to resell EMC memory products to its IBM AS/400 clients. EMC also launched a tape storage unit with a plug that made it compatible with IBM computers. By the end of 1991, these efforts had succeeded in pushing EMC's revenues even higher, as the company notched sales of $232 million, a rise of 35 percent. From these sales, EMC earned $11 million. This also represented a significant jump in net income of 47 percent. In response to these results, the price of the company's stock began to rise as well.

These gains continued in 1992, as EMC completed a $44 million two-year contract with Unisys to sell its new disk drives. The company also completed an alliance with Cambex, its former rival, to license technology for enhancing mainframe computer memory.

Overall, EMC enjoyed a strong lead in the race to implement RAID technology. Although one other competitor had announced an intention to enter the field, glitches in its technology had held up the marketing of its product, and EMC was able to enjoy a virtual monopoly. This circumstance allowed the company to make significant progress in stealing market share from IBM, which dominated the mainframe data storage market. "We've been unplugging IBM mainframe storage and installing EMC, and the choice is almost a no-brainer," one EMC customer told the *New York Times*.

In May 1992, EMC became embroiled in another legal dispute, after IBM released a statement to the press attacking EMC. The company sued IBM and IBM Credit for libel in the press release. At the time, EMC also announced that it was seeking an advertising agency to launch a $1.5 million campaign promoting its products.

One of EMC's primary advantages in competing with IBM was the small size of its products. In some cases, EMC storage devices took up one-seventh of the space of an IBM machine of equivalent capacity. In addition, EMC's practice of designing its own software linking together the parts of its storage devices, while relying on easily purchased parts from other manufacturers for its hardware, gave the company great flexibility. As advances in technology took place, it was easy for EMC to incorporate new products into its offerings. "We're riding a performance curve that is moving exponentially," an EMC software designer explained to the *New York Times*.

In the fall of 1992, EMC announced a new generation of disk storage products, predicting that this advance would power a dramatic increase in its revenues. The company's Symmetrix 5500 model, like earlier models, relied on RAID technology to store information quickly and reliably, backing up all data on more than one disk. EMC's new technology offered a 60 percent greater capacity than previous systems. The Symmetrix unit was designed to cost from $865,000 to $2.8 million. EMC completed 1992 with another big gain in sales, as revenues rose to $385 million, and profits more than doubled to reach $29 million.

Two months after rolling out its new Symmetrix line, EMC announced that it had clinched a $10 million contract with Delta Air Lines to install a Symmetrix system. By June 1993, EMC had sold more than 2,000 units of the Symmetrix system. Although EMC's memory system was more expensive than an equally large system produced by IBM, it could enable mainframe computers to perform some functions twice as fast. "We have a two-year lead over IBM today," EMC's chief executive, Michael Ruettgers told *Business Week*.

In August 1993, EMC, flush with the revenues generated by enormous sales of its Symmetrix system, began to purchase other computer companies. EMC bought Epoch Systems, Inc., as well as the Magna Computer Corporation, for about $118 million. At the end of that year, EMC reported that its revenue had reached $782 million, as income more than tripled to $127 million. On the basis of these results, EMC entered the Fortune 500 rankings for the first time.

Early in 1994, EMC acquired another company, purchasing the assets of Array Technology from Tandem Computers. As revenues and earnings continued to grow at a breakneck speed, EMC secured sales exceeding $1 billion that year. In 1995, it purchased McDATA Corp., a data switching and computer connection firm. Despite its somewhat rocky past, EMC had pushed its way into the storage market and now stood as a formidable opponent in the industry.

Gaining Market Leadership: Mid- to Late 1990s

In fact, by 1995, EMC had displaced IBM as the market leader in the mainframe data storage industry. During that year, the company continued to build upon its Symmetrix line and introduced the market's first platform-independent storage system for open systems. By 1996, it controlled a 17 percent share in the $6 billion storage system market for Unix and Windows NT servers—a market growing from 30 to 60 percent per year.

Its share of the storage market for IBM mainframes and minicomputers also continued to grow and had increased to 41 percent while IBM's fell to just 35 percent in 1996. As EMC continued its rise to the top, much of the firm's success was attributed to its new focus on customer service. According to a 1996 *Industry Week* article, "EMC's attention to its customers and their needs—the company has been ranked No. 1 in customer satisfaction in 13 independent surveys over the last two years—has paid big dividends since 1990 in revenues, profits, market share, and identifying new market opportunities."

EMC continued to launch new products into the late 1990s. In 1997, it became the leader in the open storage market and was also named to the Business Week 50 list of America's best performing companies. By 1998, revenues were climbing to the $4 billion mark and EMC received the title of "Company of the Decade" in Massachusetts by the Boston Globe. By now, nearly 90 percent of all airline reservations in the world were managed by an EMC enterprise storage and retrieval system and its other customers included large banks and financial services firms, telecommunication providers, retailers, manufactures, governments, universities, and scientific and research institutions. EMC ended the 1990s as the second-best performing stock on the S&P 500—after Dell—and the number one stock of the decade by the New York Stock Exchange.

Strategic Moves for the New Millennium

EMC entered the new millennium with great momentum. Several key storage products were launched in 2000 including the Symmetrix 8000 product line, the CLARiiON FC4500 system and the CLARiiON IP4700—both obtained by the 1999 purchase of Data General Corp.—and the EMC Celerra with HighRoad software. That year revenues grew by 32 percent over the previous year to $8.87 billion—information storage revenues contributed 93 percent of sales. It also took its Mc-DATA subsidiary public that year.

In early 2001, Ruettgers was named executive chairman while Joseph M. Tucci was elected president and CEO, and Egan was named chairman emeritus. That year, the company began an aggressive marketing push with the tagline, "EMC—Where Information Lives." It also formed a five-year, multi-billion-dollar partnership with Dell Computer Corp. Under the terms of the deal, Dell and EMC will co-brand the EMC CLARiiON product line and Dell will also market the Symmetrix line.

EMC's rampant success however, began to show signs of slowing during the latter half of 2001. In fact, its share of the storage market fell from 80 percent to 60 percent during 2001. Both IBM and Hitachi Data Systems Corp. were offering similar storage products at lower costs. To top it off, the dot-com fallout and the worsening American economy left the storage industry with small hopes for growth. EMC, which had posted a year-over-year growth rate of 37 percent since 1995, announced its first revenue decline in 48 quarters in June 2001.

By continuing to secure reseller deals—such as the one with Dell—and focusing on customer friendly sales techniques, Tucci remained confident that the firm would overcome its problems successfully, as it had in the late 1980s. Whether or not that would be enough to conquer a faltering economy and increased competition, however, remained to be seen.

Principal Subsidiaries

Avalon Consulting Group; Data General Corp.; Data General International Inc.; EMC Computer Storage Systems Israel Ltd.; EMC Computer Systems AG (Switzerland); EMC Computer Systems Argentina S.A.; EMC Computer Systems GmbH (Germany); EMC Computer Systems Mexico; EMC Computer Systems France S.A.; EMC Computer Systems Pte. Ltd. (Singapore); EMC Corporation of Canada; EMC del Peru S.A.; EMC International Holdings Inc; EMC Investment Corp.; EMC Japan K.K. (95%); Epoch Inc.; Softworks Inc.; Softworks International Ltd. (UK); Terascape Software Ltd.

Principal Competitors

International Business Machines Corp.; Hitachi Data Systems Corp.; Compaq Computer Corp.

Further Reading

Helm, Leslie, "How a Hot Company Overheated," *Business Week*, May 23, 1988, p. 126.

Keenan, Faith, "EMC Dishes Out a Little More TLC," *Business Week*, September 10. 2001.

Kirkpatrick, David, "Storage! Storage! Storage!," *Fortune*, February 15, 1999, p. 72.

Lyons, Daniel, "What's Eating EMC?," *Forbes*, November 26, 2001, p. 62.

McHugh, Josh, "When It Will Be Smart to Be Dumb," *Forbes*, May 6, 1996, p. 118.

Mulqueen, John T., "EMC Completes the Circle," *CommunicationsWeek*, August 11, 1997, p. 65.

Verespej, Michael A., "Give 'em What They Want," *Industry Week*, November 4, 1996, p. 61.

Verity, John W., "The Midgets, the Mammoth, and the Mainframes," *Business Week*, June 7, 1993, p. 31.

"What's In Store," *InternetWeek*, July 6, 1998, p. 17.

Wilke, John R., "Little EMC Challenges Leader IBM in Data-Storage," *Wall Street Journal*, July 9, 1992.

—Elizabeth Rourke
—update: Christina M. Stansell

Emerson

8000 West Florissant Avenue
St. Louis, Missouri 63136
U.S.A.
Telephone: (314) 553-2000
Fax: (314) 553-3527
Web site: http://www.gotoemerson.com

Public Company
Incorporated: 1890 as Emerson Electric Manufacturing
   Company
Employees: 123,400
Sales: $15.5 billion (2001)
Stock Exchanges: New York
Ticker Symbol: EMR
NAIC: 335312 Motor and Generator Manufacturing;
   335314 Relay and Industrial Control Manufacturing;
   335999 All Other Miscellaneous Electrical Equipment
   and Component Manufacturing

Emerson—formerly Emerson Electric Co.—operates today as one of America's most admired business success stories in the field of manufacturing. Emerson has quietly grown from a regional maker of electric motors and fans into a highly diversified international firm. During 2000, the firm was ranked among the 100 Best-Managed Companies by *IndustryWeek* magazine for the fifth year in a row. Its diverse product line is divided into eight brand segments including Emerson Network Power, Emerson Process Management, Emerson Climate Technologies, Emerson Storage Solutions, Emerson Professional Tools, Emerson Motor Technologies, Emerson Industrial Automation, and Emerson Appliance Solutions.

In 2001, Emerson operated over 60 divisions in nearly 380 manufacturing facilities across the globe. With businesses in over 150 countries, the company's international sales reached $6.2 billion in 2001—40 percent of company sales. Due to economic downturns however, Emerson ended its 43-year record of consecutive earning increases in fiscal 2001.

Company Beginnings

The company traces its roots back to the dawn of the electrical age in America. Founded in St. Louis on September 24, 1890, the firm was named for a Missouri judge, John Wesley Emerson, a descendant of the New England family of literary fame. Emerson was impressed by the ingenuity shown by a pair of brothers, Alexander W. and Charles R. Meston, in finding applications for the newly developed alternating current electric motor. In addition to lending his name, he provided the financing and became the president of the new company. The fledgling enterprise enjoyed modest success in its first three years, primarily producing small electrical and mechanical products.

In 1892, Herbert L. Parker, a Chicago railroad man, recognized the company's potential and bought Judge Emerson's controlling interest. Parker became president and general manager of Emerson, supervising the company's steady expansion until his death in 1924. During Parker's tenure, electric products developed into household and business necessities, and Emerson became a pioneer in the industry. The company produced a steady stream of innovative products by adapting its electric motors for such items as sewing machines, dental equipment, and water pumps. As electricity became an important factor in mechanized industry, Emerson supplied electric motors for office, factory and farm equipment as well.

In 1920, Parker was elected chairman of the board and T.M. Meston, the founders' younger brother, became president. During the 1920s, electric fans represented 40 percent of sales. Small electric motors for appliances and general household uses, however, were the dominant business.

Battling the Depression and Labor Issues

Emerson was hit hard by the Depression. The company paid a stock dividend in 1930, but did not do so again for ten years. In 1933, Joseph Newman took control of the company after a career as an executive at Lesser-Goldman, a St. Louis-based cotton and agricultural-products broker. Lesser-Goldman owned an interest in Emerson and was concerned about the company's financial performance during the Depression. Newman streamlined operations, focusing on lowering costs, developing new products, and broadening the company's line of fans.

While sales were uncertain, labor relations between the company and its employees were positively dismal. Convinced that the Wagner Act of 1935, which reaffirmed the right of workers to form unions, was unconstitutional, Newman refused to recognize the United Electrical, Radio and Machine Workers, C.I.O. The union called a sitdown strike in 1937 that lasted 53 days, seven days short of a record. It was 68 days before the employees went back to work, however; Newman settled only after the Supreme Court upheld the Wagner Act.

The settlement came too late for Newman. His bankers had agreed to make a new stock issue just before the strike, but the issue failed. The failure was due partly to the strike, but the company's generally poor financial picture is what ultimately led the board of directors to form a committee to seek new management.

In 1938, William Stuart Symington III was named president of Emerson Electric. A member of a prominent eastern family, Symington arrived in St. Louis facing a daunting array of problems. The company suffered a loss of $138,000 in fiscal 1938. Inventory and overhead were up, while sales had fallen substantially. Symington immediately began cleaning house, firing most of the old top management.

The new management undertook a vigorous campaign to secure new business, and landed Sears, Roebuck & Company as a promising new motor customer. Symington was willing to take risks: he bought an arc-welding business sight unseen and later took Emerson into the delicate business of manufacturing hermetically sealed motors for refrigerators.

Once Emerson was back on its feet, Symington turned his attention to solving the company's long-standing labor problems. The new president, who would later go on to a distinguished career in the United States Senate, faced a union deeply distrustful of management, believing the contract it had so bitterly won was not being honored in good faith. Symington was a realist and decided to work with the fledgling union. The ensuing agreements between Emerson Electric and the United Electrical, Radio and Machine Workers were viewed as landmark achievements for Emerson and followed the example of labor agreements in the newly unionized automobile, steel, and packing industries.

Symington also undertook a major effort to modernize Emerson's manufacturing facilities. At the time the company was housed in five separate buildings in St. Louis. Rents and taxes were high, the multi-storied structures were unsuitable for modern production methods, and none was located near a railroad siding. The company clearly had to relocate to more efficient quarters if it was to compete successfully.

The city of Evansville, Indiana, made a pitch to be the company's new home, offering a plant site and $100,000 to facilitate the move. Public officials in St. Louis declined to match the offer, fearing that it would set a precedent they would have to match for other businesses. Indicative of the changed labor atmosphere, however, the union offered to raise a similar sum through a system of wage cuts. Symington declined the union's offer, arranged independent financing, and relocated the company to a suitable location in St. Louis County.

With the advent of World War II, the company joined the war effort and manufactured a variety of war-related items. Emerson's largest contract was for the development and manufacture of the gun turrets used on Air Force bombers such as the B-17, B-25, and B-26, the major weapons in the U.S. bomber force. At the height of production during the war, the company was doing $100 million worth of defense work annually.

Emerson fell upon hard times again after the war, as defense contracts fell drastically, slipping to a low of $1.5 million in 1947. The company had been a leader in its field for most of its life, but in the postwar years large competitors like General Electric and Westinghouse saw potential in Emerson's markets. They moved quickly, building plants in low-wage areas and squeezing the company in its traditional strongholds. In 1945, Symington left the company to pursue a career in politics, boosted in no small part by the reputation he had gained as head of Emerson during the war. When his successor, a long-time company executive, died suddenly, Emerson was once again in the midst of a leadership crisis.

Reorganization Under Buck Persons: 1950s

In December 1953, Wallace R. "Buck" Persons was named president. At the time Emerson had sales of only $45 million and a host of problems that had been building for years. But Persons, who came to Emerson from Lincoln Electric, a company known for its cost-effective management, was equal to the task. He instituted an extensive reorganization of the company's commercial product line to exploit Emerson's old-line electric motor business and bring in new customers outside the household appliance market. Products were redesigned using standardized parts to allow for mass production, rather than the company's traditional job-shop lots, producing immediate and dramatic results.

Persons placed heavy emphasis on upgrading Emerson's engineering capabilities. In his first couple of years at the helm he doubled the size of the engineering staff, making a major effort to recruit top-notch engineers and develop the new Electronics-Avionics Division, which worked on fire control systems for jet bombers. He also got tough with labor. Emerson's labor costs were higher than its major competitors, who had relocated to low-wage areas. The company suffered several strikes but eventually succeeded in restructuring its labor agreements to conform with industry standards. However, Persons also emphasized planning, budgetary discipline, and a policy of open communication with employees including annual employee opinion surveys.

Key Dates:

1890: Emerson Electric Manufacturing Co. is established.

1892: Herbert L. Parker buys Judge Emerson's controlling interest.

1933: Joseph Newman takes control of the firm.

1937: Emerson workers strike for 53 days; the company's finances continue to falter.

1938: William Stuart Symington III is named president and begins a restructuring program.

1945: Defense contracts fall drastically; Symington resigns to pursue a career in politics.

1953: Wallace R. ''Buck'' Persons is named president and begins focusing on the firm's electric motor business to attract new customers.

1956: The Air Force modernizes its Bomber Fleet; military contracts account for 30 percent of sales.

1958: Emerson begins an acquisition program.

1962: Company begins to shift focus away from defense contracting.

1973: Charles F. Knight is elected CEO.

1975: Emerson enters the electric utility supply market with the purchase of A.B. Chance Company.

1986: The firm acquires Copeland Corporation and Hazeltine Inc.

1992: Fisher Controls International is acquired; sales reach $7.7 billion.

1996: Attempts to outbid Recoton for control of International Jensen Inc. fail.

1997: Net sales exceed $12.5 billion.

2000: The company's name is shortened to Emerson, and David Farr is named CEO.

Emerson also redoubled its efforts to secure defense contracts, concentrating on the engineering and development of electronics and avionics rather than on armaments production. The modernization of the Air Force's bomber fleet provided a windfall for the company's rebuilding program. By 1956 military sales accounted for 30 percent of Emerson's total sales.

While Persons' short range plans called for rebuilding Emerson's existing product lines, his long range goal was to expand into new products. To assist with this effort, Persons called in a host of management consultants. One of the first firms hired, Lester B. Knight & Associates, eventually produced Persons' successor, Charles F. Knight.

Diversification Through Acquisition: Late 1950s–60s

Beginning in 1958, Emerson embarked on an acquisition program, aiming for quality producers with strong marketing skills. Through merger or acquisition, more than ten companies were added to Emerson during the 1960s, including Day Brite Lighting, U.S. Electrical Motors, Ridge Tool Company, Thermo-Disc, White-Rodgers, Browning Manufacturing, and In-Sink-Erator. Emerson's industrial and consumer markets expanded significantly, lessening the company's dependence on uncertain defense contracts. When production of B-52 and B-58 air force bombers, for which Emerson was manufacturing tail turrets and

fire control systems, was abruptly canceled in 1962, the move away from defense contracting was accelerated. The financial impact of the cancellation was minimized, since Emerson had already heeded the advice of its military consulting experts and concentrated its defense business in helicopters and other ''limited war'' hardware, but it convinced Persons that defense would not be a consistent growth market and gave added impetus to the company's efforts to expand in commercial markets.

The wisdom of this move was underscored in 1969 when, with almost no warning, the defense department canceled Lockheed Aircraft's huge Cheyenne helicopter program, for which Emerson was the largest subcontractor. The company's defense sales skidded from $70 million to between $35 and $40 million in one day. Following the company's stringent budgetary procedures, and as a result of continued growth through acquisition, Emerson was able to avoid a loss for the year by drastically cutting expenses, but the message was clear. Emerson remained in the military market, but Persons set a cap on military business at 15 percent of total sales.

By the time the Cheyenne contract was canceled, Emerson had acquired more than a dozen companies manufacturing a wide range of commercial and industrial products. The firm's household products included lighting fixtures, kitchen waste disposers, door chimes, intercom units, power tools, heating and air conditioning, controls, and high fidelity equipment. On the industrial side, Emerson was producing power transfer equipment, industrial test equipment, and industrial tools.

By the early 1970s, Buck Persons had turned Emerson, a troubled maker of small electric motors and fans, into a company capable of competing with the industry giants. But he had no clear successor inside the company, and the time was coming for him to move on. Persons undertook an exhaustive two-year search for the right man, reviewing 150 potential candidates. The final choice was Charles F. (Chuck) Knight, Lester Knight's 37-year-old son and the lead consultant involved in helping find Person's successor. He was named Emerson's vice chairman and CEO in 1973, and chairman the following year.

Continued Growth: 1970s–80s

Knight proved an excellent choice for the job. He knew the company intimately at the highest level, since he had been an Emerson consultant for ten years and a board member of Emerson Motor Division, the company's largest division, for four years. Persons had wanted someone who would accept the company's organization and provide a sense of continuity. Knight had helped set up Emerson's management structure, and shared Persons' commitment to continued strong sales and earnings growth. Knight also had international experience, having overseen his father's European operations before becoming an Emerson consultant. Emerson had been late getting into overseas markets and now faced entrenched competition. One of Knight's main goals was to expand the company's international sales, spearheaded by specialties like its Ridgid tool line.

Knight's management philosophy kept as much decision-making responsibility as possible at the operational level; each division operated like a separate company in many respects. Managers negotiated wages and benefits according to community standards and were responsible for determining what steps must be taken at the divisional level to respond to market conditions. At this time, Emerson avoided the huge manufacturing facilities favored by some of its competitors, keeping a plant size of no more than 800 workers at most locations, and most of its plants were non-union. All these were components of what Emerson called its "best cost producer" strategy, through which it strove to manufacture the highest-quality products at their lowest relevant global cost.

Knight continued Emerson's approach of frequently entering new markets by the acquisition of an existing market leader or high-quality producer. The company entered the electric-utility supply business for the first time in 1975 with the purchase of A.B. Chance Company. Similarly, Emerson made a strong entry into the industrial measurement and process control business in 1976 by buying Rosemount, Inc.

Emerson's strategy of diversification and acquisition continued in the 1980s. Emerson acquired Copeland Corporation, the world's largest manufacturer of compressors for air conditioners and commercial refrigeration applications, in October, 1986. In December 1986, the company purchased Hazeltine, Inc., a leader in state-of-the-art defense electronics components and systems. However, in 1988, two officials at the newly acquired Hazeltine unit were indicted on charges of fraud. Emerson and Hazeltine cooperated with authorities, and in early 1989 Hazeltine pleaded guilty to the felony charge. In March 1987, Emerson acquired Liebert Corporation, a maker of computer support products.

During the late 1980s and into the 1990s, Emerson sought out companies that provided not only immediate sales and profits gains, but growth potential for years to come, and preferred to buy private firms to avoid paying the large premiums over book value that public companies demanded.

In 1988, the company posted its 31st consecutive year of earnings growth, a record that made the company a perennial Wall Street favorite. Emerson's quiet, steady growth throughout the 1980s showed no signs of faltering and its customer base had grown to include commercial and industrial buyers of a broad array of factory automation and process control equipment.

In September, 1988, James F. Hardymon was named president of Emerson. C.F. Knight remained chairman and CEO. The company continued to expand in both domestic and international markets in order to forge ahead with its plan to become a leading global manufacturer. In fact, in 1990 alone, the firm acquired ten companies including French concern Leroy-Somers SA and CESET, an Italian manufacturer of appliance motors.

Focus on International Expansion: 1990s

Along with acquisitions, Emerson also formed strategic partnerships and joint ventures in order to gain a strong foothold in the international market. In 1992, the firm entered into a joint venture with Germany-based Robert Bosch GmbH to produce power tools. Fisher Controls International was also acquired that year in a deal worth $1.25 billion, and Emerson sales reached $7.7 billion.

During this time period however, revenue growth began to slow. A 1996 *Fortune* article claimed that the firm's "market-

ing and sales forces, constrained by tight budgets, were missing critical opportunities. Innovation flagged as well, in part because division managers were opting for those investments that they knew would fatten profits in the short term." The article went on to state that "foreign expansion, long a stated corporate goal, got stuck in first gear as division chiefs, anxious to protect their home turfs, shied away from adventurism abroad." As such, Knight began to alter the company's strategy, making growth a top priority for all division managers, holding each one responsible for achieving agreed upon goals. The company also began to hold yearly two-day growth conferences where growth targets were discussed and strategies were laid out.

Back on track and with its sights firmly set on global expansion, Emerson spent the next few years gaining a strong foothold in the Eastern European market, as well as in China and India. Management eyeballed the Asia-Pacific market as highly lucrative, so the firm sought out partnerships and ventures in that region. By 1995, revenues had increased to over $10 billion.

In 1996, Emerson was outbid by Recoton for control of International Jenson Inc. That did little to dampen the firm's plans however, and the following year Computational Systems, a manufacturer of error detection equipment used by machinery in plant locations, was purchased. The company also began production at its compressor plant in Thailand. By 1997, net sales had surpassed $12.5 billion and net earnings reached $1.1 billion.

Along with purchases made during the late 1990s, including the Westinghouse Process Control Division from CBS Corp., Emerson also began to divest non-core, slow-growth businesses. During this period of acquisition and divestiture, the firm began making a name for itself as a supplier of high-tech power equipment serving both the computer and communications industries.

A New Branding Strategy for the New Millennium

Emerson made several key moves in the new millennium to reflect this new image. It adopted a new branding strategy, changing its corporate logo for the first time since 1967. It also shortened its company name from Emerson Electric Co. to Emerson, signaling the firm's expansion from an electronics firm to a global technology and engineering firm. In October of 2000, David N. Farr was named CEO while Knight remained chairman and James G. Berges was elected president. In 2000, *IndustryWeek* magazine named Emerson as one of the World's 100 Best-Managed Companies for the fifth year in a row.

The company also made several key acquisitions during 2000 and 2001. It purchased the telecommunications products business from Jordan Industries Inc., which gave it a broader reach in China, India, and Malaysia. It then went on to purchase Avansys Power Co. in October 2001 for $750 million— Emerson claims it was the largest private acquisition in China by a foreign company.

Despite these positive advances, sales in fiscal 2001 remained flat over the previous year. As many of the firm's businesses segments began to experience economic downturns, Emerson was forced to cut costs and make strategic investments, which would provide for its long-term growth. As a result, 2001 marked the end of the firm's 43-year record of consecutive earning increases. Nevertheless, Emerson management remained convinced that the company would be able to successfully combat these economic hardships. With its long-standing history of success and strong focus on securing business in developing countries, continued technological advances, and investment in fast-moving markets, Emerson appeared to be well positioned for future growth.

Principal Subsidiaries

Applied Concepts Inc.; Astec International Holdings Ltd. (United Kingdom); Avansys Power Co. (China); BI Technologies GmbH (Germany); Branson Ultrasonic S.A. (Switzerland); Clairson International Corporation; Compania do Motores Domesticos (Mexico); Computational Systems Inc.; Control Techniques USA Inc.; Copeland Corp.; Daniel Industries Inc.; Daniel Automation Company; Hytork International plc (United Kingdom); EECO Inc.; Emerson Holding Corp.; Asco Electrical Products Co. Inc.; Emerson Electric GmbH (Germany); Rosemount Inc.; Fisher-Rosemount Holding AG (Switzerland); Emerson Power Transmission Corp.; Environmental Remediation Management Inc.; Liebert Corp.; Ridge Tool Company; E.G.P. Corp.; Emerson Electric Asia Ltd. (Hong Kong); Emerson Electric RG (Russia); Emerson Electric Holdings Ltd. (China); Emerson Electric de Mexico; Leroy-Somer AB (Sweden); Fisher Controls International Inc.; High Voltage Maintenance Corp.; Kato Engineering Inc.; Vermont American Corp.

Principal Competitors

ABB Ltd.; General Electric Company; Hitachi Ltd.

Further Reading

Berman, Phyllis, "Emerson Changes Its Spots," *Forbes*, December 24, 2001, p. 66.

Deslodge, Rick, "The Remaking of Emerson," *St. Louis Business Journal*, May 15, 2000, p. 1.

Dyer, Davis and Jeffrey Cruikshank, *Emerson Electric Co.: 100 Years of Manufacturing*, St. Louis, Emerson Electric Co., 1990.

"Emerson Electric Company," *Appliance*, March 1998, p. 132.

"Emerson Electric to Invest US$1 Billion in China," *Alestron*, December 13, 2001.

"Emerson Losses Grow," *Television Digest*, November 25, 1996, p. 15.

"Emerson Unveils New Logo, Readies Print and TV Efforts," *Brandweek*, December 11, 2000, p. 5.

Henkoff, Ronald, "Growing Your Company: Five Ways to Do it Right!," *Fortune*, November 25, 1996, p. 78.

"Remedies For an Economic Hangover," *Fortune*, June 25, 2001, p. 130.

—update: Christina M. Stansell

Endemol Entertainment Holding NV

Bonairelaan 4
1213 VH Hilversu
The Netherlands
Telephone: +31 (0)35 53 99 999
Fax: +31 (0) 35 53 99 980
Web site: http://www.endemol.com

Wholly-Owned Subsidiary of Telefónica S.A.
Incorporated: 1994
Employees:
Sales: $468 million (2000)
NAIC: 512110 Motion Picture and Video Production

Endemol Entertainment Holding NV is a Dutch television production company, which in the summer of 2000 became a subsidiary of Spanish telecommunications giant Telefónica. As a result of the deal, Endemol's founders are Telefónica's largest single shareholders, together controlling a majority of its stock. Endemol operates independently, pursuing its goal of becoming a global force in multi-platform entertainment, combining television programs with the interactivity capabilities of the Internet. Rather than following the Hollywood model of producing a single version of a television show, which is then dubbed into other languages for foreign distribution, Endemol prefers to create formats that can be "localized" by domestic production companies. Although much of what it produces are traditional game shows and soap operas, Endemol has made its name with reality-based programming, in particular *Big Brother,* which stirred debate throughout Europe in its localized versions. *Big Brother* also became Endemol's first sale to the U.S. market, although the show failed to produce the kind of success enjoyed in Europe. Endemol claims to have 400 formats that it can adapt around the world. With a stronghold in Europe, Endemol has made inroads into Latin America as well as China and India. Altogether it boasts subsidiaries and joint ventures in 21 countries.

Origins

The creative force behind Endemol is its chairman, CEO, and cofounder John de Mol. He was born in The Netherlands in 1955, part of a family that was quite familiar with the entertainment business. His grandfather had his own orchestra, and his father was a popular singer, a Dutch version of Frank Sinatra. When de Mol was in high school his father served as director of Radio Noordzee. According to de Mol, "I would go hang out at the station after class. I was totally captivated by the atmosphere. He wanted me to go study law or something like that. But my mind was made up, I wanted to be in radio. So I never went to college." After getting his start as a program technician with Radio Noordzee, de Mol went to work for a pirate radio station that broadcast rock music from a ship moored in the North Sea in order to get around Dutch laws that only permitted public broadcasting. Soon pirate stations were banned and shut down, and de Mol at the age of 19 was out of work. He married singer-actress Willke Alberti, a major Dutch celebrity who was ten years older than he. During the five years of their marriage he became familiar with the glare of publicity, as the press followed his wife's every move, and he grew to resent the insinuations that he was simply living off her money. "That experience inspired me to work hard," he later wrote, "I'm very old-fashioned in the sense that I want to be the moneymaker."

De Mol became a radio sports editor of soccer broadcasts, then branched into television when he took a job with Dutch pubcaster TROS, where he learned to become a producer. He told *Variety* that in the beginning he hated working in television, remarking, "Then one day we were working on a Miss Holland program, and I felt this strange nervousness and butterflies in my stomach and realized that, in 10 minutes, 5 million people would be watching us. That's when the fever started." De Mol soon decided to strike out on his own, with the intent of selling Dutch programs to other European countries. Unable to secure bank financing he finally gained backing from entrepreneur Willem van Kooten, who he had known since his teenage years, and in 1979 established John de Mol Produkties B.V. The first major break for the company was buying the European broadcast rights of a John Denver concert in Amsterdam, which de Mol was able to sell across the Continent.

For the first few years, de Mol produced one-off special events, then in 1984 began to produce weekly television shows for TROS, including *Medisch Centrum West* and *Popformule.*

His company was now well positioned to take advantage of significant changes in European television, which for decades had been state-run and funded by taxpayers, and skewed more towards educational fare than entertainment. In 1980, there were only 25 stations operated by European Community members, but after governments in the mid-1980s began to grant commercial licenses, and cable as well as satellite operations began to make a multitude of channels available to European viewers, the need for programming increased dramatically. Although Hollywood was more than ready to fill the need, small European production companies like John de Mol Produkties were also able to find a niche producing inexpensive programming. In 1985, de Mol began to produce 30 minute shows with a $6,000 budget for Sky Channel, the first commercial broadcaster in The Netherlands. Rather than just producing original programming for the Dutch audience, however, he began to take advantage of the right to license programming formats to other countries. Seeing the Dutch audience as a perfect barometer, he believed that if a show worked in The Netherlands it would likely work elsewhere in Europe. In 1990, his show *Love Letters* was the first format to successfully cross over to Germany, where it won a number of awards for RTL TV. Other de Mol formats that spread across Europe included *Forgive Me, All You Need Is Love, Lucky Letters, Blind Date,* and *It's Your Turn.*

De Mol's prospects for becoming a European television powerhouse were greatly enhanced in 1991 when the European Community initiated "television without frontiers" mandates. Not only did all EC countries open their borders to programming from others, they now called for at least half of all air time to be devoted to programming produced by European companies. Two of the strongest players on the Continent were de Mol and another Dutch production company named JE Entertainment, which produced even more programming than its rival. The two companies often found themselves in competition with one another, and by 1994 they decided that they would be better off by combining their efforts and agreed to a merger of equals. The result was Endemol Entertainment Holding NV, the name created by combining de Mol with JE Enterainment's founder, Jan van den Ende.

1980s–90s: Going Public

In the mid-1970s Van den Ende was primarily a theatrical producer, but by the end of the decade was producing dramas for Dutch public television. In the early 1980s, he built one of Europe's largest television production facilities in Aalsmeer, converting a massive indoor flower market into a complex that included seven sound stages, editing suites, prop and storage facilities, and office space. With the rise of European commercial broadcasting in the mid-1980s he was also well prepared to take advantage of the need for entertainment programming. Like de Mol, he created formats that could be sold to other countries, including *Ron's Honeymoon Quiz* and *Soundmix Shows.* In the meantime, he continued to stay involved in theater, becoming The Netherlands' largest theatrical producer while also establishing a presence on London's West End as well as Broadway.

With the merger complete, Endemol became Europe's largest independent television production house, able to produce 2,500 hours of programming a year. The merged companies continued to operate separately in order to maintain a mix of programming and stimulate creativity by maintaining a friendly rivalry between the two operations. A long-term goal, however, was jointly held: global expansion, starting with the five top European markets of Germany, France, the United Kingdom, Spain, and Italy. Endemol initiated an acquisition program in which it purchased stakes in target production companies, working with current management teams to foster fast growth, and eventually acquiring majority interests and absorbing the companies into the fold. Over the next four years Endemol would spend $264 million for interests in production companies located in Britain, Germany, Italy, Spain, and Poland. Eventually the company would also gain a production presence in France.

To fund expansion, Endemol went public in 1996, but some disappointing ventures would prove to have an adverse effect on the performance of the company's stock, which traded on the Amsterdam Stock Exchange. Shortly before the IPO, the company's theatrical arm, Life Entertainment, overpaid for Holiday on Ice. The touring show produced poor results, as did the theatrical business in general. Endemol also suffered from an ill-advised entry into sports programming. In 1997, it attempted to launch Sport7, a pay-TV station, but its bid for Dutch soccer rights failed. Sport7 lasted just five months. To cushion the financial blow to Endemol's shareholders, van den Ende and de Mol took personal losses of $20 million each. The price of Endemol shares rebounded in 1998 as the company showed that it was returning its focus to its core TV production business by adding a distribution operation and announcing that it would spin off its live entertainment business, which was eventually sold to van den Ende in February 1999. De Mol had already become sole chairman of Endemol's Executive Board, and now van den Ende became less involved with the day-to-day operations of the company, devoting much of his time to his theatrical endeavors. In March 2000, van den Ende completely withdrew from the company, citing health concerns.

Big Brother's 1999 Launch

Although Endemol was already a powerful force in European television, it would reach an entirely new level of influence with the introduction of a reality-based television show, *Big Brother,* which premiered in The Netherlands in late 1999. Endemol was not alone in developing reality-based programming. There had been a spate of reality shows in the mid-1980s, the Japanese had long been notorious for their reality programming that was unquestionably bizarre, even bordering on the cruel, and America's MTV already had a success in its *Real World* series. Now a number of European television production companies began to develop a new wave of reality shows. At first called *The Golden Cage, Big Brother* had been in development for a couple of years, the idea triggered by a magazine article about Biosphere II. Endemol originally considered

Key Dates:

1979: John de Mol establishes John de Mol Produkties B.V.
1985: De Mol begins to produce programming for Sky Channel.
1991: European Community initiates "television without frontiers" mandates.
1994: De Mol merges with JE Entertainment to form Endemol.
1996: Endemol goes public.
2000: Telefónica acquires Endemol.

placing ten strangers in a controlled environment, following their interaction over the course of a year, but eventually opted for a more practical 100-day period. Each night the day's events in the *Big Brother* house would be summarized in an hour program. The refined game show format included assignments, such as chopping wood to keep a fire going for an entire day, in order to stimulate tension and conflict. More importantly, the audience became involved, voting on which of two contestants would be periodically removed from the house. The last person remaining won a cash prize. *Big Brother* allowed the audience to participate by using the Internet, the first step in Endemol's plan to create multi-platform programming. As the *Big Brother* format developed in other countries, and a subsequent Dutch season began, web cams were added, as were additional cable channels to follow individual contestants.

Following *Big Brother's* successful introduction in The Netherlands, Endemol was able to sell the format to a number of European countries. The show also paved the way for Endemol's entry into the United States' market. Fox, CBS, and ABC bid for the right to bring *Big Brother* to America. CBS was the winner, agreeing to pay over $20 million for a U.S. version of the show. In the end, the money was less important to Endemol than CBS's commitment to a daily show, which the company felt was an essential element of the *Big Brother* format. Earlier CBS had acquired another reality show called *Survivor,* which would premiere before *Big Brother* in the summer of 2000 and become a major success, generating the kind of national debate that was important to the *Big Brother* phenomena in other countries. Overshadowed by *Survivor, Big Brother* failed to live up to expectations in America, although CBS claimed the show to be a success because it managed to generate higher ratings than the network normally produced during a comparable period. Nevertheless, Endemol had broken through in Hollywood after years of fruitless attempts. In August 2000, the company signed a deal with NBC to provide two new reality shows, one of which would ultimately be traded for two formats that became NBC shows: *Spy TV* and *Fear Factor.*

Big Brother was also important to Endemol in attracting the attention of Telefónica, which in early 2000 agreed to pay $5.4 billion for the company, making billionaires out of de Mol and van den Ende. Telefónica hoped that by acquiring Endemol it gained content for its Internet interests, giving it a future edge when the telecommunications company believed that television and the Internet would converge. Endemol, in turn, strengthened its Internet position and gained access to Spanish-speaking markets, in particular South America, where Telefónica had established a strong presence. Telefónica also allowed de Mol to run Endemol with much the same kind of independence as before the acquisition. The company did, however, sell off its distribution operations in order to focus on content development, Telefónica's main reason for buying Endemol.

Mostly on the strength of *Big Brother,* Endemol enjoyed a strong year in 2000, with revenues growing by 57 percent over the previous year to $468 million, while posting a profit of $47 million. Attempts to spin-off new *Big Brother* concepts failed to succeed, however, and reality programming in general began to lose its edge in 2001, resulting in a drop off in ratings. In recognition of a changing environment, De Mol announced that Endemol planned to increase its fiction programming.

Nevertheless, the company continued to look forward, developing what it called "entertainment concepts" that could run on platforms other than just TV. Talk of convergence, in the meantime, had cooled considerably, and Telefónica suffered from a general downturn in the price of telecommunications stocks, opening it to criticism that it overpaid for Endemol, which had been purchased at the height of a market boom. Nevertheless, Endemol remained a valuable property that clearly established itself as an international production company with the kind of creative spirit essential in adapting to the fast-changing world of popular entertainment.

Principal Competitors

TaurusHolding GmbH & Co. KG; RL Group S.A.; United Paramount Network (UPN).

Further Reading

Andrews, Edmund L., "Europe's 'Reality' TV: Chains and Big Brother," *The New York Times,* April 11, 2000, p. A4.

De Mol, John with Vivienne Walt, "Radio Days and Reality TV," *The New York Times,* June 27, 2001, p. C6.

Echikson, William, "Striking Gold in Eurotrash TV," *Business Week,* June 15, 1998.

Edmunds, Marlene, "De Mol Is Reality's Real Thing," *Variety,* July 16, 2001, p. 17.

Flint, Joe, "CBS Wins Bid for Dutch 'Reality' Show In Effort to Keep Pace With TV Tastes," *Wall Street Journal,* February 3, 2000, p. B16.

Schlosser, Joe, "The Man Behind the Camera," *Broadcasting & Cable,* July 3, 2000, p. 16.

"Trash TV Is Going Global," *Business Week,* May 28, 2001, p. 32.

—Ed Dinger

ENDESA S.A.

Principe de Vergara 187
28002 Madrid
Spain
Telephone: (91) 566 8800
Fax: (91) 563 8181
Web site: http://www.endesa.es

Public Company
Incorporated: 1944
Employees: 29,062
Sales: EUR 15.68 billion ($14.7 billion) (2000)
Stock Exchanges: Madrid New York
Ticker Symbol: ELE
NAIC: 221111 Hydroelectric Power Generation; 221112
  Fossil Fuel Electric Power Generation; 221122
  Electric Power Distribution

ENDESA S.A., Spain's largest utility, has enjoyed phenomenal growth since its reorganization in 1983. The reorganization changed its relationship with its state parent company, Instituto Nacional de Industria (INI), by transferring all power companies under INI control to ENDESA's authority. Prior to 1983, ENDESA was one of a number of power companies controlled by the Spanish government through INI. ENDESA continued to increase in size as the Spanish utilities industry began to deregulate during the 1990s. ENDESA became fully privatized in 1998. Since that time, the company has been restructuring, making strategic partnerships, and increasing its holdings in the telecommunications industry. The firm serves over 22 million customers in 12 countries.

The INI Under Franco's Regime

If ENDESA's history was undistinguished from the time of its founding in 1944 to its reorganization in 1983, it was because it was a small, bureaucratic state organization without much decision-making power of its own. ENDESA was run by a succession of state appointees, often military or political figures close to the Spanish dictator Francisco Franco, but real power rested with INI which, in turn, had to refer all major decisions to the government.

Much of ENDESA's pre-1983 history is INI's history. INI had its origins in the Law of Protection and Development of National Industry of October 1939. It was designed to help the nation rebuild an economic infrastructure that had been, at best, weak before the devastation of three years of civil war.

The law, drafted by Juan Antonio Suanez, a close childhood friend of Franco, continued the protectionist traditions found in Spain and typically in economically weak countries that find they must compete with powerful neighbors. Every investment decision required government approval, and no industrial facility could be constructed without official sanction.

As stark and bureaucratic as this law sounds, it made sense to the new dictator Francisco Franco and his government. No foreign money and very few domestic resources were available to develop the economy. Many of these had to be diverted to national defense. Franco had won the Spanish Civil War, but the country was politically isolated. Under pressure from Nazi Germany and fascist Italy—who backed Franco in Spain's civil war—to join their side in World War II, he announced a policy of "non-belligerency." In effect, non-belligerency meant sympathetic gestures to the Axis powers, the most dramatic of which was the dispatch of the Spanish Blue Division to aid Hitler's troops on the Russian Front, while maintaining relations with Britain and the United States on the basis of Spain's neutrality. Franco had to have strong military forces to bolster this policy, and he had to quell nascent Republican support for the war. Spain was in an effective state of siege that seemed to justify strict government controls on all areas of life, including the economy.

A state economic apparatus was necessary to control the major sectors of the economy. It is no surprise that the chosen model for INI was Italy's Instituto per la Riconstruzione Industriale (IRI), created to reconstruct Italy's economy under the direct control of its dictator Benito Mussolini. Like its Italian counterpart, INI had a strong initial defense production orientation, but it was also directed to invest in enterprises that were unlikely to attract private capital and, at the government's

175

request, INI had to take over failing private companies. This last requirement, the nursing of "lame duck" companies, was a burden on INI for most of its history.

Electricity generation was one of the early major nonmilitary sectors to receive special attention and investment from INI. By 1944, Franco's government was able to look toward the end of World War II and began to take more economic initiatives. Spain remained a backward country. There was little electricity available outside major industrial areas, and even there, it was not sufficient enough to supply the industries.

The Creation of ENDESA: 1944

ENDESA was created as a public limited company, 98 percent-owned by INI, to construct badly needed power stations. Unlike most other INI companies, ENDESA was not an industrial monopoly. Two years later, in 1946, INI formed the Empresa Nacional Hidro-electrica del Ribagorzana (ENHER) to develop power generated from the River Noguera-Ribagorzana and its tributaries. Other state and private power companies were allowed to sell in local markets. Prior to the 1983 reorganization, ENDESA was responsible for less than one-third of the country's electricity output, but it was the largest generator in the sector.

INI poured investment into dams and power stations, but blackouts and electric power shortages persisted in Spain throughout the 1950s. The electricity industry, like others under INI's control, suffered from all the usual problems found in businesses run by massive state organizations. The two most prominent problems were bureaucratic inefficiency and inability to raise private and foreign capital for new investment projects. By 1948, Spanish industrial production only matched 1929 levels.

INI's empire had expanded into most of Spain's major industries, including petroleum, aviation, transportation, engineering, and manufacturing. Much of the rest of the economy was composed of small companies that had low production levels and lacked modern methods, equipment, and facilities. Spain's industrial production expanded but failed to reach the boom levels of growth in Germany, Italy, France, and other European countries that, unlike Franco's Spain, had agreed to participate in the Marshall Plan.

In the late 1950s, Spain suffered an economic crisis involving high inflation, low export levels, and insufficient growth. In 1958, the government cut off budgetary support for INI, but INI and its constituent companies borrowed heavily from private sector banks.

The government began to realize its mistake, and in 1958–60 adopted a "cold bath" stabilization plan similar to that typically favored by conservative economists today. The plan imposed ceilings on borrowing and forced ENDESA and other INI companies to become self-financing. The liberalization of business restrictions that had begun in the 1950s was speeded up to attract long-term and foreign investment.

However, little privatization was allowed. There was still a widespread fear that privatization would mean foreign domination. The fear persisted up until the 1990s. It was a major reason why Spain remained behind a protectionist wall until it moved to join the European Community (EC) in the early 1980s.

Initially, the impact was inflationary and electricity prices were allowed to rise by up to 50 percent. By 1960, however, the groundwork was laid for what has been referred to as the Spanish miracle. The so-called miracle did not extend much beyond the major metropolitan areas. Concerns about "the two Spains" caused the government to once again rely on a centralized approach to national development.

Three national development plans aimed to develop regional industry. INI's role was limited in the first two, but it was crucial to the third of these plans, which were generally successful in creating new industrialization. The government made a number of attempts to reform INI during the 1960s and 1970s in an effort to make it and INI's constituent companies more businesslike. In 1968, INI was placed under the jurisdiction of the Ministry of Industry. Claudio Boada, appointed INI president in 1970, set up a three-year reorganization plan designed to make the company more profitable and less dependent on government subsidies.

ENDESA and other subsidiaries were expected to function more like regular companies that operated on a profit-and-loss basis. A steel crisis hit INI in the early 1970s. The oil shocks of 1973 and 1979 hit Spain badly because the government continued to subsidize oil price levels until the death of Franco in 1975. INI nevertheless continued to expand and absorb loss-making companies in rescue operations.

ENDESA Reorganizes: 1980s

In 1978, a new INI president, Jose Miguel de la Rica, set significant reforms in place when he won the right not to be required by the government to take over failing companies, except by parliamentary order. From the beginning of the 1980s, this development and the general world trends that favored free market solutions and privatization encouraged INI to act more like a public sector company. INI sold all or part of its interest in a number of unprofitable companies.

The ENDESA reorganization of 1983 was part of the government's general plan to make INI more efficient and modernize Spain's institutions in preparation for full Spanish membership in the European Community. INI transferred all its power companies, Empresa Nacional Hidro-Electrica del Ribagorzana (ENHER), General Europea S.A. (GESA), Union Electrica de

Canarias S.A. (UNELCO), and Empresa Nacional Electrica de Cordoba (ENECO) to ENDESA. The reorganization did not create a monopoly, however; at least seven major power companies remained in private hands. Nevertheless, after reorganization, ENDESA became the country's largest electricity producer.

Ownership of several of the private companies was heavily concentrated in the hands of Spain's traditional elite and families who were close to General Franco. Unused to competitive pressures, these companies made some disastrous over-investments in nuclear power during the 1970s. In 1983, a government moratorium was imposed on further investment in nuclear plants.

The government called on ENDESA to bail out these companies. As a result of a 1985 asset swap, ENDESA was further strengthened. The Spanish government required heavily indebted private and public companies like ENHER, Union Fenosa, and Fuerzas Electricas de Cataluna (FECSA) to sell large parts of their power stations and market share to ENDESA. This asset swap added more than Pta5 billion to the consolidated balance sheet and caused ENDESA to double in size.

In 1988, ENDESA followed Repsol as the second of three Spanish companies to be floated in New York, which, in effect, privatized 20 percent of the company for $670 million. Telefonica was the third. ENDESA quickly became acknowledged as an appreciating stock. INI's stake in ENDESA—then 75 percent—was now one of INI's most important assets because ENDESA accounted for most of the INI group's profits.

As a result of these reorganizations, ENDESA changed from being solely a power-generating company wholesaling electricity to a more diversified—but integrated—energy production company with interests in coal, oil, nuclear, and hydroelectric-generated power.

In 1990, the company expanded into coal production with the acquisition of another INI company, ENCASUR. Traditionally, ENDESA was a wholesaler of power from generating stations. It continued in this role in the early 1990s, but its subsidiaries were full-cycle companies that could produce and sell their own products.

In 1983, however, the government also created Red Eléctrica de España or REDESA, with ENDESA as the majority shareholder, to regulate the distribution system by deciding which plants would cover the country's electric power demands. This decision was calculated according to the cost at which certain companies could produce electricity regardless of who owned the plant. The basis was strict optimization of the costs. REDESA was able to buy power from other ENDESA companies or it could buy from smaller, privately owned electricity companies. There was a complicated payment system. This in effect put ENDESA in a role sometimes played by regulatory bodies and electricity-generating boards in other countries. It must not be forgotten, however, that despite a degree of privatization, ENDESA—at the time—remained a government institution in an industry in which market forces did not fully dictate its moves.

In another important way, ENDESA continued to function through the late 1980s to the early 1990s as a government instrument. ENDESA embarked on a campaign of buying interests in private companies dictated not so much by economic self-interest as by the dictates of Spanish government policy. In early 1991, ENDESA took over the small Electra de Viesgo private utility in northern Spain and increased its stakes in other small private generators and distributors.

Overcoming Deregulation Fears

The Spanish Socialist Economy Minister Carlos Solchaga stated his intention to use ENDESA as his main weapon to restructure the Spanish energy sector. The government knew that its ability to intervene in the energy sector would be curtailed severely when EC rules for liberalizing the entire European energy network took effect at the end of 1992.

In 1990, the government warned foreign power utilities not to try to buy into their Spanish counterparts. The government feared that French utility companies would sell their cheap nuclear power in Spain after 1992, severely undercutting Spanish companies, threatening Spanish jobs, and making Spain dependent on France for her power needs.

In the early 1990s, critics claimed that ENDESA had high costs and low productivity and was kept alive by the government to buy coal from loss-making, state-owned pits. The government claimed that ENDESA would severely undermine private utilities' profits if it were allowed to compete directly in the retail market, but it also hoped that its rationalization plan for the power industry would cure any real inefficiencies before it had to compete with stronger EC firms. Solchaga wanted the power industry—including ENDESA, seven large private-sector generating and distributing companies, and several small local suppliers—to merge into, at most, three large conglomerates which would be the sole generators of electricity in the sector. The three would then supply a central network that would sell electricity to four or five distribution companies.

The mergers would also be aimed at putting Spain in a position to supply a projected 5 percent increase in annual demand. The government estimated that Spain had to spend an estimated Pta600 billion to add the further 7,500 megawatts of electricity required by the end of the decade.

In April 1991, two major private utilities, Hidroelectrica España S.A. and Iberduero, announced that they would merge to form Iberdrola. The new company controlled most of Spain's low-cost electricity generated from hydroelectric plants and challenged ENDESA's market position. The merger thwarted a possible bid by ENDESA, which then mounted a July bid to gain management control for Seville-based Compañia Sevillana de Electricidad S.A.

After a legal wrangle in which Sevillana's lawyers threatened to bring ENDESA before the European Commission on grounds of unfair competition, a compromise formula was found, enabling ENDESA to raise its stake above 20 percent without assuming management control. The deal also allowed Sevillana to buy a two percent interest in ENDESA, with a further six percent to be sold on the market. INI's stake in ENDESA would be reduced to 67 percent. The highly profitable ENDESA had been put in a privileged position by a Spanish government that was determined to build up Spanish bulwarks against foreign domination as the industry deregulated.

Privatization Continues: Mid- to Late 1990s

Indeed, ENDESA held strong to its growth strategy for much of the 1990s. In 1994, INI reduced its holding of the firm to 66.89 percent by way of a second public offering. As full privatization appeared imminent, ENDESA began to bolster as well as diversify its holdings. In 1995, it purchased 9.7 percent of Edenor S.A., the electrical distributor based in Argentina. The company also acquired 7.2 percent of Airtel, the second-largest mobile phone operator in Spain. In 1996, it increased its holding in Sevillana. That year the company reported a profit of $1 billion.

Deregulation of both the telecommunications and the electrical utilities industries in Spain went hand in hand. As such, Spain's second-largest fixed phone operator, Retevision, came under control of ENDESA and a group of investors in 1997. In August of that year, it purchased a 29 percent controlling interest in Enersis, Chile's main power group, for $1.5 billion. In September, the firm led a consortium that purchased 48.5 percent of Codensa, Columbia's electricity distributor, for $1.3 billion. By now, ENDESA had become the largest electricity group in all of Latin America. Twenty-five percent of ENDESA was offered to the public that year.

ENDESA became a private company in 1998 when the remaining 33 percent of the firm was made public. By that time, the company controlled 43 percent of its home distribution market and 47 percent of its national generation market. Management emphasized that further diversification and expansion was necessary, especially in the face of increased competition brought on by deregulation. The firm continued to make acquisitions including increasing its interest in Enersis to 60 percent. It also purchased ten percent of the Amsterdam Power Exchange, ten percent of Cable y Televisión de Catalunya, and 3.64 percent of Repsol. The company also divested certain assets including some of its holdings in Antena 3, Cepsa, and Airtel.

ENDESA entered the new millennium a much different company then it had been just five years earlier. Out from under majority government control for the first time, the company continued with its restructuring plan—which had started in 1999—so that it could compete effectively in a deregulated market. The firm created ENDESA Servicios, ENDESA Generación, and ENDESA Distribución to oversee its internal needs, electricity production, and electricity distribution, respectively. In 2000, the company's separation of its distribution and generation businesses was completed.

That year the company teamed up with Telecom Italia and Union Fenosa to create AUNA Operadores de Telecomunicaciones S.A., a firm that combined all of their holdings in Spanish telecommunications firms. It then purchased SMARTCOM PCS, a Chilean mobile phone operator. In 2001, ENDESA acquired 45 percent of Enel SpA's Elettrogen, an Italian electricity generation firm. Not all of its attempts were successful, however. In February 2001, it canceled its $13 billion bid for Iberdrola when both companies deemed the merger conditions set by the government were unacceptable.

During 2001, ENDESA launched its new corporate identity and completed streamlining its operations into six distinct business lines, including generation, distribution, commercialization of electrical energy, international lines, diversification, and services. Management felt that this new ENDESA was well positioned to compete in the ever-changing and increasingly competitive industrial market. As one of the largest companies operating in Spain, ENDESA's future in the deregulated market looked promising.

Principal Subsidiaries

Amsterdam Power Exchange (10%); Cía Operadora del Mercado Eléctrico Español, S.A. (COMEESA) (5.71%); Compañía Sevillana de Electricidad I, S.A. (SEVILLANA I); Electricidad de Puerto Real, S.A. (EPRESA) (50%); Suministradora eléctrica de Cádiz (33.5%); Electra de Viesgo I, S.A. (VIESGO I); Eléctricas Reunidas de Zaragoza I, S.A.; Gas y Electricidad I, S.A. (GESA I); Termoeléctrica del Ebro, S.A. (ELECBRO); Unión Eléctrica de Canarias I, S.A.; Distribuidora Eléctrica del Puerto de la Cruz; Eléctrica de Lijar S.L. (50%); Hidroeléctrica de Cataluya, S.L.; Nuevas Iniciativas Eléctricas del Sur, S.A., (NUINELEC); Anllares, A.I.E; Aragonesa de Actividades Energéticas, S.A. (AAESA); Carboex, S.A.; CARBOPOR (95.36%); Central Nuclear Almaraz, A.I.E (36.02%); Central Térmica Litoral Almería, A.I.E.; Central Térmica Los Barrios, A.I.E.; Empresa Carbonífera del Sur, S.A. (ENCASUR); Endesa Puertos, S.L.; Hispano-Francesa de Energía Nuclear (HIFRENSA) (52%); Nuclenor, S.A. (50%); Endesa Trading, S.A.; Endesa Gas, S.A.U.; Endesa Telecomunicaciones, S.A.; Endesa Cogeneración y Renovables, S.A. (ECYR); Endesa Chile (59.98%); Endesa Internacional Energía LTD. (Brazil).

Principal Operating Units

ENDESA Generación; ENDESA Distribución; ENDESA Energía; ENDESA Diversificación; ENDESA Internacional; ENDESA Servicios.

Principal Competitors

Hidroeléctrica Del Cantábrico, S.A.; Iberdrola S.A.; Unión Eléctrica Fenosa, S.A.

Further Reading

"Chile: Endesa Acquired 53.78% Stake in Enersis," *South American Business Information*, April 19, 1999.

Donaghy, Peter and Michael Newton, *Spain: A Guide To Political and Economic Institutions*, Cambridge: Cambridge University Press, 1989.

"Duke Still Guns for Endesa," *Oil Daily*, February 24, 1999.

"Endesa Shrinks to Grow," *Power in Europe*, October 10. 1997, p. 2.

"Enersis Clash Hits Endesa Sale," *Petroleum Times Energy Report*, November 3, 1997, p. 6.

Johnson, Keith, "Endesa Wins Bid to Acquire Italian Electricity Producer," *Wall Street Journal*, July 4, 2001, p. 4.

Robinson, Andrew, "Jockeying for Power in Spanish Electricity," *Business Week*, October 24, 2000.

"Spain Launches Her Largest Public Offer," *Privatization International*, October 1997, p. 5.

—Noel Peter Byde and Clark Siewert
—update: Christina M. Stansell

Engle Homes, Inc.

123 Northwest 13th Street
Boca Raton, Florida 33432
U.S.A.
Telephone: (561) 391-4012
Toll Free: (800) 624-3960
Fax: (561) 750-6945
Web site: http://www.englehomes.com

Wholly Owned Subsidiary of Technical Olympic USA
Incorporated: 1982
Employees: 910
Sales: $844 million (2000)
NAIC: 23321 Single Family Housing Construction;
52421 Insurance Agencies and Brokerages

Engle Homes, Inc. is one of the largest homebuilders in the United States, operating in Florida, Colorado, Texas, Georgia, Virginia, and North Carolina. Engle Homes designs, constructs, markets, and sells, detached single-family homes, condominiums, townhouses, and patio houses. Through two subsidiaries, Preferred Home Mortgage Company and Universal Land Title, the company offers financial services to its homebuyers, providing financing and title insurance services, respectively. Technical Olympic USA, a subsidiary of Greek construction giant Technical Olympic S.A., owns 100 percent of Engle Homes.

Origins

One of the United States' most prolific homebuilders during the 1990s never progressed past the fifth grade. Alec Engelstein, founder of Engle Homes, was born in Romania in 1930. The political upheaval following World War II cast Romania into communist hands, prompting Engelstein to flee Romania and find refuge in Italy—not the first time he would seek shelter from threatening political winds. After a brief stay in Rome, Engelstein moved to Canada, settling in Montreal, where he first learned the homebuilding trade. Engelstein arrived in Montreal in 1948, at the age of 18.

Engelstein spent 20 years in Montreal. He worked for a homebuilder whose projects were primarily located in the city's suburbs, gaining experience that would prove invaluable during his entrepreneurial career. That Engelstein ever decided to start his own homebuilding business was because of the relationship he enjoyed with his employer, a partnership of sorts that steered Engelstein toward his life's work. Engelstein's employer spent every winter in Florida, leaving his apprentice to sell homes and preside over the construction projects while he was away. The experience introduced Engelstein to the practicalities of working as a homebuilder, convincing the transplanted Romanian to make a career for himself in the business. Engelstein's turning point—the moment he decided to set out on his own—occurred when he was 38 years old, a decision that was triggered by an uncertain political climate.

Founder Moves to Florida in 1968

To Engelstein's thinking, the separatist movement in Quebec had created a tenuous business environment by 1968. In search of more peaceful pastures, Engelstein decided to follow the path of his employer's winter migration. He moved to Florida, intent on carving a place for himself in the homebuilding market. Engelstein spent much of 1968 looking for land, before forming his first company, A.E. Development, in 1969. Through A.E. Development, the predecessor to Engle Homes, Engelstein began his first project in Florida. Dubbed Lakeside Village, the project was located in Palm Springs, comprising a 760-unit condominium complex that included one-bedroom units selling for $9,990 and larger two-bedroom units selling for $17,900.

The completion of Lakeside Village represented the first Engelstein-inspired housing project, the first of many to follow. Once out of the gates, however, Engelstein and A.E. Development stumbled. The real estate market in southern Florida collapsed in late 1970, forcing the 40-year-old Engelstein to regroup. To contend with the precarious business climate, Engelstein merged his homebuilding interests with another developer, American Capital. The two entities worked as one until 1978, when they separated under amicable terms.

Under the conditions of the corporate divorce, Engelstein departed with one of the two projects under development by the merged companies. Engelstein's acquisition was a project con-

Company Perspectives:

For nearly a quarter century, the people at Engle Homes have dedicated themselves to offering customers a home buying and building experience that is "Simply Better." We understand that purchasing a home is one of the most important decisions you will ever make. That is why it is our mission to make this experience the best it can be. We take pride in keeping our customers involved and informed every step of the way. To make your home buying process even easier, we offer the services, strength, and expertise of our subsidiaries, Preferred Home Mortgage Company and Universal Land Title, Inc. These are just a few of the reasons why so many of our homeowners refer their family and friends to us again and again. As one of America's leading homebuilders, we've built a solid reputation by providing exceptional homes at an outstanding value. Across the nation, Engle Homes carefully selects only the finest locations in the most desirable areas.

sisting of 900 single family homes composing a development called Lakes of Sherbrooke, located in Lantanc, Florida. With this asset, Engelstein formed Engle Homes in 1978, purposefully transposing the "L" and "E" in his surname. One year later, he asked his brother Harry to join him in the business. Together, the brothers quickly fashioned the company into one of the largest three builders in the Palm Beach area. The pernicious cyclicality of the home building market again forced Engelstein to counterattack, however. By 1982, Engle Homes was bearing the brunt of recessive economic conditions in the Palm Beach market. The solution, as it would be later in his career, was for Engelstein to diversify his market, to expand geographically. Engelstein decided to broaden the scope of Engle Homes' southward—the first destination: Boca Raton.

Expansion into Southern Florida in the 1980s

As Engelstein expanded, he followed a growth strategy that evoked images of a military invasion. In a July 25, 1997 interview with *South Florida Business Journal*, Engelstein explained: "You enter a new market by creating a beach head and then you keep enlarging it. The objective is to create markets that will continue to grow and expand. We've strategically chosen regions offering strong economies with new business and employment growth." Such was the case in Engelstein's initial foray into the Palm Beach area, where he and his brother targeted first-time homebuyers. For Boca Raton, extant market conditions dictated Engelstein's actions, prompting Engle Homes to target a market niche that was under-served.

During the early 1980s, the Boca Raton housing market offered numerable buying opportunities for those wishing to spend in excess of $200,000 for a home, but less expensive new homes were hard to find. Engelstein explained, noting in a September 20, 1999 interview with *The Palm Beach Post*, "We said, all right, there are people working, young professional people who cannot afford that price range." The company's response to the untapped market was Concord Green, its first development in Boca Raton. Prices at Concord Green started at $74,000. "We hit the mother lode," Engelstein remembered in

his interview with *The Palm Beach Post.* "From there, it just went one after another."

Engle Homes grew steadily throughout the 1980s. The push southwards continued, reaching as far south as Cooper City by 1992, when Embassy Lakes, a large master planned community opened. One pressing problem that faced Engelstein at the beginning of the 1990s was a lack of capital, the money to develop projects such as Embassy Lakes. Recessive economic conditions had caused banks to grow wary, which restricted Engelstein's supply of capital, forcing him to search for alternative ways to fuel his expansion plans. Engelstein decided to sell his company to the public, filing for an initial public offering (IPO) in October 1991. Engle Homes' shares were expected to debut in November 1991, but anemic market conditions led Engelstein to cancel the offering. In 1992, his second attempt at an IPO succeeded, when 2.3 million shares were sold on the NASDAQ at $11.50 per share.

With a fresh supply of capital gleaned from the IPO, Engelstein was ready to press forward with his expansion plans. He now had shareholders to answer to and analysts to appease, forces that, to a certain extent, would direct the direction of Engle Homes' growth. The company could no longer depend entirely on developing properties in Florida, partly because it was becoming harder to find land in the company's home state and partly because of the sensitive expectations of Wall Street. Home building, perhaps more than others, was a capricious market, subject to fluctuations that could send a developer's fortunes soaring and just as quickly cause financial ruin. With all its assets tied to the southern Florida housing market, Engle Homes was exposed to the vagaries of one market, a vulnerability that sent shivers down the backs of investors and analysts alike. Engelstein realized this and began formulating an expansion strategy that would satisfy Wall Street and fuel Engle Homes' growth.

National Expansion Begins in 1993

The solution was to expand outside Florida. Engle Homes was set to become a national homebuilder with a presence in a variety of markets, using a diverse portfolio to insulate itself from the fluctuations of one particular market. Engelstein chose Dallas, Texas, as the first beach head for the company's expansion outside Florida. An Engle Homes division was established in Dallas in 1993, followed by the establishment of divisions in Tampa and Orlando before the end of the year. In 1994, the company expanded to the east, establishing divisions in the Washington, D.C., suburbs of Virginia and Maryland and in Raleigh, North Carolina. Further expansion pushed Engle Homes into Denver, Colorado, where the company's entry into the market was completed through the acquisition of Park Homes West, a local developer.

Expansion engendered appreciable gains in sales, as Engle Homes' stature swelled. In 1992, the company posted $78.2 million in sales. By 1994, the total had mushroomed to $220.9 million. The same could not be said of the company's profitability, which essentially remained flat during the growth spurt. Moreover, not every foray into a new market proved successful, the company's entry into the Raleigh market standing out as a glaring miscue. According to a February 11, 1998 article in the *Wall Street Journal*, Engle Homes "dashed into an area already overrun with national builders, started to pay too much for hilly land bypassed by others, and brought in managers unfamiliar with the area.'' There were missteps, to be sure, but overall Engle Homes was fast becoming a recognized homebuilder on the national scene. Engelstein was undeterred by the occasional foible and pressed ahead with expansion into new markets.

In 1997, Engle Homes established a presence in two of the fastest-growing housing markets in the United States. In May, the company opened an office in Atlanta, Georgia, the first step toward securing a toehold in the lucrative market. Engle Homes division president, Geoffrey Brunning, left little doubt about his company's aspirations in Atlanta. In a January 23, 1998 interview with the *Atlanta Business Chronicle,* he declared, ''Our goal is to be one of the top five home builders in the market as quickly as we can. We're intending to come in as a significant player.'' Not long after Brunning's declaration, Engle Homes controlled 623 lots in the Atlanta metropolitan area, with two developments under construction and others in the offing. Meanwhile, the company was making headway in Arizona. Engle Homes sold its first house in Arizona in 1997, realizing $136,656 in gross income. By the following year, the company had sold 234 properties, registering $47 million in gross income. In 1999, 552 houses were sold, generating $166 million in gross income, totals that ranked the company's Arizona division as the fastest-growing homebuilder in the nation.

By the end of the 1990s, Engle Homes' financial record told the tale of a rapidly growing company. Sales increased nearly ten-fold during the seven years separating the company's IPO and the end of the decade, reaching $742 million in 1999. Net income, which had languished between $6 million and $8 million during the first half of the decade, recorded strident growth during the late 1990s, surging to $28 million in 1999. Behind the numbers stood a well-balanced homebuilder operating in eight of the leading 20 home-building markets.

Diversification had carried Engle Homes into the financial services sector, where the company operated two companies to better serve its home-buying clientele. Through Preferred Home Mortgage Company, a full-service mortgage banking subsidiary, the company arranged financing for customers in all its markets. Engle Homes had also acquired a title company, Universal Land Title, which provided title insurance services to customers in Florida, Denver, and Dallas.

As Engle Homes entered its second decade as a publicly-traded concern, the strength of its operations attracted a suitor. Technical Olympic S.A., a Greek construction company with operations in Greece, the United Kingdom, the United States, and in Engelstein's native country of Romania, was the interested party. A builder of major infrastructure projects, including highway, tunnels, airports, and marine and harbor works, Technical Olympic operated in the United States through Technical Olympic USA. In October 2000, Technical Olympic USA began negotiating for the purchase of all Engle Homes' outstanding shares of common stock. Engelstein welcomed the bid, resulting in the completion of the deal in November 2000. Technical Olympic USA paid $465 million for 100 percent ownership of Engle Homes, which subsequently became an indirect, wholly owned subsidiary of Technical Olympic USA. The trading of Engle Homes' common stock ceased November 22, the day the deal closed.

Engle Homes' acquisition by Technical Olympic USA marked the beginning of a new era for Engelstein's corporate creation. A septuagenarian by the time the merger was completed, Engelstein remained in charge of the company following the merger, serving as a director and its chief executive officer. His brother Harry served as executive vice president and chief construction officer. Together, the brothers applied their considerable experience toward continued success in the new century, supported by the deep financial pockets of its Greek parent company.

Principal Subsidiaries

Preferred Home Mortgage Company; Universal Land Title, Inc.; Engle Homes/Pembroke, Inc.

Principal Competitors

Pulte Homes, Inc.; The Ryland Group, Inc.; Centex Corporation.

Further Reading

Ball, Jeffrey, ''Fallen Engle: A Builder Stumbles in Carolina Foray,'' *Wall Street Journal,* February 11, 1998, p. F2.
''Engle Homes Offers Value and Variety,'' *South Florida Business Journal,* April 23, 1993, p. 5C.
Halpern, Steve, ''The *Miami Herald* Steve Halpern Column,'' *Knight-Ridder/Tribune Business News,* January 16, 1994.
Hardy, Eric S., ''Undersized and Unloved,'' *Forbes,* December 13, 1999, p. 376.
Koppel, Dale, ''Market Diversity Helps Engle Homes Build Success,'' *South Florida Business Journal,* July 25, 1997, p. 17.
Lamm, Marcy, ''Big Fla. Home Builder Expanding in Atlanta,'' *Atlanta Business Chronicle,* January 23, 1998, p. 3A.
Lurz, William H., ''Public Builder Faces Wall Street's Mandate,'' *Professional Builder,* September 1996, p. 34.
Muellner, Alexis, ''Technical to Buy Engle Homes,'' *South Florida Business Journal,* October 27, 2000, p. 25A.
Padgett, Mike, ''Engle Homes Earns 'Triple Crown' as Fastest-Growing Start-Up Builder,'' *The Business Journal—Serving Phoenix and the Valley of the Sun,* September 22, 2000, p. 10.
Rawls, Linda, ''Greek Company to Buy Engle Homes in $465 Million Deal,'' *The Palm Beach Post,* October 13, 2000, p. 1D.
''Technical Olympic USA Completes Acquisition of Engle Homes,'' *Business Wire,* November 22, 2000, p. 13.
Van de Water, Ava, ''Engle Homes Rides Crest of Buyer's Market into Top 10,'' *The Palm Beach Post,* September 9, 1999, p. 38.

—Jeffrey L. Covell

Enron Corporation

1400 Smith Street
Houston, Texas 77002-7369
U.S.A.
Telephone: (713) 853-6161
Fax: (713) 853-3129
Web site: http://www.enron.com

Public Company
Incorporated: 1930 as Northern Natural Gas Company
Employees: 21,000
Sales: $101 billion (2000)
NAIC: 211111 Crude Petroleum and Natural Gas
    Extraction; 22121 Natural Gas Distibution; 48621
    Pipeline Transportation of Natural Gas; 221122
    Electric Power Distribution; 221119 Other Electric
    Power Generation.

Before filing for bankruptcy in 2001, Enron Corporation was one of the largest integrated natural gas and electricity companies in the world. It marketed natural gas liquids worldwide and operated one of the largest natural gas transmission systems in the world, totaling more than 36,000 miles. It was also one of the largest independent developers and producers of electricity in the world, serving both industrial and emerging markets. Enron was also a major supplier of solar and wind renewable energy worldwide, managed the largest portfolio of natural gas-related risk management contracts in the world, and was one of the world's biggest independent oil and gas exploration companies. In North America, Enron was the largest wholesale marketer of natural gas and electricity. Enron pioneered innovative trading products, such as gas futures and weather futures, significantly modernizing the utilities industry. After a surge of growth in the early 1990s, the company ran into difficulties. The magnitude of Enron's losses was hidden from stockholders. The company folded after a failed merger deal with Dynegy Inc. in 2001 brought to light massive financial finagling. The company had ranked number seven on the Fortune 500, and its failure was the biggest bankruptcy in American history.

Company Origins

Enron began as Northern Natural Gas Company, organized in Omaha, Nebraska, in 1930 by three other companies. North American Light & Power Company and United Light & Railways Company each held a 35 percent stake in the new enterprise, while Lone Star Gas Corporation owned the remaining 30 percent. The company's founding came just a few months after the stock market crash of 1929, an inauspicious time to launch a new venture. Several aspects of the Great Depression actually worked in Northern's favor, however. Consumers initially were not enthusiastic about natural gas as a heating fuel, but its low cost led to its acceptance during tough economic times. High unemployment brought the new company a ready supply of cheap labor to build its pipeline system. In addition, the 24-inch steel pipe, which could transport six times the amount of gas carried by 12-inch cast iron pipe, had just been developed. Northern grew rapidly in the 1930s, doubling its system capacity within two years of its incorporation and bringing the first natural gas supply to the state of Minnesota.

Public Offering in the 1940s

The 1940s brought changes in Northern's regulation and ownership. The Federal Power Commission, created as a result of the Natural Gas Act of 1938, regulated the natural gas industry's rates and expansion. In 1941, United Light & Railways sold its share of Northern to the public, and in 1942 Lone Star Gas distributed its holdings to its stockholders. North American Light & Power would hold on to its stake until 1947, when it sold its shares to underwriters who then offered the stock to the public. Northern was listed on the New York Stock Exchange that year.

In 1944, Northern acquired the gas-gathering and transmission lines of Argus Natural Gas Company. The following year, the Argus properties were consolidated into Peoples Natural Gas Company, a subsidiary of Northern. In 1952, Peoples was dissolved as a subsidiary, its operations henceforth becoming a division of the parent company. Also in 1952, the company set up another subsidiary, Northern Natural Gas Producing Company, to operate its gas leases and wells. Another subsidiary, Northern Plains Natural Gas Company, was established in 1954 and eventually would bring Canadian gas reserves to the continental United States.

Through its Peoples division, the parent company acquired a natural gas system in Dubuque, Iowa, from North Central Public Service Company in 1957. In 1964, Council Bluffs Gas Company of Iowa was acquired and merged into the Peoples division. Northern created two more subsidiaries in 1960: Northern Gas Products Company (later Enron Gas Processing Company), for the purpose of building and operating a natural gas extraction plant in Bushton, Kansas; and Northern Propane Gas Company, for retail sales of propane. Northern Natural Gas Producing Company was sold to Mobil Corporation in 1964, but the parent company continued expanding on other fronts. In 1966, it formed Hydrocarbon Transportation Inc. (later Enron Liquids Pipeline Company) to own and operate a pipeline system carrying liquid fuels. Eventually, this system would bring natural gas liquids from plants in the Midwest and Rocky Mountains to upper-Midwest markets, with connections for eastern markets as well.

Growth through Acquisitions

Northern made several acquisitions in 1967: Protane Corporation, a distributor of propane gas in the eastern United States and the Caribbean; Mineral Industries Inc., a marketer of automobile antifreeze; National Poly Products Inc.; and Viking Plastics of Minnesota. Also in 1967, Northern created Northern Petrochemical Company to manufacture and market industrial and consumer chemical products. The petrochemical company acquired Monsanto Corporation's polyethylene marketing business in 1969.

Northern continued expanding during the 1970s. In February 1970 it acquired Plateau Natural Gas Company, which became part of the Peoples division. In 1971, it bought Olin Corporation's antifreeze production and marketing business. It set up UPG Inc. in 1973 to transport and market the fuels produced by Northern Gas Products. UPG eventually would handle oil and liquid gas products for other companies as well.

In 1976, Northern formed Northern Arctic Gas Company, a partner in the proposed Alaskan arctic gas pipeline, and Northern Liquid Fuels International Ltd., a supply and marketing

company. Northern Border Pipeline Company, a partnership of four energy companies with Northern Plains Natural Gas as managing partner, began construction of the eastern segment of the Alaskan pipeline in 1980. This segment, stretching from Ventura, Iowa, to Monchy, Saskatchewan, was completed in 1982. About that time, it became apparent that transporting Alaskan gas to the lower 48 states would be prohibitively expensive. Nevertheless, the pipeline provided an important link between Canadian gas reserves and the continental United States. Northern changed its name to InterNorth, Inc. in 1980. That same year, while attempting to grow through acquisitions, InterNorth became involved in a takeover battle with Cooper Industries Inc. to acquire Crouse-Hinds Company, a manufacturer of electrical products. Cooper rescued Crouse-Hinds from InterNorth's hostile bid and bought Crouse-Hinds in January 1981. The takeover fight brought a flurry of lawsuits between InterNorth and Cooper. The suits were dropped after the acquisition was finalized.

While InterNorth grew through acquisitions, it also expanded from within. In 1980, it set up Northern Overthrust Pipeline Company and Northern Trailblazer Pipeline Company to participate in the Trailblazer pipeline, which ran from southeastern Nebraska to western Wyoming. Also that year, it created two exploration and production companies, Nortex Gas & Oil Company and Consolidex Gas and Oil Limited. The latter company was a Canadian operation. In 1981, InterNorth set up Northern Engineering International Company to provide professional engineering services. In 1982, it formed Northern Intrastate Pipeline Company and Northern Coal Pipeline Company as well as InterNorth International Inc. (later Enron International) to oversee non-U.S. operations.

InterNorth significantly expanded its oil and gas exploration and production activity in 1983 with the purchase of Belco Petroleum Corporation for about $770 million. Belco quadrupled InterNorth's gas reserves and added greatly to its crude oil reserves. Exploration efforts focused on the United States, Canada, and Peru.

Other acquisitions of the early 1980s included the fuel trading companies P & O Falco Inc. and P & O Falco Ltd.; their operations joined with UPG—renamed UPG Falco—in 1984 and Chemplex Company, a polyethylene and adhesive manufacturer, also acquired in 1984. InterNorth had sold Northern Propane Gas in 1983.

InterNorth made an acquisition of enormous proportions in 1985, when it bid to purchase Houston Natural Gas Corporation for about $2.26 billion. The offer was received enthusiastically, and the merger created the largest gas pipeline system in the United States—about 37,000 miles at the time. Houston Natural Gas brought pipelines from the Southeast and Southwest to join with InterNorth's substantial system in the Great Plains area. Valero Energy Corporation of San Antonio, Texas, sued to block the merger. InterNorth had entered into joint ventures with Valero early in 1985 to transport and sell gas to industrial users in Texas and Louisiana. Because these ventures competed with Houston Natural Gas, InterNorth withdrew from them when it agreed to the merger. Valero alleged that InterNorth had breached its fiduciary obligations, but the Valero lawsuit failed to stop the acquisition.

Although still officially named InterNorth, the merged company initially was known as HNG/InterNorth, with dual headquarters in Omaha, Nebraska, and Houston, Texas. In 1986, the company's name was changed to Enron Corp., and headquarters were consolidated in Houston. After some shuffling in top management, Kenneth L. Lay, HNG's chairman, emerged as chairman of the combined company. HNG/InterNorth began divesting itself of businesses that did not fit in with its long-term goals. The $400 million in assets sold off in 1985 included the Peoples division, which sold for $250 million. Also in 1985, Peru's government nationalized Enron's assets there, and Enron began negotiating for payment, taking a $218 million charge against earnings in the meantime. In 1986, Enron's chemical subsidiary was sold for $603 million. Also in 1986, Enron sold 50 percent of its interest in Citrus Corporation to Sonat Inc. for $360 million but continued to operate Citrus's pipeline system, Florida Gas Transmission Company. Citrus originally was part of Houston Natural Gas.

In 1987, Enron centralized its gas pipeline operations under Enron Gas Pipeline Operating Company. Also that year, Enron Oil & Gas Company, with responsibility for exploration and production, was formed out of previous InterNorth and HNG operations, including Nortex Oil & Gas, Belco Petroleum, HNG Oil Company, and Florida Petroleum Company. In 1989, Enron Corp. sold 16 percent of Enron Oil & Gas's common stock to the public for about $200 million. That year Enron received $162 million from its insurers for the Peruvian operations, and it continued to negotiate with the government for additional compensation.

Enron made significant moves into electrical power, in both independent production and cogeneration facilities, in the late 1980s. Cogeneration plants produce electricity and thermal energy from one source. It added major cogeneration units in Texas and New Jersey in 1988; in 1989, it signed a 15-year contract to supply natural gas to a cogeneration plant on Long Island. Also in 1989, Enron reached an agreement with Coastal Corporation that allowed the company to increase the natural gas production from its Big Piney field in Wyoming. Under the accord, Coastal agreed to extend a pipeline to the field, since the line already going to it could not handle increased volume. The same year, Enron and El Paso Natural Gas Company received regulatory approval for a joint venture, Mojave Pipeline Company. The pipeline transports natural gas for use in oil drilling.

New Markets in the Early 1990s

In the early 1990s, Enron appeared to be reaping the benefits of the InterNorth-Houston Natural Gas merger. Its revenues, at $16.3 billion in 1985, fell to less than $10 billion in each of the next four years but recovered to $13.1 billion in 1990. Low natural gas prices had been a major cause of the decline. Enron, however, had been able to increase its market share, from 14 percent in 1985 to 18 percent in 1990, with help from efficiencies that resulted from the integration of the two predecessor companies' operations. Enron also showed significant growth in its liquid fuels business as well as in oil and gas exploration.

Beginning with the 1990s, Enron's stated philosophy was to "get in early, push to open markets, position ourselves to compete, compete hard when the opening comes." This philosophy was translated into two major sectors: international markets and the newly deregulated gas and electricity markets in the United States.

Beginning in 1991, Enron built its first overseas power plant in Teesside, England, which became the largest gas-fired cogeneration plant in the world with 1,875 megawatts. Subsequently, Enron built power plants in industrial and developing nations all over the world: Italy, Turkey, Argentina, China, India, Brazil, Guatemala, Bolivia, Colombia, the Dominican Republic, the Philippines, and others. By 1996, earnings from these projects accounted for 25 percent of total company earnings before interest and taxes.

In the United States, states were given the power to deregulate gas and electric utilities in 1994, which meant that residential customers could choose utilities in the same way that they chose their phone carriers. This looked like an enormous opportunity for Enron. CEO Lay was fervently in favor of deregulation, believing it would solve problems for consumers and utilities alike. The company moved into the residential electricity market in 1996, when Enron agreed to acquire Portland General, an Oregon utility whose transmission lines would give the company access to California's $20-billion market, as well as access to 650,000 customers in Oregon. In 1997, Enron Energy Services began to supply natural gas to residential customers in Toledo, Ohio, and contracted to sell wind power to Iowa residents. Through a subsidiary, Zond Corporation, the company contracted with MidAmerican Energy Company of Houston to supply 112.5 megawatts of wind-generated electricity to about 50,000 homes, the largest single purchase contract in the history of wind energy. Zond was to build the facility in northwestern Iowa, using about 150 of its Z-750 kilowatt series wind turbines, the biggest made in the United States.

A Shaky Structure Collapses

In 1995, Enron CEO Kenneth Lay promised investors that Enron's profits would rise by 15 percent a year over the next five years. Yet the pace of growth was not uniformly smooth for Enron. By 1997, only seven states were moving ahead with deregulation of their electricity markets. Enron's profit from a national deregulated electricity market was potentially huge, and the company spent millions on advertising and lobbying for the cause. It also hired hundreds of top business school graduates to help the company define new markets. The company seemed a potential gold mine if it could successfully open up the electricity market. Meanwhile, some of its earlier projects were going badly. Its huge deal to build a power plant in India, worth $2.8 billion, was held up by embittered local politicians. Other overseas projects also faltered. Earnings had grown annually in the early 1990s by between 16 and 20 percent. The figure shrank to 11 percent for 1995, then to only 1 percent in 1996. In the second quarter of 1997, the company took a $550 million charge, representing losses on the Indian project and others.

The company continued to spend heavily to advertise and lobby for deregulation. Enron advanced into the newly deregulated California electricity market in 1998, offering consumers discounts for signing up with the company. Enron's president, Jeffrey Skilling, predicted a revolution in electricity marketing once deregulation took hold, while admitting that California residents initially would not save much money by switching to Enron. The company was bringing in $4 billion a year from electricity sales in 1998, while predicting it would have ten percent of the $300 billion domestic gas and electric retail market within ten years. Yet in 1999 the company halted its efforts to expand into California and admitted it had been losing $100 million a year in its retail push. But Enron had many other ideas for turning a profit. In 1999, it launched an Internet-based commodities trading service, EnronOnline. Enron traded gas and electricity as well as more exotic futures such as weather. This gave companies whose business was affected by weather, such as home heating companies or golf courses, a hedge against the risk of unfavorable weather. Enron also launched Enron Broadband Services, a unit that traded capacity in telecommunications bandwidth. The company invested some $1.3 billion to build a fiber optic network so that more players would be able to buy and sell bandwidth capacity. The company investigated other e-commerce markets as well, such as trading in airport landing rights. The company had made natural gas into a tradeable commodity in the 1980s, and it was looking to pull off the same trick again in these various other commodities. Wall Street began to take notice, and Enron's stock, which had languished, began to climb again. It rose 55 percent in 1999, and leapt another 87 percent over 2000.

What apparently drew investors to Enron was its aura of getting in on the ground floor of various related industries. It seemed to be a new kind of company, not a blundering old regulation-bound utility but a savvy energy trader. Though new ventures such as broadband trading were not expected to be immediately profitable, Enron supposedly had a sound core business as a gas and electricity wholesaler. In fact, Enron's core business was floundering. *Newsweek* (January 21, 2002) estimated that in the late 1990s Enron had lost "about $2 billion on Telecom capacity, $2 billion in water investments, $2 billion in a Brazilian utility, and $1 billion on a controversial electricity plant in India." An unnamed Enron insider quoted in *Business Week* (December 17, 2001) put it this way: "You make enough billion-dollar mistakes, and they add up." Yet investors were not aware of Enron's troubles. Losses were disguised in elaborate partnerships and joint ventures, keeping them off Enron's books. Enron's duplicitous bookkeeping kept the stock price high, even as Enron's top executives began selling off their own holdings. Enron's president Jeffrey Skilling abruptly resigned in August 2001, citing only personal reasons. The slowdown in technology and Internet stocks brought Enron's stock down too, and it had fallen almost by half by the third quarter of 2001. At that point the company announced a loss of $618 million. Shortly thereafter, the company announced that actually it had been misstating its earnings since 1997. While the Securities and Exchange Commission began investigating irregularities at the company, Enron tried to sell out to another Houston energy company, Dynegy. That deal collapsed when the extent of Enron's losses became clear. In December 2001, Enron filed for bankruptcy, the largest ever by an American company. Enron's collapse stirred tremendous fallout. Its executives had made millions selling off their Enron shares, while many of its employees lost their retirement savings as the stock hit rock bottom. The accounting firm Arthur Andersen, which had certi-

fied Enron's bookkeeping, was disgraced, especially as revelations surfaced that it had destroyed potentially incriminating documents. The scandal reached into the upper echelons of government as well, as Enron had given liberally to many politicians, including President George W. Bush and Attorney General John Ashcroft. CEO Kenneth Lay resigned in January 2002, while the company faced multiple congressional, criminal, and SEC investigations. The company faced liquidation, with its only valuable asset the network of natural gas pipelines it had started out with in the mid-1980s.

Principal Subsidiaries

Enron Engineering and Construction; Enron International Inc.; Enron Renewable Energy Corp.; Enron Ventures Corp.; EOG Resources Inc.; EOTT Energy Partners LP; Florida Gas Transmission Co.; Houston Pipeline Co.; Transwestern Pipeline Co.; Enron Wind Corp.; Louisiana Resources Co.; Northern Border Pipeline Co.; Northern Plains Natural Gas Co.; Northern Transportation & Storage; Linc Corp.; Azurix Corp.; Enron Capital & Trade Resource; Enron Corp.

Further Reading

Banerjee, Neela, "Trying to Salvage What Can Be Salvaged While the Creditors Line Up," *New York Times*, January 25, 2002, p. C7.

Davies, Erin, "Enron: The Power's Back On," *Fortune*, April 13, 1998, p. 24.

Eichenwald, Kurt, and Brick, Michael, "Deals that Helped Doomed Enron Began to Form in the Early 90's," *New York Times*, January 18, 2001, pp. A1, C7.

"Enron Chief Criticises U.S. Congress and World Bank," *International Trade Finance*, October 11, 1996, p. 8.

"Enron Joins West Coast Team," *ENR*, February 17, 1997, p. 12.

Fineman, Howard, and Isikoff, Michael, "Lights Out: Enron's Failed Power Play," *Newsweek*, January 21, 2002, pp. 16–24.

Fisher, Daniel, Lynn Cook, and Rob Wherry, "Shell Game," *Forbes*, January 7, 2002, p. 52.

Kemezis, Paul, "Why Enron Paid a Premium for Portland General," *Electrical World*, September 1996, pp. 57–8.

McWilliams, Gary, "The Quiet Man Who's Jolting Utilities," *Business Week*, June 9, 1997, p. 84.

Oppel, Richard A., Jr., and Jonathan D. Glater, "Enron's Chief Sold Shares After Receiving Warning Letter," *New York Times*, January 18, 2002, pp. C1, C7.

O'Reilly, Brian, "The Secrets of America's Most Admired Corporations," *Fortune*, March 3, 1997, pp. 60–4.

Palmeri, Christopher, "At the Heart of a Revolution," *Forbes*, January 12, 1998, p. 48.

——, "The Watt Hustlers," *Forbes*, September 20, 1999, p. 78.

Pechter, Kerry, "Watts In a Name? The Future of Enron's Energy Business," *Advertising Age*, October 1997, p. I14.

"Power Players," *Fortune*, August 5, 1996, p. 94.

Share, Jeff, "Massive Pipeline to Carry Bolivian Gas into Brazil," *Pipeline & Gas Journal*, August 1997, p. 34.

Wherry, Rob, "Separated at Birth," *Forbes*, December 24, 2001, p. 54.

Zellner, Wendy, "Enron Electrified," *Business Week*, July 24, 2000, p. EB54.

Zellner, Wendy, Stephanie Anderson Forrest, and others, "The Fall of Enron," *Business Week*, December 17, 2001, p. 30.

—Trudy Ring
—updates: Dorothy Kroll and A. Woodward

FAO Schwarz

FAO SCHWARZ
FIFTH AVENUE

---

767 Fifth Avenue
New York, New York 10153
U.S.A.
Telephone: (212) 644-9410
Fax: (212) 688-6053
Web site: http://www.fao.com

Wholly Owned Subsidiary of Vendex International N.V.
Incorporated: 1862
Employees: 1,400
Sales: $197 million (2000 est.)
NAIC: 451120 Hobby, Toy, and Game Stores

FAO Schwarz operates a chain of more than 40 high-end toy stores around the United States, with its flagship outlet and headquarters located on Fifth Avenue in New York City. The company is renowned for offering the most exclusive and expensive toys available, but its approach has broadened in recent years to include more mainstream items as well. The firm has been through a series of owners since the Schwarz family sold it in 1963, with the Dutch retail conglomerate Vendex International the most recent, having acquired it in 1998.

1860s Origins

FAO Schwarz traces its beginnings to the Civil War era, when German immigrant Frederick August Otto Schwarz opened a toy store in Baltimore, Maryland, that specialized in dolls. In 1870 the store, known as Schwarz Toy Bazaar, moved to a location on Broadway in New York City, where Frederick Schwarz and his three brothers made a name for themselves by importing fine European toys. The growing business needed new quarters just a decade later, when it was moved to Union Square. After several further moves, FAO Schwarz (as it had become known) settled in 1931 at 745 Fifth Avenue, in the heart of Manhattan's most prestigious shopping district. The elegant new store featured a marble staircase and a slide that went from the first floor down to the main level. Schwarz toy displays were legendary, with the Christmas season's elaborately decorated windows a tourist destination in their own right. The name FAO

Schwarz had by then become synonymous with the most exclusive, imaginative, and expensive toys available, and the store's clientele was drawn from the elite of New York.

The Schwarz family continued to run the store until the early 1960s, when a lack of interest among the younger generation led family members to decide to sell it. In 1963, it was purchased by Parent's Magazine, who just seven years later sold it to W.R. Grace & Co. Grace, too, lasted for only a short while, selling the company to toy retailer Franz Carl Weber International of Zurich, Switzerland, in 1974. By this time Schwarz had opened stores in several locations outside of New York. The chain's momentum faltered under the distant oversight of Weber, however, which saw less attention given to discovering new, innovative merchandise. Sales were also being lost to aggressive new discount toy and department store chains. By the early 1980s, Schwarz appeared to be in serious trouble. The chain of stores, which had grown to 32, soon shrank by ten as unprofitable outlets (some in hotel lobbies) were closed. The surviving stores included sites in Boston, San Francisco, Chicago, and New Orleans, as well as in a number of suburban locations. In 1985, Weber decided to abandon ship and sold the company to real estate and investment firm Christiana Companies, Inc. for $10.5 million. At this time Schwarz had annual revenues of approximately $20 million.

Just a few months later the firm's ownership changed yet again, this time when it was acquired by Christiana Companies president and CEO Peter L. Harris and a Philadelphia-based investment banker, Peter C. Morse. The 42-year old Harris was an 18-year veteran of California retail chain Lucky Stores, where he had served as president of its Gemco discount chain. He had earlier attempted unsuccessfully to acquire Schwarz on his own, before linking up with Christiana. Harris assembled a new management team of executives with retail experience at Macy's, The Gap, and other major retailers, and began to tackle Schwarz's myriad problems. One of the first ideas to be implemented was a broadening of the store's merchandise to offer a wider range of items, though the exclusive high-end toys the store was known for would not be abandoned. New trends and fashions were again sought out, the company's mothballed catalog was revived, and personal shopping services and home

187

Company Perspectives:

FAO prides itself in offering unique products in an unforgettable environment. Management designed its stores to interact with customers in a manner which distinguishes itself from other retailers. Considered the leading specialty seller of toys and collectibles in the United States, FAO is a mecca for toy lovers from all over the world.

delivery were added. Another important change was the relocation of the chain's flagship store at 745 Fifth Avenue to a space across the street at 767 Fifth. The new store would fill 2 stories and 40,000 square feet at the foot of the General Motors Building, beginning in late 1986.

A Spectacular New Flagship Store

The converted GM auto showroom, which had entrances on both Fifth and Madison Avenues, was a third larger than the old store. The new location's redesigned interior also featured a more open layout that included 80 specialty boutique areas, prominent escalators, and lots of window space. For its grand opening, the store was wrapped in red cloth and a white bow, with a large card that said "Do Not Open Until November 6." New York mayor Ed Koch presided over the opening ceremony, which featured balloons and a parade of costumed toy characters. The new store was much more fanciful and "touchable" than the previous one, though it still offered the company's trademark selection of everything from teddy bears to a $12,500 half-size Ferrari car capable of reaching 30 miles an hour. There were also children's clothes, a kids' hair salon, and even gourmet peanut-butter and jelly sandwiches. The middle of the store featured a 28-foot tall, computer-programmed animated clock tower that played a song called "Welcome to Our World of Toys" every 15 minutes, and there was a glass-walled elevator and a life-size cave, among many other child-pleasing amenities. In addition to the toys available in the store, Schwarz' catalog contained even more elaborate gift options, including a cartoon written by and starring one's child ($180,000), an African Safari adventure ($50,000) and a 14-child overnight party at the New York store that included airfare, a stretch limousine, accommodations at the Plaza, and a tour of the city led by a costumed Pinocchio character ($18,000).

The new store was a huge hit with the public, and in 1988 it was featured in a scene in the popular Disney movie Big in which characters played a huge piano by jumping on the over-sized keys. Schwarz was subsequently deluged with requests for the $15,000 instrument and a smaller model that cost $6,250. The company, which did not advertise, was frequently mentioned in children's books and movies, a testament to its reputation as the ultimate toy store in the world.

The latter half of the 1980s saw Harris and his team continuing to fine-tune Schwarz operations, with under-performing locations closed and a new superstore opened in San Francisco. The latter featured a miniature city with a drive-in theater that showed the film Godzilla on a 2-inch screen, among other imaginative details. Venture capital funding of $7 million was obtained to help with the company's evolution, and by 1990

sales had more than doubled to approximately $50 million. Schwarz, now operating solidly in the black, was also readying new stores for Beverly Hills, Chicago, and Boston.

1990 Purchase by KBB

In 1990, the company was sold yet again, this time to Dutch retail giant NV Koninklijke Bijenkorf Beheer (KBB), for an estimated $40 million. Chairman and co-owner Peter Morse left the company, while Peter Harris and the remainder of his management team remained in place. KBB had sales of $2.4 billion for 1989, and its deep pockets were expected to fund further expansion of the chain, perhaps including Europe and Japan.

The year after the sale the company announced plans to open seven more new stores, including two in the Boston area and a second, 30,000-square foot location in Chicago's North Michigan Avenue shopping district. The latter would be Schwarz's fourth in the metropolitan area. 1992 saw turnaround guru Peter Harris step down to move to the San Francisco Bay area, where he would several years later be named president of the 49ers football team. He cited family reasons for his decision to leave. His place was taken by 44-year-old John Eyler, the Harvard-educated CEO of Hartmarx Specialty Stores, Inc. of Chicago.

In the fall of 1992, Schwarz opened its first "Barbie Boutique" at the Fifth Avenue location, a store-within-a-store dedicated entirely to the venerable, hourglass-figured Mattel doll. An expanded bookstore, "Bookmonster," was added during the year as well. More new stores were opened in 1993, including 12,000 square foot "mall flagship" units in Bellevue, Washington; Costa Mesa, California; and St. Louis, Missouri. The company was in the process of upgrading its non-New York sites, trying to give each some of the glamour of the Fifth Avenue store, which the public had come to expect via its frequent appearances in movies and on television.

By the mid-1990s, Schwarz's profits were again dropping, partly due to the competitive toy marketplace, which had seen a number of chains fail under the dominance of Toys "R" Us and discounters like Target and Wal-Mart. The company was also hurt by its higher cost of doing business, which included the fanciful decorative elements each store now featured.

In 1995, the company introduced a line of exclusive licensed products in conjunction with the American Museum of Natural History. Later in the year Schwarz invested in and co-produced the Broadway musical version of the movie Big which featured a recreation of the scenes in the Fifth Avenue store. The $9 million production opened the following April.

Mid-1990s: FAO Schweetz Debuts

In 1996, Schwarz began to introduce a new concept, FAO Schweetz, an interactive store-within-a-store in some of the company's locations which offered canister-filled and bulk candy. The company had previously sold the products under a licensing agreement in New York and San Francisco, but acquired the manufacturer and set up the business as a division. The company's older store on North Michigan Avenue in Chicago was later completely converted into a Schweetz outlet.

Schwarz allied with television marketing giant QVC in 1997 to offer specialized merchandise and FAO Schwarz-branded products on a 2-hour program called "FAO Schwarz—The Premier." In the summer of the year, new "mega-flagship" stores were readied for the tourist destinations of Orlando, Florida, and Las Vegas, Nevada, while the Manhattan store prepared to expand from 40,000 square feet to 60,000. By this time the company had a total of 39 locations, including 23 mall flagship sites and 12 smaller stores. Schwarz also distributed 6 million copies of its catalog to customers worldwide, which generated 11 percent of total sales. A third of its merchandise was exclusive to the chain, while another third was considered hard to find and the remainder consisted of mass-marketed goods like Barbie. The average item cost $26, with the Mattel doll the single most popular item. During this time the company was expanding its line of house-branded toys, as well as those offered in partnership with major manufacturers, such as the "F.A.O. Barbie" which sported fashionable clothes, an F.A.O. bag, and a credit card.

In the realm of cyberspace, where the company had first established its presence with the launch of www.fao.com in 1995, Schwarz reached revenue-sharing deals with a number of Web-based companies such as Prodigy and Yahoo! to sell toys over the Internet. A marketing deal with General Motors was also signed in January of 1998 in which the GMC "Jimmy" Sport Utility Vehicle was designated the "Official Big Kids Toy" at all of the chain's stores. Schwarz would sell a toy version of the SUV and insert GM advertising literature into shopping bags with purchases. The two companies' Web sites were linked as well. In early 1998, Schwarz's ownership changed when KBB was acquired by another Dutch retailer, Vendex International.

Late 1990s Under Vendex

During the summer of the year, the hit movie Titanic spawned a series of toys that were produced by Schwarz in conjunction with film studio 20th Century Fox, including a $395 doll and a Baccarat crystal rendering of the ship priced at $2,500. Controversy arose in the fall when allegations of racist treatment of employees surfaced in a lawsuit filed by eight former workers at the Fifth Avenue store. The complaints centered upon a single manager, who subsequently left the firm. 1998 was a weak year sales-wise, with the company's heavy promotion for the film Babe: Pig in the City failing to pay off when the film did poorly. Vendex later began floating rumors that the chain was for sale, although a deal did not materialize.

Continuing to move forward, in 1999 Schwarz signed a host of new licensing agreements that brought in additional exclusive products, such as Creative Optics eyewear and lines of clothing and furniture. The company also unveiled a new corporate logo and redesigned store interiors. The rebranding was intended to impart a more playful and cartoon-like ambience, with the company's longstanding rocking horse icon retained as a design element. A new slogan, "Wish Big," replaced the previous one, "We're Serious About Play." An additional Internet marketing agreement, with San Francisco-based FamilyWonder.com, was also announced in 1999.

January of 2000 saw the company lose its top officer, John Eyler, to rival Toys "R" Us. Eyler took the positions of president and CEO with the discount chain, which was now dealing with a variety of problems. Among other achievements, Eyler was credited with greatly boosting the percentage of exclusive items offered in Schwarz stores. He was replaced by Bud Johnson, Schwarz's president and chief operating officer. Schwarz subsequently filed suit against both Toys "R" Us and Eyler, alleging "irreparable harm" would result from his changing employers. The same year, 2000, also saw a new store opened in Atlanta's Mall of Georgia, which was the first to be built around the revised brand identity. Other developments included formation of an alliance with Discovery Communications to offer its Exploration Toy Shop inside the Fifth Avenue store, and a redesign of the Schwarz Web site.

In 2001, a new concept, FAO Baby, was launched, first as a department in the Fifth Avenue store, and then as a freestanding outlet in Chestnut Hill, Massachusetts, where it replaced an older store. FAO Baby was divided into separate boutiques from different manufacturers, such as Baby Gund, Lamaze, Fisher Price, and Playskool. As in Schwarz's other stores, the emphasis was on upscale toys and clothing attractively displayed. The firm also worked during the year with Irwin Toy to develop products for preschoolers based on the PBS television series Caillou.

As the company approached the Christmas shopping season of 2001, rumors were again surfacing that owner Vendex was seeking a buyer for Schwarz, reportedly due to the Dutch firm's desire to focus on its European operations. Expansion plans were nonetheless ongoing, with new large locations expected to open in both San Francisco and Los Angeles in 2002. In the aftermath of the September 11, 2001 terrorist attacks on New York City and Washington, D.C., the firm announced it would partner with New Yorkers For Children, making a donation to that organization's special fund for children and families affected by the collapse of the World Trade Center.

Celebrating its 140th anniversary, FAO Schwarz remained the world's premier toy retailer, known for its imaginative and expensive offerings, as well as for the wonder-inspiring environments of its stores. Although the possibility of new ownership was yet again on the horizon, the company was continuing to do what it had done best for generations: satisfying the cravings of children for the toys of their dreams.

Principal Divisions

FAO Schweetz; FAO Baby.

Principal Competitors

Toys ''R'' Us, Inc.; Wal-Mart Stores, Inc.; Target Corp.; K-B Toys.

Further Reading

Barmash, Isadore, ''Christiana Diversifies, Buys FAO Schwarz,'' *Houston Chronicle*, June 23, 1985, p. 9.

Brown, Chip, ''Where the Toys Are: FAO Schwarz Opens New N.Y. Flagship Store,'' *Washington Post*, November 7, 1986, p. C1.

''FAO Schwarz on Comeback Trail—New Co-Owner Has Fun Reviving Legendary Toy Retailer,'' *Los Angeles Times*, December 8, 1986, p. 2.

''FAO Schwarz's Walking Piano Plays into the Hearts of 'Big' Fans,'' *Atlanta Journal, Atlanta Constitution*, July 26, 1988, p. E6.

Fitzpatrick, Michele, ''Old-Timer, Upstart Make a Play for Youth Market,'' *KRTBN Knight Ridder Tribune Business News*, November 23, 1999.

Foderaro, Lisa, ''FAO Schwarz Expands, With Visions of Briefer Waits,'' *New York Times*, August 26, 1997, p. 5.

Graves, Neil, ''Famed FAO Schwarz is New York's Own 'Toy Story,' '' *New York Post*, November 26, 1999, p. 2.

Gupta, Udayan, ''The Fortress Companies: FAO Schwarz Is Back on Track with New Crew,'' *Wall Street Journal*, May 21, 1990, p. B1.

Hagerty, Bob, ''FAO Schwarz's Buyer Proposes an Expansion—Dutch Firm KBB to Open More Sites in U.S., Move to Europe and Japan,'' *Wall Street Journal*, August 24, 1990.

Howard, Susan, ''At FAO Schwarz, Now, A Boutique Barbie Can Call Home,'' *Newsday*, November 11, 1992, p. 62.

Kranhold, Kathryn, ''FAO Schwarz Hopes to Woo Kids with Clothes, Chairs and Eyewear,'' *Wall Street Journal*, October 19, 1999, p. B8.

Morgan, Babette, ''Child's Play—New FAO Schwarz Stores Capture the Magic of Toys,'' *St. Louis Post-Dispatch*, October 24, 1993, p. 1E.

Mouchard, Andre, ''FAO Aims for Triple Play,'' *Orange County Register*, November 9, 1993, p. C1.

Neumeister, Larry, ''Toy Store Employee Says Company Knew of Racial Discrimination,'' *Associated Press Newswires*, September 30, 1998.

Paltrow, Scot J., ''Buyouts R Us: Dutch Acquire FAO Schwarz,'' *Los Angeles Times*, August 1, 1990, p. 1.

Rose, Michael, ''The Big Toy Story,'' *Australian Financial Review*, May 23, 1997, p. 11.

Rosenberg, Ronald, ''FAO Schwarz Polishes a New Image,'' *Boston Globe*, May 1, 1991.

Schatz, Robin, ''Retailer Working Harder at Play,'' *Newsday*, April 14, 1986, p. 5.

Strom, Stephanie, ''Palace of Toys Finds Profits Elusive,'' *New York Times*, December 23, 1993, p. D1.

''Toys 'R' Us Sued for Hiring Former FAO Schwarz Chief,'' *Dow Jones Business News*, February 17, 2000.

Wilson, Craig, ''56 Years of Toy Stories,'' *USA Today*, December 15, 1995, p. 1A.

—Frank Uhle

The First Years Inc.

One Kiddie Drive
Avon, Massachusetts 02322
U.S.A.
Telephone: (508) 588-1220
Toll Free: (800) 225-0382
Fax: (508) 583-9067
Web site: http://www.thefirstyears.com

Public Company
Incorporated: 1952 as Kiddie Products Inc.
Employees: 156
Sales: $132.1 million (2001)
Stock Exchanges: NASDAQ
Ticker Symbol: KIDD
NAIC: 42192 Toy and Hobby Goods and Supplies
Wholesalers; 42199 Other Miscellaneous Durable
Goods Wholesalers

The First Years Inc. is a developer and marketer of products for infants and toddlers. The company groups its products into three broad categories: Feeding & Soothing, Play & Discover, and Care & Safety. Feeding & Soothing products include bottles, nipples, teethers, bibs, breast-feeding accessories, and a line of spill-proof bowls and cups. The Play & Discover line includes crib toys, hand-held toys, and large playthings. The Care & Safety product group consists of home safety devices such as door and cabinet latches, monitors, toilet-training accessories, and other health and hygiene products. The First Years sells its products worldwide both under its own brand and under the licensed names ''Winnie the Pooh,'' ''Disney Mickey,'' and ''Sesame Street.'' Its customers are primarily major toy and mass-merchandising retailers, including Wal-Mart, Target, and Toys ''R'' Us. Other outlets include department stores, grocery and drug store chains, and specialty shops.

Formative Years

The First Years Inc. was founded in 1949, in Roxbury, Massachusetts, by Marshall Sidman and his wife Evelyn. Sidman, who was then in his mid-thirties, had served as a Navy ensign during World War II. After his discharge in 1945, he experimented with various careers—including piloting, baking, and selling clothing, tires, stationery, and reupholstering services. But Sidman was not content to sell someone else's products. He wanted a product of his own to promote, and ultimately, he found one—a diaper pin that a friend had developed. As Sidman approached local merchants with his diaper pins, however, he found that they were looking for full product lines rather than individual products. The Sidmans responded by adding baby items from other manufacturers to their product offering—and the company was born. The couple incorporated their business in 1952, as Kiddie Products, Inc.

The Sidmans were progressive in their approach to sales and marketing. For advice on how to best promote their products, they formed the ''Mothers Council,'' a group of local women who met every three weeks to confer. The couple was also hardworking and determined to make a go of their fledgling business. According to local rumor, Evelyn Sidman once pushed a baby carriage from door to door to sell products. And the Sidmans' son Ronald, who was two when his parents founded Kiddie Products, remembers his mother taking him along on deliveries to retail customers.

It is perhaps not surprising that the little boy who rode along on deliveries grew up to become an important force in his parents' business. In the late 1960s, Ronald—who had recently graduated from New England's Bowdoin College—went to work for Kiddie Products. In 1970, he was promoted to vice-president and in 1974 was advanced to executive vice-president.

As Ronald Sidman was assuming more responsibility in his parents' company, changes were afoot in the retail industry. Until that point Kiddie Products had functioned essentially as a distributor for other manufacturers, selling their products to independent drug stores and five-and-dimes. But by the mid-1970s, the ''big box'' stores—large chains like Kmart—were beginning to edge out those smaller, independent stores that Kiddie Products catered to. The Sidmans needed to start selling to the large chain stores—but there was a major hitch. Those stores tended to buy directly from the manufacturer, eliminating the distributor.

Company Perspectives:

At The First Years, we strive to make the first three years of life happier, healthier, and easier for children and the parents who love them.

Ronald Sidman knew that the company had to change its strategy. "It was clear that we had to develop our own product line or we would be out of business," explained Ronald Sidman in a 1997 interview with the *Boston Globe*. Sidman got to work developing products, ultimately unveiling a line of baby rattlers, bibs, teethers, and pacifiers that were sold under the brand name "The First Years." Such products were hardly revolutionary— but Kiddie Products distinguished itself by making a priority of product safety and durability. Ronald Sidman enlisted his brother, a chemical engineer, to help develop rigorous product-testing procedures. By dropping, stretching, and torque-testing toys and pacifiers, the company made sure its products could withstand the pummeling they were sure to be given by real-life babies and toddlers. Some of the tests the Sidmans developed were effective enough to be later adopted by the U.S. Consumer Product Safety Commission.

Working and Playing Well with Others

Kiddie Products had effectively distinguished itself from its competitors by emphasizing safety and durability—but that point of differentiation did not last long. Soon, other companies followed suit, and Kiddie Products had to find a new way to set itself apart. It did so by focusing on the real needs of its customers.

Much as Marshall and Evelyn Sidman sought advice from their "Mothers Council" in the early days of their business, Kiddie Products again went looking for counsel from those who were actually "in the trenches." In 1973, the company formed a small Parents Council of local expectant and new parents to offer feedback and pre-test products. The Parents Council did not stay small or local; ultimately it grew into a worldwide organization with more than 50,000 members. Members of the council provided feedback in a range of different ways—from participating in company-led "play groups" to home-testing products to responding to surveys.

However, the company was not content to simply meet the practical needs of parents. It also wanted to address the developmental needs of the children themselves. For advice on this front, Sidman approached the Child Development Unit at Boston's Children's Hospital, which was founded and directed by pediatrician and child development expert Dr. T. Berry Brazelton. Brazelton and some of his staff agreed to serve as consultants for Kiddie Products, helping the company design products that safely and effectively met the developmental needs of infants and toddlers.

In addition to going outside for advice, Kiddie Products took care to fill its internal staff with child-raising "experts" as well. "We made a point of hiring working moms with infants and toddlers at home as the lead marketing person in each [product] cateogory," Ronald Sidman said in a 1995 interview with the *Boston Globe*.

Responding to External Stimuli

By the early 1990s, Kiddie Products had established itself firmly as a leading manufacturer of children's products. For years it had exhibited a relatively conservative, "slow but steady" strategy, introducing new products at a less frenetic rate than its competitors. In 1993, however, a series of accomplishments by its nearest competitor, Safety 1st, jolted the company into reassessing its approach. Safety 1st—located in Canton, Massachusetts, just a few miles from Kiddie Products— had been founded in 1984 on the tremendous popularity of its first product: a bright yellow "Baby on Board" sign designed to hang in car windows. Building on the success of that product, the company went on to introduce an ever-increasing line of child safety products. Safety 1st moved at an aggressive pace, soon surpassing Kiddie Products and becoming Massachusetts' largest manufacturer of children's safety products. In 1993, Safety 1st went public, raising $15 million. Its sales and earnings increased significantly. Even more significantly, that same year the company introduced 111 new products—more than twice as many as Kiddie Products.

Put on the defensive, Kiddie Products scrambled to respond. The company reduced operating expenses by closing a packaging and assembly plant and outsourcing the work done there. It also dramatically stepped up product-development efforts and hired a New York-based PR firm to increase public awareness of the company. In a 1994 interview with the *Boston Business Journal*, Marshall Sidman talked about Kiddie Products' realization that it needed to regroup. "Last year was the year it was made clear we would have to improve things real fast," he said. "We've continually tried to improve what we're doing, but the urgency is certainly increased because of the intensity of the competition."

The company's efforts had the desired results. It ended 1994 with record net income of $3 million. Sales for the year were $53.2 million—up 15 percent from 1993's sales. The company also introduced 90 new products for 1995, more than twice as many as it had for the previous year and more than ever introduced in any earlier year.

A New Identity in the Mid-1990s

In the spring of 1995, Kiddie Products' 81-year-old founder died. Ronald Sidman, who had served as president since 1989, became CEO and chairman of the board as well. Shortly after Sidman was installed, Kiddie Products announced that it was changing its name to The First Years Inc. The name change capitalized upon the strength of the company's brand name, more closely aligning the organization itself with its well-known products in the minds of consumers and shareholders.

The company was flourishing—thanks, in part, to the new products it had brought to market the previous year. Especially popular were the company's new Washables and Firstronics lines. Washables products consisted of 100 percent washable, dishwasher-safe toys. Firstronics was a line of hand-held electronic toys—such as imitation remote controls and cellular phones—inspired by Ronald Sidman's young son. The company's "TumbleMates" line, which had been launched in 1992 and extended in 1994, was also a big seller. TumbleMates were

Key Dates:

1949: Marshall Sidman and his wife Evelyn begin selling diaper pins and other infant products to local retailers.

1952: Sidman incorporates his business as Kiddie Products Inc.

1968: The Sidmans's son Ronald joins the company.

1970s: Kiddie begins developing its own line of products under The First Years Brand.

1973: Kiddie forms The Parents Council.

1981: Kiddie partners with Dr. T. Berry Brazelton and the Child Development Unit of Boston Children's Hospital.

1989: Ronald Sidman becomes president of Kiddie Products.

1995: Marshall Sidman dies; Ronald Sidman becomes CEO; Kiddie Products changes its name to The First Years; company unveils new Winnie the Pooh product line.

1997: The First Years introduces new line of Sesame Street character products.

a variety of dishes and utensils designed for serving, storing, and transporting snacks and drinks.

The First Years continued to push forward with new product development. In 1995, the company added several higher-priced items to its product mix—including a new ''Nurserytronics'' line of electronic products for the nursery, such as a tape player and crib light and a rechargeable pocket monitor. Other more expensive products included odor-proof diaper pails, booster and bath seats, diaper bags, and a line of child carriers and travel tote bags.

Perhaps the most significant development on the new-product front, however, was a licensing agreement with Walt Disney Co. that allowed The First Years to develop a Winnie the Pooh line of products. By the end of 1995, the company was offering more than 40 Winnie the Pooh products, including rattles, teethers, bibs, bottles, bath accessories, and gift sets. These new products were immediate hits, generating approximately $15 million in sales for 1995, and doubling in volume in 1996. By the middle of 1997, the Winnie the Pooh line accounted for approximately one-third of The First Years' total sales revenue.

Encouraged by the success of its first licensing venture, the company quickly moved to secure another such deal—this time with the Children's Television Workshop. Signed in 1996, this new agreement allowed The First Years to develop a line of products using Sesame Street characters, and by the end of 1997, the company had introduced 30 such items. The introduction of these new products, combined with the continued expansion of existing product lines, pushed The First Years' sales up to $120.7 million for the year—a 29.6 increase over 1996's $93.1 million. Net income was $7.4 million, up from $5.2 million the year before.

The First Years continued to focus heavily on new product development, steadily rolling out between 50 and 60 new items each year. The company's licensed character products quickly proved to be its most popular lines. By the end of 1998, sales of the Winnie the Pooh and Sesame Street lines accounted for almost half of The First Years' total revenue.

Future Challenges

After almost a full decade of dramatic growth, The First Years stumbled near the end of the 1990s. In 1998, the company was forced to recall several of its products when environmental groups asserted that a chemical used in them could cause health problems in infants. The recall resulted in a $3 million charge for the company. 1999 brought more bad news. Demand for the company's licensed products, which had shown steady growth since their introduction, suddenly dropped off. Net sales for the year showed only a 3 percent increase over 1998—a significant departure from the 23 percent average growth of the previous five years.

In 2000, the company posted a decrease in both net sales and net income. It also unveiled a four-point plan for recovery—which included strengthening its management team, improving its internal processes, realigning its business structure, and finding new ways to partner with its retail customers. Toward the first point of the plan—enhancing the management team—The First Years hired three new senior managers to oversee marketing and sales, product development, and human resources. The company set about improving its internal processes by adopting a version of the Six Sigma methodology. It realigned its business structure so that marketing and product development were focused on brands rather than on product categories—that is, one group worked on The First Years brand, while another group was dedicated to the licensed products. To achieve the fourth point of the plan—which focused on customer relationships—the company began using sophisticated market analysis to customize product mix for individual retailers.

The First Years also took a look at how it was handling both its own brand and its licensed products. It made plans to more aggressively market The First Years brand, pushing for higher visibility and heightened consumer awareness. To reinvigorate the lagging sales of its licensed products, the company used new graphics to jazz up existing products. It also began working with its major retail customers to offer them exclusive versions of the licensed character graphics—so that end customers could only get a certain type of graphic on products at a certain store.

The First Years continued to struggle for the first half of 2001. At the six-month point, the company posted sales of $67.3 million and net income of $3.9 million—down from $71 million and $5.3 million respectively in the previous year. Sales of licensed products remained depressed, and sales of The First Years brand also fell of slightly, due to a general slowdown in the domestic economy.

By the third quarter of 2001, however, it appeared as though the company might be moving toward brighter days. Its quarter sales and income both showed improvement over the previous year's numbers. Sales of its licensed specialty products increased 14 percent over 2000's third quarter, and sales of The First Years Brand also picked up slightly. Even with the improvements, however, The First Years was cautious in its assessment of the future. In an October 2001 earnings release,

Ronald Sidman was quoted as saying, "While we are pleased with the sales growth and profitability achieved for the quarter, our outlook remains tempered by the continuing economic uncertainty and soft retail sales many of our customers are experiencing."

Principal Competitors

Evenflo Company, Inc.; Safety 1st Inc.; Hasbro, Inc.; Mattel, Inc.; Playtex Products, Inc.

Further Reading

Crosariol, Beppi, "The First Years Inc. Keeping Close Watch on Needs of Parents," *Boston Globe*, May 23, 1995.

Neale, Stacy, "Kiddie Grows Up Fast with New Strategy," *Boston Business Journal*, July 8, 1994, p. 3.

Pham, Alex, "First Years Inc., Maker of Infant Products Matures into Vibrant Firm," *Boston Globe*, May 20, 1997.

—Shawna Brynildssen

Florida Rock Industries, Inc.

155 East 21st Street
Jacksonville, Florida 32206
U.S.A.
Telephone: (904) 355-1781
Fax: (904) 355-0817

Public Company
Incorporated: 1945
Employees: 3,392
Sales: $715.7 million (2000)
*Stock Exchange*s: New York
Ticker Symbol: FRK
NAIC: 32732 Ready-Mix Concrete Manufacturing;
   212321 Construction Sand and Gravel Mining;
   327331 Concrete Block and Brick Manufacturing

Florida Rock Industries, Inc. and its subsidiaries make and market ready-mixed concrete; mine, process, and sell sand, crushed-stone, gravel, and other construction aggregates; and produce and sell concrete block, pre-cast and pre-stressed concrete, Portland and masonry cement, calcium products and other building materials. Although the company owns a 50 percent share in a sand and gravel plant in New Brunswick, Canada, it chiefly operates in the southeastern and mideastern United States, primarily in Florida, Georgia, North Carolina, Virginia, Maryland, and Washington, D.C. In Florida, where it is headquartered, Florida Rock has seven crushed-stone plants, nine sand pits, and one industrial sand plant. The company also maintains a plant in Kissimmee, where it manufactures pre-cast lintels and other construction products, and a Brooksville plant that produces calcium products for the animal feed industry. Outside Florida, the company owns and operates six crushed-stone plants in Georgia as well as two sand and gravel pits and two crushed-stone plants in both Virginia and Maryland. At a plant in Wilmington, North Carolina, the company also manufactures pre-stressed concrete components for highway and bridge construction. In addition, the company's marine division barges materials throughout the Chesapeake Bay and its principal estuaries. Florida Rock's chief markets include all of Florida (with the exception of the pan-

handle region) and areas in and around Atlanta, Richmond, Norfolk, Baltimore, and Washington, D.C. Through its joint venture in Canada, the company also markets products in the Caribbean and Argentina. Although it is a public company, about 29 percent of Florida Rock is owned by the Baker family, descendants of Thompson Baker, one of the company's two founders. It is also a company that enjoys a solid reputation for good management, fiscal conservatism, and stability.

The Lineage of Florida Rock Industries

Although its operations were temporarily suspended during World War II, Florida Rock Industries, Inc. descended from a business started by Thompson Baker in 1929. Baker bought a sandpit formerly owned by his father, who had defaulted on a bank loan and lost the property through repossession. Three years later, in 1932, Thompson and his partner Jim Shands formed Shands & Baker and began producing ready-mixed concrete. While the company survived the depression, it closed down during the war years, when Baker joined the Army and fought in Europe. He returned in 1945, a decorated veteran, and reopened the business. In the postwar boom, he led Shands & Baker into the crushed-stone business and oversaw the company's rapid growth throughout the 1950s and 1960s, when, almost annually, the business opened a new mine or quarry. What helped Florida Rock grow was the general population explosion in the company's market areas, especially Florida, which in the postwar years rapidly became a Mecca for both vacationers and retirees. In 1972, the company went public as Florida Rock Industries.

Throughout much of the history of the company, the Baker family remained the chief owners and managers of the business. Thompson Baker's son Edward joined the business in the 1960s, becoming president in 1969 and CEO Edward L. Baker, the son of Thompson S. Baker and grandson of founder Thompson Baker, became chairman and CEO in 1989, at which time his younger brother, John D. Baker II, was named president. In 1991, Edward Baker's son Thompson S. Baker II became vice-president. Thompson S. Baker still remained on the board of directors but retired from active management of the company in 1989. In addition to Florida Rock, the Baker family owned a

---

Company Perspectives:

The company's mission is to be an excellent construction materials company providing long-term growth and a superior return on investment. Through employees committed to continuous improvement, we will provide quality materials and superb service for our customers; operate safe, environmentally responsible facilities that are well maintained and cost effective; and develop mutually beneficial relationships with our suppliers and the communities within which we operate.

---

large share in FRP Properties Inc., a Jacksonville, Florida transportation and real estate company. Originally part of Florida Rock Industries, it was spun off in 1986. Ten years later, the family still owned about 36 percent of FRP.

Florida Rock During the Late 1980s and Early 1990s

An ever-expanding business since it was founded in 1929, Florida Rock continued its growth into the early and middle 1980s. Between 1978 and 1986, the Bakers put $210 million of the company's earnings back into the business, purchasing property, plants, and equipment, providing it with ever-increasing productivity and flexibility. By 1986, its sales had reached $259 million, and it had begun tapping into new markets by buying out competitors. Among other significant acquisitions, in 1987 it purchased Cement Products, a Florida-based company, and in the next year bought Arundel Corp., a manufacturer of construction materials operating in Maryland. Nevertheless, the company suffered from an industry slowdown that accompanied the nation's recessive economy in the late 80s and early 90s. Between 1990 and 1992, its sales dropped from $390.5 million to $271.8 million, with its net income falling off from $17.1 million to $3.9 million. Importantly, however, the company stayed profitable, even in its nadir year, 1991, when its net income fell to $2.0 million. Albeit slowly, by 1993 it had begun making what would become a steady recovery.

After the recession in the early 1990s, Florida Rock began to regain lost financial ground. 1994 was a particularly good year for the company. Its revenues rose 14.3 percent to $336.5 million, up from $294.4 million the previous year, and its net income increased to $17.2 million, up from $7.8 million. The improved financial picture resulted from the upward spiral in the company's Florida and Georgia markets, its increased cost efficiency, and its capital investment programs of the previous five years. The climb back to the 1990 sales level continued in 1995, when the company's revenues rose to $369.0 million and produced a net income of $17.2 million, which virtually matched the net income figure for 1990.

By the mid 1990s, Florida Rock had well-established operations in four eastern seaboard states—Florida, Georgia, Virginia, and, north of the Mason-Dixon Line, Maryland. Altogether, at the end fiscal 1994, it had 79 ready-mixed concrete and 11 concrete block plants in operation, a fleet of 854 ready-mixed concrete and concrete block delivery trucks, and construction aggregate operations spread across the Southeast. In Florida, it was operating

seven crushed-stone plants, eight sand plants, and one industrial sand plant. In addition, it was operating five crushed-stone plants in Georgia, one sand and gravel plant and three crushed-stone plants in Maryland, and one sand and gravel plant and two crushed-stone plants in Virginia. It was also operating aggregate distribution terminals in Norfolk and Virginia Beach, which are located in the northern part of Virginia, and in the Baltimore and Eastern Shore areas of Maryland.

The Fortunes of Florida Rock, 1996 and Beyond

Although the company had garnered many industry awards for its environmental stewardship—including four Gold Environmental Eagle Awards given by the National Stone Association—at various times specific groups targeted the company for operating its construction plants and continuing its quarrying and mining activities on land where developers were building new homes. Historically, part of Florida Rock's problem arose from the fact that Florida's explosive post-World War II population growth placed settlements closer and closer to quarries and other operational sites that had once been remote. In Dade County, for example, where Florida Rock had quarried limestone since the mid 1950s, developers moved much closer, and new homeowners, with houses built in fairly close proximity to the company's quarries, eventually began to complain about the blasting done by Florida Rock. There were also other kinds of complaints. For example, in 1997, the Haile Community Association, a neighborhood group, fought the company over the construction of its $80 million cement plant in Newberry, Florida, west of Gainesville. The group challenged the air pollution permits that the state had issued to Florida Rock, and it tried to enlist the support of the company's competitors.

Other than providing some negative publicity, such challenges did little to impede the expansion of Florida Rock, which continued to grow through both new construction and acquisitions. A particular boon for Florida Rock was the increased construction activity resulting from the preparation for the 1996 Summer Olympics in Atlanta. (It was also in 1996 that John Baker took the reins as Florida Rock's CEO. The following year, his grandfather, the company's founder, died at age 91.) In 1998 the company opened a new calcium products facility, which made calcium-based chemicals for use in animal feeds. Florida Rock also opened a crushed-stone plant in Georgia, and it added a sand and gravel plant to its operations in Maryland.

In June 1999, the year in which Florida Rock completed construction of a $100 million Portland cement plant near Brooksville, Florida, the company again expanded through two additional acquisitions. First, at a cost of $87 million, it purchased all the outstanding common stock of Harper Bros., Inc., a leading supplier of aggregates in and around its Ft. Myers home base in southwest Florida. At the time of the purchase, Harper Bros. had just doubled the size of its aggregates finishing plant. It was also engaged in aggregate mining and highway and heavy construction. Under the terms of a consent agreement with the Department of Justice permitting the sale, Florida Rock was required to divest its existing Ft. Myers Alico Road quarry lease and plant operation along with Harper Bros.'s Palmdale sand mine lease and plant operation in Glades County, Florida. Following their deal with Harper Bros.'s, Florida Rock's next purchase was the outstanding common stock of

Key Dates:

1929: Thompson Baker enters building materials business.

1932: Baker and Jim Shands found Shands & Baker.

1941: Company is temporarily disbanded because of World War II.

1945: Shands & Baker is re-founded.

1969: Baker's son Edward L. Baker becomes company president.

1972: Edward Baker is named CEO; company goes public.

1973: Company name is changed to Florida Rock Industries.

1987: Company acquires Cement Products.

1997: Founder Thompson Baker dies.

1998: Florida Stone opens calcium products plant in Florida and crushed-stone plant in Georgia; company buys sand and gravel plant in Maryland.

1999: Company finishes construction of $100 million cement plant in Florida and acquires Harper Bros. and Custom LTD.

Custom, Ltd., a ready-mixed concrete producing and sand and gravel mining company headquartered in Williamsburg, Virginia. Custom's operations, all in Virginia, included four ready-mixed concrete plants in Williamsburg, Hampton, Newport News, and Providence, and a sand and gravel mine in Charles City County. Neither party made the terms of the sale public.

In August of 1999, Florida Rock sold the highway and heavy construction assets and operations of Harper Bros., Inc. to Harper Bros. Construction Inc., a subsidiary of Superfos Construction Inc., a Denmark-based company that, in 1999, was itself acquired by Ashland Inc., the petroleum and chemical conglomerate. Then, in December 1999, Florida Rock complied with its consent arrangement with the Department of Justice by selling off its Ft. Myers Alico Road quarry lease and plant operation as well as the Palmdale Sand Mine and plant operation of its Harper Bros., Inc. subsidiary to CSR Rinker Materials Corp., itself a subsidiary of CSR America Inc. (a holding company for CSR Limited, a global construction and building materials company based in Sydney, Australia). Rinker, in business since 1926, touted itself as ''Florida's Number One Building Supplier.'' Statewide, the company had operations at over 100 locations and had been one of Florida Rock's competitors in Florida's aggregate and ready-mixed cement and concrete trade.

In April 2000, with its investment in a Canadian granite quarry and aggregate distribution operation located on the St. Croix River in Bayside, New Brunswick, Florida Rock ventured beyond the U.S. border for the first time in its history. The closest Canadian Atlantic port to the United States, Port Bayside is ice-free and open to navigation year round. The operation, in which Florida Rock bought a 50 percent share, started up in 1998. It quarries granite on a site leased from the Province of New Brunswick, with estimated reserves in excess of 100 million short tons, and sells its aggregates on the East Coast and in the Caribbean. In August of the same year, for $30 million in cash, the company also acquired 12 ready-mixed concrete plants, two concrete block plants, and two sand mines from Southern Construction Company, a private firm located in Albany, Georgia. Eleven of the ready-mix plants were located in southwest Georgia and the other in Tallahassee, Florida. The other operations were also located in southwest Georgia. Subsequently, Florida Rock sold off two of the acquired ready-mix plants to third parties and traded one plant in Georgia for a plant in Florida.

Florida Rock has historically maintained a reputation for being a stable, well-managed enterprise that has never lost its forward momentum, despite the fact that it engages in a weather-dependent, cyclical business sensitive to the state of the nation's economy. No steps it took in the 1990s seemed destined to change that assessment. It remained well positioned to respond to its industry challenges in the first decade of the new century.

Principal Subsidiaries

Arundel Corp.; Cardinal Concrete Co.; Maryland Rock Industries Inc.; Northern Concrete Group; Sadler Materials Corp.; Southern Concrete Construction; S&G Concrete Co.; S&G Prestress Co.; Tidewater Materials Corp.; Virginia Concrete Co.

Principal Competitors

Ashland Inc.; Hanson PLC; ''Holderbank'' Financiere Glaris Ltd.; Lafarge Corporation; Lehigh Portland Cement Co.; Martin Marietta Materials, Inc.; Southdown, Inc.; Vulcan Materials Company.

Further Reading

Basch, Mark, ''Chief Executive Steps Down; Brother Takes Over,'' *Knight-Ridder/Tribune Business News*, February 9, 1996.

''Florida Rock Industries, Inc. Completes Acquisition of Custom, Ltd.,'' *Business Wire*, June 11, 1999.

''Florida Rock Industries, Inc. Completes Acquisition of Harper Bros., Inc.,'' *Business Wire*, June 1, 1999.

Dorn, Chad A., ''A Fine Grind,'' *Pit & Quarry*, December 1999

Maxwell-Cook, Paul, ''We Finally Did It,'' *World Cement*, December 2000, p. 42.

Schatz, Amy, ''Florida Rock Set to Add Plant Near Brooksville, La.,'' *Knight-Ridder/Tribune Business News*, February 21, 1999.

Wilkening, David, '' 'Double Kick' from Congress?,'' *Florida Trend*, May 1997, p. 29.

—John W. Fiero

Frank Russell Company

909 A Street
Tacoma, Washington 98402
U.S.A.
Telephone: (253) 572-9500
Fax: (253) 591-3495
Web site: http://www.russell.com

Wholly Owned Subsidiary of Northwestern Mutual Life Insurance Co.
Incorporated: 1936
Employees: 1,300
Sales: $500 million (est.)
NAIC: 52392 Portfolio Management; 52393 Investment Advice; 52312 Securities Brokerage; 52311 Investment Banking and Securities; 52511 Pension Funds

The Frank Russell Company is an investment services firm that advises more than 1,000 money management clients in 35 countries who oversee $1 trillion in assets. The company also manages mutual funds, retirement plans, and other accounts worth more than $66 billion, and compiles the well-known Russell 1000, 2000, and 3000 stock indexes. Russell's clients include numerous major corporations such as AT&T, General Motors, and Compaq, and the firm also has marketing alliances with many international financial service organizations such as A.G. Edwards, Crédit du Nord, Société Générale, and the Bank of Tokyo Mitsubishi. A subsidiary of Northwestern Mutual since 1999, Russell is headquartered in Tacoma, Washington and has offices in New York, London, Paris, Tokyo, Toronto, Sydney, Australia, Auckland, New Zealand, and Singapore.

Early Years

The Frank Russell Company was founded in 1936 by a Merrill Lynch stockbroker who had retired from Wall Street and moved to Tacoma, Washington, where his son was a newspaper executive. Looking to keep busy, he began to offer investment counseling services and started a mutual fund. His small business served local investors for the next two decades, and in 1958 his grandson George joined the firm. After only three months on the job the younger Russell, a Harvard business school graduate, was left in charge when his grandfather passed away. At this time the firm, with a staff of just two, had assets of only $300,000 and 176 investors in its mutual fund, many of them friends of Frank Russell.

George Russell quickly began to take a more aggressive approach toward growing the business, and added sales representatives and other activities such as life insurance sales and real estate syndication. By 1965, there were 300 salesmen working for the firm, but Russell was still not entirely satisfied, believing that the company did nothing that distinguished it from others of its type. In 1968, he began to take a look at pension fund accounts, which at the time were typically managed by a single individual, often someone chosen for political reasons. Russell took a set of formulas developed by researcher Peter Dietz (whom he later hired) to examine the performance of different pension funds and determined that he could improve their results. He decided to take his new idea of "management of managers" to large companies by making cold calls to their treasurers. The first to sign on was J.C. Penney, and Russell soon attracted more clients, with the list eventually coming to include AT&T, General Motors, and IBM. The firm chose to limit its clients to a total of 40.

Soon after it began offering its advising service, the company opened a New York office. Russell also created two other new businesses that performed related tasks, one offering data on manager performance and the other performing securities trades for institutional investors. These later became known as Russell Analytical Services and Frank Russell Securities, respectively. In 1979 the company expanded overseas when an office was opened in London. The next year, two investment management subsidiaries were created in response to customer requests for Russell-managed funds. Expanding its presence in the pension fund consulting field, the company also began to reach out to small and medium-sized retirement plans and individual investors.

The Russell 1000, 2000, and 3000

In 1982 the firm created several indexes of stocks as a way to gauge money managers' success against the growth of the market as a whole. The lists—composed of the 1,000 largest

Company Perspectives:

Russell's multi-manager solutions offer investors a smarter choice in professional money management. The result is a tailored investment program aimed at building and preserving wealth for the long term. After more than six decades of serving investors' needs, Russell has developed a 360-degree perspective on investment managers and capital markets. Russell and its affiliates have developed the combined art and science of multi-manager investing into an advanced process imitated by many but duplicated by none. The result is a comprehensive approach that delivers goal-oriented investment programs for clients ranging from billion-dollar institutions to small individual investors around the world. Russell's competitive advantage is its continuous, in-depth money manager research and extensive knowledge of financial markets worldwide.

stocks (known as the Russell 1000, equal to about 90 percent of the market); the next 2,000 in size (the Russell 2000); and a combination of the two (the Russell 3000, covering 98 percent of the market)—were made public several years later and were quickly accepted by investors as useful tools. The indexes began to appear regularly in investment publications such as *The Wall Street Journal, Barron's,* and *Business Week.*

In 1986, the steadily growing company opened offices in Tokyo and Sydney. By 1988, Russell had 700 employees and annual revenues of approximately $100 million. The firm was then advising clients on investments totaling $240 billion. Russell's customer list included many major U.S. corporations as well as prominent foreign ones like Rolls Royce in England and the largest banks of Japan and Australia. 1988 also saw the company move into a new 12-story headquarters on the Tacoma waterfront.

In 1990 George Russell named the company's director of international consulting, Michael Phillips, to the post of president, remaining in place as chairman and CEO. He also created the Russell 20–20, which was assembled soon after the fall of the Berlin Wall. The 20–20 was a group of 20 major pension fund managers and 20 leading money managers that Russell personally led on trips to Eastern Europe and China, where they assessed the investment climate in those emerging markets. He was a strong advocate of seizing such opportunities, and doubled his 1970s-era recommendation of 10 percent foreign investment to 20. Two years later Michael Phillips took on the additional title of CEO. By 1993, the firm's clients were managing assets worth $450 billion, nearly double the amount of 5 years before.

The company was also offering other investment indexes by this time, such as the Timberlands Index, which was offered beginning in 1994 in association with the National Council of Real Estate Investment Fiduciaries. The index measured the returns on 75 percent of institutional investors' timberlands holdings in the U.S. Other real estate indexes were compiled that covered farmlands and commercial property.

In the early 1990s, a proposal was made in the Washington State legislature to place a sales tax on financial services trans-

actions. Russell fought it, threatening to leave the state if the law was passed, and changes were eventually made that mollified the company. Other tax proposals which affected Russell continued to appear from time to time, but the firm's importance to the state, and particularly to the city of Tacoma, enabled it to garner favorable treatment from legislators.

Treating Employees Right

The fact that a leading investment services firm could succeed located so far from the financial hub of New York was sometimes a surprise to people. George Russell was a strong believer that his company's employees should have a life beyond their jobs, however, and he felt that the stress of working on Wall Street precluded having a happy family life. He told the *Seattle Times,* "If you get the priorities in the right place to begin with as you run a business, and you put the people ahead of the business, then they'll eventually realize they can have fun in life, too, and the business will be fun." The company had a reputation for generosity toward its employees and was recognized by a number of different organizations for its pleasant work environment. In addition to their other benefits, in 1995 Russell began to offer a paid eight-week sabbatical leave to every employee with ten years or more of service. The company also contributed 15 percent of its employees' salaries to a profit-sharing plan.

In 1995, Russell decided to launch its first national promotional campaign, hiring Team One Advertising to handle the estimated $5 million account. The move reflected the company's growing interest in broadening its client base to include more individual investors. Introduced the following summer, the ads ran in the *Wall Street Journal* and various other publications targeted at retirees and institutions. Slogans included "Russell Knows" and "Knowledge Is Money."

In December of 1996, George Russell made his entire workforce of 1,200 part owners of the company when he announced that 5 percent of its total equity value would be transferred to them. Ownership shares were apportioned based on longevity and pay level. Over the next several years this percentage grew to 40 percent, with Russell and his wife Jane retaining the remainder. The growing company had by this time leased additional space to house its staff, the headquarters building having reached its capacity of 950.

In 1998, Russell and Mellon Trust combined forces to create Russell/Mellon Analytical Services Inc. The jointly-owned company, which was to employ 410 (280 coming from the former Russell Analytical Services), would continue to issue the Russell stock indexes, while also offering some of Mellon's investment services and taking advantage of the latter company's huge computer processing capabilities. Soon after this, an alliance was made with Société Générale Asset Management of France to offer multi-manager funds in Europe.

Sale to Northwestern Mutual

1998 was also the year that 66-year old George Russell began looking closely at the future of the Frank Russell Company. After consulting with Goldman, Sachs & Co. and considering the possibility of an IPO, he decided to sell the company to Northwestern Mutual Life Insurance in August for more than

Key Dates:

1936: Frank Russell founds a small investment firm in Tacoma, Washington.

1958: Grandson George Russell takes over business upon Frank Russell's death.

1969: The company's strategy of rating money managers is introduced, and a New York office opened.

1979: First foreign office opens in London.

1980: Russell begins offering managed funds to investors.

1982: Russell 1000, 2000, and 3000 stock indexes are created.

1986: Russell opens offices in Tokyo, Japan, and Sydney, Australia.

1988: Company moves into its new 12-story Tacoma headquarters.

1990: Russell 20–20 group founded to explore emerging markets.

1996: George Russell begins sharing company's ownership with his employees.

1997: Consulting business surpasses $1 trillion in managed assets.

1999: Russell is sold to Northwestern Mutual for $1.2 billion.

$1.2 billion. The Milwaukee-based Northwestern was the fourth-largest insurer in the U.S., with assets of more than $76 billion. The Frank Russell Co., growing annually since the mid-1970s at a rate of more than 20 percent, had itself reached $305 million in annual revenues by this time.

Following the sale, the company continued to be headquartered in Tacoma, and its management team remained intact. Northwestern Mutual insurance agents also began to offer Russell investment packages to their customers. Though the sale had been prompted in part by George Russell's concern about the impact of high estate taxes on the firm and the other complications his death might cause, he was also looking for a powerful ally. He told the *Tacoma News Tribune,* "We are relatively small globally. The model we developed is beginning to get world attention. If we don't get some muscle behind us, somebody will run over us." Noting that Northwestern had not been the highest bidder for the firm, he stated, "The criteria Jane and I had were culture, independence, and support of the community." The Russells, who were active fundraisers for such projects as the proposed $38.8 million Museum of Modern Glass on the Tacoma waterfront, planned to start a charitable foundation with some of their proceeds from the sale.

Overseas growth continued in 1999 when the company made new alliances with banks in Japan and Singapore to offer Russell investment funds in those countries. Several executives were promoted at this time to oversee the firm's international strategy. 2000 also saw further developments abroad when an alliance was formed with FTSE International Ltd. of London to jointly market both firm's products, including their stock indexes. Another agreement was reached during the year with South Africa-based Investment Solutions to distribute Russell funds in that country.

The much-debated proposal to allow Americans to invest their Social Security accounts in the stock market led Russell executives to help form the Coalition for American Financial Security to examine this option. Though it was accused by some of being motivated by greed, a coalition spokesperson declared that it was primarily engaged in fact finding and opinion polling to help gauge public sentiment about the matter. Russell also continued inking foreign alliances, partnering during 2001 with BMW Group's banking arm to sell money management programs to investors in Germany.

With its long history and sterling reputation, the Frank Russell Co. remained one of the foremost money management names in the United States. The deep pockets of Northwestern Mutual and the company's growing focus on international expansion made continued growth a good bet for some time to come.

Principal Subsidiaries

Russell Investment Group; Frank Russell Investment Management Co.; Frank Russell Insurance Fund; Frank Russell Canada, Ltd.; Russell/Mellon Analytical Services, Inc. (50%) SG/Russell Asset Management (France; 50%)

Principal Competitors

SEI Investments Co.; Merrill Lynch & Co., Inc.; Morgan Stanley Dean Whitter & Co.; The Goldman Sachs Group, Inc.

Further Reading

Blumenthal, Les, "Frank Russell Dips Hand in Political Arena," *News Tribune* (Tacoma, Wash.), July 9, 2001, p. A1.

Chernoff, Joel, "Frank Russell Dons Beret in Europe Push: Joins With Société Générale to Market Its Funds," *Investment News*, April 6, 1998, p. 5.

Dunphy, Stephen H., "Investment Oasis—Frank Russell, Highly Regarded in Global Arena, Aims to Boost Image at Home," *Seattle Times*, August 25, 1996, p. F1.

——, "Sale Reshaping Russell," *Seattle Times*, August 10, 1998, p. C1.

Eckart, Kim, "An Unruffled Russell Co. Stays the Course in Tacoma," *News Tribune* (Tacoma, Wash.), March 11, 2001, p. D1.

Fysh, Graham, and Jim Szymanski, "Frank Russell Co. Appears Headed for Alliance," *News Tribune* (Tacoma, Wash.), May 14, 1998, p. A1.

Fysh, Graham, "A Quiet Russell-Ing," *News Tribune* (Tacoma, Wash.), November 11, 1993, p. D1.

——, "Russell: A Commitment to Stay in Tacoma," *News Tribune* (Tacoma, Wash.), August 11, 1998, p. A1.

"George F. Russell Jr.," *Puget Sound Business Journal*, September 8, 2000, p. 4A.

Kelly, Bruce, "Pension Stalwart Spreads its Wings," *Investment News*, June 25, 2001, p. 15.

Lohse, Deborah, "Northwestern Mutual's Deal to Purchase Frank Russell Gives It More Wares to Sell," *Wall Street Journal*, August 11, 1998, p. A6.

Popham, Art, "Frank Russell Co. Gets Solid Response From First-Ever Ads," *News Tribune* (Tacoma, Wash.), November 2, 1996, p. B5.

Tibbits, George, "Asset Consultant Keeps Watch on Wall Street from a Distance," *Seattle Times*, August 14, 1988, p. D1.

Tucker, Rob, "Russell Develops Timberlands Index," *News Tribune* (Tacoma, Wash.), February 2, 1995, p. F1.

—Frank Uhle

GlaxoSmithKline plc

GlaxoSmithKline
Berkeley Avenue
Greenford, Middlesex UB6 0NN
United Kingdom
Telephone: (20) 8966 8000
Fax: (20) 8966 8330
Web site: http://www.gsk.com

Public Company
Incorporated: 1972 as Glaxo Holdings plc and 1989 as
    SmithKline Beecham plc
Employees: 100,000
Sales: £20.5 billion ($29.5 billion) (2001)
Stock Exchanges: New York London
Ticker Symbol: GSK
NAIC: 325412 Pharmaceutical Preparation
    Manufacturing; 325611 Soap and Other Detergent
    Manufacturing; 541710 Research and Development in
    the Physical, Engineering, and Life Sciences

GlaxoSmithKline plc (GSK) was formed from the December 2000 merger of Glaxo Wellcome plc and SmithKline Beecham plc. The $70 billion deal created the world's largest drug manufacturer and research-based pharmaceutical concern. The combined entity controlled leading market share in four of the five largest therapeutic markets—anti-infectives, central nervous system, respiratory, and gastro-intestinal/metabolic. Overall, the firm controlled nearly seven percent of the global pharmaceuticals market. Its product line includes antibiotic, antidepressant, gastrointestinal, dermatological, respiratory, cancer, and cardiovascular medications. GSK claims that every minute of every day, more than 1,100 prescriptions are written for one of its products. The company has one of the largest research and development divisions in the drug industry and spends over $450,000 every hour to research new medicine.

History of Glaxo

Glaxo began as a merchant trader. After a New Zealand partnership between Joseph Nathan and his brother-in-law was dissolved in 1873, the English-born entrepreneur started an independent company under the name Joseph Nathan & Company. Importing and exporting goods ranging from whalebone to patent medicines, Joseph Nathan prospered. He eventually returned to London in order to supervise his growing business there, while his sons remained in Wellington to manage the company activities in New Zealand.

While on a purchasing trip in London, one of the Nathan sons discovered an American process to dry milk. After securing the rights to this process, the company began production of dried milk at Bunnythorpe factory in New Zealand in 1904 and registered the product under the name Glaxo in 1906. Research on the sanitary quality of the milk soon caught the attention of the medical establishment; sales of the product, however, proved disappointing. The most promising market emerged in infant food. Thus, production of Glaxo baby food products began.

Alec, the youngest Nathan son, moved from New Zealand to London to supervise an expansion of the baby food business there. Much of the sales momentum Alec thereafter achieved is attributed to his Glaxo Baby Book, a practical guide to child care published in 1908, when the company established its Glaxo division in London. In it could be found the Glaxo slogan, "Builds Bonnie Babies," which would soon become famous. Only a year after the product registered its first impressive sales figures, Joseph Nathan died and the chair passed to his son Louis. Sales continued to grow, and within a relatively short period of time Glaxo Baby Foods had become an important UK-based manufacturer.

By the outbreak of World War I production demands compelled the company to build a more modern facility and to hire new staff. Ernest Rose joined the company to supervise manufacturing processes, and Harry Jephcott was placed in charge of Glaxo's rudimentary laboratory. With the completion of Glaxo House, the company's new headquarters, Jephcott's laboratory grew and employed a staff of eight scientists, including two women.

In the years that followed, Harry Jephcott moved up the ranks from chemist to company chair. Born in 1891, the son of a train driver, Jephcott received his education in pharmacy. When first hired by the Nathan family he was regarded as "Alec's folly," but he quickly proved his worth and became indispensable to Glaxo's success. As a top executive he was known for his firm leadership and business acumen—a perfect complement to Alec Nathan, who tended to focus on worker welfare. Jephcott's accomplishments eventually were rewarded with a knighthood.

Glaxo Baby Foods sales continued to grow in the years following World War I, and the company expanded into such markets as India and South America. Jephcott's 1923 visit to the International Dairy Congress in Washington, D.C., soon changed the course of Glaxo's history. There he observed Professor Elmer V. McCollum's and Dr. Theodore Zucker's original work in identifying and extracting vitamin D. Recognizing the huge market potential in fortifying Glaxo products with this anti-rachitic, Jephcott persuaded the company's directors to secure a process license. After achieving an immediate success with vitamin D fortified products, Glaxo moved on to produce a pharmaceutical item, Ostelin Liquid, Britain's first commercial vitamin concentrate developed in 1924. Ostelin products eventually included a comprehensive line of vitamin preparations.

In the 1930s, Glaxo's major advancements included the production of Adexolin (vitamins A and D) and Oster-milk, a retail version of Glaxo's vitamin fortified milk that soon surpassed the pharmaceutical version in sales. Because of increased business overseas, the company built a factory in India, established a company in Italy, and secured distributorships in Greece, Malaya, and China. In an effort to strengthen the company's increasing activity, Glaxo's pharmaceutical department was organized into a separate subsidiary called Glaxo Laboratories Ltd. in 1935.

During World War II, the company concentrated on producing pharmaceuticals for the war effort, including anesthetics, penicillin, and a variety of vitamin supplements. After the war, Glaxo began the mass production of penicillin in earnest, using the American process of deep fermentation. During this time, several long-time Glaxo employees retired. Harry Jephcott became chairperson of the company upon Alec Nathan's retirement. Ida Townsend, Glaxo's successful export manager, joined the board in 1947, the company's first woman director. Changes also occurred in the company's structure: Glaxo's parent company, Joseph Nathan & Company, was dissolved, and Glaxo became an independent public company in 1947. All Joseph Nathan's diversified interests, from butter importing to fencing exporting, were sold to finance Glaxo's growth.

By far the most important of Glaxo's postwar achievements was the isolation of vitamin B12 in 1948. Along with their American counterparts at Merck, who had achieved the same feat virtually simultaneously, Glaxo had made a major advance in the treatment of pernicious anemia. Of similar magnitude was Glaxo's synthesis of the hormone necessary for the treatment of hypothyroidism.

In the 1950s, Glaxo grew through acquisition and consolidation. The company acquired both a chemical and a medical supply subsidiary and established an independent veterinary department to meet the increasing demand for animal pharmaceuticals. Through a 1958 merger Glaxo joined forces with Allen & Hanbury's Ltd., one of Britain's oldest pharmaceutical manufacturers. Britain's first commercial cortisone product emerged from Glaxo's laboratories during this time. The discovery of sisal as an abundant source of an important steroid led to the commercial synthesis of a series of corticosteroids.

Glaxo's growth continued into the 1960s. To monitor this growth, the directors formed a new parent company, Glaxo Group Limited. Jephcott assumed the title of chairperson for the holding company. In 1963, he retired from this position, becoming Glaxo's first honorary president, and the physicist Sir Alan Wilson assumed the chair. Glaxo's scientists worked to develop Betnovate, a new corticosteroid. Through a licensing agreement with Schering U.S.A., a pharmaceutical company engaged in original research in corticosteroids, Glaxo developed a production process essential to the manufacture of the drug.

During the next decade, Beecham, an industry competitor, attempted the largest takeover in British history by making an unfriendly bid for Glaxo. To protect its independence, Glaxo management sought to increase its holdings through a merger with a company of similar interests. Thus Glaxo and Boots, another competitor, planned to combine their company resources. Yet neither the takeover nor the merger ever happened. The Monopolies Commissioners ruled against the proceedings on the grounds that innovation declines as companies grow above a certain size. In the wake of the aborted takeover attempt, the company was renamed Glaxo Holdings.

In 1973, Sir Alan Wilson retired and Austin Bide, a long time Glaxo employee, assumed the titles of chairperson and chief executive officer. Other changes during the 1970s included the establishment of a U.S. subsidiary through the purchase of Meyer Laboratories Inc. in 1978. Domestic consolidation brought all Glaxo's UK operations under one holding company. In pharmaceuticals Glaxo's innovative research in cephalosporins resulted in the development of Zinacef.

Near the end of the 1970s, Glaxo suffered from the effects of inflation. Citing Glaxo's continuing dependence on export trade, its failure to expand significantly beyond the British and Commonwealth markets, and its persistent reputation for poor marketing decisions, city analysts projected slower growth in the company's future. What industry observers did not foresee was the release of a drug destined to become highly successful throughout the world. Zantac, Glaxo's trade name for its anti-ulcer drug ranitidine, was still in testing during this time. However, based on the emerging results of these tests, Glaxo knew that Zantac was ready to present a competitive challenge to SmithKline's Tagamet, then the preeminent anti-ulcer medication and best-selling drug in the world.

Soon after Austin retired as chief executive officer, Zantac was launched in several European markets with a high degree of success. Paul Girolami, a long time Glaxo employee who had formerly served as Group Financial Director, assumed Sir Austin's position. Over the next several years, Girolami estab-

Key Dates:

1830: John K. Smith opens his first drugstore in Philadelphia through a company called John K. Smith & Company.

1847: Thomas Beecham begins hawking his own brand of pills in and around the town of Wigan.

1873: Joseph Nathan establishes Nathan & Company in New Zealand.

1875: Smith's company is renamed Smith, Kline & Company, ten years after Mahlon Kline joined the company, first serving as bookkeeper then moving into management.

1891: Smith, Kline acquires French, Richards & Company and changes its name to Smith, Kline & French (SK&F).

1904: Nathan begins production of dried milk in New Zealand.

1906: Nathan adopts the name Glaxo for his dried milk.

1924: Glaxo develops its first pharmaceutical product, Ostelin.

1935: Glaxo's pharmaceutical department is organized into a separate subsidiary called Glaxo Laboratories Ltd.

1947: Glaxo's parent company, Joseph Nathan & Company, is dissolved and Glaxo becomes an independent public company.

1957: Beecham researchers isolate the penicillin nucleus 6-APA, a discovery that opens the door to the manufacture of a multitude of new antibiotics.

1960: SK&F begins marketing Contac, the first all-day cold remedy.

1972: Beecham launches Amoxil, which becomes one of the most widely prescribed antibiotics.

1976: SK&F revolutionizes peptic ulcer treatment through the introduction of Tagamet.

1978: Glaxo acquires Meyer Laboratories Inc. and creates a U.S. subsidiary.

1981: Glaxo launches anti-ulcer treatment Zantac.

1989: Beecham merges with SmithKline.

1995: Glaxo and Wellcome plc merge to form Glaxo Wellcome plc.

2000: Merger between SmithKline and Glaxo Wellcome is finalized; GlaxoSmithKline is formed.

more than half of the world market in its class and became the largest-selling prescription drug in the world. The company employed a unique marketing strategy in 1981: it developed strategic partnerships with drug companies around the world to get an edge in each market. From 1980 to 1988, Glaxo's sales nearly tripled, and in 1989 profits soared 13 percent over the previous year to £1.14 billion, ensuring the company's role as the second-largest pharmaceutical company worldwide.

Over the next few years, however, Glaxo's status declined somewhat. A wave of drug company mergers in 1989 left the company fourth in worldwide sales. The company was reorganized that year, and CEO Bernard D. Taylor was replaced by Ernest Mario, formerly head of U.S. operations. Zantac sales plateaued by the start of the 1990s, when newly formulated anti-ulcer drugs threatened its commanding share, and some industry analysts doubted the company's ability to maintain its lead in new drug introductions.

In 1990, Glaxo announced worldwide regulatory trials for its new anti-migraine drug, Imigran (or sumatriptan, generically). Moreover, Zofran Injection, an important new treatment for the prevention of nausea and vomiting in cancer patients receiving chemotherapy, was approved by the United States Food and Drug Administration early in 1991. Within just over a year, the drug was available in most of the world's markets and registered sales of £259 million in Glaxo's 1991–92 fiscal year.

Glaxo tried to capture some of the entrepreneurial energy of smaller companies through joint ventures. In 1991, Glaxo entered into an agreement with Gilead Sciences Inc. In exchange for about $20 million, Glaxo purchased an equity stake in the company and its potential for creating anti-cancer drugs. The company also sold its interests outside of prescription drugs and increased its research and development allocations. One such development, Ceftazidime, an injectable antibiotic, received a strong market reception in Japan.

Zantac's arrival in Japan had involved major competition in the form of an anti-ulcer drug discovered by the Japanese Yamanouchi Company. The company's difficulties in Japan continued in the early 1990s. Corporate executives cited frequent price reductions and registration delays as impediments to greater success in this, the second-largest market in the world. Glaxo did penetrate the Chinese, Eastern European, and Russian markets in the early 1990s, opening a factory in China and establishing branches and companies in many former Communist bloc countries.

By 1992, Glaxo had captured 3.7 percent of the world's pharmaceutical market, and marked its twelfth year of continuous growth. Profits, however, did not maintain the same pace, having been eroded by research, marketing, and infrastructure costs. At the same time, Glaxo was threatened by competition from Wellcome PLC, a rival that was able to launch more than a dozen drugs during the 1980s and early 1990s, including Zovirax, a herpes treatment, and Retovir, a drug to combat AIDS. Glaxo was able to retaliate with the introduction of new asthma and hypertension treatments, in limited markets, but had yet to launch a product that could duplicate Zantac's success.

Continued industry consolidation, falling profits, and high research costs eventually led Glaxo to seek out a merger

lished himself as the architect of Zantac's marketing policy in the United States and Japan. In a joint venture with Hoffmann-La Roche, the Swiss pharmaceutical concern responsible for developing the world's two best-selling tranquilizers, Glaxo introduced Zantac to the U.S. market in 1981.

By 1984, Zantac had captured 25 percent of the new prescription market. Glaxo announced plans to build a $40 million plant in North Carolina to manufacture the drug in the United States. Joseph J. Ruvane, Jr., president of Glaxo's U.S. company, claimed Glaxo would become one of America's top ten pharmaceutical firms. The company's actively traded shares increased in price from £2.40 a share in 1980 to £10.25 after a two-for-one split. By the end of the decade, Zantac captured

partner. Eying Wellcome's growing arsenal of prescription drugs, Glaxo made a $14.9 billion bid for its competitor in 1995. Glaxo Wellcome plc was formed later that year upon completion of the deal. The merged company began to see immediate reductions in its research and development expenditures. Valtrex was introduced to replace Zovirax and the California-based combinatorial chemistry firm, Affymax, was acquired. In 1996, the company sold off its consumer business ventures to focus on prescription medicine development. The firm worked feverishly to launch a new product that could match the success of Zantac. While sales of the drug reached $1.6 billion in 1996, its patent expired the following year leaving the market wide open for cheaper, generic versions of the product. While the company expected its sales of Zantac to fall by as much as 90 percent, its pairing with Wellcome left it well positioned to diversify its product line.

In 1998, the firm launched the antidepressant Zyban, the first prescription anti-smoking drug that did not contain nicotine. It was during this time period that merger talks began with Smith-Kline Beecham. The $70 million deal fell through however, when both companies could not reach suitable terms. Robert Ingram was named CEO of Glaxo that year and pledged to focus on research and development. As he set a strategic and lofty goal of launching three new products a year, Glaxo soon realized that a merger would solidify its position in the industry and increase its new product potential.

History of Beecham

One of the first British companies to undertake intensive advertising, Beecham grew from a small regional pill-peddling operation to a multinational patent medicine company at a time when very few companies branched beyond their own communities. In 1847, Thomas Beecham began hawking his own brand of pills throughout the town of Wigan and the surrounding countryside. He soon set up shop as an herbalist and grocer in Wigan. Beecham, born the son of a farm worker in 1820, had spent his youth as a shepherd boy, and in that job he had learned a good deal about herbal remedies. Beecham was said to have had a special knack for healing sick animals and, on occasion, even humans. For several years Beecham sold his laxatives at local markets with a sales pitch that included showing off a jar of intestinal worms.

In 1859, after mixed results in Wigan, Beecham moved his operation to nearby St. Helens, where he focused on two products: a cough tablet and the famous laxative Beecham's Pills, advertised in the local newspaper as "worth a guinea a box." Both products were available through mail order and Beecham increased spending on advertising to take advantage of a rapidly growing demand for health products.

In 1881, when Thomas Beecham's son Joseph took effective control of the company, Beecham's sales were at £34,000, demonstrating average annual growth of about 18 percent, a rate it had sustained since 1865. The elder Beecham remained active in the operations of the company until his official retirement in 1895.

Joseph Beecham increased the company's advertising expenditures considerably. By 1891, annual advertising expendi-

tures had increased to £120,000, up from £22,000 in 1884, and Beecham introduced more creative ads. Advertising gimmicks included free distribution of sails printed with Beecham slogans to boat owners and inexpensive general information booklets bearing Beecham's messages.

During the 1880s, Joseph Beecham spearheaded the company's expansion overseas. First, Beecham's Pills were exported to countries throughout the British Empire. In 1888, they were distributed in the United States and Canada, and two years later a manufacturing facility was set up in New York.

Extensive advertising had made Beecham's Pills practically a household word on several continents by the end of the nineteenth century. This success was not at first duplicated after the turn of the century, however. Although Beecham remained profitable, its rate of growth slowed considerably. Joseph Beecham spent more of his time on projects unrelated to the business, including numerous philanthropic endeavors and patronage of his music-minded son, Thomas, later to become a renowned conductor. In 1913, sales remained static at £290,000, although the firm's profitability had improved.

In 1916, Joseph Beecham died, leaving a complicated estate. Beecham had never incorporated the pill business, and it remained entwined with his other affairs. Henry Beecham, Joseph's younger son, ran the business with three other executors until 1921, but had no active role after that time. Three years later, the pill business was acquired by financier Philip Hill. Hill incorporated the company as Beecham's Pills in 1928 and launched a new period of growth.

For the next ten years Hill made acquisitions broadening the product line of the company. He purchased patent medicines such as Yeast Vite, Iron Jelloids, Phosferine, and Phyllosan. In the later 1930s, the company entered the toiletries business with the acquisition of Prichard and Constance, a shampoo manufacturer that distributed the brand name Amami. In 1938, Beecham acquired Macleans Ltd., well-known for toothpaste; County Perfumery, manufacturers of Brylcreem; and Eno Proprietaries, makers of a popular antacid. In 1938, Beecham acquired Lucozade, a popular glucose drink, from its inventor W.W. Hunter, to enter the health-drink field. The company changed its name to Beecham Group Ltd. in 1945 to reflect its diversified nature.

When Beecham acquired Maclean's in 1938 it unknowingly changed its direction. With the purchase came company secretary and director H.G. Leslie Lazell. Lazell became corporate secretary of Beecham's Pills, and during the war took over as managing director of the Maclean's unit. Leslie Lazell had always been a firm believer in research, and he developed a research department at the company, which soon entered the medicines field.

Formed in 1943, Beecham Research Laboratories Ltd. employed 115 people, 34 of them graduate-level scientists. In 1947, a 27-acre facility was opened at Surrey, with Alexander Fleming, the discoverer of penicillin, presiding over the opening ceremonies. Beecham Research Laboratories started out researching both pharmaceuticals and food products but before long concentrated solely on pharmaceutical research. In 1949, Beecham's acquisition of the C.L. Bencard company, a manufacturer of allergy vaccines, paved the way for entry into the prescription drug field.

During the 1950s Beecham expanded its consumer products line and pumped the profits into drug research. It purchased new health drinks: Ribena blackcurrant juice, Shloer apple and grape drinks, and Horlicks beverages were acquired in 1969. The toiletries division also expanded, adding Vosene shampoo among others. A real breakthrough came in 1957 when company researchers isolated the penicillin nucleus 6-aminopenicillanic acid (6-APA). This discovery opened the door to the manufacture of a multitude of new antibiotics.

In 1959, Beecham marketed Broxil (phenethicillin), followed shortly by Celbenin (methicillin). The introduction of these products represented a medical breakthrough, as many bacterial strains had built up a resistance to the original penicillins—Penicillin G and Penicillin V. In 1961, Penbritin (ampicillin) hit the market, and soon Beecham's facilities were inadequate for the worldwide demand. A 35-acre complex at Worthing came on line in the early 1960s to produce 6-APA, the base for semisynthetic penicillins. Beecham's lead in antibiotics brought tremendous growth in the 1960s and 1970s.

Lazell's emphasis on marketing was also key to Beecham's growth. By 1960. the company was the second largest advertiser in the United Kingdom. Beecham was one of the first British firms to put the CEO directly in charge of the marketing team, long a standard practice in the United States.

In the mid-1960s, Beecham products penetrated the European continent. Within 20 years, this region comprised Beecham's largest single market. In the later 1960s, Beecham Pharmaceutical marketers turned their attention to the United States, where an expanding business had been built on foundations provided by Brylcreem hair dressing. In 1967, the company opened an antibiotics factory in Piscataway, New Jersey. In 1971, Beecham bought the U.S. feminine hygiene company S.E. Massengill.

In 1972, the company planned to increase the size of its prescription drug business by merging with one of its chief British competitors, the Glaxo Group. The British government blocked the merger, citing the possibility of reduced spending on research and development within the industry. Glaxo was particularly attractive because it had a large network overseas.

Also in 1972, Beecham launched Amoxil, which went on to become one of the most widely prescribed antibiotics, often used to treat bacterial infections, including those involving the ear and throat. Amoxil was the brand name for amoxycillin, which had been discovered by Beecham scientists. The company's growing antibiotic line also included Floxapen (flucloxacillin) and Ticar (ticarcillin). In the mid-1970s, new non-antibiotic drugs were introduced, such as the allergy vaccine Pollinex and the antidepressant Norval.

Acquisitions of American drug and consumer products companies accelerated toward the end of the decade and into the 1980s. In 1977 Beecham bought Sucrets throat lozenges for $76 million and acquired the floundering Calgon bath products line. Beecham turned the businesses around, revamping old products and packaging, and using aggressive marketing strategies. In 1979, Beecham purchased Jovan, the U.S. perfume manufacturer, for $85 million. Other fragrance lines were later acquired, including Diane Von Furstenberg in 1983 and the cosmetics and fragrances of BAT Industries plc in 1985. Other big acquisitions in the early 1980s included the J.B. Williams company, makers of Geritol, Sominex, Aqua Velva, and Lectric Shave among others for $100 million in 1982; DAP, Inc., manufacturer of caulk and other home improvement products for $68 million in 1983; and Norcliff Thayer, a major manufacturer of OTC drugs including the well-known antacid Tums, in the United States for $369 million in 1985. Beecham also acquired a number of European pharmaceutical companies in France, West Germany, and Italy. On the drug development front, Beecham in 1981 introduced Augmentin, an antibiotic used to treat an array of bacterial infections.

In 1984, Beecham's profits began to level off, due in part to decreased popularity of ampicillin, caused by increased antibiotic competition, and pressure from the British government to cap profits on drugs. Following Lazell's formula, Beecham's new chairman, Sir Ronald Halstead, hoped to pay for rising research and development costs through profits on consumer goods. A number of acquisitions of consumer products companies in 1984 and 1985 seemed to the company's directors too costly and out of line with Beecham's overall thrust. Halstead was let go in 1985. In 1986, Robert P. Bauman became chairman of Beecham. The company's first U.S. chairman, Bauman knew the North American market well, having worked at General Foods, Avco, and Textron. Bauman sold off some of Beecham's consumer products lines, primarily soft drinks lines, although he retained the successful Ribena, Horlicks, and Lucozade brands, and implemented cost-cutting measures worldwide. Between 1986 and mid-1989, Bauman disposed of £400 million of non-core businesses.

By the mid-1980s, Beecham had made significant headway into the U.S. marketplace and continued to hold its place as the largest over-the-counter drug producer in its home market. Beecham's pharmaceutical research focused on three general areas: cardiovascular therapy, diseases affecting the central nervous system, and anti-infectives. Demand for healthcare products increased substantially as the wealthy U.S. market grew older. Relifex, a nonsteroidal anti-inflammatory used by arthritis patients, began limited marketing in 1985 and by the late 1980s showed promise for the company. An anticlotting agent, Eminase, introduced in Europe in 1987, also appeared to be a significant breakthrough for cardiac patients. Two new antibiotics, Augmentin and Timentin, earned the Queen's Award for technological achievement in 1986. Both drugs received widespread acceptance throughout the medical community.

In July 1989, Beecham merged with an equally well established business, Philadelphia-based SmithKline Beckman Corporation. SmithKline Beckman's roots extended back to 1830, when John K. Smith opened his first drugstore in Philadelphia through a company called John K. Smith & Company. The firm soon became a leader in drug wholesaling. It was renamed Smith, Kline & Company in 1875, ten years after Mahlon Kline joined the company, first serving as bookkeeper, then moving into sales and management. In 1891, Smith, Kline acquired French, Richards & Company and changed its name to Smith, Kline & French (SK&F). At this time, SK&F produced and sold fine perfumes, liniments, tonics, hair oil, cough medicine, and various home remedies.

In 1910, SK&F expanded its product offerings through the addition of the "Blue Line," which included such standard drugs as poison ivy lotion, iron tablets, and lozenges. Around the same time as the establishment of Beecham Research Laboratories, SK&F established its own research arm called Smith Kline & French Laboratories. In the 1950s SK&F scientists developed the anti-psychotic Thorazine, which started a revolution in the treatment of mental illness. In 1952 came the launch of Dexedrine, the first time-released capsule. This was followed in 1960 by another time-release product, Contac, the first all-day cold remedy.

During the 1970s, SK&F shortened its name to SmithKline Corporation. The revolutionary peptic ulcer medication Tagamet was introduced in the United Kingdom in November 1976 and in the United States in August 1977. Tagamet went on to become, in 1989, the first drug in the world to have annual sales in excess of $1 billion. Also in 1989 SmithKline's James Black was awarded the Nobel prize in medicine for his research involving Tagamet and other beta-blockers and H2 blockers. In 1982, SmithKline acquired Allergan, a maker of eye and skin care products, and Beckman Instruments, a leading manufacturer of diagnostic and measurement instruments and supplies. On completion of the latter purchase, the company changed its name to SmithKline Beckman Corporation. By this time, SmithKline had also diversified into the clinical laboratories business. It entered that sector in the 1960s through the acquisition of seven labs in the United States and one in Canada. SmithKline Clinical Labs then merged with American Bio-Science Laboratories in 1985 to form SmithKline BioScience Laboratories, which became the industry leader in 1988 with the purchase of one of its biggest competitors, International Clinical Laboratories, Inc.

The merger of Beecham and SmithKline Beckman formed what was at the time one of the top five pharmaceutical companies in the world. The new SmithKline Beecham plc, based in London, tallied $6.9 billion in sales annually. Beecham was widely considered the healthier half of the new company. With Eminase and Relifex about to hit the U.S. market, Beecham looked solid enough to shore up its ailing American partner for at least a short time. SmithKline had failed to come up with a blockbuster product since it introduced the ulcer remedy Tagamet in the mid-1970s, despite substantial research and development expenditures. New competition from Glaxo's Zantac had eroded some of Tagamet's expected market share, and SmithKline was accused by stock analysts of lacking direction. A headline in the *Wall Street Journal*, July 7, 1989, called the merger "just what the doctor ordered" for SmithKline.

SmithKline's chairman Henry Wendt became chairman of the merged company while Robert Bauman, who became the new company CEO, faced combining two distinct corporate cultures and had little time to spare: just one week after the Beecham SmithKline merger was finalized, two U.S. giants, Squibb and Bristol-Myers, announced their own merger plans (forming Bristol-Myers Squibb Company). Beecham, with its new prescription drugs and strong presence in the over-the-counter (OTC) drug market, looked like a good partner for SmithKline, with its strong U.S. sales staff. The SmithKline

Beecham merger permitted both companies to compete on a global level neither could manage alone. In addition, the companies' R&D programs were complementary. Beecham had several new products ready for market while SmithKline was at the opposite end of the R&D cycle, promising results down the road. Geographically, Beecham's strength in Europe fit well with SmithKline's coverage in the United States and Japan. Bauman expressed his intentions to cut costs by eliminating administrative and production personnel, rather than by paring sales or research staffs.

SmithKline Expands Its OTC Business: 1990s

In the early 1990s, SmithKline Beecham concentrated on reducing the debt it had taken on to complete the merger. The company made a number of disposals, mainly in the consumer products area, including its cosmetics businesses, its adhesives unit, Brylcreem and other hair care brands, and other non-healthcare products. In early 1994, its consumer side was reorganized as the consumer healthcare division, focusing solely on OTC drugs, toothpaste and toothbrushes, and nutritional drinks. The company's OTC drug offerings were later expanded through the introduction of nonprescription versions of prescription drugs, including the launch of Tagamet HB. On the pharmaceutical side, SmithKline announced in late 1992 that it would withdraw from long-term research into gastrointestinal drugs to concentrate its R&D efforts on five areas: the central nervous system, the heart and lungs, anti-infectives, inflammation and tissue repair, and vaccines. Among the pharmaceuticals introduced by SmithKline in the early and mid-1990s were Relafen, an anti-inflammatory drug for the treatment of arthritis; Engerix B, a hepatitis B vaccine; Havrix, a hepatitis A vaccine; Kytril, an antinausea product used in treating cancer patients; and Seroxat/Paxil, an antidepressant. These introductions helped counter the plummeting sales of the prescription version of Tagamet, which went off patent in 1994.

In 1993, SmithKline spent $125 million to enter into a research collaboration agreement with and take a seven percent stake in Human Genome Sciences Inc., a newly formed enterprise actively identifying and describing the functions of human genes. The agreement gave SmithKline rights to develop drugs based on the gene sequencing information discovered by Human Genome Sciences. This collaboration was slow to pay off in terms of new medicines.

Jan Leschly, a native of Denmark who as a young man was a professional tennis player ranked as high as number ten in the world, was named CEO of SmithKline in 1994. In May of that year, the company acquired Diversified Pharmaceutical Services, Inc.—a leading U.S. pharmaceutical benefit manager (PBM)—for $2.3 billion (£1.6 billion). PBM's, which acted as drug wholesalers for managed care organizations, were growing rapidly in the United States, in tandem with the growth of health maintenance organizations and other managed care enterprises. SmithKline continued its acquisitive ways in 1994 with the August purchase of Sterling Health, a specialist in branded OTC medicines, for $2.9 billion. A few weeks later SmithKline sold Sterling's North American operations to Bayer AG for $1 billion. The net result of these moves was that SmithKline expanded its OTC presence in Western Europe significantly and even more dramatically in Eastern Europe and Asia; the company became the third largest seller of OTC products in the world, and the largest in Europe. It gained several key brands, including the analgesic Panadol and the gastrointestinal remedy Phillips Milk of Magnesia. Rounding out a year filled with large transactions, SmithKline in late 1994 sold its animal health business to Pfizer Inc. for $1.45 billion (£920 million), a move enabling SmithKline to focus further on the human healthcare market.

During the mid to late 1990s, SmithKline Beecham began marketing a number of new products. On the OTC side, the company moved into the smoking cessation sector with the launch of Nicorette gum. In 1996, the FDA approved NicoDerm CQ, a smoking cessation patch. These products held 90 percent of the OTC smoking cessation market in the United States through the late 1990s. Also in 1996 came the launch of the pharmaceutical Hycamtin, which was designed to treat ovarian cancer and small cell lung cancer. In the vaccine arena, SmithKline introduced Twinrix, the first combined hepatitis A and B vaccine; the Infanrix line of combination vaccines, which included protection against diphtheria, tetanus, and pertussis (or whooping cough) in its basic formulation, with additional protection against other diseases provided through other formulations; and LYMErix, which was introduced in 1998 as the first vaccine in the world for the prevention of Lyme disease.

SmithKline's collaboration with Human Genome Sciences had yet to pay off in terms of new medicines, but was uncovering numerous leads for potential development. SmithKline simply did not have the resources, however, to follow up on every lead. Therefore, in 1996, the company began licensing the Human Genome Sciences data to other pharmaceutical companies, including Schering-Plough Corporation, Takeda Chemical Industries Ltd., and Merck. The following year, SmithKline joined with Incyte Pharmaceuticals to create another biotechnology venture called diaDexus. This venture was focused on developing new diagnostic tests based on gene discoveries. One of its first undertakings was the development and commercializing of a new cervical cancer screening technology which had been originally conceived by Cancer Research Campaign Technology Limited.

The need for greater resources to investigate the many opportunities being uncovered by the biotechnology revolution led SmithKline to enter merger discussions, first with American Home Products Corporation, which began in 1997 and ended in early 1998, and then with U.K. rival Glaxo Wellcome. In late January 1998, Glaxo and SmithKline announced that they were on the verge of announcing a merger valued at between $65 billion and $70 billion. This would have been the largest corporate merger ever, but the deal fell apart in late February following disagreements between the two companies' CEOs over leadership of the combined company.

In the aftermath of this botched union, SmithKline refocused its operations on two core areas: pharmaceuticals and consumer healthcare. To this end, in April 1999, it sold Diversified Pharmaceutical Services to Express Scripts Inc. for £422 million ($700 million) in cash, resulting in an after-tax loss of £446 million ($740 million), which was recorded in 1998. Around this same time, the company announced a four-year restructuring plan in which it would close down excess manufacturing plants and lay off about 3,000 people, resulting in annual savings of £200 million ($332 million) by 2002. SmithKline planned to take pretax charges of up to £750 million ($1.25

billion) over the four-year period. In August, SmithKline completed the sale of its clinical laboratory unit—SmithKline Beecham Clinical Laboratories—to Quest Diagnostics, Incorporated for £618 million ($1.03 billion) and a 29.2 percent equity interest in Quest.

In mid-1999, SmithKline received FDA regulatory approval of Avandia, a diabetes drug which it began co-marketing with Bristol-Myers Squibb, and for a new use for Paxil, that of treating people suffering from severe ''social phobia''—extreme bouts of shyness that could be severely debilitating and traumatic. In December 1999, Leschly announced that he would retire as chief executive in April 2000 and be replaced by COO Jean-Pierre Garnier. Rumors instantly began to surface suggesting that the leadership change would lead to renewed merger talks with Glaxo; however, there was no immediate suggestion that SmithKline Beecham was certain to change direction with Leschly's departure. The company appeared capable of continuing on a path of organic growth, with several pharmaceuticals in advanced stages of development, including Ariflo, for chronic obstructive pulmonary disease and for asthma; Idoxifene, for osteoporosis and breast cancer; Factive, an antibiotic for the treatment of respiratory tract and urinary tract infections; Bexxar, for non-Hodgkin's lymphoma, a cancer of the immune system; and Locilex, a topical antibiotic for the treatment of infected diabetic foot ulcers.

The Formation of GlaxoSmithKline: 2000

Both Glaxo and SmithKline soon realized, however, that in order to compete in a leadership position in the fiercely competitive pharmaceuticals industry, a merger was necessary. As such, it soon became apparent that both companies wished to combine forces. Putting their differences from the 1998 proposal aside, talks resumed in early 2000, and the $70 billion deal was finalized in December of that year. Ingram was named COO and President of Pharmaceutical Operations while Garnier was named CEO of the newly merged company—GlaxoSmithKline plc. According to a July 2001 *Business Week* article, Garnier claimed that the partners would be ''the kings of science.''

Indeed, the merger created the largest drug company in the world with sales of $22.5 billion. While the company was forced to divest certain assets-including Kytril, Famvir, and Vectavir—its product line was greatly enhanced by the merger. The deal also created one of the largest sales and marketing forces in the drug industry, with over 40,000 global employees focused in that area (total employee count reached 100,000). GSK's staff of over 16,500 researchers and its R&D budget of nearly $4 billion also left the firm in a favorable position against competitors.

Under the leadership of Garnier, GSK quickly set out to capture market share in Europe's maturing drug sector. By July 2001, it had signed over 100 joint ventures with biotech firms and eyed both cancer and cardiovascular drugs as crucial to its product development strategy. This strategy included launching 15 new drugs by 2005. The company already had 23 new vaccines in the development pipeline, including an AIDS vaccine. In April, the GSK launched the asthma drug Advair in the U.S. The drug was expected to secure global sales of $2.4 billion by 2005. The firm also acquired Block Drug Company Inc., an oral health care and consumer products manufacturer.

During its first year of operation, GSK saw pharmaceutical sales increase by 12 percent. It secured savings of over $1.08 billion as a result of the merger and anticipated saving $2.59 billion by 2003 in manufacturing costs. While management felt that GSK was in an excellent position for continued growth—it claimed it was one of the fastest growing pharmaceutical companies in the U.S. market—industry analysts felt that the firm could possibly fall short of expectations if it failed to launch new products that could generate large revenues. The firm however, had nearly $6 billion in cash assets—a fact that had many in the industry wondering whether or not GSK would look to yet another deal to bolster its holdings.

Principal Subsidiaries

Glaxo Wellcome plc; Glaxo Group Ltd.; Glaxo Wellcome Export Ltd.; Glaxo Research and Development Ltd.; Glaxo Investments (UK) Ltd.; Glaxo Wellcome Vehicle Finance Ltd.; The Wellcome Foundation Ltd.; Wellcome Limited; Glaxo Operations UK Ltd.; Glaxo Wellcome UK Ltd.; Glaxo Wellcome Pharma GmbH (Austria); Glaxo Wellcome Belgium SA; Glaxo Wellcome sro (Czech Republic); Glaxo Wellcome a/s (Denmark); Glaxo Wellcome Oy (Finland); Groupe Glaxo Wellcome (France); Glaxo Wellcome GmbH & Co. (Germany); Glaxo Wellcome AEBE (Greece); Glaxo Wellcome International (Ireland); Glaxo Wellcome SpA (Italy); Glaxo Wellcome SA (Poland; 96%); Glaxo Wellcome AG (Switzerland); Glaxo Wellcome Inc. (United States); Affymax Research Institute (United States); Glaxo Wellcome Americas Inc. (United States); Glaxo Wellcome China Ltd.; Glaxo India Ltd. (51%); Glaxo Wellcome Philippines Inc.; Glaxo Wellcome (Thailand) Ltd.; GlaxoSmithKline KK (Japan; 80%); Glaxo Wellcome Mexico, SA de CV; Glaxo Wellcome Egypt SAE (89%).

Principal Competitors

Merck & Co. Inc.; Novartis AG; Pfizer Inc; Bristol-Myers Squibb Company.

Further Reading

Abrahams, Paul, ''Honeymoon Over at SmithKline: The Merged Group Must Now Increase Sales,'' *Financial Times*, October 21, 1992, p. 22.

Bauman, Robert P., Peter Jackson, and Joanne T. Lawrence, *From Promise to Performance: A Journey of Transformation at SmithKline Beecham*, Boston: Harvard Business School Press, 1997, 302 p.

Capell, Kerry, ''The Stars of Europe—Value Creators,'' *Business Week*, June 11, 2001.

——, ''Why GlaxoSmithKline Longs for Wall Street's Respect,'' *Business Week*, July 30, 2001.

De Jonquieres, Guy, ''Buying the Bactroban with the Bath Oil: Why SmithKline Beecham Has Reshaped Its Consumer Brands Side,'' *Financial Times*, January 10, 1994, p. 18.

Feinberg, Phyllis, ''Creating Joint Ventures for David and Goliath,'' *Corporate Cashflow*, May 1991, pp. 57–8.

Flynn, Julia, et al., ''Is SmithKline's Future in Its Genes?,'' *Business Week*, March 4, 1996, pp. 80–1.

Foster, Geoffrey, ''How to Make Yourself Wellcome,'' *Management Today*, July 1992, pp. 68–71.

Francis, Anne, *A Guinea a Box: A Biography*, London: Hale, 1968, 191 p.

Gerrie, David. ''Can Marketing Keep Glaxo in Pole Position?'' *Marketing* (UK), October 18, 1990, pp. 24–5.

''Glaxo Goes It Alone,'' *Chief Executive*, June 1990, pp. 22–5.

''GlaxoSmithKline Merger Completed As Trading for New Company Begins,'' *Chemical Market Reporter*, January 1, 2001, p. 11.

Green, Daniel, ''Merger of Equals Sinks into Drug-Induced Hallucination,'' *Financial Times*, February 25, 1998, p. 19.

——, ''SmithKline Awaits Results of Expansion Trial,'' *Financial Times*, December 2, 1994, p. 22.

——, ''SmithKline's Well-Sugared Pill,'' *Financial Times*, February 22, 1997, p. 5.

——, ''Team Player Leschly Likes to Prove a Point: A Competitive Streak Makes the Head of SmithKline Beecham a Tough Opponent,'' *Financial Times*, July 29, 1996, p. 7.

Guyon, Janet, ''A Mangled Merger,'' *Fortune*, March 30, 1998, p. 32.

Hindley, Diana, and Geoffrey Hindley, *Advertising in Victorian England, 1837–1901*, London: Wayland, 1972, 208 p.

Holland, Kenneth, ''Pharmaceutical Industry Profiles: Beecham Group PLC,'' *The Pharmaceutical Journal*, vol. 238, 1987.

Jackson, Tony, and Daniel Green, ''SmithKline Pays 2bn for US Group,'' *Financial Times*, May 4, 1994, p. 1.

Langreth, Robert, ''Depression Pill May Help Treat the Acutely Shy,'' *Wall Street Journal*, May 3, 1999, p. B1.

Langreth, Robert, and Steven Lipin, ''Glaxo, SmithKline Reel in Battle of Egos,'' *Wall Street Journal*, February 25, 1998, p. A3.

Lazell, H.G., *From Pills to Penicillin: The Beecham Story: A Personal Account*, London: Heinemann, 1975, 208 p.

Maremont, Mark, and Joseph Weber, ''The First Acid Test of the Drug Megamergers,'' *Business Week*, February 19, 1990, pp. 62–3.

Marion, John Francis, *The Fine Old House*, Philadelphia: SmithKline Corp., 1980, 251 p.

Moore, Stephen D., and Michael Waldholz, ''SmithKline's Science-Tech Chief, Poste, to Quit,'' *Wall Street Journal*, October 29, 1999, p. B8.

''The Mother of All Mergers,'' *Economist*, February 7, 1998, pp. 63–4.

Reekie, Duncan W., *The Economics of the Pharmaceutical Industry*, London: Macmillan, 1975.

Rosenberg, Jack, and Cynthia Starr, ''New Drugs of 1990,'' *Drug Topics*, January 21, 1991, pp. 31–43.

Savitz, Eric J., ''Glaxo's Headaches: A Remarkable Drug Company Faces Some Challenges,'' *Barron's*, June 17, 1991, pp. 8–9, 18–22.

''Science and Technology: Glaxo's Headaches,'' *Economist* (UK), November 17, 1990, pp. 111–12.

Sheeline, William E., ''Glaxo's Goal: New Wonder Cures,'' *Fortune*, November 6, 1989, pp. 101–08.

Stephens, Harrison, *Golden Past, Golden Future: The First Fifty Years of Beckman Instruments, Inc.*, Claremont, Calif.: Claremont University Center, 1985, 144 p.

Syedain, Hashi, ''SmithKline Beecham's Early Trials,'' *Management Today*, November 1989, pp. 98ff.

Tanouye, Elyse, and Robert Langreth, ''Genetic Giant: Cost of Drug Research Is Driving Merger Talks of Glaxo, SmithKline,'' *Wall Street Journal*, February 2, 1998, p. A1.

Tanouye, Elyse, and Stephen D. Moore, ''Chief Prescribes Research for SmithKline: Expected Sales of Units Set, with Big Charge, Layoffs,'' *Wall Street Journal*, February 10, 1999, p. B6.

Teitelman, Robert, ''Staying Power,'' *Financial World*, April 4, 1989, pp. 28–30.

Waldholz, Michael, Elyse Tanouye, and Gardiner Harris, ''With Executives Aging and Patents Expiring, Industry Is Ripe for Megamergers,'' *Wall Street Journal*, November 4, 1999, pp. B1, B4.

Waldholz, Michael, ''SmithKline Head to Retire After 10-Year Reign,'' *Wall Street Journal*, December 3, 1999, p. B6.

Weber, Joseph, Julia Flynn, and Karen Lowry Miller, ''SmithKline's New World Order,'' *Business Week*, September 12, 1994, p. 35.

—Thomas M. Tucker
—updates: David E. Salamie; April S. Dougal;
Christina M. Stansell

Goodrich Corporation

Four Coliseum Centre
2730 West Tyvola Road
Charlotte, North Carolina 23217-4578
U.S.A.
Telephone: (704) 423-7000
Fax: (704) 423-7100
Web site: http://www.goodrich.com

Public Company
Incorporated: 1870 as Goodrich, Tew & Company
Employees: 22,136
Sales: $4.1 billion (2001)
Stock Exchanges: New York
Ticker Symbol: GR
NAIC: 336412 Aircraft Engine and Engine Parts
Manufacturing; 332912 Fluid Power Valve and Hose
Fitting Manufacturing; 336413 Other Aircraft Parts
and Auxiliary Equipment Manufacturing

Goodrich Corporation—formerly known as The BFGoodrich Company—underwent a series of strategic changes during the 1980s and 1990s to emerge as a leading aerospace systems supplier. The company exited the performance materials market in 2001 to focus on its aircraft parts and engineered industrial products businesses. After making key acquisitions throughout the 1990s, Goodrich became the leading supplier of landing gear systems and services that are used by commercial, regional, business, and military aircraft.

Throughout most of its history Goodrich built its business on rubber production, gaining a reputation among U.S. tire makers as a leader in product development and innovation. In the early twentieth century, Goodrich used its experience in the rubber industry to diversify into chemicals and plastics, and it spearheaded the development of synthetic rubber technology during World War II. The company prospered during the postwar era but faced difficulties when the U.S. auto industry's decline in the 1970s curtailed the demand for tires. Convinced that its future lay in chemicals and plastics, the company's directors embarked on a long and often difficult restructuring plan. Goodrich finally divested itself of its tire business in 1987, emerging as a leaner, more profitable company.

Company Origins

Benjamin Franklin Goodrich followed a circuitous route into the rubber industry. Born in Ripley, New York, in 1841, Goodrich pursued an education in medicine and served as an assistant surgeon in the Union Army during the Civil War. After the war Goodrich pursued a career in business and entered into a real estate partnership with John P. Morris of New York City. In 1869, the partners found themselves investors in a small operation called the Hudson River Rubber Company. They soon acquired full ownership of the company, and Goodrich took over as its president.

Goodrich was not impressed with the company's prospects in New York and he considered moving it west, where a growing population and economy offered plenty of opportunities for expansion. After listening to a stranger praise a canal town in Ohio called Akron, he investigated it for himself. Akron's citizens were as anxious to attract business as Goodrich was to develop it. After his visit, a group of 19 potential investors sent George T. Perkins back to New York with Goodrich to examine his operations there. The group received a favorable report, and it loaned Goodrich the money he needed to move west. On December 31, 1870, Goodrich formed the partnership of Goodrich, Tew & Company with his brother-in-law Harvey W. Tew and the Akron investors. After completing a two-story factory on the banks of the Ohio Canal, Goodrich was in business as the first rubber company west of the Allegheny Mountains.

Goodrich experienced a shaky start during its first decade. The company's first product was a cotton-covered fire-hose designed to withstand the high pressures and low temperatures that often caused leather hoses to burst. While the fire-hose was a welcome innovation among the nation's firefighters, poor financing led to several reorganizations within the company. George W. Crouse, one of the original Akron investors, finally stabilized the company's finances with an additional loan in 1880, and it was incorporated in the state of Ohio as The B.F. Goodrich Company.

Goodrich died in 1888, just a few years before the bicycle craze of the 1890s revolutionized his company and the rubber industry. Among the company's early products had been the solid-band tire used on bicycles of the 1880s. The invention of the pneumatic tire in 1890 greatly increased the comfort of bicycle riding, and Goodrich began turning out bicycle tires to keep pace with the popularity of this recreation. The introduction of cord tires, which increased the speed of bicycles, and the adaptation of pneumatic tires to horse-drawn buggies, expanded the nation's rubber markets further. Goodrich increased its capacity with each addition to its tire demand, and company engineers cooperated with independent inventors to find new applications for company products.

The most important of these joint efforts was a contribution Goodrich made to the nation's infant automobile industry. In 1897, Alexander Winton of Cleveland, Ohio, organized the Winton Motor Car Company to market his horseless carriages. He asked Goodrich to develop a pneumatic tire strong enough to handle its high speeds and heavier loads. Goodrich responded with the first pneumatic tires for automobiles, beginning a long partnership with the auto industry that became the foundation for the company's profits for the next 70 years.

Early Commitment to Research and Development

From very early in its history Goodrich committed itself to research and development in rubber technology. Under the aegis of Goodrich's son, Charles Cross Goodrich, the company opened the rubber industry's first experimental research laboratory in 1895. Arthur H. Marks, one of Goodrich's engineers, was responsible for several breakthroughs in the processing of crude rubber. In its natural form, crude rubber is very sensitive to changes in temperature, becoming hard and brittle when cooled, and soft and tacky when heated. Vulcanization, a process first discovered by Charles Goodyear in 1839, mixes crude rubber with sulfur and heat to convert it to a durable material unaffected by changes in climate. At the turn of the century, Arthur Marks pioneered a procedure for de-vulcanizing vulcanized rubber, thus enabling producers to reclaim crude rubber from manufactured goods for re-use. Marks also developed methods for speeding vulcanization by adding certain organic chemical accelerators to the process. The use of such compounds reduced the time necessary for vulcanization by as much as 75 percent.

Goodrich continued to apply the latest technology to its tire production. In 1910, it introduced the first cord tire for use on U.S. automobiles. This tire, which reduced fuel consumption and increased the comfort of the ride, was developed in Silvertown, England, and marketed there as the Palmer Cord. Good-rich purchased the patent rights for it in the United States and sold it to U.S. consumers as the Silvertown Cord. Other innovations in Goodrich's tire manufacturing included the use of other organic compounds to resist deterioration by heat, oxidation, and flexing, and the inclusion in its manufacturing process of carbon black, a coloring pigment that improved the tires' resistance to abrasion.

World War I and Product Diversification

Goodrich's success in its tire business led it into product diversification. By the time of World War I, it was producing rubber for consumer goods such as shoes, boots, tennis balls, and waterproof clothing, as well as for industrial goods such as belting for power transmission and mechanical conveyors. Goodrich also expanded into chemical production. One of its first products in this field was Vulcalock, an adhesive capable of bonding rubber to metal and used to protect pipes and storage tanks from the corrosive materials they often contained. In 1926, a Goodrich engineer developed a method for plasticizing polyvinyl chloride (PVC), turning this waste chemical compound into the material recognized today as vinyl. Goodrich marketed its PVC products under the brand names Geon and Koroseal, applying them to such varied uses as floor tiles, garden hoses, and electrical insulation. Goodrich also grew with the nation's aviation industry, producing airplane tires and the first airplane de-icers, important devices used in the achievement of all-weather flying.

The automobile and aviation industries, along with the rubber demand created by World War I, powered Goodrich's expansion through the first 30 years of the 20th century. In 1912, Goodrich re-incorporated as a New York company and increased its production capacity by acquiring the Diamond Rubber Company, which owned plants adjacent to Goodrich's in Akron.

Great Depression Setbacks

On the eve of the Great Depression, Goodrich acquired two more rubber companies, the Hood Rubber Company of Watertown, Massachusetts, and the Miller Rubber Company of Akron. The depression, however, brought the company its first setbacks since the 1870s. The slowed U.S. economy reduced rubber demand, and Goodrich incurred over $24 million in net losses between 1930 and 1933. The depression also affected the company's labor relations with its 15,000 employees in Akron. The United Rubber Workers union (URW) was formed in 1934, and in 1936 national labor leader John Lewis came to Akron to rally union support. His visit sparked a five-week strike at the plants of Goodrich, Goodyear, and Firestone, temporarily shutting down the nation's three largest rubber producers.

World War II and Recovery

Recovery for Goodrich came with the nation's preparations for World War II. At the time of the war's outbreak in Europe, the United States was importing 97 percent of its crude rubber from Southeast Asia. Japanese expansion in the Pacific threatened this supply, while German advances in Europe and Africa interrupted supply routes through the Suez Canal and the Mediterranean Sea. In cooperation with the nation's rubber compa-

eral government announced plans to build its own synthetic rubber plants. Goodrich cooperated with this effort, building and operating three such plants for wartime production in Port Neches and Borger, Texas, and in Louisville, Kentucky. These plants had a combined capacity of 165,000 tons per year, making Goodrich the nation's leading synthetic rubber manufacturer by the war's end.

Postwar Return to the Consumer Market

Goodrich avoided any postwar interruptions in its growth by quickly converting to meet consumer demand. The U.S. auto industry's return to peacetime production kept the demand for tires high, and Goodrich met this demand by introducing the first 100 percent synthetic rubber tire in 1945. Two years later it developed the tubeless puncture-sealing tire that increased motorists' protection from blow-outs. The company's LifeSaver and Safetyliner tubeless tires gained wide popularity in the early 1950s, and by 1955 tubeless tires became standard equipment on new cars. Ten years later Goodrich brought another innovation to U.S. drivers, the first radial tires for passenger cars. The radial dramatically changed the U.S. tire industry by increasing tire life by up to 50 percent, and, like its tubeless predecessor, it ultimately became standard equipment on U.S. cars.

Goodrich further diversified its production in the postwar era. Continuing a long tradition of research and development, it opened a new research center in Brecksville, Ohio, in 1948. B.F. Goodrich Chemical Company, a subsidiary founded in 1943, took over the company's wartime plants and built new ones in Marietta and Avon Lake, Ohio, and in Calvert City, Kentucky. Production of Goodrich's Geon and Koroseal plastic products expanded into overseas markets with joint ventures in Britain and Japan. By 1955, Goodrich was manufacturing goods in five different areas, including tires, chemicals and plastics, footwear and flooring, industrial products, and sponge rubber goods. It had operations in 21 nations on six continents, and in 1966 its sales reached a record $1 billion.

Challenges of the 1960s and 1970s

Goodrich's fortunes declined, however, when a 1967 strike began a decade of rocky labor relations and interrupted production. In April 1967, the URW walked off of jobs at Goodrich, Firestone, and Uniroyal, and the resulting strike stalled rubber production in Akron for 86 days. That strike, along with a six-month work stoppage at one of the company's chemical plants, cost Goodrich a 27.6 percent decrease in its profits from the previous year. Three years later Goodrich was once again facing serious losses because of strikes in the rubber and related industries. The URW walked out on Goodrich plants for five weeks, while strikes by the Teamsters Union and General Motors workers also hurt the nation's tire markets. Goodrich's net income in 1970 dropped by $22 million. Continued hard times in the nation's auto and rubber industries brought Goodrich back to the bargaining table in 1976. A 141-day URW strike stopped production in all of Goodrich's domestic tire plants and finally required the intercession of U.S. Labor Secretary W.J. Usery, Jr., to settle it. These crippling experiences with labor disputes and the stagnation of the U.S. auto industry convinced Goodrich that its future was not in tires. In 1971, Goodrich's net income had fallen to $1.7 million from a high of $48.6 million in 1966.

Key Dates:

1870: Benjamin Franklin Goodrich forms the partnership Goodrich, Tew & Company with brother-in-law Harvey W. Tew and a group of Akron, Ohio-based investors.
1880: The firm is incorporated in Ohio as the B.F. Goodrich Company.
1895: The company establishes the rubber industry's first experimental research laboratory.
1897: B.F. Goodrich begins manufacturing pneumatic tires for the Winton Motor Car Company.
1910: The first cord tire for automobiles is introduced.
1930: The firm experiences losses due to a decrease in rubber demand brought on by the Depression.
1940: B.F. Goodrich introduces the first passenger-car tire in the U.S. to contain synthetic rubber.
1945: The firm develops the first 100 percent synthetic rubber tire.
1955: Tubeless tires become standard equipment on new cars.
1965: The company introduces the first radial tires for passenger cars.
1976: The firm's name is changed to the BFGoodrich Company.
1986: BFGoodrich's tire division is merged with Uniroyal.
1987: The company sells its interest in the Uniroyal venture and exits the tire industry.
1993: The PVC business is sold; Cleveland Pneumatic Co. and Rosemount Aerospace are purchased.
1999: BFGoodrich merges with Coltec Industries Inc. and moves its company headquarters to Charlotte, North Carolina.
2001: The firm changes its name to Goodrich Corporation and sells its performance materials business.

nies, the U.S. government began an intensive stockpiling and conservation effort. It also committed itself to developing synthetic rubber technology.

The rubber industry had known how to make synthetic rubber since the late 1930s. In 1937, Goodrich opened a pilot plant for producing butadiene-copolymer synthetic rubber, and within two years it was using synthetic rubber in some of its commercial products. As long as crude rubber supplies were cheap and plentiful, however, synthetic rubber remained an expensive alternative. In 1939, John L. Collyer took over as Goodrich's president after having spent ten years working for a British rubber company. Collyer returned to the United States convinced of its need to develop synthetic rubber production before it was drawn into the European conflict. Under his direction Goodrich introduced in June 1940 the first passenger-car tire in the United States to contain synthetic rubber. Called Ameripol for its use of a polymer of American materials, this tire was more expensive than one made of natural rubber, but it gained rapid consumer acceptance because it outlasted conventional tires. After Collyer's appearance before a Senate Military Affairs Committee hearing on national preparedness, the fed-

Plastics and Aerospace Instead of Tires

Ready for a drastic change, the company handed its reins to a rubber industry outsider in 1972. O. Pendleton Thomas, a former oil executive with the Atlantic Richfield Company, shook up Goodrich by having chemicals and plastics replace tires as the foundation of the company's business. At the time Thomas took over, Goodrich's position among U.S. tiremakers had fallen to a weak fourth, and the industry showed no signs of improving. The success of radials had cut consumer demand for replacement tires, while the oil crisis had lessened the U.S. taste for new cars. Thomas streamlined Goodrich's tire operations by closing unprofitable plants and retail outlets and concentrating on certain product niches, such as high-performance replacement tires. By maximizing profits in its tire business, he developed the capital necessary to increase the capacity of Goodrich's chemical and plastics production. In 1976, Thomas changed The B.F. Goodrich Company's name to The BFGoodrich Company.

Thomas's program of retrenchment and redeployment allowed his successor, John D. Ong, to develop Goodrich's chemicals business in the 1980s. Goodrich had long been the nation's number-one producer of PVC, the versatile plastic used primarily in the construction industry, as well as a producer of specialty chemicals used in products ranging from cosmetics to floor polishes. Like its tire division, Goodrich's chemical production had been hurt by the petroleum shortages and sluggish national economy of the 1970s, but when Ong took over in 1979, he maintained the course set by Thomas. The acquisition in 1979 of Tremco Inc., a producer of roofing products and construction sealants, strengthened Goodrich's position in specialty chemicals markets. Ong also announced plans to double Goodrich's PVC production by the mid-1980s, and he sank millions into the development of a plant in Convent, Louisiana. This project backfired, however, when the nation's housing industry went into its worst slump in 36 years and PVC demand plummeted. Goodrich suddenly found itself plagued by an overcapacity in its chemical production, and the company ended 1982 with a $32.8 million loss.

Goodrich's tailspin in the early 1980s led to the most dramatic changes in its history. Taking a record loss of $354.6 million in 1985, the company sold off the Louisiana plant into which it had sunk so much capital. In 1986, Ong merged Goodrich's tire division with Uniroyal, which had just fought a costly takeover battle with corporate raider Carl Icahn. The jointly owned Uniroyal-Goodrich Tire Company looked good on paper for both companies, combining Goodrich's replacement tire business with Uniroyal's original equipment market to make it the nation's second largest tire producer. Unfortunately, the relationship faltered, and in December 1987 Goodrich sold its interest in the venture for $225 million to an investment group that had already bought out Uniroyal. Shortly thereafter, Goodrich sold off its 38-acre factory complex in Akron, ending its nearly century-long association with the U.S. tire industry. In 1988, Goodrich acquired Tramco Incorporated, a provider of maintenance and repair services for commercial aircraft.

Strategic Moves in the 1990s

With the full divestiture of its tire business, Goodrich became a company devoted solely to the production of chemicals, plastics, and aerospace goods. The recovery of its PVC business and the wise investment of capital gained from its tire division sale had in the early 1990s stabilized the company. In 1993, however, chief executive John D. Ong sold off the PVC business, to the concern of investors, in favor of emphasizing the company's other chemical businesses.

Some analysts were skeptical of these strategic turns. Writer Zachary Schiller of *Business Week,* for example, noted that "the company has produced an average annual return on equity of just 1.4 percent since Ong became CEO in 1979, compared with an average of 14.4 percent for the companies in the Standard & Poors Industrials index." Moreover, the companies in the S&P index posted a 5.4 percent annual gain, but Goodrich's sales fell an average of 3.5 percent per year, Schiller observed. Stock lagged at $44, not even close to its 1989 height of $69.

Ong, however, noted for his willingness to change course, pushed into aerospace, although the industry had been sluggish for more than a decade. He built on Goodrich's aircraft parts and servicing business. Using proceeds from the sale of PVC, BFGoodrich acquired in 1993 Cleveland Pneumatic Co., a landing gear maker that complemented Goodrich's wheel-and-brake business, and Rosemount Aerospace, which made sensors that measure flight and data (speed and temperature, for example). That same year also marked the additions of the Landing Gear Division and Landing Gear Services Division and of Sanncor Industries.

Ong persisted with his current business mix, pointing out that the company was now positioned for growth opportunities. By 1994, the specialty chemical business started to show improvement, and the aerospace business held promise. The aircraft wheel-and-brake business gradually grew into aircraft parts and servicing. The following year BFGoodrich acquired QSI, Inc. in Greenville, South Carolina. In 1995, purchases included Hoskins Aviation and de-icing product lines and associated technology from Lucas Aerospace.

By 1996, BFGoodrich reported that earnings in 1996 were significantly higher than in the past three years. For the second year in a row, BFGoodrich Aerospace and BFGoodrich Specialty Chemical set records for sales and operating income. The growing demand for replacement products and service proved advantageous to the aerospace division, which also benefited from the upturn in new commercial aircraft production. BFGoodrich Specialty Chemicals acquired five businesses and increased manufacturing capacity at existing facilities. Moreover, three new plants were seen as the base for further expansion in Europe and Asia.

In the mid-1990s, Ong reflected on the last decade that took BFGoodrich from a struggling company that manufactured commodity products and sold them in highly cyclical markets to a streamlined organization focused on specialty businesses. He noted that the company's inclination for risk-taking lay within the BFGoodrich structure rather than outside. By late 1996, BFGoodrich shares reached "historic, 126-year highs" and traded at levels once thought unlikely, Ong said. He added that after challenges rocked corporate America in the 1980s and 1990s, BFGoodrich started reaching goals. Ong noted that market capitalization at the end of 1996 had increased by about 100 percent from the time the new BFGoodrich came into being at the end of 1993.

As Ong was slated to retire in 1997, David L. Burner was tapped to succeed him. Meanwhile, BFGoodrich remained focused on growth and improved returns as an aerospace and specialty chemicals company. Acquisitions that complemented and strengthened its current businesses remained at the forefront. Businesses not central to the strategy were ripe for divestment, as in the 1996 sale of Tremco to RPM, Inc., with the proceeds invested in the expansion of aerospace and specialty chemicals.

Burner continued to reshape the company through the latter half of the 1990s. As part of its aerospace strategy, the firm purchased Rohr Inc. in 1997 for $1.2 billion. The deal significantly increased the company's reach in the aircraft systems market, and by that time nearly 56 percent of BFGoodrich's revenues stemmed from its aerospace operations. That year the company also acquired Gulton Data Systems, an aerospace data acquisitions firm, and several other companies with interests in the specialty chemicals industry.

The firm continued its acquisition spree in the following year. Its most substantial purchase of 1999 was that of Coltec Industries Inc., a manufacturer of engineered products for aerospace and other industrial markets. The $2.2 billion deal signaled the firm's commitment to its aircraft-related businesses; upon completion of the purchase, company headquarters were moved to Coltec's home town of Charlotte, North Carolina. The acquisition of Coltec strengthened BFGoodrich's hold in the landing gear segment of the aerospace market and created a multi-billion company with interests in various industries, including aerospace, performance chemicals, and engineered industrial products.

A New Name for the New Millennium

BFGoodrich entered the new millennium a stronger, more focused business entity. By the end of 2000, its aerospace division accounted for 84 percent of total sales and was ranked among the top five in the United States. That year, the firm decided to divest its performance chemicals operations in order to focus on its two other business segments. It continued to make acquisitions to bolster those segments, including Barnes Engineering, IBP Aerospace, Engineering Products Company, ACI Advanced Creations Inc., Corning's Electro-Optical Instrumentation Business, Raytheon Optical Systems, and OEA Aerospace.

Changes continued into 2001, when the company announced a new name and a new corporate logo. Adopting Goodrich Corporation as its official title, the firm hoped to distance itself from its former tire-making image, promoting itself instead as a global supplier of aerospace and industrial products. Taking the transformation one step further, the company announced a possible future spin off of its engineered industrial products division. If completed, the new business would be headquartered in Charlotte and secure annual sales of approximately $800 million.

While the company continued to plan for additional growth through acquisition, factors beyond its control began to affect some of its largest aerospace customers. The terrorist attacks of September 11, 2001 initiated a major downturn in the commercial airline industry, which Goodrich served by manufacturing parts for such companies as The Boeing Company and Lockheed Martin Corp. As a result, Goodrich was forced to lower revenue expectations for the year and make employee cutbacks. Nevertheless, Goodrich management held strong to its focus on innovation, growth, and new product development. Having undergone dramatic restructuring through the past two decades, Goodrich appeared to be well positioned for future success.

Principal Subsidiaries

Goodrich Aerospace Aircraft Evacuation Systems Private Limited (India); Goodrich Aerospace Asia-Pacific, Limited (Hong Kong; 51%); Goodrich Aerospace Component Overhaul & Repair, Inc.; Goodrich Aerospace MRO Group, Inc.; Goodrich Aerospace Pte. Ltd. (Singapore); Goodrich Avionics Systems, Inc.; Goodrich China, Inc.; Goodrich Company of Japan, Ltd.; Goodrich de Mexico, S.A. de C.V.; FCC Acquisition Corporation; Goodrich FlightSystems, Inc.; Coltec Industries Inc.; Garlock Bearings Inc.; Goodrich Aerospace Europe S.A (France); Goodrich Aerospace Services S.A. (France); Goodrich Aerospace UK Limited; Rohr Aero Services Limited (United Kingdom); Rosemount Aerospace Limited (United Kingdom); Goodrich Holding Corporation; International Goodrich Technology Corporation; Rohr, Inc.; The IBP Aerospace Group, Inc.; Ithaco Space Systems Inc.

Principal Divisions

Aerospace; Engineered Industrial Products Segment.

Principal Competitors

Crane Co.; Honeywell International Inc.; Northrop Grumman Corporation.

Further Reading

B.F. Goodrich Story: Nine Stories Celebrating One Hundred Twenty-Five Years, Akron, Ohio: B.F. Goodrich Corporate Communications, 1995.

"BFGoodrich to Change Name and Logo," *Defense Daily*, March 6, 2001.

Collyer, John Lyon, *The B.F. Goodrich Story of Creative Enterprise: 1870–1952,* New York: The Newcomen Society in North America, 1952.

Deutsch, Claudia H., "Goodrich Finally Gets It Right," *New York Times*, March 12, 1989.

"Goodrich, Coltec Merger," *Chemical Market Reporter*, July 19, 1999, p. 7.

"Goodrich's Cash Cow Starts to Deliver," *Business Week*, November 14, 1977.

Jasper, Chris, "Merger Delivers for BFGoodrich," *Flight International*, August 15, 2000, p. 19.

McNulty, Mike, "Goodrich to Sell Off Materials Business," *European Rubber Journal*, June 2000, p. 12.

——, "Goodrich To Spin Off Engineered Products Unit," *European Rubber Journal*, October 2001, p. 8.

Ong, John D., *The BFGoodrich Company: A Proud Heritage, An Exciting Future,* New York: Newcomen Society of the United States, 1995.

Schiller, Zachary, "Goodrich: From Tires to PVC to Chemicals to Aerospace," *Business Week*, July 18, 1994, pp. 86–87.

Serwer, Andrew E., "How Goodrich Finally Got a Life in the Post-Industrial Age," *Fortune*, February 5, 1996, p. 29.

Sweetman, Bill, "Goodrich Re-Invents Itself," *Interavia Business & Technology*, December 2001, p. 21.

—Timothy J. Shannon
—updates: Catherine Hamrick and
Christina M. Stansell

Guerbet Group

15, rue des Vanesses
93420 Villepinte,
France
Telephone: (+33) 1-45-91-50-00
Fax: (+33) 1-45-91-51-99
Web site: http://www.guerbet-group.com

Public Company
Incorporated: 1926 as Laboratoires Guerbet
Employees: 1,040
Sales: EUR 208.94 million ($183.17 million)(2001)
Stock Exchanges: Euronext Paris
Ticker Symbol: GBT
NAIC: 325413 In-Vitro Diagnostic Substance
    Manufacturing; 325412 Pharmaceutical Preparation
    Manufacturing

Family-controlled Guerbet Group is France's leading specialist producer of contrasting agents for medical imaging procedures. The company has also built up a leading position in its specialty on the European market, and has long maintained its independence against its larger competitors. The four leading companies—Mallincrodt of the United States; Nycomed Amersham, based in Norway and the United Kingdom; Bracco; based in Italy; and Germany's Schering—control some 80 percent of the global market. A pioneer in its field, Guerbert produces chemical compounds injected into or ingested by patients undergoing medical imaging procedures (x-ray, magnetic resonance, and the like) in order to enable and enhance the visualization of internal organs and structures. The company's flagship product is Xenetix, an X-ray agent that accounts for 25 percent of its sales; Guerbert also makes Hexabrix and MRI compound Dotarem. In 2002, the company, which had been searching for a stronger entry into the United States market—its U.S. distribution had been handled by Malincrodt—reached an agreement with the United States' Cook Group to take over all assets for that company's Oxilan x-ray imaging product, similar to Xenetix. Guerbet intended to set up an American subsidiary to support this product as well as to launch its Dotarem MRI compound in the

United States. At the turn of the century, Guerbet has also been stepping up its international activity, adding new subsidiaries and affiliates in Italy, Japan, Austria, Turkey, the United Kingdom, Korea, Taiwan, and Germany. Some 30 percent of the company's 2000 sales of nearly EUR 200 million come from France; Europe as a whole accounts for 77 percent of Guerbet's sales. The company is quoted on the Euronext Paris stock exchange; the Guerbet family controls, directly and through a holding company, more than 70 percent of the company's stock. Michel Guerbet, grandson of the founder, is company chairman, while Philippe Décazes serves as CEO.

Imaging Pioneer at the Turn of the 20th Century

The discovery of x-rays in 1895 represented a revolution for medical science, allowing for the first time the imaging of the interior of a patient's body. X-rays enabled physician's to view the skeleton, but imaging of the soft tissues—and especially internal organs—remained impossible for some time.

Working in France at the turn of the 20th century, Marcel Guerbet had developed a new substance, dubbed Lipidiol, based on oil derived from pawpaw seeds. Released in 1901, the iodine-containing Lipidiol was presented by Guerbet as a treatment for cardio-vascular diseases. Together with a partner, Guerbet began producing Lipidiol for the medical market.

An important feature of Lipidiol was discovered only by chance in 1918. The compound was found to have opacifying properties when injected into the body, enabling physicians to visualize soft tissue and internal organs for the first time. Guerbet immediately recognized the potential for contrast agents and other diagnostic imaging compounds. Guerbet persuaded his son, André Guerbet, to begin conducting research into the development of contrast agents, and this market quickly became a company specialty.

In 1926, Guerbet's original partner died, giving Guerbet's son André the opportunity to purchase a 10 percent stake in the company, which was then incorporated as Laboratoires Guerbet, in Saint Ouen, north of Paris. Marcel Guerbet died in 1938, leaving André Guerbet with 60 percent control of the company. Over the next 30 years, Guerbet became one of

Company Perspectives:

We have confidence in the development of our future business given the increasingly vital contribution of imaging techniques and contrast agents in Health Economics, both in terms of diagnosis, therapeutic management and cost control. Our market is still driven by technological innovation and is increasing in volume.

France's most active developers of contrast media, producing compounds for applications including angiography (for measuring blood flow), brochography, hysterosalpingography and urography (visualization of the kidneys and urinary tract), as well as compounds for producing images of the digestive tract.

By the early 1960s, André Geurbet himself had grown terminally ill, and began preparing to transmit his share of the company to his wife and ten children, all of whom were still quite young and some of whom were still minors at the time. Guerbet's will stipulated that leadership of the company be taken over by son Michel Guerbet, a physician. The company's other shareholders were doubtful of the young Guerbet's ability to lead the company and decided to sell out their 40 percent stake to the Guerbets. The sale of property held by Marcel Guerbet's widow financed the purchase, and the Guerbet family now held 100 percent of the company. Renamed SA Laboratoires André Guerbet in 1964, the company remained small, with just 100 employees posting FFr 5 million in revenues.

Michel Guerbet, however, proved an able businessman. During the 1960s, the company developed a number of breakthrough products to establish itself as a leading developer of diagnostic contrast media in France and throughout Europe. Helping to fund the company's research and development program was a licensing agreement to develop and distribute Contrix, a compound developed in the United States, for the French market. In 1964, Geurbet released another breakthrough product developed in the company's laboratory, Telebrix.

Based on the success of Telebrix, Guerbet expanded rapidly, and began seeing a growing percentage of its sales come from its European neighbors. In 1968, the growing company moved its facilities to the Parisian suburb of Aulnay-sous-Bois. There the company operations increasingly diversified along two primary lines, those of pharmaceutical products and those of basic chemical compounds, including such active ingredients as barium for medicinal use.

In 1974, the company's laboratories launched a new imaging agent, Hexabrix, which became one of the company's leading products for more than two decades. Meanwhile, the growth of the company's two core operations led it to restructure at the end of the 1970s. In 1977, Guerbet reformed as holding company Guerbet SA, creating two principal subsidiaries, Guerbet, which took over its pharmaceuticals division, and Guerbet Chimie Aulnay, which absorbed the company's active ingredients operations.

Guerbet restructured again in 1981, creating separate export, marketing and research divisions. That same year, the company inaugurated a second production facility, in Lanester, which became a central production facility for its active ingredients division. Meanwhile, Michel Guerbet began opening up the company's capital to its employees, giving them options to buy shares in the still-private firm. This offering eventually led to listing Guerbert on the Paris stock exchange, a step the company took in 1986 when it floated on the Paris Secondary Market. As part of the offering, the Guerbet family, together with its employee-shareholders, placed much of their shares under a new holding company, Chandey, which became the company's majority shareholder, with 46 percent of the company's stock and 51 percent of its voting rights. The Guerbet family meanwhile directly controlled an additional 20 percent of the company's shares.

Guerbet's continued expansion led the company to open a new headquarters site, in Villepinte, near its main Aulnay production facility, in 1987. By then, Guerbet had captured the lead in its specialty in the French market; the success of Hexabrix, particularly in the United States, made foreign sales a growing part of the company's revenues.

Contrast Media Leader in the 21st Century

Guerbet's public offering enabled the company to step up its expansion at the end of the 1980s. In 1987, the company made two key acquisitions, Simafex, in 1987, adding fine chemicals, and another subsidiary, renamed Guerbet Biomedical, in 1988. Guerbet's product portfolio expanded as well during this period, as the company added Dotarem and Optiray x-ray contrast compounds.

The growing percentage of foreign sales in the company's revenues led it to begin opening foreign subsidiaries at the beginning of the 1990s. In 1990, the company opened a subsidiary in the Netherlands, which was followed two years later by the launch of a German subsidiary. These subsidiaries were joined by two more before the middle of the 1990s, when the company opened subsidiaries in Istanbul and London in 1994.

As the company's exclusive patent rights for Hexabrix wound down—the compound was opened to generic competition in the United States in 1995—Guerbet began preparing new products to take its place. In 1993, the company launched Lumirem. A year later, Guerbet had a new success on its hands with the launch of Xenetix. That product soon became one of Geurbet's strongest sellers, accounting for some 25 percent of its sales by the end of the decade. These products were followed by a new compound, Endorem, in 1995. By then, Guerbet's sales had risen to FFr937 million.

The company nonetheless faced disappointment at the end of the century. In 1996, Guerbert, which had held an option for the European commercialization of an ultrasound imaging product under development by an American, pulled out of the project after analysts proved skeptical about the product's performance. The company instead was forced to look elsewhere for an ultrasound product to complete its product range. Meanwhile, the company was hit hard by a doubling of the price of its core iodine ingredient during the latter half of the decade. At the same time, its four chief competitors, which together held some 80 percent of the worldwide market, had entered into a price

Key Dates:

1901: Marcel Guerbet invents Lipiodol, an oil containing iodide, intended for use in treating cardio-vascular diseases.
1918: Lipiodol is discovered to act as a contrast medium for x-ray, allowing the imaging of internal organs.
1926: The company is incorporated as SA Laboratoires Guerbet in Saint-Ouen.
1960: Guerbet acquires French license for Contrix.
1964: The company launches Telebrix.
1974: Hexabrix is developed.
1977: Guerbet restructures into two primary subsidiaries: Guerbet (pharmaceuticals) and Guerbet Chimie Aulnay (active ingredients).
1986: Guerbet goes public on Paris secondary market.
1994: The company founds subsidiaries in Turkey and the United Kingdom.
1998: Guerbet begins restructuring program.
2000: The company launches new subsidiaries in Italy, Korea, Taiwan, and opens a distribution office in Hong Kong.
2002: The company acquires distribution and development license for Oxilan.

war, forcing Guerbet to slash its prices as well. By the late 1990s, Guerbet was struggling to maintain its revenue growth, while slipping into net losses.

In 1998, Guerbet launched a radical restructuring program designed to return the company health. As part of its reorganization, the company, which had operated through its two primary branches since the restructuring at the end of the 1970s, now merged these two divisions, cutting out a great deal of redundant overhead costs. Guerbert transferred a growing share of its production to its Lanester site, which then became its main production facility. Michel Guerbet, who was preparing the succession of the company, also led the company to reorganize its executive board into a management board and a supervisory board. The company then promoted Philippe Decazes, who had been in charge of its Simafex subsidiary since 1995, as company CEO.

The restructuring, scheduled to take more than three years, quickly brought the company back to profitability, and by 1999 Guerbet was once again in the black. The strength of the restructuring effort was seen the following year, when the company's net profits rose again by nearly 67 percent. Meanwhile, Decazes and Michel Guerbet, who continued as company chairman, led the company on a new international expansion drive.

In 2000, Guerbet opened a new foreign subsidiary, in Italy, which had grown into Europe's second-largest contrast media market. The company also moved to capture a larger share of

the Asian market, opening subsidiaries in Korea and Taiwan. Guerbert also opened an office in Hong Kong to assure distribution for the company's sales in Australia, New Zealand, and elsewhere in the Pacific region.

Guerbet was also promoting its latest product launches, notably Sinerem, a contrast medium for Magnetic Resonance Imaging, and the blood pool agent P792. At the same time, Guerbet began identifying new areas of research for the company's future expansion, targeting three key areas for the decade to come: the imaging of colon cancer, detection of atheromatous plaque, and detection of a universal cancer marker.

Guerbet's shareholding structure left it protected against the wave of mergers and consolidation among its competitors in the worldwide chemicals and pharmaceuticals industry, and enabled it to maintain its strong focus on its contract media specialty. Guerbet continued to pursue its expansion in the new century as well. In January 2002, the company announced that it was acquiring the worldwide rights to develop and market Oxilan, a non-ionic x-ray imaging product, from the United States' Cook Group's Imaging subsidiary. Similar to Xenetix, the Oxilan acquisition gave Guerbet a strong entry in the United States, where the company pledged to open a subsidiary by mid-year. Guerbet clearly revealed its determination to remain a key player in the worldwide contrast media market for its next century.

Principal Subsidiaries

Simafex; Guerbet Gmbh (Germany); Guerbet Austria Ges. M.B.H; Codali Sa (Belgium); Laboratorios Farmacéuticos Guerbet Sa (Spain); Guerbet Laboratories Ltd (United Kingdom); Guerbet Spa (Italy); Guerbet Nederland Bv; Martins & Fernandes (Portugal); Guerbet Ag (Switzerland); Guerbet As (Turkey); Guerbet Produtos Radio-Logicos Ltda (Brazil); Guerbet Japan Co Ltd; Guerbet Asia Pacific Ltd (Hong Kong); Guerbet Korea Co Ltd; Guerbet Taiwan Co Ltd.

Principal Competitors

Advanced Magnetics, Inc.; Amersham plc; Berlex Laboratories; Bracco SpA; DAIICHI PHARMACEUTICAL CO., LTD; Eisai Company, Ltd.; EPIX Medical, Inc.; E-Z-EM, Inc; Mallinckrodt Inc.; Molecular Biosystems, Inc.; Schering AG.

Further Reading

Ducruet, Catherine, ''Guerbet est à la recherche d'un partenaire dans les ultrasons,'' *La Tribune*, March 31, 1998.
——, ''Guerbet met en place un plan de restructuration drastique,'' *La Tribune*, June 10, 1998.
''Guerbet a renoué avec les profits en 1999,'' *La Tribune*, March 22, 2000.
''Guerbet Is Setting Foot in the US,'' *Guerbet corporate press release*, January 16, 2002.

—M. L. Cohen

H.D. Vest, Inc.

6333 North State Highway 161, 4th Floor
Irving, Texas 75038
U.S.A.
Telephone: (972) 870-6000
Toll Free: (800) 821-8254
Fax: (972) 870-6128
Web site: http://www.hdvest.com

Wholly Owned Subsidiary of Wells Fargo & Co.
Incorporated: 1983 as H.D. Vest Investment Securities,
   Inc.
Employees: 375
Sales: $193.8 million (2000)
NAIC: 523900 Other Financial Investment Activities

Acquired in 2001 by Wells Fargo and Company, H.D. Vest, Inc. is an independently run subsidiary that manages a network of tax professionals, mostly certified public accountants, who sell a variety of financial products to their clients, including mutual funds and unit investment trusts. A large number of its representatives are located in rural areas where residents have limited investment options. The Irving, Texas, business also sells insurance and offers fee-based investment consulting services to individuals and businesses. H.D. Vest operates one of the leading online tax preparation sites, a free service that it uses to attract new customers. Now with Wells Fargo as its corporate parent, the company is expected to greatly expand its network of representatives, as well as to market new products such as home equity loans.

Herb D. Vest Goes into Business in 1973

The man who founded H.D. Vest was a maverick named Herbie Darwin Vest, the son of a West Texas refinery worker. After graduating from college, he served two combat tours in Vietnam as an infantry officer. He told *Forbes* in a 1992 article, "I didn't want to get shot at anymore, so I sought the calmest profession I could find, and became a CPA." He started his own public accounting firm in 1973, but within a few years he found himself embroiled in a different kind of conflict. While working

with clients on their tax returns, he often suggested that they consider investments to offset taxable income, plan for the future by opening IRA accounts, possibly start up college funds for their children. When asked if he could help further, all Vest could do was refer them to a banker or broker who was less knowledgeable about their individual situation. In many cases his clients would return the next tax season in the same financial condition or, even worse, had been guided into making poor investment decisions. Vest and others CPA's were prevented from selling securities by state regulations and professional guidelines set down by the American Institute of Certified Public Accountants (AICPA), which mandated that accountants could not collect commissions and were limited to a fee-based business. Such strictures made the selling of securities an unprofitable endeavor.

Deciding to challenge the system, Vest acquired a securities license and a legal opinion on the AICPA's ethics code, which he was told violated antitrust laws. In 1979, he expanded his CPA practice to include investment planning and the selling of securities on a commission basis. He also informed authorities at the Texas Board of Public Accountancy about what he was doing. "In other words," Vest told a *Dallas Morning News* reporter, "I turned myself in. I had a complaint against me from me." At first, through a broker, he only sold mutual funds and unit investment trusts to a narrow circle of friends and associates. When the venture proved successful, he included all of his clients, many of whom referred so much new business that his income increased dramatically.

Deciding to franchise his concept of combining tax advice with brokerage services, in 1983 Vest created H.D. Vest Investment Securities, Inc., a securities broker-dealer registered with the Securities and Exchange Commission. He funded his enterprise in large part by drawing on his personal credit cards. Vest purchased a mailing list of more than 300,000 tax specialists and began a letter campaign to recruit for his network of accountant/brokers. To take advantage of franchisees' contacts, Vest would also employ a pyramid selling arrangement that awarded three percent of the gross commissions of any recruit that a rep brought into the network. At the same time that he was launching his franchise business, Vest began to openly

---

Company Perspectives:

With tax professionals' understanding of financial concepts and intimate knowledge of clients' financial situations, offering financial planning is the most natural extension of a tax practice, providing the most client-centric, cost effective, and rewarding service to clients.

---

challenge the AICPA code and state laws prohibiting accountants from accepting commissions. While the Texas Board of Accountancy began an inquiry into his conduct, Vest initiated a campaign to change the laws in every state.

After two years Vest reported that he had signed up 1,000 representatives. He was also making progress in his fight against the ban on commissions. The Federal Trade Commission launched an investigation into AICPA regulations, during the course of which the Texas Board of Accountancy, in October 1986, voted to allow CPA's to receive commissions as long as they informed clients in advance about the amount of the commission. Eventually the Board also dropped its investigation into Vest. Several other states soon followed Texas in changing their laws; then in 1987 the FTC issued a letter of complaint against the AICPA, maintaining that the organization's ban on commissions violated federal anti-trust laws. The institute suspended its ethics investigation on Vest, pending a review of the entire issue by its governing council. In 1988, the AICPA council voted to lift the ban in agreement with the FTC position. Although Vest would continue his campaign until, state by state, the rules were changed, he had essentially prevailed.

H.D. Vest, Inc. Founded in 1986

In December 1986, Vest founded H.D. Vest, Inc. as a Texas corporation, which three months later acquired H.D. Vest Investment Securities, Inc. in a stock transaction, making it a wholly owned subsidiary. In July 1988, H.D. Vest went public, making an initial public offering of 214,787 shares of stock at $6 per share. By the end of 1988, H.D. Vest was reporting revenues in excess of $10 million and boasting of a network of affiliates that numbered 2,700. By the end of 1991, the company generated more than $20 million in revenues and posted a profit of almost $922,000, while the number of representatives approached 4,000. Nearly $2 million of that total came from seminars and the sale of educational materials to the company's reps. Most of the revenues, however, were the result of H.D. Vest's 30 percent share of the commissions received by reps on the mutual funds they sold to clients. In 1992, the company's revenues would grow to more than $35 million, yet H.D. Vest would lose nearly $3.2 million and the price of its stock would begin to slide, a situation that fueled internal strife.

During this period, Vest came into conflict with several of his executives over a number of issues, resulting in a swath of litigation. In April 1992, Vest fired Stephen A. Batman, president of the H.D. Vest Advisory Services Inc. subsidiary. Batman sued Vest a month later, alleging that he was fired because he questioned Vest's practice of donating money, as well as company labor, to the Republican Party. Batman later amended

the lawsuit to include allegations of misuse of the company's stock. Batman and another H.D. Vest executive, James Ainsworth, subsequently formed Global Partners, a rival broker/dealership for tax accountants, and began to lure away dozens of H.D. Vest reps with promises of higher commissions and better training. In turn, Vest sued Batman and Ainsworth for raiding his company. Then, in July 1992, Vest fired the company's president, former Navy Admiral Warren Aut, who had been on the job for only six months. Reportedly, Aut wanted to spend more money on training representatives, while Vest wanted to devote cash to direct mail efforts to grow the network even larger. The company ultimately sued Aut over his spending practices.

In October 1992, a *Forbes'* article noted, ''There is grumbling among reps about a conflict of interest in the arrangement that has given Herb Vest 3% of the firm's gross revenues and hence too much incentive to push growth over profit.'' According to critics, H.D. Vest representatives were poorly trained and that instead of earning annual commissions in a target range of $50,000, they were averaging between $11,000 and $12,000. First Global reps, on the other hand, were soon generating between $40,000 and $50,000 in annual revenues.

Aside from bad press, H.D. Vest also faced an audit from the SEC in the fall of 1992. Vest fired two more executives, who in turn sued him and the company. Not only did former strategic analyst Kenneth M. Greene allege that he was fired in retaliation for providing potentially damaging information about H.D. Vest to the SEC, the company's former legislative affairs manager, Kevin R. Greene (not related to Kenneth Greene) alleged that he was required ''to find creative ways of making large political contributions to the Republican Party in an effort to achieve Herb Vest's desire to become an ambassador.'' Both men also maintained that they were fired in part because they refused to perjure themselves in a lawsuit against Vest, although it was unclear which litigation they were referring to. Vest's lawyer insisted that these charges were groundless and merely an attempt to gain a sweetened severance package.

Problems in 1992 Lead to Changes

The company was under enough pressure in the fall of 1992 that it instituted some cost cutting measures and other changes. It cut back its recruiting staff from ten to just three in order to focus more on training, and also cut some non-core programs and downsized its office space. In all, overhead expenses were reduced by $1 million, and recruiting costs lowered from five percent of gross revenue to just two percent. Vest also changed the way he was compensated. Instead of being paid on a percentage of revenues, he would now receive a management fee of $575,000 and 8.5 percent of net income. Moreover, he agreed to have a three-member management committee fill the role of the company's president, although he would remain as chairman and CEO.

The results for H.D. Vest improved in 1993, with revenues continuing to grow in excess of $46 million, while income increased dramatically, totaling almost $3 million. Earlier controversies, however, continued to dog the company. After litigation with Kenneth Greene concluded in early 1994, when he was awarded $135,000 in actual and punitive damages,

Key Dates:

1973: Herb D. Vest launches accounting business.
1983: H.D. Vest Investment Securities, Inc. is established.
1986: H.D. Vest, Inc. is established.
1988: The company goes public.
2001: The company is sold to Wells Fargo & Co.

H.D. Vest faced renewed uncertainty in its executive ranks. One of the three people filling the office of the presidency, Lynn R. Niedermeier, resigned in April 1994, followed by a second member, Steve Hastings, in August. Then in November 1994, Niedermeier returned to the company, taking over as sole president of the firm. In the weeks that followed, four other officers of the company would leave.

Through the rest of the 1990s, H.D. Vest avoided further negative publicity. In the mid-1990s the company began a gradual shift from commission-based sales to fee-based portfolio advisory services that had a temporary adverse effect on the balance sheet. While the company lost almost $369,000 on revenues of nearly $50.3 million in 1994, it posted net earnings of $1.3 million in 1995, despite revenues falling to $44.7 million. H.D. Vest then showed steady improvement through the rest of the decade. In 1998 the company exceeded $100 million in annual revenues, and it boasted 5,900 affiliates located in all 50 states. The following year that number ballooned to 8,500 and Herb Vest received Ernst & Young's Entrepreneur of The Year Award.

In 1999, H.D. Vest once again exhibited an innovative spirit when it announced that its Web site was offering free tax return preparation. While major rivals, H&R Block and Intuit, provided free tax preparation for simple returns, H.D. Vest's offer covered all tax returns, no matter how complicated. For H.D. Vest, free tax preparation was a low cost marketing effort. The service cost the company less than $1 to process each return, while providing a chance to land new investment clients. After people completed their taxes on the H.D. Vest site, they were asked by letter if they wanted to have their 1040 analyzed, with the name and telephone number of the nearest Vest representative included. The tax preparation offer proved to be extremely successful, with the company's 260,000 filings in 2000, making it the number two online tax filing firm.

In 2000, H.D. Vest took further advantage of the Internet. It introduced MyHDVEST.com, a personal Web page, described as a consumer life-planning portal. Consumers not only gained access to educational materials on investments and estate planning, they could also interact with tax professionals or investment planners offering solutions to their particular needs. In addition, H.D. Vest formed an alliance with CompuBank to offer online banking services to its clients, such as certificates of deposit and money market accounts as well as bill paying services, that were integrated with H.D. Vest's bookkeeping and tax preparation software.

H.D. Vest's online initiatives were potentially lucrative, but the company simply did not have the infrastructure in place to support them properly. While focusing on improving its back-office operations, it was unable to devote sufficient resources in other areas like training and recruiting. In order to grow to the next level, H.D. Vest found a suitable partner in Wells Fargo & Co., the giant banking chain. In March 2001, the two parties announced that Wells Fargo would acquire H.D. Vest for $127.5 million. For Wells Fargo, the acquisition was an inexpensive alternative to buying brokerages. For each of H.D. Vest's customers, the bank paid $70, less than a third the amount spent by brokerages to recruit new clients. For H.D. Vest, the deal brought enhanced technical support for its Internet initiatives, new products to sell for its reps, and the credibility of the Wells Fargo name. The new corporate parent would also be able to devote the resources needed to grow the number of representatives. With approximately 150,000 CPA's in America, there remained plenty of opportunity to expand upon the 6,000 CPA's in the H.D. Vest network. While the Wells Fargo acquisition offered much promise for the future of H.D. Vest, and rewarded Herb Vest handsomely, it also meant that its founder's role was greatly reduced. The company's president, Roger Ochs, now ran the business, while Vest, under a long-term contract, served only as a consultant.

Principal Subsidiaries

H.D. Vest Investment Securities, Inc.

Principal Competitors

FMR Corporation; The Charles Schwab Corporation; Citigroup Inc.; Merrill Lynch & Co. Inc.; The Vanguard Group Inc.

Further Reading

Covaleski, John M., "Wells Fargo to Boost Vest's Reps, Services," *Accounting Today,* April 16, 2001, p. 1.

Hall, Cheryl, "For Vest, Breaking Law Part of Plan," *Dallas Morning News,* September 6, 1992.

Johnston, David Cay, "Small Firm Offers to Process Tax Returns Free on Internet," *New York Times,* November 12, 1999, p. C2.

Mandaro, Laura, "H.D. Vest Is Wells' Side Door to Advisory," *American Banker,* March 26, 2001, p. 1.

Pickering, John, "H.D. Vest Cuts Back Overhead," *Accounting Today,* November 23, 1992, p. 1.

Schifrin, Matthew, "Would You Buy a Mutual Fund from These Men?," *Forbes,* October 12, 1992, p. 76.

Zimmerman, Martin, "Despite Disruption, H.D. Vest in Charge," *Dallas Morning News,* March 3, 1993.

——, "CPA Battles Ban on Commissions," *Dallas Morning News,* August 30, 1998.

—Ed Dinger

The Hartz Mountain Corporation

400 Plaza Drive
Secaucus, New Jersey 07094
U.S.A.
Telephone: (201) 271-4800
Fax: (201) 271-0068
Web site: http://www.hartz.com

Private Company
Incorporated: 1926 as Hartz Mountain Pet Foods
Employees: 2,100 (estimated)
Sales: $977 million (2000 estimate)
NAIC: 311111 Dog and Cat Food Manufacturing

Since its founding, The Hartz Mountain Corporation has been instrumental in defining the pets supply industry. The Secaucus, New Jersey-based company markets approximately 1,500 different products, ranging from food to toys, for pet animals, birds, and fish. After nearly 75 years under the control of three generations of the Stern family, Hartz Mountain is now owned by the investment firm of J.W. Childs Associates, L.P., the result of a management-led buyout in December 2000.

Hartz Mountain Established in 1926

Devastated by soaring inflation and mounting unemployment, Germany during the 1920s was a country in near economic ruin and headed toward political disaster. For a vast majority of Germans, the future looked bleak: each year the economic depression worsened, leaving many of the country's citizens destitute and looking for relief from a faltering government. Some found an answer to their myriad problems in a virulent, yet magnetic political leader who promised to make Germany the greatest nation in the world, while others looked for answers elsewhere. One of those who chose to leave Germany and start life anew elsewhere was a textile manufacturer named Max Stern. In 1926, Stern left Germany and immigrated to the United States, ready to begin a career that would help create and define an American industry. Stern carried with him the products of his new trade: 2,100 canaries taken from the famous Hartz Mountain region in Germany.

Initially, Stern sold his canaries to small pet stores, but he soon expanded the scale of his business when he began selling first to mass retailers and later to supermarkets and department stores. Stern's decision to broaden product exposure through mass retailers was the first of several crucial steps that laid the foundation for the pet supply empire that would follow. This decision led the company to expand its distribution network to accommodate the delivery of a greater number of birds, and also prompted it to offer a diversified product line. The company's distribution network took time to develop, but Stern broadened his product line shortly after opening his business, when in 1930 he began selling bird food in addition to Hartz Mountain canaries. By the beginning of America's own decade-long struggle with depressed economic conditions, Stern had established the three distinctive attributes that would predicate the growth of his company and lead to its dominance of the U.S. pet supply industry.

Despite the harsh economic conditions during the 1930s and his inability to speak English, Stern was able to secure several contracts with mass retailers and, along with his brother, who had remained in Germany to purchase the canaries that Stern would sell in the United States, enjoyed considerable success over the next several decades. By the end of the 1950s, Stern's modest venture had become a formidable force in the pet supply industry, thanks largely to the growth and sophistication of the company's distribution network and the diverse assortment of products that bore the Hartz Mountain name. The company by this point sold birds, bird food, and bird accessories, products that by 1959 generated $18 million in sales, which Stern hoped to use to fund further product diversification. Following a family dispute in 1959, Stern bought out his brother's share in the company for $8 million.

Leonard Stern Joins the Company in 1959

Thereafter, Stern soon found a new partner: his son, Leonard N. Stern, who became involved in the family business during the late 1950s when his father ceded partial interest in Hartz Mountain to his three children. As a youth, Leonard Stern sold merchandise door-to-door; at age 17, he entered New York University's School of Commerce. Two-and-a-half years later he was graduated cum laude and subsequently earned his Masters of Business Administration degree at night while working days as a clerk.

In the late 1950s, Leonard and his brother Stanley purchased two failing companies involved in the fish and fish supply business—Aquarium Supply Co. and Long Life Fish Food Products—and created a new company named Sternco Industries, which they then took public in 1962 after achieving nearly the same success in the fish and fish supply business as their father had in the bird and bird supply business. Shortly after taking Sternco Industries public, Stanley Stern left the company to pursue his interests in the real estate business. Leonard bought out Stanley's shares and then turned his attention to the growth of both Sternco Industries and Hartz Mountain.

Although he would not become president and chief executive officer of Hartz Mountain until 1971, Leonard Stern wielded considerable control within the company during the 1960s. As executive vice-president and chief operating officer, he spearheaded several of its most defining marketing moves. He broadened the company's product line substantially to include dog and cat accessories—dog toys, cat litter, shampoos—which enabled the company to tap into the burgeoning growth of supermarkets at the time, yet purposely stayed away from entering into the dog and cat food business to avoid competition from entrenched pet food producers. Hartz Mountain was going to establish market dominance, both father and son had decided, and the fragmented pet supply and accessory industry provided the perfect arena in which their well-organized and diversified company could compete.

By the mid-1970s, Max and Leonard Stern were well on their way toward fulfilling their goal. Hartz Mountain by this point controlled roughly one-third of the nearly $900 million pet supply business through the company's 1,200 products, which ranged from birds, fish, hamsters, and gerbils to pet food, pet health care products, and accessories. The company that was now regarded as one of the few giants in the industry bore little resemblance to the fledgling enterprise launched by Max Stern in the mid-1920s (it could no longer sell the company's original product because the importation of canaries was made illegal in 1972). Nevertheless, by this time, canaries represented only five percent of Hartz Mountain's sales, and racks of Hartz Mountain merchandise displayed in their distinctive orange packaging occupied pet supply departments in retail outlets across the nation, in many cases being the only pet products stores stocked. The company's distribution system, by now the industry's prototype after 50 years of improvement and solidification, left competitors with little territory that was not firmly held by Hartz Mountain, leading the business press to hail the Stern organization as the General

Motors of the pet supply industry. Other accolades followed, and soon industry pundits were claiming Max and Leonard Stern had done to the pet supply industry what Kodak's George Eastman had done to the photography industry and what Henry Ford had done to the automobile industry.

Leonard Stern, by this point in full control of Hartz Mountain, had demonstrated his business acumen in other arenas as well. In addition to masterminding Hartz Mountain's rousing growth—the company recorded $135 million in sales in 1972, then nearly doubled that amount five years later despite a nationwide economic recession—Stern had purchased sizable acreage in Secaucus and Meadowlands, New Jersey, during the mid-1960s, which by the following decade had risen enormously in value. With his real estate holdings Stern formed a private company he named Hartz Mountain Industries, then shortly thereafter began reorganizing the Stern family empire into distinct segments. In order to rase the $40 million needed for the Meadowlands project, Stern took Hartz Mountain Pet Foods public in 1972. The following year Stern merged Hartz Mountain Pet Foods into Sternco Industries, the fish and fish supply company he and his brother had formed years earlier, to create Hartz Mountain Corp. Hartz Mountain stood atop its field, enjoying more than a 75 percent market share in many of its market niches and holding a nearly unassailable lead over its competitors.

Legal Challenges in the 1970s

During this time, Hartz Mountain faced several difficulties. First, in the early 1970s, a magazine article was published claiming that the chemical used in Hartz flea collars was potentially harmful; the flea collar was the company's biggest seller and contributed roughly $15 million in annual sales at the time. Then, more serious allegations were levelled at Hartz Mountain, its executive personnel, and Leonard Stern. Specifically, accusations arose concerning the company's alleged violation of antitrust laws by exerting undue pressure on distributors to deal in Hartz Mountain products exclusively. Several lawsuits were brought by competitors and distributors against Hartz Mountain during the 1970s, charging that the company's far-reaching and well-developed distribution techniques were overly aggressive, forced distributors to handle Hartz Mountain products exclusively, and involved taking the products of competitors off the shelves and replacing them with Hartz Mountain products. Ultimately, these matters were settled, and, admitting no wrongdoing, Hartz Mountain paid court settlements and a $20,000 fine to the Federal Trade Commission.

By the end of the 1970s, Stern decided to return the company to private ownership and use the funds for developing his real estate interests. When Stern bought back the publicly-held shares in Hartz Mountain, he merged Hartz Mountain Corp. into Hartz Mountain Industries, the real estate and real estate development arm of the Stern empire. Despite the legal turmoil surrounding the company at the time, Hartz Mountain had relinquished little of its dominance in the pet supply industry and continued to exert overwhelming control in many of its markets. The 75 percent market share Hartz Mountain's pet supply business reached during the 1970s continued to fuel the company's growth throughout the 1980s, as Stern turned his attention elsewhere in a bid to broaden the scope of his business interests.

Key Dates:

1926: Immigrant Max Stern founds the company to sell canaries.
1930: The company begins to sell bird food.
1972: Hartz Mountain goes public.
1979: The company returns to private status.
2000: Hartz Mountain is sold to J.W. Childs Associates in a management-led buyout.

From Pet Supplies to Publishing: Mid-1980s to 1990s

In 1985, Stern purchased the *Village Voice,* a well-known Manhattan weekly newspaper, from publisher Robert Murdoch for $55 million, then two years later launched another Manhattan weekly newspaper he christened *7 Days.* In the mid-1990s, the *L.A. Weekly* would also be added to Stern's publishing interests. In 1988, Stern formed the Harmon Publishing Company, a new division developed to oversee his real estate publications.

Also during this time, Stern formed Hartz Group Inc. to once again separate his real estate development and building operation business from his pet supply business. In the hierarchical reshuffling that followed, Hartz Group was made the parent company of Hartz Mountain Corp., and Harmon Publishing Company was organized as a division of Hartz Group. Structured as such, the conglomeration of Hartz-controlled businesses entered the 1990s cast in their separate roles.

In 1990, after failing to receive a suitable offer from bidders, Stern ceased publication of *7 Days,* which had proven to be a $10 million loser despite earning positive reviews and being nominated for a coveted National Magazine Award. Four years later, Harmon Publishing Company, which had acquired 60 publishing companies in its six years of business (all involved in publishing real estate magazines), was sold to United Advertising Periodicals for $108 million. With these business interests trimmed from his formidable corporate organization, Stern plotted his course for the mid-1990s and beyond, buoyed by the consistently strong performance of his pet supply business. The company continued as a largely family-run enterprise, with Stern's son Edward, who joined the firm in 1989, serving as executive vice-president of the Hartz Group's pet supply operations, and another son, Emmanuel, as executive vice-president of the real estate arm of the Hartz business.

With his father occupied with his media and real estate ventures, Edward was instrumental in growing the pet supply business. The company completed a number of acquisitions, including the addition of the Wardley and L/M brands. It also added manufacturing plants in America and Brazil to produce natural pet treats and rawhide for pet toys. In order to continue to develop products in line with the tastes of a new generation of pet owners, the company bolstered its research and development efforts in 1995, building new laboratories near its main New Jersey manufacturing plant. Out of these efforts came a new line of over-the-counter flea- and tick-control systems that was launched in 1998. Veterinary offices in the mid-1990s began to prescribe new squeeze-on topical flea and tick treat-ments that proved extremely popular with pet owners and severely eroded the sale of flea and tick treatments available at pet stores and other retailers. In supermarkets, where the company had experienced a slump in pet supply sales, these new and inexpensive over-the-counter products promised to restore lost revenue. Hartz Mountain also began to make a transition away from a direct-to-store distribution business model in order to reposition itself as a low cost marketer, developer, and manufacturer of pet supply products.

Hartz Relinquished as a Family Business

Edward Stern was named president of Hartz Mountain Corporation in 1997, but like his father he grew less interested in running the pet supply business. Early in 2000 he resigned his post, indicating that he preferred to devote his time to heading up the family's investment portfolio. By now the real estate business was thriving with the opening of luxury hotels in Manhattan and plans to build major television and movie production facilities in New Jersey. A year earlier Leonard Stern had put his publishing interests up for sale when none of his children expressed a desire to run them. In conjunction with Edward's resignation from Hartz Mountain, Robert Devine was named president and chief operating officer. Devine had joined the company as part of the Wardley Corporation acquisition in 1994. By July, management announced that it had retained JP Morgan to explore strategic business alternatives, indicating that it would consider selling the company.

Even as Hartz Mountain was completing a year of record revenue and profits in 2000, it was finalizing a sale of the company to J.W. Childs Associates, a leveraged buyout specialist with considerable experience investing in such consumer product companies as Snapple Beverage Corp. and General Nutrition Companies. Devine and his management team stayed on to run Hartz Mountain, holding great expectations for the future. The number of pet owners and pet households continued to rise in the United States, and the company began an initiative to expand export sales, with the goal of making them 20 percent of total sales. After nearly 75 years of family control, Hartz Mountain also made efforts to change the corporate culture, granting greater input from its employees.

Principal Subsidiaries

Hartz Canada; Hartz LTDA Brazil.

Principal Competitors

Ralston Purina Co.; Iams Company; Mars Inc.

Further Reading

"American Home Products to Buy 2 Pet-Line Firms," *Wall Street Journal,* August 19, 1971, p. 13.

Blustein, Paul, "Hartz Owner Made a Prime Target of a Big Grand Jury Investigation," *Wall Street Journal,* January 17, 1983, p. 25.

——, "Will the Canaries Come Home to Roost?," *Forbes,* April 17, 1978, pp. 59–61.

Blustein, Paul, and Richard Greene, "The Public Be Damned? In 1979?," *Forbes,* April 2, 1979, pp. 38–40.

Byrd, Edward W., "Ticked Off," *Supermarket News,* April 6, 1998, p. 51.

"Cages to Collars; Hartz Mountain Finds Pet Supplies Growth Business," *Barron's,* February 9, 1976.

"The Canaries That Laid Golden Eggs . . . , " *Forbes,* February 15, 1974, pp. 34–8.

"Developer Stern to Launch Newspaper in Manhattan," *Wall Street Journal,* July 30, 1987, p. 26.

Donaton, Scott, "*7 Days* Folds After Bidders Balk," *Advertising Age,* April 23, 1990, p. 16.

"Ex-Hartz Executive Convicted for Perjury Over Alleged Payoffs," *Wall Street Journal,* December 22, 1982, p. 7.

"Fido and His Friends," *Barron's,* March 22, 1965, p. 11.

Hammer, Alexander R., "A Billion Dollar Business Is Unleashed in Pet Sales," *New York Times,* April 7, 1968, p. F35.

"Hartz Mountain Corp. Votes to Go Private Despite Objections by Minority of Holders," *Wall Street Journal,* February 14, 1979, p. 14.

"Hartz Mountain May Go Private Via Cash Merger," *Wall Street Journal,* November 2, 1978, p. 20.

"Leonard Norman Stern," *Forbes,* October 26, 1987, p. 137.

"Leonard Stern Is Sued by Former Hartz Partner," *Wall Street Journal,* November 12, 1993, p. A5.

Mills, Joshua, "Harmon Publishing Sale to Link Ad Periodicals," *New York Times,* February 1, 1994, p. D7.

"One of the Family," *Barron's,* March 3, 1969, p. 11.

Robichaux, Mark, "Hartz Brings Back Insect Spray Some Pet Owners Fear Is Fatal," *Wall Street Journal,* September 6, 1989, p. B6.

Sandler, Linda, "Call This Business a Family Affair," *Wall Street Journal,* November 18, 1998, p. B18.

"Two Hartz Ex-Aides Sentenced on Charges from Antitrust Suit," *Wall Street Journal,* May 24, 1984, p. 24.

—Jeffrey L. Covell
—update: Ed Dinger

Hauser, Inc.

5555 Airport Boulevard
Boulder, Colorado 80301-2339
U.S.A.
Telephone: (303) 443-4662
Fax: (303) 441-5800
Web site: http://www.hauser.com

Public Company
Incorporated: 1983 as Hauser Chemical Research, Inc.
Employees: 310
Sales: $66.7 million (2001)
Stock Exchanges: Over The Counter
Ticker Symbol: HAUS
NAIC: 325411 Medicinals and Botanical Manufacturing;
    541330 Engineering Services; 541380 Testing
    Laboratories; 541710 Research and Development in
    the Physical, Engineering, and Life Sciences

Hauser Inc. is a leading producer and supplier of natural product extracts, botanical raw materials, and related products to the dietary supplement market in the United States. Hauser manufactures extracts from botanical raw materials using its proprietary extract and purification technologies. Hauser and its subsidiaries are able to process and distribute products to the dietary supplement market, including branded product sellers. The company also provides cross-disciplinary laboratory testing services, chemical engineering services, and contract research and development aimed primarily at the pharmaceutical, dietary supplement, and food-ingredient industries. These services are provided through the company's wholly owned subsidiary, Hauser Technical Services, Inc., which consist of laboratories in Boulder, Colorado and Shuster Laboratories in Quincy, Massachusetts. The laboratories provide process research and development, custom manufacturing, and testing services for the pharmaceutical industry, as well as failure analysis, material identification and suitability testing, and product design validation for the medical device industry. In addition, the laboratories provide services to the natural product field, including development of extraction and isolation processes, analytical method development, and custom

manufacturing and analysis of the chemistry of natural products. The company operates two other subsidiaries, including Botanical International Extracts, Inc., a distributor of bulk dietary supplements, and ZetaPharm, Inc., a distributor of bulk fine chemicals, excipients, and generic active ingredients. The type of products sold through ZetaPharm include bulk vitamins, dietary supplements, over-the-counter pharmaceutical ingredients, and food additives. These products are sold to various producers and processors of health food, pharmaceuticals, food and beverages, and dietary supplements.

1980s: Company Is Founded and Flourishes

The company was founded in 1983 as Hauser Chemical Research, Inc. by two research chemists, Randy Daughenbaugh and Dean Still, to provide services in contract research and development in chemical and process engineering. Although the two chemists had not selected a market niche upon founding the company, they soon developed a proprietary extraction technology for isolating and purifying plant and animal compounds at higher yields and lower costs than conventional methods. As a result, Daughenbaugh and Dean at first entered into small research and development contracts that soon led to profitable supply agreements based on their proprietary extraction technology.

In 1987 and 1988, Hauser won contracts from the National Cancer Institute (NCI) to isolate anti-tumor and anti-Aids agents from natural sources. As a result of these contracts, the company soon began supplying the National Cancer Institute with paclitaxel, a non-patented compound extracted from yew trees that first showed promising results in the treatment of ovarian, breast, and other cancers in clinical trials by NCI. Paclitaxel is an anti-tumor agent that exhibited effective activity against several types of cancer, especially refractory ovarian and refractory breast cancer. It is an anti-microtubule agent and represented the first of a new class of potential anti-tumor compounds. Microtubules are intracellular structures that serve to regulate cell division, cell shape, cell motility, and intracellular transport. Paclitaxal, which worked by attacking the cancer cell division process, constituted a new and novel compound that differed from all previously discovered cytotoxic agents.

By the late 1980s, the National Cancer Institute had spent more than $30 million on Paclitaxel research. Nonetheless, although Hauser had perfected an extraction technique to produce Paclitaxal, the product was far from being marketable. The NCI therefore decided to seek bids to produce and market a drug based on the paclitaxel compound. The rights were awarded to a partnership between Hauser and Bristol-Myers Squibb. The three-year partnership agreement between the two companies called for Bristol-Myers to spend more than $100 million to complete clinical studies and get the drug to market. Hauser, having developed the chemical extraction technology, would produce the paclitaxel for Bristol-Myers. The agreement with Bristol-Myers comprised Hauser's largest contract since its founding and provided almost all of the company's revenues until 1994, when it was terminated by Bristol-Myers Squibb.

Acquistions and Diversification in the 1990s

In January 1990, the company acquired Hauser Laboratories, Inc. for 400,000 shares of its common stock. The company's acquisition was made with the aim of expanding the interdisciplinary laboratory testing and chemical engineering skills of its technical services unit. In the same year, the company formed Hauser Northwest, a wholly owned subsidiary, to facilitate the collection of yew bark for the production of paclitaxel. In May 1994, the newly formed Hauser Northwest acquired substantially all of the net assets of Ironwood Evergreens, Inc., an Olympia, Washington-based company, to retain and expand its bark harvesting capabilities in the Northwest. This acquisition gave Hauser four business units: pharmaceuticals, natural ingredients, technical services, and secondary forest products. In July 1995, in a further effort to find new sources of revenue, the company acquired 100 percent of the stock of Shuster Laboratories, Inc., an independent consumer products research and development firm and contract labratory based in Quincy, Massachusetts, and Atlanta, Georgia.

The company pursued these acquisitions as part of a strategy to diversify its products and to become a multi-customer producer of special products from natural sources. Nevertheless, prior to 1995, virtually all of the company's revenue derived from the production and sale of paclitaxel to the Bristol-Myers Squibb Company. Taxol, the brand name drug produced from paclitaxel and marketed by Bristol-Myers, proved to be of significant use in chemotherapy treatments for ovarian and breast cancer. As a result, Taxol was enormously profitable for Bristol-Myers, becoming its second-largest seller. For tax and diversification reasons, Bristol-Myers developed its own operation in Ireland to manufacture paclitaxel and terminated Hauser as a supplier in 1994 after the agreement between the two companies had ended. The termination of the Bristol-Myers agreement sent sales plummeting, causing Hauser to reduce costs to minimize operating losses by restricting salaries, benefits, and travel.

Hauser tried to rebuild its paclitaxel business by entering into a multi-year, world-wide, and mutually exclusive supply agreement in May 1994 with the American Home Products Company. The agreement called for Hauser to supply bulk paclitaxel to American Home Products. At the same time, the two companies signed a collaborative research and development agreement, providing for the cooperative development of new products derived from naturally or synthetically produced taxanes. Under the terms of this agreement, American Home Products would fund the research and development program and be granted the option to sell exclusively throughout the world any effective product that could be used for drug therapy of human disease. In turn, Hauser would supply American Home products with any such bulk products and receive royalty payments resulting from the development and selling of the finished products.

During 1995, the company also entered into a research agreement with Dovetail Technologies, Inc. to produce research on a novel class of compounds that had demonstrated anti-cancer activity in animal studies. Hauser planned to provide chemistry and manufacturing services for Dovetail's proprietary compounds, which appeared to reinforce the body's innate ability to fight cancer by augmenting the immune system. In the same year, Hauser initiated technical and business plans to enter the nutraceutical market, which encompassed a broad range of natural products aimed at supplementing dietary intake with added nutrients. The U.S. market amounted to over $200,000 million in 1995 and was anticipated to grow at more than 20 percent per year. The company had already been producing such products as liquid and dry herbal extracts of echinacea, valerian, siberian ginseng, Panax ginseng, goldenseal, and chamomile. The company believed that its expertise in the production of special products from natural sources and extensive regulatory experience positioned it well for growth in this market. As a result, Hauser began producing nutraceutical products that could be consumed as supplements in liquids, capsules, or tablets, or as ingredients in processed foods.

In 1996, the company began producing sanguinaria extract, a natural antimicrobial, for Colgate's Viadent toothpaste and oral rinse products. The company also entered the market to produce and sell natural flavor extracts, an estimated $3 billion market per year worldwide. Hauser believed that there was a continuing trend in the United States toward the use of natural products, including the use of natural flavors and botanical extracts. The company's extracts were marketed under its brand name NaturEnhance Flavor Extracts, which encompassed fifty flavor extract products. These were used in ready-to-drink beverages, yogurt, dressings, ethnic foods, teas, and other natural products. Hauser also began producing coffee, tea, and vanilla flavor extracts for use in beverages, ice cream, yogurt, baked goods, teas, and other applications. Other extracts in this product line included black pepper, tarragon, basil, sage, thyme, oregano, and chili pepper for use in sauces, soups, stews, frozen entrees, juices, salsa, and dressings.

In 1996, Hauser also entered the natural food additives market with the goal of rapidly building a quality line of products and becoming a world leader in the development and manufacture of natural food additives. Food additives comprise products that act as preservatives, stabilizers, colorants, antioxidants, and nutritional additives. In addition, the company began manufacturing for commercial sale a line of rosemary extracts that protected the flavor and quality of foods and beverages.

In December 1996, the company was incorporated under the laws of the state of Colorado under the new name Hauser, Inc., successor company to the Delaware corporation, Hauser Chemical Research, Inc. By this time, the company's technical services division, which included Hauser Laboratories and Shuster, was providing more than 3,000 consulting and testing projects for thousands of clients each year. These project ranged from multi-year research, development, testing, and consulting programs for Fortune 100 companies to simple water tests for homeowners. The company offered clients contract research services and process and product development in a variety of chemical, engineering, and food technology applications. In addition, the company provided analytical services concerning a variety of materials, including pharmaceuticals, botanicals, and medicinals, paints and coatings, plastics, petroleum products, and metals.

Challenges in the Mid- to Late 1990s

Despite Hauser's efforts to diversify, in 1996 the company decided to sell the net assets of its secondary forest products subsidiary, Hauser Northwest, Inc., a money losing operation, in order to retain cash for its core business and improve the company's operating position. The divestiture of Hauser Northwest meant that Hauser would no longer harvest its own yew bark in the Pacific northwest and would instead rely on nursery grown, cultivated yew trees to provide acceptable raw material for processing paclitaxel. In 1997, Hauser and its customer, Yew Tree Pharmaceuticals, were named in a lawsuit filed by Bristol-Myers in the Netherlands, alleging patent infringement in Europe concerning the production of paclitaxel. The lawsuit stemmed from efforts by Bristol-Myers to maintain its monopoly over the production and marketing of its cancer fighting agent, Taxol. On July 24, 1997, the District Court in the Netherlands ruled against Bristol-Myers, denying the company's request for an injunction to halt Yew Tree from selling their paclitaxel-based product.

In 1998, Hauser set aside $1.5 million to cover product returns, development costs, and legal fees after shipments of Panax ginseng to PharmaPrint, Inc. were found to be contaminated with quintozene, an agricultural-crop fungicide that causes liver damage. The presence of the fungicide had been discovered in tests on random samples of the shipment. As a result, PharmaPrint rejected Hauser's shipment of ginseng and notified the Food and Drug Administration out of concern that the contamination could affect other ginseng products on the market. Hauser consequently halted all Panax processing and shipments until the matter was resolved with regulatory authorities.

In its continuing efforts to resurrect the paclitaxel business, in 1998 the company signed a non-exclusive agreement to supply bulk paclitaxel to Immunex and its collaborative partner, IVAX Corporation. In a related development, Hauser announced that it was terminating the exclusivity portion of its relationship with Yew Tree Pharmaceuticals for the supply of paclitaxel. This move meant that the company would continue to supply paclitaxel to Yew Tree for its product Yewtaxen, but would enable Hauser to provide the compound to other companies for marketing in Europe.

Nevertheless, the company's major focus was on expanding the herbal extracts business. In this regard, in December 1998, Hauser announced that it was merging with three subsidiaries of the Zuellig Group N.A., Inc. and Zuellig Botanicals, Inc. The merger with Zuellig Botanical Extracts, Inc., a subsidiary of Zuellig Botanicals, Inc., and with Wilcox Drug Company, Inc. and ZetaPharm, Inc, subsidiaries of Zuellig Group N.A., both quadrupled Hauser's size and created the leading U.S. supplier of herbal extracts, botanical raw materials and related products in the rapidly growing nutritional industry. At the close of the merger, Hauser issued 2,515,349 shares of its common stock to Zuellig Group N.A. and Zuellig Botanical Inc., constituting 49 percent of the outstanding shares of Hauser stock. Hauser's existing officers and public shareholders owned 51 percent of the remaining shares of the newly combined company. In connection with the merger, Wells Fargo Bank, N.A. provided a $35 million line of credit and a $10 million fixed loan in support of the merged companies. Hauser also assumed approximately $21 million in bank debt of Wilcox, ZetaPharm, and Zuellig Botanical Extracts. In addition, the merger agreement, which was finalized on June 11, 1999, called for the new organization to be headquartered in Boulder, Colorado, and operated under the Hauser name. Simultaneously with the merger, the company effected a one-for-four reverse stock split in order to increase the market price per share of common stock to comply with Nasdaq's listing requirements of at least a $5.00 minimum bid price. Because of the significance of the merger, Hauser was required to reapply for listing on the Nasdaq National Market Exchange.

With this renewed focus on herbal extracts, Hauser decided to sell its paclitaxel business, which had never regained substantial profitability after the 1994 expiration of the Bristol-Myers agreement. In fiscal years 1997 through 1999, the company's operating losses in the paclitaxel business had resulted primarily from the failure of customers to renew their purchase contracts. The company planned to use the cash from the sale of the paclitaxel operation to invest in the more promising Nutraceuticals and Technical Services units. The company also made organizational changes within its subsidiaries to improve operating costs. Hauser consolidated its raw material purchasing activities under the Wilcox division and combined its sales and marketing operations under the Botanical International Extracts unit. In addition, Hauser Laboratories and Shuster Laboratories were combined into one business unit called Hauser Technical Services, Inc.

Nevertheless, the merger and the organizational changes did little in the immediate term to bolster the company's revenues. For fiscal year ended March 31, 2000 Hauser reported a net loss of $28,374,855, compared to a net loss of $29,736,106 in fiscal year 1999. As a result of these financial struggles, the company's stock declined precipitously below one dollar per share, causing the company's common stock to be officially delisted from the Nasdaq on November 1, 2000. The delisting stemmed from the company's lack of compliance with the Nasdaq's listing requirements that call for a minimum bid price of $1.00 and a minimum public float value of $5 million. The company's common stock, however, was eligible for trading in the over-the-counter market. The company, which tried to appeal the delisting of its shares, had been experiencing significant operating losses stemming from a worldwide oversupply of dietary supplement products leading to low prices and declining revenues.

Developments and Difficulties in the New Century

In January 2001, the company announced what it considered a significant development in having reached agreement with the Whitehall-Robins Healthcare division of American Home Products Corporation to jointly develop a new dietary supplement. The agreement called for a two-year exclusive collaboration between the two companies. Whitehall-Robins was a leader in the research and development, production and marketing of a broad range of consumer health care products, with U.S. sales of approximately $1.7 billion in 2000.

Nevertheless, despite the Whitehall-Robins contract, Hauser's financial difficulties continued into 2001. Due to continuing operating losses, during fiscal year ended March 31, the company terminated the Wilcox subsidiary and liquidated its remaining inventories, exiting the sale of botanical raw materials. The decision to terminate the Wilcox operations stemmed from the significant decline in market prices for the natural product raw materials sold by Wilcox during fiscal 2000. In July, the company reported a net loss for 2001 of $33.3 million, compared with a net loss of $28.4 million in 2000. The company stated that its financial performance reflected efforts to reduce costs and re-

structure operations in order to return to profitability. To further stem the financial hemorrhaging, the company announced in August 2001 that it was selling the Hauser Contract Research division, which specialized in the extraction, purification, chemical modification, and production of fine organic chemicals from natural sources. By the first fiscal quarter of 2002, the company had begun to make progress, narrowing its net loss to $618,000 from a net loss of $1.9 million in the corresponding quarter in the previous year. By the end of 2001, the company had reorganized around three principal business segments: dietary supplements, pharmaceuticals and food ingredients, and technical services. In spite of the economic recession in 2001, Hauser's aggressive restructuring appeared to be positioning the company for possible future profitability in the herbal extracts and nutritional supplements industry.

Principal Subsidiaries

Hauser Technical Services, Inc.; Botanical International Extracts, Inc.; ZetaPharm, Inc.

Principal Competitors

Nature's Sunshine Products Inc.; Rexall Sundown Inc.; Twinlab Corp.

Further Reading

Barrett, William P., "Delaying Tactics," *Forbes*, March 23, 1998.

"Hauser Announces Intentions to Sell," *Natural Foods Merchandiser*, February 2001, p. 8.

"Hauser CEO Resigns," *Denver Business Journal*, February 2000, p. 8A.

"Hauser Seeks Sale of Contract Research Division," *Chemical Market Reporter*, September 3, 2001, p. 3.

"News Update," *Psychopharmacology Update*, August 9, 1998.

Romero, Christine L., "Colorado's Hauser Appeals to Fight Delisting from Nasdaq National Market," *Daily Camera*, September 21, 2000.

Stogner, Amy, "Hauser Consolidating Offices to Cut Costs," *Boulder County Business Report*, August 10, 2001, p. 1A.

Stogner, Amy, "Hauser Shifts Eggs to Weld Basket," *Northern Colorado Business Report*, August 10, 2001, p. 3A.

—by Bruce P. Montgomery

The Hearst Corporation

959 Eighth Avenue
New York, New York 10019
U.S.A.
Telephone: (212) 649-2000
Fax: (212) 765-3528
Web site: http://www.hearstcorp.com

Private Company
Incorporated: 1943
Employees: 18,300
Sales: $3.4 billion (2000)
NAIC: 51111 Newspaper Publishers; 51112 Periodical
Publishers; 51113 Book Publishers; 51114 Database
and Directory Publishers; 51312 Television
Broadcasters; 51321 Cable Networks; 51311 Radio
Networks; 51411 News Syndicates

The Hearst Corporation is one of the largest diversified communications companies in the world. It has interests in print, broadcasting, and the news media, including newspapers, magazines, book and business publishing, television and radio broadcasting, cable network programming, newspaper features distribution, television production and distribution, and electronic publishing. Hearst Magazines is the largest publisher of monthly magazines in the world. It publishes 16 titles in the U.S., including *Cosmopolitan, Esquire, House Beautiful, O, The Oprah Magazine,* and *Talk.* The division also puts out over 100 international editions, with distribution in more than 100 countries. A subsidiary, the National Magazine Company Limited, is one of the leading magazine publishers in the United Kingdom. The magazine division also publishes books, with titles mostly tied to its periodicals in some way. Hearst Newspapers publishes 12 daily and 16 weekly newspapers in the United States. The division also operates a subsidiary company which publishes Yellow Pages directories in Texas and is part owner of an Internet-based classified advertising company.

Hearst-Argyle TV is one of the largest independently owned broadcasting groups in the nation. It includes 26 television stations and two radio stations. Its stations reach over 17 percent of all U.S. households. Hearst Entertainment and Syndication includes the company's cable network partnerships with ABC, NBC, and ESPN; television programming and distribution activities; and the King Features group of syndication companies, which is the world's largest distributor of editorial features, comic strips, and panels to newspapers. Other business units include Hearst Interactive Media, which operates partnerships in Internet-based services such as iVillage and Hire.com, and its Business Media unit. The business media division handles a variety of business-to-business publications as well as databases and on-line services such as a used car guide and a collision database.

Founder William Randolph Hearst

The shape and history of the company's early years were intertwined with the history and designs of its founder, William Randolph Hearst. A man who inherited enormous wealth, Hearst was also a person of enormous ambition and activity whose initial interest in journalism in an era when the newspaper business could hardly be separated from the political arena led to a consuming passion for political office that was destined to end in frustration.

The company that became a behemoth in communications started out as payment for a gambling debt, when William Randolph Hearst's father, George Hearst, a self-made millionaire who had earned his fortune in mining and ranching, took possession of the *San Francisco Examiner* in 1880 after its owner had lost a wager with him. Seven years later, William Randolph Hearst, recently expelled from Harvard College for an elaborate prank, took over the running of the paper.

Newspapers in that day were, for the most part, organs of propaganda for individual politicians and political parties. Indeed, Hearst's father had accepted the paper only for the purpose of enhancing his own political career. William Randolph Hearst had big plans in mind for the money-losing four-page daily paper. Taking Joseph Pulitzer's *New York World* as his model, he began by sinking large sums into the latest printing technology and changing the paper's appearance to make it more compelling. In addition, he hired new staff members—bagging such luminaries as Ambrose Bierce—and charged them with the aggressive pursuit of stories that would improve the paper's circulation. The first big coup came with the *Examiner's* sensational coverage of a big hotel fire, just one month after Hearst took over. Slowly the paper's fortunes improved, helped along by a large dose of self-promotion. Hearst was soon referring to his paper as "A GREAT PAPER."

Hearst employees were diligent in their pursuit of shocking and titillating material to draw in more readers. In the absence of genuinely sensational news, they did not hesitate to manufacture newsworthy events, or simply to make things up. Much of the manufactured news was billed as crusading exposure of social ills, as when a woman reporter feigned illness to expose the condition of the city's ambulance corps and hospital, or when one intrepid Hearst journalist threw himself into San Francisco Bay from a ferry to test rescue procedures. Both of these stories did in fact result in improvements in the city agencies involved. In his first year, Hearst launched more than a dozen crusades, taking on such established powers as the city's political machine and the Southern Pacific Railroad. All of this activity, along with Hearst features, such as the publication of the scores of popular songs on Sunday and the introduction of a column devoted to union activities, added up to a new kind of journalism and contributed to a slowly growing circulation. Advertising revenues remained low, however, and Hearst's paper continued to consume large sums of his father's money until 1890, when it first went into the black.

By 1895, the *Examiner* was thriving, both in terms of circulation and revenue, and Hearst was ready for a new challenge. He found it in New York, taking over a decrepit daily paper, the *New York Journal.* He began by sending for the best of his San Francisco staff, dropping the price of the New York paper to a penny, and increasing its size. Hearst was going after his old ideal, Pulitzer's *World,* and his most successful tactic was the wholesale raiding of Pulitzer's staff. Waving enormous salaries, he lured some of his rival's best staff away, including the creator of the popular comic "The Yellow Kid," which would inspire the phrase "yellow journalism," used to describe the sensational and irresponsible coverage that Hearst and his rivals pioneered.

In the ensuing contest between the two papers, the techniques that Hearst's organization had first polished in San Francisco—sensationalism and crusading campaigns on behalf of the ordinary person—were taken to new heights. In addition, the paper became inextricably involved with political parties, power, and disputes, becoming heavily identified with presidential candidate William Jennings Bryan and the Democratic

Party. Since all the other large newspapers backed William McKinley, the *Journal* rapidly became the leading Democratic newspaper in the country.

Perhaps the ultimate manufactured news event was the one that started the Spanish-American War. From the start, Hearst's paper had strongly supported Cuban independence from Spain. When the American battleship Maine mysteriously blew up in Havana harbor in February 1898, Hearst and his employees printed two weeks' worth of fraudulent material blaming Spain for the attack. This coverage, which Hearst orchestrated but in which he was not alone, resulted in increased circulation for the paper—and in war.

With the dawning of the new century, Hearst's fledgling network of newspapers continued to expand. Attempting to bolster support for Bryan's 1900 presidential bid, Hearst founded the *Chicago American*, whose first issue rolled off the presses on July 4, 1900. Bryan lost once again to McKinley. Hearst's overwhelming identification in the public's mind with opposition to the president became a grave liability after McKinley was assassinated in September 1901. Some groups boycotted and banned Hearst papers. Nevertheless, his New York paper, the *Journal*, claimed the greatest number of paid subscribers in the world by the end of the year. When Hearst was elected to Congress the following year, his papers became his personal forum for conducting political activity. In 1904, the *Boston American* was added to the fold. Two years later, the 1906 San Francisco earthquake dealt a major blow to the flagship of the Hearst organization, reducing the physical plant of the *Examiner* to a ruin. Despite the devastation, the three San Francisco papers produced a joint issue on the first day after the quake and, shortly thereafter, the *Examiner* was back on its feet.

The Hearst organization branched out into magazines in 1903, with the founding of *Motor* magazine, a venture inspired by *The Car*, a British publication Hearst had come across on his honeymoon. Two years later, he bought *Cosmopolitan*, a magazine of fiction and nonfiction. Filled with the work of some of the best writers of the day, its circulation soon doubled. Hearst's most important magazine acquisition was *Good Housekeeping* in 1911. This purchase also included the laboratory facilities that would develop into the Good Housekeeping Institute and the Good Housekeeping Seal, heavily promoted under the new owners.

Hearst papers took a vigorous anti-British and isolationist stance in the era leading up to the United States's entry into World War I, bannering slogans like "America First" and "No Entangling Alliances" in fierce opposition to the policies of President Woodrow Wilson. When the United States declared war in April 1917, Hearst's opposition to the U.S. effort to aid the Allies and perceived pro-German sentiment resulted in lower circulation for his newspapers in many cities. Throughout this era, William Randolph Hearst continued his political activities in pursuit of the presidency, and Hearst papers were instruments in his crusade.

Nevertheless, throughout the second decade of the century, Hearst enterprises grew at a prodigious pace. By 1920, the print operations numbered 13 newspapers and seven magazines, including the profitable *American Weekly* newspaper insert and the British *Nash's*. As offshoots of the newspapers, the organi-

---

Key Dates:

1880: George Hearst acquires the *San Francisco Examiner* in payment for gambling debt.
1887: Son William Randolph Hearst begins running the *Examiner*.
1895: Hearst acquires the *New York Journal*.
1903: The Hearst empire moves into magazine publishing.
1923: Hearst moves into radio with purchase of WISN in Milwaukee.
1951: William Randolph Hearst dies, leaving company to be run by non-family management.
1979: The Hearst Corp. begins to expand its newspaper holdings.
1999: The publicly owned Hearst-Argyle Television formed.
2000: The company buys the *San Francisco Chronicle* and sells the *Examiner*.

---

zation also owned a money-losing newswire, the International News Service, which had emerged from World War I with its credibility badly damaged, and the King Features Syndicate, which sold the work of Hearst writers and artists to other papers.

In addition, Hearst had entered the film industry in 1913, when the first newsreel—footage of Woodrow Wilson's inauguration—was shown in movie theaters. This showing led to the establishment of the Hearst-Selig News Pictorial in 1914, which pioneered film journalism throughout the 1920s, evolving into Hearst Metrotone News with the arrival of sound in 1929. For entertainment, Hearst produced in partnership with Pathé Fréres such long-running serials as *The Perils of Pauline*. Intent both on promoting the career of his mistress, Marion Davies, and becoming a movie mogul himself, William Randolph Hearst formed Cosmopolitan Productions and in 1919 built a studio in Harlem where movies could be filmed. Hearst papers duly praised the resulting products. In time, the studio moved to Hollywood where it joined with other studios, producing musical extravaganzas like *Broadway Melody* and other films.

As William Randolph Hearst continued to seek political office in the 1920s, Hearst operations continued to grow. Papers were acquired or founded at a brisk pace, including three in 1921, six in 1922, one in 1923, and three in 1924. On the international front, Hearst expanded its magazine holdings in Britain to include *Good Housekeeping, Connoisseur,* and *Harper's Bazaar*. By the early 1930s, the tally of Hearst papers was up to 28 and the magazines numbered 13. Along with his other ventures, this necessarily gave Hearst great influence in public affairs. His influence was enhanced by the Hearst company's entry into the fledgling radio industry in 1928 with the purchase of WISN in Milwaukee, Wisconsin. By the mid-1930s, it owned ten radio stations. In 1934, the Hearst organization was restructured to give Hearst editorial control while trusted subordinates handled day-to-day business matters. By the following year Hearst had become implacable in his opposition to the policies of Franklin Delano Roosevelt, whom he had initially helped win the Democratic nomination in 1932. In the 1936 campaign Hearst papers supported Roosevelt's opponent Alf Landon. Throughout the 1930s, Hearst papers were

unstinting in their opposition to socialism and communism. This fact, combined with Hearst's love for Germany, where he traveled often, and his growing conservatism, often led his opponents to charge him with fascism.

Repercussions of the Great Depression

Throughout the years of financial turmoil and decline that began with the stock market crash in 1929, Hearst, who was accustomed to wealth of unimaginable proportions, had not significantly altered his activities. He continued to spend lavishly on art and on the construction and upkeep of his several estates. In addition, the company had used several bond issues to raise capital, resulting in debts that reached $137 million. In 1937, under pressure from the shareholders, as well as various banks and newsprint companies to whom Hearst owed money, the company tried to float another set of debentures, but was prevented from doing so by the Securities and Exchange Commission. The crash had come. Faced with the virtual bankruptcy of his vast empire, Hearst, now nearly 75 years old, turned over complete financial control of his holdings to a lawyer, one approved by his creditors, who quickly began to restructure drastically the Hearst organization. Six money-losing newspapers and seven radio stations were sold, a magazine was scrapped, and Hearst's New York flagship paper, the *New York American,* was merged with its evening counterpart. A Conservation Committee was formed to sell off assets, including two-thirds of Hearst's art collection.

Four years later, in 1941, the Hearst organization was still fighting for fiscal survival. By that time there were 94 Hearst entities with complex financial ties. With the entry of the United States into World War II, Hearst papers (reduced to a total of 18) dropped their isolationist stance and wholeheartedly supported the war effort. It was the war, opposed so staunchly by Hearst editorialists, that helped the company to regain its financial health by increasing circulation and advertising revenues.

At the end of 1943, the trustee and the Conservation Committee appointed in 1937 were succeeded by a voting trust that included two of Hearst's five sons. The trust continued to sell off property, including two-thirds of Hearst's vast San Simeon estate, and to rearrange assets, consolidating everything in 1943 within The Hearst Corporation holding company. By the end of the war in 1945, the company was on more solid financial ground once again. Three years later, the company entered a new field in communications when WBAL-TV in Baltimore, Maryland, began to broadcast.

New Leadership in the Postwar Period

By 1947, William Randolph Hearst, elderly and suffering from heart problems, had little involvement in company operations. On August 14, 1951, Hearst died, ending an era in U.S. journalism. His will stipulated that his $57 million estate be divided for tax purposes into a charitable trust and a restructured corporation. Hearst left the 100 shares of voting stock that controlled the company in the hands of a board made up of five family members and six company executives, insuring that those outside the family would have control of the corporation. One of the executives, Richard Berlin, took over as chief executive officer at Hearst's death, after 32 years with the company.

During Berlin's tenure, the company saw the collapse of its first base of operations, its newspapers, and expanded its holdings in other fields of the communications industry, such as magazines and television. The advent of television ended newspaper journalism as William Randolph Hearst had known it. No longer did the papers provide the public's primary source of news. This change in social habits resulted in a vast shake-out in the newspaper industry, in which afternoon papers in particular were hard hit, the Hearst publications included. The first paper to go was the *Chicago American*, a long-time money-loser, which was sold to its competitor, the *Tribune*, in 1956. Two years later, the Hearst newswire, International News Service, and its affiliated photo service were sold to rival United Press. Under Berlin's direction the company shed papers in San Francisco, Pittsburgh, Detroit, Boston, Los Angeles, and Milwaukee in quick succession. In 1963, Hearst sold its money-losing morning tabloid the *New York Mirror*, which had the second largest circulation in the United States. The cruelest blow came in 1966, when Hearst's flagship *Journal-American* folded in New York.

In contrast, Hearst expanded its magazine operations throughout this period, concentrating on special interest publications rather than broad, general interest titles. In 1953, the company purchased *Sports Afield* and five years later added another men's magazine, *Popular Mechanics*. Shortly thereafter, a Spanish edition of the magazine was granted the first license for a Hearst magazine foreign edition. Eventually, the company would successfully license over 100 foreign editions of its publications. In 1959, the company branched out into book publishing when it purchased Avon Publications, Inc., which produced paperbacks. In addition to new acquisitions, old publications underwent renovations, enabling them to contribute strong performances to the magazine group. *Cosmopolitan*, for instance, retooled in 1965 from a general interest magazine of fiction and nonfiction to the interests of working women and became a huge money-maker. In 1966, another venerable Hearst magazine, *Good Housekeeping*, became the leader in its field.

At his retirement in 1973, Berlin left Hearst debt-free and rich in capital, yet far poorer in publications and importance than it had once been. The following year the company was again restructured when it used the cash built up during Berlin's tenure to buy back the stock held by Hearst charitable foundations, which had been established at Hearst's death to avoid inheritance taxes. The Hearst family regained control of the company's assets, now privately owned, and the chain of command within the company was simplified. Throughout the second half of the 1970s, under the leadership of John R. Miller, Hearst experienced a huge growth in profits, as properties that had been allowed to lie dormant began to produce. For instance, the company tapped the reserve of goodwill built up in the names *House Beautiful* and *Good Housekeeping* when it successfully spun off *Colonial Homes* and *Country Living* from the older publications.

New Ventures in the 1980s and Early 1990s

In 1979, Hearst again began to expand its newspaper holdings by buying five daily papers in mid-sized cities in Michigan, Texas, and Illinois. In the early 1980s, acquisitions continued until the newspaper group was 15 strong, with publications in

Houston, Seattle, Los Angeles, and San Francisco, as well as other, smaller cities.

By the start of the 1980s, the Hearst magazine division was the largest U.S. producer of monthly magazines. It continued to perform well throughout the 1980s, adding *Redbook*, *Esquire*, a U.S. version of the British *Connoisseur*, and other titles. The Hearst magazine distribution network, which already included three subscriber services, purchased a fourth, Communications Data Services, Inc., in 1982.

During the 1980s the company's scope shifted beyond print to encompass the whole spectrum of communications enterprises. Television and radio stations were acquired, and partnerships were formed to create the Arts & Entertainment Network (A&E) and LIFETIME, a network devoted to programming for women. In late 1990 the company bought a 20 percent interest in the sports network ESPN.

In 1995, A&E launched The History Channel, devoted to historical programming and viewed by more than 37 million households in the United States. Also that year, Hearst partnered New Century Network, a national network of local online newspaper services, with eight other newspaper publishers; the company ceased, however, its CD-Rom operations that were part of Hearst New Media & Technology. In 1997, A&E teamed up with Groupe AB of France to launch La Chaine Histoire, to offer French viewers French and international history programming drawn from the History Channel International's program catalogue.

New Deals in the Late 1990s and After

The Hearst Corporation's forays into new media continued in the late 1990s. A major deal was the merger of Hearst's six television stations with Argyle Television in 1999. Argyle was a young company headed by Robert Marbut, whose career spanned the newspaper, broadcast, and direct mail industries. The combined company became a publicly traded entity, Hearst-Argyle Television Inc. The new company owned a total of 15 television stations and had assets of around $1.8 billion. The deal was spearheaded by Hearst CEO Frank Bennack, Jr., against the wishes of some of the Hearst heirs. William Randolph Hearst II filed a lawsuit protesting the plan, but the deal was completed anyway. Hearst Corp. owned 86 percent of the new company, which soon grew to blockbuster proportions. By 2002, it owned 26 television stations, claiming 17.5 percent of U.S. households as viewers. The Hearst Corp. also invested in a variety of on-line media in the late 1990s. Its business publishing division bought up a web-based electronics industry inventory database called Stocknet in 1999. The company was also part of a media consortium that bought an Internet-based classified ad distributor that year called AdOne. The company reorganized its New Media & Technology division in 1999, renaming it Hearst Interactive Media. The division collaborated with other investors and the toy company Mattel to form a new Internet company Genealogy.com. The company made many other stabs into computer-based media, many in joint ventures with other companies.

In print media, the Hearst Corporation also made major changes in the late 1990s. One of its big successes was the magazine division's launch of *O, The Oprah Magazine* in April 2000. The glossy monthly was a joint venture with television talk show hostess Oprah Winfrey. By its sixth issue, *O* had garnered 900,000 readers and was pulling in hundreds of pages of advertising. The magazine division accounted for an estimated $1.5 billion of Hearst's revenues for 1999, with $1.4 billion coming from newspapers, $900 million from its various cable holdings, and $500 million from its publicly held subsidiary Hearst-Argyle. Overall, revenue climbed 16 percent in the last two years of the 1990s, according to estimates made by *Forbes* magazine (December 25, 2000). In its march toward ever higher profitability, Hearst Corp. decided to fold William Randolph Hearst's first paper, the *San Francisco Examiner*, in 2000, and bought the city's rival paper, the *Chronicle*. Hearst Corp. paid $660 million for the *Chronicle*, a morning paper which was a stronger seller. The deal was complex. The two papers had had a joint operating agreement since 1965, but the weak performance of the afternoon *Examiner* led Hearst to announce it would shut the paper down. But when Hearst purchased the *Chronicle*, it was soon slapped with an antitrust suit alleging the single paper would form a monopoly. Though the suit was eventually dismissed, Hearst ended up selling the *Examiner* to a rival San Francisco publisher, Ted Fang. Hearst then gave Fang's company a $66 million subsidy to help get the newspaper going. Hearst hired most of the *Examiner*'s staff for the *Chronicle*, and both papers put out their first editions under new management on the same day in November 2000.

Hearst CEO Bennack retired in December 2001, after leading the company for 23 years. He was credited with having grown the company into a modern media complex, while increasing revenue sevenfold and plumping profits to thirteen times what they had been when he started. He was succeeded by Victor F. Ganzi, formerly chief operating officer, who had been with Hearst since 1970. At the time of the transition, the company seemed to be in good shape, with a sound portfolio of media properties. The Hearst Corporation had evolved from a newspaper chain known for sensationalism and irresponsible journalism, and dominated by the will of one man, to a vast and highly profitable enterprise encompassing a broad range of communications fields.

Principal Subsidiaries

Hearst-Argyle Television, Inc.; iVillage Inc. (25%); King Features Syndicates, Inc.; A&E Television Networks (37.5%); ESPN, Inc. (20%)

Principal Operating Units

Hearst Magazines; Hearst Newspapers; Hearst Entertainment & Syndication; Hearst Business Media; Hearst Interactive Media; Hearst Broadcasting.

Principal Competitors

Gannett Co., Inc.; Knight Ridder Inc.; Condé Nast Publications Inc.; Viacom Inc.

Further Reading

Adams, Mark, "Black Magic for Hearst?" *Mediaweek*, December 4, 1995, p. 5.

Chaney, Lindsay, and Michael Cieply, *The Hearsts: Family and Empire—The Later Years*, New York: Simon & Schuster, 1981.

Davis, Joel, "Here Comes Everybody," *Editor & Publisher*, April 10, 2000, p. 4.

——, "Keeping Fang at Bay," *Editor & Publisher*, November 13, 2000, pp. 26–32.

Freeman, Michael, "Hearst Gets Stations, CEO," *Mediaweek*, March 31, 1997, p. 8.

Lacter, Mark, "The Case of the Ungrateful Heir," *Forbes*, December 25, 2000, pp. 137–39.

Lundberg, Ferdinand, *Imperial Hearst: A Social Biography*, New York: Equinox Cooperative Press, 1936.

Mitchell, Greg, "Hearst Corp.'s New Chief to Take Office Next June," *Editor & Publisher*, December 10, 2001, pp. 5–6.

O'Donnell, James F., *100 Years of Making Communications History: The Story of the Hearst Corporation*, New York: Hearst Professional Magazines, Inc., 1987.

Swanberg, W.A., *Citizen Hearst: A Biography of William Randolph Hearst*, New York: Charles Scribner's Sons, 1961.

—Elizabeth Rourke
—updates: Dorothy Kroll and A. Woodward

Hops Restaurant Bar and Brewery

2701 North Rocky Point Drive, Suite 300
Tampa, Florida 33607
U.S.A.
Telephone: (813) 282-9350
Fax: (813) 282-9307
Web site: http://www.hopsonline.com

Wholly Owned Subsidiary of Avado Brands, Inc.
Incorporated: 1989
Employees: 7,290
Sales: $186.5 million (2000)
NAIC: 722110 Full-Service Restaurants; 312120
    Breweries

Hops Restaurant Bar and Brewery is the largest chain of brewpubs in the United States, with over 70 units in 16 states. As a microbrewery and a casual dining restaurant, Hops complements the meals its serves with handcrafted beers, including seasonal beer, brewed on-site with original recipes. The company emphasizes food quality, using fresh ingredients and made-from-scratch recipes. Hops' menu offers steaks, hamburgers, chicken, ribs, pasta, seafood, salads, and desserts. Signature dishes include Walker's Wood Shrimp, with Hops' proprietary sauce; Jamaican Top Sirloin, marinated for 72 hours in a sauce made with pineapple, soy, and ginger; and, for dessert, fresh Key Lime Pie.

New Restaurant Concept: 1988

David Mason and Tom Schelldorf moved from Kentucky to Florida in 1988 to open the first Hops Grill and Bar. They traveled to Tampa with many years of experience in restaurant chain operations and with the intention of developing Hops into a chain of brewpubs. Both had held management positions at Houston's Restaurant and at the Steak & Ale chains. Also, Schelldorf was involved in development of the Rafferty's Restaurant & Bar concept and chain in Kentucky. Mason and Schelldorf sold their interests in four Rafferty's units and 18 Wendy's franchises in Tennessee and Kentucky to fund the start-up of Hops.

In formulating the Hops brewpub concept, Mason and Schelldorf were inspired by George Biel, founder of Houston's Restaurant, and Norman Brinker, founder of Steak & Ale, Bennigan's Grill & Tavern, and Chili's Grill & Bar. These restaurant chain concepts involved limited menu options, meals made from scratch, and excellent service in a casual yet ambient setting. Mason and Schelldorf combined the popular casual dining concept with another new concept, the restaurant with an on-site microbrewery. While most brewpubs emphasized the handcrafted beer over the food, the Hops founders planned to serve high-quality food as well. The company used fresh ingredients, rather than from frozen or canned foods, and original, made-from-scratch recipes for everything, including soups, sauces, and salad dressings. Hops served hand-patted hamburgers prepared with freshly ground chuck beef and pork ribs smoked on the premises.

Mason and Schelldorf chose the Tampa area in which to start the Hops restaurant and microbrewery, seeing that the diversity of the population provided a good test market for the concept. The first Hops opened in a small shopping center in Clearwater in November 1989. Located in a 5,000 square-foot building, the brewpub sat up to 165 customers, mostly in booths, in a rustic yet ambient atmosphere with wood walls, soft lighting, and carpet in the dining room to minimize background noise. Open for lunch and dinner, meal prices ranged from $6.00 to $12.00 and a frosted mug of handcrafted beer cost $2.25.

Hops produced four kinds of beer from original recipes using imported Czechoslovakian hops: Clearwater Light, a low calorie beer; Alligator Ale, a full-bodied, mahogany ale; Hammerhead Red, a malt amber ale; and Lightning Bold Gold, lager style beer. The microbrewery produced 750 to 800 barrels of beer each year, over 100,000 glasses per month. Hops offered customers a tour of the brewing process led by brewmaster Tom Netolicky or a store manager. The low cost of producing beer in-house, as compared to purchasing beer from a distributor, allowed Hops to provide good value on their meals and provided financial stability against the variable cost of food products. While food sales at brewpubs usually account for 40 to 50 percent of total sales, Hops meal items accounted for about 85 percent of total sales. At Hops the beer acted as a complement to the meal, rather than as the main attraction.

Company Perspectives:

We are a casual dining microbrewery restaurant that offers high quality menu items in a relaxed atmosphere featuring signature dishes that are created from fresh ingredients and prepared in a display style kitchen that allows you to view the cooking process. We complement the made-from-scratch food by offering hand-crafted, microbrewed beer, brewed in a glass encased brewery that separates the non-smoking dining room from the bar dining area.

With the success of the first Hops Grill and Bar, Mason and Schelldorf opened new locations in the Tampa area, following a strategy of slow, profitable growth. Hops opened units in North Tampa, South Tampa, and Palm Harbor, each with its own brewmaster. A fifth unit opened in Bradenton in summer 1993. That year Hops recorded $12 million in sales and $670,000 in profits. Locations opened at least one year recorded average sales of approximately $2.75 million, with check averages at $10 per person.

The structure of the Hops' restaurants evolved with new development, channeling customers past the display kitchen as they were escorted to their tables. Hops slowly enlarged the size of each unit for added seating capacity. Each unit required approximately $1 million to develop, including $160,000 for brewing equipment. One of the tricks to opening a Hops brewpub involved beginning the brewing process one month before the scheduled opening; brewing began during the final stages of interior construction, even before hiring the staff.

In preparation for continued expansion, Hops hired John Schwaizen as vice-president of brewing operations. Schwaizen was a third generation brewmaster recently retired from the Anheuser-Busch brewing company, while most of the store-level brewmasters started making beer at home as a hobby. Hops' brewmasters met weekly to taste each other's beer as a test for consistency of taste and quality.

Hops' management planned to expand the chain both inside and outside the state of Florida. They controlled the process of expansion by company ownership of the brewpubs, rather than by selling franchises. The company formed a joint venture with another Steak & Ale veteran Camp Fitch to develop four Hops brewpubs in Jacksonville, Florida. Another partner planned to open units in Kentucky, Tennessee, and Alabama. Development outside of Florida depended on the state-by-state repeal of laws that prevented the operation of microbreweries. In 1994, Hops opened three more restaurants in Florida (one each in Lakeland, Jacksonville, and Ft. Lauderdale) and one in Bowling Green, Kentucky. Hops entered the south Florida market with a store opening in Coral Springs in October 1995 and in Boynton Beach in early 1996. Hops opened in Denver, one of the country's largest brewpub markets, in March 1996; another opened in North Carolina. By the end of 1996, Hops counted 18 brewpubs in four states. In 1997, *Nation's Restaurant News* named Hops as one of the ''Hot Concepts.''

In addition to the product they sold, Mason and Schelldorf attributed the success of Hops to a number of factors, including its treatment of employees, the restaurant's public image, and maintaining customer approval. Creating a fun work atmosphere and involving employees in decision-making led to a high rate of employee retention. Hops also offered sales incentives to servers and issued ''Smart Cards'' to both front of house and back of house employees to recognize good job performance; they used the cards for prize drawings, occasionally giving away a television or stereo. While Hops advertised in radio and print, Mason and Schelldorf preferred direct interaction with the public through sponsorship of charity golf events and ''Taste of . . .'' festivals. Word-of-mouth ultimately provided the best advertising. Perhaps most important to its success, Hops maintained repeat customer business with a changing menu, which evolved with customer tastes.

1997 Merger With Apple South

For two years Mason and Schelldorf sought to take Hops public, to raise funds for expansion, and to pay down its debt, but the market was not receptive. The reasons for this situation were various. It may have been due to the slow pace of growth at Hops; fluctuating profits, with only $1,000 net income on $24.3 million in sales in 1995; or simply saturation during a bull market. Nevertheless, Hops found capital funds and debt relief through a merger with Apple South, the largest franchisee of Applebee's Neighborhood Grill & Bar, its main territory being in the southeastern United States. Other chain restaurants owned by Apple South included Don Pablo's Mexican Kitchen, McCormick & Schmick's upscale seafood restaurants, and Canyon Café, serving southwestern cuisine. Apple South acquired Hops in March 1997 for $31.5 million, involving $15.7 million in cash and $15.8 million in stock, plus $25 million in assumed debt. In June, Mason became chairman and retained his position as CEO, while Schelldorf became president and COO, overseeing brand and divisional development. Shortly afterward Mason left the company.

Expansion of the Hops chain accelerated under new ownership. In summer and fall 1997, four new units opened in South Florida, near shopping malls in Plantation, South Dade, Pembroke Pines, and Pompano Beach. Hops surpassed Colorado-based Rock Bottom Brewery as the largest chain of brewpubs in the United States. New development followed in North and South Carolina, Tennessee, and Georgia.

In February 1998, Hops changed its name from Hops Grill and Bar to Hops Restaurant Bar and Brewery. The change followed from a dispute between Tom E. DuPree, Jr., Apple South founder and CEO, and the Applebee's franchisor. The franchisor contended that Apple South had violated development agreements in Hops similarities with Applebee's, including menu and operations as well as the words ''grill'' and ''bar'' in the name. In addition to changing the Hops name, DuPree decided to sell the Applebee's chain and focus on the company's other chains, particularly the Hops brand. Apple South then became Avado Brands.

Hops launched a new advertising campaign to cultivate recognition of its brand name and image as a brewpub chain. Radio and print ads emphasized the friendly service, the microbrewery, and fresh food preparation. A radio spot conveyed the difference in food quality by playing the sounds of frozen

Key Dates:

1989: The first Hops Grill and Bar opens in Clearwater, Florida.

1994: Hops opens its first unit outside the state of Florida.

1997: Hops merges with Apple South, a conglomerate of restaurant chains.

1998: The company's sales surpass $100 million.

1999: The 50th Hops brewpub opens in Newington, Connecticut.

2000: Avado Brands hires Ronald Macgruder as CEO of Hops.

food preparation—the thump of the frozen food item hitting the countertop and the beeps of a microwave oven being programmed—as compared to the sound of a sizzling steak which played in the background as the narrator spoke about Hops. Billboard advertising featured the Hops logo and the phrase, "America's Original Microbrewery." The menu, table-top displays, and stationary were redesigned for a consistent presentation of the Hops brand.

In 1998, Hops surpassed the $100 million sales mark, ending the year with $106.3 million in revenues, compared to $49.5 million in 1997. With per person check averages at $15.00, some restaurant sales grew five percent and averaged $3 million per unit, and profit margins hovered at 16 percent. New unit development extended Hops' reach in Florida, Colorado, Minnesota, Tennessee, and North and South Carolina. In March 1999, the 50th Hops restaurant opened, in Newington, Connecticut, which was also the first in that state. New units tended to be larger than the original Hops. For instance, a Hops in Polaris, Ohio, near Cincinnati, sat nearly 300 people in a 6,800-square-foot building. As such, development costs increased to approximately $1.4 million per unit.

While the number of units grew dramatically in 1999, with 24 new units, financial difficulties at Avado slowed new development in 2000, with only ten new units opened and the closure of two units, one in Kentucky and the other in Indiana. Hops ended 2000 with a total of 73 units in 16 states. New markets included Virginia and Rhode Island, with two units in each state, and Maryland, Indiana, Missouri, Louisiana, and Mississippi, with one unit in each state. Additional units opened in Florida, Georgia, Ohio, and Colorado. Revenues reached $186.5 million in 2000.

Changes for the New Century

While Hops prospered and expanded on the surface, behind the scenes, at Avado Brands, changes were taking place. Avado had overextended itself with debt from acquisitions and new unit development at all its subsidiaries. The situation prompted executive management at Hops, initiated by Schelldorf, to propose a buy-out. A breakdown in negotiations led to the departure of Schelldorf and other executives in April 2000.

Avado hired a new CEO in August, Ronald Macgruder. Macgruder's credentials included building the Cracker Barrel Country Store and Olive Garden chains into nationally recog-

nized restaurant brands. In particular, he oversaw Olive Garden's growth from four to 350 units. Macgruder saw in the Hops concept the same potential for national expansion. He projected the chain to grow to 500 units through expansion in existing markets, with four to five new units in each market, maximizing the cost-benefit ratio of regional advertising programs.

Hops continued to build on its success in 2000. In fall of that year, Hops introduced its first seasonal beer and its first new beer since the company began. Schwaizen, with local brewmasters, created Hoptoberfest Seasonal Brew, a medium-bodied, red-gold beer with a "mild hoppy finish." Other seasonal brews followed: Winter brews included Flying Squirrel Nut Brown Ale, produced in the warmer climate of the southern states, and the heavier Lumberjack Oatmeal Stout, for the colder climates of New England and the northern states. In 2001, Hops introduced Springtime Honey Bock, a traditional German beer produced with Pilsen and Munich malts and clover honey, evoking a mellow taste and aroma of honey. Beat the Heat Summer Wheat was the first beer Hops served unfiltered, adding a slice of citrus for summer freshness. Additions to the menu in 2001 included Seared Sea Scallops with lemon butter sauce and Banana Rum Croissant Pudding, prepared with Hops' fresh-baked croissants.

As Avado continued to repair its financial situation, new unit development slowed dramatically, with only one unit opened, in Eden Prairie, Minnesota. To pay down debt, Avado arranged for the sale and leaseback of 20 Hops properties, obtaining proceeds of $28.4 million and applying $20 million to Avado debt. A slowing economy also led to a decline in sales. In this more competitive environment, Hops initiated its first television commercials, beginning in regional areas, such as Tampa, where a concentration of Hops brewpubs existed. The ads highlighted Hops' dedicated staff, using actors to play Hops employees. In one spot a prep chef says, "I run this place. They'd be grilling air without me." In early 2002, Hops promoted new products via radio, print, and regional and cable television advertising. Hops introduced the Spicy Caribbean Trio, with three skewers of Walker's Wood Shrimp, jerk chicken, and spicy sirloin steak.

Principal Competitors

Brinker International, Inc.; Darden Restaurants, Inc.; Metromedia Company; Rock Bottom Restaurants, Inc.

Further Reading

"Apple South Completes Merger with Microbrewery," *Nation's Restaurant News*, March 31, 1997, p. 14.

Backman, Lisa, "Hops to Sell Stock," *Tampa Tribune*, October 16, 1996.

Burney, Teresa, "At Hops, They Serve No Beer Before Its Time," *St. Petersburg Times*, January 23, 1995, p. 5.

Clancy, Carole, "Hops at Center of Apple South Franchise Dispute," *Tampa Bay Business Journal*, July 18, 1997, p. 1.

Gibson, Linda, "Microbrew/Restaurant Expanding in State," *Denver Post*, October 1, 1996, p. C4.

Hayes, Jack, "Hops and Harper's Heat Up Casual Dining in Southeast," *Nation's Restaurant News*, May 17, 1993, p. 39.

——, "New Growth-Charged CEO Macgruder to Plot Hops Rollout," *Nation's Restaurant News*, August 21, 2000, p. 1.

"Hops Restaurant Bar & Brewery Opens 50th Restaurant," *PR Newswire*, March 8, 1999.

"Hops Restaurant Bar & Brewery Taps New Items For January," *PR Newswire*, January 7, 2002.

Howard, Theresa, "Hops: Brewing a Combination of Fun and Food," *Nation's Restaurant News,* May 12, 1997, p. 120.

Kane, Cheryl Heimlich, "Brew Pub Chain Hops to It; Hops Grill & Br Opening 5 New Locations in 5 Months," *South Florida Business Journal*, June 20, 1997, p. 1A.

——, "New Brew for S. Florida: Brewpub Plans up to 15 Locations," *South Florida Business Journal*, December 29, 1995, p. 1A.

Newfpoff, Laura, "Hops Considers Jumping into Local Brewpub Market," *Business Courier Serving Cincinnati—Northern Kentucky*, July 23, 1999, p. 7.

Poole, Sheila M., "A case of Heartburn at Avado; Hungry Restaurant Operator Continues to Struggle with Debt," *Atlanta Constitution and Journal,* July 5, 2001, p. 1E.

Reinan, John, "Tampa, Fla.-Based Hops Restaurant Chain to Launch Television Ad Campaign," *The Tampa Tribune,* March 18, 1999.

Simanoff, Dave, "Hops Brewpub Chain Launches First Image Advertising Campaign," *Tampa Bay Business Journal*, January 16, 1998, p. 3.

—Mary Tradii

Hydril Company

3300 North Sam Houston Parkway East
Houston, Texas 707032-3411
U.S.A.
Telephone: (281) 449-2000
Fax: (281) 985-3376
Web site: http://www.hydril.com

Public Company
Incorporated: 1933
Employees: 1,400
Sales: $239.6 million (2001)
Stock Exchanges: NASDAQ
Ticker Symbol: HYDL
NAIC: 333132 Oil and Gas Field Machinery and
    Equipment Manufacturing

Based in Houston, Texas, Hydril Company designs, manufactures, and markets products used in petroleum drilling and production. The company built its reputation in the 1930s when it produced the first hydraulically operated blowout preventer. Since that time, the company has continued to focus on blowout preventers and piping connections that undergo tremendous levels of pressure. Not only do these products save money for oil producers, they protect the environment from unnecessary oil and gas spills, both on land and in the ocean. In recent years, most of Hydril sales are related to offshore drilling and derived from outside of the United States. Among the company's other products are high torque tool joints, diverters, pressure control systems, drill stem valves and actuators, sub-sea drilling systems, high performance chokes, and custom rubber products for the oil industry. Hydril is a worldwide operation with 13 manufacturing plants and 22 sales and service offices located around the globe. Major production facilities are located in the United States as well as Canada, Mexico, Scotland, Nigeria, and Singapore. Although publicly traded, Hydril is controlled by the heirs of its founder, Frank Roger Seaver, and includes a charitable foundation in his name. His brother is the chairman of the board and his nephew the current president and chief executive officer.

The Early Career of Frank Seaver

The foundation of Hydril is very much the story of Frank Seaver, a man of varied interests who in addition to becoming a respected businessman was well known in Republican Party circles and earned a reputation as a great philanthropist, becoming a major benefactor of Pepperdine University. Born in the 1800s, the son of a banker in Pomona, California, Seaver came of age in the twentieth century, graduating from high school in 1901. He earned an undergraduate degree from Pomona College, then read law for a year in preparation for taking the bar examination, which he passed in 1906. Although he was now able to practice law, according to the custom of the day, he elected to spend a year at Harvard Law School in post-graduate study. He then moved to Los Angeles and opened his own law office. His brother Bryan soon joined him and they practiced together for nine years before World War I intervened and Seaver, a member of the National Guard since his college days, was called into military service.

During the final months of the war, Seaver served as a deck officer on a U.S. Navy cruiser, used primarily as an escort vessel for ships transporting troops and supplies to England. When hostilities ceased, he was transferred to New York City and assigned the task of disposing some 300 Navy transports. It was in New York that his wife, Blanche, made the acquaintance of industrialist and oil magnate Edward L. Doheny and his wife. The two couples began to socialize and Doheny grew so impressed by Seaver that he offered him a job. Rather than rebuild his law practice, and eager for a new challenge, Seaver agreed and began his involvement in the oil business.

After successfully completing a number of assignments, Seaver was named General Counsel and Managing General Agent for Doheny's Mexican operations. It was in Mexico that Doheny launched his often controversial business career. While Seaver lived and worked in Mexico from 1921 to 1927, Doheny was caught up in the Teapot Dome scandal, in which he was accused of making a $100,000 bribe to Secretary of the Interior Albert B. Fall. Fall was forced to resign and both men endured years of legal tribulations. Ultimately, in 1930, Doheny was acquitted of giving the bribe, although Falls was convicted of receiving it. Having lost his only son, killed by a servant in

1929, Doheny was already a broken man by the time he was free of Teapot Dome. He fell ill and was bedridden for three years before finally dying in 1935.

When he sensed that the political climate had turned against foreign investors, Seaver returned to the United States in 1927 after selling off Doheny's Mexican interests. Back in Los Angeles, he helped Doheny organize a new company, the Pacific Petroleum Products Company, which was to market gasoline through service stations it built in the San Francisco area. Doheny soon sold the business, and Seaver began to seriously consider striking out on his own. He targeted the Doheny Stone Drill Company, a subsidiary of Doheny's Petroleum Securities Company. Doheny agreed to lease some of the buildings and equipment of the business for a ten-year term.

Hydril Company Formed in 1933

Doheny Stone Drill Company, named for its founder Fred Stone, was located in Torrance, California, and struggling for survival. The number of its employees ranged from 50 to 75, depending upon sporadic demand for its heavy oil drilling machinery, threads for oil piping, and blowout preventers. Seaver decided to drop the drilling equipment in order to focus on the specialty items, but soon had to contend with the onset of the Depression. With his life savings at risk, he had no choice but to succeed in the venture. His employees, thankful to have jobs during uncertain times, were committed to helping him. Within two years they turned the company into a profitable concern. In 1933, Seaver was able to become the proprietor of the business, which he now named Hydril Company, derived from ''hydraulic drilling equipment.''

Seaver was very much a benevolent dictator who demanded a great deal from his employees while also keeping information as compartmentalized as possible. Employees knew what was important to their function, and little more than that. In this way, Seaver was able to cut out organizational clutter and operate efficiently, personally setting all policies and making all major decisions. Any matters he delegated were strictly scrutinized. He believed in simplicity and quality, as evidenced by his decision to focus on specialty products. When Hydril's blowout preventers proved to be so durable that it was costing the company replacement sales, Seaver was flexible enough to change the company's marketing efforts. Instead of selling preventers, Hydril now began to lease them.

Early on, Seaver recognized the need to have a presence in the Texas oil fields. He bought far more land in Houston than was necessary for a manufacturing plant, which some considered a waste of money. Decades later, however, it would be deemed an act of genius. All of the space was utilized by Hydril, and the company would have liked to acquire more land if only the real estate values had not grown so high. In 1937, Seaver bought a manufacturing plant in Rochester, Pennsylvania. When it opened, the large facility housed just a single machine, but Seaver anticipated that the company would soon have need for the extra space. Two years later, he was about to open a New York office when Hitler's invasion of Poland prompted him to postpone his plans. With the onset of World War II, this decision proved to be wise, since steel rationing curtailed the company's ability to manufacture oil field equipment. Now the extra capacity of the Rochester plant was put to good use, as Hydril began to manufacture war materials. In 1940, Seaver organized Hydril Company of Texas, which produced military ordnance during the war under the name of Texord Manufacturing Company.

Hydril did not profit excessively from World War II. Seaver did not care to serve as a government contractor and did not build up the business by taking advantage of available sweetheart deals for equipment and land. Moreover, Seaver was a hard-line Republican who considered the 1932 election of Franklin Roosevelt to the presidency an unmitigated catastrophe. War did not soften that belief, but Seaver remained a patriot and played his part in helping to win the conflict. As soon as hostilities ceased and steel rationing and oil drilling limitations lifted, however, he returned Hydril to its former line of business, which thrived without the benefit of government contracts.

As Seaver neared 70 years of age with no children, he settled on his brother's son, Richard C. Seaver, as the man to one day take over Hydril. Even with this endeavor, he dispensed knowledge on a need-to-know basis. For years he groomed Richard as his heir apparent without bothering to tell his nephew. Richard graduated from the Law School of the University of California in 1950 and was immediately elected secretary and a director of Hyrdil. Rather than go to work for the company, however, he accepted a position with a San Francisco law firm, heading up its Los Angeles office. His uncle subsequently hired the firm to represent Hyrdil, and Richard served as corporate counsel, which allowed Frank Seaver to familiarize him with Hydril's business. After three years of this arrangement, Frank suggested that since Richard was already doing so much work for the company he might as well become a Hydril employee. Richard declined, but over the course of the next four years his uncle slowly reeled him in, occasionally dropping a suggestion that he join the company. It was not until 1957 that Richard seriously considered accepting the offer. Realizing that if anyone other than his uncle had presented him with such an opportunity he would have readily accepted, he overcame his reluctance and finally took a job with Hydril. Still, his uncle did not reveal his intention of ultimately making Richard the president of the company, although he now familiarized him with all aspects of the business, including numerous discussions with a number of suitors interested in buying the company. Far from being possessive about Hydril, Richard claimed that about once a month he wrote his resignation from the company, none of which he actually submitted to his uncle.

Frank Seaver Dies in 1964

A month after Frank Seaver died in 1964, the board of directors of Hydril elected 42-year-old Richard Seaver to serve as the company's second president. By this point Richard was

Key Dates:

1933: Frank Seaver founds the company.
1957: Seaver's nephew, Richard Seaver, joins company.
1964: Frank Seaver dies, Richard Seaver named president.
1986: Richard Seaver relinquishes presidency but remains as chairman of the board.
1993: Richard Seaver's son, Christopher Seaver, assumes presidency.
2000: Hydril goes public.

dedicated to continuing his uncle's legacy at Hydril. He never moved into Frank Seaver's large office, preferring instead to keep it essentially the way his uncle left it, employing it only for periodic board meetings. The business continued to grow over the next 20 years, due in large part to the structure its founder put in place. Hydril also continued to devote significant resources to research and development to maintain its edge in its specialized products, although the market shifted from land drilling to deep-water operations, which placed even greater demand on blowout preventers and secure tubing. In a similar way, the source of Hydril's revenues shifted from the United States to overseas, with domestic business soon accounting for just 35 percent of revenues. Other products were also introduced to provide some diversity during the various cycles of the boom-or-bust oil industry. Moreover, the corporate offices were eventually moved to the Houston facilities. In 1986, Richard Seaver stepped down as chief executive, although he stayed on as chairman of the board, and John B. Griffiths took over as president.

The 1980s were a difficult period for the oil industry and companies like Hydril that served it. Because of the company's sound foundation and Frank Seaver's belief in not taking on debt, Hydril, unlike many other oil-field equipment companies, was able to survive two significant drilling slumps caused by the collapse of oil prices. Griffiths took over during one of these lean periods, during which the price of oil plummeted from nearly $30 a barrel to under $10. Revenues for the company that totaled $170 million in 1985 fell to $110 million over the following three years. He was forced to cut Hydril's payroll from 2,100 to less than 1,000. Some facilities were also shuttered and outside contractors hired to take over the work. These cost-cutting measures allowed Hydril to quickly regain profitability, while at the same time Griffiths invested heavily in computer-aided design systems. Although a large initial outlay, the investment paid off handsomely. Not only were engineers far more productive, they were now able to spot problems in a product before prototypes were even built. The CAD systems were also important in the development of products to serve such new techniques as horizontal drilling, which permitted a wide range of access to petroleum deposits from an extremely small footprint.

After six years Griffiths resigned, replaced as president and chief executive officer by Lynn L. Leigh. His tenure, however, would be brief. Less than two years later, in August 1993, Christopher T. Seaver, son of Richard Seaver and nephew of Frank Seaver, succeeded Leigh. He was well versed in Hydril's operations, having worked at the company for eight years. Like his father and uncle, he first pursued a legal career, serving as a corporate and securities lawyer before joining Hydril. By 1991, he was named executive vice-president and was primarily responsible for the company's tubular products. In July 1993, he was promoted to chief operating officer of Hydril, but when Leigh quit the company a few weeks later, he assumed the presidency.

With a third-generation Seaver running Hydril, and his father still serving as chairman of the board, the company had to operate in volatile conditions during the rest of the 1990s, with price swings in oil and gas having a dramatic impact on the need for the company's products. When prices were high, customers pressed Hydril to add capacity, but by the time a new manufacturing plant would come on line, the company could not be certain that conditions would permit the same level of demand. When oil prices hit their highest levels in a decade in 2000, Chris Seaver took advantage of the favorable conditions to take Hydril public, although family interests would continue to own a majority of the stock. With the money raised in the offering the company was now able to invest in capital spending, boosting capacity at a number of its facilities. In 2001, Hydril posted net profits of $25.6 million on revenues of $239.6 million. Despite the cyclical nature of drilling, the company proved to be consistently profitable. Under management of the Seaver family, Hydril harbored no grand plans for expansion, content to stay out of debt, exploit its niche operations, and maintain its reputation as a well respected, well run company that produced quality products.

Principal Business Segments

Premium Connection Segment; Pressure Control Segment.

Principal Competitors

Varco International Inc.; Grant Prideco Inc.; Lone Star Technologies Inc.; Peerless Manufacturing Co.

Further Reading

Calkins, Laurel Brubaker, "Oil Field Veteran Finds a New Home as President of Hydril," *Houston Business Journal,* January 13, 1992, p 4.

Durgin, Hillary, "Buddy, Can You Spare a Rig?," *Houston Chronicle,* May 18, 1997, p. E1.

Shook, Barbara, "Hydril Key to Survival: Fill A Need," *Houston Chronicle,* May 21, 1989, p. 1.

Smith, Aaron, "High Prices Help Two Oil Co's to Market," *IPO Reporter,* September 25, 2000.

Youngs, Bill, *The Legacy of Frank Roger Seaver,* Malibu, Calif.: Pepperdine University Press, 1976.

—Ed Dinger

Indian Airlines Ltd.

Airlines House
113 Gurudwara Rakabganj Road
New Delhi 110 001
India
Telephone: +91 (11) 371895
Fax: +91 (11) 371 0096
Web site: http://indian-airlines.nic.in/

State-Owned Company
Incorporated: 1953 as Indian Airlines Corporation
Employees: 22,500
Sales: Rs 3,755 crore ($1 billion) (2001)
NAIC: 481111 Scheduled Passenger Air Transportation;
481112 Scheduled Freight Air Transportation; 481211
Nonscheduled Chartered Passenger Air
Transportation; 481212 Nonscheduled Chartered
Freight Air Transportation

India's chiefly domestic state-owned carrier, Indian Airlines Ltd., flies passengers and cargo to 59 domestic and 16 international destinations. Its fleet numbered 52 aircraft in 2000. Indian Airlines has traditionally based its network around the four main hubs of Delhi, Mumbai (formerly Bombay), Calcutta, and Chennai (formerly Madras). The airline carries about six million passengers a year and has a substantial freight operation.

Origins

The Air Corporations Act of 1953 amalgamated India's dozen or so airlines, most of them undercapitalized, into two nationalized air carriers: Air-India Ltd., given responsibility for international routes, and Indian Airlines Corporation (IAC), the domestic airline.

The eight airlines that were amalgamated into IAC included Air Services of India Ltd., Airways (India) Ltd., Bharat Airways Ltd., Deccan Airways Ltd. (already 70 percent government-owned), Himalayan Aviation Ltd., Indian National Airways Ltd., Kalinga Airlines, Ltd., plus the domestic operations of Air-India Ltd.

IAC began operations with a fleet of 74 of the war surplus Douglas DC-3s that had founded its short-lived predecessors. The airline also had three times as many employees as it needed, writes R.E.G. Davies, a situation that was slow to change due to the government's refusal to allow layoffs. Davies also writes that the standard of maintenance was low and the airline suffered many accidents in its early years. IAC soon moved to bolster its fleet by ordering a few new de Havilland 114 Herons, retired after only a couple of years of service, and Vickers Viscount 768s, which were assigned to trunk routes. The DC-3s continued to supply feeder traffic; they soon began to be phased out by Fokker F-27s and Avro 748s. IAC began flying short-haul jets—French-made Caravelles—in the mid-1960s. The Caravelles were so popular that IAC soon needed larger jets to on the routes between Bombay (Mumbai), Delhi, Calcutta, and Madras (Chennai) that formed the India's domestic trunk network. IAC's first Boeing 737s entered service in 1971.

Between 1962 and 1972, IAC was called upon to support the military in several campaigns, first in skirmishes with China, and later with the wars with Pakistan that ultimately led to the creation of Bangladesh.

Confidence and Crisis in the 1970s and 1980s

IAC announced a Rs45 million loss for 1972. The next year, the company had several incidents of aircraft damage or loss. Labor unrest, high fuel costs, political burdens, and built-in inefficiencies added to the company's problems. However, these were met with such resolve that IAC had the confidence to order its first wide-body jets, Airbus A300s, in 1975. A program to produce ground support equipment in Indian factories was part of the deal. In 1976, new routes stretched across political divisions to Kabul, Afghanistan, in the northwest, and the Maldive Islands in the south.

The government allowed the formation of a few new limited service airlines in the 1970s: Air Works India, Huns Air, and Goldensun Aviation. None of them had long life spans. Around 1979, IAC dropped the word "Corporation" from its name.

Another national airline, Vayudoot, was formed in 1981 and tasked with carrying feeder traffic from India's smaller commu-

Company Perspectives:

Indian Airline's has been setting the standards for civil aviation in India since its inception in 1953. It has many firsts to its credit, including introduction of the wide-bodied A300 aircraft on the domestic network, the fly-by-wire A320, Domestic Shuttle Service, and Walk-in Flights. Its unique orange and white logo emblazoned on the tails of all its aircraft is perhaps the most widely recognized Indian brand symbol and over the years has become synonymous with service, efficiency, and reliability.

nities. Indian Airlines' managing director, Gerry Pais, was Vayudoot's part-time chairman. Vayudoot was serving more than 100 destinations within India by 1990. The government also set up a helicopter corporation to serve off-shore oil fields.

Britain's *Financial Times* described Indian Airlines as the world's third largest domestic carrier in the mid-1980s. With business growing at better than ten percent a year, it was increasing its capacity. Indian Airlines ordered a dozen of the new Boeing 757s in August 1984. After Rajiv Gandhi, a former Indian Airlines pilot, became prime minister, this order was changed to Airbus A320s due to what were perceived as political reasons. However, the crash of an Indian Airlines A320 in Bangalore on February 14, 1990—the type's second major crash globally in a two-year period—sorely tested management's faith in the plane, which featured new fly-by-wire flight controls and electronic cockpit instrumentation.

As part of a plan to merge Indian Airlines with Air-India, the state's international carrier, two leading young industrialists were appointed to chair the boards of the two companies in autumn 1986. Neither these plans nor the new chairmen lasted very long. In 1987, Indian Airlines carried 10 million passengers and earned a profit of Rs630 million ($48 million). However, the quality of its service was facing criticism, to be heightened by the coming entry of new carriers into the market.

New Competition in the 1990s

In a fresh wave of deregulation, nine new independent airlines were launched in India in the early 1990s. Vayudoot, the state-owned feeder airline, itself collapsed in 1993. One of the start-ups, East-West Airlines, offered such attractive wages that they prompted a pilots' strike at Indian Airlines in December 1992 during the winter tourist season. Indian Airlines had 570 pilots at the time, making an average of Rs30,000 ($962.00) a month. The airline lost Rs2.11 billion ($64.34 million) for the year.

As a result of the strike, Indian Airlines hired several Tupolev Tu-154 trijets, complete with crews, from Bulgaria and newly independent Uzbekistan. One of these, attempting to land in pre-dawn fog at Delhi on January 9, 1993, flipped over and broke into three pieces. Amazingly, all of the 165 passengers aboard survived.

After another, fatal crash and a couple of hijackings in May 1993, chairman and managing director L. Vasudev re-

signed, blaming the aviation ministry for undermining his authority. He had been hired in July 1992, filling a position vacant since the previous chairman had resigned due to the handling of yet another strike. Former Tata Iron and Steel head Russi Mody was named chairman of both Indian Airlines and Air-India in late 1994. He resigned two years later, also citing a lack of authority.

By the end of 1996, two of Indian Airlines' competitors, East-West Airlines and Modiluft, were grounded. However, Jet Airways, backed by a London-based expatriate and two Persian Gulf airlines, would soon be making a $486 million purchase of new Boeing aircraft.

In September 1997, Tata Group dropped its plans to launch an airline, citing obstruction from the ministry of civil aviation over the previous three years. Tata, whose founder had also started Air-India a half century earlier, also complained of lobbying from Jet Airways. Tata had planned to form the airline as a joint venture with Singapore Airlines.

After eight years of losses, Indian Airlines posted a Rs45 crore profit for the fiscal year ending April 1998. However, competitors like Jet Airways and Sahara Airlines continued to gnaw away at its market share, down to 60 percent by the end of 1998.

During 1998, a plan was drawn up to created a holding company in preparation for the long postponed merger of Indian Airlines with Air-India, along with Helicopter Corporation of India and Indian Airlines subsidiary Alliance Air. Both Indian Airlines and Air-India were losing money and needed to restore their aging fleets; it was hoped combining them could save some money on maintenance and other combined functions. Also in the works were plans to partially privatize Air-India. However, by the end of the year, the Civil Aviation Ministry had dismissed a joint board of directors from the two airlines.

In 1999–2000, Indian Airlines earned Rs2.8 billion ($60.2 million) from its cargo operations. During the following fiscal year, the airline considered plans to convert two of its Airbus A300 jets into dedicated freighters, a first step in making cargo a separate profit center. The company had an agreement to provide U.S.-based Emery Worldwide cargo space on its outbound flights to Singapore. It had cancelled a cargo service to the United States in 1996.

Indian Airlines trimmed a dozen positions from its managerial staff in a March 2001 reorganization. It had earlier reduced its workforce significantly by lowering its retirement age from 60 to 58. The 2000/2001 fiscal year produced a loss of Rs175.25 crore, due in large part to two 30 percent increases in the cost of fuel during the year. Indian Airlines reportedly would have earned a profit of Rs50 crore without the fuel price hikes. Though its market share had slipped to 50 percent, the company posted revenues of Rs3,755 crore, up slightly from the previous year.

To regain its profitability, the airline was planning a 10 to 15 percent increase in fares on trunk and tourist routes, reported *The Hindu*. Indian Airlines was enjoying lower fuel prices, thanks to deregulation in the fuel market.

Key Dates:

1953: Indian Airlines is formed as India's domestic airline.
1965: Short-haul Caravelle jets enter the fleet.
1972: IAC records a rare loss.
1975: The company orders its first widebody jets.
1992: India's domestic air market is deregulated.
1998: Plans to merge Indian Airlines with Air-India are drawn up but not approved.
2001: The Indian government solicits bidders for partial ownership of Indian Airlines.

When the government put Indian Airlines on the block in 2001, only two bidders came forward: Videocon International and the Hinduja Group. The latter was under investigation for an alleged scam, and Videocon had been suspended from the capital market for allegedly rigging its share price.

In November 2001, the Civil Aviation Ministry announced a plan to provide Rs9,000 crore to Indian Airlines, which was planning to reequip its fleet with around 40 new planes.

Principal Subsidiaries

Alliance Air.

Principal Divisions

Cargo.

Principal Competitors

Jet Airways; NEPC-Skyline; Sahara Airlines.

Further Reading

"Air India Loses Mody," *Financial Times* (London), December 17, 1996.

Davies, R.E.G., "Indian Airlines Corporation," *Airlines of Asia Since 1920,* London: Putnam Aeronautical Books; McLean, Virginia: Paladwr Press, 1997, pp. 33–50.

Elliott, John, "Ageing Fleets to Go," *Financial Times* (London), May 12, 1986.

——, "India Strengthens Airline Boards," *Financial Times* (London), September 22, 1986.

"Foggy Policies Responsible," *The Hindu,* December 28, 1998.

Guha, Krishna, "Tata Drops Plans for Airline," *Financial Times* (London), September 2, 1998.

Hazarika, Sanjoy, "India's Fading Airlines Store First-Class Hopes," *New York Times,* January 25, 1988, p. D8.

"Indian Airlines Cuts Down Staff Strength," *The Hindu,* March 16, 2001.

"Indian Airlines Fortunes on the Downswing," *Business Line,* December 26, 1998.

"Indian Airlines Seeks Revised Bids for Fleet Expansion," *Business Line,* December 6, 2001.

"Indian Airlines Sees Dubai as International Hub," *Gulf News,* June 10, 2001.

"Merger in the Air," *Business Line,* December 9, 1998.

Nadkarni, Shirish, "Indian Airlines Plans Cargo Boost," *Lloyd's List,* December 1, 2000.

Parsai, Gargi, "Input Costs Growing, Says Indian Airlines," *The Hindu,* April 9, 2001.

Phadnis, Ashwini, "Indian Airlines Fleet Expansion May Drag On," *Business Line,* November 29, 2001.

Rao, D. Panduranga and G. Venkata Rao, *Indian Airlines: A Study of Its Performance,* New Delhi: Inter-India Publications, 1997.

Sidhva, Shiraz, "India's New Airlines Seek Wider Horizons: A Campaign for Swifter Liberalisation of the Skies," *Financial Times* (London), August 13, 1993.

Tassell, Tony, "Jet Airways Leaves Its Indian Rivals Standing," *Financial Times* (London), January 4, 1997.

"Victim of Wrath," *Hindustan Times,* December 15, 1998.

Wagstyl, Stefan, "Indian Airlines Chief Quits After Row with Ministry," *Financial Times* (London), May 10, 1993.

——, "Pilots Strike on Indian Airlines," *Financial Times* (London), December 16, 1992.

—Frederick C. Ingram

Indianapolis Motor Speedway Corporation

4790 West 16th Street
Indianapolis, Indiana 46222
U.S.A.
Telephone: (317) 484-6747
Web site: http://www.brickyard.com

Private Company
Founded: 1909
Employees: 641
Sales: Not Available
NAIC: 711212 Racetracks

The Indianapolis Motor Speedway Corporation is a family-owned enterprise whose main business is the operation of the Indianapolis Motor Speedway and the Indy Racing League. One of the most famous races in all of motor sports—the Indianapolis 500—is run at IMS every Memorial Day weekend. The Indy Racing League began in 1996, with Tony George promoting U.S. open wheel drivers on oval tracks. The league had a slow start, but is attracting more fans and, more importantly, more sponsorship and television money.

A Tool to Sell Automobiles

The idea behind the IMS was as a marketing tool to sell cars. The original financial backers—Carl Fisher, James Allison, Frank Wheeler, and Arthur Newby—were local businessmen who envisioned people coming to see tests of the latest automobiles, then heading to the car showrooms to buy the latest models.

The track was made of crushed rock and tar and was a rectangular-shaped oval that was two and one-half miles long. The turns had 9 degrees and 12 minutes of banking. The track was built for auto manufacturers to test new car models and the owners planned races, so people could see the different manufacturers products run against each other.

The opening races of August 1909 did not go as planned, as the surface of the track was too rough on the tires and cars themselves. Soon after, the owners had over 3 million bricks brought in from western Indiana and the surface of the track was repaved in brick.

Birth of the Indy 500

In 1910, the group of businessmen scheduled three racing events, but attendance continued to be below what they had envisioned. For the next year the group decided to concentrate all of their efforts into one race. They decided to make it a long race—500 miles—and offer a large purse to the winner, $14,250.00.

The first 500 took place on Memorial Day, May 30, 1911, and was a huge success. Spectators flocked to the racetrack and the race enjoyed widespread and favorable press coverage. From 1911 until 1994, the only race ever run at IMS was the Indy 500, with the exception of one race run in September 1916.

The other business interests of the original backers of IMS grew and took their attention, so the group sold IMS to a group led by Eddie Rickenbacker in 1927. Rickenbacker was a World War I flying ace and had participated in several Indy 500s.

Although the bricks were a better surface than the original stone and tar, the surface continued to extract damage from the cars. In 1936, asphalt was used to cover rougher parts of the track and all but the main straightaway was covered in asphalt by 1941. By the fall of 1961, even that was covered, leaving only a portion of bricks at the start/finish line, hence the nickname "The Brickyard."

Soon after purchasing IMS, Rickenbacker had an 18-hole golf course built on the grounds of the Brickyard. Known as The Speedway Golf Course, most of the 18 holes were inside the famous oval and players took shots across the yard of bricks to complete the course. There was also a nine-hole course outside the oval. In 1991, the course was redesigned and renamed the Brickyard Crossing and for a time was the host site for the Brickyard Crossing Championship, a Senior PGA Tour event.

Postwar Rejuvenation

Since racing was suspended during World War II for four years, the track was shut down and fell into disrepair. Ricken-

Key Dates

1909:	Indianapolis Motor Speedway (IMS) is built.
1909:	First races held at the speedway.
1909–10:	Surface repaved with brick.
1911:	First Indy 500 held.
1917:	Racing suspended during World War I.
1927:	IMS sold to a group led by Eddie Rickenbacker.
1929:	Brickyard Crossing golf course is built.
1936:	Part of the track is covered in asphalt.
1942:	Racing suspended during World War II.
1961:	The entire track is covered in asphalt, except for a yard of bricks at the start and finish lines.
1945:	Tony Hulman, Jr., purchases IMS from Rickenbacker's group.
1990:	Tony George takes over as president and CEO of IMS.
1994:	NASCAR Brickyard 400 debuts, the first race event outside the Indy 500 since 1916.
1995:	George forms Indy Racing League (IRL), splitting from Championship Auto Racing Teams (CART).
1998:	First International Race of Champions (IROC) event at IMS
2000:	First Formula One (F1) event at IMS.

backer was concentrating on building a commercial airline, Eastern Airlines, and had little time or money to invest in IMS. The track was on the verge of being sold to real estate developers after the war, when three-time Indy 500 winner Wilbur Shaw went looking for someone to rescue the track.

Anton Hulman, Jr., better known as Tony, was a businessman from Terre Haute, Indiana. His grandfather began Hulman & Co. and developed and sold the Rumford brand of baking powder. Hulman & Co. later produced Clabber Girl baking powder. By the end of World War II, Tony was successfully running the family business, and owned newspapers, television stations, radio stations, a gas company, and Terre Haute's largest hotel.

Shaw spoke to Hulman and in 1945 Hulman purchased IMS from Rickenbacker's group for $700,000. Shaw was made president of the speedway until his death in a plane crash in 1954, when Hulman took over the day-to-day operations of IMS. Hulman died in October 1977. After Hulman's death, his daughter Mari Hulman George became Chairman of the Board and the day-to-day operations were passed to Joe Cloutier, who started as a cashier at Hulman & Co. in 1926 and went to work for IMS when Hulman purchased the business. After Cloutier's death in 1990, Tony Hulman's grandson, Tony George, assumed responsibility for the company. The new owner and president set about having the track cleaned up and repaired and the first post-World War II Indy 500 ran in May of 1946.

When Tony George took over the family business, he wanted to add races to IMS. He felt the name Indianapolis Motor Speedway was synonymous with racing and felt the potential for revenue was too great to let the track go unused 11 months of the year. George also felt that in order to provide fans

with the best in racing and facilities it would take more money than the Indy 500 brought in.

NASCAR (National Association for Stock Car Auto Racing) debuted at IMS in July 1994 with the Brickyard 400. The event was sold out—the largest crowd to watch a NASCAR event—and continued to sell out every year after. The Brickyard 400 awarded one of the top three purses in motor sports, the other two being the Indy 500 and the Daytona 500.

The stock car event was so successful the IMS began hosting an IROC (International Race of Champions) race in 1998. IROC races features drivers from different motor sports circuits, competing in identical stock cars.

Construction on a 2.606 mile Formula One (F1) track began at IMS, which is a road course, as opposed to an oval course. In September 2000, the United States Grand Prix put on the first Formula One race at IMS, the first F1 race in the United States in nine years. Although there were no American drivers in the event, about 220,000 fans (about 100,000 less than for the Indy 500), mostly from countries other than the United States, witnessed F1's return to U.S. soil.

Innovations in the 1990s

In 1995, George decided to start his own open wheel racing league in the United States, called the Indy Racing League (IRL). IRL's first race was held at the Walt Disney World Speedway in Florida, also owned by IMS.

The new league came from a philosophical disagreement with CART (Championship Auto Racing Teams) over the number of American drivers in the league. Most American racers grew up in motor sports racing on oval tracks and George felt racing on mostly road and street courses, as CART did, kept American drivers at a disadvantage. George also envisioned an open wheel league where the racing teams had nearly comparable equipment. Most big name open wheel teams and sponsors decided to stay with CART, where they felt technological development by the teams was rewarded.

The IRL did not take off in popularity as fast as George would have liked. Over the leagues first years, 1996 through 1999, the schedule of races failed to grow. Part of the reason was the IRL raced exclusively on oval tracks in the United States, limiting the number of venues the IRL could compete. Although oval tracks abound in the United States, open wheel cars needed certain conditions to race, so speeds are kept down.

Once the Indy 500 no longer featured CART drivers, beginning in 1996, television ratings dropped 30 percent for the big-time event, and fans' interest dropped as well. IMS never releases attendance figures, but media that covered the event year after year estimated attendance for all events related to the 500 had fallen after the split with CART.

In 1998, George decided to part with tradition and make the Indy 500 a two-week long event, instead of a month long event. The changes in the events leading up to the big race and cooling of tensions between CART and IRL led to larger ticket sales in 1999.

In 1999, controversy again swirled around the 500. George revoked the Indy 500 credentials of "Sports Illustrated" writer Ed Hinton. George felt that Hinton's coverage of past 500s was unfair and that the writer was insensitive in his coverage of a crash at an IRL event in May 1999 that killed three spectators. Faced with a boycott of sports writers, George finally relented, allowing Hinton to cover the 1999 Indy 500. The media commented that the boycott threat showed the 500 has lost some of its stature.

Pep Boys, an auto parts and service store chain, was a title sponsor of the IRL until the end of the 1999 season. The IRL felt that Pep Boys did not live up to its end to promote the league. The partnership dissolved in December 1999.

Northern Light, a technology company, signed a five-year, $50 million title sponsorship deal with the IRL in January 2000. The company was best known for it's Internet search engine, http://www.northernlight.com. Northern Light was pleased at the sponsorship decision after the first year. The company added web pages to its site to promote the IRL. It also hosted giveaways with other IRL sponsors on the Web site.

During the first year of the sponsorship, Northern Light CEO David Seuss took an active role in promoting IRL. Some analysts felt this helped to increase the exposure and popularity of the IRL in 2000. It was agreed the partnership was a good fit, with Northern Light promoting the league on its Web site and the IRL directing its fans to the site, increasing Northern Light's traffic by 40 percent.

The partnership was in trouble a year later as Northern Light decided not to purchase an advertising contract with ABC-TV, as the IRL deal called for. This saved Northern Light $1.5 million at a time when the U.S. economy was slowing and many dot-com companies were in financial trouble. Although Northern Light was quick to say it's support for the Indy Racing League had not diminished, some observers felt the sponsorship would continue to decline. Sponsorships fund racing leagues. For the 2000 racing season, IRL collected $143 million in sponsorship money, compared to $492 million by CART and $558 million by NASCAR.

Future of IRL

When the IRL was launched, IMS employees handled all aspects of the league. At the end of the 2000 season, IMS separated the league from itself and opened separate offices for the league. It was located on the IMS complex and staffed with employees dedicated to the league full-time.

In 2000, the IRL had nine races in ten months, with a month and a half break between the first and second races and the same break between the eighth and ninth races of the season. With the exception of two races in June, the rest of the races were scheduled about a month apart. This made it difficult in relation to marketing and television. It was also hard for the league to keep fans interested and the excitement going from one race to the next. For the 2001 season, IRL scheduled 13 races over six months, spacing the races about every two weeks or so. It was hoped this would help in building a fan base and make marketing the league easier.

In 2000, CART drivers Juan Montoya and Jimmy Vasser competed in the Indy 500 for the first time since the CART-IRL split. More CART teams were deciding to race in the IRL event in 2001, including Michael Andretti and Gil de Farran. The IRL got another boast in 2001 when CART driver Al Unser, Jr., signed up with an IRL team.

Most of the races in 2001 were at racetracks in and around the Midwest, with five within easy driving distance of Indianapolis. Several venues that had hosted races in the past—such as Las Vegas, Nevada; Charlotte, North Carolina; and Loudon, New Hampshire—did not schedule IRL events for 2001. The league scheduled a race in Miami for the first time since 1995 and aggressively marketed it, with lower ticket prices and commercials. The hope was the positive campaign would attract more fans outside of the IRL's midwestern stronghold.

George and IMS joined forces with the International Speedway Corporation, owned by Bill France (who also owns NASCAR) to form Motorsports Alliance. MA built a racetrack, a one and a half-mile oval, in Joliet, Illinois, and controls 15 other racing facilities in the United States. MA would like to build a track in the New York area, and has had discussions with Donald Trump to build one.

Officials at IMS have aggressively marketed their products and have been creative in creating partnerships. The company marketed the usual apparel and collectibles, plus the leagues and events they run. In one example, IMS signed an agreement in 2001 with Hat World to make all the hats worn by the over 4,000 Safety Patrol and Fire Crew. The promotion included cross marketing with Jiffy Lube, who displayed hats at their retail locations. Also in 2001, agreements were signed with Pepsi Cola, Infinity dealerships, and Publix supermarkets in Miami, where customers were given a chance to win a pace car. Apparel and collectibles were still the cornerstone of marketing efforts, with IMS looking to reach the casual race fan, as well as the serious one.

IMS sat on 559 acres in 2001 and continued to be a privately run family business, with Mari Hulman George as Chairman of the Board and Anton "Tony" George as President and CEO. Although rumors continued to fly about a merger with CART, IMS continued to state that George's vision of open wheel oval racing was taking off and gained momentum. IMS felt their product was a good one and they hired 30 new people in the marketing department to spread the work and gain new fans.

In order to further reduce costs for Indy League teams, the series eliminated awarding points to pole sitters and second and third place qualifiers. This meant that teams didn't need to spend so much money on engines used only for qualifying. The Indy League felt the change would also make teams concentrate on putting the best product on the oval for the race.

Principal Subsidiaries

Hulman and Company.

Principal Operating Units

Brickyard Crossing; Indy Racing League.

Principal Competitors

Championship Auto Racing Teams (CART); National Association for Stock Car Auto Racing (NASCAR); Federation Internationale de l'Automobile (FIA).

Further Reading

Andrews, Greg, et. al., "Northern Light Reduces IRL Support," *Indianapolis Business Journal,* April 2, 2001, p. 6.

Beaven, Stephen and Diana Penner, "U.S. Grand Prix Warms a Melting Pot of Fans at Indianapolis Speedway," *Indianapolis Star,* September 26, 2000.

Chengelis, Angelique, "Indianapolis 500: Q&A with Tony George," *Detroit News,* May 21, 1999.

Crowe, Steve, "Time Will Tell if F-1 and Indianapolis are Winning Formula," *Detroit Free Press,* September 21, 2000.

Dottore, Damian, "Penske Going Back to Indy," *The Orange County Register,* January 18, 2001.

Harris, Mike, "George: '. . . we don't need (CART) to have a Successful Event'," *Detroit News,* May 30, 1999.

Koenig, Bill, "Indianapolis Motor Speedway Officials Plan to Give Buildings Corporate Names," *Indianapolis Star,* July 25, 2000.

Long, Gary, "IRL Still Searching for Identity," *Miami Herald,* April 5, 2001.

——, "Some CART Stars Filtering Over to IRNLS," *Miami Herald,* April 5, 2001.

Pedley, Jim, "Andretti Works to Bridge IRL, CART Gap," *Kansas City Star,* March 28, 2001.

Saward, Joe, "Tony George Interview," *Inside F-1,* March 1, 1999.

Schoettle, Anthony, "IRL in Groove with Northern Light," *Indianapolis Business Journal,* October 23, 2000, p. 3.

Sullivan, Tim, "Tony George's Diluted Indy 500," *Tennessean,* May 30, 1999.

Underwood, Stephen, "Creative Partnering for IMS," *Sporting Goods Business,* March 9, 2001, p. 40.

—Lisa Musolf Karl

Industrial Services of America, Inc.

7100 Grade Lane
Louisville, Kentucky 40232
U.S.A.
Telephone: (502) 366-3452
Toll Free: (888) 494-4472
Fax: (502) 368-1440
Web site: http://www.isa-inc.com

Public Company
Incorporated: 1953 as Tri-City Scrap Baling
Employees: 135
Sales: $89.2 million (2000)
Stock Exchanges: NASDAQ
Ticker Symbol: IDSA
NAIC: 541618 Other Management Consulting Services;
53249 Other Commercial and Industrial Machinery
and Equipment Rental and Leasing

Industrial Services of America, Inc. is multi-faceted waste management and recycling company based in Louisville, Kentucky. The company operates in four main segments: metals recycling, solid waste management services, waste equipment sales, and software and hardware support services. ISA's metals recycling business, ISA Recycling, consists of two recycling facilities that handle ferrous, non-ferrous, and fiber waste. The recycling division also brokers deals between buyers and sellers of scrap metal around the world. The company's solid waste management business, Computerized Waste Systems (CWS) provides waste disposal services, including contract negotiations with independent hauling companies, centralizing dispatch services, and centralized billing for large, multiple-location companies. CWS's main clients are Home Depot and Office Depot. ISA's WESSCO (Waste Equipment Sales and Services Company) division leases, sells, and services equipment for the waste handling and recycling industries. The company's fourth and newest division, iR2, is a provider of information technology solutions to ISA's other divisions and to external clients, both domestic and international.

Beginnings: From Detroit to Louisville

The company that would eventually be called Industrial Services of America was founded by Harry Kletter, the son of immigrant parents who had come to the United States from Russia and Austria. Kletter grew up on Detroit's east side, where his father had established his own business to clean up foreclosure properties, preparing them to be resold. When he collected scrap materials from these foreclosure sites, he often hauled them to his brother's salvage yard, also in Detroit. In the late 1930s, Kletter's father, along with Harry and his brother Sam, started a new business—a scrap company called Illinois Waste Materials Co. With the onset of World War II and the growing demand for steel, the scrap industry flourished, and the Kletters' business flourished along with it. In 1945, however, Kletter was taken away from the family enterprise when he joined the Navy.

Returning from his Navy duty, Kletter first located in Detroit with his family, but soon moved to Cincinnati. In the early 1950s, Kletter started his own scrap business—Tri-City Baling Company—in Louisville, Kentucky. He later changed the company's name to Tri-City Industrial Services. Tri-City bought, processed, and sold ferrous and non-ferrous scrap metal. Kletter proved an aggressive entrepreneur with a hunger for expansion and diversification. In 1956, just three years after establishing his company, he formed Tri-City Trash and Sanitation Company, a waste-hauling business. In 1961, he moved into manufacturing by acquiring Anchorpac, a maker of compactors for the waste industry. Kletter broadened his manufacturing base in 1965, forming the Tri-Pak division to produce a complete line of waste-handling equipment: containers, hoists, and transfer stations, in addition to the compactors the company was already producing.

Part of Tri-City's rapid expansion was due to what started out as a hobby for Kletter. In the 1950s, the company founder took up aviation, negotiating flying lessons as part of a deal he was making for some scrap airplanes and engines. Eventually receiving his pilot's license, Kletter was able to travel more broadly than he otherwise would have. In the September 2000 issue of *Recycling Today*, he explained how this increased mobility affected his business. "If we had not flown, we would never have grown the way we did," he said. "We were every-

---

Company Perspectives:

Our objective is to reduce your waste expense, increase your recycling revenues, recommend equipment and finance options and utilize our technology division to better prepare your company for the Second Industrial Revolution. As the first public company in the waste industry, our personnel are committed and focused to deliver quality service and total satisfaction to our customers.

---

where so easily in the '50s. We were able to get to remote places and make deals for pipeline scrap and surplus.''

Whatever the cause for its growth, Tri-City was soon established as one of the leaders in its field. In 1969, it became the first company in the waste industry to go public, when it acquired and merged with Alson Manufacturing, a publicly held, but inactive, corporate shell. Upon merging with Alson, Tri-City changed its name to Industrial Services of America, Inc.

1970–80: Ups and Downs

In 1979, ISA acquired Computerized Waste Systems (CWS), a Boston company that managed solid waste and recycling services for companies. At the time of the acquisition, CWS had a limited client base. What it did have, however, was a good concept and the software program needed to implement it. ISA relocated CWS to Louisville and quickly set about building the business. Soon, the company began acquiring significant new clients, including Home Depot, which contracted with CWS to provide waste management services for its locations all over the United States. Companies using CWS's services phoned their service requests to a central call center in Louisville. From that center, the company dispatched its network of third-party vendors, which included waste-hauling companies, recycling companies, and equipment manufacturing and maintenance companies.

The early 1980s proved difficult for ISA. As the country slid into an industrial recession, the scrap business fell off dramatically. ISA, which was highly leveraged at the time, was hit hard. Ultimately, the company filed for Chapter 11 reorganization and sold off a number of its assets as part of the necessary restructuring. Among the assets it sold were Tri-Pak, the equipment manufacturing division, which by that time had several production facilities around the United States, and Tri-City Trash and Sanitation Company, its hauling business. Another asset ISA sold at that time was a non-ferrous scrap processing facility, which adjoined its headquarters in Louisville. Although the company did not sell its scrap yard, it did close it down for a time.

These divestitures allowed ISA to emerge from bankruptcy in 1985. They also left the company tightly focused on its most profitable, highest growth business: waste management services. The mid-1980s also saw the formation of a new ISA division to sell, lease, and service a range of solid waste handling and disposal equipment. While ISA no longer produced its own equipment, its reputation in the industry left it ideally positioned as a representative for other manufacturers. The division formed to handle that business, Waste Equipment Sales

and Services Company, was commonly known by its acronym: WESSCO.

1990: Acquisitions and Leadership Changes

By the mid-1990s, ISA was again ready to expand. In 1995, it upgraded its facilities, increasing productivity by adding new scrap processing and recycling equipment. The company also refurbished its offices.

In 1997, the company acquired The Metal Center, a metals recycling facility operated by TMG Enterprises, of Louisville. The business, which purchased, processed, and sold non-ferrous scrap metal, was renamed ISA Recycling. This acquisition was particularly interesting in that until the mid-1980s, The Metal Center had been a part of ISA; it was one of the assets the company sold off to emerge from bankruptcy. The business had grown under its interim ownership and had made improvements in the form of new, state-of-the-art recycling equipment. When ISA re-acquired it, it had more than $10 million in annual revenues.

In 1998, Harry Kletter, who had led ISA through the more than 30 years since its founding, stepped down from his post as president. He retained his positions of CEO and chairman. The office of president was filled by Sean Garber, a five-year veteran of the waste industry. Garber had joined ISA in 1996, coming from a vice-president's position at OmniSource Corp., a metal recycling business in Fort Wayne.

Garber's plans were to pursue new acquisitions in the waste and recycling fields, as well as to expand its existing businesses. One of his first moves toward expanding ISA's recycling capabilities was the acquisition of a metals recycling operation previously owned by R.J. Fitzpatrick Smelters. The facility, located in Seymour, Indiana, had estimated annual revenues of $4 million a year. ''We are growing ISA's metal recycling capabilities to capitalize on the profit potential of the metal business,'' Garber said in an August 1998 press release, adding, ''Fitzpatrick Smelters' operations in scrap metal, ferrous and non-ferrous materials make an excellent fit with our core capabilities.''

ISA's revenues increased significantly in 1998, jumping up 44 percent from the previous year's. This increase stemmed from double-digit growth in both the waste management services division and the recycling division. But despite the higher revenues, the company was adversely affected by a drop in commodity prices in the ferrous and non-ferrous markets and a decline in domestic steel production. With this steel industry slowdown, many of the mills that bought product from ISA severely curtailed their scrap purchasing, leaving the company with a glut of inventory. The excess inventory, which was devalued by the falling commodity prices, hurt ISA's bottom line, and the company posted a year-end loss of $543,000.

ISA rebounded in 1999, however. Not only did the company enjoy record annual revenues, but it moved back into profitability, posting a net income of $827,000. Sales increased in all of the company's business segments, most significantly in management services segment, which grew by 24 percent.

New Century, New Directions

In early 2000, Kletter resigned from his position as CEO of ISA. Rather than replace him with a new CEO, the company

Key Dates:

1953: Harry Kletter forms Tri-City Scrap Baling Company.
1956: Tri-City Waste and Sanitation Company is founded.
1965: Tri-Pak is formed as a division of Tri-City.
1969: Tri-City becomes a publicly held company and changes its name to Industrial Services of America (ISA).
1979: ISA acquires Computerized Waste Systems.
1980: Bankruptcy reorganization forces ISA to sell Tri-Pak, Tri-City Waste and Sanitation, and a metals recycling facility in Louisville.
1997: ISA re-acquires "The Metal Center" in Louisville.
2001: ISA completes Phase 1 of a major facilities renovation.

chose to eliminate that position and have the president report directly to board of directors. Kletter remained the board chairman and at the same time acquired a new, somewhat unusual title, becoming the company's Chief Visionary Officer. Kletter's retirement from active leadership was to be short-lived, however. In May 2000, after slightly more than two years in the office, Sean Garber resigned from his position as president. Kletter once again assumed the day-to-day guidance of the company.

Management changes aside, ISA started the new century on a progressive note. In mid-2000, the company announced that it was forming a new division to leverage information technology opportunities. Named iR2, which stood for "Second Industrial Revolution," the new division offered software development and support to ISA's other divisions with the aim of streamlining the transaction processing and increasing overall efficiency and capability. IR2 also offered hardware and software consulting services to external clients, primarily in the waste and recycling industry. Later in 2000, the company ventured a step further into the new economy when it announced that it planned to begin selling waste management products and services online via the Ariba B2B eCommerce Platform. The Ariba system was a large e-commerce network that brought together business buyers and sellers from around the world.

Also in 2000, ISA formed a new service division to work in tandem with its recycling business: ISA Brokerage. The broker-age served as an intermediary for large-scale buyers and sellers of scrap, negotiating deals for customers in North American, Europe, Asia, and India.

As ISA upgraded and expanded its service offerings, so too did it upgrade and expand its facilities. In 2001, the company completed the first phase of a major renovation that included a new call center and expanded Internet platform for the CWS division. Phase 2 and Phase 3, upon completion, would add a waste equipment sales and leasing showroom for the WESSCO division and expand the company's iR2 division to enable Internet hosting and other technical services to its customers in the waste and recycling industries.

As ISA positioned itself for the 21st century, it appeared to be placing a great deal of emphasis on its management services businesses. According to company sources, however, the physical operations side of the business—the scrap yard and recycling facilities—were also potential targets for growth. During the 1990s, consolidation in the scrap industry, followed by a plunge in commodity prices, had caused a number of scrap yards across the United States to be shut down. The vacuum's created by these closures appeared to be likely areas of expansion for ISA Recycling. Further plans for the recycling division included using the scrap yard and recycling facility as a "model" where potential customers could view waste handling and recycling equipment in action.

Principal Competitors

Allied Waste Industries, Inc.; Avalon Holdings Corporation; Casella Waste Systems, Inc.; Envirosource, Inc.; IMCO Recycling Inc.; Metal Management, Inc.; Republic Services, Inc.; Safety-Kleen Corp.; Waste Connections, Inc.; Waste Holdings, Inc.; Waste Management, Inc.

Further Reading

Conn, Jennifer, "Scrap Has Long Area History," *Waste News,* March 17, 1997, p. 11.
"Industrial Services of America," *Solid Waste Report,* December 21, 2001.
"Sean M. Garber–Industrial Services of America Inc.," *Wall Street Transcript Digest,* January 17, 2000.
Taylor, Brian, "A Perpetual Pioneer," *Recycling Today,* September 2000.

—Shawna Brynildssen

Ingenico—Compagnie Industrielle et Financière d'Ingénierie

9 Quai de Dion Bouton
92816 Puteaux Cedex
France
Telephone: (+33) 1-46-25-82-00
Fax: (+33) 1-47-72-56-95
Web site: http://www.ingenico.fr

Public Company
Incorporated: 1980
Employees: 930
Sales: EUR 380 million ($304 million)(2001)
Stock Exchanges: Euronext Paris
Ticker Symbol: ING
NAIC: 333313 Office Machinery Manufacturing

France's Ingenico—Compagnie Industrielle et Financière d'Ingénierie is the world's leading manufacturer of electronic payment terminals and systems, beating out Hypercom and Verifone of the United States. Founded in 1980 by chairman and CEO Jean-Jacques Poutrel, who still owns about 14 percent of the company, Ingenico's products include debit, credit card and "smart" card point-of-sale payment terminals, smart card readers, front office servers for magnetic-strip cards and transactions, as well as software and e-commerce payment solutions. Ingenico ships more than one million terminals per year in the fast-growing electronic payment market. The company has also been quick to integrate emerging technology into its products, including communication with GSM-based mobile telephones and groundbreaking infrared-based secure payment integration with the popular Palm Pilot personal digital assistant. With its 1999 acquisition of IVI Checkmate, third-largest in the United States market and subsequently renamed Ingenico Corp., Ingenico not only boosted itself to the global market leadership, it also gave itself a prime entry in the United States—a market set to explode as it converts to the micro-chip based smart cards at the beginning of the twenty-first century. As a result of that acquisition, the company was able to win a $200 million contract from First Data Corp. in 2002 to develop its multifunction terminals for the U.S. market over the next five years. Ingenico

is listed on the Euronext Paris stock exchange. Gemplus, the world's leading manufacturer of smart card, owns nearly 30 percent of Ingenico through its founder Marc Lassus; the two companies have not ruled out a possible merger in the future.

Electronic Payment Pioneer in the 1980s

France was one of the pioneers of electronic payment systems during the 1970s and 1980s and played a leading role in introducing this technology to the rest of the world. Stimulating the country's interest in secure electronic payment systems was the enormous success of the Minitel network, which placed Internet-like services in French homes in the early 1980s. France was also the birthplace of so-called smart cards, which, unlike magnetic-based credit cards, featured microchips to enable quick processing of customer purchases. The early acceptance of smart cards in France and in much of the rest of Europe encouraged the emergence of a new market devoted to the design and manufacture of payment and other financial transaction terminals.

In 1980, Jean-Jacques Poutrel and partner Michel Malhouitre established their own business, Compagnie Industrielle et Financière d'Ingénierie Ingenico, dedicated to the development and manufacturing of card-based payment terminals. Ingenico quickly rose to the top of the French market, and by 1985 the company went public, listing its stock on the Parisian bourse's Secondary Market. A year later, Ingenico switched its listing to the Paris exchange's Monthly Settlement market.

The company had grown quickly, in part because of the high margins it was able to command at a time when the electronic terminals market was just beginning to take off in Europe and elsewhere. Early on, Ingenico eyed a place in the international market, launching a subsidiary in Australia in 1988 in order to position itself for entry into the Asian Pacific markets. Ingenico opened a subsidiary in Spain at the end of the decade. The company was also quick to recognize the potential of smart cards, invented in the early 1970s, and in 1988 became an early investor in newly formed Gemplus, which was set to become the leader of the global smart card market in the 1990s.

Ingenico launched its Euromos "multiple application" terminal in 1990, hoping to establish an industry standard. Two

Company Perspectives:

The world of electronic payments is constantly changing. Electronic purses are proliferating, and Internet payment is a reality. Many different methods of payment are now available and terminals must be capable of handling these different scenarios. The objective which Ingenico has set itself is to enable electronic transactions to be carried out in all these contexts, in total security, and to facilitate the use of these systems, including in the Internet environment.

years later the company rolled out its line of Elite terminals. By then, the company had also signed a partnership agreement with Italy's Olivetti, and had acquired a contract, with French petroleum company Total, to place terminals in its network of service stations. The early part of the decade held its share of difficulties for the company, however. As its core French and European markets suffered through an extended economic crisis, Ingenico too saw its immediate prospects dwindle, to the point where stock market analysts had come to consider the company somewhat of a has-been that had run out of breath.

Ingenico set out to prove those analysts wrong. The company quickly recognized that its future lay in its expansion on the international market. In 1992, international sales accounted for just 16 percent of the company's total revenues of nearly FFr185 million. Just one year later, however, the company had boosted its foreign sales to 34 percent of sales, and included fast-growing China among its new markets. By 1994, international sales accounted for more than half of Ingenico's revenues. Yet the company continued to suffer the extended crisis in its core French and European markets.

In 1994, Ingenico began plans to move into the lucrative North American market—the United States alone represented some 40 percent of the worldwide market for payment terminals. Instead of attacking the United States directly, and thereby finding itself in head-to-head competition with market giants Verifone and Hypercom, Ingenico chose to move into neighbors Mexico and Canada. In that year, the company placed its first terminals in Mexico, with two contracts for a total of 12,000 machines. At the same time, the company decided to sell of its 13.5 percent holding in Gemplus, generating some FFr75 million.

Global Leader in the 21st Century

The year 1995 proved to be a turning point for Ingenico. Growing acceptance of the smart-card technology, and the development of the so-called "electronic purse," led to a major increase in demand for Ingenico's multiple application-capable terminals and systems. A big boost for the company, and the industry in general, was the adoption of smart card technology by the world's largest credit card companies, including Visa, MasterCard, and Europay. If the United States remained resistant to the new technology, the rest of the world had quickly recognized the value of the microchip-based smart cards. Ingenico Pacific, the company's Australia-based subsidiary, grew especially strongly as the fast-growing Asian markets readily adopted the new technology. The Chinese market, still in the

beginnings of its conversion to capitalism, turned directly to the use of smart cards.

In 1995, the company's revenues were once again on the rise, reaching FFr 190 million, and by 1996 the company's sales had swelled to FFr 280 million. In that year, the company took a major step into the U.S. market when its created a joint-venture with Canada's International Verifact Inc. (IVI), in an agreement which gave Ingenico a 16 percent share of IVI. The joint-venture provided for mutual distribution agreements of the company's complementary products, giving Ingenico's product an entry into both the U.S. and Canadian markets, but also strengthened the company's entry into the South American market.

Meanwhile, Ingenico began a series of external growth operations—indeed, acquisitions were to account for a strong share of the company's rise in the late 1990s. In 1996, the company acquired Innovatron Data Systems in France, and then moved across the border, purchasing EPOS, based in Germany. That year, also, Ingenico debuted its latest product innovation, the Elite 700 range of mobile terminals. By the end of 1997, Ingenico's sales had grown to more than FFr 450 million.

In 1998, Ingenico made two new acquisition that enabled the company to climb to the number two position worldwide, behind U.S.-based leader Hypercom. In May of that year, De La Rue Ltd., of the United Kingdom, the world's leading banknote printer, agreed to merge its Fortronics electronic terminals division into Ingenico, in a deal that transferred 20 percent of Igenico's stock to De La Rue. The acquisition, which reduced Ingenico founder Poutrel's position in the company to that of minority shareholder, was also seen as a means to prepare for his retirement from the company. With the completion of the acquisition in 1999, the new subsidiary was renamed Ingenico Fortronics.

The acquisition of the De La Rue division boosted Ingenico into the position as second largest in its market. That deal was soon followed up by the announcement in September 1998 that Ingenico was acquiring Bull's electronic terminals division, including its Spain-based Telesincro subsidiary. Under the terms of that acquisition agreement, Bull became Ingenico's new majority shareholder, with more than 29 percent of its stock. The deal gave Ingenico Telesincro a 70 percent share of the Spanish market and also boosted the company to more than FFr 1 billion in revenues.

IVI merged with the U.S. company Checkmate, forming IVI Checkmate, the third-largest terminals supplier in the United States. The merger reduced Ingenico's position in the larger company to just 9 percent, but placed it in a prime position for an eventual acquisition of that company. Back in Europe, the company also acquired a 40 percent stake in Veron, the Italian market leader.

Ingenico continued its expansion into 1999, setting up a subsidiary in Sweden and launching a new subsidiary, Ingenico Software. The company also rolled out two new product lines, the Elite 790 GSM and the Ingenico smart card reader for Internet-based transactions. Parallel to that launch, the company formed a new subsidiary, Ingenico.com, dedicated to secure online transactions, especially transactions made through next-

---

Key Dates:

1980: Jean-Jacques Poutrel and Michel Malhouitre establish Compagnie Industrielle et Financière d'Ingénierie Ingenico.

1985: Ingenico goes public on Paris Stock Exchange's Secondary Market.

1986: Company transfers its listing to Monthly Settlements Market

1988: The company creates subsidiary Ingenico Pacific.

1990: Ingenico launches ''multiple application'' Euromos terminal.

1994: The company enters the North American market with its first Mexican terminals contracts.

1996: Ingenico acquires Innovatron Data Systems and EPOS (Germany) and forms a strategic alliance with IVI in Canada.

2002: Company is awarded largest-ever contract from First Data Corporation.

---

generation mobile telephones, a market expected to explode during the early years of the new century.

Bull restructured its operations at the end of 1999 and sought a buyer for its nearly 30 percent stake in Ingenico. In December 1999, that share was sold to Marc Lassus, founder and head of Gemplus, which by then had grown into the world's leading smart card maker. One month later, Ingenico stepped up to the acquisition plate, buying French-based IT services and consultancy firm EAC. In April 2000, Ingenico acquired Lexem, a leading French secured internet transaction specialist. Then in June of that year, Ingenico turned to the United Kingdom, acquiring software publishing and payment application hosting services provider Saunders & Jeffries. Not all of the company's activities were positive, however. At the end of 2000, the company decided to sell off its 40 percent stake in struggling Veron.

Ingenico nonetheless had good reason to cheer at the turn of the century. In January 2001, the company debuted its latest transaction coup. The company partnered with Palm, the maker of the highly successful Palm Pilot personal digital assistant, to enable Palm user to complete purchasing transactions using the Pilot's infrared port and specially equipped Ingenico terminals.

A more important moment for the company came in August 2001, when Ingenico announced its agreement to takeover IVI Checkmate for $55 million. The deal not only gave Ingenico a strong position in the United States, it also boosted it to the number one position worldwide. By November of that year,

Ingenico was cheering as it saw its sales top the FFr 2 billion mark for the first time. Yet by the end of the year, the company had outperformed even its own forecast, topping EUR 380 billion. At that time, Poutrel, who was said to be preparing to retire soon after, announced the company's plan to boost its sales to EUR 600 million by 2003.

The company's prominence in the fast-growing Chinese market was certain to aid the company in reaching its goal. Meanwhile, Ingenico seemed on its way toward dominating the United States market as well. In January 2002, Ingenico announced that it had been awarded a five-year, $200 million contract to develop and implement a multiple-technologies terminals network, including smart-card capacity, for First Data Corporation. The contract represented Ingenico's largest ever, and confirmed its rise to market leader.

Principal Subsidiaries

I.D.S.—Sofracin SA; DSI International SA; S.C.I. du 5 Parc Floral; INGENICO International (PACIFIC) PTY Ltd (Australia); INGENICO SINGAPOUR; INGENICO Fortronic Ltd (UK); Ingenico Iberia SL (Spain); TELESINCRO S.A. (Spain); INGENICO Hansea GmbH (Germany); EPOS SERVICE GmbH (Germany); INGENICO GmbH (Germany); EPC GmbH (Germany); INGENICO AB (Sweden); IVI INGENICO (76%); INGENICO TRANSACTION SYSTEMS Ltd (United Kingdom); LEXEM; INGENICO ITALIA (95%); Ingenico do Brasil LTDA (97.91%).

Principal Competitors

Hypercom Corporation; Verifone, Inc.; V-Star; Thales SA; Schlumberger SA; Lipman plc; NCR Corporation.

Further Reading

Anderson, Simon, ''De La Rue Rejig After Deal with Ingenico,'' *Daily Telegraph*, April 2, 1998.

Besses-Boumard, Pascale, ''Ingenico change de taille et organise son avenir avec le britannique De La Rue,'' *Les Echoes*, March 30, 1998, p. 14.

Bremer, Catherine, ''Ingenico Sees Operating Profit Doubling,'' *Reuters*, June 26, 2001.

''Ingenico entend dépasser ses objectifs de croissance,'' *La Tribune*, August 27, 2001.

''Le jackpot chinois profite encore à Ingenico,'' *La Tribune*, August 13, 2001.

Lorenzini, Frédéric, ''Ingenico profite de ses projets Internet,'' *La Tribune*, January 19, 2000.

—M.L. Cohen

iVillage

iVillage Inc.

500-512 Seventh Avenue
New York, New York 10018
U.S.A.
Telephone: (212) 600-6000
Web site: http://www.ivillage.com

Public Company
Founded: 1995
Employees: 309 (2001)
Sales: $76.35 million (2000)
Stock Exchanges: NASDAQ
Ticker Symbol: IVIL
NAIC: 541512—Computer Systems Design Services;
　　541519 Other Computer Related Services

iVillage Inc. is an Web-based media company dedicated to serving the needs of adult women through online communities and content areas focused on such topics as Astrology, Babies, Beauty, Books, Computing, Diet & Fitness, Food, Games, Health, Home & Garden, Lamaze, Money, News & Issues, Parenting, Pets, Relationships, Shopping, and Work. A free iVillage membership allows members to use features such as email, instant messaging, and personal homepages. At the end of 2000, iVillage reported, it was receiving about 214 million monthly visits to its sites. The lion's share of iVillage revenues are derived from advertising and sponsorships.

1990s Start Up

iVillage was conceived and created by Candice Carpenter, a complex woman, lauded by some as a visionary genius, damned by others as a pushy manipulator. A graduate of Stanford and Harvard, Carpenter served as president of both Time-Life Video and Q2, a subsidiary of QVC, before going to work as a consultant for America Online in 1995. Although she knew next to nothing about computers or the nascent Internet—she admitted to *Crain's New York Business* that she was "technophobic"— Carpenter immediately grasped the possibilities inherent in online culture. She found a wealth of communities lurking beneath the surface at AOL, brought together by the common interest of their members: a community for gay people, for example, one for people interested in quilt-making, another for pet owners. Carpenter's insight was that virtual communities were the future of the Internet. Her genius was to take that idea and from it create a branded media firm.

Carpenter put together a three-person team to create a business plan based on her idea. She brought in two friends who also had experience in the media sector: Nancy Evans, the founder and editor of *Family Life* magazine, and Robert Levitan, the ex-president of video publisher YearLook Enterprises. In September 1995, in Evans' Manhattan apartment, the three sketched out some ideas for their new network on a drawing pad that belonged to Evans' daughter. The company that came out of the brainstorming sessions was based on slogans like "Internet for the rest of us" and Humanize cyberspace." At its core would be three communities, focused on family, health, and career, but targeted at the general public, not specifically at women. They thought of the communities as virtual village greens where everyone gathered and knew everyone else. An "i" was added simply because it was the Internet prefix of choice at the time.

iVillage attracted its first major investor, Carpenter's former employer, America Online, in September 1995. The investment was a significant one for AOL—it was the first time the firm gave major support to an independent company, rather than merely an online project. iVillage agreed to develop five communities for AOL, including groups on health and work. Its first AOL channel, Parent Soup, debuted in January 1996. Other investors lined up quickly. By spring 1996, TCI Interactive, the venture capital firm Kleiner, Perkins, Caulfield & Byers, and the Tribune Company had put money into Carpenter's company.

iVillage's sharp focus also led to partnerships with companies that specialized in iVillage content areas. In June 1996, it entered an agreement to sell KidSoft's software products for children in the Parent Soup General Store. The general store was iVillage's foray into e-retailing and represented a broadening of the company's mission to giving its community members access not only to information and experts, but to "quality products from leading online merchants," as one press release put it." Later in 1996, two alliances were forged intended to make Parent Soup the preeminent site for parents on

Company Perspectives:

iVillage Inc. is a media company, which operates iVillage.com, Women.com, Lamaze Publishing, the New-born Channel, iVillage Solutions, and Astrology.com. iVillage.com is a leading women's online destination providing practical solutions and everyday support for women 18 and over. Lamaze Publishing produces advertising-supported educational materials for expectant and new parents. The Newborn Channel is a satellite television network in over 1,000 hospitals nationwide. iVillage.com is organized into branded communities across multiple topics of high importance to women and offers interactive services, peer support, content and online access to experts and tailored shopping opportunities.

the Web. First, it merged with another Web site for parents, ParentsPlace.com. Then it set up an advertising deal with MomsOnline, another channel on AOL.

Ultimately, though, what made Parent Soup most attractive to web surfers was not its advertising or retailing, it was its content. There were directories of experts, articles of interest, forums and online chats on topics of interest to parents and access to advice on the most pressing problems, such as childhood illness, development, and nutrition, as well as interactive surveys and polls. iVillage continued to develop its other special interest networks. About Work, a community focused on career and workplace, went online in late 1996. Better Health & Medical followed in September 1997. The most significant, in the end, was the oddly-named Life Soup, a Web community where women in the prime of their lives could discuss all the problems that touched them, from finance, fitness, food, sex, and relationships.

Late 1990s Web Site for Women

By 1998, the introduction of an iVillage community specifically for women was inevitable. Although the company's first communities were planned as virtual meeting halls where any interested parties could participate, it was soon evident that visitors to the sites were overwhelmingly women. What's more, iVillage sites were powerful magnets to high-income, well-educated women, a market segment advertisers considered difficult to reach. iVillage was drawing more women than any other Web site. It had more than twice as many women visitors as its nearest competitor, Women.com, and it promised to attract even more in the short-term future. At the time, it was projected that 34 million women would go online for the first time in the next two and a half years, that the number of women using the Internet would increase five times over from 1996 to 2000.

If it could draw together this vast and influential group, iVillage was clearly on to something of interest to advertisers. Its Better Health & Medical site, the first to include content aimed specifically at women, attracted $3 million in sponsorships from Tenet Healthcare and pharmaceutical companies Merck and Astra-Merck. Making its new direction explicit, the company modified its name to iVillage.com: The Women's Network. It began pursuing revenue from three different

sources, advertising, e-retailing, and sponsorships of specific areas of iVillage sites. Candice Carpenter predicted that iVillage would turn its first profit by the end of 1998.

A spring 1998 investment drive showed that iVillage was riding the wave. A diverse group of ten companies that included Tenet Healthcare Corp., the National Bank of Kuwait, and Technology Crossover Ventures, a California venture capital firm, pitched in about $32.5 million, $12 million more than the iVillage had hoped to raise. The sum brought the total already invested in the company to $67 million. iVillage planned to use the latest funds to raise its profile through an advertising campaign on television and radio.

In November 1998, iVillage signed two-year deal with AT&T to establish a new Internet access service, called iVillage Online. It would be on the order of America Online but geared specifically to the Web needs of women. It was a project iVillage had been looking to pursue for the better part of a year. In return, AT&T became the exclusive provider of communications services to members of iVillage.com. iVillage closed a third big deal the same month, when NBC obtained an equity share in iVillage of undeclared value. The agreement involved no cash, it was an swap of services. In exchange for iVillage content on NBC.com, NBC agreed to advertise iVillage on its TV networks, NBC and MSNBC, as well as on NBC.com and the MSNBC pages of the MSN.com site. The NBC deal was seen as an important one for iVillage, even though no money was involved. TV was the only way to reach the mass of untapped mainstream users and was expected to draw even more women to the iVillage sites.

Going Public in 1999

By the beginning of 1999, iVillage and its investors were ready to take the service public and an offering was scheduled for mid-March 1999. Investors were attracted to the fact that iVillage's membership base made it so attractive to advertisers. Its $9.1 million in advertising revenue outweighed income from sponsorships and product sales by a wide margin, accounting for 82 percent of iVillage's income during in the first nine months of 1998. The relationships with NBC and AOL were critical too; some Wall Street analysts believed the company needed to raise its public profile, particularly through exposure on prime-time TV, if the stock offering was to be successful.

Other factors, though, were working against the company. Although membership had increased dramatically during 1998—from 170,000 members to nearly three-quarters of a million in just ten months time—dollar losses were multiplying just as quickly. The 1997 $14.5 million in red ink had more than doubled to $32.4 million loss in 1998. Just days before the offering, iVillage lost one of its fastest growing sites, Armchair Millionaire. The site for beginning investors, which reportedly accounted for ten percent of visitor traffic at iVillage, had been bought back by its founder Lewis Schiff. Some analysts believed the loss of Armchair Millionaire would hurt iVillage's value on Wall Street. Others observed that 70 percent of the visitors to Armchair Millionaire were men, which cut against the grain of iVillage's core constituency. They reasoned that the loss of Armchair Millionaire would merely tighten iVillage's demographics and make it all the more attractive to advertisers.

Key Dates:

1995: Candice Carpenter, Nancy Evans, and Robert Levitan establish iVillage; America Online buys a minority stake in iVillage.

1996: Parent Soup, the first iVillage site, debuts on AOL; the Tribune Company invests in iVillage.

1997: Life Soup, iVillage's first site specifically for women, goes online.

1998: Total investments in iVillage reach $67 million; NBC partners with iVillage.

1999: iVillage goes public and raises over $1 billion.

2001: iVillage merges with Women.com to form the largest site for women on the Web and acquires control of Business Women's Network.

Even darker shadows were cast over the IPO by lawsuits against iVillage that were made public just days before the stock offering. One former employee charged the firm with reneging on a promise to give him the stock options he had been promised with hired. Joanne O'Rourke Hindman, an ex-iVillage Chief Financial Officer, made the same accusation, but went even further. She alleged that when she was hired as CFO in September 1997, she became aware of irregularities in iVillage accounting practices. She told Candice Carpenter that the company was claiming revenues in its financial statements prematurely, sometimes even before letters of intent were signed. As a result, Hindman claimed, Carpenter demoted her shortly afterwards and fired her two months later. Hindman's allegations drew attention to the unusually high rate of employee turnover at iVillage, a problem laid at the door of Carpenter's mercurial personality. However, neither the lawsuits nor the charges of financial impropriety, nor iVillage's employee attrition rate was expected to hurt the stock offering.

Candice Carpenter's reportedly abrasive temperament was interpreted as a sign of the business genius that had made iVillage possible in the first place. Some observers went as far to say that the allegations were timed to hurt the stock offering. However, two years later, when iVillage's stock price was already hitting the skids, more suits were brought against iVillage by former employees for deceptive recruiting practices, such as offering compensation packages that included stock options that were never delivered.

Despite such apparent setbacks, the iVillage public offering was one of the most spectacular debuts in Wall Street history. A week earlier, Goldman, Sachs, the underwriters, were planning to price the shares at about $14. Two days before the offering, Goldman, Sachs raised the opening price range to $22 to $24— at that price iVillage would have a market value of about $588 million. However, when trading began on NASDAQ, the opening bid was $95.875, valuing iVillage, a three and half year old company that had never had a profitable year, at $2.22 *billion*. By the time the day had ended the firm had sold 3.65 million shares. The share price finally settled at $80.125, but not before soaring as high $100.

By the end of 1999, iVillage had pumped its membership up to nearly two million and was registering about 5.5 million visits to its sites every month. It had acquired a lucrative online shop for baby goods called iBaby and announced a deal to promote and sell Ralston-Purina products. The deals helped boost e-commerce revenues to 28 percent of total revenues, which had grown to $25.3 million. Losses kept pace, however, climbing to $86.7 million for the first three quarters of 1999.

The ongoing losses did not tarnish iVillage's glittery appeal to other firms. In February 1999, it announced a major partnership with Unilever, the Dutch producer of consumer brands such as Dove, Vasoline, Q-Tips, Wisk, Lipton, Ragu, and Breyers Ice Cream. iVillage was attractive to Unilever, because 85 percent of its products were purchased or used by women. The two firms each chipped in $100 million to start a new Web site, called Substance.com, devoted to women's personal care and beauty issues. Although Unilever cosmetics and beauty products would be prominently featured on the site, the firms claimed the primary purpose of the site was not to sell goods— in fact, Unilever refused outright to sell its products on the Web site. Its purpose was to help women solve specific problems and provide Unilever with consumer feedback. The site finally launched in spring 2001.

Reality was beginning to catch up with iVillage's share price by spring 2000, plunging from highs around $100 to less than $10. The company reacted by naming Doug McCormick, the former CEO of the cable TV Lifetime network and a member of iVillage's Board of Directors, as president, a new position at iVillage. According to Candice Carpenter, the post was created to oversee international growth and iVillage bandwidth expansion. However, most outside observers were convinced that McCormick's appointment was part of a management shake-up meant to wrest the company out of its financial doldrums. McCormick's first public action was to sell the iBaby online store off to BabyGear.com, a move intended to make iVillage even more attractive to advertisers by not competing with them for sales. As such, it also represented a move away from e-retailing and back to a pure media orientation at iVillage.

The management shake-up continued in iVillage's uppermost rank in July 2000, when founder Candice Carpenter stepped aside as Chief Executive Officer and was replaced by McCormick. Various reasons were given for Carpenter's departure: there was the company's poor earnings record—it had never reported a profitable quarter; there was Carpenter's abrasive, frequently alienating management style—the firm had one of the highest employee turnover rates in the online industry; there was the apparent lack of vision at the company—iVillage had started out as a group of general communities, then focused on women, swerving from a pure media orientation into e-commerce and then back again; and finally there were questions about Carpenter's handling of the firm's finances— iVillage had gone through a whopping five Chief Financial Officers in just four years time. Carpenter denied being forced out as CEO, and she remained as a member of the iVillage board. Within a year, though, Carpenter had left the board and the company she created.

The media questioned the wisdom of saving a Web site for women by appointing a man its head and public face. Man or woman, McCormick had his work cut out for him. The company was perceived to be in such bad shape that its share price had dropped to around $1 and NASDAQ was threatening the company with delisting. McCormick took decisive action. In February 2001, he oversaw the "merger" of iVillage and its main Web competitor, Women.com, a move that consolidated the two into the largest sites for women on the Web. It was a complicated deal. iVillage purchased Women.com for $25 million in stock. At the same time, however, the Hearst Corporation, Women.com's largest stockholder, made a $20 million cash payment to iVillage and received a 30 percent interest in the combined company, which continued to go by the name iVillage. Hearst also promised another $15 million for production and advertising, and put many of its women's magazine titles online at iVillage.

In October 2001, iVillage reported the first profitable quarter in its history. Largely responsible for the scant $0.4 million in earnings was the July acquisition of the Women's Business Network, a profitable operator of fee-based databases of women's organizations and Web sites.

Principal Competitors

Lifetime Entertainment Services; Martha Stewart Living Omnimedia Inc.; Oxygen Media Inc.

Further Reading

"America Online Partners with iVillage, an Independent Programming and Marketing Studio," *Business Wire*, September 28, 1995.

Barlas, Pete, "It Takes iVillage To Gather Investors," *Investor's Business Daily*, May 1, 1998, p. A9.

——, "It Takes NBC To Build iVillage," *Investor's Business Daily*, November 30, 1998, p. A10.

Bohning, Stacy, "Ivillage.Com Co-Founder Entered The World Of Dot-Com Out Of Frustration," *St. Louis Post-Dispatch*, May 11, 2000, p. C1.

Brookman, Faye, "Millionaires of Silicon Alley: Candice Carpenter," *Crain's New York Business*, November 29, 1999, p. 52.

Chernoff, Allan, "iVillage, Chairman & CEO," *Market Call*, CNNFN, July 25, 2001.

Colford, Paul, "Ex-'Lifetime' Chief To Head Ivillage / Shake-Up At Dot-Com That Caters To Women," *Newsday*, April 21, 2000, p. A51.

DeNitto, Emily, "Top Cats: 25 Players Shaping Silicon Alley," *Crain's New York Business*, November 24, 1997, p. 26.

"Former iVillage Officials Sue the Company," *New York Times*, January 18, 2000, p. C8.

Gerena-Morales, Rafael, "Unilever, Ivillage Form Co. To Run Beauty Web Site," *Newsday*, February 16, 2000, p. A42.

Green, Heather, "Douglas McCormick: A Way with the Ladies?," *Business Week*, February 19, 2001, p. 46.

Guida, Tony, "iVillage CEO & Unilever President," *Capital Ideas*, CNNFN, February 15, 2000.

Hansell, Saul, "Chief Executive of iVillage Gives Up Title to President," *New York Times*, July 29, 2000.

——, "Accounting Is Questioned In Lawsuit Against iVillage," *New York Times*, March 10, 1999, p. C2.

"iVillage and AT&T to Launch First Women's Internet," *Business Wire*, November 18, 1998.

"iVillage Announces Online Network for Women," *PR Newswire*, September 8, 1997.

"iVillage Confirms Plans To Sell Its Baby Products Unit," *New York Times*, June 3, 2000, p. C4.

Kaufman, Joanne, "iVillage; Learning the Hard Way," *Fortune Small Business*, March 2000.

Lacey, Stephen, "iVillage Puts Laser To Community Model," *IPO Reporter*, December 21, 1998.

Li, Kenneth, "Online Network's Stock Offer in Doubt with Popular Site's Departure," *New York Daily News*, March 12, 1999.

Molineaux, Charles, "iVillage European Deal," *The N.E.W. Show*, CNNFN, July 19, 2000.

Napoli, Lisa, "A Focus on Women at iVillage.com," *New York Times*, August 3, 1998, p. D6.

Sabga, Patricia, "CEO Shake Up at iVillage," *The N.E.W. Show*, CNNFN, July 28, 2000.

Schaffler, Rhonda, and Jim Waggoner, "CEO, iVillage," *Market Call*, CNNFN, February 6, 2001.

Schwardron, Terry, "Parenting Sites a Step Ahead in Infancy of Net Communications," *Los Angeles Times*, December 9, 1996 p. D4.

Seo, Diane, "Rivals Battle To Be New Online Force," *Los Angeles Times*, July 23, 1999, p. C1.

Siwolop, Sana, "A Shifting Landscape At the iVillage Offering." *New York Times*, March 21, 1999, Sect. 3, p. 9.

—Gerald E. Brennan

Japan Tobacco Inc.

2-1, Toranomon 2-chome
Minato-ku
Tokyo 105-8422
Japan
Telephone: (81) 3-3582-3111
Fax: (81) 3-5572-1441
Web site: http://www.jtnet.ad.jp

Public Company
Incorporated: 1949 as Japan Tobacco and Salt Public
    Corporation
Employees: 15,590
Sales: $35.6 billion (2001)
Stock Exchanges: Tokyo
NAIC: 312221 Cigarette Manufacturing; 312111 Soft
    Drink Manufacturing; 311412 Frozen Specialty Food
    Manufacturing; 325412 Pharmaceutical Preparation
    Manufacturing.

Japan Tobacco Inc., known as JT, is the world's third-largest tobacco company. JT controls about 75 percent of the Japanese cigarette market, and about 8 percent of the cigarette market worldwide. Its leading brands are Mild Seven, Japan's number-one seller, and Cabin, Caster, Seven Stars, and Peace. The company also owns international rights to the key brands Winston, Salem, and Camel, which it acquired from RJ Reynolds in 1999. These three brands, along with Mild Seven, are marketed through the company's JT International subsidiary, headquartered in Geneva, Switzerland. Japan Tobacco is a diversified company with substantial interests in pharmaceutical development and sales, and in the sale and distribution of packaged foods and beverages. The company markets drugs that fight cancer and HIV, and operates joint ventures with pharmaceutical companies in Japan, the United States, and Europe. JT markets Green Giant brand frozen foods in Japan, as well as other prepared foods, and acquired the food operations of Asahi Chemical in 1997. JT also sells several leading packaged soft drinks and teas under the brand names Green's, Roots, and others. In addition, the company has interests in printing,

agribusiness, and real estate. Japan Tobacco was a state-owned monopoly until 1985. The Japanese government still owns two-thirds of the company, with the rest publicly traded on the Tokyo Stock Exchange.

Roots in the 19th Century

Japan Tobacco's origins date back to 1898 when a government bureau was established within the Ministry of Finance to operate a monopoly on tobacco production within Japan. The tobacco industry in Japan can, however, be traced back to 1869, when Yasugoro Tsuchida, a Tokyo merchant, began the production of rolled cigarettes on a small scale. This represented the introduction of locally produced cigarettes and came less than 20 years after the first introduction of cigarettes to Japan as imports from Britain and the United States. In 1883, Iwatani Co. Ltd., a trading company, began the production and sale of Japan's first popular cigarette brand, Tengu. In 1888, the government responded to the increase in tobacco smoking by placing a special tax on the products, with varying rates for rolled tobacco and cigarettes. Around this time the Murai Brothers Company began producing and selling Sunrise cigarettes and importing Hero cigarettes from the United States. In 1896, the company expanded into the Tokyo market, thus prompting a price war with Iwatani Co. Ltd.

At the time Japan was undergoing an accelerated period of industrialization. The Tokyo Stock Exchange opened in 1878, the Bank of Japan began operations in 1882, and the state-owned Yamato Iron and Steel Works began operation in 1901. In 1895, Japan established itself as a military power with the defeat of China in the Sino-Japanese War. Operations such as these needed funding, and the government realized that a tobacco monopoly such as existed in several European countries could be a lucrative source of revenue. In 1898, a tobacco bureau was established within the Ministry of Finance to operate this monopoly. In 1905, a salt monopoly was added to the bureau's responsibilities. The bureau began marketing Cherry cigarettes in 1904, a brand still sold in Japan. In 1906, it began producing and selling its most popular brand at the time, Golden Bat. In 1900 Japan became one of the world's first countries to pass a law forbidding the consumption of cigarettes by minors—those under the age of 18. For

---

Company Perspectives:

By circulating and expanding funds (''cash flow'') generated by high-quality business activities, JT is committed to fulfill—to the best of its ability and in a fair and balanced manner—its responsibilities to its shareholders, customers, employees, and society and to ensure their satisfaction with JT's performance.

---

the next 30 years tobacco and salt production in Japan continued to be administered by this bureau within the Ministry of Finance. Profits went directly into state coffers and were regarded as a kind of tax by the authorities. The prices charged by the government on tobacco were relatively low while those on salt were minimal, and the monopoly was in some ways used as a means of controlling the nation's economy, providing a regular source of income for the government.

Postwar Production

By 1940, Japan was heading towards war with the Allied Powers. The supplies of raw tobacco leaves from the West, notably from North and South America, were becoming less and less reliable. The government was forced to implement rationing of cigarettes in 1943. Following Japan's defeat and subsequent occupation, the country's economy was restructured by the Allied Powers. They felt it reasonable to keep the monopoly in place as a source of income for the cash-starved Japanese government. In 1949, the government bureau traditionally responsible for tobacco production became a public company, known as the Japan Tobacco and Salt Public Corporation. Although still a wholly government-owned concern, tobacco production and sales in Japan were now to be operated on a commercial basis and as a self-accountable business concern. The company began afresh, and in 1949 commenced the retailing of two brands—Peace and Corona, the former of which is still a top seller in Japan. In 1950, rationing of tobacco products was halted, and in 1952 finished tobacco products were exported from Japan for the first time, mostly to Southeast Asian nations. In 1954, a new consumption tax was established on sales of cigarettes with the proceeds going directly to the government rather than the Japan Tobacco Corporation. In 1957, the company introduced its most popular brand, Hope, and also set up a research center to study the effects of cigarette smoking on health. This came at a time when scientists in the United States were beginning to publicize the link between smoking and lung cancer. Japan, with its lower incidence of cancer, was more concerned with its very high rate of stroke- and stress-related deaths, and the research center studied the causes of these illnesses. The Japanese population continued to take up smoking at a prodigious rate, and by 1967 Japan Tobacco's best selling cigarette brand, Hope, was also the world's best selling brand. In the following year the company established a factory for producing cigarette paper and filters to cater for increased demand in Japan. Following reports of the health risks of smoking from both the West and to a lesser extent within Japan, Japan Tobacco began to issue health warnings on its cigarette boxes. The warnings were fairly low-key, however, and only advised the smoker not to overindulge in the habit.

Since the salt monopoly was established in 1905, Japan Tobacco in its various forms had been entrusted by the Japanese government with full responsibility for the country's salt supply. The salt business had traditionally been conducted with the aim of maintaining stable salt supplies and prices. As Japan does not have any salt mines, Japan Tobacco has had to import most of its salt, mainly from China and Korea. In 1972, Japan Tobacco introduced a new method of producing salt in which sea water is separated from fresh water by membranes, and the salt allowed to permeate across the membrane. This method was introduced into all Japan Tobacco salt-making facilities.

In 1973, Japan Tobacco began the sale of Marlboro cigarettes under license from Philip Morris Co. Ltd. of the United States. As the largest tobacco company in the world, the latter was determined to make inroads into the lucrative Japanese market but was bewildered by Japan's complex distribution system. Most of Japan Tobacco's products were sold in small kiosks and vending machines, presenting an importer of cigarettes with a difficult and arduous task in cracking the market— a competitor would require a huge capital investment to set up such a network, and supply staff and maintenance staff would be required. Japan Tobacco at the time controlled almost 100 percent of Japan's cigarette market. In 1974, the company began its paradoxical ''smoking clean'' advertising campaign. The advertisement featured models in outdoor surroundings, smoking Japan Tobacco cigarettes. The irony of the suggestion that smoking is a clean habit and results in good health was obvious, but it was nonetheless built into a national campaign. In 1977, Japan Tobacco introduced its current best-selling brand, Mild Seven.

In the 1980s, Japan Tobacco faced increasing pressure from foreign cigarette manufacturers to allow them to sell their products more freely on the Japanese market. The Japanese government was under pressure to cut its huge trade surplus with the United States and therefore exerted pressure on Japan Tobacco to cooperate with foreign importers and allow them the use of distribution channels, notably Japan Tobacco's large network of automatic vending machines. Philip Morris and RJ Reynolds were the first to make inroads, with Lark, a Philip Morris brand especially designed for the Japanese market, becoming a best-seller. In 1985, Japan Tobacco underwent a fundamental restructuring. The government reorganized the company by privatizing it and re-establishing it as Japan Tobacco Incorporated, a joint stock company with its shares fully owned by the Japanese government. In the face of increasing competition from foreign imports, the move was intended to make the company more competitive, while still giving the government a monopoly on cigarette manufacture in Japan. In 1987, import tariffs on cigarettes were lifted, making it possible for importers to sell cigarettes at approximately the same price as Japan Tobacco. Since 1987, as a consequence, both Japan Tobacco's total sales and its share of the Japanese market have been declining. The company's management realized that the new Japan Tobacco would have to diversify in order to sustain growth. Japan Tobacco International Corporation (JATICO) was established in 1985 to export cigarettes. First year sales were 7.5 billion cigarettes, which compared with the 270 billion sold domestically. The United States and Southeast Asia were the chief targets of JATICO's products.

Key Dates:

1898: A tobacco bureau is established by the Japanese government.

1949: The company is incorporated as Japan Tobacco and Salt Public Corporation.

1967: JT is the producer of Hope, the world's best-selling cigarette brand.

1985: The company begins exporting cigarettes.

1987: Import tariffs are eased, opening Japanese the market to foreign tobacco companies.

1994: The Japanese government sells one-third of JP to the public.

1999: JT buys non-U.S. operations of RJ Reynolds.

Japan Tobacco entered the pharmaceutical business in 1986, with the formation of JT Pharmaceutical Co. Ltd. This subsidiary took advantage of its parent company's extensive research and development facilities. The main areas of the pharmaceuticals business on which the company focused at first were over-the-counter (OTC) cough remedies and nutritional supplement drinks. One of the company's successes was Kakimaro, marketed as a hangover remedy. Through international strategic alliances, JT Pharmaceutical also entered the field of OTC ethical drugs.

Through other subsidiaries formed between 1985 and 1990, Japan Tobacco entered the food, fertilizer and agribusiness, and real estate businesses. The latter made use of Japan Tobacco's real estate holdings which, like many Japanese companies in the real estate boom years of the late 1980s, it used to its full financial advantage through office letting, land sales, and renting.

Growth and Diversification in the 1990s and After

By the mid-1990s, Japan Tobacco was the fourth-largest cigarette maker in the world. It faced increasing competition at home from European and U.S. imports and at the same time eyed the opening of the potentially huge market in China. The company's pharmaceuticals division grew rapidly, and JT invested some hundreds of billions of yen in diversified interests such as the beverage business, real estate, and health clubs. But tobacco remained the pillar of the company, accounting for almost 90 percent of the firm's revenue. A significant proportion of Japan's population continued to smoke, and the kind of class-action lawsuit that dogged U.S. tobacco companies was unheard of in Japan. Though growth in domestic cigarette sales was small, company managers maintained an optimistic outlook. Consequently the Japanese government arranged to sell one-third of the company to the public in 1994 to raise money. The government had previously privatized portions of other state-owned companies, including the telecommunications company Nippon Telegraph & Telephone and its East Japan Railways. The shares were first offered to large investors and then made available through a lottery system to individual investors. Yet in the midst of a falling stock market, response to the public offering was dull.

JT went ahead with various diversification projects in the mid-1990s. In 1996, the company entered a joint venture with the British company Grand Metropolitan PLC, owner of Burger King, to expand the Burger King franchise in Japan. Burger King was a distant third in the Japanese burger market, but both firms saw plenty of room for expansion. In 1997, JT acquired the food operations of the Asahi Chemical Industry Co., Ltd. This gave JT access to a wider market for its food business. Previously, the firm had reached primarily commercial customers with its frozen foods, but the Asahi purchase gave the company some well-known consumer brands. The company also sold beverages through a network of vending machines. JT reorganized its vending machine operating companies in order to widen its beverage market. In pharmaceuticals, the company also pursued joint ventures and made acquisitions. One significant acquisition was that of the Torii Pharmaceutical Co. Ltd. in 1998. JT bought up 53 percent of the company and then beefed up the company's marketing.

The biggest coup for Japan Tobacco was its acquisition in 1999 of the non-U.S. operations of RJ Reynolds. The company shelled out $7.8 billion for Reynolds' international operations. The deal established JT as the world's third-largest tobacco company (behind Philip Morris and British American Tobacco) and made Japanese history as the largest foreign acquisition to date by a Japanese company. JT gained RJR's three leading brands, Camel, Winston, and Salem. These brands were big sellers in places where JT had little inroad, including Eastern Europe and the former Soviet Union. Sales of brands with a global presence were growing at an estimated five percent annually, while overall cigarette sales growth was just one percent.

The acquisition was expensive and cut heavily into JT's earnings, but the company saw its future in global expansion. Though 35 percent of Japanese adults smoked, a much higher percentage than in Europe and the United States, the smoking population was expected to peak in 2007. And although JT had not been sued over health issues, an awareness of smoking's health risks was beginning to penetrate in Japan. The company looked to the opening of China's market to cigarettes as a source of revenue and hoped to concentrate other foreign sales in Pacific Rim countries that still had growing markets for tobacco. By 2000, the company was pushing its leading Mild Seven brand in Malaysia, Thailand, and Singapore. The company gained a new president in late 2000, Katsuhiko Honda. Honda had negotiated the acquisition of the RJ Reynolds' brands. International sales made up close to 40 percent of the company's business by the turn of the century. The company also worked closely with its two global rivals, Philip Morris and British American Tobacco. Documents leaked by *Advertising Age* in 2001 showed that the three top companies had agreed to work together to limit their marketing around the world. Japan Tobacco and the others proposed to voluntarily limit advertising in publications with a substantial readership under age 18, to keep tobacco ads 100 meters away from schools, and in other ways restrict their advertising.

Principal Subsidiaries

JT International S.A.; Torii Pharmaceutical Co. Ltd. (53%); J.T. Agris Co., Ltd.; J.T. Canning Co., Ltd.; J.T. Drinks Co., Ltd.; J.T. Foods Co., Ltd.; Chicago Foods Co., Ltd.; Lifix Co., Ltd.; My Circle Co., Ltd.; J.T. Real Estate Co., Ltd.; Your Factory Co., Ltd.; J.T. Enoshima Prince Hotel Co., Ltd.; J.T. Engineering Co., Ltd.; Tokyo Clinical Testing Co., Ltd.; Tokyo Establishment Enterprises Co., Ltd.; Murajo Production Centre; Enkai Enterprises Co., Ltd.; G-Tech Co., Ltd.; J.T. Anlits Co., Ltd.; Japan Tobacco I-Mex Co., Ltd.; Hokkaido Tobacco Services Co., Ltd.; Tokyo Tobacco Services Co., Ltd.; Chubu Tobacco Services Co., Ltd.; Kansai Tobacco Services Co., Ltd.; Kyushu Tobacco Services Co., Ltd.; Uny-Tobacco Services Co., Ltd.; Tohoku Filter Enterprises Co., Ltd.; Japan Filter Enterprises Co., Ltd.; Osaka Filter Enterprises Co., Ltd.; Neo-Filter Enterprises Co., Ltd.; J.T. CMK Co., Ltd.; J.T. Okamura Co., Ltd.; J.T.S. Electric Co., Ltd.; J.T. Nifco Co., Ltd.; Napps Co., Ltd.; J.T. Soft Services Co., Ltd.; J.T. Fashions Co., Ltd.; J.T. Kokubu Co., Ltd.; J.T. Act Co., Ltd.; J.T. Creative Co., Ltd.; J.T. Travel Co., Ltd.; S.K. Services Co., Ltd.; Planzart Co., Ltd.; C B One Co., Ltd.; Fuji Flavour Co., Ltd.; Japan Metallising Industries Co., Ltd.; Alpack Services Co., Ltd.; Nitto Industries Co., Ltd.; Tohoku Plant Services Co., Ltd.; Kanto Plant Services Co., Ltd.; Tokai Plant Services Co., Ltd.; Hachisendai Production Co., Ltd.; Kyushu Factory Services Co., Ltd.; Tobacco Benefit Association.

Principal Competitors

Philip Morris Companies Inc.; British American Tobacco p.l.c.

Further Reading

Bentley, Stephanie, ''Euro Launch for Japanese Cigarettes,'' *Marketing Week*, August 16, 1996, p. 7.

Coleman, Joseph, ''Big tobacco Still Calls the Shots in Japan,'' *Marketing News*, August 4, 1997, p. 12.

Dawson, Chester, ''Smoke Alarm,'' *Far Eastern Economic Review*, June 22, 2000, pp. 50–2.

Friedland, Jonathan, ''Thank You for Not Smoking,'' Far *Eastern Economic Review*, August 4, 1994, p. 66.

''Japanese New Issues: Down in Smoke,'' *Economist*, October 22, 1994, p. 91.

McKegney, Margaret, and Madden, Normandy, ''Tobacco Report Reveals Global Retreat,'' *Advertising Age*, August 13, 2001, pp. 1, 27.

Updike, Edith Hill, ''Burger King Wants to Build a Kingdom in Asia,'' *Business Week*, November 25, 1996, p. 52.

—Dylan Tanner
—update: A. Woodward

The Jean Coutu Group (PJC) Inc.

530 Bériault Street
Longueuil, Québec J4G 1S8
Canada
Telephone: (450) 646-9760
Fax: (450) 646-5649
Web site: www.jeancoutu.com

Public Company
Incorporated: 1969 as Jean Coutu Discount Pharmacy
Employees: 17,650
Sales: C$2.92 billion ($1.9 billion) (2001)
Stock Exchanges: Toronto
Ticker Symbol: PJC.A
NAIC: 446110: Pharmacies and Drug Stores; 621498 All Other Outpatient Care Centers

The Jean Coutu Group (PJC) Inc., headquartered in Longueuil, Quebec, was founded in 1969 by pharmacist-entrepreneur Jean Coutu, whose unique vision of the pharmacist's role has redefined the profession. The Jean Coutu Group is the largest retailer of pharmaceutical and parapharmaceutical products in Quebec, ranks second in Canada and, after the major acquisition of 80 Osco Pharmacies in January 2002, is in seventh place among the top 10 pharmaceutical retailers in North America. The firm manages three subsidiaries and 544 establishments. In Canada, the Jean Coutu Network (JCN) consists of 293 franchised outlets located chiefly in Quebec, Ontario, and New Brunswick. The Jean Coutu Group (PJC) U.S.A., a subsidiary, operates the Brooks Pharmacy Network (BPN) of 251 corporate outlets situated in the six New England states and the state of New York. Each outlet is organized in four sections: clients go to the *Pharmaceutical Center*, the main focus of The Jean Coutu Group, for professional consultation, prescriptions, and laboratory services. The *Boutique Photo Center* sells photography supplies and equipment, develops over 3.5 million rolls of film annually, and ranks as the leading film developer in Quebec. Cosmeticians in the *Beauty Section* are available for consultation; customers may choose from a large array of beauty products and accessories, treatments, perfumes, etc. The

Commercial Section contains health and beauty aids, baby supplies, household items, natural products, and confections—to name but a few retail products. Another subsidiary, RX Information Center Ltd., develops and implements the technological services related to management of professional and business activities. In Canada, the systems of subsidiary Services Sécurivol Inc. provide rigorous management of security.

In both Canada and the United States—over and above supporting the professional advancement of its pharmacists and catering to customers—The Jean Coutu Group provides support and financing for many social and charitable causes related to public health, including help for indigent persons and the ongoing fight against drug abuse, alcoholism, and family violence. The National Awards Institute awarded two trophies to The Jean Coutu Group: a trophy for Entrepreneurship and another for Marketing. For three consecutive years, a poll conducted for *Commerce* magazine found that The Jean Coutu Group is "The Most Admired Company in Quebec." In 2001, the editors of *Drug Topics* magazine selected the Brooks Pharmacy Network as the "Pharmacy Chain of the Year."

The Early Years

Jean Coutu, eldest child of pediatrician Dr. Lucien Coutu, was born in Montreal in 1927. After obtaining degrees in the liberal arts and in science (physics, biology, and chemistry), he enrolled at the University of Montreal for a degree in medicine. However, after an unfortunate experience as student leader, he had second thoughts about a medical career. Recalling "the good smell" of the pharmacies belonging to his cousin, Jean Locas, Coutu thought about how this successful and esteemed businessman managed many employees and also participated in a variety of professional and civic activities. "As a pharmacist, it will be easier for me to be actively involved with many people in the very place where I conduct business," Coutu said to himself, according to Cardinal and Lapierre's essay in the 1996 issue of the Canadian magazine *Gestion*. Coutu then registered for a pharmacology degree at the University of Montreal.

Jean Coutu's background in academic medicine facilitated his pharmaceutical studies; he took part-time work in a branch of

---

Company Perspectives:

From the outset, we grounded our success on two basic principles: our partnership culture and our ability to adapt. Consequently, we have continuously ensured that our company fosters value not only for our customers but also for all those involved in the company: our franchisees, our employees, our suppliers, and our shareholders. Moreover, we have never lost sight of our primary mission: meeting consumers' needs by continual monitoring of current markets and adapting our product selection to the special needs of every generation we serve in all the areas where our stores are located.

Pharmacies Leduc, the most important pharmacy chain of the era. As clerk, assistant manager, and then manager at the age of 23, Jean moved his Leduc branch from tenth to first place in the network. Flush with his success, pharmaceutical diploma in hand, he approached the chain's owner with a proposal: "I've worked for you for five years," said he to Mr. Leduc, "and I like the work. In the branches of your network, five of us young pharmacists would like to enter into a partnership with you." The astonished owner replied that Pharmacies Leduc was, and always would be, a family business. Jean saw the handwriting on the wall and within six months had resigned from the Leduc store.

During the 1950s, pharmaceutical research was making rapid strides in Montreal; patented medicines and discoveries in endocrinology and virology were opening up new markets. In 1955, he enthusiastically agreed to partner with his cousin, Jean Locas, to open three pharmacies in Montreal. At the end of the five-year contract with his cousin, Jean struck out on his own. By year-end 1965, Jean owned and managed four pharmacies in Montreal.

1966–89: A Pharmacist-Entrepreneur

Consumer attitudes toward the purchase of medication were slowly changing. After obtaining information from pharmacists who prepared prescriptions, customers often went elsewhere to buy comparable patented products at prices lower than those of pharmacies. A realist and entrepreneur, Jean asked Louis Michaud, another pharmacist, to accompany him to Toronto to visit the chain of Top Discount stores, Gérard Virthe reported in the December 1980 issue of *Revue Commerce*. Reportedly, the owner of one of the discount stores commented, "You pharmacists will succeed when you no longer think about 'big fat profits.'" Challenged by these words, Jean and Louis returned to Montreal to experiment with a new kind of establishment: a "Farmateria," that is, a store that could not be called a pharmacy because it did not offer prescription services but stocked and sold at discount prices all the other products available in traditional pharmacies. This venture was so successful that within two years the partners opened 17 Farmaterias. However, similar stores quickly surfaced as strong competitors. Jean and Louis liquidated the Farmaterias and returned to management of their traditional-style pharmacies.

Still, Jean persisted in his desire to operate a "total service" discount pharmacy; in short, he thought of setting up "a Farmateria within a pharmacy," reported Cardinal and Lapierre

in *Gestion*. Assisted by Jacques Masse, in 1969 Jean invested his life savings of C$250,000 to open Quebec's first Pharm-Escompte Jean Coutu (Pharm-Discount Jean Coutu; Canadian law did not allow use of the word *pharmacy* with the word *discount*). In this new store, customers could not only obtain prescriptions from an ever-present licensed pharmacist but also buy over-the-counter drugs and all the retail products previously offered in the Farmaterias. Pharm-Escomptes were open till late at night and remained open on weekends. Jean's goal was to have the commercial side of the enterprise take in enough money to supplement the cost of always having a certified pharmacist present in the store—as mandated by Canadian law. "Other pharmacists were skeptical about the future of an establishment that operated on such a slim profit margin, but Jean was banking on mass merchandising," wrote Cardinal and Lapierre.

Skeptics notwithstanding, the first Pharm-Escompte was a resounding success. In 1971, Jean and Louis renewed their partnership and opened a second discount pharmacy in Verdun. Then Louis converted his Côte-des-Neiges drugstore to the new format; Jean did likewise for his Mont-Royal store and sold his other pharmacies. In 1973, the partners opened their fifth discount pharmacy in Montreal—and incorporated as Services Farmico, Inc. (SFI). Having persuaded Pharmacie Montreal's owner that discount drugstores were the pharmacies of the future and that bulk-buying allowed for very low prices that attracted more customers, Louis Michaud won SFI's first franchisee: the renowned Pharmacie Montreal. This pharmacy, commented Jean Coutu in *Gestion*, was a "central downtown institution having 250 employees, 35 trucks making deliveries on a 24-hour basis throughout Montreal, and no doors, because it was open day and night."

The franchising of Pharmacie Montreal was a turning point for Services Farmico. Noticing the obvious success of the "Jean Coutu prototype," many pharmacists wanted to be franchised; the SFI network soon spread all over Quebec. In 1974, SFI bought a warehouse in Longueuil, on the south shore of the island of Montreal, and organized a wholesale-delivery service for the franchisees. A year later, SFI established its headquarters in Longueuil and expanded the center to further facilitate the wholesaling and distribution activities required of a franchiser. By year-end 1980, the SFI network consisted of 50 pharmacies and reported revenues of more than C$150 million dollars.

Jean then discussed the future of the company with his partner, Louis Michaud. "We've been in business together for 13 years," the *Gestion* writers reported Jean as saying. "All is well. My children are interested in the firm and yours are not. For you, the pharmacy is an investment; for me it's a reason for living and a way of life. . . . Either you buy me out or I buy you out." Louis sold his shares of stock to Jean, who was then the sole owner of the SFI network; in 1982, he opened a store in New Brunswick, and in 1983 expanded into Ontario. In 1986, completion of an Initial Public Offering brought additional capital to Services Farmico, which was then listed on the Montreal and Toronto stock exchanges as The Jean Coutu Group (PJC) Inc. The Jean Coutu Group (PJC) Inc. U.S.A. was incorporated as a subsidiary.

1987–94: Expansion into the U.S. Market

During 1987, JCG Canada built a 280,000-square-foot distribution center near its headquarters in Longueuil. Ever-

Key Dates

1969: Jean Coutu and Louis Michaud open Quebec's first discount pharmacy: Pharm-Escompte.

1973: Coutu and Michaud incorporate their venture under the legal name of Services Farmico Inc. (SFI)

1974: SFI develops a franchise system and acquires a distribution center in Longueuil, Quebec. Pharmacie Montreal is the first franchisee.

1980: Jean Coutu buys out Louis Michaud's share of SFI.

1986: SFI goes public and is traded on the Montreal and Toronto Stock Exchanges as The Jean Coutu Group (PJC) Inc.

1987: The Jean Coutu Group creates an American subsidiary: The Jean Coutu Group (PJC) U.S.A. Inc.

1995: JCG USA acquires 30 pharmacies from Rite Aid Corporation.

2002: JCG USA acquires 80 Osco stores from Boise, Idaho-based Albertson Inc.

mindful of the health and leisure of its employees, the company also put up a Sports Center for them—thereby introducing a ''first'' for employees in the pharmaceutical industry. During the healthy economy of the 1970s and 1980s, the company seized every opportunity not only to define professional and marketing practices in the Canadian pharmaceutical industry but also to establish itself as one of the most dynamic and profitable firms in its sector in North America. In 1987, the Jean Coutu Network (JCN) integrated the 12 stores of the Cloutier Pharmacy Network into its franchise network.

Creation of PJC USA, the U.S. subsidiary, was a first move toward the realization of what reporter Virthe, in *Revue Commerce,* had quoted as Jean Coutu's hope of ''covering North America with his pharmacies.'' Jean, who had insisted on the best possible professional education for his children, placed his son Michel in charge of the new venture. Michel had watched the U.S. market since the age of 19. After earning a degree in law from the University of Sherbrooke, he had practiced law for three years before obtaining, at his father's insistence, a Master of Business Administration degree from the University of Rochester in New York. In 1987, The Jean Coutu Group acquired the 22 branches of Maxi Drug pharmacies and gradually launched five Maxi Drug pharmacies (later converted to Brooks Pharmacies), in the United States.

In 1990, Jean Coutu withdrew from some of his administrative responsibilities but remained active as chairman of the board and chief executive officer; his youngest son, François, was named president and chief operating officer. François, after matriculating in business at McGill University, had earned a degree in pharmacology from Samford University in Alabama. He then interned for eight months at a Walgreen Pharmacy in Hollywood before returning to Montreal to manage a pharmacy, buy a few pharmacies for himself, and then work his way through the administrative ranks of JCG Canada. Jean Coutu gave Louis, his eldest son who also had a flair for business, the position of Vice-President of Commercial Policies.

The Jean Coutu Group acquired 16 pharmacies in Rhode Island from Douglas Drug, Inc., thereby raising the number of U.S. outlets to 21. The following year, JCG Canada established a division for acquisitions and real-estate development and purchased 11 properties housing Jean Coutu outlets. Furthermore, to favor the needs of its growing number of employees—many of whom were women—in 1992 the firm opened a day-care center next to its Sports Center. The new building could accommodate up to 60 children ranging in age from newborn babies to six-year-old youngsters.

During the 1990s, a lethargic economy began to reduce the buying power of consumers, thereby affecting the break-even point of some franchised outlets. JCN opened 15 new outlets, including three new Maxi Drug stores in Ontario. So that franchisees could have purchasing options that would allow them to sell at lower prices, JCG Canada completely restructured the operation of its distribution centers. Thus, in accordance with its internal partnership philosophy, The Jean Coutu Group voluntarily reduced its profit margins in order to increase sales and ensure the network's financial stability.

The financial and marketing landscapes were changing: consumers were more aware of quality and prices; a lower inflation rate and the emergence of new competitors were shifting market share within the retail industry. Like major corporations in the United Sates, The Jean Coutu Group sought to maintain profitability by increasing sales volume. ''There is only one way to achieve this objective: sharpening our competitive edge and outperforming the competition,'' wrote Chairman Jean and President François in their *1994 Annual Report.* ''Variety [of products], quality of customer service, and a competitive price policy,'' they maintained, would distinguish the company from ''the new forms of competition, including warehouse-stores, department-store chains, and mail-order drugstore services.''

However, part of the solution still slept in Jean Coutu's hope of becoming the North American leader of the pharmaceutical industry. In 1994, at a cost of C$204.7 million, subsidiary JCG USA purchased 221 pharmacies and 16 commercial properties from Ohio-based Revco D.S. Inc.'s Brooks Drug Stores. This purchase placed The Jean Coutu Group among the 15 largest North American organizations in its industry. The newly acquired stores, ideally located in the six New England states, ranked high in the prescription-drug sector; prescriptions generated 45 percent of sales and Brooks salespeople were expert merchandisers: precisely the pharmaceutical and commercial combination Jean Coutu had envisioned. The U.S. subsidiary also leased a warehouse-distribution center in Dayville, Connecticut.

The Brooks acquisition created an unusual challenge for JCG USA: management of some 4,000 new employees and administration of the 221 outlets added to the 21 stores already installed in New England. Fortunately, the Jean Coutu Group had resources for in-house management. Another JCG subsidiary—Le Centre d'information Rx lté (Rx Information Center Ltd)—set up information systems for the U.S. network. In fewer than four months, a completely new infrastructure was designed, implemented with new software that included a prescription allocation package, and integrated with the information system at Longueuil headquarters.

Furthermore, the U.S. subsidiary established a management system and purchased a new building to set up headquarters in Warwick, Rhode Island. Canadian colleagues joined the U.S. team to reorganize the overall storage and distribution activities of the Dayville distribution center, which already had state-of-the-art equipment and space for storing 18,000 different items. Within four months, the Dayville center was fully operational and running at a normal pace with standard turn-around times. The Dayville center had 300,000 square feet of storage space and 50 docks for receiving merchandise. The information systems were completely overhauled and equipped with cutting-edge technology, including expansion of an electronic data interchange (EDI) system.

1996 and Beyond: Financial Challenges and Reorganization

During 1996 and 1997, The Jean Coutu Group outperformed its industry because its uniquely centralized management structure enabled franchisees to buy products at highly competitive prices. JCG Canada bought and integrated eight Quebec-based Mayrand pharmacies into its franchise network. Reacting to the trend for ambulatory care, the company also installed an Orthopedics Department in its pharmacies. Moreover, the Rx Information Center began to implement a POS (point-of-sale) management system and installed a wireless (radio frequency) communication system. Next, JCG Canada's purchase and integration of 19 Cumberland Pharmacies and POS systems marked the largest transaction in the history of retail pharmacies in Quebec.

JCG USA strengthened its position in Massachusetts and Rhode Island with the acquisition of 30 drugstores from Pennsylvania-based Rite Aid Corporation. In exchange, eighteen of the Brooks outlets in Maine—the region furthest from the American distribution center—were transferred to Rite Aid, thereby optimizing JCG USA's advertizing budget and reducing transportation costs, since 80 percent of the BPN outlets were then within a 93-mile radius of the Dayville distribution center. JCG USA also designed a computerized Rx Watch system for its customers: a personalized card gave clients free access to the information stored in their patient files—a great help in emergencies. The network developed its parapharmaceutical sector by increasing the range of private-label products to 800 items, of which 50 were new "Brooks" brands. Furthermore, JCG USA opened two outlets modeled on a new design that included areas reserved for pharmacist-customer consultations and a drive-in service window.

During 1998, The Jean Coutu Group began to reap further benefits from its focus on modernization. Introduction of commercial POS management proceeded apace in Canada; 25 percent of the corporate pharmacies had implemented POS capabilities by the end of 1998. Five new outlets were added to the Canadian network, which also concentrated on the renovation, expansion and relocation of existing establishments. Standardized computer equipment and use of Intranet, a private corporate network, further increased efficiency and performance.

Although an increase in U.S. corporate tax rates reduced JCG USA's contribution to consolidated earnings, the increased profitability of the U.S. subsidiary's corporate pharmacies made up for minimized earnings. The U.S. network opened eight new pharmacies and began to modernize its existing outlets; 25 establishments benefitted from expansions, as well as from in-store and exterior improvements. On the legal front, JCG USA joined other pharmacy chains in Massachusetts to counteract the near monopoly certain pharmacies exercised through exclusive contracts with insurance companies. Patients whose medication was covered by these contracts had to bring their prescriptions to the pharmacy designated by the insurer. In February 1998, an out-of-court settlement freed consumers from this authoritarian situation and BPN registered an average increase of 3,000 prescriptions per week for the months of March, April, and May 1998.

During 1999, an additional 38 of JCN's franchised establishments adopted the POS system, bringing to 100 the number of outlets using this form of financial management, and 50 POS venues were renovated. The network honed its competitive advantages by expanding its range of products: franchisees had access to more than 1,000 private-label products. In the United States, all the BPN outlets operated with POS systems, and close to half of the establishments offered the Interactive Vocal Response (IVR) system that allowed consumers to renew prescriptions by telephone.

At the beginning of the 21st century, after some 30 years of in operation, The Jean Coutu Group defined itself as "a modern organization with experience." Efficiency of operation enabled the company not only to cope with increased competition but also, in many instances, to implement new procedures to meet the needs created by rapid changes in health-care access and the delivery of professional services. According to its *Annual Report 2000*, the company's ongoing modernization program remained focused on three principal objectives: highly professional customer services, improvement of the outlets of both networks, and optimized use of state-of-the-art technologies. During 2000, 45 pharmacies in Canada and 17 U.S. corporate outlets underwent major retrofitting and, in some instances, relocation.

Demographic changes, such as urban development and an aging population, created a client base needing new services and greater professional attention. All Brooks Pharmacies in the United States could access the new IVR system; in Canada, the system was in its pilot phase. For the third consecutive year, The Jean Coutu Group was named "Most Admired Company in Quebec," according to the results of a poll published in the March 2000 issue of *Commerce* magazine.

The year 2001 was outstanding for the corporate development of The Jean Coutu Group, which continued its ongoing quest for greater efficiency in all areas of the company. A strong synergy existed between the various Canadian and U.S. teams through optimal use of state-of-the-art technologies and innovative business management. Never before had a Canadian retail company succeeded in establishing itself profitably in the United States. To ensure that both of its pharmacy networks remained among "the best known and the most efficient," the company enhanced professional services by continuing its training programs for all levels of personnel and by broadening the range of services available to customers. The Jean Coutu Network retrofitted 38 pharmacies and moved four of them to locations conducive to better sales growth.

In 2001, Jean Coutu Group USA's revenues peaked at $1 billion (C$1.53 billion). These results strongly testified to the business acumen in Michel Coutu's strategy for the U.S. subsidiary. With a 6.8 percent increase in the number of prescriptions filled (close to 3 million), Brooks Pharmacy outlets maintained their above-average ranking among all pharmacies in the U.S. market. Since the 1995 acquisition of the Brooks Pharmacies, BPN outlets were thoroughly overhauled to optimize sales: some 50 outlets were relocated, 120 were retrofitted, and 130 new outlets were added.

Michel Coutu's strategy was "to create a new consistent personality for the Brooks chain . . . to move [it] from a dispensing facility to a provider of health-care services," Sandra Levy reported in the April 16, 2001 issue of *Drug Topics*. "Among the changes were a separate drop-off area for prescriptions, a separate area for pick-up, a RxCare Center, . . . [and] a glass-enclosed consultation center next to the pharmacy." The consultation center allowed privacy for counseling, patient education, screenings, and immunizations. By the end of 2001, RxCare Centers were installed in 70 Brooks outlets and all other outlets were slated for installation of the Centers within three years.

At the end of 2001, The Jean Coutu Group's revenues skyrocketed to $1.9 billion (C$2.92 billion). The company managed a total of 544 establishments within its two networks. The Jean Coutu Network consisted of 252 outlets, 40 clinics, and one PJC Santé Beauté for a total of 293 franchised outlets operating in the provinces of Quebec, Ontario, and New Brunswick. The Brooks Pharmacy Network consisted of 251 corporate outlets in the six New England States and New York.

During the first half of 2002, The Jean Coutu Group declared a two-for-one stock split and attained new heights in operating efficiency and revenues. In Quebec, JCN opened four large-scale outlets; the Candiac outlet included a private office for consultations about medication and health-related concerns.

The most important event of this period, however, was JCG USA's purchase of 80 Boston-area Osco drugstores from Boise, Idaho-based Albertson, Inc., one of the world's largest food and drug retailers.

According to *The Gazette* of Montreal, president and COO François Coutu said that almost all the 800 stores of the Osco chain were in the West and the Midwest. The 80 New England stores, the oldest retail drug chain in New England, "were 'a solitude' being supplied from distribution centers as far away as Chicago." These stores, however, were "a perfect fit for the Brooks chain, allowing the company to finally get a foothold in Boston," commented François, who estimated that the company would invest "between $2 million and $3 million a year in each of the next four years to upgrade the Osco stores," and, in February 2002, to begin replacing the Osco banner with that of Brooks Pharmacy. *The Gazette* reporter added that, at the time of the Osco acquisition, the Brooks Pharmacy Network accounted "for more than 60 percent of The Jean Coutu Group's business." The $240-million Osco deal added another dimension of possibility to founder Jean Coutu's hope of "covering North America with his pharmacies."

Principal Subsidiaries

The Jean Coutu Group (PJC) U.S.A.; Le Centre d'information Rx Lté; Sciences Sécurivol Inc.

Principal Competitors

CVS Corporation; Eckerd Corporation; The Katz Group; Pharmaprix.; Rite Aid Corporation; Shoppers Drug Mart Inc.; Wal-Mart Stores Inc.; Walgreen Co.

Further Reading

Bouchard, Jean-Maurice, "François Jean Coutu: la nouvelle âme du Groupe Jean Coutu," *Québec Entreprise,* February 1999, pp. 8–18.

Cardinal, Jacqueline, and Laurent Lapierre, "Jean Coutu et le Groupe PJC," *Gestion,* December 4, 1996, pp. 51–6.

Dupaul, Richard, "Le Groupe Jean Coutu poursuit son offensive américaine," *La Presse* (Montréal), December 7, 2001, pp. D1–2.

"Les 60 entreprises les plus admirées au Québec," *Revue Commerce,* March 2000, p. 19.

Levy, Sandra, "Brooks Pharmacy: a Winner," *Drug Topics,* April 16, 2001.

"Prescription Filled! Jean Coutu Finally Gains Foothold in Boston With Osco Stores," *Gazette,* December 7, 2001, p. C1.

Soulié, Jean-Paul, "La Personnalité de la Semaine," *La Presse* (Montréal), January 30, 2002.

Tremblay, Jacinthe, "François Jean Coutu," *Revue Commerce,* March 1999, p. 20

Virthe, Gérard, "L'homme du mois: Jean Couru, Président, les Services Farmico Inc.," *Revue Commerce,* December 1980, pp. 3, 6.

—Gloria A. Lemieux

Ledcor Industries Limited

1000, 1066 West Hastings Street
Vancouver, British Columbia V6E 3X1
Canada
Telephone: (604) 681-7500
Fax: (604) 895-0801
Web site: http://www.ledcor.com

Private Company
Founded: 1947
Employees: 1,000
Sales: Not Available
NAIC: 231390 Telecommunications Transmission Lines,
Construction; 231 Prime Contracting; 2312 Building
Construction; 23121 Residential Building
Construction; 23122 Non-Residential Building
Construction; 2313 Engineering Construction; 23131
Highway, Street and Bridge Construction; 23133 Oil
and Gas Pipelines and Related Industrial Construction;
2314 Construction Management

Ledcor Industries Limited, based in Vancouver, British Columbia, is a construction company with more than 50 years of general contracting experience throughout North America. In 2000, Ledcor described itself as the second largest contractor in Canada and the largest open shop contractor. Ledcor is active in building construction, civil construction, telecommunications and industrial construction. It has branches in Vancouver, Toronto, Edmonton, Calgary, Denver, Seattle, Reno, Washington, and Quebec City. Senior employees are shareholders in the privately owned company.

1940s Beginnings

Ledcor Industries was founded in 1947 in Edmonton, Alberta. Founder William Lede dreamed about building a global company through consistently excellent performance, top-notch construction, responsible fiscal management, outstanding customer service, rigorous safety training, and accountability in every corporate practice. Lede dedicated his company to quality workmanship and personalized service.

In the beginning, Ledcor was an earthmoving contractor providing services in Edmonton and surrounding area. The company's first significant project was to build the access road and well site for Imperial Oil's oil discovery, Leduc No. 1.

After successfully completing work on this historical project, the company enlarged its construction operations and began providing services to the resource industries and to the public sector. Public sector activity was in a growth period at that time.

Gradually, Ledcor moved from earthmoving contracts to civil contracting. It built highways, buildings, dams, as well as carrying out rock blasting and excavation. It also tackled utility construction, and by early seventies was moving into pipeline construction. In 1971, Ledcor started a small inch gathering system contractor that was later to become the pipeline division.

By the early 1980s, David W. Lede was chairman and chief executive officer. Under his leadership, the company undertook a strategic review and planning initiative. The outcome was the decision to expand geographically and to diversify into other construction operations. Over the next few years, Ledcor expanded throughout North America. They opened offices in Vancouver, Toronto, Calgary, Seattle, and Reno. The corporate head office moved from Edmonton to Vancouver.

During this time, Ledcor broke into the building construction market by purchasing a small company. Thus began the Industrial and Mining Construction Divisions of the company. Ledcor also entered the oil and gas well servicing business, while the Civil Division expanded to include underground installation of fiber-optic cable. They created six construction divisions: Civil, Mining, Telecommunications, Pipeline, Industrial, and Building Construction.

This restructuring process was initiated during one of the most severe construction slumps ever to occur in western Canada. Thanks to the restructuring, Ledcor was able to accomplish substantial growth despite the economic downtimes of the period.

Challenges in the 1980s

However, not everything was smooth sailing. In 1985, Ledcor was awarded two government contracts worth $12 mil-

---

Key Dates:

1947: The company's first project is to build the access road and well site for Imperial Oil's famous oil discovery, Leduc No. 1.

1971: The company starts a small inch gathering system contractor that later becomes the pipeline division.

1985: Ledcor is awarded contract to work on the Coquihalla Highway in British Columbia.

1987: Ledcor establishes a telecommunications division and merges with Consolidated General Western Industries.

1998: A communication division is spun off as a subsidiary under the name Worldwide Fibre; Ledcor teams with Fonorola to install a fiber optic cable across Canada.

2000: Worldwide Fibre is renamed 360networks; Ledcor wins the top category at VRCA (Vancouver Regional Construction Association Awards) in the General Contractor Award of Excellence.

---

lion to work on BC's Coquihalla Highway. Controversy erupted regarding Ledcor's hiring practices, initiating one of the very few scandals ever to touch Ledcor. According to Peter Comparelli's article published in the Vancouver Sun, NDP Labour Critic Colin Gableman argued that Ledcor had recruited employees from Alberta, despite a contractual obligation to hire BC workers for the project. Ledcor denied the allegations, saying that only four out of five supervisors were Albertans and that other workers were from BC. Gableman retorted that, "All Ledcor did was to encourage the Alberta workers to switch their Alberta plates to BC license plates." Gableman also alleged that Ledcor was trying to keep union organizers out of the work site. Alberta is generally viewed as being friendly to industry while BC is thought to be friendly to organized labor. In time, the controversy died down and work on the highway continued.

In 1987, Ledcor Industries and Consolidated General Western Industries, also from Vancouver, agreed to merge their operations through a share exchange. At that time, Ledcor's primary operations were in British Columbia, Alberta, and Ontario. It owned 30 percent of Consolidated General and indirectly owned 25 percent of Inter Cable Communications Inc. Consolidated General was a public diversified investment and holding company. The transaction gave Ledcor 75 percent controlling interest in GWI. The latter changed its name to Ledcor Industries Limited.

Also, in 1987, Ledcor launched its communications division. The Ledcor division designed, engineered and built communications networks for telephone companies throughout North America.

The 1990s and Beyond

Ledcor's growth continued in the nineties. In 1996, *Public Construction News* rated the company as Canada's fifth largest general contractor according to volume of work. Also in 1996, Ledcor was awarded the contract for the Ekati diamond mine in the Northwest Territories. This project presented special chal-

In September 1996, a highly significant event occurred in Ledcor's history. Long distance carrier Fonorola announced intent to join with Ledcor Industries to build a 48-strand fiber-optic cable between Vancouver, Calgary, Edmonton, Winnipeg, and Toronto. The $120 million cable was to be constructed along a CN Rail right-of-way. Ledcor planned to sell 75 percent of the installed capacity to third party users, such as communities, governments, and large industries in North America. The ambitious plan raised eyebrows and generated considerable speculation as to Ledcor's long range vision. As Peter Aggus wrote in IMC's *Telecom Advisor*, "This company has displayed amazing confidence in the profitability of a totally independent optical fiber networking spanning the continent. Figures like $1.2 billion of investment in an 18,000 km network are enough to make anyone take this company seriously."

Some speculated that Ledcor had ambitions to operate a telecommunications network. However, according to Ledcor's web site, this was not the strategy. Their plan was to franchise deliver fiber strands to companies like BC Tel and Telus. They described it as a "condominium-style approach" and likened it to laying down the asphalt for others to drive on.

Ledcor's role in the project was as developer and builder. Fonorola was to act as carrier and sell the bandwidth capacity to interested parties. Over the following months, other carriers joined the project, including AT&T and Metronet. Construction progressed smoothly until reaching Longlac in northern Ontario. The rocky environment of the Cambrian Shield of Northern Ontario presented special challenges in the area reaching from Longlac to southern Ontario. However, by then, Ledcor had experience in installing fiber optic cable in all sorts of environments—in everything from rock to seawater. Alex Navarro, a project design engineer described the situation: "You have the hardest rock in the world." Other challenges involved having to provide generators or electrical lines from the nearest source to power repeater stations located every 120 kilometers along the line. Despite the challenges, the cable was laid.

In 1998, the telecommunications division spun off as a subsidiary and was renamed Worldwide Fiber (WFI). It had acquired a percentage of the 8,300-kilometer Canadian Fiber Optic Telecommunications system and had a patented rail-mounted system that had been used in various locations across North America. Worldwide Fiber also obtained a subsidiary, Pacific Fiber Link Inc., which participated in the construction of a fiber optic backbone network between Sacramento, California, and Portland, Oregon.

Also, in 1998, after four years of planning, construction work started on the SEA-Van One, a project to provide a diversity route between Vancouver, BC and Seattle, Washington. Ledcor opted to incorporate Vancouver Island in the link. This involved a substantial investment in submarine cable. Completed after one year of construction, the project involved a fast-tracked state-of-the-art cable installation procedure. It provided advanced communications links to several remote communities, at a relatively economic price. BC Tel, Sprint Canada, and Metronet were among those companies that purchased capacity on Sea-Van.

However, the project was not without setbacks. Peculiarly, although Ledcor reached agreement with 89 municipalities and property owners for the right to cross their land, it could not make a deal with Vancouver, its own city. The dispute centered upon what the city could charge Ledcor Industries for the right to run underground fiber cables through city property. According to William Boei, business writer for the *Vancouver Sun*, Ledcor reported that the city had threatened to tear up 175 metres of fiber-optic cable that crossed city land. The city denied this, but in turn accused Ledcor of building without permission and of trespassing on city property. After 15 months of negotiations, Ledcor asked the CRTC (the federal regulatory agency) to help work out a long-term solution. The city in turn asked the CRTC to clarify whether municipalities could charge telecom companies a fee for laying cable across municipal property.

Years ago, prior to deregulation, the CRTC had ruled that public utilities could share in rights-of-way. However, with deregulation, municipalities were complaining of an escalation of private companies wanting rights-of-way for profit. The Ledcor situation was a test case with far-reaching implications. If CRTC found in favor of the City of Vancouver, the ruling could lead to new policies that would have made it much more expensive for data carriers to build new networks.

Although no one involved in the dispute would estimate how many dollars could be at stake, Lis Angus, executive vice-president of Angus Telemanagement, said it could be a "horrendous amount of money."

As CRTC warned it would, the resulting investigation took a long time. On January 25, 2001, after several appeals, the CRTC ruled that Ledcor had the right to construct, maintain, and operate transmission lines that Ledcor had constructed in 18 street crossings in Vancouver. It was a major breakthrough.

Meanwhile, Worldwide Fiber Inc.'s fiber became a hot commodity. In 1999, Bell Canada, AT&T Canada/Metronet and Call-Net each bought 12 strands of WFI's 48-strand fiber, while BCT.Telus contracted to build a separate network into Bell Canada's central Canadian heartland.

However, Worldwide Fiber opted to keep the remaining 12 strands of fiber for itself and announced its intent to move from a contractor into a telecommunications carrier. In early 1999, WFI contracted with Level 3 Communications, a U.S. network company, to build 800 route-km of fiber linking Buffalo, Toronto, and Montreal. As part of the deal, WFI retained additional dark fiber strands for its own use. "It's an innovative strategy that helps WFI keep the cost of its own networks down," said George Karidis, associate research director with telecom consultants, The Yankee Group in Canada. Karidis went on to remark that over the last few years, Ledcor had built most of the fiber networks in Canada and many of the U.S. builds as well.

In March 2000, Worldwide Fibre was renamed 360networks inc. According to the company website, "The new name better reflects our shift beyond our historic business of constructing networks to providing a broad range of high-bandwidth services on those networks." 360networks was a public company listed on NASDAQ.

In 2000, 360networks completed a 29,000-km North American telecommunications network. Construction of a transatlantic network was underway, with completion date set for 2001.

Ledcor's other divisions enjoyed similar successes. Ledcor Construction had participated in the construction of projects as diverse as cinemas, hotels, office buildings, casinos, institutional projects, manufacturing facilities and warehouses, and a number of special projects, including the interior of Vancouver Regional Airport and a Revenue Canada Taxation Centre.

Ledcor Mining had worked on a number of major contracts in Canada, the United States, and Mexico. Activities included topsoil stripping, dam construction, contract mining, plant site grading and portal construction, layback of highwall, leach pad construction, and reclamation.

The heavy civil and highway component provided the private and public sectors with earthmoving, drill, blast, and excavation of solid rock, as well as the construction of bridges, highways, dams, container port facilities, and major concrete structures. Projects completed include the Vancouver Island Highway and the Alaska Highway.

The pipeline division had worked throughout varied terrain, including prairie, muskeg, heavily forested areas, and mountains. Ledcor had developed its own semi-automatic welding procedures to complement its work in other semi-automatic and in manual processes. Additionally, the company maintained a state-of-the-art maintenance and transportation facility in Edmonton, Alberta.

Major projects there included river crossings at Peace River, North Saskatchewan River, Athabasca, Red Deer, and the Brazeau River. Larger pipeline projects included Enbridge in Camrose, Alberta; TCPL in Chinchaga, Alberta; TCPL in St. Paul, Alberta; and Syncrude in Fort McMurray, Alberta.

Ledcor's Industrial division consisted of seven sub-components: construction, electrical, rigging, maintenance, module assembly, pipe fabrication, and construction management. The company had worked on a wide array of projects across North America.

Into the new millennium Ledcor's reputation was low profile and private. Company executives rarely consented to interviews and not a lot of reference material was available about Ledcor Industries. Still, the company was known for its commitment to excellence and for bringing in projects on time and on budget.

Ledcor was also known for its excellent safety record. Over the years, they had been recognized many times with safety awards and publicly stated that they are committed to the safety of their work force. According to *WorkSafe BC*, co-owners Cliff and David Lede witnessed the death of their father in a workplace accident in 1980. "Although Ledcor's management and workers were already committed to workplace safety, the tragedy had a lasting effect on the way they do business," wrote *WorkSafe BC*.

WorkSafe BC further acknowledged Ledcor's commitment to safety when their model Blood and Body Fluids Precautions Policy was implemented in 1998. "Workers increasingly reported finding discarded needs on or near construction sites,'' wrote *WorkSafe BC*. ''Ledcor worked with a WCB (Workers Compensation Board) prevention officer to incorporate the precaution policy into its project-specific safety program—the company now trains every one of the approximately 1,000 workers on its Canadian and U.S. projects in these precautions before they begin working with the construction firm.''

Although Ledcor Industries did not make its financial status readily available, one could surmise that the company was doing well based on its growth, the number and size of its projects, and its reputation. In particular, the communication division seemed on the brink of great success given the decision brought down by CRTC and given the current global interest in broadband technologies.

Principal Subsidiaries

360networks inc (69%).

Principal Divisions

Telecommunications; Building; Civil; Industrial.

Principal Competitors

Centex Construction Group; Morrison Knudsen Corporation.

Further Reading

Aggus, Peter, ''Anatomy of a Long Distance Resource Supplier,'' *IMC's Telecom Advisor*, Spring, 1999.

Anglen, Robert, ''Pickets Result in Second Reno Regal Cinema Construction Shutdown,'' *Reno Gazette-Journal*, October 13, 1999.

Boei, William, ''B.C. Firm Joins Big League,'' *Vancouver Sun*, September 25, 1999.

——, ''Company Wants Same Deal as Utilities,'' *Vancouver Sun*, December 4, 1999.

——,'' Ledcor, City Turn to CRTC to Settle Fibre-Optic Scrap,'' *Vancouver Sun*, April 3, 1999.

''Companies Merging,'' *Province*, January 4, 1987.

Comparelli, Peter, ''Albertans Get BC Work, MLA says,'' *Vancouver Sun*, April 16, 1985.

''Consolidated General to Merge with Ledcor,'' *Globe & Mail*, January 3, 1987

''Decision CRTC: 2001–23,'' *CRTC*, January 25, 2001.

Huneault, Greg, ''New 'Highway' Under Construction,'' *Northern Ontario Business*, May, 1998.

''Ledcor, CGWI Agree to Share Exchange,'' *Vancouver Sun*, January 3, 1987.

''Puget Sound Plan Began 5 Years Ago,'' *Vancouver Sun*, February 4, 1999. p. F15.

''Workplace Fatalities Take Devastating Tool New WCB Report Shows,'' *WorkSafe Online*, 1999.

—June Campbell

London Drugs Ltd.

12831 Horseshoe Place
Richmond, British Columbia V7A 4X5
Canada
Telephone: (604) 272-7400
Web site: http://www.londondrugs.com

Private Company
Incorporated: 1945
Employees: 6,000
Sales: C$1.26 billion (US$792 million) (2000 est.)
NAIC: 44611 Pharmacies and Drug Stores

London Drugs Ltd. is one of the largest operators of drug store chains in Canada. Like mass merchandisers, the stores cover a broad range of product mix. While pharmacy remains the core business, stores also offer computers and accessories, cameras, photo-finishing services and supplies, household appliances, audio-video equipment, and other high-end consumer electronics.

Company Beginnings: 1945–63

In 1945, Sam Bass, a controversial British Columbia pharmacist bought a 1,000-square-foot pharmacy store on Main Street in Vancouver, British Columbia. At that time, the business was bringing in C$25,000 a year. The economic climate was right for opening a new business. With the end of World War II, Canada was entering a period of economic optimism. Sam Bass named his new store London Drugs because he thought that the name sounded patriotic.

At the time that Bass bought the drug store on Main Street in Vancouver, he had no cash and no credit rating. However, the owner of the drug store was eager to sell, so he agreed to sell the store on June 1 and collect payment on July 1. That gave Bass one month to raise the cash. He promptly offered a clearance sale and initiated a policy of low-percentage markup on prescription drugs, instead of a flat fee as was used by other pharmacists. Also, as owner of the pharmacy, Bass found he had lines of credit available to him from manufacturers, thereby allowing the pharmacist to restock the store after the sale.

Business boomed when customers discovered that the low prescription prices were permanent and not loss leaders. By July 1, the cash was available to make the purchase payment. At the end of his first year, Bass's store had brought in C$80,000. Customers were coming from all over Vancouver to take advantage of the economically priced prescription drugs.

Bass understood that his store needed a competitive advantage over other pharmacies. The pharmacist thus implemented what was viewed at the time as an outrageous new idea. He offered extended shopping hours from 9:00 a.m. to midnight, seven days a week. The move initiated a battle with the Pharmaceutical Association and with city hall, the first of many such battles that have occurred throughout the course of London Drugs' history.

By 1953, Canada was in a period of postwar recession. Many competitors were operating with modest business plans, but Sam Bass opted instead to diversify his product mix, another strategy that became standard operating procedure for London Drugs. The corporate Web site reports that the company ''sent shockwaves through the pharmaceutical industry by offering discount photographic equipment and supplies.'' In 1958, Bass once again startled the pharmaceutical industry by price-cutting dispensing fees on prescriptions. He also began advertising on CJOR radio. The ad campaign was effective and sales increased accordingly.

In 1961, Bass implemented the first of London Drug's Optical Departments. Bass had been interested in the concept since 1957, when the income tax appeal board ruled that substantial sums of monies received as kickbacks from optical firms must be taxed as income and not as capital gains, as the doctors had been claiming. (In mid-1959, the British Columbia Supreme Court ruled that the doctors in question had acted ethically.) It took Bass until 1964 to persuade two opticians to utilize the same concept of merchandising that had worked so well for London Drugs—that is, using a low-percentage markup in dispensing a prescription. The idea proved equally successful. Bass supervised the pricing and quality of the merchandise in the Optical Departments, but Western Optical Ltd. manufactured the lenses. Ten years later, nine London Drugs' stores in the Lower Mainland offered Optical Departments.

Expansion and Struggles: 1963–70

In 1963, London Drugs entered a period of expansion when Bass opened a new store in downtown Vancouver at the corner of Georgia and Granville. This store eventually achieved the highest per-square-foot sales of any drugstore in Canada. In 1968, Bass sold his company to a U.S. firm, the Daylin Corporation. Bass himself remained on as president until 1976. Under Daylin's ownership, the company continued to grow. The third store opened in 1969 in New Westminster, British Columbia. At 9,000-square-feet, the store was thought to be among the most spacious drug stores in Canada.

London Drugs wanted to offer its customers good quality at low prices. To defend his right to offer prescription drugs at low costs, Sam Bass fought his way to the Supreme Court of Canada. When a federal government implemented a commission to investigate the cost of drugs, Bass went to Ottawa to appear before the commission. He offered several proposals to reduce drug costs. Of the five subsequent recommendations that the commission made, three were found in Bass's brief. *The New Westminster Columbian* quoted Bass as saying, "There's a large group of people in the world who think everyone should look after Number One—himself. I want to do that by making a success of my business, but I can't do it without looking after the interests of everyone else who needs anything in a drugstore. I believe drug prices could be lowered a great deal. I try to help by intelligent buying in large quantities and selling at the smallest possible profit margin. And everything we sell is top quality."

In June 1969, the Teamsters' Union organized the employees of London Drugs, a move that proved to be far from problem-free for all concerned. When the company and the union were unable to negotiate a first contract, the Teamsters twice called for a strike vote, and twice London Drugs' employees voted against strike action. The Labour Relations Board (LRB) made use of its power to impose a first contract, one that was not supported by the company's employees. Shortly thereafter, the employees lost a bid in the courts to quash the decision. A bitter struggle continued between the union officials and London Drugs' management. In 1973, the Teamsters and the Retail-Wholesale Union gave London Drugs a "hot" designation. Promptly, London Drugs sued the two unions for damages. According to the *Vancouver Sun,* the company "asked damages under the Trade Unions Act against the unions for allegedly persuading people not to do business with the store and for inducing breach of contract between the store and its suppliers."

Strike action was declared at London Drug's warehouse in 1973. Five of 17 employees picketed outside while the remaining 12 daily crossed the picket line to report for work. Shortly thereafter, those who crossed the picket line filed a decertification application. LRB vice-chairman Jack Moore threw out the application, saying, "I am not satisfied that the trade union has ceased to represent the majority of the employees in the unit."

When an LRB-imposed contract expired in 1975, the Teamsters argued that the agreement should remain in effect unless terminated by a strike or lockout. London Drugs disagreed, and the dispute was again taken to the LRB for settlement This time, the Board upheld London Drugs' position, leaving the employees without a contract. By this time, the employees had filed for decertification three times, and many had begun refusing to pay union dues to protest the board's reluctance to decertify the Teamsters. An arbitration board subsequently ordered the workers to pay their dues. Labor strife continued for years to come.

The Formative Years: 1970–80

In 1970, Mark Nussbaum had joined London Drugs, an event that London Drugs' newsletter, *London Bridge,* described as "a significant turning point in London Drugs' history. He brings with him a dynamic American-style of retail merchandising that forever redefines what London Drugs is." Nassbaum's first major project was to mark the company's 25th anniversary by opening the company's largest store to date. Situated on West Broadway, Vancouver, the store introduced another addition to the product mix—consumer electronics.

In 1971, London Drugs' large store in downtown Vancouver closed and relocated to the newly built Pacific Center Mall. The original offices and warehouse in Vancouver also closed and relocated to a new 80,000-square-foot facility in Richmond, British Columbia. In the same year, London Drugs opened a store in North Vancouver, and entered an ongoing period of strife with the North Vancouver City Council. One week following London Drugs' opening, North Vancouver City Council changed its shops regulation bylaw to cut back the store's Sunday and evening operations. The bylaw also barred London Drugs from selling items such as major appliances, electronics, furnishings, automotive supplies, and paint and hardware supplies during hours when other retail stores were closed. Bass promptly launched legal action against the council, claiming the new bylaw to be discriminatory. A period of decisions and appeals followed, with London Drugs ultimately achieving the legal right to operate their stores on Sundays and evenings in North Vancouver.

In the years to follow, the company pursued a strategy of expansion, opening new stores in various locations in the Lower Mainland of British Columbia. In 1976, London Drugs opened its first out-of-province store in Edmonton, Alberta. It opened a second store in that city a few months after.

In 1976, Sam Bass was replaced as president of London Drugs by the senior vice-president, Stanley H. Glazier. Few details are known regarding the reasons for Bass's leaving. Spokespersons from Daylin Inc. reported that Bass had left for "personal reasons," while Glazier reported that Bass's leaving was "the result of a decision by the board of directors." Around the same time as Bass's exit from the company, Daylin Inc. initiated bankruptcy proceedings and offered Pay Less Drug Stores of Oakland, California, the option to purchase London Drugs for C$9 million. The Pay Less deal did not come to fruition, however, and London Drugs was sold to Tong Louie of

Key Dates:

1945: Pharmacist Sam Bass opens the first London Drugs.

1953: Bass diversifies product mix by offering discount photographic supplies.

1958: Bass cuts dispensing fees on prescriptions.

1963: London Drugs opens a second store in downtown Vancouver.

1968: Sam Bass sells London Drugs to Daylin Corporation.

1969: Daylin opens third London Drugs situated in New Westminster.

1970: Mark Nussbaum takes over management of London Drugs; London Drugs 25th Anniversary marked by opening of large new store in Vancouver.

1971: London Drugs begins opening new stores in western Canada, including sites in North Vancouver, Burnaby, and Edmondton.

1976: Tong Louis buys London Drugs from Daylin Corporation.

1982: London Drugs opens new stores, one each in Alberta and British Columbia, and moves its head office moved to Richmond, B.C.

1985: The company celebrates its 40th anniversary and opens three new stores.

2000: LDHealth.com is launched.

H.Y. Louie Co. Ltd., a B.C. owned and operated firm. Louie continued to strengthen the company's commitment to providing customers with quality products at the lowest prices.

Expansion and Innovation: 1980–90

During the 1980s, London Drugs continued to expand. Stores were opened in British Columbia on Vancouver Island, the Lower Mainland, and Kamloops, while in Alberta new stores opened in Edmonton, Red Deer, Calgary, and Grande Prairie. In the spring of 1981, London Drugs opened a new distribution center in Richmond, British Columbia. Encompassing 137,000-square-feet, it was automated with a conveyer belt system, replacing the former manual operations. In 1982, the head office relocated to this complex as well.

In 1981, London Drugs added a new product to its marketing mix—a one-hour photo-finishing service. The service was piloted at the West Broadway store in Vancouver, but in time labs were installed in every existing outlet. The company soon dominated the photo-finishing market in Western Canada. Two years later, in 1983, the company entered the home computer business, offering computer departments in four locations in the Lower Mainland. In 1985, London Drugs celebrated its 40th anniversary. At year's end, it had a total of 25 stores. Expo 86 provided London Drugs with a new opportunity to promote itself by sponsoring a first-aid station on the fairgrounds. Also in 1986, London Drugs responded to consumer complaints and banned "adult sophisticated" magazines from its shelves. The move followed a similar decision by 7-Eleven stores when they pulled adult magazines a month earlier, instigating a flurry of media discussion regarding the role of private industry in censorship.

In the spring of 1987, London Drugs' store in North Vancouver became British Columbia's first drug store to sell wine, wine-based coolers, and alcoholic cider. This innovation, which occurred after ongoing negotiations with the Liquor Control Board (LCB), was intended as a four-month pilot project, with an expansion into wine outlets to follow if deemed feasible. As expected, the move generated considerable controversy: competing merchants, government officials, elected representatives, and groups against alcoholically impaired drivers engaged in a heated debate. At the end of the trial period, executive vice-president Mark Nassbaum was quoted as saying that the project was overwhelmingly successful, as indicated by mounting sales volume and a poll conducted in the community. However, a governmental liquor-policy review committee recommended that the service be discontinued, claiming that the public did not want wines sold in private stores.

A Challenging Decade: 1990–2000

The *London Bridge* newsletter describes the 1990s as being economically more challenging than the 1980s. Nevertheless, expansion continued, and by the end of the 1980s London Drugs was operating 34 stores. This figure grew to 54 stores by the end of the 1990s. New stores opened in British Columbia in Chilliwack, White Rock, West Vancouver, Colwood, Maple Ridge, and Kelowna, and in Alberta in Edmonton and Calgary. Other stores were renovated. Never far from controversy, London Drugs generated publicity in 1992 when breast-feeding groups in British Columbia organized a boycott against the company to protest the sale of formula products. Later, in 1999, local residents failed in an attempt to block the building of a new complex in the Kerrisdale community of Vancouver.

In 1995, the company's 50th anniversary, London Drugs launched London Drugs Insurance Services. In the latter part of the decade, more innovations were introduced at selected stores, including a temporary Ticketmaster outlet, a full service Royal Bank, Internet cafes, Sound Rooms in the Audio Visual Departments and a Photo Station where customers could view and edit their photos online.

2000 and Beyond

As the new century commenced, London Drugs appeared poised for continued success. In 2000, the chain opened a new store at the site of its roots in the 1960s. Located at the corner of Georgia and Granville in downtown Vancouver, this new store is a two level, 22,000-square-foot retail outlet. President Wyneth Powell remarked in an interview with the *Vancouver Sun* that more than one million cruise ships pass through Vancouver annually, and that comprises an excellent market for photo finishing and cosmetics. Also in 2000, London Drugs launched LDHealth.com, a Web site that allows consumers to order prescription refills by email. According to an article published in the *Vancouver Sun,* the company plans to become a health provider and will dispense information on a wide series of medical topics.

Like previous London Drugs executives before him, Powell declined to provide annual sales figures but did report that the company achieved one of the highest sales-per-square-foot figures of any retailer in Canada. The company planned to operate 100 stores across Canada by the end of the decade.

Principal Competitors

Finlandia Consultants Ltd.; Pharmasave; Shoppers Drug Mart.

Further Reading

Cheveldon, Belinda, ''Sam Bass Fights to Lower Prices,'' *New Westminster Columbian,* January 16, 1969.

''Constantineau, Bruce, ''London Drugs Returns to Its Roots,'' *Vancouver Sun,* 2000, p.D2

''Drug Firm Sues Unions,'' *Vancouver Sun,* October 30, 1973.

''Drug Store Closing Law Upheld,'' *Vancouver Sun,* January 7, 1972.

Fayerman, Pamela, ''Druggist Says Wine Right Prescription,'' *Vancouver Sun*, March 17, 1987.

Gram, Karen, ''Free Baby Formula Nets Boycott,'' *Vancouver Sun,* September 11, 1992.

''London Drugs in New Mall: Instant Success Expected,'' *Vancouver Sun*, October 26, 1971, p.3A

''London Drugs Makes Statement,'' *Chain Drug Review,* January 1, 2001.

''London Drugs, Richmond, BC An Early Adaptor of E-Comm,'' Ministerial Conference on Economic Conference, October 7, 1998.

''London in Expansion Mode,'' *Chain Drug Review,* April 23, 2001.

McBurnie, George, ''Price Espionage Denied,'' *Vancouver Sun,* June 6, 1975.

Mickleburgh, Rod, ''Board Rules Union Pact Is Over at Warehouse,'' *Vancouver Sun,* November 20, 1975.

Parton, Nicole, ''Chain Bans Explicit Magazines,'' *Vancouver Sun*, June 27, 1986.

——, ''Drugstore Wine Shop Opens Today,'' *Vancouver Sun*, March 16, 1987.

''A Perspective on Our Fabulous Fifty,'' *London Bridge,* Autumn 1995, pp. 22–31.

''Pharmacy Merchandising,'' *Vancouver Sun*, October 26, 1971.

''Playboycotting of pornography,'' *Vancouver Sun,* June 30, 1986.

Thomas, Lew, ''North Van City Limits Drug Store Sale,'' *Vancouver Sun,* July 16, 1971.

Volick, Heather, ''London Drugs Runs with ActiveStore,'' *Pharmacy Connects*, January 1998.

Ward, Doug, ''Views on Booze Called Confusing,'' *Vancouver Sun,* August 8, 1987.

—June Campbell

L'Oréal SA

41, rue Martre
92117 Clichy
France
Telephone: (1) 47 56 70 00
Fax: (1) 47 56 80 02
Web site: http://www.loreal.com

Public Company
Incorporated: 1939
Employees: 48,222
Sales: Euro 12.6 billion ($11.9 billion) (2000)
Stock Exchanges: Paris
Ticker Symbol: OR
NAIC: 32562 Toilet Preparation Manufacturing

L'Oréal SA, one of the largest companies in France, is the world's largest manufacturer of high-quality cosmetics, perfumes, hair care, and skin care products. Its brands are found in over 150 countries and include such well-known names as Lancôme, Maybelline, Garnier, Redken, and Matrix. The company is known for its involvement in research and development—it spent 3 percent of sales on cosmetology and dermatology research in 2000—and owns a 19.5 percent stake in the pharmaceutical firm Sanofi/Synthélabo. Liliane Bettencourt and her family control 51 percent of Gesparal, a holding company that owns 54 percent of L'Oréal. The Swiss food giant, Nestlé S.A., owns the remaining 49 percent of Gesparal.

Early 19th Century Origins

L'Oréal's story begins in turn-of-the-century Paris, at a time when women of the demimonde dyed their hair, their choice restricted to fiery red or coal black. In 1907, Eugène Schueller, a young chemist, began to concoct the first synthetic hair dyes by night in his kitchen and sell them to hair salons in the morning under the brand name of Auréole. His strategy was successful; within two years he established the Société Française des Teintures Inoffensives pour Cheveux, which soon afterward became L'Oréal.

In 1912, the company extended its sales to Austria, Holland and Italy and by 1920 its products were available in a total of 17 countries, including the United States, Brazil, Chile, Peru, Equador, Bolivia, and the Soviet Union, and in the Far East. At this stage, L'Oréal consisted of three research chemists and ten sales representatives.

Rapid Growth: 1920s–50s

Schueller's timing had been singularly fortunate. The end of World War I was celebrated by the Jazz Age, when short hairstyles became fashionable, with a new emphasis on shape and color. By the end of the 1920s, there were 40,000 hair salons in France alone and L'Oréal's new products O'Cap, Imédia Liquide, and Coloral captured the growing market. In 1928, the company made its first move toward diversification, purchasing the soap company Monsavon.

In the 1930s and 1940s, platinum-haired screen idols such as Jean Harlow and Mae West made blond hair especially popular and bleaches such as L'Oréal Blanc sold well. L'Oréal was quick to make use of both old and new media to promote its products. In 1933, Schueller commissioned famous artists of the time to design posters and also launched his own women's magazine, *Votre Beauté*. Dop, the first mass-market shampoo, was promoted through children's hair-lathering competitions at the highly popular French circuses. and by 1938 L'Oréal was advertising its hair products with radio jingles.

During this period, L'Oréal demonstrated its ability to meet new consumer demands. When the Front Populaire won the 1936 elections and introduced the first paid holidays for French workers, L'Oréal's Ambre Solaire was ready to capture the new market for suntan lotions. Meanwhile, the company's sales network was expanding on both a national and an international scale. Products began to be sold through pharmacies and perfumers and new Italian, Belgian, and Danish subsidiaries were established between 1936 and 1937.

Even the outbreak of World War II in 1939 failed to curb the company's growth. At a time of strict rationing, women permed their hair and bought cosmetics to boost their morale. L'Oréal launched the first cold permanent wave product, Oréol, in 1945.

Company Perspectives:

Our Professional Products Division strives to promote the global development of highly innovative and exclusive hair care products for salon use, and the expansion of the salon profession through a policy of active partnership centered on hairdresser training. The mission of our Consumer Products Division is to develop beauty products for the widest possible range of customers by offering highly innovative products at competitive prices through mass-market retail channels. The Luxury Products Division devotes itself to maintaining the highest possible quality in its products, packaging, merchandising, and communications, thus confirming the brands as world-renowned signatures. And our Active Cosmetics Department strives to create and develop dermo-cosmetic healthcare brands that meet the highest standards of skin care safety and effectiveness, as proven by clinical tests.

At the same time, the company continued to expand; by the end of the war there were 25 research chemists and distribution had been extended to the United Kingdom, Argentina, and Algeria.

During this period, François Dalle and Charles Zviak joined the group, both recruited by Monsavon at a time when the cosmetics industry held far less attraction for graduate chemical engineers than the atomic-energy or oil industries. Both men would play an important role in the company's future; by 1948, Dalle had already been appointed joint general manager of L'Oréal.

The consumer boom of the 1950s and the arrival of new blond screen idols Marilyn Monroe and Brigitte Bardot (originally a brunette) meant further expansion for L'Oréal. By 1950, a research-and-development team of 100 chemists had created further innovative products, including the first lightening tint, Imédia D, introduced in 1951, and the first coloring shampoo, Colorelle, introduced in 1955, which answered an increasing demand for subtlety. The company advanced further into the field of skin care, entering into technological agreements with the company Vichy, in 1954. Vichy was to become part of the L'Oréal group in 1980.

Eugène Schueller's promotional talents were recognized in 1953 when he was awarded an advertising Oscar. Schueller died in 1957 and François Dalle took over as chairman and CEO at 39 years of age.

Focus on R&D and Acquisitions: 1960s–70s

The 1960s were years of revolution, both cultural and commercial. As music and fashion became increasingly teen-oriented, there was a growing interest in conserving—or simulating—youthful looks. At the same time hundreds of new boutiques, supermarkets, and chain stores sprang up to supply this rapidly growing market. L'Oréal made a growing commitment to capital investment. In 1960, a new research-and-production center was established in Aulnay-sous-Bois, bringing the number of research staff up to 300. In 1963 and 1964, the company opened new cosmetological and bacteriological facilities, evidence of a highly scientific approach to skin care.

Another production unit, Soprocos, opened in St. Quentin in 1965, and over the decade new distribution outlets were established in Uruguay, Algeria, Canada, Mexico, and Peru. L'Oréal was listed on the French stock exchange in 1963, during a period of restructuring within the group. In 1962, owing to the boom in hair-product sales, L'Oréal sold Monsavon in order to concentrate on its core business. At the same time it bought the hair-hygiene specialist Cadoricin. In 1964, L'Oréal bought Jacques Fath perfumes and a year later Lancôme thereby gaining a significant entry into the high-quality skin-care, make-up, and perfume market and gaining increased access to perfumery outlets. Garnier, a hair-product company, and Laboratoires d'Anglas were also added to the group. In 1968, the company took major stakes in Golden in the United Kingdom and in Ruby, a personal hygiene and household products manufacturer. In the same year, L'Oréal bought the fashion and perfumes house André Courrèges.

With increased resources and expertise, L'Oréal launched a number of successful products, many of which are market leaders to this day. These included the hair spray Elnett, Récital hair dyes, and the perfume Fidji. Fidji was launched under the Guy Laroche brand name.

In 1969, L'Oréal recruited a young Welshman, Lindsay Owen-Jones, from the prestigious Fontainebleau business school INSEAD. An Oxford languages graduate, he would go on to become the fourth chairman and managing director of L'Oréal. At the age of 25, he became general manager of L'Oréal's public-products division in Belgium and turned around unprofitable subsidiaries in France and Italy, before going to the United States to take charge of L'Oréal's distributor, Cosmair Inc. in 1980.

L'Oréal benefited from the emphasis on health and fitness in the 1970s. From this time onwards, L'Oréal's earnings outstripped those of any other French blue chip and grew twice as fast as the cosmetics-industry average. L'Oréal's success permitted further commitment to research and development; the number of research staff rose from 500 in 1970 to 750 in 1974. New production facilities were opened in France and in 1979 the International Centre for Dermatological Research was established at Sofia-Antipolis, in the south of France, for the treatment of skin disorders and aging.

Over the decade, structural and tactical changes were made within the group, based on the findings of the 1969 management study done by McKinsey & Co. The year 1970 saw the establishment of new operational divisions and management structure. A few years later, the company began to speed up the process of internationalization, with particular emphasis on New Zealand, Australia, Japan, and Hong Kong. In 1976, L'Oréal signed a technical-assistance contract with the Soviet Union.

Expansion into overseas markets—particularly Japan—was aided greatly by the company's new alliance with the Swiss foods giant Nestlé S.A., to whom Eugène Schueller's daughter, Madame Liliane Bettencourt, sold nearly half of her L'Oréal stock in 1974. The two allies established a French holding company, Gesparal—51 percent-owned by Bettencourt and 49 percent-owned by Nestlé. Gesparal controlled 72 percent of L'Oréal's voting rights, while Bettencourt remained largest individual shareholder of Nestlé, holding roughly 5 percent.

Key Dates:

1907: Eugène Schueller begins to concoct the first synthetic hair dyes and sells them under the brand name of Auréole.

1912: The company expands to Austria, Holland, and Italy.

1920: The firm's products are now available in the U.S., Brazil, Chile, Peru, Ecuador, Bolivia, the Soviet Union, and the Far East.

1928: Monsavon, a soap company, is acquired.

1933: Famous artists are commissioned to design L'Oréal posters; the magazine *Votre Beauté* is launched.

1938: The company advertises its hair products on the radio.

1945: L'Oréal launches the first cold permanent wave product, Oréol.

1950: The firm develops a research and development team of 100 chemists.

1955: The first coloring shampoo, Colorelle, is introduced.

1963: The company lists on the French stock exchange.

1969: Lindsay Owen-Jones joins the firm.

1973: L'Oréal purchases a 53.4 percent interest in Synthélabo.

1974: Eugène Schueller's daughter, Madame Liliane Bettencourt, sells nearly half of her L'Oréal stock to Nestlé S.A.

1977: The company buys stakes in magazines *Marie-Claire Album* and *Interedi-Cosmopolitan*.

1988: The firm acquires Helena Rubenstein Inc.; Owens-Jones is named chairman and CEO.

1994: Control of Cosmair Inc. is purchased from Nestlé S.A. and Bettencourt.

1995: The Maybelline brand is acquired.

1996: L'Oréal Retail is formed from the merger of the U.S. hair-care and cosmetics groups.

1998: Soft Sheen Products Inc. is acquired.

1999: Elf Aquitaine and L'Oréal merge their pharmaceutical subsidiaries to create Sanofi-Synthélabo.

Throughout the 1970s, L'Oréal continued to make purchases within the cosmetics and hair-care industry: Biotherm in 1970; Gemey, Ricils, and Jeanne Piaubert in 1973; and Roja in 1975. The latter merged with Garnier in 1978. This was also a time for diversification for L'Oréal. In 1973, it took a controlling stake of 53.4 percent in the pharmaceutical company Synthélabo, a specialist in the production of cardiovascular drugs and hospital materials, followed in 1979 by the purchase of Metabio-Joullie, manufacturer of aspirins, over-the-counter drugs, veterinary, cosmetic, and dietary items. Metabio-Joullie and Synthélabo were merged in 1980 under the latter's name. In 1977, L'Oréal ventured into another complementary field, magazine publishing, taking stakes in *Marie-Claire Album* and *Interedi-Cosmopolitan*.

Meanwhile, in the new division Parfums et Beauté International, several of L'Oréal's most successful products were launched—Vichy's moisturizer Equalia and the Cacharel perfume Anais Anais, reckoned to be the world's best-selling perfume. In addition, the well-known Kérastase hair products were redesigned.

Continued Success: 1980s

The 1980s were particularly favorable for L'Oréal. François Dalle won the post of first vice-president on Nestlé's administrative council, the title of Man of the Year in the chemicals and cosmetics sector from the Fragrance Foundation of the United States, and title of Manager of the Year from the *Nouvel Economiste*. In 1984, he gave up the leadership of L'Oréal, although he continued to act as chairman of the group's strategic committee. The position of chairman and CEO went to Charles Zviak. Lindsay Owen-Jones became vice-president and Marc Ladreit de Lacharrière, joint vice-president, soon to take control of the company's financial policy.

This event was followed by some restructuring within the group; in 1985 the Parfums et Beauté division was split into three departments—Lancôme/Piaubert, perfumes, and active cosmetics—and five geographical areas. At the same time the new management clearly felt it necessary to centralize control of the company's finances, and in 1987 a financial bulletin was issued announcing the creation of L'Oréal Finances, which would implement the financial strategy established approximately ten years before.

In 1986, L'Oréal's shares were distributed to investors outside France for the first time when the company raised FFr1.4 billion through a one-for-ten rights issue, offering new shares to stockholders. This was followed, in 1987, by a one-for-five stock split.

At this time, L'Oréal began to play an increasingly active role in the management of Synthélabo, which, after merging with Metabio-Joullie, had become France's third-largest pharmaceutical company. Synthélabo's research-and-development budget was increased considerably, allowing the company in 1982 to become the first private laboratory to participate in the World Health Organization's project for research and education in neuroscience.

During the 1980s, Synthélabo enhanced its international status, setting up joint marketing affiliates in the United States and Britain with the U.S. company G.D. Searle, and establishing joint ventures in Japan with Fujisawa and Mitsubishi Kasei. The company also took controlling stakes in Kramer of Switzerland, in 1982, and LIRCA of Italy in 1983. Nevertheless, Synthélabo continued to report poor sales figures, owing to difficulty in updating its product line and unfavorable market conditions in France. L'Oréal subsequently reiterated its commitment to Synthélabo, keeping restructuring to a minimum and increasing its holding from 63 percent to 65 percent after October 1987's Black Monday, when the shares fell considerably. L'Oréal saw that the solution to Synthélabo's problems lay in extending its overseas sales, thereby offsetting unfavorable domestic pricing and reimbursement policies. By the end of the decade, profitability had improved and some promising new drugs were ready to be approved for marketing in the 1990s.

Meanwhile, L'Oréal's research-and-development facilities continued their steady growth, with research staff reaching 1,000 by 1984. L'Oréal's enormous commitment to research resulted in the success of products such as Lancôme's Niosôme, launched in 1986, one of the few anti-aging creams found to be effective by independent dermatologists.

If this was the age of high-tech skin care, it was also the era of designer brands. In 1980, a new distribution company, Prestige et Collections, was created for Cacharel, whose perfume Loulou, launched in 1987, went on to become a best seller. In 1984, Nestlé took over Warner Cosmetics of the United States on behalf of L'Oréal's U.S. agent Cosmair, thereby acquiring for the group the prestigious names of Ralph Lauren, Paloma Picasso, and Gloria Vanderbilt. At this stage, however, L'Oréal was interested only in the perfumes and cosmetics divisions of the designer brands. In 1983, the company sold its 49.9 percent stake in the couture house Courrèges to Itokin of Japan, although it retained 100 percent of Courrèges Parfums.

A further addition to the L'Oréal group was the Helena Rubenstein skin-care and cosmetics range. In 1983, L'Oréal began by taking major stakes in Helena Rubenstein's Japanese and South American subsidiaries, the former integrated with Lancôme in the new Japanese affiliate, Parfums et Beauté, in 1984. In 1988, L'Oréal bought Helena Rubenstein Inc., a U.S. company that was in financial difficulties as a result of the sharp drop in sales following the founder's death. It would not be an easy matter to bring the company back into profit. Bought in the same year, Laboratoires Goupil, a dental-care-products manufacturer whose toothpastes held over 90 percent of the French market, was also unprofitable, but it was felt that L'Oréal's skillful marketing could remedy the situation. L'Oréal's last acquisition of the 1980s was the skin-care specialist Laboratoires Roche Posay.

While making acquisitions, L'Oréal also took the opportunity to sell off unwanted components of the group. These included the personal hygiene and comfort products of Laboratoires Ruby d'Anglas and Chiminter, which were felt to be too far outside the group's main area of interest and not in accord with L'Oréal's policy of internationalization.

L'Oréal was keen to diversify into communications. In 1984, the company took a 10 percent stake in the French pay-TV company, Canal Plus, with the stake raised to 10.4 percent in 1986. In 1988, L'Oréal took a 75 percent stake in Paravision International, an organization charged with the creation, production, and distribution of audiovisual products for an international audience. The following year, L'Oréal entered by way of Paravision into a joint venture with the U.S. company Carolco Pictures Inc., to handle foreign television-distribution and programming rights.

New Leadership in 1988

In 1988, Lindsay Owen-Jones became the new chairman and chief executive officer of L'Oréal at the age of 42. Marc Ladreit de Lacharrière became director and executive vice-president while Charles Zviak moved on to the chairmanship of Synthélabo. Zviak died the following year, having been one of the few chemists to attain leadership of a major French company. The end of the decade was marked further by rumors of L'Oréal's involvement in a proposed joint takeover bid for the French luxury-goods company Louis Vuitton Moët Hennessy, together with Vuitton's head, Monsieur Racamier, and Paribas/Parfinance. Although the existence of such a plan was denied by L'Oréal, the company joined with Orcofi, a Vuitton-controlled

holding company, to buy 95 percent of the perfume and couture house Lanvin.

L'Oréal explained that although Vuitton owned Dior and Givenchy, competitors in the perfume and cosmetics market, L'Oréal had no Vuitton shares and no intention of attacking the company. On the contrary, the Vuitton alliance would give L'Oréal an entrée into the field of luxury goods. Although Lanvin lost money since L'Oréal's acquisition, company officials remained optimistic, declaring that the experience gained from running a luxury boutique was valuable in itself.

In 1991, L'Oréal found itself embroiled in a bitter dispute with Jean Frydman, a former director of Paravision. Frydman—who held dual Israeli-French citizenship—had filed suit against the company, charging it with "fraudulent behavior and racial discrimination" stemming from the 1989 sale of the Frydman family's 25 percent share of Paravision—L'Oréal's film distribution division—after being pressured by François Dalle. Frydman alleged that L'Oréal violated a 1977 French law prohibiting companies from participating in an Arab boycott against Israel when the company forced his resignation and the sale of the family's stake at an unfair price because of his business ties to Israel. The ensuing investigation created a minor scandal in France by digging up unsavory facts about founder Eugène Schueller's anti-Semitic, fascist politics during World War II. Later that year, however, Frydman dropped the suit in exchange for a letter of apology from Dalle.

During the 1990s, the cosmetics industry experienced growth, but with increasing rivalry. While L'Oréal's alliance with Nestlé protected it from corporate marauders, it continued to be vulnerable to competition in Western markets in the early 1990s from the likes of Japanese competitors Shiseido and Kao—although 90 percent of the turnover of both companies come from their home market—and from Unilever, following the latter's takeover of Elizabeth Arden and Fabergé.

International Expansion: Late 1980s–90s

In the years following his appointment as chairman and CEO, Owen-Jones set about making L'Oréal a genuinely international company. He began cultivating an integrated international team of top managers, enabling the company to quickly respond to and capitalize on consumer trends worldwide. Owens-Jones also supported greater cooperation between L'Oréal's numerous brand names and divisions. After Lancôme Niosôme was developed in 1986, L'Oréal then translated the new technology into a mass market L'Oréal skin-care line sold under the name Plentitude. Plentitude was launched in Europe and Australia in the late 1980s, and within two years of its U.S. launch in 1989, it had captured a 10 percent share of the market.

It was precisely this kind of synergy between subsidiaries, analysts say, that led to L'Oréal's 15 percent overall profit growth in the 1980s. In the boom years of the 1980s, high-end lines such as Lancôme and Helena Rubenstein performed extremely well. When the prestige market slumped in the early 1990s, such mass market lines as L'Oréal were poised to pick up the slack.

L'Oréal also eyed the U.S. market, which represented one-third of the world market, as one with opportunities for further profit growth. At the time, despite having full control of strategy, management, and marketing in this region, L'Oréal reaped only 5.5 percent from the profits of its sole U.S. agent Cosmair Inc. One advantage of this system for L'Oréal was protection from the weakness of the U.S. dollar and from high marketing costs—Cosmair handled a sales volume of over $1 billion that provided the company with the flexibility to launch new products which could then be transferred to L'Oréal affiliates worldwide. Other markets targeted for expansion during the early 1990s included Japan.

L'Oréal was also one of the first western companies to set up shop in the former Soviet Union, forming Soreal, a joint-venture with the Russian chemical company Mosbytchim. L'Oréal invested $50 million in the venture to produce approximately 40 million units of deodorant, perfume, shampoos, and hair sprays annually. Soreal products were sold in 1992 at a mere 100 outlets in Moscow and at an additional ten throughout Russia. Hard currency was difficult to come by as banks either collapsed or were unaccustomed to dealing with Western businesses. In order to obtain the equipment necessary to upgrade production, Soreal created Maroussia, a women's fragrance that was imported to Western Europe in exchange for machinery and materials.

L'Oréal's structure during this time remained unchanged, with the group consisting of a federation of competitive companies, including 147 production and distribution facilities worldwide, divided into five divisions. Only research and development facilities and overall management control were centralized. There was speculation as to the fate of L'Oréal when Bettencourt, in her mid-60s in 1990, relinquishes her corporate involvement. The French government took a strong interest in the issue. French government agreements restricted foreigners from taking over French companies before 1994. However, by 2001 Bettencourt still controlled her interest in the firm: should she decide to sell, Nestlé would have first option to purchase, and Bettencourt remained tight-lipped about her future plans.

As consumers became more environmentally aware, L'Oréal fell under increasing pressure to conform to new standards of product safety. The company was forced to phase out the use of chlorofluorocarbons which are said to be harmful to the ozone layer. L'Oréal also came under attack from the animal-rights lobby, which accused the company of subjecting laboratory animals to inhumane tests, although L'Oréal claimed that animal testing of new products was down to 5 percent from 50 percent in 1985. By 1989, the firm stopped animal testing altogether.

As L'Oréal entered the mid-1990s, the company found itself engaged in a battle with rivals Proctor & Gamble and Unilever for worldwide domination of the mass cosmetic and fragrance markets. L'Oréal seemed determined to remain the leader, hiking its advertising budget by as much as 50 percent for some products, and creating a whole new image for most of its color cosmetics. The company was also reaching out to customers by repackaging its merchandise and making display cases more accessible and user-friendly.

L'Oréal also made several strategic moves to solidify its market position. In 1994, it purchased control of Cosmair from Nestlé and Bettencourt. The following year, it acquired the

Maybelline brand for $600 million. The company also purchased two drug companies that year including Germany-based Lichtenstein Pharmazeutica and Irex, based in France.

As part of its continued focus on the U.S. market, the firm formed L'Oréal Retail division in 1996, merging its U.S. hair care and cosmetics businesses under one umbrella. It continued to introduce new products in this market, including the Garnier hair care brand. By that time, its Cosmair subsidiary accounted for 23 percent of L'Oréal's entire cosmetics business.

Strategic Acquisitions: Late 1990s and Beyond

In 1998, the company launched a global advertising campaign with the tagline, "Because I'm worth it." Under the leadership of Owen-Jones, L'Oréal began making a series of acquisitions that would bring it closer to its goal of becoming one of the world's top four brands. It also renewed its focus on its emerging markets including Asia and Eastern Europe. In China, Maybelline was sold in 40 cities and the company hoped to up that number to 80. Owen-Jones stated in a 1998 *Women's Wear Daily* article, "It's the beginning of the Chinese snowball. There have been three million Maybelline lipsticks sold. Our aim is to make sure every Chinese woman has a lipstick in her hand instead of the Little Red Book." Latin America also became a key market focus, especially after an economic crisis shook the Asian region in the latter half of the 1990s.

In 1998, Cosmair acquired Soft Sheen Products Inc., a leading ethnic hair care firm. The ethnic market was now considered to be among the top growth opportunities in the cosmetics industry. The following year, Elf Aquitaine and L'Oréal merged their pharmaceutical subsidiaries to create Sanofi-Synthélabo, creating the second-largest pharmaceutical company in France. Long-known for its dedication to research and development, L'Oréal continued forging ahead on that front. The company signed a five-year partnership agreement with the United Nations Organization for Education, Science, and Culture (UNESCO) entitled "For Women in Science." As part of the program, female researchers would be given grants to pursue scientific research. During 1999, sales continued to increase—up 12.1 percent over the previous year. Western Europe accounted for 56.1 percent of company sales, while North America accounted for 27.1 percent. That year, the company reported the strongest profit growth of the decade.

L'Oréal entered the new millennium with continued success. It purchased Carson Inc., the leading ethnic cosmetics firm, cementing L'Oréal's position in that market. It also acquired Ylang Laboratories Ltd., an Argentine cosmetics firm, and the Scandinavian Respons brand from Colgate Palmolive Inc. Kiehl's Since 1851 Inc. was also purchased along with Matrix Essentials Inc. In order to take advantage of its parent company's strong brand recognition, Cosmair's name was changed that year to L'Oréal USA.

The company had a record year in sales and profits during 2000, and L'Oréal remained the market leader in the cosmetics industry with a 16.8 market share. In Japan, sales increased by 46 percent and Maybelline became the leading mass-market cosmetics brand in the country. Along with its acquisitions, L'Oréal launched several new products, including Maybelline's

Water Shine lipstick and Full 'n' Soft Mascara, Age Perfect Skincare by L'Oréal Paris, Garnier's Fructis Style product line, and fragrances Ralph by Ralph Lauren and Miracle by Lancôme.

During 2001, the company continued to divest non-core, slow-growth businesses. L'Oréal announced plans to sell its interest in its *Marie-Claire* magazine holdings along with its Lanvin S.A. subsidiary. It also strengthened its position in the dermatological cosmetics market with the purchase of the Bio-Medic's brand name from CosMedic Concepts Inc.

Attributing much of its prosperity to its global branding strategy, L'Oréal remained confident that its success would continue into the future. "Blink an eye, and L'Oréal has just sold 85 products around the world, from Redken hair care and Ralph Lauren perfumes to Helena Rubinstein cosmetics and Vichy skin care," claimed a 1999 *Business Week* article. With its strong market position, L'Oréal seemed poised to continue its dominance in the cosmetics industry well into the future.

Principal Subsidiaries

Carson Holdings Ltd. (South Africa); Kiehl's Since 1851 Inc. (United States); Matrix Essentials Inc. (United States); Lancôme Parfums et Beauté & Cie; Lancôme Institute et Cie; Helena Rubenstein Inc; Laboratoire Garnier Paris; L'Oréal UK Ltd.; L'Oréal USA; Maybelline Ltd. (Hong Kong); Parfums Cacharel et Cie; Parfums Guy Laroche; Parfums Ralph Lauren; Redkin Laboratories GmbH (Germany).

Principal Competitors

The Estée Lauder Companies; Proctor & Gamble Co.; Shiseido Company Ltd.

Further Reading

Benjamin, Patricia, "Sitting Pretty," *Business,* January 1987.

Dang, Kim-Van, "L'Oréal's Integration: What a Difference a Year Makes," *Women's Wear Daily,* April 25, 1997, p. 8.

Deeny, Godfrey, "L'Oréal Execs Probed by Magistrate for Joining Arab Boycott of Israel," *Women's Wear Daily,* May 15, 1991, p. 27.

Dorn, Pete, "Lindsay Owen-Jones: A World Vision for L'Oréal," *Women's Wear Daily,* October 12, 1990, pp. 10–11.

Echikson, William, "L'Oréal: Aiming at High and Low Markets," *Fortune,* March 22, 1993, p. 89.

Fearnley, Helen, "L'Oréal—Not Just A Pretty Face," *Financial Weekly,* May 5, 1988.

"Owen-Jones Satisfied With Remarkable Success," *Cosmetics International,* April 25, 1999, p. 5.

"L'Oréal Announces Two Key Acquisitions in the U.S.," *Chemical Market Reporter,* April 24, 2000, p. 16.

"L'Oréal Drops Lanvin as Recent Acquisitions Prove Profitable," *Cosmetics International,* August 15, 2001, p. 5.

"L'Oréal Goes For Ethnicity," *Soap Perfumery & Cosmetics,* March 2000, p. 7.

"L'Oréal Keeps Going Strong and Helps Women in Science," *Cosmetics International,* October 25, 1999, p. 5.

"L'Oréal Says Progress Is History in the Making," *Cosmetics International,* March 10, 2001, p. 6.

"L'Oréal: The Beauty of Global Branding," *Business Week,* June 28, 1999.

"L'Oréal's Dark Roots," *Time,* July 1, 1991, p. 56.

Raper, Sarah, "Ex-L'Oréal Head Settles Race Bias Case," *Women's Wear Daily,* December 23, 1991, p. 3.

——, "Taking Russia: Tough Times at the Factory," *Women's Wear Daily,* August 7, 1992, p. 4.

Rummell, Tara, "What's New At L'Oréal?," *Global Cosmetic Industry,* February 1999, p. 18.

Sauer, Pamela, "A Makeover of Global Proportions," *Chemical Market Reporter,* December 3, 2001.

Tosh, Mark, "L'Oréal's 1990 Net Rises 15.2%; Sales Gain 11.7%," *Women's Wear Daily* April 17, 1991, p. 21.

Weil, Jennifer, and Janet Ozzard, "L'Oréal's New Focus on Emerging Markets," *Women's Wear Daily,* April 10, 1998, p. 11.

—Jessica Griffin
—updates: Maura Troester and Christina M. Stansell

M.H. Meyerson & Co., Inc.

525 Washington Street
Jersey City, New Jersey 07310
U.S.A.
Telephone: (201) 459-9500
Toll Free: (800) 888-8118
Fax: (201) 459-9521
Web site: http://mhmeyerson.com

Public Company
Founded: 1960
Employees: 182
Sales: $72.4 million (2001)
Stock Exchanges: NASDAQ
Ticker Symbol: MHMY
NAIC: 52311 Investment Banking & Securities Dealing;
  52312 Securities Brokers

M.H. Meyerson & Co., Inc. is a market maker in more than 4,000 securities traded on the NASDAQ exchange and over the counter (unlisted on exchanges). In addition to executing trades for retail customers and brokerages (mainly the latter), this broker-dealer also buys and sells securities on its own behalf and is a full-service financial and investment-banking firm, with individual and institutional accounts. As an investment banker, it makes private placements of equity securities and assists in the structuring of public offerings of such securities. M.H. Meyerson also participates in municipal-bond offerings, offers clients the ability to participate in such placements on a syndicated basis, prepares research reports, and renders financial advice.

Profiting in the ''Go-Go'' Years

Marty Myerson was selling cars for Baron Motors, a Lincoln-Mercury dealership in Great Neck, Long Island, during the late 1950s when he noted, as he told George M. Taber of *BUSINESS News New Jersey,* that some of his young customers came in ''every 90 days and bought a new car just to change the color.'' After finding that all these high rollers were stock traders on Wall Street, he decided to try the financial district

himself, starting out in 1959 at the bottom, as a messenger at the age of 28. A year later, with $3,000 borrowed and $2,000 of his own money, he opened a Manhattan brokerage office with one employee, a bookkeeper. Meyerson saved start-up costs by not paying himself a salary, relying on his wife, a kindergarten teacher, to make ends meet.

Meyerson's company, M.H. Meyerson, moved across the Hudson River to Jersey City, New Jersey, in 1967 to avoid an increase in the stock-transfer tax by the state of New York. This action was believed to be the first of its kind following the imposition of the controversial increase, which went into effect in mid-1966. The firm was buying and selling over 300 low-priced securities for its own account at this time and had 19 employees. Interviewed by the *Wall Street Journal,* Meyerson conceded, ''We have private wires to 40 Big Board firms and over-the-counter houses. Each wire costs us $4 a month here, and will cost $25 in Jersey City.'' He said that his firm's capitalization was more than $200,000 and its trading volume about 1.6 million shares a month. By the mid 1970s many other OTC brokers had followed Meyerson to Jersey City.

Before early 1971, the over-the-counter (OTC) market, consisting of securities not listed on any of the six U.S. exchanges, was virtually impossible to monitor. In *The Go-Go Years,* John Brooks' popular account of Wall Street in the 1960s, the author explained that before the introduction of the NASDAQ computerized system, ''There was no such screen on the trader's desk; to get the best price on a thinly traded stock . . . he might have to telephone a dozen other firms to get their quotes, engage in shouted conversations with other traders in his own firm to find out what kind of bids and offers they were getting, and finally agree to a price that would never be reported to the public at all. In such a market, the opportunities for manipulation were endless.''

M.H. Meyerson thrived in this climate. At its peak during the late 1960s the company employed some 360 people, mostly in paperwork backroom operations, and opened offices in several big U.S. cities. According to Michael Silvestri, later the company's president, Martin Myerson introduced one of the first traders' contracts on Wall Street in 1968, a practice that he described as ''common place'' to Patricia A. Meding of *Today's Investor.* ''We did that,'' Meyerson added, ''because all

Key Dates:

1960: Founding of M.H. Meyerson & Co.
1967: The firm is trading in 300 low-priced securities when it moves to Jersey City.
1971: In the wake of a bear market, Meyerson closes its offices elsewhere.
1983: M.H. Meyerson is found guilty of bribery to inflate the price of a stock.
1994: Meyerson's initial public offering of stock allows it to retire its long-term debt.
2000: A subsidiary begins Internet trading, but this unit is sold the following year.

too often, traders would take positions with exposure to themselves that cost their firms a lot of money. . . . We felt they would trade more wisely if they were personally involved and responsible for their losses. . . . That philosophy has worked.''

A More-Regulated Marketplace: 1970–90

The unregulated period of OTC trading ended in February 1971, when the National Association of Securities Dealers introduced the NASDAQ computerized communications system, which collected, stored, and disseminated price quotations from a nationwide network of dealers, thereby narrowing the spread between bid and asked prices. In addition to losing some of their profit margins, the wholesalers were suffering from the bear market that struck Wall Street in 1970 and from competition for orders from full-service brokerage firms. By late 1971 M.H. Meyerson & Co. had closed its Swiss branch and was poised to shutter its offices in Boston, Chicago, Los Angeles, Philadelphia, San Francisco, and Washington. In November of that year Meyerson said that his company, which was making markets in some 500 to 600 unlisted securities, planned to reduce that number by 50 to 60 percent. (As a market maker, M.H. Meyerson was dealing primarily with other securities houses, buying and selling OTC securities for them in return for assuming the obligation to maintain an orderly market–that is, finding sellers to meet a sudden buying spree and, conversely, buyers to meet a flood of sell orders, even if the firm had to put up its own capital.)

The OTC wholesalers were again shaken by the 1973–74 bear market and federal legislation, intended to protect employee pension investments, that led many institutions to sell thinly capitalized OTC stocks. M.H. Meyerson appeared in the pages of the *Wall Street Journal* in 1977, when the federal Securities and Exchange Commission filed a suit alleging that the company, and Meyerson personally, had bribed Swiss bankers to inflate the stock price of Micro-Therapeutics Inc. for the purpose of making a public offering at the manipulated price. The SEC also accused M.H. Meyerson of destroying brokerage records that the agency sought to inspect. Micro-Therapeutics, which had ceased operations in 1976 and whose stock was later described by a federal judge as ''worthless,'' made a hair tonic alleged to be a remedy for baldness. This judge found the defendants guilty in 1983 and ordered the company and Meyerson to pay as much as $1.6 million. The case was settled the following year. Later M.H. Meyerson also

agreed to pay fines in order to settle violations for entering stock quotations with excessive spreads between the buy and sell prices, and for allowing a customer to sell shares short without first checking if the stock could be borrowed.

Because, according to Meyerson, of the restraints his company imposed on its brokers, during the stock-market crash of October 1987, ''This firm had only seven margin calls,'' he told Meding. The company's director of research quoted Meyerson in these words, ''In October 1987 when the market dropped over 500 points in one day, we not only knew that evening where the firm stood, but we had our plan of action in place the next morning by 9 a.m. before the market even opened. We did the same thing again in February 1988 when the market had a correction. . . . We have the facts and information readily available, and we have structured the firm to survive.''

The National Association of Securities Dealers, however, took a dimmer view of the activities of OTC market makers such as M.H. Meyerson during the October crisis, finding that during the blizzard of selling orders many of them simply became incommunicado, reneging on their obligation to maintain orderly markets. In 1988 the association established new rules that required its members to continue executing orders even in the face of a giant sell-off. Orders made through NASDAQ's Small Order Execution System would now be distributed among market makers on the basis of the highest bid and the lowest asking price. Those firms that did not execute the orders would be suspended as a market maker for 20 trading days.

Public Company: 1994–2000

M.H. Meyerson was trading about 80 million shares of stock a month in early 1994, when it was a market maker for about 2,200 securities. In what were usually dealer-to-dealer (wholesale) transactions, the company, on behalf of its proprietary trading accounts, carried long or short trading positions in these securities. Its 40 traders were compensated by receiving a fixed percentage of the profits from trading after deduction of general expenses. Their contracts provided for individual liability for any funds owed the company relating to losses, if any, incurred from trading activities. Retail customer accounts were being serviced by 35 registered representatives. The investment-banking division had, since 1990, been the managing or co-managing underwriter of nine initial public offerings and two private placements that raised in excess of $68 million. M.H. Meyerson's revenues came to $16.04 million in fiscal 1993 (the year ended January 31, 1993), of which securities transactions accounted for 70 percent, underwriting for 22 percent, and commissions for 6 percent. Revenues rose to $18.74 million in fiscal 1994, of which securities transactions accounted for 87 percent, underwriting for 11 percent, and commissions for 2 percent. Net income came to $822,607 in fiscal 1993 and $1.43 million in fiscal 1994.

M.H. Meyerson made its initial public offering of stock in January 1994, selling 2.3 million units for $4 each, with each unit consisting of one share of stock and one redeemable warrant. Net proceeds to the firm came to $7.58 million, allowing it to retire its long-term debt of $8.52 million. Three months after the offering, the Meyerson family retained 45 percent of the stock. *Forbes* staffer Amy Feldman took a jaundiced view of the offering, noting the firm's previous disciplining by federal authorities and the checkered career of its underwriter, Stratton Oakmont, Inc., which was being sued by the Securities and Exchange Commission for securities fraud and coercive sales tactics. Stratton Oakmont subsequently went out of business.

In fiscal 1995, M.H. Meyerson's revenues fell to $14.47 million, and the firm lost $597,854, an outcome Meyerson blamed on the failure of a clearing house and to "erratic markets." Its stock never traded above $2.88 during the calendar year and fell as low as 88 cents–well below book value. The firm bought back some 300,000 of its own shares about this time. One believer in its future was *Today's Investor,* which called the company "the best kept secret on Wall Street" and gave it a strong buy recommendation during the first part of 1996. M.H. Meyerson returned to profitability in fiscal 1996, when its revenues rose more than 50 percent. Revenues almost doubled in fiscal 1997, reaching $41.89 million, and net income soared to $1.82 million. In 1996 the firm moved from Montgomery Street to bigger quarters on two floors of the Newport Tower, affording its founder a marvelous view of lower Manhattan from his corner office on the 34th floor. Meyerson was not inclined to let the altitude go to his head, however. Asked by a shareholder at the annual meeting whether the company was going to leverage itself to increase its potential for profits, he replied that in his 36 years in the business more than half of all brokerage houses had failed, usually because they had gone heavily into debt.

Martin Meyerson's caution was well advised, for in fiscal 1998 the firm's revenues dropped by about 50 percent, and it suffered a loss of $1.72 million. Management called new order-handling rules a significant factor in the company's loss of trading revenue. (During 1997, the Securities and Exchange Commission mandated changes in NASDAQ trading that had the effect of reducing the spread brokers maintained between bid and asked prices.) A partial recovery the following year brought M.H. Meyerson back into the black. In February 1999, the company issued a press release announcing plans to offer trading over the Internet by year's end. Suddenly the firm's stock, which had been trading at below $1 a share as recently as three months earlier, shot up as high as $21.88. Two days after the announcement, Meyerson's two sons, the firm's president, and its controller sold $1.2 million worth of stock, while the founder told *Business Week* that he had himself sold "several hundred thousand" shares. Two weeks later, the value of the stock had retreated to about $5 a share. (It was trading at about $1 a share in the summer of 2001.)

Meyerson enjoyed its best year ever in fiscal 2000, earning $3.04 million on revenues of $62.12 million–almost double the previous year's total. Management attributed its great increase in volume in part to the stimulus inspired by trading on the Internet. The company also reported that during the 1990s it managed or co-managed more than 30 initial and second public offerings of stock and over 20 private placements, thereby raising more than $460 million in capital. In addition, its syndication activities resulted in being included in nearly 200 additional equity underwritings during this time period. In fiscal 2001, however, the company lost $508,272 on revenues of $72.39 million. Clearing charges rose by 55 percent–over $10 million, which management attributed to increased trading volume.

M.H. Meyerson in 2000 and Beyond

Wholesale trading and market making remained the major part of Meyerson's business in fiscal 2001, accounting for 92 percent of its revenue. As of April 1, 2001, the firm was a market maker in over 4,000 NASDAQ and over-the-counter securities, standing ready to buy or sell a particular security at the national best bid or offer. Underwriting accounted for 3 percent of revenue. Among Meyerson's activities in investment banking, the company structured public offerings and made private placements of equity securities. Commissions comprised another 3 percent of revenue. The firm was handling about 14,500 retail customer accounts, consisting of both individuals and institutions. Meyerson also was providing execution services, primarily to retail service firms, online securities brokers, banks, and hedge funds seeking to purchase or sell securities on behalf of their retail customers.

In addition to these functions, since 1997 Meyerson had been acting as manager or co-manager of municipal bond offerings and as participants in selling groups. It also advised clients on bonds and offered them the ability to participate in syndicate placements of these securities. Another division was maintaining accounts with hundreds of investment and mutual funds, banks, investment trusts, and other institutional investment vehicles. This division also was preparing and disseminating research reports on publicly traded companies that Meyerson believed represented special opportunities for purchase and investment by its clients and others.

The electronic-brokerage subsidiary formed in 1999, eMeyerson, began offering online brokerage and investment information and related data in 2000. This subsidiary also offered other financial institutions Internet-based business-to-business financial products and solutions. M.H. Meyerson owned 54 percent of the capital stock but sold it in July 2001 to ViewTrade Holding Corp.

M.H. Meyerson & Co. had no long-term debt in fiscal 2001. As of April 2001, Martin H. Meyerson, who was still chairman and chief executive officer, owned 27.9 percent of the company's shares, and Jeffrey E. Myerson owned 5 percent. Electronic Trading Group, L.L.C. owned 13.8 percent.

Principal Competitors

Bernard L. Madoff Investment Securities Inc.; Herzog, Heine Geduld Inc.; Knight Trading Group Inc.; Mayer & Schweitzer, Inc.; Spear, Leeds & Kellogg, LLC.

Further Reading

Brooks, John. *The Go-Go Years.* New York: Weybright and Talley, 1973.

Donlan, Thomas G., "Crash Course in Market Reform," *Barron's,* July 18, 1988, pp. 13, 24, 26.

Du Bois, Peter C., "Over-the-Counter Bids," *Barron's,* July 18, 1977, pp. 11, 16–17, 24.

Feldman, Amy, "A New Issue with Baggage," *Forbes,* January 3, 1994, p. 268.

Foust, Dean, "How Real Is That E-Broker?," *Business Week,* March 8, 1999, pp. 96–97.

Hershman, Arlene, "Over the Counter: Frantic, Frenetic, Frazzled," *Dun's Review,* August 1968, pp. 32, 37.

Meding, Patricia A., "M.H. Meyerson & Co., Inc: The Best Kept Secret on Wall Street," *Today's Investor,* November 1995, pp. 6–7, 27.

"M.H. Meyerson & Co., Officer Face Judgment Of Up to $1.6 Million," *Wall Street Journal,* February 8, 1983, p. 5.

"M.H. Meyerson & Co., Inc. Transfers Subsidiary eMeyerson.com Inc., to ViewTrade Securities, Inc.," *PR Newswire,* July 26, 2001 (on ProQuest database).

"Micro-Therapeutics, Others Are Named In SEC Securities Suit," *Wall Street Journal,* August 18, 1977, p. 5.

Morgenson, Gretchen, "Why Traders Die Broke," *Forbes,* June 16, 1997, pp. 246, 248.

Rustin, Richard E., "Meyerson to Cut Market Making Activity; Says Firm Strong but Economy Uncertain," *Wall Street Journal,* November 15, 1971, p. 4.

Schifrin, Matthew, and Scott McCormack, "Free Enterprise Comes to Wall Street," *Forbes,* April 6, 1998, pp. 114–15, 118.

"Securities Firm Plans To Leave New York, Blaming Stock Levy," *Wall Street Journal,* November 1, 1966, p. 12.

Taber, George M., "Market Maker on the Move," *BUSINESS News New Jersey,* June 26, 1996, p. 14.

—Robert Halasz

THE MAY DEPARTMENT STORES COMPANY

The May Department Stores Company

611 Olive Street
St. Louis, Missouri 63101-1799
U.S.A.
Telephone: (314) 342-6300
Fax: (314) 342-4473
Web site: http://www.maycompany.com

Public Company
Incorporated: 1910
Employees: 137,000
Sales: $14.5 billion (2001)
Stock Exchanges: New York
Ticker Symbol: MAY
NAIC: 45211 Department Stores

The May Department Stores Company is the second-leading upscale department store chain operator in the United States, just behind Federated Department Stores. The St. Louis-based company operates 11 department store chains and David's Bridal, the largest retailer of wedding apparel and accessories in the United States. Included in its holding are the well-known names of Lord & Taylor, Robinson's-May, Kaufmann's, Foley's, Filene's, Hecht's, Meier & Frank, Strawbridge's, L.S. Ayres, The Jones Store, and Famous-Barr. With nearly 600 retail outlets in 43 states, May recorded its 26th year of consecutive record sales and earnings during fiscal 2001.

The Early Years

The beginnings of The May Department Stores Company can be traced to 1877, when company founder David May opened his first store in the mining town of Leadville, Colorado, at the age of 29. An immigrant from Germany, May had settled in Indiana during his teen years, where he earned his living as a salesman in a small men's clothing store. Diligence and marketing flair won him a quarter-interest in the business, but ill health forced him to sell his stake and seek a drier, healthier climate in the West, where he tried prospecting. Inexperience brought swift failure, though, and thus he returned to the field he knew and opened a men's clothing store with two partners.

The firm of May, Holcomb & Dean supplied the miners with red woolen underwear and copper-riveted overalls. The store was an instant success, but a real estate disagreement dissolved the partnership, leaving May alone to put up a building on newly purchased ground. This second venture was called The Great Western Auction House & Clothing Store, an enterprise that was soon large enough to welcome a partner, Moses Shoenberg, whose family owned the local opera house. By 1883, the new partnership was flourishing, for the town's population had become sophisticated enough to demand clothing for many purposes. May and Shoenberg kept pace with the demand, ensuring success with aggressive advertising methods and conservative fiscal management.

Before long, The Great Western Auction House & Clothing Store was financially able to expand its merchandise to include women's apparel, after testing the market with a huge stock of expensive dresses bought from an overstocked Chicago store. Two years later, despite a post-boom depression that would doom Leadville's prosperity by the end of the decade, May bought out Shoenberg's interest in the store in 1885. He went on to add a branch store in Aspen, Colorado, and then another called the Manhattan Clothing Company in Glenwood Springs, Colorado.

Corporate strategy was already firmly established by this time. Print advertising that trumpeted genuine bargain prices lured an ever-escalating, middle-class clientele, while frequent sales kept the merchandise moving. Fast stock turnover kept the customers in the height of fashion. Energy and swift management decisions were David May's trademarks. A frequently-quoted story tells that he paid $31,000 for the stock of a bankrupt clothing store he spied during an 1888 visit to Denver, Colorado. By the end of the day, he had installed a brass band out front to help sell out the existing stock. It only took him one week to clear the inventory, remodel the store, and establish the property anew as The May Shoe & Clothing Company.

May's expansion efforts continued through the 1890s. First came the 1892 purchase of the Famous Department Store in St. Louis, Missouri, for which he and three Shoenberg brothers-in-law paid $150,000. Six years later, spreading his interests to Cleveland, Ohio, he spent $300,000 to buy the aging Hull & Dutton store, renaming it May Company. In order to more easily manage his many holdings spread across the country, in 1905 May moved the company headquarters to St. Louis, Missouri, where it remained into the 1990s.

Expansion in the Early 1900s

In 1911, one year after the May Department Stores Company was incorporated in New York, it was listed on the New York Stock Exchange. May used proceeds to purchase a second St. Louis chain, the William Barr Dry Goods Company. To consolidate the firm's Missouri holdings, he merged the two St. Louis chains, forming the Famous-Barr Company. In spite of the large investment this move demanded, sales for the year reached $14.8 million, with net profits of $1.5 million.

By 1917, David May was ready to hand the company presidency over to his son, Morton. He named himself as the company's chairman of the board, but did not reduce his active interest in business affairs; in 1923, at the age of 75, he bought a Los Angeles department store, A. Hamburger & Sons, for $4.2 million cash. He then personally supervised its renovation and its energetic promotion. Renamed The May Company, the store opened new avenues in California and helped to produce 1926 sales figures that surpassed the $100 million mark for the first time in the company's history. It was a final triumph for David May, who died in 1927 at the age of 79.

That same year, the company acquired Bernheimer-Leader Stores, Inc., of Baltimore, Maryland. At a price of $2.3 million, the new acquisition was also renamed The May Company, and, by newly established company policy, was the last acquisition for some time to follow. Top priorities then became consolidation, improvement in performance, and store remodeling. Systematic modernization plans to update delivery systems and to provide customer parking began in 1928 and were completed in 1932.

May's sales reached $106.7 million in 1929. During the bleak years that followed, the company maintained its stability with strict financial planning and a greater focus on inventory. Buyers had always maintained large stocks of merchandise, regardless of the external economic climate. This practice now proved to be profitable, for higher purchase costs were not a problem; the company simply added the old and the new prices of an item, averaged the two, and held one of its famous sales. Large inventories thus became an asset, leaving the stores unaffected by the Depression-era foundering of distressed suppliers.

A distinct advantage to the company lay in the wide geographical spread of May's subsidiaries. Each store had its own buying department, allowing it to cater to its individual needs. Since the Depression's depth likewise varied from area to area, buyers could gauge their stock requirements with accuracy. Additional centralized buying facilities, however, allowed buyers to take advantage of mass-purchasing practices to keep their

costs down. Careful planning paid off—although sales dipped to $72.5 million by 1932, they slowly recovered, rising to $89.2 million by the end of 1935.

Post-Depression Diversification

By 1939, the company was ready to expand once again. Foreshadowing a 1940s trend toward suburban shopping centers, May opened a Wilshire Boulevard branch of its Los Angeles store, stocking it with merchandise for the upper-income customer. Then, in 1946, May organized a merger with Kaufmann Department Stores, Inc., of Pittsburgh. With a history stretching back to 1871, Kaufmann's was western Pennsylvania's largest department store and had cordially shared several May buying offices for many years. Together, the two operations were large enough to produce combined 1945 sales of $246.4 million. Kaufmann's brought to the partnership a higher-income clientele, seven new units, and its own brand of paint, linens, and toiletries. In 1948, there was another important acquisition: the Strouss-Hirshberg Company of Youngstown, Ohio. This gave the company stores in Youngstown and Warren, Ohio, and New Castle, Pennsylvania.

The company founder's formula of aggressive promotion, competitive pricing, and wide selection gave it dominance in five of the eight cities that were now home to May stores. Liberal salaries and incentive plans ensured staff loyalty, as exemplified by several department store heads who had been with the company for numerous years. The different elements made a successful mix, resulting in 1949 sales that reached $392.9 million, despite population shifts to the suburbs, competition from discount houses, and increases in customer spending for food and gasoline.

In 1951, Morton D. May succeeded his father as company president, and Morton J. May moved on to the company chairmanship, just as his own father had done previously. Continuing in his father's expansion and consolidation footsteps, the younger May held the reins of 25 stores by the end of 1953; the lineup now consisted of ten large downtown stores, five large branch stores, and ten smaller branch stores. Sales for that year topped off at $447.5 million, and the company could well afford the $10 million it spent over the 1954–55 period to remodel, modernize, and enlarge suburban stores. Additional potential for suburban expansion spurred construction of the firm's first shopping plaza, The Center of Sheffield. Covering 55 acres near Lorain, Ohio, the development contained about 40 retail stores as well as parking for 3,000 cars. It proved so popular that another center was constructed in Los Angeles within the next two years.

Other new ventures in the 1950s included the 1957 purchase of Denver's Daniels & Fischer Stores Company, which was subsequently merged with existing Denver operations and renamed May D&F. Hecht Company of Washington, D.C., was also acquired in 1959, with branch operations in Baltimore. Though start-up costs and refurbishing usually curbed earnings in an acquisition's first year, Hecht's merger did not affect profits. May finished the decade with record sales reaching $645.1 million.

The 1960s–70s: Social and Demographic Influences

As the 1960s began, demographic research, used to track present and future buying patterns, showed two new trends. On

Key Dates:

1877: David May opens his first store in Leadville, Colorado.
1892: The Famous Department Store is acquired.
1898: May purchases the Hull & Dutton store and renames it May Company.
1905: The company's headquarters are moved to St. Louis.
1911: The firm lists on the New York Stock Exchange; the Famous-Barr Company is formed.
1926: Sales surpass $100 million.
1946: The company merges with Kaufmann Department Stores.
1954: May begins a $10 million modernization of its stores.
1959: The Hecht Company of Washington, D.C. is acquired.
1965: May completes the purchases of Meier & Frank Co. Inc. and G. Fox & Company.
1978: The firm's Venture subsidiary buys 19 Turn-Style stores from Jewel Companies.
1986: May acquires Associated Dry Goods for $2.5 billion.
1990: The company buys the 26-store chain, Thalhimers; sales surpass $10 billion.
1992: May begins to implement a consolidation strategy.
1996: Thirteen Strawbridge & Clothier Stores are purchased; the company spins off its Payless ShoeSource holdings.
2000: The David's Bridal chain of stores is acquired.

one hand, there was a shift to discount merchandising, bringing the company into competition with drugstores, supermarkets, and discount houses. On the other hand, the more expensive end of the spectrum was now showing an increased emphasis on fashion in clothes, linens, and other May staples. To move inexpensive staples more efficiently, the company increased automation in most units. At the specialty merchandise end, the company upgraded its merchandise to include even more exclusive brands.

Two important acquisitions were negotiated in 1965, both of which were finalized the following year. One was a merger with Meier & Frank Co., Inc., of Portland, Oregon. Another acquisition, G. Fox & Company, brought May into Hartford, Connecticut. Both of these mergers were scrutinized by the Federal Trade Commission (FTC), whose restrictive powers were broadened early in 1966. As both transactions had been initiated before the new restrictions came into force, the acquisitions were allowed, although the company had to agree to make no further acquisitions for ten years unless specifically permitted by the FTC.

When Morton D. May became chairman of the board in 1967, to be succeeded as president by Stanley J. Goodman, a disturbing new trend appeared: the vigorous acquisitions program and its concomitant store renovations and expansions began to eat into profits. Downtown stores were waning in popularity, and customer demand at the new suburban branches

was not yet enough to compensate. Labor costs also rose significantly. Year-end figures told their own story: in 1966 total sales reached $869.1 million, yielding a profit of $45.9 million, while 1967 total sales reached $979 million but brought a profit of just $38.4 million. The following year, although total sales passed the $1 billion mark for the first time, profit sank to $36.2 million.

Nevertheless, plans involving the discount end of the market continued. In 1968, the company hired John F. Geisse, an experienced discount merchandiser, to head its new discount subsidiary; he soon became a vice-president. The new enterprise, called Venture, started in St. Louis in 1970. Achieving quick success, it burgeoned to a 12-unit chain by 1972. Three years later there were 20 stores, serving a population of over eleven million.

In 1975, the Venture subsidiary contributed an estimated 9 percent of May's $1.75 billion in sales. Focusing on the Midwest market, the company had eight Chicago-area Venture stores, a number too small to give the advantages of increased productivity or warehousing and distribution savings. To remedy this problem, in 1978 the subsidiary purchased 19 Turn-Style stores with a combined annual sales figure of about $180 million from Jewel Companies. The units were then redesigned and restocked at a cost of $27 million. Further expansion had to be temporarily shelved, however, because existing distribution and inventory monitoring systems were unable to cope with the sudden increase in the Chicago-area activities.

Catalog shopping, accommodating the ever-swelling numbers of working women, was another new enterprise of the 1970s. In a 50–50 partnership with Canadian Consumers Distributing Company, Ltd., May opened 18 catalog showrooms in the mid-1970s, planning an eventual 150 more. Unlike other catalog stores that offered merchandise that was dispatched from separate warehouses, these supplied catalog-ordered items from storage facilities on the premises. Although hopeful that the new enterprise would at least break even by the end of 1976, this was not the case, and May sold its 70 U.S. showrooms to Consumers Distributing Company (CDC) in 1978.

In November 1979, the company bought Volume Shoe Corporation for about $150 million in stock. A family-owned chain of more than 800 self-service stores in Topeka, Kansas, Volume was then enjoying annual sales totaling more than $200 million. The following year, a recession combined with negative effects of start-up costs for an enlarged shoe distribution center and cut deeply into profits. Between 1979 and 1983, however, the chain showed the biggest earnings increase of any May Department Store Division. Moving purposefully toward its goal of establishing a Payless Shoe Outlet chain nationally, Volume purchased 83 stores from HRT Industries as well as 38 from Craddock-Terry Shoe and was eyeing possibilities in east coast cities.

At the same time, a new May president, David Farrell, instituted a program of refurbishments to renovate some of the company's more outdated units and rejuvenate their image as trendy fashion outlets. The company spent $117 million on the Famous-Barr chain alone, although other stores were also remodeled. Farrell also instituted stringent cost-cutting means, which included the installation of new telephone and energy-management systems for all 138 department stores. Merchandise was upgraded to tempt the upscale customer, for the company was competing against specialty stores whose fashion reputations were already established.

Maintaining Market Share in the 1980s

A significant threat to market share appeared in the mid-1980s, in the form of warehouse stores and off-price outlets. Offering brand-name merchandise at discount prices, they forced retailers to rethink their customary strategy. May's answer, to fulfill its requirements of upgrading merchandise at one end of their market niche and meeting the off-price challenge at the other, was the 1986 acquisition of Associated Dry Goods (ADG) at a cost of $2.5 billion. This steep purchase price brought the company the quality Lord & Taylor chain, J.W. Robinson department stores, L.S. Ayres units, Caldor discount operations, and Loehmann's off-price apparel shops. As was the case with the other May subsidiaries, each chain continued to operate independently.

In 1987, May formed a 50–50 partnership with PruSimon, called May Centers Associates (MCA). May transferred its shopping center operations to MCA. Two partners owned PruSimon: Melvin Simon & Associates, Inc., of Indianapolis, Indiana, and the New York-based Prudential Insurance Company of America. PruSimon paid $550 million in cash for its share of the partnership. May's chief benefit was to disengage from management functions unrelated to the stores, which increased in number once again with the $1.5 billion acquisition of Filene's of Boston and Foley's of Houston in 1988.

After spending two years acquiring a huge chunk of the upscale department store market, the company then decided to narrow its retailing focus, and made moves to discontinue its discount operations. Loehmann's was sold in 1988, two years after it was acquired. Offered next were Venture and the Caldor chain that had been part of the ADG acquisition. Unfortunately, there were a large number of retail operations for sale at the end of the 1980s, and the company was unable to reach its asking price of almost $600 million for Caldor. Consequently, it sold this unit to an investor group, which formed a company called Odyssey Partners L.P., to buy an 80 percent share. In 1990, Venture was spun off to shareholders in a tax-free distribution. That same year, May acquired Thalhimers, a 26-store group based in Richmond, Virginia, which helped May's sales surpass $10 billion.

Continued Expansion: 1990s and Beyond

In the early 1990s, The May Department Stores Company continued to expand its reach through the acquisition of stores around the country, consolidating them into one of May's own companies, depending on the geographic region in which they were situated. Thalhimers was consolidated with Hecht's, and Rochester, New York-based Sibley's was consolidated with Famous-Barr. Furthermore, in 1993 Los Angeles' May Company and Robinson's were combined to form Robinson's-May, which remained one of the area's premiere upscale department stores into the late 1990s.

Many critics began to wonder whether May's quick takeovers would backfire. Because the company was purchasing stores with names that were already established and then changing each store into one of its own, the possibility existed that customers would become confused and once-prosperous stores would lose business. Fortunately for May, however, this did not seem to be the case, and the company continued to post record earnings throughout the acquisition phase. Furthermore, the company actually saved itself money by controlling its marketing expenses; rather than spend money to promote many different individual stores from city to city, the company instead was able to advertise regionally once new stores were transformed into one of May's namesakes.

The aggressive acquisition and transformation practice continued throughout the mid-1990s. Engulfed by the rapidly expanding May holdings were ten Hess's in Pennsylvania and New York in 1994, and 16 Wanamaker and Woodward & Lothrop stores in Philadelphia and Washington, D.C., in 1995. All in all, throughout 1995 the May Company either acquired or opened a total of 37 new department stores. It also acquired two large discount shoe store chains, Kobacker Company and The Shoe Works, in Columbus, Ohio. Together, these two chains numbered 550 stores.

The company followed its impressive expansion efforts with another key acquisition of 13 Strawbridge & Clothier stores in Philadelphia in 1996. The stores continued to be operated under the name Strawbridge's, and May opened another 15 throughout the year. May also decided to spin off its Payless Shoe-Source holdings to the public in mid-1996, listing the newly-freestanding company on the New York Stock Exchange that year and achieving annual sales of $11.7 billion.

Toward the end of the century, May stores continued to face keen competition, but the company thrived on the strength of its stellar reputation and its on ongoing efforts to upgrade products and maintain its position as marketer of high-visibility brands. The company continued to build on these strengths with innovative merchandising ideas, while retaining a focus on expansion throughout the country. During 1998, Jerome Loeb was named chairman and Eugene Kahn took over as president and CEO. Under the leadership of these two retail veterans, May logged its 24th consecutive year of record sales and earnings that year and added 11 Dillard's Inc. stores to its arsenal.

During 1999, May divested its consumer electronics interests in order to make way for additional floor-space for its higher-margin items such as housewares, furniture, gift merchandise, and textiles. It acquired the Utah-based Zions Cooperative Mercantile Institution and consolidated those stores into its Meier & Frank operations. Profits reached $927 million that year on sales of $13.86 billion.

May moved into the new millennium determined to continue its success. As part of its strategy to secure a younger customer base, the company purchased the David's Bridal Inc. chain of wedding apparel and accessories stores in 2000. David's Bridal was the largest wedding apparel and accessories chain in the United States and had a solid customer base of 18 to 34-year-olds—the exact demographic May began to target for its department stores. As such, the company began implementing new programs that would entice young bride-to-be's to shop at both David's and May-owned department stores. For instance, a

David's Bridal customer would receive a wedding gift card if she registered at a May department store.

May also opened 23 new department stores in 2000 and expanded into nine new markets. The following year, it acquired 13 stores from bankrupt Wards and nine stores from Saks Inc. In December, it announced plans to purchase After Hours Formalwear Inc., the largest tuxedo rental and sales retailer in the United States Kahn commented on the purchase in a 2001 *Daily News Record* article, stating, ''After Hours is a very exciting acquisition and a highly strategic complement to our David's Bridal business. There are tremendous marketing and other business synergies between David's stores, After Hours' stores, and the wedding registry business in our department store divisions.''

As May forged ahead with its growth plans in the new millennium, the American economy slowed and the retail sector began to feel the pains of overgrowth. In fact, by 2001, the United States had 5.6 billion square feet of retail space—20 square feet per person. May however, remained confident that even during difficult economic times, it would continue to secure record growth. With its strong position in the retail industry and its long-standing successful business strategy, May appeared to be well positioned to combat increased competition and economic hard times well into the future.

Principal Subsidiaries

Leadville Insurance Company; Snowdin Insurance Company; May Merchandising Company; May Department Stores International; May Capital Inc.; Grande Levee Inc.; David's Bridal, Inc.; Lord & Taylor; Hecht's; Strawbridge's; Foley's; Robinson's-May; Kaufmann's; Filene's; Famous-Barr; L.S. Ayres; The Jones Store; Meier & Frank.

Principal Competitors

Federated Department Stores Inc.; Dillard's Inc.; Saks Inc.

Further Reading

''ADG Acquisition Turns May into Super Power,'' *Chain Store Age Executive*, September 1986.

Berner, Robert, ''Too Many Retailers, Not Enough Shoppers,'' *Business Week*, February 12, 2001.

''A Discounter Bids for Power in Chicago,'' *Business Week*, August 28, 1978.

La Monica, Paul R., ''May Department Stores; The Shoe Doesn't Fit,'' *Financial World*, April 8, 1996, p. 16.

''May Department Stores,'' *Barron's*, March 29, 1954.

''May Exits CE, Beefs Up Home Furnishings,'' *HFN: The Weekly Newspaper for the Home Furnishing Network*, March 29, 1999, p. 3.

''May Stores: Watch Them Grow,'' *Fortune*, December 1948.

''May Wraps Dillard's Buy,'' *HFN: The Weekly Newspaper for the Home Furnishing Network*, September 14, 1998, p. 4.

''Retailers Discover Their Real Estate Riches,'' *Business Week*, January 19, 1981.

Rutberg, Sidney, and Valerie Seckler, ''May Co. Aims to Spin Off Payless Shoes,'' *WWD*, January 18, 1996, p. 2.

Weitzman, Jennifer, ''May Co. Buys After Hours Formalwear,'' *Daily News Record*, December 24, 2001.

Yaeger, Don, ''High-end Goods the Ticket,'' *HFN: The Weekly Newspaper for the Home Furnishing Network*, June 10, 1996, p. 9.

—Gillian Wolf
—updates: Laura E. Whiteley and Christina M. Stansell

Milnot Company

100 South Fourth Street, Suite 1010
St. Louis, Missouri 63102
U.S.A.
Telephone: (314) 436-7667
Fax: (314) 436-7679
Web site: http://www.milnot.com

Private Company
Incorporated: 1916
Employees: 65
Sales: $200 million (2000 est.)
NAIC: 311514 Dry, Condensed, and Evaporated Dairy
    Product Manufacturing; 311422 Specialty Canning

Milnot Company, headquartered in St. Louis, Missouri, produces canned milk goods, baby food under the Beech-Nut brand, canned chilli under the Chilli Man brand, and several private-label products. For most of the company's history, its signature product was its evaporated milk, but through diversification, starting in the mid 1970s, it expanded its line of products. It almost doubled in size when, in 1998, it purchased Beech-Nut. Three years later, the company's attempt to merge with the H.J. Heinz Company was blocked by the Federal Trade Commission. Milnot remains a private company and is owned by Madison Dearborn Partners, a Chicago-based capital investment firm.

1912–40: Milnot Begins as a Dairy

Martin Jensen founded Milnot Company as the Litchfield Creamery Company in 1912. It was located in Litchfield, Illinois, and was initially a dairy. In 1915, Jensen was joined in the enterprise by Charles Hauser, then somewhat later by William Hartke. These three men incorporated the company and, in 1916, built a new plant at what would remain the company's Litchfield milk-canning location for the rest of the century.

World War I helped the company develop because it produced an increased demand for processed dairy products. The United States, even before its entry into the war in 1917, was shipping these products and other goods to its future allies. In 1919, after the armistice, the Litchfield plant processed 23 million pounds of milk, most all of which it marketed as sweetened, condensed, and evaporated milk.

In the next decade, the company continued to grow, albeit slowly. Thereafter, despite the impact of the Great Depression, its growth accelerated. One reason for its growth was the introduction of Milnot in 1930, a new, canned-milk product. Although at first sales of Milnot were slow, they soon picked up, and in 1932, under Hauser's leadership, Milnot production began a rapid expansion. In 1936, to accommodate the growing demand for Milnot, the company acquired an additional production plant located in Indiana. Three years later, in 1939, the product was renamed Milnot. By 1940, the company had grown to be about the same size as Pet, its major competitor.

1946–90: Milnot Grows and Diversifies

Although World War II curtailed Milnot's production, the post-war boom years spurred the company's additional growth. It built a new plant in Warsaw, Indiana, in 1946. Production started there in 1947. Next, in 1948, after buying land on the Missouri-Oklahoma border, the company opened another plant in Seneca, Missouri, where, eventually, all of its canned milk production would be consolidated.

Over the next few decades, Milnot expanded and diversified. In 1975, it purchased rights to a proprietary chili recipe from Joe DeFrates, who had twice been named world champion in a chili cook-off competition. The company then began producing and marketing its Chilli Man canned chili, using the unique "chilli" spelling because it was an abbreviated rendering of DeFrates' home state of Illinois. Eight years later, in 1983, Milnot also added a sweetened condensed milk to its line. Dubbed Dairy Sweet, it was made by adding sweeteners to its evaporated milk, the staple product in the company's early development.

Still, despite its new product lines, Milnot's growth slowed. It remained profitable, but after it sold out to TW Services in the 1980s, its sales simply stagnated from a lack of adequate strategic planning and sufficient capital investment. In 1990, Michael Osborne, then working for TW Services, put together

an investment group that, for $25 million, bought Milnot from
the parent company, which was then selling off properties. The
investment group consisted of Osborne; Ingles Capital Corp.,
headed by Greg Ingles of Dallas, Texas; and Eli Jacobs, owner
of the Baltimore Orioles. At that time, Milnot had annual sales
of around $35 million, and Osborne and the other investors
knew that the company had a strong base and had an excellent
opportunity to increase its line of brands and develop new
markets.

1991–95: Milnot Further Diversifies and Its Sales Rapidly Climb

Osborne brought substantial experience to his new position
as Milnot's president and CEO. He had worked in Pet's dairy
division for several years, from about 1972 to 1983, when Pet
sold that division. In his new job at Milnot, Osborne took that
company in some of the same directions that Pet itself had gone.

Within three years after Osborne took over the helm at
Milnot, the company's sales nearly tripled, reaching about $110
million, including revenues generated by its Mexican food
division. About half its sales came from it nationally distributed, private label products, including it signature evaporated
milk, which was competing in the same market as Osborne's
old employer's product, Pet evaporated milk. In St. Louis,
where Osborne moved Milnot's headquarters in 1990, the company's strong selling, regional brands–Chilli Man Chilli and
Dairy Sweet–competed, respectively, with Armour's canned
chili and Borden's Eagle Brand condensed milk.

Under Osborne's leadership, Milnot, using its size to advantage, succeeded in attracting executives from larger, competitive companies like Kraft, Con Agra, and Anheuser-Busch,
which made Eagle Snacks. It was also able to compete with
such larger companies through its strong and efficient regional
distribution, primarily in the Northwest, Southwest, and Southeast, but it also was able to maintain a good national distribution
volume of its private label products.

Osborne also spearheaded the growth of Milnot's Mexican
food line through acquisitions. In Fort Worth, Teaxs, the company bought the strong-selling Jimenez brand from Quality
Foods. It also acquired Fiesta, a Mexican food company in
Dallas. It then combined two plants in the Dallas-Fort Worth
area to give the company a full line of Mexican foods and put it
in direct competition with Pet's Old El Paso line.

By the mid-1990s, Milnot's most familiar products were still
its signature evaporated milk and strong regional food brands,
chief among which were Chilli Man Chilli and Dairy Sweet, the

sweetened condensed milk which continued to compete for a
larger market share against Borden's market-leading Eagle
Brand. The company still had one of its six operations in its
home base of Litchfield. The corporate hub was in St. Louis,
however, where most of the managerial staff was headquartered, though some of the major owners were in Dallas.

1996–98: Change in Ownership Leads to Major Acquisition

In December 1995, Osborne had a fatal heart attack. Under the
leadership of interim president James Tappan, Milnot began
searching for a suitable replacement for Osborne. The company's
board named Robert Pizzuti to the CEO and president posts in the
spring of 1996. Before his appointment, Pizzuti was serving as
president of RJP Associates, a Greenwich, Connecticut-based
management consulting firm. He also brought food industry
experience to his new job, having previously served as president
of Whitman Chocolates from 1991 to 1994, and, prior to that, as a
vice-president of Maxwell House Coffee Co. What he came to
was a company that had only about 125 employees, some 25 of
whom were at the company headquarters in St. Louis and another
30 at its Litchfield plant 60 miles to the northeast. The rest
worked at the company's facilities in Joplin, Missouri, and Denver, Colorado.

When Pizzuti took charge, he began looking to acquire other
product lines, even outside the canned milk and canned meat
industries. He was also interested in developing new markets.
The problem he faced was an industry stagnation that had lasted
for several years. Sales of evaporated milk, Milnot's chief
staple, had suffered industry-wide declines. In 1995, for example, they had dropped by 10 percent over 1994, not a promising
trend for a company that had built its reputation in the canned
milk business. There were also mounting problems, including
the rising cost of milk, itself driven up by the rising cost of cattle
feed. Also, as a result of varying taste preferences across the
nation, the canned chili industry was highly fragmented, making it difficult for Milnot to move into new markets for its Chilli
Man line. The company's annual revenues had stagnated in a
range between $70 million and $80 million, and Pizzuti knew
that his challenge was to spur them up, if need be by diversifying the company's product line. That, however would require new capital.

Fortunately, Milnot was bought out by Chicago-based Madison Dearborn Partners, an investment firm that had been formed
by John Canning, Jr., in 1992. Madison Dearborn specialized in
management buyout transactions as well as a wide range of
private refinancing and recapitalization investments. The acquisition by Madison Dearborn was significant because it assured
Milnot of adequate capitalization for continued growth. Significantly, it allowed Milnot to make a major acquisition in 1998
when it purchased Beech-Nut Nutrition Corp., the branded baby
food subsidiary of Ralcorp Holdings, Inc., a St. Louis, Mis-
souri-based maker of private-label ready-to-eat cereals, crack-
ers, cookies, and snack nuts. The $68 million investment more
than doubled Milnot's revenue base, which jumped from about
$90 million to $230 million. Beech-Nut, which dated back to
the 1930s, had been passed around from one parent company to
another over the previous four decades before its purchase by
Milnot. Besides Ralcorp, its owners included Nestlé, Ralston-

Key Dates:

1912: The company is founded as Litchfield Creamery Company.

1916: Charles Hauser and William Hartke incorporate Litchfield and build new plant.

1930: The company begins manufacturing MILNUT.

1936: Litchfield buys another plant in Indiana.

1939: Creamery changes its name to Milnot.

1946: Milton builds a new plant in Warsaw, Indiana, beginning production the next year.

1948: Company opens another facility at Seneca, Missouri, right on the Missouri-Oklahoma state line.

1975: Milnot purchases a proprietary chili recipe from Joe DeFrates, two-time chili cook-off champion.

1983: The company introduces Dairy Sweet sweetened condensed milk.

1990: Michael Osborne heads investment group that buys Milnot from TW Services; company moves from Litchfield into MCI Building in St. Louis.

1995: Osborne dies and is succeeded by interim president James Tappan.

1996: Robert Pizzuti is named company CEO and president.

1998: Milnot acquires Beach-Nut from Ralcorp.

2001: Heinz efforts to purchase company thwarted on anti-trust grounds.

Purina, and Bristol-Myers (which later became Bristol-Myers Squibb). With the acquisition of Beach-Nut, Milnot entered an entirely new market.

1999 and Beyond: Plans New Growth Strategies

Towards the end of the 1990s, Milnot made repeated efforts to buy Pet Milk from The Pillsbury Company, Pet's corporate parent. Scott Meader, who had replaced Pizzuti as Milnot's CEO, was actively seeking to double the company's annual revenue to $500 million through another major acquisition. Its last bid on Pet came six moths after it had completed its purchase of Beech-Nut, As before, the company's efforts were frustrated by what Meader and his colleagues saw as an overvalued price tag on Pet. In any case, after Pet Milk sales took a nosedive, and Pillsbury took Pet off the auction block, at least temporarily. Although Milnot was the logical buyer for Pet, no deal could be struck, leaving Milnot to look for other options.

In 2000, it thought it found one: a merger deal with H.J. Heinz Co. In the baby-food market, Heinz ranked second and Milnot's Beach-Nut brand third, but they were far behind the industry's frontrunner, Gerber Products, which commanded a 73 percent share of the market and had annual revenues closing in on $600 million. Some analysts saw the proposed buyout of Milnot by Heinz as an effort by the two companies to gang up on the leader, and, in fact, executives at Milnot said as much, claiming that, combined, Heinz and Milnot could give Gerber a better market place battle. In any case, the merger attempt was eventually blocked by the Federal Trade Commission, which saw in the deal a monopolistic threat to the baby-food market. The merger collapse occurred in 2001 and left Milnot to devise new strategies for expansion or another buy out alternative.

Principal Subsidiaries

Fiesta-Jimenez Co.

Principal Competitors

Dairy Farmers of America; H.J. Heinz Company; Nestlé S.A.; Novartis AG.

Further Reading

Anderson, Tom, ''Milnot Will Fight FTC's Attempt to Block Merger,'' *St. Louis Business Journal*, July 17, 2000, p. 9.

''Beech-Nut Is Acquired by Milnot,'' *Supermarket News*, August 10, 1998, p. 51.

Conrad, Lee, ''Milnot Looks Outside As Canned Milk Market Sours; New President Faces Challenge of Rising Costs of Products,'' *St. Louis Business Journal*, May 13, 1996, p. 7A.

Desloge, Rick, ''Milnot Co. Finds Its Niche in the Land of Giants,'' *St. Louis Business Journal*, April 13, 1992, p. 8A.

——, ''Milnot Wants to Buy Pet,'' *St. Louis Business Journal*, March 29, 1999, p. 1.

Lee, Thomas, ''St. Louis-Based Firm Frustrated with Failed H.J. Heinz Merger,'' *Knight-Ridder/Tribune Business News*, May 19, 2001.

Murray, Barbara, ''Milnot, Heinz Abandon Baby Food Merger Bid,'' *Supermarket News*, May 7, 2001, p. 119.

—John W. Fiero

Minuteman International Inc.

111 South Rohlwing Road
Addison, Illinois 60101
U.S.A.
Telephone: (630) 627-6900
Fax: (630) 627-1130
Web site: http://www.minutemanintl.com

Public Company
Incorporated: 1951 as American Cleaning Equipment
   Corp.
Employees: 414
Sales: $85.2 million (2000)
Stock Exchanges: NASDAQ
Ticker Symbol: MMAN
NAIC: 333319, 551112

Based in Addison, Illinois, Minuteman International Inc. develops and manufactures equipment and products used for floor maintenance, including walk-behind and rider-operated floor scrubbers; burnishers and floor machines; indoor/outdoor sweepers; carpet care machines; and critical care vacuums for removing hazardous waste. The company serves both commercial and industrial clients in more than 40 countries through an established network of distributors.

Laying the Foundation: 1951–80

Minuteman's roots go back to July 1951 when the company was incorporated under the name American Cleaning Equipment Corp. Its founders, Jim McSheehy and Mat Zmudka, decided to focus the organization's efforts on industrial customers, because commercial clients already were being served by much larger competitors. In keeping with this strategy, American Cleaning became a pioneer by unveiling the very first vacuum attached to a 55-gallon drum in 1952. Additionally, it also was one of the first manufacturers to produce critical filter vacuums for hazardous waste removal. Over time, this niche proved to be valuable for American Cleaning. In 1981, it controlled about half of the market for such devices, which larger

manufacturers often overlooked because they were highly specialized. American Cleaning mostly served clients in the midwestern United States. Its product line essentially included machines for cleaning walls and polishing floors, wet/dry vacuums for commercial and contractor use, and wet/dry vacuums used for boiler and industrial cleaning.

After Jim McSheehy passed away and Mat Zmudka decided to sell American Cleaning, a consultant from Cleveland named Bob O'Brien bought half of the company and became its president in 1974. Prior to that time, O'Brien, who held an engineering degree from Purdue University, had worked for several leading enterprises, including automotive giant Chrysler and consulting firm Booz, Allen & Hamilton. By the late 1970s, O'Brien and the McSheehy family, which maintained part ownership, were interested in selling American Cleaning because of factors like rising interest rates and an unfavorable climate for expansion.

Changing Hands in the 1970s

It wasn't long before Hako Werke, a West German company that manufactured complementary products, expressed an interest in acquiring American Cleaning. In 1978, Hako Werke President Tyll Necker approached O'Brien in Atlanta at the International Sanitary Supply Association trade show. A period of discussions and negotiations followed, and in June of 1980 Hako Werke acquired American Cleaning. The new company was renamed Hako Minuteman Inc. Hako Werke had the resources to take Minuteman to a new level and made sure proper attention was given to supporting, marketing, and growing the enterprise.

In 1981, Jerome E. Rau was named president and chief executive officer of Hako Minuteman Inc. Until his death on September 20, 2000, Rau successfully led the company through an era of growth, development, and expansion. During his tenure, the firm's sales grew from $4.5 million to more than $85 million.

Rau was born in Cincinnati, Ohio, on December 11, 1932 to Arthur and Kathryn Rau. In 1944, he moved to Prior Lake, Minnesota, and attended Shakopee High School, graduating in 1951. Rau graduated from the University of Minnesota, where he played football. Rau then joined the Reserve Officers Training Corps (ROTC) and spent two years at Fort Sill, Oklahoma.

Company Perspectives:

The core of Minuteman International is anchored by a single, straightforward vision—to deliver exceptional floor cleaning equipment and chemicals combined with a single-minded focus to anticipate and answer our customers' needs. Answering those needs is just the beginning of a performance-driven philosophy to help our distributors maximize profit and provide outstanding service, products, and training to each Minuteman customer. That philosophy is combined with the ongoing development of new and more cost effective methods of manufacturing and product design to keep our customers on the leading edge of floor care technology into the next century.

Prior to entering the business world, he taught at the junior high school level for eight years, and at the same time coached high school football and refereed basketball games. His business career began with Spring Park, Minnesota-based Advance Machine Co. in 1967, where he worked in sales and eventually was named vice-president of the company's industrial division.

In November 1984, Minuteman made its first acquisition when it purchased the Minnesota-based Multi-Clean Products Division of H.B. Fuller Co. The acquisition was very positive and allowed Minuteman to expand its distribution network and add an already established line of carpet cleaning equipment to its offerings, along with chemical coating and cleaning products. Prior to the acquisition, Multi-Clean had been in operation since 1934, and had been producing chemicals since 1946.

By 1987, Minuteman was serving a broad range of industrial, institutional, and commercial end-users—including supermarkets, hotels, factories, churches, retail stores, offices, schools, convalescent centers, hospitals, and nursing homes. Its product line included floor and carpet care equipment, and commercial and industrial vacuums manufactured in Addison, Illinois. Additionally, the company's products for chemical cleaning and coating were produced in St. Paul, Minnesota. In March of 1987, Minuteman became a public corporation, and its shares were traded on the NASDAQ.

The following year, Minuteman completed a 46,000-square-foot addition to its plant in Addison, Illinois, which gave the company approximately twice the factory and warehouse space it had previously. In Minuteman's 1988 annual report, Rau announced that the company would move its engineering and development departments into the new space and that Minuteman would invest in new equipment for them the following year so the company could stay on the cutting edge from a technology standpoint.

Growth and Expansion in the 1990s

Following the expansion of its Addison, Illinois, plant, Minuteman obtained 40,000-square-feet of new space for its Minnesota-based Multi-Clean division and moved it from St. Paul to Shoreview. The new facility would allow Multi-Clean to increase production, and improve the safety and efficiency of its operations.

In 1991, Minuteman made its second major acquisition and purchased Parker Sweeper Co., a manufacturer of equipment used for sweeping lawns and turf. By doing so, it assimilated more than 100 years of history into the organization. The story of Parker Sweeper reveals a rich and interesting heritage. In 1878, a pattern maker named William Henry Thomas Parker left England for America. He moved to Springfield, Ohio, which at the time was a hub for agricultural equipment manufacturing, and established a pattern-making shop there in 1884 called the W.T. Parker Manufacturing Co. His son, Edwin D. Parker, joined him in 1915 and the business was renamed Parker Pattern Works Co. It was the younger Parker's idea to create a lawn-sweeping device that resulted in the birth of the lawn sweeping industry. Prior to the invention of lawn sweepers, grass clippings and other debris were removed manually with hand rakes. Sweeping devices made the task of removing debris easier and more efficient.

A Chicago firm by the name of Hibbard, Spencer, and Bartlett was the first recorded customer to purchase a sweeper in 1921. After that initial sale, Parker began developing and producing lawn sweepers on a larger scale. In the late 1920s and 1930s it marketed two models, the "Everwear" and the "Springfield," to parks, cemeteries, and other customers with large lawns. When the lawn sweeping business boomed, Parker split into two separate companies. Pattern making continued under the already established company name, while the Springfield Lawnsweeper Co. concentrated on making lawn sweepers. The advent of World War II temporarily changed the operations of both companies. They were joined back together to form the Parker Pattern and Foundry Co., which manufactured military parts.

In 1944, Edwin Parker's son, Richard, was named the company's general manager. He previously had worked for an engineering firm in Indianapolis, but opted to join the family business because his father was going to divest it. After the war, the company returned its focus to lawn sweepers and introduced machines suitable for domestic lawn care use. In 1948, the company changed its name to the Parker Sweeper Co. Richard Parker became company president in 1959.

During his affiliation with Parker, the company experienced a period of growth and expansion. Parker eventually acquired the Lawn Beauty Spreader Division of Schneider Metal Manufacturing Co. On the international front, its products reaching South American, European, African, and Far Eastern markets by the mid-1950s. By the late 1960s, Parker's product line included indoor and outdoor vacuums, mass-debris removal equipment, power rakes, lawn spreaders, and powered and trailing lawn sweepers. By the late 1970s, international sales accounted for 20 percent of the 120-employee firm's sales, and its reach had grown to include the Soviet Union and Japan. Parker became a supplier to Sears Roebuck & Co. in 1977, and received the Sears Symbol of Excellence Award three years later. The company celebrated 100 years of operation in 1984. At that time, it controlled 85 percent of the U.S. lawn sweeper market, and four smaller firms controlled the remainder. Richard Parker died in 1989 at the age of 80, three years before his company was acquired by Hako Minuteman.

In 1994, Minuteman moved Parker's operations to its Hampshire, Illinois, facility, where a new 200,000-square-foot

Key Dates:

1951: Company incorporated in July under the name American Cleaning Equipment Corp.

1952: American Cleaning unveils a vacuum attached to a 55-gallon drum, which was the first of its kind.

1974: Bob O'Brien buys half of the company and is named president.

1980: Hako Werke acquires American Cleaning in June, and the company is renamed Hako Minuteman Inc.

1981: Jerome E. Rau named president and CEO.

1984: Minuteman Canada is established; company makes its first acquisition, of the Multi-Clean Products Division of H.B. Fuller Co.

1987: Minuteman goes public on the NASDAQ.

1991: Company makes its second major acquisition by purchasing Parker Sweeper Co.

1994: The company name is changed to Minuteman International Inc.

1997: Minuteman's sales exceed $50 million for the first time in company history, reaching $53 million.

2000: Jerome Rau dies from a heart attack at the age of 67; Gregory Rau named president and CEO.

foundation had been created to accommodate expansion. It could be expanded in 50,000-square-foot increments, the first of which was finished in the third quarter of 1994. Also in 1994, Minuteman changed its official name from Hako Minuteman to Minuteman International. An aggressive international expansion followed, and Minuteman began marketing its products in Belgium, Central America, Iceland, Sweden, the United Kingdom, and the Philippines. In the company's 1994 annual report, CEO Jerome Rau indicated that during 1995 Minuteman would attempt to increase its reach in Europe, as well as in Asia, Canada, Latin America, the Middle East, and the Pacific Rim.

In 1995, the growth and expansion that had started earlier in the decade was unfolding with considerable momentum. Exciting developments were happening on several fronts. First, Minuteman increased the size of its engineering staff by 25 percent in response to demand and the time required to roll out new products. The company's international presence grew when it introduced products in five new markets, bringing the number of countries it served outside of the United States to 40.

In September 1995, the second 50,000-square-foot module of the company's Hampshire, Illinois, plant became operational. This happened ahead of schedule and would lower handling costs and increase efficiency in the area of manufacturing. Along with its expanded infrastructure, Minuteman installed a new laser system, which it used to cut sheet metal more precisely, as well as a unit that washed parts more effectively before they were painted.

In 1995, Minuteman President and CEO Jerry Rau was selected as vice-president/president-elect of the International Sanitary Supply Association (ISSA). According to Minuteman's 1995 Annual Report, Rau was the first equipment manufacturer to head up the trade organization since 1959. At that time, only five equipment manufacturers had served on the

association's board since the end of World War II. According to the report, Rau had several goals for ISSA. They included "marketing, building, and enhancing the ISSA for greater exposure to new markets, developing active ISSA representation for chemical and equipment manufacturers faced with continuous regulations, and developing new educational opportunities which offer members new ways to enter and take advantage of new markets and products."

In 1996, Minuteman celebrated its tenth anniversary of being a public company. That year, the company experienced even greater international expansion. A sales manager was hired to coordinate sales activity in Europe, and a warehouse was secured in the Netherlands so products could be delivered more quickly. The appearance of Minuteman's products also changed when a new charcoal and rich wine color scheme was introduced. The move was intended to provide a more modern look than the orange colors it used previously.

In 1997, Minuteman's sales exceeded $50 million for the first time in the company's history, reaching $53 million. That year, Multi-Clean was made a separate company division. In Minuteman's 1997 annual report, Rau called this "a challenge and a source of satisfaction." To make the unit more specialized, the company had to hire and train a sales force dedicated to cleaning chemicals and coating products. The new sales force was separate from the sales force that sold Minuteman's equipment.

Nearing the decade's end, Minuteman made its third major acquisition when it purchased Aberdeen, North Carolina-based AAR PowerBoss Inc. in 1998. The addition allowed Minuteman to bolster its already strong lineup of products with large, industrial, rider-operated scrubbers and sweepers, which were different from the mostly walk-behind, commercial units Minuteman had been producing. According to *Crain's Chicago Business*, "The merger gave Minuteman, which sold its products mostly to big retail chains, its first real entree into the industrial market and a broader lineup of products to compete against market leader Tennant Co. of Minneapolis." In addition to expanding its product offerings, Minuteman also was able to improve efficiency by moving the production of some products, such as its 3800 rider scrubber, to the PowerBoss plant. The successful integration of PowerBoss into Minuteman allowed sales to reach an all-time high of $76 million in 1999, ending the decade on a high note.

Into The Millennium

In January 2000, Jerome Rau's son, Gregory J. Rau, was named Minuteman's president and chief operating officer. The elder Rau maintained his status as chairman and CEO. Prior to the promotion, Gregory Rau served Minuteman for 16 years in a variety of sales positions before becoming vice-president of sales and later executive vice-president. An established succession plan was for the younger Rau to become CEO in January 2001. However, Jerome Rau's unexpected death during a business trip to Buenos Aires caused Gregory Rau to assume the role sooner. Jerome Rau died from a heart attack at the age of 67 on Wednesday, September 20, 2000.

According to the September 24, 2000 *Chicago Tribune*, Gregory Rau said his father "was known most for his willingness to counsel and offer guidance to his numerous employees and friends." The company's 2000 annual report summarized the extent of their loss. It read: "When Jerry Rau delivered a message, people heard it. It was hard to ignore his passion for details and getting things right, every time. Because to Jerry Rau, every detail mattered—especially those details that stood for quality, integrity, and performance. Jerry Rau's dynamic management style brought the company's product line to an industry breadth and depth challenged by few. In addition, Rau ushered in an era of innovative engineering and cutting edge technology which led to over 33 patents for the company and 'first time ever' products such as the Ultra Violet Single Floor Coat System. Rau's intuitive vision continued to drive the company into new markets such as industrial cleaning, outdoor cleaning, and lawn cleaning."

Although the elder Rau's death was a dark shadow on the year 2000 for Minuteman, the company's sales reached a record high of $85 million. Additionally, *Forbes* ranked Minuteman among America's 200 best small companies. Furthermore, *Crain's Chicago Business* called Minuteman "an acquirer in a consolidating business," and indicated that Gregory Rau was expected to carry on this strategy, painting a bright picture for the firm's future.

Principal Subsidiaries

Multi-Clean; Minuteman PowerBoss Inc.; Minuteman Canada Inc.; Minuteman European B.V. (The Netherlands); Minuteman International Foreign Sales Corp.

Principal Competitors

Electolux (U.S.); HMI Industries; Tennant Co.

Further Reading

Carter, Ron, "Parker Sweeps Up in Lawn Vacuuming Business," *Springfield News-Sun* (Ohio), October 21, 1984, p. 10B.

"Jereome E. Rau," *Chicago Tribune,* September 24, 2001.

"Jereome E. Rau of Hoffman Estates," *Daily Herald,* September 23, 2000.

Miller, Edward, "Parker Sees Production of Own Parts as Vital," *Springfield News-Sun* (Ohio), July 2, 1978, p. 5B.

Murphy, H. Lee, "Minuteman Eyeing Smooth Transition After CEO's Death," *Crain's Chicago Business,* October 23, 2000, p. 23.

—— "Minuteman International Inc.," *Crain's Chicago Business,* June 7, 2000, p. 68.

"Parker Sweeper Swept, De-Thatched and Scrubbed Its Way to Success," *Springfield News-Sun* (Ohio), January 20, 1997.

Rosenbaum, Michael, "The New Owners Speak German," *Inc.,* September 1981, p. 120.

"Springfield Industries. The Parker Sweeper Co.," *Springfield News-Sun* (Ohio), May 24, 1959.

Stafford, Tom, "Parker Sweeper Sale Nearly Complete," *Springfield News-Sun* (Ohio), April 28, 1992, pp. 1, 4.

—Paul R. Greenland

Misys plc

Burleigh House
Chapel Oak
Salford Priors
Evesham WR11 8SP
United Kingdom
Telephone: + 44 (0) 1386 871373
Fax: + 44 (0) 1386 871045
Web site: http://www.misys.com

Public Company
Incorporated: 1979
Employees: 7,000
Sales: $1.2 billion (2001)
Stock Exchanges: London
Ticker Symbol: MSY
NAIC: 511210 Software Publishers

As of 2002, Misys plc was one of the world's largest independent applications software products groups. The United Kingdom-based company had operations in more than 30 countries. Its principal activities were the development and licensing of application software products to customers in well-defined vertical markets. Founded in 1979 to provide computer systems to insurance brokers in the United Kingdom, the company expanded in the 1990s through acquisitions to reduce its reliance on a single market and began providing software solutions to the banking and securities, healthcare, and financial services markets. While Misys's banking and securities division serves global markets, its healthcare division serves the U.S. market only, and its financial services division serves insurance brokers and independent financial analysts in the United Kingdom.

Rapid Growth and Diversification: 1979–95

Kevin Lomax, the chairman of Misys, was the lead investor when Misys was founded in 1979 with private capital. He served as non-executive chairman until 1985, when he became the firm's full-time executive chairman. As a supplier of computer systems to insurance brokers in the United Kingdom,

Misys grew rapidly. In 1987, it gained access to public capital by floating its stock on the Unlisted Securities Market. In 1989, the company's stock became listed on the main London Stock Exchange.

Toward the end of the 1980s, Misys decided to broaden the range of its activities and reduce its dependence on a single market. It began a series of acquisitions designed to strengthen its market position and increase its presence through consolidating different market segments. In 1992, Misys acquired a 20 percent interest in Countrywide IF Network, a collective of independent financial analysts (IFs). Misys subsequently acquired all of Countrywide and used it to become a dominant presence in the IF market. In 1994 Misys acquired Kapiti, a financial services software firm with 15 international offices, giving Misys a significant presence outside the United Kingdom. Kapiti was subsequently renamed Midas-Kapiti International Ltd. (MKI).

Although Misys was still considered a "little-known software company," according to *Computer Weekly,* its 1995 takeover of ACT Group plc made it Great Britain's largest software supplier. Misys's 212-million-pound acquisition of banking software developer ACT Group gave it control of three of the five principal banking software products in the world: Equation, Bankmaster, and Midas. The ACT Group had been troubled by an expensive and overly complicated research and development project called DBA, which was costing it many millions of pounds and involved 20 man-years. Following the acquisition, Misys renamed the subsidiary ACT Financial Systems and replaced its managing director and finance director.

Entering U.S. Healthcare Market: 1997–98

By 1997, Misys had operations in 50 countries, with more than half of its revenue coming from outside the United Kingdom. The company's 1997 annual report noted that 22 percent of its revenue came from emerging markets. For fiscal 1997 ending May 31, the company had net revenue of $477 million (£325 million) and earnings before taxes of $99 million. It had nearly 4,000 employees, including more than 350 in Ireland and about 1,000 in offices around the world.

Company Perspectives:

Today, Misys is one of the world's largest independent applications software products groups and the UK's biggest. Its main activities include selling software solutions to banks, transaction processing and claims administration for physicians in the U.S., systems for insurance brokers in the U.K., and administrative and compliance services for Independent Financial Advisors, or IFs.

Toward the end of 1997, Misys expanded into supplying software solutions for the U.S. healthcare market with the acquisition of Medic Computer Systems for $923 million. Based in Raleigh, North Carolina, Medic provided practice management information systems for physicians and was considered one of the top five health care information technology companies in the United States. Its product line consisted of three software suites: + Medic PM was targeted toward smaller physician practices; the recently launched + Medic Vision served larger physician groups and was especially appropriate for managed care; and AutoChart was designed for use by individual physicians to access and maintain patient clinical records. For fiscal 1996, Medic had revenue of $192 million and net income before taxes of $39 million.

Following the acquisition, Medic became the corporate headquarters for Misys's healthcare division. The healthcare division consisted of Medic, which operated exclusively in the United States, and ACT Medisys, which operated in the United Kingdom and some overseas regions. ACT Medisys sold hospital and laboratory systems to private and public customers.

The newly created healthcare division was the company's fourth. Its other divisions were banking and securities, insurance, and information systems. The company's banking and securities division was the world's largest independent supplier of software products to this sector and had more than 1,600 customers in 100 countries. The division had 24 branch offices in addition to those in the United Kingdom and Ireland. It served the wholesale banking market, the retail banking market, and provided software for corporate banking activities.

Misys's insurance division supplied computer systems, software, and related services to the General and Life & Pension markets in the United Kingdom. It also provided transaction processing services. During 1997 and 1998, the insurance division was involved in developing a retail Web site for insurance products through Misys Interactive Trading.

The information systems division provided software products and services to a variety of vertical markets in the United Kingdom, including contracting and construction, the hotel and leisure industry, and manufacturing and distribution.

For fiscal 1998 ending May 31, Misys reported revenue of £448 million and an operating profit of 98 million pounds. The banking and securities division contributed £252 million toward revenue and had an operating profit of £71 million. The healthcare division had revenue of £83 million and an operating profit of £13 million. The insurance division reported revenue of £50 million and had an operating profit of £13 million, while the information systems division had revenue of £47 million and an operating profit of £5 million. During fiscal 1998, Misys disposed of Misys Computer Services and Misys Integrated Solutions, which comprised its support services businesses, for £10 million. The two companies joined with Zygal Dynamics, which sold printers to banks, to form a desktop management company, Cyberdesk.

Growth Through Acquisitions: 1999–2001

At the beginning of 1999, Misys acquired C-ATS Software Inc. for about $60 million in cash. C-ATS was based in Palo Alto, California, and developed risk management and other sophisticated financial software. C-ATS had become a takeover target following substantial losses in 1997 and 1998. Its flagship software product, Carma, served large banks and other financial institutions by helping them manage their risks and exposure to interest rate fluctuations and other market swings. Following the acquisition C-ATS was renamed and became a subsidiary of Misys subsidiary Midas-Kapiti International Ltd. (MKI), which also provided software applications to the securities and banking industries. Midas-Kapiti had 1,200 customers in 90 countries and provided software to 18 of the world's 20 largest banks.

In addition to acquiring C-ATS Software during fiscal 1999, Misys also sold all of its operations in the information systems division to a group of investors that included their management for about £32 million. As a result of disposing of those non-core assets, Misys was now focused entirely on financial services—including insurance—and healthcare. For fiscal 1999, Misys reported revenue of £582 million and an operating profit of £135 million.

Believing that the Internet would be a catalyst for a fundamental restructuring of many financial services internationally, Misys was determined to establish a pivotal position in Web-based financial services. It planned to build twin Web portals that would serve both independent financial analysts (IFs) and consumers in the United Kingdom. During fiscal 2000, Misys invested £11 million in its portal initiative.

The company's Internet strategy also extended to healthcare and insurance. In the United States, Misys and Medic entered into an alliance with Healtheon/WebMD, a leading healthcare e-commerce business. The terms of the alliance were finalized in January 2000, resulting in Misys gaining up to 4.4 million warrants in Healtheon/WebMD and revenue sharing from new Internet services to be offered to Medic's physician base. In the United Kingdom, Misys's newly established Internet services division was pursuing an investment and marketing program to establish Screentrade as the dominant insurance portal. Screentrade provided U.K. consumers with comparative insurance quotations and the ability to purchase car, home, and travel insurance over the Internet.

In fiscal 2000, Y2K issues affected Misys's banking and securities division as well as its healthcare division. In banking and securities, Misys checked every customer's system for Y2K compliance and, where necessary, provided the required upgrades. This massive project involved systems spread across 110 countries. In the U.S. healthcare market, Y2K concerns resulted in an anticipated slowdown in activity. The healthcare division reported sluggish demand for its larger systems, while demand for small and medium-size systems was strong in the early part of 1999 as old systems were replaced. During fiscal 2000, Misys strengthened its position in the retail financial services market with the acquisition of Financial Options Group and the i.e. group, which owned the 850-member IF Network. Following these acquisitions Misys created the subsidiary Misys IF Services to consolidate its position in the IF market. Overall Misys reported revenue of £708.8 million for fiscal 2000 ending May 31 and an adjusted operating profit of £130.2 million.

Following several months of testing, Misys's business-to-business portal for IFs, called m-link, launched in July 2000. Later in the year, a free Web builder service was added to m-link that enabled individual IFs to have their own Web site without a set-up cost. IFs could then promote their own Web site to their clients. With the success of m-link dependent on companies offering their insurance and investment products online through the service, Misys signed up seven of the United Kingdom's largest life insurance companies in October 2000.

During fiscal 2001 ending May 31, the Misys insurance division was renamed the financial services division. Its operations were boosted by two acquisitions in the previous year, the i.e. group and the Financial Options Group. In healthcare, Misys disposed of its U.K.-based health businesses, the ACT Medisys group of companies, in February 2001 for £24 million.

Finding that consumer adoption of the Internet for purchasing personal finance products was slower than expected, Misys closed down its consumer portals, Screentrade and theformula.com, in June 2001. Theformula.com, which was still in development, was to be a consumer financial services portal offering insurance, investments, and mortgages. Misys had been unable to find a suitable partner to share development and marketing costs. The Internet Services division was discontinued, and the company's business portals m-link and i2i-link were consolidated into the financial services division.

Revenue for fiscal 2001 ending May 31 reached record levels again. Misys reported revenue of £849 million from continuing operations and an adjusted operating profit of £140 million. The banking and securities division accounted for 41 percent of the firm's 2001 revenue and 59 percent of its operating profit. The healthcare division contributed 22 percent of Misys's revenue and 24 percent of its profit, while the financial

services division contributed 37 percent of the company's revenue and 17 percent of its profit.

In June 2001, Misys announced it would acquire DBS Management plc, a principal competitor in the IF market, and Arizona-based Sunquest Information Systems Inc., which provided clinical systems to hospitals and other acute care facilities in the United States. The acquisition of DBA Management was valued at £75 million and resulted in a Misys-controlled network of 7,250 IFs and 3,700 member firms. That made Misys the largest IF network with 25 percent of all IFs as members. Sunquest Information Systems was headquartered in Tucson, Arizona. Its acquisition by Misys was valued at $404 million. Following the acquisition Sunquest became a subsidiary of Misys and part of its healthcare division.

According to Misys chairman Kevin Lomax, the acquisition of DBS Management marked the end of Misys's acquisitions in the United Kingdom. For the future, the company planned to examine acquisition and development opportunities in Germany, which it considered a mature market similar to the United Kingdom.

For 2002, Misys embarked on a major rebranding strategy to take advantage of the Misys name. Although the company remained committed to the philosophy of individual business units with delegated authority and responsibility, Misys planned to bring most of its banking and healthcare subsidiaries under the Misys name. As part of its rebranding strategy, Midas-Kapiti International Ltd. and related MKI operating units were renamed Misys International Banking Systems. In the healthcare division, Medic Computer Systems and Sunquest Information Systems were both renamed Misys Healthcare Systems.

Principal Divisions

Banking and Securities; Healthcare; Financial Services.

Principal Subsidiaries

Misys International Banking Systems Ltd.; Misys Asset Management Systems; Misys Securities Trading Systems; Kindle Banking Systems (Ireland); Summit Systems, Inc. (United States); Physicians Systems, Inc. (United States); Hospital Systems, formerly Sunquest Information Systems, Inc. (United States); Misys IF Services plc; DBS Management plc; Countrywide Insurance Marketing Ltd.; CWA Claims Services Ltd.; Misys Financial Systems Ltd.

Principal Competitors

Applied Systems, Inc.; DST Systems, Inc.; The Sage Group plc; Sun Life Financial Services of Canada, Inc.

Further Reading

Bazzoli, Fred, "Misys Quietly Preparing to Grow," *Internet Health Care,* January–February 2002, p. 33.

"B2C Portal Closures Set to Cost Misys," *New Media Age,* June 28, 2001, p. 8.

Boles, Tracey, "The Bankhall of Fame," *Money Marketing,* September 28, 2000, p. 19.

——, "Gale to Be Misys IF Chief Executive," *Money Marketing,* September 21, 2000, p. 3.

Essick, Kristi, "U.K. Company Acquires Medic," *Computerworld,* September 15, 1997, p. 42.

Gallagher, Rosemary, "Industry Won't Make a Drama out of Misys," *Money Marketing,* February 1, 2001, p. 18.

——, "Misys Ends UK Buys and Turns to Germany," *Money Marketing,* July 26, 2001, p. 2.

——, "Misys Goes Mega in DBS Deal," *Money Marketing,* June 21, 2001, p. 1.

——, "Rise in IF Business Lifts Gloom at Misys," *Money Marketing,* July 26, 2001, p. 10.

Inman, Phillip, "Can Misys Get Its ACT Together?," *Computer Weekly,* February 23, 1995, p. 14.

——, "Misys Gets in on ACT and Boots out Bosses," *Computer Weekly,* June 15, 1995, p. 4.

——, "The Man Who Would Be King of Software," *Computer Weekly,* March 9, 1995, p. 112.

McKenna, Ian, "The Missing M-Link," *Money Marketing,* October 5, 2000, p. 34.

"Misys Ploughs £50m into Virtual Broking Web Site," *Retail Finance Strategies,* December 2000, p. 2.

"Misys to Set up Consumer Site," *Money Marketing,* November 30, 2000, p. 8.

"Misys Welcomes the Age of the Cyber Desk," *Computer Weekly,* February 5, 1998, p. 6.

Morrissey, John, "Consolidation Continues: Misys to Acquire Medic Computer for Nearly $1 Billion," *Modern Healthcare,* September 15, 1997, p. 20.

"No Delay, Says M-Link, after Crash Clash," *Money Marketing,* June 29, 2000, p. 3.

O'Connell, Joanne, "Tennis Champ Cash Serves up Misys Deal," *Money Marketing,* July 6, 2000, p. 10.

Stevenson, Rachel, "M-Link in Net Deal with Big Life Firms," *Money Marketing,* October 19, 2000, p. 3.

Stones, John, "Davy Set to Net £6.6m," *Money Marketing,* June 21, 2001, p. 3.

Taylor, Dennis, "British Software Firm to Eat C-ATS," *San Francisco Business Times,* January 15, 1999, p. 43.

—David P. Bianco

The Morgan Group, Inc.

2746 Old U.S. 20 West
Elkhart, Indiana 46515
U.S.A.
Telephone: (219) 295-2200
Toll Free: (800) 289-7565
Fax: (800) 285-0828
Web site: http://www.morgrp.com

Public Company
Incorporated: 1942 as Morgan Drive Away, Inc.
Employees: 289
Sales: $108 million (2000)
Stock Exchanges: American
Ticker Symbol: MG
NAIC: 48423 Specialized Freight (Except Used Goods)
Trucking, Long-Distance; 484121 General Freight
Trucking, Long-Distance, Truckload

The Morgan Group, Inc. is an Elkhart, Indiana-based company that delivers manufactured and modular homes, office trailers, trucks, and recreational and specialty vehicles through its main subsidiary, Morgan Drive Away. Contracting with major manufactured housing producers—such as Oakwood Homes and Fleetwood Enterprises—and makers of recreational and commercial vehicles—such as Winnebago Industries and Thor Industries—Morgan Drive Away provides transportation from the manufacturer to the end customer. The company outsources its delivery services through a network of more than 1,300 independent truck owner-operators and more than 1,400 other drivers. Drivers are dispatched from Morgan's 98 offices in 32 states. Morgan Group also provides insurance and financial services to its contract drivers through two other subsidiaries: Interstate Indemnity Company and Morgan Finance, Inc.

1930s: Servicing a New Industry

The foundation for the Morgan Group was laid in 1934, in Elkhart, Indiana, a small town just a few miles from the Michigan border. That year, an Elkhart businessman named Wilbur

Schult had opened a new company to build house trailers—compact, practical affairs, inspired by the covered wagon and designed as portable homes for Depression-era families moving cross-country. Two years after, Schult founded his business, he was a approached by a 20-year-old man named Ralph Morgan. Morgan was looking for work, offering as past experience a job as a kitchen gadget salesman. Schult put Morgan to work selling his house trailers.

Morgan proved to be an excellent salesman, selling a large number of trailers and towing them to the customers himself with his $25-a-month Ford. After five years working for Schult, Morgan decided to form his own business to deliver house trailers. However, there was one major flaw in his plan: at that time, the Interstate Commerce Commission did not allow independent drivers to haul trailers. Not to be deterred, Morgan put his sales skills to work on the ICC, lobbying for a change in regulation. In 1941, he got his way, and, with that hurdle crossed, formed his company in 1942: Morgan Drive Away, Inc. Morgan himself served as president; two colleagues, Floyd Cosper and Ralph Miller, served as vice-president and secretary-treasurer respectively.

As the Great Depression gave way to World War II, Morgan's new business got a boost. The government purchased thousands of mobile homes to set up temporary camps for workers near factories that contributed to the war effort. Morgan Drive Away became the primary delivery company for these mobile homes, transporting them to "trailer towns" all over the nation. With the end of the war, the government donated or sold its trailers to colleges and universities—and Morgan again made the deliveries.

1950s–70s: Industry and Ownership of Company Changes

The mobile home industry flourished in the years following the war, and Morgan Drive Away flourished along with it. As more and more people began to view trailers as an acceptable housing option, the trailers themselves evolved to become longer, wider, and more like actual homes. With the longer trailers, however, it was impossible for Morgan to use the tractor rigs it

---

had previously used; the tractor and trailer together would violate state road restrictions on total length. To solve this problem, Morgan helped redesign the tractors, cutting their length down from 15–16 feet to 8–10 feet. He also continued to be an active voice for his industry, lobbying state and federal policy-makers for better and more consistent regulations.

During the 1950s, Morgan began hauling recreational vehicles, travel trailers, and trucks, as well as mobile homes. While transporting these types of vehicles would never play as large a role as the transportation of mobile homes, the diversification did pay off. By the end of the century, vehicle transportation—which Morgan called "Driver Outsourcing"—accounted for approximately one-quarter of Morgan Drive Away's total business.

In 1958, at the age of 42, Ralph Morgan died. Ralph Miller, who had been with the company from the start, became president. He held that position until 1962, when the company was sold to CLC of America—a Chicago-based conglomerate whose primary business was transporting freight on river barges.

During the years of CLC ownership, Morgan forged some key customer relationships. In the 1960s, the company developed a relationship with Fleetwood—a rapidly growing California company that produced manufactured homes and recreational vehicles. By the end of the century, Fleetwood would be the largest manufacturer of RVs in the nation, and one of Morgan'a biggest customers. In the 1980s, the company established a relationship with another important customer: Oakwood Homes. More than 40 years old, the North Carolina-based Oakwood was one of the nation's largest producers of factory-built homes.

Late 1980s–Early 1990s: Lynch Corp.

Toward the end of the 1980s, Morgan's parent company, CLC of America, ran into financial trouble. The company filed for bankruptcy in early 1986, then emerged at the end of 1987 with a plan for reorganization. In the spring of 1988, CLC was purchased by agricultural commodity processor Archer-Daniels-Midland Co., but the acquisition did not include Morgan. Instead, the company was acquired in a leveraged buyout by Lynch Corp., a Connecticut-based conglomerate that owned primarily broadcasting and telecommunications companies. Morgan Drive Away formally became a subsidiary of The Morgan Group, Inc., a corporation formed by Lynch. The Morgan Group, in turn, was held under Lynch's Services subsidiary.

In 1992, four years after the acquisition, Lynch installed new management at Lynch Services and at Morgan. Charles Baum, a former securities analyst, became the chairman and CEO of Lynch Services. Phil Ringo, a transportation industry veteran,

became the President of Lynch Services and the CEO of Morgan Drive Away. The change in leadership foreshadowed more changes ahead.

One of Baum and Ringo's first steps was to take Morgan public. In the summer of 1993, the company made an initial offering of 1.1 million shares at $9 per share. According to an article in the July 23, 1993 edition of the *South Bend Tribune*, the IPO proceeds were earmarked for paying off debt, buying up small transportation companies, and diversifying into such related business lines as insurance and truck leasing. Two small acquisitions followed right away: Transamerican Carriers and Low Transportation Inc. Both Transamerican and Low were regional providers of manufactured housing transportation. In a December, 1993 interview with the *Wall Street Transcript*, Charles Baum explained that there would likely be similar acquisitions in the future. He said that Morgan was operating in a very fragmented industry, and even though it had the dominant market share, that still was only one-fifth of the total. "So what that means is that there are a great many of what might be called 'moms and pops,' or smaller regional companies in the $2 to $10 million range," he explained. "We think that this is an area ripe for an acquisition program for us."

In that same 1993 interview, Baum unveiled plans for another area of expansion. The company was preparing to enter the financial services market, providing financing to its contract drivers who were buying their own equipment. "We are seeking to form a finance subsidiary and, along with a provider of capital, service the purchase of those vehicles," Baum said.

1993 and 1994 were good years for Morgan. Both the manufactured housing and the RV industries experienced high sales, which translated into lots of deliveries. The company posted operating revenues of $82.8 million in 1993—up 23 percent from 1992. Earnings more than doubled, growing from $645,000 in 1992 to $1.6 million in 1993. Revenues and earnings both continued to climb in 1993 and 1994, increasing to $101.89 million and $2.21 million respectively.

Mid- to Late 1990s: Diversification

The middle of the decade brought more acquisition and expansion for Morgan. The company put into action its plan for branching into financial services. Forming a subsidiary, Morgan Finance, it began offering financing to selected contract drivers for equipment purchases. Then, in May of 1995, the company acquired Transfer Drivers, Inc. (TDI), an Osceola, Indiana transportation company. With more than 400 drivers and $7 million in revenues, TDI was a market leader in outsourced hauling of rental and new equipment and vehicles. Its major customers included Ryder Systems, Budget Rentals, and Bluebird Bus. This acquisition was significant for Morgan because it served as an entrance into a broader transportation market, a move Baum and Ringo saw as critical to the company's future. "Our vision is to expand into being an outsourcing provider for other industries shipping other products, not just manufactured housing and recreational vehicles," Baum said in a June 1995 interview with *Equities* magazine.

In 1996, Morgan made another important acquisition: Transit Homes of America, Inc. Like Morgan, Transit Homes was

Key Dates:

1936: Ralph Morgan goes to work for Wilbur Schult.
1941: Morgan decides to go into business for himself and gets permission from the ICC to haul house trailers on highways.
1942: Morgan Drive Away, Inc. is formed.
1958: Ralph Morgan dies.
1962: Morgan Drive Away is acquired by CLC of America.
1988: Morgan is acquired by Lynch Corp.
1993: Morgan makes an initial public offering.
1995: The company acquires Transfer Drivers, Inc.
2000: Anthony Castor is appointed CEO of The Morgan Group.

a national provider of transportation services to manufactured housing producers. The acquisition added some 350 drivers to Morgan's growing driver base, as well as annual revenues of more than $20 million.

At the end of the 1990s, Morgan's revenues and earnings, which had climbed steadily through most of the decade, suffered a sudden decline. Revenues fell 3 percent, from $150.46 million in 1998 to $145.63 in 1999. Earnings dropped more precipitously—from $903,000 in 1998 to $19,000 in 1999. The decreases were due largely to a downturn in the manufactured housing industry. Throughout the nation, higher interest rates and oversupply led to an extreme slowdown in manufactured housing shipments. With manufactured housing accounting for two-thirds of Morgan's total business, the slowdown had an immediate impact on revenues.

2000 and Beyond

Their losses in 1999 made Morgan's keenly aware of its vulnerability to fluctuations in the industries it served. It realized that to reduce the impact of such fluctuations—to hedge against industry cycle—it needed to more tightly control its expenses and make better and more diverse use of its resources. As a first step toward those aims, in January of 2000, the company appointed a new CEO: Anthony Castor, III. Castor, who had previously served as CEO of Precision Industrial Corp., a New Jersey-based company, had a strong track record in business development. As new CEO, one of Castor's first moves was to reduce Morgan's expenses by reducing its workforce. In March of 2000, the company cut approximately 25 percent of its administrative staff at its Morgan Drive Away facility.

As the company moved into the new decade and new century, it continued to be plagued by softness in the manufactured housing industry. For 2000, Morgan posted revenues of $108 million, a decrease of 26 percent from the previous year, and a net loss of $4.8 million. Revenues remained on a downward spiral into the middle of 2001, with the company posting a 22 percent decrease for the first six months over the same period in 2000. Due to continued cost-cutting measures, however, Morgan was able to dramatically improve its bottom line; net income for the six-month period rose to $85,000 compared with a loss of $599,000 for the first half of the previous year.

In the summer of 2001, Lynch Corp., which still owned slightly more than half of Morgan, came to the company's rescue with a $2 infusion of badly needed capital. The investment increased Lynch's stake in Morgan to almost 70 percent. Soon thereafter, Lynch announced that it planned to spin off Morgan to its shareholders.

As Morgan prepared to move into 2002, its near-term success appeared to hinge largely upon a rebound in the manufactured housing industry. In an August 13, 2001 press release, Castor noted that the demand for manufactured housing had shown a slight improvement in the second quarter. He also said that although the company hoped to see that trend continue, its long-range plan for turnaround was not dependent upon on conditions in the manufactured housing industry. "Our objectives remain the same," he said. "To produce positive earnings and cash flow in 2001 despite the lower revenue base and, of course, allow for improved revenue and profitability when industry conditions improve."

Principal Subsidiaries

Morgan Drive Away, Inc.; Interstate Indemnity Company; Morgan Finance, Inc.

Principal Competitors

Allied Holdings, Inc.; American Homestar Corporation; Arkansas Best Corporation; Consolidated Freightways Corporation; Landstar System, Inc.; P.A.M. Transportation Services, Inc.; Trism, Inc.; Yellow Corporation.

Further Reading

"CEO Interview, The Morgan Group," *Wall Street Transcript*, December 13, 1993.
"Morgan Group Narrows Fourth-Quarter Loss," *South Bend Tribune*, March 18, 1998, p. C9.
"Proxy Court: The Morgan Group Inc.," *Indianapolis Business Journal*, February 11, 2002.

—Shawn Brynildssen

Münchener Rück
Munich Re Group

Munich Re (Münchener Rückversicherungs-Gesellschaft Aktiengesellschaft in München)

Königinstrasse 107
D-80791 Munich
Germany
Telephone: (49) (89) 3891-0
Fax: (49) (89) 3990-56
Web site: http://www.munichre.com

Public Company
Incorporated: 1880
Employees: 36,481
Total Assets: EUR 31.1 billion ($29.1 billion) (2000)
Stock Exchanges: Frankfurt am Main Berlin
Ticker Symbol: MUV
NAIC: 52413 Reinsurance Carriers; 524128 Other Direct
   Insurance (Except Life, Health, and Medical) Carriers

Munick Re (known as Münchener Rückversicherungs-Gesellschaft Aktiengesellschaft in München in Europe) is the world's largest reinsurance company. Munich Re's reinsurance division, whose subsidiary American Re is third in the American non-life insurance market, reinsures more than 5,000 insurance companies in about 150 countries and has leading market positions in Italy, Scandinavia, the Netherlands, Canada, and Japan. Focusing solely on reinsurance for most of its history, almost half of the company's premium income is now generated from direct insurance. In direct insurance, Munich Re focuses on insurance for individuals, such as life and health insurance, as well as on insurance for small and medium-sized businesses. The company's major direct insurance subsidiary is ERGO Insurance Group, Germany's second largest direct insurer. Munich Re's investment arm, MEAG Munich ERGO AssetManagement GmbH manages the group's own EUR 158 billion investment portfolio and offers its services to third parties. Munich Re also developed a strategic partnership with HypoVereinsbank, a private bank based in Munich that has a 13.3 percent stake in Munich Re. The company holds a 20 percent stake in Allianz, Germany's leading direct insurer,

which in turn owns about the same amount of Munich Re shares. Another 7.5 percent of the company's shares is owned by Deutsche Bank.

Origins

Quiet strength has been one of Munich Re's hallmarks throughout the company's 120-year history. The German insurance industry of the nineteenth century had few of the inhibitions about reinsurance that characterized the then-leading country in the insurance industry, the United Kingdom. German Munich Re was not the first reinsurance company to be established; Cologne Re preceded it by 34 years. However, it was the first to be totally independent of a primary insurance operation and soon became a driving force of this new branch of insurance.

The company's founder, Carl Thieme, a native of Erfurt in Thuringia, had reached the sound but—in the 1870s—unfashionable conclusion that dependence on a primary insurer meant reinsurance operations had to take on a narrow range of often poor quality risks with frequently disastrous financial results. Instead, Thieme sought to set up an independent reinsurance company which could choose its risks according to their quality and spread the risks by operating in all extant classes of insurance.

Thieme, already an experienced and successful insurance agent in Munich, had developed good connections with the leading figures of the Bavarian financial world of the time. Chief among these was Theodor Cramer-Klett, who had been instrumental in developing in Bavaria a modern banking system capable of servicing the rapid industrialization that was going on in Germany under the protectionist policies of Otto von Bismarck.

Undeterred by the perilous state of the German insurance industry in the 1870s—Bismarck had even considered nationalizing it—Thieme and Cramer-Klett, along with four others, decided to set up a joint-stock operation with a capital of the then-large sum of DM 3 million. The share capital, partly paid, was

Company Perspectives:

We are developing modern insurance solutions: *In a world characterized by change, insurers are faced with ever-new challenges. We support our business partners by identifying future trends, generating future knowledge and developing joint products for the challenges of tomorrow. In this central task, our longstanding tradition of innovation repeatedly stands us in good stead: for example, in evaluating know-how from sophisticated insurance markets for application in less developed markets. Thus Munich Re is currently supporting private initiatives to establish new export credit insurers in Eastern Europe, Latin America and Asia—areas in which the globalization of trade is opening up new business opportunities for reinsurers as well.*

subscribed by eight shareholders, most of whom were the co-founders of the new company. On April 19, 1880, Münchener Rückversicherungs-Gesellschaft Aktiengesellschaft in München was formed. Thieme also favored the conclusion of mutually binding treaties between insurer and reinsurer instead of the hitherto traditional individual placement of risks. He regarded treaties as both more efficient and more secure from the point of view of both insurance and reinsurance companies. The new company's first treaty was with the Thuringia Insurance Company, whose Bavarian agent Thieme was and remained until 1886.

By the end of the first year's trading, gross premium income had passed one million marks. In 1888, Munich Re shares were offered for the first time on the Munich stock exchange by the bankers Merck, Finck & Company, themselves founded by the ubiquitous Cramer-Klett, and competition for shares was intense. The firm's capital base was expanded several times in the closing years of the century and by 1914 stood as some 20 million marks. In that year Munich Re was able to offer its shareholders a 40 percent dividend on profits from a turnover which had grown to nearly DM 177 million—a powerful statement of the company's financial soundness. At its founding in 1880, Thieme had employed just five employees. By 1914 the staff numbered 450.

Internationalization Delayed by World Wars

Thieme had been anxious from the start to see Munich Re establish itself not only in other parts of Germany but also in foreign countries. Thus the establishment of offices in Hamburg and Vienna in the year of founding was matched by Munich Re's first reinsurance treaty with a foreign insurance company, the Danish Almindelinge Brand-Assurance-Compagni of Copenhagen. During the 1880s the company used an office in St. Petersburg.

Thieme, however, realized that the greatest reinsurance opportunities lay in Britain and, increasingly, in North America. To exploit these markets a London branch office was set up in 1890. London was regarded as a notoriously difficult insurance market for foreign firms to penetrate, but Munich Re managed to do this under the able and energetic leadership of the London manager, Carl Schreiner. In 1892, Schreiner also founded Mu-

nich Re's first U.S. operation by putting up the required security of $500,000.

Thieme was astute enough to realize that if new classes of insurance could be created, then Munich Re would be well placed to secure the resulting reinsurance treaties. As Thieme wished Munich Re to retain its status as a reinsurer, he chose to help set up new insurance operations rather than risk the wrath of his clients by attempting to take Munich Re into the field of primary insurance.

In 1890, Thieme's efforts to introduce personal accident insurance into Germany led to the founding of Allianz, and his interest in export credit insurance resulted in the creation of Hermes in 1917, a large proportion of whose initial share capital was provided by Munich Re. At the turn of the century, Munich Re was one of several insurers introducing machinery and luggage insurance. Munich Re pioneered machinery insurance in association with Allianz and at about the same time introduced luggage insurance into central Europe.

The risks as well as the potential profits of an international spread of business became apparent in the first two decades of the next century. The Baltimore fire of 1904 and the San Francisco earthquake and fire in 1906, the latter costing Munich Re DM 11 million, demonstrated the size of losses which the reinsurance industry could now face. The promptness of Munich Re's settlement of its primary insurers' claims contributed much to the establishment of reinsurance as an industry on an equal footing with primary insurance.

The outbreak of World War I in Europe in 1914 again proved the double-edged nature of international coverage. Munich Re, with its comparatively large commitments in the United Kingdom and North America, found its business in the United Kingdom suspended, a blow compounded by the growing anti-German feeling in the United States and the eventual total loss of its U.S. business in 1917 when the United States entered the war on the Allied side.

Hard on the heels of Germany's military defeat in 1918 came occupation, reparation payments, and, most damaging of all, the ruinous hyper-inflation of 1923, when the German mark plummeted out of control. In 1924–25, after the stabilization of the mark, Munich Re's turnover amounted to only DM 127 million, less than two thirds of its 1914 turnover in real terms.

In 1917, Munich Re had helped found the Hermes Kreditversicherungsbank by providing share capital and accepting the reinsurance of risks. Hermes was an export-credit-insurance operation designed to offer wartime protection to German exporters, but in the postwar period it was used to help stimulate German export trade back to recovery. Gains made in this sector, however, were offset almost immediately by the onset of the Depression in 1929. Munich Re was forced to cut both salary and staffing levels in the early 1930s—in 1932 staff numbers sank to 342 against a 1920 total of more than 600. Munich Re also found it necessary to assist a number of ailing primary insurance companies—a far-sighted move at a time of great financial difficulty. During the difficult interwar years, control of Munich Re was largely in the hands of Wilhelm Kisskalt, who succeeded Thieme as chief executive in 1922. He in turn was succeeded by Kurt Schmitt in 1938, another former employee who had transferred to the Allianz in 1914 and had become general manager there in 1921.

In 1933, Schmitt became minister of economic affairs in the new National Socialist government of Adolf Hitler. According to Munich Re, Kisskalt and Schmitt hoped that Schmitt's acceptance of the post would enable him to exercise a moderating influence on the extremist policies of the new Nazi government. When this hope proved illusory, Schmitt resigned of his own accord in 1934. This episode did not appear to harm the fortunes of Munich Re—in the mid-1930s its turnover exceeded prewar levels for the first time.

During World War II, as in World War I, Munich Re lost its position in the huge insurance markets of the Allied nations. Although this had a considerable impact on its growth, Munich Re's turnover still reached DM 230 million by the end of the conflict in 1945. In spite of the briefness of Schmitt's official association with the former German leadership, Munich Re found it expedient to appoint a new chief executive that year, at the start of the Allied occupation. The new chief executive was an Austrian, Eberhard von Reininghaus. Although he may have been regarded with more favor than his predecessor, this did not prevent the Allies from occupying Munich Re's headquarters in Munich's Königinstrasse until 1951. More seriously, Munich Re found itself banned from operating abroad in common with all other German companies. This compounded the damage already caused by the massive economic dislocation in Germany in the immediate postwar period. Munich Re was once again forced to cut its staff—by 1950 only 302 were left—and turnover for the 1949–50 fiscal year amounted to only half that of 1945.

A Leading Reinsurer in Postwar Years

Munich Re adopted a policy of concentrating on whatever gaps remained in the home insurance market. The impact of the Marshall Plan and the reorganization of the German currency began that process of economic recovery now known as the German "economic miracle" of the 1950s and 1960s. Insurance and reinsurance benefited from the economic upturn, and by the middle of the 1950s Munich Re's turnover had surpassed all previous levels at nearly a third of a billion deutsche marks. Eberhard von Reininghaus died in 1950, and his place was taken by Alois Alzheimer, who had joined Munich Re in 1929. Alzheimer, general manager for the next 18 years, oversaw the restoration of the company's fortunes and its reestablishment as a leading player in the world's reinsurance industry. At the time of his retirement in 1969, Munich Re's annual turnover exceeded DM 2 billion.

General manager Horst K. Jannott became the second-longest serving chief executive of Munich Re after Thieme. A lawyer by training, he joined Munich Re in 1954, made his name in balance sheet mathematics, and progressed rapidly to the top of the corporate ladder. During his stewardship, Munich Re's gross premium income increased nearly sixfold to stand at DM 12.4 billion in 1989.

Profits Decline in the 1970s and 1980s

The mid-1970s marked a significant shift in the balance of the company's profits away from reinsurance toward what the company called its "general business," primarily investment income. Reinsurance profitability began to decline rapidly in the early years of the decade, and the company recorded a loss for the first time in 1977 of about DM 15 million. By 1981, this figure had increased to DM 116 million, and by 1989 had reached DM 381 million. Munich Re's increasingly large losses in this part of its business, however, were spectacularly offset by the growth of profits in its general business. In 1977, this brought in about DM 49 million, and in 1989, DM 900 million.

Munich Re was able to turn in consistently strong and rising net profits. The decline in reinsurance underwriting results were caused largely by overcapacity in the reinsurance industry and consequent severe rate competition, plus the growing tendency of primary insurers to organize their own reinsurance cover, ceding to the established reinsurance companies a growing proportion of the more volatile risks. Against this background, Munich Re's ability to offer regular dividends of 18 to 20 percent was quite an achievement.

During the 1970s and 1980s, Munich Re's proportion of foreign business increased continuously, despite the effects of a strong deutsche mark in the same period. At the end of the 1970s, about 40 percent of its business originated outside West Germany and foreign business was outperforming domestic business. Half of these foreign earnings came from other European countries, the remainder from the rest of the world. The early 1980s registered a slowdown in the growth of foreign premium income, partly due to an appreciating deutsche mark and partly due to setbacks in the transport and life insurance sectors. Disasters such as the 1985 Mexico earthquake and Hurricane Gilbert—the latter cost Munich Re between 100 million and 120 million deutsche marks—and the increasingly high cost of U.S. liability claims further cut into foreign profits. At the end of the decade, the foreign sector picked up as the deutsche mark began to depreciate against both dollar and sterling. By 1989, about half of Munich Re's earnings came from abroad.

This upturn was not solely the result of external factors such as the deutsche mark rate of exchange. Munich Re's wisdom in declining to provide coverage on war risks was proved during the 1980–88 war between Iran and Iraq, which cost other underwriters heavily.

Acquisitions, New Products, and Disasters in the 1990s

In the 1990s, three major trends had a strong impact on the world's reinsurance market. First, the decade started out with devastating winter storms, hurricanes, and typhoons, and a trend towards increasing risks of major natural catastrophes became evident. For reinsurers, that meant an increasingly volatile business with more significant losses. Second, primary insurance companies were consolidating on a global level, thereby reducing the number of reinsurance clients and boosting their own financial strength. Third—besides an intensifying competition among reinsurers—some large banks and primary insurers entered the market for reinsurance. Munich Re's management reacted in different ways. It strengthened the company's reinsurance business through several mergers and acquisitions and a strong foothold in the German direct insurance market; it established a new asset management subsidiary and invested in new product development; and it reorganized its shareholdings and took measures to attract new investors. As a result, Munich Re more than quadrupled its premium income within a decade, while profits multiplied by a factor of 38 and dividends were raised eight times.

In a $3 billion deal, Munich Re acquired North America's third largest property-casualty reinsurer, American Re based in Princeton, New Jersey, in November 1996. In October 2000, the company bought the life insurance division of Chicago-based CNA Financial Corporation and established a new holding company for its North American business, Delaware-based Munich-American Holding Corporation. Munich Re also strengthened its presence in Western Europe and expanded into Eastern Europe, Asia, and Latin America. The company acquired Italian Reale Ri in 1998 and a new office location in the inner city of Paris in spring 2001. New branch offices opened in China in 1997 and in Poland and Chile two years later. To counteract declining reinsurance profits, Munich Re invested heavily in the European direct insurance market. In 1997, Munich Re merged Hamburg-Mannheimer AG, a direct insurer in which the company held an 80 percent stake, with the VICTORIA group, another large direct insurer of which Munich Re owned 23 percent, to form ERGO Versicherungsgruppe, which instantly became Germany's second biggest direct insurance company. In 1999, the two companies established MUNICH ERGO AssetManagement GmbH (MEAG), a joint venture to manage their assets. Two years later, Munich Re took over more

than 90 percent of ERGO's shares. The company also acquired a 60-percent stake in Bad Homburg-based Alte Leipziger Europa Beteiligungsgesellschaft AG (AL Europa), a holding company with majority stakes in 14 insurance companies in eight Central and Eastern European countries, including Poland's third biggest insurer, Hestia. In addition, the company supported private initiatives to establish independent export credit insurers in Eastern Europe, Latin America, and Asia.

In the area of new product development, Munich Re, together with Swiss Re, Internet Capital Group, and Anderson Consulting launched London-based ''inreon,'' an Internet-based reinsurance exchange where standardized reinsurance risks could be traded between insurance companies and reinsurance companies or brokers, in December 2000. In the first half of 2001, Munich Re promoted a new agricultural insurance scheme for European farmers, who in general were not covered against drought, floods, or storms by state-supported insurance, as they were in the United States. The company partnered with European insurer AXA Colonia in developing a new kind of cancellation coverage for major sporting events and provided earthquake coverage for FIFA's soccer World Cup in 2002 in Japan and Korea. Munich Re's Geoscience Research Group closely watched global trends for the occurrence of natural disasters and published reports and a *World Map of Natural Hazards*.

Beginning in the late 1990s, Munich Re started restructuring its shareholdings involving Allianz, Germany's number one direct insurance group. Allianz had been co-founded by Munich Re founder Carl Thieme in 1890, which resulted in a close connection between the two companies and in a number of joint and cross-shareholdings. The two companies exchanged their shares in American Re and Allianz of America. Munich Re became the sole owner of American Re and Allianz the sole owner of Allianz of America. Munich Re lowered its stake in life insurer Allianz Lebensversicherungs-AG to 40 percent and sold its stakes in Dresdner Bank AG, Bayerische Versicherungsbank AG, and Frankfurter Versicherungs-AG to Allianz. In turn, the company acquired 6.5 percent of Allianz' shares in ERGO and health insurer DKV, and the shares that Allianz and Dresdner Bank held in Hypo-Vereinsbank (HBV), raising Munich Re's share to 25.7 percent. In addition, Munich Re planned to take over Allianz shares in Karlsruher Lebensversicherung AG, raising its stake in the life insurer to 90.1 percent by July 2002. Munich Re and Allianz also reduced their cross-holdings from 25 to roughly 20 percent. These measures were aimed at making Munich Re more attractive to investors. The company took another step in that direction when it converted the existing bearer shares, which represented about two percent of its share capital, into registered shares in January 1999.

While 1999 had been Munich Re's worst year in its history in terms of losses caused by natural disasters, a man-made disaster of, to date, unimaginable proportions dwarfed those losses when on September 11, 2001, two hijacked planes hit the twin towers of New York's World Trade Center, causing them to collapse. While claims cost from aviation, building, business interruption, life and worker compensation insurance to American Re were estimated at EUR 1 billion at first, that amount was soon doubled to a ''conservative estimate'' of EUR 2.1 billion—approximately $1.89 billion or 11.5 percent of the group's reinsurance premiums in 2000. Only two months later, another plane crashed into a residential neighborhood in New York's borough Queens, causing another loss of around $50 million. While this would have been the end for many reinsurers, Munich Re expected to be able to cope with these, the biggest losses in its history.

In accordance with German regulations, Munich Re had consistently practiced extremely conservative accounting policy which undervalued the worth of its assets. It was estimated that the stock exchange transactions with Allianz would uncover hidden reserves of over EUR 4 billion and that, in addition, Munich Re could expect equalization payments in cash of about EUR 700 million from Allianz in 2002. In November 2001, Munich Re announced a capital boost for American Re of over $1 billion. For the future the company was expecting a revitalized re-insurance market in the attack's aftermath, an increase in direct insurance sales through its partnership with HBV, growing profits from asset management generated by MEAG, and a potentially huge new market for private pension plans supported by the German government.

Principal Subsidiaries

ERGO Versicherungsgruppe AG (91.7%); Karlsruher Lebensversicherung AG (54%); Europäische Reiseversicherung AG; MEAG Munich ERGO AssetManagement GmbH (85.1%); American Re Corporation (United States); American Re-Insurance Company (United States); Munich American Reassurance Company (United States); Munich Reinsurance Company of Africa (South Africa); Munich Reinsurance Company of Canada; Munich Reinsurance Company of Australasia (Australia); Münchener Rück Italia S.P.A.; New Insurance Company (Switzerland); Great Lakes Reinsurance (UK) PLC.

Principal Competitors

General Cologne Re; Swiss Reinsurance Company; ''Winterthur'' Swiss Insurance Company; Hannover Re.

Further Reading

Dönch, Uli, and Matthias Kowalski, ''Ende der Bescheidenheit: Der unheimliche Gigant Münchener Rück drängt ins Rampenlicht,'' *Focus,* August 5, 1996, p. 136.

1880–1980: 100 years of Munich Re, Munich: Munich Re, 1980.

''Münchener Rück kauft American Re,'' *Frankfurter Allgemeine Zeitung,* August 15, 1996, p. 16.

''Münchener Rück kündigt weitere Entflechtung von Allianz an,'' *Frankfurter Allgemeine Zeitung,* December 6, 1997, p. 17.

''Münchener Rück landet Milliarden-Coup in USA,'' *Süddeutsche Zeitung,* August 16, 1996.

''Münchener Rück realisiert stille Reserven in Milliardenhöhe,'' *Frankfurter Allgemeine Zeitung,* July 19, 2001, p. 17.

—D. H. O'Leary
—update: Evelyn Hauser

News Corporation Limited

2 Holt Street
Sydney, New South Wales 2010
Australia
Telephone: (02) 9288-3000
Fax: (02) 9288-3292
Web site: http://www.newscorp.com

Public Company
Incorporated: 1979
Employees: 31,400
Sales: A$25.5 billion ($13.8 billion) (2001)
Stock Exchanges: Australia London New York New
    Zealand
Ticker Symbol: NWS
NAIC: 51111 Newspaper Publishers; 51113 Book
    Publishers; 51223 Music Publishers; 51312 Television
    Broadcasting; 51321 Cable Networks; 51211 Motion
    Picture and Video Production

News Corporation Limited is the holding company for the large range of enterprises created or acquired since the 1950s by the Australian-American businessman Rupert Murdoch. It operates as one of the five largest media conglomerates in the world with assets totaling $43 billion in 2001. The company's holdings include businesses involved in filmed entertainment, television, satellite and cable network programming, newspapers, magazines, book publishing, music, digital television technology, and online programming. News Corp. also owns 85 percent of the Fox Entertainment Group, 40 percent of the STAPLES Center—the home of the Los Angeles Lakers basketball team and the Los Angeles Kings ice hockey team—and major league baseball team the Los Angeles Dodgers. Nearly 75 percent of the firm's revenues stem from its U.S. operations, while Canada, Europe, the United Kingdom, Australia, Latin America, and the Pacific Basin region account for the remaining 25 percent.

Beginnings of News Coporation

Rupert Murdoch was born in Melbourne in 1931, the son of Sir Keith Murdoch, managing director of the *Herald* and *Weekly Times* newspaper group. Sir Keith did not own many shares in the group, but was the major shareholder in News Ltd., which published the *Adelaide News* and *Sunday Mail,* and in a Brisbane company whose two newspapers he amalgamated into one, the *Courier-Mail.*

Sir Keith died in 1952. After graduating that year, his son spent some months as a junior subeditor at the *London Daily Express* and returned to Australia in 1953 to take over the Adelaide newspapers. His father's executors sold the *Courier-Mail* to the *Herald* and *Weekly Times* group. In 1956, News Ltd. acquired the *Perth Sunday Times*; in 1957, it launched *TV Week*—inspired by the American *TV Guide*—which was to be the most profitable of all its Australian publications. In 1958, control of Channel 9, one of two TV channels in Adelaide, was awarded to Southern Television Corporation, in which News Ltd. had 60 percent of the shares. Murdoch's empire-building had begun.

The Building of an Empire: 1960s–1970s

The year 1960 was a watershed for News Ltd. It bought Cumberland Newspapers, a group of local papers in the Sydney suburbs, then acquired the *Sydney Daily* and *Sunday Mirror* from the Fairfax group. Rohan Rivett, the editor of the *Adelaide News,* became the first of many editors to be fired from Murdoch newspapers. Five weeks before his dismissal he had been celebrating his acquittal on charges of seditious libel. These had arisen out of the *News'* criticisms of a state government inquiry into the case of an Aborigine found guilty of a murder that Rivett, and Murdoch, thought he had not committed. His departure marked the end of Murdoch's leanings toward anti-establishment views.

In 1964, News Ltd. launched *The Australian,* Australia's first national newspaper, based in Canberra. Murdoch considered the venture prestigious enough to be worth a loss of A$30 million, over the course of 20 years, to keep going. Typesetting in Canberra and flying the matrices to Melbourne and Sydney for printing were difficult, and in 1967 the paper was moved to Sydney. In 1969, its latest editor oversaw its re-adoption of opposition to the Vietnam War, a return to the stance first espoused by the paper in 1965 when Australian troops were initially assigned there.

Company Perspectives:

We strive to produce and distribute the most compelling content to the farthest reaches of the globe.

Murdoch, meanwhile, was in London. In October 1968, Robert Maxwell had offered to buy the United Kingdom's News of the World Organization (NOTW) for £26 million. The company owned the Sunday newspaper *News of the World,* the Bemrose group of local newspapers, the papermaker Townsend Hook, and several other publishing companies. It had been run since 1891 by the Carr family, which had now split into two factions, one led by NOTW's chairman, Sir William Carr, with 32 percent of the shares, the other by his cousin, Derek Jackson, whose decision to sell his 25 percent stake had precipitated the crisis. Maxwell, born in Czechoslovakia, was then a Labour member of Parliament. Maxwell's foreign origin, combined with his political opinions, provoked a hostile response to his bid from the Carrs and from the editor of the *News of the World,* Stafford Somerfield, who declared that the paper was—and should remain—as British as roast beef and Yorkshire pudding. News Ltd. arranged to swap shares in some of its minor ventures with the Carrs and by December it controlled 40 percent of the NOTW stock. In January 1969, Maxwell's bid was rejected at a shareholders' meeting where half of those present were company staff, temporarily given voting shares. Illness removed Sir William Carr from the chairmanship in June 1969, and Murdoch succeeded him. In 1977, just before his death, Carr wrote to Maxwell to express regret that he had spurned his original offer for NOTW. The *News of the World* remained the biggest-selling English-language newspaper in the world.

Murdoch next sought a British daily to accompany the *News of the World.* He found it in 1969, when IPC decided to sell off *The Sun,* which had been launched in 1964 but had never been profitable, with sales of about one million copies. Under Murdoch, by contrast, *The Sun*'s circulation reached two million in 1971 and three million in 1973.

NOTW had added television to its list of interests in 1969, when it bought eight percent of the voting shares in London Weekend Television (LWT), a company created in 1968 to run commercial television from Friday evening to Sunday night in a large and lucrative region centered on the capital city. The holding was rapidly built up to 36 percent of the voting shares and Murdoch became a non-executive director of LWT. He promptly saw to the dismissal of its managing director and took the chair of the executive committee in charge of scheduling, thus running the station without having been awarded a franchise. The Independent Television Authority ordered LWT to put its affairs in order without Murdoch in charge. The controversy over this incident was revived in 1977 when the government-appointed Committee on the Future of Broadcasting made severe criticisms of the authority's failure to enforce its own rules. By that time, however, Murdoch had moved to the United States, and NOTW's shares in LWT were sold in 1980.

Back in Australia, Murdoch found that *The Australian* had become too liberal for his liking. In 1971, he dismissed its

editor, Adrian Deamer, who had been in the post for three years—a remarkable record, considering that the paper would have 13 editors in its first 16 years. In 1972, News Ltd. bought the *Sydney Daily* and *Sunday Telegraph* from Packer's Consolidated Press, which had been losing circulation to the three Fairfax papers, the *Sydney Morning Herald,* the *Sun,* and the *Sunday Sun-Herald.* The ailing *Sunday Australian* was absorbed into the *Sunday Telegraph* soon afterward.

Murdoch had become close to Gough Whitlam, then leader of the Australian Labor Party, and gave A$75,000 to the party's advertising campaign in 1972. If this was a return to Murdoch's earlier radicalism, it was short-lived. Within three years his papers were attacking the Labor Party again, with *The Australian,* for example, using raw figures, rather than seasonally adjusted ones, to suggest, wrongly, that unemployment was rising. After the 1975 election, in which Whitlam was defeated, Murdoch himself, using a "special correspondent" byline, wrote a report for *The Australian* on the Labor Party's secret—and eventually fruitless—appeal to Saddam Hussein, the dictator of Iraq, for financial aid, which resulted in a meeting in Sydney between Whitlam and Saddam's nephew. Ironically, what appeared to be just more anti-Whitlam propaganda was true.

In 1973, the News group made its first American acquisitions, purchasing three newspapers in San Antonio, Texas. One of these, the *San Antonio News,* achieved brief but worldwide notoriety in 1976 with the striking but inaccurate headline "Killer Bees Move North." The next American acquisition, in 1976, was the *New York Post,* the city's only evening paper. This was swiftly followed, early in 1977, by the purchase of the New York Magazine Company, which published the magazines *New York* and *Village Voice.* The acquisitions were, in fact, accomplished so quickly that *New York*'s proposed comment on the Post purchase, a picture of Murdoch as a killer bee, had to be dropped.

Murdoch's personal supervision of the *Post* led to an increased circulation, most notably through a series of reports on the "Son of Sam" serial killings, culminating in the misleading headline "How I Became a Mass Killer" over a selection of old and innocuous letters from the murderer to a girlfriend. The *Post* did especially well in the summer of 1979 when, armed with separate agreements with the unions, a long-running strike kept its rivals closed. The paper continued to suffer from financial problems, caused partly by the reluctance of the large department stores to advertise in such a down-market publication.

Murdoch did not neglect the Australian sector of his growing empire. In 1978, News Ltd. joined forces with the Packer's group and the British football pools company Vernons to start a New South Wales lottery. In 1979, it built up a 48.2 percent stake in Channel TEN-10, a Sydney television station. At the Australian Broadcasting Tribunal hearings into its purchase, Murdoch praised the work of its chairman and promised that the station would retain total independence without interference. Two weeks after the tribunal approved the change of ownership, the chief executive was replaced by a News Ltd. director with no television experience; two months later the chairman resigned.

A much bigger acquisition followed, also in 1979, when News Ltd. gained control of ATI, a group of airlines and other transport firms. Its founder, Sir Reginald Ansett, stayed on as chairman of

Key Dates:

1953: Rupert Murdoch takes over his father's business.
1957: News Ltd. launches TV Week.
1960: Cumberland Newspapers, the *Sydney Daily,* and the *Sunday Mirror* are acquired.
1964: The firm establishes Australia's first national newspaper, *The Australian.*
1969: Murdoch acquires *The Sun,* a British daily.
1973: News Ltd. enters the U.S. market with the purchase of three newspapers based in Texas.
1976: The firm buys the *New York Post.*
1979: News Corp. is reorganized as a holding company.
1981: The *London Times, the Sunday Times, the Times Literary Supplement,* and the *Times Educational Supplement* are purchased.
1983: News Corp. gains majority interest in Satellite Television PLC and purchases a stake in Twentieth Century Fox Film Corp.
1984: The *Chicago Sun-Times* is acquired.
1988: Murdoch acquires *TV Guide* and Triangle Publications; Fox Broadcasting Company begins operation.
1989: Sky Television is launched in the United Kingdom.
1990: Faltering under a huge debt load, News Corp. begins restructuring efforts.
1998: Murdoch sells *TV Guide* and offers 18.6 percent of the Fox Entertainment Group to the public.
1999: News Corp. gains full control of Fox/Liberty Networks by acquiring Liberty Media's 50 percent interest.
2001: Fox Family Worldwide Inc. is sold; Chris-Craft Industries is purchased for $4.4 billion.

ATI, but Murdoch became chief executive. Murdoch agreed with Sir Peter Abeles, the chairman of the TNT transport group, that News Ltd. and TNT should have 50–50 ownership of ATI and that Abeles should become joint chief executive. There then followed lengthy public hearings before the Australian Broadcasting Tribunal on whether or not News Ltd. should be allowed to own a Melbourne television station, the original goal of the ATI/TNT dealings. The tribunal decided against granting approval, mainly on the grounds that a Sydney-Melbourne combination under one company would have too big a role in network operations. By the time of the ruling, however, News Ltd. had paid for the station and the statutory six months allowed for ordering divestment had passed; the tribunal's decision had no effect. The ruling was eventually reversed on appeal.

The current structure of Rupert Murdoch's group of companies also dates from the creation of News Corp. as the main holding company in 1979. In 1990, Murdoch owned only 7,200 shares in News Corp. itself, but he also had control of Cruden Investments Pty Ltd., which owned more than 116 million shares, about 54 percent of the total. In 2001, the Murdoch family controlled nearly 30 percent of the firm.

Focus on Publishing: Early 1980s

In 1981, News International, the British arm of the Murdoch group, acquired 42 percent of the voting shares in the British

publishers William Collins and Sons and bought the *London Times, the Sunday Times, the Times Literary Supplement,* and the *Times Educational Supplement* from what is now The Thomson Corporation. Fifteen years earlier, Lord Thomson's own purchase of *The Times* and its supplements had been investigated by the Monopolies Commission, as Lonrho was to be investigated when it made a bid for the *London Observer* later in 1981. Yet the government of the day waived this requirement in News International's case.

At the same time as News Corp.'s image was being pushed up-market by these ventures, its down-market newspapers were all engaged in attracting more readers with an adaptation of bingo. In Britain, *Sun* bingo cards were sent to every household, and rival papers all picked up the game. It then spread to the *Sydney Daily Mirror* and to the *New York Post,* where it had to be renamed Wingo for copyright reasons. The rival *Daily News* responded with its own version, Zingo. Murdoch then went on to acquire the *Boston Herald*—formerly the *Herald-American*—in 1982 and the *Chicago Sun-Times* in 1984.

The *Sun*'s editors Larry Lamb and, from 1981, his successor Kelvin McKenzie, brought the paper into line with Murdoch's political views. Thus in 1982, the paper offered enthusiastic support to the British forces in the Falklands War (as almost all the national newspapers did), but characteristically went further, marking the sinking of the Argentine cruiser General Belgrano with the headline "Gotcha!" and calling the BBC's defense correspondent and two rival newspapers traitors. The *Sun* remained the biggest-selling daily newspaper in the U.K. in 2001 with nearly four million more readers each issue than its nearest competitor.

Murdoch's up-market papers could be tempted by sensationalism as well. In 1983, News Corp. was severely embarrassed by the revelation that the much-publicized secret diaries of Adolf Hitler, which the *Sunday Times* planned to serialize under an arrangement with the German magazine *Stern,* were forgeries. Lord Dacre, better known as the historian Hugh Trevor-Roper, who served as one of the "national" non-executive directors of Times Newspapers, first declared that the samples he had seen were genuine, then told the editor of the *Sunday Times* that they were forgeries just as the printing of the world exclusive story began. Murdoch decided to go ahead with the printing; *Stern* had to return the money it had paid for the diaries, and the *Sunday Times* actually retained some of the extra readers the story had attracted to it.

The appointment of Andrew Neil as editor of the *Sunday Times* later in 1983 negated the guarantees exacted from News International by the British government two years before, since the required consultation with the newspaper's staff did not take place. Harold Evans had reluctantly resigned from the editorship of the *Times* in 1982, at Murdoch's request. Evans could have appealed over Murdoch's head to the "national" directors but chose not to do so, leaving the guarantees untested.

Diversifying Into Satellite Television: 1983

News Corp. first ventured into satellite television in 1983. It acquired majority holdings in Satellite Television PLC (SATV), which had been set up in 1980 to supply a U.K.-based service to northern Europe, and in the Inter-American Satellite Television Network, which was renamed Skyband Inc. and had its head office moved from California to New York. It was largely to gain access to a supply of feature films and television programs that News Corp. bought into the Twentieth Century Fox Film Corporation also in 1983. Within two years, with the News International papers all featuring articles attacking the BBC, SATV, renamed Sky Channel, had about three million subscribers in 11 European countries and was available in Britain on cable.

During 1985, Murdoch and his closest advisers planned the removal of all the News International papers from the Fleet Street area, the traditional base for national newspapers, to a plant at Wapping, in east London, where troubled relations with the print unions could be superseded by a single union agreement with the Electrical, Electronic, Telecommunications and Plumbing Union (EETPU). Electronic typesetting equipment was ordered, but kept hidden from the print workers; the EETPU recruited new production staff, and then, when the plant was ready, the journalists on the four newspapers were given from one to three days to move or to leave the company and the plant began producing papers in January 1986. It was not only the 5,500 sacked print workers who felt somewhat betrayed after this dramatic move. The EETPU never did get a single union agreement, and News International did not recognize any trade unions. In 1987 the British company acquired a fifth newspaper, *Today,* from the company Lonrho—which had bought out the newspaper's founder, Eddy Shah—soon after its launch in 1986.

Growth Through Acquisition: Late 1980s

While 1986 was a year of triumph for Murdoch in Britain, in Australia it was a year of retreat. News Ltd. sold off both Channel TEN-10 in Sydney and ATV 10 in Melbourne, as well as radio stations, a record company, and three newspapers. However, 1987 was the year of the acquisition of the *Herald* and *Weekly Times* group once run by Murdoch's father. Shortly before the deal went ahead, Murdoch had a private meeting with the prime minister, Bob Hawke, and the treasurer, Paul Keating, and his Australian newspapers all switched political allegiance to Labor, the governing party. The purchase of the *Herald* and *Weekly Times* group cost A$2.3 billion, was the biggest single takeover of newspapers ever accomplished, and made News Corp. the largest publisher of English-language newspapers in the world. Shortly afterward the chairman of the Australian Press Council resigned in protest at the government's failure to invoke the Foreign Takeovers Act against Murdoch, for by this time Murdoch had become an American citizen. It was not until 1989 that newly released government documents revealed that the Foreign Investment Review Board had opposed the acquisition, although Prime Minister Hawke declared that it had not.

News Corp. ended 1987 with two more purchases, the *South China Morning Post,* the most important English-language newspaper in Hong Kong, and the American publishing house Harper & Row. It then sold 50 percent of Harper & Row to William Collins and Sons. This arrangement lasted only until April 1989, when News International bought Collins outright. HarperCollins Publishers, created as a merger of these and other book and map publishers, is now the largest English-language publisher in the world.

In 1988, three decades after he had borrowed its format for his own publication on television, Murdoch bought the American magazine *TV Guide* and the company that published it, Triangle Publications, for $2.83 billion. Fox Broadcasting Company started up during the same year as the first new television network in the United States to challenge the long-established trio of ABC, CBS, and NBC. Its huge initial costs were reduced, fortuitously, when a Hollywood writers' strike allowed it to run a large number of repeats, and it broadcast at first only on Saturdays and Sundays.

Financial Woes: 1989–1990

In February 1989, Sky Television was launched in the United Kingdom as a four-channel service available at first only on cable but increasingly via satellite receiver dishes. By the summer of 1990, it was reaching 1.6 million households, but the losses incurred in its development were a major cause of declining profits for News Corp., along with the eight-month-long airline pilots' strike in Australia. It was claimed that profits would have been higher than in the financial year 1988–1989 if these two factors were excluded. Profits were also being eroded by the rising cost of interest payments on the group's rising level of debts.

Murdoch had once said that he never gave anyone shares but just borrowed to finance expansion. The next year or two revealed the disadvantages of that policy, as the sale of his Australian book publishing and distribution companies in June of 1989 proved to be the start of a trend, though revenue and profits from most of News Corp.'s subsidiaries continued to grow. In 1990, it sold 49 percent of South China Morning Post (Holdings) Ltd., parts of its minority holdings in the news agency Reuters and in the publishers Pearson plc, the American publishing firm J.B. Lippincott, the British papermaker Townsend Hook, the Fox subsidiary DeLuxe Laboratories and the U.S. magazines Star and Sportswear International. Its acquisitions that year—25 percent of the Spanish publisher Grupo Zeta; the whole of F.F. Publishing and Broadsystem Ltd. in Britain; and 50 percent holdings, with Hungarian partners, in two publishing companies, Mai Nap Rt and Reform Rt—were relatively minor.

One way around the group's increasing financial problems was to juggle the figures in News Corp.'s annual reports. For example, the 1988 losses by News Ltd., the Australian division of the group, were shown as A$202 million in the 1989 report but as A$83 million in 1990, although the overall impact on group profits was said to be the same in both reports. Another way was to restructure the subsidiaries so that a higher proportion of group profits could be made in tax havens, such as Bermuda. In 1989, 25 percent of profits were attributed to tax haven companies; in 1990 the proportion was 54.5 percent, and News Corp.'s effective tax rate was 1.76 percent rather than the statutory 39 percent.

The merger of Sky Television with its smaller rival, BSB, in November 1990 did nothing to stem the continuing losses from satellite television, since it meant that BSB's pound 380 million loan facility was withdrawn. It also turned out that neither company had consulted the Independent Broadcasting Authority, which licensed BSB's operations, and had thus breached the contract. Once again, as with ATV 10 in Melbourne, Murdoch presented the regulatory body with a fait accompli. By mid-1991, Sky, now renamed BSkyB, had swallowed up pounds 1.5 billion in investments from various shareholders, among whom News Corp. was the largest, with a 49 percent stake. Between August and December 1990, the value of News Corp. shares fell by two-thirds. The firm's debts, to 146 banks, stood at more than $8.2 billion, and Murdoch had to promise to repay $1.2 billion by June 1992.

In 1990, Murdoch began a well-planned, controlled restructuring of News Corp.'s massive debt. After months of foot-dragging, his banks arranged a refinancing package dubbed "Project Dolphin" that called for $7.6 billion to be repaid by 1994. In return, the interest rate on the debts was raised by a full percentage point, and Murdoch agreed to a fire sale on many of his recent acquisitions. Between February 1991 and February 1992, Murdoch parted with $800 million worth of businesses, including most of News Corp.'s United States magazines—*New Woman, New York,* and *Premier*—and equity in Group Zeta. In the process, Murdoch's equity in News Corp. was reduced to about 30 percent, thereby reducing his volatile influence on the company but retaining his marketing savvy.

As News Corp.'s stock price rose, it sold $180 million of convertible preference shares (a type of equity) to three American companies, then divested itself of 55 percent of its Australian printing and magazine businesses. The resulting new company, called Pacific Magazines and Printing, took A$300 million in debt from News Corp.'s balance sheet and raised A$382 million from investors via a rights issue.

By the end of 1991, Murdoch had won back the confidence of his banks. They agreed to extend News Corp.'s repayment schedule by three years, allowing him to carry $3 billion of debt that had been due in February 1994 until 1997. The banks also permitted News Corp. to pay some dividends and keep some of the proceeds of its asset sales.

Success After Financial Restructuring: Early-to-Mid 1990s

Against all odds, and to the surprise of many observers, Murdoch and News Corp. not only survived the largest restructuring outside bankruptcy court in history, but went on to reach new highs in the early 1990s. By third quarter 1991, News Corp.'s net profits had skyrocketed to A$107.5 million ($84.3 million). The 315 percent increase from the previous year may have salved the pain of Murdoch's divestment in the magazine industry.

Although News Corp.'s British and Australian tabloids continued to bring in steady profits, Murdoch turned his attention to movies and television in the early 1990s, having sold nearly all the company's American newspapers and magazines except *TV Guide.* During that time, News Corp.'s Fox network topped ratings charts with shows such as *The Simpsons* and *Beverly Hills 90210,* Twentieth Century Fox's *Home Alone* became one of the most popular movies in history, and even BSkyB began to show promise. By the end of 1992, BSkyB had subscriptions of 3.4 million households in Great Britain and Ireland, amounting to approximately 19 percent of the total population of the United Kingdom.

Although Murdoch was discouraged from going on another acquisitions spree, he did forge an alliance with French TV giant Canal Plus to develop pay television services throughout Europe. With only 6 percent of West European homes equipped with cable, the market for pay-TV was regarded as a largely untapped one and analysts predicted that the News Corp./Canal Plus deal would create a formidable opponent in the battle for subscribers.

News Corp.'s enormous commercial weight, coupled with its accompanying social influence, made both the group and Murdoch, its chief executive, long-time subjects of significant controversy. This is usually presented in personalized terms. For example, while there are several biographies of Murdoch himself available, there is no history of the group as such. This approach often distorted the allocation of responsibility for the activities of a group whose admirers regarded as a great achievement and its detractors as a dangerous concentration of power.

Emerging As a Powerhouse: Mid-to-Late 1990s

Conflict surrounding Murdoch continued into the mid-to-late 1990s, as the media mogul once again began rebuilding his empire—this time focusing on global dominance in the entertainment, television, satellite, and cable network industries. The financial problems of the late 1980s and early 1990s a thing of the past, Murdoch began a whirlwind of activity, first saving the *New York Post* from financial ruin, then purchasing a majority interest in Star TV, Hong Kong's satellite network. The broadcasting rights to the National Football League were also purchased.

In late 1996, News Corp. teamed up with Softbank Corp. to create Japan Sky Broadcasting Company Ltd. (JskyB), a digital satellite broadcasting services firm. The company also acquired the remaining shares of New World Broadcasting Group—Fox had originally acquired a 20 percent interest in New World in 1994. That year, News Corp.'s revenues increased by 10 percent over the previous year to $9.9 billion, but operating profits fell by 24 percent.

Murdoch continued making deals despite faltering profits. During 1997, News Corp. completed its purchase of Heritage Media Corp. It also acquired International Family Entertainment Inc. in a $1.9 billion deal. The firm continued to pay close attention to its Fox interest, launching both Fox Sport Americas in Latin America and the Fox News Channel. News Corp. also began satellite ventures in Mexico and Brazil.

Murdoch's feverish pace continued in the latter half of the 1990s. The professional baseball team, the Los Angeles Dodgers, was purchased for $300 million. In April of 1998, News Corp. also landed the rights to the new series of *Star Wars* films. Management hoped that the success of the series would keep pace with the highly successful and profit-boosting *Titanic* film. The company sold its *TV Guide* to Universal Video Satellite Group for $2 billion and sold 18.6 percent of the Fox Entertainment Group to the public. The IPO raised $2.7 billion. Not all of Murdoch's acquisition attempts were successful however. The media giant failed to successfully team up with EchoStar Communications Corp., a large concern in the satellite industry.

In 1999, News Corp. purchased Liberty Media Corporation's 50 percent interest in Fox/Liberty Networks. The firm also bought 224.8 million non-voting shares from MCI WorldCom, worth $1.4 billion. Net profit for the year however, fell by 35 percent over the previous year. Management cited investments in digital technology at BskyB as well as in various other satellite operations as culprits in the falling profits.

Alliances for the New Millennium

News Corp. entered the new millennium with continued focus on its entertainment, satellite, and cable operations. The original foundation of the firm, its newspaper segment, continued to prosper. During 2001, the company made several key moves to better position itself during an economic slowdown in the U.S. During the dot-com fallout of 2000 and 2001, News Corp. was forced to forego several Internet-related ventures. In fact, it ended its $1 billion partnership with WebMD Corp., an Internet-based healthcare services and information provider—WebMD shares had fallen from a high of $75 per share to just $5 per share.

The firm also sold its Fox Family Worldwide Inc. to Walt Disney Company for $5.3 billion in 2001. It also set plans in motion to merge its Italy-based Stream pay television operations with Vivendi Universal. Stream had been losing approximately $360 million per year. Murdoch's attempts to gain control of a major satellite concern were spoiled once again after negotiations with DirecTV Inc.—owned by General Motors Corp.—fell through.

News Corp. did score a coup however, when it completed the $4.4 billion purchase of Chris-Craft Industries Inc. The deal added 10 new U.S. television stations to the firm's arsenal. The acquisition, coupled with station trades with ClearChannel Communications Inc. and Viacom International Inc., gave News Corp. duopolies in seven markets including New York, Los Angeles, Dallas, Houston, Washington, Phoenix, and Minneapolis.

According to a December 2001 AsiaPulse News article, Murdoch addressed concerns related to the faltering American economy in a December staff email stating, "momentous events beginning on September 11—and economic conditions beginning long before that—have forced every News Corp. company to find ways to streamline its operations. I have very little doubt that next year will be another very difficult one—which should make us only more determined to succeed at every level." This determination and News Corp.'s history of success would no doubt leave it standing as a leading media conglomerate in the years to come.

Principal Subsidiaries

Fox Broadcasting Co. (United States); Fox Television Stations Inc. (United States); Fox Entertainment Group Inc. (United States; 85%); HarperCollins Publishers Inc. (United States).

Principal Operating Units

Filmed Entertainment; Television; Newspapers; Book Publishing; Magazines and Inserts; Cable Network Programming.

Principal Competitors

AOL Time Warner Inc.; Bertelsmann AG; Walt Disney Company.

Further Reading

"Back From the Brink," *Economist,* December 7, 1991.

"Chris-Craft Sale Approved," *Los Angeles Business Journal,* July 30, 2001, p. 70.

Crainer, Stuart, *Business The Rupert Murdoch Way,* Oxford, Eng.: Capstone Publishing Ltd., 1998.

Egan, Jack, "Murdoch Scores a Big Goal," *U.S. News & World Report,* September 21, 1998, p. 60.

Harris, Robert, *Selling Hitler,* London: Faber and Faber, 1986.

Higgins, John M., "News Corp. Finally Gets Family Deal," *Broadcasting & Cable,* June 16, 1997, p. 12.

Leapman, Michael, *Barefaced Cheek,* London: Hodder and Stoughton, 1983.

McClellan, Stephen, "News Corp. Revenue Up, Profit Down," *Broadcasting & Cable,* August 26, 1996, p. 10.

Michaels, James W., "Rapping With Rupert," *Forbes,* September 28, 1992.

Munster, George, *A Paper Prince,* Ringwood, Penguin Books Australia, 1985.

"News Corp. Buys New World," *Television Digest,* July 22, 1996, p. 8.

"100 Leading National Advertisers: Monsanto Co. Montgomery Ward & Co. Nestle SA; News Corp.; Nike Inc.," *Advertising Age,* September 25, 1991.

Regan, Simon, *Rupert Murdoch,* London: Angus and Robertson, 1976.

"Rupert Murdoch Warns News Corp.'s Staff of Difficult Year Ahead," *AsiaPulse News,* December 24, 2001.

Schwartz, Matthew, "WebMD, News Corp. End $1 Billion Partnership," *B to B,* January 8, 2001, p. 4.

Serafini, Dom, "Looking Into Murdoch's Plans: A Blueprint for World Conquest," *Video Age International,* October 1997, p. 1.

Williams, Michael, "Giant Tag Team for Pay-TV," *Variety,* October 12, 1992.

Wintour, Charles, *The Rise and Fall of Fleet Street,* London: Hutchinson, 1989.

—Patrick Heenan
—updates: April Dougal and Christina Stansell

NORTH FORK BANK

North Fork Bancorporation, Inc.

275 Broad Hollow Road
Melville, New York 11747
U.S.A.
Telephone: (516) 844-1000
Toll Free: (800) 223-9363
Fax: (516) 694-1536
Web site: http://www.northforkbank.com

Public Company
Incorporated: 1905 as Mattituck Bank
Employees: 2,300
Total Assets: $1.18 billion (2000)
Stock Exchanges: New York
Ticker Symbol: NFB
NAIC: 551111 Offices of Bank Holding Companies;
52211 Commercial Banking

North Fork Bancorporation, Inc. is a bank holding company that principally operates commercial banks on Long Island, New York, and in the New York City area. It runs over 150 North Fork Banks, and maintains a telebanking operation through its Superior Savings of New England subsidiary. North Fork is a relatively small bank in a market dominated by large players, yet it has consistently outperformed its higher profile peers. It maintains a somewhat old-fashioned, low-tech image, emphasizing face-to-face customer contact. The company offers traditional banking products such as checking and savings accounts, and provides commercial and consumer loans and commercial and residential mortgages. It maintains branches in small communities up and down Long Island and does substantial business in Brooklyn and the Bronx. North Fork was rated number one among banks and thrifts by industry journal *U.S. Banker* in 2000, and it has been noted since the 1980s for its remarkable efficiency and high level of return on equity. The bank grew aggressively through acquisitions beginning in the late 1980s, and has also expanded by building new branches.

Early Years

The company was founded in 1905 in Mattituck, New York, a small Long Island town in Suffolk County on the north fork of eastern Long Island. The area was primarily rural and home to many duck farms. Suffolk County was also a popular summer vacation spot for New Yorkers. The company operated as Mattituck Bank until 1950, when it became the North Fork Bank and Trust Company. North Fork Bank and Trust grew slowly, over the 1950s consolidating with three other banks also located on the north fork of the island. The four banks combined under the North Fork Bank and Trust name, and opened new branches in other parts of Long Island. By 1963, there were 31 banks based on Long Island. These combined and consolidated over the next decades, until there were only 11 by 1984. North Fork managed to survive in large part because of high real estate values in Suffolk County's Hamptons district, where many New Yorkers kept summer homes.

There seemed little else to distinguish North Fork until it met up with John Kanas, who became its president at age 29 and spearheaded its phenomenal transformation into one of the country's leading banks. Kanas was a native Long Islander, the son of a duck farmer. He had owned a deli and been a school teacher when, in 1971, North Fork Bank and Trust announced plans to open a branch in his home town, East Moriches. The bank at the time had just $20 million in assets. It offered a training program for new branch managers. Kanas quit his teaching post to enter the training program, learning the banking business while the branch was being built. Kanas was attracted to banking almost by his contempt for it. He told a story to *Forbes* explaining the origin of his yen to work in the industry. While he was still a deli owner, Kanas's wife went to the bank to withdraw $5,000. She was turned away because she needed her husband's signature to take that large an amount from their joint account. Kanas suggested she go back the next day and see if she could get out $10,000 instead, which would close the account. Apparently the bank's policy for withdrawal was different than its policy for closing an account, and Mrs. Kanas got the full amount. This seemed ludicrous to John Kanas. "I thought, hey, these people don't know what they're doing," he told *Forbes*. ''This is the industry for me.'' Despite his scant background in banking, Kanas quickly made an impression at North Fork. He went from branch bank manager in 1971 to president of the company in 1977. At the former president's death, Kanas was promoted, though he was only 29 years old. He was the youngest bank president in the entire country.

Kanas quickly made changes at North Fork. He fired managers who were not pulling their weight and hired younger people to replace them. These he lured with incentives tied to the bank's future profitability. Three years after taking over the top job, Kanas reorganized North Fork as North Fork Bancorp. This then became the holding company for North Fork Bank and Trust in 1981. North Fork Bancorp went public in 1982 and began trading on the NASDAQ. Kanas was exceedingly adept at bringing in new business. Between 1979 and 1984, assets tripled, and over 1982 alone, deposits increased over 80 percent. The bank had a healthy business in commercial real estate loans, primarily in hotels, condominiums, and co-op apartments. The real estate market in the Hamptons was thriving, and North Fork attracted many wealthy customers for home mortgages. The bank had been paying dividends to shareholders since 1971. After the company reorganized, dividends increased every year through the early 1980s. In 1983, North Fork became one of only a few banks to make it onto *Forbes* magazine's annual list of the country's best small public companies. The bank's assets had grown to $260 million, and its return on assets (1.7 percent in 1984) ran at twice the industry norm for banks of North Fork's size.

Banking in the Late 1980s and Early 1990s

Bank deregulation in the 1980s let North Fork expand into new financial areas, such as securities. But it also threatened the small bank with direct competition from big New York banks. Kanas voiced a variety of possible schemes to enlarge North Fork, including moving into suburban Connecticut, New Jersey, or Florida. But eventually North Fork settled on an acquisition campaign that gave it more branches in its native Long Island, and then in other areas of suburban New York.

In 1988, North Fork Bancorp had 22 Long Island branches and about $696 million in assets. That year it bought a neighboring institution, the oldest savings bank in Suffolk County, Southold Savings Bank. Southold had $603 million in assets, and operated through five Long Island branches. The acquisition, in cash and stock, cost North Fork something over $110 million. Southold continued to operate under its old name, as a subsidiary of the North Fork Bancorp holding company, until 1992.

North Fork switched its stock from the NASDAQ to the New York Stock Exchange in 1990, increasing its visibility by

trading on the most prestigious exchange. Shortly after, North Fork announced plans to acquire the Eastchester Savings Bank, headquartered in White Plains, New York. Eastchester had nine branches in suburban Westchester and Rockland counties, and assets of $531 million. But the local real estate market began to sour shortly after the deal was announced. North Fork took a second quarter loss, stung by bad loans, and the bank had to cut costs by letting 100 employees go. Eastchester too announced a loss, and the merger was temporarily scuttled. Eventually North Fork picked up Eastchester for about $62 million, rather than the $80 million it had originally offered. Eastchester became part of North Fork's Southold subsidiary.

This was a rough period for North Fork Bancorp. The turn down in the real estate market led to a large percentage of bad, or ''nonperforming,'' loans. Nonperforming loans rose from $154 million by the end of 1991 to over $171 million by the next quarter. The bank's management was scrutinized by federal regulators over how it had disclosed the bad loans. North Fork lost over $40 million between 1990 and mid-1992. The bank ultimately hired a team of specialists from Texas to remedy North Fork's hemorrhaging loan portfolio. Kanas himself took a pay cut until the bank went back in the black. The company also merged its two subsidiaries, North Fork Bank and Trust and Southold Savings Bank, into one subsidiary company. All Southold and Eastchester branches took the North Fork name.

Acquisition Spree in the 1990s

By late 1992, the amount of North Fork's bad loans had fallen substantially, and the bank returned to profitability. With this bad patch behind it, North Fork began expanding rapidly through more acquisitions. In 1994, it bought the Bayside Federal Savings Bank, and the next year acquired the Bank of Great Neck. North Fork acquired certain branches of Extebank in 1996, which gave it its first foothold in Manhattan. It also acquired 10 branches of First Nationwide. The next year, it moved into New York's borough of the Bronx with its acquisition of North Side Savings Bank, and began doing business in Brooklyn in 1998 when it bought Home Federal Savings Bank.

North Fork followed a pattern when it made these acquisitions. Generally, top management at the acquired bank was let go. But North Fork made every effort to retain tellers, so that customers did not notice or resent the change in ownership. And most of North Fork's personnel worked for incentive pay, something rare in the banking industry. Some employees worked purely on commission, while branch managers, for example, could earn big bonuses in addition to their salary, based on the branch's profitability. North Fork also emphasized customer service and face-to-face interaction, even as its competitors added high-tech services like on-line banking. One analyst who followed North Fork described the bank's customers to the *Wall Street Journal* as being '' . . . more like people 20 years ago.'' Many branches were in blue-collar neighborhoods, and many loan customers were small businesses. North Fork persuaded a good percentage of its customers to hold their money in so-called demand deposit accounts, which were interest-free checking accounts. These were cheaper for the bank to maintain. North Fork operated relatively few automated teller machines and built them primarily in high-

---

Key Dates:

1905: Mattituck Bank founded.
1950: Name changed to North Fork Bank & Trust Co.
1971: John Kanas joins the bank as a branch manager.
1977: Kanas becomes president of the bank.
1982: North Fork goes public.
1988: North Fork buys Southold Savings Bank, marking the first of several acquisitions.
1990: North Fork stock moves to New York Stock Exchange.
1999: The company announces two acquisition deals in two weeks.

---

traffic locations that tended to generate fees from non-North Fork customers.

This rather unconventional approach seemed to work. By the mid-1990s, North Fork had consolidated its reputation as a remarkable money machine. It consistently bested bigger area banks in efficiency. A bank's efficiency is measured as a ratio of how much money it must spend to generate one dollar of operating income. In 1997, North Fork's efficiency ratio was 39.54, meaning it spent less than 40 cents to generate each dollar of income. Its competitor Chase Manhattan, by comparison, had an efficiency ratio of 59.

North Fork had assets of $4.1 billion by 1997, and it continued to expand by acquiring smaller banks. It bought Branford Savings Bank that year for $38 million, giving it its first territory in Connecticut. Branford had struggled with bad loans in the early 1990s but was profitable again by the time of the merger. John Kanas told *American Banker* that he hoped to use Branford as a base "to pursue a vigorous campaign of deposit-gathering throughout New England." In March 1998, North Fork closed on a deal to acquire New York Bancorp, a 35-branch bank based on Long Island, with $3.3 billion in assets. In 1999, North Fork made two deals within two weeks of each other. First it spent $570 million to acquire JSB Financial Inc., which was the parent company of Jamaica Savings Bank, with 13 branches in the New York metropolitan area. Jamaica had a strong customer base among immigrants, many of them small businessmen. Then North Fork announced it had picked up Reliance Bancorp, based in Garden City, New York. Reliance had 29 branches, mostly in Queens and elsewhere on Long Island. North Fork paid $352 million to acquire Reliance. Reliance had assets of $2.5 billion. These two deals together swelled North Fork to 152 branches and gave it a total of $9.2 billion in deposits and $15.5 billion in total assets. North Fork continued to manage to integrate its newly acquired banks into its operations. Its efficiency ratio remained very low. At 35 in 1998, North Fork's efficiency ratio was about half the average for the top 50 banks in the country. North Fork's earnings per share also rose rapidly, outpacing bigger banks like Chase Manhattan.

Aiming for the Manhattan Market

North Fork's various acquisitions had given it branches throughout Long Island, including Brooklyn and Queens, by the late 1990s. But it only had two branches in the lucrative market of Manhattan. One it had acquired when it bought certain assets of Extebank in 1995, and another North Fork opened in 1999. Building its own branches, called "de novo" branching, was a more difficult and expensive way to enter the Manhattan market than to take over an existing Manhattan bank. But three times since 1997 other banks had beat out North Fork in acquiring Manhattan targets. Astoria Financial Corp. snatched Greater New York Savings Bank away from a potential North Fork merger in 1997, and then the next year got to Long Island Savings Bank, scuttling North Fork's plans. In 1999, North Fork lost out again, this time to Roslyn Bancorp, when it attempted to buy T R Financial Corp. So that year North Fork announced it would go the de novo route, with plans to build 12 branches in Manhattan and Brooklyn. A series of mergers and consolidations had left Manhattan banking mainly in the hands of giant banks, which spelled an excellent opportunity for a smaller, service-oriented bank like North Fork. Chemical Bank, Manufacturers Hanover, and Chase Manhattan had all become part of Chase Manhattan Corp., which had an almost 40 percent share of the deposits in Manhattan by early 2000. Another 16 percent share of deposits was held by Citibank. North Fork had less than half of one percent of the Manhattan deposit market. Nevertheless, its two Manhattan branches accounted for close to 20 percent of all business checking accounts at North Fork. It was not a market North Fork could afford to be shut out of.

In March 2000, North Fork offered to buy Dime Bancorp, a bank twice its size, with nine branches in Manhattan. Dime was on the eve of a takeover deal with Hudson United Bancorp, a New Jersey bank, and North Fork's offer was unwelcome. Dime fought off North Fork's takeover, selling a stake to a private equity firm and hiring an esteemed retired banking executive as its new chairman. After six months, North Fork backed off. It continued to work on its de novo branches, and then in June 2001 announced that it would acquire another bank with several Manhattan branches, Commercial Bank of New York.

Principal Subsidiaries

North Fork Bank; Superior Savings of New England; Amivest Corp.; Compass Investment Services Corp.

Principal Competitors

Citigroup Inc.; Chase Manhattan Corp.; Independence Community Bank.

Further Reading

Barthel, Matt, "Superefficient North Fork Keeps Its Eye on the Prize," *American Banker*, January 6, 1997, p. 4A.

Beckett, Paul, and Deogun, Nikhil, "In Manhattan, an Upstart Bank Moves in on Giants' Home Turf," *Wall Street Journal*, March 9, 2000, pp. B1, B4.

Beckett, Paul, "North Fork Drops Bid for Dime Bancorp, Plans to Buy Back 10% of Its Own Stock," *Wall Street Journal*, September 29, 2000, p. A4.

Condon, Bernard, "Shirtsleeve Banking," *Forbes*, October 4, 1999, pp. 66–68.

Epstein, Jonathan, "N.Y.'s North Fork Plans New England Entry with $38M Purchase of Connecticut Bank," *American Banker*, July 31, 1997, p. 5.

Frank, Stephen K., "North Fork Bancorp Ruffles Feathers in Bank Circles," *Wall Street Journal*, July 31, 1996, p. B4.

Kallen, Barbara, "Is Being Good, Good Enough?" *Forbes*, February 27, 1984, p. 97.

Lazo, Shirley A., "Speaking of Dividends," *Barron's*, January 2, 1989, p. 49.

Milligan, John W., "Mini-Merger Mogul," *US Banker*, May 1998, p. 50.

Moyer, Liz, "North Fork of N.Y. to Pay $570M for Long Island Thrift," American Banker, August 17, 1999, p. 24.

——, "2 Weeks, 2 Deals: N.Y.'s North Fork in Growth Spurt," *American Banker*, August 31, 1999, p. 1.

——, "North Fork to Invade Big Apple the Hard Way—From Scratch," *American Banker*, February 23, 1999, p. 1.

"North Fork Bancorp to Acquire Southold for Cash and Stock," *Wall Street Journal*, December 22, 1987, p. 31.

"North Fork to Buy Eastchester Financial Under Revised Pact," *Wall Street Journal*, October 9, 1990, p. C14.

Sidel, Robin, "Dime's Novel Twist: Its Defenses Worked," *Wall Street Journal*, July 10, 2001, pp. C1, C14.

Talley, Karen, "North Fork Challenged," *LI Business News*, May 11, 1992, p. 1.

——, "North Fork Is Back in the Black," *LI Business News*, November 2, 1992, p. 3.

——, "North Fork Plans to Prevail in a Turbulent Marketplace," *LI Business News*, August 6, 1990, p. 1.

—A. Woodward

Opinion Research Corporation

P.O. Box 183
Princeton, New Jersey 08542
U.S.A.
Telephone: (908) 281-5100
Toll Free: (800) 444-4672
Fax: (908) 281-5103
Web site: www.opinionresearch.com

Public Company
Incorporated: 1938
Employees: 1,900 full-time; 4,000 part-time (2000)
Gross Billings: $160.91 million (2000)
Stock Exchanges: NASDAQ
Ticker Symbol: ORCI
NAIC: 541613 Market Consulting Services; 541618
Other Management Consulting Services; 54191
Marketing Research and Public Opinion Polling;
561499 All Other Business Support Services

Primarily through acquisitions, Opinion Research Corporation (ORC) has evolved into a leading global measurement-based, marketing-services firm to provide businesses and governments with sophisticated market research and teleservices. The company functions as three complementary businesses: ORC International conducts research in global marketing; ORC Macro specializes in research, social marketing, and information technology; and ORC ProTel provides premium-quality teleservices. The company has conducted studies in over 100 countries, supports 31 offices across the United States, Latin America, Europe, Asia, and Africa and operates ten research call centers located in the United States, the United Kingdom, Korea, and Taiwan. ORC's blue-chip multinational clients include 28 of *Financial Times Global* 100 companies and 27 of *US Fortune* 100 companies, including 6 of the top 10. The company's services and products include advanced analytics and data modeling, market and social research, demographic and health surveys, data collection and processing, management consulting, information technologies, public-sector research, and premium-quality teleservices. Most of its commercial pro-

jects are for businesses selling to other businesses and address issues such as customer loyalty and retention, market demand and forecasting, corporate image, and competitive positioning. Public-sector clients represent virtually every department of the U.S. government, many state and local governments, and non-government organizations around the world. *Fortune Small Business* magazine lists ORC as one of its "100 Fastest-Growing Small Companies" and *Forbes* magazine places the company among its "200 Best Small Companies."

1938–67: Pioneering Corporate Market Research

Claude Everett Robinson, while still in his early thirties, published an influential book on the 1928 presidential election, and during 1936–38 developed new scientific sampling techniques for the Gallup Poll. On October 26, 1938, for the purpose of applying the principles of general-public opinion polling to the marketing issues facing America's largest companies, Robinson founded and began to operate Opinion Research Corporation (ORC) in a two-room suite of New York City's Chrysler Building. During that first year, the company's clients included Sears & Roebuck, Standard Oil of New Jersey, *The New York Times*, Hoover, Time Inc., and General Motors. In 1939, rapid increase of business and a growing staff necessitated the company's move to Princeton, New Jersey. Billings for 1938–39 totaled $41,043; expenses amounted to $46,292. However, ORC had a backlog of work with which to begin a new year.

Seventeen new clients requested more than 60 surveys in 1940. ORC, one of the first organizations to conduct pre-election polling, completed its first political survey in 1941. The company also tested advertising copy and convinced a group of U.S. business leaders of their need to know about social and economic trends. To this end, in 1943 the company introduced the *ORC Public Opinion Index* which, for 40 years, included monthly surveys of how basic opinion trends affected business and commerce. In 1945, ORC initiated research on how consumers accepted new products and services and began biennial studies of how financial-security analysts evaluated industries and companies in the United States. Additionally, ORC conducted its first benchmark studies of trademark design, brand image, and product placement—and, for General Motors, conducted its first-ever survey of employee attitudes.

In the early 1960s ORC launched CARAVAN, a weekly shared-cost telephone survey that allowed multiple clients to gather the best of timely information at a relatively low cost. By 2001, CARAVAN was a twice-weekly national survey and the oldest continually running consumer omnibus survey in the nation. The company also became the leading polling firm for the U.S. Republican Party and its presidential candidates. Members of ORC's highly qualified professional staff—many of whom held advanced university degrees—were drawn from many disciplines and specializations. When Robinson died in 1961, the company he founded had expanded its offerings to mirror changing social conditions in the United States; for instance, studies about controlling air and water pollution, about judging the impact of inflation on the public, and about finding ways of attracting youth to business careers.

1968–91: Prosperity, Decline, and Resurgence

In 1968, ORC expanded its services by opening offices in Canada and Mexico. At the end of that year, the company was purchased by the New York-based publishing firm of McGraw-Hill. According to Michael R. Cooper's comment in the October 1998 issue of *The ORaCle,* an ORC International Associates publication, the companies were not complementary. (Cooper served as ORC's President in 1989 and later also as Chief Executive Officer and Chairman.) "The trade publication *Advertising Age,*" wrote Cooper, "reported 'poor communications' between the companies and quoted an industry source that 'McGraw-Hill really didn't know what it was getting itself into when it acquired ORC.' " In 1975 McGraw-Hill sold ORC to Cambridge, Massachusetts-based Arthur D. Little Inc., a consulting firm also based in Cambridge.

The companies were optimistic about mutual development of their potential: ADL strategy and ORC fact-based analysis. However, 14 years later, ORC had grown either slightly or not at all. The company had prospered "in the '40s, '50s, and '60s [but declined] in the '70s and '80s," Cooper noted in the *ORaCle* source cited above. When he, John Short (who succeeded Cooper in 1998), and others joined ORC in 1989, they "saw a Company with a rich heritage and a premier pedigree—but without direction. Neglect from its then-owner had left it

without motivation and without reason to succeed. The company was bleeding and going nowhere but down," Cooper emphasized.

The new managers, however, saw the possibility for "a new company—[one] with the same name, a new spirit of innovation and devotion to quality performance—but with a new corporate *raison d'être,*" Cooper wrote. Management infused energy into the company and defined a strategy to return it to profitability by providing clients with research-based knowledge—market intelligence that would help companies define their strategic direction and overall profitability. To bring about this turnaround, in 1991 ORC's top management bought the company back from Arthur D. Little, reinstated it as an independent firm, and went public in 1993 by successfully completing an initial public offering (IPO).

1992–97: Strategic Acquisitions and Organic Growth

ORC's top management refined and implemented the vision that had brought the company through the end of the 1980s and the beginning of the 1990s. Founder Robinson had defined the field of corporate market research; however, to stay at the forefront of the industry, ORC needed to increase its national visibility and establish a strong worldwide presence to deal with issues emerging for corporations intent on globalization. During 1992, the company acquired London-based Research by Telephone and in 1993 purchased Gordon Simmons Research Group (GSR), also headquartered in London. GSR was a market-research firm conducting studies for companies, such as Ford Motor Company, Marks and Spenser, and Woolworth, plc.

Next, ORC's 1994 acquisition of Toledo-based Strategic Research and Consulting, Inc. gave it access to the U.S. auto industry; first-ever clients included General Motors, Chrysler Corporation, and Harley Davidson, Inc. The company also opened an office in Detroit and a European Information Centre in London. In 1994, ORC created two syndicated global-research products: CORPerceptions and BrandPerceptions. These programs quantified and compared the value of brand equity and corporate equity for clients throughout Asia/Pacific, Europe, and North America. Furthermore, the development of an international network of preferred-partner research firms increased ORC's marketing power by connecting the company to local-service providers.

In 1995 the company opened ORC Asia as its Hong Kong-based headquarters on that continent; the company also built a new telephone-interviewing call center in Tucson, Ohio. Then, the acquisition of Marketing Information Quest in Korea, of Chicago-based Quality Expectations, and of SIA (a public sector/technology company operating in London and Manchester) further extended ORC's global presence. By year-end 1996, ORC, now known as ORC International, offered many services and products, including measurement and tracking of customer satisfaction, image assessment and competitive positioning, advertising evaluation and tracking, assistance for the introduction of new products, and business panels for executives and professionals. The company focused on client projects that required periodic updating and tracking of information, thereby creating the potential for higher-margin recurring revenues. For fiscal 1996, net revenues increased to $47.27 million from $44.10

Key Dates:

1938: Claude E. Robinson founds Opinion Research Corporation (ORC).

1943: ORC introduces its *Public Opinion Index*, monthly surveys of how basic opinion trends affect business and commerce.

1960: ORC launches CARAVAN, a weekly shared-cost telephone survey.

1968: The company expands to Canada and Mexico; McGraw-Hill purchases ORC.

1975: McGraw-Hill sells ORC to Arthur D. Little, Inc., a consulting firm.

1991: ORC's top management buys back the company.

1993: ORC goes public and acquires London-based Gordon Simmons Research.

1994: Company opens an office in Detroit and opens the European Information Centre in London.

2000: For the fifth consecutive year, ORC posts record earnings.

2001: Eurostat awards ORC a contract for social research projects throughout the European Union.

million in 1995; net income reached $810,000, compared to a net-income loss of $1.67 million in 1995.

With the acquisition of Korea-based Marketing Information Quest, Taiwan-based Tripro, and Mexico-based Strategic Insight, ORC increased its offices abroad. According to its *1997 Annual Report*, ORC's outreach was based on a four-point strategy: 1. globalization of its market-research business; 2. strategic extension of modeling and analytics into teleservices; 3. building of differentiated value; and 4. implementation of targeted resource-allocation focused on globalization, teleservices, and differentiation. ORC created TeleScience, an innovative teleservice capability through which in-depth experience in advanced analytics and modeling techniques was applied to superior telemarketing. Furthermore, to add differential value to its products, ORC developed proprietary specialties—such as Market Demand Analysis and Forecasting—which assisted clients for the introduction of new products and, if relevant, the preparation of an Initial Product Offering.

For fiscal 1997, ORC's revenues reached $56.67 million and net income peaked at $1.15 million. Revenues from overseas accounted for 31 percent of ORC's these results. According to Flaherty and Arnaldo's story in the December 13, 1998 issue of *Equities,* ORC also established longstanding relationships with affiliate companies in major markets around the world.

1998–2000: Expanding Services and Solidifying Global Infrastructure

In 1998, ORC Chairman/CEO/President Michael R. Cooper resigned and was succeeded by John F. Short, the company's former vice-chairman and chief financial officer. The $11-billion market research industry was still "highly fragmented with thousands" of small companies, observed Flaherty and Arnaldo in their *Equities* essay. "About 90 percent of research firms . . . were 'data suppliers' focusing on branded consumer goods (the low end of the industry). ORC, however . . . did business-to-business research, applying sophisticated mathematical models and quantitative analysis in order to provide clients with unique market insight.''

The 1998, purchase of Lansing, Illinois-based ProTel Marketing, Inc. (renamed ORC ProTel, Inc.) extended the company's core business into teleservices. ORC combined its market-research expertise in segmentation modeling and database management with ProTel's quality teleservices to quantify buyer behavior, optimize targeting of customers, and provide feedback to improve sales. This breakthrough capability, named ORC TeleScience, applied sophisticated modeling techniques to cutting-edge teleservices, thereby lowering the costs of increased sales and the acquisition of customers. "A year-long beta test conducted by a major credit-card company showed that ORC's model resulted in an activation rate 100 percent higher than that of its competitors,'' noted Flaherty and Arnaldo.

The desire to serve clients in new markets abroad fueled ORC's 1998 acquisition of Macro International Marketing Inc. (renamed ORC Macro International Inc.), a firm supporting businesses and governments worldwide. ORC Macro's substantial government-client business and social research expertise complemented ORC's leading position with corporate clients to create an organization having expanded international capabilities and innovative offerings for government agencies. Continuing integration of ORC's social and business-to-business operations also improved overall efficiency. In September, ORC Macro won an estimated $50 million in new contracts from various federal agencies and in October received a five-year contract, worth up to $14.2 million, from the Department of Health and Human Services.

Outbound telemarketing services for Cendant Corporation, ORC's largest single client, accounted for 18 percent of the company's 1998 revenues. The offering of "global-market research that provides consistent, comparable intelligence across borders and cultures corresponds exactly to marketplace demands,'' Short commented in the company's *1998 Annual Report.* Revenues increased 29 percent to $73.17 million in 1998, from $56.67 million in 1997. This increase was due principally to $15.92 million in revenues generated by ORC ProTel and ORC Mexico, as well as by an increase in market-research revenues in the United States and Great Britain.

The company—with 1999 Internet-related revenues of $6.6 million—also benefitted from owning The Quantum Research Corporation (now a division of ORC Macro), a firm that specialized in delivering Internet-based survey research, data analysis, and dynamic databases for some of the nation's leading science, health, and education organizations. ORC introduced e.Tr@ck—a nationally syndicated research study of online shoppers—that provided e-commerce companies with vital consumer insights gleaned from a complete demographic portrait of the nation's adults, whether or not they shopped online.

In fiscal 1999, ORC posted record financial results for the fourth consecutive year. Revenues peaked at $118.62 million, a 62 percent increase over fiscal 1998 revenues of $73.17 million. The increase resulted principally from revenues generated by

ORC Macro, and from improvements in ORC's teleservices business. Net income rose to $2.42 million, compared to a loss of $170,000 in 1998. A Macro client since 1989, the United States Agency for International Development (USAID) accounted for 11 percent of the company's revenues.

2000 and Beyond

In response to a Fortune 1000 financial institution's contract for an Internet-based business panel, ORC developed an Internet B2B (business-to-business) panel, which it began to manage and maintain in February 2000. The panel, consisting of 1,000 executives from small- and medium-sized businesses across the United States, collected and updated information to help the client make decisions about marketing and sales strategies. ORC also created a Syndicated Business Panel consisting of 1,400 middle-market companies; a client could contract for unrestricted access to a panel, but ORC owned the panel and could use it with other clients.

The July ISO 9001 Certification of ORC's offices in Ohio and Michigan placed ORC among the few in its industry to be thus recognized for the quality standardization mandated by ISO 9001. In September, ORC acquired C/J Research, a premier market-research organization with a blue-chip client list that included Walt Disney Company, Wendy's International, Sprint Corporation, and *The Chicago Tribune*. Furthermore, C/J improved ORC positioning for work with companies dealing with fast-moving consumer goods (FMCG).

In the following month, ORC announced a $17-million increase to its contract with USAID. In November, ORC Macro acquired Maryland-based Social & Health Services, Ltd. (SHS), a leading communications and information-management company. At this time, *Forbes* magazine recognized ORC "for financial performance over a five-year period in five key criteria, including sales and profit growth, net income, and return on equity," listing the company among its "200 Best Small Companies." Furthermore, in December ORC announced that its SHS unit was among the first organizations to be awarded a subcontract in the federal government's new school-violence-prevention program.

In fiscal 2000, for the fifth consecutive year, ORC reported record earnings. United States market research, in rounded numbers, amounted to 24 percent of revenues, United Kingdom market research to 11 percent, teleservices to 13 percent, and social research to 53 percent. Annual revenues increased 36 percent to $160.91 million and net income grew 31 percent to $3.30 million. Internet-related revenues were $11 million, an increase of 57 percent compared to 1999.

As 2001 got underway, ORC was recognized as one of the few organizations with the skills, technology and systems to effectively administer worldwide social research projects when Eurostat, the Statistical Office of the European Communities, contracted for a series of social research projects across Europe in order to obtain data about social welfare throughout the European Union.

Furthermore, at the request of several government offices, ORC created "fourth generation" search engines, also known as "Deep Search" engines, that probed narrowly and deeply

into the Web. At regular intervals, these engines automatically updated all materials available at each site. These Web sites, searchable in several languages, included www.health.org (articles on the prevention of alcohol, tobacco, and illicit drug use) and www.parentsmart.com (over 21,000 articles parents could use to help their children with school work). In March 2001, ORC introduced www.enterpriseworks.org, a powerful, first-of-its-kind search engine for information on efforts to fight poverty and promote sustainable development in Africa, Asia, and Latin America. ORC also won database-management contracts— valued in excess of $14 million over a period of three to four years—from government agencies in both the United States and the United Kingdom. The contracts stipulated that ORC would develop new error-pattern identification technology, design and code record-matching algorithms, and build web portals with multiple layers of embedded access control.

Further recognition was published in the July issue of *Fortune Small Business* magazine, which listed ORC as one of its "100 Fastest-Growing Small Companies." The choice of companies was based on several key financial criteria, including earnings growth, revenue growth, and total stock return.

When ORC was awarded a $7-million contract by the Centers for Disease Control and Prevention to support the new "Healthy Passages" initiative, the company agreed to serve as the coordinating center for data collected by three prominent universities. CDC also gave ORC a $4.7-million, five-year contract, to implement National Youth Risk Behavior Surveys (YRBS), a project ORC had supported since 1988. At the end of the third quarter of 2001, ORC's Social Research Business had won approximately $85 million in new contracts, thereby providing a foundation for solid growth in fiscal 2002, Chairman Short observed in an early October news release.

Since its inception in 1938, Opinion Research Corporation had known good times and hard times but nothing quite so bad as the events of 2001. The effects of an economic recession, an era of terrorism introduced by the demolition of New York City's World Trade Center and part of Washington D.C.'s Pentagon, and continuing war in Afghanistan brought many companies to either the brink of bankruptcy or total destruction. Nevertheless, as Chairman Short commented in an October 25 news release, ORC was "able to sustain revenue growth and positive cash flow during these challenging times," although weakness in national market research and teleservices made for lower-than-expected financial results.

For the first nine months of 2001, revenues were $132.9 million, or 13 percent, when compared to $117.2 million for the first nine months of 2000. Chairman Short continued his October comment by saying he strongly believed that "our diversification in the products we offer, the markets we serve and the worldwide geographies in which we operate, will provide a strong foundation and help the company achieve long-term growth and succeed in this difficult economic environment." Indeed, judging from the company's past history, it is possible to believe that ORC, with its wealth of intellectual capital and sophisticated technological infrastructure, would continue to thrive as it lived up to its motto and provided "Insight Beyond Measure."

Principal Subsidiaries

European Information Centre Limited (United Kingdom); Macro International Inc.; Opinion Research Corporation, S.A. de C.V. (United Kingdom); O.R.C. International Ltd. (United Kingdom); ORC Consumer, Inc.; ORC Holdings, Ltd. (United Kingdom); ORC Korea, Ltd.; ORC International Holdings, Inc. (Cayman Islands); ORC Protel, Inc.; ORC Teleservices Corp.; Social & Health Services, Ltd.

Principal Competitors

Harris Interactive; Information Resources, Inc.; Market Facts, Inc.; NFO WorldGroup, Inc.; The NPD Group, Inc.; Taylor Nelson Sofres plc.

Further Reading

"BT Ignite Solutions: UK and German Businesses Bring in the E-Business Experts for Ongoing Success," *M2 Communications Presswire,* May 3, 2001.

"Celebrating 60 Years: 1938–1998," *The Oracle*, Princeton, N.J., October 1998, pp. 1–9.

Fellman, Michelle Wirth, "A New World for Marketers," *Marketing News*, May 10, 1999.

Flaherty, Robert J., and Arnaldo Arroyo, "Opinion Research Corporation," *Equities Special Solutions*, December 13, 1998, pp. 1 and 7.

"Opinion Research Corporation," *Marketing News*, June 5, 2000.

—Gloria A. Lemieux

Pakistan International Airlines Corporation

PIA Head Office
Quaid-E-Azam International Airport
Karachi 75200
Pakistan
Telephone: +92 (21) 4579 4763
Fax: +92 (21) 457 0147
Web site: http://www.piac.com.pk/

Public Company
Incorporated: 1955
Employees: 19,000
Sales: PkR 47.11 billion ($966 million) (2001)
Stock Exchanges: Karachi
Ticker Symbol: PIAC; PIAB
NAIC: 336411 Aircraft Manufacturing; 336412 Aircraft
Engine and Engine Parts Manufacturing; 481111
Scheduled Passenger Air Transportation; 481112
Scheduled Freight Air Transportation; 481211
Nonscheduled Chartered Passenger Air
Transportation; 481212 Nonscheduled Chartered
Freight Air Transportation; 48819 Other Support
Activities for Air Transportation

Pakistan International Airlines Corporation (PIA) is the flag carrier of Pakistan, whose government owns 85 percent of its shares. PIA's route network stretches to Asia, the Middle East, Africa, Europe, and North America. It connects 35 cities within Pakistan. Six million people flew the airline in 2000, when passenger traffic accounted for 85 percent of revenues. Engineering and charter services accounted for nine percent. PIA also conducts some contract work for aerospace manufacturers.

Origins

Pakistan's first airline pre-dated the creation of the country itself on August 14, 1947. Merza Ahmad and Merza Abol Hassan Ispahani, two brothers from a wealthy textile family in Bengal, had formed Orient Airways on October 23, 1946. Using the same type of war surplus Douglas C-47s that had launched so many other airlines, Orient established a Calcutta-Akyab-Rangoon route on June 30, 1947. The company's headquarters was moved from Calcutta to Chittagong due to the war that accompanied the Partition of India that summer. In October 1947, Orient began connecting the eastern half of the country (now Bangladesh) with the west, 1100 miles across India.

Pakistan's Ministry of Defense created Pakistan International Airlines (PIA) as a government department in 1951. The government combined Orient with PIA on October 1, 1953, but continued flying under its own name. PIA took over one of Orient's routes, Karachi-Dacca, on June 7, 1954 using a new Lockheed Super Constellation. In February 1955, PIA began flying to London via Cairo using another of its three Constellations. Older planes such as the DC-3 and the Convair continued to form the basis for the domestic fleet, though turboprop powered Vickers-Armstrong Viscounts were being phased in by the end of the decade.

PIA became a state corporation on March 11, 1955. After this, Orient's planes were repainted in PIA's green livery; Orient's shareholders received a 40 percent interest in PIA. A route between Karachi and Delhi, the capital of India, was launched on March 15. Pakistan International Airlines Corporation was incorporated on April 18, 1956 under the Pakistan International Airlines Corporation Act; it listed on the Karachi Stock Exchange on November 5, 1957.

In spite of technical assistance from Pan American Airways, PIA suffered a couple of crashes in the late 1950s. Zafarul Ahsan, the civil servant who had guided the airline's early development, was blamed for these and replaced by Air Commodore (later Air Marshall) Malik Nur Khan in 1959.

Jet-Powered in 1960

In 1960, PIA became Asia's first jet operator, flying a weekly service to London using a Boeing 707 leased from Pan Am. This route was extended to New York the next year but was suspended in 1963 due to a lack of traffic. At the same time, PIA was offering low-priced "Airbus" service in its domestic markets. For a couple of years between 1963 and 1966, PIA operated a scheduled helicopter network.

A number of unique international air links were established in the mid-1960s. PIA began flying to Kabul, Afghanistan and in 1964 became the first non-communist airline to fly to the People's Republic of China. It also flew to Moscow and, briefly, Teheran. By the end of the decade, its international network included Paris, Istanbul, Dubai, Bangkok, Manila, and Tokyo.

PIA also suffered some atrocious setbacks. A Boeing 720 jet crashed at Cairo in 1965, killing 123 people. Nur Khan was replaced as managing director by Asghar Khan. In the same year, armed conflict erupted in the Punjab. In 1966, PIA lost one of its three Sikorsky S-61 helicopters in a fatal accident. Violent uprisings in East Pakistan led to the formation of the independent state of Bangladesh and scuttled the flights that had connected Pakistan's two widely separated wings. This effectively cut PIA's traffic in half, notes aviation historian R.E.G. Davies.

New Ventures in the 1970s

Routes were redrawn and the fleet was trimmed in response to PIA's loss of territory. However, the reduction in traffic was only temporary. Pakistani immigration to Great Britain and demand for labor in the Gulf States pushed loads past projections. PIA was also doing a brisk cargo business.

R.E.G. Davies notes a couple of interesting side ventures during this period. PIA had its own nursery for stocking its cabins with fresh flowers. It also operated its own poultry farm to meet its own catering needs as well as those of other airlines passing through Karachi.

PIA ordered its first wide-body jets in April 1973. However, this order for three Douglas DC-10s was marred by a bribery scandal. Air Marshal Nur Khan returned as PIA chairman in 1974 and was joined by Enver Jamall, a veteran of the Tata airline in India, as managing director.

After losing money in 1971–72, PIA showed a profit of $3 million in 1974. Its ancillary services to other airlines brought in $4 million a year, while its annual budget was about $200 million. Operating profits reached $5.5 million in 1975–76 on revenues of $206.6 million.

In 1976, PIA began operating Boeing 747 jumbo jets, leased from TAP of Portugal, for the first time. The increase in capacity allowed PIA to carry 20,000 pilgrims to Jeddah every year. In 1977, service resumed to Bangladesh, formerly East Pakistan.

In a pattern more typical of western airlines' involvement with those of developing countries, PIA acquired a 20 percent interest in Air Malta in April 1977 and supplied it with technical staff. PIA also helped Air China set up its flight kitchens.

Jamall was named PIA chairman in 1978; M.M. Salim, one of the company's earliest managers, returned as managing director two years later. Expansion of the fleet continued.

Difficult Times in the 1980s and 1990s

Jamall and Salim were replaced by Major General Rahim Khan and Air Marshall Wigar Azim as chairman and managing director, respectively, in 1981. The company had suffered a couple of serious aircraft mishaps. With the prospect of financial losses looming near, the new management cut four thousand jobs, reducing the total to 20,000, while unions were banned by martial law. A $60 million bailout package gave the government an equity shareholding. Revenues rose 17 percent to PkR7,702 million ($570 million) in 1982–83, with after-tax profits doubling to Rs411 million.

The PIA fleet now included 23 jets and nine Fokker turboprops. PIA ordered several new short-range Boeing 737 jets in the mid-1980s to carry its feeder traffic. Other propeller-driven planes rounded out its domestic fleet. However, in contrast to PIA's earlier growth periods, much of the fleet seemed outdated by 1995, noted *Air Transport World*.

PIA initiated a unique Islamabad-London flight via Moscow in the mid-1980s. By 1990, three Pakistan cities were linked to England, and Manchester was added as an English destination.

The prospect of a partial privatization of 15 percent of the airline was being raised by 1990. PIA was making profits, but was hampered by certain government mandates, such as artificially low domestic fares, high jet fuel taxes, and a ban on serving or selling alcoholic drinks. A couple of years later, the government would increase duty on aircraft and parts as well as airport fees.

The collapse of the Soviet Union in late 1991 created new opportunities for PIA with several newly independent Muslim states. PIA's western fleet and technical expertise made it unique in the region. In 1993, the domestic air market in Pakistan was opened to competition from private airlines for the first time in 40 years. A dozen tiny carriers soon sprang up.

PIA posted its first loss during fiscal 1991 due to the spike in insurance premiums and fuel prices caused by the Gulf War. It lost an estimated $40 million on domestic service alone. However, the next year saw record profits of $41 million on revenues of $880 million. Air Marshall Farooq Umar, managing director, introduced a restructuring program after net profits slipped to $4.5 million in 1993–94. Umar had been the first CEO of Shaheen Air, a former cargo airline that was now competing with PIA for passengers, even international ones, after being allowed to fly to the Persian Gulf in the mid-1990s.

By this time, ancillary projects provided an important part of PIA's revenues, though the chicken farm had been sold. The company conducted maintenance and training for other airlines. One unit even manufactured parts for aerospace companies such as Boeing, GE, and SNECMA. The company invested heavily in automation and computer systems, selling some

Key Dates:

1946: Orient Airways is formed.
1955: Pakistan International Airlines is formed and merges with Orient.
1959: ''Golden Years'' of the company begin with appointment of Nur Khan as managing director.
1964: PIA begins service to China.
1970: Flight Kitchen is set up.
1973: The company orders its first wide-body jets.
1981: Pakistan approves a $60 million bailout package.
1991: The company tallies a rare annual loss due to factors arising out of the Gulf War.
1994: A restructuring program is introduced.
2000: The government approves a Rs 20 billion bailout for PIA.

software to third parties. PIA also had interests in hotels in Karachi and abroad.

Challenges Continue in 2000

In the late 1990s, former prime minister Benazir Bhutto was accused of illegally giving out jobs at PIA during her second term in office, between 1993 and 1996. Sher Afghan Malik, managing director in 2001, had to deal with a ticket sales scandal that he estimated may have been costing the airline up to PkR2.8 billion ($45 million) a year. There were also complaints of inefficiency and poor customer service, reported the *Financial Times*. PIA had lost international stature and was considered by some to be primarily an ''ethnic carrier'' devoted to ferrying expatriates home, rather than a competitive choice for tourists or business travelers.

Hamid Nawaz, a retired lieutenant general who was PIA's chairman, urged management to help turn the airline around. By July 2001, PIA had a PkR20 billion financial package from the government and the trade unions were once again effectively suspended. Malik had earlier expressed hope that making changes to the computer reservations system would help restore profits.

PIA lost PkR11 billion in 2000. Management expected the company to break even by the end of 2001. Although national pride was an important part of PIA's mission, there was a limit on the price the government was willing to pay for the prestige of having an international air carrier. As in the past, there was the implicit threat that unless the airline could operate on its own, it would simply cease to exist.

The U.S.-led campaign against the Taliban in neighboring Afghanistan resulted in most foreign airlines canceling their scheduled flights to Pakistan. Twenty-nine of them closed their offices in Pakistan in September 2001. The air campaign against Taliban forces also affected PIA negatively, due to the closing of seven of Pakistan's airports and declaration of its airspace as a war zone. PIA lost PkR2.09 billion on sales of PkR47.11 billion in the year ended December 2001.

Pakistan's intensifying dispute with India again curtailed PIA's extensive connections with that country in 2001. After

India banned PIA from its airspace in January 2002, Cathay Pacific stepped in to carry PIA traffic to Bangkok, Hong Kong, and Singapore. PIA had earlier lent Cathay Pacific assistance during a pilots' strike. The political and military volatility in the Middle East and Central Asia continued to affect the operations of PIA and would perhaps do so for some time to come.

Principal Subsidiaries

Midway House (Pvt) Ltd.; PIA Hotels Ltd.; PIA Shaver Poultry Breeding Farms (Pvt) Ltd.; Skyrooms (Pvt) Ltd.

Principal Divisions

Automation; Cargo Sales & Services; Flight Kitchen; Flight Operations; Ground Handling; Precision Engineering Complex; Telephone Sales; The Training Centre.

Principal Competitors

Emirates Group; Gulf Air; Saudi Arabian Airlines; Shaheen Air International.

Further Reading

Aftab, Mohammed, ''PIA Braced for Harsher Climate,'' *Financial Times* (London), January 14, 1986.
——, ''Taking a New Flight Path,'' *Financial Times* (London), January 10, 1984.
Bokhari, Farhan, ''Ailing Pakistani Airline Looks for Uplift,'' *Financial Times* (London), Companies & Finance Sec., April 12, 2001, p. 31.
''Cathay Pacific to Help Pakistan International Airlines Beat Indian Ban,'' *Business Recorder*, January 9, 2002.
Coleman, Herbert J., ''Capacity Boost Spurs Pakistani Carrier,'' *Aviation Week & Space Technology*, July 21, 1975, p. 32.
——, ''Pakistan Hopes to Double Airline Services Revenue,'' *Aviation Week & Space Technology*, August 25, 1975, p. 71.
Davies, R.E.G., ''Airlines of Pakistan,'' *Airlines of Asia Since 1920*, London: Putnam Aeronautical Books; McLean, Virginia: Paladwr Press, 1997, pp. 63–83.
Hill, Leonard, ''Jump Starting PIA,'' *Air Transport World*, July 1997, pp. 169ff.
Khomne, Ranjit, ''PIA Chief Heads Back Home,'' *The Times of India*, December 31, 2001.
Mirza, Iqbal, ''PIA Chief Unfolds 10-Year Plan to Make Airline Financially Stable,'' *Business Recorder*, September 23, 2001.
——, ''PIA's 10 Aircraft Grounded for Want of Spares,'' *Business Recorder*, July 14, 2001.
——, ''With Foreign Carriers Shying Away from Pakistan, Heavy Responsibility Falls on Pakistan International Airlines,'' *Business Recorder*, October 9, 2001.
''Over Meddling Led to Pakistan International Airline's Decline: Enver Jamall,'' *Business Recorder*, October 31, 2001.
''Pakistan Drops Restrictions, Pursues International Flights,'' *Aviation Week & Space Technology*, April 12, 1993, p. 28.
''Pakistan International Airlines: Eager to Establish Direct Air Links with Korea,'' *Business Korea*, August 1992, p. 47.
''Pakistan International Airlines Suffered Losses Worth Rs11 Billion in 2000,'' *Business Recorder*, August 15, 2000.
''Pakistan New Entrants Line Up Against Barriers,'' *Airfinance Journal*, May 1994, p. 16.
''PIA Invests in Automation, Sells Software to Other Airlines,'' *Aviation Week & Space Technology*, August 10, 1992, p. 38.

"PIA Management Urged to Help Rescue Airline," *Business Recorder,* July 19, 2001.

Proctor, Paul, and Irtaza Malik, "Liberalization Spurs New Pakistan Airlines," *Aviation Week & Space Technology,* April 12, 1993, p. 38.

Proctor, Paul, "PIA Moves to Capture Growth in Central Asian Business," *Aviation Week & Space Technology,* August 10, 1992, p. 38.

Rao, N. Vasuki, "India, Pakistan Ban Overflights," *Journal of Commerce—JoC Online,* January 2, 2002.

"Rs51.8bn Budget Approved for PIA," *DAWN Internet Edition,* December 13, 2001.

Vandyk, Anthony, "Growing Pains," *Air Transport World,* March 1995, p. 83.

Westlake, Michael, "Local Turbulence: PIA Aims for Partial Privatisation," *Far Eastern Economic Review,* January 18, 1990, p. 39.

—Frederick C. Ingram

&. PanAmSat.

PanAmSat Corporation

20 Westport Road
Wilton, Connecticut 06897
U.S.A.
Telephone: (203) 622-6664
Fax: (203) 622-9163
Web site: http://www.panamsat.com

Public Company
Incorporated: 1984
Employees: 800
Sales: $1.02 billion (2000)
Stock Exchanges: NASDAQ
Ticker Symbol: SPOT
NAIC: 51322 Cable and Other Program Distribution;
    51334 Satellite Telecommunications

PanAmSat Corporation is a leading provider of satellite operations, serving markets in all parts of the globe. The company keeps aloft a fleet of over 20 satellites, which allow hundreds of customers to broadcast television and video programming to millions of households worldwide. PanAmSat serves prominent news organizations such as the BBC, the Associated Press, Bloomberg, and many more, and carries cable programming for Disney, AOL Time-Warner, Viacom, China Central Television, and many others. The company's satellites carry over 500 channels of so-called direct to home television programming. PanAmSat's satellites also provide telecommunications service to communications companies on five continents, and provides streaming video capacity over the Internet to computer networks in countries such as Australia, Japan, Korea, Taiwan, Peru, Chile, and Argentina. The company has eleven offices worldwide, and seven technical ground facilities. The company was founded by a maverick television executive, Reynold Anselmo, who was the first to challenge the existing satellite monopoly, Intelsat. PanAmSat is now 80 percent owned by Hughes Electronics, a subsidiary of General Motors.

1980s: Abandoning Television for Satellites

PanAmSat was founded in 1984 by Reynold (''Rene'') Anselmo, who had made his career bringing Spanish-language television programming to the United States. He was born in 1926 in Bedford, Massachusetts, a community outside Boston. His father was born in Italy but raised in Chile and Argentina, and eventually became postmaster of Quincy, Massachusetts. Anselmo was apparently restless and headstrong as a youth. When he was 16 in 1942, his high school principal offered to lie about Anselmo's age in order to get him into the military, as school clearly did not suit him. Anselmo fought in the South Pacific, and after leaving military service attended the University of Chicago. Upon graduating in 1951, he went to Mexico, where he began producing and directing both theater and television. His various jobs included writing for the Voice of America, dubbing ''I Love Lucy'' into Spanish, and producing a Spanish-language version of the U.S. Broadway comedy *The Boy Friend*. Anselmo made friends with Emilio Azcarraga Milmo, whose father was the head of Mexico's largest media and television company, Televisa. By 1954, Anselmo was working for Televisa, marketing its programs to other countries in Latin America. In 1963, he moved to New York to become president of Spanish International Network, known as SIN. SIN built up a network of Spanish-language TV stations, which showed programming predominantly from Televisa. By the early 1980s, SIN had grown to be a major presence in the Spanish-language market in the United States, with the lion's share of advertising dollars. Anselmo owned 24 percent of SIN's holding company, and had large stakes in several of its stations. But the company had problems. Tension between Anselmo and his business partners led to a lawsuit in the mid-1970s, which finally came to a head in the early 1980s. The Federal Communications Commission (FCC) investigated the company after competitors alleged that SIN was controlled by Televisa. Foreign ownership in a domestic network was limited by law to only 20 percent, and SIN appeared to violate this. Anselmo wanted to keep going with SIN despite the legal tangles. But his partners overruled him, and the company was sold for $600 million in 1986 to Hallmark Cards Inc. Though he had been against the sale, Anselmo personally gained $100 million for his share of the company.

Company Perspectives:

PanAmSat Corporation is a leading provider of global video and data broadcasting services via satellite. The company builds, owns, and operates networks that deliver entertainment and information to cable television systems, TV broadcast affiliates, direct-to-home TV operators, Internet service providers, and telecommunications companies and corporations. With 21 spacecraft in orbit today, PanAmSat has the world's largest commercial geostationary satellite network.

Even before the final breakup of his company, Anselmo had founded PanAmSat. In 1984 he applied to the FCC for permission to launch a private satellite, to be used to carry television and video into parts of South America. This was an extraordinary thing to try to do, since satellite transmissions had been provided since 1964 by only one company, the International Telecommunications Satellite Organization, or Intelsat. Intelsat was jointly owned by a consortium of over 100 governments. Intelsat built and operated the satellites, while marketing was done by individual member-owners. The United States had a 25 percent share in the consortium, which was headquartered in Washington, D.C. Federal laws favored Intelsat, requiring, for instance, that long distance phone companies to send a percentage of their signals over the satellite network. The company made handsome profits on huge markups, and it had successfully battled for years to keep potential competitors away. But Anselmo was determined to fight his way into the satellite market. While Intelsat was armed with top lobbyists, Anselmo battled with his own wits, sending members of Congress and others antic letters featuring his dog Spot. Then a 1985 FCC ruling authorized private satellites, and Anselmo was on his way.

Building a Solid Customer Base

Anselmo was sole owner of PanAmSat, and he used his own fortune to bring the satellite venture off. He bought a cut-rate satellite, paying $45 million to RCA Astro Space Electronics for one that another customer had cancelled. Full price would have been about $80 million. He had some prospective customers, but none who would commit. It took until 1987 for the FCC to approve the satellite's launch, and Anselmo scheduled the satellite to lift off in June 1988. Again he had to take the cheapest route. The United States had shut down its satellite launch program after the space shuttle Challenger blew up in January 1986. Anselmo went to the European launching consortium, Arianespace, instead. But Arianespace's reputation was not as solid as it might have been—four rockets since 1981 had failed after liftoff. The June 1988 launch was billed as the maiden voyage of a new series of rockets. Ordinarily, the test flight would not have had any paying customers. But PanAmSat signed up. And Anselmo gambled on the success of the flight, insuring the satellite for only half its replacement value. PanAmSat still had to negotiate with individual governments who were members of the Intelsat consortium for something called "landing rights," guaranteeing that his satellite would not interfere with Intelsat signals. Anselmo had won agreements with West Germany and about six other countries by the time of the launch.

Luckily for Anselmo, the launch went perfectly, and PAS-1, as it was called, was up and functional. PanAmSat soon signed up cable broadcasters such as CNN, ESPN, and a sports cable network, as well as the news corporation Reuters, and many customers in Latin America. The satellite went up just as the communist regimes in Eastern Europe were breaking down, and news organizations hungry for reports from Prague and Berlin were happy to use PanAmSat's services. Gross revenues for 1989 were already $17 million, and it looked like the venture would soon pay for itself. By 1991, the PAS-1 was at about full capacity. The Persian Gulf War also brought a burst of news material, and a corresponding rise in satellite use, for PanAmSat as well as Intelsat. Besides news organizations, PanAmSat also signed up universities, such as the University of Florida; telecommunications customers like Chile's Compania de Telefonos; and private companies. With business going so well, the company began raising money to launch more satellites. In August 1991, PanAmSat announced it had made a deal with Hughes Communications Inc. to buy three of its satellites. These would be launched over the next several years and placed in orbit over the Atlantic, the Pacific, and the Indian Ocean. The company promised Hughes $300 million for building the satellites.

By 1993, PanAmSat was bringing in a profit of close to $17 million on sales of $50 million. Still, it did not have anything near the capital it needed to pay Hughes. Rene Anselmo resorted to his old friend Emilio Azcarraga, who now headed Televisa. The two men had not spoken since the mid-1980s, when Azcarraga demanded Anselmo go ahead with the sale of the embattled SIN. But apparently the bad blood was behind them. Azcarraga forked over $200 million, giving his Grupo Televisa a 50 percent stake in PanAmSat. Then through a junk bond offering, PanAmSat raised another $420 million, enough and then some to pay for the building and launching of the new satellites. The first of the new batch went up in July 1994, again on an Arianespace rocket.

The company's next satellite, PAS-3, failed at launching. PanAmSat had had plans to make a public stock offering, but the bad news abut PAS-3 made that seem not such a good idea. But the company went on and launched its next satellite, PAS-4, on schedule. This orbited over the Indian Ocean and primarily served customers in South Asia and Africa. PanAmSat made plans for more satellites, particularly ones for serving television audiences in Latin America.

Rene Anselmo died in September 1995, at the age of 69. The company was left in the hands of Fred Landman, Anselmo's son-in-law. Landman continued as president even after the company made a major change by merging with the satellite unit of Hughes Electronics, Hughes Communications, in 1996. Hughes paid $3 billion for a little over 70 percent of PanAmSat. Televisa reduced its stake in the new company to under ten percent. The combination made a much bigger company, which was publicly held, and still called PanAmSat Corp. Hughes ran a fleet of ten satellites, which served U.S. markets. PanAmSat at the time of the merger had four satellites up, and seven more scheduled for launching over the next two years. Both Hughes and PanAmSat had focused primarily on television markets, instead of telephony or other business communications. After the merger, the new company continued this trend. PAS-6 went up in August 1997, completely dedicated to digital direct-to-

Key Dates:

1984: Rene Anselmo founds the company.
1988: The company's first satellite is launched, the PAS-1.
1995: Anselmo dies.
1996: The company merges with Hughes Electronics and goes public.

home broadcasting in Latin America through a customer company called Sky Latin America. About 80 percent of the newly merged company's business was in television, and most of the remaining 20 percent was dedicated to private business communication networks. Large corporations such as General Motors and Wal-Mart used the satellite link to carry their intracorporate information. Less than one percent of PanAmSat's business was devoted to telephony, and less than 1 percent as well went to Internet hookups in 1997.

A Bigger Network in the Late 1990s and After

One of PanAmSat's satellites failed in orbit in mid-1998, and months later another one was wrecked when the rocket launching it exploded after lift-off. These accidents depressed PanAmSat's stock price, and revenue stayed flat that year. Yet the company announced that it would add nine more satellites over the next three years. By 1999, PanAmSat had successfully launched three of the nine. In April of that year, President and CEO Fred Landman was replaced by the company's former chief operating officer, Douglas Kahn. Kahn had founded his own Internet consulting firm and had also worked in the software industry. He believed the logical direction for PanAmSat was in relaying voice, video, and data for new Internet companies. Though this still represented only a small fraction of PanAmSat's business, it was a rapidly growing category. In 2000 the company set up an Internet access service called Net-36, which was to provide video, such as movies on demand, over the Internet. PanAmSat also kept up with its proposed satellite launch schedule. In 2000, it sent up four new satellites in less than five months. It replaced the PAS-1, the satellite Rene Anselmo had bought for half price in the late 1980s, with a more powerful craft, the PAS-1R. The company's fleet ran to 21 satellites, with two more launches expected for 2001.

However, PanAmSat's revenue did not increase as the company had expected. By the first quarter of 2001 it was clear that the Internet market was not nearly as strong as it had been. The company cut its spending on Net-36, and sharply reined in its revenue expectations for that project. Industry-wide, prices for leasing of satellite time seemed to be falling too. As total revenue fell, PanAmSat struggled to control its costs. In July 2001, the company announced that it was trimming its staff, and consolidating its four Connecticut headquarters into one office in Wilton, Connecticut. Weeks after this news, president and CEO Kahn resigned. He was replaced by a board member, Joseph Wright, Jr., who had been a director of the Federal Office of Management and Budget. Despite its economic woes, the company stuck to its plan to increase its fleet.

Principal Competitors

Intelsat, Ltd.; Loral Space and Communications, Ltd.; Lockheed Martin Corp.

Further Reading

Anderson, Karen, "PanAmSat's Galaxy X Goes Up . . . in Flames," *Broadcasting & Cable*, August 31, 1998, p. 12.
——, "The Path of Kahn," *Broadcasting & Cable*, April 5, 1999, p. 38.
Andrews, Edmund L., "More Orbits Planned by Mr. Anselmo," *New York Times*, August 4, 1991, p. F10.
——, "New Competition in the Sky, and Just in Time for the War," *New York Times*, February 10, 1991, p. F12.
——, "Success With a Satellite Leads to a Space Network," *New York Times*, July 9, 1994, pp. 35, 37.
Dickson, Glen, "As Technologies Grow, So Grows PamAmSat," *Broadcasting & Cable*, August 25, 1997, pp. 44–48.
——, "Post-Merger PanAmSat on Course," *Broadcasting & Cable*, August 25, 1997, pp. 42–44.
Johnston, David Cay, "Rene Anselmo, 69, the Founder of a Satellite Network, Is Dead," *New York Times*, September 21, 1995, p. B12.
Kuznik, Frank, "A Piece of Outer Space to Call His Very Own," *New York Times Magazine*, April 1, 1990, pp. S47, S54–56.
Pasztor, Andy, "PamAmSat's Net, Revenue Drop, And It Trims Growth Forecasts," *Wall Street Journal*, April 17, 2001, p. B14.
Payne, Seth, "Earth to Intelsat: The Party's Over," *Business Week*, September 5, 1988, pp. 94–98.
Stephens, Guy M., "PanAmSat: Fighting the Good Fight," *Satellite Communications*, November 1990, p. 19.
"Upfront," *Satellite Communications*, August 1995, p. 18.

—A. Woodward

Pancho's Mexican Buffet, Inc.

3500 Noble Avenue
Fort Worth, Texas 76111-0407
U.S.A.
Telephone: (817) 831-0081
Fax: (817) 838-1480
Web site: http://www.panchosmexicanbuffet.com

Public Company
Incorporated: 1968, in Delaware
Employees: 2,001
Sales: $56 million (2000)
Stock Exchanges: NASDAQ
Ticker Symbol: PAMX
NAIC: 722211 Limited-Service Restaurants

Pancho's Mexican Buffet, Inc., based in Fort Worth, Texas, owns and operates 47 restaurants, principally in Texas, but also in Arizona, Louisiana, New Mexico, and Oklahoma. It is the only publicly owned company offering Tex-Mex food served in a cafeteria-style, all-you-can-eat buffet. It offers sit-down table service for customers after they have gone through its restaurants' service lines, and it also provides take-out service. Recently, in an attempt to bolster its sales, Pancho's started converting some of its units into a new, upscale restaurant format dubbed Pancho's Buffet & Grill, featuring an expanded menu, newly refurbished and redecorated interiors, and kitchens open to public view. It also introduced a scaled-down version of its traditional restaurants named Pancho's Express Buffet, offering fewer food choices and smaller portions at a quicker service pace and lower prices. Costs at these were cut by replacing the labor-intensive serving lines with a self-service operation. Additionally, it converted a few of its regular restaurants into self-service units and scaled-down its prices. In the spring of 2001, the company completed plans to merge Pancho's Restaurants, Inc., into an affiliate of Stephen Oyster. That step did not involve any immediate changes in the company's operations.

Jesse Arrambide, Jr., Turns Family Business into a Chain

Jesse Arrambide, Jr., founded the first of the company's restaurants in El Paso, Texas. Arrambidie learned to make Mexican specialities–tamales, enchiladas, and tacos—from his mother, but he also learned the art of ''commodity'' or large-quantity cooking while serving onboard a naval troopship in World War II. Years later, he put what he learned to good use, starting first in 1958, when he began using the commodity cooking technique in Pancho's, his family's El Paso bar. Offering a selection of a few Mexican staples served buffet style, Arrambide was soon drawing a dining crowd, and in a few years his success encouraged him to start up a new restaurant chain.

In the 1970s, Pancho's introduced two full-service restaurant concepts that it later abandoned. The first was a seafood restaurant dubbed Spanish Galleon and opened as a three-unit mini chain. The other, like Pancho's traditional restaurants, was a Mexican eatery named Emiliano's, which never grew larger than two units.

In was not until 1979 that Pancho's failed to turn a profit for the first time. At that juncture, founder Arrambide elected to turn over the chain's operating reins to president Hollis Taylor, who became the company's CEO. Although he was a topnotch restaurateur, Arrambide knew that other skills were needed to direct the company and that his hands-on, personal style of running things was no longer appropriate. Taylor was his logical replacement because Taylor had the right credentials for the job–years of experience in finance and accounting.

Pancho's Fares Well Despite 1980s Oil Industry Bust in Its Market Area

By 1982, Pancho's had grown into a chain of 28 restaurants, some located outside of Texas, although the company's epicenter remained there. Over the next five years, the chain would increase to 45, which included the conversion of its Spanish Galleon and Emiliano's restaurants into Pancho's.

The company simply fared well during the 1980s. In fact, unlike most restaurant chains with their business locus squarely in the oil patch, Pancho's was turning a good profit. Only Dallas-based Chili's seemed to be keeping pace with it. In 1986, the chain earned $2.5 million, up 33 percent from the previous year. In the same period, its total sales jumped to $43.1 million, up from $36 million in 1985, almost a 20 percent increase. And that was at a time when oil prices were collapsing and driving the company's market area into a serious recession.

In part, Pancho's survived the oil industry debacle of the mid-1980s because of its pricing strategies. In 1987, Pancho's all-you-can-eat buffet was still just $3.99, which, considering the quantity and variety of food available to customers, was a solid bargain. Children between 6 and 11 ate for half price, and those under 6 ate free. The average lunch ticket totaled just $4, and the average dinner ticket just $4.50. However, bargain meal prices do not tell the whole success story. Taylor and his management team played a vital role, both by improving operational margins and accelerating the company's expansion. By 1987, the company was adding about a dozen units a year and hoped to double its size by 1990, staying mostly within its four-state market—Texas, Louisiana, New Mexico, and Arizona—but also venturing into Oklahoma.

Rapid Expansion Leads to Problems and Strategies in the 1990s

In the new decade of the 1990s, Pancho's found the financial road a little rockier than it had been in the mid-1980s. The company took a reported loss of $3.5 million in 1991, principally arising from its aborted attempt to open three new units in Colorado and, also, its adoption of a different workmen's compensation plan. More troubling was the fact that sales were stagnating. In fiscal 1992, although the company returned to profitability, its revenues, $73.1 million, were slightly down from the previous year's $73.6 million. In order to boost sales, in 1993 Pancho's planned to begin increasing the number of its all-you-can eat cafeteria-style restaurants at an annual rate of 10 percent. It would prove to be a more ambitious plan than circumstances would allow.

Also in 1993, Pancho's founder, Jesse Arrambide, Jr., died. He was succeeded as the company's chairman by his son, Jesse Arrambide III, who inherited the chain's growing problems. Pancho's rapid expansion brought with it new and persistent bottom-line problems, compelling the company to cut back by closing down several unprofitable units. It total number of restaurants in 1994 was 77, but that figure dropped to 70 in 1995. Still, Pancho's continued to open new units up until the third quarter of its fiscal 1995 year, when its losses for the first 9

months had reached $6.07 million. While it had closed some units during that period, it had also opened three new ones in the Texas cities of Galveston, Pasadena, and Baytown, and it was on the verge of opening another in Guadalajara, Mexico, but the disappointing fiscal situation brought a temporary moratorium on further expansion. Of the 70 units remaining open at the end of 1995, 66 were company owned and the remaining four were franchises.

Between 1993 and 1996, the company took some strategic steps designed to improve its efficiency and enhance customer appeal. For one thing, in 1994, it entered into a distribution service agreement with SYGMA Network Inc. Pancho's determined that SYGMA, a unit of Sysco Corp. specializing in distributing foods and supplies for restaurant chains, would both increase delivery frequency and reduce Pancho's distribution costs. The agreement also held the promise of facilitating the distribution of necessities to future Pancho's restaurants located outside its existing network. Despite this change, the rising cost of food compelled the company to raise its own prices somewhat, from $4.69 at lunch and $4.99 at dinner to $4.99 for both lunch and dinner on week days and $5.49 on weekends. To offset the negative impact of its increased prices, the company used an aggressive advertising campaign centered on its unique ''raise the flag'' method of calling for table service. Although all customers went through the cafeteria-style buffet line, once seated they could signal waitresses and waiters for second portions by holding up the small Mexican flags that adorned each table. The scheme had family-dinning appeal and, boosted by a 30-second television commercial, was for a time quite successful. In one period in 1994, it helped increase comparable-store sales by more than 92 percent. Pancho's pushed the family eating idea in other ways as well, granting, for example, a senior-citizen discount of 20 percent and still allowing children under five to eat free.

Working to Develop New Strategies and Concepts

These measures stemmed but did not turn the tide, though, and net losses continued to plague Pancho's. In 1996, the company lost $415,000 on sales of $71.5 million, and in the next year lost $4.71 million on sales of $67 million. However, the loss for the 1997 fiscal year included a pre-tax restructuring charge of $5.1 million. The charge resulted from the shut down costs involved in 11 restaurants and the cost of disentangling the company from its joint Mexican venture. The loss looked worse on paper than it was, and, in fact, in 1997 the average-restaurant sales figure improved to $1.12 million, which was slightly better that the figure from the previous year. However, the next year the picture turned gloomier. Pancho's ended fiscal 1998 with a $12.5 million loss, despite the fact that it had a year-end earnings rise that resulted from the sale of some of its closed restaurant sites. The company's poor stock performance—it was unable to sustain a market value over $5—also forced it to move from the NASDAQ National Market to the NASDAQ Small Cap Market. To prepare for the change, Pancho's used a one-for-three reverse stock split so that it could build the value of its stock above the mandatory minimum trading price of $1 per share.

In 1998, Hollis Taylor indicated that in 1999 the company would try to further reduce its debt and develop new concept

Key Dates:

1966: Jesse Arrambide, Jr., opens Pancho's first restaurant in El Paso, Texas.
1979: Arrambide turns over operational control of company to Hollis Taylor.
1993: Founder Arrambide dies; Jesse Arrambide III is named company's chairman.
1994: Company enters distribution agreement with SYGMA Network Inc.
1998: Pancho's tries out its first Pancho's Express Buffet.
2000: Company rolls out its new Pancho's Buffet & Grill concept.
2001: Company merges with Stephen Oyster affiliate Pancho's Restaurants, Inc.

changes. Between 1996 and 1998, Pancho's had reduced its debt service by 50 percent, bringing down its notes payable to $1.4 million. The net proceeds of $973,000 realized from the sale of two restaurants in October 1998 were primarily used to help pay down that debt. By 1999, the company could thus point with pride to its sound financial condition in addition to its good record of promoting people based on performance, its annual allocation of funds to all its properties, its centralized accounting system, and its reporting requirements that allowed its 48 units a fair degree of autonomy.

2000 and Beyond

One new concept that emerged from planning strategies near the end of the century was Pancho's Express Buffet. Early in 2000, Pancho's announced plans to convert, within a year, four of its units in selected markets into new Pancho's Express Buffet restaurants. Its aim, based on a pressing need to increase its customer base, was to broaden its appeal by reducing meal prices and speeding up its service. The concept, featuring a new logo and signage, a modified interior decor, and a smaller kitchen, was designed to establish a price point of $3.99 per person, $2 below that of its traditional restaurants. Pancho's had tested the new format late in 1998, in Fort Worth, converting one of its established restaurants for the purpose. In 1999, without using any advertising to punch up its business, the unit increased its same-store sales by a very encouraging 30 percent over the previous year and set in motion the plan to convert additional selected units into the new format. It was a new basket into which Pancho's was clearly planning to put more and more of its financial eggs.

To balance the Express Buffet with a pricier alternative, the company also began converting some of its units into a new, Pancho's Buffet & Grill concept. These upscale restaurants offered an expanded buffet menu, with more specialty grill items and a salsa bar, as well as new decor and a new logo and signage. The new Express Buffet and Buffet & Grill concepts were rolled out as part of the company's strategic efforts to regain the momentum it had lost in the industry over the latter part of the 1990s.

In 2001 Pancho's was purchased by fast-food veteren Stephen Oyster. Oyster, who before buying the company held about 9.6 percent of its stock, paid approximately $7.35 million for the chain, purchasing outstanding shares at $5 each, about $1.50 higher than the market price then current. At the time of the buyout, Pancho's chain consisted of 48 owned and operated restaurants in Texas, Arizona, Louisiana, New Mexico, and Oklahoma, just three more units than it had back in 1987. Whether the financial reorganization of Pancho's would have any impact on its growth strategies or major changes in its operations remained to be seen.

Principal Subsidiaries

PAMEX of Texas Inc.; PMB Enterprise West Inc.; PMB INTL Inc.

Principal Competitors

El Chico Restaurants, Inc.; Luby's, Inc.; Mexican Restaurants, Inc.; Prandium, Inc.; Taco Bell Corp.; Taco Cabana, Inc.

Further Reading

Carlino, Bill, "Pancho's: Dramatic Changes Set for '99," *Nation's Restaurant News*, January 11, 1999, p.1.
Cochran, Thomas N., "Pancho's Mexican Buffet Inc.," *Barron's*, August 29, 1988, p.31.
Nichols, Don, "Pancho's: Success in a Slack Market," *Restaurant Business*, June 10, 1987, p.142.
Rodda, Kelli, "Pancho's to Display Its New Concept at Mesquite Eatery," *Fort Worth Business Press*, January 12, 2000, p. 4.
Ruggless, Ron, "Pancho's Poised to Test Climate South of Border," *Nation's Restaurant News*, January 11, 1993, p. 4.
Silver, Deborah, "Small Change," *Restaurants & Institutions*, April 15, 2000, p. 65.
Sullivan, R. Lee, "Raise the Flag," *Forbes*, April 25, 1994, p. 84.

—John W. Fiero

PAYCHEX®

Paychex, Inc.

911 Panorama Trail South
Rochester, New York 14625-0397
U.S.A.
Telephone: (716) 385-6666
Fax: (716) 383-3428
Web site: http://www.paychex.com

Public Company
Incorporated: 1979
Employees: 7,300
Sales: $869.9 million (2001)
Stock Exchanges: NASDAQ
Ticker Symbol: PAYX
NAIC: 541214 Payroll Services; 54121 Data Processing
Services

Paychex, Inc. is the second-largest payroll accounting service in the United States, just behind competitor Automatic Data Processing Inc. (ADP). The company processes payrolls for over 375,000 businesses nationwide. Paychex finds its clients mostly among small businesses with fewer than 200 employees, and its typical client has just 14 employees. Though payroll processing is its main service, Paychex also provides an array of human resource compliance and benefits administration services, including payroll tax and workers' compensation insurance administration, 401(k) plan record-keeping, and section 125—individual health care planning—administration. The firm also offers various employee pay options that include direct deposit. With headquarters in Rochester, New York, the company operates out of more than 100 offices across the United States.

Paychex was founded by B. Thomas Golisano, who still heads the company. In 1971, Golisano worked as a sales manager at Electronic Accounting Systems (EAS), a payroll processing company based in Rochester, New York. EAS aimed its services at large companies with at least 50 employees. Its minimum charges were generally too much for smaller companies to afford, and EAS did not pursue the small-company market. But Golisano, then 29 years old, speculated that small companies had as much need for a payroll accounting service as large companies. A little research at the library confirmed Golisano's suspicions that the potential market was enormous—in 1971, 95 percent of the nation's 3.5 million businesses had fewer than 50 employees. Golisano's father ran his own small heating contracting firm, and Golisano knew firsthand that making out payroll checks was a big headache for the small businessman. Golisano decided to market a payroll service that would be cheap enough for small businesses like his father's to afford.

Early Growth: 1970s

When Golisano first took his idea to EAS, the company was not interested in pursuing small clients. But EAS did agree to rent Golisano an office for his venture, and in 1971 Golisano started his own company, then called PayMaster. His service was offered to companies for only a $5 minimum charge per pay period, and the total fee was proportional to the number of employees. Not only was the price reasonable, but Golisano made his service extremely convenient. Whereas clients of EAS had to fill out forms each pay period and turn them in to the company, Golisano's clients only had to make one phone call. The client simply called in the hours each employee worked, and any changes, and the company did the rest. The process only took about four minutes.

It took Golisano a year to attract 42 clients, and Paychex did not break even for three more years. During that time, Golisano kept the business afloat, somewhat precariously, with borrowed money and credit card loans. Because Paychex clients were small, the company needed a lot of accounts to keep going. Golisano marketed to CPA's, and increasingly got referrals from satisfied customers. After five years, Paychex had attracted about 300 clients in Rochester, and the business was relatively stable.

The impetus to expand the company came from two friends of Golisano, who approached him independently in 1974. One suggested opening a branch office in Syracuse, and he and Golisano would be co-owners. The second asked Golisano to sell him a franchise, and he started up a branch in Miami. Then Golisano began to recruit people to open branches in other

Company Perspectives:

Paychex was founded in 1971 with an objective of providing timely, accurate, and affordable payroll-related services to American business. Focused on that goal, the company and its employees have been successfully serving clients and their employees while achieving consistent growth and strong financial performance for shareholders.

cities. By 1979, he had 17 partners, 11 of them joint ventures and six franchises. These operated in 22 cities spread across the country. Golisano's partners came from various backgrounds—teaching, sales, engineering. Some were high school friends or friends of the family; some were his softball buddies. Golisano gained one partner on a trip to Florida—the doorman of the Boca Raton Hotel. They were all trained them at the company's Rochester base, after which they received help to set up business elsewhere.

By 1979, it began to be apparent that there were problems with the looseness of the organization. Paychex had 200 employees, 5,700 clients, and 18 principals. Different partners had different skills and different aims. Some locations offered different services from others, so that the Paychex product was not consistent. There was little central planning, and little input from one office to another. Golisano decided he wanted to consolidate Paychex into one company. For this he needed the acquiescence of his partners. It was difficult to persuade people who had headed their own branches that they would be better off as part of a more traditional company organization. Golisano came up with an equitable stock distribution formula and presented a five-year plan for the future of the company, which included taking it public. After a tense two-day meeting in the Bahamas, all the principals agreed to the consolidation. In 1979, the company incorporated as Paychex, Inc.

Adjusting to Reorganization and Product Expansion: 1980s

The company began to change quickly. People who had been president of their own branches became vice-president of the new corporation. The company immediately began hiring and training a crew of sales professionals. The branches, which had previously operated more or less independently, were now subjected to management controls such as location-by-location comparisons of productivity. The company also strove to standardize its services. This was extremely important as the company grew. Most of its new business came from referrals from satisfied clients. It was crucial that if one company praised the way its account was handled by, for example, the Syracuse office, a company in New York could also expect the very same service. Golisano himself kept careful track of his growing organization, lugging around a three-ring notebook with hundreds of pages of relevant figures wherever he went.

Paychex initially experienced financial difficulties as a result of the reorganization, and at one point in 1980 cash-flow problems caused the company to suspend salaries. But this crisis was quickly resolved, and Paychex did grow as expected. With its

new professional sales team in place, Paychex began to attract clients in numbers much higher than anticipated. By 1982, the average salesperson was bringing in 100 clients a year. This figure rose steadily. In August 1983, Paychex made its initial public offering. The company raised $7.7 million, which was used to fuel further expansion. By 1986, Paychex had close to 60,000 clients. The company had 58 offices in 32 states. Sales doubled to $51 million in the three years since the public offering. The company was far bigger than Golisano's former employer, EAS.

Revenues close to doubled again in the next three years. In 1989, the company brought in $101 million from its client base of 115,000 accounts. Some of the growth came from acquisitions, such as the 900 clients acquired when Paychex bought a Minneapolis company, Purchase Payroll, in 1987. Paychex also began to expand its services. In 1987, Paychex opened a division of Benefit Services, to keep track of clients' employee benefit plans. The next year, the company opened a Personnel Services division. The new services under this rubric included preparation of employee handbooks, providing information on new laws affecting the workplace, and updating clients on equal-employment regulations. In 1989, Paychex began offering a new service called Taxpay. For clients selecting Taxpay, Paychex prepared payroll tax returns, made the payments, and actually filed the returns with the government. Taxpay provided a real revenue boost to Paychex for two reasons. For each client who selected Taxpay, Paychex gained about a 45 percent increase in revenue on that account due to the fact that this service required only a little additional work. Paychex also benefited from Taxpay because it accepted money in advance to pay the taxes. Before the taxes came due, Paychex could collect interest on this "float" money. Paychex invested the float money, an average daily balance of $4,000 per customer, in tax-free municipal securities, and earned an average annual return of three to four percent. In just a few years, almost half of Paychex payroll clients were also using Taxpay, and Paychex experienced a vital boost in revenue.

Paychex had experienced growth of around 20 percent annually in the 1980s, and the company was consistently featured on lists such as Forbes' "Best Small Companies in America" and the OTC Review list of "100 Most Profitable NASDAQ Companies." The company's success did not go unnoticed, and Paychex began to face competition from the leading payroll accounting service firm, Automatic Data Processing Inc. ADP began a separate sales division to try to hook small business accounts. By 1989, ADP had 400 sales representatives in this division, versus Paychex's 310. In that year, companies with fewer than 50 employees made up 60 percent of ADP's accounts and brought in about twice as much revenue as did Paychex. Even so, the small business market was enormous, and there was still room for growth. And about 80 percent of Paychex's clients renewed every year. Most of the clients the company lost did not turn to another provider. The rate of failure among small businesses is very high, and most lost clients simply went out of business. But to keep up with this turnover, Paychex sales representatives had to bring in an average of 160 new clients a year, or over three a week.

To train salespeople to keep up with this demanding quota, Paychex opened its own school at its Rochester branch. In 1991,

Key Dates:

1971: B. Thomas Golisano establishes PayMaster.
1979: The firm incorporates as Paychex Inc.
1983: Paychex goes public and raises $7.7 million in the IPO.
1998: The firm is added to the S&P 500.
2001: Paychex posts its eleventh consecutive year of record revenues and net income.

Paychex spent approximately $3,500 per trainee to put its new salespeople through a seven-week course in tax law, accounting principles, and selling skills, and to send them on rounds with experienced sales representatives. The expense of the school, which had 11 full-time instructors, was far less than it cost Paychex to recruit a replacement for sales reps who quit or were fired. And new hires who had come through the training school started making money for the company twice as fast as before. Paychex had started in the 1970s with people who had little or no background in either selling or payroll accounting; in the 1990s, the company was operating with a highly professional and well-prepared staff.

Success with New Services: Early to Mid-1990s

By 1990, Paychex had 335 sales representatives and around 125,000 clients. But a recession in the autumn of that year set back the number of paychecks the company was processing, and sales representatives found it hard to meet their ambitious quotas. Nevertheless, the Taxpay service was increasingly successful. At the end of fiscal 1991, Paychex estimated it had lost several million dollars due to recessionary cutbacks, but it more than made up the difference with revenue from Taxpay. That year saw record sales of $137 million, as well as record earnings of $9.6 million. At this time the company had around 26,000 Taxpay customers, and that number rose to over 50,000 by 1993.

Paychex added other services as well. In 1991, the company formed a Human Resource Services division, offering clients a package of employee evaluation and testing tools, employee handbooks, insurance services, customized job descriptions, and other benefits. Paychex used its expertise to help its Human Resource clients keep abreast of government regulations affecting the workplace and took over time-consuming administrative procedures. The company then introduced Paylink in 1993. Paylink appealed to businesses that used personal computers, allowing clients to send payroll information in to the Paychex database via computer modem. In 1994, Paychex added a similar service, Reportlink. After a client's payroll was computed, Reportlink sent the figures back to the client's computers for use in internal reports and accounting.

Paychex continued to roll out new services, though in 1994 over 80 percent of its revenue still came from its basic payroll accounting service. And enrolling new payroll clients was still the key to the company's growth. According to CEO Golisano in a June 13, 1994 *Barron's* article, Paychex aimed to expand its client base by 11 to 12 percent a year in order to keep revenue growing at close to 20 percent annually. This actually meant

bringing in even more new clients than it seemed, because Paychex always had to make up the 20 percent of clients it lost each year. And though in 1994 there were still more than 4.6 million businesses with fewer than 100 employees, more than 60 percent of these had only one to four employees, and thus were too small to be likely potential clients. Paychex also had to contend with increasing competition from software manufacturers. Business owners with personal computers had an array of cheap software packages to choose from that made doing their own payroll relatively cheap and convenient.

But Golisano was confident the company could meet its goal. He took time off in 1994 to run for governor of New York as an independent party candidate. Golisano had become increasingly interested in trying to solve Rochester's urban problems, working with city youths on running their own businesses and heading a city campaign to lower the rate of teen pregnancies. Golisano also had an in-depth knowledge of government regulations and tax codes that he believed harassed small businesses. Though Paychex had made its living dealing with government red tape for its clients, Golisano claimed he would work for tax reform and simplification if elected. A long shot at best, Golisano did not win the governorship, but Paychex flourished. In 1995, the company increased its client base by 11.8 percent, exactly as Golisano had wished. Paychex had over 200,000 clients, and half of these were using the lucrative Taxpay service. Earnings were up almost 40 percent, with net income of $39 million. The company increased its penetration in the California market with two acquisitions—Pay-Fone and Payday. The Human Services division introduced a 401(k) record-keeping service, and other human resources services, as well as Paylink and Taxpay, continued to grow significantly.

Continued Growth: Late 1990s and Beyond

Paychex aimed to expand even more through the remainder of the 1990s. Its market penetration was still low enough to leave room for growth. The company also committed to make use of blossoming technologies in computer networking and digital communications to enhance its service and capabilities. In 1996, Paychex acquired California-based Olsen Computer Systems Inc. and National Business Solutions of Florida. The firm celebrated its 25th anniversary that year and was ranked number two on the "Industrial & Commercial Services" segment of the *Wall Street Journal*'s Shareholder Scoreboard ranking of 1,000 companies.

By 1997, the company had secured five consecutive years of over 30 percent earnings growth. It continued to expand its product and services offerings, including the addition of the Paychex Access Card. In a partnership with First Chicago NBD Corp., the firm developed the card to allow wages to be deposited into a Paychex Access Card account. These wages could then be withdrawn using a MasterCard-branded debit card, thus eliminating the need for paper paychecks. The firm's success continued to be recognized throughout the industry and during 1998, the company was added to Standard and Poor's 500 Index (S&P 500).

Paychex looked for continued expansion in the United States, eyeing the domestic market as a lucrative avenue for increased revenues and earnings. When questioned about whether his company could continue to secure such solid results, Golisano replied in a 1999 *Business Week* article that Paychex only had five percent of the payroll processing market and the entire industry had just 13 percent overall penetration. "So there is no reason that we shouldn't grow at relatively the same rates, as long as we continue to do our job," Golisano stated firmly.

Paychex did just that as it entered the new millennium. In fiscal 2001, the company posted its 11th consecutive year of record revenues and net income. The firm continued to invest in new technology as well as develop new services that catered to its small business clientele. Paychex also held strong to its long-standing belief that employee training was key in its success. In fact, during the year 2000, 5,000 employees were trained at the University of Paychex, and 750,000 hours were spent on field training and ongoing training programs. The firm's focus on its employees led to its first-time ranking in *Fortune*'s 2002 list of "100 Best Companies to Work For" in the United States.

As Paychex forged ahead in the payroll industry, it remained committed to serving small business. According to the company's 2001 annual report, the firm was dedicated to achieving success in the future by focusing on its growth strategy which included increasing its client base, obtaining higher utilization of ancillary services, developing new services, and leveraging its infrastructure. With 30 years of success under its belt, Paychex appeared to be well positioned to secure positive earnings well into the future.

Principal Competitors

Automatic Data Processing Inc.; Administaff Inc.; Ceridian Corp.

Further Reading

Barrier, Michael, "The Power of a Good Idea," *Nation's Business*, November 1990, pp. 34–6.

Burlingham, Bo, and Michael S. Hopkins, "How to Build an Inc. 500 Company," *Inc.*, December 1988, pp. 41–56.

Cowan, Alison Leigh, "Getting Rich on Other People's Paychecks," *Business Week*, November 17, 1986, pp. 148–49.

Gold, Howard R., "Lofty Paychex," *Barron's*, October 24, 1994, p. 13.

"An In-House Sales School," *Inc.*, May 1991, pp. 85–6.

Golisano, B. Thomas, and Robert J. Warth, "Managing After Startup," *Management Accounting*, February 1989, pp. 27–30.

Jaffe, Sam, "Time to Cash in on Paychex?," *Business Week*, August 17, 2001.

Johnson, Heather, "Training Pays Off at Paychex," *Training*, December 2001, p. 50.

Martin, Douglas, "New York's Answer to Ross Perot," *New York Times*, October 2, 1994, Sec. 3, p. 7.

Meeks, Fleming, "Tom Golisano and the Red Tape Factory," *Forbes*, May 15, 1989, pp. 80–2.

Meeks, Fleming, with Jean Sherman Chetzky, "Hear, Watch, and Sell the Customer," *Forbes*, November 11, 1991, pp. 218–20.

Montgomery, Leland, "Business Services," *Financial World*, January 5, 1993, pp. 53–4.

"Newer Services Promise Sharp Gains in Growth," *Barron's*, March 12, 1990, pp. 52–3.

"New Paychex System Pays Without Checks," *American Banker*, April 20, 1998, p. 18.

"Paychex Inc. to Post 3% Increase in Profit for Fiscal 4th Quarter," *Wall Street Journal*, July 7, 1987, p. 36.

"Paychex Posts Record for Annual Earnings," *Business First of Buffalo*, July 2, 2001, p. 6.

"Q&A With Paychex's Thomas Golisano," *Business Week*, March 29, 1999.

Welles, Edward O., "Tom Golisano Goes Public," *Inc.*, November 1992, pp. 126–30.

Yakal, Kathy, "Paychex Founder Ranks High in Innovation, Service, Results," *Accounting Today*, May 19, 1997, p. 22.

Zipser, Andy, "Burning Bright," *Barron's*, April 6, 1992, pp. 18, 40–1.

—A. Woodward
—update: Christina M. Stansell

Pearson plc

80 Strand
London WC2R 0RL
United Kingdom
Telephone: (20) 7411 2000
Fax: (20) 7010 6060
Web site: http://www.pearson.com

Public Company
Incorporated: 1897 as S Pearson & Son Ltd.
Employees: 27,000
Sales: £3.87 billion ($5.7 billion) (2000)
Stock Exchanges: London New York
Ticker Symbol: PSO
NAIC: 51111 Newspaper Publishers; 51112 Periodical
Publishers; 51113 Book Publishers

Since the mid-1990s, Pearson plc has transformed itself from a industrial holding company with a large and sometimes confusing group of interests to the world's largest publisher of educational materials with three major business groups. Pearson Education provides textbooks, learning tools, and testing programs to over 100 million people. The Penguin Group publishes both fiction and non-fiction under the imprints Allen Lane, Avery, Berkley Books, Dutton, Hamish Hamilton, Michael Joseph, Plume, Putnam, Riverhead, and Viking. The Financial Times Group publishes the *Financial Times* newspaper, *Les Echos* in France, *Expansion* in Spain, and a host of personal finance magazines, including *Investors Chronicle*. The restructuring, led by CEO Majorie Scardino and chairman Dennis Stevenson, proved successful as the company's revenues doubled from 1996 to 2000 while its operating profit tripled.

Early Growth As a Building and Contracting Firm

In its early years, the business was dominated by Weetman Dickinson Pearson, and later First Viscount Cowdray, who transformed it into an international contracting concern, which he subsequently converted to an investment trust-type operation. Pearson's roots can be traced to Weetman's grandfather,

Samuel Pearson, who in 1844 became an associate partner in a Huddersfield-based building and contracting firm. In 1856, his eldest son, George, entered the business, which became known as S Pearson & Son, "sanitary tube and brickmakers and contractors for local public works in and around Bradford."

Contracts undertaken at this time were locally based and were for railway companies and, more frequently, for the provision of water supply, drainage, and sewerage facilities to expanding industrial cities. The business developed rapidly, moving its head office in 1857 to nearby Bradford, Yorkshire, and expanding its associated brick-making, glazed tile, and sanitary pipe activities. In 1873, Weetman Pearson entered the business and received a share in its ownership on the retirement of Samuel in 1879.

Pearson, increasingly under the direction of Weetman, began to make a quick metamorphosis into an internationally based concern. In the late 1870s, contracts outside the north of England were undertaken for the first time, and the head office was moved to London in 1884. Five years later projects were in progress as far afield as Egypt, the United States, Canada, and Mexico with port works, railway construction and tunneling, and water supply and drainage predominating. Between 1884 and 1914 some 67 projects, with a total value of almost £43 million, were undertaken. Of these, 36—valued at £16.5 million or 38 percent of the total—were located outside Great Britain and Ireland; with 10 percent in the United States and Canada; 45.5 percent in Central and South America; and 7 percent in Egypt, Spain, China, Malta, and Bermuda.

The British government was a major client, as were municipalities, railway and harbor companies, and water utilities. Contracts of particular note included the Admiralty Harbour at Dover; the Blackwall Tunnel under the River Thames in London; the East River Railway Tunnels, New York, for which a U.S. subsidiary, S Pearson & Son Inc., was formed to carry out the work; Malta Dry Docks and Breakwaters; and Halifax Dry Dock in Canada.

However, Mexico was the country where Pearson made its greatest mark, to the extent that Weetman Pearson, by now a member of Parliament, was dubbed in the House of Commons

Company Perspectives:

We have a simple strategy that we all understand and believe in—we will steadily increase value for Pearson's shareholders. We want to make outstanding returns for our shareholders by creating, owning, applying, and exploiting intellectual property and we want to do this in a way that is brave, imaginative, and decent.

and elsewhere as the "Member for Mexico." The first contract for the Mexican government, which ran from 1890 to 1896, was for the construction of the Mexican Grand Canal to drain Mexico City and its surrounding area. A succession of other government-owned or sponsored projects followed—the £3 million conversion of Vera Cruz harbor into a modern seaport; the £2.5 million reconstruction of the Tehuantepec Railway and its associated terminal ports, linking the Atlantic and Pacific Oceans; and the Salina Cruz harbor and docks, at £3.3 million.

Expansion Into Oil and Electric Power: Early 1900s

A growing confidence between Mexican dictator Porfirio Díaz and Weetman Pearson consolidated Pearson's Mexican interests. Under the Tehuantepec Railway contract, Pearson built the facilities at cost, provided part of the capital, and then managed the railway and ports, taking part of the profits as remuneration. This entry into the mainstream of Mexican business soon led to other interests, most importantly oil. In 1901, Pearson began to acquire oil-bearing land and by 1906 owned 600,000 acres and had royalty leases over about another 250,000. Oil refining began, and in 1908 Pearson entered the Mexican oil retail trade in direct competition with Walter Pierce Oil Company, mostly owned by Standard Oil Company, resulting in severe price competition.

However, it was not until 1910 that the business was transformed into an international oil concern with the discovery of the Potrero de Llano oil field. The Aguila (Mexican Eagle) Oil Company Ltd. was formed to take over most of Pearson's oil interests and make a public issue of securities. In 1912, as a means of extending this business, the Eagle Oil Transport Company Ltd. and the Anglo Mexican Petroleum Company Ltd. were formed to focus on international distribution and sales. Some £12 million of Pearson capital had by now been committed to Mexican oil. During World War I, an immense trade was done in supplying the British government. In 1919, the Royal Dutch group acquired a large shareholding in the Aguila and took over management control, although for many years Pearson continued to own a large part of the company. In 1919, Whitehall Petroleum Corporation Ltd. was formed to take over Pearson's oil interests and prospect—mostly unsuccessfully—for oil worldwide. Its most notable action was the establishment of the Amerada Corporation, a major U.S. oil company, in 1919.

Another feature of Pearson's diversification after 1900 was the generation, supply, and application of electric power in Latin America. This began when Díaz invited Weetman Pearson to electrify and then manage the tramway system—later extended to electricity supply generally—in Vera Cruz, a service which was carried into effect by the Vera Cruz Electric Light, Power, and Traction Company Ltd. Soon Pearson developed similar schemes elsewhere in Mexico. After World War I, these developments were extended outside Mexico, when undertakings in Chile were acquired. The Chilean interests were subsequently modernized and managed by Pearson's Cia. Chilena de Electricidad. All these electrical interests were consolidated into Whitehall Electric Investments Ltd. in 1922.

In 1897, Pearson, which was then reckoned to be the world's leading contractor, was converted into a limited company with an issued share capital of £1 million, all of which was owned by the Pearson family or by non-family directors. In 1907, Whitehall Securities Ltd. was formed to take over all of Pearson's non-contracting activities, while in 1919, S Pearson & Son (Contracting Department) Ltd. took over the firm's contracting interests. S Pearson & Son Ltd. became the group's holding company.

Postwar Expansion

During World War I, the contracting company was preoccupied with military contracts, of which the huge munitions plant at Gretna Green in Scotland—worth £9.2 million—was the largest. However, in the late 1920s the construction business was closed down, not sold, as a going concern apparently as a result of family whim. By now, however, Pearson had diversified well beyond the supplying of oil and electricity. In 1908, Weetman Pearson was a member of a large syndicate which acquired the London evening newspaper *The Westminster Gazette*. After the war, he acquired total control of the newspaper, converted it into a morning daily, and began to build around it a group of provincial newspapers. In 1919, the company established Whitehall Trust Ltd. as a finance and issuing house, and at about the same time its principal asset, a substantial interest in Lazard Brothers & Company, the London merchant bank, was acquired. A partnership was formed with Dorman Long & Company Ltd. to develop a coal mining and iron and steel industry in Kent, although this project was not to figure prominently in Pearson's affairs,

When Lord Cowdray died in 1927, he had completely reshaped his family's business. He was succeeded as chairman by his second son, Clive, while his eldest son, Harold, played a significant part in the development of Westminster Press Ltd. The management philosophy was to develop and extend the core businesses through local management. In 1929, the electricity businesses in Mexico and Chile were sold, but similar electricity undertakings were developed in southwest England. The company played a substantial role in establishing British Airways Ltd.—not the state-owned business that came to be known as British Airways PLC—in 1935.

The most significant result of World War II was the purchase of strategic Pearson assets by the British government. These included the airline interests but, much more significantly, the interest in the Amerada Petroleum Corporation, which was compulsorily acquired in 1941. The year 1948 saw the nationalization of the electricity undertakings in the west of England.

In the 1950s, the general strategy of Pearson, which from 1954 was under the chairmanship of the Third Lord Cowdray, was to concentrate on well-defined sectors and within them

Key Dates:

1844: Samuel Pearson becomes an associate partner in a building and contracting firm.
1910: The Aguila Oil Company Ltd. is created to oversee most of Pearson's oil interests.
1919: Whitehall Petroleum Corporation Ltd. is formed to take over Pearson's oil interests; Whitehall Trust is created as a finance and issuing house.
1957: Pearson acquires an interest in Financial News Ltd.
1969: The company goes public.
1979: A controlling interest in Camco Inc. is purchased.
1984: The company's name is changed to Pearson plc.
1985: Subsidiary Penguin Publishing Co. Ltd. acquires Viking of the U.S. and the Michael Joseph and Hamish publishing houses.
1987: U.S.-based publisher Addison Wesley is purchased.
1988: The firm buys Les Echos Group.
1989: Pearson begins divesting its oil businesses.
1993: The company begins to focus on its media businesses related to information, education, and entertainment.
1994: Software Toolworks is purchased and renamed Mindscape.
1996: HarperCollins Educational, Twenty-First Century Business Publications, and Putnam Berkeley are acquired; Westminster Press is sold.
1998: Pearson acquires Simon & Schuster's education, reference, and business and professional publishing division.
2002: Pearson sells its 22 percent stake in RTL Group to Bertelsmann AG.

build up specialist niche businesses producing quality products, with much decision-making devolved to local management. This was to be a successful and enduring philosophy. The five legs on which the business now stood were financial services, publishing, oil, manufacturing, and investment trusts.

Acquisitions and Divestitures: 1950s–80s

In 1945, the surviving oil interests were largely confined to oil and gas properties owned by Rycade Corporation of the United States. In the 1950s, the activities of this company were extended, while particularly successful expansion also occurred in western Canada through Whitehall Canadian Oils Ltd. In addition, a small interest in Amerada was reacquired. Publishing was strengthened in 1957 when a substantial interest was taken in Financial News Ltd., which in turn owned a large interest in the *Financial Times* and a small range of quality periodicals. In 1960, the last of the overseas electricity utilities was disposed of when the business of Athens Piraeus Electricity Company, which had operated under a concession granted in 1925, was sold to the Greek state, although a smaller trolley bus operation in Athens was retained until about 1970. In manufacturing industry, a substantial interest in Acton Bolt Ltd., makers of nuts and bolts, was sold to GKN Ltd. in 1959, and another in Saunders-Roe Ltd., builder of helicopters, was sold to Westland Aircraft Company Ltd. in 1959.

In 1969, for tax and fiscal reasons, the business was converted into a quoted company and 20 percent of the equity was sold to the public. The company was then valued at £20 million, and profits before tax, attributable to shareholders, totaled almost £7 million. About 25 percent of profits came from financial services which largely consisted of Lazard Brothers & Co. Ltd., which was now almost fully owned by Pearson and Whitehall Securities Corporation, which provided services to the group. An additional 30 percent of profits were generated from a 51 percent holding in the publicly quoted S Pearson Publishers Ltd., owner of the *Financial Times*; Westminster Press Ltd., controller of about 60 local and provincial newspapers; and the Longman Group Ltd., a general publishing house. Oil interests in North America, which were reorganized at the end of the 1960s, provided about 20 percent of profits. Manufacturing, where the chief asset was a 59 percent interest in Standard Industrial Group Ltd., another publicly quoted company, included interests in pottery, glass, engineering, and warehousing. This contributed about 7 percent of profits. Finally, 15 percent of profits were contributed by investment trusts.

In the 1970s, the North American interests of Pearson were mostly represented by the holding in Ashland Oil, held by Midhurst Corporation. This holding was slowly reduced and the proceeds used to acquire other North American interests, especially in oil exploration and production services, as part of an effort to extend Pearson's interests outside the United Kingdom and into North America. The most significant move was the acquisition of Camco Inc., supplier of services and equipment to the oil industry on a worldwide basis, in which a controlling interest had been purchased by 1979. This business was subsequently built up by acquisition. Lignum Oil Co. and Hillin Oil, involved in the acquisition and development of oil producing properties, were also acquired, but were sold in 1989 as part of a divestment of oil exploration activities which also included the sale of Whitehall Petroleum.

Financial services remained grouped around the merchant bank of Lazard Brothers in which Pearson, in 1990, had a 50 percent interest, reduced from 79 percent. This decrease followed an ownership reorganization in 1984 when, as an early response to increasing internationalization of the securities industry, Lazard of London and two other Lazard houses, in Paris and New York, became more closely linked. An exchange of ownership interests resulted in Pearson having a 10 percent profit interest in both these houses. Notwithstanding the acquisition in 1976 of the unowned part of Embankment Trust Ltd., investment trust and other portfolio-type investments were decreased in order to fund acquisitions.

At time, Pearson's interests in manufacturing were concentrated in the Doulton fine china business, which emerged as a world leader with a strong overseas distribution network. The engineering interests were strengthened in 1980 by the acquisition of the high technology businesses of Fairey Industries Ltd., and their merging with Pearson's other engineering interests in 1982. However, these relatively minor activities were disposed of in 1986 as part of group policy to focus more on core activities. Similarly, involvement in the manufacture of specialist glass, which had expanded rapidly in the 1970s, was terminated in 1982 with the sale of Doulton Glass Industries Ltd.

The minority interest in Pearson Longman Ltd. was acquired in 1982. Publishing, the division of Pearson with the highest proportion of profits, embraced financial publications that included not just the *Financial Times*—the world's leading financial newspaper—but also a host of important financial periodicals, including *The Economist*, in which Pearson had a 50 percent interest, and the *Investor's Chronicle*, as well as on-line electronic publications. Longman by acquisition and organic expansion, emerged as a major publisher of professional, educational, medical, and general reference publications. Penguin also held a strong international position in publishing both paper- and hard-back fiction and expanded its operations through the acquisition, among others, of Viking of the United States and the Michael Joseph and Hamish Hamilton publishing houses in 1985. Westminster Press expanded into newspapers distributed free of charge and disposed of several newspapers paid for by readers, as it concentrated resources in areas where it was a clear market leader. In 1987, the acquisition of Addison Wesley of the United States, with a strong schools and college list, confirmed Pearson as a major international publishing group. The global holdings increased in 1988 by a share swap with Elsevier, a leading Dutch publishing company, and through the acquisition of the French Les Echos Group. The swap with Elsevier was undone in 1991, when the two companies were unable to devise merger terms acceptable to all parties.

One new interest, since the mid-1980s linked to the publishing division, was the expansion into daytime family entertainment. Although Pearson had owned Chessington Zoo for many years, this area was fully established through the acquisition of Madame Tussauds in 1978. Since then a number of acquisitions were made and developed, virtually all U.K. based. Further developments in this general sector included the acquisition of a 25 percent holding in Yorkshire Television Ltd. in 1981, and a less than successful involvement, which was terminated, in filmmaking. It also gained a 16 percent share in BSkyB, the first satellite television service in the United Kingdom, in 1990.

While Pearson's shares became much more widely held, the Pearson family continued to hold a large—but not controlling—share of the equity in the late 1980s. The Third Lord Cowdray retired from the chairmanship in 1977 and was succeeded by Lord Gibson and then by Lord Blakenham in 1983, both of whom were family members. The company's name was changed to Pearson plc in 1984, and by the early 1990s, the company could claim to be one of the most successful British-based companies.

Focus on Media-Related Businesses: 1990s and Beyond

Indeed, Pearson had become quite large with considerable holdings spread across many industries. In an attempt to increase profits, the company began its migration towards focusing solely on its media businesses related to information, education, and entertainment. For the remaining years of the 1990s, Pearson accelerated its acquisition and divestiture activity to mold itself into a publishing industry giant.

Pearson's purchases included Extel Financial Ltd. for £74 million in 1993, Thames Television, and Software Tool-works—renamed Mindscape—for £312 million in 1994. The company also acquired the Register Group Ltd. and Future Publishing Ltd. that year, along with Interactive Data Corporation in 1995. The firm beefed up its entertainment holdings by purchasing stakes in several television concerns along with Grundy Worldwide Ltd. and ACI. At the same time, the company sold off its interest in Camco International Inc., Yorkshire Tyne-Tees TV, its 9.75 percent direct holding in BSkyB for £560 million, and Westminster Press.

Pearson added to its publishing arsenal in 1996 by acquiring HarperCollins Educational, Twenty-First Century Business Publications, and Putnam Berkeley, which was renamed Penguin Putnam Inc. The most dramatic changes however, came in 1997 with the appointment of Majorie Scardino as CEO. The first woman to lead a major British concern, Scardino immediately set plans in motion to increase revenue growth and bolster the firm's reputation in the media industry. She was joined by Lord Dennis Stevenson, the company's first non-family chairman, who had replaced Blakenham earlier in the year.

In an attempt to boost U.S. sales of its *Financial Times* newspaper, Pearson began heavily investing in advertising and printing, hoping to capitalize on the paper's global business coverage—coverage that its competitors lacked. The duo also stepped up the pace of the firm's restructuring program, and divested its Troll, TVB, and Churchill Livingstone holdings in 1997. The following year its sold the famed Tussauds Group, Capitol Publishing, Future Publishing, Mindscape, and its Law and Tax publishing concerns. The company also made several key purchases, including All American Communications Inc., Resource Data International, and several newspaper concerns. The most significant acquisition however, was that of Simon & Schuster's education, reference, and business publishing arm for $4.6 billion. The deal secured Pearson's position as the world's largest educational publisher.

In 1999, the company continued to trim its portfolio with the sale of its Lazard holdings for £410 million. It also sold its Macmillan Library and General reference businesses, Jossey-Bass, and various other non-core holdings. It also purchased E Source Inc. and Thomson Financial Securities Management.

Pearson entered the new millennium looking much different then it had just five years earlier. Scardino's strategy of streamlining company operations appeared to be paying off as revenues had doubled since 1996 and were climbing to the £4 billion mark. Operating profit had also tripled during that time period to £686 million. The company continued to make strategic purchases to complement its media holdings. In 2000, National Computer Systems Inc. was acquired for $2.5 billion and merged into its Pearson Education unit. Dorling Kindersley plc was also purchased and its operations were folded into The Penguin Group. Pearson then combined its asset valuation business with Data Broadcasting Inc. In July 2000, the company merged its television holdings with CLT-Ufa to form the RTL Group S.A. It made its final exit from television however, when it sold its 22 percent stake in RTL to Bertelsmann AG in 2002. By now, the company stood as a global media company with its businesses concentrated on education, business information, and consumer publishing.

While Pearson had made great strides in becoming a leading media concern, the company faced economic challenges. During 2001, the firm was forced to cut its Internet spending related to the *Financial Times* Web site. The Penguin Group was also hit by an industry wide drop-off in backlist sales. The Latin American market weakened and advertising sales in company's publications fell dramatically. As such, profits in the Financial Times Group fell by nearly 40 percent in 2001. As economic hard times continued, Pearson cut costs and revised its business strategies in order to combat the financial downturn. Nevertheless, Scardino remained optimistic about the company's future. Having accomplished what she set out to do, the CEO held firm to her belief that Pearson would remain a leader in the publishing industry.

Principal Subsidiaries

Addison-Wesley Longman Inc. (U.S.); Addison Wesley Educational Publishers Inc. (U.S.); Pearson Education Ltd.; Prentice Hall Inc. (U.S.); NCS Pearson Inc. (U.S.); Financial Times Group Ltd.; Financial Times Business Ltd.; Data Broadcasting Inc. (U.S.; 60%); Les Echos SA (France); Recoletos Compania Editorial SA (Spain; 78.97%); Penguin Putnam Inc. (U.S.); The Penguin Publishing Co. Ltd.; Penguin Books Australia Ltd.; Doring Kindersley Holdings Ltd.

Principal Operating Units

Pearson Education; The Penguin Group; The Financial Times Group.

Principal Competitors

Dow Jones & Company Inc.; The News Corporation Ltd.; Vivendi Universal Publishing.

Further Reading

Colby, Laura, ''Yankee Expansionist Builds British Empire,'' *Fortune*, March 16, 1998, p. 102.

Jeffrey, Don, ''All American Acquired by Pearson,'' *Billboard*, October 11, 1997, p. 96.

Milliot, Jim, ''Acquisitions Boost Pearson Book Sales to $1.5 Billion,'' *Publishers Weekly*, April 28, 1997, p. 11.

Morais, Richard C., ''The U.S. Is a Very Noisy Place,'' *Forbes*, June 16, 1997, p. 54.

''Pearson Is Slashing Its Spending On the *Financial Times* Web Site,'' *Marketing*, March 15, 2001, p. 2.

''Pearson Plc Issues Trading Update,'' *Business Wire*, December 18, 2001.

Spender, J.A., *Weetman Pearson. First Viscount Cowdray*, London: Cassell & Co. Ltd., 1930.

''Weetman Dickson Pearson. 1st Viscount Cowdray,'' *Dictionary of Business Biography: A Biographical Dictionary of Business Leaders Active in Britain in the Period, 1860–1980*, Vol. IV, edited by David Jeremy, London: Butterworth & Co. Ltd., 1985.

Young, Desmond, *Member for Mexico. A Biography of Weetman Pearson, First Viscount Cowdray*, London: Cassell & Co., Ltd., 1966.

—John Orbell
—update: Christina M. Stansell

Peek & Cloppenburg KG

Berliner Allee 2
D-40212 Düsseldorf
Germany
Telephone: (49) (211) 3662-0
Fax: (49) (211) 3662-697
Web site: http://www.peekundcloppenburg.de

Private Company
Incorporated: 1901 as Peek & Cloppenburg
Employees: 8,800
Sales: DM 2 billion ($957 million, 2000)
NAIC: 44814 Family Clothing Stores; 44811 Men's
   Clothing Stores

Based in Düsseldorf, Peek & Cloppenburg KG is among Germany's leading apparel retailers. The company owns 65 large fashion stores in big cities, offering clothing for the whole family in the middle and upper price range. Peek & Cloppenburg is also present with two stores in Vienna and with one in Warsaw. The company's subsidiary Anson's Herrenhaus KG sells menswear in 16 sales outlets, including stores in Belgium and the Netherlands. Peek & Cloppenburg and Anson's stores carry upscale designer labels such as Armani, Bugatti, Cerruti, Joop, Ralph Lauren, Hugo Boss, S. Oliver, Bugatti, Esprit, and Strenesse in a shop-in-shop system. The company also sells clothing under its own labels such as McNeal and Savannah. Peek & Cloppenburg is majority-owned and run in the fourth generation by members of the Cloppenburg family.

Beginnings in the 19th Century

The roots of Peek & Cloppenburg go back to the 19th century. In 1869, Johann Theodor Peek and Heinrich Cloppenburg established their first fashion store in the Dutch city of Rotterdam. The two German apparel merchants had moved from Westphalia to the Netherlands, as many others had done, including the Brennikmeyer family, which later founded Germany's leading textile retail group and Peek & Cloppenburg's foremost competitor. However, Heinrich Cloppenburg's son James moved back to Germany, and in March 1901 founded Peek & Cloppenburg in Germany. In the same year the first

Peek & Cloppenburg stores opened in Düsseldorf's Schadow-strasse and in Berlin's Gertraudenstrasse.

From the Turn of the Century to World War II

In the beginning, Peek & Cloppenburg stores carried only men's apparel. At the turn of the century, it was still most common for clothes to be tailored to the customer's specifications, which made industrial manufacturing of clothes impossible. However, with the appearance of industrial sewing machines apparel makers thought about ways to overcome this obstacle. Peek & Cloppenburg came up with a uniform size system for men's clothes which enabled them to order and stockpile larger batches of a certain style. In 1907, the company started printing and mailing catalogues to potential customers to promote its self-produced high-quality menswear. In the early days the catalogues included drawings—not photographs—of the available models and their price. After 1910, Peek & Cloppenburg started offering a line of clothes suitable for the tropics, catering to the needs of Germans who lived in the country's African colonies. In 1911, James Cloppenburg's brother-in-law Paul Schröder founded his own company in Hamburg and opened a first store there in the same year. In order to distinguish the two independent firms, they were later referred to as "P&C North" for the company in Hamburg and "P&C West" for the Düsseldorf-based firm, the history of which is the main focus of the following sections.

In 1926 James Cloppenburg, Jr., the son of James Cloppenburg, entered the business. After the economic downturn following World War I had been overcome, Germany enjoyed a short period of economic growth in the second half of the 1920s. During that time, Peek & Cloppenburg provided Düsseldorf's and Berlin's upper-class families with elegant clothes. Over time Peek & Cloppenburg expanded its product range, starting with clothing for boys. In the mid-1930s the company also started carrying women's apparel. In 1936, another Peek & Cloppenburg store opened in Frankfurt's Zeil boulevard, followed by another one in Essen one year later.

Recovery after World War II

World War II once again interrupted the development of the business—and it could have been the end for Peek & Clop-

Company Perspectives:

Social Awareness: *It is of utmost importance to P&C to offer our customers goods produced under human conditions with concern for environmental protection while respecting the industrial safety regulations of the respective country. We therefore only work with companies who practice fair remuneration, social security, and protective health measures, prohibit child labor and take measures to protect the environment. These companies in turn are obligated to only accept materials from suppliers who are obligated by contract to fulfill these same requirements.* Product Safety: *P&C requires each supplier to adhere to German law by obtaining chemical analyses before each delivery especially regarding the "Food and Items of Usage Law." In addition P&C randomly tests goods received at different European laboratories for forbidden Azo dyes and other substances (e.g. pesticides, heavy metals, PCP, formaldehyde, nickel and now also TBT, etc.).*

penburg. All of its stores, centrally located in inner cities, were destroyed during the war. But the company owners decided to live up to the challenge and started making plans for new stores in Düsseldorf, Frankfurt, Essen, and Berlin. Reconstruction went slowly since raw materials and equipment were scarce. However, that didn't stop the company from selling clothes again right after the war. A provisional store was opened near Frankfurt's Kaiserstrasse, and in October 1945 on the Zeil boulevard. Finally, in 1950, the old location in the city of Frankfurt was opened again, starting out with a limited store size. Two new Peek & Cloppenburg stores opened in the 1950s: one in Recklinghausen, a city in the Ruhr, in 1955, and one in Berlin in 1956.

Because of the prevailing shortage of supplies of all kinds, including apparel, Peek & Cloppenburg decided to set up their own clothing production. By 1963 about 650 people worked at the company's menswear factory in Herne. At that time Peek & Cloppenburg was considered to be among Germany's leading manufacturers of men's clothes. However, at the end of the 1960s Peek & Cloppenburg decided to discontinue its production arm which was sold and later became known as the firm Dressmaker. While rebuilding and modernizing old stores, the company focused on expanding its distribution network. In the 1970s, Peek & Cloppenburg also invested in advertising, establishing the image of a modern, high-quality brand fashion retailer. The 1970s also marked the beginning of a period of business expansion which lasted for about two decades. Peek & Cloppenburg opened six new stores in the 1970s and eleven in the 1980s, many of them located in newly opened shopping malls. The company also started buying up its competitors. In 1969, Peek & Cloppenburg acquired the Mannheim-based firm Neugebauer and Wuppertal-based Klischan. In 1973, Peek & Cloppenburg bought the firms Vetter in Karlsruhe and Hettlage in Krefeld. In the late 1970s, the company acquired two more competitors: Lünen-based Kepa and Römer located in Offenbach. In the mid-1980s Peek & Cloppenburg took over three department stores from the German Hertie chain, located in Dortmund, Herne, and Castrop-Rauxel. By 1986, Peek & Cloppenburg had become one of Germany's leading textile retailers, generating total sales of DM 1 billion annually in 32 sales outlets.

Expansion Under New Leadership Begins in 1986

After steering Peek & Cloppenburg for 60 years, James Cloppenburg died in 1986 at age 84. His son Harro Uwe had worked in the family business since 1968 and became CEO at age 45. He kept expanding the business in the early 1990s. When the Peek & Cloppenburg store in Essen moved to a new location in 1989, the old store was re-opened as a special store for meanswear under the brand name "Anson's" which was managed by the newly-founded Anson's GmbH. The company decided that in every city where a Peek & Cloppenburg store already existed, the second store would be an Anson's. The concept was to offer a wide range of menswear, including special sizes, from classical to high fashion. With a focus on the middle price range, Anson's offered more expensive designer brands as well as less expensive clothes under the store's own labels. While there was a lot of redundancy with the menswear offered at Peek & Cloppenburg stores in the beginning, Anson's started developing its own profile.

In early 1993, Peek & Cloppenburg acquired 15 stores from Bernward Leineweber GmbH & Co. KG, adding 1,100 employees to its payroll. Many of the former Leineweber stores were located in northern Germany, especially in Hamburg. In order to avoid problems with the Hamburg-based Peek & Cloppenburg group, the company decided to push the Anson's concept and converted most Leineweber stores into Anson's stores. Anson's GmbH was transformed into Anson's Herrenhaus KG which operated independently from its parent company. Harro Uwe Cloppenburg's son Hendrik became Anson's purchasing director. Later his younger son John became part of Anson's management team.

Harro Uwe Cloppenburg was mainly responsible for everything connected with buying and selling clothes, including personnel. All other business functions such as accounting, controlling, IT, logistics, and public relations he handed over to Hartmut M. Krämer, a manager whom he had hired on recommendation of a common friend. In 1989, Krämer became a co-owner of the company—at that time the only one who was not a member of the Peek or Cloppenburg families. Harro Uwe Cloppenburg avoided public appearances. He rarely attended industry events and maintained relationships by entertaining a few selected business partners at his home. Krämer represented the company at the obligatory trade shows and other public events such as the opening of new Peek & Cloppenburg stores. At the same time the influence of the Peek family diminished. By the mid-1990s only one family member had remained in the Peek & Cloppenburg management: Walter Peek, who directed the company's women's apparel department.

In the mid-1990s Peek & Cloppenburg kept opening new fashion stores for the whole family. As early as 1987, the company was planning to tear down the old building in West-Berlin's Tauentzien that housed Peek & Cloppenburg's flagship store in Berlin. However, U.S. retail group W. Woolworth, which ran a store right next to Peek & Cloppenburg and who at first wanted to cooperate with the company, later changed their mind. The location was mainly frequented by upscale clientele while Woolworth targeted less moneyed consumers and didn't want to risk a huge investment in the wrong place. Finally, in the early 1990s Woolworth gave up its location, and Peek & Cloppenburg built a new store within 14 months. The new store

Key Dates:

1901: The first Peek & Cloppenburg stores open in Berlin and Düsseldorf.
1911: Peek & Cloppenburg North is founded.
1936: Peek & Cloppenburg stores start carrying women's clothes.
1945: All of the company's stores are destroyed.
1986: Harro Uwe Cloppenburg takes over as CEO after his father's death.
1991: Anson's is established as a second store concept.
1995: Peek & Cloppenburg's flagship store in Berlin opens its doors.
1997: Two Peek & Cloppenburg stores open in the Austrian capital, Vienna.
1998: Dutch P&C Groep becomes a wholly owned subsidiary.
1999: The company launches an image campaign under the slogan: ''We Are family.''
2001: The first Peek & Cloppenburg store in Poland opens in Warsaw.

with six levels and 450 employees opened in spring 1995. The second-largest Peek & Cloppenburg store—only the company's Frankfurt location was larger—was the biggest investment in the company's history to date. For the first time the store offered fashion for young people, including the Levi's, Diesel, and Chevignon labels as well as its own Review label. Another innovation was the ''Fashion Sport'' section. New Peek & Cloppenburg stores were also opened in big eastern German cities such as Potsdam, Leipzig, Dresden, and Stralsund. Between 1986 and 1995, the number of Peek & Cloppenburg stores grew from 32 to 47.

Activities in Western Europe in the 1990s

While the company had successfully expanded against the industry trend in Germany up until the mid-1990s, Peek & Cloppenburg was less fortunate with its ventures abroad. Through its subsidiary Gerhard Horn KG, Peek & Cloppenburg held a 42.3 percent share in the Dutch P&C Groep N.V. P&C Groep generated about DM 400 million in sales, employed 1,600 people and owned 42 stores in the Netherlands and 14 in Belgium, including Peek & Cloppenburg stores; the Somebody outlets that sold the company's own brand; and the Mac&Maggie stores. The group's second major shareholder was Amsterdam-based firm Vendex International N.V. which held almost 25 percent of the shares. The remaining P&C Groep stock was traded at the Amsterdam stock exchange.

Beginning in 1994, Peek & Cloppenburg continuously increased its interest in P&C Groep. By January 1995, Peek & Cloppenburg had acquired the share majority of more than 68 percent; in May 1998, the company took over the Vendex shares and bought the remaining 5 percent of the shares which were publicly traded. By December 1998, P&C Groep had become a wholly owned Peek & Cloppenburg subsidiary. However, while P&C Groep had turned up profits until 1993, the group started generating losses in the following years. To turn

around the trend of decreasing sales, P&C Groep introduced the shop-in-shop system in six of its Peek & Cloppenburg stores such as in Brussels and Antwerp. Besides the company's own brands such as Somebody, No Matter, and Sideway, P&C Groep started selling designer brands, including Bugatti, Esprit, Levi's, S. Oliver, and Marc Aurel, and also introduced baby clothing under the Beebies label. However, P&C Groep's efforts to stop the downward trend were not successful. With consumers in the Netherlands and Belgium holding back on clothing purchases, the cost for advertising and reorganization didn't turn into higher profits. Consequently Peek & Cloppenburg sold off most of P&C Groep's stores in the late 1990s. Between November 1995 and February 1996, the Mac&Maggie stores in the Netherlands and Belgium were sold; the two German stores in Essen and Cologne were sublet. Another 22 stores were sold to the German Charles Vögele Group. By spring 2001, the number of Peek & Cloppenburg stores in the Netherlands and Belgium had decreased to less than ten. All of the remaining stores were planned to be transformed into Anson's stores.

Besides its activities in Belgium and the Netherlands, Peek & Cloppenburg also ventured into neighboring Austria. In spring 1997, Peek & Cloppenburg announced that it had teamed up with Hamburg-based Peek & Cloppenburg North to expand into Western Europe. The two independent companies which already cooperated in purchasing, personnel and advertising, founded a subsidiary in Austria in which the Düsseldorf-based group had a majority interest. In 1998, two Peek & Cloppenburg stores opened in Vienna which were stocked with women's fashion by Peek & Cloppenburg North, while Peek & Cloppenburg West managed the menswear department. In 2001, Peek & Cloppenburg opened its first store in a shopping mall in Warsaw. The company planned to open more stores in Austria and Poland and to expand into Hungary after 2001.

Reorganization and A New Image

The late 1990s were a hard time for Germany's fashion department store chains. Many of them, such as long-time market leader C&A, were struggling with declining sales. Others went out of business or were bought up by larger competitors. Peek & Cloppenburg managed to resist the trend mainly by opening new stores, thereby generating more volume. However, sales per square meter were stagnating and even declining in some locations. The variety of Peek & Cloppenburg stores—from big houses with over 16,000 square meters of shopping area in big cities such as Frankfurt and Berlin to small stores with only about one sixth that size in small cities—became more and more of a management challenge. In addition, smaller competitors with marketing concepts that were high fashion oriented and well-targeted, such as Swedish Hennes & Mauritz and Kiel-based New Yorker, as well as outlets competing with low prices, were luring customers away from bigger stores such as Peek & Cloppenburg. The company reacted in two major ways.

First, it reorganized its structure, partly to keep the company from being split up by family shareholders, partly to avoid becoming large enough to be required by the law to publicize key financials. Peek & Cloppenburg's major company, James Cloppenburg KG, was split up into three smaller ones while the number of shareholders actively involved in management was diminished. The newly founded Harro-Uwe-Cloppenburg-Stiftung based in Liechtenstein became the second largest shareholder after James Cloppenburg's widow Elisabeth. Second, the company tried to cut cost in different ways. When sales were declining in the mid-1990s the company reduced its workforce through layoffs.

However, despite relatively rigid German labor laws, Peek & Cloppenburg managed to significantly reduce the number of full-time employees by giving some part-time contracts instead. Soon about one quarter of Peek & Cloppenburg personnel was employed on an ''on-call'' basis and did not receive a fixed salary. Peek & Cloppenburg also refused to pay the license fee charged by Germany's national recycling company Duales System Deutschland and set up their own recycling system to comply with German law. When German banks pushed an electronic payment system with high fees, Peek & Cloppenburg refused to participate. Instead, the company pioneered a system of electronic charge card purchases based on the commonly used Euroscheck check banking card which was later adopted widely throughout the retail landscape. Another way to cut cost was to increase the percentage of house label sales, which traditionally yielded higher profits, while keeping a high profile through selling top designer brands. To reach that goal the company started improving the coordination of collection design, logistics, and marketing and strengthening the visibility and image of its own brands. At the other end, Peek & Cloppenburg reduced the number of vendors.

A second measure to counteract the market trend, Peek & Cloppenburg executed a general image overhaul. Starting with a new typeface especially developed for the company, the modernization of Peek & Cloppenburg's own ''outfit'' also included the architecture and interior design of the company's new flagship stores to be built in Dusseldorf, Cologne, and Stuttgart, which were planned by international star architects. The company's traditional advertising method—catalogues included in major general interest, news, and fashion magazines—was continued with a fresh, more modern image oriented on the standards of upscale fashion magazines such as Vogue and Elle, including the booking of top models such as Claudia Schiffer. These measures were accompanied by an image campaign under the slogan ''We are family,'' showing VIP testimonials such as singers Nina Hagen and Ute Lemper in Peek & Cloppenburg clothes.

In 1998, managing director Hartmut M. Krämer left Peek & Cloppenburg to become the new CEO of French retail group La Redoute. One year later with the retiring Hans Peek, the last member of the Peek family left Peek & Cloppenburg's manage-

ment. By the end of the 20th century Peek & Cloppenburg had almost reached its limits of growth within Germany and was preparing for further expansion into Europe.

Principal Subsidiaries

James Cloppenburg KG West; Anson's Herrenhaus KG; P & C Groep N.V. (Netherlands); Peek & Cloppenburg G.m.b.H. (Austria); Peek & Cloppenburg BV (Belgium); P&C Sp.z.o.o. (Poland).

Principal Competitors

H&M Hennes & Mauritz AB; Otto Versand GmbH & Co.; C&A; Karstadt Quelle AG.

Further Reading

''Deutsche Kontrolle bei P & C in Holland,'' *TextilWirtschaft,* January 5, 1995, p. 3.

''Die Rheinländer gehen nach Norden,'' *TextilWirtschaft,* February 18, 1993, p. 14.

Edelmann, Heike M., ''P&C lässt Image aufwerten,'' *TextilWirtschaft,* September 16, 1999, p. 72.

''Hans Peek beendet Tätigkeit,'' *TextilWirtschaft,* April 1, 1999, p. 98.

''In Berlin mächtig aufgetrumpft,'' *TextilWirtschaft,* April 6, 1995, p. 16.

''Mainstream mit modischen Spitzen,'' *TextilWirtschaft,* September 5, 1996, p. 14.

''Mehr Profit mit Eigenmarken; Niederlande: P & C mit neuer Sortimentsstategie,'' *TextilWirtschaft,* February 15, 1996, p. 31.

Müller, Jürgen, ''Auch wir müssen uns anstrengen,'' *TextilWirtschaft,* March 22, 2001, p. 50.

Müller, Jürgen, Sabine Spieler, and Michael Werner, '' P&C wird vertikaler,'' *TextilWirtschaft,* July 29, 1999, p. 130.

''Niederländische P & C wird 100% deutsch,'' *TextilWirtschaft,* November 19, 1998, p. 44.

''Peek & Cloppenburg geht in die Schweiz,'' *TextilWirtschaft,* July 21, 1998, p. 12.

''Peek & Cloppenburg/La Redoute: Hartmut M. Krämer wechselt nach Frankreich,'' *TextilWirtschaft,* December 25, 1997, p. 13.

''P&C Baut an der Zukunft,'' *Werben und Verkaufen,* February 4, 2000, p. 196.

''P & C Düsseldorf: Flexibler Einsatz, weniger Kosten,'' *TextilWirtschaft,* February 15, 1996, p. 2.

''P&C: Vereint auf Europa-Kurs,'' *TextilWirtschaft,* May 1, 1997, p. 4.

''Peek & Cloppenburg verschiebt Expansion,'' *Wirtschaftsblatt,* October 16, 1999, p. 5.

Schumacher, Harald, ''Peek & Cloppenburg Im Namen des Vaters,'' *Wirtschaftswoche,* March 21, 1996, p. 80.

''Sehen uns als Konkurrenz zu P&C,'' *TextilWirtschaft,* October 7, 1993, p. 16.

—Evelyn Hauser

Pizza Inn

Pizza Inn, Inc.

3551 Plano Parkway
The Colony, Texas 75056
U.S.A.
Telephone: (469)384-5000
Fax:
Web site: http://www.pizzainn.com

Public Company
Incorporated: 1961
Employees: 211
Sales: $63.5 million (2001)
Stock Exchanges: NASDAQ
Ticker Symbol: PZZI
NAIC: 422490 Other Grocery and Related Products
    Wholesalers

With its corporate headquarters located near Dallas, Pizza Inn, Inc. franchises and services some 450 Pizza Inn Restaurants, both in the United States and overseas. Domestically, Pizza Inns are found in 21 states, primarily in the south, with strong concentrations in Texas, Arkansas, and North Carolina. Only three of the restaurants are company owned, all located in Dallas, where they are used to train new employees and franchisees, as well as for research purposes. Pizza Inn has been especially aggressive in franchising outside of the United States, with restaurants located in 12 countries, from Iceland to the Philippines. Pizza Inn features four types of restaurants. Full service Pizza Inns seat 130 to 185 customers, and generally offer additional carry out and delivery services. In addition to pizza, these operations offer pasta, sandwiches, and desserts, as well as beer and wine in select locations. A second category of Pizza Inns are dedicated solely to pizza delivery and carry-out. Some Pizza Inns employ a self-serve buffet concept, offering essentially the same items as the full service restaurants, but seating between 60 to 70 customers. These units also offer pizza delivery and carry out. A final type of Pizza Inn operation is the Express Serve unit, which can be found in a convenience store, airport terminal, or within a college campus facility. Seating is limited if offered at all, and the menu is kept to a minimum. Eschewing delivery, the express operation focuses on quick carry-out service. In addition to franchise fees, Pizza Inn makes money through its Norco Distributing Co. unit, which sells food and paper products and restaurant equipment to its chain of restaurants.

Pizza Inn's 1960s Origins

Although pizza had been offered for a number of years, mostly in the major East Coast cities with large concentrations of Italian-Americans, a pizza craze swept the country after World War II, resulting in a large number of mom-and-pop operations and eventually entrepreneurs with bigger plans. In 1958, Frank and Dan Carney opened the first Pizza Hut in Wichita, Kansas, and a year later they incorporated and opened their first franchise unit in Topeka, Kansas. While Pizza Hut was devoted to a table and chairs concept for pizza, Detroit native Tom Monaghan founded Domino's Pizza in 1960 and pioneered the delivery chain. A short time later Michael Ilitch, also from Detroit, founded Little Caesars, which focused on the carry-out of inexpensive pizza. Each of the three future pizza magnates unknowingly carved out a unique share of the future market and for many years were dominant among pizza chains. Pizza Inn, another early entrant in the industry, competed with Pizza Hut in the restaurant category. The company originated in Dallas, Texas, in 1961, a year after one of its co-founders, Francis J. Spillman, had opened a storefront pizza business close to the campus of Southern Methodist University. Before entering the restaurant business, Spillman had worked for Boeing Aircraft and American National Insurance Company. The company began franchising in 1963, employing a territorial concept that permitted franchisees to operate a minimum number of Pizza Inns in a particular area.

Pizza Inn grew at a steady rate over the next several years, so that by 1970 the company owned approximately 100 restaurants while franchising another 125. In addition to Pizza Inns, the company operated and franchised a small number of Papa's Pizza Parlors, Pepe Taco Restaurants, and der Chees n' Wurst outlets. Pizza Inns' efforts to achieve rapid expansion, however, were derailed when the U.S. economy began to sputter in the early 1970s. Pizza Inn's poor financial health, in fact, precipitated a March 1971 merger agreement with Pizza Hut. Under terms of the proposed deal, eight Pizza Inn shares of common stock would be exchanged for one Pizza Hut share. Two months later, after Pizza Inn and its franchisees were unable to resolved some territorial conflicts with Pizza Hut, the deal was scuttled. To alleviate its poor financial condition, Pizza Inn management was forced to institute a cost reduction program. The company sold off the Kubler Sausage Company and 11 restaurant operations, and closed another ten, including all of its Pepe Taco restaurants. To pay off a loan that Pizza Hut had made in anticipation of the two companies merging, Pizza Inn transferred 21 restaurants it owned through subsidiaries. Moreover, the company cut staff and agreed to a repayment plan with creditors that would greatly restrict its ability to merge, borrow additional money, or increase compensation to officers. As a result of all these changes in 1971, Pizza Inn posted a net loss of nearly $500,000, despite generating record sales of nearly $12 million.

Pizza Inn Rebounds in the 1970s

Pizza Inn recovered quickly and renewed its pattern of growth through the rest of the 1970s. Annual revenues topped $50 million in 1976 and $100 million by 1978, while net profits ranged from $1.7 million to $2.3 million. The number of new restaurant openings also kept pace, so that by the end of the decade Pizza Inn, which totaled 745 units, was second only to Pizza Hut among U.S. pizza restaurant chains. Pizza Inns could be found in 33 states, mostly in the South, with a third of the units located in Texas. Nearly 350 of the restaurants were company owned, including two in Monterrey, Mexico. Furthermore, Pizza Inn now had other franchised restaurants located in Mexico, as well as Puerto Rico, Japan, the Philippines, and South Africa. Pizza Inn first became involved with franchising outside of North America when it opened units in U.S. military bases in Japan.

The fortunes of Pizza Inn began to decline in the 1980s as the company faced increased competition from other pizza chains. After many years of turning a profit, Pizza Inn lost $590,000 in 1985. Its stock, which two years earlier had traded at $17.50 now fell to around $6 at the start of 1986. Spillman announced that Pizza Inn needed to open new units that focused on home delivery, as well as to remodel existing stores, but the company was already $57 million in long-term debt and simply lack the wherewithal to finance Spillman's reported goal of opening as many as 150 restaurants in 1986. Following further losses in the first quarter of 1986, Pizza Inn sold off its meat manufacturing subsidiary, Quality Sausage Company, for $23.7 million in cash and the assumption of $5.4 million in debt. Rumors began to circulate that the company was a ripe takeover target.

Spillman's critics accused him of mismanaging Pizza Inn, maintaining that he ran the public corporation as if it were a private firm. In the summer of 1986, Spillman assembled an investor group to, indeed, take the company private, fending off

a possible takeover bid and presumably shielding it from Wall Street pressure to produce short-term results. Spillman offered to buy all Pizza Inn shares for $10.50 each. A revised price of $11 per share was subsequently approved by a special committee of two independent directors. A bid of $12 per share was also made by a pair of investors, but the offer was quickly rejected after Spillman indicated that his group would not sell their 39 percent stake in Pizza Inn, thereby preventing rival bidders from gaining the two-thirds shareholder vote required in Texas mergers. A great deal of controversy ensued, with critics charging that Spillman was underestimating the value of Pizza Inn, in particular the worth of a cheese subsidiary and the real estate on which a large number of company-own restaurants were located.

Spillman's group increased its bid to $12.50 per share, but ultimately failed to arrange the necessary financing to close the deal. After securing an option to buy over one million Pizza Inn shares from Spillman, Pantera's Corp., a St. Louis-based pizza restaurant operation, offered $48 million in cash and stock for the company in March 1987. Pizza Inn shareholders were set to receive approximately $14.50 in cash and Pantera's stock. Although Spillman engineered a last-second bid, Pantera's finally gained shareholder approval in July 1987, took over control of Pizza Inn, and assumed its corporate name. With the addition of 120 Pantera's restaurants, the new Pizza Inn became the fourth largest overall pizza chain in the country.

It was announced that Spillman would be kept on as president of Pizza Hut under the terms of a five-year contract. In fact, he only stayed as a consultant for just three months then left to create companies to franchise Pizza Inn restaurants. When he failed to pay royalty fees for food bills, however, his relationship with Pizza Inn was severed. He changed the names of his restaurants to Oregano's Pizza, but made only a gesture of disassociating himself from Pizza Inn, resorting to taping over Pizza Inn signs and blotting out logos on menus. Pizza Inn took Spillman to court, resulting in a two-year ban on Spillman operating a restaurant anywhere within five miles of a Pizza Inn. The presiding federal judge called Spillman's acts ''the most egregious case of deliberate trademark infringement ever heard by this court.''

Pizza Inn's new management had more serious issues to address that its conflict with the chain's founder. It sold off the J.T. McCord's hamburger and chili restaurants that Spillman had created under Pizza Inn and slashed a third of the company's administrative work force. The company also introduced a new Italian-style buffet format to a large number of units in order to distinguish Pizza Inn from the competition in the highly competitive pizza industry, which was now being rocked by price wars between Pizza Hut, Domino's, and Little Caesars. Aside from conversion costs to a buffet operation, the debt Pantera's incurred in acquiring Pizza Inn proved overly burdensome, so that by the summer of 1989 the company was in difficult straits. After failing to meet several deadlines to make interest payments, Pizza Inn was unable to arrange a refinancing plan and faced the prospect of selling off units in order to pay its bills. By September 1989, the bottom fell out, and Pantera's stock fell to just 37.5 cents. With assets of $76.7 million and liabilities of $81.7 million, the company had no choice but to file for Chapter 11 bankruptcy protection. The court was instru-

Key Dates:

1960: Francis J. Spillman opens a pizza business near the Southern Methodist University campus.
1961: Pizza Inn is incorporated.
1963: Franchising of the company begins.
1971: A bid to merge with Pizza Hut fails.
1987: Pantera's Corp. acquires Pizza Inn.
1989: The company is forced to declare bankruptcy.
1990: Jeff Rogers is named president.
1993: Pizza Inn returns to profitability.

mental in the hiring of long-time fast food executive Jeff Rogers to serve as a consultant in the liquidation of the company. After becoming familiar with Pizza Inn, he became convinced that the company's problems were far from insurmountable, and rather than selling the operation the better course would be to attempt a turnaround. In January 1990 he was hired as Pizza Inn's chief executive officer in order to do just that.

Rogers was well suited to rescuing an ailing fast food chain, having recently turned around the Bonanza steak restaurant business. While earning a undergraduate degree in Hotel and Restaurant Management at the University of Denver, he began his business career in the marketing department of International Industries, which was the parent company of International House of Pancakes, Orange Julius, and other franchise chains. After serving five years as International Industries' marketing director, Rogers became president of Communications-200, a Los Angeles advertising agency that did work for A&W Restaurants and other restaurant clients. In 1979, he moved to Dallas to take over marketing for Bonanza, which had been losing money and market share. By 1983, he became president of Bonanza's parent company, USACafes, and was instrumental in the chain tripling in value and gaining a slot on the New York Stock Exchange during the six years he was in charge. In 1989, however, Metromedia Restaurant Group acquired the Bonanza chain and Rogers was let go.

Revitalization in the 1990s

Out of work in Dallas, Rogers accepted the top position at Pizza Inn, a company that was over $32 million in debt. Even before he began the task of selling off Pizza Inn's 190 company-owned restaurants, he arranged to have the corporate headquarters spruced up. Hallways dark from burned-out light bulbs and hallways cluttered with stacks of file boxes, dirty bathrooms, and dingy drapes were indicative of a company that had lacked leadership for a long period of time. By simply cleaning up and painting the walls, Rogers instantly boosted employee morale. "People thought I was the turnaround king strictly because I cleaned the place," he told the *Dallas Business Journal*. Rogers also began to repair relations with franchisees, whom he learned had not been in contact with the home office for an entire year. With Pizza Inn selling off units, franchising would now be the life blood of the company. In effect, the franchisees would finance the future growth of the company, since they would be the ones making the major capital investments. Rogers also came to rely on the franchises to conduct the chain's research

and development, believing that because they were on the front lines they would be better able to recognize what worked and what failed. One area that he felt strongly about was delivery, which was the fastest-growing segment of the pizza market. Little more than a third of all Pizza Inns offered delivery, a situation that Rogers began aggressively to address.

Pizza Inn lost money in 1991 and 1992. It was in 1992 that he hired one of his key executives at USACafes, Ronald Parker, to become Pizza Inn's chief operating officer. Improved customer service, cleaner restaurants, and a better menu resulted in Pizza Inn turning a profit of $2.2 million in 1993, which increased to $2.6 million the following year, and $3.2 million in 1995, as systemwide sales improved to $218 million. Pizza Inn turned to the convenience store market, opening Pizza Inn Express units inside Coastal Marts. Its full service restaurants moved into North Carolina, gaining a toe hold for Pizza Inn in the east. Moreover, Pizza Inn renewed its overseas efforts, franchising restaurants in Brazil, the Philippines, and the Middle East. At the same time, the company did not sacrifice control of the chain for sheer size. When its South Korean franchisee, who operated 40 stores, failed to use proper ingredients and offered poor service, the company did not hesitate to terminate the licensing agreement and seek new partners.

For his efforts in revitalizing Pizza Inn, Rogers was named *Inc.* magazine's Entrepreneur of the Year in the "turnaround category" in September 1994. To maintain momentum in the mid-1990s, Rogers greatly increased Pizza Inn's marketing budget, more than doubling the money spent on television advertising. The size of the Pizza Inn chain continued to grow each year, with new units more than offsetting under-performing ones that were shut down. In 1998, for instance, Pizza Inn opened 66 domestic units and 16 international units, while at the same time closing 54 units domestically and five overseas.

The fortunes of Pizza Inn peaked in 1997 when the company generated revenues of $69 million and posted a net profit of $4.5 million. Over the next few years, sales would stagnant, although the company would remain consistently profitable in the highly competitive pizza industry. In July 2000, Parker took over as president of the company to focus on operational issues and franchise service, allowing Rogers, who remained CEO, to concentrate on unit growth and profitability. The company continued its international growth, signing franchise deals in new territories such as Romania, Honduras, and Iceland. In 2001 Pizza Inn launched new initiatives to improve sagging sales trends, including store remodelings and the rolling out of the buffet format to new units. Although now fiscally healthy, Pizza Inn was not large enough to challenge its main rival, Pizza Hut, on a head-to-head basis. Rather, the chain had to continue to carefully target its markets in the southern portion of the United States while adding to its very successful overseas franchising program.

Principal Subsidiaries

PIBCO, ltd.; Barko Realty, Inc.; Pizza Inn of Delaware, Inc.; Pizza Inn, Servicos de Gestao de Franchising, Lda.; R-Check, Inc.

Principal Competitors

Domino's Pizza Inc.; Godfather's Pizza Inc.; Little Caesar International Inc.; Papa John's International Inc.; Pizza Hut Inc.; Sbarro Inc.; Uno Restaurant Corporation.

Further Reading

Alpert, William M., "Pie with Crust," *Barron's National Business and Financial Weekly,* September 15, 1986, p. 15.

Genusa, Angela, "Turnaround: Corporate Cleanup Leads to Pizza Inn Turnaround," *Dallas Business Journal* June 24, 1994, p. C21.

Mehegan, Sean, "Mighty Mice," *Restaurant Business,* November 1, 2000, pp. 26–30.

——, "Picking Up the Slices: Five Years After Bankruptcy, Pizza Inn Strives to Make Its Turnaround Stick," *Restaurant Business,* February 10, 1996, p. 34.

Opdyke, Jeff D., "Pizza Inn Cooks Up Turnaround and Grabs Bigger Slice of Market," *Wall Street Journal,* November 10, 1993, p. T2.

Warner, Rick Van, "Pantera's Takes Control, Slashes Staff at Pizza Inn," *Nation's Restaurant News,* September 28, 1987, p. 1.

Weil, Jonathan, "Little-Noticed Pizza Inn Shares May Soon Have a Higher Profile," *Wall Street Journal,* January 14, 1998, p. T2.

Zipser, Andy, "Pantera's Says Chapter 11 Filing is Expected Soon," *Wall Street Journal,* September 20, 1989, p. 1.

—Ed Dinger

The PNC Financial Services Group Inc.

One PNC Plaza
249 Fifth Avenue
Pittsburgh, Pennsylvania 15222-2707
U.S.A.
Telephone: (412) 762-2000
Fax: (412) 762-7829
Web site: http://www.pnc.com

Public Company
Incorporated: 1983 as PNC Financial Corporation
Employees: 24,900
Total Assets: $69.88 billion (2001)
Stock Exchanges: New York
Ticker Symbol: PNC
NAIC: 551111 Offices of Bank Holding Companies;
52211 Commercial Banking; 523991 Trust, Fiduciary,
and Custody Activities

The PNC Financial Services Group Inc. is the 13th largest bank in the United States and a leading diversified financial services firm operating in Delaware, Kentucky, New Jersey, Ohio, and Pennsylvania. PNC grew rapidly in the 1980s and 1990s mainly through a series of acquisitions, the largest being the 1995 purchase of Midlantic Corp. and the 1999 purchase of First Data Investment Services Group. In an era of heavy bank consolidation brought on by increasing competitive pressures and deregulation, PNC's aggressive acquisition program enabled it to stay a leading force in the banking industry. PNC's main businesses include community banking, corporate banking, real estate finance, asset-based lending, wealth and asset management, and global fund services.

Origins

PNC Bank Corp.'s immediate forerunner was PNC Financial Corporation, formed in 1983 from the merger of two Pennsylvania banking concerns, the Pittsburgh National Corporation and the Provident National Corporation. The Pittsburgh National Bank was incorporated in 1959, but its roots can be traced back to 1852, when steel magnates James Laughlin and B.F. Jones opened the Pittsburgh Trust and Savings in downtown Pittsburgh. PNC Financial's other predecessor, the Provident National Bank, headquartered in Philadelphia, can also be traced to the mid-1800s. In 1847, the Tradesmens National Bank of Philadelphia opened its doors. After more than a century of banking and a series of name changes and acquisitions, it became the Provident National Bank in 1964. The Pittsburgh National Bank and the Provident National Bank combined their extensive banking experience in 1983. At that time, the newly formed bank holding company was no more than a medium-sized regional concern, but it rapidly developed into one of the nation's most powerful super-regional banks.

PNC's first chief executive, Merle E. Gilliand, had already served as CEO at Pittsburgh National Bank for 11 years by the time PNC Financial was formed. Gilliand set the tone of PNC's management style, which has been described as "bottom-up management." He surrounded himself with competent senior executives and allowed them to make decisions on their own. This grass roots approach was rare in banking. Gilliand, however, contended that this method provided better service and, over the long run, a better bank. Under Gilliand's leadership, PNC emphasized quality, not size. Nonetheless, this strategy also proved very conducive to growth in the changing markets of the 1980s.

PNC's chief rival in the 1980s was the Mellon Bank. For years, Mellon controlled the large corporate accounts of Pittsburgh's many companies (the city ranked third in the nation in number of corporate headquarters). As a result, PNC was forced to cater to mid-sized companies and to businesses outside of Pittsburgh. But, when Pittsburgh's big companies experienced difficulties in the late 1970s and 1980s, PNC was not as exposed to the "rust belt" problems as the Mellon Bank. PNC, under Gilliand, was content to operate on a smaller scale than its rival, striving to provide all the same services with greater quality.

Deregulation Prompts Growth: 1980s

Banking deregulation allowed, and to some extent encouraged, mergers between banks. As the 1980s wore on, a number

Company Perspectives:

PNC comprises several distinct businesses designed to provide our customers with the best in a broad range of products and services. This specialization, along with PNC's overarching entrepreneurial spirit, enables each business to focus on anticipating and fulfilling your individual financial needs. We are hardworking, high energy, innovative, and committed to operating at the highest levels of service and profitability so that we are successful in our highly competitive industry and marketplace.

of well-run banks found it in their interest to join forces with the PNC group. PNC's acquisition strategy focused on purchasing healthy banks, which would add to the corporation's overall strength. In 1984, PNC acquired the Marine Bank of Erie, Pennsylvania. A year later, it acquired the Northeastern Bancorp of Scranton, Pennsylvania. PNC's criteria for acquisitions were strict by industry standards. Acceptable banks were mid-sized, with assets of between $2 and $6 billion, had a solid market share in their operating regions, earned excellent return on equity and on assets, and ideally had expertise in a specific area of financial services which would benefit the entire group. Close attention was also paid to whether or not the bank's management philosophy was compatible with PNC's.

In 1985, Thomas H. O'Brien replaced the retiring Merle Gilliand as CEO at PNC. At 48, O'Brien was the youngest CEO of any major U.S. bank. Ironically, he had started his banking career at PNC's archrival, the Mellon Bank, before earning his MBA at Harvard. O'Brien had risen quickly through the ranks of the Pittsburgh National Bank, eventually heading PNC's merchant banking activities, and finally becoming chairman and chief executive. As the top executive at PNC he continued Gilliand's bottom-up management style. O'Brien would let executives at affiliates implement their own ideas at their own bank without a great deal of interference from the top. As a result of the autonomy PNC gave its affiliated banks, the banking group was an attractive merger partner for exactly the healthy regional banks it wished to acquire. PNC could grow, and the new affiliates could take advantage of the extended services offered by the group. PNC became known for its friendly takeovers of already successful banks.

Under O'Brien's conservative yet aggressive leadership, PNC grew at a tremendous rate. In 1986, the Hershey Bank joined the group. The following year, with the acquisition of Citizen's Fidelity Corporation of Louisville, PNC grew larger than its rival, the Mellon Bank. In 1988, PNC acquired the Central Bancorp of Cincinnati and the First Bank and Trust of Mechanicsburg. While acquisitions normally diluted the value of a corporation's stock for some time, PNC's careful planning allowed it to quickly make up for the dilution. By the late 1980s, Wall Street analysts were so confident in PNC's management that acquisition announcements did not seriously reduce the stock's price.

The relaxation of interstate banking regulations in the United States during this time created a new kind of bank: the

super-regional. Super-regionals operated in a number of states, and began in the late 1980s to compete with the money center banks for a greater share of large corporate business. As mid-sized companies needed more services in the international trade arena, the super-regionals became more and more involved there as well. With its network spread throughout Pennsylvania, Kentucky, Ohio, and Delaware, PNC was the premier super-regional in the United States by 1987 and had become the nation's twelfth largest banking group. Its assets had more than doubled since 1983, and its earnings were among the highest in the industry.

Like many banks throughout the world, PNC was forced to set aside huge sums as a provision against bad debt in Third World countries in 1987. Unlike many banks, however, the PNC group still earned a substantial profit that year, despite its $200 million increase in loan loss reserves. While two-thirds of U.S. banks actually showed losses, PNC netted more than $255 million for its shareholders that year.

The banking group was very conservative in its lending throughout the 1980s. It set limits for the number of loans allowed to any particular industry and enforced stringent credit criteria. At the same time, PNC was energetic in its marketing. The corporation went after trust and money management business as well as corporate lending. PNC affiliates also showed higher than average earnings from fee income.

Diversification Through Acquisition: 1990s

PNC suffered a slight setback in 1989 and 1990 when it was caught with millions in nonperforming commercial real estate loans—part of them inherited through its late 1980s acquisitions—resulting in reduced earnings. The company responded by tightening its loan policies and beginning an effort to reduce its dependence on riskier commercial loans in favor of the more dependable consumer sector. A restructuring in 1991 further reflected PNC's desire to diversify its holdings by focusing company operations on four core businesses: corporate banking, retail banking, investment and trust management, and investment banking. The following year, with assets reaching $45.5 billion, PNC began a program of consolidation in which all its banks and most of its affiliated companies would take on the name PNC Bank. PNC Financial Corporation itself changed its name to PNC Bank Corp. in early 1993.

PNC's desire to diversify was evident in its nonbank acquisitions of the early 1990s. In 1993, PNC acquired the Massachusetts Company to boost its financial services offerings. That year it also acquired the Sears Mortgage Banking Group, a major home mortgage lender, from Sears Roebuck & Co. for $328 million in cash. The move immediately quadrupled PNC's mortgage business, pushing it into the top ten nationwide. In 1994, a third major nonbank acquisition bolstered the bank's asset management area. The purchase of BlackRock Financial Management for $240 million in cash and notes increased PNC's amount of assets under management to $75 billion, the sixth-largest amount among bank asset managers.

These acquisitions, however, would pale in comparison to those overseen by chairman and CEO O'Brien in the mid-1990s. As a prelude, in 1993 PNC purchased First Eastern Corp.

of Wilkes-Barre, Pennsylvania, for $330 million, solidifying its holdings in northeastern Pennsylvania. In keeping with his strategy of expanding only within or adjacent to PNC's existing retail banking territory, O'Brien then shifted his attention to the Philadelphia area and New Jersey, long a target for PNC growth. Early in 1995, PNC purchased 84 branches in southern and central New Jersey from Chemical Banking Corp. for $504 million. Then in July of that year, the bank announced it would acquire Midlantic Corp. of Edison, New Jersey, through a $2.84 billion stock swap. Midlantic's $13.7 billion in assets would give PNC a total of $75.8 billion in assets, making it the eleventh largest bank in the country. More importantly, PNC had purchased the third largest bank in New Jersey and had achieved a significant presence there.

Through its acquisitions in the early and mid-1990s, PNC Bank Corp. had in many ways created a unique type of bank that could provide a model for others to emulate. It was considered one of the top super-regionals in the country with more than 800 branches in the contiguous area of Indiana, Kentucky, New Jersey, Pennsylvania, and Ohio. At the same time, it was building a national and in some cases international presence in the areas of asset management services and investment banking. Its strong regional retail banking operations coupled with its diversified financial services businesses were designed to help it weather banking downturns that inevitably beset PNC's and other banks' earnings in the past. And as barriers to interstate banking continued to fall and bank consolidation continued, PNC was forced to look for ways to remain competitive among its peers.

As such, PNC eyed the expansion of its consumer mortgage business as a potentially lucrative avenue. Through this unit, PNC put plans in motion in 1997 to expand its product offerings. During 1996, its customers had purchased $5.6 billion in mortgages. By cross-selling home equity loans, credit cards, and investment services to these customers, PNC hoped to tap into a niche market that most banks had failed in. A 1997 *American Banker* article reported that "banks have failed at cross-selling in the past because they embraced mass marketing,

instead of a targeted approach, and did not follow up." PNC however, felt that its mortgage business was well positioned to excel at this new approach. Its efforts proved fruitless, however, and PNC sold its consumer mortgage business in 2000 to Washington Mutual Home Loans Inc.

The company also began a restructuring effort during the late 1990s in order to pare back less profitable operations. In 1997, it closed nine branches and the following year sold 16 Western Pennsylvania-based branches to First Western Bancorp Inc. It also announced that it would sell off its credit card business—3.3 million accounts—to MBNA Corp. in order to focus on its investment services and other product lines. The company then made a $1.1 billion purchase of First Data Investor Services Group, a mutual funds and retirement plans services provider. The deal strengthened PNC's investment services subsidiary PFPC Worldwide, making it the leading full-service mutual fund transfer agent and the second largest full-service mutual fund accounting services provider. PNC also spun off 30 percent of its BlackRock subsidiary in 1999 at $14 per share. Its restructuring efforts appeared to pay off, and in 1999 the company secured $1.3 billion in profits, a 13 percent increase over the previous year. Revenue also increased by six percent to $52 billion.

Adopting a New Image for the New Millennium

Signaling the firm's commitment to its diversified services, PNC adopted a new brand image and changed its name to The PNC Financial Services Group in 2000. That year, O'Brien retired leaving James E. Rohr at the helm. While under new leadership, the company forged ahead in its plans to invest in high-growth business ventures as it maintained a strong hold on its consumer banking activities. Automated Business Development Corp. was acquired and became part of PFPC's operations. The company also teamed up with Perot Systems to create BillingZone, an electronic bill payment platform.

By this time however, PNC not only faced increased competition as the industry continued to consolidate but rough economic times as well. A January 2002 *Institutional Investor* article claimed that both Rohr and PNC were "suffering in a generally difficult climate for banks; the recession has crimped loan growth, pushed credit losses higher and hurt the valuations in securities and venture capital portfolios." Indeed, as PNC continually restructured and streamlined operations to battle the challenging economic climate, it was forced to post a $615 million fourth-quarter charge in 2001 in order to write down loans, restructure its venture capital business, and exit the auto leasing market. PNC also came under fire during 2002 as the Federal Reserve Board and the Securities Exchange Commission announced that it was investigating PNC's accounting practices. To top it off, the company was named in a shareholder class action lawsuit that claimed that PNC and its auditor Ernst & Young LLP had violated the Securities Exchange Act of 1934 by misrepresenting PNC's financial results from July 19, 2001 to January 29, 2002. The claim also stated that both parties had not used proper accounting standards and therefore had misled investors about the financial condition of the firm.

As PNC battled litigation and turbulent economic times, management remained confident that the restructuring of its banking operations would lead to future earnings and profit growth. With a new corporate tagline–"The Thinking Behind the Money"—PNC was focused on remaining a leader among its peers. Whether or not it would succumb to industry consolidation or partner in a merger of equals, however, remained to be seen.

Principal Subsidiaries

PNC Bank, N.A.; PNC Bancorp, Inc.; PNC Advisors, N.A.; PNC Bank Capital Securities, LLC; PNC Commercial Management, Inc.; BlackRock, Inc.; PNC Leasing, LLC; PNC Capital Leasing, LLC; PNC Holding, LLC; PFPC Worldwide Inc.; PNC Funding Corp.; PNC Investment Corp.

Principal Competitors

Citigroup Inc.; Mellon Financial Corp.; Wachovia Corporation.

Further Reading

Chase, Brett, "Protégé Succeeds Mentor at PNC's Flagship Bank," *American Banker*, June 2, 1997, p. 5.

Crockett, Barton, "Has PNC Picked the Wrong Time to Grow in Investment Management?," *American Banker*, October 5, 1994, p. 8.

"Forging a New Bank at PNC," *United States Banker*, July 1993, pp. 22–4.

Gold, Jacqueline S., "Bank to Basics," *Institutional Investor*, January 2002, p. 91.

"Hail to the Chief," *US Banker*, March 2000, p. 14.

"In Brief: PNC Bank Selling Card Business to MBNA," *American Banker*, December 28, 1998.

Lombaerde, Geert De, "PNC Bank Beat Goals to Boost 1999 Profits," *Business Courier Serving Cincinnati*, February 11, 2000, p. 4.

Murray, Matt, and Timothy L. O'Brien, "PNC Bank Corp. Agrees to Purchase Midlantic in a $2.84 Billion Stock Swap," *Wall Street Journal*, July 11, 1995, p. A3.

——, "PNC Is Acquiring Chemical Branches for $504 Million," *Wall Street Journal*, March 9, 1995, p. A6.

O'Brien, Timothy L., and Steven Lipin, "In Latest Round of Banking Mergers, Even Big Institutions Become Targets," *Wall Street Journal*, pp. A3–4.

Olson, Thomas, "PNC Ensures New Market by Selling Insurance Products," *Pittsburgh Business Journal*, July 25–31, 1994, p. 15.

——, "PNC's Purchase of Sears Mortgage Offers Market Clout," *Pittsburgh Business Times*, May 17, 1993, p. 5.

"PNC Bank to Buy First Eastern Corp. in $330 Million Deal," *Wall Street Journal*, p. B4.

"PNC Chairman: We Won't Be Forced to Merge," *American Banker*, August 7, 1998, p. 24.

Rieker, Matthais, "PNC 'Repositions' Itself, Taking $615M Charge," *American Banker*, January 4, 2002, p. 20.

Schroeder, Michael, "A Pittsburgh Bank That's Dazzling the Street," *Business Week*, February 29, 1988, p. 84.

——, "Maybe This Bank Should Have Cried Wolf," *Business Week*, September 17, 1990, p. 140.

Stern, Gabriella, and Robert McGough, "PNC Agrees to Acquisition of BlackRock," *Wall Street Journal*, p. A4.

Talley, Karen, "PNC Unit's Expansion Plan Includes Cross-Selling Push," *American Banker*, January 30, 1997, p. 81.

Tascarella, Patty, "PNC Trims Branches and Workers As Part of Major Restructuring Plan," *Pittsburgh Business Times*, February 27, 1998, p. 4.

Winokur, Cheryl, "PNC Unveils $1.1B Deal for First Data Subsidiary," *American Banker*, July 21, 1999, p. 1.

—updates: David E. Salamie and Christina M. Stansell

Raytheon Aircraft

Raytheon Aircraft Holdings Inc.

9079 East Central
Wichita, Kansas 67206
U.S.A.
Telephone: (316) 676-7111
Fax: (316) 676-8867
Web site: http://www.raytheonaircraft.com

Wholly-Owned Subsidiary of Raytheon Company
Incorporated: 1994 as Raytheon Aircraft Co.
Employees: 18,000
Sales: $3.22 billion (2000)
NAIC: 336411 Aircraft Manufacturing; 54171 Research
and Development in the Physical, Engineering, and
Life Sciences

Raytheon Aircraft Holdings Inc. owns the Raytheon Aircraft Company and related enterprises. Raytheon Aircraft includes Beech Aircraft and Hawker corporate jets. Beech is known for its popular King Air series of business turboprops and the piston-powered A36 Bonanza, of which more than 3,000 examples have been built. Beech also produces a small jet transport for civil and military use, and the 1900 series of regional turboprop airliners. Hawker's well regarded jets include the Horizon, 800XP, and Premier I. Raytheon Aircraft aims to shift more of its production to jets in the coming years. It has led the industry in switching from aluminum to composite construction. Its Starship, though a commercial flop, was the first all-composite business aircraft certified by the FAA. Based in Wichita, Kansas, Raytheon Aircraft has plants in eleven US states.

Buying Beech in 1980

Beech Aircraft Corporation, one the best known producers of propeller-driven aircraft in the United States, became a subsidiary of Raytheon Company in February 1980. Raytheon traded about $800 million worth of stock for Beech, whose line of market-leading planes included the twin-engine Baron, the King Air turboprop, and the single-engine Bonanza.

Beech brought nearly 11,000 workers into the company, which employed 78,000 around the world. It had earned $43 million on 1979 sales of $626 million, compared to Raytheon's $197 million profit on sales of $3.7 billion.

Raytheon's takeover of Beech was mirrored elsewhere in the industry. By 1985, when General Dynamics Corp. bought Cessna Aircraft Co. and Chrysler Corp. bought Gulfstream Aerospace Corp., all U.S. business aircraft manufacturers were owned by larger, stronger corporations. The rising cost of developing new aircraft was one reason why, new Beech CEO James Walsh told *Industry Week* in 1986.

Sales for both Raytheon and its new Beech Aircraft unit slid in the next few years. In 1984, Beech laid off 500 workers at plants in Kansas, Alabama, and Colorado. The entire business jet industry would only sell 239 new planes in 1985 as older planes were remaining in service for decades. Sales of Beech's propeller-driven offerings were also suffering due to rising product liability premiums and impending tax reforms, noted *Industry Week*.

These last two conditions proved so troubling for the aircraft manufacturers that Cessna had all but stopped producing the piston-engine planes that had made it famous. Beech, which was spending $20 million a year to insure against product liability claims, diversified into jet aircraft after acquiring Mitsubishi Aircraft International. Its Beechjet had formerly been named the Misubishi Diamond II.

Unfortunately, the lower end of the business jet market was becoming overcrowded. Besides segment leaders Cessna and Learjet, Beech faced competition from a number of overseas firms such as British Aerospace and France's Dassault.

Beech had already dominated the turboprop market with its King Air series. These planes used a jet engine to turn a propeller, allowing them to outperform piston engine planes while using considerably less fuel than pure jet aircraft. While weathering new competition from Piper Aircraft, which was plugging its new $2.8 million Cheyenne 400LS with ads featuring famed test pilot Chuck Yeager, Beech was developing a radical new composite design featuring a canard wing and pusher propellers that would sell (or not sell) for more than $3 million a plane. Beech eventually spent $500 million to develop the Starship.

Company Perspectives:

Any time, any place. That's the philosophy of Raytheon Aircraft. We offer a complete line of aviation solutions. If it deals with business aircraft, we provide it.

After three years of dismal sales for both Beech and its parent, 1988 brought something of a turnaround. Raytheon reported record sales ($8.2 billion) and earnings ($489.6 million) while Beech's sales rose 35 percent to $948.3 million. In 1989, profits for the Aircraft Products segment rose more than 40 percent to $44 million on sales approaching $900 million.

Beech Aircraft had produced primarily commercial aircraft until it teamed with McDonnell Douglas and Quintron to win an Air Force contract for a tanker transport pilot trainer in February 1990. Beech's share of the contract, for delivery of up to 211 Beechjets, had a potential to be worth $1 billion over six years. In addition, noted *Barron's,* the military contract spurred additional commercial sales of the Beechjet, as well as military sales to other nations. As a result of the contract, Beech planned to double the size of its Kansas facilities.

The first Starship turboprops were not delivered until March 1990. In spite of the advanced avionics, stable design, and smooth ride, they did not sell well.

Buying British in 1993

Along with rival Dassault, Raytheon made a bid for Cessna after it went up for sale in October 1991. Raytheon was considering whether to enter the medium to heavy corporate jet business. It did so not through the August 1993 purchase of Cessna, but by acquiring Corporate Jets, Inc., a unit of British Aerospace PLC with operations in Wales (U.K.) and Arkansas, for $273 million (£250 million). The company, which manufactured the Hawker 800 and Hawker 1000 business jets (also known by the names BAe 800 and BAe 1000)—the best-selling mid-sized jets in history—was renamed Raytheon Corporate Jets.

The sale of these operations and the subsequent closure of the UK plants drew protests. After the eventual removal of Hawker production to Wichita, Kansas, there would be no business jet manufacturers left in England. Yet Hawker Siddeley was one of the most beloved names in British aviation; its famed Hurricanes had defended the country during the Battle of Britain, and the original company had been founded by no less an aerospace icon than Tommy Sopwith.

Raytheon Aircraft Products Group, which comprised Beech and Raytheon Corporate Jets, announced sales of $1.47 billion for 1993, producing segment income of $182 million. The two units merged in September 1994 to form Raytheon Aircraft Company. The restructuring trimmed 940 workers in the U.S. and UK from the payroll. Former United Technologies Corp. executive Arthur E. Wegner, who had succeeded Max E. Bleck as Beech Aircraft CEO in July 1993, was picked to lead the newly merged entity.

With the power of strong brands like Beech and Hawker, Raytheon Aircraft was accustomed to leading the market segments in which it participated. Yet the market was toughening, noted Britain's *Financial Times,* as executive jets came to be widely perceived as a high-dollar perk rather than an essential corporate tool.

On account of poor sales, Raytheon Aircraft cancelled the Starship turboprop program in December 1994 after building 50 of the planes. In 1995, Raytheon Aircraft implemented a $30 million modernization program at its Wichita facilities as it relocated Hawker production there. In the middle of the year, Beech won a $7 billion contract to build trainers for the U.S. military in collaboration with Pilatus Aircraft Ltd., a Swiss company specializing in high-performance turboprops. The JPATS (Joint Primary Aircraft Training System) contract called for Beech to build 711 PC-9 MKII planes in the next 20 years as the Air Force and Navy began training student pilots together. Later in the year, Raytheon Aircraft won a contract to supply the Pentagon with 103 drones (very small unmanned aircraft) and spares worth $30 million for use in air defense training.

By 1996, Raytheon was marketing an improved version of the Hawker 800. The company had taken the BAe 1000/Hawker 1000 out of production as it redesigned that model. The slightly larger plane that would replace it, the Hawker Horizon, bore only a superficial resemblance and would not begin deliveries until 2001, later pushed back to 2003. Raytheon was able to price the Horizon at $14.5 million fully equipped (later raised to $17 million), relatively low for its category, due to the implementation of low-cost manufacturing techniques and composite materials, which allowed for a reduced number of parts. Raytheon contracted out the wing construction to Japan's Fuji Heavy Industries.

The year 1996 turned out to be a banner year. Raytheon Aircraft sales increased 15 percent to $2.3 billion; income showed a similar increase to $284 million (later reported as $181 million). Deliveries in most categories were up, though the company began to wind down production of its 19-seat Beech 1900D regional airliner, essentially a larger version of the King Air turboprop, as U.S. airlines replaced them with regional jets. Sales to foreign airlines later revived this program, however.

The company sold 480 civilian planes and another 51 military trainer derivatives of its Beechjet in 1996. The company's comprehensive restructuring continued with the aim of reducing the seven to ten years it took to bring new planes into production by 25 percent.

Raytheon Aircraft entered the fractional ownership business in 1997 with the creation of Raytheon Travel Air. The concept, pioneered by companies such as Executive Jet, Inc. (EJI), sold timeshares in business jets, complete with pilots and maintenance and, in Raytheon's case, even catering. (EJI was also a very important customer, placing a $2 billion order for Horizons in June 1999.)

The Beech Bonanza celebrated its fiftieth anniversary in 1997. The twin-engine Baron, derived from the Bonanza, remained a very popular plane. Results for Raytheon Aircraft continued to improve in 1997, with sales of $2.45 billion and

Key Dates:

1980: Beech becomes a subsidiary of Raytheon.
1986: Beech enters jet business through purchase of Mitsubishi Aircraft International.
1990: U.S. Air Force chooses Beechjets to train tanker pilots.
1993: Raytheon buys BAe's line of Hawker business jets.
1994: Beech and Raytheon Corporate Jets merged into Raytheon Aircraft Company.
1996: Raytheon Aircraft posts record sales.
2000: Raytheon Aircraft again posts record sales as divestment rumors abound.
2001: Nearly 1700 jobs are cut as economy slows.

income of $239 million. Its backlog grew to levels not seen in a dozen years. By mid-1998, the company had 100 orders for its new $4.2 million Premier mid-size business jet, which had not yet begun deliveries. The stunning results even prompted the company's Massachusetts parent to hold its annual shareholder meeting in Wichita.

Raytheon Aircraft announced a unique joint marketing agreement with Jaguar Cars in early 1998. The deal produced a series of Special Edition aircraft, including a $2.65 million King Air C90B with a Jaguar-inspired luxury interior. Raytheon also began offering an active noise suppression system on its King Air 350 model.

Sales Peak in 2000

Business aircraft manufacturers had one of their best years in 1999. In September of the year, Raytheon Aircraft appointed Hansel Tookes II, a former Navy and airline pilot and head of a Pratt & Whitney engines group, as president and chief operating officer. He was named chairman and CEO after Wegner retired a year later. Raytheon Aircraft had another year of record sales in 2000.

Rumors of an impending divestiture of Raytheon Aircraft abounded around the turn of the century. Its parent company reportedly would use the $4 billion it expected from the sale to reduce its total corporate debt of $10 billion, a legacy of its 1990s buying spree. General Dynamics Corp., which bought Gulfstream Aerospace in 1999, was named as a likely buyer since Raytheon Aircraft would fill in the lower end of its product line. Dassault Aviation, a French manufacturer of business jets, also expressed interest, largely due to the Beech piston-engine and turboprop lines.

In April 2001, Raytheon Co. announced the sale of 70 percent of Raytheon Aerospace Co., Raytheon Aircraft's support services subsidiary, to New York investing firm Veritas Capital for $153 million. Raytheon Aerospace had 5,300 employees and revenues of about $400 million a year.

Also in April, Raytheon Aircraft announced it was cutting 450 white-collar jobs as a preemptive move in the context of a weak stock market. Two months later, 470 hourly employees in Kansas were let go as the company lowered its production

estimates. Yet another 750 jobs were cut in October 2001; the company cited a slowing economy exacerbated by the September 11 terrorist attacks as reasons for reducing production. Jim Schuster had become CEO of Raytheon Aircraft in June 2001 after Tookes left to head Raytheon's international operations.

The $5.3 million Premier I entry-level business jet did not begin deliveries until the end of 2001; at the time, the company had 300 customers lined up for it. In fact, the company's total backlog, most of it for Raytheon's newest jets, was worth $4 billion.

Principal Subsidiaries

Raytheon Aircraft Company; Raytheon Aircraft Charter and Management Company; Raytheon Travel Air Company; Raytheon Aircraft Services, Inc.

Principal Competitors

Cessna Aircraft Company; Gulfstream Aerospace; Israeli Aircraft Industries; Northrop Grumman Corporation; Rockwell International Corporation.

Further Reading

Anderson, Curt, "Raytheon to Sell Shared Ownership in Aircraft," *Arizona Republic,* June 5, 1997, p. E10.

Atchison, Sandra D., "Why Beech Is Floating on Cloud 9," *Business Week,* March 19, 1990, p. 128.

Betts, Paul, "Raytheon's UK Jet Plants Set to Close," *Financial Times,* September 16, 1994, p. 1.

——, "Weighed Down by High-Flying Image," *Financial Times,* September 28, 1994, p. 24.

Biddle, Frederic, "Will Diversification Last at Rocketing Raytheon?" *Boston Globe,* January 24, 1989, p. 39.

Braham, James, "Maybe They Made 'Em Too Well," *Industry Week,* March 31, 1986, p. 70.

Byrne, Harlan S., "Raytheon Co.; In Diversifying Years Ago, 'We Did the Right Thing'," *Barron's,* April 2, 1990, pp. 61–62.

Cox, Bob, "CEO of Raytheon's Beech Aircraft Corp. Breathes New Life into Company," *Wichita Eagle,* September 21, 1997.

——, "In Wichita, Kan., Raytheon Aircraft Makes Up for Lost Time," *Wichita Eagle,* September 21, 1997.

——, "Raytheon Aircraft Co. Stars in Parent Company's 1996 Results," *Wichita Eagle,* January 21, 1997.

Dinell, David, " 'Sound of Silence' New Feature for Raytheon's King Air 350," *Wichita Business Journal,* March 27, 1998, p. 13.

Donlan, Thomas G., "Poised for Takeoff," *Barron's,* January 26, 1987, p. 14.

Hedrick, Frank E., *Pageantry of Flight: The Story of Beech Aircraft Corporation,* New York: Newcomen Society in North America, 1967.

Higdon, Dave, "GAO Backs Raytheon Aircraft Co. in Military's Choice of Flight Trainer," *Wichita Eagle,* February 6, 1996.

Johnson, Maryfran, "Raytheon Aims to Build Aircraft Quicker," *Computerworld,* March 17, 1997, pp. 75, 79.

Kirchofer, Tom, "Raytheon Cuts 750 More; Economy, Attacks Force Decrease in Aircraft Jobs," *Boston Herald,* October 2, 2001.

McMillin, Molly, "New Raytheon Chief Shuffles Management," *Wichita Eagle,* July 13, 2001.

——, "Raytheon Aircraft: Re-Engineering, JPATS Breed Optimism," *Wichita Business Journal,* August 4, 1995, p. 1.

——, "Raytheon Executive Works to Improve Production at Wichita, Kan., Facility," *Wichita Eagle,* June 17, 2001.

——, "Raytheon Unveils New Super-Size Business Jet in Wichita, Kan.," *Wichita Eagle,* April 18, 2001.

——, "Wichita, Kan.-Based Raytheon [Aircraft] Appoints Heir for Retiring CEO," *Wichita Eagle,* September 9, 1999.

McMillin, Molly, and Jessica Marshall, "Raytheon Announced 750 Job Cuts by the End of the Year," *Wichita Eagle,* October 2, 2001.

Mason, Francis K., *Hawker Aircraft Since 1920,* Annapolis, Md.: Naval Institute Press, 1991.

Muller, Joann, "Raytheon Unit Is Accused of Industrial Espionage; Florida Firm Alleges Foul in $450 Million Aircraft Pact," *Boston Globe,* January 22, 1997, p. E2.

——, "Soaring Unit Finally Gets Its Day in the Sun," *Boston Globe,* May 26, 1998, p. D1.

North, David M., "Executive Jet to Spend $2 Billion for Horizons," *Aviation Week & Space Technology,* June 21, 1999, p. 41.

Pearce, Dennis, "Lexington, Mass.-Based Raytheon Enjoys High Aircraft Unit Profits," *Wichita Eagle,* January 27, 1999.

——, "Raytheon Develops Business Jet Made Mostly from Composite Materials," *Wichita Eagle,* March 8, 1999.

Pelletier, A.J., *Beech Aircraft and Their Predecessors,* Annapolis, Md.: Naval Institute Press, 1995.

Phillips, Edward H., "Premier I Aims for Top Spot in Small-Bizjet Arena," *Aviation Week & Space Technology,* September 17, 2001, pp. 60–67.

——, "Raytheon Still Improving Venerable A36 Bonanza," *Aviation Week & Space Technology,* July 29, 1996, pp. 53ff.

——, "Raytheon Unveils Hawker Horizon," *Aviation Week & Space Technology,* November 18, 1996, pp. 55ff.

Proctor, Paul, "Raytheon Restructures Merged Aircraft Units," *Aviation Week & Space Technology,* June 5, 1995, pp. 58ff.

"Raytheon Jet Production Takes Off," *Quality,* May 2001, pp. 59–60.

Ripley, Tim, "France's Dassault Aviation Considers Buying Raytheon Aircraft," *Defense Daily International,* December 22, 2000, p. 1.

Scott, Gerald, "The Cat's Pajamas; Jaguar-Raytheon Venture Gives a New Meaning to Bonnet Leaper," *Chicago Tribune,* Auto Show Sec., February 8, 1998, p. 7.

Sutton, Oliver, "Premier Set to Change the Bizjet Mindset," *Interavia,* October 1998, pp. 32–34.

Vartabedian, Ralph, and James F. Peltz, "Beech Wins $7 Billion US Trainer Derby," *Los Angeles Times,* June 23, 1995, p. D1.

Velocci, Anthony L., Jr., "Raytheon Aircraft May Be Candidate for Divestiture," *Aviation Week & Space Technology,* March 13, 2000, p. 51.

Zitner, Aaron, "Raytheon Says It May Expand Commercial Aircraft Operation," *Boston Globe,* May 27, 1993, p. 45.

—Frederick C. Ingram

Renishaw plc

New Mills	
Wotton-under-Edge	
Gloucestershire GL12 8JR	
United Kingdom	
Telephone: (+44) 1453-524-524	
Fax: (+44)1453-524-901	
Web site: http://www.renishaw.com	

Public Company
Incorporated: 1973 as Renishaw Electrical Ltd.
Employees: 1,512
Sales: £125.35 million ($177.3 million) (2000)
Stock Exchanges: London
Ticker Symbol: RSW
NAIC: 334519 Other Measuring and Controlling Device Manufacturing; 334515 Instrument Manufacturing for Measuring and Testing Electricity and Electrical Signals

Renishaw plc is the world's leading manufacturer of test-probe and measurement equipment for Co-ordinate Measuring Machine (CMM) systems offering precision sensitivity up to one-third of a micron. The company, based in Gloucestershire, England, is structured into six divisions, each focusing on a specific CMM product applications: Machine tools, Lasers, Calibration, Encoders, Digitizers, and Spectroscopy. Three additional divisions, Technical Services, Manufacturing Services, and Corporate Services offer support to the company's product divisions. Renishaw, led by founders David R. McMurtry, chairman and CEO, and John Deer, deputy chairman—who together own more than 50 percent of the company's stock—not only leads its market but has long functioned as its chief pioneer. The company holds a large array of patents, many of which are under Mc-Murty's name, protecting its products and technologies, and is well known for defending its patents against infringements. The company operates on a worldwide basis, with one-third of its sales coming from the United States. The United Kingdom represents 11 percent of sales, and the company generates more than 35 percent of its revenues in Europe. Japan is another of the company's major markets, generating 12 percent of its revenues, which topped £125 million in 2001. The company is present in more than 20 countries worldwide.

Inventing an Industry in the 1970s

David McMurty worked as an engineer at Rolls-Royce during the 1970s, and, as Assistant Chief of Engine Design, was closely involved in developing the Olympus engine used to power the Concorde jet then under development. In 1972, McMurty was asked to come up with a solution for measuring the tiny tubes—as small as one-quarter inch in diameter—used in the Olympus engine design. Traditional measuring devices were unable to provide post-production measurement—a necessary step for ensuring the safety and viability of the engine—because they tended to deflect the thin tubes. McMurty took the problem home with him, and, over the weekend, developed the world's first "touch-trigger" probe, using materials that included six ball bearings and even a piece of his bedroom carpet. Mounted on a standard measuring machine, the touch-trigger probe offered a far more sensitive reading than any other available technology and was to remain an industry standard into the next century.

Rolls-Royce instantly saw the potential of McMurty's invention, and protected it with a patent, listing McMurty as the inventor. The patent was owned by Rolls-Royce, however. Yet McMurty already looked forward to adapting the probe for use in other industrial applications. In this, McMurty was encouraged by his first third-party order, for ten probes from CMM maker Notsa.

McMurty had already gained some commercial and manufacturing experience, having formed with a partner a small company, Shepherd and Adams (the name came from his wife's and his partner's wife's maiden names), to design and build components based on other McMurty inventions. In 1973, McMurty joined with another Rolls-Royce engineer, John Deer, who specialized in power plant aerodynamics and had experience in machine shop engineering, to acquire a license from Rolls-Royce to develop new products based on the touch-trigger patent.

In order to secure the license, Deer and McMurty acquired a dormant limited liability company, Renishaw Electrical Ltd.

Company Perspectives:

Renishaw will design, manufacture, and supply metrology systems of the highest quality and reliability to enable customers worldwide to carry out dimensional measurements to traceable standards. Our product offerings will enhance quality and productivity, and we will strive for total customer satisfaction through superior customer service.

Our aim is to provide leading edge technology by encouraging innovation to address our customers' needs. We are committed to sustained growth through continued investment in product development and manufacturing methods. Renishaw wishes to be recognized collectively and individually as leaders and contributors in our field and our community. We wish to achieve our aims in a way that is caring, open, and honest. Renishaw is an environmentally conscious and responsible company. We will strive to ensure that all aspects of the business have the least harmful effect on the environment.

Through Renishaw, Deer and McMurty were granted the license agreement with Rolls-Royce and began developing their first touch-trigger products, under the S&A name, in McMurty's garage. Both McMurty and Deer remained employed at Rolls-Royce, producing their prototype probes in their spare time. In order to fill the Notsa order, production was moved to Deer's home. Notsa then included the probe as part of its display at a trade fair, and the device attracted interests and orders from other CMM manufacturers. The new business encouraged Deer to leave Rolls-Royce and became Renishaw's first full-time employee in 1974.

Renishaw had a growing business but did not own its own product. In 1976, Deer convinced Rolls-Royce to sell a 50 percent interest in the touch trigger patent to Renishaw. The company then bought its first dedicated facility, a former ice-cream factory in Wotton-under-Edge, in Gloucestershire, and began manufacturing under the Renishaw trade name. By then, Renishaw had nine employees and had already gained its primary position among the world's CMM manufacturers. The company soon extended its range, adapting its technology for use on CNC machinery.

McMurty continued to move up in the Rolls-Royce ranks, and by 1977 he had been promoted to Deputy Chief Designer. However, McMurty chose instead to pursue Renishaw's development, reducing his role at Rolls-Royce to that of a two-day-per-week consultant. McMurty was a prime force behind development of Rolls-Royce's M45 "Quiet Engine" and remained with that company through the completion of that project. At last, in 1979, McMurty left Rolls-Royce to join Renishaw full time.

The arrival of McMurty signaled the start of a new era of product development at Renishaw, as McMurty turned his design genius to adapting and expanding the company's technology to a wider range of applications. McMurty's designs not only improved Renishaw's product line, it also kept new products at the forefront of the company's growing industry niche. From the outset, however, Renishaw distinguished itself by its careful safeguarding of its technology. The company maintained a strict policy of pursuing patents for its new designs. As McMurty told the *Financial Times:* "The first patent set us off on a track we have continued with. We develop only products that are patentable and that can be commercialized." Renishaw also proved itself an aggressive combatant when it came to protecting its patents against copyright infringement, to the point where, by the late 1990s, the company's legal department was a steady contributor to the company's profits.

International Expansion in the 1980s

Renishaw began to grow quickly at the start of the 1980s. After expanding its first manufacturing facility in 1980, the company, which by 1981 was posting nearly £3 million in sales, purchased a 14-acre site in a former wool mill outside of Wotton. This site, New Mills, became the company's headquarters and, after an extensive renovation, opened officially in 1985.

By then, Renishaw had already become an internationally operating company. In 1981, Renishaw set up its first foreign subsidiary, in Chicago, Illinois, bringing it close to the U.S. automotive and other industries. The United States was quickly to become Renishaw's primary market—by the turn of the century the company posted some one-third of it sales in the United States market alone. That same year, the company launched Renishaw Electronics (Ireland) Ltd., later renamed Renishaw (Ireland) Ltd., in order to add manufacturing capacity.

In 1982, Renishaw turned to Japan, establishing the subsidiary Renishaw KK in Tokyo and opening a regional office in Nagoya. The following year, Renishaw went public, taking a listing on the London Stock Exchange's Unlisted Securities Market. By 1984, Renishaw had stepped up to a full listing on the London main board. Nonetheless, McMurty and Deer maintained majority control of the company, leading the *Financial Times* to the describe the company as being "in a no-mans land between public and private."

Yet with McMurty and Deer at the helm, Renishaw often flouted current-day management wisdom. The company insisted on maintaining strong cash stock piles, and, in times of economic recession, refused to consider laying off employees as a means of maintaining its profitability levels. The company also insisted on maintaining full control of its manufacturing process, to the point where it designed its own continuous unmanned production system, dubbed Ramtic, giving the company still tighter control of its just-in-time manufacturing process. Renishaw's insistence on self-reliance even led the company toward developing its own in-house travel agency, responsible for coordinating travel within the company's growing international network. in 1986, the company moved into Germany, launching its Renishaw GmbH subsidiary.

An important step in Renishaw's history came in 1987, when the company purchased the remained 50 percent of its original touch-trigger probe patent from Rolls-Royce. By then, that patent had given the company virtual monopoly control of its market niche, with its market share estimated to range up to 80 percent. The company had meanwhile continued to build strongly on that foundation, adapting its technology to a variety of industrial applications. Renishaw also entered other, related

Key Dates:

1972: David McMurty invents the world's first touch-trigger probe.
1973: McMurty and John Deer acquire Renishaw Electrical Ltd and acquire license to produce touch-trigger probes.
1983: Renishaw lists on the London Stock Exchange's Unlisted Securities Market.
1984: Renishaw lists on LSE main board.
1990: The company's international expansion includes Italy, Spain, Switzerland, and Hong Kong.
2001: Renishaw forms joint-venture distribution agreement with RLS of Slovenia to enter Eastern Europe.

fields, such as the development of spectroscopy products, including Raman and photoluminescence-based microscope and spectroscopes. Other patents gave the company leading positions in areas such as microchip inspection devices; systems for testing aircraft wing response to turbulence; and a system, developed in the 1990s, for using computer-controlled scanners to provide more accurate measurements of gaps between teeth.

Renishaw made its first and only acquisition in 1988, acquiring France's Périféric SARL, a maker of terminals for CNC machine tools. Renishaw's interest in that company, renamed Renishaw SA in 1990, was especially in its established distribution network, giving Renishaw a strong introduction into the French market.

World Leader in the 21st Century

At the end of the 1980s and the beginning of the 1990s, Renishaw stepped up its international expansion, launching subsidiaries in Italy in 1989, Spain and Switzerland in 1991, and Hong Kong in 1993. The company was also expanding its manufacturing base, opening a new facility, the Technology Centre, on its Wotton headquarters and manufacturing campus in 1990. A further addition to that facility was made with the completion of a new machine shop in 1993. By 1997, the company was expanding again, in the first phase of what was seen as a long-term expansion program designed to double the size of the company's Gloucestershire campus.

In the late 1990s, Renishaw continued to build on its commanding world leadership position, opening a number of new offices around the world. The company entered South America, with a subsidiary in Sao Paulo, Brazil, in 1996. By then, the company had also begun to build its interests in the Pacific and Far East, opening representative offices in Singapore and Beijing, China, in 1994, then in Jakarta, Indonesia, in 1995. Renishaw added a new office in Shanghai in 1997, while adding a presence in Seoul, South Korea, in 1999 and in India through new subsidiary Renishaw Metrology Systems Private Ltd. in 2000. The company also strengthened its position in the Pacific region, launching subsidiary Renishaw Oceania, based in Australia.

In 2001, the company made its first moves into the Eastern European market, establishing a 50–50 joint venture agreement with RLS merilna tehnika d.o.o., of Slovenia. As part of that agreement, RLS was to handle the marketing of Renishaw's products in Slovenia, Croatia, Hungary, Romania, and Bulgaria, while Renishaw agreed to introduce RLS's products in its own markets. In that year, also, Renishaw established a new Dutch subsidiary, Renishaw International BV, to support its business in the Benelux market.

Renishaw suffered from the economic downturn at the turn of the century, particularly as its largest market, the United States, struggled to throw off a possible recession in 2001. The company continued to boast revenues gains, however, boosting its sales past £125 million for that year. With a portfolio of more than 700 patents, many of which were signed by chairman and CEO McMurty, Renishaw seemed certain to continue its tradition of technological inventiveness into the twenty-first century.

Principal Subsidiaries

Renishaw Inc. (United States); Renishaw GmbH (Germany); Renishaw KK (Japan); Renishaw International BV (Netherlands); Renishaw Metrology Systems Private Ltd (Bangalore); Renishaw Oceania Pty Ltd. (Australia); Renishaw SA (France); Renishaw (Hong Kong) Ltd; Renishaw SpA (Italy); Renishaw Iberica S.A (Spain); Renishaw A.G (Switzerland); Renishaw Latino Americana Ltda (Brazil); Renishaw (Ireland) Ltd.

Principal Competitors

Badger Meter, Inc; Controlotron Corporation; Euro Tech Holdings Company Limited; HORIBA, Ltd; ILX Lightwave Corporation; Marpos SpA; Mesa Laboratories, Inc; RADCOM Ltd.; Rohde & Schwarz GmbH & Co. KG.

Further Reading

"Investment Column: Renishaw," *Independent*, January 25, 2002, p. 21.
Marsh, Peter, "Technology Entrepreneur Has the Measure of His Markets," *Financial Times*, September 1, 1999.
Potter, Ben, "How Renishaw Measures Up," *Daily Telegraph*, October 1, 1999.
Renishaw Group Profile 2001, Renishaw Plc, Wotton: 2001.
Swann, Christopher, "Six Ball Bearings and a Piece of Bedroom Carpet," *Financial Times*, October 23, 1998.

—M. L. Cohen

rotork

Rotork plc

Rotork House
Brassmill Lane
Bath, Avon BA1 3JQ
United Kingdom
Telephone: (+44) 1225-733-200
Fax: (+44) 1225-733-381
Web site: http://www.rotork.com

Public Company
Incorporated: 1968 as Rotork Controls plc
Employees: 1,021
Sales: £107.88 million ($161 million)(2000)
Stock Exchanges: London
Ticker Symbol: ROR
NAIC: 333995 Fluid Power Cylinder and Actuator
Manufacturing

Rotork plc is the world's leading manufacturer of valve actuators—devices that provide remote control of valves for pipelines and other systems. The company's products combine electronic control capabilities with mechanical, hydraulic, pneumatic, and other systems to provide on-off and graduated control of typically fluid flow systems. The company also manufacturers companion process control systems and components, but actuators remain its primary product, accounting for nearly all of its £108 million in revenues. Based in Bath, England, Rotork has long been active internationally, with manufacturing facilities, service and sales centers, and other subsidiaries located in the United States, Canada, Venezuela, Japan, Singapore, China and Malaysia, Australia, France, Germany, and elsewhere. Approximately half of the company's sales are achieved outside of the United Kingdom. The company's principal market has long been the oil and gas industry; since the late 1990s the company has sought to protect itself from that industry's cycles by stepping up its activity in other industries, notably in the water and wastewater sector, power generation industry, and pulp and paper industry. Rotork is traded on the London Stock Exchange and is led by CEO William H. Whiteley.

Specialization and Innovation in the 1950s and 1960s

Rotork operated as a small electrical and mechanical engineering workshop in Bristol, England, during the mid-1940s, when it was acquired by the Frenchay Products Group, owned by the Fry brothers, David and Jeremy. Under Frenchay, the Rotork company was given the task of developing valve motorization devices, a more or less undeveloped market at the time. Yet Rotork soon came under the wing of Jeremy Fry himself, who saw the potential in building a company focused on valve actuators. Rotork was reformed as a separate company, Rotork Engineering Company Ltd., and began buying and motorizing valves in the early 1950s. Soon after the company began designing its own valve actuators, and in 1952 released the first design featuring the Rotork name. In 1957, Fry brought Rotork to new quarters, a workshop established in his own home. The company continued to operated primarily on the research and design side, contracting out for its manufacturing requirements.

Fry's intuition was quickly validated. The massive increase in demand for oil products in the postwar era, stemming not only from a dramatic increase in automobile use but also in the rebuilding and modernization of Europe's industry, had created a vast new market for actuators. Rotork's steady innovation, including the development of flameproof actuators in the mid-1950s, gave it an edge on competitors and the company was soon winning large-scale orders from such petroleum industry heavyweights as BP and Shell.

The nature of Rotork's products made it an international company from the start as it sought out customers in the world's major port cities. The company established its first foreign sales agent in 1958, in Australia. By then, it was producing nearly 600 actuators per year, not only from oil companies but from a growing number of valve manufacturers. The company now began to take on its own production needs, establishing a manufacturing facility in an old mill.

Rotork achieved a breakthrough in 1960 when it introduced an O ring seal that enabled the company to produce its first environmentally sealed actuators. Another breakthrough at the time was a simplified switching mechanism, dubbed the Syncroset. These innovations were incorporated into Rotork's

new A range of Syncroset actuators, which was to remain the
company's core product line for many years.

By 1962, orders for the A range forced the company to
expand its manufacturing capability, and the company built a
new plant, in Bath, which quickly became Rotork's headquarters site as well. By then, the company had entered the European
continent, drumming up sales in Germany and France. One of
the company's largest-ever orders came from France, where the
government's Atomic Energy Authority placed an order for
1,000 actuators for a new uranium isotope production plant.
This order led the company toward setting up a dedicated
service facility in that country.

The next major step in Rotork's actuator design was the
introduction of the Syncropak in 1964. This design built on the
company's O ring seal—which protected components from
harsh environmental condition—to feature integrated starter
and control systems. With reduced installation and operation
costs, as well as greater reliability and control, the Syncropak
became the company's next big seller. By 1966, Rotork's production had ramped up to 4,000 units per year, and by the end of
the decade had topped 6,000 devices per year, more than half of
which featured Rotork's Syncropak technology.

Rotork continued to eye international expansion in the late
1960s. The company found a manufacturing partner in Japan,
then in the midst of a industrial boom. Rotork also began to eye
entry into the highly lucrative U.S. market, the site of much of the
world's oil and petroleum industry. In 1968, the company opened
its first United States, Rotork Inc., in New York. In order to
finance its expansion in the United States, Rotork went public in
1968, listing on the London stock exchange as Rotork Controls
Ltd. The successful stock offering gave the company an initial
value of more than £2 million. The majority of Rotork's shares
remained controlled, however, by Jeremy Fry.

Growth in the 1970s; Microelectronics in the 1980s

The company's steady growth had led it to add new manufacturing space at its Bath facility. By 1970, that plant had
doubled its original size—by 1975 the facility had grown again
by another 50 percent. Meanwhile, Rotork was adding manufacturing capacity elsewhere, especially in the United States,
where it opened a dedicated facility in Maryland in 1970. At the
same time, Rotork offered the next step in its actuator design,
releasing a double-sealed actuator that provided superior environmental protection.

The company faced new problems during the 1970s, however,
as the number of its competitors—many of which were now
imitating Rotork's own designs—sprang up, offering lower
priced but lower quality products. Rotork's own commitment to
quality, highlighted by its quality assurance program called Controlled Manufacturing System, helped win approval for use of its
actuators in the nuclear power program in the United States.
Meanwhile, despite unrest at home and a gloomy economic
climate, Rotork continued to book increases in orders. By 1974,
the company had reached an annual production of 13,000 units,
building up its actuator sales to more than £5 million per year.
Nonetheless, the economic turmoil of the second half of the
decade, notably within the company's core petroleum market, hit
the company hard and Rotork struggled to stay profitable.

In 1977, the company entered a new market, quickly indus-
trializing India, where it entered a joint-venture manufacturing
agreement. Two years later, Rotork opened a manufacturing
subsidiary in Germany. The company was also expanding its
actuator range to include smaller, lower-cost and lower-margin
electrical actuators. They then added large-scale electrical actuators and a series of partial-turn actuators, enabling it to extend
its product range to include nearly the entire spectrum of actuator demand.

Despite continued difficulties in a number of its markets in
the early 1980s—including the accident at Three Mile Island
which placed a pall of the nuclear power industry in the United
States—Rotork continued to record steady increases in product
orders. Part of this increase came in the company's continued
international expansion. In 1983, the company entered a number of new markets, including Spain and Singapore. The following year, it opened a subsidiary in Saudi Arabia, marking its
presence in 11 countries.

In 1984, however, Rotork achieved a new breakthrough. The
launch of the newest A range actuator, the 1600 Series, introduced the company's first product incorporating solid-state
electronics as part of its control systems. The success of the
1600 Series encouraged the company to abandon its attempt to
cover the lower-end of the market and instead concentrate its
efforts on developing high-end and high-margin lines. By the
end of 1984, nearly half of all new orders were for the solid state
1600 Series. That year, Jeremy Fry retired, having built Rotork
into a business producing revenues of £21 million per year.

Rotork had been developing its own dedicated control systems for its valve actuators, a process which was speeded up in
1985 with the acquisition of a company specializing in instrumentation and control systems. By 1986, Rotork was ready to
launch its latest product, Pakscan, which offered microproces-
sor-based control over multiple actuator arrays. Pakscan
quickly became one of Rotork's principal products, generating
roughly a quarter of its sales. Other new products turned out
during the 1980s were the AQ quarter-turn actuator, which was
followed up the by smaller Q range, both of which incorporated
electronic control technology.

Boosting IQ for the Turn of the Century

During the 1980s, Rotork's international expansion continued, now with an emphasis on the booming Asian Pacific

Key Dates:

1945: Rotork, a small mechanical and electrical engineering firm, is acquired by Frenchay Products, owned by David and Jeremy Fry.

1952: Jeremy Fry orients Rotork toward the design of valve actuators, releasing the first Rotork-branded actuator.

1960: Rotork develops an O ring seal and Syncroset.

1962: The company builds a manufacturing facility and its headquarters in Bath, England.

1968: Rotork goes public as Rotork Controls plc.

1970: The company opens a manufacturing plant in the United States.

1984: Rotork launches 1600 Series A range actuator, the first featuring solid state electronics.

1992: The release of the IQ range represents the company's biggest product breakthrough since the 1960s.

1999: The company acquires Fluid System Srl, based in Italy, and the U.K. firm the Valvekits Group.

2002: Rotork acquires the U.S. company Jordan Controls.

region. The company established a dedicated subsidiary in Australia, replacing its former sales agent. The company's Singapore office became the hub for Rotork's expansion into Malaysia, Thailand, Indonesia, Hong Kong, and then later into China as well.

In 1992, Rotork achieved a new product breakthrough with the release of its new IQ range. This new product range represented a step forward in the integration of microprocessor technology, enabling the company to reduce the number mechanical components by more than half over the A range. The IQ actuators also featured such innovations as hand-held infrared setting tools, which enabled actuators to be commissioned from a distance and under otherwise hazardous conditions.

The IQ series represented the most significant event in Rotork's history since the launch of the A range nearly three decades early. The new product line quickly asserted itself, establishing Rotork at the forefront of the world's actuator technology and enabling Rotork to boost its sales past the £100 million mark by decade's end. The IQ series gave the company a long head start on its competition, and it was not until later in the decade that Rotork began to meet serious competitive response.

In the meantime, Rotork moved to expand its operation a bit, in part to reduce its reliance on the petroleum industry by attracting more business from other sectors, especially the water and wastewater management industry and the power generation industry. As part of this effort, Rotork established a specialized Fluid Power Division, operating from manufacturing plants in Rochester, New York; Leeds, England; and Singapore in 1995.

In the late 1990s, Rotork took advantage of the strength of the British pound and the economic turmoil affecting Asia and South America to make a series of acquisitions in 1998 and 1999, including Exeeco Ltd., Alecto Valve Actuators (based in the Netherlands), and Fluid System Srl (based in Italy). The

company was also building up its interests in gearboxes as it sought to extend its reach across a wider array of components touching its core actuator business, buying up Valvekits Group Ltd. in 1999. That year, the company's sales topped £117 million. The following year, Rotork bundled its gear manufacturing business under a new division, Rotork Gears.

Rotork closed out the century with a number of developments, including the construction of a new manufacturing plant in Rochester, New York. The company also established its first wholly-owned subsidiary in China in 2000, as that market took on growing importance to the group. That year the company acquired the actuator division of Skil Controls Ltd., bringing the company a new line of Skilmatic actuators. This acquisition fit in with the company's determination to extend its actuator expertise across a wider range of applications. Rotork continued to work toward this objective with the launch of a new line of electro-hydraulic actuators, the EH range. By the end of 2000, the company had successfully launched the latest generation of IQ actuators. Nonetheless, as many of its major markets slowed down in what was feared to be the start of a new global recession, Rotork's sales slumped as well, dipping back to £108 million for the year.

Rotork bounced back at the beginning of 2002, announcing the acquisition of Jordan Controls, based in the United States. That company's process control actuators, allowing control over both valve opening range and timing, fit in with Rotork's ambition to establish itself as an across-the-board actuator supplier. Given the company's long history at the forefront of actuator innovation, Rotork seemed certain to retain its leadership position well into the new century.

Principal Subsidiaries

Rotork Controls Ltd; Exeeco Ltd; Valvekits Ltd; Rotork Controls Inc. (United States); Rotork Controls (Canada) Ltd; Rotork Motorisation SA, (France); Rotork Controls (Italy) Srl; Rotork Fluid System Srl (Italy); Rotork Controls (Singapore) Pte Ltd,; Rotork Ltd, (Hong Kong); Rotork Japan Co Ltd; Rotork Controls (Germany) GmbH; Rotork Controls (Spain) SL; Rotork Controls (Singapore) Pte Ltd; Rotork Australia Pty Ltd; Rotork BV (Netherlands); Alecto Valve Actuators BV (Netherlands); Rotork Arabia Ltd (Saudi Arabia); Rotork Controls Ltd (India); Rotork-Controls de Venezuela SA; Rotork Ltd (Hong Kong); Rotork Controls Co, Ltd. (South Korea); Rotork Controls Ltd, (China); Shenzhen Sinopec-Rotork Actuation Co, Ltd, (China; 35%); Rotork Africa (Pty) Ltd (South Africa); Rotork (Thailand) Ltd; Rotork Sdn Bhd (Malaysia); Rotork Japan Co Ltd; Rotork Control & Safety Ltd; Rotork Inc (United States); Rotork Overseas Ltd; Graphics Interface Ltd. (25%).

Principal Competitors

Asco Joucomatic Ltd; British Engines Ltd; Technologies Ltd; Crane Stockham Valve Ltd; Dairy Pipe Lines Ltd; FCX Manufacturing U.K. Ltd; Fisher-Rosemount Ltd; Goodwin International Ltd; Guest & Chrimes Ltd; Holdings Ltd; Hender Ltd; Hopkinsons Ltd; IMI Bailey Birkett Ltd; Kent Introl Ltd; Keystone Valve (UK) Ltd; Metso Automation Ltd; Reiss Engineering Ltd; Severn Glocon Group PLC; Engineering PLC; Truflo Marine Valves Ltd; Tyco Valves Ltd.

Further Reading

Anderson, Simon, "Shares Rise on Rotork's Confident Forecasts," *Daily Telegraph*, March 28, 1998.

Blackwell, David, "Rotork Acquires US Valves Group," *Financial Times*, January 9, 2002.

Foley, Stephen, "Rotork," *Independent,* August 9, 2001, p. 17.

Murray-West, Rosie, "Stay a Spell with Rotork's Wizardry," *Daily Telegraph*, August 9, 2001, p. 38.

Pickard, Jim, "Rotork Benefits from Recovery in Oil Industry," *Financial Times*, August 9, 2001.

Rotork: 40 years in Control, UK: Rotork Plc, 1997.

—M.L. Cohen

RSA Security Inc.

36 Crosby Drive
Bedford, Massachusetts 01730
U.S.A.
Telephone: (781) 301-5000
Fax: (781) 301-5170
Web site: http:/www.rsasecurity.com

Public Company
Founded: 1982 as RSA Data Security
Employees: 1,093
Sales: $282.7 million (2001)
Stock Exchanges: NASDAQ
Ticker Symbol: RSAS
NAIC: 51121 Software Publishers; 334119 Other
    Computer Peripheral Equipment Manufacturers

RSA Security Inc. develops, manufactures, and distributes a wide range of security equipment and software. RSA's BSAFE public-key encryption software has been the de facto industry standard for data protection for over a decade. The firm's SecurID authentication systems use tokens and smart cards to guarantee that only authorized individuals can gain access to buildings and computer networks. Its Keon public key infrastructure software provides business with the means to produce private and legally binding electronic communications and transactions.

Technology Origins and Company Start-Up

The discoveries behind RSA's most important technological breakthroughs were made possible in the mid-1970s. Computer scientists were concerned then about finding a secure way to encrypt data, that is to reduce data to an unreadable code in order to prevent unauthorized persons from having access to it. At the time only one type of encryption had been developed, single-key encryption. In a single-key system, a single mathematical formula or key was used both to encode and decode. If an encrypted email were sent using a single-code technology, both the sender and the receiver would have to know the same mathematical key. If the sender wanted to send encrypted email to a number of recipients, *all* of them would have to know the key. The more widespread the

key was, of course, the more likely it would fall into the hands of someone would who *should not* have it. Once it fell into the wrong hands, the key was all but useless.

Scientists at Stanford University proposed a solution to the problem in 1976. The theory, called public-key encryption, was perfected a year later by Ronald Rivest, Adi Shamir, and Leonard Adleman, three students at MIT. Their system used a mathematical formula to generate two related keys: the private-key was known only by a single individual, call him John Doe; the public-key was freely available to anyone who wanted it. Each key was a one-way key and was useless without the other. For example, the public key was used to encode data being sent to Doe, but only Doe's private key could be used to read the data. Since he was the only one who knew it, or had to know it, chances were much slimmer that it would become known to persons who should not have it. Doe could also use the private key to encode messages which could be opened using his public key. Because only Doe was in possession of the private key, such messages bore a kind of electronic signature, guaranteeing that it was Doe who sent them.

Rivest, Shamir, and Adleman obtained a patent through MIT for their development, and in 1982 they set up a company in Adleman's apartment. It was called RSA Data Security, the name an acronym formed by the partners' initials. Unfortunately, RSA encryption was performed using sophisticated and complex mathematics. Most computers in the 1980s were simply not powerful enough to perform the calculations quickly, and soon the company was facing bankruptcy. In 1986, Jim Bidzos, a Florida businessman, was hired to save the Silicon Valley business. Bidzos lived and breathed business, and it wasn't long before he started getting results. Lotus Development bought a license for its Lotus Notes in 1987. Motorola, Apple, and Novell would soon follow. By 1988 the turnaround was in full swing. That year Rupert Murdoch made a multi-million dollar offer to buy the company. Murdoch and Bidzos were unable to agree on a price and, in the end, the deal collapsed.

Attempts to Impose Government Control in the 1980s

As more and more of the economy began to depend on computers to conduct daily affairs, data security became an

---

Company Perspectives:

RSA Security, the most trusted name in e-security, helps organizations build secure, trusted foundations for e-business through its RSA SecurID two-factor authentication, RSA BSAFE encryption, and RSA Keon digital certificate management systems. With approximately one billion RSA BSAFE-enabled applications in use worldwide, more than eight million RSA SecurID users, and almost 20 years of industry experience, RSA Security has the proven leadership and innovative technology to address the changing security needs of e-business and bring trust to the new online economy.

---

increasingly pertinent issue. Bidzos hoped to make RSA's software the standard for encryption in the Untied States and the rest of the world. It would prove to be an up and down game that lasted years, but it was a game Jim Bidzos was uniquely qualified to play. A major milestone was achieved in February 1989 when the technical committee at a large but obscure government/academic computer network called Internet designated RSA to certify encryption keys for its members. Two months later Digital Equipment Corp. and RSA forged a strategic alliance in which they agreed to share technology. Perhaps most significant was a Defense Department license of RSA encryption software taken out in February 1990. The contract was not merely an acknowledgment of the power of RSA's technology, it also seemed to open the door to acceptance of the RSA standard by the entire federal government and the 300,000 companies that did business with it.

Hopes that the rest of the government would follow the Defense Department's example were premature however. In 1990, the National Security Agency (NSA), one of the most powerful and secretive bodies in the U.S. government, started to flex its muscle against RSA. One of NSA's most important tasks is the interception and decoding of encoded transmissions sent by foreign governments and spies. NSA opposed the spread of RSA software on national security grounds. The software's level of sophistication was so high its codes were virtually unbreakable, even by the government's own codebreakers. The Federal Bureau of Investigation (FBI) joined its voice in opposition, maintaining that it would not be able to monitor the activity of terrorists and criminals in the United States who had access to RSA encryption. Under the influence of the NSA and the FBI, the government established as its position that any public-key encryption system should include a *third* key—one the government could use to gain access to encoded data and data transmissions. The NSA and FBI also urged the government to impose tight restrictions on the dissemination of the software at home and abroad.

RSA claimed that NSA interest in blocking the spread of its technology dated back to 1982, when the firm was first founded. The Commerce Department had expressed interest in adopting RSA encryption as the standard for public-key cryptography in the United States. At the request of Commerce, RSA submitted technical information but never heard back from the government. According to the *Wall Street Journal*, it was NSA that persuaded the Commerce Department to cut its ties with RSA.

NSA came out again against government acceptance of RSA software in the early 1990s. Jim Bidzos told *Fortune* about a deal he had with a major software manufacturer that NSA wanted to kill—until Bidzos threatened to go to the *New York Times* and his congressman with the full details. The agency backed down. A few months later, RSA announced a contract with Microsoft. Bidzos seemed to relish going head-to-head with the government. When the government was putting together its alternative to RSA, an encryption package called DSS, it hesitated to pay a $2 million licensing fee to the German holder of a key patent. Bidzos zoomed in. Within an afternoon's time, he persuaded the man to accept a royalty package from RSA. Bidzos killed two birds with that deal: RSA got a key technology, and he blocked the government's access to technology they needed for their alternate encryption package.

Bidzos was outspokenly opposed to any government attempt to control encryption technology. In 1993, when the government released the ''Clipper Chip,'' its approved encryption scheme that would give government access to all coded voice and data transmissions, Bidzos mounted a campaign calling on business to reject any system with ''Big Brother inside.'' Most in the computer industry believed that the government's efforts to block acceptance of RSA software were futile anyway. For one thing, because RSA's most important patent was not enforceable outside the United States, foreign companies could use it to develop their own public-key packages, which would provide encryption just as impermeable to NSA and other government snoops as RSA's. Rather than blocking the spread of effective encryption technology, the computer industry felt the government's actions would simply rob the initiative from U.S. firms and give it to foreign companies.

Early 1990s Acceptance by American Computer Industry

If it still wasn't the official standard, by 1993 RSA's technology was the de facto standard for the American computer industry. Every major computer manufacturer had licensed it. In January 1994, following a conference on data security organized by RSA, a group of leading firms that included Apple, Novell, Lotus, Microsoft, Sun Microsystems, Digital Equipment, Hewlett Packard, National Semiconductor, General Magic, the Bankers Trust Company, and a consortium of five cellular data companies, defied the government by rejecting the Clipper Chip outright and formally adopting RSA's software as their encryption package of choice. There was good reason the industry to embrace RSA. It's products were able to operate in many computer environments; the company's reputation was unassailable—no weak spots had been discovered in RSA's encryption; finally, RSA held all the important encryption patents.

RSA was the victim of an act of industrial espionage in 1994. An unidentified individual posted the code for firm's software on the Internet. The suspected culprits called themselves the Cypherpunks, an online group opposed to government control of encryption technology. The Cypherpunks had also been engaged in a running feud with RSA, whom they accused of monopolistic behavior that interfered with the dissemination of encryption software. RSA immediately announced that the disclosure did not in any way compromise the security of systems protected by RSA software. Bidzos por-

ogy and a roster of high-powered clients was a natural for a public offering.

Mid-1990s Acquisition by Boston Firm

Hence, it came as a great surprise on Wall Street in April 1996 when RSA let itself be acquired by Security Dynamics Technologies, Inc., a small, relatively unknown computer security firm in the Boston, Massachusetts, area. Security Dynamics had earned $34 million in 1995 producing credit-card sized devices known as smart cards that controlled access to computers and computer networks, as well as to buildings. The firm was founded in 1984 and went public in 1994. Security Dynamics CEO Charles Stuckey first initiated talks with RSA in 1995 about the possibility of licensing its encryption technology. Stuckey eventually came to believe that Security Dynamics needed a line of encryption products of its own, and RSA fit the bill perfectly. The idea of an acquisition by the Boston firm was attractive to Bidzos because of the synergies their complementary product lines were likely to generate, as well as the fact that Security Dynamics would not be perceived as a rival to RSA'a other licensees.

Security Dynamics paid out four million shares of stock to RSA's three stockholders. Investors considered the deal a bargain for Security Dynamics, and they showed it with their pocketbooks, sending the firm's share value soaring over $13 to $49.62. Based on that price, the company had paid $251 million for RSA, more than 20 times its 1995 earnings. With e-commerce on the verge of exploding, the deal looked even better considering that RSA seemed to hold the key to secure transactions. Although Security Dynamics was headquartered in Massachusetts, RSA remained based in California.

RSA Data Security opened another foreign subsidiary in January 1999. RSA Data Security Australia was established in Brisbane to develop encryption software which the company planned to market internationally. It hired two Australian researchers to work on technology compatible with RSA's existing line. Critics postulated that the establishment of RSA Data Security Australia in Brisbane was another ploy to evade U.S. export regulations. However, the deal was concluded after only months of negotiations with the Commerce Department over its provisions. In the end, the government okayed RSA's activity in Australia, as long as no U.S. workers or U.S. technology were involved.

RSA Data Security's Jim Bidzos was a marketing genius who knew how to generate the maximum positive publicity for his company and his products. One example was the regular conferences on computer security of the sort that bred the computer industry's rejection of the Clipper Chip. Another was the RSA's DES Challenge, held regularly in the late 1990s, whose purpose was to show up the flaws in the DES encryption standard that the Clinton administration was promoting. In the form advocated by the government, DES utilized a 56-bit system which meant the numerical keys it generated were fifty digits in length. By contrast the keys used on RSA's most powerful systems used keys of 100 digits or more. The difference, according to Bidzos, was that every time another digit was added to a key, the code became twice as difficult to break. In the DES Challenge, cash awards were given to the contestant

---

Key Dates:

1977: Public-key encryption is developed by Ronald Rivest, Adi Shamir, and Leonard Adleman at the Massachusetts Institute of Technology.

1982: Rivest, Shamir, and Adleman found RSA Data Security.

1989: RSA encryption software adopted by fledgling Internet.

1990: RSA software adopted by Defense Department, a move that the National Security Agency opposes.

1993: U.S. government introduces its Clipper Chip technology; group of leading computer, banking, and electronics firms reject Clipper Chip in favor of RSA software.

1994: RSA code is published anonymously on Internet.

1996: RSA Data Security acquired by Security Dynamics Technologies Inc.

1999: RSA Data Security and Security Dynamics Technologies offer joint product line for first time and parent adopts the RSA name.

2001: RSA Security acquires Xcert International, Inc., 3G International, and Securant Technologies

---

trayed it primarily as an infringement of the firm's intellectual property rights and promised to prosecute the offenders. Some analysts believed the affair could have a negative financial impact on RSA. Others, however, speculated the disclosure could have a positive effect. The publication of the code would prove once and for all that RSA systems included no so-called trapdoors that would allow the government to eavesdrop on private communications.

Export restrictions, instigated and enforced by the NSA, were relaxed in 1992 by the first Bush administration. RSA was not allowed to ship its most powerful software abroad, but its less powerful, 40-bit systems, specifically the RC2 and RC4, were exempted from controls. Three and a half years later, in February 1996, Jim Bidzos began testing government export regulations. He organized RSA subsidiaries in the People's Republic of China and in Japan to develop programs more powerful than those permitted under NSA restrictions. For example, the Chinese firm, organized in collaboration with the Chinese Ministry of Foreign Trade and Economic Cooperation and its Academy of Sciences, was given the NSA-approved 40-bit software, but was expected to develop new encryption software from it on their own. Bidzos said RSA in the United States would further develop any promising leads developed in China. The Japanese deal involved RSA cooperation with Nippon Telephone & Telegraph Corporation on the development of powerful new encryption chips, chips that RSA was not permitted to sell directly to a Japanese company.

In the mid-1990s, RSA was still a privately owned company. It had been an attractive takeover target ever since Rupert Murdoch tried to buy it in the 1980s—between 1992 and 1994, Bidzos had received no fewer than five written offers. In 1996, as the dot-com IPO frenzy was getting underway on Wall Street, investors felt that RSA with its widely accepted technol-

who was able to most quickly decode a bit of data coded in DES. In 1997, it took 96 days to crack the test message; in 1998, 41 days; finally, the time fell to just 56 hours. The competitions succeeded in demonstrating the ultimate weakness of the 56-bit standard and resulted in endorsements from computer trade associations in favor of standardizing more powerful systems like RSA's.

RSA and its nominal parent Security Dynamics offered their first joint line of products, the Keon product group, in June 1999. Keon included a Web-based certificate server. Just three months later, Security Dynamics took the name of its California subsidiary, becoming RSA Security Inc. The new name reflected a compete restructuring of the two companies' management that had taken place at the firm, essentially uniting RSA and Security Dynamics as a single company. That company had 800 workers spread through California, Massachusetts, and an office in Sweden. Its revenues in September 1999 were up 21 percent over the previous year.

A battle for patents that Security Dynamics had brought to RSA Security Inc. erupted in February 2000. Kenneth Weiss, who had founded Security Dynamics in 1984, left in 1996 after internal disagreements with other board members. He claimed that under the terms of his employment contract with Security Dynamics he was entitled to the return of patents that were not being commercially exploited by the company. He demanded the return of up to ten patents for security techniques for data compression, data encryption, and biometric identification. Weiss requested that the claim go to arbitration. As of fall 2001, the question had not been settled.

RSA released the code to its most important encryption patent two weeks before it was scheduled to pass into the public domain. The 1983 patent, held by the Massachusetts Institute of Technology and licensed to RSA, made RSA the unquestioned leader of the American encryption field for two decades. With the expiration of its patents, RSA's encryption software suddenly faced competition from domestic and foreign companies. The company believed that its strong customer base and new technology in development would enable it to maintain its position of leadership in the data security field. Lost licensing fees would not hurt the firm's bottom line greatly. Of $218 million in 1999 revenues, royalties made up only $550,000 or so.

RSA Security saw its business slow to a trickle in the wake of the September 11, 2001 attacks on the World Trade Center and Pentagon. Orders to the firm were cut back significantly, taking a bite of about $15 million from revenues. A stock buy-back plan backfired on the company around the same time when the slowing business caused its share price to plunge. They had fallen to $10.90 from the year's high of $44.33. RSA expected to have to pay out about $43 million in stock options it had sold as part of the buy-back scheme.

Principal Subsidiaries

RSA Australia; RSA Japan, Xcert International, Inc.

Principal Divisions

RSA Capital.

Principal Competitors

Check Point Software Technologies Ltd.; Network Associates, Inc.; Secure Computing Corporation.

Further Reading

Clark, Don, "Bay Firm's 'Scrambler' To Guard U.S. Computers," *San Francisco Chronicle*, February 15, 1990, p. A1.
——, "RSA Data May Be Sold In Stock Deal," *Wall Street Journal*, April 15, 1996, p. A3.
——, "RSA Picked to Provide Computer Lock," *San Francisco Chronicle*, February 1, 1989.
——, "RSA Data Security Will Fund China Encryption Software Effort," *Asian Wall Street Journal*, February 9 1996, p. 12.
Kerber, Ross, "RSA Security to Release Software Code Early—Firm Seeks to Reassure Investors as Patent Ends," *Boston Globe*, September 7, 2000, p. C6
Kirchofer, Tom, "Buyback of Shares Gives RSA Big Blow," *Boston Herald*, October 2, 2001, p. 30.
Kutler, Jeffrey, "Another RSA Turkey-Shoot At U.S. Encryption Standard," *American Banker*, January 5, 1999, p. 19.
Markoff, John, "A Secret Computer Code Is Out," *New York Times*, September 17, 1994, p. A37.
——, "Industry Defies U.S. on Data Encryption," *New York Times*, January 14, 1994, p. D3.
——, "Profit and Ego in Data Secrecy," *New York Times*, June 28, 1994, pp. D-1.
Ranalli, Ralph, "Security Dynamics Takes New Name from Calif. Unit," *Boston Herald*, September 13, 1999, p. 31.
Rogers, Amy, "RSA, Security Dynamics Launch Cert Server," *Computer Retail Week*, June 28, 1999.
"RSA Data to Form Foreign Unit for Encryption," *Boston Globe*, January 7, 1999, p. C7.
Stipp, David, "Techno-Hero Or Public Enemy? James Bidzos of Rsa Data Security Wants to Go Global With a Potent Shield Against Computer Break-Ins," *Fortune*, November 11, 1996, p. 172.
Syre, Steven, and Charles Stein, "On Outs, Founder Still Tries to Crack RSA Security," *Boston Globe*, February 23, 2000, p. D1.
Zachary, G. Pascal, "U.S. Agency Stands in Way Of Computer-Security Tool," *Wall Street Journal*, July 9, 1990, p. B1.

—Gerald E. Brennan

Snecma Group

2, boulevard du Général Martial-Valin
75724 Paris Cedex 15
France
Telephone: (33) 01 40 60 80 80
Fax: (33) 01 40 60 81 02
Web site: http://www.snecma.com/

State-Owned Company
Incorporated: May 29, 1945 as Société nationale d'étude
et de construction de moteurs d'aviation
Employees: 36,000
Sales: EUR 5.65 billion; FFr 36.9 billion; $3.67 billion
(2000)
NAIC: 336412 Aircraft Engine and Engine Parts
Manufacturing; 54171 Research and Development in
the Physical, Engineering, and Life Sciences

Snecma Group is considered the world's oldest manufacturer of aircraft engines. It is the fourth largest after GE, Pratt & Whitney, and Rolls-Royce. Of Snecma's two core businesses, Propulsion accounts for a little more than two-thirds of total business. Equipment—a category including landing gear, braking systems, nacelles and thrust reversers, and power transmission—provides the remainder. Revenue from engine and landing systems support services accounts for about 13 percent of sales. The company's CFM International joint venture with GE Aircraft Engines brings Snecma $500 million a year for its share of spare parts business alone.

Pioneering Origins

France has produced its share of aviation pioneers; no less important than the airframe designers and the pilots were the people who produced engines powerful enough and light enough for powered flight to finally take wing.

The technology for the first airplane engines was developed at the same time as early automotive engines. A steam engine powered an early flight attempt by Clément Ader in 1890. Internal combustion engines provided a better power-to-weight ratio, yet most of the early engines sold to aircraft designers were derived from those found in automobiles.

In 1906, Santos Dumont made the first gasoline-powered flight in Europe using a V-8 Antoinette engine producing up to 50 horsepower. Anzani, the Renault brothers, and other firms produced workable engines. According to Snecma's official history, the first airplane motor to be considered a true worldwide success was 50 horsepower Omega, a seven cylinder rotary engine produced by Gnôme. The famed aviator Henri Farman flew a Voisin aircraft powered by an Omega engine to set a 1909 distance and endurance record (180km in 3 hours and 15 minutes).

Snecma traces its origins to the Société des Moteurs Gnôme, founded in 1905 by Louis Seguin. In 1915, this firm merged with the Société des Moteurs Le Rhône, founded three years earlier by Louis Verdet, to form Gnôme & Rhône. While Gnôme had continued to produce rotary engines in the 50 to 100 horsepower range, Rhône had refined its fixed-cylinder engines to produce 200 horsepower. However, both these lines of engines were being outclassed in terms of reliability, economy, or power by several contemporary engine manufacturers.

Nevertheless, the two merged companies were quite successful commercially, thanks to licensed production in Great Britain, Russia, the United States, Sweden, Germany, and Japan, as well as joint ventures in Italy and elsewhere.

Retooling Between the Wars

A number of factors hit Gnôme & Rhône (G&R) hard after the war. A huge tax burden was levied based on the firm's previous international success. At the same time, a mass of war surplus engines glutted the market.

Unlike its other domestic rivals, Gnôme & Rhône lacked experience in areas apart from aero engines, a market now glutted by thousands of surplus motors. A variety of schemes, from making sewing machines to engines for farm tractors or cars, all failed. In constant francs, the company's sales in 1921 were almost half those of 1913, though the factories were five times larger, notes one scholar in the journal *Entreprise et Histoire*. In that year, the already legendary company reduced its employment from 6500 workers to 1200.

Production of motorcycles under the Gnôme & Rhône was one area that produced quite satisfactory results in the marketplace; in fact these machines gained a devoted following. In 1922 the English firm Bristol licensed to G&R the right to produce its powerful air-cooled radial engines producing up to 450 horsepower, as well as the freedom to sell them anywhere in the world except for the United States and the territories of the British Empire. With the support of its banks, G&R was able to retool its workshops to build engines, including the new Jupiter introduced in 1923. At the time, G&R had also taken a significant holding in a French-Romanian airline, which helped establish its engines in Eastern Europe.

Between 1924 and 1928, sales increased more than sixfold. At the same time, the air, sea, and land branches of the French military were deciding their outdated equipment was in need of replacement, hence, another blossoming market at home. Expanding commercial fleets produced still more demand. The radial Jupiter engines earned a reputation for being simple to run and easy to fix, even if in-line and V-8 engines made by Hispano-Suiza and Lorraine-Dietrich were more powerful. A novel program, instituted in 1924, allowed for the lease of the engines for a given number of flight-hours, which relieved designers and manufacturers some of the financial strain associated with bringing out new models of aircraft. The popular Jupiter engine was subsequently licensed for production in several European countries as well as the Soviet Union and Japan.

G&R introduced its K family of engines in 1928. In terms of power, this series culminated in the 750 horsepower 14K licensed to a Soviet factory for eventual use in Antonov transports. G&R's designers evolved L, M, and N families of engines by 1939; one of the latter achieved 1150 horsepower.

Air power played a determining role World War II, and G&R engines had a significant part to play. The Soviet Union's Molotov factory was producing 300 licensed G&R engines a month in 1940 for use in biplanes and Sukhoi fighters. In Japan, Mitsui illegally copied the 850 h.p. 14K engine, producing the "Suizei" powerplant found in the Mitsubishi Zeroes that attacked Pearl Harbor. During the Nazi occupation of France, G&R became a subsidiary of BMW. Emmanuel Chadeau writes in *Entreprises et Histoire* that G&R thereby influenced 16 manufacturers in 14 countries during the war; this off-shore production nearly equaled G&R's own output of 8,000 motors a year—together accounting for a quarter of the worldwide market.

SNECMA Created in 1945

The high share price that G&R commanded prevented it from being nationalized before the war. However, this did come to pass after the Liberation. SNECMA, la Société nationale d'étude et de construction de moteurs d'aviation, was thus created on May 29, 1945. The company was an amalgamation of diverse design bureaus and workshops; it inherited a work force of 10,000 mostly part-time employees. Along with G&R, Snecma was given some of the factories of the Société des moteurs et automobiles Lorraine, formerly Lorraine-Dietrich, which had been nationalized as la Société nationale des moteurs and had been relegated to making parts for tanks. Some of Snecma's other facilities had been devoted to the production of German Junkers engines by the thousands during the Nazi occupation. G&R also owned a factory of the Aéroplanes Voisin firm, which had gone bankrupt in 1938.

Unfortunately, the British government preferred to grant licenses for the newly acquired jet engine technology to rival Hispano-Suiza in the immediate postwar period. Snecma immediately after World War II suffered many of the same disadvantages as G&R had immediately after WWI. It was not until 1950, writes Chadeau, that budgetary crisis forced a restructuring that closed unproductive plants and reequipped modern ones to give the firm some hope of a future.

Given their already apparent importance in the future of military aviation, jet engines were the prime focus of Snecma's development in the 1950s. However, the company did not abandon propeller-driven aircraft. In 1951, the firm acquired a license from the Bristol firm to produce the 2,080 h.p. Hercules engine for use in Noratlas military transports; nearly 1,400 of these were produced by 1964.

The creation of jet engines in the World War II propelled planes allowed a huge leap in aircraft performance. However, in the period immediately after the war, the devastated nations of Europe were unable to match American and Soviet research into jet engine design until the middle of the 1950s. A group of 120 former BMW engineers were assembled in the French controlled sector of Germany in 1946 and integrated into the Snecma team in France in 1950. From their efforts sprang the ATAR series of military engines, the first of which was created in 1948. Their first test of an engine equipped with afterburner came in 1953. The SO-4050 Vautour was the first plane powered by these engines; other better-known fighters such as the Mystère and Super-Mystère, and Mirage III, IV, and V. Planes powered by these engines set several speed records and enjoyed a lively export trade.

Meanwhile, Hispano-Suiza had been producing jet engines under license from Rolls-Royce, including the famous Tay engine, which it began building in 1954. The next year, it introduced its own turbojet, known as the Verdon, which was installed in Mystère IV aircraft.

Another French firm, Turboméca, was making quite low-powered jet engines, though in 1960 it began producing the Adour engine for the Jaguar fighter in cooperation with Rolls-Royce. Turboméca also produced engines for turboprops and, most notably turbine-driven helicopters, which it supplied to a variety of French and foreign firms. Yet another firm, Microtubo, was launched in 1961 to produce small turbojets.

While Hispano-Suiza and Turboméca were signing deals with Rolls-Royce, in November 1959 Snecma entered a contract to produce Pratt & Whitney's popular JT8-D engine in

Key Dates:

1905: Société des Moteurs Gnôme founded.
1915: Gnôme merges with Le Rhône to form Gnôme & Rhône.
1922: G&R begins producing Bristol radial engines under license.
1945: Snecma created.
1959: Snecma begins producing Pratt & Whitney engines under license.
1968: Snecma acquires control of Hispano-Suiza.
1971: Snecma enters into longstanding partnership with General Electric.
1985: Snecma merges with rocket engine producer SEP.
1994: Messier-Bugatti landing gear unit merges with Dowty of Britain.
2000: Labinal and Hurel-Dubois are acquired.
2001: French government plans, then postpones Snecma privatization.

France. The JT8-D powered several American military jets as well as the DC-8 and Boeing 707 airliners. Snecma signed an agreement with Bristol Engines in November 1962 to develop the Olympus engines for the Concorde supersonic transport.

In 1968, Snecma took control over Hispano-Suiza, which included the mechanical engineering firm Bugatti, the landing gear manufacturer Messier, and the engine maker Berthiez. All of these were at the edge of ruin.

Revitalized in the 1970s–80s

A couple of initiatives would result in Snecma recapturing a leading place among aircraft engine makers by the end of the 1970s. Even though only a few examples of the Concorde would be produced, Snecma gained considerable experience and prestige through its participation. In 1969, the firm had begun development of its M56 engine, which would first appear on the market in 1976. An even more far-reaching program was launched in 1971 with General Electric, which was eager to break Pratt & Whitney's domination of the U.S. market.

In this agreement, Snecma was to produce 20 percent of GE-s type CF6 engines (CF meaning ''commercial fan''), which were destined for use in several Boeing airliners. In addition, they would also be used in the first planes made by Airbus Industrie, the new European consortium created to challenge U.S. control of the industry. A second contract provided for the joint production of the CFM 56 engine. The CFM International joint venture was formally created in 1974.

Snecma expanded its role in the CFM program after the CF6 engine was chosen for both the Airbus A310 and Boeing 767. In late 1980 Snecma and GE began planning a new $30 million plant in France to accommodate its production.

The French government mandated the merger of the Société Européenne de Propulsion (SEP) with Snecma in 1984. SEP produces rocket engines used in the Ariane space program and was merged with Snecma due to concerns it could not meet

increasing production demands. By 1985, Snecma was taking a half share of CFM contracts, including a $2.7 billion order for 137 engines to re-equip the U.S. Air Force's aerial refueling fleet.

Consolidation in the 1990s

The unprecedented airline industry downturn recession in the early 1990s resulted in consolidation among suppliers. In early 1994, Snecma merged its Messier-Bugatti landing gear subsidiary with Dowty, owned by the United Kingdom's TI Group. Messier-Bugatti was effectively privatized for the merger. However, the two cultures of the merged parties clashed; TI Group exited the Messier-Dowty joint venture by the end of 1997.

In the mid-1990s, Snecma's engine business was encountering its first civil market downturn ever, according to CEO Gerard Renon. It lost $100 million on sales of $1.8 billion in 1993. Workforce cuts and other measures were taken to increase productivity and shorten production cycles. Employment was reduced from 14,000 in late 1990 to 11,500 in December 1996.

A unique four-way alliance between Snecma, GE, Pratt & Whitney, and MTU to develop a small jet engine fell apart in September 1994. Meanwhile, CFM's market share of engines for larger jets approached 70 percent.

When Jean-Paul Bechat became Snecma's new head in the summer of 1996, following the brief reign of Bernard Dufour, he stated the company was close to bankruptcy and full of conflict. However, within a year things were closer to normal—operating profit rose 70 percent, to Ffr 440 million in 1996.

After losing Ffr 280 million in 1996, Snecma posted a net profit of Ffr 750 million ($122 million) for 1997. Exports accounted for about 70 percent of turnover, with more than three-quarters of these coming from the civil sector.

As the lifespan of jet engines increased, scheduled maintenance became a more important source of business. A new division, Snecma Services, was created in January 1997, which offered support services for landing systems and engines. By 1999, it had sales of $400 million and 2,000 employees. The Snecma group as a whole reported revenues of $5.3 billion for 1999. That year, CFM International celebrated the delivery of its 10,000th engine; the joint venture was widely held to be the most successful Europe-U.S. collaboration ever.

Snecma was converted into a holding company in January 2000. Snecma Moteurs was created to consolidate its air and space propulsion operations. Later in the year, Snecma acquired Labinal group for $1.1 billion but sold off its automotive businesses. Part of Labinal's holdings included Turbomeca, which produced nearly $1 billion worth of turbine engines for helicopters and fixed-wing military planes. Snecma also acquired the British engine nacelle/thrust reverser manufacturer Hurel-Dubois in 2000, which it soon consolidated with Hispano-Suiza to form Hurel-Hispano.

Between 1995 and 2000, sales rose 100 percent, reaching FFr 36.9 billion (EUR 5.65 billion), mostly on the strength of acquisitions. Exports accounted for most of the increase, while rapidly growing commercial sales accounted for 84 percent of the total.

Preparing for Privatization in 2001

Plans to privatize Snecma were developed throughout 2001. A merger of Snecma's ballistic propulsion activities with those of rocket engine and munitions manufacturer SNPE, was also under consideration. The French government planned to sell off a quarter of Snecma in an Initial Public Offering if market conditions were favorable, hoping to garner EUR 1.5 billion from the sale. These plans were put on hold after the September 11 terrorist attacks against the United States produced a downturn in the markets. The EUR 500 million SNPE merger, dubbed the Herakles project, had begun to fall apart over the question of leadership.

During the year, Snecma entered a joint venture with Rolls-Royce to produce engines for the next generation of European military aircraft. It had also tapped low-cost, quality Russian engineering talent from NPO Saturn to develop a new engine for regional jets. A collaboration between Snecma and FiatAvio (Italy), ITP (Spain), MTU Aero Engines (Germany), Rolls-Royce, and Techspace Aero (Belgium) was developing a turboprop engine for the Airbus A400M military transport. Meanwhile, Snecma Services entered a maintenance, repair, and overhaul venture with Sabena Technics.

Principal Subsidiaries

CFM International (United States; 50%); Messier-Dowty International, Ltd. (United Kingdom).

Principal Divisions

Cinch; Globe Motors; Hispano-Suiza; Hurel-Hispano; Labinal; Messier Bugatti; Messier-Dowty; Messier Services; Snecma Control Systems; Snecma Moteurs; Snecma Services; Techspace Aero; Turbomeca.

Principal Operating Units

Propulsion; Equipment.

Principal Competitors

General Electric Co.; Pratt & Whitney; Rolls-Royce plc.

Further Reading

Boyer, Michael, "CFM International Flying High," *Cincinnati Enquirer,* January 23, 1995, p. D1.

——, "French Partnership Lifts GE; Venture's Health Appears Robust," *Cincinnati Enquirer,* March 13, 2001, p. B5.

Burt, Tim, "Two Months to Light on the Right Logo: Tim Burt on the Marriage of Landing Gear Makers Dowty and Messier," *Financial Times,* Companies & Finance Sec., August 13, 1996, p. 18.

Chadeau, Emmanuel, "Contraintes technologiques et stratégies internationales: le moteur d'aviation, 1920–1970," *Entreprises et Histoire,* April 1992, pp. 61–78.

Cox, Bob, "Grand Prairie Copter Firm Sold; Turbomeca's French Parent Company Is Bought," *Fort Worth Star-Telegram,* May 6, 2000, p. 2.

Edgecliffe-Johnson, Andrew, "TI Ends French Aerospace Link-Up; Three-Year-Old Venture Halted by £207m Disposal," *Financial Times,* Companies & Markets Sec., December 11, 1997, p. 23.

"Flourishing Snecma Shrugs Off State-Ownership Stereotype," *Interavia,* May 1999, p. 30.

"General Electric, Snecma Plan New Plant in France," *Aviation Week & Space Technology,* November 3, 1980, p. 218.

"Herakles: un enjeu capital pour Snecma," *Le Figaro,* September 11, 2001.

Jasper, Chris, "SNECMA Services Seeks Partner to Expand On-Wing Engine Repairs," *Flight International,* October 17, 2000, p. 30.

Macrae, Duncan, and Antony Angrand, "Snecma Enjoys View from the Top," *Interavia,* February 2001, pp. 10–12.

Macrae, Duncan, "Restructured Snecma Flying Out of Turbulence," *Interavia,* July/August 1997, p. 21.

Mallet, Victor, "France to Sell Off a Quarter of Snecma," *Financial Times,* Companies & Finance International, June 25, 2001, p. 24.

——, "Snecma to Delay Listing While Markets Suffer," *Financial Times,* Companies & Finance International, September 18, 2001, p. 32.

Marsh, David, "Snecma Takes Half Share in $2.7 Billion US Air Force Order," *Financial Times,* January 17, 1985.

Norris, Guy, "Overhauls Bolster a Strong Market," *Financial Times,* Survey—Aerospace, June 18, 2001, p. 9.

"Reversing the Flow," *Flight International,* January 26, 1994.

"SEP Modifying Programs After Merger," *Aviation Week & Space Technology,* August 13, 1984, p. 81.

Shifrin, Carole A., "TI Group, Snecma Combine Landing Gear Businesses," *Aviation Week & Space Technology,* March 14, 1994, p. 28.

Skapinker, Michael, "French Inherit Dowty Spirit," *Financial Times,* Companies & Finance Sec., December 12, 1997, p. 26.

"Snecma Prepares for Privatization," *Aviation Week & Space Technology,* January 1, 2001, p. 43.

"Snecma Seeks Larger Role in Engine Project," *Aviation Week & Space Technology,* January 25, 1982, p. 36.

"Snecma Set for More Consolidation," *Interavia,* July/August 2001, pp. 28–29.

"Snecma Sets Recovery Plan for CFM56 Engine Production," *Aviation Week & Space Technology,* May 30, 1988, p. 27.

Sparaco, Pierre, "Snecma Program to Cut Engine Operating Costs," *Aviation Week & Space Technology,* April 8, 1996, p. 58.

——, "Snecma Sabena Joint Venture Seeks Engine MRO Growth," *Aviation Week & Space Technology,* May 21, 2001, pp. 70–71.

——, "Snecma Seeks Efficiency Gains to Counter Declining Sales," *Aviation Week & Space Technology,* May 16, 1994, p. 35.

——, "Snecma Services Completes Extensive Restructuring," *Aviation Week & Space Technology,* April 2, 2001, pp. 98–99.

Sutton, Oliver, "Snecma Chief Looks to Future, and Partner?," *Interavia,* July/August 1999, p. 22.

Taverna, Michael A., "Snecma Pins Growth on New Service Set-Up," *Aviation Week & Space Technology,* March 29, 1999, pp. 81f.

——, "Snecma, Russian Partners Plan Regional Airliner Engine," *Aviation Week & Space Technology,* October 4, 2001, p. 69.

——, "Turbomeca Buy Gives Snecma a Foothold in the Turboshaft Market," *Aviation Week & Space Technology,* September 4, 2000, p. 41.

—Frederick C. Ingram

Sprint Corporation

2330 Shawnee Mission Parkway
Westwood, Kansas 66205
U.S.A.
Telephone: (913) 624-3000
Fax: (913) 624-3088
Web site: http://www.sprint.com

Private Company
Incorporated: 1986 as US Sprint Communications
    Company, L.P.
Employees: 84,000
Sales: $23.6 billion (2000)
NAIC: 51331 Wired Telecommunications Carriers;
    513322 Cellular and Other Wireless
    Telecommunications.

Sprint Corporation is the private holding company for two publicly traded firms, Sprint FON and Sprint PCS. Sprint FON ("fiber optic network") operates a wire-based telecommunications business, providing local and long-distance telephone service, integrated voice, data, and Internet connections, and a phone directory publishing arm. Sprint PCS ("personal communications services") maintains the largest digital wireless network in the nation. The unit is the fourth-largest wireless company in the United States. Long a distant number three in the nation's long-distance telephone market, Sprint was responsible for a series of technological innovations in the 1980s and 1990s, including installing the first coast-to-coast fiber optic transmission network in the United States. It continues to innovate with new communications technology, deploying new forms of high-speed data transmission networks. Sprint also has a sizable international telecommunications market.

Predecessors in the Early 20th Century

Sprint traces part of its origin to the Southern Pacific Communications Corporation, a division of the Southern Pacific Railroad. During the early years of electronic communication, it was common for railroads to install telegraph wire on poles along its tracks. This enabled dispatchers to monitor trains and relay track conditions to locomotive engineers. With the advent of telephony, these wires were converted to voice communications. The complex nature of railroad communications necessitated the installation of telephone switches and multiplexing equipment, which allowed several conversations to be carried over the same pair of wires. By the 1940s, these railroads had established enormous long-distance networks that were independent of the Bell System and other telephone companies.

The Southern Pacific Railroad operated its telephone system as an independent company, called the Southern Pacific Communications Corporation, or SPCC. Like all telephone systems, this network used copper wire as its transport medium. But by the late 1950s, the Southern Pacific and other railroads started to use radio systems, which eliminated the need to maintain thousands of miles of aerial wire and enabled dispatchers to communicate directly with engineers. SPCC continued to operate its "switched private network" for official interoffice communications. But during the 1970s, maintenance costs for the wireline system were no longer economical.

In 1983, the GTE Corporation offered to purchase SPCC, which included a satellite company and the Switched Private Network Telecommunications group, known as "Sprint." GTE, parent company of General Telephone, the United States' largest non-Bell telecommunications company, hoped to add the system to its own toll office network to form the backbone for a new long-distance unit to compete with AT&T. Federal antitrust action obliged AT&T to divest itself of its 22 local Bell companies by 1984. In addition, AT&T's long-distance monopoly was ended, clearing the way for competition.

GTE knew that a long-distance network would be relatively simple to create and extremely profitable once in operation. It had the engineering and switching capability but lacked the long-distance corridors in which it could install wiring. While Sprint came with a dilapidated wire network, it offered hundreds of miles of open easements between major cities. GTE completed its acquisition of SPCC later in 1983, rechristening the operation GTE Sprint Communications.

Sprint's second parent was a Kansas phone company that began in 1899 as the Brown Telephone company. It controlled a local Kansas and a midwestern market. In the 1950s, the company was one of the top alternatives to Ma Bell in the country. It changed its name in the 1940s to United Utilities and again in 1972 to United Telecommunications. United Telecom was a $1 billion company by the mid-1970s, with over 3.5 million telephone lines in markets across the country. With the break-up of AT&T in 1984, United Telecom began development of its own long-distance company, called US Telecom. Hundreds of long-distance companies had emerged at the same time, each looking for just a piece of AT&T's hugely profitable business. Few of these actually operated alternative networks, choosing instead to simply aggregate traffic over AT&T's high-capacity data lines.

The Nation's First Complete Fiber Optic Network

GTE Sprint installed fiber optic cable along its routes—a process begun by SPCC—because the transmission medium operated at extremely high frequencies, used virtually incorruptible digital signals, and was impervious to electronic interference. A single cable, the size of a common electrical cord, could carry as many calls as a three-foot thick copper cable.

The technology was not lost on US Telecom, whose president, Bill Esrey, announced that the company would construct its own nationwide fiber optic network and fight for a position in the long distance market along with GTE, MCI, and AT&T. To bolster the small network, United Telecom purchased U.S. Telephone Communications, a fledgling Dallas-based long-distance carrier, and easements along key routes of the Consolidated Rail Corporation between cities in New England, mid-Atlantic, and midwestern states.

Esrey's plan for a long-distance company was denounced as impossible by experts quoted in *Telephony*, *TE&M*, and other trade publications. The critics would probably have been proven correct—the costs of assembling such a network were astronomical. But Esrey, who was named president and CEO of United Telecom in 1985, believed his goal could be attained—before competitors gained a lock on the market—by taking on a partner. In GTE Sprint, Esrey saw a well-capitalized partner with an identical strategy and a largely complementary network. He organized discussions with GTE and in 1986 announced the merger of US Telecom and GTE Sprint. The 50–50 joint venture (technically a limited partnership) was created on July 1, 1986 under the name US Sprint. Commensurate with the creation of US Sprint, the company introduced its distinctive logo, a diamond split by a series of horizontal lines. The lines, reportedly meant to represent fiber optic channels, become thicker from left to right.

Because United Telecom and GTE operated hundreds of local exchanges, they had to guarantee that their customers would have equal access to AT&T and MCI. This would prevent US Sprint from gaining a long-distance monopoly among United Telecom and GTE customers. In October 1986, the new company introduced an imaginative advertising campaign, featuring a tiny pin that was dropped on a table in front of a telephone receiver. As it hit, the "ting" could be heard on a phone thousands of miles away. The ad maintained that this clarity was made possible by US Sprint's fiber optic network, implying that it was superior to AT&T's wireline system and MCI's microwave network. The image in the advertisement was so powerful and the campaign so successful that the tiny pin came to symbolize the superiority of US Sprint's network.

Within nine months, US Sprint had doubled its number of customers. However, the company was ill-prepared for this growth. Bell companies, which dominated the nation's population centers, were slow to establish equal access to US Sprint, MCI, and other competitors of AT&T. Often, customers had difficulty using US Sprint. Many who got through reportedly received wildly inaccurate bills. These problems took months to iron out, inspiring AT&T to launch a massive ad campaign to woo customers back.

United Telecom and GTE channeled more than $2 billion into US Sprint, mostly for construction and marketing. The company issued millions of "FON Cards" containing dialing instructions that would enable callers to gain access to US Sprint from any telephone. The company also built a National Operations Control Center (NOCC) in Kansas City that joined up with another such center in Atlanta. The NOCC managed call routing nationwide and enabled US Sprint to offer the nation's first non-AT&T long-distance operator services. US Sprint equipped its network almost entirely with switches built by Northern Telecom, a major competitor of AT&T in the manufacturing market.

In planning its long-distance network, US Sprint adopted a flat architecture in which calls were passed from center to center, and routed around congested switching offices. By contrast, AT&T's network used a hierarchical design, in which calls of only a few dozen miles were routed over a bottom-tier network. Calls of a few hundred miles were passed along to a higher-tier network, and calls of a thousand miles or more were carried on yet another network.

The simplicity of US Sprint's network enabled engineers to make changes in its switching software instantaneously. AT&T's system required a series of staggered cut-overs. One of the changes US Sprint made was the conversion in 1988 to Signaling System 7, a highly efficient routing technology that improved network management and speeded call completion. The system also enabled US Sprint to begin offering its own 800 services in competition with AT&T.

In a spirited demonstration of the obsolescence of the microwave networks operated by AT&T and MCI, US Sprint blew up one of the last of its own microwave towers in February 1988. This action inspired AT&T and MCI to speed efforts to convert their systems over to fiber optic cable. By May 1988, US Sprint completed the last cut-over of traffic from the old US Telecom and GTE Sprint networks to the fiber optic system. The company was now 100 percent fiber optic.

Key Dates:

1899: Brown Telephone is founded in Kansas.
1983: GTE acquires the Southern Pacific Communications Corporation (SPCC) and renames the company GTE Sprint Communications.
1984: United Telecom enters long-distance phone market.
1986: GTE Sprint and US Telecom merge.
1992: Following reorganization, the company is renamed Sprint Corp.
2000: Proposed merger of Sprint with WorldCom falls through.

Evolving Technologies in the Early 1990s

In November 1988 US Sprint completed construction of its third transcontinental route. This helped US Sprint to win a contract to handle 40 percent of the federal government's long-distance business through a system called FTS2000. AT&T won the remaining 60 percent. The division of service between the two companies ensured that the government could maintain long-distance communications in the event either company suffered a network failure. The government became US Sprint's largest customer. Companies such as Grumman, Calvin Klein, Elizabeth Arden, Chesebrough-Pond's, and National Starch also became major US Sprint accounts.

In April 1989, US Sprint won its battle to gain access to millions of Bell company telephones whose long-distance service could be provided only by AT&T. U.S. District Court Judge Harold Greene, who presided over the break-up of the Bell System, ordered pay phone franchisees to select a long-distance company or be assigned one at random. This provided US Sprint with an opportunity to gain thousands of new accounts, handling long-distance calls placed from Bell company pay phones. Also in April, US Sprint reported its first profitable quarter, earning $27.5 million.

GTE, however, had encountered financial difficulties resulting from a battle with another party for control of options on US Sprint. The company also needed cash to pay down debts and finance other areas of its business. GTE's chairman, Rocky Johnson, announced that his company wanted out of US Sprint. United Telecom purchased a 30.1 percent interest in US Sprint from GTE in July 1989, leaving Johnson's company with a 19.9 percent stake until such time that United Telecom could generate the funds to complete the buyout. In August, US Sprint acquired Long Distance/USA, a Honolulu-based company whose bilingual agents handled calls between Hawaii and Japan. The acquisition left US Sprint with a 50 percent market share of call traffic out of Hawaii. Telenet, a satellite communications division that evolved from the SPCC's original satellite operations, was merged with US Sprint's international voice services in January 1990 and renamed Sprint International.

Expanding its presence in the global telecommunications market, US Sprint purchased a 50 percent interest in PTAT-1, a transatlantic fiber optic cable system run in conjunction with Britain's Cable & Wireless. The relationship was later expanded to allow US Sprint to engage in joint marketing efforts in Britain with Cable & Wireless. The company established another marketing arrangement with Maryland National Bank (later called MBNA America) to issue Visa and MasterCard charge cards. The "Priority Card" provided all the features of the FON Card, while enabling users to build bonus rebates from credit purchases. It was also intended to match a similar card from AT&T.

US Sprint launched a new advertising campaign in October 1990 featuring Candice Bergen, star of the television series "Murphy Brown." Bergen's effectiveness as a spokesperson grew with the show's popularity, eventually making her the most valuable spokesperson in advertising. By 1991, US Sprint had garnered a seemingly small nine percent of the nation's long-distance business, placing it behind MCI, with 14 percent, and AT&T, with 64 percent. This was, however, 9 percent of a $70 billion market, and it provided United Telecom with about half of its total annual revenue. Hard-earned market share gains of only a tenth of a percent represented $70 million in revenue.

To win those bits and pieces of the market, US Sprint inaugurated its Priority marketing program, extending discounts to customers with monthly billing of $20 or more. But much of the company's efforts were concentrated in the business market. US Sprint operated more than 1,200 video-conferencing centers, enabling business customers to conduct visual presentations without having to fly and lodge their participants. In addition, US Sprint was the first major carrier to offer public frame relay data service, a high-speed digital transmission service unencumbered by standard error-correction, thus allowing more information to be transmitted in less time. This was followed by worldwide virtual private network services, in which a customer could communicate between offices in different countries as easily as between offices in the same building.

Continuing its international growth, US Sprint was licensed to construct a fiber optic network in the United Kingdom, using canal and river routes owned by the British Waterways Board. It began planning partnership agreements for several more submarine cable projects spanning the Atlantic and Pacific Oceans and the Caribbean. The company branched into Canada and established interconnection arrangements with TelMex, the Mexican telephone authority, and the Russian telephone network. US Sprint also entered the Unisource partnership with Swedish and Dutch firms, enabling it to win over another major customer, Unilever.

United Telecom completed its acquisition of US Sprint from GTE in 1992. The long-distance group's revenues dwarfed those of United Telecom's other operations, necessitating a corporate reorganization. Bill Esrey led an effort to drop "US" from the Sprint name in order to better reflect the globalization of the company. He also suggested changing United Telecom's name to Sprint, thereby making more efficient use of promotional budgets. Thus, US Sprint became Sprint Communications, and United Telecom was renamed the Sprint Corporation. Later that year the parent company successfully bid to acquire Centel, a company with local telephone operations in 13 states and numerous cellular properties. The Centel operations were folded into Sprint. By 1993 the company served over 6 million customers. It was the third-largest long-distance provider in the United States, but it remained far behind the top two, AT&T and MCI. Revenue was just under $13 billion by 1994, compared to $75 billion for AT&T.

Strategies in the Late 1990s and After

The company continued to push for long-distance customers, while also providing local service, primarily in rural areas. By 1997, Sprint's customer base had grown to seven million local service customers, giving it about 10 percent of the nation's long-distance market. This territory was fiercely fought over, particularly by AT&T and MCI, which ran hundreds of television ads touting their superior long-distance service and bashing competitors. Continuing its more restrained advertising, Sprint seemed destined never to catch up. In the late 1990s, the company began looking for new ways to set itself apart. In 1998, Sprint began advertising a new generation of telecommunications. It hoped to offer high-speed digital connections that would allow simultaneous transmission of voice, data, and video, as well as providing Internet connections, called an Integrated On-Demand Network, known as ION. The company first marketed ION to business customers, who could be more easily persuaded than consumers to shell out for expensive new equipment. Sprint started selling ION to residential consumers in 1999, beginning in its home city of Kansas City and in other southwestern locales. The high-speed ION service bundled local, long-distance, and Internet service charges onto a single bill.

The company's wireless division also grew through the late 1990s. It was in fourth place among wireless communications providers, behind Verizon, Cingular, and AT&T. It had just over 8 million customers, slightly more than it claimed for local telephone service. Yet the wireless division did not make money. Another growing but money-losing venture was Sprint's Internet transport (or "backbone") service, which gave support, monitoring, and performance reporting to web sites. Not a leader in any of its major service areas, the company was ripe for a takeover. The telecommunications industry had seen a wave of consolidation after 1996, when the Telecommunications Act of that year set the stage for increased competition for long-distance customers between the regional Bell companies (which had formed after the break-up of AT&T in 1984) and other carriers. Several smaller or little-known companies became blockbusters, including the new parent of MCI, WorldCom Inc. In October 1999 WorldCom offered $115 billion for Sprint, an enormous price considering Sprint's 1998 revenues were just over $17 billion. But WorldCom, which had been on an acquisition spree since 1995 and had bought parts of AOL and CompuServe in 1997, was eager to get hold of Sprint's wireless business, which had some promising new technology in the pipe. The merger would have created an enormous new company, and regulators in the U.S. and Europe alike raised questions about the anti-competitive implications of the deal. Sprint's stockholders approved the merger in April 2000. Yet in July 2000 federal regulators ruled that the merger should not go through. Sprint had put many of its plans on hold for the nine months when the deal was pending, and meanwhile many top executives cashed out and left.

The collapse of the WorldCom merger set back some of Sprint's plans, particularly for international expansion. Yet it still had a unique portfolio of properties. Unlike most of its competitors, Sprint was spread among four main business areas, with its local phone, long-distance, internet, and wireless operations. The company hoped to be able to cross-sell its services to existing customers, bundling its various services. However, by late 2001 it was clear that the telecommunications market was down. Sprint laid off over 6,000 employees in October, while the industry as whole shed 225,000 workers that year. Despite the soft economy, Sprint kept on with investments in new technology. It shut down its ION project, which had debuted in some cities in 1999, citing technological and economic difficulties with the deployment. But it then contracted with equipment-maker Nortel Networks Corp. to deploy a new switching technology known as "packet" network. The packet-based system allowed more traffic on telecommunications lines. Sprint vowed to put all its phone lines on the packet system eventually, which would both save the company money and allow it to offer more services to its customers. Sprint invested in upgrades of its wireless network and continued to gain customers for its new Wireless Web service. The company seemed prepared to ride out falling revenues and a stagnant market in the early 2000s, as it continued to plan new products and services.

Principal Subsidiaries

Sprint FON Group; Sprint PCS Group; Call-Net Enterprises Inc.

Principal Divisions

Sprint Global Markets; Sprint North Supply; Sprint Publishing and Advertising.

Principal Competitors

Verizon Communications Inc.; Cingular Wireless; AT&T Corp.; Qwest Communications International Inc.

Further Reading

Chakravarty, Subrata N., "Nimble Upstart," *Forbes*, May 8, 1995, pp. 96–9.

Crockett, Roger, " 'Only Sprint Has It All'—Or Does It?," *Business Week*, June 15, 1998, p. 51.

Fierman, Jaclyn, and Suzanne Barlyn, "When Genteel Rivals Become Mortal Enemies," *Fortune*, May 15, 1995, p. 90.

Heinzl, Mark, "Nortel Wins $1.1 Billion Contract from Sprint to Upgrade Network," *Wall Street Journal*, November 6, 2001, p. B6.

Kupfer, Andrew, "The Telecom Wars," *Fortune*, March 3, 1997, pp. 136–42.

"Let's Celebrate!," *Sprint Monthly*, July 1991, pp. 14–17.

Marcial, Gene, "Sprint's Phone Could Ring Again," *Business Week*, September 10, 2001, p. 139.

Schiesel, Seth, "Sprint Still Aspires to Offer One-Stop Communications," *New York Times*, January 15, 2001, pp, C1, C6.

Sloan, Allen, and Anjali Arora, "Behind the Phone Frenzy," *Newsweek*, October 18, 1999, p. 58.

—John Simley
—update: A. Woodward

Sun Communities Inc.

31700 Middlebelt Road, Suite 145
Farmington Hills, Michigan 48334
U.S.A.
Telephone: (248) 932-3100
Fax: (248) 932-3072
Web site: http://www.suncommunities.com

Public Company
Incorporated: 1985
Employees: 513
Sales: $151.3 million (2000)
Stock Exchanges: New York
Ticker Symbol: SUI
NAIC: 52593 Real Estate Investment Trusts

Sun Communities Inc. operates as a real estate investment trust (REIT) that owns, operates, and develops manufactured housing communities. In 2001, the company had over 110 communities with over 39,000 developed sites and nearly 5,000 sites available for development. Sun's manufactured communities typically maintain an occupancy level of nearly 95 percent and have an average monthly rent of $288 per site. The firm operates in 15 states with the majority of sites in Michigan, Florida, Indiana, Ohio, and Texas.

Origins and the Escalating Popularity of the REIT

Milton M. Shiffman began investing in real estate in 1964. Working at the time as a doctor, Shiffman was involved in the development, acquisition, and construction of commercial property in his spare time. In 1975, he established the predecessor to Sun Communities Inc.

In 1981, Shiffman retired from his medical practice to concentrate fully on his growing company. He and his son, Gary A. Shiffman, began focusing on acquiring and then either expanding or renovating manufactured housing communities. In 1985, the pair incorporated the firm in order to pursue further growth options.

During the late 1980s, however, the real estate industry began to experience a decline. In fact, by the early 1990s, commercial property values dropped from between 30 and 50 percent. As a consequence, the Shiffmans began toying with the idea of launching a real estate investment trust. Congress created the REIT in 1960 to enable small investors to take a stake in large real estate investments. REITs were designed to pool the resources of many investors into a single entity that was focused on producing income through commercial real estate ownership and finance. Ninety percent of a REIT's taxable income was then paid out to its shareholders each year.

REITs did not become popular until the early 1990s, however, because of certain tax and ownership restrictions. At first, a REIT could only own real estate, but the Tax Reform Act of 1986 laid the groundwork for change and enabled a REIT to own, operate, and even finance income-producing real estate. The Act also restricted the use of real estate investments as tax shelters. When REITs were created, laws in the U.S. allowed taxpayers to take significant interest and depreciation deductions that reduced their taxable income. REITs on the other hand, were based on creating taxable income. Up until the Reform Act—which limited the amount an investor could deduct on their taxes—REITs had difficulty securing capital because many investors looked for tax-sheltering investment opportunities.

During the early 1990s, many private real estate companies began utilizing the REIT structure to gain capital. At the same time, investors also began to eye the commercial real estate industry as a lucrative investment and were confident that the market would recover from the troubles of the 1980s.

Going Public as a REIT: 1993

The Shiffman's followed suit and in December 1993 took Sun Communities Inc. public as a REIT, offering 5.7 million common shares. At the time of the initial public offering (IPO), the company operated 31 manufactured communities with 9,036 sites in six states.

Sun Communities began expanding rapidly after its IPO, which raised $145.8 million. In January 1994, it acquired Timberline Estates, a manufactured community with 296 sites

---

Company Perspectives:

Sun Communities is committed to being the premier provider of quality community lifestyles by offering individualized housing and residential services. We aspire to be the industry leader in meeting the unique wants and needs of our customers. We dedicate ourselves to excellence by acting with integrity and honesty, exploring new revenue sources, emphasizing caring and fairness, encouraging the entrepreneurial spirit, providing accountability through specialization, and fostering teamwork.

---

located near Grand Rapids, Michigan. In March, the firm purchased Meadow Lake Estates for $12 million, increasing the number of its Michigan-based holdings to twelve.

By July of that year, Sun had acquired seven more communities and set plans in motion to sell an additional 3.5 million shares of its common stock. Chateau Properties Inc., a competing REIT based in Clinton Township, Michigan, took notice of Sun's activities. According to *Crain's Detroit Business*, Jeffrey Kellogg, CEO of the competitor, "speculated that Sun Communities maybe figured out they're not big enough and wanted to hurry up and grow while REITs are still popular with investors." Kellogg also stated in the 1994 article that there was "a certain amount of do-it-while-you-can philosophy" among REITs.

That philosophy certainly held true for Sun, who by the end of 1994 had the best-performing stock among manufactured housing REITs—Chateau Properties' stock was second in the ranking. In its first year of operating as a public REIT, Sun had acquired 15 properties for $92 million, and had expanded into Florida and St. Louis, Missouri. It also secured revenues of $32.3 million, and net income of $7.8 million.

Expansion and Acquisition: Mid- to Late 1990s

Sun continued to expand in 1995, adding 3,900 new sites to its arsenal. In April of that year, the firm acquired Scio Farms of Ann Arbor, Michigan, for $23.6 million. At the time, Scio—with 853 sites—was the largest single community that Sun had ever acquired. Sun then went on to purchase Kensington Meadows, also located in Michigan. The company funded the deal through the issuance of 51,678 operating partnership units (O.P. Units). This was the company's fifth purchase using O.P Units. In a 1995 company press release, president Gary Shiffman explained the benefits of the units, stating, "The issuance of O.P. units creates opportunities to acquire quality communities that would not otherwise be available because of tax ramifications to the seller. In addition, Sun has the ability to fund acquisitions without the costs associated with raising equity in the public marketplace."

During the mid-1990s, manufactured housing was the fastest-growing segment of the U.S. real estate industry. Investors were encouraged by their financial planners to buy shares in manufactured housing REITs, leaving Sun well positioned for continued growth. In fact, by the close of 1995, Sun had acquired two new communities in Florida and as well as two in Austin, Texas, which was considered the fastest growing area in

the state in terms of population and job creation. Revenues for the year increased by 39 percent to $45.1 million, while net income reached $11.7 million.

Sun became involved in significant merger activity in 1996. In March of that year, the company announced plans to purchase 25 new manufactured housing communities from Aspen Enterprises Ltd. The $226 million deal increased Sun's holdings by nearly 60 percent, secured the company's hold on the Michigan market, and expanded the firm's reach in both the Florida and Arizona markets.

Acting as a white knight, Sun made an $380 million stock offer for competitor Chateau Properties in August 1996. Two days before Sun's bid, Chateau had received a hostile $387 million cash bid from Manufactured Home Communities Inc. (MHC). At the time of the offers, Chateau had plans in the works to merge with ROC Communities Inc. A merger of Sun and Chateau however, would secure Sun's position as the largest community owner in the United States, as well as rescue Chateau from the MCH bid—Chateau management felt a deal with MCH would not be beneficial for the firm.

While many analysts felt that both companies had offered too much for the Chateau—Sun's bid was the highest tax-free offer—the firms argued that it was a lucrative opportunity to get a step ahead of competition in the industry. During the mid-1990s, the industry was filled with companies that owned a relatively small amount of communities. In fact, "manufactured housing companies say they have no choice but to acquire each other because it is getting harder to find large groups of property for sale," reported *The New York Times* in August 1996.

The bids made by both Sun and MHC also marked the first unsolicited offers made among manufactured housing REITs. In the end though, Chateau opted to merge with ROC. The deal created the largest manufactured home community REIT in the United States.

Despite its failed attempt to acquire its largest competitor, Sun continued to expand and, by the end of 1996, operated 79 communities. Its revenue increased again, reaching $73.2 million, up 62 percent over the previous year. The company's net income also rose to $18.6 million.

The firm continued its acquisition strategy in 1997, with the purchase of nine communities from Park Realty Inc. for approximately $93 million. The deal strengthened Sun's foothold in the Southwest, Indiana, and Florida. Throughout the year, Sun acquired a total of 14 communities and developed 917 new sites. Through its Sun Home Services subsidiary, the company also sold 548 new homes and was involved in the resale brokerage of 555 additional homes. Sun also spun off Bingham Financial Services Corp. in 1997 as a financial services firm that offered financing and insurance to Sun's residents.

Revenues continued to grow in 1998, reaching $120.6 million. The company acquired ten communities that year, bringing its holdings to 106 communities. During 1999, Sun partnered with Champion Development Corp., a subsidiary of Champion Enterprises Inc., to develop manufactured housing communities in new growth markets. Operating under the name SunChamp, the venture developed nine communities in Texas, North

Key Dates:

1975: Milton M. Shiffman begins acquiring manufactured housing communities.
1981: Shiffman retires from his medical practice to concentrate fully on his growing company.
1985: The company incorporates in order to expand further.
1993: The firm goes public as Sun Communities Inc.
1994: Sun has the best-performing stock among manufactured housing REITs.
1996: The company purchases 25 new manufactured housing communities from Aspen Enterprises Ltd.
1997: Nine communities are acquired from Park Realty Inc.
1999: Sun partners with Champion Development Corp. to develop manufactured housing communities in new growth markets.
2000: The company launches its ''Residents First'' program.

Carolina, Indiana, and Ohio during its first year of business. Sun also purchased nine existing communities and developed 1,125 new sites. Revenue for the year increased by 12 percent over 1998 and the firm's funds from operations (FFO) grew by 9.1 percent per share.

Continued Success in an Unstable Market

During its first six years of operating as a public REIT, Sun experienced good fortune. The company's earnings grew at an average annual growth rate of 10 percent. Its acquisition record was strong, homesite demand was high, and finance companies eased up on lending restrictions, allowing more people to finance homes. In fact, homes were selling at a record pace and according to the company, nearly 20 million people in the United States lived in manufactured housing, representing eight percent of the American population.

During 2000, however, the manufactured housing industry began to experience a decline. Finance companies had set credit standards too low during the 1990s and were now stuck with unpaid loans as well as repossessed homes. Many lenders then raised credit qualifications, leaving many buyers unable to obtain home loans. With the flood of repossessed homes on the market, sales of new homes began to falter and the number of new manufactured home buyers dropped.

While Sun's growth slowed during 2000, the company still recorded positive revenues of $134.4 million and net income of $29.1 million. The firm acquired three new communities that year and developed 751 new sites. It sold five slow growth communities in Florida as part of its strategy to focus on those communities with stronger earnings potential. Sun also launched its ''Residents First'' program, which was designed to improve its customer relations, reduce turnover in communities,

attract new residents, and create demand for Sun properties. Founder Milton M. Shiffman died that year while son Gary remained at the helm of Sun as chairman and CEO.

Even as the manufactured home market remained unstable in 2001, Sun's future continued to look promising. The company's favorable occupancy levels and low tenant turnover coupled with a strong balance sheet left it well positioned for future growth. Shiffman commented in the company's 2000 annual report, ''When the economic wind shifts from your back into your face, you must work harder and smarter to achieve your objectives.'' Sun management pledged to do just that in order to secure the firm's position as a leading owner and operator of manufactured housing communities.

Principal Subsidiaries

SCF Manager Inc.; SCN Manager Inc.; Sun Acquiring Inc.; Sun Florida QRS Inc.; Sun Houston QRS Inc.; Sun QRS Inc.; Sun Texas QRS Inc.; Sun Communities Operating Limited Partnership.

Principal Competitors

Chateau Communities Inc.; Manufactured Home Communities Inc.

Further Reading

Breskin, Ira, ''Sun Communities Inc.,'' *Investor's Business Daily*, December 16, 1996, p. A4.
Gargaro, Paul, ''All of New REIT's Holdings Will Be Michigan Properties,'' *Crain's Detroit Business*, May 6, 1996, p. 166.
——, ''Sun Communities Rises by $226 M: 25 Sites Make It 60% Bigger,'' *Crain's Detroit Business*, March 25, 1996, p. 36.
——, ''Sun Continues to Rise,'' *Crain's Detroit Business*, November 11, 1996, p. 2.
Halliday, Jean, ''Investment-Trust Thrust: 2 Housing Communities File Initial Offerings,'' *Crain's Detroit Business*, October 4, 1993, p. 2.
——, ''Sun Seeks New Shares to Fund Home Deals,'' *Crain's Detroit Business*, July 25, 1994, p. 1.
Maletz, Kate, ''Higher Bids Expected for Chateau,'' *Mergers and Acquisitions Report*, August 26 1996.
''Manufactured Home REIT Plans to Expand,'' *National Mortgage News*, March 13, 1995, p. 20.
''Manufactured Housing REITs Hot Sector,'' *National Mortgage News*, June 19, 1995, p. 35.
National Association of Real Estate Investment Trusts, ''The REIT Story,'' Washington, D.C.: National Association of Real Estate Investment Trusts, 2001.
''Sun Communities Bid Creates a Battle for Chateau Properties,'' *New York Times*, August 22, 1996, p. D4.
''Sun Communities in $93 Million Deal with Park Realty,'' *New York Times*, September 12, 1997, p. D4.
''Sun Communities Inc. Reports a 6.3 Percent Increase in Third Quarter FFO Per Share,'' *Business Wire*, October 23, 2001.
''Sun Will Stay Aggressive on Buys,'' *National Mortgage News*, November 14, 1994, p. 22.

—Christina M. Stansell

Swiss Reinsurance Company (Schweizerische Rückversicherungs-Gesellschaft)

Mythenquai 50/60
CH-8022 Zürich
Switzerland
Telephone: (01) 285 21 21
Fax: (01) 285 29 99
Web site: http://www.swissre.com

Public Company
Incorporated: 1863
Employees: 9,585
Total Assets: $19.5 billion (2000)
Stock Exchanges: Swiss
Ticker Symbol: RUKN
NAIC: 52413 Reinsurance Carriers

Schweizerische Rückversicherungs-Gesellschaft, known as Swiss Reinsurance Company, or Swiss Re in English-speaking countries, is the oldest professional reinsurance firm in Switzerland and one of the largest reinsurance companies in the world. It is notable for the range of its international activities, the fine reputation of the services it offers, and its powerful financial base. The company's main business segments include risk transfer, risk retention financing, and asset management. Swiss Re operates with over 70 offices in 30 countries across the globe.

Professional reinsurance began in the 1840s in Cologne, where the first company specializing in this kind of insurance was set up in 1846. Switzerland was the first country outside Germany to take up the idea, which was put into effect when the Swiss Reinsurance Company was founded. The Swiss have contributed to the development of reinsurance by providing it with a theoretical foundation, as well as by taking the first steps towards internationalization and setting an early example of how to survive through times of crisis.

Birth of Swiss Insurance Industry: Mid- to Late 1800s

The insurance industry got well under way in Switzerland soon after the middle of the 19th century. The moving spirit was Alfred Escher, statesman and entrepreneur, who laid the foundation of Zürich's development as a financial center with the establishment of the Schweizerische Kreditanstalt. In 1857, it played a decisive part in the creation of the Schweizerische Lebensversicherungs- und Rentenanstalt, the first major life insurance company in Switzerland. The evolution of fire insurance in Switzerland was given impetus by a conflagration in the cantonal capital of Glarus on May 10 and 11, 1861. With victims receiving very little in the way of compensation payment, the disaster exposed the deficiencies of existing insurance arrangements. On November 7, 1861, there was a general meeting of the Allgemeine Versicherungs-Gesellschaft Helvetia, founded in 1858 at St. Gall. It was the first Swiss company to sell marine insurance and also had provision in its statutes for the supplying of fire insurance. The meeting resulted in a decision to set up the Helvetia Schweizerische Feuerversicherungs-Gesellschaft St. Gallen. The purpose of the new company was to provide fire insurance coverage for buildings and movables in Switzerland and other countries. M.J. Grossman was appointed managing director of the new venture and remained at the head of both companies until 1910—nearly half a century. The insurance companies that started up in Basel in 1863–64 also owe their existence directly to the Glarus fire.

This market situation and the possibility of extending into neighboring countries were seen as offering a good basis for the introduction of professional reinsurance into Switzerland. The initiative was taken by M.J. Grossmann, who reckoned that the reinsurance yield alone of the two Helvetia companies justified a separate company, especially as in previous years over 20 percent of insurance premium was earned by foreign reinsurers. At the beginning of July 1863, Grossmann put his ideas on the subject into a memorandum addressed to the Schweizerische Kreditanstalt in Zürich and proposing the establishment of a reinsurance company in conjunction with the Helvetia. This memorandum is a landmark in the history of insurance, offering the first clear formulation of the fundamental principles underlying professional reinsurance.

Grossman began by mentioning the first independent reinsurance company in Cologne. He suggested that the emergence of modern reinsurance was due to growing competition, which obliged insurers to make constantly increasing efforts to satisfy customers, with ever-larger amounts of money being involved, a considerable portion of it—the excess, in terms of the trade—going into the pockets of reinsurers. Reinsurance arrangements, he continued, could not be made with companies supplying insurance cover to the same clientele, so the best thing would be to have reinsurance supplied by firms that did nothing else, since they had greater experience and more specialized knowledge of that branch of the business, and there would be no danger of their using inside information to poach business. Here was an allusion to a vital element in insurance practice: the safeguarding of trust. The document also stressed the need for internationality. The company should provide cover for Swiss insurance firms, but it also should enter into reinsurance relations with foreign firms.

This memorandum led to the establishment of the Swiss Reinsurance Company. It was hoped from the start that the company would be set up in collaboration with the Schweizerische Kreditanstalt, which would supply the necessary capital and confer special prestige on the new company. It was assumed that, as regards organization, it was much easier to start a reinsurance company than a direct insurer. On July 10, 1863, the Helvetia board of directors agreed to the plan, and to the memorandum being sent on to the Kreditanstalt, with which negotiations could begin. Under the chairmanship of Alfred Escher, the board of directors of the bank looked at the proposal and on September 18, 1863, set up a committee to examine it more closely.

The Formation of the Swiss Reinsurance Company: 1863

The Swiss Reinsurance Company was finally established with participation of the Schweizerische Kreditanstalt, the Helvetia, and the Handelsbank of Basel. Swiss Re's share capital was SFr6 million, with a payment of 15 percent from stockholders. Its purpose, according to its statutes, was to provide reinsurance cover to domestic and foreign insurance companies and private insurers in the fields of marine, fire, and life insurance. As a joint-stock company, the Schweizer Rück (Swiss Re) needed authorization from the Zürich cantonal government. Its charter, dated December 19, 1863, bears the signature of Gottfried Keller, the famous Swiss writer, who drew up the document in his capacity as official clerk to the canton from 1861 to 1876.

The board of directors of the Swiss Re, chaired by M.J. Grossmann and including among its members well-known figures from the Swiss insurance and banking worlds, met on December 26, 1863, to draw up its constitution. It was decided to send a circular letter, written in French and German, to insurance companies considered to be desirable potential customers. Georg Schmidt was asked to become managing director of the new enterprise, with effect from May 1, 1864. He had begun his career with the Aachener und Münchener Feuer-Versicherungs-Gesellschaft. In 1859, as a senior official of the Dresdner Feuer-Versicherungs-Gesellschaft, he had been responsible for setting up its subsidiary, the Oësterreichischer Phönix in Wien.

The early history of professional reinsurance in Switzerland showed some of the structural features peculiar to this security system between insurers. These first years showed the necessity of adequate capital backing and of commitment between partners to a shared purpose, in order to insure long-term balance of risks. Like the basic principles outlined in Grossmann's memorandum, the importance of these requirements was demonstrated by the new company's practical experience.

Individual classes of insurance were tackled in the order in which they appeared in the statutes. On January 1, 1864, Swiss Re carried out is first contract, taking on part of Helvetia General's direct and indirect marine insurance business, as stipulated when the new company was founded. Next came fire and finally—in 1865—life reinsurance. It seems that the business prospered from the very beginning, with showers of proposals for reinsurance deals, but the first annual report notes that extreme care should be taken in selecting reinsurance customers, on the principle of "better no deal at all than a bad one."

In spite of this cautious policy, the company was soon incurring considerable losses, and the founders' optimistic expectations about the earning potential of reinsurance were at first unfulfilled. In December 1864, at the end of the first year of trading, realizing that a contract he had concluded on behalf of the firm was going to result in a loss, Georg Schmidt committed suicide.

Fire insurance had produced particularly unsatisfactory results on account of a markedly worsening trend in direct insurance damage claims. Reinsurers also had to cope with heavy commission payments. Remedial measures adopted by the company seemed to bring about a rapid improvement, and a plan to drop fire insurance business was abandoned. At the general meeting of May 14, 1869, a decision was made to cover the losses by reducing the share capital from SFr6 million to SFr4.5 million. The company's faith in the future of reinsurance in Switzerland, in spite of its early difficulties, paid off in the end. Not only were the losses made up, but the firm even managed to achieve profits and was able to pay a dividend.

Key Dates:

1863: The Swiss Reinsurance Company is established.
1881: The company signs its first accident reinsurance contract.
1901: The firm expands into motor-vehicle third-party reinsurance.
1906: Swiss Re loses SFr8.4 million after the San Francisco Earthquake.
1910: The U.S. branch opens in New York City.
1923: The North American Reassurance Company is founded.
1924: Swiss Re acquires Bayerische Rückversicherung AG of Munich.
1938: The company organizes its holdings under Neue Holding AG.
1940: The predecessor to the North American Reinsurance Corp. is created.
1960: The Swiss Insurance Training Centre is created to help train employees.
1968: Swiss Re begins publishing *Sigma*, a journal that analyzes trends in the industry.
1977: A majority interest in the Schwweiz Allgemeine Versicherungs-Aktien-Gesellschaft is purchased.
1987: A finance holding company, Schweiz Allgemeine is established.
1988: Swiss Re acquires the Harald Quant Group's 50 percent holding in the Augsburger Aktienbank.
1991: The firm acquires a majority interest in the ELVIA Swiss Insurance Company.
1994: The company initiates a restructuring program with a renewed focus on reinsurance.
2001: Swiss Re reorganizes into three business groups; the company announces plans to acquire Lincoln Re.

Expansion: 1900–40s

The four decades from the beginning of the 20th century to the outbreak of World War II saw Swiss Re develop into the leading reinsurer of its time. The period is colored by the influence of Charles Simon, one of the leading entrepreneurial personalities in the history of reinsurance. A native of Alsace, he entered the company in 1895, became deputy director and—until 1919— managing director, and finally served until his death as chairman of the board of directors. He did not confine his activities to the world of insurance. He was an expert mountaineer and a respected art collector, and the University of Zürich gave him an honorary doctorate in recognition of his literary studies. He was succeeded by Erwin Hürlimann, who became a member of the board of management in 1904, took over as managing director in 1919, and was on the board of directors from 1930 to 1966, serving as its chairman from 1942 to 1958. The two men worked together in close collaboration for nearly 40 years, making decisions that shaped the future of Swiss Re.

Improved profits enabled the company to extend its activities into other classes of insurance. Having signed its first accident reinsurance contract in 1881, Swiss Re went on to take on motor-vehicle third-party insurance in 1901, and engineering

reinsurance in 1904. It now had over 100 employees. In 1893, a relief fund started in 1885 was turned into an independent scheme to assist white-collar workers; it was further extended in 1913, when the company celebrated its 50th anniversary. In addition, profits were being reinvested to strengthen the firm's reserves. This far-sighted funding strategy proved its worth when Swiss Re's foreign business was severely affected by the 1906 San Francisco Earthquake. The company suffered a gross loss of SFr8.4 million, SFr4.3 million of which it had to bear itself. Half the loss could be met by the additional reserves that had been built up and the rest came out of the profits of other sections of the business; the result was a temporary reduction of dividends. The company's generous treatment of claims enhanced its world reputation and brought a compensatory increase of business. As well as fire reinsurance, life, accident, and liability reinsurance grew steadily in importance.

On October 25, 1913, after 15 years of operating from various sites, the company moved into prestigious and imposing new head offices on the Mythenquai beside the lake at Zürich. This is still the headquarters of Swiss Re, which over the years has acquired a number of other buildings, old and new.

The 1920s saw a considerable expansion of Swiss Re's foreign activities. Ever since it was founded, the firm had done business abroad. Its presence in the main insurance markets was strengthened by the steady creation of branches and subsidiaries all over the world. Its first overseas base was the U.S. branch of the Swiss Re, opened in New York City in 1910. In 1916 the parent company acquired a majority holding in the English Mercantile & General Insurance Company, founded in 1907.

At the outbreak of World War I, only about 20 percent of Swiss Reinsurance's premium income was coming from Switzerland. When the war ended, the company was able to press ahead with its policy of foreign expansion, assisted by its strong financial base and the stability of the Swiss currency. In 1923, it founded in New York the North American Reassurance Company, the first firm in the U.S. market to specialize in life reinsurance. Subsequent expansion was concentrated principally in Europe, where Swiss Re did business in 11 countries with 31 insurance companies, mainly direct insurers and most of them in Germany. Some were well-known, long-established companies forced by the economic collapse brought on by inflation to seek a partner with strong capital resources. The explanation of direct insurance's large contribution to Swiss Re's premium income can be traced back to this point.

In 1924, in the course of the development of its foreign reinsurance business, Swiss Re acquired the Bayerische Rückversicherung AG of Munich, founded in 1911, which had gone up for sale after its parent company, the Bayerische Versicherungsbank, was acquired by Allianz. In the years following World War II, this company proved to be extremely valuable, since during the Allied occupation of Germany Swiss firms could not maintain direct links with their German partners. Erich R. Prölss, the long-serving head of Bayerische Rück, is one of the most important names in German insurance law. In 1940, restrictions placed on foreign insurers led to the founding under U.S. law of a company that was to become the North American Reinsurance Corporation and that took over the major part of the business of Swiss Re's U.S. branch.

Focus on International Business: 1960s–80s

Thanks to Switzerland's neutrality and the security offered by its currency and laws, Swiss Re's worldwide reinsurance connections survived World War II, and the company used the universal trust it inspired to extend those connections. Its overseas activities were boosted by new branches and subsidiaries set up mainly in the United States, Canada, South Africa, and Australia. In 1968, in the interest of clear market definition, Swiss Re parted company with its U.K. associate, renamed Mercantile & General Reinsurance, and in 1969 set up the Swiss Reinsurance Company (UK) Ltd. in London. Consultancies were opened in Central America, South America, and East Asia.

In Germany, Swiss Re reorganized the direct insurance companies within its sphere of influence. Whereas formerly they had been loosely linked in what was called the Swiss Club, the groups were fitted now into a tighter structure. Since 1938, subsidiaries and associated companies had been owned by the Neue Holding AG, which changed its name in 1970 to Schweizer Rück Holding AG. In 1974, Swiss Re used the Schweizer Rück Holding subsidiary to set up the SR Beteiligungen Aktiengesellschaft, with offices in Munich. On January 1, 1975, Swiss Re transferred to the Munich company its majority holding in the Magdeburger Versicherungsgruppe of Hannover, and its major stake in Vereinte Versicherungen, formerly the Vereinigte Versicherungsgruppe, formed in 1974 from a number of older companies and renamed in 1987. It all amounted to a process of separation of functions and relocation from Switzerland to Germany. At the same time, these measures would extend Swiss Re's direct insurance business, which alongside reinsurance plays its own important part in the activities of the group.

In addition to the company's business activities in Germany, a start had been made on setting up a financial-service group. In 1987, with this aim in view, a finance holding company, the Schweiz Allgemeine was established in Munich, to which the mh Bausparkasse AG, previously part of the Magdeburg Insurance Group, was incorporated, while in 1988 Swiss Re acquired the Harald Quant Group's 50 percent holding in the Augsburger Aktienbank. At the same time the Schweiz Allgemeine Direkt Versicherung AG was started in Augsburg for the sale of insurance direct to the client.

Swiss Re strengthened its direct insurance by acquisitions in other European countries besides Germany. In 1977, it bought a majority interest in the Schweiz Allgemeine Versicherungs-Aktien-Gesellschaft of Zürich, founded in 1869, a major international insurer with foreign subsidiaries of its own, and in 1988, it became the owner of Lloyd Adriatico S.p.A., Trieste, a prominent Italian direct insurer, as well as acquiring the third-largest reinsurance firm in Switzerland, the Union Rückversicherungs-Gesellschaft of Zürich.

With its extensive international activities Swiss Re made reinsurance an important Swiss export. Over 90 percent of the company's reinsurance premiums came from abroad, the largest markets being North America and Germany. Most of its direct insurance business came from Germany, mainly from health, automobile, and liability insurance. The volume of direct insurance business done by the group was likely to increase further.

Reinsurance being a complex international operation, the company has always been very much concerned with employee training. In 1960, the Swiss Insurance Training Centre was set up in the form of a trust to provide instruction for insurance workers from all over the world, especially from developing countries. Entrepreneurial initiative has led to clients being offered, in addition to actual reinsurance cover, a wide range of services relating to the assessment and avoidance of risks. In this connection, the Swiss Re Group included consultancy firms that advise on damage assessment and claims adjustment.

The company also carried out scientific investigations into general and specific problems of direct insurance and reinsurance; the results, published in its own documentation series, constitute important contributions to the theory and practice of the industry. One publication, *Sigma*, which has been appearing regularly since 1968, analyzes trends and structural changes and sets out international comparisons; another, *Experiodica*, started in 1973, printed useful excerpts from specialist literature. Thus Swiss Reinsurance Company used the knowledge and experience gained through its international business to propagate reinsurance expertise and the requisite high degree of professionalism.

Renewed Focus on Reinsurance: 1990s and Beyond

During the 1990s, Swiss Re continued to make strategic acquisitions, along with refocusing its core efforts on reinsurance. In 1991, a majority stake in ELIVA Swiss Insurance Company was acquired. ELIVA then took over the Swiss insurance business of Schweiz Allgemeine Versicherungs AG. The following year, Swiss Re moved into the Baltic region by establishing Swiss-Baltic Reinsurance Advisors in Tallinn, Estonia.

In 1994, the company underwent a reorganization that placed its reinsurance business at the forefront of its strategy. The firm began divesting its direct insurance businesses that year. In 1995, Swiss Re secured a 53 percent increase in net income over the previous year, due in part to its successful restructuring.

Swiss Re made several important purchases over the next few years as part of its plan to fully penetrate the life and health segment of the reinsurance industry. The Dutch-based Alhermij Group was acquired in 1995, and the Mercantile & General Re Group followed in 1996. The latter purchase secured Swiss Re's leading position in the life and health segment of the insurance industry. As such, the company combined its related businesses to form Swiss Re Life & Health with headquarters based in London.

During 1997, the company took 100 percent control of Unione Italiana de Riassicurazione and renamed it Swiss Re Italia. Then, in 1998, the company acquired Connecticut-based Life Re Corp. for $1.8 billion. The purchase gave Swiss Re a foothold in the administrative reinsurance market and also a leading position in the U.S. reinsurance market. Brian Shea, a London-based Salomon Smith Barney analyst, stated in a 1998 *National Underwriter Life & Health* article that the acquisition was "another deal in a string of deals which have been strategically very, very sensible for Swiss Re." The company also purchased Reaseguros Alianza S.A. of Mexico and acquired a majority stake in Dutch-based NCM Holding.

The operations of Union Re Zurich were merged into those of Swiss Re during that year as well. The company had purchased a majority interest this firm in 1988 from Swiss Bank Corp., Swiss

National Insurance Co., and Zurich Insurance Co. Union Re—a well-known brand in Europe and the Asia region—took on the Swiss Re name. In fact, at the start of 1999, all of Swiss Re's businesses were unified under the Swiss Re brand name.

During the late 1990s, Swiss Re began to eye the investment banking market as a lucrative growth avenue. In 1999, investment banking firm Fox-Pitt, Kelton Group was purchased. Swiss Re management felt that in order to succeed in the years to come, reinsurance companies would have to offer both reinsurance and investment banking services. Walter Kielholz—company CEO since 1997—claimed in a 1999 *Business Insurance* article that "as securitization gains momentum, having access to investors, trading expertise, etc., will become an increasingly essential factor for success in reinsurance."

While 1999 proved to be the second-least profitable year for reinsurers across the board, Swiss Re continued to fare well. The drop in profits however, was linked to a decline in policyholder surplus for two straight years—policyholder surplus is the amount greater than liabilities that the insurer has available to meet future policyholder claims. Insurers can either raise premium prices to generate more surplus or invest to create additional surplus. With a weakening stock market in the late 1990s and into 2000, surplus was declining.

The weakening market conditions, however, did not put a damper on Swiss Re's growth plans. In 2000, the firm acquired California-based Underwriters Re Group. The purchase strengthened the company's leading position in the non-life segment of the industry. The following year, the company restructured its operations, establishing three business groups including: Life—Swiss Re Life & Health; Non-Life—Americas, Asia, and Europe Divisions; and Financial Services—New Markets, Investors, and Capital Partners. During 2001, the company also announced plans to purchase Lincoln Re, a business of Lincoln National Corp., for $2 billion.

Disaster struck in September 2001, though, when the World Trade Center was attacked and destroyed by terrorists. According to the company's *Sigma* report, the insured property and business interruption losses were estimated at $19 billion, one of the largest property losses in the history of the insurance industry. Total losses related to the attacks were estimated at $90 billion. As the Trade Center's largest insurer, Swiss Re would, no doubt, feel the financial strains of this loss well into 2002. Whether or not these strains would affect the firm's growth strategy remained to be seen.

Principal Subsidiaries

European Reinsurance Company of Zurich; Schweiz Allgemeine Versicherungsgesellschaft; Swiss Re Investors Zurich; Swiss Re Partnership Holding AG; Xenum Finance AG (42.5%); Bavarian Reinsurance Company Limited (Germany); Bayerische Rück-Holding Aktiengesellschaft (Germany); European Credit and Guarantee Insurance PCC Limited (UK); Fox-Pitt; Kelton Group Limited (UK; 66.6%); Palatine Insurance Company Limited (UK); SR International Business Insurance Company Ltd. (UK); Swiss Re Asset Management Ltd. (UK); Swiss Re Capital Markets Limited (UK); Swiss Re GB Limited (UK); Swiss Re Life & Health Limited (UK); Swiss Re New

Markets Ltd. (UK); Swiss Re (UK) House Ltd.; Swiss Reinsurance Company U.K. Limited; The Mercantile & General Reinsurance Company (UK); Swiss Re International Treasury Ltd. (Ireland); Bavarian Reinsurance Ireland Ltd. (Ireland); Swiss Re Italia S.p.A.; Rück Treasury & Management (Luxembourg) S.A.; Swiss Re Treasury (Luxembourg) S.A.; NCM Holding N.V. (Netherlands); Bayerische Rück Norge AS (Norway); Atlantic International Reinsurance Company Ltd. (Barbados); European International Holding Company Ltd. (Barbados); Englewood Reinsurance Company Ltd. (Bermuda); Swiss Reinsurance Company Canada; Facility Insurance Holding Corporation (U.S.); Allied Life Financial Corporation (U.S.); Life Reassurance Corporation of America (U.S.); Swiss Reinsurance America Corporation; Swiss Re America Holding Corporation; Swiss Re Life and Health America Inc.; Swiss Re Management Corporation (U.S.); Swiss Re New Markets Corporation (U.S.); Swiss Re México, S.A. (94.78%); Swiss Re Australia Ltd.; Swiss Re Southern Africa Limited; Swiss Re Investors Asia Limited (Hong Kong).

Principal Competitors

GeneralCologne Re; Hannover Re; Munich Re.

Further Reading

Buckley, Keith M., "Strategic Acquisitions Help Swiss Re Earn 'AAA' from DCR," *National Underwriter Property & Casualty-Risk & Benefits Management*, March 6, 2000, p. 14.

De Mestral, Aymon, *Charles Simon Humaniste et Réassureur 1862–1942*, Zürich: Compagnie Suisse de Rénaissance à Zürich, 1947.

Eisenring, Max E., *Skizzen aus 125 Jahren Geschichte der Schweizerischen Rückversicherungs-Gesellschaft in Zürich*, Zürich, 1989.

Gerathewohl, Klaus, *Reinsurance Principles and Practice*, Volume II, Karlsruhe, 1979.

Howard, Lisa S., "Swiss Re Acquires Life Re to Expand Administrative Reinsurance Line," *National Underwriter Life & Health-Financial Services Edition*, August 3, 1998, p. 3.

"Insured Losses Drop in 2000 Despite More Catastrophes," *Best's Review*, March 2001, p. 78.

Jennings, John, "Refocused Strategy Seen Paying Off at Swiss Re," *National Underwriter Property & Casualty-Risk & Benefits Management*, August 26, 1996, p. S36(2).

Koch, Peter, "Über die Anfänge der professionelle Rückversicherung in der Schweiz," *Zeitschrift für Versicherungswesen*, 1990.

Lonkevich, Dan, "Swiss Re Buys Underwriters Re," *National Underwriter Property & Casualty-Risk & Benefits Management*, December 13, 1999, p. 1.

Mazier, E.E., "Swiss Re Presses 'One Attack' Theory," *National Underwriter Property & Casualty-Risk & Benefits Management*, October 29, 2001, p. 5.

Schweizerische Rückversicherungs-Gesellschaft Rückblick 1863–1963, Zürich, 1963.

"Swiss Re CFO: Hard Market Is Around the Corner," *A.M. Best Newswire*, March 16, 2001.

"Swiss Reinsurance Company—A Century of Progress: 1863–1963," *Post Magazine*, 1964.

Unsworth, Edwin, and Rodd Zolkos, "Lincoln Re Buy Would Boost Scale of Swiss Re Book," *Business Insurance*, August 6, 2001, p. 3.

Zolkos, Rodd, "Swiss Re Purchase to Expand Services," *Business Insurance*, January 4 1999, p. 2.

—Peter Koch translated from
the German by Olive Classe
—update: Christina M. Stansell

T-Netix, Inc.

67 Inverness Drive East
Englewood, Colorado 80112
U.S.A.
Telephone: (303) 790-9111
Toll Free: (800) 531-4245
Fax: (303) 790-9540
Web site: http://www.t-netix.com

Public Company
Incorporated: 1986 in Colorado as Tele-Matic Corp.
Employees: 441
Sales: $103.3 million (2000)
Stock Exchanges: NASDAQ
Ticker Symbol: TNTX
NAIC: 4813 Telephone Communications

T-Netix, Inc. is a leading provider of specialized call processing, billing, and other services primarily to the corrections industry. The company delivers these services through direct contacts with correctional facilities and through relationships with leading telecommunications companies, including AT&T, Verizon, Quest, and SBC Communications. T-Netix operates two principal units: the Corrections Division and the Internet Services Division. The Corrections Division primarily processes telephone calls for prison inmates. The company provides customized call processing services to telephone companies that serve more than 1,600 correctional facilities in 43 states. T-Netix employs specialized software and systems that allow telecommunications providers and prison operators to control telephone use by restricting the length of an inmate's call, blocking unauthorized or fraudulent calls, and monitoring and recording calls. T-Netix's advanced call control software and services also enable correctional facilities to control calls by facility, cellblock, telephone, and in some cases, each inmate. The Corrections Division primarily manages its specialized telecommunications hardware and software systems for long distance and local exchange carriers on a contractual basis and sells inmate calling systems. In addition, the Corrections Division provides other inmate–related products, including an elec-tronic monitoring system for low-risk offenders, a prison information management system, and software for inmate accounting, product inventory, and commissary management. The Internet Services Division provides interLATA Internet services to internet subscribers and buys and resells Internet bandwidth.

The Mid-1980s: Company Beginnings

Terry Johnson founded Tele-Matic in 1986 after the federal government dismantled AT&T's telephone monopoly and deregulated the communications industry. The company primarily made pay telephones until 1991 when it released Strike Three!, a three-way call detection technology that prevented inmates from making fraudulent calls. Due to Strike Three!'s success, in 1992 president and chief operating officer Tom Huzjak changed Tele-Matic's marketing strategy by focusing on processing calls for the corrections industry. As a result, Tele-Matic bought eight inmate-focused telephone companies and acquired approximately 33 percent of Tele-Matic UK, purchasing the rest in 1994 for 40,000 shares of common stock. The acquisitions enabled Tele-Matics to provide call and processing services to inmates at 368 correctional facilities in 34 states. To service this many correctional facilities, by 1995 the company installed more than 10,500 phone lines and planned to install additional lines in the future. Although inmate calling represented more than a billion dollar opportunity, it also was fraught with credit card fraud and running scams over the network. Nevertheless, the company entered the inmate calling business with the aim of providing specialized call processing and monitoring services to jails and prison systems throughout the country. The rapidly growing prison population, which tripled between 1980 and the mid-1990s, spawned the company's growth. Tele-Matic's growth also stemmed from allowing inmates greater access to telephones by jails and prisons, which received commissions from the calls.

The Mid-1990s: Expansion into Voice Verification

In 1994, Thomas Huzjak became Tele-Matic's president and chief executive officer. In 1995, the company changed its name to T-Netix, and in October of that same year acquired all of the

Company Perspectives:

T-Netix, Inc. provides specialized call processing and bill services for correctional institutions to the telecommunications industry, direct local and long-distance call processing for correctional facilities, value-added telecommunications services such as pre-connection restrictions, digital recording, jail and inmate management systems, video booking, and sales to call-processing systems hardware. Through its Contain product, T-Netix provides parolee and home detention monitoring services using the Internet and SpeakEZ, its patented voice verification technology. The company services more than 1,600 corrections facilities and justice departments nationwide.

outstanding stock of SpeakEZ, Inc., a privately held development-stage company. T-Netix bought the SpeakEZ for $3 million in company stock, cash, and notes payable, and thereafter operated it as a wholly owned subsidiary. The acquisition of SpeakEZ led the company to an increased focus on new technology, specifically biometric identification or speaker verification technologies. This technology used voiceprints or speech patterns as a way of verifying an individual's identity. T-Netix believed that this technology had particular applicability in curbing fraud in the financial services, telecommunications, and security industries. The company's main objective was to be a leading provider of innovative fraud prevention and identification products and services to these specific industries in the international arena. Thus, virtually all of the company's revenue stemmed from its corrections industry call processing services.

The company anticipated that the emerging market for voice verification offered significant growth opportunities. T-Netix CEO, Thomas Huzjak, believed that such security technologies as data encryption, digital certificates, server firewalls, and certificates of authority helped to secure networks, but fell short of true identification of the person making a transaction. The company's voice print technology addressed the weak link in the secured system chain. As a result, by 1998 the SpeakEZ division had developed a suite of products and several strategic relationships to address the voice verification market. T-Netix introduced several verification products to protect Web sites, LANs, and personal computers. The company introduced its VoicEntry product as a biometrics-based alternative to typed password protection for individual and shared computer users. T-Netix's VeriNet product provided network security for web and internet-based applications through the use of speaker verification technology. The company sought the rapid introduction of VeriNet by entering into a distribution relationship with and investing in a start-up venture called Sentry Systems, Inc., which was developing a turnkey security system for e-commerce transactions. T-Netix also established distribution relationships with network security technology companies, including several facial imaging firms, such as Miros and Visionics, and the fingerprint company BioNetrix. For the financial services industry, the company introduced its Customer Verification Service (CVS), designed for use by banks, brokerage houses, insurance companies, and other financial institutions to authenticate customer transactions through a voice

recognition system. The company also developed and installed for GTE Telecommunications System, Inc., its Verifi-Air product to address wireless telecommunications fraud. This product compared a cellular caller's password voice with the stored voice print of the authorized caller.

In 1998, the company also purchased a 15 percent stake in Cell-Tel Monitoring, Inc. (Cell-Tel), a provider of software for offender caseload management by community corrections, probation, and parole agencies. Cell-Tel's product, Contain, utilized SpeakEZ's voice print speaker verification technology for the community or home-based corrections market. Management of parole and probation programs had been a growing concern among local, county, state, and federal criminal justice agencies. During 1995, five states had reported increases of more than 10 percent in their probation populations and 10 states had reported similar increases in their parole populations. With the increase of this population, the corresponding national average caseload per probation/parole officer had risen to about 117 offenders. Because of these burdensome case loads, the company marketed Contain as a cost effective and efficient means of monitoring people on probation and parole. The product worked by calling the subject's home, or other agency approved locations, and prompting the individual via automated speech to say a password. SpeakEZ's voice print technology then verified the speaker's identity by comparing the voice prints of the speaker with the subject's. If the speaker failed to be verified, Contain automatically notified the corrections officer by telephone, fax, or email. The Contain system also enabled officers to confirm failed verifications and to send voice mail to individuals on parole or probation. As a result, the system allowed officers to detect parole and probation violations faster and with more accuracy than more traditional methods and at lower cost.

The Late 1990s: Corporate Changes and Acquisitions

In 1998, Thomas Huzjak resigned as chief executive officer and chairman of the board of directors. Alvyn Schoop, the company's chief financial officer, was named the new chief executive officer and continued as president of the company's T-Netix Inmate Calling Services Division. Daniel Carney, co-founder and former chairman of Pizza Hut, and a member of T-Netix's board since 1991, accepted the chairmanship of the company's executive board. Huzjak's departure stemmed from differences over strategic and operating philosophies, particularly over the need to refocus operations with an emphasis on core capabilities. As the new CEO, one of Schoop's first major moves was to streamline the SpeakEZ Division to bring operating expenses more in line with revenue opportunities. Schoop consolidated the division's Piscataway, New Jersey operations into the company's Englewood, Colorado headquarters location. The major problem stemmed from the lack of significant sales of its SpeakEZ products, despite the company's sales and distribution agreements with such corporations as Lucent, IBM, and OTG. The absence of broad based sales also derived from the market for speaker verification technology still being in its infancy. Nevertheless, Schoop moved to reposition T-Netix to focus on its core inmate calling services business, and on reducing non-core operating expenses that had adversely affected earnings for the past several years. In addition, he attempted to address the research and development costs associated with

Key Dates:

1986: Company is incorporated in Colorado as Tele-Matic Corp.

1992: The company acquires eight inmate-focused telephone companies and purchases a 33 percent stake in Tele-Matic U.K.

1994: Remaining shares of outstanding common stock of Tele-Matic Corp. are purchased.

1995: The company acquires SpeakEZ, Inc. for $3 million; changes name to T-Netix, Inc.

1999: The company acquires chief rival Gateway Technologies, Inc.

2001: T-Netix acquires Telequip Labs. Inc. and realigns corporate organization to focus on core business.

the SpeakEZ Division by curtailing development costs and operating losses. To accomplish this aim, the company shifted marketing away from a direct customer sales strategy to licensing its voice print technology to other companies.

In January 1999, the company announced that it was acquiring main rival Dallas-based Gateway Technologies, Inc., a privately held provider of inmate telecommunications services, for $35.2 million in stock and debt. The acquisition, completed in June, made T-Netix the largest inmate calling services provider in the country. The agreement included the issuance of approximately 4.05 million shares of T-Netix common stock to Gateway shareholders, plus options and T-Netix's assumption of $10 million in Gateway debt. Although the two companies had been main competitors, each had developed a specialty in the inmate calling services market. T-Netix had primarily served larger facilities with 50 or more phone lines, while Gateway had specialized in facilities with 75 or fewer phone lines. The merger enabled T-Netix to serve the entire corrections facilities market, and provided the company with Gateway's established billing services, managers, and a sales force.

On August 25, 2000, Alvyn Schoop resigned after two years as CEO and director. Daniel Carney, chair of the board, was appointed interim CEO until a new chief executive officer could be appointed. Under Schoop's direction, T-Netix had become the leading provider of inmate telecommunications and other services in the country. Schoop also had put the company on solid financial ground with year end 2000 results showing total revenues of $103.3 million, an increase of 41 percent compared with $73.2 million in 1999. On November 16, 2000, the company announced that Tom Larkin would assume the additional title of chief executive officer in addition to his responsibilities as company president. Larkin had joined the company in 1999 as executive vice-president of sales and had been serving as president since March 2000.

On January 19, 2001, the company completed the purchase of 100 percent of the outstanding stock of Telequip Labs, Inc., a small, strategically based provider of inmate telecommunications calling services with headquarters in Dallas. The company anticipated that the acquisition would enable it to expand services to smaller corrections facilities with 20 or fewer phone lines. At the same time, T-Netix entered into an agreement with Telus Corporation, allowing Telus to become the exclusive provider of T-Netix inmate call processing services in Canada. T-Netix expected the agreement to generate revenues from $18 million to $40 million over the life of the six-year contract. Under the terms of the agreement, T-Netix would extend services to Telus's long distance correctional facilities customers. In return, T-Netix would receive a percentage of the billed monthly revenues for Telus's accounts.

In December 1999, the company had announced that its wholly owned subsidiary T-Netix Internet Services, Inc. executed a master service agreement with US West (now called Quest America, Inc.) to provide interLATA internet services to Quest customers. The agreement, which commenced December 1, 1999, called for T-Netix to serve as a middleman in buying, reselling, and processing billing of Internet bandwidth to these customers. The contract stipulated an initial minimum term of sixteen months until March 2001. The company's Internet Services Division accounted for about 25 percent of T-Netix's total revenue for the year 2000. Based on this agreement, T-Netix anticipated that the opportunities presented by its procurement and management of ISP bandwidth offered far-reaching positive implications for future business growth. Nevertheless, by the end of 2001 this initial enthusiasm gave way to disappointment as all operations under the contract with Quest ceased in November 2001 and the company failed to make substantial headway in the Internet services market.

2000 and Beyond: Corporate Restructuring

The poor performance of the Internet Services Division and other business inefficiencies and redundancies led the company to realign its organizational structure. Despite its 1999 merger with Gateway, the company determined that duplication remained in the organization after the two firms joined forces. The company therefore sought to cut costs by reducing its workforce, eliminating inefficient business segments, and consolidating its operations and closing excess facilities. Pursuant to this restructuring strategy, the company announced plans to discontinue its internet service unit and to sell the SpeakEZ Division, both money losing divisions. As a result, T-Netix entered into a definitive agreement on September 27, 2001 to sell all of the assets of the SpeakEZ Division for approximately $3 million in cash and other considerations. Also in 2001, the company opened a national service center in Carollton, Texas to consolidate most of its support centers into one operation near Dallas. The new center was designed to handle nationwide service and support for the company's 1,600-plus customer facilities and the more than 20,000 calls from inmate families that the company processed each month. With these changes aimed at re-focusing and enhancing its core businesses, the company appeared to have repositioned itself for future growth.

Principal Divisions

Corrections Division; Internet Services Division.

Principal Competitors

Evercom Inc.; Lucent Technologies Inc.; Nuance Communications Inc.

Further Reading

Cantwell, Rebecca, "Cell Phone Deal Locked Up, T-Netix Buys Gateway, Creates Largest Inmate Calling Service," *Rocky Mountain News*, February 12, 1999.

Fillon, Roger, "US West Deal Lets T-Netix Branch Out," *Denver Post*, December 17, 1999.

Form 10-K For Fiscal Year Ended December 31, 1997, United States Securities and Exchange Commission.

Form 10-K For Fiscal Year Ended December 31, 1998, United States Securities and Exchange Commission.

Form 10-K For Fiscal Year Ended December 31, 1999, United States Securities and Exchange Commission.

Form 10-Q For Quarter Ended September 30, 2001, United States Securities and Exchange Commission.

Kaplan, Charles, "Captive Audience," *Equities,* January 1995, p. 36.

"T-Netix and Cell-Tel Launch Commercial Version of Contain Product Line," *PR Newswire,* September 3, 1998.

"T-Netix Announces CEO Alvyn Schopp to Step Down; Chairman Daniel Carney to Serve as Interim CEO," *PR Newswire*, August 25, 2000.

"T-Neetix Announces New Chief Executive Officer," *PR Newswire*, November 16, 2000.

"T-Netix Announces the Opening of A New State-of-the-Art National Service Center," *PR Newswire*, April 26, 2001.

"T-Netix Appoints Thomas Larkin President," *PR Newswire*, March 17, 2000.

"T-Netix Broadens Market Reach in Telecommunications Services by Acquiring Key Inmate Calling Services Provider," *PR Newswire*, February 11, 1999.

"T-Netix Enters Internet Services Market," *PR Newswire*, December 17, 1999.

"T-Netix, Gateway Complete Previously Announced Merger," *PR Newswire*, June 15, 1999.

"T-Netix Introduces VeriNet (SM) Products for Voice Verification Over Internet and Lans," *PR Newswire*, June 12, 1998.

"T-Netix Names New Chief Executive Officer, Chairman," *PR Newswire*, December 9, 1998.

T-Netix Purchases Telequip Labs, Inc." *PR Newswire*, January 24, 2001.

"T-Netix Realigns Its Organizational Structure," *PR Newswire*, July 23, 2001.

"T-Netix Reports Fiscal First Quarter Earnings: Discusses Streamlining of SpeakEZ Dvision," *PR Newswire*, December 10, 1998.

"T-Netix Signs Agreement for Inmate Call Processing Services with TELUS Corporation," *PR Newswire*, January 23, 2001.

"T-Netix VeriNet (SM) Judged Must See Technology by *PC Week* Magazine at PC Expo," *PR Newswire*, June 26, 1998.

—Bruce P. Montgomery

TAKE2interactive

Take-Two Interactive Software, Inc.

575 Broadway, 6th Floor
New York, New York 10012
U.S.A.
Telephone: (212) 334-6633
Fax: (212) 334-6644
Web site: http://www.take2games.com

Public Company
Incorporated: 1993
Employees: 658
Sales: $387 million (2000)
Stock Exchanges: NASDAQ
Ticker Symbol: TTWO
NAIC: 511200 Software Publishers

Take-Two Interactive Software, Inc. is a New York-based developer, publisher, and distributor of interactive software games. A leader in its field, Take-Two has global reach, with publishing and distribution operations located in Canada, the United Kingdom, France, Germany, Denmark, Italy, Australia, and Japan. The company offers products, either created internally or acquired through third party developers, for all major game consoles (including Sony's PlayStation2, Nintendo's GameCube, and Microsoft's Xbox), as well as for personal computers and handheld computing devices. Take-Two's distribution subsidiary, Jack of All Games, is America's top console game distributor, selling to such major customers as Wal-Mart, Toys 'R' Us, Target, Kmart, Blockbuster, and Amazon. In recent years Take-Two has established a presence in online multi-player gaming, which promises to be a future growth area in the highly competitive gaming industry.

Take-Two Founded in 1993

Take-Two's founder was Ryan Brant, the son of Peter Brant, newsprint heir and co-owner of *Interview* magazine. While earning a degree in economics at the University of Pennsylvania's Wharton School of Business—from which he graduated in May 1992—Brant gained practical business experience working for his father. He served as the chief operating officer of illustrated book publisher Stewart, Tabori & Chang from

May 1991 until August 1993, but anxious to forge his own business career he decided to leave the traditional publishing world. In a 1996 *Forbes* profile, he explained, ''I wanted to get into a business where I could raise capital as a younger guy. In technology people expect you to be a younger person.'' Through family and private investors the 21-year-old entrepreneur was able to raise $1.5 million and establish Take-Two in the fall of 1993.

Early on, Brant forged a relationship with Bob Fish, a partner in charge of the entrepreneurial practice of major accounting firm PriceWaterhouseCoopers. PWC offered a significant discount on its services for the start-up, in anticipation of Take-Two becoming a profitable business that in the future could afford to pay a standard rate. According to Brant, ''We were looking for somebody who could handle the company as a small firm and grow with us.'' The much older Fish would play a significant role in helping to shape the structure of Take-Two.

At the outset Take-Two was simply another computer and video game developer in search of a hit product. It was one of the first developers to invest in well-known actors to star in its live-action products. The trend was started by Mechadeus, a San Francisco game developer that had used an unknown actress in its 1993 offering, *Critical Pass*. As a follow-up to that modest success, in order to appeal to the target audience of 16 to 35-year-old males, the company hired Tia Carrere, known for her work in the films *Wayne's World* and *True Lies*. The resulting game, The Daedalus Encounter, became an immediate success. Take-Two hired acting legend Dennis Hopper to star in its game *Hell: A Cyberpunk Thriller*. Released in December 1994, the game would sell 300,000 copies worldwide over the next six months and generate a healthy profit for the company. For its Ripper game, Take-Two then devoted $625,000 of a $2.5 million production budget to sign veteran actors Christopher Walken, Karen Allen, and Burgess Meredith. Not only did the use of name brand talent boost sales, it made it easier for companies like Take-Two to pre-sell its games to overseas distributors in order to raise money to cover production budgets.

In March 1995, Take-Two was established enough to negotiate a four-year licensing arrangement with Sony, allowing it to develop games for Sony's popular PlayStation game console. Take-Two's early success then attracted the attention of Acclaim

---

Company Perspectives:

Take-Two Interactive Software, Inc. is a leading worldwide publisher, developer and distributor of interactive software games.

Take-Two's product offerings include titles for the leading hardware platforms, such as PlayStation, PlayStation2, Xbox, Game Boy Advance as well as for PCs. Games are published under the Take-Two, Rockstar Games, Gathering of Developers, TalonSoft, Pop-Top and Global Star labels.

Distribution Inc., the powerhouse distribution operation of Acclaim Entertainment that boasted a 10,000 store network. In February 1996, Take-Two reached an agreement with Acclaim to distribute its titles, starting with *Ripper* and followed by *Hell: A Cyberpunk Thriller* and *Star Crusader*. Despite forging this important alliance, Brant was dissatisfied with the state of Take-Two, which at this point was generating around $10 million in annual revenues. As quoted in a 1999 *Crain's New York Business* article, Brant observed, "One day we woke up and said, 'We're going to get killed here unless we get bigger.' "

Goint Public in 1997

Three years after starting Take-Two, Brant initiated a string of acquisitions that would dramatically expand the company's business, turning to Fish for help with the resulting accounting and tax issues. Take-Two's first purchase was completed in September 1996 when it paid nearly $1.75 million in cash and stock for Mission Studios Corporation, a flight simulation game developer whose only product to date was *JetFighter III*. The game was subsequently released by Take-Two two months later. In order to fund further purchases, Brant then took steps to take the company public. With Whale Securities acting as its underwriter, Take-Two, in April 1997, completed an initial public offering of stock, priced at $5 a share and netting close to $6.5 million. An additional $4 million was raised late in the year through the issuance of promissory notes to venture capitalists.

Although far from an imposing war chest, these funds were sufficient enough for Take-Two to begin to widen its focus from software development to include publishing and distributing games, as well as to extend the company's reach overseas. In July 1997, Take-Two acquired GameTek (U.K.) and its operation that distributed computer software games in Europe and other international markets (renamed Take-Two Interactive Software Europe Limited). In addition, Take-Two acquired game developer Alternative Reality Technologies, Inc. from GameTek, in the process gaining a number of games, including *Dark Colony, The Quivering,* and *The Reap*. As part of the GameTek transaction, Take-Two hired Kelly Sumner, an executive officer of GameTek. Sumner would ultimately become Take-Two's chief executive officer. Keeping on experienced management would also become part of Brant's strategy for external growth. Furthermore, in July 1997, Take-Two acquired Inventory Management Systems, Inc. and Creative Alliance Group, Inc. Both companies were involved in the domestic distribution of software games for both game consoles and PCs. In December 1997, Take-Two acquired Alliance Inventory Management, a wholesale distributor of games and hardware in the United States. By building a distribution

business, Brant was ensuring additional outlets for Take-Two games and, more importantly, establishing a more consistent revenue base than could be expected from the hit or miss existence of a game developer.

Take-Two continued to grow its business in 1998. In addition to its earlier licensing arrangement with Sony, Take-Two signed a three year deal to develop games for the Nintendo game console, followed by a similar agreement with Sega and its Dreamcast system. In March 1998, Take-Two strengthened itself in a number of areas by acquiring the BMG Interactive unit from Bertlesmann AG for approximately $14.2 million in stock. Take-Two gained a sales, marketing, and distribution operation in France and Germany, as well as a product publishing and distribution business in the United Kingdom. In addition, Take-Two gained a back catalogue of games and the distribution and sequel rights to twelve video and PC game titles. Out of this collection would come Take-Two's first major worldwide hit, the Sony PlayStation car game *Grant Theft Auto*, which over the course of the next 18 months would sell over 1.5 million copies. Take-Two also bolstered its game development business by acquiring the UK studio Spidersoft, which it renamed Tarantula and devoted to the development of products for the Nintendo GameBoy Color platform, and the U.S. developer Talonsoft, which was devoted to the creation of historical strategy games (a deal not completed until early 1999).

Take-Two added other important properties to its distribution business in 1998. In June it acquired DirectSoft Australia in a $256,000 stock transaction that added distribution operations in Australia and New Zealand. Domestically, Take-Two took a major step in August 1998 when it acquired Cincinnati-based of All Games Inc., which greatly expanded the company's distribution channels in the United States and contributed handsomely to the bottom line. For the year, Take-Two more than doubled its revenues over 1997, growing to $191 million; net profit grew to $7.1 million, a significant improvement over the company's $3.6 million profit in 1997. Take-Two was one of the few companies located in Manhattan's Silicon Alley to actually make money, yet investors remained somewhat skeptical, viewing it as a collection of companies with no discernable long-term strategy for the future. As a result, the price of the Take-Two's stock showed little movement, despite the company's respectable balance sheet.

In 1999, Take-Two continued to reach out in a number of directions. It greatly increased its spending on research and development of new games, from $1.7 million during the previous year to $5.2 million. Take-Two firmed up its hold on the profitable *Grand Theft Auto* game by acquiring the outstanding capital stock of its developer, DMA Design Holdings Limited. The company acquired Bungie Software Products, maker of software games for PCs, and Telstar Electronics Studios, the interactive software division of U.K. music publisher Telstar Group plc. Moreover, Take-Two purchased a 19.6 percent stake in a game start-up called Gathering of Developers (GoD) and signed a five-year deal to distribute the company's PC titles in the United States and Europe. GoD was created by a group of established Texas game developers, some of whom were responsible for the creation of the highly popular *Quake* and *Doom* games. They formed GoD as a way to gain more leverage

Key Dates:

1993: Take-Two is incorporated.
1995: The company is licensed to produce games for Sony PlayStation.
1996: Acclaim Distribution agrees to distribute Take-Two games.
1997: The company goes public.
2001: Kelly Sumner replaces Ryan Brant as CEO.

for independent game developers in an industry increasingly dominated by non-creative entertainment industry executives. For Take-Two, forging a relationship with the talent included in GoD was considered a major coup. Recognition of the creative people behind interactive games was also a major factor in the company forming its Rockstar Games label, part of an attempt by a number of companies to begin marketing game authors—in effect, to make rock stars out of engine programmers.

Building an Online Presence in 1999 and Beyond

Take-Two made a number of purchases in 1999 to build up its distribution business. In February, it acquired L.D.A. Distribution, which distributed interactive games in both the United Kingdom and France. In addition, Take-Two picked up a video game accessories manufacturing subsidiary, Joytech Europe Ltd. In March 1999, Take-Two added the budget software publishing and distribution operations in Norway, Sweden, and Denmark of FunSoft Nordic A.S., which was renamed of All Games Scandinavia. Later in the year, Take-Two paid $2.2 million to acquire Verte Italia Spa, a publisher of software and video games with a major distribution operation in Italy. Take-Two also began to look to the Internet in 1999, an area that held great promise for the future of interactive gaming. The company began development of an multiplayer online version of *Grand Theft Auto,* which the company anticipated would become the first in a number of its titles to be converted. Take-Two also gained a toehold in online commerce with the acquisition of DVDWave.com, retailer of DVD movies, a site on which the company hoped to soon start selling games. Investors took some notice of Take-Two activities in 1999, bidding up its stock above $13, although the price would again sink to the $7 level before finding a middle ground. Nevertheless, Take-Two continued to grow its balance sheet at a furious pace. Revenues in 1999 increased by more than 57 percent over the previous year, topping $300 million, while net income more than doubled to $16.3 million.

In 2000, Take-Two acquired the outstanding shares of GoD, making the game developer into a wholly-owned subsidiary, and also purchased PopTop Software. Aside from these investments, Take-Two devoted much of its cash to growing its online endeavors. In February, it acquired a stake in eUniverse, a major online gaming and entertainment network that boasted more than 6 million unique visitors each month. The investment paved the way for Take-Two to promote its games on the site, including the creation of online communities created around the company's titles. In March 2000, Take-Two purchased the Israeli video technology company, Pixel Broadband Studios, developers of software that transmitted video games across high-speed Internet access networks. Also in 2000, Take-Two bolstered its online presence by signing a deal with Freeloader, a free downloadable games portal. Furthermore, the company established a London-based subsidiary, Broadband Studios, to focus on the development of online games.

After acquiring more than two dozen companies in the past four years, not all of which lived up to expectations, Take-Two had taken on considerable debt, a situation that troubled investors. Take-Two, however, continued to increase sales at a steady rate despite a general downturn in the tech sector, posting revenues of $387 million in 2000 and income of almost $25 million. For Take-Two, 2001 was a transitional year. Kelly Sumner took over as chief executive, while Brant remained as chairman of the board. Sumner announced that his focus would be on further international expansion. The company enjoyed a run-up of its stock, topping out at $24.50 in June. It fell to the $13 range by early September when the terrorist attacks on the World Trade Center temporarily shut down the business and caused a precipitous decline in Take-Two stock. The company soon regained its balance, and actually looked to benefit from the attacks, with consumers expected to stay home and engage in activities such as interactive games rather than venture outside, a situation that occurred a decade earlier during the Gulf War. Moreover, the gaming industry expected that Microsoft's Xbox entry in the gaming console business would also spur game sales. As the year came to a close, however, rumors began to circulate that Microsoft was interested in establishing itself in the software side of the gaming industry. To many, Take-Two, with its relatively low stock price and diversified business, was clearly a prime candidate. Whether independent or part of a behemoth like Microsoft, Take-Two appeared destined to remain a major force in the interactive gaming industry.

Principal Subsidiaries

Mission Studios, Inc,; Take-Two Interactive Software Europe Limited; Inventory Management Systems, Inc.; Jack of All Games; Gathering of Developers, Inc.

Principal Competitors

Activision Inc.; Acclaim Entertainment Inc.; Capcom Co.; Eidos plc; Electronic Arts Inc.; Hasbro, Inc.; Konami Co. Ltd.; Midway Games, Inc.; Microsoft Corporation; Mattel Inc.; Namco Ltd.; THQ Inc.

Further Reading

Aron, Laurie Joan, ''Fatherly Advice on Facts of Financial Life,'' *Crain's New York Business,* October 12, 1998, p. 34.

Darlin, Damon, '' 'Your turn to die, sucker!','' *Forbes,* July 17, 1995, p. 108.

''Game Boy,'' *Forbes,* May 20, 1996, p. 276.

Marcial, Gene G., ''A Second Chance for Take-Two?,'' *Business Week,* July 26, 1999, p. 135.

''A Play for Take-Two?,'' *Business Week,* December 17, 2001, p. 149.

Vargas, Alexia, ''Fun Plus Games Equal Profits,'' *Crain's New York Business,* March 26, 2001, p. 30.

Walsh, Mark, ''NY's Game Boy: Take-Two Rolls Up Rivals, But Stock Lags,'' *Crain's New York Business,* March 29, 1999, p. 3.

—Ed Dinger

Takeda Chemical Industries, Ltd.

1-1 Doshomachi 4-Chome
Chuo-ku, Osaka 540-8645
Japan
Telephone: (81) 6 6204-2111
Fax: (81) 6 6204-2880
Web site: http://www.takeda.co.jp

Public Company
Incorporated: January 1925
Employees: 15,900
Sales: ¥963.4 billion ($7.7 billion) (2001)
Stock Exchanges: Tokyo Osaka Nagoya Fukuoka
Sapporo
NAIC: 325412 Pharmaceutical Preparation
Manufacturing; 325411 Medicinal and Botanical
Manufacturing; 325413 In-Vitro Diagnostic Substance
Manufacturing; 325414 Biological Product (Except
Diagnostic)

Takeda Chemical Industries, Ltd. is Japan's largest pharmaceutical company as well as one of the largest drug firms worldwide. Until the late 1980s, Takeda's name was virtually unrecognized outside the borders of its own nation. However, with the increasing presence of Japanese companies on the U.S. market during the 1990s, Takeda's reputation gained wider recognition.

The company operates as a research-based pharmaceuticals firm with operations in over 90 countries. Its products include ethical drugs, over-the-counter (OTC) drugs, bulk vitamins, food additives, chemical products, plant protection products, animal health products, and life-environment products. During 2001, its pharmaceutical operations accounted for 75.5 percent of total sales. Some of its original products include the anti-prostatic cancer agent Lupron Depot, the anti-peptic ulcer agent Prevacid, and the blood pressure reduction product Blopress.

Takeda's corporate headquarters are located in the same city of its origins—Doshomachi, Osaka. In the mid-18th century this urban center was the focus of the nation's drug business.

Ohmiya Chobei, the company founder, established a small firm in 1783 to sell Japanese and Chinese medicines. During the Meiji Era (1886–1912) the firm's products expanded to include imported medicines from the west. After the company's first factory was completed in 1895, production began on manufactured pharmaceuticals. Fine chemicals were added to the production line in 1909, and four years later a modern factory was constructed to facilitate growth.

Expansion Begins in the 1920s

From the start of the Showa Era in 1925, the company's operations expanded significantly and transformed it from a local business to a major pharmaceutical concern. An important innovation during this period of growth was the successful synthesis of vitamin C in 1937 and vitamin B1 in 1938. Takeda marketed the product of this innovative research under the name Metabolin-Strong and became the manufacturer of Japan's first synthetic vitamin preparation. During the postwar years Japanese citizens expressed a new health consciousness. A vigorous orientation toward health and hygiene found Takeda's products in great demand. By 1962, 30 percent of the nation's drug sales were generated from the sale of vitamin preparations; Takeda supplied nearly 50 percent of the total, earning the title of "Takeda of Vitamin Fame."

In the 1940s, the company changed its name to Takeda Chemical Industries, Ltd. and absorbed two other firms, Konishi Pharmaceutical and Radium Pharmacy, into its operations. The company's experience with vitamin production increased with the successful synthesis of a thiol derivative of thiamine, otherwise known as a long-acting vitamin B1 preparation. Alinamin, the brand name of this synthesized product, became one of Takeda's most popular items. In 1952, Takeda's food division was established under the name Takeda Food Industry. This division grew to include the manufacture of enriched foods, food additives and beverages. Six years later Takeda's research activity was strengthened by the completion of new laboratory facilities.

Besides the manufacture of synthetic vitamins, Takeda's pharmaceutical products included tranquilizers, treatments for nervous disorders, and antibiotics. In the food product division,

Company Perspectives:

Takeda's corporate philosophy is to contribute to better health and quality of life for people throughout the world. This philosophy forms the basis of Takeda's identity, and it has not varied with the passage of time or changes in the business environment. All our activities must satisfy this criterion.

manufactured items included Plussy, a soft drink enriched with vitamin C, and Ino-Ichiban, a popular condiment. Takeda's formidable expansion allowed the company to invest unprecedented amounts of money into new equipment and facilities. Even more significant was Takeda's role in the inception of the drug export trade; by exporting manufacturing techniques for Alinamin, Takeda led the Japanese pharmaceutical industry towards international expansion.

In the early 1960s, the Japanese drug industry experienced an annual growth rate exceeding 20 percent, making it one of the fastest growing industries in the nation. In addition, sweeping changes in government regulation would soon make the industry one of the most profitable. Takeda was well-positioned to capitalize on these changes; no one single industry competitor came close to challenging Takeda's preeminence in sales and marketing.

Changes in Japanese Policy Lead to Explosive Growth: 1960s

The 1961 implementation of the Japanese National Health Insurance system marked an important date for the pharmaceutical industry. Under this system the patient's prescription costs were almost completely covered by the insurance program. In addition, the official drug pricing system allowed doctors full reimbursement for the cost of dispensing drugs. This structure, therefore, encouraged the generous prescription of drugs because doctors profited from the difference between the price at which they purchased drugs and the higher official price, set by the Ministry of Health and Welfare, at which they were reimbursed. For this reason the pharmaceutical industry experienced unprecedented financial success.

Takeda's growth matched the expansion of the industry and the health insurance system. Under the leadership of Ohmiya Chobei Takeda VI, descendant of the company founder, Takeda operated as a holding company for numerous subsidiaries, including Yoshitomi Pharmaceutical, Teikoku Hormone, and Biofermin Pharmaceutical. As profits increased the company established subsidiaries in Taiwan, Hong Kong, Thailand, the Philippines, Indonesia, West Germany, the United States, and Mexico. By 1970, 10 percent of the total national production of pharmaceuticals was traceable to Takeda operations. Moreover, while Japan's industry share of drug exports remained only 2.9 percent of total sales, export figures increased 34.7 percent between 1968 and 1970 with Takeda's business accounting not only for 25 percent of total pharmaceutical exports but also for 25 percent of food additives and industrial chemicals exports.

Despite movement toward export expansion, the trade deficit in pharmaceuticals remained sizeable; as late as 1982, 80

percent of the drugs sold in Japan continued to be manufactured overseas or with technology developed abroad. It was precisely this trade deficit that compelled the government to implement changes. One cause for this imbalance was traceable to Japan's lack of strict patent laws in the industry which, in turn, made research and innovation unprofitable. To encourage the industry to be less reliant on foreign technology the government passed stronger patent protection laws and altered the drug pricing system. By establishing high prices for innovative products, the development of new drugs suddenly became a highly lucrative business. Pharmaceutical companies immediately invested money in research and development and for the first time technology began moving from Japan to foreign markets. By 1977, Japan had received 1,700 drug and related product patents in the United States alone, ranking it second among all foreign recipients of U.S. drug patents.

Focus on R&D, Licensing Agreements: 1970s–80s

Takeda participated actively in this new orientation toward innovation. Between 1970 and 1974, research expenditures increased and a new plant in Kashima was built to strengthen these efforts. The number of patents received locally and abroad for products developed in Takeda laboratories surpassed 3,000. As leadership passed from Chobei Takeda to Shinbei Konishi, the new company president made the development of pharmaceuticals a priority along with the continued expansion into foreign markets. In addition, a new food company was established with the intent of raising the company's food industry market share to 12 percent. Konishi's strategy proved successful. While the sales of vitamins increased nearly four times between 1960 and 1964, the 1970s found Takeda instrumental in developing innovative antibiotics. A majority of Takeda's $1.8 billion in sales was generated from the sale of vitamins and antibiotics in the early 1980s. By 1982, cephalosporins—a powerful third-generation antibiotic—accounted for 24 percent of Japan's domestic drug sales.

The Japanese pharmaceutical industry's increasing emphasis on research served not only to strengthen the domestic market but also to facilitate growth overseas. On the one hand, because large expenditures were now needed to support the industry-wide effort, drug companies initiated a concerted expansion into foreign markets as a means of recouping the millions of dollars necessary to develop one drug. On the other hand, Japan's innovation in antibiotics compelled foreign companies to solicit their expertise. Thus began the popular trend of securing foreign licensing agreements between Japanese drug companies and their foreign counterparts. Between 1970 and 1980, drug-licensing increased nearly four times. The enactment of the Pharmaceutical Affairs Act, effectively extending the time a Japanese company can market a drug under exclusive license, encouraged further agreements. Takeda, representing the largest of the Japanese pharmaceutical concerns, contributed largely to this increase. By 1983, the company was involved in agreements with over 20 companies, including the licensing of a cephalosporin antibiotic with Abbott Laboratories.

As industry analysts were keen to observe, licensing agreements with foreign companies were often just the first step in establishing independent foreign operations. Since agreements generally paid the licensee an initial fee and between 2 and 7

Key Dates:

1783: Ohmiya Chobei establishes a small firm to sell Japanese and Chinese medicines.

1895: The company establishes a factory.

1909: Fine chemicals are added to the company's product line.

1925: The firm begins expansion.

1937: Vitamin C is synthesized.

1938: The firm synthesizes vitamin B1 and markets the product under the name Metabolin-Strong; the company becomes the manufacturer of Japan's first synthetic vitamin preparation.

1952: Takeda Food Industry is formed.

1961: The Japanese National Health Insurance system is implemented.

1970: By now, 10 percent of the total national production of pharmaceuticals are traceable to Takeda operations, and its business accounts for 25 percent of total pharmaceutical exports.

1974: Due to changing Japanese laws, Takeda begins to invest heavily in research and development.

1983: Takeda secures a licensing agreement for a cephalosporin antibiotic with Abbott Laboratories.

1985: The firm forms a joint venture with Abbott Laboratories, forming TAP Pharmaceuticals Inc.

1988: Tsukuba Research Laboratories is established.

1995: Ulcer drug Prevacid is approved for sale by the FDA.

1998: Takeda Pharmaceuticals America Inc. is established in the United States.

1999: The firm and six other pharmaceutical concerns agree to pay $1.7 billion to settle a price-fixing class action suit.

2001: BASF AG and Takeda form a joint venture to combine their bulk vitamin operations.

percent in royalties, a more lucrative endeavor was often pursued as a next step in securing overseas markets. Therefore, in 1985, Takeda initiated a joint venture with Abbott Laboratories where profits were split 50–50. Calling the venture Takeda Abbott Products—the named was eventually changed to TAP Pharmaceutical Products Inc.—the two partners worked to develop and market four new products, including a treatment for diabetes. Takeda's efforts to gain access to the U.S. market were not always easy. The Food and Drug Administration's long approval process often frustrated company officials. Similarly, Takeda experienced difficulty securing a U.S. producer for Nicholin, a treatment for unconsciousness caused by brain damage.

For the most part, however, Takeda's foreign expansion was successful and the company received further impetus to pursue overseas partners when the National Health Insurance system was reformed in the 1980s. By 1982, the per capita drug bill for Japanese citizens reached $95, making the Japanese drug market the second largest in the world. In an effort to halt escalating healthcare costs, the government reduced official drug prices by a total of nearly 50 percent and required elderly and insured workers to carry some of the costs of treatment. To maintain

their respective market shares, companies reduced prices while continuing to allot generous sums for research. Thus foreign markets as a means of alleviating deteriorated domestic profit margins offered even greater appeal. In 1985, for example, Takeda opened a North Carolina plant to produce vitamin B1 in the United States.

Even as Takeda continued pursuing foreign ventures, domestic sales were hurt drastically by the government reforms. Two of the best selling antibiotics, Pansporin and Bestcall, were given between a 12 and 13 percent price reduction and total sales of antibiotics dropped from 18.4 to 16 percent. Similarly, vitamins, once accounting for close to 40 percent of sales, represented a mere 9 percent of the total. To ameliorate this trend, company president Ikushiro Kurabayashi shifted Takeda's domestic market orientation toward the growing population of aged people.

According to a government sponsored research study, one of every four Japanese would be at least 65 in the year 2020. For this reason Takeda's research started to concentrate on drugs for geriatric diseases. One such drug, called Avan, treated senile dementia. Having entered the market in early 1987, Avan generated ¥1 billion a month. Following Avan, Takeda planned to release an anti-osteoporosis drug aimed at treating the 4.3 million sufferers of this disease.

Takeda's research and development expenditures for 1985 reached ¥31.5 billion. This represented the highest budget allotment among all Japanese pharmaceutical companies. In 1988, the company opened its second research base, Tsukuba Research Laboratories. Aside from the drugs for geriatric diseases, the company began developing an anti-diabetic agent and a high blood pressure treatment drug. Furthermore, Takeda's research made the company a world leader in biotechnology. Due to the fact that Takeda also excelled in fermentation technology, foreign companies began to pursue this expertise as a means of manufacturing products of biotechnology on a large scale. Although company profits suffered from the changes in the health insurance program, Takeda remained on the right track to securing its position as one of the world's most successful pharmaceutical manufacturers.

International Expansion: 1990s and Beyond

During the 1990s, Takeda continued to expand its research and development efforts, secure strategic partnerships, and expand its presence in the United States. During 1991, the company launched Lansoprazole, which was used to treat ulcers. Developed along with Abbott Laboratories, the drug was approved by the FDA in 1995. Selling under names Prevacid, Ogast, and Takepron, it quickly became the firm's best-selling product.

In 1995, the firm teamed up with SmithKline Beecham PLC to research, develop, and market pharmaceuticals in the genome field. The company then formed a joint venture with Human Genome Sciences (HGS) in which Takeda received sole rights to license certain HGS products in Japan. Takeda also joined with Novo Nordisk to research diabetes.

During the mid-1990s, Japan's Ministry of Health and Welfare continued to cut pharmaceutical prices. Takeda responded to the cutbacks and increased foreign competition by restructuring its business operations and focusing on its international operations. In 1997, the company established a marketing subsidiary, Takeda UK Ltd., along with establishing a manufacturing facility in Ireland. Takeda America Holdings Inc., a holding company for its U.S. business, was also created. The following year, it purchased 100 percent interest in its marketing subsidiary in Italy as well as in France. It also created a pharmaceutical marketing subsidiary in Switzerland and a development subsidiary in the U.K.

As part of its strategic push into the U.S. market, the company created Takeda Pharmaceuticals America Inc. in 1998 as a marketing subsidiary. The move was seen by many as the beginning of its separation from Abbott Laboratories. A 1999 *Crain's Chicago Business* article claimed that "the bonds began to loosen in 1997 when Takeda decided not to renew a contract giving North-Chicago-based Abbott a right of first refusal to distribute Takeda's new drugs." The TAP venture secured over $2 billion in 1998, however, and $3.5 billion in 2001. By that time, it was the one of the fastest-growing pharmaceutical firms in the world. Amid speculation, Takeda held strong to its 50 percent ownership.

The company's growth into international markets did not leave it unscathed. In 1999, the firm—along with six other pharmaceutical concerns—settled a $1.17 billion class-action suit brought against them by U.S. buyers. Together, the companies had banded together to raise the prices of certain vitamins by 7 to 15 percent. Takeda pled guilty to the suit and apologized for its role in the vitamin price-fixing scandal. It came under public fire once again during 2001, when it settled a lawsuit that was filed under the Racketeer Influenced and Corrupt Organizations (RICO) Act. The suit claimed that Takeda and its TAP subsidiary failed to act when finding out that certain physicians were billing and over-billing insurance companies for the drug Lupron, when they had received the drug for free or at highly discounted prices. Takeda agreed to pay out $875 million to settle the case.

Despite its legal problems, Takeda continued to develop new drugs including Actos, an insulin sensitizer. It was sold in the United States in collaboration with Eli Lilly and Company. The company also launched its blood pressure drug, Blopress. During 2000, the firm's animal health businesses were consolidating into a new joint venture subsidiary, Takeda Schering-Plough Animal Health K.K.

Takeda also formed a joint venture with BASF AG during 2001 in which the two companies merged their bulk vitamin business to form BASF Takeda Vitamins K.K. Takeda then transferred control of its vitamin operations outside of Japan to BASF. Together, the venture controlled nearly 30 percent of the global vitamin market. Takeda also partnered with Mitsui Chemicals Inc. to form Mitsui Takeda Chemicals Inc., a urethane chemicals and composite materials firm.

Takeda's ability to develop new drugs left it with substantial profit gains. During 2001, the company posted a record profit of $2.86 billion; this was a 32 percent increase over the previous year and marked the tenth straight year of pre-tax profit increases. The company continued to focus on its research and development efforts that year. It added a new genetic research facility at its Tsukuba Research Center in Ibaraki, Japan, and also created Takeda Research Investment Inc., a subsidiary that invested in bioventure firms. With its business strategy fixed on research and new product development, Takeda appeared to be well positioned for future growth.

Principal Subsidiaries

Wako Pure Chemical Industries Ltd. (68.93%); Nihon Pharmaceutical Co. Ltd. (84.49%); Takeda Healthcare Products Co. Ltd.; Wyeth Lederle Japan Ltd. (40%); Shimizu Pharmaceutical Co. Ltd. (32.5%); Amato Pharmaceutical Products Ltd. (30%); Takeda America Holdings Inc.; Takeda Pharmaceuticals North America Inc.; TAP Pharmaceutical Products Inc. (United States; 50%); Takeda Europe Holdings Ltd. (United Kingdom); Takeda Europe Research & Development Centre Ltd. (United Kingdom); Laboratoires Takeda (France); Takeda UK Ltd.; Takeda Italia Farmaceutici S.p.A. (76.92%); Takeda Pharma GmbH (Germany; 50%); Takeda Pharma Ges.m.b.H. (Austria; 50%); Takeda Pharma AG (Switzerland; 50%); Takeda Ireland Ltd.; Tianjin Takeda Pharmaceuticals Co. Ltd. (China; 75%); Takeda Chemical Industries Taiwan Ltd. (99.88%); Boie-Takeda Chemicals Inc. (Philippines; 50%); Takeda Thailand Ltd. (48%); P.T. Takeda Indonesia (70%); BASF Takeda Vitamins Ltd. (34%); Takeda Food Products Ltd.; Mitsui Takeda Chemicals Inc. (49%); Takeda Schering-Plough Animal Health K.K. (40%).

Principal Competitors

Eli Lilly and Company; Sankyo Co. Ltd.; Schering-Plough Corporation.

Further Reading

"British Authorities Approve BASF Deal," *Feedstuffs*, July 23, 2001, p. 18.

"Japan's Takeda Chemical Sees Record Pretax Profit For 10th Year," *AsiaPulse News*, November 7, 2001.

Klein, Sarah A., "Abbott Joint Venture Faces More Lawsuits," *Crain's Chicago Business*, September 24, 2001, p. 62.

Mertens, Brian, "Healthy Player in a Vulnerable Industry," *Asian Business*, July 1996, p. 8.

Moore, Samuel K., "Vitamins Makers Settle U.S. Civil Suit for $1.17 Billion," *Chemical Week*, November 10, 1999, p. 15.

"Pharma Japan: Takeda Creates New U.S. Subsidiary to Invest in Bioventures," *Chemical Business Newsbase*, November 27, 2001.

Somasundaram, Meera, "Hey, Abbott! Your Ally Goes it Alone: Takeda's U.S. Drive Starts Here," *Crain's Chicago Business*, March 1, 1999, p. 1.

"U.S. Scandal Cost Drug Giant Takeda 105 Bil. Yen," *Mainichi Daily News*, October 5, 2001.

—update: Christina M. Stansell

TAP—Air Portugal Transportes Aéreos Portugueses S.A.

<table>
<tr><td>

Edifício 25, Aeroporto de Lisboa
P-1704 Lisbon Codex
Portugal
Telephone: (+351) 1 841 5000
Fax: (+351) 1 841 5095
Web site: http://www.tap-airportugal.pt

State-Owned Company
Incorporated: 1945 as Transportes Aéreos Portugueses
Employees: 8,500
Sales: $900 million (2000)
NAIC: 481111 Scheduled Passenger Air Transportation;
    481112 Scheduled Freight Air Transportation; 49211
    Couriers; 48819 Other Support Activities for Air
    Transportation; 611512 Flight Training

</td></tr>
</table>

Lisbon-based TAP—Air Portugal Transportes Aéreos Portugueses S.A. (TAP) is a national air carrier with routes to Europe, North, South, and Central America, and Africa. In 2000, TAP flew five million people to 58 destinations. TAP belongs to that class of European state-owned airlines that has constant difficulties turning a profit, although the carrier has seen considerable revenues and traffic growth. From its beginnings, TAP has retraced the steps of Portuguese explorers with far-flung routes across Africa, and later the Atlantic. The airline loses money on these flights. TAP also has significant cargo and maintenance operations.

Origins

TAP Air Portugal was created on March 14, 1945 with the original name of Transportes Aéreos Portugueses. TAP was not Portugal's first airline; Aero Portuguesa, half owned by Air France until 1943, had been created before the war. It flew a single route to Tangier until it was closed down in 1953.

Lisbon had been an important airport for trans-atlantic air crossings during World War II, though the Portuguese aviation industry was too small to exploit it. TAP would later benefit from the wartime construction of an airfield at Sal Island in the

Cape Verde group. As a division of the Secretariat of Civil Aeronautics, TAP's first mission was to explore possible commercial air routes.

TAP's first planes were the Douglas DC-3s that started many an airline after World War II. The first commercial service of Lisbon to Madrid, operated in conjunction with Iberia Airlines, began on September 19, 1946, when TAP became a scheduled airline in its own right. The "Imperial Line" from Lisbon to Luanda (Angola) and Lourenzo Marques (now Maputo, Mozambique) was initiated on the last day of the year. This route, one of the longest undertaken by DC-3s on a scheduled basis, required twelve overnight stops.

Uniquely, scheduled international services commenced in force before domestic services. A Lisbon-Oporto route had been operated briefly in 1945 by a small airline that had been started late in the war, Companhia de Transportes Aéreos (CTA). TAP took over these operations in July 1947. A new plane type, the C-54 Skymaster, was delivered the same year. Routes to Paris, Seville, and London were added between 1947 and 1949.

The airline soon needed more cash to maintain its expanded network. The government partially privatized TAP in 1953, attracting investments from banking, shipping, and mercantile firms. Routes to Tangier and Casablanca were started the same year. The C-54s soon replaced the DC-3s on these flights, which now traversed the Sahara, dramatically shortening flying time.

A pair of Lockheed L-1049G Super Constellations were put into service on the Imperial Route in November 1955. Even with these state-of-the-art aircraft, the flight between Lisbon and Mozambique took 22 hours. By 1957, the Super Connies were being used on the Paris and London Routes, and TAP had ordered three Vickers Viscount plans for medium-length routes. The Douglas DC-3s that had launched the airline were taken out of service in 1959. Historian R.E.G. Davies's May 1962 listing of world airline fleets allots TAP three Douglas DC-4s, three DC-6s, and five Lockheed Super Constellations.

TAP was a rather small airline in the early 1960s. Its share of the intra-European air market was less than one percent. However, the carrier's operations were far-reaching. TAP began service to Brazil in cooperation with Panair do Brasil in the 1960s. Its routes to Africa were supplied feeder traffic by two local airlines, DTA and DETA.

TAP in the Jet Age

TAP briefly leased Comet 4B jets from British European Airways (BEA) in 1961 for use on the London-Lisbon route. It soon switched to French Caravelle jets, however, which were first used on the Lisbon-Madrid route in 1962. By the next year, the jets were replacing the Super Constellations on the African line. Caravelles also launched new routes to Frankfurt, Geneva, and Munich. TAP installed its first flight simulator to train crews for the Caravelle but ordered another model jet in the same year, the Boeing 707.

In 1964, TAP established or regularized operations to Sal, Bissau, and Funchal (Santa Catarina). Flights to the U.S. began in 1965 with the delivery of TAP's first Boeing 707. These planes also took over the Johannesburg route while Caravelles were switched to Lisbon-Brussels. Finally, the B707s were used briefly on the "Friendship Flight" service from Lisbon to Rio, which ended in 1967.

By the end of 1967, TAP had retired all of its propeller-driven planes, creating Europe's first all-jet commercial fleet. Zurich, Copenhagen, Buenos Aires, Salisbury, Amsterdam, and Sao Paulo were added to the network as the airline adopted the industry trend of computerized yield management. A Boeing 707 simulator was installed in 1969.

Also in 1969, TAP launched a new subsidiary, Transportes Aéreos Continentais for air taxi services (this closed in 1985). TAP became half owner of the airline SATA, based in the Azores, when it was restructured in 1972.

A suite of new facilities was opened at Lisbon Airport in 1971, including TAP's new headquarters, a new hangar, and training centers. Montreal was added to the route network. In 1972, TAP's first Boeing 747 jumbo jets were delivered; within two years, TAP was the only European airline capable of overhauling the JT 9-Ds engines that equipped its 747s.

TAP was nationalized in 1975. Boeing 727 airliners entered its fleet the same year. In 1976, TAP began flying to Caracas, Venezuela, and Milan, Italy, with the Boeing 707s and 727s, respectively, while Kinshasa was added to the African route. Unfortunately, TAP suffered a horrific accident in November 1977 when a Boeing 727 overran a wet runway in Funchal, Portugal, killing 131 people. Nevertheless, *Air Transport World*

gave TAP its "Technical Management Award" in 1978 as Lyon and Luxembourg were added to the European network.

A New Image for the 1980s

TAP became known as TAP Air Portugal as part of a corporate identity makeover in 1979. A new logo, a new aircraft paint scheme, and new uniforms were part of the package. A unique exhibit of all the airline's uniforms opened at the Costumes Museum in 1981.

New destinations for 1980–1981 included Rome, Barcelona, and Manchester. The airline began a refleeting program. The Boeing 707 and 727 aircraft were replaced with more advanced and more flexible Boeing 737s and Lockheed L-1011 Tristars in 1983. The massive Boeing 747s proved difficult to fill to capacity and were also replaced. The same year, the U.S. Federal Aviation Administration certified TAP as a full service maintenance provider; a contract to overhaul 35 of Federal Express Corporation's Boeing 727s soon followed. Meanwhile, a hospitality subsidiary was created, dubbed Hotel and Restaurant Management, S.A., or "ESTA." Air Portugal Tours was created the next year (1984). TAP carried more than two million passengers in 1984 and introduced the new Navigator business class.

In January 1986, TAP announced plans to float 49 percent of charter subsidiary Air Atlantis on the Lisbon Stock Exchange. However, these did not come to fruition, and the unit was later dissolved at a loss.

In 1987, TAP ordered more Boeing 737s, but also ordered A310s from Airbus. These planes began arriving in 1989. A slew of new destinations were added in 1987 through 1989: Athens, Munich, Vienna, Toronto, Dublin, Hamburg, Nice, Stockholm, Stuttgart, Curaçao, Newark, Toulouse, Dakar, and Abidjan. TAP ordered two extra long haul airliners, A340s, from Airbus in 1989, and installed a Boeing 737 flight simulator.

Restructuring in the 1990s

The annual passenger count exceeded 3 million in 1990, and the fleet continued to expand to accommodate this growth. In 1991, TAP was reorganized as a Sociedade Anónima, or public limited company, with the Portuguese government holding most of the shares.

New routes added between 1991 and 1993 included Berlin, Bordeaux, Bologna, Oslo, Stockholm, and Tel Aviv. However, the global recession that erased airline profits worldwide in the early 1990s did not spare TAP, which accumulated losses of Esc 100 billion. In 1993, TAP was spending Esc 15 billion a year on lease payments for its 38 planes. After experiencing cash shortages, TAP cancelled an order for four Airbus A340s and shut down its Air Atlantis charter subsidiary.

Government plans to sell up to 49 percent of the airline did not materialize just yet, however, although United Air Lines and others expressed some interest. Plans to reduce the workforce from 10,500 to 9,000 by the end of 1993 were met with strikes.

The Strategic and Economic-Financial Plan (PESEF) was initiated in 1994. The development of new products was a

---

Key Dates:

1946: TAP begins flying to Spain and Mozambique.
1953: Portugal partially privatizes TAP.
1961: New jets begin to extend TAP's route network to the Americas.
1975: TAP is nationalized.
1983: Overhaul and maintenance operations are certified by the FAA.
1994: Cash-starved TAP launches a turnaround plan.
1997: TAP sees its first profit in 20 years.
2000: SairGroup agrees to take an equity stake in TAP, but later rescinds.

---

central part of the turnaround. TAP took a stake in the Air Macau start-up airline. TAP also cut some routes and began flying North Atlantic routes in cooperation with Delta Air Lines of the U.S. A new food service subsidiary, Cateringpor, was launched. By this time, TAP had thoroughly overhauled 150 aircraft for Federal Express.

To help turn the airline around, the Portuguese government agreed to inject Esc 180 billion ($1 billion) into the carrier over four years, a proposal that was approved by the European Commission contingent upon TAP's restructuring. Project TAP 2000 was launched in 1995 with the aim of modernizing the company; i.e., making it more efficient while simultaneously upgrading the fleet. Manuel Ferreira Lima became TAP's new chairman in February 1996.

In 1996, TAP ordered 22 Airbus aircraft worth Esc 70 billion ($456 million) to update its medium haul fleet. In 1997, it installed a flight simulator for its Airbus A319, A320 and A321 planes. The total fleet was cut to 31 planes, and staff had been reduced 30 percent to 7,400 employees.

In 1997, TAP entered a strategic alliance with Swissair, which promised a stream of steady traffic from a successful partner. As part of TAP Air Portugal's repositioning within the European market, Chairman Manuel Ferreira Lima in 1997 hinted at dropping the "TAP" moniker from the airline's name, a plan which was not immediately adopted.

The restructuring efforts and Portugal's recovering economy were showing results in the form of profits for the year 1997— the airline's first in nearly two dozen years. TAP earned $8 million after accumulating $730 million in losses since the beginning of the decade.

In 1998, TAP logged its second consecutive profit, Esc 1.6 billion on operating revenue of Esc 155 billion. This came in the face of striking pilots' demands for higher wages.

TAP continued to order new Airbus aircraft in 1998. The carrier was a founding member of the Qualiflyer Group alliance with Swissair and Austrian Airlines. The airline also began code-share operations over the South Atlantic with upstart Transbrasil. Cooperative marketing agreements proliferated in the following year. A new route to Cuba was added in 1998 as talk of privatization began in earnest. Merger talks with domes-

tic rival Portugalia were unproductive, and that carrier announced its public stock offering in September 1998.

Refinements such as new traditional Portuguese dishes upgraded TAP's in-flight service in 1999. At the beginning of the year, the carrier banned smoking on all European and North American routes. TAP placed a half a dozen new Airbus aircraft into service in 1999.

The "Modernization of the Organization" Project (MOP) of 2000 reorganized TAP into Airline, Handling, and Maintenance business units. A new charter company, Linhas Aéreas Charter, was created in January 2000 in partnership with Abreu Viagens. TAP created alliances with LAM (Mozambique Airlines), PGA-Portugália, and Finnair during the same year. Portugália was a privately owned airline that also competed with TAP on certain domestic and international routes. Traffic counts pushed past 5 million passengers in 2000.

In February, the government announced a privatization plan in which SairGroup—Swissair's parent—would take a 34 percent holding in TAP. Swissair agreed to pay Esc 31 billion ($150 million) for the stake. Pilots and other employees were also to be given 10 percent ownership in the airline modification to the deal announced in June 2000. However, in February 2001, SairGroup withdrew from the agreement.

Fernando Pinto, a former chairman of Brazil's VARIG airline, was given that post at TAP in November 2000. Losses for the year were $100 million. TAP was aiming to halve these in 2001 and break even in 2002.

Principal Subsidiaries

Air Portugal Tours; Linhas Aéreas Charter (51%).

Principal Operating Units

Airline; Handling; Maintenance.

Principal Competitors

Iberia Líneas Aéreas de España S.A.; Portugália.

Further Reading

"Airline Q&A: TAP Air Portugal," *Ground Handling International,* September 1999, p. 40.

Barnett, Chris, "TAP Upgrades JFK-Lisbon Service," *Journal of Commerce—JoC Online,* April 12, 2001.

Boland, Vincent, "Airlines Prepare to Hit Runway to Privatisation," *Financial Times,* Companies & Markets, January 26, 1998, p. 19.

Bowman, Louise, "Portugalia Floats Solo," *Airline Business,* September 1998, pp. 2f.

Cameron, Doug, "Turn Off the TAP," *Airline Business,* December 1997, pp. 54+.

Davies, R.E.G., *A History of the World's Airlines,* London: Oxford University Press, 1967.

Gibson, Marcus, "TAP Still Flying on a Wing and a Prayer," *European,* February 3, 1995, p. 28.

Gill, Tom, "Pilots Hamper TAP Privatisation," *Airline Business,* May 1999, p. 19.

Hall, William, and Peter Wise, "SairGroup Pulls Out of TAP Deal," *Financial Times,* February 2, 2001, p. 32.

Hill, Leonard, "TAP-Dancing to Profits," *Air Transport World,* March 1998, pp. 50–51.

Lennane, Alexandra, "TAP Prepares to Break Loose," *Airfinance Journal,* June 1998, pp. 38–41.

"Southern Europe's Airlines: On a Prayer," *Economist,* July 30, 1994, p. 59.

"State Aid: TAP Can Have Subsidies, Says Commission," *European Report,* Business Brief, July 11, 1994.

"TAP Sale Gives Portugal Flying Start," *Privatisation International,* March 2000, p. 74.

"TAP Wins Strong Market Approval," *Airfinance Journal,* December 1996, p. 6.

Wise, Peter, "TAP Chief Seeks Cash Injection," *Financial Times,* June 22, 1993, p. 29.

——, "Restructuring Scheme for TAP-Air Portugal Agreed," *Financial Times,* January 19, 1994, p. 14.

——, "Swissair Buys 34 Percent of TAP in Rescue Move," *Financial Times,* February 4, 2000, p. 30.

—Frederick C. Ingram

TaurusHolding GmbH & Co. KG

Robert-Bürkle-Strasse 2
D-85737 Ismaning
Germany
Telephone: (49) (89) 9956-0
Fax: (49) (89) 9956-2123
Web site: http://www.kirchgruppe.de

Private Company
Incorporated: 1956 as Sirius Film
Employees: 5,626
Sales: DM 6.5 billion ($3.1 billion) (2000)
NAIC: 51312 Television Broadcasting; 51211 Motion
   Picture and Video Production; 33422 Radio and
   Television Broadcasting and Wireless
   Communications Equipment Manufacturing

TaurusHolding GmbH & Co. KG, known as KirchHolding or Kirchgruppe until 2002, is a German media conglomerate with a leading position in movie and TV entertainment in Germany and Europe that supplies TV stations in over 130 countries from its extensive library of movies and TV programs. The group is organized into three business divisions: KirchMedia, the movie and TV division in which KirchGruppe has a 72 percent stake; the group's pay-TV arm KirchPayTV, of which it owns over 69 percent; and the KirchBeteiligungs division which bundles the group's various media and digital technology shareholdings, such as its 40 percent interest in one of Germany's leading publishing houses, Axel Springer Verlag AG, and its music publishing arm F.K.M. KirchMedia trades movie and TV rights, produces films and TV programs, and owns about 52 percent of ProSiebenSat.1 Media AG, Germany's biggest private television group, which runs four TV and cable channels with a cumulative market share of approximately 30 percent. KirchPayTV operates the digital pay-TV channel Premiere World and offers digital TV services through its BetaDigital subsidiary. Over 90 percent of the group's sales come from commercial TV advertising revenues and from movie and broadcasting license trading. Founder and CEO Leo Kirch owns TaurusHolding and his son Thomas holds a 6.54 percent share in KirchMedia.

1956–78: Trading Films and Making Music

Leo Kirch grew up on his parents' vineyard in the German town of Würzburg. But instead of learning how to grow grapes and make wine, he went to Würzburg University and studied mathematics and business administration. In 1956, Kirch went on to found his first enterprise, Sirius Film, a company that traded film rights. At a time when television was taking the world by storm, he envisioned the enormous demand for movies and other programs that would be shown on television. Kirch started making contacts with Hollywood studios, with Germany's young public TV broadcaster ARD, and with other players in the European movie scene. It turned out that Kirch had a knack for choosing popular movies and a sense for business opportunities. The first film rights he bought in 1956 included Carlo Ponti's and Dino di Laurentis' production of Federico Fellini's *La Strada.* It turned out to be very popular among German TV broadcasters, where it has been showed 47 times. Two years later, Kirch landed his first deal with public TV broadcaster ARD, selling them a movie that hadn't been showed in movie theaters before. Kirch purchased seven more movies by Italian director Luchino Visconti, and his company co-produced another Italian movie. In 1959, Kirch started acquiring movies in the United States with William Wyler's *The Best Years of Our Lives.* In the same year, he made his first package deal and bought 100 movies from United Artists/ Warner Brothers.

In 1959, Kirch took the first step to market his movies outside of Germany, founding the international distribution company Beta Film. In 1960, KirchGruppe received the rights for a package of film comedian Buster Keaton movies and acquired another package of Japanese movies, documentaries, and short movies. In the same year KirchGruppe was able to sell a 700-movie package to ARD. In 1963, the TaurusFilm subsidiary was founded. The company marketed movies and programming to German TV stations. Its first deal was a 300-film package sold to Germany's second public broadcaster ZDF. After 1966, KirchGruppe was represented in the United States by International Television Trading Corp. (ITTC). In 1968, IdunaFilm, another movie and TV-production company that later became TaurusProduktion, was founded. Other major movie acquisitions followed in 1969 when KirchGruppe pur-

Company Perspectives:

It is our basic principle to try consistently to anticipate new markets and not to limit ourselves to existing distribution channels, but to use all means of distribution and sales opportunities that expand our value chain in a useful way. The demand for programming and services will grow nationally and abroad, in particular through digital technologies and the resulting convergence of television, multimedia applications, and the Internet. Thereby, nothing less than a new infrastructure for programs and services is emerging. Digital television will become the door-opener for new interactive services extending from the ordering of products and services to banking services and games at the home-based TV set. To be successful, the Internet requires new forms of offers. Since 1999 we have been preparing for this future market in our new company Kirch New Media AG.

chased the RKO Library of Howard Hughes, the wealthy American inventor and film mogul, with almost 1,000 titles, and in 1971 when the company acquired the library of 1920s-30s Hollywood director Hal Roach Library with over 1,200 titles.

In 1964, Kirch got involved in music. His new company Cosmotel, co-founded that year with German star-director Herbert von Karajan, started producing classical music programs. Three years later the company made its first opera-movie *La Bohème,* directed by Herbert von Karajan and movie director Franco Zeffirelli. Kirch's second classical music production company Unitel was founded in 1966. In 1970, Unitel started an exclusive cooperation with star composer and conductor Leonard Bernstein which lasted until Bernstein's death in 1990 and yielded over 110 hours of programming. In 1972, Unitel signed with the Vienna Philharmonic Orchestra, another high-profile performer in the international classical music scene. In 1974, there began a fruitful cooperation between Unitel and the Public Broadcasting Network (PBS) in the United States. Together they developed the first weekly classical music program on American television, *Great Performances,* which started out with a Unitel-produced performance of Johann Sebastian Bach's *Mass in B-Minor* with Karl Richter. Another cooperative venture between Unitel and the renowned annual classical music festival Bayreuther Festspiele began in 1978. Unitel acquired the rights to videotape all of Bayreuth's Richard Wagner stagings, starting out with the filming of *Tannhäuser.* In 1990, Leonard Bernstein awarded Leo Kirch with a "personal Emmy" as a token of appreciation for two decades of "making music."

1984–93: Making Television

The year 1984 marked the beginning of commercial television in Germany and for the KirchGruppe the beginning of its TV-era. With the group's expanding movie archive, it was in a good position to provide TV with content it had already been providing to public TV stations. Owning TV stations, however, was the next step in the commercial exploitation of the entertainment assets that were stockpiled in a gigantic film warehouse in Unterföhring near Munich. Consequently, in 1984 KirchGruppe got involved in pay and cable TV. Pay TV station Teleclub started broadcasting in Switzerland in 1984 and in

Germany four years later. In 1990, KirchGruppe co-founded German pay-TV channel Premiere World with German publishing house Bertelsmann and French pay-TV operator Canal+ and became a 25 percent holder in the new company. Three years later the channel started broadcasting and took over the 100,000 German Teleclub subscribers. In 1991, KirchGruppe acquired an 8 percent share in Italy's first pay-TV firm Telepiù which increased to 45 percent by 1997.

In 1984 KirchGruppe also got involved in cable TV channel PKS, one of the first commercial TV channels in Germany. To get PKS off the ground, KirchGruppe provided the channel, which was broadcast in Germany's first cable TV project Kabelprojekt Ludwigshafen, with content free of charge for two years. PKS then became SAT.1, one of Germany's first commercial general interest channels, in which KirchGruppe acquired a 43 percent share. The other shares were held by the big names of German publishing, including Axel Springer, Holtzbrinck, Bauer, Burda, and Aktuell-Presse-Fernsehen (APF), a company owned by over 150 mid-sized newspapers with the vision to create news shows on private TV. SAT.1 went on air in 1985. Four years later, Kirch's movie channel ProSieben started broadcasting for nine hours a day. ProSieben emerged from former channel Eureka TV and was majority owned by Leo Kirch's son Thomas.

Leo Kirch's third area of interest besides entertaining movies and music programs was Germany's most popular sport—soccer—which drew large TV audiences. In 1991, Kirch-Gruppe together with Axel Springer Verlag founded the international sports rights marketing firm ISPR in which each group held 50 percent. In the same year ISPR acquired the rights to broadcast the German national soccer league games. In 1992, KirchGruppe bought a 24.5 percent stake in commercial TV channel Tele 5 which was transformed into commercial sports channel Deutsches SportFernsehen (DSF) the following year.

1993–98: Making Headlines

Right from the beginning, Leo Kirch preferred to build his empire quietly, and avoided publicity. In 1993, for the first time, KirchGruppe published a little brochure giving an overview of the group. Although the publication called "Facts and Figures" did not contain key financials, insiders estimated the group's annual sales at about DM 800 million—over $425 million. Kirch's empire had grown to a diverse group of over 40 national and international subsidiaries and shareholdings. By 1993, KirchGruppe had become the largest entertainment program provider for German-speaking countries, including Switzerland and Austria. The group was involved in all areas of the movie and TV entertainment business, such as production, synchronization, distribution, rights and licensing trade, movie and video rental, and merchandising. Besides owning about 15,000 movies and 50,000 hours of TV shows, Kirch's many production firms put out about 400 hours of new movies and TV programs per year. The group delivered content to all but one German TV channel—news channel n-tv was the exception. KirchGruppe had not only become a full service provider for the entertainment industry, but also an owner of 70 movie theaters in Austria and a shareholder in five German commercial TV stations. Moreover, beginning with the 10 percent share in 1984, KirchGruppe had continuously bought shares of Germany's largest publisher Axel Springer Verlag. By 1993 Kirch owned 35 percent of the company and made his way into Springer's

Board of Directors. Movie TV channel Pro 7, majority-owned by Leo Kirch's son Thomas, broke even in 1993.

Kirch's activities in the TV market and his active interest in Axel Springer, publisher of the two national newspapers *Die Welt* and *Bild Zeitung,* was watched suspiciously by the Springer management. Because of Leo Kirch's lion's share of 43 percent in SAT.1, he dominated the management decisions and used the TV channel to broadcast movies, soap operas, and sports shows for which he owned the rights. While Kirch cashed in, other shareholders, including Axel Springer Verlag, had to account for the station's losses. Because of Kirch's hegemony and the network's constant losses, two other major shareholders, Bauer and Burda, left SAT.1. In 1990, Axel Springer Verlag drafted a 195-page suit against Kirch and another shareholder, Holzbrinck, another major publisher. Springer accused Kirch and Holtzbrinck of having a secret agreement that handed Holtzbrinck's voting rights over to Kirch; that SAT.1 productions were produced almost exclusively by Kirch subsidiary PKS and Holtzbrinck subsidiary AVE; and that Kirch reimbursed Holtzbrinck for possible losses from SAT.1 activities. However, Springer abandoned the lawsuit. Instead, in December 1996 Springer offered to buy out all APF shareholders, hoping to gain more influence with a 40 percent share. To Springer's displeasure, in January 1997 a new German law allowed media groups to own a majority in private TV stations. A change in Axel Springer's top management at the end of 1997 ended the tension between Springer and Kirch, and Holtzbrinck sold his shares again to Leo Kirch for about DM 200 million, which made Kirch the majority shareholder.

KirchGruppe's dominance of German commercial TV stirred up the interest of Germany's media and cartel authorities. According to German law, every player in the German TV market was allowed to dominate no more than two commercial channels. However, eagerly escorting commercial TV stations and dominated by the major political parties, Germany's state-owned Landesmedienanstalten were unable to take concerted action. An attempt to shut down sports channel DSF in which Axel Springer and KirchGruppe together held over 50 percent, led nowhere. Even the German cartel authority finally ceased its investigations.

1999: Reorganizing an Empire

In the late 1990s, the battle for market share in the entertainment industry became more and more global and more capital-intensive. The prices for movie and broadcasting rights were going up and financing high-quality movie and TV productions that were marketable worldwide also became more expensive. Competition among the 20 or so commercial and about a dozen public TV stations for the German TV advertising market was stiff. If KirchGruppe wanted to stay in the game, it would have to broaden its capital base for future investments and look for international partners. Going public seemed to be the next natural step, and KirchGruppe reorganized its network of over 50 subsidiaries to prepare for outside investors.

The company was reorganized into three major business divisions. KirchPayTV bundled all of the group's riskier enterprises, its pay-TV, digital TV, and new media activities. The pay-TV business was still sluggish in Germany and it was not clear yet if it would take off eventually. All Internet and multimedia activities were organized under the umbrella of the newly founded Kirch New Media AG. KirchBeteiligungs GmbH tied together Kirch's various media and digital technology shareholdings, including its 40 percent interest in Axel Springer Verlag. Kirch's main business was presented as the bait for new investors. Under the holding company KirchMedia it integrated the areas free-TV, rights trading, production, and film technology. Thomas Kirch traded his majority share in ProSieben Media AG for a 6.54 percent stake in KirchMedia. Germany's most profitable commercial TV station became the flagship of Kirch's ''family of channels.'' Four European investors jumped on the boat in 1999: Capital Research Management Funds, Fininvest S.p.A., Lehman Brothers Merchant Banking and Kingdom Holdings 8 B.V. In 2000, KirchHolding GmbH & Co. KG was founded as the new holding company of the restructured group. KirchHolding's share in KirchMedia was 81.14 percent while the rest was held by Thomas Kirch and the four new investors.

2000 and Beyond

Besides consolidating KirchGruppe as an entertainment content provider through long-term license agreements with major American and European studios, the company had to take steps to prepare for battle on an international level. In a first step, the group entered a strategic alliance with long-time Italian business partner Mediaset in which KirchGruppe had acquired a 1.3 percent share in 1995. Founded and partly owned by Italian Prime Minister Silvio Berlusconi, Mediaset owned Italy's three biggest commercial free-TV channels—Canale 5, Italia 1, and Rete 4—and was active in license trading and TV advertising marketing. Together they founded the new Eureka holding (later renamed Epsilon Mediagroup) targeted at the European movie and TV market. The group's subsidiaries included BetaFilm, by then the largest international distribution company for movies and TV programs outside the United States, which held a 3.95 percent share in Hollywood studio New Regency Productions; Publieuros, a TV advertising marketing firm including Mediaset's Publieurope International that marketed advertising time for 16 European commercial TV stations; the international TV holding European Television Network ETN; upscale movie production firm Emotion; and TV rights and co-production firm Evision.

The second way for KirchGruppe to become more competitive and stay in the game against its major rival CLT-Ufa was to utilize synergies within the group to cut costs. In June 2000, KirchSport GmbH was founded as KirchMedia's new holding for its sports rights and marketing activities, including the agencies Prisma Sports & Media, ISPR, and Swiss CWL Telesport and Marketing AG, the group's latest acquisition in that area. Only one month later KirchGruppe announced the planned merger of SAT.1 and ProSieben Media AG to form ProSiebenSat.1 Media AG, Germany's largest television group with roughly DM 4 billion in sales. The company's shares were publicly traded for the first time in October 2000. Axel Springer Verlag exchanged its 41 percent share in SAT.1 for 11 percent in the new company. Cologne-based retail trade group REWE gave up its 41.6 percent share in ProSieben and received a 5.71 percent share in KirchMedia instead. Through the merger, KirchGruppe expected to create synergies in the area of TV-advertising marketing by merging the Pro 7 agency Media Gruppe München (MGM) and the SAT.1 agency Media 1. The group's "family of channels" offered advertising customers four distinct audiences for their messages: SAT.1 was targeted at the family market; Pro 7 fed movies and comedy shows to a younger audience while Kabel 1 focused on an audience age 30 and up; N24 delivered news to more educated audiences, and DSF drew mainly men to its sports program. Another area was TV news production where Pro 7's new subsidiary, news TV station N24, was getting ready to produce TV news for all four Kirch channels including Pro 7, SAT.1, DSF, and Pro 7 subsidiary, movie channel Kabel 1.

In January 2001, Rupert Murdoch's global media and entertainment group The News Corporation Ltd. acquired a 2.48 share in KirchMedia. Was that the first sign that the world was finally taking notice? In a brief portrait of the 74-year-old, media-shy founder of KirchGruppe in March 2001, Germany's weekly news magazine *Der Spiegel* questioned the media cliché of Leo Kirch, the emperor, using his power to influence German politics at his will. Instead, the magazine emphasized his obsession with putting the visions he had for his enterprise into practice—sometimes with the use of politics, if need be. Kirch's business vision, though, the magazine concluded, was always to have a monopoly. Kirch's next planned step was to take KirchMedia public.

Such aggressive expansion, however, had left the holding company burdened with a heavy debt load. Moreover, its pay TV segment was faring poorly and a slump had hit the advertising market. A proposed merger with ProSiebenSat.1 fell through as KirchHolding's financial picture worsened. A new name, TaurusHolding GmbH & Co. KG, adopted in 2002, could not disguise a very uncertain future for the media giant, according to some analysts.

Principal Subsidiaries

TaurusLizenz GmbH & Co. KG; TaurusSport GmbH; TaurusTV GmbH; DSF GmbH; TaurusTV International GmbH; Taurus Produktion GmbH (Germany); TaurusMedia-Technik GmbH; Kirch New Media AG; PayTV Rechtehandel GmbH & Co. KG; Unitel GmbH & Co. KG; F.K.M. GmbH; Beta Film GmbH; KirchMedia WM AG; BetaBusinessTV GmbH; BetaResearch GmbH; BetaDigital Gesellschaft für digitale Fernsehdienste mbH; CBM GmbH; Glücksrad GmbH; Filmproduktion Janus GmbH; Johannisthal Synchron GmbH.

Principal Divisions

KirchMedia; KirchPayTV; KirchBeteiligungs.

Principal Competitors

RTL Group; CANAL + ; Groupe AB S.A.; The News Corporation Ltd.

Further Reading

44 Jahre KirchGruppe—eine Erfolgsgeschichte, Ismaning, Germany: KirchHolding GmbH & Co. KG, June 11, 2001.
Brychcy, Ulf, "Ein Medienmogul setzt sich immer besser ins Bild," *Süddeutsche Zeitung,* February 27, 1993.
"Die Kirch-Gruppe darf die Mehrheit am Sender Sat 1 übernehmen," *Frankfurter Allgemeine Zeitung,* October 14, 1998, p. 17.
"Eine Medien-Monopoly auf bayerische Art," *Frankfurter Allgemeine Zeitung,* April 19, 1993, p. 17.
Geldner, Wilfried and Thomas Schuler, "Wenn wir Inzucht betrieben, wären wir längst tot," *Süddeutsche Zeitung,* November 16, 1993.
"Größter deutscher TV-Konzern peilt Notierung im Dax an," *Welt* (online edition), August 21, 2000.
Herrgesell, Oliver, "Kirch im Dorf lassen," *Woche,* February 18, 1993, p. 31.
"Kirch hält nun mehr als ein Drittel der Springer-Aktien," *Süddeutsche Zeitung,* March 9, 1993.
"Kirch und Springer wollen keine Sat 1-Anteile abgeben," *Süddeutsche Zeitung,* May 14, 1993.
"Leo Kirch," *Der Spiegel,* March 12, 2001, p. 115.
"Leo Kirch gibt Einblick in seine Firmenstruktur," *HORIZONT,* March 12, 1993, p. 23.
Ott, Klaus, "Der Juniorchef im Imperium Kirch. Thomas Kirch's Sonderaufgaben verstoßen gegen geltende TV-Konzentrationsregeln," *Süddeutsche Zeitung,* March 16, 1993.
——, "Kirch bekommt Mehrheit bei Sat 1," *Süddeutsche Zeitung,* January 8, 1997.
——, "Kirch hält nicht die Mehrheit an Sat 1," *Süddeutsche Zeitung,* November 5, 1997.
——, "Leo Kirch steigt bei Radio Arabella ein," *Süddeutsche Zeitung,* December 4, 1993.
"Privatsender Pro 7 an der Gewinnschwelle," *Frankfurter Allgemeine Zeitung,* July 2, 1993, p. 25.
Riehl-Heyse, Herbert, "Das Medien-Imperium des Leo Kirch," *Süddeutsche Zeitung,* August 5, 1992.
"Verwaltungsgerichtshof: Lizenz für DSF nicht statthaft," *Frankfurter Allgemeine Zeitung,* March 27, 1993, p. 25.
"Von der musicbox zum Deutschen Sportfernsehen," *Frankfurter Allgemeine Zeitung,* April 19, 1993, p. 21.

—Evelyn Hauser

TDL Group Ltd.

874 Sinclair Road
Oakville, Ontario L6K 2Y1
Canada
Telephone: (905) 845-6511
Fax: (905) 845-0265
Web site: http://www.timhortons.com/

Wholly Owned Subsidiary of Wendy's International, Inc.
Incorporated: 1964
Employees: 42,000
Sales: C$1.7 billion ($1.29 billion) (2000)
NAIC: 72211 Full-Service Restaurants; 72221 Limited-
   Service Eating Places

TDL Group Ltd. is the licensing company for the Tim Hortons donut chain, Canada's largest purveyor of coffee and baked goods. Acquired by the Wendy's International, Inc. hamburger chain in 1995, Hortons has 1900 mostly franchise-owned stores in Canada and more than 130 in the United States. The *Toronto Star* has called Tim Hortons arguably the most successful franchising company in Canada, the country with the highest per capita concentration of doughnut shops in the world.

Origins

Tim Horton, namesake for the donut chain, was born January 12, 1930 in Cochrane, Ontario. In 1949, he joined the Toronto Maple Leafs, for whom he played during most of his 22-year career in the National Hockey League. Towards the end of his career, the defenseman played for the New York Rangers, Pittsburgh Penguins, and Buffalo Sabres.

Ohio's *Columbus Dispatch* detailed Horton's early fast food career in a 1999 article. It was meant as a kind of retirement plan for Horton in the days before colossal salaries were routine for hockey stars. A hamburger stand venture failed in the 1950s. Eventually, Horton's cousin, Dennis Grigg, along with other Toronto-area partners, suggested opening a doughnut shop.

The first Tim Horton Donut Shop opened in Hamilton, Ontario, in May 1964. The partners chose the steel town due to a lack of competition from what they perceived to be their princi-

pal threat, the Mister Donut chain. The new store took in $34,100 in its first year but made little profit. The menu was initially limited to donuts and coffee (ten cents a cup). Two of the chain's proprietary yeast donuts, the Apple Fritter, with apple and cinnamon, and the Dutchie, featuring raisins, were its largest sellers in the 1960s.

Ronald V. Joyce, taken by the idea of using Horton's name to pitch donuts, took over the first Tim Horton store in 1965. Joyce was a former Navy man and—quite appropriately, given the popular association of doughnuts and law enforcement personnel—a police officer for nine years. Born in Tatamagouche, Nova Scotia, in 1930, he left home at age 15 and spent the next few years working menial jobs and otherwise "surviving," recorded the *Toronto Star* in a 1995 article. He then spent five years in the Canadian Navy before a nine-year term as a motorcycle cop with the Hamilton Police. Joyce and Horton became full partners in 1967, when Joyce was running three stores. Eventually, the company established an office in Oakville, midway between Hamilton and Horton's Toronto-area home.

Lonely at Top after 1974

Horton died in an auto accident on February 21, 1974 while returning from a hockey game. Joyce soon created the Tim Horton Children's Foundation in his honor, which operated camps for underprivileged children from the communities in which the donut chain operated. Joyce acquired the remaining shares in the licensing company, Tim Donut Ltd., from Horton's widow, Lori Horton, for $1 million. (She later unsuccessfully sued to reverse the transaction, claiming alcohol and drug abuse had made her mentally incompetent.) The doughnut chain consisted of 40 stores at the time.

One of the most significant and enduring new products the chain introduced was its bite-sized donut "hole," called the TIMBIT, which was added to the menu in 1976. A number of new products were rolled out in the 1980s, including muffins and cakes, pies, croissants, cookies, soups, and chili. Sandwiches and bagels were introduced in the mid-1990s.

The chain opened its 100th store in December 1978. It took only another six years to open its next 100 stores. Among its first efforts south of the border, Hortons opened four stores in

Buffalo, New York, in 1985. By 1997, the company had 21 stores in the area. A foray into Joyce's vacation area of Fort Lauderdale, Florida, did not fare as well, since the company had trouble supplying those stores.

In the late 1980s, one franchisee, Scott's Hospitality Ltd., first joined Tim Horton donuts with Wendy's hamburgers when it set up nine joint restaurants at highway service stations. This gave the hamburger units the breakfast menu they lacked while filling the donut section's off-peak hours with burger sales. The Wendy's-Hortons connection was cemented by the golf course friendship of Joyce and Wendy's founder Dave Thomas, who owned neighboring houses in Florida.

At the time of Hortons twenty-fifth anniversary in 1989, the company stated that every year it was selling 145 million cups of coffee (110 million to go) as well as 550,000 pounds of ground coffee in tins. Total sales were about $325 million in 1990, and the company was opening about 50 stores a year. In the middle of the decade, Hortons was adding new types of outlets, setting up counters or kiosks in Tiger Express gas stations, Great Atlantic & Pacific Tea Co. grocery stores, and Shoppers Drug Mart drug stores.

Growing with Wendy's After 1995

With 1994 sales of C$603 million, Hortons handily eclipsed rival doughnut chains Dunkin' Donuts, a unit of Allied Domecq PLC, and Robin's Donuts, owned by Robin's Foods Inc. (and acquired in 1999 by Afton Food Group). Its third largest rival, Country Style Donuts, was a unit of giant food processing giant Maple Leaf Foods Inc.

Hortons opened its 1,000th store in August 1995. In the final days of the year, the TDL Group Ltd., the chain's licensing company, signed a merger agreement with Wendy's International, Inc., the third-largest hamburger chain in the United States. The chain was to operate as an independent division of Wendy's, lead by Joyce's deputy, company president Paul House, a former Dairy Queen executive.

The merger would help expand Tim Hortons in the United States, where it had encountered some difficulty in its previous attempts to take root. Wendy's was itself looking to expand and raise its profile in Canada. The deal was worth $540 million in Wendy's stock and the assumption of $125 million of Hortons debt.

The merger was the largest in Wendy's history. The deal made Hortons chief Ronald Joyce the burger giant's largest shareholder, with 13.5 percent of the company's outstanding

stock, or 17 million shares—more than twice the number then owned by Wendy's founder Dave Thomas.

System-wide sales exceeded $1 billion in 1997. Though Hortons was second in sales only to McDonald's on its home turf, its expansion into the United States brought it into a glutted market where it faced competition from players ranging from Starbucks Coffee to corner convenience stores and supermarket bakeries.

As it expanded, the chain preferred to take on franchisees who were interested in operating their own stores. Much of the growth was coming from existing owners adding new stores. After opening a few new company-owned stores in Michigan, Ohio, and West Virginia—many in 80 converted Rax and Hardee's restaurants acquired by Wendy's—Hortons planned to begin opening franchised ones in the United States in late 1997. The doughnut chain then had about 25,000 employees system-wide.

By August 1998, Tim Hortons had 100 stores in the United States, and 1700 overall, though three of its West Virginia stores closed. Hortons had also sold several company-run restaurants in Massachusetts and Minnesota, and cut franchise fees and rents. The company then focused on expanding the chain on the I-95 corridor between Providence, Rhode Island, and Portland, Maine. Tim Hortons' U.S. business had yet to turn a profit by the end of 1998. The company was also expanding in Quebec, which was culturally perhaps more different from Hortons' home base in English Canada than was the United States.

The late 1990s saw the reintroduction of sandwiches under the "Tim's Own" label. Hortons took part in the "cappuccino economy" by introducing a range of espresso-based drinks, including Café Mocha and Iced Cappuccino. The company also sold canned ground coffee via Canadian supermarkets. In a pilot program with proceeds earmarked for a local children's hospital, cans of "Ron and Dave's Special Blend" had appeared on Kroger shelves in central Ohio in 1996. In 2000, Hortons' food menu expanded with the introduction of chicken stew, served in a bread bowl, and coffee cake.

Hortons celebrated its 2000th store opening in December 2000. With a slower-growth strategy than it had in its earlier southerly expansion attempts, the company planned to be profitable in the United States by the end of 2002. However, besides suffering from a name recognition problem south of the border, it faced the intrusion of a powerful new entrant into its motherland. Krispy Kreme Doughnut Corporation soon opened several stores in the Vancouver area, and Krispy Kreme's average per-store sales (approaching $3 million) dwarfed those of competitors like Dunkin' Donuts ($650,000) and Tim Hortons ($700,000). Tim Hortons president Paul House dismissed Krispy Kreme's stature, saying the chain's total number of stores at the time (166) was little more than the number Hortons had in the United States alone. He also pointed out Hortons' broad menu of food items, while Krispy Kreme was strictly doughnuts and coffee. Dunkin' Donuts, which had 175 of its 200 Canadian restaurants located in Quebec, was also increasing its branding and renovation budget, planning to spend $40 million over five years to stave off rivals.

The IAWS Group plc, based in Ireland, announced plans for a 50–50 joint bakery venture with Tim Hortons in March 2001.

<table>
<tr><td colspan="2">Key Dates:</td></tr>
</table>

1964:	Hockey player Tim Horton opens a donut shop.
1965:	Ronald Joyce takes over the first store in Hamilton, Ontario.
1967:	Joyce and Horton become equal partners.
1974:	Horton dies, and Joyce buys out his family's share in the business.
1995:	Wendy's International, Inc. buys Hortons.
2000:	Hortons celebrates its 2,000th store opening.

The bakery, built in Brantford, Ontario, was to supply European style breads to Tim Hortons as well as to IAWS's own Cuisine de France outlets in the United States beginning in 2002. The partners were initially investing £75 million ($125 million) in the venture, with plans to eventually build two more bakeries as demand warranted.

Principal Subsidiaries

T.H.D. Donut (Delaware), Inc. (USA).

Principal Competitors

Coffee Time Corporation; Country Style Food Services Inc.; Dunkin' Donuts Inc.; Krispy Kreme Doughnut Corporation; Robin's Foods Inc.

Further Reading

Baglole, Joel, "Doughnut War Getting Hot: Krispy Kreme, Tim Hortons About to Square Off in Each Other's Territory," *Gazette* (Montreal), August 24, 2001, p. C9.

Diekmeyer, Peter, "Dunkin' Rolls Out the Dough: $40-Million Campaign Aimed to Thwart Rivals—Especially Tim Hortons," *Gazette* (Montreal), November 6, 2001, p. C1.

Dow, Alastair, "Man Behind Tim Horton Donuts Keeps a Low Profile," *Toronto Star,* October 13, 1990, p. C3.

Farkas, David, "Hortons Hears a 'Who?'," *Chain Leader,* September 2000, pp. 68–74.

"If You Think There Are Lots of Doughnut Shops Here, Check Out Canada," *Los Angeles Times,* July 3, 1995, p. D4.

Ko, Marnie, "Bribery by Donut? The Toronto Police Are Accused of Conflict of Interest After Accepting Freebies from Tim Horton's," *Report Newsmagazine,* December 18, 2000, pp. 22–3.

Kuller, Betsy, "Why Fried Dough Is Our National Passion; Cold Winters and Long Commutes Make Canada a Doughnut Mecca," *Toronto Star,* August 21, 1995, p. B3.

Leger, Mark, "Holey War," *This Magazine,* May/June 1997, p. 6.

Libin, Kevin, "Holey War," *Canadian Business,* August 21, 2000, p. 34.

Lietzke, Ron, "Wendy's Gobbles Up Canada Doughnut Chain," *Columbus Dispatch,* August 9, 1995, p. 1H.

McGrath, Brendan, "IAWS Seeks £100m in Sales from Canadian Bakery," *Irish Times,* Business & Finance, March 7, 2001, p. 20.

McHutchion, John, "After 31 Years, They Aren't Stale Yet; Hortons Chief Won't Slow Down After Merger—Except for Golf," *Toronto Star,* August 10, 1995, p. B1.

McHutchion, John and Drew Hasselback, "Expansion Sparked Fast Food Merger," *Toronto Star,* August 9, 1995, p. C1.

Murray, Matt, "Wendy's Makes a Date with Tim Hortons to Go South; Some Marketers in U.S. Find Holes in Strategy," *Ottawa Citizen,* April 17, 1997, p. C5.

North, David, "King Cruller," *Canadian Business,* Entrepreneur of the Year Sec., December 31, 1999, p. 127.

Pilieci, Vito, "Canadian Giant Says It Will Rise to Challenge: Tim Hortons Has Long Been Ready for War," *Ottawa Citizen,* December 30, 2000, p. H1.

Surette, Louise, "Food for Thought from Thomas: Wendy's Founder Says Shared-Restaurant Premises Is a Good Way to Go," *Gazette* (Montreal), January 26, 1999, p. D4.

"Tim Hortons Franchises Aren't Easy to Come By," *Ottawa Citizen,* May 20, 1997, p. F3.

"Tim Hortons Plans Expansion as Wendy's Merger Deal Signed," *Toronto Star,* January 4, 1996, p. C7.

"Wendy's Pays Big Dough for Tim Hortons," *Gazette* (Montreal), August 9, 1995, p. D1.

Whittington, Les, "Soaking Up the Profits," *Ottawa Citizen,* October 14, 1997, p. B1.

Williamson, Douglas, "Wendy's and Tim Hortons Made for Each Other: Happy Couple Taking Corporate Marriage Abroad," *Ottawa Citizen,* May 20, 1997, p. F3.

Wolf, Barnet D., "Brewing Success Slowly; After a Too-Ambitious Start in the United States, Tim Hortons Now Measures Progress One New Restaurant at a Time," *Columbus Dispatch,* September 30, 2001, p. 1E.

——, "Sweetness Made Right; Tim Hortons' Moves in U.S. Not Half-Baked," *Columbus Dispatch,* July 4, 1999, p. 1H.

——, "Tim Hortons' Coffee Could Percolate into Groceries," *Columbus Dispatch,* December 18, 1998, p. 1G.

——, "Tim Hortons Is Using Local Expansion to Test Potential for U.S. Success," *Columbus Dispatch,* August 2, 1998, p. 1H.

Young, Lisa, "Coffee Talk: WMS Helps Tim Hortons Manage Success," *Materials Management & Distribution,* January 1999, pp. 22–24.

—Frederick C. Ingram

Telefonaktiebolaget LM Ericsson

S-126 25 Stockholm
Sweden
Telephone: (08) 719 00 00
Fax: (08) 18 719 1976
Web site: http://www.ericsson.com

Public Company
Incorporated: 1918 as Allmänna Telefonaktiebolaget L.M.
Ericsson
Employees: 105,129
Sales: SKr 273.6 billion ($29 billion) (2000)
Stock Exchanges: Stockholm NASDAQ Swiss
    Düsseldorf Frankfurt Hamburg London Paris
Ticker Symbol: ERICY
NAIC: 33421 Telephone Apparatus Manufacturing;
    33429 Other Communications Equipment
    Manufacturing

Telefonaktiebolaget LM (Ericsson) is one of the world's largest telecommunications concerns with the largest customer base across the globe. With operations in over 140 countries, Ericsson has three main divisions—Mobile Systems, Multi-Service Networks, and Consumer Products—that focus on providing products and services related to network management tools, data backbone and optical networks, and Internet applications. During 1999 and into the new millennium, Ericsson was involved in major restructuring efforts due to increased competition and falling revenues.

Growth During the Late 1800s and Early 1900s

The company bears the name of Lars Magnus Ericsson, an engineer who founded a workshop to repair telegraph machines in Stockholm in 1876. At first, Ericsson only worked with telegraph equipment, but that changed in 1877 when the newly invented telephone reached Sweden. LM Ericsson began producing telephones the next year, but sales were disappointing because the American Telephone and Telegraph Company (AT&T) had a virtual monopoly on telephone service in Swe-

den and used its own equipment. AT&T's Bell subsidiaries faced no serious competition in Sweden until 1883, when engineer Henrik Tore Cedergren founded Stockholms Allmänna Telefonaktiebolag (SAT) to provide telephone service and purchased his equipment from LM Ericsson.

Another boost to LM Ericsson's fortunes appeared in the 1880s in the form of an expanding export market. In 1881, the company's international business was very small and limited to other Nordic countries. By the end of the decade, however, its telephones were appearing in western Europe, Great Britain, and Russia. If LM Ericsson's export business expanded in the 1880s, it exploded in the 1890s. The company began selling telephones in Australia and New Zealand. Late in the decade it sold telephone exchanges that switch calls, as well as telephones in South Africa. During the Boer War, LM Ericsson supplied field telephones to the British armed forces. In 1899, LM Ericsson opened its first foreign factory, in St. Petersburg, Russia; by the turn of the century it had begun selling telephones in China and the South Pacific.

In 1900, exports accounted for about 90 percent of LM Ericsson's total sales. Contraction of demand in the domestic market and rapidly expanding foreign markets were partly responsible for this dominance of exports. Telegrafverket, the state-run telephone company, and SAT had been Ericsson's principal customers in Sweden, but both decided to set up their own manufacturing subsidiaries. Telegrafverket did so in 1891 and SAT in 1896. Nonetheless, Ericsson's annual sales went from SKr 500,000 in 1890 to SKr 4 million in 1900.

Ericsson incorporated in 1896 as Aktiebolaget LM Ericsson & Company, with Ericsson serving as chairman, president, and sole shareholder. He retired as president in 1900 and was succeeded by Axel Boström, his former office manager. Ericsson stepped down as chairman the next year and died in 1926.

Even without the guiding hand of its founder, Ericsson continued to conquer international markets in the years leading up to World War I. It began selling equipment in Egypt and set up manufacturing subsidiaries in Great Britain, the United States, France, and Austria-Hungary. It also began installing telephone exchanges, joining with SAT to set up a network in Mexico in

Company Perspectives:

We believe in an "all communicating" world. Voice, data, images, and video are conveniently communicated any-where and anytime in the world, increasing both quality-of-life, productivity, and enabling a more resource-efficient world. We are one of the major progressive forces, active around the globe, driving for this advanced communication to happen. We are seen as the prime model of a networked organization with top innovators and entrepreneurs working in global teams.

1905. Relations with SAT, all but severed in 1896 when it began manufacturing its own equipment, were repaired in 1901 after SAT acquired telephone concessions in Moscow and Warsaw. Realizing that his production capacity was inadequate to supply these new markets, Henrik Cedergren agreed to merge his manu-facturing operations with Ericsson's. SAT sold its subsidiary, AB Telefonfabriken, to Ericsson in exchange for Ericsson stock.

Ericsson suffered during World War I as hostilities cut off most of its foreign markets. Exports were limited to Russia and neutral countries. The Russian market dissolved in 1918 when the new Bolshevik government nationalized Ericsson's Soviet operations, seizing about SKr 20 million worth of assets. De-spite these setbacks, the company's sales continued to rise, from about SKr 9 million in 1913 to SKr 14 million in 1920.

The most important event of the World War I years was Ericsson's merger with SAT in 1918. The two companies had been allied for decades, with a short separation after the establish-ment of AB Telefonfabriken. The companies decided to pool their assets in the uncertain war years. The new entity was called Allmänna Telefonaktiebolaget L.M. Ericsson. Arvid Lindman of Ericsson was appointed chairman, with Hemming Johansson of Ericsson and Gottlieb Piltz of SAT serving as co-presidents.

The Kreuger Debacle: 1930s

In 1921, an attempt to hammer out a worldwide telephone cartel agreement between Allmänna Telefonaktiebolaget L.M. Ericsson, AT&T's Western Electric subsidiary, and a German engineering firm, Siemens & Halske, fell through, and the three giants of the telephone business spent the rest of the decade battling with each other along with a U.S. firm, International Telephone and Telegraph Corporation (ITT), in the world's markets. In 1926, the company dropped Allmänna (general) from its name and became known by its present name. Ericsson had become one of the most important players in its chosen arena, but by 1930, the company would find its survival in doubt as it was caught in the machinations of Ivar Kreuger, the notori-ous Swedish financier and confidence man. Kreuger rose to prominence in the 1920s, trying to forge an international mo-nopoly in the production and sale of matches. He acquired the necessary financing, however, through fraud; he lied about the extent of his assets and the profitability of his previous ventures to gain credit. For years his deceits went undetected, and his empire grew. In the late 1920s he began to diversify, and he purchased Ericsson stock in 1926 and 1927. By 1930, Kreuger

controlled Ericsson. Kreuger's takeover had little effect on Ericsson's operations, but the company's assets became another token in his pyramid financing scheme.

By 1931, the Great Depression had made it all but impossible to raise capital through the securities markets, so Kreuger was forced to take desperate measures to meet his debt obligations and keep his gossamer empire from disintegrating. In one last effort, he approached ITT chairman Sosthenes Behn and proposed to sell his Ericsson stock to ITT. He would sell ITT a controlling interest in Ericsson for $11 million, which he needed to make interest payments on his own bonds. Early in 1932, however, ITT backed out of the deal as doubts about Kreuger's solvency began to emerge. ITT demanded its money back, but Kreuger had already spent it. Kreuger killed himself in March 1932.

After Kreuger's death, an independent audit revealed that he had also embezzled $5 million in cash from Ericsson by replacing the money with illiquid French telephone bonds. His looting had bankrupted the company, and furthermore, he had delivered it into the hands of ITT, one of Ericsson's major foreign competi-tors. Sweden's three major banks—Skandinaviska Kredit, Stockholms Enskilda Bank, and Svenska Handelsbanken—moved quickly to restore Ericsson's liquidity and restructure the company. They also negotiated with ITT over its share of Ericsson, a process made delicate by the fact that Swedish law forbade foreign interests from exercising a voting majority in Swedish companies. Under agreements reached later that year, ITT was allowed a large, but not a majority, share of re-issued Ericsson stock, and Behn was given a directorship. The new Ericsson board met for the first time in May 1933, with former National Power Administration official Waldemar Borgquist as chairman. Marcus Wallenberg, Jr., of Stockholms Enskilda Bank was also appointed to head a special committee over-seeing Ericsson's finances. This marked the beginning of Wal-lenberg's long association with the company—he became chairman in 1953—and effectively added Ericsson to the Wal-lenberg family business empire.

The so-called Kreuger crash made the Depression doubly hard for Ericsson. Abroad, the company secured its market share by entering into cartel agreements with its competitors. At home, it cut back its work force and did not pay a dividend from 1932 until 1936. The outbreak of World War II did not make things any easier. The German invasion of Poland eliminated a foreign market that had been an important source of revenue, and Ericsson once again omitted its dividend in 1939. The company lost about a third of its export sales during the war as well as foreign assets that were destroyed or nationalized. On the other hand, Ericsson did benefit from Sweden's military buildup and manufacturing of telephones, aircraft instruments, machine-guns, and ammunition for the military.

Focus on Core Operations and International Expansion: 1950s–60s

Only after World War II ended was Ericsson able to put the troubles of the 1930s behind it. Once again, Ericsson concen-trated on its core telephone manufacturing business, and export markets played their traditional leading roles. During the war, domestic orders had accounted for a peak 80 percent of all sales, but this began to decrease steadily in 1946. By 1973, the ratio

Key Dates:

1876: Lars Magnus Ericsson establishes a workshop to repair telegraph machines in Stockholm.
1878: LM Ericsson begins manufacturing telephones.
1883: Telephone service provider Stockholms Allmänna Telefonaktiebolag (SAT) is created and buys its equipment from LM Ericsson.
1886: The firm incorporates as Aktiebolaget LM Ericsson & Company.
1899: The first foreign factory is opened in Russia.
1901: Ericsson acquires SAT's manufacturing operations.
1918: The company merges with SAT to form Allmänna Telefonaktiebolaget L.M. Ericsson.
1926: The firm officially adopts the name Telefonaktiebolaget LM Ericsson.
1931: Ivar Kreuger proposes to sell a controlling interest in Ericsson to competitor ITT.
1951: Ericsson acquires a majority interest in North Electric Company of Ohio.
1960: Wallenberg Jr. purchases ITT's stake in Ericsson.
1963: The company begins selling assets in an effort to focus on its telephone businesses.
1976: Ericsson introduces the AXE switching system.
1985: The company is awarded its first AXE contract from British Telecom.
1988: Nokia Corp. buys Ericsson's computer business.
1994: Ericsson is now operating as one of the world's largest manufacturers of telephone apparatus, radio communications instruments, cellular mobile phone telephone switching systems, and cables.
1998: Sven-Christer Nilsson is elected president and CEO.
1999: Ericsson and Qualcomm Inc. settle a patent dispute and Ericsson purchases the firm's wireless infrastructure business.
2001: Ericsson announces a mobile phone business joint venture with Sony Corp.

would be reversed; exports would account for about 75 percent of Ericsson's sales, just as they had during the early 1920s. Despite the nationalization of its Mexican subsidiary in 1958, sales in Latin America and Australia boomed in the 1950s. Profits grew, and the company expanded steadily throughout the postwar years.

In 1951, Ericsson expanded its manufacturing capacity in the United States by acquiring a majority interest in North Electric Company of Ohio for $1.7 million. In the early 1960s, however, North Electric's orders from General Telephone Corporation and the U.S. Air Force fell off sharply and the company began to lose money. In 1966, Ericsson sold a 52 percent interest in the subsidiary to United Utilities, a telephone and utilities concern that had become North Electric's main customer. Ericsson sold its remaining interest to United Utilities in 1968.

In 1960, Ericsson finally rid itself of Ivar Kreuger's legacy. After several years of negotiation, Marcus Wallenberg, Jr., purchased an option on ITT's entire stake in the company, which consisted of almost 1.1 million shares of preferred and

common stock worth a total of $22.7 million. All of the common shares were subsequently sold through underwriting syndicates, and 200,000 of the preferred shares were sold on the open market, with the remaining 438,000 divided between Providentia, a Swedish trust company, Svenska Handelsbanken, Skandinaviska Enskilda Banken, and Ericsson itself.

Ericsson pared back its non-telephone business in the 1960s. In 1963, it sold off ERMEX AB, a subsidiary that produced electric cattle fences and locks. In 1968, it divested its electricity-meter operations when it sold another subsidiary, Ericsson Mätinstrument, to the Swiss engineering concern Landis & Gyr. At the same time, it savored its reputation as the world's premier non-U.S. telecommunications company. The crossbar switching system, which it had pioneered in the early 1950s, formed the basis of telephone networks in many countries. In 1973, Ericsson attempted to expand its share of the British market by entering into a joint venture with electrical manufacturer Thorn Electrical Industries to produce telephone exchanges.

Development of the AXE System: Mid-1970s

Ericsson fell behind competitors like ITT, GTE, and Siemens in technological development in the late 1960s and early 1970s. That changed in 1976, however, when Ericsson introduced its AXE switching system. The AXE was the first fully digital switching system, converting speech into the binary language used by computers. Its competitors still used the slower and less-reliable analog system, in which electric currents conveyed the vibrations of the human voice. The AXE's modular software and hardware gave it another edge over its rivals, making it easier to manufacture and test as well as easier for customers to repair and modernize. The system was an immediate success, winning virtually every major international telecommunications contract for two years after its introduction. Björn Svedberg, the young engineer who led the AXE development team, was appointed president of the company in 1978.

In 1980, Ericsson purchased a controlling interest in Datasaab, a struggling computer manufacturer that had been jointly owned by Saab-Scania and the Swedish government. Ericsson used this acquisition as the starting point of a major effort to enter the U.S. office automation market. Ericsson also modified its powerful MD-110 PBX switch, a central-office switch, to suit the needs of U.S. customers, and in 1983, it entered into a joint venture with Honeywell to market the MD-110 in the United States and to develop other telecommunications products. Previously a bit player in the United States, Ericsson realized that it needed to play a major role there to ensure its prosperity.

In 1985, however, Ericsson discontinued the sale of personal computers in the United States after selling only 3,000 units, or one-fifth of its goal for the year, and technical problems with the MD-110 suggested that it had been brought to market too quickly. Ericsson laid off 500 employees—one-quarter of its work force—from its money-losing U.S. operations.

At the same time, however, the AXE system continued to prove a tremendous success; in 1985 Ericsson won its first AXE contract from British Telecom, worth $140 million. Also in 1987, Ericsson gained 16 percent of the French telephone-switching market when the French government accepted its bid for Compagnie Générale Constructions Téléphoniques, an ailing switch-maker. This coup was especially prestigious because Ericsson bested its two largest international competitors, AT&T and Siemens.

Profits Rise: Late 1980s to Mid-1990s

Faced with the vitality of its core switching business and the relative torpor in its data-processing business, Ericsson decided to divest the latter and refocus on the former in 1988, abandoning its vision of producing its own automated office system. It sold its computer and terminal operations to Nokia Corporation, a Finnish concern, for $217 million. With this sale, Ericsson prospered. It laid the groundwork for future profits by winning contracts for switching equipment from the U.S. regional Bell companies that were formed when AT&T was broken up. Ericsson also benefited from a surge in the demand for cellular phone service, and the quality of its products enabled Ericsson to capture 40 percent of the world's cellular systems market. The company's position solidified in 1989 when an Ericsson-backed design for digital mobile radio transmission was selected over entries from AT&T and Motorola as the U.S. standard by the Cellular Telecommunications Industry Association.

In 1988, Ericsson amassed gross profits of Skr 1.2 billion, a 60 percent increase over the previous year. Profits continued to grow throughout the end of the decade, and the company continued to expand its position in overseas markets. In 1990, telecommunications giant Nippon Telephone and Telegraph chose Ericsson, Motorola, and AT&T to be its partners in a plan to jointly develop a digital mobile telephone system. The move was expected to give Ericsson valuable access to Japan's burgeoning mobile phone market. In 1991, the company strengthened its position in Europe's cellular phone market when it acquired 50 percent of Orbitel Mobile Communications, the manufacturing subsidiary of British concern Racal Telecom PLC. The following year it purchased a majority interest in Fuba Telekom, a German telecommunications concern.

By now, Ericsson had risen a long way from the nadir of the Kreuger crash. As a large corporation with a small domestic market, it relied heavily on export markets for most of its revenues and despite its size disadvantage relative to international competitors, Ericsson worked its way to the top of the telecommunications industry by the early 1990s. In fact, it stood as one of the world's largest manufacturers of telephone apparatus, radio communication instruments, cellular mobile phone switching systems, and cables by 1994. Income for 1995 rose by 36 percent over the previous year to SKr 7,610 million—$1.1 billion—while orders rose by 25 percent.

Ericsson spent the next few years determined to remain a market leader. During 1996, the firm launched two new cellular phones that utilized digital control channel technology and were supported by Time Division Multiple Access (TDMA), an operating standard used by nearly all U.S. markets. Ericsson also purchased the remaining interest in Oribitel and the remaining stake in its joint venture with Raychem Corp. that had been formed two years earlier. The venture, entitled Ericsson Raynet, was created to develop and market fiber networks for phone access networks.

That year, Ericsson logged record results. Orders, sales, and earnings increased—as they had for the past five years—and the firm had grown to serve the world's largest customer base. The company attributed much of its success during this time span to its focus on research and development. During 1996, the company increased research and development spending by 50 percent over 1995 spending and employed 18,000 R&D engineers in factories across the globe. The following year, Ericsson announced that it would restructure operations into three business segments—Mobile Phones and Terminals, Mobile Systems, and Infocom Systems—a move that signaled the firm's commitment to its mobile phone business.

Success continued in 1997 as the company focused efforts on expanding its research in third-generation mobile telephone systems and Wideband Code Division Multiple Access (WCDMA). WCDMA was defined by Ericsson in its 2000 annual report as "a technology for wideband digital radio communications of Internet, multimedia, video, and other capacity-demanding applications." This technology, developed by Ericsson and other telecommunication firms, was selected for the third generation of mobile phone systems in Europe, Japan, Korea, and the United States. The company also continued to work with Intel Corp., IBM Corp., Toshiba Corp., and Nokia Ltd. on the Bluetooth system, a new technology based on radio signals that eliminate the need for wires when transmitting signals between phones, computers, and other devices.

Restructuring in the Late 1990s and Beyond

Sven-Christer Nilsson was elected president and CEO in 1998 while Lars Ramqvist succeeded Svedberg as chairman. Under the direction of Nilsson, Ericsson reorganized business operations again, forming three new business segments. Network Operators included the firm's wireless and fixed solution for data and telecommunications and those operations that had fallen under the previous Mobile Systems division as well as the Infocom Systems division; the Consumer Products segment included the firm's mobile phone operations; and Enterprise Solutions offered solutions for business communications. As part of the restructuring, Nilsson also planned to cut 11,000 jobs over the next two years.

Along with reorganizing, Ericsson made several key acquisitions. In 1998, the firm purchased U.S.-based Advanced Computer Communications Inc., a leading routing and remote access technology firm. The following year, Torrent Network Technologies Inc. and Touch Wave Inc.—both U.S. firms—were purchased. During 1999, Ericsson also settled a two-year patent dispute concerning Wireless Code Division Multiple Access (CDMA) technology with Qualcomm Inc. As part of the settlement, Ericsson acquired Qualcomm's wireless infrastructure business.

At the same time, however, Ericsson's financial success of the past was dwindling. Despite its efforts, its share of the mobile handset market was faltering, due in part to fierce competition by market leader Nokia. From 1998 to 1999, Ericsson's share fell from 15.1 percent of the market to just 10.5 percent. Its share of the mobile infrastructure market however, remained strong with more than a 30 percent share. By the end of the decade, 70 percent of Ericsson's revenues stemmed from infrastructure sales, while 21 percent came from the sale of handsets.

Nilsson's stint as Ericsson's president and CEO was short-lived. In July 1999, he was forced to resign when his restructuring efforts were deemed ineffective. Ramqvist eventually took over as chairman and Kurt Hellström, the executive vice-president of the firm's Asia operations, was named president and CEO.

During 2000, Ericsson continued its $1 billion restructuring effort. Several strategic moves were put in place to return the company to profitability across all of its business segments. It entered the Internet Protocol (IP) telephony market with the launch of its WebSwitch 2000 product line targeted at the U.S. businesses. It also divested several non-core businesses including its interest in Jupiter Networks. While Ericsson faced many obstacles in 2000—including increased competition, slowing economies, and the weakening of the Swedish Krona against the U.S. dollar—it was able to increase sales and net income. Ericsson shares, however, lost value for the first time in 10 years.

The firm's faltering Consumer Products division reported a loss in 2000 of SKr 24 billion due in part to a factory fire and quality issues. The company claimed that during 2000, only one out of ten handsets bore the Ericsson name, while four out of ten mobile telephone calls traveled over an Ericsson network. As such, Ericsson announced in 2001 that it would outsource production of its mobile phones to Flextronics International Ltd., cutting its Consumer Products division workforce from 18,000 in 2000 to just 7,000 in 2001. It also announced plans to form a joint venture with Sony. The deal created Sony Ericsson Mobile Communications, a company that would include both firm's mobile phone businesses. As the firm continued to shift its major focus from mobile handsets to wireless infrastructure, Ericsson also began a new advertising campaign slogan—"Ericsson can grow your business"—in hopes of gaining recognition in the increasingly competitive telecommunications industry.

While Ericsson's financial results remained lackluster, management concluded that it would overcome its obstacles. In its October 2001 third quarter report, Hellström boasted that "in these challenging times, our customers rely more that ever on our ability to deliver better solutions faster. With our dedicated people, strong cash position, premier customer base, and technological lead, I am confident that we will deliver on our customers' expectations better than any competitor." Whether or not the company would quickly return to profitable during the years to come however, remained to be seen.

Principal Subsidiaries

Ericsson Utvecklings AB; Ericsson Enterprise AB; Ericsson Microwave Systems AB; Ericsson Radio Systems AB; Ericsson Telecom AB; Ericsson Gamsta AB; Ericsson Mobile Communications AB; Ericsson Radio Access AB; Ericsson Software Technology AB; SRA Communication AB; LM Ericsson Holding AB; Ericsson Austria AG; Ericsson France S.A.; Ericsson GmbH (Germany); Ericsson S.p.A. (Italy; 72%); Ericsson AG (Switzerland); Teleindustria Ericsson S.A. (Mexico); Ericsson Company Ltd. (China); Ericsson Communication Private Ltd. (India); Ericsson Taiwan Ltd.; Ericsson Cables AB; Ericsson Inc. (United States); Nippon Ericsson K.K. (Japan; 90%); Ericsson Australia Pty. Ltd.

Principal Divisions

Network Operators; Consumer Products; Enterprise Solutions.

Principal Competitors

Nokia Corporation; Motorola, Inc.; Siemens AG.

Further Reading

Attman, Artur, Jan Kuuse, and Ulf Olsson, *LM Ericsson 100 Years,* 2 vols., Stockholm: Telefonaktiebolaget LM Ericsson, 1976.

Darby, Ian, "Ericsson Starts Global Telecoms Push," *Campaign*, October 26, 2001, p. 8.

"Ericsson: A Tale of Two Fronts," *Wireless Insider*, April 23, 2001.

"Ericsson Agreed to Acquire Remaining 49% of Ericsson Raynet," *Communications Daily*, January 18, 1996, p. 7.

"Ericsson Aims to Be More Resilient," *New Straits Times*, November 13, 2001.

"Ericsson and Sony Agree to Mobile Merger," *Electronics Weekly*, September 5, 2001, p. 10.

"Ericsson Appoints New CEO," *EDGE, on & about AT&T*, February 2, 1998.

"Ericsson's New Organization," *EDGE, on & about AT&T*, October 5, 1998.

Evers, Joris, "Ericsson Restructures Business and Hires COO," *Network World*, August 17, 2001.

Harbert, Tim, "A Tale of Two Mobile Phone Telephone Makers," *Electronic Business*, May 2000, p. 88.

Meyers, Jason, "Here, There, and Everywhere," *Telephony*, October 21, 1996, p. 42.

Reed, Stanley, "In Need of a Recharge," *Business Week*, May 7, 2001.

Reed, Stanley, "Q&A with Ericsson CEO Hellstrom," *Business Week*, May 7, 2001.

"Resignation: Ericsson Chief Ousted in Face of Financial Crunch," *InfoWorld*, July 12, 1999.

Shaplen, Robert, *Kreuger: Genius & Swindler*, New York: Alfred A. Knopf, 1960.

Thompson, Robert, "Bluetooth Bites Into Wireless Marketplace," *Computer Dealer News*, June 22, 1998, p. 1.

—Douglas Sun
—update: Christina M. Stansell

Telefónica S.A.

Gran Via 28
28013 Madrid
Spain
Telephone: (34) 91 584-4700
Fax: (34) 91 531-9347
Web site: http://www.telefonica.es

Public Company
Incorporated: 1924 as Compañia Telefónica Nacional de España S.A.
Employees: 148,000
Sales: $27.9 billion (2000)
Stock Exchanges: Madrid Barcelona Bilbao Valencia London Paris Frankfurt Tokyo New York Lima Buenos Aires Sao Paulo
Ticker Symbol: TEF
NAIC: 51331 Wired Telecommunications Carriers; 513322 Cellular and Other Wireless Telecommunications; 51321 Cable Networks

Until the 1990s the government-controlled public company known since May 1988 as Telefónica de España, S.A. (Telefónica), was the dominant player in the Spanish telecommunications industry. Like many of its international counterparts, however, Telefónica was fully privatized in 1997 and became known as Telefónica S.A. the following year when basic telephony in Spain was deregulated. By 2001, Telefónica S.A. operated as the leading telecommunications concern in the Spanish and Portuguese-speaking regions of the globe. Acting as a parent company for ten major subsidiary companies, including the likes of Telefónica de España, Telefónica Latinoamericana, Telefónica Móviles S.A., Terra Lycos S.A., Telefónica DataCorp S.A., Atento, and Admira, the company had business interests in fixed telephony, mobile telephony, Internet content and services, audiovisual media content, and various other telecommunications and e-commerce-related services.

Early History: Late 1800s through the 1920s

Compañia Telefónica Nacional de España S.A. (CTNE), as it was officially called until 1988, was founded in Madrid on April 19, 1924, with capital of Pta1 million, divided into 2,000 ordinary shares. Until then, the Spanish telephone service had been a muddle, supplied since its inception in 1877 by private individuals and small French and Spanish companies holding government concessions. These companies operated incompatible and inefficient manual systems under severe government restrictions, paying heavy royalties to the state. In the first decade of the twentieth century, Barcelona, with 3,000 telephones, possessed the largest of such systems. Successive royal decrees from 1882 onward had failed to bring order out of the chaos created by these concession holders, so the Spanish government decided that the responsibility for Spain's telephones should be entrusted to a single body. On August 25, 1924, the government was empowered by another royal decree to sign a contract with the new Compañia Telefónica Nacional de España, conferring upon it the monopoly for operating the national telephone service. CTNE's task was to acquire the telephone operations and premises belonging to the existing private companies, or those that had reverted to the state, and to organize, integrate, develop, and modernize—in particular by a drive toward automation—Spain's urban and trunk telephone networks. One condition of the contract was that at least 80 percent of CTNE's employees must be Spanish nationals.

CTNE came into being as a result of a takeover by the International Telephone & Telegraph Corporation (ITT) of one of the existing Spanish telephone companies, created in 1899. The brothers Sosthenes and Hernand Behn, who had previously operated telephone companies in Puerto Rico and Cuba, set up ITT in 1920 as a U.S. holding company for their current and future enterprises. The companies were destined to become an international telephone system with corporate headquarters in New York. When in 1924 Spain was chosen for ITT's entry into Europe, local investors came forward, influential Spaniards were invited to serve on the board of the new subsidiary, and the goodwill of Miguel Primo de Rivera's authoritarian government was secured. As a private-sector company providing a public service, CTNE would be subject to tensions between nationally

Company Perspectives:

Telefónica S.A. strives to satisfy the customer's every need, offering a global range of services whose priority is that of providing the highest quality on the market.

and shareholder-oriented strategies. Telefónica is still accountable to the Ministry of Transport, Tourism and Telecommunications, and a nonvoting government delegate sits on the Telefónica board. Although it is government controlled, Telefónica has benefited from a high degree of autonomy. The Spanish telephone service was never hampered by being linked, as in some countries, with postal services, or by being administered directly by the state civil service.

In CTNE's early years, its efforts were concentrated on the arduous task of extending and improving the existing telephone service. It was operating in a largely agricultural, undercapitalized economy, and its geographical context was a vast mountainous central region, sparsely populated and difficult to access, bordered by coastal strips and plains containing most of the population. Prosperity varied sharply between regions and classes. The political background was unstable and would eventually erupt into the Spanish Civil War of 1936 to 1939. The new company set to work briskly in September 1924 and by the end of 1925 had 1,135 exchanges and "centers," nearly twice as many as it originally had. Some that were very small were operated by a family or individual, and some village centers consisted of a single pay phone in a private house. In 1925, CTNE's first underground cable was laid in the Escorial Palace near Madrid, and the site of the company's imposing headquarters in Madrid's Gran Via was purchased. In 1926, new manual exchanges were built in 48 cities, and in 37 other cities existing exchanges were refurbished. When King Alfonso XIII opened the new Spanish intercity telephone network in December, its 3,800-kilometer circuit constituted a European long-distance telephone record. By then, the number of manual exchanges in operation had risen to 1,397.

In 1926, the company's long-term drive toward the full automation of Spain's telephone system was under way. The automation process, which had actually begun just before CTNE's time, in 1923, with an automatic exchange in Balaguer, would be finally completed in 1988. Between 1926 and 1929, automated rotary switching systems were installed first in San Sebastián—an L.M. Ericsson AGF type with 5,300 lines—and then in 19 other city exchanges. Rotary switching systems are electromechanical devices—at first semi-automatic, later automatic—using rotating shafts to effect telephone connections. They superseded manual operators. At the same time the company was extending the basic network by opening hundreds of large and small manual exchanges. In Madrid, one manual exchange and two automatic Rotary 7-A exchanges with 10,000 lines came into use at the opening of the CTNE main offices in July 1929.

In 1928, Madrid had acquired its first prepaid call token-operated telephones. In the same year, telephone communication had been established between Spain and Cuba, and the

telephone link was made with Argentina and Uruguay in 1929. In 1930, the two main islands of the Canaries, Tenerife and Gran Canaria, were telephonically linked by underwater cable, while the next year a radiotelephone service was established between the Canaries and the Iberian Peninsula. Mallorca's telephone link with the mainland was also established in 1931. Between 1936 and the early 1950s, CTNE's development suffered severely, first from the upheaval and destruction of the civil war and then from Spain's political and economic isolation, both during World War II and after the defeat of the Axis powers, which had been favored by the government of General Francisco Franco. Until 1945, most of CTNE's capital was held by ITT. At that point, Franco's government (1939–75) nationalized the company, taking over its stock from ITT and retaining 41 percent of the share capital, the rest going to more than 700,000 shareholders. In 1946, the state renewed CTNE's contract. The company kept its monopoly over all civil domestic telephone services in Spain and was obligated to develop and extend them according to certain state requirements. This state contract remains in force, although it was extended and varied subsequently by governmental decrees and orders.

Expansion and Modernization:
Late 1940s through the 1970s

Under the chairmanship—from 1945 to 1956—of José Navarro Reverter y Gomis, the Compañia Telefónica expanded its facilities and continued the modernization of its equipment. In 1952, Madrid and Barcelona saw their first in-city radio car phones. The next year the company installed its first pulse code modulation (PCM) radiolink, between Madrid and the Escurial, and in 1955 connected its millionth telephone. In 1957, a coaxial cable carrying 432 telephone circuits went into service, linking Madrid, Saragossa, and Barcelona, and the following year it became possible for Spaniards to telephone to ships at sea and planes in flight. The company's installations—telephone sets, lines and cables, switchboards, and exchanges—were meanwhile keeping pace with, and often pioneering, the industry's rapid technological advances. The company was no longer concerned only with telephones. Telecommunications technology was proliferating all over the world, permitting the transmission, emission, and reception not only of voice messages, but also of other sound signals, visual data, texts, and images via optical and other electromagnetic systems, including satellites, beginning in 1960. Noise and other interference with transmission of signals could be reduced by digital communications systems—PCM's—in which voice, picture, and other data were coded in binary form. International standard-setting and regulatory bodies had by this stage been set up.

From the early 1960s until the first oil crisis in 1973, Spain and CTNE enjoyed the *años de desarrollo,* or years of development. During most of this period, Telefónica was headed by Antonio Barrera, who was chairman from 1965 to 1973. There was a rise in the national standard of living. During the years from 1963 to 1964, the country passed the $500 annual per capita income mark and was no longer to be counted as a developing nation according to the United Nations definition. Industrialization gathered speed, and there was a shift of population from the country to the towns. The demand for telephone services rose steeply and with it, especially in rural areas, the

Key Dates:

1924: Compañia Telefónica Nacional de España S.A. (CTNE) is established.
1964: CTNE inaugurates Spain's first experimental earth station.
1985: CTNE becomes the first Spanish company to list on the London Stock Exchange.
1988: Spain passes the telecommunications law, Ley de Ordenación de las Telecomunicaciónes (LOT); the company's telephone service becomes fully automated.
1990: The firm acquires a stake in Telefónica de Argentina.
1994: The company begins to reorganize in preparation for deregulation.
1998: Telefónica S.A. is formed to act as a parent company; basic telephony in Spain is deregulated.
1999: The domestic telecommunications business is transferred to a subsidiary, which adopts the name Telefónica de España.
2000: The firm begins purchasing additional shares in its Latin American holdings; Terra Networks S.A. acquires Lycos Inc.

large backlog of would-be customers waiting to be connected or put within reach of a public phone. The crossbar automatic switching system was introduced into the company's telephone exchanges in 1962. Crossbar systems are much faster than rotary ones and involve less friction and therefore less wear.

In 1964, CTNE took another pioneering step when it inaugurated Spain's first experimental earth station, designed to work in conjunction with international communication satellites Relay and Telstar. This was followed by other such ventures, notably in 1970 the company's earth station at Buitrago, to be used for telephone communication, data transmission, telegraphy, and black-and-white and color television, via the INTELSAT satellites (International Organization for Telecommunications via Satellites), or a combination of satellite and submarine cable. The goal of total automation was close to being accomplished. Automatic trunk dialing was introduced in 1960, and international trunk dialing appeared in 1972. In July 1971, a telephone service to the former Soviet Union was established, routed manually via Paris, and later the same year the company opened Europe's first dedicated public packet-switched data transmission network. Toward the end of 1978, the first computer-controlled electromagnetic network exchange was installed in Madrid. In 1980, the first digital exchange systems were installed, and in the early 1990s, the digitalization of lines and exchanges continued to advance rapidly. By 1985, Telefónica was providing a network for the transmission of national and international television.

Changes in the Telecommunications Industry: 1980s

As the range of products and services grew and competition increased, there was a tendency for European countries to deregulate their telecommunications industries. Spain began plan-

ning to depart from its protectionist tradition at the end of the 1950s. Events contributing to this liberalizing tendency and paving the way for a more outward looking policy for the Compañia Telefónica included the election of the first socialist government in 1982, the entry of Spain into the European Economic Community (EEC) in 1986, the 1987 EEC Green Paper proposing the deregulation of the newer parts of the European telecommunications market, and Spain's 1988 telecommunications law, the Ley de Ordenación de las Telecomunicaciónes (LOT). The LOT implemented some of the EEC proposals, but the Spanish government contested some of the Green Paper's provisions, being particularly reluctant to see inroads made on its revenue from data transmission services.

At the end of 1982, the new Socialist government brought in the energetic Luis Solana as president of the Telefónica board. His objectives were to float the company on world markets, reduce the formidable backlog of telephone customers waiting to be connected, and make the company profitable after the recession of the late 1970s and early 1980s. In 1983, net profits were up 11 percent over the previous year, and by 1985 Luis Solana could claim that Telefónica was recovering. By adopting a four-year purchasing plan aimed at procuring over 90 percent of hardware from Spanish suppliers, he helped save jobs in Telefónica's subsidiaries. He announced various projects for research and development and promotion of exports, as well as for cooperative agreements and joint ventures, Spanish and international, involving both industrial production and technology transfers. In 1984, Telefónica celebrated its 60th anniversary by adopting a new logo, ten dots arranged in the shape of a T within a circle. When in June 1985 the Compañia Telefónica became the first Spanish company to be listed on the London Stock Exchange, it was able to state that in the previous 20 years it had increased the number of telephone lines in service more than sixfold and the telephone penetration per capita more than fivefold. Spain, with 13 million telephones—35 per hundred inhabitants—and 8 million lines installed, had the ninth-largest network in the world.

In 1986, Luis Solana reaffirmed the company's international orientation, announcing initiatives that included strategic agreements and joint ventures with American Telephone and Telegraph (AT&T) Technologies Inc. of the United States for ATT Microelectrica España—application-specific integrated circuits, 70 to 80 percent for export; SysScan of Norway for Maptel (digital mapping); British Aerospace, Olivetti, Brown Boveri, Philips, Saab-Scania, and Telfin for European Silicon Structures ES2 (integrated circuits); and Fujitsu of Japan for Fujitsu España (DP hardware and software). Through the late 1980s, profits and development continued their upward trend. World financial markets were opening up to Telefónica, which had shares quoted in Europe, the United States, and Japan. In 1988, Telefónica increased the number of seasonal telephone booths—booths installed at resorts and in population centers during tourist seasons to meet increased telephone traffic—and prepared for the introduction of cardphones. In that same year, steps were taken to reverse the decline in the quality and efficiency of the telephone service arising from failure to keep pace with the surge in demand—there was 2 percent average growth in demand in the 1970s, rising to 12 percent in 1989. Telefónica invested in new ventures, including the pan-European company Locstar and Geostar (U.S.), set up to develop radiopaging via satellite in their respective continents. The first Spanish-Soviet enterprise was set up to produce telephones of Spanish design. International cooperation agreements were signed with other public networks operators, including France Telecom, British Telecom, STET of Italy, and, in the United States, NYNEX, Bell Atlantic, Ameritech, and Southwestern Bell. In May 1988, the firm officially adopted the name Telefónica de España S.A.

The year 1989, during the chairmanship of Cándido Velazquez, formerly head of the Spanish state-owned tobacco industry and the successor of Luis Solana in January, brought improved service quality, management restructuring (decentralization), and investment in the urgently needed expansion of the network infrastructure. The company set Pta582 billion aside for investment, 62.7 percent more than in 1988. Telefónica Servicios (TS-1) was created to provide VANS (value-added network services), including radiopaging, electronic mail, voice mail, electronic data interchange, videotext, and international corporate communications. Telefónica installed nearly 1.5 million telephone lines in 1989, more than 87 percent of them digital. Spain now had over 15 million telephones. The waiting list had been reduced under Cándido Velazquez, but it still stood at 600,000 at the end of 1989. At 30 lines per 100 inhabitants, Spain had a lower level of telephone service penetration than any other European Economic Community member. Telefónica's good financial performance culminated in 1989 in a 16 percent increase in annual revenue to Pta703 billion ($5.1 billion) and an 8 percent increase in profits to Pta68.5 billion.

During this time period, Telefónica ensured a strong hold over its supplies of telecommunications equipment, with an interest in Spain's largest manufacturers of telecoms hardware, a 21.14 percent share in Alcatel Standard Electrica S.A., and a 12 percent in Amper S.A., the main Spanish manufacturer of telecommunications terminals. Telefónica's Plan Industrial de Compras (PIC) put a severe limit on imports, thus protecting its native suppliers, which were largely its own subsidiaries.

Because of the government's controlling interest, Telefónica's policies were closely linked with those of the state, and its strategies were influenced by national unemployment and inflation figures. Government restrictions were evident in staffing policy—the company was obliged to maintain a larger work force than it otherwise would—and in the fixing of telephone tariffs which resulted, until the late 1980s, in a constant cross-subsidy from international calls to local ones. The latter were traditionally very cheap by European standards, with some private domestic subscribers never exceeding their allowance of free calls and paying only the rental charge. Local tariffs were raised—by 14 percent in 1990—but such increases required government approval. Governmental trends also had an effect on the company's funding, investment, and marketing policy. Telefónica had traditionally been able to rely on the Spanish Bourses for a large part of its funding, but until LOT it was inhibited from raising capital abroad by government policy, which constrained exports. Telefónica's tax liabilities were met by a government levy, based on its net profits, and were usually a set minimum of 6 percent of total revenue.

Until the late 1960s, the company had left most of its research to its main supplier, SESA. Once properly started, however, Telefónica's research and development took off and by 1971 was employing about 100 people in this area. In 1989, Telefónica, with the participation of Pacific Telesis and AT&T's Bell Communications Research, opened its new $53 million research and development center. This center, occupying 21,000 square meters and employing, at the end of 1989, a staff of 500, had developed a second-generation packet-switching system and was engaged in projects on optical communication, speech technology, and various European Economic Community and European Space Agency projects. Throughout its history, the company has been attentive to the quality and concerned for the welfare of its employees. In August 1924, the same month that its first contract with the government was authorized by royal decree, a company training department was set up. In 1989, over 43,000 of the 71,155 employees were given training or refresher courses, and over 55 percent of 1,930 new recruits were university graduates. Since 1925, employees were offered the opportunity of becoming shareholders in the company.

As well as maintenance and extension of the basic telephone services, Telefónica's activities in the early 1990s covered data transmission; VANS (value-added network services), including radiopaging, electronic mail, electronic data interchange, videotext, and international corporate communications; and satellite communications. There was also development of the supporting infrastructures—digitalization of transmission services, installation of optical fiber cables, extension of ISDN (integrated services digital network), and maintenance of Telefónica's position among world leaders for submarine cable networks. In the early 1990s, Telefónica was aimed at expansion into European and Latin American markets by acquisition. The telephone network also benefited from a program completed in 1993 that commercialized the first Spanish satellite, Hispasat, and saw the launch of an additional satellite as well. In Spain, Telefónica also made large-scale preparations to meet the extra calls on its telephone and telecommunications services that were made during 1992, the year Barcelona hosted the Olympic Games. The company also adopted the Cellular Access Rural Telephony system that year, which was designed to allow for cellular telephone service in rural areas.

During the 1990s, Telefónica continued to invest in international expansion as well as in developing technologies. In 1990, the firm acquired an interest in telecommunication network providers in Chile and in Telefónica de Argentina. The following year, it gained majority control over Telefónica Larga Distancia of Puerto Rico. The company also began to develop its mobile telephony service, the operations of which were organized under Movistar and eventually fell under control of the Telefónica Móviles subsidiary.

Privatization and Deregulation: 1990s and Beyond

During the 1990s, the landscape of the telecommunications industry began to change dramatically. As such, the business operations of Telefónica were deeply affected. Beginning in 1994, the company began to reorganize itself in preparation for privatization as well as deregulation of basic telephony. The following year, the Spanish government began the privatization movement, selling off 12 percent of its holdings in the company by offering 100 million shares on the market.

The company also began its foray into the Internet arena in 1995 by launching InfoVia. The firm's mobile service offerings also began to develop rapidly, and by 1996 had secured three million users—eight out of every 100 Spaniards. The government fully privatized Telefónica in 1997, selling off its remaining 20.9 percent interest in the company. The $4.4 billion offering—the largest in Spanish history—was followed by the creation of the Telecommunications Market Commission, which was developed to promote competition in the rapidly deregulating telecommunications industry.

Led by Juan Villalonga—elected chairman and CEO in 1996 by Spain's Prime Minister Jose Maria Aznar—Telefónica quickly began to create ventures that would ensure its stature in the competitive market. One such venture was formed in 1998, when the company teamed up with what was then known as MCI Communications Corp. to provide product and services to U.S.-based consumers and small businesses. This venture would ultimately lead to Villalonga's departure in 2000, after he was linked to a 1998 insider trading scandal relating to the MCI Worldcom Inc. merger.

During 1998, basic telephony in Spain was deregulated. As part of Telefónica's reorganization, its domestic telecommunications business was transferred to a subsidiary, which took on the name Telefónica de España. Telefónica S.A. was then created to act as a parent company for the firm's business lines. As a result of facing new competition in its home market, the company continued to focus its efforts on its international expansion. The company entered the Brazilian market when that country's telephone company, Telebras, was privatized. During 1998, the firm secured $18.2 billion in revenues with nearly 26 percent stemming from operations outside of Spain. By this time, over 50 percent of its 37 million fixed lines were outside of its home country, 54 percent of its 14.4 million cellular phone customers did not reside in Spain, and 86 percent of its 2.3 million pay-television subscribers were international. Telefónica had also invested nearly $10.9 billion in the Latin American region by the late 1990s and controlled nearly 40 percent of its telecommunications.

Along with its international phone operations, Telefónica was also focused on its Internet and media-related businesses. In 1999, the firm's Terra Networks S.A. Internet subsidiary went public. On the first day of trading on the NASDAQ, Terra's stock price increased by as much as 198 percent. The firm then strengthened its Internet holdings in 2000, when Terra acquired Lycos Inc. in a $12.5 billion purchase. After the deal was finalized, the company became known as Terra Lycos S.A.

Telefónica made several other strategic moves upon entering the new millennium. As part of its quest to become a leading global telecommunications firm, the company began purchasing additional shares in its Latin American holdings. Entitled Operation Verónica, the strategy allowed Telefónica gain stronger control of Telefónica de Argentina, Telesp, Telefónica de Peru, and Tele Sudeste. Telefónica Móviles S.A., the company's cellular subsidiary, went public in 2000 and also began marketing mobile Internet services. By March of that year, it had secured over 10 million customers and laid the groundwork to acquire four Mexican cellular companies owned by Motorola Inc.

Telefónica did not emerge from both privatization and deregulation unscathed, however. In June 2000, a popular Spanish newspaper, *El Mundo,* published articles that claimed Villalonga had used privileged information about the MCI and Worldcom merger to buy and sell Telefónica stock at an advantage in 1998. While both Telefónica and Villalonga denied the insider trading accusations, Cesar Alierta was named to replace Villalonga as chairman. The company also became target of a virus that sent email text messages to cellular telephones belonging to Telefónica customers. The message text claimed Telefónica was a ruthless monopoly. The virus, named Timofonica—*timo* means "scam" in Spanish—did not damage any phones and was deemed harmless by the company.

Meanwhile, an economic crisis in Argentina made investors wary of Telefónica's strong involvement in that country as well as the rest of Latin America. While its stock price fell, the company remained in a stronger position than other European telecommunications firms because of its low debt. In fact, a 2001 *Business Week* article claimed that "while investors are generally leery right now about European telecoms, Telefónica's basic business looks solid, despite current jitters about Latin America. The telecom is assured of revenues from its Latin American subsidiaries, thanks to their leadership positions in most of their markets." It was this leadership that left Telefónica management confident that its success would continue into the future. With a strong focus on remaining a leading global telecommunications firm, Telefónica appeared to be well positioned for continued growth.

Principal Subsidiaries

Telefónica de España S.A.; Telefónica Latinoamericana; Telefónica Móviles S.A.; Terra Lycos S.A.; Telefónica DataCorp; Atento Holding Telecomunicaciones S.A.; Admira S.A.; Telefónica Publicidad e Información S.A. (59.87%); Emergia (Uruguay); Adquira S.A.

Principal Competitors

Auna Operadores de Telecomunicaciones S.A.; Jazztel p.l.c.; Retevisión S.A.

Further Reading

Automización integral de España, Madrid: Servicio de Publicaciones de Telefónica, 1989.
Edmondson, Gail, and Margaret Popper, "Spain's Success," *Business Week, International Edition*, August 3, 1998.
Hooper, John, *The Spaniards,* Harmondsworth: Penguin Books, 1986.
Koerner, Brendan I., "A Telephone Spam Scam," *U.S. News & World Report*, June 19, 2000, p. 45.
Lalaguna, Juan, *Spain,* Gloucestershire: Windrush Press, 1990.
"Largest Privatization in Spanish History," *Privatization International*, February 1997, p. 40.
Parry, John N., "Telefónica Finds the Game Has Changed," *European*, April 24, 1997, p. 19.
"Results of MCI/Worldcom/Telefónica Agreements," *Telephony*, March 16, 1998, p. 1.
Schmidt, Philip, "The Wrong Call on Telefónica?," *Business Week*, June 25, 2001.
"Spain-Adios Don Juan?," *Economist*, July 1, 2000, p. 49.
"Telefónica's Bid to Be a Cyberstar," *Business Week*, May 29, 2000.

"Telefónica Cranks Up Profits," *Fiber Optic News*, November 22, 1999.

"Telefónica Shells Out 1.78 Billion Dollars for Motorola Mexico Mobile Holdings," *InfoLatina S.A. de C.V.*, October 12, 2000.

"Telefónica to Undergo Name Change, Restructuring Moves," *Telecommunications Reports*, March 23, 1998, p. 13.

Tomlinson, Richard, "Dialing In on Latin America," *Fortune*, October 25, 1999, p. 259.

—Olive Classe
—update: Christina M. Stansell

Texas Instruments Inc.

12500 TI Boulevard
Dallas, Texas 75243-4136
U.S.A.
Telephone: (972) 995-2011
Toll Free: (800) 995-4360
Fax: (972) 995-4360
Web site: http://www.ti.com

Public Company
Incorporated: 1930 as Geophysical Service, Inc.
Employees: 42,400
Sales: $11.8 billion (2000)
Stock Exchanges: New York Swiss
Ticker Symbol: TXN
NAIC: 334413 Semiconductor and Related Device
Manufacturing; 335314 Relay and Industrial Control
Manufacturing

Texas Instruments Inc. (TI) operates as one of the largest semiconductor manufacturers in the world. By 2001, it had a leading market share in the analog chip and digital signal processor (DSP) industries. In fact, over half of the world's wireless phones have TI's DSPs. The company's main businesses include semiconductors, which accounted for 87 percent of revenues in 2000; educational and productivity solutions; sensors and controls; and digital light processing (DLP) products. While TI experienced record financial results in 2000, the company's profits were significantly impacted during 2001, when the semiconductor industry experienced one of worst downturns in its history.

Origins

The history of Texas Instruments is intimately related to the history of the American electronics industry. TI was one of the first companies to manufacture transistors, and it introduced the first commercial silicon transistors. It was a TI engineer—Jack Kilby—who developed the first semiconductor integrated circuit in 1958, and TI's semiconductor chips helped fuel the modern electronics revolution. (Kilby won a Nobel Prize in 2000 for his contributions.) After a disappointing performance in the 1980s, the corporation abandoned its long-held, but unfulfilled dream of becoming a consumer electronics powerhouse in favor of specialization in high-tech computer components.

Texas Instruments' roots can be traced to Geophysical Service, a petroleum-exploration firm founded in 1930 by Dr. J. Clarence Karcher and Eugene McDermott. Headquartered in Dallas, Texas, Geophysical Service used a technique for oil exploration developed by Karcher. The technique, reflection seismology, used underground sound waves to find and map those areas most likely to yield oil. When Karcher and McDermott opened a research and equipment manufacturing office in Newark, New Jersey—to keep their research and their seismography equipment operations out of view of competitors—they hired J. Erik Jonsson, a mechanical engineer, to head it.

Focus on Defense Contracts, Electronics: 1940s–50s

Toward the end of the 1930s, Geophysical Service began to change its business focus because of the erratic nature of the oil exploration business. The company was reorganized: an oil company, Coronado Corporation, was established as the parent company, and a geophysical company, Geophysical Service, Inc. (GSI), was formed as a subsidiary. McDermott and Jonsson, along with two other GSI employees, purchased GSI from Coronado in 1941. During World War II, oil exploration continued, and the company also looked for other business opportunities. The skills GSI acquired producing seismic devices were put to use in the development and manufacture of electronic equipment for the armed services. This experience revealed marked similarities in design and performance requirements for the two kinds of equipment. Jonsson, encouraged by GSI's expansion during the war, helped make military manufacturing a major company focus. By 1942, GSI was working on military contracts for the U.S. Navy and the Army Signal Corps. This marked the beginning of the company's diversification into electronics unrelated to petroleum exploration.

After the war, Jonsson coaxed a young naval officer named Patrick E. Haggerty—a man of exceptional vision—to join

418

GSI. At a time when many defense contractors had shifted their focus from military manufacturing to civilian markets, Haggerty and Jonsson firmly believed that defense contracts would help them establish GSI as a leading-edge electronics company. They won contracts to produce such military equipment as airborne magnometers and complete radar systems. Haggerty, who was general manager of the Laboratory and Manufacturing (L&M) division, also set about turning GSI into a major electronics manufacturer. He and Jonsson soon won approval from the board of directors to build a new plant to consolidate scattered operations into one unit. The new building opened in 1947.

By 1951, the L&M division was growing faster than GSI's Geophysical division. The company was reorganized again and renamed General Instruments Inc. Because its new name was already in use by another company, however, General Instruments became Texas Instruments that same year. Geophysical Service Inc. became a subsidiary of Texas Instruments in the reorganization, which it remained until early 1988, when most of the company was sold to the Halliburton Company.

The next major change came late in 1953, when Texas Instruments went public by merging with the almost-dormant Intercontinental Rubber Company. The merger brought TI new working capital and a listing on the New York Stock Exchange and helped fuel the company's subsequent growth. Indeed, the postwar era was a heady time for Texas Instruments. In 1953 alone, TI acquired seven new companies. Sales skyrocketed from $6.4 million in 1949 to $20 million in 1952 to $92 million in 1958, establishing TI as a major electronics manufacturer.

An important factor in TI's astronomical growth in the 1950s was the transistor. In 1952, TI paid $25,000 to Western Electric for a license to manufacture its newly patented germanium transistor. Within two years, TI was mass-producing high-frequency germanium transistors and had introduced the first commercial silicon transistor. The silicon transistor was based on research conducted by Gordon Teal, who had been hired from Bell Laboratories to head TI's research laboratories. Teal and his research team had developed a way to make transistors out of silicon rather than germanium in 1954. Silicon had many advantages over germanium, not least of which was its resistance to high temperatures. The silicon transistor was a critical breakthrough.

It was Patrick Haggerty who was convinced that there was a huge market for consumer products that used inexpensive transistors. In 1954, TI, together with the Regency division of Industrial Engineering Associates, Inc., developed the world's first small, inexpensive, portable radio using the germanium transistors TI had developed. The new Regency Radio was introduced in late 1954 and became the hot gift item of the 1954 Christmas season. The transistor soon usurped the place of vacuum tubes forever.

During all this, Haggerty and Mark Shepherd Jr.—then manager of TI's Semiconductor Components division and later chairman of TI—had been trying, with little success, to persuade IBM to make TI a supplier of transistors for its computers. But Thomas Watson Jr., president and founder of IBM, was impressed with the Regency Radio, and in 1957 IBM signed an agreement that made TI a major component supplier for IBM computers. In 1958, Patrick Haggerty was named to succeed Jonsson as president.

From 1956 to 1958, Texas Instruments' annual sales doubled from $46 million to $92 million. In 1957, TI opened its first manufacturing facility outside the United States—a plant in Bedford, England, to supply semiconductors to Britain and Western Europe. In 1959, TI's merger with Metals and Controls Corporation—a maker of clad metals, control instruments, and nuclear fuel components and instrument cores—gave TI two U.S. plants as well as facilities in Mexico, Argentina, Italy, Holland, and Australia.

The Integrated Circuit: 1958

One of Texas Instruments' most important breakthroughs occurred in 1958 when a newly hired employee, Jack S. Kilby, came up with the idea for the first integrated circuit. The integrated circuit was a pivotal innovation. Made of a single semiconductor material, it eliminated the need to solder components together. Without wiring and soldering, components could be miniaturized, which allowed for more compact circuitry and also meant huge numbers of components could be crowded onto a single chip.

To be sure, there were manufacturing problems to be overcome. The chips had to be produced in an entirely dust-free environment; an error-free method of "printing" the circuits onto the silicon chips had to be devised; and miniaturization itself made manufacturing difficult. But Texas Instruments realized the chip's potential and, after two years of development, the company's first commercial integrated circuits were made available in 1960. Although the electronics industry initially greeted the chip with skepticism, integrated circuits became the foundation of modern microelectronics. Smaller, lighter, faster, more dependable, and more powerful than its predecessors, the chip had many advantages; however, it was expensive—$100 for small quantities in 1962. But integrated circuits were ideally suited for use in computers. Together, chips and computers experienced explosive growth.

Semiconductors quickly became a key element in space technology, too, and early interest by the military and the U.S. space program gave TI and its competitors the impetus to improve their semiconductor chips and refine their production techniques. Under Jack Kilby, TI built the first computer to use silicon integrated circuits for the air force. Demonstrated in 1961, this ten-ounce, 600-part computer proved that integrated circuits were practical.

Chip prices fell to an average of $8 per unit by 1965, making the circuits affordable enough to use in consumer products.

Key Dates:

1930: Geophysical Service Inc. (GSI) is founded by Karcher and McDermott.
1939: Coronado Corp. is formed as a parent company for GSI.
1941: McDermott, Jonsson, and two GSI employees purchase the GSI from Coronado.
1942: GSI secures military contracts for the U.S. Navy and Army Signal Corps.
1946: Patrick E. Haggerty joins the company; the Laboratory and Manufacturing (L&M) division is created.
1951: The L&M is renamed Texas Instruments Inc. (TI).
1953: TI goes public by merging with the Intercontinental Rubber Company.
1954: Industrial Engineering Associates and TI develop the world's first small portable radio.
1958: Kilby creates the first integrated circuit.
1961: TI builds the first computer to use silicon integrated circuits for the Air Force.
1967: Company engineers invent a hand-held calculator.
1969: IBM begins using integrated circuits in all of its computers.
1970: The single-chip microprocessor is developed.
1976: TI introduces an electronic digital watch that retails for $19.95.
1978: Speak & Spell, an educational device using TI's new speech-synthesis technology, is launched.
1979: The firm begins selling home computers.
1983: TI posts its first-ever loss of $145 million.
1988: The company forms a partnership with Hitachi Ltd. to develop 16-megabit DRAM technology.
1991: The firm joins with Canon, Hewlett-Packard, and the Singapore government to construct a semiconductor facility in Singapore.
1999: Butterfly VLSI Ltd. is acquired.
2001: Sales and profits drop dramatically due to a fallout in the semiconductor industry.

Another important breakthrough came in 1969, when IBM began using integrated circuits in all its computers. Soon the government was no longer TI's main customer, although defense electronics remained an important part of its business. Within ten years of Kilby's discovery, semiconductors had become a multi-billion-dollar industry. Early on, TI's management anticipated a huge world demand for semiconductors, and in the 1960s the company built manufacturing plants in Europe, Latin America, and Asia. TI's early start in these markets gave the company an edge over its competitors.

In 1966, Haggerty was elected chairman of TI's board when Jonsson left to become mayor of Dallas. Haggerty had already challenged a team of engineers to develop a new product—the portable, pocket-sized calculator—to show that integrated circuits had a place in the consumer market. In 1967, TI engineers invented a prototype hand-held calculator that weighed 45 ounces. It was four years before the hand-held calculator hit the stores, but once it did, it made history. Within a few years, the once-ubiquitous slide rule was obsolete.

Entering the Consumer Electronics Industry: 1970s

In 1970, TI invented the single-chip microprocessor, or microcomputer, which was introduced commercially the next year. It was this breakthrough chip that paved the way not only for small, inexpensive calculators but also for all sorts of computer-controlled appliances and devices. TI formally entered the consumer-electronic calculator market in 1972 with the introduction of a four-ounce portable calculator and two desktop models, which ranged in price from $85 to $120. Sales of calculators soared from about 3 million units in 1971 to 17 million in 1973, 28 million in 1974, and 45 million in 1975.

Despite this early success, TI was to learn many bitter lessons about marketing to the American consumer. Even early success was hard won. Bowmar Instruments had been selling a calculator that used TI-made chips since 1971. In 1972, when TI entered the calculator market and tried to undercut Bowmar's price, Bowmar quickly matched TI and a price war ensured. TI subscribed to learning-curve pricing: keep prices low (and profits small) in the early stages to build market share and develop manufacturing efficiencies, and then competitors who want to enter the market later will find it difficult or impossible to compete. But after a few years, competitors did begin to make inroads into TI's business; by 1975, as increased competition in the market led to plummeting prices; the calculator market softened, leading to a $16 million loss for TI in the second quarter.

However, TI rebounded and again sent shock waves through the consumer-electronics world in 1976 when it introduced an inexpensive, reliable electronic digital watch for a mere $19.95. Almost overnight, TI's watches grabbed a large share of the electronic watch market at the expense of long-established watch manufacturers. A little more than a year later, TI cut the price of its digital watch to $9.95.

When low-cost Asian imports flooded the market in 1978, however, Texas Instruments began to lose its dominant position. TI also failed to capitalize on liquid crystal display (LCD) technology, for which it held the basic patent. It had not anticipated strong consumer demand for LCD watches, which displayed the time continuously rather than requiring the user to push a button for a readout. When sales of LCD watches exploded, TI could not begin mass-production quickly enough. The company's digital watch sales dropped dramatically in 1979, by the end of 1981 TI had left the digital watch business.

Meanwhile, in TI's mainstay business, semiconductor manufacturing, orders for chips became backlogged. Texas Instruments had spread its resources thinly in order to compete in both the consumer and industrial markets, and worldwide chip demand had soared at the same time. Despite these problems, TI grew at a rapid rate during the 1970s. Defense electronics continued to be highly profitable and semiconductor demand remained strong, buoyed by the worldwide growth in consumer-electronics manufacturing. The company reached $1 billion in sales in 1973, $2 billion in 1977, and $3 billion in 1979.

Mark Shepherd was named chairman of the board upon Patrick Haggerty's retirement in 1976, and J. Fred Bucy, who had worked in almost all of TI's major business areas, was named president and remained chief operating officer. Haggerty continued as general director and honorary chairman until his death in 1980.

In 1978, Texas Instruments introduced Speak & Spell, an educational device that used TI's new speech-synthesis technology, which proved quite popular. That same year, TI was held up as *Business Week's* model for American companies in the 1980s for its innovation, productivity gains, and phenomenal growth and earnings records.

In mid-1979, TI introduced a home computer that reached the market in December. Priced at about $1,400, the machine sold more slowly at first than TI had predicted. In 1981, sales began to pick up, though, and a rebate program in 1982 kept sales—and sales predictions—very strong. In April 1983, TI shipped its one millionth home computer.

Challenges in the 1980s

Suddenly, however, sales of the TI-99/4A fell off dramatically. By October, TI's overconfident projections and failure to predict the price competitiveness of the market had driven the company out of the home computer business altogether. By the time the 99/4A was withdrawn from the market, TI's usual competitive-pricing strategy had reduced the computer's retail price below the company's production cost, causing TI's first-ever loss, $145 million, in 1983.

TI's consumer electronics never managed to become a consistent money-maker. The company was often accused of arrogance—of trying to find mass markets for new TI inventions rather than adapting its product lines to accommodate customers' needs—and TI's aggressive price-cutting was often insensitive to dealers and customers alike. In addition, TI's pursuit of both consumer and industrial markets often caused shortages of components resulting in backlogged or reduced shipments.

After experiencing its first loss, TI found regaining its former footing difficult. A slump in semiconductor demand during the recession of the early 1980s made TI's heavy losses in home computers particularly painful. Cost-cutting became a high priority, and TI trimmed its work force by 10,000 employees between 1980 and 1982. In addition, management decided that its matrix management structure was strangling the company and so began to modify the system to revive innovation. Although the company's engineers continued to lead the semiconductor field in innovations, increased competition both in the United States and overseas meant that technological superiority was no longer a guarantee of success. The company recorded yet another $100 million-plus loss in 1985.

TI President Fred Bucy was roundly criticized for being abrasive and autocratic, and the disappointments of the early 1980s hastened his departure. In May 1985, Bucy abruptly retired and Jerry Junkins was elected president and CEO. Junkins, a lifetime TI employee with a much cooler and more conciliatory management style, proved a popular chief executive.

TI's aggressive defense of its intellectual property rights— the exclusive use of the patented technological developments of its employees—highlighted activities in the late 1980s. In 1986, TI filed suit with the International Trade Commission against eight Japanese and one Korean semiconductor manufacturers

who were selling dynamic random-access memories (DRAMs) in the United States without obtaining licenses to use technology that belonged to TI. TI reached out-of-court settlements with most of the companies but, more importantly, demonstrated that infringements on its patents would not be tolerated. Royalties from these decisions proved an important source of revenue (over $250 million annually) for TI.

In late 1988, Texas Instruments announced plans to join Japan's Hitachi, Ltd. in developing 16-megabit DRAM technology. Although this decision came as quite a surprise to the electronics industry, given TI's successful Japanese subsidiary and its manufacturing plant there, TI explained that the move was necessary to spread the mounting risks and costs involved in producing such an advanced chip.

Back in 1977, TI had boldly set itself a sales goal of $10 billion by 1989; not long after, it upped the ante to $15 billion by 1990. The company actually entered the 1990s some $9 billion short of that extraordinary goal. After watching its share of the semiconductor market slide from 30 percent to a meager 5 percent over the course of the decade, Junkins took a decisive step. In 1989, the CEO inaugurated a strategic plan to radically reshape Texas Instruments, dubbed "TI 2000." A key aspect of the plan was to loosen the corporation's traditionally tight corporate culture and encourage innovation. This fundamental change was intimately linked to a shift in manufacturing focus from cheap, commodity-based computer chips to high-margin, custom-designed microprocessors and digital signal processors. For example, in 1989 TI embarked on a partnership with Sun Microsystems Inc. to design and manufacture microprocessors, sharing engineering personnel and proprietary technology in the process. TI garnered vital contracts with Sony Corporation, General Motors Corporation, and Swedish telecommunications powerhouse L.M. Ericsson. The company promoted its repositioning with new business-to-business advertising. From 1988 to 1993, the specialty components segment increased from 25 percent of annual sales to nearly 50 percent. In 1993, Junkins told *Business Week* that TI was "looking for shared dependence" in these partnerships. He also hoped to parlay technological gains into mass sales.

Rebounding Under the TI 2000 Plan: 1990s

Under Junkins, TI also increased its global manufacturing capacity through a number of joint ventures in Europe and Asia. A 1990 partnership with the Italian government allowed the shared construction expenses of a $1.2 billion plant. In 1991, the firm joined with Canon, Hewlett-Packard, and the Singapore government to construct a semiconductor facility in Singapore. By 1992, TI had forged alliances with Taiwanese manufacturer Acer, Kobe Steel in Japan, and a coterie of companies in Singapore. Texas Instruments planned to invest $1 billion in Asian plants by the turn of the century. Joint ventures with Samsung Electronics Co., Ltd. and Hitachi, Ltd. in 1994 split the costs of building semiconductor plants in Portugal and the United States, respectively. TI 2000 also set a goal of increasing the company's high-margin software sales five times, to $1 billion, by the mid-1990s.

Although Texas Instruments recorded net losses in 1990 and 1991, the company's sales and profits rebounded in 1992 and

1993. Profitability, in terms of sales per employee, increased dramatically from $88,300 in 1989 to $143,240 in 1993. In 1992, the firm won the coveted Malcolm Baldrige National Quality Award in manufacturing and adopted the Baldrige criteria as its quality standards. Wall Street noticed the improved performance: TI's stock price more than doubled from 1991 to early 1993.

The firm continued to develop new products, invest in strategic alliances, and divest non-core, slow-growth businesses. In 1994, it launched the multimedia video processor, the first single chip processor to become available commercially that combined multiple parallel DSP and RISC chips. The following year, it won both the prestigious Singapore Quality Award and the European Quality Award. It was during this time period that the company began to focus on DSP chips, which could convert analog signals into digital form in real time. Eyeballing the market as a lucrative growth avenue, TI invested heavily in this area. During the 1990s, DSP chips began to be used in such as products as modems, cellular phones, PC peripherals, and television sets. By 1997, TI controlled 45 percent of the market.

Reshaping TI: Late 1990s and Beyond

While TI worked hard to get itself back on track in the 1990s, it continued to face hardships. During 1996, the price of its memory chips dropped by nearly 80 percent. Then, during an overseas business meeting in May, Junkins died suddenly of heart failure. Long-time TI employee Tom Engibous took over as president and CEO and stepped up the company's acquisition and divestiture plan. In 1997, several of the firm's business units were sold including Defense Systems & Electronics, Mobile Computing, Software, MulTIpoint Systems, Inspection Equipment, the Mold Manufacturing businesses, the Chemical Operations department, the Telecommunications Systems division, and the Power semiconductor unit. The company also made several key acquisitions including Intersect Technologies, Amati Communications Corp., and GO DSP Corp.

When questioned about the company's rapid movements in a 1997 *Electronic Business* article, Engibous commented "a tragedy like that—referring to Junkins' death—causes you to spend time reflecting. We concluded that what we were doing was in the right direction, but we thought we needed to do it at a much more rapid pace." As such, the company continued to acquire firms related to its DSP focus including Spectron Microsystems, Adaptec Inc., Oasix Corp., and Arisix Corp. TI also sold its memory chip business to Micron Technologies Inc. for $880 million.

The acquisitions continued into the following year. TI added Butterfly VLSI Ltd., Integrated Sensor Solutions, Telogy Networks, ATL Research A/S, Libit Signal Processing Ltd., Unitrode Corp., and Power Trends to its arsenal. The firm continued to develop new products as well, including a DSP chip that facilitated high-speed Internet access. Along with leading the DSP market with a 48 percent share, TI held the top position in the analog semiconductor market for the second year in a row. All in all, TI launched 191 analog products in 1999, nearly seven times more than it developed in 1996.

TI entered the new millennium on solid ground. The company's financial performance appeared to be back on track with revenues of $11.8 billion and profits of $2.7 billion. During 2000, the firm purchased Toccata Technology ApS, Burr-Brown Corp., Alantro Communications, and Dot Wireless Inc. It also formed a partnership with Qualcomm Inc. in which both companies were allowed to supply integrated circuits for all wireless standards without infringing on patent rights. TI partnered with four China-based manufacturers to develop and distribute wireless handsets and consumer electronics. The company also teamed up with Imax Corp. to develop digital projectors for movie theaters as well as IMAX theaters. Under the terms of the deal, Imax became the exclusive licensee of TI's DLP Cinema technology.

The tide quickly changed, however, when in the latter half of 2000 and into 2001 the semiconductor industry became embroiled in its worst downturn to date due to high customer inventories and weakening demand. Heavily dependent on that segment, TI's profits began to drop off dramatically and were not expected to return until sometime in 2003. Sales also fell throughout the year, down by as much as 40 percent.

"Despite the challenges," claimed a 2001 *Business Week* article, "few doubt that TI will remain one of the chip industry's leading players in 2003. TI also has a reputation for excellent service, something that impresses long-term customers looking for more participation and input from suppliers." The company's history of overcoming challenges left Engibous confident that TI would emerge from this downturn successfully. With a strong focus on developing technologies, TI appeared to be well positioned to withstand these hardships.

Principal Subsidiaries

Amati Communications Corporation; Auto Circuits, Inc.; Automotive Sensors & Controls Dresden GmbH (Germany); Benchmarq Microelectronics Corporation of South Korea; Burr-Brown AG (Switzerland); Burr-Brown Europe Limited (England); Burr-Brown Pte Ltd. (Singapore); Butterfly Communications Inc.; European Engineering and Technologies S.p.A. (Italy); Fast Forward Technologies Limited (England and Wales); GO DSP Corporation (Canada); ICOT International Limited (UK); Intelligent Instrumentation GmbH (Germany); Intelligent Instrumentation, Inc.; JMA Information Engineering Ltd.; Power Trends, Inc.; Silicon Systems (Singapore) Pte Ltd.; Telogy Networks, Inc.; Texas Instrumentos Eletronicos do Brasil Limitada; Texas Instruments A/S (Denmark); Texas Instruments Asia Limited; Texas Instruments Automotive Sensors and Controls; Texas Instruments Business Expansion GmbH (Germany); Texas Instruments Canada Limited; Texas Instruments (China) Company Limited; Texas Instruments de Mexico, S.A. de C.V.; Texas Instruments Deutschland GmbH (Germany); Texas Instruments Equipamento Electronicl Lda. (Portugal); Texas Instruments France S.A.; Texas Instruments Holland B.V.; Texas Instruments Hong Kong Limited; Texas Instruments (India) Limited; Texas Instruments Italia S.p.A.; Texas Instruments Japan Limited; Texas Instruments Korea Limited; Texas Instruments Ltd.; Texas Instruments Malaysia Sdn. Bhd.; Texas Instruments Inc. (Philippines); Texas Instruments Singapore (Pte) Ltd.; Texas Instruments Taiwan Ltd. Texas Instruments Limited (United Kingdom); Unitrode Corporation.

Principal Competitors

Analog Devices Inc.; Motorola Inc.; STMicorelectronics N.V.

Further Reading

Boitano, Margaret, "Burn, Baby, Burn," *Fortune*, March 20, 2000, p. 254.

Burrows, Peter, "TI Is Moving Up in the World," *Business Week*, August 2, 1993, pp. 46–47.

Josifovska, Svetlana, "Deep in the Heart of Texas Instruments," *Electronic Business*, October 2000, p. 116.

Kharif, Olga, "Texas Instruments' Long Road Back," *Business Week*, October 26, 2001.

Lineback, J. Robert, "Rebuilding TI," *Electronic Business Buyer*, March 1994, pp. 52–7.

Palmeri, Christopher, "Chips Ahoy!," *Forbes*, April 7, 1997, p. 48.

——, "Faster, Faster: TI's Signal Processors Make Possible Lots of New Gifts for Gadget Geeks," *Forbes*, March 6, 2000, p. 60.

Ristelhueber, Robert, "Texas Tornado," *Electronic Business*, December 1997, p. 35.

Rogers, Alison, "Texas Instruments: It's the Execution that Counts," *Fortune*, November 3, 1992, pp. 80–3.

"TI, IMAX Partner," *Dallas Business Journal*, June 9, 2000, p. 20.

Williams, Elisa, "Mixed Signals," *Forbes*, May 28, 2001, p. 80.

—updates: April Dougal Gasbarre; Christina M. Stansell

Thorntons plc

Thornton Park
Somercotes
Alfreton
Derbyshire DE55 4XJ
United Kingdom
Telephone: (+44) 1773-540-550
Fax: (+44) 1773-540-066
Web site: http://www.thorntons.co.uk

Public Company
Incorporated: 1921 as JW Thornton Ltd.
Employees: 4,539
Sales: £153.5 million ($232.8 million)(2000)
Stock Exchanges: London
Ticker Symbol: THT
NAIC: 311330 Confectionery Manufacturing from
  Purchased Chocolate

Thorntons plc is one of the United Kingdom's leading manufacturer and retailer of chocolate and other confectionery products. Founded in 1911, the company remains more than 30 percent owned by the Thornton family. Yet the company's day-to-day operations are led by chief executive Peter Burdon, who joined the company in 2000. Thorntons' products, which focus on chocolates, fudge, and toffee but also include other candies, target the high-quality, high-end market. This commitment to quality has gained the company a strong reputation throughout the United Kingdom and made it one of the country's most popular brands. Most of Thorntons' sales come through its network of more than 500 retail shops—some 400 or which are directly owned by Thorntons, while the rest operate as franchises. The company's products are also available through such large-scale department store chains as Marks and Spencers. In 2001, the company also began rolling out a line of products to be sold through the supermarket channel. In addition to its retail shops, Thorntons operates a growing number of Thornton Cafes, which sell coffee and other desserts in addition to the company's chocolates. Many of these cafes are located within existing Thornton stores. The company also began pilot testing selling fresh coffee and other beverages and snacks at its retail stores, a program begun in 2000. Despite steady sales gains, Thorntons has been struggling with its profitability since the late 1990s. The company's difficulties have seen its share price plunge from a high of nearly 300 pence in 1998 to as low as 85 pence at the turn of the century. This development has in turn sparked suggestions that the company may be a strong takeover candidate. A more likely scenario, given the company's proud history as an independent chocolate manufacturer, may be a management buyout of the company. In the meantime, the Thornton family remain present in the company's direction, with John Thornton, formerly CEO with the company, serving as its chairman.

"In Chocolate Heaven Since 1911"

Thornton's was established in 1911 when Joseph Thornton, who had been working as a traveling candy and confectionery salesman, opened his own shop in Sheffield. Joining Thornton to help run the store was his eldest son Norman, then only 14 years old. The Thornton shop was a success, and in 1913 the family opened a second store. The new store included a kitchen where the family began making their own candies. By the time Joseph Thornton became ill in 1917, Norman Thornton had begun establishing a reputation for the Thornton name as a maker of quality sweets, while opening two more stores, plus a store selling fresh fruit, by the end of the decade. The younger Thornton took over the business's operations entirely after his father's death in 1919. Two years later, Thornton was joined by his younger brother, and together they began to expand the business, which was then incorporated as JW Thornton Ltd.

The success of the Thorntons' chocolate and other confectionery products soon spread beyond Sheffield, and by the middle of the 1920s the family began to prepare to expand across the Midlands region. In 1927, the company opened its first full-fledged factory in Sheffield. The production from this facility, while still relatively small, enabled the company to supply a growing number of stores. By 1935, the company had opened 15 stores. By the end of that decade, the company's retail network had expanded beyond the Midlands region and into the North of England, reaching a total of 35 stores.

The end of World War II, and the resulting economic boom as England reconstructed throughout the 1950s, proved a profitable time for Thorntons. The Thornton brothers continued to lead the company and were now by the third generation of the Thornton family, including Michael Thornton, who joined in 1957 and remained active in the company's affairs until the end of the century. Thornton's chocolates and other confectionery goods became a favorite of the British sweet tooth. The company underwent a rapid expansion, and by the 1960s operated more than 200 stores, not only across the Midlands and Northern regions, but in Scotland as well.

During the mid-1960s, the company added another family member, John Thornton, who was named managing director in 1982, then took on the roles of chief executive and chairman in 1987. The following year, the company went public, listing 25 percent of the company's share—with the rest held by the Thornton family—on the London exchange. Over the next decade, the Thornton family continued to reduce its shareholding, which decreased to just 30 percent at the end of the 1990s.

Meanwhile, expansion of the company's retail network had slowed somewhat, so that by the mid-1990s the company's operations had grown to 260 company-owned stores. At the same time, Thornton's began franchising its shops, which, although representing less than 10 percent of sales, allowed it to expand its retail network by more than 100 stores. Thorntons also began to expand beyond the United Kingdom, entering Belgium and France, where it built up a chain of some 21 stores.

Struggling for Profits in the New Century

In 1995, John Thornton retired from day-to-day management of the company, hiring Roger Paffard, formerly with the office supply retailer Staples. The company now exited the Belgium and French markets, where it had never successfully imported its retail formula. As a spokesman for the company itself described its inability to penetrate these markets, Thorntons "did not invest enough time and effort to understand the differences between the U.K. and the French and Belgian markets." In 1996, the company sold off its Belgian subsidiary, Gartners-Pralines, to chocolatier Pauwels, then sold its 21 French stores to a rival retailer in that market, Jeff de Bruges.

Instead, Paffard led Thorntons on a new expansion drive in the United Kingdom. In October 1996, the company announced its intention to step up its number of new stores, backed by a £30 million investment program, with the intention of opening 90 new stores by 2000. The following year, the company became still more ambitious, forecasting the opening of its 500th company-owned store by the year 2001. In order to reach this goal, the pace of new store openings went into overdrive. In March 1998, the company announced its intention to open as many as 100

stores in that year alone. Supporting the company's new growth was the beginning of construction of a new manufacturing and warehouse facility in Derbeyshire, to be completed by early 1999, part of a new £53 million investment plan. The stock market responded positively to the company's buoyant forecasts, sending its stock price to a high of nearly 300 pence.

Yet it soon became apparent that Thortons had overextended itself. The company first stumbled in 1999 during the crucial Easter season, when it ran out of stock—sending customers to its competitors. By May 1999, the company was forced to make its first profit warning, admitting that: "We didn't have the right product range. We changed as little as possible because we were concentrating on improving other parts of the business, be we underestimated just how unforgiving our customers would be."

The company's customers continued to withhold their forgiveness through the next year, despite the company's efforts to correct the previous year's mistakes. Thorntons now rolled out a range of novelty products—such as chocolate-scented tee shirts and body lotions. The company also pressed on with its new store openings, especially among its franchise network, hoping to open another 200 stores. Thorntons also began looking for new retail outlets, such as through the Internet, interactive television, and mail-order sales channels. Meanwhile, the rising popularity of coffee shops, such as Starbucks, inspired the company to begin developing its own coffee shops, most of which were to be located within its existing stores.

None of these efforts was able to stop the company's profits slide. Another Easter stock error—which saw the company forced to deep-discount some £1.4 million of unsold Easter eggs—forced the company to make its third profit warning in 18 months. The company's sagging profits continued to sink its share price, sparking fears that the company might offer itself up as a takeover target. At last, John Thornton asked Paffard to resign in March 2000.

Watching the company's troubles was Peter Burdon, a former McKinsey consultant then working for the Boots retail chain. Burdon told the *Daily Telegraph:* "For the past 10 years it has been my ambition to run a medium-sized food company. When I read about (Paffard's) departure I immediately thought 'this is my job.' I wrote to John Thornton saying these are the issues your firm is facing, this is me, and suggesting we got together for a chat." Burdon was hired two months later.

Burdon immediately began implementing a three-year plan to restore the company to stability. Among his first moves was to slow the rate of new store expansion. The company then went to work rebuilding its product line, repositioning its stores toward the less seasonally dependent gift market and refurbishing its stores. The company also replaced its long-running "In Chocolate Heaven Since 1911" advertising campaign. Meanwhile, the success of its café format encouraged the company to continue rolling out coffee shops, reaching 23 shops by the end of 2000, with plans to increase that number to nearly 100 at the turn of the century. By then, the company had succeeded in stabilizing its profits, and was once again returning to sales growth, posting £153.5 million for the year.

In 2001, Thorntons began plans to roll out a new line of Thorntons branded dessert products for the U.K.'s supermarket branch, signing on customers including Sainsburys, Safeway, and Asda. By the end of his first year as company CEO, Burdon

had successfully turned the company around and continued to point it in new directions. One of these was the roll-out of a new pilot program, that of offering hot drinks and pastries as carry-out items at its stores. The company planned a full-scale roll out of this new concept to all of its stores if the pilot program proved successful. Despite the company's renewed optimism, it remained frustrated by the continued low course of its share price—which valued the company at just £56 million, compared to a high of nearly £400 million—so much so that by the summer of August 2001 the company acknowledged that it might consider a management buyout to remove it from the public market—and the possibility of a hostile takeover.

Principal Competitors

Cadbury Schweppes PLC; Nestlé Holdings (UK) PLC; Mars UK Ltd; Kraft Foods UK Ltd; The Wrigley Company Ltd; Ferrero UK Ltd; Swizzels Matlow Ltd; Leaf (UK) Ltd; Bendicks (Mayfair) Ltd.

Further Reading

Finch, Julia, "Thorntons' New Recipe," *Guardian*, March 7, 2001.
——, "Family Ousts Sweet Empire Chief," *Guardian,* March 1, 2000.
——, "Thorntons Profits Crack In," *Guardian*, May 6, 1999.
Lee, John, "Chocs Away with Company High Flyer," *Financial Times*, May 12, 2001.
Jenkins, Patrick, "Thorntons Eyes Expansion in Hot Drinks and Pastries," *Financial Times,* September 19, 2001.
Simon, Emma, "Hard Nut with a Sugar Coating Thorntons," *Daily Telegraph*, April 23, 2000.
Smith, Alison, "Thorntons Aims to Get Up Close and Personal," *Financial Times*, March 7, 2001.
——, "Thorntons' Chief Hopes to Taste Seasonal Success," *Financial Times*, December 14, 2000.
Treanor, Jill, "Thorntons Profit Meltdown Continues," *Guardian*, June 3, 2000.

—M. L. Cohen

Total Entertainment Restaurant Corporation

9300 East Central Suite 100
Wichita, Kansas 67206
U.S.A.
Telephone: (316) 634-0505
Fax: (316) 634-6060
Web site: http://www.tentcorp.com

Public Company
Incorporated: 1997
Employees: 1,850
Sales: $56 million (2000)
Stock Exchanges: NASDAQ
Ticker Symbol: TENT
NAIC: 72211 Full-Service Restaurants

Total Entertainment Restaurant Corporation is a Wichita, Kansas-based company consisting of three restaurant chains: Fox and Hound, Bailey's Sports Grille, and Bailey's Pub and Grille. The Fox and Hound chain is the company's largest, containing approximately 25 restaurants located in more than a dozen states. TEC's Bailey's Sports Grille chain consists of approximately nine locations in five states, and its Bailey's Pub & Grille is a four-unit chain with locations in three states. All three chains combine dining and entertainment in the form of both televised sporting events and onsite games of skill like billiards, darts, and shuffleboard. Total Entertainment's restaurants are located in both major urban areas and in smaller regional markets—in most cases in shopping centers. The average unit is 9,000 to 10,0000 square feet in size and contains between 175 and 200 seats. Total check amounts average between $10 and $12.

Early 1990s: Two Separate Chains

The company that was ultimately to become Total Entertainment Restaurant Corp. started as two small restaurant chains developed separately. The oldest of the two, Bailey's Sports Grille, began in a strip mall in Charlotte, North Carolina, in November 1989. Its founder, Dennis Thompson, was a veteran restaurateur, who had previously been a Godfather's Pizza franchisee and had gone on to found the Lone Star Steakhouse chain.

In 1989, Thompson owned and operated Creative Culinary Concepts, a parent company for his small chain of Lone Stars.

Reportedly, Thompson's decision to open a new sports bar stemmed in part from a question he put to his Lone Star employees: What did they like to do for fun after work? Their answer—go to bars to play pool or watch sports—indicated a market for a combination drinking-dining-entertainment establishment. So Thompson designed Bailey's as a casual sports bar and restaurant with decent but simple food, numerous televisions carrying satellite and cable coverage of sporting events, and games of skill like pool and darts.

After operating Bailey's for four years, Thompson decided to expand. In 1994, he opened two additional Bailey's, one in Little Rock, Arkansas, and another in Greenville, South Carolina. The new locations were modeled after the original one—with a central dining area, a gaming area around the perimeter, and dozens of TVs.

While Thompson was getting his second and third restaurants up and running, two Texans—Steve Hartnett and Mark Lee—were in the process of launching the other chain that would eventually be part of Total Entertainment: the Fox and Hound. Like Thompson, Hartnett and Lee had backgrounds in restaurant management. The 44-year-old Hartnett had originally run pubs geared to college students. Then, in the 1980s, working as a stock trader and money manager, he had developed an intense interest in billiards. It was through pursuit of this hobby that he met Mark Lee, a 29-year-old former restaurant manager who shared Hartnett's passion for the game. Together, the two men decided to open an upscale pool hall and pub. They styled their new bar/restaurant to resemble an English pub, naming it Fox and Hound English Pub and Grille. The first Fox and Hound opened in August 1994 in a shopping mall in Arlington, Texas, and almost immediately Hartnett and Lee added two more locations to their small venture. In September, the duo opened a Fox and Hound in College Station, Texas, the home of Texas A&M University. Just a few months later, in December 1995, a third Fox and Hound was opened, in Dallas.

Through the remainder of 1995 and 1996, Hartnett and Lee's venture stalled at three units. Meanwhile, Thompson was expanding his chain aggressively, more than doubling its size In April 1995, Bailey's moved into Tennessee, establishing a location in Nashville. Two more Tennessee locations—Knoxville and Johnson City—followed in December 1995 and May 1996. In October, Thompson opened his seventh Bailey's, in Columbia, South Carolina. For that year, Bailey's posted $9.3 million in sales and $1.5 million income.

1997: Jamie Coulter and Total Entertainment

In late 1996, Steve Hartnett was approached by Jamie Coulter, a well-known restaurateur based in Wichita, Kansas. Coulter headed up his own company, Coulter Enterprises, a restaurant-management group that operated a string of Pizza Hut franchises. But he was best known as the CEO and Chairman of the highly successful Lone Star Steakhouse chain, which had been founded in the 1980s by Dennis Thompson.

Coulter had a long and impressive history in the restaurant business. He had become a Pizza Hut franchisee in 1965, going on to open more than 170 Pizza Hut locations in the course of fifteen years. In 1980, he dissolved his original franchise operation and opened Coulter Enterprises, which managed a smaller number of Pizza Huts. In 1991, he had become involved with the Lone Star brand, and expanded it exponentially.

Coulter offered $5 million in cash and $20 million in IPO stock for Hartnett's three-unit Fox and Hound chain, which had annual sales of around $5.5 million. Hartnett, who had been looking for a way to expand the concept, saw the offer as just the opportunity he needed. Coulter's next move was to acquire the Bailey's chain, which he did in February 1997. Coulter already had a working relationship with Thompson. In 1991, he had teamed with Lone Star founder to grow the chain and ultimately to take it public. Thompson had remained involved with the company, serving as a director and vice-president.

When Coulter acquired the two chains, he created a new entity, Total Entertainment Restaurant Corp., to serve as a parent company them, and arranged for his other company, Coulter Enterprises, to handle their accounting and administrative duties. Total Entertainment was headquartered in Dallas and had a seasoned management team that included some of Coulter's long-time colleagues. While Coulter held the chairman's position, the new company's CEO and president was Gary Judd, formerly vice president of special projects for Coulter Enterprises. Dennis Thompson served as a member of the board of directors.

Although developed independently of one another, Total Entertainment's two chains had much in common. Both mar-

keted themselves as ''social gathering places'' rather than just restaurants—locations that joined dining and entertainment, in the form of games and televised events. Both were considered to be ''upscale casual,'' which meant dress codes, stylish decor, and better-than-average pub food.

The two chains also shared an important feature that distinguished them from much of their competition: a kitchen that stayed open until 3:00 a.m. The restaurants' late-night hours proved to have quite an appeal for patrons. In a May 1999 interview with *Restaurant Hospitality*, Gary Judd explained, ''It's a great part of our business because when the malls, retail outlets, and other restaurants shut down, we're the place people go. The 11 p.m. to 3 a.m. period is lucrative.''

No sooner had Coulter formed Total Entertainment than he began preparing to take it public. In spring 1997, the company filed a prospectus, and in July made an initial public offering (IPO) of two million shares. The IPO generated approximately $19.5 million. The remainder of 1997 was a characterized by expansion for Total Entertainment. In September, the company opened a fourth Fox and Hound, in Memphis, Tennessee, the first of that chain to be located outside Texas. In October, a Bailey's opened in Nashville, and in December 1997, two more Fox and Hounds were launched, in Chicago and Omaha.

1998–99: Expansion and Leadership Changes

At the beginning of 1998, Total Entertainment consisted of six Fox and Hounds and nine Bailey's Sports Bars. Together, the chains had locations in eight states. The company spent the new year in a whirlwind of growth, opening 12 new Fox and Hounds. The expansion dramatically broadened the chain's geographic presence, adding locations in Alabama, Ohio, Missouri, Pennsylvania, Kansas, Louisiana, and North Carolina. The company also opened three additional Bailey's locations, in Atlanta, Detroit, and Chapel Hill, North Carolina. These new restaurants were named Bailey's Pub & Grille, rather than Bailey's Sports Grille, and were styled more along the lines of the Fox and Hound units.

By the end of 1998, Total Entertainment operated 32 restaurants, twice as many as it had just 12 months earlier. The growth spurt had increased the company's sales significantly—from $18.56 million in 1997 to $34.11 million in 1998. In addition, income almost doubled, growing from $1.08 million in 1997 to $2.08 million in 1998.

The beginning of 1999 brought with it major shifts in leadership for Total Entertainment. Jamie Coulter, who had headed up the company for less than two years, resigned from his position as chairman of the board to focus his attention on his Lone Star Steakhouse chain. At the same time, Gary Judd stepped down as CEO, although continuing to serve as the company's president. Steve Hartnett and Dennis Thompson became co-chairs of Total Entertainment, and the CEO's office was filled by Steven Johnson, who had previously been the chief operating officer of Coulter Enterprises. With the changes in leadership, the company's headquarters moved from Dallas to Wichita, Kansas.

Under Hartnett and Thompson's guidance, Total Entertainment suspended its focus on new unit development. A handful of new locations—those that were already in development—

Key Dates:

1989: Dennis Thompson opens the first Bailey's Sports Grille.

1994: Steven Hartnett and Mark Lee open the first Fox and Hound.

1996: Well-known restaurateur Jamie Coulter purchases the Fox and Hound chain.

1997: Coulter acquires the Bailey's Chain, forms Total Entertainment Restaurant Corporation as parent company for the two chains, and takes the new company public.

1999: Jamie Coulter resigns as CEO of Total Entertainment; Dennis Thompson and Steve Hartnett become co-chairs.

opened for business during the first quarter of 1999. In January, two new Fox and Hounds opened in Pittsburgh and in Winston-Salem, North Carolina; in February, two more opened, in Indianapolis and Houston; and in March, one began operations in Baton Rouge, Louisiana. With the end of the first quarter, however, came the end of new store openings for the year. In an August 2001 interview with the *Wall Street Transcript*, Total Entertainment's president, Steven Johnson explained the rationale for this self-imposed growth expansion hiatus. "We had grown very rapidly since going public and at the expense of some of our existing operations," he said. "We felt like we needed to step back, take a look at our operations, and get our ducks in a row before we started growing again."

Total Entertainment spent 1999 and 2000 implementing a range of measures to make their operation run more efficiently and more profitably. They increased the number of district managers from four to six, reducing the number of locations each manager was responsible for and thereby allowing for more hands-on and time-intensive management. They also attempted to reduce turnover in their unit-level management—a problem notorious in the restaurant industry—by introducing a new compensation and rewards plan. Finally, they reworked the menus, adding 19 new selections designed, in part, to appeal to lunch patrons. The company's efforts were rewarded almost immediately by same-store sales growth throughout the remainder of 1999 and all of 2000.

Future Expansion

By the end of 2000, the company once again began to grow—albeit at a much more conservative pace than it previously had—opening new units in Parma, Ohio, Dearborn, Michigan, and Lewisville, Texas. In 2001, it moved into two new states, developing two restaurants in Denver, Colorado, and one in Phoenix, Arizona. It managed to maintain the positive sales trend begun in early 1999, posting higher than 5 percent growth in same-store sales for the first half of 2001.

Going forward, it appeared as though Total Entertainment would continue to grow at a measured pace. In an August 2001 interview with the *Wall Street Transcript*, Total Entertainment's president, Steven Johnson, said that the company planned to open at least seven new locations per year for the next few years. This manageable rate of expansion, he said, would allow for selectivity in site location. "Since we have limited growth plans we're not just putting sites on so that we can meet our development quota," he explained.

Principal Operating Units

Bailey's Sports Grille; Bailey's Pub and Grille; Fox and Hound English Pub and Grille.

Principal Competitors

Champps Entertainment, Inc.; Dave & Buster's, Inc.; Hooters of America, Inc.

Further Reading

"CEO Interview, Total Entertainment Restaurant Corp." *The Wall Street Transcript*, August 20, 2001.

Hayes, Jack, "Coulter Cues Up New Entertainment Chain," *Nation's Restaurant News*, May 26, 1997, p. 3.

"Total Challenges," *The IPO Aftermarket*, August 18, 1997.

—Shawna Brynildssen

**new york
sports clubs**

Town Sports International, Inc.

888 Seventh Avenue
New York, New York 10106
U.S.A.
Telephone: (212) 246-6700
Fax: (212) 246-8422
Web site: http://www.nysc.com

Private Company
Incorporated: 1973 as St. John Squash Racket Inc.
Employees: 6,400
Sales: $225 million (2000)
NAIC: 713940 Fitness and Recreational Sports Centers

Town Sports International, Inc. runs a network of over 120 health and fitness clubs from its Manhattan headquarters. The company has experienced rapid growth since the late 1990s, becoming one of the largest health club chains in the United States, with more than 250,000 members. The primary focus of TSI is the Northeast corridor that runs from Boston to Washington, D.C. TSI clubs operate under four brand names: New York Sports Clubs, Washington Sports Clubs, Boston Sports Clubs, and Philadelphia Sports Clubs. Augmenting its locations in the boroughs of New York City, New York City Sports Clubs has a strong presence in the suburbs of Westchester County, New Jersey, and Connecticut. Philadelphia Sports Clubs has one Southern New Jersey location. In addition to the District of Columbia, Washington Sports Clubs has units in Maryland and Virginia. Boston Sports Clubs has locations in outlying areas of Boston, as well as one club in Nashua, New Hampshire. Moreover, TSI operates three Swiss Sports Clubs, with two units in Basel, Switzerland, and one in Zurich. Since its origin, TSI has been in the forefront of the health club industry, creating a sound business model that has provided strong profits and allowed the company to build new clubs and acquire many underperforming mom-and-pop operations.

Original Company Formed in 1973

TSI grew out of the commercial squash club business created by Harry Saint in the early 1970s. Saint grew up in Pennsylvania,

graduated from Haverford College, and did some graduate work in philosophy studies in Germany. Saint's intention was to become a writer, and in fact he sold a short story to Esquire before his father died, and he returned home to Pennsylvania to look after his family's real estate interests. Saint was also an avid squash player of admittedly modest ability. After tennis enjoyed a boom in the late 1960s and early 1970s, squash appeared to be the next racket sport ready to gain broad popularity. To that time, the sport in America had been generally limited to private clubs and Ivy League colleges. Squash had several characteristics that made it seem even more commercially attractive than the tennis business. Because a squash court was only one-tenth the size of a tennis court, it cost in the neighborhood of $50,000 to build, as opposed to $150,000 for an indoor tennis court. Because there were more courts available in a similar size facility, a squash center could charge significantly less per hour than tennis. It was also felt that squash was the perfect urban sport, because the game was fast paced and customers could receive a good workout in a short period of time.

After the first commercial squash facility in North America was opened in Toronto, Saint looked to bring commercial squash to the New York City market. He created St. John Squash Racket Inc. in 1973, raising $300,000 from private investors, including his wife Gerarda, who came from a prominent European family with royal lineage. Saint also recruited a team that included attorney Michael Johnston and architect John Copelin, who went on to enjoy a significant career designing sports facilities. In October 1973, Saint was looking for someone to manage the club he was opening in New York. An assistant introduced him to her brother, Marc Tascher, who had recently graduated from college. Tascher would become the first employee of the club and eventually succeed Saint as the head of the company.

Like Saint, Tascher wanted to be a writer, although he had also been a subscriber and avid reader of the *Wall Street Journal* since his early teens when he dreamed of attending the Wharton School of Business and forging a career on Wall Street. Instead the Long Island native became an English major and after graduating from SUNY in Binghamton, New York, had no definite plans for a job. According to Tascher, the main reason Saint hired him to run his squash club was precisely because he had no experience and, therefore, no preconceived notions about how the business should operate. It was that spirit of trailblazing that the company would maintain even after Saint departed.

Squash Enjoys a Boom in the Mid-1970s

The Fifth Avenue Squash Club, located at the intersection of 37th Street in Manhattan, opened early in 1974. It is uncertain whether it or the Berwyn Squash Club located outside of Philadelphia deserves the honor of being the first commercial squash club in the United States. Regardless, Fifth Avenue was an immediate success. According to Tascher, it was cash flow positive in its first month, and in its second year generated revenues of $375,000 with a $150,000 profit. The squash boom was on, and Saint and Tascher from their New York location quickly became key figures in the promotion of the sport. They helped get publicity and were instrumental in making squash a trendy activity, bringing women to the game and supporting a nascent professional tour. For the next decade, they were the major promoters of professional squash in the United States.

Saint opened new clubs and changed the name of the company to Town Squash Inc. His wife's family also became the majority shareholders as the company raised money for expansion. In 1975, the site for a second club was purchased on 86th Street in Manhattan. Four floors were added to a one-story building, and a slice of the first floor was taken over to create a street level entrance. In exchange, the first-floor tenant received a mezzanine. The facility, Uptown Racket Club, opened on October 1976 and included a restaurant and sporting goods store. It was a combination of businesses that was many years ahead of its time. In 1977 Town Squash opened a third club in a Manhattan hotel, the Doral Inns Squash Club.

Although Town Squash was successful, it became apparent in the late 1970s that squash was not the gold mine it had once appeared to be. The enthusiasm for squash had waned, surpassed in popularity by racket ball. Squash was difficult for beginners, particularly because the ball required long rallies in order to heat its rubber to give it bounce. Many beginners simply became frustrated and quit playing the game. Squash clubs were no longer creating new players as much as they were cannibalizing each other's members. More troubling to the squash business was the underlying economic fact that time was the actual commodity. If court times were not sold, inventory was lost forever. When the Fifth Avenue Squash Club was the only commercial facility on the island of Manhattan, demand for the space far outpaced available time, so as a result the club had no difficulty selling its

inventory. When the squash boom brought competition, however, the economics changed radically.

Town Squash, saddled with high debt from its recent expansion, began to adapt to these business realities in two major ways. As early as 1979, Nautilus equipment and exercise classes were introduced. Not only did Town Squash take advantage of the growing interest in fitness, it was able to generate revenue to lower the burden on squash. The company also began to sell monthly memberships (as opposed to charging nominal yearly dues and per use rentals) that permitted unlimited use of the club. In effect, the time burden was transferred to the members. If they failed to use the facilities, it was their loss and not the club's.

Briefly in the 1970s, Saint took on some partners to develop two Manhattan locations as well as one in Washington, D.C. After a falling out, the partners retained the Manhattan facilities (which would eventually become part of TSI several years later), and Town Squash became the sole operators of what would become the company's first venture outside of New York, Capital Hill Squash Club, which opened in 1980. Also in 1980 Town Squash became one of the first health clubs to use electronic fund transfer, after Tascher learned of a New Jersey club that was using it. Electronic transfers soon became the backbone of the industry, lessening the need for collection and eventually providing 90 percent of TSI's monthly revenues.

In 1981, Town Squash advertised for a new manager to run the Fifth Avenue club. One of the applicants was Robert Giardina, who had recently moved to the city from Florida, where he had worked for European Health Spa, which at the time was the nation's largest health chain. Giardina was disillusioned with the business, believing that there was too much emphasis on selling memberships and not enough on backend service. Instead of the manager's position, however, Giardina was offered a job as the Town Squash sales manager. According to Giardina, the main reason he accepted the position was because he recognized that the company had an upscale clientele that might provide good networking possibilities for getting into another line of work. When Saint left the company a short time, however, Giardina became an increasingly more important partner for Tascher, who now took over as the chief executive.

By 1981 Saint was divorced and found it difficult to run a company that was owned by his ex-wife's family. Moreover, he still wanted to pursue his dream of writing. He cashed in his share of Town Squash and five years later sold a novel, *Memoirs of an Invisible Man,* that created a stir when it became the object of a heated Hollywood bidding war for the movie rights. Giardina encouraged Tascher to focus on the health club side of the business. The company began to position its facilities as "racket and fitness" clubs. Doral received the first retrofit, then Town Squash applied the concept to a new facility on 62nd Street. In 1985, it became partners in a Brooklyn club, Cobble Hill Racket & Fitness.

Town Squash Inc. Becomes Town Sports Inc. in Mid-1980s

Squash was undergoing a fundamental change in the mid-1980s that would also make it an even less attractive business.

Interest shifted from the American game with its hard ball and narrow courts to the European game with its softer ball and wider courts. Squash courts had to be rebuilt to keep up with customers' tastes, resulting in fewer courts and less revenue. The company's involvement with squash culminated in a major tournament it organized at Manhattan's Hunter College in 1986. Also in that year, Town Squash partnered with some doctors to open a combination medical facility and health club on 34th Street and Second Avenue in Manhattan. The TSI Fitness Training Facility was not only the company's first club that did not feature squash courts, it was the first time that the initials TSI were used. In short order, it would stand for Town Sports International, rather than Town Squash Inc. For Giardina, responsible for overseeing print ads, it was becoming increasingly difficult to maintain continuity, with each club having an individual name. Moreover, the ''racket and fitness'' tag proved cumbersome. The company was also developing plans for more aggressive growth and the requirements for simplicity would eventually lead to the New York Sports Club concept, which would be shortened further to NYSC and eventually applied to operations in other cities.

TSI expanded to Switzerland in 1987. Saint's ex-wife Gerarda had tried to transfer the company's model to Europe and opened health clubs in Basel and Zurich. After traveling to Switzerland to meet with her, Tascher and Giardina convinced her to let them take over the clubs, installing their own managers. Her family then extended a financial commitment to TSI to make further growth possible. In 1990, the company added four new clubs, three in New York and one in Washington, D.C. While three were acquisitions of existing businesses, a Manhattan facility located at 151 Reede Street was a greenfield operation that would serve as a model for future clubs.

Long before this time, Tascher began to see the possibilities of creating a major brand out of New York Sports Clubs. He built a management team, bringing in people from other fields, and developed a long-term plan. The company became especially aggressive in taking over the management of underperforming clubs, but always as partners. Eventually TSI would acquire the interests of its partners. By 1995, the company operated 26 fitness clubs with 56,000 members, and Tascher presented a long-term plan to be the family that continued to be majority shareholders but, in fact, were not as personally committed to the business as Tascher and the rest of management. Initially, the family's representative agreed to his plan to raise

institutional capital in order to add 20 new clubs in a five year period. The family then changed its representation and rescinded its approval, putting Tascher in what he felt was an untenable position with both his management team and the investment community.

Although Tascher quit as the company's chief executive, he remained the second largest shareholder and retained a seat on the board. Behind the scenes he worked to interest potential buyers in TSI, resulting in two offers. It was in this environment that the TSI management team went to the investment firm of Bruckmann, Rosser, Sherrill & Co. to finance a leveraged buyout offer that was eventually accepted by the majority shareholders. Tascher was not a part of this team and went on to open several New York area health clubs on his own. Giardina, on the other hand, remained at TSI, becoming president and chief operating officer. Succeeding Tascher as chief executive officer was Mark Smith, a former professional squash player who had joined the company in 1985 and had been responsible for the operation of the Swiss clubs. Essentially, TSI would carry out the plan that Tascher had presented to previous ownership and expanded upon it as the company grew at a tremendous pace in the late 1990s.

TSI began to expand north of New York City into Westchester in October 1995, when it took over an All Pro Fitness Center located in a Scarsdale shopping center. A year later it acquired the Soundview Fitness Center in Mamaroneck and in 1997 acquired a Club Fit's location in White Plains. Late in 1997 TSI moved into the Connecticut market with a club in Stamford. Four more New York Sports Clubs would open in Connecticut over the next two years. A major attraction to building clubs in communities surrounding New York City was the ability to attract members, many of whom were employed in Manhattan, by allowing them to use TSI facilities that were close to both home and work. Although the first New Jersey club dated back to 1990, it wasn't until 1997 and 1998 that TSI moved aggressively into that market, fueled in large part by the acquisition of four Ovox Fitness Clubs and five Lifestyle Fitness Clubs. TSI also bought existing clubs and opened greenfield operations on Long Island, adding five locations by 2000.

TSI grew its Washington Sports Clubs franchise, not only adding clubs to the District of Columbia, but also opening facilities in North Bethesda and Germantown, Maryland. It opened six clubs in nearby Virginia communities. Moreover, TSI entered entirely new markets. In September 1999 it gained a toehold in Philadelphia by acquiring the well established Society Hill Health Club. In the next year, TSI added four more clubs in the city, as well as the nearby communities of Chalfont, Pennsylvania, and Cherry Hill, New Jersey. A club in Bryn Mawr, Pennsylvania, opened in 2001 and a facility in Philadelphia's Rittenhouse Square was scheduled to open in 2003. The Boston area was entered in November 1996, followed by the opening of five more area clubs by May 1999. The 2000 acquisition of Health Development Corp. added 11 new clubs to the Boston Sports Club brand, making it the second largest TSI brand. In addition, TSI expanded its Swiss operation in 2001, opening a second club in Basel as part of a soccer stadium.

For 2000 TSI generated sales of $225 million and posted a profit of $4.8 million. Because the company had incurred a good deal of debt during its rapid expansion, a more accurate indicator of TSI's financial picture was its cash flow before debt service, which produced a robust 30 percent margin. Clearly TSI had found a viable model for the fitness business, which had seen a large number of casualties over the years. The industry remained highly fragmented, offering numerous takeover opportunities for TSI in its continued effort to grow into a super-regional concern and the possibility of gaining a national foothold. Moreover, the market for fitness clubs was growing as aging baby boomers turned to exercise and insurers worked with businesses to provide employees with club memberships in order to save medical costs by improving health through exercise. The outlook for TSI appeared bright for some time to come.

Principal Divisions

Boston Sports Clubs; New York Sports Clubs; Philadelphia Sports Clubs; Swiss Sports Clubs; Washington Sports Clubs.

Principal Competitors

Bally Total Fitness Holding Corporation; Gold's Gym Enterprises Inc.; The Sports Club Company Inc.

Further Reading

Gault, Ylonda, ''Survival of the Fittest Among Health Clubs,'' *Crain's New York Business,* May 9, 1994, p. 3.

King, Maxwell, ''Squash Everyone?,'' *Forbes,* August 1, 1977, p. 56.

Martin, Douglas, ''Fitness Clubs Vie for Market Share,'' *New York Times,* February 1, 1993, p. B4.

Pristin, Terry, ''Health Clubs Consolidating as Membership Grows,'' *New York Times,* August 16, 1998, p. 35.

Radosta, John S., ''Squash Racquets, Anyone? Definitely Yes,'' *New York Times,* November 21, 1977, p. 67.

Singer, Penny, ''Place for Getting Fit That Offers Baby-Sitting,'' *New York Times,* April 7, 1996, p. 6.

—Ed Dinger

Travelocity.com, Inc.

15100 Trinity Boulevard
Fort Worth, Texas 76155
U.S.A.
Telephone: (817) 785-8000
Fax: (817) 785-8003
Web site: http://www.travelocity.com

Public Company
Incorporated: 1996
Employees: 1,380
Sales: $301.8 million (2001)
Stock Exchanges: NASDAQ
Ticker Symbol: TVLY
NAIC: 454110 Electronic Shopping and Mail-Order
  Houses; 514191 On-Line Information Services

Travelocity.com, Inc. operates a leading online travel Web site where travelers can take control of their bookings and reservations and research information about potential destinations. The site provides reservation information for more than 700 airlines, more than 50,000 hotels, and more than 50 car rental companies. It also offers more than 6,500 vacation packages as well as tour and cruise departures. Internationally, Travelocity.com operates Web sites for customers in Canada in both French and English, as well as in the United Kingdom and Germany. During 2001, it finalized arrangements to launch Travelocity Europe in partnership with Otto, a German direct marketing firm. Also during 2001, the company logged more than $3.1 billion in gross travel bookings and posted revenue of $301.8 million.

Steady Growth Following Launch: 1996–98

Travelocity.com was launched in March 1996 as a joint venture of two travel companies, Sabre Interactive and Worldview Systems Corp. Sabre Interactive was a unit of AMR Corp., the parent company of American Airlines, while Worldview was a partnership formed by publisher Random House and Ameritech, a regional Bell operating company (RBOC). Sabre was the leading travel reservation system used by travel agents. Its principal business was to develop and install travel agents'

computer reservation systems. Sabre booked Travelocity.com's airline reservations, while Worldview provided travel-related content for the site.

At first Travelocity's strategy was to offer compelling content and sell airline tickets. Destination information provided at the site included hotel recommendations, restaurant reviews, entertainment listings, weather reports, video clips, photos, maps, news, chat forums, and other information about specific destinations. Travelocity provided this information on its Web site directly from Worldview's databases. After Sabre Interactive bought out Worldview's interest in Travelocity in February 1997, Worldview remained the featured content provider for the Travelocity Web site.

In its first three months of operation, Travelocity reported 1.2 million visits and had 144,000 people register at the site. Registration was required to make a purchase through Travelocity. The site soon added more features, including hotel reservations, car rentals, and vacation packages. It was able to provide street maps for specific U.S. attractions through an agreement with Vicinity Corp. The Travelocity site was refined to make it easier to use, and by the end of 1996 it offered travel information for more than 200 destinations internationally and had more than 400,000 registered members. During 1996, Travelocity was selected to be the travel content provider for Time Warner's experimental online service, Road Runner.

Travelocity grew steadily during its first two years in business. Together with Expedia, an online travel site launched by Microsoft Corp. in October 1996, it was one of the leading travel sites on the Internet. While purchases were made online, tickets were delivered either to a local travel agency or through Travelocity's own travel agency, the Travelocity Service Center. Sabre and Travelocity built 12,000 customized Web sites for travel agents to help them handle online bookings. This helped position Travelocity as an ally, rather than a competitor, to travel agents. Travelocity was a key component in Sabre's strategy to capture the biggest possible share of overall travel bookings, both on and off the Web. For 1997, Travelocity handled more than $100 million in gross travel bookings, a significant percentage of the estimated $900 million booked in online travel reservations that year.

Merger Results in Dramatic Growth: 1999–2000

In October 1999, Travelocity announced it would merge with Preview Travel, another leading online travel service. The new combined company was called Travelocity.com, Inc., and was headquartered in Fort Worth, Texas. The merger made Travelocity.com a category leader in online travel services. It also had the effect of making Travelocity.com a public company, with access to public equity markets, because Preview Travel was already a public company.

Following the merger, which was completed in March 2000, Travelocity was separated from its parent company, Sabre. Sabre retained a 70 percent ownership interest in Travelocity, while Preview shareholders owned the remaining 30 percent. Sabre also continued to be Travelocity's principal technology partner, handling its online transactions. In the future Sabre would also provide technology for other online travel services, including Priceline.com and Hotwire.

As a result of the merger Travelocity was the third most-visited electronic commerce site in the world following Amazon.com and eBay. The new Travelocity had about 17 million registered members and 8 million monthly visitors. It was the preferred travel provider for all of the major Internet portals, including America Online, Excite, Go Network, Lycos, Netscape, USA Today, and Yahoo!.

Prior to their merger, both Travelocity and Preview Travel were pursuing a strategy of building market share. As a result, both companies sustained losses in 1998 and 1999, with Travelocity reporting a loss of $21 million in 1998 and Preview a loss of $27 million. For 1999, Travelocity and Preview Travel reported combined revenue of $90.9 million and a combined loss of $49.8 million. Competing travel site Expedia went public in November 1999 and, according to Media Metrix, had slightly more traffic than Travelocity during the 1999 holiday season.

Around this time, Travelocity and Preview Travel entered into an agreement with Priceline.com, the name-your-own-fare online service. Together, the three companies agreed to refer customers to each other's sites and collect referral fees when purchases were made. The arrangement enabled Travelocity and Preview Travel to expand its audience and serve customers who were looking for the cheapest fares. Expedia countered by announcing it would develop its own name-you-own-price plan for airline tickets.

Once the merger between Travelocity and Preview Travel closed in March 2000, the new Travelocity launched a $50 million print and television advertising campaign to gain new customers. The ad campaign positioned Travelocity as the place where people could take control of their travel arrangements. The radio spots noted that Travelocity's online site listed 45,000 hotels, 700 airlines, and 50 car rental companies. Meanwhile, Travelocity had combined online traffic of more than eight million visitors in February 2000, according to Media Metrix, making it the top online travel site in terms of traffic. Expedia had 5.3 million visitors, while Travelocity by itself had 5.1 million.

By mid-2000, Travelocity completed its integration with Preview Travel and introduced a redesigned Web site. New features included a group shopping tool that made travel planning for groups easier. Also added to the site were customer reviews and a message board. The home page was redesigned, and wireless travel services were offered. At the end of June 2000, Travelocity had 21.6 million registered members, up from 19.2 million at the end of March.

In the second half of 2000, Travelocity and American Airlines Publishing launched *Travelocity Magazine,* a bimonthly periodical with a controlled circulation of 250,000. The new magazine was part of Travelocity's strategy to extend its brand, and it enhanced the company's position as a provider of tools for travelers who wanted to take control of their travel planning. The company sold its ten millionth airline ticket in October 2000.

To serve customer outside of the United States, Travelocity supported Web sites in Canada, the United Kingdom, and Germany by the end of 2000. The company first began serving international customers in September 1997, when it gained the infrastructure to support global pricing and taxation. At first international customers were served by Travelocity's main online site in the United States, with tickets delivered through Sabre's international network of more than 10,000 travel agents. The company ventured into the United Kingdom market in mid-1998 and established a customer service center in Cardiff, Wales. It then partnered with a U.K. travel agency to develop a Web site specifically for British customers. Travelocity Canada was established in April 1999, followed by a bilingual customer service center in Ottawa and then English and French Web sites for Canadian customers. Travelocity then launched Travelocity Germany, and in 2000 the company entered into an agreement with Japan Airlines, All Nippon Airways, and 11 other international carriers to launch Travelocity Japan in 2001.

Seeking Profitability in 2001

Travelocity's gross travel bookings reached $2.5 billion in 2000, more than double that of 1999 and more than 22 percent of the estimated $11 billion spent in online travel during 2000. At the beginning of 2001, Travelocity was the top-ranked online travel provider with 8.72 million visitors in January, equal to an 18 percent market share, according to Nielsen/NetRatings and Harris Interactive. The other top four online travel providers in terms of visitors were Southwest Airlines with 5.1 million visitors; Expedia, with 4.8 million visitors; Priceline.com, with 3.4 million visitors; and Delta Airlines, with 3.0 million visitors.

Travelocity began 2001 by predicting it would achieve profitability by the end of the year. During 2001, the company faced new competition from the airlines, which launched two new online ticketing services Hotwire.com and Orbitz.com. The airlines also capped commissions at $10 per ticket for all airlines tickets sold online or offline, and some airlines—notably Northwest and KLM—eliminated commissions for airline tickets sold online. In March 2001, Travelocity stopped booking flights on Southwest Airlines after the two companies experienced customer service problems. Travelocity also began charging customers $10 commissions on Northwest and KLM tickets.

Part of Travelocity's strategy to achieve profitability was to introduce new services during the year. For its fifth anniversary in March 2001, it launched several new services, including the Travelocity Preferred Traveler travel club, and Goodbuy, a negotiated fare service for 20 airlines and rooms at 2,500 hotels. Option Finder was a new feature that searched for alternate airports and departure dates. For the first quarter ending March 31, 2001, Travelocity reported a pro forma profit of $618,000 before special items and a positive cash flow. However, special items totaling $26.4 million resulted in a quarterly net loss of $22.1 million, compared to a net loss of $9 million for the same quarter in 2000. Nevertheless, Travelocity's stock rallied on the news and increased more than 134 percent from January through the end of April 2001. Travelocity's second quarter of 2001 was also profitable on a pro forma basis, excluding the write-off of goodwill.

During the rest of the year, Travelocity added more new products and services. Through an investment in Viator, Travelocity added a database of sightseeing tours, attractions, and other destination activities in 33 countries. A partnership with American Classic Voyages Co. enabled Travelocity to offer Hawaiian cruises. In July, Travelocity introduced its Bon Voyage e-mail service, which recommended activities, events, and personalized special offers to its members. A new specialty content area for golf travel was added, and later in the year a new content area for ski and snowboarding vacations was introduced. The company also increased its offline support, opening a third customer service center in Virginia and improving the technology in all of its customer service centers.

Internationally, Travelocity entered into agreements with Lufthansa and British Airways, and it began offering the entire range of 73 European rail passes. The company announced it would acquire Air Tickets Direct, a United Kingdom-based online travel agency that also had a dedicated call center for offline customer support. Before the end of the year it finalized arrangements with Otto, a German direct marketing firm, to launch Travelocity Europe.

For the third quarter ending September 30, Travelocity reported a pro forma profit of $4.9 million before special items. Membership increased to 30.4 million. While the online travel industry was the best performing sector of the Internet economy for the first eight months of 2001, the terrorist attacks of September 11 had a devastating effect on online travel providers. Online bookings dropped to only 30 to 40 percent of their previous levels. At the beginning of October Travelocity announced it would close its call center in Sacramento, California, and reduce its workforce by 19 percent, or 320 jobs. The company had about 1,700 employees before the cutbacks and planned to institute a hiring freeze.

The economic slowdown of 2001 and the lingering effects of September 11 made the fourth quarter of 2001 a difficult one. Travelocity's gross travel bookings for the quarter were $630.2 million, down 9.5 percent for the same quarter of 2000. For the year 2001, Travelocity reported gross travel bookings of $3.1 billion, an increase of 27 percent over 2000. While the company was able to report a pro forma quarterly profit of $4.9 million, it recorded a net loss of $24.4 million for the fourth quarter, more than double the loss of the same quarter in 2000. For all of 2001, Travelocity had a net loss of $85 million. While Travelocity did not achieve profitability in 2001, it was able to report pro forma net income of $15.6 million for the year, and membership at the end of the year rose to 32 million.

Principal Competitors

American Express Co.; Cendant Corp.; Expedia, Inc.; Hotwire; Lowestfare.com, Inc.; Orbitz; Priceline.com, Inc.

Further Reading

Anderson, Karen M., ''Gloves Are off in Fight Between Expedia and Travelocity,'' *Travel Agent,* January 10, 2000, p. 114.

Beirne, Mike, ''Upping the Ante,'' *Brandweek,* September 10, 2001, p. 31.

Biesada, Alexandra, ''Travelocity.com,'' *Texas Monthly,* February 2001, p. 26.

Bittle, Scott, ''Travelocity Site Gets Lots of Bites,'' *Travel Weekly,* July 11, 1996, p. 15.

Black, Jason, ''Terrell Jones of Travelocity,'' *Internet World,* September 15, 2001, p. 37.

Blakey, Elizabeth, ''Travelocity Cuts Jobs, Closes Call Centers,'' *E-Commerce Times,* October 5, 2001.

Butterman, Eric, ''Profits for Travelocity and Expedia Put More Pressure on Orbitz Debut,'' *Travel Agent,* April 30, 2001, p. 4.

——, ''Standing Alone,'' *Travel Agent,* September 10, 2001, p. 32.

Caulfield, Brian, ''A Balancing Act for One Travel Site,'' *Internet World,* April 27, 1998, p. 13.

Cronin, Mary J., ''The Travel Agents' Dilemma,'' *Fortune,* May 11, 1998, p. 163.

Fisher, Daniel, ''Parental Ingratitude,'' *Forbes,* June 12, 2000, p. 64.

Fredericks, Alan, ''Old-Fashioned Service,'' *Travel Weekly,* September 13, 2001, p. 82.

Goetzi, David, ''Travelocity Voyage Puts the Consumer in Charge,'' *Advertising Age,* April 17, 2000, p. 54.

Goodridge, Elisabeth, ''Travelocity Overcomes Barriers in Its Global Expansion,'' *Information Week,* December 11, 2000, p. 76.

Hibbard, Justin, ''Airlines, Online Agencies Battle for Customers,'' *Information Week,* November 9, 1998, p. 30.

''Japanese Airlines Join with Travelocity.com on New Web Venture,'' *Airline Industry Information,* August 16, 2000.

Jones, David, and Jennifer Perez, ''Travelocity Gets in the Airline Web Site Game with Japanese Deal,'' *Travel Agent,* August 28, 2000, p. 8.

Kornik, Joseph, "Sabre Interactive Buys Travelocity," *Travel Weekly,* February 6, 1997, p. 1.

Mack, Ann M., "Travelocity Takes off with New Tools," *Mediaweek,* July 10, 2000, p. 52.

McGee, William J., "Travelocity-Preview Merger Creates Online Powerhouse," *Travel Agent,* October 11, 1999, p. 8.

Meehan, Michael, "Online Travel Deals Make for Strange Bedfellows at Sabre," *Computerworld,* August 14, 2000, p. 20.

"Radio Helps Travelocity Take Off," *Mediaweek,* September 18, 2000, p. 10.

"SWA-Travelocity Split," *Travel Agent,* March 12, 2001, p. 92.

Tanner, Lisa, "Travel Heavy-Hitters to Publish Travelocity Mag," *Dallas Business Journal,* June 9, 2000, p. 24.

Taylor, Catharine P., "Waiting and Seeing," *Advertising Age,* September 24, 2001, p. 28.

"Travelocity Buys Stake in Viator," *Travel Weekly,* May 21, 2001, p. 8.

"Travelocity Redesigned," *Travel Agent,* July 3, 2000, p. 4.

"Travelocity Sells 10 Millionth Ticket," *Travel Weekly,* October 9, 2000, p. 1.

"Travelocity Turns Five," *Travel Agent,* April 9, 2001, p. 116.

"Where the Net Delivers: Travel," *Business Week,* June 11, 2001, p. 142.

Wilson, David, "Internet Travel Sites Take Flight Amid Internet Chaos," *Los Angeles Business Journal,* May 7, 2001, p. 40.

—David P. Bianco

VIVENDI UNIVERSAL

Vivendi Universal S.A.

42 avenue de Friedland
75380 Paris Cedex 08
France
Telephone: (1) 71 71 10 00
Fax: (1) 71 71 10 01
Web site: http://www.vivendiuniversal.com

Public Company
Incorporated: 1853 as Compagnie Générale des Eaux
Employees: 290,000
Sales: $40.1 billion (2000)
Stock Exchanges: Paris New York
Ticker Symbol: V
NAIC: 513322 Cellular and Other Wireless Telecommunications; 51331 Wired Telecommunications Carriers; 51321 Cable Networks; 51312 Television Broadcasting; 22131 Water Supply and Irrigation Systems; 56292 Materials Recovery Facilities; 51211 Motion Picture and Video Production; 512199 Other Motion Picture and Video Industries; 51121 Software Publishers; 51223 Music Publishers

Formerly known as the Générale des Eaux Group, Vivendi Universal S.A. operates as a leading entertainment conglomerate with interests in music, publishing, television and film, telecommunications, Internet-related businesses, and the environment. Through its 2000 purchase of Seagram Company Ltd., it gained control of Universal Music Group and Universal Studios, securing its position as the leading music company with a 22 percent share of the world music market. Vivendi Universal Publishing is the third largest concern in the global publishing market and holds the number two position in the educational publishing segment of the industry. The company also owns CANAL+, the leading European pay-television firm with over 15 million subscribers, and Groupe Cegetel, the leading private telecommunications operator in France. The firm also holds a 63 percent share in Vivendi Environnement, a leading environmental services subsidiary that operates the number one water company in the world.

Origins

Compagnie Générale des Eaux was founded in 1852 during the reign of Napoleon III and is often described as France's first capitalist venture. The company was authorized by imperial decree on December 14, 1853, and from the start benefited enormously from the emperor's personal interest, as well as from support and investment from the international business community in Paris, London, and Lyons, which had studied the water supply companies of the United States and the United Kingdom and realized rich pickings could be had. The list of founders included the Rothschild family, a Fould, a Lafitte, the Duc de Morny—the emperor's half brother—and a large proportion of the imperial nobility. Shareholders included James de Rothschild, who had the largest single subscription of 5,000 shares, and a cross-section of members of the nobility, stockbrokers, and bankers. The initial capital was FFr 20 million which was raised from an 80,000 share subscription.

Early History: Late 1800s

The political and financial influence of its founders and shareholders gave the new company a high profile from the start, but the company also caught the mood of the day with its declared objective of providing "assistance for municipal authorities in implementing schemes of fundamental importance to public health." Not only was the notion of water-for-all part of a new municipal socialism which had already taken root in the United Kingdom and Germany, but also France's growing industries were becoming insatiable in their need for water and power. Without an industrial base, France could not compete with its neighbors, the United Kingdom and Germany. If the foundation of Compagnie Générale des Eaux was a calculated political move, it was also an astute financial one. "We shall be opening up a mine, the wealth of which has not been explored," reported the first board of management to the shareholders, which claimed that "as the first occupants of this mine, it will be our privilege to select and exploit the best seams." The shareholders were not disappointed.

Projected returns of 4 percent were realized at 25 percent from the first year of business. Lyons and Nantes headed the list of municipal authorities anxious to receive Générale des Eaux

Company Perspectives:

Our vision is to be the world's preferred creator and provider of entertainment, education, and personalized services to consumers anywhere, at any time, and across all distribution platforms and devices.

water. Within months, a 99-year agreement had been concluded with Lyons to provide water for domestic and industrial consumption. For an initial investment of FFr 6 million and operating costs of FFr 80,000 per year, Générale des Eaux guaranteed a gross annual income of FFr 381,500 before a drop of water had even flowed through the pipes. A contract with Nantes followed in 1854, with Générale des Eaux undercutting the haphazard services of current suppliers, but still managing to make a healthy 20 percent profit.

Securing the contract for the Paris water supply took a little longer. Initially turned down for the bid to supply the capital's water, Générale des Eaux began buying into small local water companies in the suburbs. When in 1860 the suburbs were annexed to the city, the company was in a strong position to negotiate with the prefecture of the Seine and the city of Paris authorities. Slow penetration into and around the desired market was a clever strategy, and became something of a hallmark of Générale des Eaux's acquisition policies thereafter. The seven-year wait was worth it. Générale des Eaux won a 50-year contract to supply Paris and the suburbs. The city of Paris, for its part, took possession of all water machinery and installations which had previously belonged to the company. Générale des Eaux guaranteed a supply of water which they charged back to the authorities. As the population of Paris grew and the demand for both domestic and industrial water increased, the water supplier saw its profits grow.

The character of Générale des Eaux was beginning to emerge. The company preferred to deal with large municipal authorities which would contract agreements for long periods of time and sought out projects which would bring high profits to enable greater investment. It also displayed a strong speculative and entrepreneurial streak, the latter of which is particularly remarkable. Générale des Eaux anticipated the growth of the Côte d'Azur and the so-called Emerald Coast of Brittany some 20 to 30 years before the resorts became fashionable, installing water supplies and drainage systems in Nice and the surrounding areas from the 1860s and subsequently supplying Antibes, Menton, Hyères, and Monaco in the 1870s and 1880s. Towards the end of the century, the coastal towns and large cities of Brittany and Normandy were supplied by Générale des Eaux.

Despite heady successes in the company's first 50 years, the end of the century brought an unforeseen problem. In 1892, there was a major typhoid epidemic in Paris. The authorities acted by ordering a systematic sampling of water for laboratory analysis, and in 1902 the Public Hygiene Act laid down standards for public health in relation to the water supply. The connection between water supply and cholera and typhoid was finally understood. From now on municipal authorities demanded not just efficiency but guarantees that the water being delivered for domestic consumption was clean and disease-free. For Générale des Eaux, the Public Hygiene Act meant hefty investment in research and new machinery. Treating waste water before it ran back into the clean water supplies also became a priority.

There was, too, a new competitor in the field. Société Lyonnaise des Eaux et de L'Eclairage was founded in 1880 and by the start of the 20th century had established itself as a force to be reckoned with. From then on, something of a race developed between the two companies to acquire market shares in the supplying of water to unserviced municipalities. Between 1900 and 1940 the rate at which water supply networks spread through France accelerated with each decade. Both companies expanded their areas of influence by buying up local water companies and overhauling their operations, so that by the outbreak of World War II Compagnie Générale des Eaux and Société Lyonnaise des Eaux et de L'Eclairage supplied 50 percent of all town dwellers.

Guy Dejouany Joins the Firm: 1950

Dominating the fortunes of Compagnie Générale des Eaux in the postwar years was the personality of Guy Dejouany. An engineer by profession, he was educated at the Ecole Polytechnique and, after appointments in Metz and Paris, joined Générale des Eaux in 1950. His rise through the company was swift. A director in 1960, he became deputy director general in 1965, director general in 1972, and president and director general in 1976. In the 1960s he was instrumental in the development of a thermal energy program, showing himself to be a strong advocate of diversification beyond the traditional water concerns. Moreover, he turned the company from a fairly institutional concern into a dynamic, highly diversified group which, in 1991, was one of the most successful companies on the Paris Stock Exchange. Dejouany has remained a decidedly nonpublic figure, declining to give interviews and running an unusually small headquarters with only 15 managers. Dejouany was involved in the first tentative moves, in the 1970s, into urban cleaning and maintenance, waste, electrical contracting, house building, and construction.

By 1981, Compagnie Générale des Eaux was beginning to make the headlines with its profits of FFr 331 million. Ironically, its attractiveness nearly brought about its downfall. At the start of the 1980s, 75 percent of shares were held by small investors, headed by Dejouany. In March 1981, Compagnie Générale d'Electricité announced a 15 percent stake, a significant interest held by a large company. Two years later Saint-Gobain, the glass and pipe manufacturer, which had already bought enthusiastically into Olivetti and Bull CH Honeywell only to have the government insist that it pull out, announced a 33 percent holding in Compagnie Générale des Eaux. Months of complicated maneuvers on the Paris Stock Exchange had been necessary, but Générale des Eaux had exposed itself to the risk of a buying by a large company when it issued new shares at the start of 1983 to raise capital for investment. The announcement brought crises within the water company and within the government. Dejouany and a number of government critics complained that Saint-Gobain, one of France's six major companies nationalized in 1982, was attempting a creeping nationalization of the water company. Saint-Gobain replied that it was merely

---

Key Dates:

1852: Compagnie Générale des Eaux is founded.
1860: The company secures a 50-year contract to supply water to Paris and its suburbs.
1981: Profits reach FFr 331 million; Compagnie Générale d'Electricité purchases a 15 percent stake in Générale des Eaux.
1983: Saint-Gobain is forced by the French government to cut its stake in the firm.
1996: Jean-Marie Messier is named chairman and begins a reorganization program.
1998: The company changes its name to Vivendi.
2000: After merging with CANAL+ and Seagram Company Ltd., the firm takes on the name Vivendi Universal S.A.
2001: Mp3.com Inc. and Houghton Mifflin Company are acquired; plans are set in motion to purchase USA Networks Inc.

---

seeking to expand its business by ordinary means, but was soon requested by the government to cut its stake to 20.7 percent. Dejouany further redressed the balance by asking Schlumberger, the Franco-American service and electronics group, to buy a 10 percent share at a cost of FFr 550 million to offset Saint-Gobain's interest.

Expansion: 1980s–90s

This share purchase ended the crisis and signaled the end, too, of the growing pains of Générale des Eaux. From this moment on, the company went from strength to strength, multiplying its interests abroad and buying into some of France's leading companies at home. The results were dramatic. The 1980s, as a whole, saw sales at home increase seven and a half times, from FFr 11.5 billion to FFr 76.5 billion, and sales abroad multiply 35 times, from FFr 630 million to FFr 22 billion. Net profits rose from FFr 331 million in 1981 to FFr 766 million in 1986 and then took off sharply to finish at FFr 1.8 billion in 1989.

The weighty program of investment and activity abroad produced both admiration and controversy in countries targeted for Générale des Eaux treatment. By 1991, Générale des Eaux was the second largest water distributor in Spain and the third largest distributor of bottled water in the United States, and also supplied water in Portugal, Malta, and Italy. It collected waste in Bogota and Prague, cleaned the streets and underground system of Madrid, supplied cable television in Montreal, and managed industrial waste and thermal power from California to Benelux.

Générale des Eaux also moved across the English Channel. Britain in the late 1980s, with a water industry heading for privatization and local authorities beginning to put many of their service contracts out for tender, was ripe for investment. Lyonnaise des Eaux and Société d'Aménagement Urbain et Rural (SAUR) made large tenders for the ten regional water companies, Lyonnaise paying £47.6 million for Essex Water in June 1988, and SAUR paying £58.6 million for Mid Southern Water in January 1989. Générale des Eaux, in contrast, focused

on buying shares in a number of smaller companies, including Three Valleys, Folkestone & District, Mid-Kent, Severn and Trent, and Bristol, and looked to the wider areas of energy, waste, healthcare, construction, and cable television to establish a foothold in Britain. The foothold was designed to be flexible. When British electricity companies were privatized in 1990, Générale des Eaux dropped some of its water interests and bought into Associated Electricity. Similarly, when television franchises were put up for bids in 1991, Générale des Eaux bought shares in a number of cable television operations. Less expected was the purchase of American Medical International's chain of private hospitals in Britain in March 1990 and an 83 percent stake in Norwest Holst. In June 1991, Générale des Eaux's U.K. waste company Onyx announced a seven-year rubbish collection contract with the city of Liverpool, the latest of twenty such contracts with municipalities all over Britain.

The progress of Générale des Eaux in Britain mirrored the development of the company in France during its early days in the 19th century. The profits were just as rich—in 1990, the company made £900 million in Britain, which now represents almost one-tenth of total group sales revenue worldwide. In the general spread of its international and home operations there were similarities, too, to company behavior in the previous century and during the early 1990s. Générale des Eaux was responsive to current environment issues. In May 1990, it paid $100 million for a 16 percent stake in Air and Water Technologies, a major pollution-control company based in New Jersey in the United States. Air, water, and soil pollution prevention was high on the list of priorities for Générale des Eaux in the 1990s and its activities by that time had already earned it attention from Europe's press for its environmental concerns.

By 1991, Générale des Eaux's interests in cable television and cellular car phones included a 21.6 percent share in CANAL+, 90 percent of Générale d'Images, and 80 percent of Compagnie Générale de Vidéo-communications, making Générale des Eaux the leading operator of cable networks in France. Although the 1991 Gulf War boosted viewing figures, cable television had yet to take off in a big way. It was thought, however, that the mid-1990s would see a large increase in the subscription base. The launch of cellular phones showed quicker returns. Between the inception of the service in March 1989 and the end of the year, there were 10,000 subscribers. At a European level, the carphone subsidiary, Compagnie Financière pour le Radio Téléphone, worked with BMW and Veba in Germany to install telephones directly.

In addition to entering the communications sector, Générale des Eaux had bought into a number of French blue chip companies including, since 1986, Saint-Gobain. Saint-Gobain's major subsidiary, Société Générale d'Entreprise, which had in turn been acquired from Compagnie Générale d'Electricité, was bought out by Générale des Eaux in 1988, thereby giving it a major position in France's construction industry. Phenix, Seeri, and Sari added to Générale des Eaux's command in this area, with projects such as the La Defense building in Paris. In Paris, the company cleaned the Louvre, the Métro, the Ministry of Finance, and the Museé d'Orsay art gallery, and collected waste for Peugeot, Air France, the SNCF (Société Nationale des Chemins de Fer Français), and Nestlé.

Changing Focus; Changing Names:
Mid- to Late 1990s and Beyond

Continuing with its expansion efforts, Générale des Eaux underwent a series of strategic changes during the mid-to-late 1990s that turned the company into a major entertainment and environmental concern. In 1996, Dejouany retired, leaving Jean-Marie Messier to take over the helm. The 39-year-old executive quickly began a hard core restructuring effort with a focus on its environmental and communication-related businesses and began selling off over $25 billion in holdings. At the time, Générale des Eaux was referred to as a "corporate octopus" with over 2,200 subsidiaries involved in the property, construction, health, energy, mobile phones, amusement parks, cable television, and railway industries. A 1996 article in *The European* claimed that the company had "begun to spin out of control following reckless investment, mainly in property, the disappointing performance of the private healthcare division, and problems in maximizing investments in mobile phones and cable TV, which have lagged behind in France." The article went on to state that "there have also been complaints about high prices and low service in the water sector."

As part of Messier's grand scheme, he implemented a strategy on which the company was focused on gaining world leadership in the environmental services industry, as well as in both the media and communications industries. During 1996, plans were set in motion to create the Groupe Cegetel, a subsidiary that would cover fixed and mobile phone businesses in France—the telecommunications market in France was deregulated in 1998. As part of its push into publishing, the company acquired a 30 percent interest in Havas in 1997 and then merged with Havas the following year. It afterward purchased Cendant Software Corp., an electronic publishing firm. It was also during 1998 that the firm adopted a new name, Vivendi, chosen to suggest life and vitality.

Vivendi marked its entrance into the new millennium with a $34 billion stock purchase of Seagram Company Ltd. The deal added Universal Music Group and Universal Studios to Vivendi's holdings, giving it control of the world's largest music company. It also purchased the remaining shares of CANAL+ and then changed its name once again to Vivendi Universal. During this time period, companies that had traditionally focused on either content or distribution began seeking out strategic purchases that would align both content and distribution holdings. The merger of America Online Inc. and Time Warner was one such purchase that signaled the industry's changing landscape. Messier commented on the AOL deal in a 2001 Time International article, stating that "nothing in the world of communications would ever be the same again. Being strong in content is not enough. You also need to own part of your own distribution network."

As such, Vivendi began to seek out a distribution partner that would give it a stronger foothold in the U.S. market. Along with its purchases of U.S.-based publisher Houghton Mifflin Company and Internet music service provider mp3.com Inc., the company announced its intent to purchase the entertainment assets of USA Networks Inc. for over $10 billion in December 2001, along with a ten percent stake in EchoStar Communications Corp., the second largest satellite-television operator in the U.S. The USA Network deal would give Vivendi access to over 84 million U.S. television viewers and bring it closer to competing with the likes of rival AOL Time Warner.

In just seven years, Messier had transformed the Générale des Eaux Group of the 1800s into a leading entertainment conglomerate with net income of $2.1 billion in 2000 and sales of nearly $50 billion in 2001. While the company's recent acquisition spree left it with debt equaling $18 billion—a 50 percent debt-to-equity ratio which was higher than most of its competitors—management was confident that the firm was on the right track to securing future growth. Messier, in fact, held strong to his belief that Vivendi Universal would become the world's preferred creator and provider of entertainment.

Principal Subsidiaries

Universal Music Group; Vivendi Universal Publishing; CANAL+; Groupe Cegetel; Vivendi Telecom International; Vivendi Universal Net; Vivendi Environnement S.A. (63%); MP3.com Inc.

Principal Competitors

AOL Time Warner Inc.; Viacom Inc.; Bertelsmann AG.

Further Reading

"All Vivendi Wants for Christmas," *Business Week*, December 24, 2001.

Guyon, Janet, "Can Messier Make Cash Flow Like Water?," *Fortune*, September 3, 2001, p. 148.

"Master of the Universe," *Time International*, August 6, 2001, p. 32.

McClellan, Steve, "Vivendi Deal Makes It Truly Universal," *Broadcasting & Cable*, December 31, 2001, p. 8.

Tillier, Alan, "Golden Boy Dips His Toe in the Water," *European*, May 23, 1996, p. 32.

——, "Vivendi Makes its Multimedia Play," *European*, November 30, 1998, p. 19.

"Veni Vidi Vivendi," *Economist*, December 22, 2001.

"Why Vivendi's Shuffling Has Only Just Begun," *Fortune*, July 10, 2000, p. 38.

—Catriona Luke
—update: Christina M. Stansell

WACHOVIA

Wachovia Corporation

One First Union Center
Charlotte, North Carolina 29288-0013
U.S.A.
Telephone: (704) 374-6565
Toll Free: (800) 413-7898
Fax: (704) 374-3425
Web site: http://www.wachovia.com

Public Company
Incorporated: 1958 as First Union National Bank of
    North Carolina; 1968 as The Wachovia Corporation
Employees: 84,000
Total Assets: $330 billion (2001)
Stock Exchanges: New York
Ticker Symbol: WB
NAIC: 551111 Offices of Bank Holding Companies;
    52211 Commercial Banking; 52221 Credit Card
    Issuing

The new Wachovia Corporation was formed from the September 2001 merger of First Union Corporation and Wachovia Corporation. The deal created the fourth-largest bank holding company in the U.S. based on assets and the fifth-largest U.S. broker/dealer based on registered representatives. By combining forces, the new company offered financial services in 12 states through 2,800 branches, and also provided full-service brokerage in 49 states. Wachovia caters to nine million households and 900,000 businesses by offering such services as banking, brokerage, asset management, wealth management, treasury services, corporate and investment banking, international banking, credit and debit card products, trust services, mortgage banking, and home equity lending.

History of First Union

Before its merger with Wachovia, First Union ranked as the nation's sixth largest bank holding company, based on total assets of $254 billion in 2000. Its employee base—71,262 strong—served a customer group of more than 7 million peo-

ple. The firm's 2,200 banking branch offices along the East Coast made it the nation's third largest bank branch network. The company provided full-service investment banking, retail banking, commercial banking, and trust services. First Union also had 375 diversified offices throughout the United States that provided its customer base with brokerage services.

First Union traces its founding to 1908 as the Charlotte-based Union National Bank. The First Union name made its initial appearance in 1958 following the merger between Union National Bank and Asheville, North Carolina-based First National Bank. At the time of the merger, the new bank became the first Charlotte bank to own branch offices in another city.

Union National Bank's founder, H.M. Victor, would have a difficult time recognizing the bank he founded in 1908. The company's first offices were in the modest Buford Hotel on Charlotte's main downtown thoroughfare of Tryon Street. Victor raised funds to start Union National Bank by selling 1,000 shares of stock at $100 each. Next, he set up his office at a roll-top desk in the hotel's main lobby. Soon, Victor had earned a reputation as a conservative banker who always confirmed his customers' creditworthiness prior to issuing them any loans. For many years, Victor even refused to make loans for the then newly invented automobile. Finally, he relented with a loan to a customer for a Model-T Ford. Just to be safe, however, he held the owner's keys and title until the loan was repaid in full.

As Union National grew, the company maintained the reputation Victor had established as being an institution of high credit quality, strong financial performance, and excellent customer service. It was this image and visibility that kept the bank open during the troubled 1930s. The Great Depression forced many of Union National's competitors to shut their doors permanently during that era.

In the successful decades the followed the depression, Union National Bank stood out as a pioneer and leader in many areas of the banking industry, and it developed an innovative approach to growth and diversification. For example, in 1947 Union National became the first Charlotte-based bank to open a branch office. Later, it was the first bank to offer a flat-fee checking account. Even before the development of MasterCard

Company Perspectives:

Completion of this merger is a defining moment for Wachovia and First Union, providing the opportunity to create of the finest companies in the world. We look forward to leveraging combined strengths to realize the potential of our new company and to build sustained value for our shareholders, customers, employees, and communities.

and Visa, Union National was the first bank to offer a charge card. Through the years, First Union has followed this legacy of leadership, becoming the first bank in the United States to link all of its branches by satellite for data transmission in 1993.

In 1958, a visionary leader at Union National by the name of Carl McCraw, Sr.—then serving as president of the bank—recognized that the future of U.S. banking lay in a strong branching network. With a young manager by the name of C.C. Hope, McCraw traveled to New York to study mergers in depth. McCraw was in very good company with the young Mr. Hope. Hope was later to become vice chairman of the corporation, president of the American Bankers Association, and director of the Federal Deposit Insurance Corporation before his death in 1993.

McCraw and Hope studied bank mergers diligently, and their research paid off later that year when Union National merged with First National Bank and Trust Company of Asheville. The merger created the First Union National Bank of North Carolina. By 1964, the company had further diversified by acquiring the Raleigh-based Cameron-Brown Company. Cameron-Brown was one of the Southeast's leading mortgage banking and insurance companies. The acquisition propelled First Union to become one of only a few banking companies that was legally empowered to offer a full line of insurance and mortgage products to its customers in all 50 states. Cameron-Brown changed its name to First Union Mortgage Corporation in 1986. By 1994, the mortgage company stood as one of the nation's 11 largest mortgage banking companies based on mortgage servicing volume.

The late 1960s brought more organizational change to First Union. During that time, the company formed a bank holding company, and C.C. Cameron, the founder of Cameron-Brown, became chairman of the newly formed holding company. By December 31, 1968, First Union formed a bank holding company with total assets of nearly $1 billion. In 1973, Edward E. Crutchfield, Jr., became the nation's youngest president of a major banking company when he was named president of First Union at age 32.

From the 1960s to the mid-1980s, First Union expanded across the state, merging with more than thirty banks and adding branches to its statewide system. In 1985, the Supreme Court approved regional interstate banking, and First Union was among the first U.S. banks to take advantage of this decision. At that time, the company expanded into other states and acquired banks in North and South Carolina, Georgia, Florida, and Tennessee.

Also in 1985, Crutchfield succeeded Cameron as chairman and chief executive officer of First Union Corporation. That year, he conducted an expansion program that encompassed Northwestern Financial Corporation of Greensboro, North Carolina. The merger was the largest in North Carolina's history, and it created the state's second largest bank. It also established First Union's flagship banking operation.

In 1988, First Union's national presence was sufficient to warrant listing its stock on the New York Stock Exchange. Prior to this event, the stock was traded only over the counter. Between 1985 and 1994, First Union used its powerful statewide foundation to complete 40 acquisitions and mergers with banks in North and South Carolina, Georgia, Tennessee, and Florida. In 1993, the company expanded its banking operations into Virginia, Maryland, and Washington, D.C. The corporation grew from $8.2 billion in assets on June 30, 1985, to $70.8 billion on December 31, 1993.

First Union's basic business strategy was to seek out other banking organizations with compatible management and philosophies. By merging with such similar companies, First Union maintained the reputation established by Victor at the original Union National. The bank held firmly to its image of strong financial performance and quality products and service. As the company consolidated the operations of its acquired banking partners, First Union managed to achieve efficiencies by standardizing products, policies, and procedures and by making full use of high technology automation systems.

During its growth years, First Union's transition was strengthened by such leaders as Frank H. Dunn, Jr., chairman and chief executive officer of First Union National Bank of North Carolina; Byron E. Hodnett, chief executive officer of First Union National Bank of Florida; Harald R. Hansen, chairman, president, and chief executive officer of First Union National Bank of Georgia; Sidney B. Tate, chairman, president, and chief executive officer of First Union Bank of South Carolina; Robert L. Reid, chairman, president, and chief executive officer of First Union National Bank of Tennessee; and Benjamin P. Jenkins, president and chief operating officer of First Union National Bank of Virginia. The banks' mergers also added the talents of B. J. Walker, formerly of Atlantic Bancorporation and by 1994 vice-chairman of First Union Corporation, to First Union's arsenal.

Through the early 1990s, management of First Union's sales, marketing, and customer service fell under the jurisdiction of John R. Georgius, president of the corporation. Georgius helped develop the Quality Customer Service (QCS) program, which by 1994 had become an industry-wide model. Under the Quality Customer Service program, First Union constantly trained employees on improved techniques for customer service and sales. Employees earned cash incentives for achieving the program's high standards of service. The corporation's incentive program was just one example of its full commitment to providing quality service to its more than seven million customers. It also served as a baseline for attracting new customers. As Georgius stated in First Union's Corporate Overview, "In the 1990s, there should be no question that First Union is one of the finest sales-driven, service-oriented organizations in the United States."

Other people took notice of First Union's success, on both the customer service front and the financial front. First Union Corporation was profiled as one of the *101 Companies That Profit from Customer Care*, a book that cited role models "for the new American manager." The book praises First Union for its Quality Customer Service program, for its aggressive "mystery shopping" program by an independent firm, and for its in-depth market research into customer definitions of service.

In the 1990s, First Union also continued to build its product inventory. For example, the company built the most competitive foreign exchange operation in the southeastern United States, with a team of experienced traders who provided pricing and advice 24 hours a day. The foreign exchange operation assisted more than 350 corporate customers in some 54,000 transactions in 1993. This exchange operation became increasingly important in the North Carolina region as it attracted foreign-owned corporations at a rate that outpaced the rest of the nation.

Also, after nearly a decade of using derivatives to manage interest rate risk, First Union established a "derivatives products" business in 1993. That year, the company assisted 300 corporate customers in nearly 500 transactions to manage interest-rate risk, reduce the cost of financing their businesses, and expand the financing opportunities available to them. The "capital partners" group was established in 1987 to provide merchant banking services to its southeastern communities. First Union also had financing specialists in such fields as trade finance, communications, health care, energy, lease finance, transportation, mortgage banking, and insurance.

That same year, First Union launched an aggressive new strategy to compete head-on with major brokerage and investment banking firms. The company estimated there were more than 100,000 corporations and entrepreneurs at the time who need alternative financing solutions to traditional bank loans. Among those products First Union offered were syndicated loans, private placements, securitization of assets, mezzanine financing, and equity capital. The company had recruited more than 60 capital markets experts from top money centers to spearhead the initiative.

After eight years of offering its own proprietary mutual funds, First Union began rapidly developing a licensed sales force to sell mutual funds in 1993. The company increased its range of financial offerings with the acquisition of Lieber & Company, advisor to the Evergreen Funds.

One element on First Union's side for future growth and success was its home region. The South Atlantic region of the United States witnessed continued movement, or "in-migration," of people into the area from other parts of the nation. During the last decade, the South Atlantic states gained 3.3 million people in population in-migration. First Union's experts predicted that the rate would rise to 4.1 million people over the next decade. This rate is significantly better than any other region in the United States. Between 1991 and 1993, the South Atlantic region attracted more than 3,300 new or expanded plants and offices, 35 percent more than any other region and 29 percent of all new corporate locations in the United States. The South Atlantic region also attracted 45 percent of all new and expanded foreign-based facilities during this same time period. All of these statistics were even more remarkable because the region represented only 18 percent of the total United States population.

As banking opportunities increased with rapid regional growth, First Union's banking region was projected to continue to outpace the rest of the nation in population, employment, and personal income growth throughout the 1990s. This situation, plus First Union's inherent financial strength, meant that the company was well positioned for growth, with resources, management talent, technological advantage, market position, and products to continue to lead the pack in the banking world.

During the mid-1990s, Chairman Crutchfield described First Union's mission "to be the best place for companies and individuals to obtain the financial services and products they want—and then to delight them with our efforts to help them achieve their financial goals." He continued, "When an individual wants an equity mutual fund, or a corporate treasurer seeks to hedge foreign currency exposure, or a state or municipality wants to issue general obligation bonds, or any customer has any financial need, our vision is for them to think, 'I bet First Union offers that.' "

As such, First Union sought to build its product and services portfolio as well as boost brand recognition through acquisitions as the banking industry continued to consolidate into the late 1990s. By now, the company had made nearly 40 purchases since 1985 and continued with this strategy. In 1996, the bank expanded into the New Jersey market with the purchase of First Fidelity Bancorp. The following year, First Union announced its $17 billion offer for Philadelphia, Pennsylvania-based CoreStates Financial Corp. Upon completion of the deal, First Union became the number one bank in both New Jersey and Pennsylvania. In 1998, investment bank First Wheat Butcher Singer, Bowles Hollowell Conner & Co., Covenant Bancorp, and consumer finance company Money Store Inc. were also purchased. Then, in 1999, the firm set its sights on Chicago-based Everen

Capital Corp. The acquisition bolstered the firm's retail brokerage services by 46 percent and increased its number of brokers by 42 percent.

The company's activities proved costly, and by 1999 revenue growth was declining. The company also began to post lower than expected earnings that, in turn, caused First Union's stock price to fall. In February of that year, the bank announced that it would cut up to 10 percent of its work force. The company also began to close unprofitable branches and divest slow growth holdings. After he was diagnosed with cancer in 2000, Crutchfield turned over his CEO post to G. Kennedy Thompson and retired from the firm in March 2001. That same year, the firm announced a $2.8 billion restructuring effort that included shutting down the home equity lending operations of the Money Store and selling its mortgage servicing and credit card portfolios.

The firm's new focus was on three core businesses: the general bank, capital management, and capital markets. Under the leadership of Thompson, First Union claimed that its acquisition spree had ended in order to control costs and foster internal development. Revenue growth continued to elude the bank, however, and analysts began to speculate that First Union was prime for takeover. The company then shocked the banking industry when it made a $14 billion bid for competitor Wachovia Corp.—just a few short months after it announced its departure from the acquisition arena.

History of Wachovia

Before its merger with First Union, Wachovia operated as a southeastern interstate bank holding company with dual headquarters in Atlanta, Georgia, and Winston-Salem, North Carolina. The company's Retail Financial Services unit had approximately 668 banking offices in Florida, Georgia, North and South Carolina, and Virginia, and served 3.8 million customers. Its services included checking and savings, mortgage lending, consumer loans, and credit cards. Wachovia's Corporate Financial Services division provided commercial lending, leasing and leveraged finance, treasury consulting, payments and information services, investment banking, debt and equity capital markets services, executive services, commercial insurance, and asset management. Its clients included over 28,000 businesses in the United States and 40 other countries. The firm's Asset and Wealth Management business provided full service brokerage and a host of asset management services to over 40,000 wealth management customers and 260,000 investment client households. In 2000, Wachovia's assets reached $74 billion.

While the banking industry was marked by fierce competition and volatility in the early 1990s, Wachovia managed to maintain its prominence in both size and reputation. In 1994, Wachovia was listed by Financial World magazine as the most financially stable of the nation's largest bank companies holding assets greater than $30 billion. A September 15, 1992 article in the *American Banker* attributed the bank's "enviable performance record" to "one of the lowest loss experiences in the industry and its place as one of the highest and most stable earners."

Wachovia's preeminence in the banking industry and its broad range of services was secured by a strategic merger in the mid-1980s. Within a week of the June 10, 1985 Supreme Court decision to uphold regional reciprocal interstate banking, Wachovia and First Atlanta Corp. merged their respective strengths and market coverage into a new company, First Wachovia Corporation. In May 1991, the organization moved to employ a single identity for all its constituent parts: The First National Bank of Atlanta became Wachovia Bank of Georgia; Wachovia Bank and Trust Company became Wachovia Bank of North Carolina; and the parent company, First Wachovia Corporation, was renamed Wachovia Corporation. Then on December 6, 1991, South Carolina National Corporation joined the bandwagon and added its member bank, South Carolina National Bank (SCN) to the Wachovia family. Following the trend toward a common corporate identity, SCN changed its name to Wachovia Bank of South Carolina in May 1994.

In 2000, the company's main subsidiaries included Wachovia Bank N.A., Wachovia Securities Inc., The First National Bank of Atlanta, and OFFITBANK. Its original subsidiaries were secured under one common parent company by the mid-1990s, and each bank remained a separate legal entity with its own board of directors, management, and staff. Moreover, each of the three original banks—Wachovia Bank of Georgia, Wachovia Bank of North Carolina, and Wachovia Bank of South Carolina—were invested with a long history of its own, adding yet another layer of complexity—and interest—to Wachovia's past.

Wachovia Bank of Georgia traces its history to the Civil War, the subsequent financial rebuilding of Atlanta, and the determination of one prominent civic leader, General Alfred Austell, who gained banking experience at Atlanta's Bank of Fulton. After this bank closed at the end of the war, Austell played a significant role in both redeeming the Bank of Fulton's Confederate notes and in plying influential contacts in Washington, D.C., toward securing a national bank charter for Atlanta. On September 14, 1865, a federal charter was granted to the Atlanta National Bank making it the first national bank in the Southeast. Austell became president.

Other Georgia entrepreneurs made the best of reconstruction and formed banks that would eventually branch into the Wachovia tree. Joining forces with his father, Colonel Robert J. Lowry founded the state-chartered Lowry Banking Company. Changing to a national charter, that bank became the Lowry National Bank in 1900.

Colonel Robert Flournoy Maddox and his partner, Jett Rucker, established a planters' warehouse that eventually became a lending business, using tobacco and cotton as collateral. In 1879, the partners moved exclusively into banking with the establishment of a private bank, Maddox-Rucker & Company, which obtained a National Charter and changed its name to American National Bank in 1908. Their enterprise continued to grow over the next several decades, converting to a state-chartered bank—the Maddox-Rucker Banking Company—in 1891, and finally obtaining a national charter and changing its name to American National Bank in 1908.

From his post as mayor of Atlanta in 1880, Captain James W. English was well connected to start yet another influential Georgia bank. By 1889, he had become one of the founders and in 1890 was named the president of state-chartered American Trust and Banking Company. By 1896, the bank had adopted a federal charter as the Fourth National Bank of Atlanta.

Though these early Georgia banks continued to prosper beyond the turn of the century, they were constrained by a state law prohibiting banks from expanding beyond their city limits. A series of mergers that began just before World War I, however, provided an alternative means of growth. In 1916, Atlanta National Bank merged with American National and kept the Atlanta National name. In 1923, Lowry National Bank merged with Trust Company of Georgia to become the Lowry Bank and Trust Company of Georgia; a year later, the new entity merged with Atlanta National to become the Atlanta and Lowry National Bank. Finally, in 1929, the Atlanta and Lowry National Bank merged with the Fourth National Bank to become The First National Bank of Atlanta, making it the largest and the oldest national bank in the Southeast.

While banking in postbellum Georgia was undergoing rapid change and consolidation, important predecessors to Wachovia were also evolving in North Carolina. In 1804, the state's General Assembly chartered North Carolina's first two banks— the Bank of Cape Fear and the New Bern Bank. Though organized banking came relatively late to North Carolina, its charter offered one main advantage over other state banking charters: statewide branch banking was permitted. By 1847, with Israel Lash as cashier, the bank had its first full-time branch in Salem.

Although the Bank of Cape Fear, like many of its peers, did not survive the Civil War, Lash used it as the groundwork for the First National Bank of Salem, which opened in 1866 with Lash as president and his nephew, William Lemly, as cashier. When Lash died in the late 1870s, Lemly helped implement new growth and change at the bank. After choosing a new site in the adjoining town of Winston and signing a new charter, he established Wachovia National Bank on June 16, 1879. Wyatt Bowman served as the bank's first president until his death in 1882, when Lemly took the helm.

Meanwhile, economic growth in the Piedmont region precipitated the development of trust companies. In 1891, a group of local financiers proposed legislation to permit the new innovative combination of banking services with the responsibilities of trust management. The North Carolina General Assembly voted favorably, and on June 15, 1893 Wachovia Loan and Trust Company became the state's first chartered trust company.

The Loan and Trust Company's early success was largely attributable to the unusual perseverance and innovation of its chief management; Francis Henry Fries served as president, and his nephew, Henry Fries Shaffner, served as secretary-treasurer. Fries and Shaffner distinguished Wachovia Loan and Trust as a financial innovator.

The new bank's name reflected its regional bent. Salem and Winston were situated in the Piedmont region, primarily settled by Moravian colonists of German descent in the 1750s. Their benefactor, Count Zinzendorf, traced his ancestral roots to a region along the Danube known as Der Wachau. In deference to that lineage, the Moravians called their new home and many of its businesses ''Wachovia.''

In 1910, that name was again put to use, this time to describe a third Wachovia, the merger between Wachovia National Bank and Wachovia Loan and Trust Company. The new institution, Wachovia Bank and Trust Company, opened its doors for business on January 1, 1911.

With deposits of $4 million and a total capital base of $7 million, the consolidated bank stood out as the largest bank in the South and one of the largest trusts in the East. Management of the institutions also merged: Francis Fries was elected president, and James Gray—former president of Wachovia National Bank—became vice-president. The new bank distinguished itself with innovations across the financial board. Over the next several decades, the bank continued to grow, joining the Federal Reserve System in 1918, opening a second Winston-Salem office in 1919 (the two towns became a single civic entity in 1913), and merging with Forsyth Savings to establish a third Winston-Salem location in 1930.

While the turn-of-the-century predecessors to Wachovia Corp. were taking shape in Georgia and North Carolina, South Carolina saw the development of other financial institutions that would eventually join Wachovia. In 1792, the Bank of the United States opened a branch bank in the port city of Charleston. The branch also served as a depository for federal taxes and duties. On December 17, 1834, the state approved an act chartering the Bank of Charleston. In July, the stockholders appointed James Hamilton, Jr., president, and, by late November, the Bank of Charleston had replaced the public Branch Bank of the United States as a major new private financial institution in the region.

Early growth of the Bank of Charleston was attributable to Henry Workman Conner, who became president in 1841. Connor gained a reputation for his hard work and initiative, and under his leadership the bank instituted an early interstate banking venture by creating a network of financial agencies from Augusta, Georgia, to New Orleans, Louisiana, and beyond. By 1848, the agency department accounted for $7.5 million in transactions, up from $300,000 only seven years earlier. As Charleston became an even more important trading hub, the bank's operations continued to grow until the Civil War. After Gordon Rose was elected president in 1850, the bank consistently managed to declare dividends that averaged 8 to 10 percent of its capital stock per year, while keeping total assets well ahead of liabilities.

The Civil War temporarily interrupted the Bank of Charleston's upward trajectory. In fact, by 1869, the bank was insolvent. Nevertheless, under the guidance of president Archibald S. Johnson, the Bank of Charleston became the only antebellum South Carolina bank to revive itself during Reconstruction. After stockholders approved the conversion to a national charter, the bank reopened its Broad Street office in 1872; and even though its national charter prohibited branch banking, it remained a strong presence in the industry for decades.

In 1914, as Europe became embroiled in war, the Bank of Charleston joined the newly formed Federal Reserve System, designed to stabilize the national banking system. In 1922, the Comptroller of the Currency authorized two branch banks, allowing for greater volume of accounts for small businesses and individuals, and paving the way for further expansion.

The bank's development reached a new plateau in 1926, when its twelfth president, Robert S. Small, oversaw the consolidation of the Carolina National Bank of Columbia and the Norwood National Bank of Greenville with the Bank of Charleston to form The South Carolina National Bank. By the early 1930s, The South Carolina National Bank was present in 19 cities and communities across the state and provided a broad range of services.

From World War I to the 1980s, The South Carolina National Bank, The First National Bank of Atlanta, and Wachovia Bank and Trust Company responded to industry-wide trends in ways that would influence their eventual alliance. As the banking industry grew at unprecedented rate, one major problem faced by all banks—including Wachovia's ancestors—was that of currency control. The result was a boom-and-bust trend: panics in 1837, 1873, 1893, 1903, 1907, for example, undermined credit stability and set both banks and their clients on edge—if not in the red.

In 1912, Congressman Carter Glass proposed a system to improve mobility of bank reserves and provide a standard for controlling checking deposits. On December 24, 1913, the Federal Reserve Act was signed into law. Creating a system of regional Federal Reserve Banks, the law required all national banks to become members and keep a portion of their reserves on deposit in a Federal Reserve branch. State banks were given the option of joining the system. Incentives were introduced to entice national banks into keeping their federal charters: banks holding such charters were permitted, for the first time, to offer trust services, real estate loans, and mortgage loans. Passage of the McFadden Act of 1927 further empowered existing banks to engage in intrastate branch banking.

After the Great Depression mandated a national bank holiday that forced all banks to close, the federal government outlined new standards to assess the readiness of banks to reopen. Wachovia Bank and The First National Bank of Atlanta were among the first banks to pass the test. Shortly thereafter, the Banking Act of 1933 established more permanent controls. Strict federal insurance of deposits became the rule, and state-chartered banks were strongly encouraged to participate. Moreover, commercial banking was separated from most securities underwriting and trading, an area that was thereafter regulated by the new Securities and Exchange Commission.

Just as the effects of the Depression began to subside, World War II began, launching Wachovia's precursors into an all-out campaign to help finance the Treasury Department by selling defense bonds and providing other financial services. Wachovia, The First National Bank of Atlanta, and SCN all helped finance the war effort.

The postwar era saw a surge in economic growth, spurring new and expanded bank services. New term installment loans replaced the more volatile "call-loan" approach. No longer permitted to underwrite stocks or bonds of private enterprise, banks joined a massive "T-loan" program to implement corporate lending. And a sweeping Social Security system introduced in the 1930s began manifesting itself in the growing number of retirement and pension plans, many of which were funded by trust institutions and the trust departments of banks. Wachovia

and SCN offered new financial services to accommodate these changes.

With the advent of heightened competition in the 1960s, banks introduced more flexible financial products and services. More and more savings were flowing out of banks and into other institutions—so-called nonbank banks—that were not controlled by such restrictions as interest-rate ceilings or reserve requirements. To compete with these investment firms, insurance companies, and retailers with financial subsidiaries, banks called for regulatory reform. After 1962, interest rate ceilings were slightly relaxed, giving banks a bit more competitive ground, especially with the development of such products as negotiable certificates of deposit and variable-rate mortgages linking rates on loans to the prime rate, reserve-free foreign investments, and Eurodollar investing. The First National Bank of Atlanta, SCN and Wachovia Bank—like many others—established formal international departments in the 1960s.

Banks also found other creative solutions to existing regulations. The Bank Holding Company Act of 1956, for example, prohibited bank holding companies from expanding across state lines. However, that provision did not apply to holding companies with only one bank, and, consequently, many commercial banks established themselves as subsidiaries of "one-bank holding companies." Not surprisingly, Wachovia's three relatives established their own holding companies: The Wachovia Corporation in 1968; First National Holding Corporation in 1969; and South Carolina National Corporation in 1972.

The 1970s were marked by further bank deregulation, permitting greater diversification in the industry. In 1970, an amendment to the Bank Holding Company Act permitted bank holding companies to engage in a far wider range of banking-related businesses. Diversification became the order of the day. First Atlanta established an overseas office in London and, at home, capitalized on new statewide banking privileges to acquire 13 banks across Georgia. In the 1970s, Wachovia introduced its Personal Banker program to augment retail customer banking using computerized account management and in 1980 forged ahead in its introduction of adjustable mortgages. SCN's Common Trust Fund reflected a new rise in trust services, also carried out by Wachovia's master trust service and First Atlanta's Timberland Fund.

Nevertheless, overall economic malaise in the United States strained financial markets. Factors such as inflation and foreign oil dependency—culminating in the Arab oil embargoes of 1973 and 1978—prompted Congress to consider revisions of federal fiscal policy. Wachovia's conservative policies—such as high loan loss reserves and low loan-to-deposit ratios—helped the bank weather the recession almost unscathed, while its largest competitor in the Southeast, NCNB Corp., suffered significant losses. "We are going back to a more purist view of banking," CEO John G. Medlin Jr. told *Business Week* magazine on November 1, 1976.

Legislation passed in 1980 continued the trend toward bank deregulation. That year, the Financial Institutions Deregulation and Monetary Control Act lifted interest-rate ceilings on savings accounts linked to transaction accounts, phasing out regulation and interest-rate ceilings within two years. Banks were thus better able to compete head-on with the likes of money market mutual funds.

Bank holding companies gained still greater freedom to compete more equitably with the U.S. Supreme Court passage, in June 1985, of legislation upholding their right to reciprocal interstate banking. Within days of the court ruling, leading financial institutions moved to realize the mutual benefits of a new era in banking. Wachovia Corporation merged with First Atlantic on December 5, 1985, and on December 6, 1991, they were joined by SCN.

A concerted effort was made to establish a joint identity for the growing holding company. On May 31, 1994, SCN began operating as Wachovia Bank of South Carolina. A campaign of advertisements and celebrations heralded the common name, embodied by the blue Wachovia sign and logo. The program to adopt a unifying corporate identity—which had begun in 1990—was completed in just under four years.

Much of Wachovia's success could be attributed to the corporation's use of technology to connect its widespread network of members and to provide new, sophisticated services. As early as the 1970s, automated teller machines provided 24-hour-a-day account information and cash. Tape-driven computers were eventually replaced by electronic machines capable of unprecedented processing power.

By the 1980s and 1990s, new technologies helped Wachovia achieve a whole new level of information management and service delivery. First Atlanta and Wachovia were early leaders in highly automated lockbox centers to process receivables and provide cash management services to corporations. SCN helped pioneer debit card electronic transaction banking, while First Atlanta contributed to anti-fraud systems designed for merchants using VISA or MasterCard. In tandem with state-of-the-art operational centers to coordinate general operations across all three states, Wachovia collaborated with the Federal Reserve to develop date encryption systems to maximize transmission security. In addition, from 1991 to 1993, Wachovia spent more than $3 million on computer-aided software engineering, known as CASE, to set the groundwork for a competitive edge in the design and maintenance of new banking products. "If CASE delivers even a fraction of what we feel comfortable it will do," Walter E. Leonard Jr., president of Wachovia Operational Services Inc., told the *American Banker* on July 6, 1993, "this is a very important thing for us over the long haul."

On January 1, 1994, L.M. Baker, Jr., stepped up as CEO of Wachovia, succeeding John G. Medlin, Jr., who remained the board's chairperson. Along with Baker, a new management team set ambitious goals for the corporation's transition into the twenty-first century. Following an industry trend toward increased centralization, Wachovia Corp. created a General Banking Division to manage retail and home-market commercial operations across its three states. The new division was headed by G. Joseph Prendergast. "All we've done here is taken the three banks and put me in the position of trying to facilitate the coordination of an agenda," Mr. Prendergast told the *American Banker* on November 14, 1994. That agenda included a number of measures, including scaling back the branch networks in all

three states, consolidating Wachovia's back office, and automating processes for greater efficiency.

Indeed, efficiency was a key factor for a corporation that had grown out of a myriad of banks to become one of the Southeast's largest financial institutions in the 1990s. One risk of consolidation and closing branches would be a loss of customers to competitors. The proper implementation of technological systems, on the other hand, could enable the corporation to reach a far wider client base with fewer conventional branches. In this regard, Wachovia's aggressive investment in CASE technology could pay off handsomely in the long term. Still, Wachovia's complexity remained somewhat daunting. In the *Winston-Salem Journal* of March 21, 1994, Mr. Baker summarized a jocular exchange with his recent predecessor: "John Medlin came in the other day and said, 'How are things going,' and I said, 'I haven't the slightest idea. . . .'" As the leader of one of the world's most reputable banks, Baker epitomized the sort of humor derived from deep-set confidence, yet at the same time acknowledged uncertainty in a volatile and quickly changing industry.

While its rivals were making headlines with major acquisitions, Wachovia had taken a different approach to remaining competitive during the mid-1990s. Its last major purchase being that of SCN in 1991, Wachovia held firm to its belief that consistent, solid, and reputable services were key to survival. The company was eventually forced, however, to begin making acquisitions as consolidation continued. The bank began to build an international presence by forming partnerships with London-based HSBC Holdings plc and Bank Mendes Gans from Amersterdam. In 1997, the firm made its first global acquisition by purchasing Banco Portugues do Atlantico-Brazil S.A. A 1997 *American Banker* article explained the company's strategy as a company executive commented that "what's very clear is that international capabilities and global services will be a key determinant of a bank's ability to maintain and develop large corporate relationships. Clients want to do business with a smaller number of people with a broader array of services."

Wachovia also acquired Virginia-based Jefferson Bankshares Inc. for $542 million and Central Fidelity Banks Inc. for $2.3 billion in 1997. Both deals brought Wachovia leadership in the Virginia market with 335 branches and $9.9 billion in deposits. The purchases continued into the late 1990s and included Florida-based Ameribank Bancshare Inc., Interstate Johnson Lane Inc., OFFITBANK Holdings Inc., and Berry, Evans, Josephs & Snipes Inc. The company's buying spree appeared to have paid off—Wachovia's revenues increased 10 percent in 1997 and 15 percent in 1998.

Wachovia entered the new millennium intent on growth. Acquisitions for 2000 included the credit card business of Partners First Holdings LLC, Atlanta-based B C Bankshares Inc., Florida-based Commerce National Corporation, and DavisBaldwin Inc. of Tampa, Florida. The company began to experience problems, however, when loan losses peaked and the U.S. economy faltered. As a result, profits and stock price fell dramatically for the firm. As such, Wachovia was forced to sell off certain assets. Unable to compete among the larger banks formed from the recent bank mega-mergers, it agreed to be acquired by longtime competitor First Union in 2001.

Wachovia-First Union Merger: 2001

In April 2001, First Union made its $14 billion bid for Wachovia. At the time, First Union was facing possible takeover threats and Wachovia's profits were tumbling. As both companies suffered, they eyed the benefits of merging. For Wachovia, a purchase by First Union meant its name would stay intact, and it would have seats on half of the board. That held much weight with the bank, a company known for its rich history and proud heritage. For First Union, an acquisition would bolster its assets to $329 billion, making it a much less attainable takeover target, and position it as the fourth-largest bank in the United States behind Citigroup Inc., J.P. Morgan Chase & Co., and Bank of America Corp.—all of whom were involved in mega-merger activity.

The bid for Wachovia however, was met with opposition from Sun Trust Banks Inc. Sun Trust had originally approached Wachovia in December 2000 about a possible merger. The proposal had failed, but Sun Trust had held onto hope that talks would eventually resume. After First Union made its move in April, Sun Trust launched a $30 million proxy battle in May in an attempt to persuade Wachovia shareholders to reject the First Union bid. All three companies became embroiled in a very public battle that included lawsuits, rival merger applications, and advertising in newspapers, radio, and television that both First Union and Sun Trust used to try to gain shareholder approval. All in all, Wachovia and First Union spent nearly $75 million to fend off Sun Trust. Sun Trust's efforts proved fruitless, and on July 31, First Union shareholders approved the deal. On August 3, Wachovia shareholders followed suit, and the merger was finalized in September 2001. Thompson was named president and CEO, and Baker held the chairmanship.

The merged company kept the Wachovia name and became the largest financial holding company along the East Coast with 19 million customers. While the integrated company reported a third-quarter loss, it posted a 2000 fourth-quarter profit of $730 million. As results of the merger looked favorable, the new Wachovia had yet to prove it would be the success both Thompson and Baker touted it to be. In an investor conference, Thompson described the firm as "on track, on time, and on budget."

Principal Subsidiaries

Wachovia Bank N.A.; Wachovia Securities Inc.; The First National Bank of Atlanta; OFFITBANK; ABCA, Inc.; Capital Finance Group Inc.; Corestates Holdings Inc.; Everen Capital Corp.; First Union Securities Inc.; First American Service Corp.; First Union Commercial Corp.; First Union Community Development Corp.; First Union Development Corp.; First Union FPS Inc.; First Union Genesis Holdings Inc.; First Union Insurance Services Inc.; First Union Investors Inc.; First Union Life Insurance Company; First Union Mortgage Corp.; First Union National Bank; First Union National Bank of Delaware; First Union Private Capital Inc.; First Union Services Inc.

Principal Competitors

Bank of America Corp.; Citigroup Inc.; Sun Trust Banks Inc.; J.P. Morgan Chase & Co.

Further Reading

"Caution Works At Wachovia," *Business Week*, November 1, 1976, p. 57.

Cline, Kenneth, "Q and A: Wachovia's Medlin: Buying Branches May Mean Investing in Obsolescence," *American Banker*, September 2, 1993, p. 5.

——, "The Back Office: Systems Development—Wachovia Puts Its Money on Automated Software Development," *American Banker*, July 6, 1993, p. 12A.

——, "Wachovia Creates General Banking Division," *American Banker*, November 14, 1994, p. 5.

Cope, Debra, "Wachovia Launching a Fund that Invests in Forests," *American Banker*, April 14, 1994, p. 20.

"Don't Give Up on the Old Wachovia," *US Banker*, May 2001, p. 12.

Epper, Karen, "Wachovia Deploys New Software to Automate Its Indirect Lending," *American Banker*, May 10, 1994, p. 14.

A History of Banking and Wachovia, A Course Well Charted, Winston-Salem: Wachovia Corp., 1994.

Hochstein, Marc, "New First Union Says Its Appetite Is Curbed," *American Banker*, June 27, 2000, p. 1.

Holliday, Karen, "Staying Power, but Too Staid?," *US Banker*, May 1997, p. 51.

Kraus, James R., "Wachovia, Buying Brazil Bank," *American Banker*, January 9, 1997, p. 8.

Milligan, Jack, "Thompson On a Short Rope," *US Banker*, March 2001, p. 34.

Moore, Pamela, "Wachovia's New CEO is a Man of Many Interests," *Winston-Salem Journal*, March 21, 1994, p. 13.

"Review 2001: This Summer's Cliffhanger: the Battle for Wachovia," *American Banker*, December 26, 2001, p. 4.

Rogoski, Richard R., "Merger Media Blitz Turned into Negative Political-Style Ads," *Business First-Columbus*, August 31, 2001, p. B8.

Svare, Christopher J., "Entry into South Carolina Strengthens Wachovia's Base," *The Magazine of Bank Management* January 1992, p. 16.

Talley, Karen, "Wachovia Called Solid Bet," *American Banker*, April 8, 1999, p. 28.

Tully, Shawn, "First Union Buys Retail—And Pays the Price," *Fortune*, June 21, 1999, p. 43.

"Wachovia-Ameribank Merger Is Complete," *American Banker*, April 3, 1998, p. 22.

"Wachovia Announces Major Cash Management Technology Investment," *Business Wire*, December 3, 1992.

"Wachovia Paying $2.3B for Central Fidelity of Va.," *American Banker*, June 25 1997, p. 1.

Zack, Jeffrey, "Seems Like a Seamless Transition at Wachovia," *American Banker*, January 9, 1995, p. 8A.

—Wendy Johnson Bilas and Kerstan Cohen
—update: Christina M. Stansell

WARNACO

The Warnaco Group Inc.

90 Park Avenue
New York, New York 10016
U.S.A.
Telephone: (212) 661-1300
Fax: (212) 687-0480
Web site: http://www.warnaco.com

Public Company
Incorporated: 1874
Employees: 21,440
Sales: $2.25 billion (2000)
Stock Exchanges: New York (Delisted 2001)
NAIC: 315212 Women's, Girls', and Infants' Cut and
Sew Apparel Contractors; 315231 Women's and
Girls' Cut and Sew Lingerie, Loungewear, and
Nightwear Manufacturing

The Warnaco Group Inc. is a major international apparel company operating out of New York City. Along with its subsidiaries, the company designs, manufactures, and markets women's intimate apparel, women's and junior's apparel, men's apparel, and swim accessories and fitness apparel. It has licensing deals with such prominent brands as Calvin Klein, Fruit of the Loom, and Chaps by Ralph Lauren. A subsidiary, Authentic Fitness, is the North American distributor of Speedo swimwear. In 1994, Warnaco distinguished itself as the only Fortune 500 industrial company with a female chief executive, Linda Wachner. After several successful years, she would be ousted in 2001, leaving the company saddled with debt, operating under bankruptcy protection, and in the shadow of an Securities and Exchange Commission (SEC) investigation.

Warnaco's Origins: 1874

Brothers DeVer and Lucien Warner started what would become Warnaco in 1874. Both men had been trained as doctors, but each also had an entrepreneurial bent, as evidenced by their ventures ranging from traveling medical lecture series to snake-oil remedies. Among the latter was ''Warner's Safe Kidney and Liver Cure,'' a bottled formula prescribed for urinary disorders and malaria, among other afflictions. Another of the brothers' projects was a replacement for the corset, which they felt was hazardous to women's health. They had devised a less constricting ''waist pattern'' in the 1860s, but it did little to shape women's waists. In 1874, though, DeVer invented an improved version that sported shoulder straps. Manufactured samples were met with enthusiasm in New York. The brothers quit their other jobs and, with $2,550 in start-up capital, began selling their ''Dr. Warner's Health Corset. Problems were numerous during the start-up phase. A competing manufacturer threatened to sue the Warner's for copying its design, and the brothers were forced to change the original name of their corset (Dr. Warner's Sanitary Corset) because somebody else already owned the name. Understandably, they also suffered from a dearth of pattern-making experience. While DeVer learned the necessary pattern-making skills, Lucien used his contacts in New York City to begin developing distribution channels for their corset. Lucien's wife, Karen, pitched in and the three labored in Lucien's home. Once they got the operation up-and-running, sales were swift. They moved the company out of the Warner residence in 1875, and by 1876 had already outgrown their small manufacturing plant in McGraw, New York.

As word of Warner's comfortable corset spread, sales soared at an astonishing rate. In 1876, the Warner's moved to Bridgeport, where they built a four-story factory. They continued to redesign and improve their corsets with considerable success. They even introduced new products like an innovative folding bustle (used to support the rear of a dress). Particularly successful was the Coraline Corset line, which was manufactured in part with Tampico grass imported from Mexico. In 1883, in fact, *Harper's Bazaar* identified the four most popular corsets in the U.S. as Warner corsets, three of which were Coralines. The incredible success of the Coraline and other Warner designs made both brothers millionaires by the early 1880s. By the mid-1880s, the Warners employed more than 1,500 workers, most of whom were immigrant women or poor New England farm girls. During the remainder of the late 1880s, Warner Brothers, as the company was called, continued to flourish. The brothers introduced a steady stream of designs, usually based on European fashions, and began importing products from England

Key Dates:

1874: Brothers DeVer and Lucien Warner found the company.
1894: The Warners' business is incorporated.
1915: The bra is patented.
1968: The company changes its name to Warnaco.
1986: Linda Wachner gains control of company in hostile takeover.
1991: The company goes public.
1996: Annual revenues top $1 billion.
2001: Warnaco declares bankruptcy; Wachner resigns.

for resale. Some ideas languished. Failed efforts included wool underwear, a chemical business, a Florida orange grove operation, and an attempt to manufacture baseballs.

The corset company constantly prospered and both brothers amassed considerable wealth. Besides building opulent homes for themselves and their families, they heaped their fortunes on a number of beneficiaries. For instance, they established the Seaside Institute, a type of boarding house for poor women that served meals at cost and offered a reading and music room, among other amenities. Lucien also donated large sums to his alma mater, Oberlin College. By the end of the century the Warner brothers had effectively retired from the day-to-day operations of the company. DeVer married a 26-year-old woman after his wife died in 1895. He then purchased a succession of yachts that he sailed up and down the East Coast. DeVer wintered in Augusta, Georgia, where he established a strong friendship with John D. Rockefeller. Lucien, a frequent White House guest who cultivated friendships with Presidents Cleveland, Taft, Harrison, and Roosevelt, became a world traveler after his secession from the business, vacationing in China, Japan, New Zealand, Egypt, and elsewhere throughout the world.

Company Incorporated in 1894

With its originators no longer active in the company, Warner Brothers was legally changed from a partnership to a corporation in 1894. DeVer's son, D.H., took control of the company around that time. D.H. differed from his father and uncle in that he had little formal education. He started working at the company in 1887 when he was 19 years old and worked as an apprentice in every department in preparation for his father's departure. Despite his lack of education, D.H. was a savvy businessman with multiple talents and a flair for leadership. As a young man, he had been an amateur boxer, flute player, and yachtsman, among other credits. By the time he took over Warner Brothers, he was also acting as the president or director of several other concerns, including the Bridgeport National Bank, a gas company, and a department store. When he finally focused his intensity on Warner, the company profited handsomely.

Between 1894 and 1913, Warner's sales vaulted more than three-fold to $7 million and profits averaged $700,000 annually. The gains were largely the result of ongoing innovation. Warner introduced rust-proof steel boning as a replacement for more

expensive whalebone in corsets, and introduced a successful corset that doubled as a hose supporter. The latter innovation is recognized as an important evolutionary step in the development of the brassiere in the 1910s. Indeed, Mary Phelps Jacob patented the bra in 1915, and shortly thereafter sold the invention to Warner. The purchase of the bra proved to be an excellent move at the time, and during the late 1910s Warner achieved steady sales and profit growth, with revenues hitting $12.6 million in 1920.

Contributing to the success of the company during the early 1900s was Lucien's son, L.T. He was very different from D.H. in both background and personality. The two often clashed, but their skills were complementary and their combined efforts were ultimately beneficial to the company. The Warners' fortunes began to change, however, after 1920. Corsets quickly fell out of fashion early in the decade and were replaced with the "wraparound." The company scrambled to adapt its products with only tepid success. Throughout the Roaring Twenties, Warner's performance waned. Sales fell to a pitiful $2.5 million by the end of the decade. During the Great Depression, moreover, Warner began to lose money. By 1932, its balance sheet was bleeding more than $1 million in red ink.

Augmenting the company's downfall was the personal deterioration of D.H. Although an energetic businessman and leader as a young man, D.H. was a dissolute womanizer throughout his adult life. His decline hastened after his wife died in 1931. He continued to spend lavishly and drink to excess before his death in 1934 at the age of 66. D.H.'s son-in-law, John Field, became the new chief executive and L.T. became chairman of the board. A Yale graduate, Field had worked with D.H. and L.T. at Warner for several years. Under Field's control, Warner tightened its belt and revamped its product line during the 1930s, barely escaping bankruptcy. Vital to Warner's survival were inventions like the "Two-Way-One-Way" girdle, an elastic undergarment that wrapped around the body and flattened the hips yet still allowed full body movement.

By the early 1940s, Warner's sales had surged back up to about $4 million, approximately $300,000 of which was retained as profit. The lean war years were followed by solid growth as the U.S. economy boomed. Warner's revenues topped $12 million and profits roared back to $1 million by 1947. John Field's son, John Jr., joined the company and was placed in charge of advertising, among other duties. Warner continued to prosper during the 1950s by selling its popular Warner brand lines of bras, girdles, and "corselettes." Sales rocketed to more than $25 million by 1956, growing at more than three times the industry average. Beginning in the mid-1950s, though, Warner Brothers lost focus and became too unwieldy. Frustrated by his 73-year-old father's authoritative, non-progressive management style, John Field, Jr., wrested control of the company from the elder Field by persuading the board of directors to oust him.

New managers worked to whip Warner Brothers into shape during the late 1950s. In addition to restructuring, they grew the company at a rapid rate by diversifying, acquiring other companies, and expanding distribution channels. Specifically, Warner broadened its product lines to include menswear and accessories, and both men's and women's sportswear. It expanded distribution by selling through large chain stores like Sears and

J.C. Penney, and by opening production facilities in Europe and South America. Importantly, Warner purchased C.F. Hathaway Company, America's oldest shirt manufacturer, and Lady Hathaway, a well-known women's sportswear division. That buyout instantly made Warner a major player in those respective industries. Warner went public in 1961, and by the early 1960s was generating annual revenues in the $100 million range.

During the 1960s, Warner Brothers continued to grow through acquisition and merger. It purchased the popular Puritan and Thane brands in 1964, and then bought out White Stag, a casual sportswear maker. Sales increased to an impressive $185 million in 1968, and profits reached an all-time high of $77 million, reflecting annual growth since 1960 of more than 25 percent. By the late 1960s, the company had unarguably become a leader in the U.S. apparel industry.

In the early 1970s, the company stepped up its rampant expansion strategy. In an effort to keep up with rapidly changing fashions during this period, Warner tried to assemble a diverse group of holdings that would allow it to capitalize on consumer whims as they emerged. Brands accumulated in the 1970s included Speedo, Playmore, Rosanna, Jerry Silverman, and High Tide. Warner also branched into retail stores and launched a more aggressive international agenda.

Mid-1970s Missteps

The company had changed its name to Warnaco in 1968 and in 1974 celebrated its 100th anniversary with record sales and profits. By the mid-1970s, though, the company had again grown unwieldy, ballooning into a diversified, international apparel conglomerate with nearly 20 divisions. The aggressive diversification strategy had made Warnaco a big player, but was failing to generate profit growth. In fact, Warnaco's profitability began to slip in the mid-1970s. During 1975 and 1976, the company experienced severe stress as a result of various mishaps. Warnaco's entry into the leisure suit business, for example, brought crushing losses when that short-lived style faded. Its retail store division also suffered, contributing to hefty losses. Distressed by Warnaco's mounting difficulties, Field offered to allow a new, fresh management team to pick up the ball and carry Warnaco into the 1980s.

Warnaco's board brought in two outside managers—Philip Lamoureux and James Walker—to work with Field and eventually assume leadership of the company. They immediately clashed with Field, assuming control of day-to-day operations, but then edging him out of the decision-making process. The situation deteriorated to the point where Field, like his father, had to be forced out of his leadership role. Warnaco's balance sheet improved significantly under the new management. Walker and Lamoureux jettisoned several of Warnaco's non-performing units, restructured management, and labored to improve the profitability of its successful core apparel lines. Profits soon recovered to record levels during the late 1970s. Even during the recession of the early 1980s, Warnaco's sales and profits boomed.

After successfully reviving the embattled Warnaco, Lamoureux left Warnaco in 1982. The following year, Walker died unexpectedly from a kidney-related virus. The company itself, however, remained healthy to all appearances, and in 1983 hit a record net income of $28.3 million. Furthermore, the company's balance sheet was strong, with relatively little debt and a vigorous cash flow. But Warnaco's balance sheet failed to reflect some underlying problems. During the late 1970s and early 1980s, the company had reduced spending on research and development and cut back on its marketing efforts. These moves reduced costs but boded poorly for Warnaco's long-term growth. In 1984, the company's profits again started to slide. Performance continued to slip into the mid-1980s, despite the purchase of the successful Olga Co. in 1984. Warnaco began to review its alternatives.

Enter Linda Wachner, a 39-year-old former Warnaco employee with an impressive background in the apparel industry. Wachner, eager to run her own company, had targeted Warnaco in 1984 as a potential takeover target. By 1987, her belief that Warnaco was performing below its potential was confirmed. She joined forces with Los Angeles investor Andrew Galef in a month-long battle for control of the company. Wachner and Galef, through their newly-formed W. Acquisition Corp., won the bid and Wachner stepped in as chief executive in April of 1987, with Galef as chairman. Wachner quickly replaced Warnaco management with her own team and reorganized the company. Her strategy was to streamline the corporation, pay down the debt incurred as a result of the leveraged buyout, and build Warnaco into a dominant force in its key market niches.

Wachner, one of just a few women heading Fortune 500 companies, was a force to be reckoned with. She had known since her childhood in Forest Hills, New York, that she wanted to run something. She came to that conclusion at the age of 11, lying in a full-body cast after undergoing surgery to correct severe scoliosis. Facing the possibility that she may never walk again, she became determined to take charge of whatever she did in her life. "The focus I have today comes from when I was sick," she explained in a June 15, 1992 *Fortune* interview. "When you want to walk again, you learn how to focus on that with all your might, and you don't stop until you do."

Wachner translated her intensity into career success beginning in 1966. She graduated from the University of Buffalo in that year at the age of 20 and went to work in the retail industry with a division of Federated Department Stores. She immediately began telling her superiors how they could improve the operation, earning a reputation as an aggressive business woman. Wachner accepted a position in Warnaco's marketing department in 1974. Within less than a year she was promoted to vice-president. In 1978, she was recruited to head the sagging Max Factor division of Norton Simon, and in two years turned the operation from a $16 million loss to a $5 million profit. Wachner unsuccessfully attempted a leverage buyout of Max Factor in 1984, after which she resigned. She tried to buy Revlon in 1986 before setting her sights on Warnaco.

Warnaco Group, Inc. was a troubled apparel company in the 1990s, but it grew into an industry powerhouse under the leadership of Linda Wachner. Wachner assumed an aggressive stance at Warnaco. She pared the company's 15 divisions down to two main categories: intimate apparel and menswear. She dumped other units, including the large women's apparel and sportswear businesses, and initiated widespread cost-cutting programs. She brought a new customer and cash-flow focus to Warnaco that resulted in significant gains. In addition, she broadened Warnaco's core product lines with new ventures, such as a deal to supply the popular Victoria's Secret retail chain. In 1990, she organized a separate company, Authentic Fitness, to acquire the Speedo swimwear brand from Warnaco for $85 million plus debt, then took on the additional role as CEO of this separate company. She began to build a national chain of Speedo stores, funded by taking Authentic Fitness public in 1992. Wachner also raised capital for Warnaco with a successful public offering in 1991. By 1992, Wachner had slashed the company's burdensome debt load by 40 percent, boosted the company's stock price by a hefty 75 percent, and increased cash flow from $50 million to $90 million annually. To this point in her tenure at Warnaco she was given high marks for turning the company into a rising star of the apparel industry. The only criticism of her performance came from former employees who chafed at her tough, hard-nosed management style.

Few people, however, were able to criticize Warnaco's financial performance during the early 1990s. Despite a recession during much of that time, Warnaco's sales steadily grew from $518 million in 1989 to more than $700 million by 1993. Warnaco experienced losses during the late 1980s, but was netting income of about $50 million by 1992. More importantly, the company had reduced its long-term debt from more than $500 million in the late 1980s to less than $250 million by 1993. Furthermore, the company was positioned for future growth. Warnaco had plowed capital into its important Warner and Olga brands, allowing it to cash in on the growing upscale lingerie market in the mid-1990s. In addition, in 1994 Warnaco purchased the rights to produce Calvin Klein men's underwear, following by Calvin Klein's women's underwear a year later, and North American rights for Calvin Klein jeans in 1998. To widen its channels of distribution, the company also acquired well-known labels for sale to the discount chains. In the early 1990s, Warnaco launched a line of bras under the Fruit of the Loom label for such mass merchants as Kmart and Wal-Mart, followed by a distribution agreement with Avon Products. In 1994, Warnaco acquired the Van Raalte label for apparel sold to Sears Roebuck.

Wachner was especially aggressive in 1996, completing three major acquisitions: GJM Group, Hong Kong maker of private label sleepwear; Body Slimmers Inc., makers of shapewear; and Lejaby-Euralis, French manufacturer of bras and swimwear. She also sold off the Hathaway men's shirt business, which had been underperforming. Although Warnaco surpassed the $1 billion mark in annual revenues in 1996, it posted a $8 million loss, due in large part to costs associated with the Hathaway sale and a restructuring effort.

The success of Warnaco under Wachner reached a high-water mark in 1998, when the price of the company's stock topped $44. By the middle of the year, however, Warnaco began to lose its footing, as demand for its products fell and the company began to take on excessive debt, much of which was incurred in order to buy back stock that had peaked in value. The situation was aggravated in 1999, when Warnaco brought Authentic Fitness, which had been previously sold off, back into the fold at a cost of $600 million. Critics charged that while the deal added greatly to Wachner personal wealth, it hurt Warnaco's balance sheet, a transaction that *Time* magazine characterized as "financial gymnastics."

Wachner had benefited from positive press coverage in her early years at the helm, resulting in a celebrity and social standing that she put to good use in building Warnaco. The Fruit of the Loom deal was reportedly struck on the ski slopes of Aspen, and the Calvin Klein men's underwear agreement was broached at dinner in the Hamptons. Now Wachner was becoming increasingly the subject of severe press criticism, much of which centered on an abrasive personality and a hefty compensation package. Her board was also attacked as being weak, its members too dependent on Wachner's social connections that helped them to land other lucrative board positions. A public relations nightmare would ensue in 2000, when designer Calvin Klein sued Warnaco and publicly declared that Wachner was a "cancer" on his label. At the heart of the matter was his contention that Warnaco was violating its licensing agreement by selling Calvin Klein jeans to warehouse clubs like Costco and Sam's Club, thereby undercutting the value of the brand. In general, Warnaco was accused of dumping product in order to boost sales and make financial targets.

Although Klein and Warnaco settled its differences in January 2001, shortly before the matter was to go to trial, Warnaco was already in deep financial trouble in the spring of 2001. Despite generating revenues of nearly $2.25 billion in 2000, the company lost $344.2 million. As a result, the price of the company's stock began to plummet. By June 2001, Warnaco was forced to declare bankruptcy, and was soon forced to restate its number for the previous three years. The company entered the autumn of 2001 under the cloud of an SEC investigation and a stock price that continued to drop until it was worth just pennies, resulting in Warnaco being removed from the ranks of the Fortune 500 and ultimately delisted from the New York Stock Exchange.

On November 16, 2001, Wachner was ousted as chairman of Warnaco's board, then resigned as chief executive. Antonio C. Alvarez, Jr., brought in months earlier to serve as the company's chief restructuring officer, was appointed the new CEO. With the company burdened by nearly $2.5 billion in debt, he immediately announced an intention to sell off a number of assets, and possibly the entire company. Whatever actions that were taken to deliver the business from bankruptcy, it was clear that Warnaco was about to begin an entirely new, and uncertain, chapter in its corporate history.

Principal Subsidiaries

Calvin Klein Jeanswear Company Inc.; The Bra Company Limited; Warnaco Inc.; Warnaco International Inc.

Principal Competitors

Benetton; Danskin; Donna Karan; Jockey International; Liz Claiborne; Maidenform; NIKE; Nautica Enterprises; Tommy Hilfiger.

Further Reading

Agins, Teri, and Erin White, "Saddled by Debt, Clothing Maker Warnaco Seeks Bankruptcy Protection," *Wall Street Journal*, June 12, 2001, p. B1.

Cainiti, Susan, "America's Most Successful Businesswoman," *Fortune*, June 15, 1992, p. 102.

Donlon, J.P., "Queen of Cash Flow," *Chief Executive,* January/February 1994, p. 38.

Field, John W., *Fig Leaves and Fortunes: A Fashion Company Named Warnaco,* West Kennebunk, Maine: Phoenix Publishing, 1990.

Furman, Phyllis, "Refocusing Warnaco Paying Off for Wachner," *Crain's New York Business,* November 21, 1994, p. 51.

Govoni, Steve, "Garment Centered," *Financial World,* June 10, 1986, p. 8.

Jaffe, Thomas, "What's in a Label," *Forbes,* September 24, 1984, p. 238.

Kaufman, Leslie, "Calvin Klein Suit Against Warnaco Is Settled," *New York Times,* January 23, 2001.

"After 15 Years, Executive's Short Goodbye," *New York Times,* November 17, 2001, p. A1.

Lunzer, Francesca, "Big Shoes to Fill," *Forbes,* December 5, 1983, p. 264.

Monget, Karyn and Ricki M. Young, "As Linda Exits Warnaco, VF, PVH Lead Suitors For Brands," *WWD,* November 19, 2001, p. 1.

Taylor, Alex, "New Outfit for a Queen of Beauty: Linda Wachner," *Fortune,* January 5, 1987, p. 56.

—Dave Mote
—update: Ed Dinger

Waste Connections, Inc.

620 Coolidge Drive, Suite 350
Folsom, California 9563
U.S.A.
Telephone: (916) 608-8200
Fax: (916) 351-0249
Web site: http://www.wasteconnections.com

Public Company
Incorporated: 1997
Employees: 2,010
Sales: $304.4 million (2000)
Stock Exchanges: NASDAQ
Ticker Symbol: WCNX
NAIC: 56211 Waste Collection

Waste Connections, Inc. is the fourth-largest, publicly-held solid waste services company in the United States. The company provides solid waste collection, transfer, disposal, and recycling services in 15 states west of the Mississippi River, serving more than 700,000 commercial, industrial, and residential customers in suburban and rural communities. Waste Connections owns and operates 64 collection operations, 21 transfer stations, 14 landfills, and 16 recycling facilities. Additionally, the company manages, but does not own, another nine transfer stations and six landfills.

Founder's Background

Not long after its formation, Waste Connections earned the reputation as a fast-growing company destined for national prominence, a fitting description for a company founded by a young, fast-rising executive headed for national recognition himself. Ron J. Mittelstaedt, the architect of Waste Connections' formation, achieved success in the corporate world at a young age, enjoying the power and the responsibilities typically conferred upon someone ten years his senior. A graduate of the University of California at Santa Barbara, where he earned a bachelor of science degree in economics at the age of 20, Mittelstaedt joined the transportation industry after completing his studies. He spent roughly three years working for Airborne Express in New York City, before being selected to manage the company's operations in San Francisco. Mittelstaedt's promotion brought him into contact, for the first time, with the waste disposal industry.

While working in operations management in San Francisco, Mittelstaedt was approached by an executive recruiter. Browning-Ferris Industries, Inc., a massive waste disposal firm on a never-ending acquisition spree, was looking outside the waste disposal industry for someone to manage some of the companies it had purchased. Specifically, Browning-Ferris needed an executive skilled in managing transportation logistics, and the then 24-year-old Mittelstaedt stood out among the list of candidates. An offer was made to Mittelstaedt, offering him a post in Tucson, Arizona, but he declined, not wanting to relocate to that area. Browning-Ferris was not to be denied the services of the youthful Mittelstaedt, however. Three months after Mittelstaedt refused the company's offer, Browning-Ferris came back with another offer; a similar position, but this time in Sacramento. Mittelstaedt accepted the job offer, and entered an industry in which he would exert considerable influence.

Mittelstaedt was hired as a sales manager at Browning-Ferris, charged with overseeing the company's commercial and industrial selling activity in the Sacramento Valley. By the time he was 26 years old—two years after joining Browning-Ferris—Mittelstaedt earned a promotion, becoming general manager of the company's operations in the Sacramento area. He spent roughly another four years working for the industry giant, learning the Browning-Ferris approach to growth within the waste disposal industry. The lessons he learned during his tenure would be put to use roughly a decade later, forming the strategic basis for Waste Connections' prolific growth.

Browning-Ferris was the product of a Houston accountant's perspective on an industry set to undergo sweeping change. Tom Fatjo, Jr., who kept financial records for a number of garbage collectors in Houston, foresaw the effect looming federal legislation would have on a highly-fragmented industry populated by thousands of small, independent garbage collection companies. During the 1960s, the U.S. Congress mandated that garbage collection trucks meet higher standards of sanitation. Further, legislation stipulated that, owing to concerns

Company Perspectives:

Our growth is being accomplished by aggressively acquiring selected companies in high growth markets and enhancing their operations through the introduction of modernized fleets, technology, management support, and the capital that comes from being part of a publicly traded company. We look to grow rapidly within a market through expanding the range of services we offer and by helping our local managers to continue the success they have built locally by expanding into adjacent regions. As we grow, whether by acquisition or by internal growth, we seek to constantly upgrade our level of customer service. At the same time we look to retain the local name and goodwill associated with the companies and the entrepreneurs who helped to build them.

related to air pollution, the incineration of garbage would give way to landfill burial. For the sundry independent garbage collectors, the new proclamations sounded the death knell of their existence. To comply with the new standards, large capital investments would be needed to establish the garbage business as a modern, sanitary, and technologically competent industry. Most of the small companies were in no position to raise the money needed to survive in the new industry. Accordingly, Fatjo assembled an investment team to take advantage of the opportunity. His company, Browning-Ferris, began acquiring local garbage collection companies at a frenetic pace, devouring hundreds of local operators a year to create a large, integrated, multi-jurisdictional waste disposal company.

Browning-Ferris' aggressive acquisitive activity had not slackened by the time Mittelstaedt joined the firm. When he left Browning-Ferris in 1993, he became part of the great shuffle of waste disposal companies that created industry stalwarts. He joined Sanifill, an upstart company that later merged with other waste disposal operators, eventually joining another industry behemoth, Waste Management, Inc. The change in employers forced Mittelstaedt to move to Chicago, a move he quickly regretted. He resigned and moved back to El Dorado Hills, northeast of Sacramento. Several small public companies in the waste disposal industry approached Mittelstaedt, offering him leadership positions as chief executive officer of their firms, but he declined. In his early 30s at the time, Mittelstaedt had decided to leave the waste disposal industry and to pursue interests in other business areas.

The Late 1990s Birth of Waste Connections

Mittelstaedt's departure from the waste disposal industry was stopped by an enticing bit of information. The source of the news was Browning-Ferris. The ever-expanding company had decided to sell its operations in Idaho and Washington to raise capital. Mittelstaedt heard about the proposed divestiture in July 1997 and quickly decided that he wanted to buy the properties. He submitted a bid in August and assembled a management team to lead the company that would control the Browning-Ferris assets. Mittelstaedt solicited the help of former colleagues at Browning Ferris, as well as several executives who

worked for USA Waste Services. As Waste Connections' leadership was being assembled, Mittelstaedt turned to the task of raising the money needed to make his company a viable corporate entity. He raised $8.5 million in private capital from his business contacts and invested his own money into the concern, ranking as the largest single investor. Next, Mittelstaedt secured a $10 million line of credit from an unnamed bank in Seattle, which was used to pay for the Browning-Ferris assets. Mittelstaedt was in business, selecting Roseville, California, as the home for his new company.

Waste Connections, incorporated on September 9, 1997, commenced operations on October 1, 1997, the day after the Browning-Ferris deal closed. Combined, the operations acquired by Waste Connections, which had been acquired by Browning-Ferris at various times in 1995 and 1996, generated $13.4 million in revenue in 1996. Mittelstaedt and his executive team would add to this total, quickly and considerably, assiduously adhering to an acquisition strategy that constituted the basis of Waste Connections' success.

From its inception, Waste Connections strove to become the dominant company in the secondary, non-urban markets located west of the Mississippi. The company shunned large metropolitan markets, opting instead to build an integrated, clustered presence in the suburban and rural west. Further, waste disposal companies were only considered as acquisition candidates if they controlled a leading market share in their communities, generally needing to rank either first or second in their markets. Waste Connections officials also made sure the acquisition targets had access either to their own landfill or to a municipal dump, thereby avoiding dependence on a local competitor. Lastly, Waste Connections preferred to acquire a company with an exclusive right to operate in its market, either through a franchise agreement, a long-term municipal contract, or a governmental certificate.

Few industry observers chose to argue against Waste Connections' acquisition strategy. The company focused exclusively on the western United States because, compared to the East, the competition was less intense, there were stronger projections for economic growth, and a greater number of number of independent companies suitable for acquisition. Mittelstaedt's decision to operate in rural and suburban markets appeared prudent as well, sheltering the company from the more intense competitive pressures in metropolitan markets and providing a greater opportunity to secure exclusive operating rights within a particular market. In theory, Waste Connections' operating strategy was sound; the company's success, however, would depend on the execution of its strategy. In the years ahead, the diligent selection of acquisition targets and the efficient integration of the acquired companies into the company's fold would determine the success of Mittelstaedt's bid to become an industry giant.

Growth through Acquisition in the Late 1990s

Roughly a half-year after its formation, Mittelstaedt could point to an unruffled start to Waste Connections' rise to dominance. The company had successfully integrated a number of waste disposal firms in Washington, California, Idaho, Wyoming, and South Dakota. Through nine collections operations,

Key Dates:

1997: Ron Mittelstaedt founds company to acquire Browning-Ferris assets.
1998: Waste Connections completes its initial public offering of stock.
1999: Acquisition of International Environmental Industries Inc. makes Waste Connections one of the largest waste disposal companies in the country.

three transfer stations, one landfill, and one recycling facility, the company served approximately 140,000 commercial, industrial, and industrial customers. Such was the stature of the company when Mittelstaedt decided to convert to public ownership. On May 22, 1998, Waste Connections completed its initial public offering (IPO), offering two million shares of common stock at $12 per share. The net proceeds from the IPO were used to reduce the company's debt and to accelerate its expansion program.

The process of selecting acquisition targets, acquiring the companies, and integrating them into the company's existing operations progressed following the IPO. Waste Connections adopted a pace of expansion that averaged nearly 40 acquisitions a year during its first four years of business. In October 1998, the company signed a definitive merger agreement with four waste collection companies in Washington. The companies—Murrey's Disposal Company, Inc.; American Disposal Company, Inc.; D.M. Disposal Co.; and Tacoma Recycling Company, Inc.—were collectively known as The Murrey Companies, generating roughly $33 million in annual revenue and ranking as one of the largest independent companies in the Pacific Northwest. The transaction was completed in January 1999, making Waste Connections one of the largest waste collectors in the suburban Seattle/Tacoma area. The acquisition increased Waste Connections' revenue base by more than 40 percent.

The addition of The Murrey Companies marked the beginning of a prodigious acquisition spree. In 1999, when corporate headquarters were moved to Folsom, California, Waste Connections acquired 51 businesses, including the largest since its inception two years earlier. In August 1999, the company purchased International Environmental Industries Inc. (IEII), an operator of four landfills and three collection operations in markets surrounding El Paso and southern New Mexico. The acquisition made Waste Connections one of the largest hauling and disposal firms in the country, the significance of which was not lost on Mittelstaedt. In an August 12, 1999 interview with *The Sacramento Bee,* he remarked, "It's an enormous milestone. It represents the largest transaction we've ever done in terms of revenues, cash flow, and number of employees." The addition of IEII positioned Waste Connections for continued expansion in Texas, Oklahoma, and New Mexico, with El Paso serving as a regional headquarters.

Although Waste Connections' pace of expansion slowed in 2000, the vitality of the company intensified decidedly. During the year, 25 businesses were acquired, increasing revenues from $184 million to $304 million. Waste Connections' net income, a measure of how successfully the company integrated its new assets, soared, jumping from $9.2 million in 1999 to $28.2 million. Equally as important, the company's esteem among investors was at an all-time high. In 2000, Waste Connections' stock ranked as the top performer in the environmental sector, appreciating 129 percent. After hovering at $9 per share at the end of 1999, the company's stock was trading at $34 per share by August 2001.

At the time of Waste Connections' robust stock valuation, Mittelstaedt presided over a vibrant solid waste empire. Between the company's IPO and August 2001, roughly 135 private businesses were acquired, giving Waste Connections a customer base of nearly 800,000. Four years after its creation, the company ranked as the fourth largest, publicly-owned solid waste company in the United States, larger than the four companies ranking fifth through eighth combined. In the coming years, Waste Connections' strident expansion was expected to continue forward. According to the company's calculations, there were approximately 2,000 private solid waste companies located west of the Mississippi. Mittelstaedt and his team estimated there were roughly 450 companies suitable for inclusion within Waste Connections' operations. The years ahead promised to see the acquisition and integration of these companies into one of the industry's powerhouses.

Principal Subsidiaries

WCI Acquisition Corporation.

Principal Competitors

Waste Management, Inc.; Republic Services, Inc.; Allied Waste Industries, Inc.

Further Reading

Lamb, Celia, "Waste Firm Buys Nine More," *Sacramento Business Journal,* October 13, 2000.
Schmidt, Bob, "Ron Mittelstaedt," *Sacramento Business Journal,* March 3, 2000, p. 29.
Walter, Bob, "Sacramento, Calif.-Area Firm Creates Solid Waste Empire," *Sacramento Bee,* August 17, 2001, p. 14.
"Waste Connections, Inc. and The Murrey Companies Announce Merger Agreement," *PR Newswire,* October 22, 1998, p. 26.
"Waste Connections, Inc. Announces Its Initial Public Offering," *PR Newswire,* May 22, 1998, p. 3.
"Waste Connections Trades Idaho Holdings," *Sacramento Business Journal,* April 21, 2000, p. 3.

—Jeffrey L. Covell

WestLB

Westdeutsche Landesbank Girozentrale

D-40217 Düsseldorf
Herzogstrasse 15
Germany
Telephone: (49) (211) 826-01
Fax: (49) (211) 826-6119
Web site: http://www.westlb.com

State Owned Company
Incorporated: 1969 as Westdeutsche Landesbank
    Girozentrale
Employees: 11,390
Total Assets: EUR 400 billion ($374 billion) (2000)
NAIC: 52211 Commercial Banking

Westdeutsche Landesbank Girozentrale—WestLB for short—is a major force in the German economy and a strong competitor of the Big Three German banks. WestLB is the central bank of West Germany's most populous region, North Rhine-Westphalia, the clearing bank for the *Sparkassen* or savings associations in the states of North Rhine-Westphalia and Brandenburg, and a specialist wholesale bank with offices in 35 countries around the globe. The bank provides a full range of financial services such as project and real estate financing, investment banking, and electronic banking to corporate and public sector clients as well as institutional and private investors. The State of North Rhine-Westphalia owns roughly 43 percent of WestLB. Another combined stake of about 28 percent is held by regional savings associations and municipalities. WestLB's strength is in part the result of its structure—joint ownership between the state government, regional banks, and local authorities—a structure that can be traced to its origins in two seventeenth-century provincial banks.

1832–1969: From Assistance Bank to State Bank

In 1818, the Swedish government stunned Europe by offering 160,000 taler to the German province of Westphalia as reparation for the damages incurred when Swedish and Dutch soldiers marched through the province during the Napoleonic Wars. This money was decreed the property of all Westphalia by its president, Freiherr von Vincke. The funds were used to develop the region's economy and pay for public-works projects, but some formal policies were needed to distribute the money. In 1832, the Westphalian Provinzialbank-Hülfskasse was founded to accomplish this task. The bank was the first *hilfskasse*, or assistance bank, in Prussia and played a pivotal role in developing the region's economic potential throughout the 19th century.

Frederick William IV, the king of Prussia, was impressed by the advantages the *hilfskasse* offered Westphalia and ordered that a similar bank be created in the Rhineland in 1847. Its government, influenced by the economic success of the Aachener Union already in business within the province, founded the Provinzial-Hülfskasse of the Rhineland in 1854.

The two banks were instrumental in making the Rhine-Westphalia region one of the biggest and most productive industrial areas in Europe by the time World War I began. Both banks had become *landesbanks* before the end of 19th century, which greatly increased their range of services, since *hilfskasse* banks had more restricted charters. Their new names were Landesbank für Westfalen Girozentrale, Münster, and Rheinsche Girozentrale und Provinzialbank, Düsseldorf.

Both *landesbanks* endured the boom-bust economic cycle of Germany during the military buildup of the World War I years, the hyperinflation of the Weimer Republic, the second buildup as the Nazis assumed power in 1933, and the economic chaos of the immediate postwar years. Finally, with the Marshall Plan and the currency reforms of 1948, Germany's postwar recovery began. At about this time both banks expanded their services to include clearing transactions for savings banks, thus adding the generic term *girozentrale* to their names. With the economic miracle of the 1950s, there was talk of combining the two *landesbank girozentrale* institutions, since the North Rhine and Westphalia provinces had become politically unified under the British occupation. For political reasons, however, this merger was not feasible until the late 1960s.

On January 1, 1969 the two local banks were combined at last, ostensibly to fight the economic domination of the Big Three banks—Deutsche Bank, Dresdner Bank, and Commerzbank. The new institution, based in one of Germany's most populous and wealthy states, could hope to rival the leading international banks

Company Perspectives:

On the strategic front, as a commercial bank WestLB AG will be in a better position to fulfill growing competitive and profitability requirements. The legal status of a joint-stock company and the related structures under German Stock Corporation Law will make the commercial bank transparent and understandable to international clients, investors, and employees in the long term. This will support the strategic focusing of the bank as a leading European wholesale bank and open up several options with regard to capital procurement and strategic partnerships. Independent status will also help to create a clear market profile. In addition, there will be a strategic refocusing of the bank's business activities. WestLB AG will expand business segments such as Special Finance and Equity Investments, in which WestLB has widely accepted expertise. On the other hand, the bank will discontinue some other businesses, for example Private Banking, where a wholesale bank has only limited scope for expansion.

and pose a challenge to the Big Three, which exercised overwhelming economic control over West Germany and showed relative insensitivity to regional needs, especially for capital for the large export industries in the region.

Thus, the Landesbank für Westfalen Girozentrale, Münster, and the Rheinsche Girozentrale und Provinzialbank, Düsseldorf, became a new entity, the Westdeutsche Landesbank Girozentrale, and Ludwig Poullain was named chairman of the management board. He committed the bank to a policy of growth and expansion that would enable it to challenge, and occasionally surpass, the Big Three banks in total assets.

The 1970s: Outside Expansion and In-House Trouble

During its first few years, WestLB prospered. Because of its unusual flexibility, the bank could, for instance, offer tailor-made long-term loans to customers. Also, because of the increased capital which WestLB controlled, its commercial-loan operations expanded to include larger companies, which meant larger loans and greater profits.

In 1970, WestLB made international news by joining the Chase Manhattan Bank and two other banks in starting up Orion Bank Ltd., an international merchant bank. The bank, in which WestLB held a minority interest, had an initial capitalization of $24 million.

In 1973, WestLB made news when it posted more than $150 million in foreign-exchange losses, the result of unauthorized speculative trading by employees who were subsequently fired.

During the mid-1970s, WestLB did indeed reach its goal of joining the Big Three banks, becoming Germany's third-largest lending institution in 1976. That year, WestLB proposed a merger with the troubled Hessische Landesbank. The resulting firm would have been Europe's largest bank, but the merger eventually fell through for political reasons.

Moreover, a drawn out scandal soon began to tarnish the bank's image. It began when Ludwig Poullain, the bank's founding chairman, announced his resignation in December 1977,

claiming that his chairmanship was untenable. The WestLB supervisory board refused his resignation and fired him for "gross neglect of his duties." Poullain successfully sued to force the bank to pay his remaining contractual wages of $230,000 a year for six years. Over the next several years, Poullain was charged with bribery, fraud, and malfeasance regarding a $465,000 consulting fee he received from Josef Schmidt, a financial broker who himself was charged with embezzlement, tax evasion, breach of trust, and criminal bankruptcy.

Poullain had not fully disclosed to WestLB management the terms of the consulting fee that Schmidt gave him, nor had he informed WestLB that he granted Schmidt a loan for the coincidental sum of $465,000 and neglected to tell the WestLB management board that Schmidt was under investigative arrest when it granted him another loan for $930,000, again at the behest of Poullain himself. Poullain later claimed that the charges against him were politically motivated because his steering the bank into an international presence had allegedly upset some state politicians. In 1981 he was found not guilty of the charges.

The 1980s: Heightened International Focus Under New Leadership

In 1980, the bank reported that it had made huge profits in foreign currency for 1979. Even so, total earnings were down by almost 68 percent and the bank stopped paying dividends until 1986.

Profits were down by two-thirds for fiscal 1980, and some called for the resignation of Johannes Völling, who had replaced Poullain. WestLB was suffering from a rise in interest rates. The bank was forced to finance fixed-rate long-term loans with higher-cost short-term funds. Since WestLB was North Rhine-Westphalia's central bank and the clearing bank for the area's 159 savings associations, any dip in WestLB's profits affected the region.

Eventually Völling did resign, in July 1981, stating that the bank's low profits had eroded confidence in his ability. Friedel Neuber, formerly head of the Rhineland Federation of Savings Banks, was appointed the new chairman. Neuber's appointment drew criticism, as he had never worked at a bank. However, he would head WestLB for the next 20 years. Neuber's priorities were to restructure, review operations for profitability, and expand the bank's international business.

In late 1981, WestLB sold its stakes in two industrial companies, Philipp Holzmann and Preussag, raising some DM 700 million, part of it to cover anticipated losses for the year. In mid-1982, WestLB raised DM 1.12 billion in new capital from its shareholders; the North Rhine-Westphalia state government contributed the most, raising its stake in the bank to 43 percent. This increase was designed to provide WestLB with capital for future growth and to help mitigate the higher degree of risk involved in its loans to Third World countries. WestLB began to strengthen its loan-loss reserves following Mexico's suspension of debt payments in August 1981; by 1988, its reserves covered more than 50 percent of its exposure. These measures soon paid off; WestLB's earnings rose sharply in 1982—enough to allow it to repurchase a 35 percent stake in Preussag.

In 1984, WestLB, along with four other German banks, combined forces to create a new venture-capital company. The

---

Key Dates:

1832: Westphalian Provinzialbank-Hülfskasse is founded.
1969: Westdeutsche Landesbank Girozentrale is established.
1981: Friedel Neuber becomes WestLB chairman.
1995: WestLB receives banking licenses for Poland and Russia.
2001: The German government agrees to revoke the special status of state-owned banks; WestLB's shareholders agree to transform the bank into a public stock company.

---

same year at least one top credit official on the management board resigned because of his role in the bank's involvement with Deutsche Anlagen Leasing GmbH, a lending concern that lost huge amounts of money due to over-extension, weak management controls, and devaluation of its assets. Nevertheless, WestLB again experienced high earnings in 1986 and that year was able to resume the payment of dividends.

In 1985 and 1986, WestLB increased its international business, as Neuber had long planned. In 1985, Owens-Illinois Inc. sold a 58 percent share of Gerresheimer Glas AG to the bank, which syndicated the glass manufacturer for other German investors. In 1986, WestLB dramatically heightened its international profile by taking part in an arrangement with the Japanese to sell securities on the Tokyo exchange. In exchange for access to the deutsche mark bond market in Europe, the Japanese allowed WestLB and three other large German banks to deal securities under certain limited circumstances.

This strong international position allowed WestLB to lead a banking syndicate that bought a one-fourth share in the Deutsche Babcock AG engineering group from the government of Iran in 1987. The bank again profited from selling the shares to institutional investors after syndicating its interest in the acquired firm.

As part of the improvement of economic and political relations between Eastern and Western Europe, in May 1988 WestLB joined most of the other major German banks in offering sizable loans to the Soviet Union. WestLB also played a historic role in furthering open trade when a Swiss subsidiary of the bank brought to market Moscow's first foreign bond issuance since the 1917 revolution, a formal acknowledgment of the close economic ties that existed between the two countries.

WestLB also revived its plan to merge with Hessische Landesbank. Though the proposed merger caused much excitement, the plan fell through in December 1988 when the state of Hessen, Hessische's home region, decided to sell its 50 percent stake in Hessische to the Hessen savings banks, which disapproved of the proposal.

The 1990s: Tourism and Other Expansion Projects

By the beginning of the 1990s, WestLB had become the fourth-largest West German bank in total assets. The following decade was characterized by the liberalization of the European and global financial markets, which brought about growing competition, intensified consolidation, and the rising influence of the European Union's legislation on German law. The reunification of the two German states in 1990 opened up new growth opportunities for WestLB. The bank helped establish Deutsche Industrie- und Handelsbank (DIHB), a new bank for corporate clients from the eastern German states, became the central clearing bank for the *Sparkassen* in Brandenburg, the state surrounding Berlin, and acquired a 50 percent stake in Investitionsbank Brandenburg.

Looking for lucrative growth markets, WestLB turned to tourism and helped carry out a remarkable coup that would change Germany's tourism landscape forever. The bank's major industrial shareholding, Preussag, was struggling with competitive pressures and the cyclical nature of the steel market. WestLB helped Preussag with its complete turnaround from the second largest German steelmaker to Europe's leading tourism empire. In 1992, the bank acquired Thomas Cook, a leading British tourism group, in which it already owned a 10 percent stake. In the same year a consortium lead by WestLB bought a majority share in Kahn KG, which in turn held a 40 percent stake in Touristik Union International (TUI), Germany's largest tour operator. In January 1993, WestLB established its new tourism holding company, TCT Touristik Beteiligungs GmbH & Co. KG. When it became apparent that WestLB was about to dominate TUI, the other TUI shareholders resisted fiercely. However, later in the year TUI's shares were redistributed. German charter airline LTU, another one of WestLB's major shareholdings, and German logistics concern Hapag Lloyd AG, held each 30 percent in TUI. When Hapag Lloyd AG went up for sale in 1997, WestLB helped Preussag acquire the company in a DM 2.8 billion deal. After the takeover, WestLB transferred LTU's 30 percent share in TUI to Preussag. With a 60 percent stake in TUI, Preussag announced that tourism would become its new major focus. The deal passed the German cartel authorities when WestLB agreed to sell its interest in LTU. Finally, in 2000, Preussag succeeded in a friendly takeover of the largest British tourism group, Thomson Travel Group plc. after WestLB had agreed to the EU Commission's requirement to sell its stake in Thomas Cook Holdings Ltd. The "new" Preussag—with the help of WestLB—had become a leading shipping company and Europe's number one tourism group.

In an effort to enhance its business, WestLB invested heavily in its national and international infrastructure during the 1990s, expanded its portfolio of shareholdings, and focused on special project financing. The company, together with bank partners, founded the mortgage bank Immobilienbank, based in Mainz, and security bank Wertpapierservice-Bank in Frankfurt. The British Standard Chartered Bank, West Merchant Bank, and brokerage firm Panmure Gordon were among WestLB's international acquisitions. In 1995, WestLB received banking licenses for doing business in Poland and Russia. By that time, international business accounted for roughly one-third of the bank's total revenues. Besides central and eastern Europe, WestLB strengthened its foothold in Asia.

In the second half of the decade, WestLB experienced growing difficulties. Contrary to the increasing risk the bank carried, WestLB's financial reserves declined. Margins in the lending business shrunk while administrative cost rose. The bank had to swallow losses in the billions in connection with the Asian financial crisis and some risky adventures in Russia. Investments were necessary to prepare for the advent of the new European currency. All those factors caused profits to grow much slower than revenues. On top of that, German tax authorities started investigating WestLB for transferring billions of deutsche marks out of the country to avoid taxes.

1999 and Beyond: Unexpected Reorganization

In the late 1990s, WestLB, according to *American Banker* the twentieth largest bank in the world, worked on refocusing its strategy to concentrate on core competencies when an earlier business transaction with the state North Rhine-Westphalia took on a life of its own. In 1992, to meet the European Union's higher requirements for capital assets for banks, the state had transferred its residential construction support arm Wohnungsbauförderanstalt (WFA) to WestLB. The transaction boosted WestLB's capital base by DM 4 billion that the state did not have to pay out of its budget. However, the Bundesverband Deutscher Banken, the trade association of German banks, filed a complaint with the EU, claiming that the transaction had given WestLB an unfair advantage. In 1999, the EU ruled that WestLB had to pay North Rhine-Westphalia EUR808 million in interest on the deal for the period from 1992 until 1998. This sum equaled the interest a commercial lender would have charged, but which WestLB had not been charged by the state. WestLB appealed the ruling and in early 2002 the case was still pending.

Besides the WFA deal, WestLB was affected by the fact that the EU was not willing to further tolerate the special status of German state-owned banks. By law, state-owned banks were provided with state guarantees for their liabilities. At the same time, these banks competed with commercial banks that could not rely on such financial backup. In 2001, the German government agreed to revoke the special status of state-owned banks by 2005.

In December 2001, WestLB's shareholders approved a new corporate structure for the bank. WestLB's commercial activities, which accounted for about 80 percent of the bank's business, were to be spun off as WestLB AG, a public stock company that competed in the financial markets, in the second half of 2002. The state-owned parent company was to be renamed Landesbank NRW and to take on all public-interest activities.

Jürgen Sengera, ex-gatekeeper of the German national handball team and longtime member of the bank's management board, succeeded Friedel Neuber in September 2001 as WestLB chairman. To get the bank ready for a new chapter in its history, he planned to hire new top managers, reorganize WestLB's operations which had become more costly and less profitable, radically cut down the number of the bank's sales offices and shareholdings, and focus on investment banking and international trade and special project financing. He also planned to discontinue private banking services.

Principal Subsidiaries

WestLB Europa Holding AG; WPS WertpapierService Bank AG (99.97%); Westdeutsche Spielbanken GmbH & Co. KG; WestLB UK Ltd.; West Merchant Bank Ltd. (United Kingdom); Westdeutsche Landesbank (France) S.A.; Banque d'Orsay S.A. (France); Westdeutsche Landesbank (Ireland) plc; Westdeutsche Landesbank (Italia) S.p.A.; Banque Européenne pour l'Amérique Latine (BEAL) S.A. (Belgium); WestLB International S.A. (Luxembourg; 75%); WestLB New York Capital Investment Ltd. (United States); Criterion Investment Management LLC (United States); WestLB Asset Management (USA) LLC; Westdeutsche Landesbank Polska S.A. (Poland); SAO Westdeutsche Landesbank Vostok (Russia); Westdeutsche Landesbank (Hungaria) Rt. (99.99%); WestLB Asia Pacific Ltd. (Singapore); WestLB Asset Management (Japan) Co. Ltd.; WestLB Asset Management (Australia) Pty. Ltd. (51%).

Principal Competitors

Commerzbank AG; Deutsche Bank AG; Dresdner Bank AG.

Further Reading

"Die Bank bleibt Global Player," *Focus,* September 3, 2001, p. 254.

"Die WestLB verliert Millionen und einen Vorstand," *Frankfurter Allgemeine Zeitung*, May 23, 2001, p. 22.

"Engere Süd-Partnerschaft der WestLB; Düsseldorfer Institut mit viel Dynamik, aber wenig Gewinn," *Süddeutsche Zeitung*, May 16, 1991.

"Missmanagement; Eine Bank bricht ein," *Focus,* February 12, 2001, p. 196.

Pohl, Hans, *Von der Hülfskasse von 1832 zur Landesbank*, Düsseldorf: WestLB, 1982.

"Rückenwind für die WestLB flaut ab. Neuber will 50 Prozent an zu gründender Immobilienbank," *Süddeutsche Zeitung*, May 18, 1994.

"SAir wird größter Eigentümer der LTU," *Süddeutsche Zeitung*, November 13, 1998.

"Schlappe für die WestLB bei TUI. Beteiligung an Europas größtem Reiseriesen verhindert, "*Süddeutsche Zeitung*, December 14, 1992.

Schragl, Bettina and Robert Gillinger, "WestLB als Touristikgigant," *Wirtschaftsblatt*, September 3, 1997, p. 3.

"WestLB; Aufbruch in Düsseldorf," *Focus,* May 28, 2001, p. 260.

"WestLB baut Cook in Touristik-Holding ein," *Süddeutsche Zeitung*, January 5, 1993.

"WestLB beugt sich dem Wunsch der Sparkassen," *Frankfurter Allgemeine Zeitung*, December 4, 2001, p. 18.

"WestLB blickt immer weiter über Europa hinaus," *Süddeutsche Zeitung*, May 15, 1996.

"WestLB bringt Briten in die Luft," *Süddeutsche Zeitung*, October 7, 1998.

"WestLB geht gegen Brüssel vor Gericht," *Süddeutsche Zeitung*, July 9, 1999.

"WestLB hält trotz ungünstiger Einflüsse Kurs," *Süddeutsche Zeitung*, May 17, 1995.

"WestLB mit höherem Ergebnis," *Süddeutsche Zeitung*, November 4, 1996.

"WestLB profitiert von guter Börsentendenz," *Süddeutsche Zeitung*, May14, 1997.

"WestLB verzeichnet Bremsspuren," *Süddeutsche Zeitung*, November 19, 1998.

—update: Evelyn Hauser

Whatman plc

Whatman House
St Leonard's Road
20/20 Maidstone
Kent ME16 0LS
United Kingdom
Telephone: (+44) 1622 676670
Fax: (+44) 1622 677011
Web site: http://www.whatman.co.uk

Public Company
Incorporated: 1740
Employees: 1,064
Sales: £98.66 million ($147.3 million)(2000)
Stock Exchanges: London
Ticker Symbol: WHM
NAIC: 541710 Research and Development in the
    Physical, Engineering, and Life Sciences

Formerly a renowned maker of fine papers, Whatman plc has consistently reinvented itself to meet the emerging needs of its times. The Whatman plc entering the 21st century has redirected itself to become a specialist in separation and filtration media for the healthcare, life science, and biomedical research markets, with a particular emphasis on DNA filtration technologies. As part of its reorientation, Whatman sold off its industrial filtration arm—which represented one-third of its revenues—in 2000 and has been actively expanding its biomedical and DNA technology, notably through acquisitions such as the purchase of the United States' HemaSure Inc. and the DNA apparatus product line from Invitrogen (formerly known as Life Technologies Inc.), both in 2001. Despite the company's transformation, paper-making remains at the heart of the company's products: Whatman's research efforts have developed a number of technologies for the production of multi-layer and chemically active papers used in such applications as paper chromatography, diagnostic test kits, and DNA storage. The company also produces a range of filtration products for the healthcare and laboratory and biomedical markets, including microfiltration products, nucleopore membranes, and other filtration products

and systems. More than half of Whatman's sales come from the United States and Canada; Europe, including the United Kingdom, is the company's second-largest market, generating some 33 percent of its sales, while the Asia-Pacific region accounts for 12 percent of sales. The company posted revenues of nearly £100 million in 2000. David Smith, chief architect of the company's transformation at the end of the 1990s, was replaced as CEO by Tim Coombs at the end of 2001.

Paper Making Innovator in the 18th Century

James Whatman was born into a family of tanners based around Kent, England in 1907. Whatman learned the tanners trade, but, as the tanning process produced a gelatin by-product used by paper makers, Whatman was in close contact with paper makers, and notably the Harris family. In 1733, Whatman built a paper mill for his friend, Richard Harris. Harris then began building a new, larger mill, Turkey Mill, near Maidstone. When Harris died in 1739, Whatman married his widow, and took over paper-making operations at Turkey Mill.

Whatman quickly distinguished himself a maker of quality paper. As with most of the European paper industry, Whatman's early production was of so-called "laid" paper, which had a somewhat coarse feature. Printer John Baskerville approached Whatman with the request for a paper with a finer finish in order to show off his new serif font. Whatman complied, developing a new wire mesh to produce what became known as "wove" paper (because it was similar in appearance to woven linen). Whatman is commonly credited with producing the first wove paper in 1756, and Baskerville became the first to print on the new paper type in 1757. The technique eventually became a standard in the paper-making industry, representing some 99 percent of all paper.

The Whatman paper—the Whatman name was to become synonymous with wove paper—retained a monopoly for some 30 years on the technique, and was instrumental in enabling the British papermaking industry to compete against larger rivals in France and Holland. Yet Whatman himself did not live to see the results of his innovation. Whatman died in 1759, stipulating that his business be turned over to his son, James II, then 17 years old, when the younger Whatman reached 23 years of age. By the time of Whatman's death, Turkey Mill had become England's largest paper mill.

James Whatman II proved a ready businessman, however, and by the age of 21 his mother had turned the family business over to him. The younger Whatman inherited his father's gift for innovation as well. In 1765, Whatman discovered a means of whitening paper by adding laundry blue to the typically yellowed paper pulp. The resulting paper and further improvements in the wove process helped the Whatman name become world-renowned, especially among the world's watercolor artists, but also among such personalities as Napoleon, who used Whatman paper to compose his will in 1821. Whatman success led him to expand, building a second mill and producing, in addition to wove paper, marbled paper, and paper for copper plate engravings.

Whatman, who also had a son named James, began instead to groom protegé William Balston, who had entered the Whatman household as a schoolboy, to take over his business. When Whatman suffered a stroke in 1790, Balton, then 31 years old, took over running the family's paper mills. In 1794, however, Whatman sold off his business for £20,000. Balston remained a partner in the business, however. James Whatman II died in 1798.

The partnership dissolved in 1805, and Balston struck out on his own. While his partners kept Turkey Mill, and continued production of Whatman-branded watercolor papers until the mid-nineteenth century, Balston built his own mill, the Springfield Mill, nearby. Balston had inherited his mentor's gift for innovation. Despite its location on the River Medway, the Springfield Mill became the first in the world to install the steam-powered Fourdrinier machine. That machine remained in operation on the site for more than 90 years.

Balston's interest in chemistry led him to establish a small research laboratory on the Springfield Mill site, and the Balston company quickly became one of the country's largest. By 1835, Balston's operation had grown to ten vats and employed more than 100 people. Balston himself became a prominent personality in British paper-making world. By the 1850s, Balston was joined by two of his ten children, sons William and Richard. In 1959, the Balstons bought out the original Whatman partners and acquired all rights to the use of the Whatman name. By then, Whatman was often listed in dictionaries and reference books as a generic term for wove paper.

William and Richard Balston took over the paper company's operation after their father's death and changed the company's

name to W&R Balston in 1861. By then the company had grown to more than 250 employees. In 1862, a fire destroyed nearly all of the Springfield Mill, sparing only the Fourdrinier steam engine. The Balston brothers quickly rebuilt the business and were back in operations after only three months. The Balstons continued to expand, and by the end of the century the Springfield site operated 18 vats, while the company had built a second mill, with an additional four vats, nearby. By then, Richard Balston had become the sole leader of the family business.

Following the Trends in the 20th Century

W&R Balston remained true to the Whatman tradition of innovation as it moved into the twentieth century. The outbreak of World War I gave the company a new opportunity—and a new direction. Until then, much of the filter papers used by the British arms and steel industries had been imported from Germany. With the two countries in conflict, the British government sought a new source for the important material and approached W&R Balston.

The company quickly realized that the coming years were to see a huge increase in the demand for paper-based filtration products, not only for industrial applications but for the scientific community as well. The company turned more and more of its production and research efforts toward developing filter papers for the health care, research, schools, and other industries. With much of trade in continental Europe disrupted by the war years, W&R Balston also began seeking out new markets, and particularly North America. In 1914, the company contracted with fellow British firm Harry Reeve Angel, which had opened an office in New York, to serve as its North American sales agent.

W&R Balston was hard hit by the depression years, and by the 1930s was forced to cut back its production to just three days per week during a period lasting some five years. That decade nonetheless saw vast advances in scientific and medical research, which in turn stepped up demand for Balston's filter paper products. The company's flair for innovation made history again in 1944 when its Whatman No. 1 filter paper was used in experiments that led to the development of paper chromatography—a ground-breaking technique for separating compounds that was to revolutionize the medical research community. W&R Balston's role in that development encouraged the company to expand its production in that field and the company quickly became one of the world's leading makers of analytical papers.

By the 1950s, W&R Balston's production had turned almost entirely toward its filter and analytical paper production. The company began phasing out its remaining fine quality papers production. In 1955, it ended its line of handmade watercolor paper, and, in 1962, shut down production of mold-made papers as well. The company meanwhile expanded its range of filter products beyond paper to incorporate the variety of new materials then being produced, such as glass and quartz microfibers. The company's filters became as successful as its fine papers had been, and by the end of the 1960s the Whatman brand name was once again known throughout the world.

Facing new economic challenges in the 1970s, as the world slumped into a recession following the Arab Oil Embargo of

Key Dates:

1733: James Whatman sets up a paper mill.
1756: Whatman is credited with inventing ''wove'' paper-making process.
1765: Whatman son, James II, who took over after his father's death, invents paper whitening process using laundry blue.
1790: William Balston takes over mill operations after Whatman has a stroke.
1805: Balston establishes a new mill, which is the first paper mill to be powered by a steam engine.
1859: Balston and sons acquire full rights to Whatman brand name
1861: Balston's sons William and Richard Balston take over mill and company is renamed W&R Balston.
1914: Balston begins supply filter paper to British military and steel industry, causing company to phase out papermaking to focus on filters for scientific and industrial applications.
1955: Balston ends production of watercolor paper.
1974: W&R Balston merges with Angel Reeve International to form Whatman Angel Reeve, listing on the London Stock Exchange.
1984: The company establishes subsidiaries in France and Singapore as part of international expansion during the 1980s.
1990: The company changes its name to Whatman PLC and restructures operations.
1993: Whatman acquires Cyclopore, based in Belgium, as the company begins focus on filtration and purification technologies for health care research and related industries
1999: Whatman launches improved paper-based DNA storage and retrieval product and acquires DNA filtration specialist Cambridge Molecular Technologies, paying £4 million.
2002: Whatman begins consolidation of manufacturing sites, with plans to shut down eight plants by 2003.

1973, Whatman turned toward long-time North American sales agent and publicly listed Reeve Angel International, which by then had built up its own successful filtration materials business. The two companies merged, becoming Whatman Reeve Angel Ltd. The new, larger company retained the former Reeve Angel's listing on the London stock exchange.

New Directions in the 21st Century

The company continued to market under both Whatman and Balston brand names. Yet it was the Whatman name that proved the most durable. The company expanded quickly during the 1980s, moving into new international markets. In 1984, the company created subsidiaries in France and Singapore. Elsewhere, the company expanded its industrial filters operations to the point where it was said that, in some countries, Whatman had become considered a synonym for certain filter types. The company's industrial park expanded to include manufacturing sites in the United Kingdom, the United States, Germany, and

elsewhere. Whatman Reeve Angel also flirted with a return to paper production, reintroducing Whatman's mold-made paper in 1982.

The company restructured its operations in 1990 and renamed itself Whatman Plc. The decade to come was to see the company transform itself once again. Whatman's filtration products were now at the forefront of emerging technologies in the health care and scientific research fields. More and more emphasis was being placed, on the one hand, on sophisticated blood filtration techniques—particularly given the AIDS epidemic of the 1980s and 1990s—and, on the other, on the rapid and ongoing breakthroughs in DNA and genetic technologies. While the company's industrial filtration business continued to play a prominent role on its books—accounting for as much as one-third of the company's revenues—Whatman's interests increasingly turned toward the new technologies.

The company began making a series of acquisitions boosting its strengths in analytical filtration and separation technologies, including the 1993 purchase of Belgium's Cyclopore, a filter membrane specialist, and the 1997 acquisition of Polyfiltronics, based in the United States. Leading the company's charge was David Smith, who joined Whatman in 1994 and became its CEO. In 1997, Smith led Whatman on a small but significant acquisition, that of Fitzco, a company based in the United States that had patented a process for storing DNA on paper.

The match seemed a perfect meeting of Whatman's historical background as a paper innovator and its new role as a research industry specialist. Yet when Whatman attempted to sell the paper based on Fitzco's research, it met with market resistance: while storing DNA on paper eliminated the costly need to maintain stocks of refrigerated blood samples, analyzing the paper-based DNA was extremely difficult.

Whatman once again revealed its heritage for innovation. After two years of development, the company brought out a new and revolutionary product. By adapting the composition of the paper itself, the company had found a way to separate the stored DNA from the paper. The launch of the product heralded the beginning of a new era for Whatman as a leading filtrations and separations technology company. In that year, the company boosted its DNA-oriented business with the acquisition of DNA filtration specialist Cambridge Molecular Technologies, paying £4 million.

The rise of Whatman's high-tech genetics component led it to restructure again in 2000. As part of that restructuring the company sold off its industrial filtration business—which accounted for one-third of the company's revenues—to Parker Hannifin, telling the *Financial Times:* ''We had to bite the bullet and sell [the industrial unit]. For a small company that's quite a brave move—to sell a third of its business.'' Soon after, the company set up a strategic marketing alliance with U.S.-based HemaSure, a blood filtration specialist, to market Whatman's DNA filtration, purification, storage, and related technology for blood-transfusion and blood bank applications in the United States. The companies were also collaborating on an improved leucocyte blood filter product.

Whatman's alliance with HemaSure proved merely a step toward acquiring the Massachusetts-based company the following year. Despite shareholder protests—because HemaSure was hamstrung by a patent lawsuit and was losing money—the acquisition went through for a total price of $25 million. The acquisition, proposed in February 2001, was completed by May of that year. Less controversial for the company was its agreement to purchase the DNA Apparatus Product Line from Invitrogen Corporation (formerly Life Technologies Inc.) for $1.5 million. That acquisition was added to Whatman's Germany-based Biometra molecular biology subsidiary.

Whatman's newest transformation had not gone as smoothly as the company had hoped, however. By September 2001, the company was being criticized for what some considered a "botched" reorganization. Hit hard by the worldwide economic slowdown of that year, and particularly in its key U.S. market, which had come to account for 53 percent of company revenues by 2000, Whatman was forced to issue a profits warning. The fallout from the reorganization came to bear on CEO David Smith, who tendered his resignation and was replaced as CEO by Tim Coombs.

Coombs immediately led Whatman on a strategic review of its business. In December 2001, the company enacted a reorganization of its business structure, replacing its formerly separated business units of Laboratory, Healthcare Components, Process Filtration, and BioScience with a single unified structure. The company also announced a consolidation of its manufacturing park, including the shutting down of eight of its manufacturing facilities by 2003. Upon completion, the company expected to have just four main production facilities and four specialized production facilities. These moves were expected to begin generating extra profits by the end of 2002. Meanwhile, the strategic review included a commitment to the company's shift toward DNA extraction, purification and storage, along with the creation of a new division, Filtration and Separations Technology, which was to focus on such biotechnology areas as multiwells and proteomics. Whatman had come a long way from its origins as a papermaker, yet, after more than 250 years, continued its founder's flair for innovation.

Principal Subsidiaries

Aquilo Gas Separations BV (Netherlands); Arbor Technologies Inc. (United States); Biometra Biomedizinische Analytik GmbH (Germany); Cambridge Molecular Technologies Limited; Fitzco Inc. (57%; United States); Gerbermembrane GmbH (Germany); Polyfiltronics Inc. (United States); Wex Filtertechnik GmbH (Germany); Whatman Asia Pacific Pte Limited (Singapore); Whatman BioScience Inc. (United States); Whatman Bioscience Ltd; Whatman Canada Limited; Whatman Finance Limited (Ireland); Whatman GmbH (Germany); Whatman Inc. (United States); Whatman International Limited; Whatman Japan KK; Whatman Nucleopore Canada Limited; Whatman Reeve Angel Inc. (United States); Whatman SA (Belgium); Whatman Sarl (France).

Principal Competitors

Qiagen Corporation; APBiotech Inc.; Beckman Coulter, Inc.; Bio-Rad Laboratories, Inc.; Celltech Plc.; Cepheid; Ciphergen Biosystems, Inc.; Genometrix Incorporated; Genset S.A.; Innogenetics S.A.; Invitrogen Corporation; Neurosearch AB; Millipore Corporation; Packard BioScience Company; Stratagene Holding Corporation; Visible Genetics Inc.

Further Reading

Anderson, Simon, "Whatman Leaps into Cutting Edge," *Daily Telegraph*, October 16, 1999.

Firn, David, "Whatman Benefits from Shift to DNA Handling," *Financial Tiems*, September 2, 2000.

Gledhill, Dan, "Investors Claim DNA Firm's Bid Is a Born Loser," *Independent on Sunday*, February 11, 2001, p. 2.

Grande, Carlos, "Whatman Hurt by Botched Reorganization," *Financial Times*, September 4, 2001.

Larsen, Peter Thal, "Whatman Leaps from Napoleon's Memoirs to DNA Test Paper," *Financial Times*, July 1, 1999.

—M. L. Cohen

Zila, Inc.

5227 North 7th Street
Phoenix, Arizona 85014-2800
U.S.A.
Telephone: (602) 266-6700
Toll Free: (800) 922-7887
Fax: (602) 234-2264
Web site: http://www.zila.com

Public Company
Incorporated: 1980
Employees: 241
Sales: $77.6 million (2000)
Stock Exchanges: NASDAQ
Ticker Symbol: ZILA
NAIC: 325412 Pharmaceutical Preparation Manufacturing

Zila, Inc., based in Phoenix, Arizona, is a manufacturer and marketer of pharmaceutical, biomedical, dental, and nutraceutical products. Its operations have been organized into three groups—Pharmaceuticals, Professional Products, and Nutraceuticals—which manufacture and distribute the company's line of products through its principal subsidiaries. The Pharmaceutical Group consists of the wholly-owned subsidiary Zila Pharmaceuticals, Inc. and produces over-the-counter (OTC) and prescription mendicants, including its Zilactin line (its signature OTC products for treating canker sores, chapped lips, toothaches, and teething pain), Peridex prescription mouth rinse (for treating gingivitis), and the OraTest oral cancer detection system. The Professional Products Group operates through Bio-Dental Technologies Corporation, a wholly-owned subsidiary that, in turn, is the parent company of Ryker Dental of Kentucky, Inc. (dba Zila Dental Supply), a national distributor of professional dental supplies. Zila Dental markets the products of dental supply manufacturers, selling about 500 items via mail-order, telemarketing, and direct sales operations. The Nutraceuticals Group consists of Oxycal Laboratories Inc. and its two subsidiaries: Inter-Cal Corporation and Oxycal Export, Inc. The Nutraceutical Group makes and distributes Ester-C (a

unique form of Vitamin C) and a line of botanical ingredients, including Palmettx (a saw palmetto product). Zila sells its nutraceutical products in over 40 countries.

1980–87: Dr. James Tinnell Founds Company and Begins Marketing Zilactin

Zila Pharmaceuticals, Inc., which would later be transformed into Zila, Inc., was organized and incorporated in Nevada on September 12, 1980. It effectively went into research and development operations the following year. The company's founder, Dr. James E. Tinnell, who graduated from the University of Arkansas School of Medicine, had been in private practice since 1965, but in 1979 he had begun limiting his work to the treatment of herpes virus patients at the Herpes Clinic in Las Vegas, Nevada. Between 1974 and 1979, he had served as the resident physician for a major casino and hotel in that city. Tinnell's interest in developing a medicine for fighting herpes was a major incentive for starting up the company.

In 1983, Zila named Joesph Hines president and CEO. Hines came over from Desert Valley Cos. Inc., a Phoenix-based, management consulting firm, which, from 1976 until 1983, he both owned and operated. He also brought pharmaceutical industry experience to his new job. Between 1966 and 1976, he had served as CEO of several subsidiaries of Dart Industries, formerly named Rexall Drug and Chemical Co.

Until the late 1980s, Zila relied almost exclusively on Zilactin for its revenues. Introduced in 1985, Zilactin, the company's first product, was a patented, non-prescription mendicant initially used for treating various mouth and lip sores, including canker sores and fever blisters as well as abrasions caused by orthodontic devices. It was a medicated gel that created a protective film in the mouth and helped ease the pain of such sores. Relief lasted up to six hours, which was much longer than relief afforded by competing products, even such long-established salves as Sterling Winthrop's Campho-Phenique and Del Pharmaceutical's Orajel. Through professional detailing and sampling, Zilactin soon established itself as a very solid base for the development of Zila's whole line of products. The national introduction and marketing of Zilactin in 1985 was financed by Daleco Zila Partners, a California limited partnership, which put up about $3.3 million, and its general partner Daleco Technology Management Inc.

1988–90: Expansion and New Products

Under a reorganization plan, in 1988 Zila Pharmaceuticals, Inc., reincorporated in Delaware, became a wholly-owned subsidiary of the newly created Zila, Inc. and was merged with and into it. The surviving corporation, Zila, Inc. would thereafter serve as parent company to additional subsidiaries, including Zila International Inc., Zila Ltd., and Zila Merger Corporation.

Investors in Zila anticipated a favorable outcome to the company's efforts to increase the sales of Zilactin. Among other things, in that year the firm sought FDA permission to market Zilactin with additional applications as an approved ointment for treating genital herpes and shingles. It also anticipated receiving permission to place the American Dental Association's seal of approval on its product. Expecting a surge in future sales, the company filed a registration statement with the SEC for a secondary offering of 7,125,023 shares of stock to be offered by more than 100 individual and institutional investors, including Hines and the company's financial backers, Daleco Zila Partners and Daleco Technology Management Inc.

At that time, Zila was still a developer and marketer, not a manufacturer. It had only nine full-time employees. A California company actually made its products. It was also a small operation, selling only about $3 million in ointments in the fiscal year that ended on July 31. It was also just treading water, having logged losses over the previous five years. Its estimates were that it had gained only a 4 percent share of the oral hygiene market by 1989. But its future was certainly looking up.

Events justified the optimism. Among other things, the company turned the financial corner by the end of its 1989 fiscal year, realizing a net income of $124,118 on sales of $2.56 million. The previous year it had inked a loss of $264,975 on revenues of only $1.22 million. In 1990, Zila negotiated an agreement with Bausch & Lomb Inc., giving that company the exclusive rights to manufacture its line of oral health care products outside the United States. It also had new products on the market: ZilaBrace, a gel for abrasions on the inner cheek; and ZilaDent, for treating gum sores caused by dentures. It was also readying another product for the market, Zilactol, a liquid for treating HSV-1, an oral virus infection.

1991–95: Growth Through Increased Sales in Zilactin

Until 1991, Zila leased a Phoenix facility on Thomas Road in Phoenix, but in that year it bought a 16,000 square-foot building at 5227 N. Seventh Street in the same city. According to records, Zila paid $600,000 for the two-story structure. The company began using only a third of the space and leased out the remainder to the Center Against Sexual Assault and other tenants. The building continued as Zila's headquarters into the next century.

By the year it moved, Zila had achieved some financial stability. It held $1.1 million in cash assets, was completely free of long term debt, and had a net working capital of $1.44 million. It was, Hines assured company shareholders, poised for yet stronger growth. Strategies to achieve it called for developing more new products and markets as well as expanding and diversifying through acquisitions and mergers. Still, into 1996, Zila's primary focus remained on producing and marketing its four major OTC items in its Zilactin family line of mendicants:. Zilactin, a protective gel for canker sores, cold sores and fever blisters; Zilactin-B, a protective, benzocaine based film for relieving the pain of mouth sores; Zilactin-L, a liquid version for treating developing fever blisters and cold sores; and Zilactin-Lip, a lip salve used to prevent sun blisters and to treat cold sores and chapped lips.

1996–97: Diversifying Through Mergers and Acquisitions

Iin August 1996, Zila entered into a merger agreement with Bio-Dental Technologies Corporation. Under its terms, Bio-Dental merged into Zila Dental Supply, a wholly-owned subsidiary of Zila created for the purpose. Bio-Dental was a dental supply firm which, through its own subsidiaries, marketed a wide range of professional dental supplies and computer-based dental technology systems. Basically, the parties to the merger viewed it as a "pooling of interests" transaction.

In January of the next year, 1997, The Supply House also became part of Zila Dental Supply. The Supply House had started operations in 1990, when it purchased San Diego Dental Supply, a small dental products distributor in San Diego, California. The new company began marketing on a larger, nationwide scale, using field sales representatives as well as telemarketing and direct mail advertising to extend its market coverage. In 1994, The Supply House acquired Ryker Dental, which, because Ryker was located in Lexington, Kentucky, increased the company's marketing efficiency. Until Zila Dental Supply emerged, Zila had still only had its single, Zila Pharmaceutical division.

Zila also acquired Peridex from Proctor & Gamble in November 1997. Peridex, first introduced by P & G in 1987, was a prescription antibacterial oral rinse used for treating gingivitis and reducing plaque. It was the first such rinse to receive the American Dental Association seal of approval for its use. Although terms of the sale were not disclosed, P & G decided to sell off the successful product in order to focus the dental product segment of its business on toothpaste.

Key Dates:

1980: Dr. James E. Tinnel founds Zila Pharmaceuticals, Inc. as a Nevada corporation.
1983: Joseph Hines is elected company president and CEO.
1985: Company introduces and begins marketing Zilactin.
1988: Zila Pharmaceuticals is merged with and into Zila, Inc., incorporated in Delaware.
1991: Company purchases two-story Phoenix building for its operation.
1993: Zila introduces OraScan in Canada.
1995: Company enters a 56-country product distribution agreement with Proctor & Gamble Co.
1996: Company acquires Bio-Dental Technologies Corporation, which becomes a wholly-owned subsidiary of Zila.
1997: Zila acquires Peridex oral rinse from Procter & Gamble and The Supply House.
1998: Zila acquires Oxycal Laboratories and its Inter-Cal marketing subsidiary.
1999: The company sells Cygnus Imaging to Procare Laboratories, Inc. and Integrated Dental Technologies to InfoCure Corporation.
2001: Zila acquires Innovative Swab Technologies from National Healthcare Manufacturing Corporation.

Despite its fairly bold acquisition strategy, Zila experienced some growing pains in the 1990s, even in 1997, when its annual revenue soared way above what it had ever been before. It reached $38.7 million that year, up from just $6.8 million the year before, roughly six times as much. But the company also logged a $6.5 million net loss. It would rebound though, first in 1998, when its revenue took another big jump, reaching $62.1 million, which gave Zila its first profitable year since 1993.

1998–99: Going Online and Focusing on Core Divisions

It was also in 1998 that Zila Dental Supply took to the Internet, launching an online order entry system designed to provide customers with a quick and easy means of ordering products from any location. Included among its features was the Personal Shopping List, which facilitated the replenishing of supplies by providing users with a log of their previous orders.

Two measures taken near the end of 1999 positioned Zila for continued expansion through its acquisition strategy for growing its core divisions–its pharmaceutical, nutraceutical, and dental supply businesses. In October, the company sold its Cygnus Imaging unit; then, in December, it sold its Practice Works software division. Cygnus Imaging, with a price tag of about $4.0 million, went to Procare Laboratories, Inc. of Scotsdale, Arizona; while Practice Works, for about $4.65 million, went to InfoCure Corporation of Atlanta. In addition to intensifying its business focus, the combined sales of almost $8.7 million gave Zila new capital for its growth plans.

Some of the funds were to used on Zila's Inter-Cal Corp.'s new 65,000-square-foot manufacturing facility, which got un-

der construction in Prescott, Arizona, in the fall of 1999. Growth in Zila's nutraceutical area was being fueled the health industry's increasing demand for a Vitamin C product line. But some of the funds were also slated for Zila's pharmaceutical and dental supply subsidiaries, still the mainstays of the company. Among its principal investments were funds spent on developing and producing OraTest, the company's new and extremely promising oral cancer detection system.

2000 and Beyond

In 2000, while waiting for FDA approval of OraTest, Zila was busy revving up sales of that product abroad, where it already had obtained permission for its sale and distribution in 16 countries. The company's plan was to develop professional respect for the diagnostic product worldwide. Meanwhile, at home, Zila contracted with ILEX Oncology Services, Inc. to act as its representative of the product with the FDA. ILEX Oncology Services conducts clinical tests and has a well established reputation as a leader in the field of cancer research. If approved, OraTest holds the promise of producing annual revenues in excess of $500 million, with no competitive product even on the market horizon. In July 2001, the company got a boost from a study conducted on OraTest at Johns Hopkins University and reported on in the American Association for Cancer Research's *Journal of Clinical Cancer Research,* which found that OraTest was a very powerful oral cancer detection product.

Zila also developed other products at the turn of the century, including Zila Pro-Wash and Zila Pro-Scrub, antiseptic hand washes and scrub for use by healthcare professionals. The roll out of these two products commenced in May 2001, with plans for marketing them through exhibits at major dental and medical shows and through major telemarketing campaigns.

While growth and diversification created difficulties for Zila through the 1990s, particularly in 1997, by 2000 the company's financial situation had considerably improved. Its sales rose to $77.6 million that year, producing a net income of $2.9 million, its best on record. Furthermore, although it recorded a loss in its 2001 fiscal year, in its fourth quarter its revenues were up from the previous fiscal year. Zila, it seemed, had finally reached the financial stability that partially eluded the company through the previous decade. Thanks to the prospects of OraTest as well as the increased sales of its other new and established lines, Zila's future growth potential looked extremely promising. However, it should also be noted that the company was seriously considering selling off its dental supply subsidiary, a move that would bring major changes in Zila's corporate complexion and focus. As of the fall of 2001, that divestment, if not a certainty, remained a strong possibility.

Principal Subsidiaries

Oxycal Laboratories Inc.; Zila Pharmaceuticals Inc.; Zila Dental Supply; Zila Technologies, Inc.; Innovative Swab Tech Inc.

Principal Divisions

Pharmaceutical Group; Nutraceuticals Group; Professional Products Group.

Principal Competitors

Advanced Nutraceuticals, Inc.; Darby Group Companies, Inc.; Del Laboratories, Inc.; Henry Schein, Inc.; Patterson Dental Company.

Further Reading

Gonzales, Angela, " Phoenix Pharmaceuticals Maker Buys Headquarters Building," *Business Journal-Serving Phoenix & the Valley of the Sun*, February 4, 1991, p. 10.

——, "Zila Inc. Entering Toothpaste Market, Negotiating with ADA," *Business Journal-Serving Phoenix & the Valley of the Sun*, May 4, 1992, p 2.

——, "Zila Zeros in on Growth Plans after Selling 2 Units," *Business Journal-Serving Phoenix & the Valley of the Sun*, November 5, 1999, p. 7.

Luebke, Cathy, "Zila Reaping Reward of Work on Oral Cancer Aid," *Business Journal-Serving Phoenix & the Valley of the Sun*, November 26, 1993, p. 19.

Stern, Jonathan, "Phoenix Firm Betting Its Future on Medicine to Fight Herpes," *Phoenix Business Journal*, January 27, 1986, p. 17.

Tigner, Rochelle, "Zila Shareholders Register to Sell 7.12 Million Shares," *Business Journal-Serving Phoenix & the Valley of the Sun*," April 17, 1989, p. 7.

"Toothache Swabs a Hit for Zila," *Chain Drug Review*, June 7, 1999, p. 174.

"Zila," *On Wall Street*, June 2000, p. 87.

"Zila Prepares to Launch Oral Cancer Screening System," *Chain Drug Review*, July 3, 1995, p. 271.

"Zila's Teething Gel a Success," *Chain Drug Review*, June 29, 1998, p. 214.

—John W. Fiero

INDEX TO COMPANIES

INDEX TO COMPANIES

Index to Companies

Listings in this index are arranged in alphabetical order under the company name. Company names beginning with a letter or proper name such as Eli Lilly & Co. will be found under the first letter of the company name. Definite articles (The, Le, La) are ignored for alphabetical purposes as are forms of incorporation that precede the company name (AB, NV). Company names printed in bold type have full, historical essays on the page numbers appearing in bold. Updates to entries that appeared in earlier volumes are signified by the notation **(upd.)**. Company names in light type are references within an essay to that company, not full historical essays. This index is cumulative with volume numbers printed in bold type.

Meade County Rural Electric Cooperative Corporation, **11** 37
Meade Instruments Corporation, 41 261–64
Meadow Gold Dairies, Inc., **II** 473
Meadowcraft, Inc., 29 313–15
Means Services, Inc., **II** 607
Mears & Phillips, **II** 237
Measurex Corporation, **8** 243; **14** 56; **38** 227
Mebetoys, **25** 312
MEC - Hawaii, UK & USA, **IV** 714
MECA Software, Inc., **18** 363
Mecair, S.p.A., **17** 147
Mecca Leisure PLC, **I** 248; **12** 229; **32** 243
Mechanics Exchange Savings Bank, **9** 173
Mechanics Machine Co., **III** 438; **14** 63
Mecklermedia Corporation, 24 328–30; **26** 441; **27** 360, 362
Medal Distributing Co., **9** 542
Medallion Pictures Corp., **9** 320
Medar, Inc., **17** 310–11
Medco Containment Services Inc., 9 346–48; 11 291; **12** 333; **44** 175
Medcom Inc., **I** 628
Medeco Security Locks, Inc., **10** 350
Medfield Corp., **III** 87
Medford, Inc., **19** 467–68
Medi Mart Drug Store Company. *See* The Stop & Shop Companies, Inc.
Media Arts Group, Inc., 42 254–57
Media Exchange International, **25** 509
Media General, Inc., III 214; **7** 326–28; **18** 61; **23** 225; **38** 306–09 **(upd.)**
Media Groep West B.V., **23** 271
Media News Corporation, **25** 507
Media Play. *See* Musicland Stores Corporation.
MediaBay, **41** 61
Mediacom Inc., **25** 373
Mediamark Research, **28** 501, 504
Mediamatics, Inc., **26** 329
MediaOne Group Inc. *See* U S West, Inc.
Medic Computer Systems LLC, **16** 94; **45** 279–80
Medical Care America, Inc., **15** 112, 114; **35** 215–17
Medical Development Corp. *See* Cordis Corp.
Medical Development Services, Inc., **25** 307
Medical Economics Data, **23** 211
Medical Expense Fund, **III** 245
Medical Indemnity of America, **10** 160
Medical Innovations Corporation, **21** 46
Medical Marketing Group Inc., **9** 348
Medical Service Assoc. of Pennsylvania, **III** 325–26
Medical Tribune Group, **IV** 591; **20** 53
Medicare-Glaser, **17** 167
Medicine Bow Coal Company, **7** 33–34
Medicine Shoppe International. *See* Cardinal Health, Inc.
Medicor, Inc., **36** 496
Medicus Intercon International, **6** 22
Medifinancial Solutions, Inc., **18** 370
MedImmune, Inc., 35 286–89
Medinol Ltd., **37** 39
Mediobanca Banca di Credito Finanziario SpA, **II** 191, 271; **III** 208–09; **11** 205
The Mediplex Group, Inc., **III** 16; **11** 282
Medis Health and Pharmaceuticals Services Inc., **II** 653
Medite Corporation, **19** 467–68

Meditrust, 11 281–83
Medlabs Inc., **III** 73
MedPartners, **36** 367
Medtech, Ltd., **13** 60–62
Medtronic, Inc., 8 351–54; **11** 459; **18** 421; **19** 103; **22** 359–61; **26** 132; **30** 313–17 **(upd.); 37** 39; **43** 349
Medusa Corporation, 8 135; **24** 331–33; **30** 156
Mees & Hope, **II** 184
The MEGA Life and Health Insurance Co., **33** 418–20
MEGA Natural Gas Company, **11** 28
MegaBingo, Inc., **41** 273, 275
Megafoods Stores Inc., 13 335–37; 17 560
MegaKnowledge Inc., **45** 206
Megasong Publishing, **44** 164
Megasource, Inc., **16** 94
Meggitt PLC, 34 273–76
MEI Diversified Inc., **18** 455
Mei Foo Investments Ltd., **IV** 718; **38** 319
Meier & Frank Co., 23 345–47
Meijer Incorporated, 7 329–31; **15** 449; **17** 302; **27** 312–15 **(upd.)**
Meiji Commerce Bank, **II** 291
Meiji Fire Insurance Co., **III** 384–85
Meiji Milk Products Company, Limited, II 538–39
Meiji Mutual Life Insurance Company, II 323; **III** 288–89
Meiji Seika Kaisha, Ltd., I 676; **II 540–41**
Meikosha Co., **II** 72
Meinecke Muffler Company, **III** 495; **10** 415
Meineke Discount Muffler Shops, **38** 208
Meis of Illiana, **10** 282
Meisei Electric, **III** 742
Meisel. *See* Samuel Meisel & Co.
Meisenzahl Auto Parts, Inc., **24** 205
Meissner, Ackermann & Co., **IV** 463; **7** 351
Meister, Lucious and Company, **13** 262
Meiwa Manufacturing Co., **III** 758
N.V. Mekog, **IV** 531
Mel Farr Automotive Group, 20 368–70
Mel Klein and Partners, **III** 74
Melaleuca Inc., 31 326–28
Melamine Chemicals, Inc., 27 316–18
Melbourne Engineering Co., **23** 83
Melbur China Clay Co., **III** 690
Melco, **II** 58; **44** 285
Meldisco. *See* Footstar, Incorporated.
Melkunie-Holland, **II** 575
Mellbank Security Co., **II** 316
Mello Smello. *See* The Miner Group International.
Mellon Bank Corporation, I 67–68, 584; **II** 315–17, 342, 402; **III** 275; **9** 470; **13** 410–11; **18** 112
Mellon Financial Corporation, 42 76; **44 278–82 (upd.)**
Mellon Indemnity Corp., **III** 258–59; **24** 177
Mellon-Stuart Co., I 584–85; 14 334
Melmarkets, **24** 462
Mélotte, **III** 418
Meloy Laboratories, Inc., **11** 333
Melroe Company, **8** 115–16; **34** 46
Melville Corporation, V 136–38; 9 192; **13** 82, 329–30; **14** 426; **15** 252–53;, **16** 390; **19** 449; **21** 526; **23** 176; **24** 167, 290; **35** 253. *See also* CVS Corporation.

Melvin Simon and Associates, Inc., 8 355–57; 26 262
Melwire Group, **III** 673
MEM, **37** 270–71
Memco, **12** 48
Mcmorex Corp., **III** 110, 166; **6** 282–83
Memphis International Motorsports Corporation Inc., **43** 139–40
The Men's Wearhouse, Inc., 17 312–15; 21 311
Menasco Manufacturing Co., **I** 435; **III** 415
Menasha Corporation, 8 358–61
Menck, **8** 544
Mendelssohn & Co., **II** 241
Meneven, **IV** 508
Menka Gesellschaft, **IV** 150; **24** 357
The Mennen Company, **I** 19; **6** 26; **14** 122; **18** 69; **35** 113
Mental Health Programs Inc., **15** 122
The Mentholatum Company Inc., IV 722; **32 331–33**
Mentor Corporation, 26 286–88
Mentor Graphics Corporation, III 143; **8** 519; **11** 46–47, 284–86, 490; **13** 128
MEPC plc, IV 710–12
Mepco/Electra Inc., **13** 398
MeraBank, **6** 546
MERBCO, Inc., **33** 456
Mercantile Agency, **IV** 604
Mercantile and General Reinsurance Co., **III** 335, 377
Mercantile Bancorporation Inc., **33** 155
Mercantile Bank, **II** 298
Mercantile Bankshares Corp., 11 287–88
Mercantile Credit Co., **16** 13
Mercantile Estate and Property Corp. Ltd., **IV** 710
Mercantile Fire Insurance, **III** 234
Mercantile Mutual, **III** 310
Mercantile Property Corp. Ltd., **IV** 710
Mercantile Security Life, **III** 136
Mercantile Stores Company, Inc., V 139; 19 270–73 **(upd.)**
Mercantile Trust Co., **II** 229, 247
Mercator & Noordstar N.V., **40** 61
Mercedes Benz. *See* Daimler-Benz A.G.
Mercedes Benz of North America, **22** 52
Merchant Bank Services, **18** 516, 518
Merchant Co., **III** 104
Merchant Distributors, Inc., **20** 306
Merchants & Farmers Bank of Ecru, **14** 40
Merchants Bank, **II** 213
Merchants Bank & Trust Co., **21** 524
Merchants Bank of Canada, **II** 210
Merchants Bank of Halifax, **II** 344
Merchants Dispatch, **II** 395–96; **10** 60
Merchants Distributors Inc. *See* Alex Lee Inc.
Merchants Fire Assurance Corp., **III** 396–97
Merchants Home Delivery Service, **6** 414
Merchants Indemnity Corp., **III** 396–97
Merchants Life Insurance Co., **III** 275
Merchants National Bank, **9** 228; **14** 528; **17** 135
Merchants National Bank of Boston, **II** 213
Merchants Union Express Co., **II** 396; **10** 60
Merchants' Assoc., **II** 261
Merchants' Loan and Trust, **II** 261; **III** 518
Merchants' Savings, Loan and Trust Co., **II** 261
Mercier, **I** 272

INDEX TO INDUSTRIES

Index to Industries

CONSTRUCTION

CONTAINERS

DRUGS/PHARMACEUTICALS

ELECTRICAL & ELECTRONICS

ENGINEERING & MANAGEMENT SERVICES

FINANCIAL SERVICES: BANKS

FINANCIAL SERVICES: NON-BANKS

FOOD PRODUCTS

FOOD SERVICES & RETAILERS

INSURANCE

LEGAL SERVICES

MANUFACTURING

PAPER & FORESTRY

PERSONAL SERVICES

PETROLEUM

PUBLISHING & PRINTING

REAL ESTATE

RETAIL & WHOLESALE

RUBBER & TIRE

TELECOMMUNICATIONS

WASTE SERVICES

GEOGRAPHIC INDEX

Geographic Index

Korea

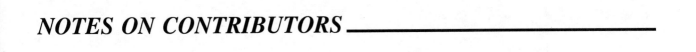

NOTES ON CONTRIBUTORS

Notes on Contributors

BIANCO, David. Freelance writer, editor, and publishing consultant.

BRENNAN, Gerald E. Freelance writer based in California.

BRYNILDSSEN, Shawna. Freelance writer and editor based in Bloomington, Indiana.

CAMPBELL, June. Freelance writer and Internet marketer living in Vancouver, Canada.

COHEN, M. L. Novelist and freelance writer living in Paris.

COVELL, Jeffrey L. Seattle-based freelance writer.

DINGER, Ed. Brooklyn-based freelance writer and editor.

FIERO, John W. Freelance writer, researcher, and consultant.

GREENLAND, Paul R. Illinois-based writer and researcher; author of two books and former senior editor of a national business magazine; contributor to *The Encyclopedia of Chicago History* (University of Chicago Press) and *Company Profiles for Students.*

HALASZ, Robert. Former editor in chief of *World Progress* and *Funk & Wagnalls New Encyclopedia Yearbook*; author, *The U.S. Marines* (Millbrook Press, 1993).

HAUSER, Evelyn. Researcher, writer and marketing specialist based in Arcata, California; expertise includes historical and trend research in such topics as globalization, emerging industries and lifestyles, future scenarios, biographies, and the history of organizations.

INGRAM, Frederick C. Utah-based business writer who has contributed to *GSA Business, Appalachian Trailway News,* the *Encyclopedia of Business,* the *Encyclopedia of Global Industries,* the *Encyclopedia of Consumer Brands,* and other regional and trade publications.

KARL, Lisa Musolf. Freelance editor, writer, and columnist living in the Chicago area.

LEMIEUX, Gloria A. Freelance writer and editor living in Nashua, New Hampshire.

MONTGOMERY, Bruce P. Curator and director of historical collection, University of Colorado at Boulder.

STANSELL, Christina M. Freelance writer and editor based in Farmington Hills, Michigan.

TRADII, Mary. Freelance writer based in Denver, Colorado.

UHLE, Frank. Ann Arbor-based freelance writer; movie projectionist, disc jockey, and staff member of *Psychotronic Video* magazine.

WOODWARD, A. Freelance writer.